MANAGERIAL ECONOMICS IN A GLOBAL ECONOMY

Third Edition

Managerial Economics in a Global Economy

DOMINICK SALVATORE
Professor of Economics and Business
Fordham University, New York

The McGraw-Hill Companies, Inc.
Primis Custom Publishing

New York St. Louis San Francisco Auckland Bogota
Caracas Lisbon London Madrid Mexico Milan Montreal
New Delhi Paris San Juan Singapore Sydney Tokyo Toronto

MANAGERIAL ECONOMICS IN A GLOBAL ECONOMY

ISBN 0-07-233712-5

Printed in the United States of America

1 2 3 4 5 6 7 8 9 0 BBC 0 9 8

Printer/Binder: Braceland Brothers, Inc.

About the Author

Dominick Salvatore is Professor of Economics and Business at Fordham University. He is co-chairman of the New York Academy of Sciences, and consultant to the Economic Policy Institute in Washington and the United Nations in New York.

Professor Salvatore is the author of more than 30 books, among which are: *Microeconomics* (1994) and *International Economics* (5th ed., 1995). He has also written Schaum's Outlines in *Managerial Economics, Microeconomics,* and *Statistics and Econometrics.*

Professor Salvatore is the editor of the *Handbook Series in Economics* for the Greenwood Press. He is the co-editor of the *Journal of Policy Modeling* and *Open Economies Review,* and associate editor of the *American Economist.* His research has been published in more than 100 journal articles in leading business and economics journals and presented at numerous national and international conferences.

Contents in Brief

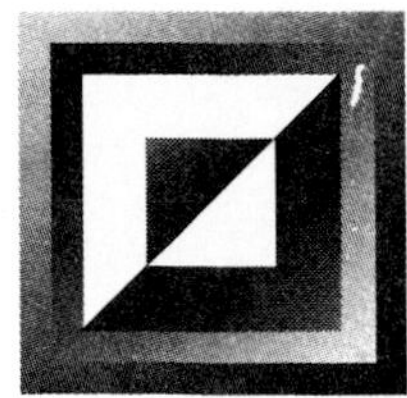

Contents

PART FIVE: REGULATION, RISK ANALYSIS, AND CAPITAL BUDGETING 503

Case Studies

Preface

This is a textbook for the traditional course in managerial economics offered in most business and economics programs. The organization of the text and the topics covered follow the traditional way the course is being taught, but they have been greatly extended in many new and exciting directions to reflect *modern* managerial tools and methods.

The primary aims of this text are:

- *To provide a unifying theme of managerial decision making around the theory of the firm.* This text shows how managerial economics is not the study of unrelated topics but the *synthesis* of economic theory, decision sciences, and the various fields of business administration studies, and it examines how they interact with one another as the firm attempts to reach optimal managerial decisions in the face of constraints.
- *To introduce an international dimension into managerial economics to reflect the globalization of production and distribution in today's world.* Most managerial economics texts on the market today approach managerial economics almost as if the international economy did not exist. However, many of the commodities we consume are imported, and firms today purchase many inputs abroad and sell an increasing share of their outputs overseas. Even more important, domestic firms face more and more competition from foreign producers. While little of this is reflected in current managerial economics texts, an increasing number of instructors feel that it is time to rectify such deficiencies by incorporating international ramifications throughout the managerial economics course.
- *To present many new topics and managerial tools not discussed at all or discussed only superficially in other managerial texts.* These include strategic behavior, the economics of information, international risks, the new (international) economies of scale, and learning curves, as well as the virtual corporation, total quality management, reengineering, benchmarking, the learning organization, the digital factory, bundling, and the business use of the Internet.
- *To show how managerial decisions are actually made in the real world.* The text includes 115 *real-world case studies (far more than in most other texts)*, as well as 5 longer *integrating case studies* at the end of each of the five parts of the text. Since managerial economics is by nature an applied field, this

feature can hardly be overstated. The case studies in this text cover a broad range of topics: competition and profits in the personal computer industry, benchmarking at Xerox, reengineering at General Electric, Gillette introducing the Sensor razor, the world car by Ford, micromarketing, forecasting the demand for air travel over the North Atlantic, General Motors deciding small is better, Xerox losing and regaining international competitiveness, tomorrow's factory, logistics at Compaq, the depreciation of the dollar and the profitability of U.S. firms, Wal-Mart's preemptive marketing strategy, Kodak's antidumping victory over Fuji, transfer pricing by multinational corporations, antitrust and the new merger boom, risk-metrics (J.P. Morgan's method of measuring risk), and capital budgeting techniques of major U.S. firms.

OTHER UNIQUE FEATURES

The text has other unique features, among which are the following:

- It offers *complete coverage of all the topics* usually encountered in actual managerial decision making and covered in any managerial economics course. Thus, the text allows a great deal of *flexibility in the choice of the topics* that any instructor may wish to cover.
- *The text can be used in courses with or without calculus.* In-depth coverage of the full range of calculus and optimization techniques used in managerial decision making is presented in the optional sections of Chapter 2. In all subsequent chapters, calculus is used only in the mathematical appendixes at the end of most chapters and in footnotes.
- *While applied in nature, this text rests on sound analytical foundations.* This addresses the common criticism that texts in this field either are overly theoretical, or are applied in nature but resting on weak theoretical foundations.

THE SUBJECT MATTER OF MANAGERIAL ECONOMICS

Managerial economics refers to the application of economic theory and the tools of analysis of decision science to examine how a firm can make optimal managerial decisions in the face of the constraints it faces.

This is a text for the standard upper-level undergraduate and graduate course in managerial economics offered in most business and some economics programs. This text uses the theory of the firm to integrate and link economic theory (microeconomics and macroeconomics), decision sciences (mathematical economics and econometrics), and the functional areas of business (accounting, finance, marketing, personnel or human resource management, and production) and shows how all of these topics are crucial components of managerial decision making. The functional areas of business administration studies examine the business environment in which the firm operates and, as such, they provide the background for managerial decision making. Economic theory provides the analytical framework for optimal decision making, while decision science provides the tools for optimization and for the estimation of economic relationships. As an overview course, managerial economics integrates and links all of these topics and shows their crucial importance in managerial decision making.

As stated above, the text exhibits *four unique features. First,* it uses the theory of the firm as the unifying theme to examine the managerial decision-making process. *Second,* it introduces a global view into managerial economics to reflect the internationalization of production and distribution in today's world. *Third,* it introduces many new and exciting topics into the study of managerial economics, such as strategic behavior, the economics of information, the virtual corporation, reengineering, the learning organization, and the digital factory. *Fourth,* it shows how managerial decisions are actually made today in the real world with 115 real-world case studies (more than any other text) and five more extensive cases at the end of each of the five parts of the text.

ORGANIZATION OF THE BOOK

The text is organized into five parts.

- *Part One* (Chapters 1 and 2) examines the nature and scope of managerial economics, presents the theory of the firm, and reviews optimization techniques. Chapter 1 shows in a clearer and more convincing manner than in other texts how the theory of the firm provides the unifying theme to the study of managerial economics and why a global view of managerial economics is required as a result of the rapidly increasing trend toward the internationalization of production and distribution in the world today. A brief review of the basics of demand and supply is also included. Chapter 2 then reviews optimization techniques, or the way a firm seeks to achieve its aims and objectives, subject to some constraints, most efficiently. Chapter 2 also discusses several of the new managerial tools.
- *Part Two* (Chapters 3 to 5) analyzes demand. Separate chapters deal with the theory of demand, the empirical estimation of demand, and demand forecasting. Other texts generally do not have a separate chapter for each of these important topics and are, as a result, less complete and somewhat confusing.
- *Part Three* (Chapters 6 to 8) presents the theory and measurement of the firm's production and costs. It also presents linear programming and examines its uses in managerial economics. The presentation of input substitution in production in Chapter 6, the discussion of short-run and long-run cost curves in Chapter 7, and the presentation of linear programming in Chapter 8 are all more complete and clearer than in any other text.
- *Part Four* (Chapters 9 to 11) brings together demand analysis (examined in Part Two) and production and cost analysis (examined in Part Three) in

order to analyze how price and output are determined under various forms of market organization. Chapter 9 deals with perfect competition, monopoly, and monopolistic competition; Chapter 10 examines oligopoly and strategic behavior; while Chapter 11 deals with pricing practices under various forms of market organization.

- *Part Five* (Chapters 12 to 14) examines regulation and antitrust, the role of government in the economy, risk analysis, and long-term investment decisions or capital budgeting.

PEDAGOGICAL FEATURES

In addition to the 115 real-world case studies presented in the text (six to ten per chapter), there is a more extensive integrating real-world case study at the end of each of the 5 parts, which provides an overview of the type of managerial decision making examined in the particular part.

Important pedagogical features of the text are as follows:

- The sections of each chapter are numbered for easy reference, and longer sections are broken into two or more subsections.
- All of the graphs and diagrams are carefully explained in the text and then summarized briefly in the captions.
- Diagrams are generally drawn on numerical scales to allow the reading of the answers in actual numbers rather than simply as distances. Also, the judicious use of color and shading in the illustrations aids the student's understanding.
- Important terms are presented in boldface in the chapters, and a glossary giving the definition of each important term, arranged alphabetically, is provided at the end of the book.

Each chapter also contains the following teaching aids:

1. An *Outline* of each chapter, giving an overview of the material.
2. A *Summary,* which reviews the main points covered in the text.
3. *Discussion Questions.* The ability to answer these questions indicates that the student has fully absorbed the material covered in the chapter.
4. *Problems.* These ask the student to actually apply and put to use what he or she has learned from the chapter. Answers to selected problems, marked by an asterisk (*), are provided at the end of the book for the type of quick feedback that is so essential to effective learning. The floppy disk symbol indicates the solutions that can be computer-generated.
5. *Supplementary Readings.* These include the most important references on the various topics covered in each chapter. A separate name index is included at the end of the book.

FOR THE INSTRUCTOR

The following ancillaries are available to the instructor:

1. An *Instructor's Manual prepared by the author* is available which provides the answers to all end-of-chapter questions and problems. The *Manual* was prepared with as much care as the text itself and is the most extensive of any text presently on the market.
2. A separate *Test Bank,* which contains a total of 1200 items (800 multiple-choice questions with answers, 150 true-and-false questions with answers, and 250 numerical problems fully worked out). This comprehensive *Test Bank* is more extensive than any competing text on the market.

FOR THE STUDENT

The student will find the following supplements invaluable:

1. A *Study Guide,* prepared by Professor Robert Brooker of Gannon University, is available from McGraw-Hill to assist students in reviewing and applying the material covered in the text. A software package that runs on IBM-PC and IBM-PC compatible computers in a Microsoft Windows 3.1, Excel 5.1 environment is *fully integrated* with the text and study guide, and contains routines for regression analysis, forecasting, linear programming, capital budgeting, risk analysis, and all other important techniques of analysis presented in the text. The problems at the end of each chapter that can be solved using this software package are marked by .
2. A *Schaum Outline* on the *Theory and Problems of Managerial Economics,* prepared by the author, is also available to students from McGraw-Hill. This presents a problem-solving approach to the topics presented in the traditional way in any managerial economics text, including this one. This outline contains a brief statement of the theory, with examples, as well as 156 multiple-choice questions with answers and 266 solved problems.
3. Numerous, recent, and original selections from *Business Week* are available from McGraw-Hill through Primis. Adopters of the text can create a reader from a list of articles which appeared recently in *Business Week.* A new reader can be created by the instructor at the beginning of each new semester.

ACKNOWLEDGMENTS

This text grew out of the undergraduate and graduate courses in managerial economics that I have been teaching at Fordham University during the past 20 years.

I was very fortunate to have had many excellent students in my classes, who with their questions and comments contributed much to the clarity of exposition of this text.

I owe a great intellectual debt to my brilliant former teachers: William Baumol (New York and Princeton Universities), Victor Fuchs (Stanford University and the National Bureau of Economic Research), Jack Johnston (University of California at Irvine), and Lawrence Klein (University of Pennsylvania and the Wharton School of Business). It is incredible how many of the insights that one gains as a student of a superb economist and teacher live on for the rest of one's life.

Many of my colleagues in the School of Business and Department of Economics at Fordham University made numerous suggestions that significantly improved the final product. Among these are Victor M. Borun, George C. Logush, Katherin Marton, Marta W. Mooney, James A. F. Stoner, David P. Stuhr, and Robert M. Wharton from the Business School; and Joseph Cammarosano, Clive Daniel, Edward Dowling, Nicholas Gianaris, James Heilbrun, and Greg Winczewski from the Department of Economics. My former colleague, Frank Fabozzi, now a visiting professor at the Sloan School of Management at M.I.T., also made many valuable suggestions.

The following professors reviewed the first and second editions of the text and made many useful suggestions for improvements: Saul Barr, University of Tennessee; John Beck, Indiana University, South Bend; Trent E. Boggess, Plymouth State College; Robert Brooker, Gannon University; Barrington K. Brown, Bowie State University; John Bungum, Gustavas Adolphus College; John E. Connor, LaSalle University; John Gregor, Plymouth State College; Simon Hakim, Temple University; James Horner, Cameron University; Nicholas Karatjas, Indiana University of Pennsylvania; Demitrius Karenteli, Assumption College; Douglas J. Lamdin, University of Maryland, Baltimore; Louis Lopilato, Marcy College; Wilfred McAloon, Fairleigh Dickinson University; Warren Machone, University of Central Florida; Philip S. Mahoney, University of Northern Colorado; Daniel Marsh, University of Dallas; Don Maxwell, Central State University; Marshall H. Medoff, California State University, Long Beach; Patrick O'Sullivan, State University of New York, Old Westbury; Robert Pennington, University of Central Florida; Walter Rice, California Polytech Institute; Janet M. Rives, University of Northern Iowa; John Rodgers, University of North Carolina, Greensboro; William J. Simeone, Providence College; Michael Szenberg, Pace University; John Wade, Western Carolina University; James N. Wetzel, Virginia Commonwealth University; and Richard Winkelman, Arizona State University.

I am grateful to the following professors for making numerous useful suggestions for the third edition of the text: Dean Baim, Pepperdine University; Richard Hannah, Middle Tennessee State University; Dean Hiebert, Illinois State University; Robert Nicholson, University of Richmond; and David Riefel, University of North Carolina at Charlotte.

Robert Derrell, Joseph Grana, Jenifer Moll, Vidyotham Reddi, Shalini Sharma, and Catherine Skelly assisted me throughout this project. No professor could ask for better graduate assistants. I am grateful to the literary executor of the estate of the late Sir Ronald A. Fisher, F.R.S., to Dr. Frank Yates, F.R.S. and to the Longman Group Ltd., London, for permission to reprint Table C.2 from their book, *Statistical Tables for Biological, Agricultural and Medical Research,* 6th ed. (1974).

Finally, I would like to express my gratitude to the entire staff of McGraw-Hill, especially to Gary Burke, Lucille Sutton, Victoria Richardson, and Curt Berkowitz, for their kind and skillful assistance, and to Angela Bates and Marie Sundberg (the departmental secretaries at Fordham) for their efficiency and skillful disposition.

Dominick Salvatore

MANAGERIAL ECONOMICS IN A GLOBAL ECONOMY

PART ONE

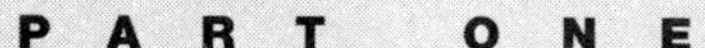

Introduction

Part One (Chapters 1 and 2) examines the nature and scope of managerial economics and presents the optimization techniques that will be used in the rest of the text. Chapter 1 defines the subject matter of managerial economics and examines its relationship to other fields of study; it presents the theory of the firm and examines the nature and function of profits; finally it examines the importance of introducing an international dimension into managerial economics; the appendix reviews the basics of demand, supply, and equilibrium. Chapter 2 presents the techniques for maximizing or minimizing an objective function, such as profits or costs, respectively, and examines new management theories.

CHAPTER 1

The Nature and Scope of Managerial Economics

KEY TERMS
(in order of their appearance)

Managerial economics
Economic theory
Microeconomics
Macroeconomics
Model
Mathematical economics
Econometrics
Functional areas of business administration studies
Firm
Transaction costs
Circular flow of economic activity
Theory of the firm
Value of the firm
Constrained optimization
Principal-agent problem
Satisficing behavior
Business profit
Explicit costs
Economic profit
Implicit costs
Internationalization of economic activity

CHAPTER OUTLINE

In this chapter we examine the nature and scope of managerial economics. We begin with a definition of managerial economics and a discussion of its relationship to other fields of study. We then go on to examine the theory of the firm. Here, we discuss the reason for the existence of firms and their functions, and we define the value of the firm, examine the constraints faced by firms, and examine the limitations of the theory of the firm, including the so-called principal-agent problem. Subsequently, we examine the nature of profits by distinguishing between economic and business profits and by analyzing their function in a free-enterprise system. Finally, we examine the importance of introducing an international dimension into managerial economics to reflect the globalization of production and distribution in today's world. In the appendix, we review the basics of demand, supply, and equilibrium.

Each section of the chapter includes one or more real-world case studies which clearly illustrate the major concept introduced in the particular section. This is an important chapter because it defines the subject matter of managerial economics, it clearly shows its relationship to other fields of study, and it examines the great importance and relevance of managerial economics in all business and economic decision-making situations and programs in today's global economy.

1-1 THE SCOPE OF MANAGERIAL ECONOMICS

In this section we define the function of managerial economics and examine its relationship to economic theory, management decision sciences, and functional areas of business administration studies.

Definition of Managerial Economics

Managerial economics* refers to the application of economic theory and the tools of analysis of decision science to examine how an organization can achieve its aims or objectives most efficiently. The meaning of this definition can best be examined with the aid of Figure 1-1.

Management decision problems (see the top of Figure 1-1) arise in any organization—be it a firm, a not-for-profit organization (such as a hospital or a university), or a government agency—when it seeks to achieve some goal or objective subject to some constraints. For example, a firm may seek to maximize profits subject to limitations on the availability of essential inputs and in the face of legal constraints. A hospital may seek to treat as many patients as possible at an "adequate" medical standard with its limited physical resources (physicians, technicians, nurses, equipment, beds) and budget. The goal of a state university may be to provide an adequate education to as many students as possible, subject to the physical and financial constraints it faces. Similarly, a government agency may seek to provide a particular service (which cannot be provided as

*The definition of all boldfaced terms, arranged alphabetically, is provided in the Glossary at the end of the book.

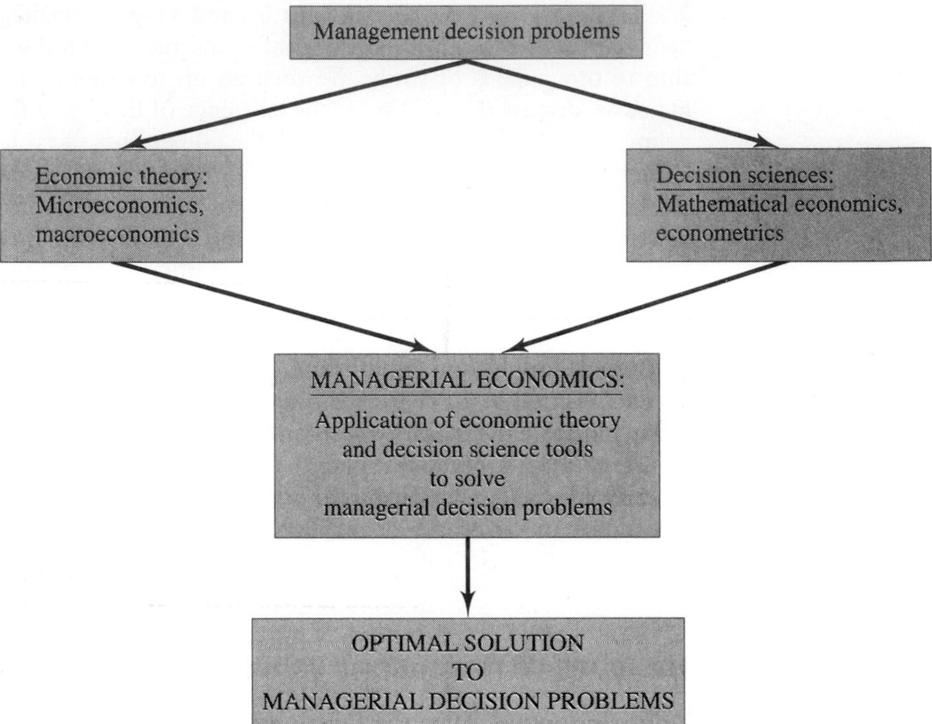

Figure 1-1
The Nature of Managerial Economics
Managerial economics refers to the application of economic theory and decision science tools to find the optimal solution to managerial decision problems.

efficiently by business firms) to as many people as possible at the lowest possible cost. In all these cases, the organization faces management decision problems as it seeks to achieve its goal or objective, subject to the constraints it faces. The goals and constraints may differ from case to case, but the basic decision-making process is the same.

Relationship to Economic Theory

The organization can solve its management decision problems by the application of economic theory and the tools of decision science. **Economic theory** refers to microeconomics and macroeconomics. **Microeconomics** is the study of the economic behavior of *individual* decision-making units, such as individual consumers, resource owners, and business firms, in a free-enterprise system. **Macroeconomics,** on the other hand, is the study of the total or aggregate level of output, income, employment, consumption, investment, and prices for the economy *viewed as a whole.* While the (microeconomic) theory of the firm is the single most important element in managerial economics, the general macroeconomic conditions of the economy (such as the level of aggregate demand, rate of inflation, and interest rates) within which the firm operates are also very important.

Economic theories seek to predict and explain economic behavior. Economic theories usually begin with a **model.** This abstracts from the many details surrounding an event and seeks to identify a few of the most important determinants of the event. For example, the theory of the firm assumes that the firm seeks to maximize profits, and on the basis of that it predicts how much of a particular commodity the firm should produce under different forms of market structure or organization. While the firm may have other (multiple) aims, the profit-maximization model accurately predicts the behavior of firms, and, therefore, we accept it. Thus, the methodology of economics (and science in general) is to accept a theory or model if it predicts accurately and if the predictions follow logically from the assumptions.[1]

Relationship to the Decision Sciences

Managerial economics is also closely related to the decision sciences. These utilize the tools of mathematical economics and econometrics (see Figure 1-1) to construct and estimate decision models aimed at determining the optimal behavior of the firm (i.e., how the firm can achieve its goals most efficiently). Specifically, **mathematical economics** is used to formalize (i.e., to express in equational form) the economic models postulated by economic theory. **Econometrics** then applies statistical tools (particularly regression analysis) to real-world data to estimate the models postulated by economic theory and for forecasting.

For example, economic theory postulates that the quantity demanded (Q) of a commodity is a function of or depends on the price of the commodity (P), the income of consumers (Y), and the price of related (i.e., complementary and substitute) commodities (P_C and P_S, respectively). Assuming constant tastes, we may postulate the following formal (mathematical) model:

$$Q = f(P, Y, P_C, P_S) \tag{1-1}$$

By collecting data on Q, P, Y, P_C, and P_S for a particular commodity, we can then estimate the empirical (econometric) relationship. This will permit the firm to determine how much Q would change by a change in P, Y, P_C, and P_S, and to forecast the future demand for the commodity. This information is essential in order for management to achieve the goal or objective of the firm (profit maximization) most efficiently.

To conclude, "managerial economics" refers to the application of economic theory and decision science tools to find the optimal solution to managerial decision problems.

[1]See M. Friedman, "The Methodology of Positive Economics," in *Essays in Positive Economics* (Chicago: University of Chicago Press, 1953), and M. Blaug, *The Methodology of Economics and How Economists Explain* (Cambridge, England: Cambridge University Press, 1980).

Relationship to the Functional Areas of Business Administration Studies

Having defined the subject matter of managerial economics and its function, we can now examine the relationship between managerial economics and the **functional areas of business administration studies.** The latter include accounting, finance, marketing, personnel or human resource management, and production. These disciplines study the business environment in which the firm operates and, as such, they provide the background for managerial decision making. Thus, managerial economics can be regarded as an overview course that *integrates* economic theory, decision sciences, and the functional areas of business administration studies; and it examines how they interact with one another as the firm attempts to achieve its goal most efficiently.

Most students taking managerial economics are likely to have some knowledge (from other courses) of some of the topics presented and tools of analysis utilized in managerial economics. While reviewing these topics and studying the others, the student should pay particular attention to the overall decision-making process by which the firm can achieve its objective, since this is the ultimate goal of managerial economics.

In short, managerial economics is not the study of a number of topics but the utilization of economic theory and management science tools to examine how a firm can achieve its objective most efficiently within the business environment in which it operates. If all students in a managerial economics course had already taken courses in microeconomic and macroeconomic theory, in mathematical economics and econometrics, and in the functional areas of business, then managerial economics could concentrate exclusively on its integrating and synthesizing role in analyzing the decision-making process. As it is, most students have had some of those courses but not all. Thus, a managerial economics course, while stressing the process of reaching optimal managerial decisions, must also present the theories and tools required to make such optimal managerial decisions.

Business decisions have been likened to military strategy (see Case Study 1-1) and are now being revolutionized by the rapid globalization of the world economy and by the widespread use of computers and information technology (see Case Study 1-2).

Case Study 1-1
Decision Making in Business and Military Strategy

According to William E. Peackock, president of two St. Louis companies and former Assistant Secretary of the Army under Jimmy Carter, decision making in business has much in common with military strategy. While business managers' actions are restricted by laws and regulations to prevent unfair practices and the objective of managers, of course, is not to literally destroy the competition, there is much that they can learn from military strategists. Peackock points out that, down through history, military conflicts have produced a set of Darwinian basic principles that are an excellent guideline to business managers in meeting the competition in the marketplace. Neglecting these principles can make the difference between business success and failure.

In business as in war, it is crucial to have a clear objective as to what the organization wants to accomplish and to explain this objective to all employees. The benefits of a simple marketing strategy that all employees can understand are clearly evidenced by the success of McDonald's. Both business and warfare also require the development of a strategy for attacking. Being aggressive is important because few competitions are ever won by being passive. Furthermore, both business and warfare require unity of command to pinpoint responsibility. Even in decentralized companies with informal lines of command, there are always key individuals who must make important decisions. Finally, in business as in war, the element of surprise and security (keeping your strategy secret) is crucial. For example, Lee Iacocca stunned the competition in 1964 by introducing the immensely successful Mustang. Finally, in business as in war, industrial espionage to discover a rival's plans or steal a rival's new technological breakthrough is becoming increasingly common.

More than ever before, today's business leaders must learn how to tap employees' ideas and energy, manage large-scale rapid change, anticipate business conditions five or ten years down the road, and muster the courage to steer the firm in radical new directions when necessary. Above all, firms must think and act strategically in a world of increasing global competition.

Source: W. E. Peackock, *Corporate Combat* (New York: Facts on File Publication, 1984); W. B. Wriston, "The State of American Management," *Harvard Business Review*, vol. 90, January–February 1990, pp. 78–83; and "The Valley of Spies," *Forbes*, October 26, 1992, pp. 200–204.

Case Study 1-2

The Management Revolution

Business and society are today in the midst of a revolution comparable to the Industrial Revolution in both scale and consequence. Today's revolution has four components: the globalization of markets, the spread of the information technology and computer networks, the dismantling of traditional managerial hierarchies, and the creation of a new information economy. These four components are all occurring fast and at the same time, and are affected by and affect one another. Globalization (the first component of today's revolution) once meant simply exporting some goods and services to other nations and maybe setting up a few production facilities abroad. Today, globalization means that more and more managerial decisions must consider the world as a whole, rather than the region or the nation, as the relevant marketplace. Because of the tremendous improvement in communications and transportation, tastes are converging internationally, many more products than in the past are now imported and most others have parts of components made abroad, and domestic producers face ever-growing competition from abroad. The second component of today's revolution is the spread of the information technology and computer networks. Practically every bank teller, post office worker, retail clerk, telephone operator, bill collector, and so on works with a computer today. This greatly speeds up the delivery of goods and services, cuts waste, reduces inventory, and generally increases productivity. The computer has also dismantled traditional managerial hierarchies and decimated the ranks of middle management (the third component of today's revolution). In the past, middle managers were the transmission lines for information between top management and workers. Today, information can in most instances be transmitted from top management directly to workers and viceversa by a simple tap of a computer key and without any need of middle management. The fourth component of today's revolution is the rapid spread of the information economy where the creation of value is increasingly based on knowledge and communications rather than as in the past on natural resources and physical labor. For example, many auto repairs will soon be made not by a mechanic with a wrench but by a technician who fixes an engine knock by reprogramming a computer chip, and goods and services will increasingly be marketed and distributed electronically. Today's four-pronged revolution affects drastically not only how traditional products and services are produced and distributed but also the entire organization of production, consumption, and management in ways that are not yet fully evident or understood.

Source: "Welcome to the Revolution," *Fortune,* December 13, 1993, pp. 66–78.

1-2 THE THEORY OF THE FIRM

In this section, we examine first the reason for the existence of firms and their principal functions. Then we define the value of the firm and the constraints under which it operates. Finally, we discuss the limitations of the theory of the firm. This is a most important section since the theory of firm behavior is the centerpiece and central theme of managerial economics.

Reasons for the Existence of Firms and Their Functions

A **firm** is an organization that combines and organizes resources for the purpose of producing goods and/or services for sale. There are millions of firms in the United States. These include proprietorships (firms owned by one individual), partnerships (firms owned by two or more individuals), and corporations (owned by stockholders). Firms produce more than 80 percent of all goods and services consumed in the United States. The remainder is produced by the government and not-for-profit organizations, such as private colleges, hospitals, museums, and foundations.

Firms exist because it would be very inefficient and costly for entrepreneurs to enter into and enforce contracts with workers and owners of capital, land, and other resources for each separate step of the production and distribution process. Instead, entrepreneurs usually enter into longer-term, broader contracts with labor to perform a number of tasks for a specific wage and fringe benefits. Such a general contract is much less costly than numerous specific contracts and is highly advantageous both to the entrepreneurs and to the workers and other resource owners. The firm exists in order to save on such **transaction costs.** By internalizing many transactions (i.e., by performing many functions within the firm), the firm also saves on sales taxes and avoids price controls and other government regulations that apply only to transactions among firms.

On the other hand, firms do not continue to grow larger and larger indefinitely because of limitations on management ability to effectively control and direct the operation of the firm as it becomes larger and larger. It is true that up to a point, a firm can overcome these internal disadvantages of large size or diseconomies of scale by establishing a number of semiautonomous divisions (i.e, by decentralizing). Eventually, however, the increased communication traffic that is generated, coupled with the further and further distancing of top management from the operation of each division, impose sufficient diseconomies of scale to limit the growth of the firm. Furthermore, the firm will reach a point where the cost of supplying additional services within the firm exceeds the cost of purchasing these services from other firms. An example is provided by some highly technical (legal, medical, or engineering) service that the firm may need only occasionally.

The function of firms, therefore, is to purchase resources or inputs of labor services, capital, and raw materials in order to transform them into goods and services for sale. Resource owners (workers and owners of capital, land, and raw materials) then use the income generated from the sale of their services or other resources to firms to purchase the goods and services produced by firms. The **circular flow of economic activity** is thus complete.[2] In the process of supplying the goods and services that society demands, firms provide employment to workers and pay taxes that government utilizes to provide services (such as national defense, education, and fire protection) that firms could not provide at all or as efficiently.

The Objective and Value of the Firm

Managerial economics begins by postulating a theory of the firm, which it then uses to analyze managerial decision making. Originally, the theory of the firm was based on the assumption that the goal or objective of the firm was to maximize current or short-term profits. Firms, however, are often observed to sacrifice short-term profits for the sake of increasing future or long-term profits. Some examples of this are expenditures on research and development, new capital equipment, and an enhanced promotional campaign.[3] Since both short-term as well as long-term profits are clearly important, the **theory of the firm** now postulates that the primary goal or objective of the firm is to maximize the wealth or **value of the firm.** This is given by the present value of all expected future profits of the

[2]For a more extensive discussion, see D. Salvatore, *Microeconomics,* 2nd ed. (New York: HarperCollins, 1994), pp. 6–7.

[3]Many managers, however, complain that the pressure to report profits every year or every quarter forces them to take actions which are detrimental to the long-term profitability of the firm.

firm. Future profits must be discounted to the present because a dollar of profit in the future is worth less than a dollar of profit today.[4]

Formally stated, the wealth or value of the firm is given by

$$PV = \frac{\pi_1}{(1+r)^1} + \frac{\pi_2}{(1+r)^2} + \cdots + \frac{\pi_n}{(1+r)^n} \tag{1-2}$$

$$= \sum_{t=1}^{n} \frac{\pi_t}{(1+r)^t} \tag{1-2a}$$

where PV is the present value of all expected future profits of the firm, π_1, $\pi_2, \ldots, \pi_n$ represent the expected profits in each of the n years considered, and r is the appropriate discount rate used to find the present value of future profits. In Equation 1-2a, Σ refers to "the sum of" and t assumes the values from 1 up to the n years considered. Thus, $\Sigma_{t=1}^{n}$ means "sum or add" all the $\pi_t/(1 + r)^t$ terms resulting from substituting the values of 1 to n for t. Hence, Equation 1-2a is an abbreviated but equivalent form of Equation 1-2. The introduction of the time dimension in Equations 1-2 and 1-2a also allows for the consideration of uncertainty. For example, the more uncertain is the stream of expected future profits, the higher is the discount rate that the firm will use, and, therefore, the smaller is the present value of the firm.

Since profits are equal to total revenue (TR) minus total costs (TC), Equation 1-2a can be rewritten as

$$\text{Value of firm} = \sum_{t=1}^{n} \frac{TR_t - TC_t}{(1+r)^t} \tag{1-3}$$

Equation 1-3 provides a unifying theme for the analysis of managerial decision making and, indeed, for this entire text. Specifically, TR depends on sales or the demand for the firm's output and the firm's pricing decisions. These are the major responsibility of the marketing department and are discussed in detail in Part Two (Chapters 3 through 5) and Part Four (Chapters 9 through 11), respectively. The TC depends on the technology of production and resource prices. These are the major responsibility of the production and personnel departments and are discussed in detail in Part Three (Chapters 6 through 8). The discount rate (r) depends on the perceived risk of the firm and on the cost of borrowing funds. These are the major responsibility of the finance department and are discussed in detail in Chapters 13 and 14 (in Part Five).

Equation 1-3 can also be used to organize the discussion of how the various departments within the firm interact with one another. For example, the marketing department can reduce the cost associated with a given level of output by promoting off-season sales. The production and personnel departments can stimu-

[4]A $1 investment today at 10 percent interest will grow to $1.10 in one year. Therefore, $1 is defined as the present value of $1.10 due in one year. For the purpose of this chapter, this is all that needs to be known. A detailed presentation of the concepts of present value and compound interest, which are required for understanding Chapter 13 on risk analysis and Chapter 14 on long-term investment decisions, is given in Appendix A at the end of the book.

late sales by quality improvements and the development of new products. The accounting department can provide more timely information on sales and costs. All these activities increase the efficiency of the firm and reduce its risk, thereby allowing the firm to use a lower discount rate to determine the present value of its expected future profits (which increases the value of the firm).

Constraints on the Operation of the Firm

We have seen above that the goal or objective of the firm is to maximize wealth or the value of the firm. In trying to do this, however, the firm faces many constraints. Some of these constraints arise from limitations on the availability of essential inputs. Specifically, a firm may not be able to hire as many skilled workers as it wants, especially in the short run. Similarly, the firm may not be able to acquire all the specific raw materials it demands. It may also face limitations on factory and warehouse space and in the quantity of capital funds available for a given project or purpose. Government agencies and not-for-profit organizations also face similar resource constraints. Besides resource constraints, the firm also faces many legal constraints. These take the form of minimum wage laws, health and safety standards, pollution emission standards, as well as laws and regulations that prevent firms from employing unfair business practices. In general, society imposes these constraints on firms in order to modify their behavior and make it more nearly consistent with broad social welfare goals.

So important and pervasive are the constraints facing firms that we speak of **constrained optimization.**[5] That is, the primary goal or objective of the firm is to maximize wealth or the value of the firm subject to the constraints it faces. The existence of these constraints restricts the range of possibilities or freedom of action of the firm and limits the value of the firm to a level that is lower than in the absence of such constraints (unconstrained optimization). Within these constraints, however, the firm seeks to maximize wealth or its value. While government agencies and not-for-profit organizations may have goals other than wealth or value maximization, they also face constraints in achieving their goals or objectives, whatever these goals or objectives might be. Most of the discussion in the rest of the text will be in terms of constrained optimization, and we will develop and use powerful techniques such as linear programming to examine how the firm achieves constrained optimization.

Limitations of the Theory of the Firm

The theory of the firm which postulates that the goal or objective of the firm is to maximize wealth or the value of the firm has been criticized as being much too narrow and unrealistic. In its place, broader theories of the firm have been proposed. The most prominent among these are models that postulate that the primary objective of the firm is the maximization of sales, the maximization of management utility, and satisficing behavior.

[5]We refer to "optimization" rather than "maximization" in order to allow for cases where the firm wants to *minimize* costs and other objectives, subject to the constraints it faces.

According to the sales-maximization model introduced by William Baumol and others, managers of modern corporations seek to maximize sales after an adequate rate of profit has been earned to satisfy stockholders.[6] Indeed, some early empirical studies found a strong correlation between executives' salaries and sales, but not between salaries and profits. More recent studies, however, found the opposite.

Oliver Williamson and others have introduced a model of management utility maximization, which postulates that with the advent of the modern corporation and the resulting separation of management from ownership, managers are more interested in maximizing their utility, measured in terms of their compensation (salaries, fringe benefits, stock options, etc.), the size of their staff, extent of control over the corporation, lavish offices, etc., than in maximizing corporate profits.[7] This is referred to as the **principal-agent problem.** That is, the agent (manager) may be more interested in maximizing his or her benefits than maximizing the principal's (the owner's) interest. This principal-agent problem can be resolved by tying the manager's reward to the firm's performance in relation to other firms in the same industry. Managers who maximize their own interests rather than the corporation's profits are also more likely to be replaced either by the stockholders of the corporation or as a result of the corporation's being taken over (merged) with another firm that sees the unexploited profit potential of the first.

Finally, Richard Cyert and James March, building on the work of Herbert Simon, pointed out that because of the great complexity of running the large modern corporation—a task complicated by uncertainty and a lack of data—managers are not able to maximize profits but can only strive for some satisfactory goal in terms of sales, profits, growth, market share, and so on. Simon called this **satisficing behavior.** That is, the large corporation is a satisficing, rather than a maximizing, organization.[8] This, however, is not necessarily inconsistent with profit or value maximization, and, presumably, with more and better data and search procedures, the modern corporation could conceivably approach profit or value maximization.

While these alternative and broader theories of the firm stress some relevant aspect of the operation of the modern corporation, they do not provide a satisfactory alternative to the theory of the firm postulated in Section 1-2. Indeed, the stiff competition prevailing in most product and resource markets as well as in managerial and entrepreneurial talent today forces managers to pay close attention to profits—lest the firm go out of business or they be replaced. As a result, we retain our theory of the firm (in terms of profit or value maximization) in the rest of the text as the basis for analyzing managerial decisions, because it is from this vantage point that the

[6]See W. J. Baumol, *Business Behavior, Value and Growth* (New York: Macmillan, 1959).

[7]See O. E. Williamson, "A Model of Rational Managerial Behavior," in R. M. Cyert and J. G. March, eds., *A Behavioral Theory of the Firm* (Englewood Cliffs, N.J.: Prentice-Hall, 1963).

[8]See R. M. Cyert and J. G. March, eds., *A Behavioral Theory of the Firm,* and H. A. Simon, "Theories of Decision-Making in Economics," *American Economic Review,* vol. 49, June 1949.

behavior of the firm can be studied most fruitfully. The assumptions of the theory may be somewhat unrealistic, but the theory predicts the behavior of the firm more accurately than any of its alternatives.

Case Study 1-3

The Objective and Strategy of Firms in the Cigarette Industry

The objective of firms in the cigarette industry seems to be to maximize profits over the long run or the value of the firm, as postulated by the theory of the firm. Different firms, however, pursue these goals differently. The doubling of the federal excise tax on each pack of cigarettes, which came into effect on January 1, 1983, as well as the rise in other state taxes since then, resulted in a sharp increase in cigarette prices and a reduction in consumption. In order to lure customers from rivals and maintain profit levels, the weaker three of the nation's six major producers introduced generic cigarettes. These contain cheaper tobacco, come in plain black-and-white packages, are advertised very little, and sell at less than half the price of name brands.

The other three major producers, instead, followed the more traditional marketing strategy of brand proliferation. That is, they introduced a large number of new brands to appeal to every conceivable taste or consumer group and spent hundreds of millions of dollars on advertising. They resisted the introduction of generic cigarettes because these cigarettes have very low profit margins. But as sales of generic cigarettes rose, these other major producers responded with the introduction of discounts—brand-name cigarettes that cost more than generics but less than the traditional brands. Then on Friday, April 2, 1993 (which became known as the infamous Marlboro Friday), Philip Morris took the unusual step of cutting the price of Marlboro cigarettes (one of the world's best-known and profitable brands) and its other premium brands by 20 percent (about 40 cents per pack) in an effort to contain continued loss of market share to generic cigarettes. RJR Nabisco, Philip Morris's main competitor, quickly matched the price cut.

Thus, while the goals of both groups of cigarette producers was the same (i.e., long-term profit maximization or maximizing the value of the firm), their strategy was different. Those companies that suffered very large declines in sales and profits as a result of increased cigarette prices and declining consumption introduced generic cigarettes. The others adopted a more traditional strategy and introduced discount brands but eventually had to cut prices on their brand names also. At the same time, both groups of cigarette producers greatly expanded sales abroad, where antismoking campaigns are either in their infancy or still nonexistent and cigarettes can still be advertised on television. As a result, sales of American cigarettes abroad are growing rapidly at the same time that they are declining domestically.

Source: "Big Tobacco Toughest Road," *U.S. News & World Report,* April 17, 1989, p. 26; "Philip Morris Cuts Cigarette Prices, Stunning Market," *New York Times,* April 3, 1993, p. 1; and "The Smoke Clears at Marlboro," *Business Week,* January 31, 1994, pp. 76–77.

Case Study 1-4
The Virtual Corporation

Today's joint ventures and strategic alliances provide early glimpses of the virtual corporation—the firm of the future. This is a temporary network of independent companies (suppliers, customers, and even rivals) coming together with each contributing its core competence to quickly take advantage of fast-changing opportunities. In today's world of fierce global competition, the window of opportunity to take advantage of fast-moving opportunities is often so frustratingly brief as to make it impossible for a single firm to have all the in-house expertise to quickly launch complex products in diverse markets. By temporarily banding together to take advantage of a specific market opportunity and with each company bringing what it is best at, the virtual firm is a "best-of-everything organization." Informational networks and electronic contracts will permit far-flung partners to work together on a particular project and then disband when the opportunity has been fully exploited.

In a virtual firm, one of the partners may have the idea for a new product, another may design the product, another may produce it, and still another market it. For example, IBM, Apple Computer, and Motorola have come together to develop a new operating system and computer chip for a new generation of computers. MCI Communications has entered into partnerships with as many as 100 companies to provide a one-stop package of telecommunications hardware and services based on MCI competencies in network integration and software development with the strength of other companies making all kinds of telecommunications equipment.

Although power, flexibility, and quickness are crucial advantages, the virtual corporation model does face two real risks. First, a company joining such a network may lose control of its core technology. Second, by abandoning manufacturing, the company may become "hollow" and become unable to resume the manufacture of its traditional product in the future when the network dissolves. Some observers point out that IBM's desire to quickly enter the personal computer (PC) market in 1981 by relying on Intel for computer chips and Microsoft for the operating software left IBM without control of the market and encouraged hundreds of clone makers to eventually enter the market with lower prices and better products.

Thus, not everyone is sold on the virtual firm model. In order to work, the virtual firm will have to be formed by partners that are dependable and are the best in their field, the network will have to serve the interest of all partners in a win-win situation, each company must put its best and brightest people in the network to show its partners that its link with them is important to the company, the objective of the network and what each partner is expected to gain must be clearly defined, and the network must build a common telecommunications network and other infrastructures so that each partner can be in constant touch with one another to anticipate problems and review progress. Creating and successfully operating a virtual firm is not easy but it may very well be the way of the future.

Source: "The Virtual Firm," *Business Week,* February 8, 1993, pp. 98–102.

1-3 THE NATURE AND FUNCTION OF PROFITS

In this section we examine the nature and function of profits. We distinguish between business and economic profits, present various theories of profits, and examine the function of profits in a free-enterprise economy.

Business versus Economic Profit

To the general public and the business community, profit or **business profit** refers to the revenue of the firm minus the explicit or accounting costs of the firm. **Explicit costs** are the actual out-of-pocket expenditures of the firm to purchase or hire the inputs it requires in production. These expenditures include the wages to hire labor, interest on borrowed capital, rent on land and buildings, and the expenditures on raw materials. To the economist, however, **economic profit** equals the revenue of the firm minus its explicit costs and implicit costs. **Implicit costs** refer to the value of the inputs owned and used by the firm in its own production processes.

Specifically, implicit costs include the salary that the entrepreneur could earn from working for someone else in a similar capacity (say, as the manager of another firm) and the return that the firm could earn from investing its capital and renting its land and other inputs to other firms. The inputs owned and used by the firm in its own production processes are not free to the firm, even though the firm can use them without any actual or explicit expenditures. Their implicit costs are what these same inputs could earn in their best alternative use outside the firm. Accordingly, economists include both explicit and implicit costs in their definition of costs. That is, they include a normal return on owned resources as part of costs, so that economic profit is revenue minus explicit and implicit costs. While the concept of business profit may be useful for accounting and tax purposes, it is the concept of economic profit that must be used in order to reach correct investment decisions.

For example, suppose that a firm reports a business profit of $30,000 during a year, but the entrepreneur could have earned $35,000 by managing another firm and $10,000 by lending out his capital to another firm facing similar risks. To the economist this entrepreneur is actually incurring an economic loss of $15,000 because, from the *business* profit of $30,000, he would have to subtract the implicit or opportunity cost of $35,000 for his wages and $10,000 for his capital. A business profit of $30,000, thus, corresponds to an economic loss of $15,000 per year. Even if the entrepreneur owned no capital, he would still incur an economic loss of $5,000 per year by continuing to operate his own firm and earning a business profit of $30,000 rather than working for someone else in a similar capacity for $35,000. Thus, the entrepreneur should close his firm and work in his best alternative occupation. In other words, it is the economic, rather than the business, concept of profit that is important in directing resources to different sectors of the economy. In the rest of the text we will use the term *profit* to mean economic profit and *cost* to mean the sum of explicit and implicit costs.

Theories of Profit

Profit rates usually differ among firms in a given industry and even more widely among firms in different industries. Firms in such industries as steel, textiles, and railroads generally earn very low profits both absolutely and in relation to the profits of firms in pharmaceutical, office equipment, and other high-technology industries. Several theories attempt to explain these differences.

Risk-Bearing Theories of Profit According to this theory, above-normal returns (i.e., economic profits) are required by firms to enter and remain in such fields as petroleum exploration with above-average risks. Similarly, the expected return on stocks has to be higher than on bonds because of the greater risk of the former. This will be discussed in greater detail in Chapter 13.

Frictional Theory of Profit This theory stresses that profits arise as a result of friction or disturbances from long-run equilibrium. That is, in long-run, perfectly competitive equilibrium, firms tend to earn only a normal return (adjusted for risk) or zero (economic) profit on their investment. At any time, however, firms are not likely to be in long-run equilibrium and may earn a profit or incur a loss. For example, at the time of the energy crisis in the early 1970s, firms producing insulating materials enjoyed a sharp increase in demand, which led to large profits. With the sharp decline in petroleum prices in the mid 1980s, many of these firms began to incur losses. When profits are made in an industry in the short run, more firms are attracted to the industry in the long run, and this tends to drive profits down to zero (i.e., it leads to firms earning only a normal return on investment). On the other hand, when losses are incurred, some firms leave the industry. This leads to higher prices and the elimination of the losses.

Monopoly Theory of Profit Some firms with monopoly power can restrict output and charge higher prices than under perfect competition, thereby earning a profit. Because of restricted entry into the industry, these firms can continue to earn profits even in the long run. Monopoly power may arise from the firm's owning and controlling the entire supply of a raw material required for the production of the commodity, from economies of large-scale production, from ownership of patents, or from government restrictions that prohibit competition. The causes, effects, and control of monopoly are examined in detail in Chapters 9, 11, and 12.

Innovation Theory of Profit The innovation theory of profit postulates that (economic) profit is the reward for the introduction of a successful innovation. For example, Steven Jobs, the founder of the Apple Computer Company, became a millionaire in the course of a few years by introducing the Apple Computer in 1977 (see Case Study 1-5). Indeed, the U.S. patent system is designed to protect the profits of a successful innovator in order to encourage the flow of innovations. Inevitably, as other firms imitate the innovation, the profit of the innovator is reduced and, eventually, eliminated. This is, in fact, what happened to the Apple Computer Company in the early 1980s.

Managerial Efficiency Theory of Profit This theory rests on the observation that if the average firm tends to earn only a normal return on its investment in the long run, firms that are more efficient than the average would earn above-normal returns and (economic) profits.

All of the above theories of profit have some element of truth, and each may be more applicable to some industries. Indeed, profits often arise from a combination of factors, including differential risk, market disequilibrium, monopoly power, innovation, and above-average managerial efficiency. This was, for example, the case of the Apple Computer Company when it was established.

Function of Profit

Profit serves a very crucial function in a free-enterprise economy, such as our own. High profits are the signal that consumers want more of the output of the industry. High profits provide the incentive for firms to expand output and for more firms to enter the industry in the long run. For a firm of above-average efficiency, profits represent the reward for greater efficiency. On the other hand, lower profits or losses are the signal that consumers want less of the commodity and/or that production methods are not efficient. Thus, profits provide the incentive for firms to increase their efficiency and/or produce less of the commodity, and for some firms to leave the industry for more profitable ones. Profits, therefore, provide the crucial signals for the reallocation of society's resources to reflect changes in consumers' tastes and demand over time.

To be sure, the profit system is not perfect, and governments in free-enterprise economies often step in to modify the operation of the profit system to make it more nearly consistent with broad societal goals. For example, governments invariably regulate the prices charged for electricity by public utility companies to provide shareholders with only a normal return on their investment. Governments also pass minimum wage legislation and pollution emission controls to internalize to polluting firms the social cost of the pollution they create. While not perfect, the profit system is the most efficient form of resource allocation available. In societies such as the former Soviet Union and the People's Republic of China, where profits were not allowed, a committee of the party performed this function in a much less efficient manner.

Case Study 1-5

Profits in the Personal Computer Industry

In 1976, Steven Jobs, then 20 years old, dropped out of college and together with a friend developed a prototype desktop computer. With financing from an independent investor, the Apple Computer Company was born, which revolutionized the computer industry. Sales of Apple Computers jumped from $3 million in 1977 to over $1.9 billion in 1986, with profits of over $150 million. The immense success of Apple was not lost on potential competitors, and by 1984 more than 75 companies had jumped into the market. Even IBM, which had originally chosen not to enter the market, soon put all its weight and muscle behind the development of its own version of the personal computer—the IBM PC. Because of increased competition, however, many of the early entrants had dropped out by 1986 and profits fell sharply. For example, profit margins for the 11 largest U.S. computer companies averaged 11.5 percent from 1980 to 1985 but only 6.5 percent from 1986 to 1990. Since 1991, PC makers have been engaged in a brutal price war in which PC prices fell by as much as 20 to 40 percent per year, and this cut profit margins even further.

This is a classic example of the source, function, and importance of profits in our economy. While Jobs is not doing as well today as he did in the early 1980s (he actually was ousted from the company in 1985 after a power struggle with the company's president, John Scully, and he unsuccessfully tried a comeback with his NeXT computer), he is still a multimillionaire. His huge rewards resulted from correctly anticipating, promoting, and satisfying an important type of market demand. Competitors, attracted by the huge early profits, were quick to follow, thereby causing profits in the industry to fall sharply. In the process, however, more and more of society's resources were attracted to the computer industry, which supplied consumers with rapidly improving personal computers at sharply declining prices.

Source: "Steve Job's Vision So On Target At Apple, Now Is Falling Short," *The Wall Street Journal,* May 25, 1993, p. A1; "Echoing Compaq, IBM Sets Sizeable Price Cuts," *The New York Times,* August 25, 1994, p. D3; and "Apple's Choice: Preserve Profits or Cut Prices," *The Wall Street Journal,* February 22, 1995, p. B1.

1-4 THE INTERNATIONAL FRAMEWORK OF MANAGERIAL ECONOMICS

Many of the commodities we consume today are imported, and American firms purchase many inputs abroad and sell an increasing share of their products overseas. Even more important, domestic firms face increasing competition from foreign firms in the U.S. market and around the world. The international flow of capital, technology, and skilled labor has also reached unprecedented dimensions. In short, there is a rapid movement in the world today toward the internationalization of production and consumption. Thus, it is essential to introduce an international dimension in the study of managerial economics to reflect these present-world realities.

Specifically, as consumers, we purchase Japanese Toyotas and German Mercedes, Italian handbags and French perfumes, Hong Kong clothes and Taiwanese hand calculators, English Scotch and Swiss chocolates, Canadian fish and Mexican tomatoes, Costa Rican bananas and Brazilian coffee. Often, we are not even aware that the products we consume, or parts of them, are in fact made abroad. For example, imported cloth is used in American-made suits, many American brand-name shoes are entirely manufactured abroad, and a great deal of the orange juice we drink is imported. American multinational corporations produce and import many parts and components from abroad and export an increasing share of their output. For example, most of the parts and components of the IBM PC are in fact manufactured abroad and more than one-third of IBM revenues and profits are generated abroad. The strongest competition and challenge faced by Boeing in commercial aircraft production is not from American McDonnel-Douglas but from European Airbus Industrie. General Motors, Ford, and Chrysler face increasing competition from Toyota, Nissan, and Honda. United States steel companies almost collapsed during the 1980s as a result of increasing foreign competition and rising steel imports and survived only after merging with foreign steel producers, mostly Japanese and French. Case Study 1-6 gives a sample of global corporations and the proportion of their sales outside the home country.

In view of such an **internationalization of economic activity,** it would be entirely unrealistic to study managerial economics in an international vacuum, as if U.S. firms did not in fact face serious and increasing competition from foreign firms. This requires the development of a new type of global executive (see Case Study 1-7). In fact, the business leader of the future will require many new skills that are not easy to acquire (see Case Study 1-8). This text will explicitly introduce and integrate this essential international dimension into the study of managerial decision making and will examine the new skills required of the future business leader. All the topics examined in traditional managerial economics are covered, but the focus is broadened to reflect the globalization of most economic activities and the management revolution taking place in the world today.

Case Study 1-6

The Rise of the Global Corporation

One of the most significant business and economic trends of the late twentieth century is the rise of global or "stateless" corporations. These are companies that have research and production facilities in many countries, are run by an international team of managers, and sell their products, finance their operation, and are owned by stockholders throughout the world. The trend toward global corporations is unmistakable and is accelerating. Going global has become an essential competitive strategy. Global corporations maintain a balance between functioning as a global organism while customizing products to local tastes. Both geographic and product managers report to top managers at the companies' headquarters, who reconcile differences. Companies that were entirely domestic and merely exported some of their output as late as a decade ago are now finding that in order to remain competitive, they have to become global players. The necessity to be insiders in most major world markets rather than mere exporters is rapidly growing. Even smaller companies are often finding it necessary to form joint ventures with foreign companies in order to expand abroad and remain competitive at home. Today a large number of corporations with headquarters in the United States, Europe, and Japan sell more of their products and earn more profits abroad than in the country where the corporation headquarters are located. Table 1-1 shows a sample of such corporations.

Table 1-1
Global Corporations

Company	Home Country	Total 1989 Sales (billions)	Sales Outside Home Country (%)	Assets Outside Home Country (%)	Shares Held Outside Home Country (%)
Nestlé	Switzerland	$39.9	98.0	95.0	Few
Phillips	Netherlands	30.0	94.0	85.0	46.0
Electrolux	Sweden	13.8	83.0	80.0	20.0
Volvo	Sweden	14.8	80.0	30.0	10.0
ICI	Britain	22.1	78.0	50.0	16.0
Michelin	France	9.4	78.0	NA	0.0
Canon	Japan	9.4	69.0	32.0	14.0
Sony	Japan	16.3	66.0	NA	13.6
Bayer	Germany	25.8	65.4	NA	48.0
Gillette	United States	3.8	65.0	63.0	10.0
Colgate	United States	5.0	64.0	47.0	10.0
Honda	Japan	26.4	63.0	35.7	6.9
Daimler Benz	Germany	45.5	61.0	NA	25.0
IBM	United States	62.7	59.0	NA	NA
Coca-Cola	United States	9.0	54.0	45.0	0.0
Digital	United States	12.7	54.0	44.0	NA
Dow Chemical	United States	17.6	54.0	45.0	5.0
Saint-Gobain	France	11.6	54.0	50.0	13.0
Xerox	United States	12.4	54.0	51.8	0.0
Caterpillar	United States	11.1	53.0	NA	NA
Hewlett-Packard	United States	11.9	53.0	38.6	8.0

Source: "The Stateless Corporation," *Business Week,* May 14, 1990, pp. 98–105.

Case Study 1-7

Training Global Executives

A Harvard University survey of 929 senior executives who work for more than 500 different companies in 30 countries ranked IBM the world's best company in developing global executives, ahead of the Royal Dutch/Shell Group (headquartered in the Netherlands/United Kingdom) in second place, Unilever (the Netherlands/United Kingdom) in third place, Procter & Gamble (United States) in fourth place, and BBC Brown Boveri (Switzerland) in fifth place. IBM attributed its number 1 ranking in the survey to the personal involvement of its chairman in top managers' career development and the company's heavy reliance on foreign nationals for overseas posts. Developing global executives is becoming increasingly important in our rapidly globalizing world. More than half of IBM's income and more than two-thirds of Colgate's income are now generated outside the United States. It is not surprising, therefore, to find that 94 percent of the executives surveyed said that developing global executives was vitally important to their business and that 69 percent said that their company was formulating strategies for global career development.

Most large multinational corporations in the United States and abroad are also providing global career training much sooner in their managers' careers. For example, Procter & Gamble established the P&G College in 1992 to train midlevel managers in global issues. Also in 1992, General Motors set up a program to send 30 U.S. middle managers abroad for three months in order to provide them global marketing experience. In 1990, the Travel Related Services unit of the American Express Co. inaugurated a global-management exchange program under which junior managers with at least two years' experience are sent overseas for 18 months. In 1987, Colgate established one of the most elaborate global marketing-management programs lasting 24 months, after which the trainees become associate product managers in the United States or abroad. The typical participant in Colgate's program holds an M.B.A. degree, speaks a foreign language, has already lived abroad, and has both strong computer skills and some prior business experience. This program has become such a powerful recruiting tool that more than 15,000 people apply for the 15 slots each year.

Source: R. Ely and J. McCormick, *The New International Executive: Business Leadership for the 21st Century* (Amrop International: Cleveland, December 1993); and "Younger Managers Learn Global Skills," *The Wall Street Journal,* March 31, 1993, p. B1.

Case Study 1-8

The Business Leader of the Future

Besides the traditional hard skills of accounting, marketing, and finance, the business executive of the future will be a leader and a visionary rather than merely a manager, he will have a global outlook and be knowledgeable of information systems and technology, he will capitalize on diversity and be a master of teamwork, he will be creative and show initiative, he will be able to discern patterns and opportunities in apparent chaos and have the ability to synthesize information rather than just analyze it, and, above all, he will be strong on interpersonal skills and be able to communicate effectively. In short, being smart and well trained in traditional business areas will no longer be enough for the business leader of the twenty-first century.

Specifically, the ideal business leader of the future must be cross functional, or have the ability to combine disparate skills to solve problems. She must be a visionary and a leader; that is, she must combine hard work and a deep understanding of the business in which she is in with the ability to inspire others to also work hard to make the vision a reality. She must work effectively on teams, be accepted by others as the person with the best sense of the challenge confronting the group, and be able to break problems into manageable, status-free tasks that others are willing to focus on. She must have a deep understanding of global issues and the ethical aspects of her business decisions. For example, is it OK to promote smoking in developing countries now that we know how harmful it is to health and at a time when it is declining in the United States? She must be familiar with and be able to use information technology and be comfortable with technology in general. She does not have to be a scientist, but she must understand in detail how the technology incorporated in the product or service that the firm sells works and avoid calling the experts every time she has to make a decision. She must have some experience with excellence—in whatever field—so as to recognize it and encourage it in others when she sees it.

Sounds impossible? Maybe it is, but those who come closer to this ideal will rise to the pinnacles of business leadership in the future. Having an M.B.A. from a good school is important, but in today's world no one is automatically impressed. The business leader of the future must sell herself and above all must perform. Today's corporations have enormous expectations from its newly minted M.B.A.s, often expecting them to have talents and abilities that few chief executives possess. Most of the 700 or so business schools, from Harvard to the most modest, understand this and are striving to reengineer the training of M.B.A.s to reflect the qualifications that the future business leader must possess for the new, competitive, dynamic world of the twenty-first century. The difficulty is that many of the new required skills are hard to measure and teach in the classroom, and that is why many business schools are taking in students who already have some business and real-world experience.

Source: "Reengineering the MBA," *Fortune,* January 24, 1994, pp. 38–47; and "Harvard B-School," *Business Week,* July 19, 1993, pp. 58–65.

SUMMARY

1. "Managerial economics" refers to the application of economic theory (microeconomics and macroeconomics) and the tools of analysis of decision science (mathematical economics and econometrics) to examine how an organization can achieve its aims or objectives most efficiently. The functional areas of business administration studies (accounting, finance, marketing, personnel, and production) provide the environmental background for managerial decision making.

2. Firms exist because the economies that they generate in production and distribution confer great benefits to entrepreneurs, workers, and other resource owners. The theory of the firm postulates that the primary goal or objective of the firm is to maximize wealth or the value of the firm. This is given by the present value of the expected future profits of the firm. Since the firm usually faces many resource, legal, and other constraints, we speak of "constrained optimization." Alternative theories of the firm postulate other objectives for the firm, but profit or value maximization predicts the behavior of the firm more accurately than does any of its alternatives.

3. "Business profit" refers to the revenue of the firm minus its explicit costs. The latter are the actual out-of-pocket expenditures of the firm. Economic profit equals the revenue of the firm minus its explicit and implicit costs. The latter refer to the value of the inputs owned and used by the firm in its own production processes. Economic profit can result from one or a combination of the following: risk bearing, frictional disturbances, monopoly power, the

introduction of innovations, or managerial efficiency. Profits provide the signal for the efficient allocation of society's resources.

4. Many of the commodities we consume today are imported, and American firms purchase many inputs abroad, sell an increasing share of their output to other nations, and face increasing competition from foreign firms operating in the United States. Furthermore, the international flow of capital, technology, and skilled labor has also reached unprecedented dimensions. In view of such internationalization of economic activity in the world today, it is essential to introduce an international dimension into the study of managerial economics.

DISCUSSION QUESTIONS

1. What is the relationship between the field of managerial economics and (*a*) microeconomics and macroeconomics? (*b*) Mathematical economics and econometrics? (*c*) The fields of accounting, finance, marketing, personnel, and production?
2. Managerial economics is often said to help the business student integrate the knowledge gained in other courses. How is this integration accomplished?
3. What is the methodology of science in general and of managerial economics in particular?
4. What might be the objective of a museum?
5. Why do firms exist? Who benefits from their existence?
6. How does the theory of the firm differ from short-term profit maximization? Why is the former superior to the latter?
7. How does the theory of the firm provide an integrated framework for the analysis of managerial decision making across the functional areas of business?
8. What effect would each of the following have on the value of the firm? (*a*) A new advertising campaign increases the sales of the firm substantially. (*b*) A new competitor enters the market. (*c*) The production department achieves a technological breakthrough which reduces production costs. (*d*) The firm is required to install pollution-control equipment. (*e*) The work force votes to unionize. (*f*) The rate of interest rises. (*g*) The rate of inflation changes.
9. How is the concept of a normal return on investment related to the distinction between business and economic profit?
10. What factors should be considered in determining whether profit levels are excessive in a particular industry?
11. Why does the government regulate telephone and electric power companies if the profit motive serves such an important function in the operation of a free-enterprise system?
12. Why is it crucial to introduce an international dimension into managerial economics?

PROBLEMS

The symbol indicates problems that can be solved using the Analytical Software Diskette, provided free to adopters of the text.

1. Find the present value of $100 due in one year if the discount rate is 5 percent, 8 percent, 10 percent, 15 percent, 20 percent, and 25 percent.

2. Find the present value of $100 due in *two* years if the discount rate is 5 percent, 8 percent, 10 percent, 15 percent, 20 percent, and 25 percent.

*3. The owner of a firm expects to make a profit of $100 for each of the next two years and to be able to sell the firm at the end of the second year for $800. The owner of the firm believes that the appropriate discount rate for the firm is 15 percent. Calculate the value of the firm.

4. A firm is contemplating an advertising campaign that promises to yield $120 one year from now for $100 spent now. Explain why the firm should or should not undertake the advertising campaign.

*5. Determine which of two investment projects a manager should choose if the discount rate of the firm is 10 percent. The first project promises a profit of $100,000 in each of the next four years, while the second project promises a profit of $75,000 in each of the next six years.

6. Determine which of the two investment projects of Problem 5 the manager should choose if the discount rate of the firm is 20 percent.

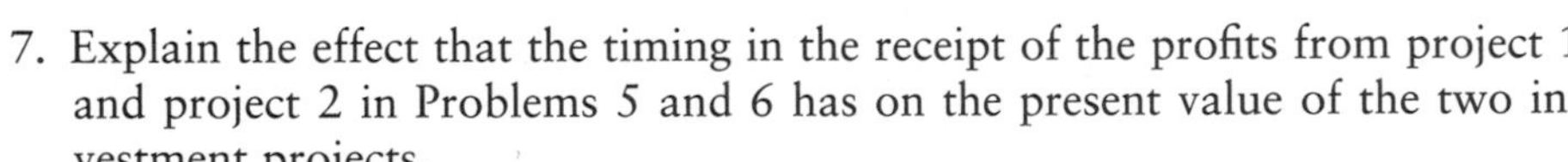

7. Explain the effect that the timing in the receipt of the profits from project 1 and project 2 in Problems 5 and 6 has on the present value of the two investment projects.

*8. The cost of attending a private college for one year is $6,000 for tuition, $2,000 for the room, $1,500 for meals, and $500 for books and supplies. The student could also have earned $15,000 by getting a job instead of going to college and 10 percent interest on expenses he or she incurs at the beginning of the year. Calculate the explicit, implicit, and the total economic costs of attending college.

9. A woman managing a duplicating (photocopying) establishment for $25,000 per year decides to open her own duplicating place. Her revenue during the first year of operation is $120,000, and her expenses are as follows:

Salaries to hired help	$45,000
Supplies	15,000
Rent	10,000
Utilities	1,000
Interest on bank loan	10,000

Calculate (*a*) the explicit costs, (*b*) the implicit costs, (*c*) the business profit, (*d*) the economic profit, and (*e*) the normal return on investment in this business.

10. According to Milton Friedman, "Business has only one social responsibility—to make profits (as long as it stays within the legal and moral rules of the game established by society). Few trends could so thoroughly undermine the very foundations of our society as the acceptance by corporate officials of a social responsibility other than to make as much money for their stockholders as possible." Explain why you agree or disagree with such a statement.
11. Apply the decision-making model developed in this chapter to your decision to attend college.
12. **Integrating Problem**
    Samantha Jones has a job as a pharmacist earning \$30,000 per year, and she is deciding whether to take another job as the manager of another pharmacy for \$40,000 per year or to purchase a pharmacy that generates a revenue of \$200,000 per year. To purchase the pharmacy, Samantha would have to use her \$20,000 savings and borrow another \$80,000 at an interest rate of 10 percent per year. The pharmacy that Samantha is contemplating purchasing has additional expenses of \$80,000 for supplies, \$40,000 for hired help, \$10,000 for rent, and \$5,000 for utilities. Assume that income and business taxes are zero and that the repayment of the principal of the loan does not start before three years. (*a*) What would be the business and economic profit if Samantha purchased the pharmacy? Should Samantha purchase the pharmacy? (*b*) Suppose that Samantha expects that another pharmacy will open nearby at the end of three years and that this will drive the economic profit of the pharmacy to zero. What would the revenue of the pharmacy be in three years? (*c*) What theory of profit would account for profits being earned by the pharmacy during the first three years of the operation? (*d*) Suppose that Samantha expects to sell the pharmacy at the end of three years for \$50,000 less than the price she paid for it and that she requires a 15 percent return on her investment. Should she still purchase the pharmacy?

APPENDIX

THE BASICS OF DEMAND, SUPPLY, AND EQUILIBRIUM

In this appendix, we present an overview of the functioning of markets. We begin by reviewing the concepts of market demand and market supply curves and then show how the equilibrium price is determined at their intersection. Afterward, we examine the effect on the equilibrium price resulting from a change in demand and/or supply. This appendix can be skipped by students who remember all of this from their principles of economics course.

The Demand Side of the Market

Every market has a demand side and a supply side. The demand side can be represented by a *market demand curve,* which shows the amount of the commodity buyers would like to purchase at different prices. For example, the market demand curve for aluminum in Figure 1-2 shows that 4 million pounds of aluminum would be demanded annually at the price of \$1.50 per pound (point *A*), 6 million pounds would be demanded at the price of \$1.00 per pound (point *E*), and 8 million pounds would be demanded at the price of \$0.50 per pound (point *B*). Note that more aluminum would be demanded annually at lower prices; that is, the demand curve for aluminum slopes downward to the right. This is true for practically all commodities and is referred to as the *law of demand.* Demand curves are drawn on the assumption that buyers' tastes, buyers' incomes, the number of consumers in the market, and the price of related commodities (substitutes and complements) are unchanged. Changes in any of these factors will cause a demand curve to shift. For example, if consumers' tastes for aluminum products or consumers' incomes increase, the entire demand curve for aluminum shifts to the right, indicating that buyers will purchase more aluminum at each price annually. More will be said on market demand in Chapter 3.

The Supply Side of the Market

The supply side of a market can be represented by the *market supply curve.* This shows the amount of a commodity that sellers would offer for sale at various prices. For example, the market supply curve for aluminum in Figure 1-3 shows that 2 million pounds of aluminum would be offered for sale annually at the price of \$0.50 per pound (point *C*), 6 million pounds would be offered at the price of

Figure 1-2
The Market Demand Curve for Aluminum

The market demand curve for aluminum shows that at lower aluminum prices, buyers would purchase greater quantities of aluminum.

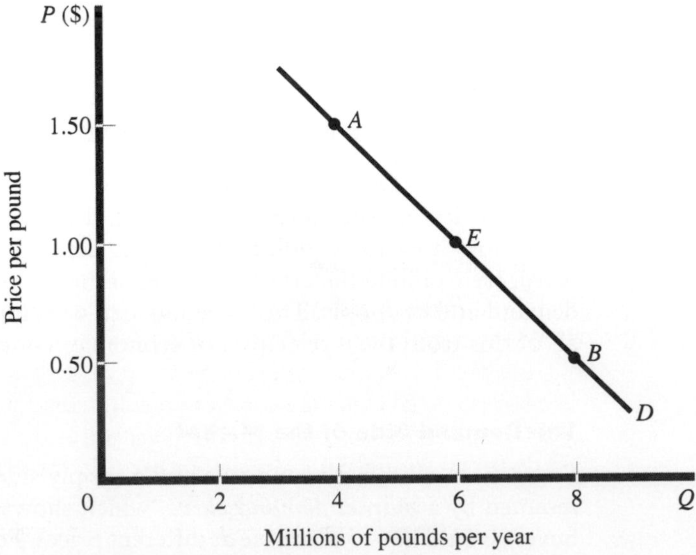

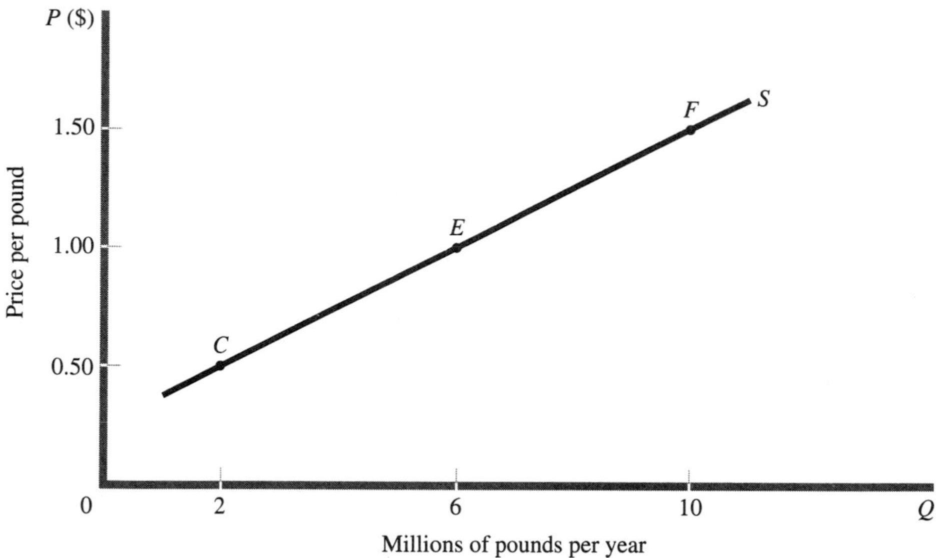

Figure 1-3
The Market Supply Curve for Aluminum

The market supply curve for aluminum shows that at higher aluminum prices, sellers would sell greater quantities of aluminum.

$1.00 per pound (point *E*), and 10 million pounds at the price of $1.50 (point *F*). Note that a higher aluminum price will induce sellers to sell more (i.e., the supply curve of aluminum slopes upward to the right). This is usually true for most products. Supply curves are drawn on the assumption of constant technology and input or resource (labor, capital, and land) prices. An improvement in technology and/or a reduction in input prices would make it possible to produce a commodity, such as aluminum, at a lower cost and cause the entire supply curve of aluminum to shift to the right, indicating that sellers would sell more aluminum annually at each price. On the other hand, an increase in resource prices would cause the supply curve to shift to the left. More will be said on production, costs, and supply in Chapters 6–9.

The Equilibrium Price

The *equilibrium price* of a commodity is determined at the intersection of the market demand curve and the market supply curve of the commodity. For example, in Figure 1-4, the equilibrium price of aluminum is $1.00 per pound and is given at point *E* where the market demand curve for aluminum (from Figure 1-2) and the market supply curve (from Figure 1-3) intersect. At the price of $1.50, the quantity supplied of aluminum exceeds the quantity demanded, and the resulting *excess supply or surplus* (AF = 6 million pounds) induces sellers to lower their price to get rid of unwanted aluminum inventories. On the other hand, at

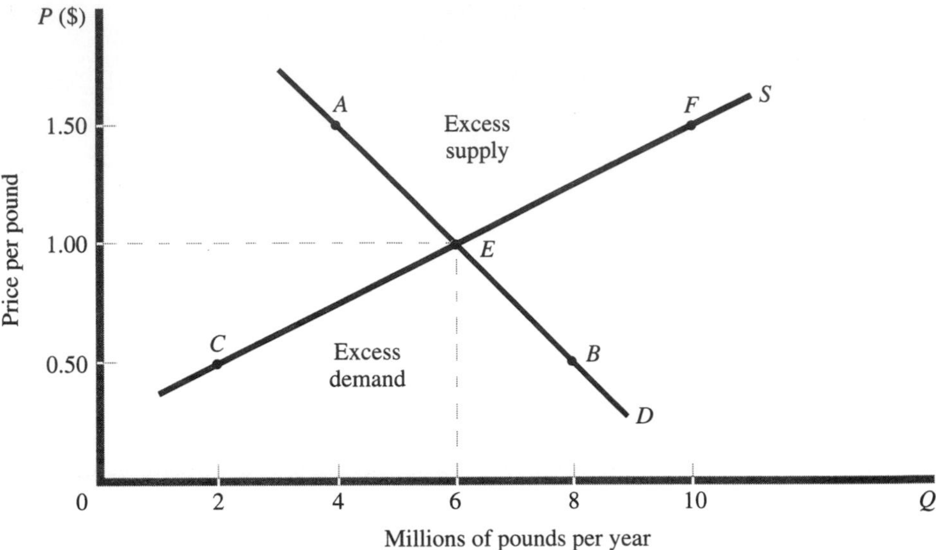

Figure 1-4
The Equilibrium Price of Aluminum
The equilibrium price of aluminum is $1.00 per pound and is given at the intersection of the market demand and the market supply curve of aluminum.

the price of $0.50 per pound, the quantity demanded of aluminum exceeds the quantity supplied, and the resulting *excess demand or shortage* ($CB = 6$ million pounds) allows sellers to increase price. Only at the price of $1.00 per pound does the quantity demanded of aluminum match the quantity supplied and there is no tendency for the price to change. Thus, the equilibrium price of aluminum is $1.00 per pound. This is the price that would persist in time as long as the demand and/or the supply curve of aluminum do not change (shift). At a particular point in time, the actual or observed market price may or may not be the equilibrium price. We know, however, that market forces always push the market price toward the equilibrium level. This may occur rapidly or slowly. Before a market price reaches a particular equilibrium level, the demand curve and/or the supply curve may shift defining a new equilibrium price.

Shift in the Demand Curve and Equilibrium

If the demand curve for a commodity increases or shifts to the right as a result, for example, of growth in the economy, the equilibrium price will rise. For example, Figure 1-5 shows that an increase in the demand curve for aluminum from D to D' results in an excess demand of aluminum of $EE' = 6$ million pounds per year at the original equilibrium price of $1.00 per pound. As a result, the equilibrium price of aluminum rises from $1.00 to $1.50 per pound and is determined at the intersection of D' and S at point F. The opposite occurs for a reduction in demand.

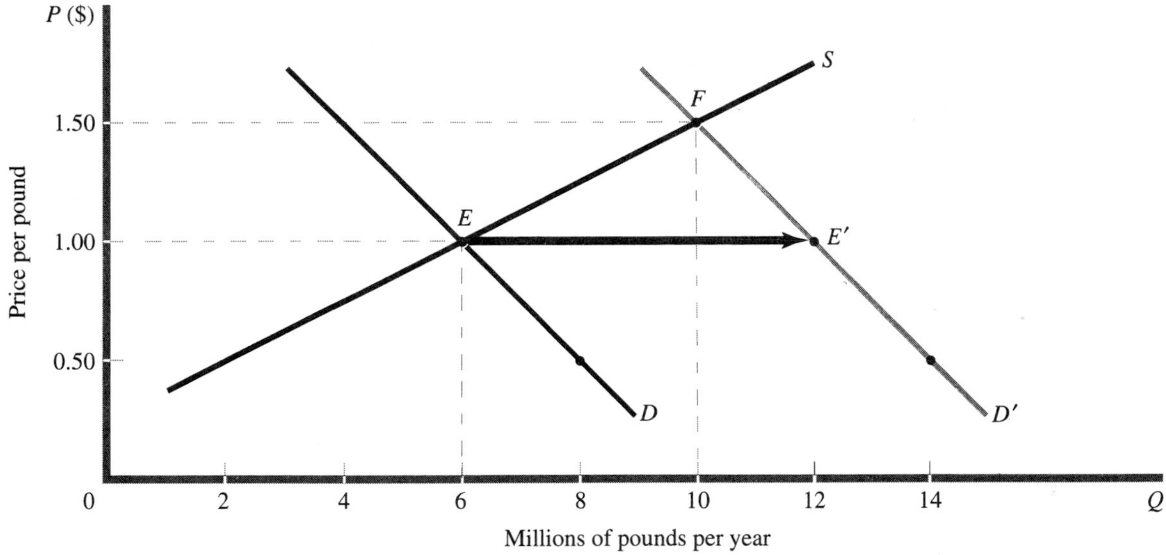

Figure 1-5
The Effect of a Rightward Shift of the Demand Curve for Aluminum
A rightward shift in the demand curve of aluminum results in an increase in the equilibrium price of aluminum.

Problem 1 Draw a figure similar to Figure 1-4, and show on it the change in the equilibrium price of aluminum resulting from a parallel leftward shift in the market demand curve for aluminum of 4 million pounds.

Shift in the Supply Curve and Equilibrium

If the supply curve of a commodity increases or shifts to the right as a result, for example, of an improvement in technology or a reduction in resource prices, the equilibrium price will fall. For example, Figure 1-6 shows that an increase in the supply curve of aluminum from S to S' results in an excess supply of aluminum of $EE' = 6$ million pounds per year at the original equilibrium price of \$1.00 per pound. As a result, the equilibrium price of aluminum falls from \$1.00 to \$0.50 per pound and is determined at the intersection of D and S' at point B. The opposite occurs for a reduction in supply. If both the demand and supply curves of aluminum shift to the right to D' and S', respectively, the equilibrium price of aluminum will remain at \$1.00 per pound, but the equilibrium quantity increases from 6 million pounds to 12 million pounds (you should be able to sketch this on Figure 1-6).

Problem 1 Draw a figure similar to Figure 1-4, and show on it the change in the equilibrium price of aluminum resulting from a parallel leftward shift in the market supply curve for aluminum of 3 million pounds.

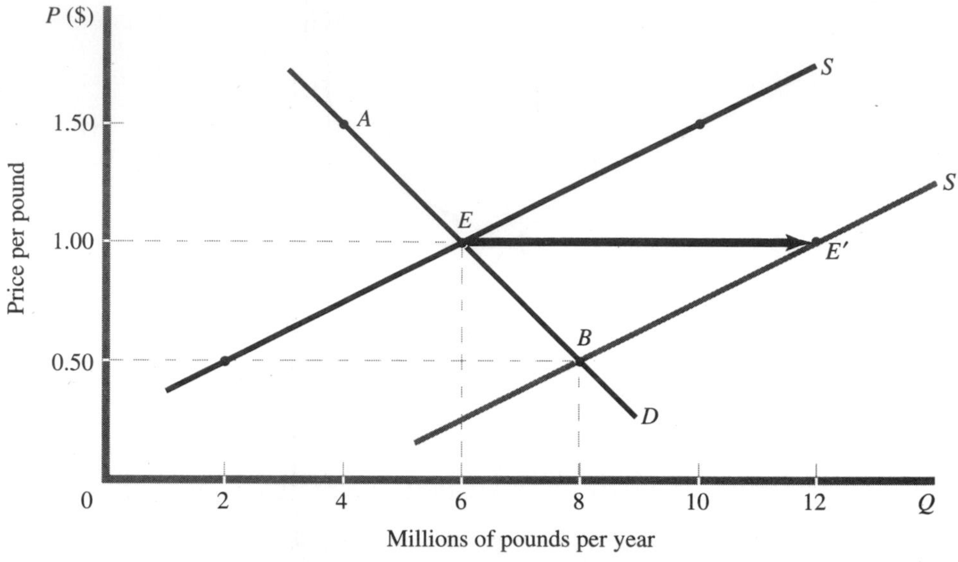

Figure 1-6
The Effect of a Rightward Shift of the Supply Curve for Aluminum
A rightward shift of the supply curve of aluminum results in a reduction in the equilibrium price of aluminum.

Problem 2 Draw a figure similar to Figure 1-4, and show on it the change in the equilibrium price of aluminum resulting from a shift in the market demand curve of aluminum from *D* to *D′* (as in Figure 1-5) and in the market supply curve of aluminum from *S* to *S′* (as in Figure 1-6).

Case Study 1-9
Changes in Demand and Supply and the Price of PCs

From 1986 to 1996, the demand for personal computers (PCs) increased sharply in the United States, but the supply increased much more. As a result, the price of PCs adjusted for inflation and quality changes fell sharply in the United States. This can be visualized with Figure 1-7, where *D* and *S* are the U.S. demand and supply curve of PCs, respectively, in 1986, and *D′* and *S′* are the U.S. demand and supply curve of PCs in 1996. *D* and *S* intersect at point *E* in Figure 1-7 and give the equilibrium price of P_E in the United States in 1986, while *D′* and *S′* intersect at point *E′* and give the much lower equilibrium price of P'_E in 1996. We can expect the trend toward more computing power at lower prices to continue and even accelerate in the future.

Source: "Computer Chaos," *U.S. News & World Report,* July 26, 1993, pp. 44–49; and "Wonder Chips," *Business Week,* July 4, 1994, pp. 86–92.

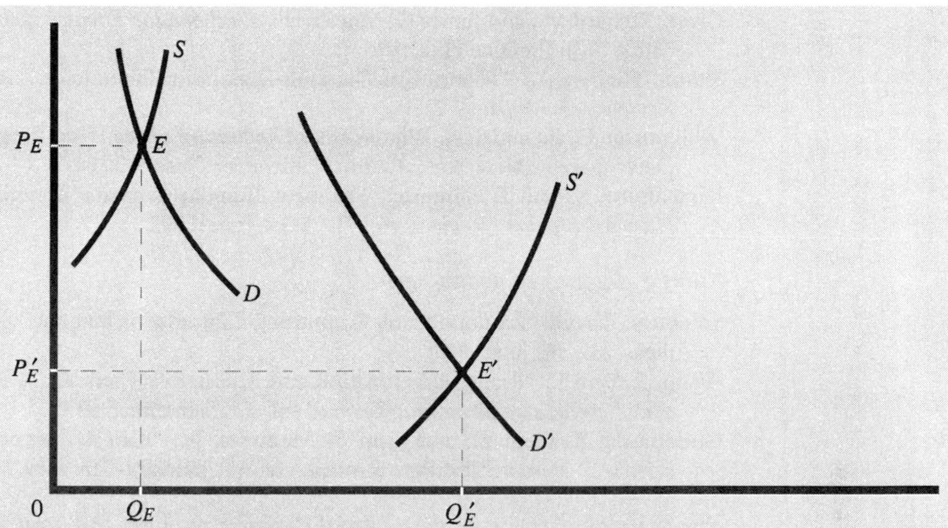

Figure 1-7
Shifts in Demand and Supply and the Price of PCs
With *D* and *S*, the equilibrium price of PCs in the United States is P_E in 1986. With *D′* and *S′*, the equilibrium price of PCs in the United States is P_E' in 1996.

SUPPLEMENTARY READINGS

A paperback in the Schaum's Outline Series in economics that presents a problem-solving approach to managerial economics and that can be used with this and other texts is:

Salvatore, Dominick: *Theory and Problems of Managerial Economics,* Schaum Outline Series (New York: McGraw-Hill, 1989).

For a general description of the scope of managerial economics and its relationship to other fields of study, see:

Anderson, K.: "The Purpose at the Heart of Management," *Harvard Business Review,* vol. 70, May–June 1992.

Beasley, Howard W.: "Can Managerial Economics Aid the Chief Executive Officer?" *Managerial and Decision Economics,* vol. 2, September 1981.

Baumol, William J.: "What Can Economic Theory Contribute to Managerial Economics?" *American Economic Review,* vol. 51, May 1961.

Bazerman, M.: *Judgment in Managerial Decision Making* (New York: Wiley, 1990).

A more extensive discussion of the theories of the firm is found in:

Baumol, William J.: *Business Behavior, Value and Growth* (New York: Macmillan, 1959).

Williamson, Oliver F.: "A Model of Rational Managerial Behavior," in R. M. Cyert and J.G. March, eds., *A Behavior Theory of the Firm* (Englewood Cliffs, N.J.: Prentice-Hall, 1963).

Cyert, Richard M., and **James G. March**, eds.: *A Behavior Theory of the Firm* (Englewood Cliffs, N.J.: Prentice-Hall, 1963).

Simon, Herbert A.: "Theories of Decision-Making in Economics," *American Economic Review,* vol. 49, June 1959.

Williamson, O. E., and **S. G. Winter**, eds.: *The Nature of the Firm: Origins, Evolution, and Development* (New York: Oxford University Press, 1991).

Hirschhorn, L., and **T. Gilmore**: "The New Boundaries of the 'Boundaryless' Company," *Harvard Business Review,* vol. 70, May–June 1992.

On the theories of profit, see:

Solomon, David: "Economic and Accounting Concepts of Income," *The Accounting Review,* vol. 36, July 1961.

Wong, Robert E.: "Profit Maximization and Alternative Theories: A Dynamic Reconciliation," *American Economic Review,* vol. 65, September 1975.

Goodpaster, Kenneth E., and **John B. Mathews, Jr.**: "Can a Corporation Have a Conscience?" *Harvard Business Review,* vol. 60, January–February 1982.

For the globalization of managerial decision making and qualification for the future business leader, see:

Salvatore, D.: *International Economics,* 5th ed. (Englewood Cliffs, N. J.: Prentice-Hall, 1995), Chap. 1.

Davidson, William H., and **José de la Torre**: *Managing the Global Corporation: Case Studies in Strategy and Management* (New York: McGraw-Hill, 1989).

Zalenik, A.: "Managers and Leaders: Are They Different?" *Harvard Business Review,* vol. 70, March–April 1992.

CHAPTER 2

Optimization Techniques and New Management Tools

KEY TERMS

Marginal cost
Marginal revenue
Marginal analysis
Derivative of *Y* with respect to *X* (*dY/dX*)
Differentiation
Second derivative
Partial derivative
Constrained optimization
Lagrangian multiplier method
Lagrangian function
Benchmarking
Total quality management (TQM)
Reengineering
Learning organization
Broadbanding
Networking

CHAPTER OUTLINE

In Chapter 1 we defined "managerial economics" as the application of economic theory and the tools of decision science to examine how an organization can achieve its aims and objectives most efficiently. In the case of a business firm, the objective is usually to maximize profits or the value of the firm or to minimize costs, subject to some constraints. Accordingly, in this chapter we present optimization techniques, or methods for maximizing or minimizing the objective function of a firm or other organization. These techniques are very important and will be used frequently in the rest of the text. In this chapter we also describe many of the new management tools that have been introduced in recent years and examine how they are revolutionizing the way firms are managed.

The first step in presenting optimization techniques is to examine ways to express economic relationships. This is done in Section 2-1. In Section 2-2, we examine the relationship between total, average, and marginal concepts and measures, such as revenue, product, cost, or profit. In Section 2-3, we then examine the process of optimization by a firm graphically. Since differential calculus is extremely important and useful in finding the optimal solution to complex problems, we review the concept of the derivative and the rules of differentiation in Section 2-4. We then apply the rules of differential calculus to find the optimal solution to unconstrained and constrained optimization problems (Sections 2-5, 2-6, and 2-7, respectively). Sections 2-4 to 2-7 can be omitted for courses in which calculus is not used. In the rest of the text, more advanced material utilizing calculus will be presented only in footnotes and appendixes.

Finally Section 2-8 discusses many of the new management tools that are revolutionizing the way firms are managed and examines their relationship to the traditional functional areas of managerial economics. At the end of the chapter, there is an extensive integrating real-world case study which illustrates, integrates, and shows the relationship among the various concepts presented in this chapter and in Chapter 1.

2-1 METHODS OF EXPRESSING ECONOMIC RELATIONSHIPS

Economic relationships can be expressed in the form of equations, tables, or graphs. When the relationship is simple, a table and/or graph may be sufficient. When the relationship is complex, however, expressing the relationship in equational form may be necessary. Expressing an economic relationship in equational form is also very useful because it allows us to use the powerful techniques of differential calculus in determining the optimal solution of the problem (i.e., the most efficient way for the firm or other organization to achieve its objectives or reach its goal).

For example, suppose that the relationship between the total revenue (TR) of a firm and the quantity (Q) of the good or service that the firm sells over a given period of time, say, one year, is given by

$$TR = 100Q - 10Q^2 \tag{2-1}$$

Table 2-1
The Total-Revenue Schedule of the Firm

Q	$100Q - 10Q^2$	TR
0	$100(0) - 10(0)^2$	\$ 0
1	$100(1) - 10(1)^2$	90
2	$100(2) - 10(2)^2$	160
3	$100(3) - 10(3)^2$	210
4	$100(4) - 10(4)^2$	240
5	$100(5) - 10(5)^2$	250
6	$100(6) - 10(6)^2$	240

By substituting into Equation 2-1 various hypothetical values for the quantity sold, we generate the total-revenue schedule of the firm, shown in Table 2-1.

Plotting the *TR* schedule of Table 2-1, we get the *TR* curve in Figure 2-1. Note that the *TR* curve in Figure 2-1 rises up to $Q = 5$ and declines thereafter. Thus, we see that the relationship between the total revenue of the firm and its sales volume can be expressed in equational, tabular, or graphical form.

Figure 2-1
The Total Revenue Curve of a Firm

The total-revenue curve shows the total revenue (*TR*) of the firm at each quantity sold (*Q*). It is obtained by plotting the total-revenue schedule of Table 2-1. Note that *TR* rises to $Q = 5$ and declines thereafter.

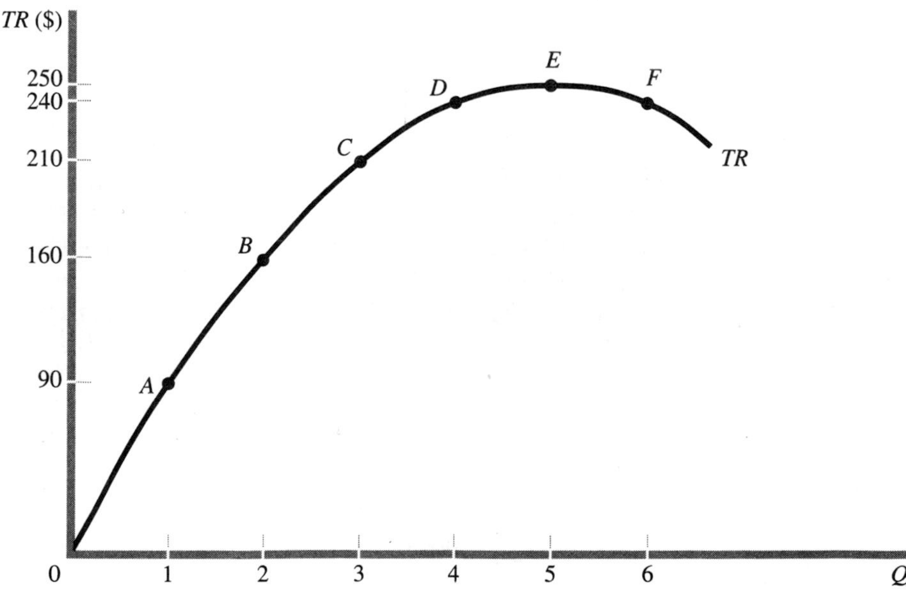

Table 2-2
Total, Average, and Marginal Costs of a Firm

Q	*TC*	*AC*	*MC*
0	$ 20	—	—
1	140	$140	$120
2	160	80	20
3	180	60	20
4	240	60	60
5	480	96	240

2-2 TOTAL, AVERAGE, AND MARGINAL RELATIONSHIPS

The relationship between total, average, and marginal concepts and measures is crucial in optimization analysis. This relationship is basically the same whether we deal with revenue, product, cost, or profit. In what follows, we examine the relationship between total cost, average cost, and marginal cost. This, together with the revenue concepts examined in the previous section, will be utilized in the next section to show how a firm maximizes profits (a most important example of optimizing behavior on the part of the firm).[1] In the following section, we examine the relationship between total, average, and marginal cost, and then we show how average- and marginal-cost curves are derived geometrically from the total-cost curve.

Total, Average, and Marginal Cost

The first two columns of Table 2-2 present a hypothetical total-cost schedule of a firm, from which the average- and marginal-cost schedules are derived (columns 3 and 4 of the table). Note that the total cost (*TC*) of the firm is $20 when output (*Q*) is zero and rises as output increases.[2] Average cost (*AC*) equals total cost divided by output. That is, $AC = TC/Q$. Thus, at $Q = 1$, $AC = TC/1 = \$140/1 = \$140$. At $Q = 2$, $AC = TC/2 = \$160/2 = \$80$, and so on (see the third column of Table 2-2). Note that *AC* first falls and then rises. Marginal cost (*MC*), on the other hand, equals the change in total cost per unit change in output. That is, $MC = \Delta TC/\Delta Q$, where the symbol Δ (delta) refers to "a change in." Since output increases by 1 unit at a time in column 1 of Table 2-2, the *MC* (in the last

[1]The relationship between total, average, and marginal revenue, product, and profit will be examined in Problems 1 to 3 at the end of the chapter, with the answer to Problem 3 provided at the end of the text for feedback.

[2]The reason that the total cost is positive when output is zero is that the firm incurs some costs in the short run, such as rent on buildings during the life of the contract, which are given and fixed whether the firm produces or not. The theory of cost will be examined in detail in Chapter 7. At this point, we are interested only in the relationship between total, average, and marginal concepts and measures in general, as exemplified by the relationship between total, average, and marginal costs.

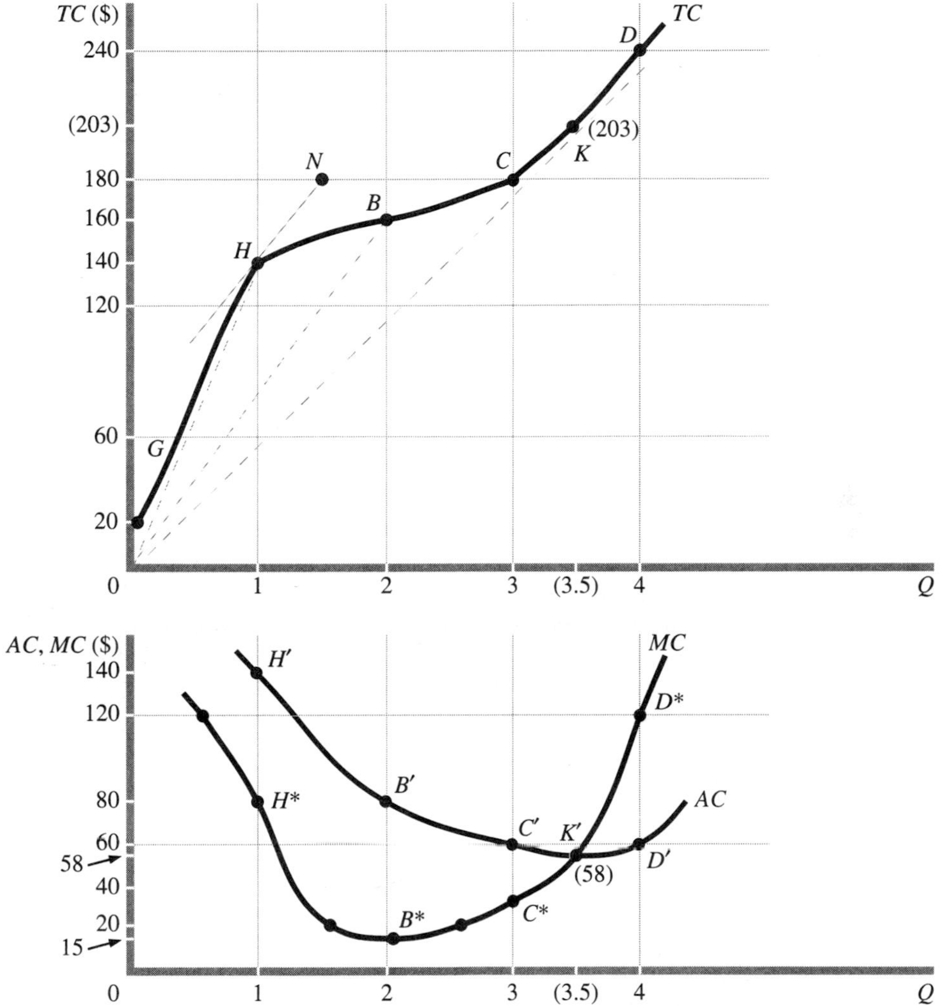

Figure 2-2
Total-, Average-, and Marginal-Cost Curves and Their Relationship

AC is given by the slope of a ray from the origin to the *TC* curve. Thus, *AC* falls to point *K* (Q = 3.5) and rises thereafter. *MC* is given by the slope of the *TC* curve. Thus, *MC* falls to point *B* (the point of inflection at $Q = 2$) and then rises. When *MC* is less than *AC*, *AC* falls; when *MC* is larger than *AC*, *AC* rises; $MC = AC$ at the lowest *AC*.

column of the table) is obtained by subtracting successive values of *TC* shown in the second column of the table. For example, *TC* increases from \$20 to \$140 when the firm produces the first unit of output. Thus, $MC = \$120$. For an increase in output from 1 to 2 units, *TC* increases from \$140 to \$160, so that $MC = \$20$, and so on. Note that, as for the case of the *AC*, *MC* also falls first and then rises.

Plotting the total-, average-, and marginal-cost schedules of Table 2-2 gives the corresponding cost curves shown in Figure 2-2. The shape of the *TC* curve (in the top panel) is explained in Chapter 7. Note that the *AC* curve (in the bottom panel) is U shaped. Since marginal cost is defined as the change in total cost per unit change in output, the *MC* values of Table 2-2 are plotted (as an approximation) halfway between successive levels of output in the bottom panel of Figure 2-2. Thus, the *MC* of \$120, which results from increasing output from 0*Q* to 1*Q* in Table 2-2, is plotted at 0.5*Q* in the bottom panel of Figure 2-2; the *MC* of \$20, which results from increasing output from 1*Q* to 2*Q*, is plotted at 1.5*Q*; and so on. Note that the *MC* curve is also U shaped but reaches the lowest point at a smaller level of output than the *AC* curve, and it intercepts (i.e., it goes through) the lowest point of the latter. This is always the case (for the reason explained below).

Geometric Derivation of the Average- and Marginal-Cost Curves

The *AC* and *MC* cost curves in the bottom panel of Figure 2-2 can be derived *geometrically* from the *TC* curve in the top panel. The *AC* corresponding to any point on the *TC* curve is given by the slope of a ray from the origin to the point on the *TC* curve. For example, the *AC* corresponding to point *H* on the *TC* curve in the top panel is given by the slope of ray 0*H*, or \$140/1 = \$140 (point *H*′ in the bottom panel). The *AC* corresponding to point *B* on the *TC* curve is given by the slope of ray 0*B*, or \$160/2 = \$80 (point *B*′ in the bottom panel). The *AC* for both points *C* and *D* on the *TC* curve is given by the slope of ray 0*CD*, or \$180/3 = \$240/4 = \$60 (points *C*′ and *D*′, respectively, in the bottom panel). These correspond to the *AC* values shown in Table 2-2. *AC* is minimum at point *K* on the *TC* curve and is given by the slope of ray 0*K*, or \$203/3.5 = \$58 (point *K*′ in the bottom panel). By joining points *H*′, *B*′, *C*′, *K*′, and *D*′ in the bottom panel, we generate the *AC* curve corresponding to the *TC* curve in the top panel. Note that the slope of a ray from the origin to the *TC* curve in the top panel falls to point *K* and then rises. Thus, the *AC* curve in the bottom panel falls to point *K*′ (at *Q* = 3.5) and then rises.

From the *TC* curve we can also derive geometrically the *MC* curve. The *MC* curve corresponding to any point on the *TC* curve is given by the slope of the tangent *HN* to the *TC* curve at that point. For example, the slope of the tangent to the *TC* at point *H* in the top panel, or *MC*, is \$80 [from (\$180 − \$140)/0.5] and is plotted as point *H** in the bottom panel. The slope of the tangent (not shown) to the *TC* curve at points *B*, *C*, *K*, and *D*, or *MC*, is \$15, \$40, \$58, and \$120, respectively, and is plotted as points *B**, *C**, *K*′, and *D** in the bottom panel. By joining points *H**, *B**, *C**, *K*′, and *D** in the bottom panel, we generate the *MC* curve corresponding to the *TC* curve in the top panel. Note that the slope of the *TC* curve in the top panel declines to point *B* (the inflection point) and rises thereafter. Thus, the *MC* curve in the bottom panel falls to point *B** (at *Q* = 2) and then rises. Note also that the slope of the *TC* curve, or *MC*, at point *K* is equal to the slope of the ray from the origin to point *K* on the *TC* curve, or *AC*. Since this is the lowest *AC*, *MC* = *AC* at the lowest point on the *AC* curve (see Figure 2-2).

The bottom panel of Figure 2-2 shows an important relationship between the *AC* and *MC* curves. That is, as long as the *MC* curve is below the *AC* curve, the *AC* curve falls, and when the *MC* curve is above the *AC* curve, the *AC* curve rises. When *AC* is neither falling nor rising (i.e., at the point where the *AC* is at its minimum), the *MC* curve intersects the *AC* curve from below, and $AC = MC$. This makes sense. For example, for a student to increase his or her cumulative average test score, he or she must receive a grade on the next (marginal) test that exceeds his or her average. With a lower grade on the next test, the student's average will fall. If the grade on the next test equals the previous average, the average will remain unchanged.

In this section we have dealt only with marginal cost. Marginal revenue and marginal profit are similarly defined (as the change in total revenue and total profit, respectively, per unit change in sales or output) and are equally important. In the next section, we will show how the concept of the margin is crucial in determining the optimal behavior of the firm.

Case Study 2-1

Total, Average, and Marginal Cost in the U.S. Steel Industry

The total-cost function of the U.S. steel industry in the 1930s was estimated to be

$$TC = 182 + 56Q \tag{2-2}$$

(with all decimals rounded to the nearest whole number), where *TC* is the total cost in millions of dollars, and *Q* is output in millions of tons. Substituting various hypothetical values for *Q* into Equation 2-2, we get the *TC* schedules shown in the third column of Table 2-3. $AC = TC/Q$ in the fourth column of the table, and $MC = \Delta TC/\Delta Q$ in the fifth column. The *TC*, *AC*, and *MC* schedules are then plotted in Figure 2-3. Note that the *TC* curve is linear, with fixed costs of \$182 million per year, and slope (*MC*) of \$56 million for each million tons of steel produced. Thus, the *AC* curve declines continuously, and the *MC* curve is horizontal. These curves are a simplified version of the average- and marginal-cost curves shown in Figure 2-2. More recently (1989),* the total-cost function for Springs Industries, a leading producer of textile and home furnishings in South Carolina, was estimated to be

$$TC = 10.65 + 0.94S \tag{2-2a}$$

where *S* is millions of dollars of sales. Thus, the total-cost curve of Springs is linear, with fixed costs of \$10.65 million, declining *AC*, and constant *MC* at 0.94 (i.e., \$940,000) per million dollars of additional sales (the slope of the *TC* curve). Thus, these curves look very much like those for steel in Figure 2-3 (the student should be able to sketch the curves for Springs on his or her own).

*Ronald P. Wilder, "Empirical Cost Analysis in Managerial Economics: A Short-Run Cost Estimation Exercise," November 1989. Mimeographed.

Table 2-3
Total-, Average-, and Marginal-Cost Schedules of the U.S. Steel Industry in the 1930s

Q (In Millions of Tons)	182 + 56*Q*	*TC* (In Millions of Dollars)	*AC* (In Millions of Dollars)	*MC* (In Millions of Dollars)
0	182 + 0	$182	—	—
1	182 + 56	238	$238	$56
2	182 + 112	294	147	56
3	182 + 168	350	117	56
4	182 + 224	406	102	56

Source: Based on T. Yntema, in Committee on the Judiciary, U.S. Senate, 85th Congress, *Administered Prices: Steel* (Washington, D.C.: Government Printing Office, 1940).

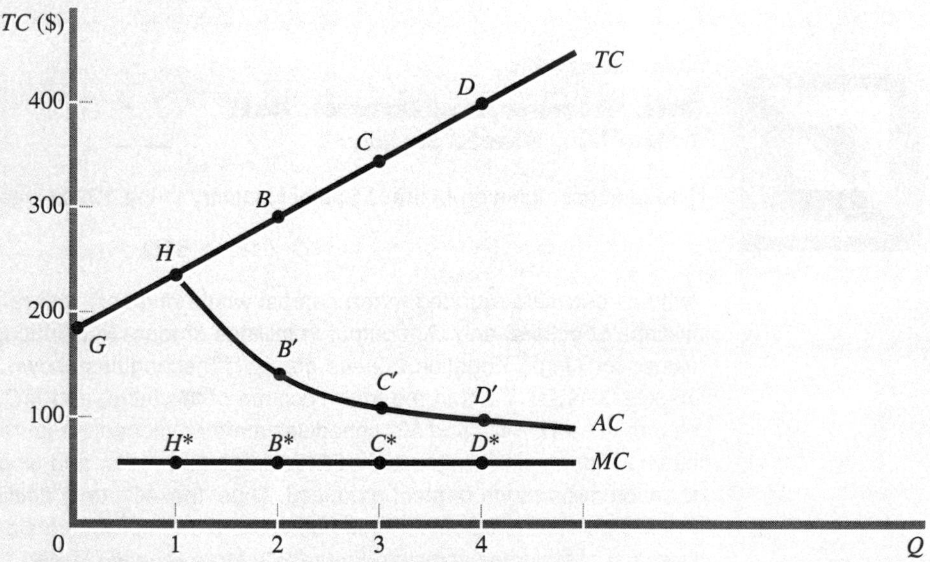

Figure 2-3
***TC, AC,* and *MC* Curves of the U.S. Steel Industry**
The total-cost curve of the U.S. steel industry in the 1930s was estimated to be linear, with fixed costs of $182 million per year. Thus, *AC* declines continuously and *MC* is constant at $56 million per additional million tons of steel produced (the slope of the *TC* curve).

2-3 OPTIMIZATION ANALYSIS

Optimization analysis can best be explained by examining the process by which a firm determines the output level at which it maximizes total profits. We will start by using the total-revenue and total-cost curves of the previous sections in order to set the stage for the subsequent marginal analysis, with which we are primarily concerned.

Profit Maximization by the Total-Revenue and Total-Cost Approach

In the top panel of Figure 2-4, the *TR* curve is that of Figure 2-1, and the *TC* curve is that of Figure 2-2. Total profit (π) is the difference between total revenue and total cost. That is, $\pi = TR - TC$. The top panel of Figure 2-4 shows that at $Q = 0$, $TR = 0$, but $TC = \$20$. Therefore, $\pi = 0 - \$20 = -\$20$ (point G'' on the π function in the bottom panel). This means that the firm incurs a loss of $20 at zero output. At $Q = 1$, $TR = \$90$ and $TC = \$140$. Therefore, $\pi = \$90 - \$140 = -\$50$ (the largest loss, given by point H'' in the bottom panel). At

Figure 2-4
Profit Maximization as an Example of Optimization
The firm maximizes total profit at $Q = 3$, where the positive difference between *TR* and *TC* is greatest, $MR = MC$, and the π function is at its highest point.

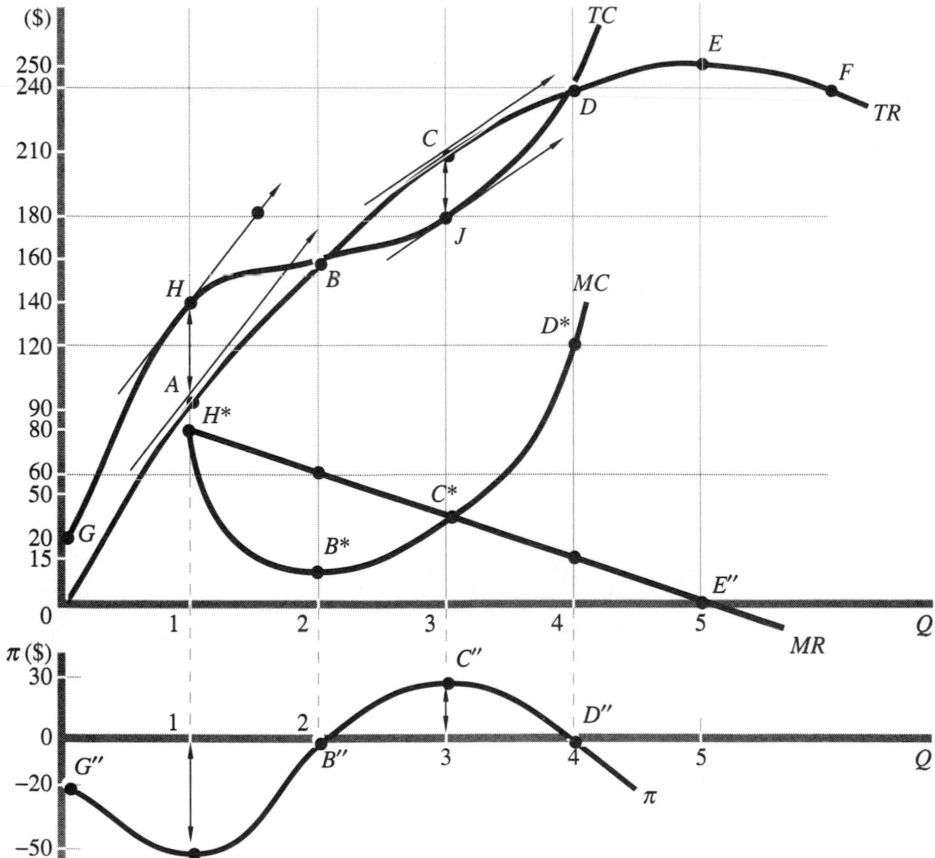

$Q = 2$, $TR = TC = \$160$. Therefore, $\pi = 0$ (point B'' in the bottom panel), and the firm breaks even. The same is true at $Q = 4$, at which $TR = TC = \$240$ and $\pi = 0$ (point D'' in the bottom panel). Between $Q = 2$ and $Q = 4$, TR exceeds TC, and the firm earns a profit. Total profit is greatest at $Q = 3$, at which the positive difference between TR and TC is greatest. At $Q = 3$, $\pi = \$30$ (point C'' in the bottom panel).

Optimization by Marginal Analysis

While the process by which the firm maximized total profit was determined above by looking at the total-revenue and total-cost curves, it is more useful to use marginal analysis. Indeed, marginal analysis is one of the most important concepts in managerial economics in general and in optimization analysis in particular. According to marginal analysis, the firm maximizes profits when marginal revenue equals marginal cost. **Marginal cost (*MC*)** was defined earlier as the change in total cost per unit change in output and is given by the slope of the *TC* curve. The slope of the *TC* curve in the top panel of Figure 2-4 falls up to point *B* (the point of inflection) and rises thereafter. Thus, the *MC* curve (also in the top panel of Figure 2-4) falls up to point B^* (at $Q = 2$) and then rises (as in Figure 2-2). **Marginal revenue (*MR*)** is similarly defined as the change in total revenue per unit change in output or sales and is given by the slope of the *TR* curve. For example, at point *A*, the slope of the *TR* curve or *MR* is \$80 (point H^* on the *MR* curve in the top panel of Figure 2-4). At point *B*, the slope of the *TR* curve or $MR = \$60$. At points *C* and *D* the slope of the *TR* curve, or *MR*, is \$40 and \$20, respectively. At point *E*, the *TR* curve is highest or has zero slope, so that $MR = 0$. Past point *E*, *TR* declines and *MR* is negative.

According to marginal analysis, as long as the slope of the *TR* curve or *MR* exceeds the slope of the *TC* curve or *MC*, it pays for the firm to expand output and sales. The firm would be adding more to its total revenue than to its total costs, and so its total profit would increase. In Figure 2-4, this is true between $Q = 1$ and $Q = 3$. On the other hand, between $Q = 3$ and $Q = 4$, the slope of the *TR* curve or *MR* is smaller than the slope of the *TC* curve or *MC*, so that the firm would be adding less to its total revenue than to its total cost, and total profits would be less. At $Q = 3$, the slope of the *TR* curve or *MR* equals the slope of the *TC* curve or *MC*, so that the *TR* and *TC* curves are parallel and the vertical distance between them (π) is greatest. At $Q = 3$, $MR = MC$ (point C^* in the top panel of Figure 2-4) and π is at a maximum (point C'' in the bottom panel). This is an extremely important concept and is of general applicability. That is, according to **marginal analysis,** as long as the marginal benefit of an activity (such as expanding output or sales) exceeds the marginal cost, it pays for the organization (firm) to increase the activity (expand output). The total net benefit (profit) is maximized when the marginal benefit (revenue) equals the marginal cost. Although the example discussed above involves profit maximization, marginal analysis can also be applied to decisions involving maximization of utility, cost minimization, and so on.

Two additional points must be noted with regard to Figure 2-4. The first is that the slope of the TR curve or MR equals the slope of the TC curve or MC (see point H^*) at $Q = 1$ also. However, at $Q = 1$, TC exceeds TR, and the firm incurs a loss. Indeed, at $Q = 1$, the loss is greatest (at \$50, see point H″ and the π curve in the bottom panel of Figure 2-4). Thus, for the firm to maximize its total profits, MR must not only be equal to MC but the MC curve must also intersect the MR curve from below, which occurs in Figure 2-4 only at $Q = 3$. This difference between the intersections at $Q = 3$ and $Q = 1$ distinguishes between the profit-maximizing and the loss-maximizing level of output and leads to our second point. That is, that the slope of the total profit (π) function in the bottom panel of Figure 2-4 is zero both at point H'' (where the total loss of the firm is greatest) and at point C'' (where the firm maximizes total profit). But the π function faces up (so that its slope increases, from being negative to the left of point H'', to zero at point H'', to positive to the right of point H'') where the losses are maximum, while it faces down (so that its slope declines) in the neighborhood of point C'', where the firm maximizes its total profit. As it will be seen in what follows, marginal analysis is conducted much more expediently with the use of differential calculus in the rest of the chapter.

Case Study 2-2
Optimal Pollution Control

To a stout environmentalist, the optimal level of pollution is probably zero. However, as long as pollution is a by-product of the production and consumption of commodities that we want, it does not make much economic sense to try to reduce pollution to zero. The optimal level of pollution is the one at which the marginal *benefit* of pollution (in the form of avoiding more costly methods of waste disposal) equals the marginal cost of pollution (in terms of higher cleaning bills, more respiratory illnesses, and so on).

This is shown in Figure 2-5, where the horizontal axis measures levels of pollution per year and the vertical axis measures the marginal cost and benefit of pollution to society. Note that with increasing levels of pollution, the marginal cost (MC) increases while the marginal benefit (MB) declines. In the absence of any pollution control, firms and individuals would dump wastes until the benefit of pollution equals zero (point A in the figure), and pollution would be excessive. From society's point of view, the optimal level of pollution is Q^* given by point E, where the MB curve intersects the MC curve, and $MB = MC$. While the optimal solution is clearcut, however, it is often difficult to estimate the MB and MC in the real world.

Source: M. L. Cropper and W. E. Oates, "Environmental Economics: A Survey," Journal of Economic Literature, June 1992; and "Economists Strive to Find Environment's Bottom Line," The New York Times, September 8, 1992, p. C1.

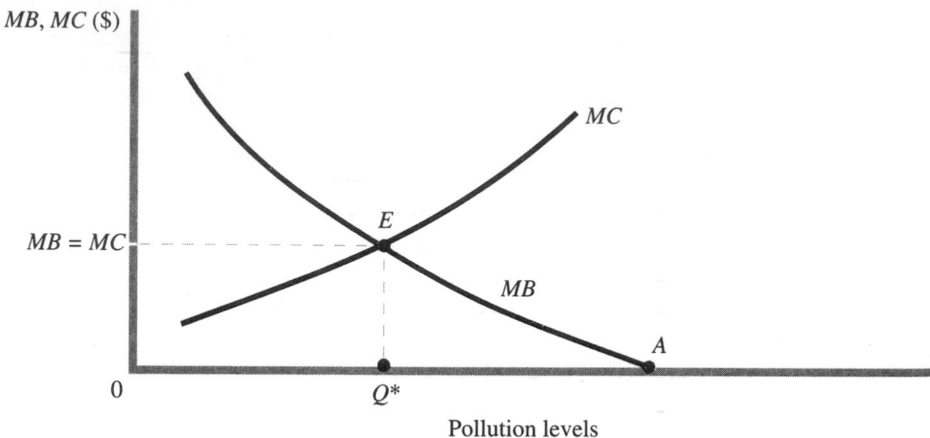

Figure 2-5
The Optimal Level of Pollution

The *MC* curve shows the rising *MC* or loss to society from increasing levels of pollution. The *MB* curve shows the declining marginal benefit to the polluter (and to society) by being able to freely dump increasing amounts of waste. Without controls, dumping will take place at point *A*, where $MB = 0$. The optimal level of dumping is Q^*, at which the *MB* and *MC* curves intersect and $MB = MC$.

2-4 DIFFERENTIAL CALCULUS: THE DERIVATIVE AND RULES OF DIFFERENTIATION*

Optimization analysis can be conducted much more efficiently and precisely with differential calculus, which relies on the concept of the derivative. In this section, we examine the concept of the derivative and present some simple rules of differentiation.

The Concept of the Derivative

The concept of the derivative is closely related to the concept of the margin examined earlier. These can be explained in terms of the *TR* curve of Figure 2-1, reproduced with some modifications in Figure 2-6.

In the previous section, we defined the marginal revenue as the change in the total revenue per unit change in output. For example, when output increases from 2 to 3 units, total revenue increases from \$160 to \$210. Thus,

$$MR = \frac{\Delta TR}{\Delta Q} = \frac{\$210 - \$160}{3 - 2} = \frac{\$50}{1} = \$50$$

*This section and Sections 2-5 to 2-7 can be skipped in managerial economics courses that do not use calculus. In the rest of the book, calculus will be used only in footnotes and appendixes.

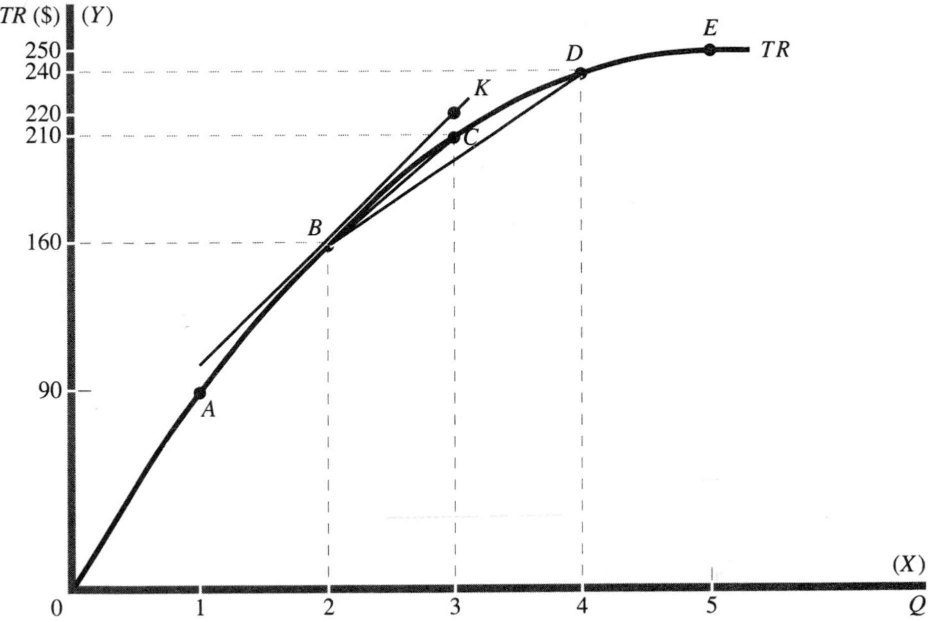

Figure 2-6
The Concept of the Derivative
The derivative of *TR* with respect to *Q* measures the limit of $\Delta TR/\Delta Q$, as ΔQ approaches zero. Geometrically, this is given by the slope of the *TR* curve, or *MR*, at the point at which we want to find the derivative. More generally, letting $TR = Y$ and $Q = X$, the derivative of *Y* with respect to *X*, $dY/dX = \lim_{\Delta X \to 0} \Delta Y/\Delta X$.

This is the slope of chord *BC* on the total-revenue curve. However, when the quantity is infinitesimally divisible (i.e., when ΔQ assumes values smaller than unity and as small as we want, and even approaching zero in the limit), then *MR* is given by the slope of shorter and shorter chords, and it approaches the slope of the *TR* curve at a point, in the limit. Thus, starting from point *B*, as the change in quantity approaches zero, the change in total revenue or marginal revenue approaches the slope of the *TR* curve at point *B*. That is, $MR = \Delta TR/\Delta Q = \$60$ (the slope of tangent *BK* to the *TR* curve at point *B*) as the change in output approaches zero in the limit.

To summarize, between points *B* and *C* on the total-revenue curve of Figure 2-6, the marginal revenue is given by the slope of chord *BC* ($50). This is the *average* marginal revenue *between* 2 and 3 units of output. On the other hand, the marginal revenue at point *B* is given by the slope of line *MK* ($60), which is tangent to the total-revenue curve at point *B*. The marginal revenue or slope of the total-revenue curve varies at every point on the total-revenue curve. For example, at point *C*, the marginal revenue is $40 and is given by the slope of the tangent (not shown) to the total-revenue curve at point *C*. Similarly, at point *D*, *MR* = $20, while at point *E*, *MR* = $0. Thus, *MR* declines as we move farther up the total-revenue curve to reflect its concave shape and declining slope.

More generally, if we let $TR = Y$ and $Q = X$, the **derivative of Y with respect to X** is given by the change in Y with respect to X, as the change in X approaches zero. That is,

$$\frac{dY}{dX} = \lim_{\Delta x \to 0} \frac{\Delta Y}{\Delta X} \tag{2-3}$$

This reads: The derivative of Y with respect to X is equal to the limit of the ratio $\Delta Y/\Delta X$, as ΔX approaches zero. Geometrically, this corresponds to the slope of the curve at the point at which we want to find the limit. Note that the smaller the change in X, the closer is the value of the derivative to the slope of the curve at a point. For example, for ΔX between 2 and 4 in Figure 2-6, the average $dY/dX = \$40$ (the slope of chord BD). For the smaller ΔX between 2 and 3, the average $dY/dX = \$50$ (the slope of chord BC), which is closer to the slope of the curve at point B (that is, $dY/dX = \$60$). The concept of the limit is extremely important in marginal and optimization analysis. However, before we can actually utilize the concept, we must define the rules by which we can find the derivative of any mathematical function (equation) in general and of any economic function in particular.

Rules of Differentiation

Differentiation is the process of determining the derivative of a function, i.e., finding the change in Y for a change in X, when the change in X approaches zero. In this section, we present the rules of differentiation.[3]

Constant Function Rule The derivative of a constant function, $Y = f(X) = a$, is zero for all values of a (the constant). That is, for the function

$$Y = f(X) = a$$

$$\frac{dY}{dX} = 0$$

For example, for the function

$$Y = 2$$

$$\frac{dY}{dX} = 0$$

This is graphed in the left panel of Figure 2-7. Since Y is defined to be a constant, its values does not change for any value of X, and so dY/dX (the slope of the Y line) is zero.

[3]A more extensive treatment of these rules as well as their proofs is presented in any introductory calculus text, such as John B. Fraleigh, *Calculus and Analytic Geometry* (Reading, Mass.: Addison-Wesley, 1985).

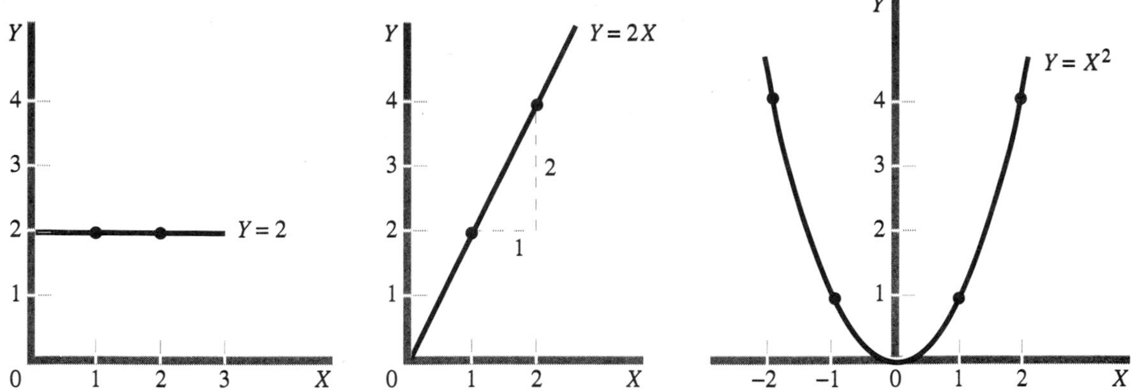

Figure 2-7
Differentiating Constant and Power Functions
The derivative (slope) of the constant function $Y = 2$ is zero. The derivative (slope) of the power function $Y = 2X$ is 2 for any range of X values. For $Y = X^2$, $dY/dX = 2X$. Thus, dY/dX (slope) changes at every value of X and is negative for $X < 0$, is zero for $X = 0$, and is positive for $X > 0$.

Power-Function Rule The derivative of a power function, $Y = aX^b$, where a and b are constants, is equal to the exponent b multiplied by the coefficient a times the variable X raised to the $b - 1$ power. That is, for the function

$$Y = aX^b$$

$$\frac{dY}{dX} = b \cdot a \cdot X^{(b-1)}$$

For example, given the function $Y = 2X$, where $a = 2$, $b = 1$ (implicit), $dY/dX = 1 \cdot 2 \cdot X^{(1-1)} = 2X^0 = 2(1) = 2$. That is, for

$$Y = 2X$$

$$\frac{dY}{dX} = 2$$

This is graphed in the middle panel of Figure 2-7. Note that the slope of the line (dY/dX) is constant at the value of 2 over any range of X values. As another example, for the function $Y = X^2$, $dY/dX = 2 \cdot 1 \cdot X^{(2-1)} = 2X^1 = 2X$. That is, for the function

$$Y = X^2$$

$$\frac{dY}{dX} = 2X$$

This is graphed in the right panel of Figure 2-7. Note that the slope of the curve (dY/dX) varies at every value of X and is negative for $X < 0$, zero at $X = 0$, and positive for $X > 0$.

Sums-and-Differences Rule The derivative of a sum (difference) is equal to the sum (difference) of the derivatives of the individual terms. Thus, if

$$U = g(X) \qquad \text{and} \qquad V = h(X)$$

where U is an unspecified function, g of X, while V is another unspecified function, h of X,[4] then for the function

$$Y = U \pm V$$

$$\frac{dY}{dX} = \frac{dU}{dX} \pm \frac{dV}{dX}$$

For example, if $U = g(X) = 2X$ and $V = h(X) = X^2$, so that

$$Y = U + V = 2X + X^2$$

$$\frac{dY}{dX} = 2 + 2X$$

Since $dU/dX = 2$ and $dV/dX = 2X$ (by the power-function rule), the derivative of the total function (dY/dX) is equal to the derivative of the sum of its parts ($2 + 2X$). As another example, for

$$Y = 0.04X^3 - 0.9X^2 + 10X + 5$$

$$\frac{dY}{dX} = 0.12X^2 - 1.8X + 10$$

Note that the derivative of the first three terms of the Y function are obtained by the power-function rule, while the derivative of the constant, 5, is equal to zero, by the constant-function rule.

Product Rule The derivative of a produce of two expressions is equal to the first expression multiplied by the derivative of the second, *plus* the second expression times the derivative of the first. Thus, for the function

$$Y = U \cdot V$$

where $U = g(X)$ and $V = h(X)$,

$$\frac{dY}{dX} = U\frac{dV}{dX} + V\frac{dU}{dX}$$

For example, for the function

$$Y = 2X^2(3 - 2X)$$

[4]In the equations $U = g(X)$ and $V = h(X)$, or more generally, $Y = f(X)$, the variable to the left of the equals sign is called the "dependent variable" while the variable to the right of the equals sign is called the "independent variable." The reason for this terminology is that the value of the dependent or left-hand variable depends on the value of the independent or right-hand variable or variables. On the other hand, the independent or right-hand variable or variables is or are determined outside, or independently, of the relationship expressed by the equation.

and letting $U = 2X^2$ and $V = 3 - 2X$

$$\frac{dY}{dX} = 2X^2\left(\frac{dV}{dX}\right) + (3 - 2X)\left(\frac{dU}{dX}\right)$$
$$= 2X^2(-2) + (3 - 2X)(4X)$$
$$= -4X^2 + 12X - 8X^2$$
$$= 12X - 12X^2$$

Quotient Rule The derivative of the quotient of two expressions is equal to the denominator multiplied by the derivative of the numerator, *minus* the numerator times the derivative of the denominator, all divided by the denominator squared. Thus, for the function

$$Y = \frac{U}{V}$$

and letting $U = g(X)$ and $V = h(X)$,

$$\frac{dY}{dX} = \frac{V(dU/dX) - U(dV/dX)}{V^2}$$

For example, for the function

$$Y = \frac{3 - 2X}{2X^2}$$

and letting $U = 3 - 2X$ and $V = 2X^2$

$$\frac{dY}{dX} = \frac{2X^2(-2) - (3 - 2X)4X}{(2X^2)^2} = \frac{-4X^2 - 12X + 8X^2}{4X^4}$$
$$= \frac{4X^2 - 12X}{4X^4} = \frac{4X(X - 3)}{4X(X^3)} = \frac{X - 3}{X^3}$$

Function-of-a-Function (Chain) Rule If $Y = f(U)$ and $U = g(X)$, then the derivative of Y with respect to X is equal to the derivative of Y with respect to U multiplied by the derivative of U with respect to X. That is, if

$$Y = f(U) \qquad \text{and} \qquad U = g(X)$$

then

$$\frac{dY}{dX} = \frac{dY}{dU} \cdot \frac{dU}{dX}$$

For example, if

$$Y = U^3 + 10 \qquad \text{and} \qquad U = 2X^2$$

then

$$\frac{dY}{dU} = 3U^2 \qquad \text{and} \qquad \frac{dU}{dX} = 4X$$

Therefore,

$$\frac{dY}{dX} = \frac{dY}{dU} \cdot \frac{dU}{dX} = (3U^2)4X$$

Substituting the expression for U (that is, $U = 2X^2$) into the previous expression, we get

$$\frac{dY}{dX} = 3(2X^2)^2(4X) = 3(4X^4)4X = 48X^5$$

As another example, to find the derivative of

$$Y = (3X^2 + 10)^3$$

let $\quad U = 3X^2 + 10 \quad$ and $\quad Y = U^3$

then $\quad \frac{dY}{dU} = 3U^2 \quad$ and $\quad \frac{dU}{dX} = 6X$

Thus, $\quad \frac{dY}{dX} = \frac{dY}{dU} \cdot \frac{dU}{dX} = (3U^2)6X$

Substituting the value of U (that is, $3X^2 + 10$) into the previous expression, we get

$$\frac{dY}{dX} = 3(3X^2 + 10)^2(6X) = 3(9X^4 + 60X^2 + 100)(6X)$$
$$= 162X^5 + 1{,}080X^3 + 1{,}800X = 2X(81X^4 + 540X^2 + 900)$$

Table 2-4 summarizes the above rules for differentiating functions.

Table 2-4
Rules for Differentiating Functions

FUNCTION	DERIVATIVE
1. Constant function	
$Y = a$	$\frac{dY}{dX} = 0$
2. Power function	
$Y = aX^b$	$\frac{dY}{dX} = b \cdot a \cdot X^{(b-1)}$
3. Sums and differences of functions	
$Y = U \pm V$	$\frac{dY}{dX} = \frac{dU}{dX} \pm \frac{dV}{dX}$
4. Product of two functions	
$Y = U \cdot V$	$\frac{dY}{dX} = U\frac{dV}{dX} + V\frac{dU}{dX}$
5. Quotient of two functions	
$Y = \frac{U}{V}$	$\frac{dY}{dX} = \frac{V(dU/dX) - U(dV/dX)}{V^2}$
6. Function of a function	
$Y = f(U)$, where $U = g(X)$	$\frac{dY}{dX} = \frac{dY}{dU} \cdot \frac{dU}{dX}$

2-5 OPTIMIZATION WITH CALCULUS

In this section we examine the process of optimization with calculus. First we examine how we can determine the point at which a function is maximum or minimum. We then show how to distinguish between a maximum and a minimum.

Determining a Maximum or a Minimum by Calculus

Optimization often requires finding the maximum or the minimum value of a function. For example, a firm may want to maximize its revenue, minimize the cost of producing a given output, or, more likely, it may want to maximize its profits. For a function to be at its maximum or minimum, the derivative of the function must be zero. Geometrically, this corresponds to the point where the curve has zero slope. For example, for total-revenue function (2-1),

$$TR = 100Q - 10Q^2$$

$$\frac{d(TR)}{dQ} = 100 - 20Q$$

Setting $d(TR)/dQ = 0$, we get

$$100 - 20Q = 0$$

Therefore, $$Q = 5$$

That is, for total-revenue function (2-1), $d(TR)/dQ = 0$ (i.e., its slope is zero) and total revenue is maximum at the output level of 5 units (see Figure 2-1). Similarly, the derivative or slope of the marginal-cost and average-cost functions of Figure 2-2 is zero at $Q = 2$ and $Q = 3.5$, respectively, where these functions (curves) are minimum.

Distinguishing between a Maximum and a Minimum: The Second Derivative

We have seen in the previous section that the derivative (slope) of a function (curve) is zero at both a minimum and a maximum point. To distinguish between a maximum and a minimum point, we use the **second derivative.** For the general function $Y = f(X)$, the second derivative is written as d^2Y/dX^2. The second derivative is the derivative of the derivative and is found by applying again to the (first) derivative the rules of differentiation presented in Section 2-5 and summarized in Table 2-4. For example, for

$$Y = X^3$$

$$\frac{dY}{dX} = 3X^2$$

and $$\frac{d^2Y}{dX^2} = 6X$$

Similarly, for $TR = 100Q - 10Q^2$,

$$\frac{d(TR)}{dQ} = 100 - 20Q$$

and

$$\frac{d^2(TR)}{dQ^2} = -20$$

Geometrically, the derivative refers to the slope of the function, while the second derivative refers to the *change* in the slope of the function. The value of the second derivative can thus be used to determine whether we have a maximum or a minimum at the point at which the first derivative (slope) is zero. The rule is *if the second derivative is positive, we have a minimum, and if the second derivative is negative, we have a maximum.* We have already encountered the geometric equivalent of this rule when dealing with the total profit (π) function in the bottom of Figure 2-4. That function has a zero slope (that is, $d\pi/dQ = 0$) at $Q = 1$ and $Q = 3$. But in the neighborhood of $Q = 1$, the slope of the π function increases (that is, $d^2\pi/dQ^2 > 0$) from being negative at $Q < 1$, zero at $Q = 1$, and positive at $Q > 1$, so that the π function faces up and we have a minimum. On the other hand, in the neighborhood of $Q = 3$, the slope of the π function decreases (that is, $d^2\pi/dQ^2 < 0$) from being positive first, then zero, and then negative, so that the π function faces down and we have a maximum. A few applications follow.

First, given the following total-revenue function,

$$TR = 45Q - 0.5Q^2$$

$$\frac{d(TR)}{dQ} = 45 - Q$$

Setting the first derivative equal to zero, we find that the TR function has a zero slope at $Q = 45$. Since $d^2(TR)/dQ^2 = -1$, this TR function reaches a maximum at $Q = 45$.[5]

As another example, consider the following marginal-cost function:

$$MC = 3Q^2 - 16Q + 57$$

Then

$$\frac{d(MC)}{dQ} = 6Q - 16$$

Setting the first derivative equal to zero, we find that the MC curve has zero slope at $Q = 2\frac{2}{3}$. Since $d^2(MC)/dQ^2 = 6$, this MC curve reaches a minimum at $Q = 2\frac{2}{3}$ so that the MC curve looks similar to the MC curve in Figure 2-2.

[5]Note that for the function $TR = 100Q - 10Q^2$ examined earlier, we found that $d(TR)/dQ = 100 - 20Q$. Therefore, $d(TR)/dQ = 0$ at $Q = 5$, and $d^2(TR)/dQ^2 = -20$, so that this TR function reaches a *maximum* at $Q = 5$ (see Figure 2-1). If plotted, the above TR curve would look like the one in Figure 2-1, but it reaches a maximum at $Q = 45$.

A final, more comprehensive and important example is provided by profit maximization by the firm. Suppose that the total-revenue and total-cost functions of the firm are, respectively,

$$TR = 45Q - 0.5Q^2 \qquad TC = Q^3 - 8Q^2 + 57Q + 2$$

Then

$$\begin{aligned} \pi &= TR - TC \\ &= 45Q - 0.5Q^2 - (Q^3 - 8Q^2 + 57Q + 2) \\ &= 45Q - 0.5Q^2 - Q^3 + 8Q^2 - 57Q - 2 \\ &= -Q^3 + 7.5Q^2 - 12Q - 2 \end{aligned}$$

To determine the level of output at which the firm maximizes π, we proceed as follows:

$$\begin{aligned} \frac{d\pi}{dQ} &= -3Q^2 + 15Q - 12 = 0 \\ &= (-3Q + 3)(Q - 4) = 0 \end{aligned}$$

Therefore,

$$Q = 1 \quad \text{and} \quad Q = 4$$

$$\frac{d^2\pi}{dQ^2} = -6Q + 15$$

At $Q = 1$, $(d^2\pi/dQ^2) = -6(1) + 15 = 9$, and π is minimum. At $Q = 4$, $(d^2\pi/dQ^2) = -6(4) + 15 = -9$, and π is maximum. Therefore, π is maximized at $Q = 4$, and from the original π function we can determine that

$$\begin{aligned} \pi &= -(4)^3 + 7.5(4)^2 - 12(4) - 2 \\ &= -64 + 120 - 48 - 2 \\ &= \$6 \end{aligned}$$

The geometric equivalent of the above analysis is similar to Figure 2-4.[6]

2-6 MULTIVARIATE OPTIMIZATION

In this section, we examine multivariate optimization, or the process of determining the maximum or minimum point of a function of more than two variables. To do this, we first introduce the concept of the partial derivative, and then we use it to examine the process of maximizing a multivariable function.

Partial Derivatives

Until now we have examined the relationship between two variables only. For example, variable Y (say, total revenue, total cost, or total profit) was assumed to

[6]Note that if we set the $d(TR)/dQ$ or MR equal to $d(TC)/dQ$ or MC, we would find that $MR = MC$ at $Q = 1$ and $Q = 4$. However, only at $Q = 4$ does the MC curve intercept the MR curve from below so that π is maximized.

be a function of or to depend on only the value of variable X (total output or quantity). Most economic relationships, however, involve more than two variables. For example, total revenue may be a function of or depend on both output and advertising, total costs may depend on expenditures on both labor and capital, and total profit on sales of commodities X and Y. Thus, it becomes important to determine the marginal effect on the dependent variable, say, total profit, resulting from changes in the quantities of each individual variable, say, the quantity sold of commodity X and commodity Y, *separately*. These marginal effects are measured by the **partial derivative,** which is indicated by the symbol ∂ (as compared to d for the derivative). The partial derivative of the dependent or left-hand variable with respect to each of the independent or right-hand variables is found by the same rules of differentiation presented earlier, except that all independent variables other than the one with respect to which we are finding the partial derivative are held constant.

For example, suppose that the total profit (π) function of a firm depends on sales of commodities X and Y as follows:

$$\pi = f(X, Y) = 80X - 2X^2 - XY - 3Y^2 + 100Y \tag{2-4}$$

To find the partial derivative of π with respect to X, $\partial\pi/\partial X$, we hold Y constant and obtain

$$\frac{\partial \pi}{\partial X} = 80 - 4X - Y$$

This isolates the marginal effect on π from changes in the quantity sold of commodity X only (i.e., while holding the quantity of commodity Y constant). Note that the derivative of the third term of the π function is $-Y$ (since the implicit exponent of X is 1) and that Y is treated as a constant. The fourth and the fifth terms of the π function drop out in the partial differentiation because they contain no X term. Similarly, to isolate the marginal effect of a change of Y on π, we hold X constant and obtain

$$\frac{\partial \pi}{\partial Y} = -X - 6Y + 100$$

We can visualize geometrically the concept of the partial derivative with a three-dimensional figure, with π on the vertical axis and with the X axis and the Y axis forming the (plane surface, rather than the line) base of the figure. Then, $\partial\pi/\partial X$ measures the marginal effect of X on π, in the cross section of the three-dimensional figure along the X axis. Similarly, $\partial\pi/\partial Y$ examines the marginal effect of Y on π in the cross section of the three-dimensional figure along the Y axis. Note also that the value of $\partial\pi/\partial X$ depends also on the level at which Y is held constant. Similarly, the value of $\partial\pi/\partial Y$ depends also on the level at which X is held constant. This is the reason that the expression for the $\partial\pi/\partial X$ found above also contains a Y term, while $\partial\pi/\partial Y$ also has an X term.

Maximizing a Multivariable Function

To maximize or minimize a multivariable function, we must set each partial derivative equal to zero and solve the resulting set of simultaneous equations for the optimal value of the independent or right-hand variables.[7] For example, to maximize the total-profit function (2-4, repeated below for ease of reference),

$$\pi = 80X - 2X^2 - XY - 3Y^2 + 100Y \tag{2-4}$$

we set $\partial\pi/\partial X$ and $\partial\pi/\partial Y$ (found earlier) equal to zero and solve for X and Y. Specifically,

$$\frac{\partial \pi}{\partial X} = 80 - 4X - Y = 0$$

$$\frac{\partial \pi}{\partial Y} = -X - 6Y + 100 = 0$$

Multiplying the first of the above expressions by -6, rearranging the second, and adding, we get

$$\begin{array}{r} -480 + 24X + 6Y = 0 \\ 100 - \quad X - 6Y = 0 \\ \hline -380 + 23X \qquad = 0 \end{array}$$

Therefore, $X = 380/23 = 16.52$.

Substituting $X = 16.52$ into the first expression of the partial derivative set equal to zero, and solving for Y, we get

$$80 - 4(16.52) - Y = 0$$

Therefore, $Y = 80 - 66.08 = 13.92$.

Thus, the firm maximizes π when it sells 16.52 units of commodity X and 13.92 units of commodity Y. Substituting these values into the π function, we get the maximum total profit of the firm of

$$\begin{aligned} \pi &= 80(16.52) - 2(16.52)^2 - (16.52)(13.92) - 3(13.92)^2 + 100(13.92) \\ &= \$1{,}356.52 \end{aligned}$$

[7]The condition for distinguishing between a maximum and minimum is based on the value of the second-order partial derivative. This condition is much more complex than for a function of a single independent variable and is beyond the scope of this text. In the rest of this book, the context of the problem will tell us whether the point at which all partial derivatives are zero is a maximum or a minimum, and we implicitly assume that the second-order condition for maximization or minimization is satisfied. For the interested reader, the second-order condition to distinguish between a maximum and a minimum for a multivariate function is examined in any calculus text.

Case Study 2-3

Optimal Product Quality and Total Profits at Hewlett-Packard

In the late 1970s and early 1980s, the Hewlett-Packard Computer Company suffered serious quality problems, and these problems cut sharply into the company's sales and profits. The company's response was a much improved quality-control program based on increased inspection, training, and rewards for quality improvements. The program was highly successful as evidenced by the fact that within a few years, service and repairs for the company's products declined 35 percent and inventories by nearly 25 percent. The quality-control program cost money, however, and the question faced by top management was how much of the company's resources were to be devoted to improving product quality and how much to spend on other functions, such as product development, advertising, and diversification. So successful was Hewlett-Packard in solving these problems and in developing, introducing, and marketing new high-tech products that the company quadrupled in size over the past decade.

These are the types of choices that most firms face almost daily. The optimal solution or the amount of resources that a firm should devote to each of the many activities that affect its sales and profits can be analyzed with the partial derivative concepts examined in this section. That is, the firm should pursue each activity until the marginal *net* benefit from the activity (i.e., until its partial derivative) is zero. While the firm may not have sufficient data to apply this rule precisely, the concept and the rule themselves are very clear. The firm should strive to come as close as possible to the optimal solution and, in the meantime, collect more and better data on the cost and benefits of pursuing each activity, so as to be able to get even closer to the optimal solution in the future.

Source: "One Company's Quest for Improved Quality," *The Wall Street Journal*, July 25, 1983, p. A10; "From Dinosaur to Gazelle," in *Reinventing America, Business Week*, 1992, p. 65; and "How H-P Continues to Grow and Grow," *Fortune*, May 2, 1994, pp. 90–100.

2-7 CONSTRAINED OPTIMIZATION

Until now in this chapter we have examined unconstrained optimization, or the maximization or minimization of an objective function subject to no constraints. Most of the time, however, managers face constraints in their optimization decisions. For example, a firm may face a limitation on its production capacity or on the availability of skilled personnel and crucial raw materials. It may also face legal and environmental constraints. In such cases, we have a **constrained optimization** problem, i.e., the maximizing or minimizing of an objective function subject to some constraints. The existence of such constraints reduces the freedom of action of the firm and usually prevents attainment of its unconstrained optimum. Constrained optimization problems can be solved by substitution or by the Lagrangian multiplier method. These are examined in turn.[8]

Constrained Optimization by Substitution

A constrained optimization problem may be solved by first solving the *constraint equation* for one of the decision variables, and then substituting the expression for this variable into the *objective function* that the firm seeks to maximize or minimize. This procedure converts a constrained optimization problem into an unconstrained one, which can then be solved as indicated in the previous section.

For example, suppose that the firm seeks to maximize its total-profit function given by Equation 2-4 in the previous section (and repeated again below for ease of reference),

$$\pi = 80X - 2X^2 - XY - 3Y^2 + 100Y \tag{2-4}$$

but faces the constraint that the output of commodity X plus the output of commodity Y must be 12. That is,

$$X + Y = 12 \tag{2-5}$$

To solve this optimization problem by substitution, we can solve the constraint function for X, substitute the value of X into the objective function (π) that the firm seeks to maximize, and then apply the procedure for maximizing an unconstrained objective function shown in the previous section. Specifically, solving the constraint function for X, we get

$$X = 12 - Y$$

Substituting the above constraint expression for X into the objective profit function, we obtain

$$\begin{aligned}\pi &= 80(12 - Y) - 2(12 - Y)^2 - (12 - Y)Y - 3Y^2 + 100Y \\ &= 960 - 80Y - 2(144 - 24Y + Y^2) - 12Y + Y^2 - 3Y^2 + 100Y \\ &= 960 - 80Y - 288 + 48Y - 2Y^2 - 12Y + Y^2 - 3Y^2 + 100Y \\ &= -4Y^2 + 56Y + 672\end{aligned}$$

To maximize the above (unconstrained) profit function, we find the first derivative of π with respect to Y, set it equal to zero, and solve for Y. That is,

$$\frac{d\pi}{dY} = -8Y + 56 = 0$$

[8]In this chapter, we examine only equality constraints, or constraints that can be expressed as equations. In Chapter 8, we present linear programming, which is a constrained optimization method in which the constraints are expressed as inequalities (i.e., the constraints impose only an upper or lower limit on the actions of the decision maker).

Therefore, $Y = 7$.

Substituting $Y = 7$ into the constraint function, we get $X = 12 - Y = 12 - 7 = 5$. Thus, the firm maximizes total profits when it produces 5 units of commodity X and 7 units of commodity Y (as compared with $X = 16.52$ and $Y = 13.92$ when the firm faced no output constraint—see p. 55). With $X = 5$ and $Y = 7$,

$$\begin{aligned}\pi &= 80(5) - 2(5)^2 - (5)(7) - 3(7)^2 + 100(7) \\ &= \$868\end{aligned}$$

as compared with \$1,356.52 found earlier in the absence of any output constraint.

Constrained Optimization by the Lagrangian Multiplier Method

When the constraint equation is too complex or cannot be solved for one of the decision variables as an explicit function of the other(s), the techniques of substitution to solve a constrained optimization problem can become burdensome or impossible. In such cases we may resort to the **Lagrangian multiplier method.** The first step in this method is to form a **Lagrangian function.** This is given by the original objective function that the firm seeks to maximize or minimize plus λ (the Greek letter lambda that is conventionally used for the Lagrangian multiplier) times the constraint function set equal to zero. Because it incorporates the constraint function set equal to zero, the Lagrangian function can also be treated as an unconstrained optimization problem, and its solution will always be identical to the original constrained optimization problem.

As a way of illustration, we show how the constrained profit maximization problem that was solved in the previous section by substitution can be solved by the Lagrangian multiplier method. To do so, we first set the constraint function (that is, $X + Y = 12$) equal to zero and obtain

$$X + Y - 12 = 0$$

We then multiply this form of the constraint function by λ and add it to the original profit function we seek to maximize (i.e., to $\pi = 80X - 2X^2 - XY - 3Y^2 + 100Y$) to form the Lagrangian function (L_π). That is,

$$L_\pi = 80X - 2X^2 - XY - 3Y^2 + 100Y + \lambda(X + Y - 12) \tag{2-6}$$

The above Lagrangian function (L_π) can be treated as an unconstrained function in three unknowns: X, Y, and λ. Now, the solution that maximizes L also maximizes π.

To maximize L_π, we set the partial derivative of L_π with respect to X, Y, and λ equal to zero, and solve the resulting set of simultaneous equations for the values of X, Y, and λ. Finding the partial derivative of L_π with respect to X, Y, and λ, and setting them equal to zero, we get

$$\frac{\partial L_\pi}{\partial X} = 80 - 4X - Y + \lambda = 0 \tag{2-7}$$

$$\frac{\partial L_\pi}{\partial Y} = -X - 6Y + 100 + \lambda = 0 \tag{2-8}$$

$$\frac{\partial L_\pi}{\partial \lambda} = X + Y - 12 = 0 \tag{2-9}$$

Note that Equation 2-9 is equal to the constraint imposed on the original profit function of the firm (Equation 2-4). Indeed, Lagrangian function (2-6) was specifically set up so that when the partial derivative of L_π with respect for λ (the Lagrangian multiplier) is set equal to zero, not only the constraint of the problem is satisfied but the Lagrangian function (L_π) reduces to the original unconstrained profit function (π), so that the optimal solution of both functions is identical.

To find the value of X, Y, and λ that maximizes L_π and π, we solve simultaneously Equations 2-7, 2-8, and 2-9. To do this, subtract Equation 2-8 from Equation 2-7 and get

$$-20 - 3X + 5Y = 0 \tag{2-10}$$

Multiplying Equation 2-9 by 3 and adding to it Equation 2-10, we obtain

$$\begin{array}{r} 3X + 3Y - 36 = 0 \\ \underline{-3X + 5Y - 20 = 0} \\ 8Y - 56 = 0 \end{array}$$

Therefore, $Y = 7$ and $X = 5$, so that $\pi = \$868$ (as in the previous section). Finally, by substituting the value of $X = 5$ and $Y = 7$ into Equation 2-8, we get the value of λ. That is,

$$-5 - 42 + 100 = -\lambda$$

Thus, $\lambda = -53$.

The value of λ has an important economic interpretation. It is the marginal effect on the objective-function solution associated with a 1-unit change in the constraint. In the above problem, this means that a decrease in the output capacity constraint from 12 to 11 units or an increase to 13 units will reduce or increase, respectively, the total profit of the firm (π) by about \$53.

Case Study 2-4

Constrained Profit Maximization at Fast-Food Restaurants

Most fast-food restaurants cook french fries and other foods in beef tallow. This is a flavorful shortening high in saturated fat, which has been linked to heart disease. Chicken, which is low in fat, in a fast-food sandwich has been found to contain more fat than a pint of ice cream. The reason fast-food restaurants used beef tallow is that it makes food more flavorful and it is cheaper than alternative ways of cooking food. Using beef tallow, therefore, was consistent with fast-food restaurants' goal of profit maximization.

A few years ago, however, with the public's increased concern and knowledge about the relationship between food and health, and under pressure from the American Medical Association, the two largest chains, McDonald's and Burger King—seeking to enhance their reputation for wholesome food—switched from animal fat to unsaturated fat in frying their chicken and fish. This is an example of constrained profit maximization.

Although more people were expected to eat at fast-food restaurants if their food became more "healthy," the total profits of these restaurants were expected to fall. We can only presume that McDonald's and Burger King, being very alert profit maximizers, would have cooked their foods in unsaturated fat rather than in animal fat in the first place if that would have led to higher profits. Competition forced other fast-food restaurants to follow, and so costs rose and profits fell in the entire fast-food industry. But just about when most fast-food restaurants started to provide less fatty food on their menus, consumers' tastes began to change back again to more rich and fatty food because of their better taste.

Source: "Fast Fries Fried in What?" *The New York Times*, June 27, 1986, p. 34; "McDonald's Will Put Nutritional Data for Menu on Wall Posters, Tray Liners," *The Wall Street Journal*, June 11, 1990, p. B6; and "Too Skinny a Burger Is a Mighty Hard Sell, McDonald's Learns," *The Wall Street Journal*, April 15, 1994, p. A1.

2-8 NEW MANAGEMENT TOOLS FOR OPTIMIZATION

During the past two decades many new management tools have been introduced that are revolutionizing the way firms are managed. The most important of these new management tools are: benchmarking, total quality management, reengineering, and the learning organization. In this section we discuss each of these and examine how they are related to the traditional functional areas of managerial economics.

Benchmarking

Benchmarking refers to the finding out, in an open and aboveboard way, how other firms may be doing something better (cheaper) so that your firm can copy and possibly improve on its technique. Benchmarking is usually accomplished by field trips to other firms. The technique has now become a standard tool for improving productivity and quality at a large number of American firms, including some of the best-known, such as IBM, AT&T, Ford, Du Pont, and Xerox.

Benchmarking requires (1) picking a specific process that your firm seeks to improve and identifying a few firms that do a better job and (2) sending on the benchmarking mission the people who will actually have to make the changes. Benchmarking can result in dramatic costs reductions. For example, through benchmarking, Xerox was able to cut the cost of processing each order from $95 to $35 and, as a result, save tens of billions of dollars. Similarly, benchmarking allowed Ford to reduce the number of employees handling accounts payable from 500 to less than 200 in a few months. Through benchmarking, the Mellon Bank cut complaints by

60 percent and was able to resolve them on the average in 25 days instead of 45 days. Benchmarking has now become a standard tool to increase productivity and minimize costs at many U.S. and foreign firms. The explosion in interest in benchmarking has led to the formation of many benchmarking associations, councils, conferences, courses, data, and consultants.

Case Study 2-5

Benchmarking at Xerox and Ford

The first benchmarking mission by a U.S. firm was undertaken by Xerox in 1979, when it realized that the Japanese were selling copiers for less than Xerox's production costs. At first Xerox management thought the Japanese were dumping (i.e., selling copiers in the United States at prices below their production costs) in order to establish a foothold in the American market. But a benchmarking mission to Japan led Xerox to the shocking realization that Japanese production costs were in fact much lower than Xerox's. Responding to the challenge eventually led Xerox to imitate Japanese producers, thus recapturing some of its lost market. Xerox has successfully used benchmarking ever since.

The highly successful Ford Taurus introduced in the early 1980s was also the result of benchmarking. Ford first set out to identify about 400 features that U.S. car buyers considered most important, then it identified the competitive cars (mostly Japanese) which embodied those features, and finally, it built a car (the Taurus) incorporating those features at competitive costs by copying the production methods of its competitors. The new redesigned 1992 Taurus was, once again, based on a new round of benchmarking. Ford benchmarked door handles and fuel economy against the Chevy Lumina, the halogen headlamps and tilt wheel against the Honda Accord, the easy-to-change taillight bulbs and express window control against Nissan's Maxima, and the remote radio controls against the Pontiac Grand Prix.

Source: "How to Steal the Best Ideas Around," *Fortune,* October 19, 1992, pp. 102–106.

Total Quality Management

One movement that swept U.S. corporations in the 1980s involves maximizing quality and minimizing costs through **total quality management (TQM).** This refers to constantly improving the quality of products and the firm's processes so as to consistently deliver increasing value to customers. TQM constantly asks, "How can we do this cheaper, faster, or better?" It involves worker teams and benchmarking. In its broader form, TQM applies quality-improvement methods to all firm processes from production to customer service, sales and marketing, and even finance. By improving quality and reducing costs in all these areas Hewlett-Packard achieved spectacular results. Other companies that have successfully used TQM are Xerox, Motorola, Marriott, Harley-Davidson, and Ford.

Five rules determine the success of a TQM program:

1. The corporate executive officer (CEO) must strongly and visibly support it with words and actions.
2. The TQM program must clearly show how it benefits customers and creates value for the firm.
3. The TQM program must have a few clear strategic goals; that is, it must ask, "What is the firm trying to accomplish?"
4. The TQM program must provide quick financial returns and compensation—people need to see early and concrete results to continue to support the program.
5. The TQM program should be tailored to a particular firm; that is, one firm cannot simply copy someone else's TQM program.

Despite some glaring successes from using TQM programs (e.g., Motorola was able to cut $700 million in manufacturing costs over five years), only about a third of American corporations polled indicated that their TQM program had a significant impact on increasing the quality of their products, reducing costs, and increasing their competitiveness. The most frequent reason for failure for TQM programs is the failure of upper management to show a strong personal involvement and commitment to the program. Other reasons for failure were that TQM programs often were not strongly linked to the overall business strategy of the firm or aimed at delivering increasing value to customers.

Case Study 2-6

Total Quality Management at Johnson & Johnson, Motorola, and Tenneco

Johnson & Johnson's TQM program identified three quantifiable goals: increasing customer satisfaction, reducing the time it takes to introduce new products, and cutting costs. One total quality initiative, by encouraging the sharing of responsibility rather than resistance to it, reduced the time required by Johnson & Johnson to prepare customized retail displays for chain drugstores and supermarkets from 120 days to 30 days, and this contributed to an increase in sales from $25 million to $90 million in one year. Motorola's TQM program has had two basic aims. One is defect prevention, and the other is cycle-time reduction (i.e., the time it takes to get a job done). Past success in achieving the first goal has led the company to set the goal of two defects per *billion* operations by the year 2000. The second goal has led to a reduction in the time required to close the books each month from 11 days five years ago to just 2 days now, and this has led to a 50 percent saving in external auditors' cost. The TQM program at Tenneco was based on sharply cutting internal failures (such as unscheduled downtime), external failures (which resulted in a flood of warranty claims), prevention of defects (project planning), and appraisal (testing and inspection). As a result of its TQM program, Tenneco was able to turn a $732 million loss in 1991 to a $215 million profit in 1992. The TQM successes at Johnson & Johnson, Motorola, Tenneco, and at other firms were achieved by management answering three basic questions: Who is the customer, what service is the firm providing, and what strategy is the firm following?

Source: "TQM—More than a Dying Fad?" *Fortune,* October 18, 1993, pp. 66–72; and "Report Card on TQM," *Management Review,* January 1994, pp. 22–25.

Reengineering

Reengineering is the hottest new trend in management of the 1990s. Reengineering seeks to completely reorganize the firm. It asks, "If this were an entirely new firm, how would you organize it? Or if you were able to start all over again, how would you do it?" And then it requires going out and completely restructuring the firm to conform to that vision. Reengineering involves the radical redesign of all of the firm's processes to achieve major gains in speed, quality, service, and profitability. While total quality management (TQM) seeks how to do something faster, cheaper, or better, reengineering asks first whether something should be done at all, and so it is more likely than TQM to come up with novel solutions.

There are two major reasons to reengineer: (1) fear that competitors may come up with new products, services, or ways of doing business that might destroy your firm or (2) greed if you believe that by reengineering, your company can obliterate the competition. The best candidates for reengineering are firms that face major shifts in the nature of competition such as financial and telecommunications firms after deregulation. Reengineering involves reorganizing the firm horizontally around cross-functional core processes managed by teams that seek to maximize customers' satisfaction. Profits are likely to come and be maximized at dramatically higher levels in the long run if the reengineering is successful. For example, instead of product development being handled by different departments as in traditional firms (where the marketing department comes up with an idea for a new product, hands it to the engineering department, which then hands it to the production department), in a successfully reengineered horizontal firm, a team of key people will handle all aspects of product development, from the idea, to the production, to the marketing of the product, thus eliminating layers of management, bureaucracy, and waste and providing cheaper and better products to customers.

Although reengineering makes a great deal of sense on paper, it is extremely difficult to carry it out in the real world, and not all firms are capable or need to reengineer. Even those that have been most successful have not completely eliminated functional specializations. That is, there will always be a need for experts in production, finance, marketing, human resource development, and so on. What reengineering does is to make them work together in teams. Few firms, however, are likely to ever become entirely horizontal or boundaryless. Most are likely to be hybrids, or less vertically organized than in the past but not fully horizontal or boundaryless.

Case Study 2-7
Reengineering at GE

When Jack Welch became corporate executive officer (CEO) in 1981, General Electric (GE) had a strong balance sheet, but modest earnings and technology, and was almost an entirely nonglobal business. By 1990, Welch had entirely redesigned (read: reengineered) GE into a wholly new and much more efficient, dynamic, global, and profitable organization. The reengineering involved first of all brutally awakening GE to the need to change for survival in the dramatically transformed competitive situation of the 1980s. Secondly, it involved envisioning a new boundaryless firm based on cross-functional teamwork capable of constantly reinventing itself. Finally, it required the actual redesign of the firm into one in which information flowed freely across functional and business boundaries, from where it was developed to where it was needed, and capable of continuous change.

Actual reengineering at GE involved the adoption of a new strategy, revolutionizing its organizational structure and entirely changing its human resource management. The strategy was for GE to aim for high-growth businesses. This meant that GE had to be number 1 or number 2 in each segment of the market; otherwise it had to fix, sell, or close the business. The organizational structure was reorganized into 13 businesses that shared the best practices and reported to a central CEO team. In human resource management, GE made rewards very flexible, had employees' appraisal from above as well as from below, and made training and development a continuous process. Needless to say, Welch had to overcome tremendous resistance from traditional vested interests all down the chain of command. But he was able to carry out over the past decade one of the most far-reaching programs of innovation in business history, a program that has turned GE into one of the most efficient and dynamic firms in the world.

Source: "Revolutionize Your Company," *Fortune,* December 13, 1993, pp. 114–118; "Reengineering: The Hot New Management Tool," *Fortune,* August 23, 1993, pp. 41–48; "The Horizontal Corporation," *Business Week,* December 20, 1993, pp. 76–81; and "Reengineering Tales from the Front," *Management Review,* January 1995, pp. 13–18.

The Learning Organization

The learning organization may be the new hot management tool of the next decade. A **learning organization** is one that values continuing learning, both individual and collective, and believes that competitive advantage derives from and requires continuous learning in our information age. According to Peter Senge, its intellectual and spiritual champion, a learning organization is based on five basic ingredients. The first is for people to develop a *new mental model* by putting aside old ways of thinking and being willing to change. The second is to achieve *personal mastery* by learning to be open with others and listen to them rather than telling them what to do. The third is to develop *system thinking,* or an understanding of how the firm really works. The fourth is to develop a *shared vision* or a strategy for the firm that all its employees share. And the fifth, and most important, is to strive for *team learning,* or seeing how all of the firm's employees can be made to work and learn together to realize the shared vision and carry out the strategy of the firm. To be sure, none of these five concepts is new; however, what is original and promises to provide major benefits is how the concepts are linked together to create a learning organization.

Although the five ingredients on which the learning organization is based may be clear in theory, they are very difficult to carry out in practice. It is to make the learning organization more accessible to management that Senge formed the Center for Organizational Learning at the Massachusetts Institute of Technology (MIT) in 1990. This research center has 18 sponsors (among them are, Ford, AT&T, Motorola, and Federal Express), each paying $80,000 per year and striving to create a pilot program for transforming their firm into a learning organization with the help of the center. These leading corporations believe that by becoming learning organizations, they can dramatically increase their efficiency and dynamic competitiveness. For now, the learning organization is, for the most part, a management vision of the future. It is possible, however, that the concept may storm corporate American in the next decade, as total quality management did in the 1980s and reengineering in the 1990s.

Case Study 2-8

Applying Learning-Organization Principles at Ford

One of the earliest successful uses of learning-organization principles was in the launching of the new Lincoln Continental at Ford. The first step was to induce people involved in the Lincoln project to come forward early on and admit that they had a problem that needed to be solved. This went smack against Ford's culture, where problems were hidden as long as possible to avoid charges of incompetence. The new openness allowed people working on the Continental project to work together more readily, to engage in systems thinking and thereby solve more effectively systems problems.

For example, the project manager found that because the engineers who designed the air-conditioning system, the headlights, the power seats, and the CD player traditionally worked separately, they did not realize that the simultaneous operation of these car systems drained the car battery. Under Ford's traditional management system, when this problem came to light, the engineers from the various departments would fight with one another to determine who had to make the adjustment to lower the power requirement. The impasse would then have to be broken by a decision from the overall project manager. The engineers in the department that had to give in would then feel like losers, and a great deal of time would be lost in controversy and hard feelings. Because of the management shift to using learning-organization principles, the engineers for the various car systems of the new Lincoln Continental were all working together, and realizing the problem early on, they decided to raise the car idle to increase the battery charge. This, however, required increasing fuel efficiency. Since the engineers working on that problem did not feel like losers but rather knew that they were working for the good of the car, they solved the problem much more quickly and in a spirit of cooperation and appreciation by all the other departments. By looking at the problem as a systems problem and addressing it by systems thinking, the Lincoln Continental engineers avoided blaming each other and finger pointing, which greatly increased production efficiency.

Source: "Mr. Learning Organization," *Fortune,* October 17, 1994, pp. 147–158.

New Management Tools and Functional Specialization in Managerial Economics

The past decade has seen the introduction of many new management tools and trendy remedies that seek to improve efficiency and productivity while maximizing profits subject to the constraints faced by the firm. Some of these new management tools are *benchmarking, total quality management* (*TQM*), *reengineering,* and the *learning organization.* Others are *skill-based pay, worker empowerment,* **broadbanding** (the elimination of multiple salary grades to foster movement among jobs within the firm), **networking** (the forming of temporary strategic alliances where each firm contributes its best competency), and *capturing synergies* (by the firm diversifying into related businesses). The labels abound and so do the promises of major benefits. The results to date, however, have been mixed. Most leading American firms now use benchmarking, but only about a third successfully adopted TQM programs. Fewer have tried reengineering, and the learning organization is for the most part still in its blueprint stage. Failure to receive major benefits by the firms that tried some of these new management tools often resulted from lack of conviction and effort, however. Applied with more conviction, their success rate is likely to increase, and when success does come, it can provide some major benefits.[9]

Be that as it may, the new management tools and ideas have already changed drastically the way many firms are being managed, and many more firms are likely to be forced to change their management ways in the future. The increasing use of these new management tools, however, is not likely to eliminate functional specializations and the need for specific expertise in production, finance, marketing, human resource development, and so on. One reason for this is that some of the new management tools and ideas do not provide a completely worked out and cohesive set of guidelines that most firms can easily understand and implement. For example, learning-organization principles are based on some brilliant ideas that some firms can implement and some cannot and that can sometimes lead to major benefits and sometimes cannot. To be sure, under the pressure of global competitiveness, firms will have to be constantly looking for new as well as traditional ways to increase their productivity and competitiveness.

[9] "Many Companies Try Management Fads, Only to See Them Flop," *The Wall Street Journal,* July 6, 1993, p. A1; "Total Quality Is Termed Only Partial Success," *The Wall Street Journal,* October 10, 1992, p. B1; and "Hopelessly Seeking Synergy," *The Economist,* August 20, 1994, p. 53.

Some universal truths stemming from the new management tools and ideas that would consistently benefit any organization are (1) explaining the firm's corporate strategy to employees, suppliers, and customers, (2) improving and simplifying development and production processes, and (3) reducing cycle time, that is, how long it takes to get any task done, by paying more attention to processes and teamwork than to functions and individualism.

SUMMARY

1. Economic relationships can be expressed in equational, tabular, or graphical form. Expressing an economic relationship in equational form is very useful because it allows the use of the powerful techniques of differential calculus to determine the optimal behavior of the firm.
2. The relationship between total, average, and marginal concepts and measures is crucial in optimization analysis. The relationship is basically the same whether we deal with revenue, product, cost, or profit. The average value is equal to the total value divided by the quantity. The marginal value is equal to the change in the total value per unit change in the quantity.
3. Optimization analysis can best be explained by examining the process of profit maximization by the firm. The firm maximizes its total profit at the output level at which the positive difference between its total revenue and its total cost is greatest, and its marginal revenue equals its marginal cost. More generally, according to marginal analysis, optimization occurs where the marginal benefit of an activity equals the marginal cost.
4. Optimization analysis can be conducted much more efficiently and precisely with differential calculus. This relies on the concept of the derivative, which is closely related to the concept of the margin. The derivative of total revenue with respect to output is given by the limit of the ratio $\Delta TR/\Delta Q$, as ΔQ approaches zero. Geometrically, this corresponds to the slope of the total-revenue curve at the point at which we want to find the derivative and is equal to the marginal revenue at that point. More generally, the derivative of Y with respect to X, $dY/dX = \lim_{\Delta X \to 0} (\Delta Y/\Delta X)$. The rules of differentiation are summarized in Table 2-4.
5. For a function (curve) to be at its maximum or minimum, the derivative (slope) of the function must be zero. To distinguish between a maximum and a minimum, we use the second derivative. This is the derivative of the derivative and is found by the same rules of differentiation used to find the (first) derivative. If the second derivative is positive (so that the curve faces up and its slope increases), we have a minimum at the point where the derivative of the function (slope of the curve) is zero. If the second derivative is negative (so that the curve faces down and its slope increases), we have a maximum.
6. The partial derivative of a multivariate function measures the marginal effect on the dependent or left-hand variable resulting from changing one of the independent or right-hand variables, while holding all the others constant.

With this in mind, partial derivatives are obtained by applying the same rules of differentiation presented earlier. A function is optimized (i.e., maximized or minimized) at the point where all its partial derivatives are zero.

7. Firms often face constraints in their optimization decisions. When the constraint function is relatively simple, we can solve a constrained optimization problem by substitution. This involves (1) solving the constraint equation for one of the decision variables, (2) substituting the expression for the constraints variable into the objective function that the firm seeks to maximize or minimize, and then (3) treating the problem as an unconstrained problem. When the constraint equation is complex, we may use the Lagrangian multiplier method. The Lagrangian function is given by the original objective function that the firm seeks to maximize plus λ (the Lagrangian multiplier) times the constraint function set equal to zero. The Lagrangian function can then be solved as an unconstrained function.

8. During the past two decades many new management tools have been introduced that are revolutionizing the way firms are managed. "Benchmarking" refers to the finding out how other firms may be doing something better so as to copy and possibly improve on it. "Total quality management (TQM)" is the effort to constantly improve the quality of products and the firm's processes by benchmarking and teamwork. "Reengineering" is the radical redesign of all of the firm's processes to achieve major gains in speed, quality, service, and profitability. A "learning organization" is one that values continuing learning and believes that competitive advantage derives from and requires continuous learning in our information age.

DISCUSSION QUESTIONS

1. What is the meaning of the average and marginal (*a*) revenue, (*b*) product, (*c*) cost, and (*d*) profit?
2. (*a*) What is the shape of the marginal-revenue curve if the total-revenue curve has a concave shape? (*b*) What is the value of the marginal revenue when total revenue increases? When total revenue is maximum? When total revenue decreases? (*c*) What is the shape of the marginal-revenue curve if the total-revenue curve is a positively sloped straight line?
3. If the total-product curve first increases at an increasing rate (i.e., it faces up) and then increases at a decreasing rate (i.e., it faces down), (*a*) what is the shape of the corresponding average-product and marginal-product curves? (*b*) What is the relationship between average product and marginal product? (*c*) What is the relationship between the above total-product curve and the total-cost curve of Figure 2-2? (*Hint:* Sketch the above total-product curve.)
4. (*a*) How does a firm determine the profit-maximizing level of output? (*b*) How would you react to a sales manager's announcement that he or she has in place a marketing program to maximize sales?

5. How should a firm determine the best level of (*a*) advertising? (*b*) Input use? (*c*) Investment?
6. (*a*) How does the value of a businessperson's time affect his or her decision to fly or drive on a business trip? (*b*) How much time should a consumer spend on shopping (searching) for lower prices? (*c*) For which type of good would you expect consumers to spend more time on comparative shopping, or shopping for lower prices?
7. (*a*) What is meant by the "concept of the derivative"? (*b*) Why are the concept of the derivative and the use of differential calculus so important to marginal analysis?
8. (*a*) What is meant by the "second derivative"? (*b*) How is the second derivative used in distinguishing between a maximum and a minimum point?
9. (*a*) What is meant by the "partial derivative"? How is it determined? (*b*) Can the partial derivative of a function with respect to one independent variable depend also on the value of the other independent variable? Why?
10. (*a*) Why is the concept of the partial derivative important in managerial economics? How can we use partial derivatives to optimize a multivariate function? (*b*) If the total revenue of a firm depends on the amount sold of both commodity 1 (Q_1) and commodity 2 (Q_2), how can the partial derivative of the total revenue with respect to Q_1 and Q_2 be expressed? (*c*) Suppose that commodity 1 and commodity 2 face identical cost conditions in production. What is the marginal condition for the firm to maximize its total profit from the sale of each commodity?
11. (*a*) What is meant by "constrained optimization"? (*b*) How important is this to managerial economics? (*c*) How can a constrained optimization problem be solved?
12. (*a*) What is meant by the "Lagrangian multiplier method"? (*b*) How is the Lagrangian function formed? (*c*) How can a constrained optimization problem be solved by the Lagrangian multiplier method? (*d*) What is the economic meaning of the Lagrangian multiplier, λ?
13. Do the new management tools eliminate the need for the functional areas of managerial economics? Why?

PROBLEMS

1. Given the following total-revenue function:

$$TR = 9Q - Q^2$$

(*a*) Derive the total-revenue, average-revenue, and marginal-revenue schedules from $Q = 0$ to $Q = 6$ by 1's. (*b*) On the same set of axes, plot the total-revenue, the average-revenue, and the marginal-revenue schedules of part (*a*). (*c*) With reference to your figure in part (*b*), explain the relationship among the total-, average-, and marginal-revenue curves.

2. Given the following total-product schedule:

Q	0	1	2	3	4	5	6	7	8
TP	0	2	5	9	12	14	15	15	14

(*a*) Derive the average-product and marginal-product schedules. (*b*) On the same set of axes, plot the total-, average-, and marginal-product schedules of part (*a*).

*3. (*a*) Derive the average- and marginal-profit schedules for the total-profit curve in the bottom panel of Figure 2-4 in the text. (*b*) Plot the total-profit curve of Figure 2-4, and below it, on a separate set of axes, plot the corresponding average- and marginal-profit schedules of part (*a*). (*c*) With reference to your figure in part (*b*), explain the relationship among the total-, average-, and marginal-profit curves in part (*b*).

4. Given the following total-cost schedule:

Q	0	1	2	3	4
TC	1	12	14	15	20

(*a*) Derive the average- and marginal-cost schedules. (*b*) On the same set of axes, plot the total-, average-, and marginal-cost schedules of part (*a*). (*c*) With reference to your figure in part (*b*), explain the relationship among the total-, average-, and marginal-cost curves in part (*b*).

5. With the total-revenue curve of Problem 1 and the total-cost curve of Problem 4, derive the total-profit function and show how the firm determines the profit-maximizing level of output.

*6. (*a*) Draw on the same set of axes the marginal-revenue curve derived in Problem 1 and the marginal-cost curve derived in Problem 4, and use them to explain why the best level of output of the firm is 3 units. (*b*) Explain why your answer to part (*a*) is an example of marginal analysis and optimizing behavior in general.

7. Find the derivative of the following functions:

(*a*) $Y = f(X) = a$
$TC = f(Q) = 182$

(*b*) $Y = 2X^2$
$Y = -1X^3$
$Y = \frac{1}{2}X^{-2}$
$TR = f(Q) = 10Q$
$TR = f(Q) = -Q^2$

(*c*) $Y = 45X - 0.5X^2$
$Y = X^3 - 8X^2 + 57X + 2$
$TR = 100Q - 10Q^2$ (Equation 2-1)
$TC = 182 + 56Q$ (Equation 2-2)

(*d*) $Y = X^3 - 2X^2$
$Y = 8X^4 - 20X^3$
$Y = 4X^3(2X - 5)$

(e) $Y = \dfrac{3X^3}{X^2}$

$Y = \dfrac{5X^3}{4X + 3}$

(*f*) $Y = U^5$ and $U = 2X^3 + 3$
$Y = U^3 + 3U$ and $U = -X^2 + 10X$
$Y = (2X^3 + 5)^2$

*8. Given the following total-revenue and total-cost functions of a firm:

$$TR = 22Q - 0.5Q^2$$
$$TC = \tfrac{1}{3}Q^3 - 8.5Q^2 + 50Q + 90$$

determine (*a*) the level of output at which the firm maximizes its total profit; (*b*) the maximum profit that the firm could earn.

9. A firm's total-revenue and total-cost functions are

$$TR = 4Q$$
$$TC = 0.04Q^3 - 0.9Q^2 + 10Q + 5$$

(*a*) Determine the best level of output. (*b*) Determine the total profit of the firm at its best level of output.

10. Given the following cost functions, determine the level of (nonzero) output at which the cost functions are minimized and the level of those costs.

(*a*) $AC = 200 - 24Q + Q^2$
(*b*) $MC = 200 - 48Q + 3Q^2$

*11. For the following total-profit function of a firm:

$$\pi = 144X - 3X^2 - XY - 2Y^2 + 120Y - 35$$

determine (*a*) the level of output of each commodity at which the firm maximizes its total profit; (*b*) the value of the maximum amount of the total profit of the firm.

12. **Integrating Problem**
The Warren & Smith Company manufactures commercial zippers of two kinds, kind X and kind Y. Its production department estimates that the average-cost function of the firm is

$$AC = X^2 + 2Y^2 - 2XY - 2X - 6Y + 20$$

(*a*) The manager of the firm would like to know the level of output of zipper X and zipper Y at which the average cost of the firm is minimized and the level of this minimum average cost. (*b*) The firm expects an order of both zippers that will require it to produce a total output of 6 units of both kinds of zippers (each unit may be a large number of zippers), and so the manager would also like to know how many of each type of zipper the firm must produce to minimize its average cost, and what its minimum average cost would be if it receives the order. The manager gives this assignment to two researchers who use different methods to obtain their answer. (*c*) While the firm expects the order to be of 6 units, it may be as large as 7 units or as small as 5 units. Determine the minimum average cost of the firm with these different order sizes.

SUPPLEMENTARY READINGS

For a problem-solving approach to the topics covered in this chapter, see:

Salvatore, Dominick: *Theory and Problems of Managerial Economics,* Schaum Outline Series (New York: McGraw-Hill, 1989), Chap. 2.

For a review of differential calculus, see:

Dowling, Edward T.: *Mathematics for Economists* (New York: McGraw-Hill, 1992).

Chiang, Alpha: *Fundamental Methods of Mathematical Economics,* 3rd ed. (New York: McGraw-Hill, 1984).

Mathematical optimization techniques are presented in:

Salvatore, Dominick: *Microeconomics,* 2nd ed. (New York: HarperCollins, 1994), mathematical appendix.

Baumol, William J.: *Economic Theory and Operations Analysis,* 4th ed. (Englewood Cliffs, N.J.: Prentice-Hall, 1977).

Silberberg, Eugene: *The Structure of Economics: A Mathematical Analysis* (New York: McGraw-Hill, 1990).

The new management tools are discussed in:

Walton, M.: *The Denning Management Method* (New York: Dodd and Mead, 1986).

Garvin, D. A.: *Managing Quality: The Strategic and Competitive Edge* (New York: Free Press, 1988).

Grant, R. M., R. Shani, and **R. Krishnan:** "TQM's Challenge to Managerial Theory and Practice," *Sloan Management Review,* Winter 1994, pp. 25–35.

Hammer, R. M., and **J. Champy:** *Reengineering the Corporation: A Manifesto for Business Revolution* (New York: HarperBusiness, 1993).

Nevis, E. C., A. J. DiBella, and **J. M. Gould:** "Understanding Organizations as Learning Systems," *Sloan Management Review,* Winter 1995, pp. 73–85.

Senge, P.: *The Fifth Discipline* (New York: Doubleday, 1990).

Senge, P.: *The Fifth Discipline Fieldbook* (New York: Doubleday, 1994).

INTEGRATING CASE STUDY ONE

The Decision to Invest in Wendy's Restaurants

Introductory Comment The following selection illustrates most of the concepts presented in this part of the text, and, thus, it serves as an excellent integrating case study. It clearly shows the nature and scope of managerial decisions in a current real-world situation. In addition, it illustrates the theory of the firm in actual operation and the importance and function of profits in providing the signal for the efficient allocation of society's resources. It also shows the firm's optimizing behavior as it attempts to minimize costs and maximize profits. Finally, it shows why increased competition and lower profit margins in the United States are driving the fast-food industry to expand abroad, where competition is weaker and profit margins are higher.

In less than 18 hours, Peter Salg will open a new Wendy's restaurant here, next to the University of Colorado campus. Mr. Salg plans to serve tomorrow morning's breakfast in the restaurant that today looks somewhat like a war zone, with hammers, drills, and saws littering the tables restaurant patrons will soon use.

Wendy's International Inc., expects to see at least 400 more operations like Mr. Salg's completed by the end of the year. Last year, 450 were opened, the most in any year since 1978. By 1989, the Wendy's chain will comprise 5,000 restaurants, 1,500 more than it has today. "The last fifteen years have been times of ever-increasing demand for restaurant services," Mr. Salg explains. Indeed, from 1970 to 1983 the number of franchised restaurants in the United States increased by 116 percent. Total sales, adjusted for inflation, soared 257 percent over the same period. Mr. Salg attributes the rapid growth to significant changes in demographic conditions.

"When I was a kid, you went out to eat once a month," he recalls. "Now people eat out four or five times a week." Higher incomes and the rapid flow of women into the work force account for a large part of the increased demand for eating out. "But all of that is slowing down," Mr. Salg says. "In the past you could open a restaurant and manage it well, and you'd do well. Now if you want more customers, you have to take them away from other restaurants. We have to take customers away from McDonald's, take them away from Burger King, take them away from the Mom-and-Pop restaurant down the street." Mr. Salg confirms a hunch of Wendy's executives—that the key to surviving is being big. "That's the attraction of franchising," he says. "Without the millions—sometimes billions—spent on marketing, a restaurant just won't be able to survive. Just being good isn't enough anymore. You have to be big and good."

For restaurant owners like Mr. Salg, this boils down to a growing competitive fervor with an increased awareness of the factors that affect the demand for meals at their restaurants, including demographic conditions, location, income levels, and prices. Many of the planning decisions that stem from analyses of these factors are made at Wendy's International in Dublin, Ohio. Detailed feasibility studies, prepared by analysts there, discuss data such as median income, population, and average age of the people working and living in a given area. They then estimate the number of fast-food restaurants the area can sustain and decide upon a number of Wendy's restaurants to build in the area. Executives then discuss the results of the studies with people like Mr. Salg, who have "area agreements" with the corporation. In 1985, for example, Wendy's analysts determined that Mr. Salg's area, which includes a four-county area north of Denver, could sustain at least 10 more Wendy's restaurants. Mr. Salg agreed to build them. Had he refused to build the restaurants, Wendy's would have offered the rights to build them to individual buyers.

The price of an established franchise varies with the revenue the restaurant is expected to generate. A restaurant near a college campus, for example, commands a higher price than a similar restaurant away from the heavy flow of fast-food restaurant patrons. A franchise that is expected to generate $17,000 per week earned by a typical Wendy's restaurant will cost more than the average $500,000 purhcase price—a price that does not include the physical asset of the building. Before construction can begin on a new restaurant, an owner must pay Wendy's headquarters a $25,000 franchise fee and sign a contract pledging to turn over 10 percent of the restaurant's total sales to the corporation. "This is the price," Mr. Salg comments, "of being part of the family." In addition, an owner signs a detailed agreement that outlines what products the restaurant will sell, how the products will be prepared and served, and the hours the store will operate. Over 60 percent of the money pledged by individual owners makes up Wendy's advertising budget, providing television commercials, billboards, and flashy brochures for audiences at national, regional, and local levels.

Another benefit of "being part of the family" is the discount rates on food and paper products available to individual restaurant owners. Wendy's International does not supply Mr. Salg with the beef, potatoes, and paper cups he uses in operating his restaurants. But the corporation does make national contracts with large-scale distributors for the benefit of franchise owners. "We don't have to use those distributors, but we get enormous cost cuts if we do," Mr. Salg says. Owners may purchase products from any vendor whose products fulfill Wendy's specifications. Beef served at the restaurants must have a fat content that falls within a 19 to 20 percent range, for example. For owners who do not wish to purchase products from the contracted suppliers, Wendy's provides a list of other large distributors whose products are satisfactory.

The cost of the products he uses are the basis for Mr. Salg's pricing strategy. "Wendy's does not tell us what we can charge for our meals," he explains. "They would be violating every federal franchise law if they did." To determine the prices of menu items, Mr. Salg looks at his costs, particularly his food costs. His "target food cost" lies between 28.7 and 29 percent of the retail price of the meal. Mr. Salg charges food prices that will yield food costs within his target. For some items, such as beverages, food costs are only 20 percent of the price of the item. For others—hamburgers, for example—food costs comprise 45 percent of the sale price. The overall food cost for a typical meal, however, must fall within his 28.7 to 29 percent target range. If Mr. Salg notices that his food costs are going over 29 percent of total sales, he considers raising his prices. Before he decides to do so, he "takes a walk to McDonald's to see what they're doing." The McDonald's restaurant nearest him generally charges 5 to 10 cents more for menu items comparable to Mr. Salg's. "So I always have a margin," he says. If Mr. Salg discovers a 10-cent spread between the price of a single hamburger at his restaurant and a comparable burger at McDonald's, he will experiment with a 5-cent increase in the price of his burger. If the extra nickel fails to produce enough additional revenue to put him within his target, he will increase the price of side items. "Running the price down the menu makes the increase less noticeable," Mr. Salg says.

"I don't raise my prices unless I have to," Mr. Salg says. "Every time we raise prices, we lose customers." The number of customers he loses depends on the degree to which he increases prices. With a 5-cent (4 percent) increase in the price of a single hamburger, Mr. Salg expects only a small loss of customers. "Those customers usually come back," he says. "But an increase in the price of a burger by 15 cents (12 percent) causes a tremendous reduction of customer traffic." Mr. Salg turns a trained ear to comments made by customers after he changes the price of any of his menu items. "I always listen very closely to what the customers say. I am very sensitive to their reactions." Mr. Salg has been listening to restaurant patrons for nearly 40 years. Restaurant management, the only career he's ever known, is second nature to him. He got his first job, he recalls, when he was 14—flipping hamburgers at an innovative young restaurant named McDonald's.

In early 1990, Wendy's introduced a mini-menu of "super value" items costing less than $1 and so did Burger King, Taco Bell, Pizza Hut, and Kentucky Fried Chicken (the latter three owned by PepsiCo Inc.). Late in 1990, McDonald's, the world's largest fast-food chain, was forced to respond and decided to mark down several of its menu items to well below $1 in a desperate effort to win back customers that it lost to competitors because of their lower prices. The move intensified an already brutal price war in the industry. While demand continued to grow, so did competition, and a shakeout in the fast-food industry is in the making with only the big chains probably surviving. Increased competition and lower profit margins at home are also driving the large fast-food chains to expand abroad, where competition is weaker and profit margins are higher. For example, almost 5,000 of the nearly 15,000 McDonald's restaurants are now in more than 70 countries outside the United States and McDonald's is now opening two restaurants abroad for every new one it opens at home. Indeed, the largest McDonald's (serving about 40,000 people per day) is now in Beijing. Burger King, the second largest fast-food chain (which is owned by Grand Metropolitan, the large British multinational), and Wendy's International are also expanding abroad.

Source: Adapted and reprinted with permission from Suzanne Tregarthen, "Pricing of Beef at Wendy's Restaurant," *The Margin,* March 1986, pp. 9–10; "Discount Menu Is Coming to McDonald's as Chain Tries to Win Back Customers," *The Wall Street Journal,* November 11, 1990, p. B1; "Overseas Sizzle for McDonald's," *The New York Times,* April 17, 1992, p. D1; "McDonald's Conquers the World," *Fortune,* October 17, 1994, pp. 103–116; and "Wendy's Expects Growth to Continue, Earnings Will Meet Analysts' Forecasts," *The Wall Street Journal,* February 22, 1994, p. B5C.

PART TWO

Demand Analysis

Part Two (Chapters 3 through 5) analyzes demand. This is one of the most important aspects of managerial economics since no firm could exist or survive if a sufficient demand for its product did not exist or could not be generated. Chapter 3 deals with demand theory and examines the forces that determine the demand for the firm's product. Chapter 4 then shows how a firm can estimate the demand for its product. Finally, Chapter 5 examines how a firm can forecast demand. The increasing importance of global products and global competition is examined throughout.

CHAPTER 3

Demand Theory

KEY TERMS

Consumer demand theory
Normal goods
Inferior goods
Individual's demand schedule
Individual's demand curve
Law of demand
Substitution effect
Income effect
Giffen good
Change in the quantity demanded
Change in demand
Market demand curve
Market demand function
Bandwagon effect
Snob effect
Monopoly
Perfect competition
Oligopoly
Monopolistic competition
Durable goods
Demand function faced by a firm
Derived demand
Producers' goods
Price elasticity of demand (E_P)
Point price elasticity of demand
Arc price elasticity of demand
Total revenue (TR)
Marginal revenue (MR)
Income elasticity of demand (E_I)
Point income elasticity of demand
Arc income elasticity of demand
Cross-price elasticity of demand (E_{XY})
Point cross-price elasticity of demand
Arc cross-price elasticity of demand

CHAPTER OUTLINE

In this chapter, we begin our analysis of consumer demand. Demand is one of the most important aspects of managerial economics since a firm would not be established or survive if a sufficient demand for its product did not exist or could not be created. That is, a firm could have the most efficient production techniques and the most effective management, but without a demand for its product that is sufficient to cover at least all production and selling costs over the long run, it simply would not survive. Indeed, many firms go out of business soon after being set up because their expectation of a sufficient demand for their products fails to materialize even with a great deal of advertising. Each year also sees many previously established and profitable firms close as a result of consumers' shifting their purchases to different firms and products. Demand is, thus, essential for the creation, survival, and profitability of a firm.

In this chapter we examine *demand theory,* or the forces that determine the demand for a firm's product. We also introduce the important concept of elasticity. These measure the responsiveness in the quantity demanded of a commodity to changes in each of the forces that determine demand. The forces that determine consumers' demand for a commodity are the price of the commodity, consumers' incomes, the price of related commodities, consumers' tastes, and all the other important but more specific forces that affect the demand for a particular commodity. In Chapter 4 we will show how a firm can actually estimate the demand for the product it sells, and in Chapter 5, we will examine how the firm can forecast future demand for the product. We will see that in order to properly estimate and forecast demand, we need to be familiar with the theory of demand presented in this chapter as well as with the estimating techniques presented in Chapter 4.

The strength and stability of present and future demand for the firm's product are also crucial in determining the most efficient methods of producing and selling the product, as well as in planning for the expansion of production facilities, and for entering new markets and other product lines. For example, if the demand for the firm's product is forecasted to grow but to be unstable, the firm may need to build a larger plant (to meet the growing demand) but may also have to carry larger inventories (because of the volatility of demand), and may want to increase its promotional effort to make demand less volatile (for example, by trying to increase off-season demand, finding new uses for its product, and so on). In any event, demand analysis is essential to the firm and to its profitability.

3-1 THE DEMAND FOR A COMMODITY

In this section, we begin by examining the determinants of an individual's demand for a commodity. By then aggregating or summing up the individual consumer's demands for the commodity, we obtain the market demand curve for the commodity. The share of the total market or industry demand for the product that a particular firm faces depends on the number of firms in the industry and on the structure or the form of market organization of the industry. Finally, in order to show how the abstract concepts of demand theory are applied in the real world, we examine the demand for Big Macs and the demand curve for sweet potatoes in the United States (see Case Studies 3-1 and 3-2).

An Individual's Demand for a Commodity

In managerial economics we are primarily interested in the demand for a commodity faced by the firm. This depends on the size of the total market or industry demand for the commodity, which in turn is the sum of the demands for the commodity of the individual consumers in the market. Thus, we begin by examining the theory of consumer demand in order to learn about the market demand, on which the demand for the product faced by a particular firm depends. The analysis is general and refers to almost any type of commodity (good or service).

The demand for a commodity arises from the consumers' willingness and ability (i.e., from their desire or want for the commodity backed by the income) to purchase the commodity. **Consumer demand theory** postulates that the quantity demanded of a commodity is a function of, or depends on, the price of the commodity, the consumer's income, the price of related (i.e., complementary and substitute) commodities, and the taste of the consumer. In functional form, we can express this as

$$Qd_X = f(P_X, I, P_Y, T) \tag{3-1}$$

where Qd_X = quantity demanded of commodity X by an individual per time period (year, month, week, day, or other unit of time)
P_X = price per unit of commodity X
I = consumer's income
P_Y = price of related (i.e., substitute and complementary) commodities
T = tastes of the consumer

Even the most unsophisticated of managers has probably had occasion to observe that when the firm increases the price of a commodity, sales generally decline. He or she also knows that the firm would probably sell more units of the commodity by lowering the price. Thus, he or she expects an inverse relationship between the quantity demanded of a commodity and its price. That is, when the price rises, the quantity purchased declines, and when the price falls, the quantity sold increases.

On the other hand, when a consumer's income rises, he or she usually purchases more of most commodities (shoes, steaks, movies, travel, education, automobiles, housing, and so on). These are known as **normal goods.** There are some goods and services, however, of which the consumer purchases less as income rises. For example, when a consumer's income rises, he or she usually consumes fewer potatoes, hot dogs, and hamburgers since he or she can now afford steaks and other higher-quality foods. Potatoes, hot dogs, hamburgers, and similar "cheap" foods are then **inferior goods** for the consumer. Most goods are normal, however, and we will be dealing primarily with these in the analysis that follows.

The quantity demanded of a commodity by an individual also depends on the price of related commodities. The individual will purchase more of a commodity

Table 3-1
An Individual's Demand Schedule for Commodity *X*

Price of commodity *X* per unit (P_X)	\$2	\$1	\$0.50
Quantity demanded of *X* per time period (Qd_X)	1	3	4.5

if the price of a substitute commodity increases or if the price of a complementary commodity falls. For example, a consumer will purchase more coffee if the price of tea (a substitute for coffee) increases or if the price of sugar (a complement of coffee) falls (since the price of a cup of coffee *with sugar* is then lower). Even more importantly, the quantity of a commodity that an individual purchases depends on tastes. For example, today's typical consumer purchases leaner meats than he or she did a generation ago because of heightened concern with the level of blood cholesterol and body weight (a change in tastes).

To summarize, then, consumer demand theory postulates that the quantity demanded of a commodity per time period increases with a reduction in its price, with an increase in the consumer's income, with an increase in the price of substitute commodities and a reduction in the price of complementary commodities, and with an increased taste for the commodity. On the other hand, the quantity demanded of a commodity declines with the opposite changes.

For the purpose of analysis it is often useful to examine the relationship between the quantity demanded of a commodity per unit of time and the price of the commodity only (i.e., independently of the other forces that affect demand). This can be accomplished by assuming, for the moment, that the individual's income, the price of related commodities, and tastes are unchanged. The inverse relationship between the price and the quantity demanded of the commodity per time period is then the **individual's demand schedule** for the commodity, and the plot of data (with price on the vertical axis and the quantity on the horizontal axis) gives the corresponding **individual's demand curve.**[1]

For example, Table 3-1 gives a very simple hypothetical demand schedule for an individual, and Figure 3-1 presents the corresponding individual's demand curve (d_X). Commodity X could refer, for example, to hamburgers. The table and the figure show that at the price of \$2 per unit the individual purchases 1 unit of the commodity per time period. At $P_X = \$1$, the individual purchases 3 units of X, and at $P_X = \$0.50$, $Qd_X = 4.5$. Note that the individual's demand curve, d_X in Figure 3-1, is negatively sloped, indicating that the individual purchases more of the commodity per time period at lower prices (while holding income, the price of related commodities, and tastes constant). The inverse relationship between the price of the commodity and the quantity demanded per time period is referred to as the **law of demand.**

The reason for the negative slope of d_X, or inverse relationship between P_X and Qd_X, is not difficult to find. When P_X falls, the quantity demanded of the commodity by the individual (Qd_X) increases because the individual substitutes

[1]Note that, by convention, quantity per unit of time (the dependent variable), rather than price (the independent variable), is plotted on the horizontal axis.

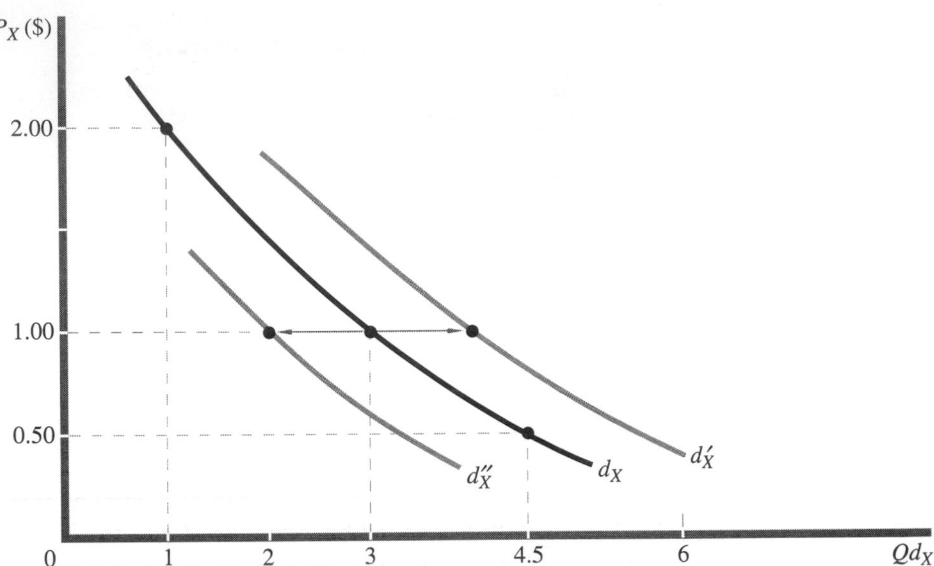

Figure 3-1
An Individual's Demand Curve for Commodity *X*

At the price of $2, the individual purchases 1 unit of the commodity per time period. At $P_X = \$1$, the individual purchases 3 units of *X*, and at $P_X = \$0.50$, $Qd_X = 4.5$. The inverse relationship between P_X and Qd_X (negative slope of d_X) is called the "law of demand." d_X shifts to the right, say, to d'_X, with an increase in the consumer's income, in the price of a substitute commodity, in tastes for the commodity, and with a reduction in the price of a complementary commodity. d_X shifts to the left, say, to d''_X, with the opposite changes.

in consumption commodity *X* for other commodities (which are now relatively more expensive). This is called the **substitution effect.** In addition, when the price of a commodity falls, a consumer can purchase more of the commodity with a given money income (i.e., his or her real income increases). This is called the **income effect.** Thus, a fall in P_X leads to an increase in Qd_X (so that d_X is negatively sloped) because of the substitution effect and the income effect.[2]

If any of the things held constant in drawing a demand curve change, the entire demand curve shifts. The individual's demand curve shifts upward or to the right (so that the individual demands more of the commodity at each commodity price) if the consumer's income increases, if the price of a substitute com-

[2]The demand curve shown in Figure 3-1 is derived with indifference curve analysis in the appendix to this chapter. If commodity *X* were an inferior good, the increase in real income resulting from the reduction of P_X would lead the consumer to purchase less, not more, of commodity *X*. Thus, the income effect would be negative, while the substitution effect would continue to be positive (i.e., to lead the consumer to purchase more of *X* when its price declines). Only in the very rare case when the consumer spends so much on commodity *X* that the negative income effect overwhelms the positive substitution effect will Qd_X fall when P_X falls (so that the demand curve would be positively sloped). Commodity *X* is then called a **Giffen good** (after the nineteenth-century English economist, Robert Giffen, who first discussed it). This is extremely rare in the real world, and we disregard this possibility in what follows.

modity increases or the price of a complementary commodity falls, and if the consumer's taste for the commodity increases. This gives d'_X in Figure 3-1. With opposite changes, d_X shifts to the left to, say, d''_X.[3] To clearly distinguish between a movement along a given demand curve (as a result of a change in the commodity price) from a shift in demand (as a result of a change in income, price of related commodities, and tastes), we refer to the first as a **change in the quantity demanded** and to the second as a **change in demand.**

From Individual to Market Demand

The **market demand curve** for a commodity is simply the *horizontal summation* of the demand curves of all the consumers in the market. For example, in the top part of Figure 3-2, the market demand curve for commodity X is obtained by the horizontal summation of the demand curve of individual 1 (d_1) and individual 2 (d_2), on the assumption that they are the only two consumers in the market. Thus, at $P_X = \$1$, the market quantity demanded of 5 units of commodity X is the sum of the 3 units of X demanded by individual 1 and the 2 units of X demanded by individual 2. If there were 100 individuals in the market, instead, each with demand curve d_X, the market demand curve for commodity X would be D_X (see the bottom part of Figure 3-2). D_X has the same shape as d_X, but the horizontal scale refers to hundreds of units of commodity X.[4]

The market demand curve for a commodity shows the various quantities of the commodity demanded in the market per time period (QD_X) at various alternative prices of the commodity, while holding everything else constant. The market demand curve for a commodity (just as an individual's demand curve) is negatively sloped, indicating that price and quantity are inversely related. That is, the quantity demanded of the commodity increases when its price falls and decreases when its price rises. The things held constant in drawing the market demand curve for a commodity are: the number of consumers in the market (N), consumers' incomes (I), the price of related (i.e., substitute and complementary) commodities (P_Y), and tastes (T). A change in any of these will cause the market demand curve of the commodity to shift in the same direction (and as a result) of the shift in the individuals' demand curves. Thus, we can express the general **market demand function** for commodity X as

$$QD_X = F(P_X, N, I, P_Y, T) \tag{3-2}$$

Finally, it must be pointed out that a market demand *curve* is simply the horizontal summation of the individual demand curves *only* if the consumption

[3]A change in expectations about the future price of a commodity will also result in a shift in the individual's demand curve. For example, if the individual expects prices to be lower in the future, he or she will postpone purchases in the anticipation of the lower prices in the future. Thus, the individual's demand curve for the commodity in the current period shifts to the left. On the other hand, if the individual expects prices to rise in the future, his or her demand curve for the present period shifts to the right, as the consumer increases present purchases to avoid future price increases.

[4]Note that the demand curves are curvilinear in the top part of Figure 3-2 but straight lines in the bottom part of the figure. Either form is possible, with the linear form perhaps more common.

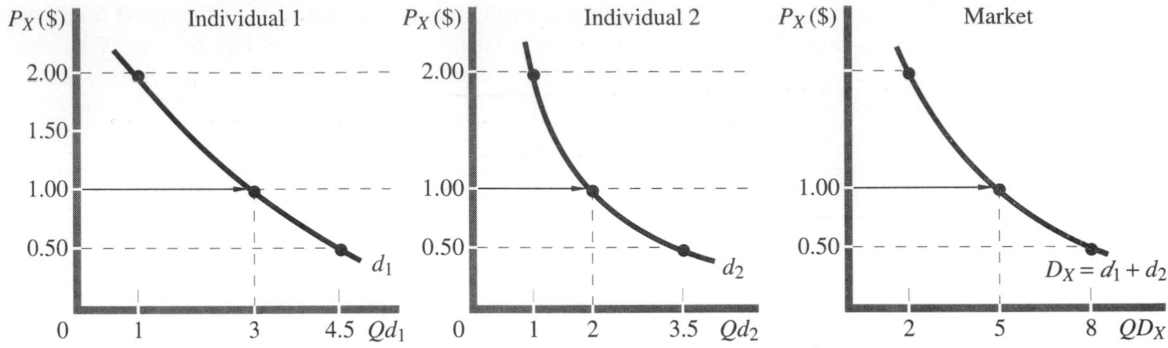

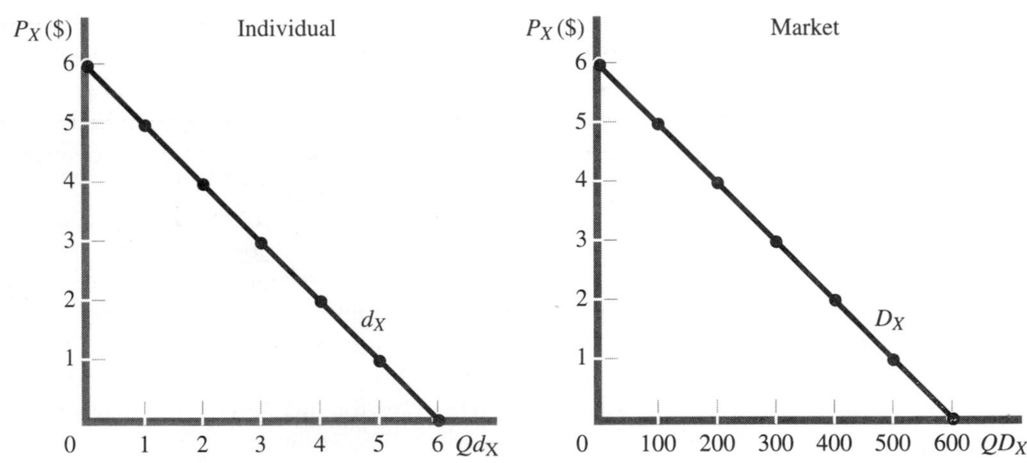

Figure 3-2
From Individual to Market Demand

The top part of the figure shows that the market demand curve for the commodity, D_X, is obtained from the horizontal summation of the demand curve of individual 1 (d_1) and individual 2 (d_2). The bottom part of the figure shows an individual's demand curve, d_X, and the market demand curve, D_X, on the assumption that there are 100 individuals in the market with demand curves identical to d_X.

decisions of individual consumers are independent. This is not always the case. For example, people sometimes demand a commodity because others are purchasing it and in order to be "fashionable." The result is a **bandwagon effect** to "keep up with the Joneses." This tends to make the market demand curve flatter than indicated by the simple horizontal summation of the individuals' demand curves. At other times, the opposite, or **snob effect,** occurs as many consumers seek to be different and exclusive by demanding less of a commodity as more people consume it. This tends to make the market demand curve steeper than indicated by the horizontal summation of the individuals' demand curves. For simplicity, however, we assume the absence of such bandwagon and snob effects in what follows.

The Demand Faced by a Firm

Since the analysis of the firm is central to managerial economics, we are primarily interested in the demand for a commodity faced by a firm. The demand for a commodity faced by a particular firm depends on the size of the market or industry demand for the commodity, the form in which the industry is organized, and the number of firms in the industry.

If the firm is the sole producer of a commodity for which there are no good substitutes (i.e., if the firm is a monopolist), the firm is or represents the industry and faces the industry or market demand for the commodity. **Monopoly** is rare in the real world, and, when it does occur, it is usually the result of a government franchise, which is accompanied by government regulation. Examples of this are the local telephone, electricity, public transportation, and other public utility companies. At the opposite extreme is the form of market organization called **perfect competition.** Here, there are a large number of firms producing a homogeneous (i.e., identical) product, and each firm is too small to affect the price of the commodity by its own actions. In such a case, each firm is a price taker and faces a horizontal demand curve for the commodity (i.e., the firm can sell any amount of the commodity without affecting its price). This form of market organization is also very rare. The closest we may have come to it in the United States was in the growing of wheat at the turn of the century when millions of small farmers raised wheat of the same type.

The vast majority of the firms operating in the United States and in other industrial countries today falls between the extremes of monopoly and perfect competition, into the forms of market organization known as "oligopoly" and "monopolistic competition." In **oligopoly,** there are only a few firms in the industry, producing either a homogeneous or standardized product (e.g., cement, steel, and chemicals) or a heterogeneous or differentiated product (e.g., automobiles, cigarettes, and soft drinks). The most striking characteristic of oligopoly is the interdependence that exists among the firms in the industry. Since there are only a few firms in the industry, the pricing, advertising, and other promotional behavior of each firm greatly affect the other firms in the industry and evoke imitation and retaliation. This is a very common form of market organization in the production sector of the economy, where efficiency requires large-scale operation (production).

The other very common form of market organization is **monopolistic competition.** Here, there are many firms selling a heterogeneous or differentiated product. As the name implies, monopolistic competition has elements of both competition and monopoly. The competitive element arises from the fact that there are many firms in the industry. The monopoly element arises because each firm's product is somewhat different from the product of other firms. Thus, the firm has some degree of control over the price it charges (i.e., the firm faces a negatively sloped demand curve). However, because the products of the many other firms in the industry are very similar, the degree of control that a firm has over the price of the product it sells is very limited. That is, each firm faces a demand curve which, though negatively sloped, is fairly flat, so that any increase in price would lead to a very large decline in sales. This form of market organization is very common in the service sector of the economy—witness the very large number of gasoline stations and barber shops in a given area, each selling similar but not identical products or services.

A detailed discussion of market organization will be presented in Chapters 9 and 10, but what has been said above is sufficient to allow us to identify the most important forces that determine the demand for a commodity faced by a firm. Under all forms of market organization, except perfect competition, the firm faces a negatively sloped demand curve for the commodity it sells, and this demand curve shifts with changes in the number of consumers in the market, consumers' incomes, the price of related commodities, consumers' tastes, as well as with changes in other more specific forces that may affect the firm's demand in the particular industry or market.

These other forces may be price expectations, the level of advertising and other promotional efforts on the part of the firm, the pricing and promotional policies of other firms in the industry (especially in oligopoly), availability of credit, the type of good that the firm sells, and so on. The demand curve for a product faced by a firm will shift to the right (so that the firm's sales increase at a given price) if consumers expect prices to rise in the future, if the firm mounts a successful advertising campaign, or if the firm introduces or increases credit incentives to stimulate the purchase of its product. On the other hand, the demand curve faced by a firm shifts to the left if consumers expect prices to fall in the future, if competitors reduce their prices, undertake a successful advertising campaign of their own, or introduce credit incentives.

The demand for a firm's product also depends on the type of product that the firm sells. If the firm sells **durable goods** (such as automobiles, washing machines, and refrigerators that provide services not only during the year when they are purchased but also in subsequent years, or goods that can be stored), the firm will generally face a more volatile or unstable demand than a firm selling nondurable goods. The reason is that consumers can run their cars, washing machines, or refrigerators a little longer by increasing their expenditures on maintenance and repairs, and they can postpone the purchase of a new unit until the economy improves and their income rises or credit incentives become available. They can also reduce inventories of storable goods. When the economy improves or credit incentives are introduced, the demand for durable goods can then increase (i.e., shift to the right) substantially.

We can specify the linear form of the **demand function faced by a firm** as

$$Q_X = a_0 + a_1P_X + a_2N + a_3I + a_4P_Y + a_5T + \cdots \tag{3-3}$$

where Q_X refers to the quantity demanded of commodity X per time period faced by the firm, and P_X, N, I, P_Y, and T refer, as before, to the price of the commodity, the number of consumers in the market, consumers' incomes, the price of related commodities, and consumers' tastes, respectively. The a's represent the coefficients to be estimated by regression analysis, which is the most used technique for estimating demand. Regression analysis will be examined in the next chapter. Here we simply examine the meaning and use of the estimated coefficients (i.e., the a's). The dots in Equation 3-3 refer to the other determinants of demand that are specific to the firm in a given industry and which can only be identified by an in-depth knowledge of the particular industry and firm.[5]

The demand faced by a firm will then determine the type and quantity of inputs or resources (producers' goods) that the firm will purchase or hire in order to produce or meet the demand for the goods and services that it sells. Since the demand for the inputs or resources that a firm uses depends on the demand for the goods and services it sells, the firm's demand for inputs is a **derived demand.** The greater the demand for the goods and services that the firm sells, the greater will be the firm's demand for the inputs or resources that are required to produce those goods and services. In fact, the firm's demand for **producers' goods,** such as capital equipment and raw materials that can be stored, is also more volatile and unstable than the firm's demand for perishable raw materials. These and other aspects of the demand for inputs or factors of production are examined in Chapter 6 (which deals with production) and in subsequent chapters.

Thus, we have a number of demands. There is the individual's demand for a commodity, the market demand for the commodity, the demand for the commodity that the firm faces, and the firm's derived demand for the inputs it needs to produce final commodities, and it is important to clearly distinguish among these different demand concepts.

[5]If tastes or other determinants of demand remain approximately constant during the period of the analysis, they can safely be omitted from Equation 3-3. This would be particularly useful in the case of tastes since it is often difficult to obtain reliable quantitative measures of changes in tastes. One way to capture changes in tastes is to include a time trend in the estimating regression (see Case Study 3-2).

Case Study 3-1

The Demand for Big Macs

McDonald's holds nearly a 30 percent share of the $65 billion U.S. restaurant business and 46 percent of its $2.6 billion burger business. It serves more than 22 million customers per day and, with sales of nearly $15 billion in 1993, dwarfs its competitors. After nearly three decades of double-digit gains, however, domestic sales at McDonald's have been growing slowly since 1986 as a result of higher prices, changing tastes, slow growth of the domestic economy, demographic changes, and increased competition from other fast-food chains and other forms of delivering fast foods.

Price increases at McDonald's exceeded inflation in each year since 1986 and in 9 of the last 17 years. The average check at McDonald's is now $4—a far cry from the 15-cent hamburger on which McDonald's got rich—and sent customers streaming to lower-pricing competitors. Concern over cholesterol and calories, as well as a slowing down of growth of the economy and in personal incomes, have also reduced growth. In addition, the proportion of the 15- to 29-year-olds (the primary fast-food customers) in the total population has shrunk from 27.5 to 22.5 percent during the past decade. Increased competition from other fast-food chains, other fast-food options (pizza, chicken, tacos, and so on), frozen fast foods, mobile units, and the vending machines have also slowed down the growth of demand for Big Macs.

McDonald's did not sit idle and tried to meet its challenges head on by introducing a "value menu" in 1990 with small hamburgers selling for as little as 59 cents (down from 89 cents) and a combination of burger, french fries, and soft drink for as much as half off. In response to increased public concern about cholesterol and calories, McDonald's began publicizing the nutritional content of its menu offerings, substituted vegetable oils for beef tallow in frying its french fries, replaced ice cream with lowfat yogurt, introduced bran muffins and cereals to its breakfast menu, and even (unsuccessfully) introduced the MacLean Deluxe—a new reduced-fat, quarter-pound hamburger on which McDonald's spent from $50 to $70 million to develop and promote. Furthermore, in response to increased competition from frozen fast foods, mobile units, and vending machines, an increasing number of McDonald's franchises have drive-throughs, from which they now generate almost half their business. McDonald's is also expanding very rapidly abroad, where it faces much less competition and where there is much more room for growth.

Source: "An American Icon Wrestles with a Troubled Future," *The New York Times,* May 12, 1991, Sec. 3, p. 1; and "Too Skinny a Burger Is a Mighty Hard Sell, McDonald's Learns," *The Wall Street Journal,* April 15, 1994, p. A1.

Case Study 3-2

The Demand for Sweet Potatoes in the United States

Using the technique of regression analysis presented in Chapter 4, Schrimper and Mathia estimated the following demand function for sweet potatoes in the United States for the period of 1949 to 1972:

$$QD_S = 7{,}609 - 1{,}606P_S + 59N + 947I + 479P_W - 271_t \qquad (3\text{-}4)$$

where QD_S = quantity of sweet potatoes sold per year in the United States per 1,000 hundredweight (cwt)

P_S = real-dollar price of sweet potatoes per hundredweight received by farmers

N = two-year moving average of total U.S. population, in millions

I = real per capita personal disposable income, in thousands of dollars

P_W = real-dollar price of white potatoes per hundredweight received by farmers

t = time trend ($t = 1$ for 1949, $t = 2$ for 1950, up to $t = 24$ for 1972)

The above estimated demand function indicates that the quantity demanded of sweet potatoes per year in 1,000-cwt (i.e., in 100,000-pound) units in the United States (QD_S) declines by 1,606 for each $1 increase in its price (P_S), increases by 59 for each 1 million increase in population (N), increases by 947 for each $1,000 increase in real income (I), increases by 479 for each $1 increase in the real price of white potatoes (P_W), but falls by 271 with each passing year (the coefficient of t, the time trend variable). Thus, the demand curve for sweet potatoes is negatively sloped, and it shifts to the right with an increase in population, in income, and in the price of white potatoes, but shifts to the left with each passing year. Since the demand for sweet potatoes increases (i.e., shifts to the right) with an increase in income, sweet potatoes are a normal good (even though we usually think of potatoes as being an inferior good). Since QD_S increases with an increase in P_W and declines with a reduction in P_W, white potatoes are a substitute for sweet potatoes. Finally, the negative coefficient of t can be taken to reflect the declining tastes for sweet potatoes over time.

If we now substitute into Equation 3-4 the actual values of $N = 150.73$, $I = 1.76$, $P_W = 2.94$, and $t = 1$ for the United States for the year 1949, we get the following equation for the U.S. demand curve for sweet potatoes in 1949:

$$\begin{aligned} QD_S &= 7{,}609 - 1{,}606P_S + 59(150.73) + 947(1.76) + 479(2.94) - 271(1) \\ &= 7{,}609 - 1{,}606P_S + 8{,}893 + 1{,}667 + 1{,}408 - 271 \\ &= 19{,}306 - 1{,}606P_S \end{aligned} \tag{3-5}$$

By then substituting the value of \$7 for P_S into Equation 3-5, we get $QD_S = 8{,}064$. If $P_S = \$5.60$ (the actual real price of sweet potatoes in the United States in 1949), $QD_S = 10{,}312$. Finally, if $P_S = \$4$, $QD_S = 12{,}882$. This demand schedule is plotted as D_X in Figure 3-3.

On the other hand, if we substitute into Equation 3-4 the values of $N = 208.78$, $I = 3.19$, $P_W = 2.41$, and $t = 24$ for the year 1972, we get Equation 3-6 for the U.S. demand curve for sweet potatoes in 1972:

$$QD'_S = 17{,}598 - 1{,}606P_S \tag{3-6}$$

Figure 3-3
The Market Demand Curve for Sweet Potatoes in the United States

By substituting into Equation 3-5 the values for P_S of \$7, \$5.60, \$4 and plotting, we get market demand curve D_X for sweet potatoes in the United States for 1949. On the other hand, by substituting the same values for P_S into Equation 3-6, we get D'_X as the U.S. demand curve for sweet potatoes in 1972. Since the constant term is smaller for 1972 than for 1949, D'_X is to the left of D_X.

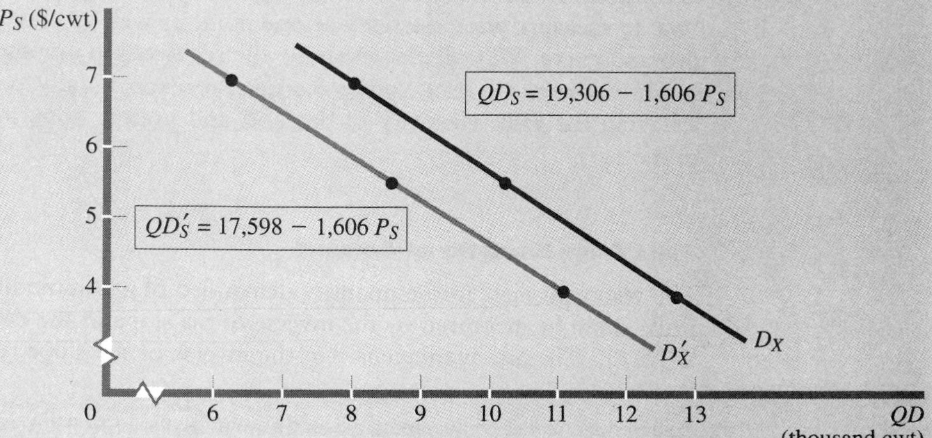

By then substituting the same values as above for P_S into Equation 3-6, we get market demand curve D'_X in Figure 3-3. Note that the reduction in tastes for sweet potatoes between 1949 and 1972 and in P_W tends to shift D_X to the left, while the increase in N and I tends to shift D_X to the right. Since the first set of forces overwhelms the second, D'_X is to the left of D_X. In general, it is the average value of the independent or explanatory variables over the entire period that is substituted into the estimated demand equation to get the equation of the *average* demand curve for the period (see Problem 2, with the answer at the end of the text).

Finally, it must be pointed out that each producer of sweet potatoes shares in the total market demand for sweet potatoes. Therefore, for a given change in the market price of potatoes or other variable, the quantity response by a firm will be some fraction of the total market response. Furthermore, in order to estimate demand correctly, a producer would have to include explanatory variables in addition to those used to estimate the market demand—as indicated in the previous section. Practically all the available estimates of demand, however, refer to market demand because firms do not want to disclose their knowledge of the market and their strategies and plans to competitors. An example of the demand faced by a firm is given in Problem 2 (with the answer at the end of the text).

Source: Ronald A. Schrimper and Gene A. Mathia, "Reservation and Market Demands for Sweet Potatoes at the Farm Level," *American Journal of Agricultural Economics,* vol. 57, February 1975.

3-2 PRICE ELASTICITY OF DEMAND

The responsiveness in the quantity demanded of a commodity to a change in its price is very important to the firm. Sometimes, lowering the price of the commodity increases sales sufficiently to increase total revenues. At other times, lowering the commodity price reduces the firm's total revenues. By affecting sales, the pricing policies of the firm also affect its production costs, and thus its profitability. In this section, we introduce measures of the responsiveness (elasticity) in the quantity demanded of the commodity to a change in its price. We will show how to measure price elasticity at one point as well as over a range (arc) of the demand curve. We will also examine the relationship among price elasticity, the total revenue of the firm, and its marginal revenue. Finally, we discuss the factors affecting the price elasticity of demand and present some real-world estimates of it.

Point Price Elasticity of Demand

The responsiveness in the quantity demanded of a commodity to a change in its price could be measured by the inverse of the slope of the demand curve (i.e., by $\Delta Q/\Delta P$).[6] The disadvantage is that the inverse of the slope ($\Delta Q/\Delta P$) is expressed

[6]Since price is plotted on the vertical axis and quantity on the horizontal axis, the quantity response to a change in price could be measured by $\Delta Q/\Delta P$, which is the inverse of the slope of the demand curve.

in terms of the units of measurement. Thus, simply changing prices from dollars to cents would change the value of $\Delta Q/\Delta P$ one hundredfold. Furthermore, comparison of changes in quantity to changes in prices across commodities would be meaningless. In order to avoid these disadvantages, we used instead the price elasticity of demand.

The **price elasticity of demand (E_P)** is given by the percentage change in the quantity demanded of the commodity divided by the percentage change in its price, holding constant all the other variables in the demand function. That is,

$$E_P = \frac{\Delta Q/Q}{\Delta P/P} = \frac{\Delta Q}{\Delta P} \cdot \frac{P}{Q} \tag{3-7}$$

where ΔQ and ΔP refer, respectively, to the change in quantity and the change in price. Note that the inverse of the slope of the demand curve (that is, $\Delta Q/\Delta P$) is a component, but only a component, of the elasticity formula and that the value of $\Delta Q/\Delta P$ is negative because price and quantity move in opposite directions (i.e., when P rises, Q falls, and vice versa).[7]

Equation 3-7 gives the **point price elasticity of demand,** or the elasticity at a given point on the demand curve. For example, for D_X (the market demand curve for commodity X in Figure 3-2, repeated above for ease of reference) in Figure 3-4, $\Delta Q/\Delta P = -100/\$1$ at every point on D_X (since D_X is linear), and so price elasticity at point B is

$$E_P = \frac{\Delta Q}{\Delta P} \cdot \frac{P}{Q} = \frac{-100}{\$1} \cdot \frac{\$5}{100} = -1\left(\frac{5}{1}\right) = -5$$

This means that the quantity demanded declines by 5 percent for each 1 percent increase in price, while holding constant all the other variables in the demand function. At point C on D_X, $E_P = -1(\frac{4}{2}) = -2$; at point F, $E_P = -1(\frac{3}{3}) = -1$; at point G, $E_P = -1(\frac{2}{4}) = -\frac{1}{2}$; and at point H, $E_P = -1(\frac{1}{5}) = -\frac{1}{5}$.[8]

As the above calculations show, the price elasticity of demand is usually different at different points on the demand curve.[9] For a linear demand curve, such as D_X in Figure 3-4, the price elasticity of demand has an absolute value (that is, $|E_P|$) that is greater than 1 (i.e., the demand curve is elastic) above the geometric midpoint of the demand curve; $|E_P| = 1$ at the geometric midpoint (that is,

[7]In terms of calculus,

$$E_P = \frac{\partial Q}{\partial P} \cdot \frac{P}{Q}$$

We take the partial rather than the regular derivative of Q with respect to P in order to remind ourselves that the other variables included in the demand function are to be held constant in measuring the effect of a change in P on Q.

[8]Sometimes the absolute value of E_P (that is, $|E_P|$) is reported. This creates no difficulty as long as we remember that price and quantity move in opposite directions along the demand curve. Note that at point J, $E_P = -1(\frac{0}{6}) = 0$, while at point A, $E_P = -1(\frac{6}{0}) = -\infty$. Thus, E_P can range anywhere from 0 to $-\infty$.

[9]Since the slope and its inverse are constant for a linear demand curve, but P and Q vary at different points on the demand curve, E_P varies at different points on the demand curve.

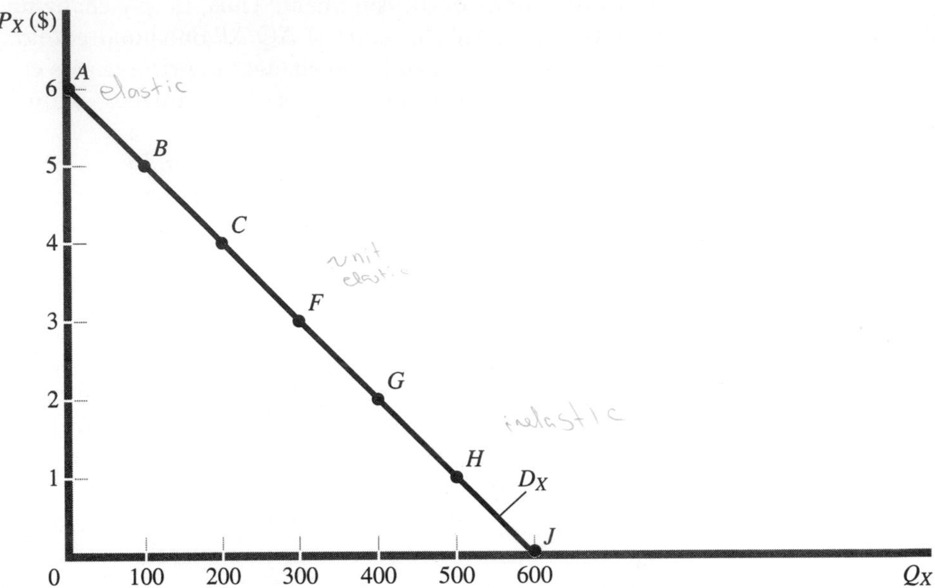

Figure 3-4
The Point Price Elasticity of Demand
At point *B* on D_X,

$$E_P = \frac{\Delta Q}{\Delta P} \cdot \frac{P}{Q} = \frac{-100}{\$1} \cdot \frac{\$5}{100} = -1\left(\frac{5}{1}\right) = -5$$

At point *C*, $E_P = -1(\frac{4}{2}) = -2$; at point *F*, $E_P = -1(\frac{3}{3}) = -1$; at point *G*, $E_P = -1(\frac{2}{4}) = -\frac{1}{2}$; and at point *H*, $E_P = -1(\frac{1}{5}) = -\frac{1}{5}$.

D_x is unitary elastic), and $|E_P| < 1$ below the midpoint (that is, D_X is inelastic). This is confirmed by examining the values of E_P found above for D_X.[10]

Note that the value of $\Delta Q/\Delta P$ is given by a_1, the estimated coefficient of *P* in regression Equation 3-3.[11] Therefore, the formula for the point price elasticity of demand can be rewritten as

$$E_P = a_1 \cdot \frac{P}{Q} \tag{3-8}$$

where a_1 is the estimated coefficient of *P* in the linear regression of *Q* on *P* and other explanatory variables. For example, with $a_1 = -1{,}606$ cwt/$1 in regression

[10]The point price elasticity of demand can also be obtained geometrically by dividing the price of the commodity (*P*) at the point on the demand curve at which we want to find the elasticity by $P - A$, where *A* is the price at which the quantity demanded is zero (i.e., the price at which the demand curve crosses the vertical axis). For a curvilinear demand curve, we draw a tangent to the demand curve at the point at which we want to measure E_P and then proceed as if we were dealing with a linear demand curve (see Problem 5, with the answer at the end of the text).

[11]In terms of calculus, $\Delta Q/\Delta P = \partial Q/\partial P$. Since the exponent of *P* is 1 in Equation 3-3, $\partial Q/\partial P = a_1$ (the coefficient of *P*).

Equation 3-4, and $Q_S = 8{,}064$ cwt at $P_S = \$7$, $E_P = -1{,}606(7/8{,}064) = -1.39$. This means that a 1 percent increase in P_S leads to a 1.39 percent decline in Q_S.

Arc Price Elasticity of Demand

More frequently than point price elasticity of demand, we measure **arc price elasticity of demand,** or the price elasticity of demand between two points on the demand curve, in the real world. If we used Formula 3-7 to measure arc price elasticity of demand, however, we would get different results depending on whether the price rose or fell. For example, using Formula 3-7 to measure arc price elasticity for a movement from point C to point F (i.e., for a price decline) on demand curve D_X in Figure 3-4, we would obtain

$$E_P = \frac{\Delta Q}{\Delta P} \cdot \frac{P}{Q} = \frac{100}{-\$1} \cdot \frac{\$4}{200} = -2$$

On the other hand, using Formula 3-7 to measure arc price elasticity for a *price increase* from point F to point C, we would get

$$E_P = \frac{\Delta Q}{\Delta P} \cdot \frac{P}{Q} = \frac{100}{-\$1} \cdot \frac{\$3}{300} = -1$$

To avoid this, we use the average of the two prices and the average of the two quantities in the calculations. Thus, the formula for arc price elasticity of demand (E_P) can be expressed as

$$E_P = \frac{\Delta Q}{\Delta P} \cdot \frac{(P_2 + P_1)/2}{(Q_2 + Q_1)/2} = \frac{Q_2 - Q_1}{P_2 - P_1} \cdot \frac{P_2 + P_1}{Q_2 + Q_1} \tag{3-9}$$

where the subscripts 1 and 2 refer to the original and to the new values, respectively, of price and quantity, or vice versa. For example, using Formula 3-9 to measure the arc price elasticity of D_X for a movement from point C to point F, we get

$$E_P = \frac{Q_2 - Q_1}{P_2 - P_1} \cdot \frac{P_2 + P_1}{Q_2 + Q_1} = \frac{300 - 200}{\$3 - \$4} \cdot \frac{\$3 + \$4}{300 + 200} = \frac{7}{-5} = -1.4$$

We now get the same result for the reverse movement from point F to point C:

$$E_P = \frac{Q_2 - Q_1}{P_2 - P_1} \cdot \frac{P_2 + P_1}{Q_2 + Q_1} = \frac{200 - 300}{\$4 - \$3} \cdot \frac{\$4 + \$3}{200 + 300} = \frac{-7}{5} = -1.4$$

This means that *between* points C and F on D_X, a 1 percent change in price results, on the average, in a 1.4 percent *opposite* change in the quantity demanded of commodity X. Note that the value of $E_P = -1.4$ for arc price elasticity of demand is between the values of $E_P = -2$ and $E_P = -1$ obtained by the use of Formula 3-7 for the point price elasticity of demand.

While we have been examining the price elasticity of the market demand curve for a commodity, the concept applies equally well to individuals' and firms' demand curves. In general, the price elasticity of the demand curve that a firm faces (i.e., the absolute value of E_P) is larger than the price elasticity of the corresponding market demand curve because the firm faces competition from similar commodities from rival firms, while there are few if any close substitutes for the *industry's* product from other industries.

Price Elasticity, Total Revenue, and Marginal Revenue

There is an important relationship between the price elasticity of demand and the firm's total revenue and marginal revenue. **Total revenue (*TR*)** is equal to price (P) times quantity (Q), while **marginal revenue (*MR*)** is the change in total revenue per unit change in output or sales (quantity demanded).[12] That is,

$$TR = P \cdot Q \tag{3-10}$$

$$MR = \frac{\Delta TR}{\Delta Q} \tag{3-11}$$

With a decline in price, total revenue increases if demand is elastic (i.e., if $|E_P| > 1$); TR remains unchanged if demand is unitary elastic, and TR declines if demand is inelastic.

The reason for this is that if demand is elastic, a price decline leads to a proportionately larger increase in quantity demanded, and so total revenue increases. When demand is unitary elastic, a decline in price leads to an equal proportionate increase in quantity demanded, and so total revenue remains unchanged. Finally, if demand is inelastic, a decline in price leads to a smaller proportionate increase in quantity demanded, and so the total revenue of the firm declines. Since a linear demand curve is elastic above the midpoint, unitary elastic at the midpoint, and inelastic below the midpoint, a reduction in price leads to an increase in TR down to the midpoint of the demand curve (where total revenue is maximum) and to a decline thereafter. MR is positive as long as TR increases; MR is zero when TR is maximum, and MR is negative when TR declines.

For example, suppose that a firm is a monopolist and faces the market demand curve for commodity X shown in Figure 3-4. The market demand schedule that the firm faces is then the one given in the first two columns of Table 3-2. The price elasticity of demand at various prices is given in column 3 and equals those found on page 92 for demand curve D_X. The total revenue of the firm is given in column 4 and is obtained by multiplying price by quantity. The marginal revenue of the firm is given in column 5 and is obtained by finding the change in total revenue per unit change in output. Note that TR increases as long as $|E_P| > 1$, TR is maximum when $|E_P| = 1$, and TR declines when $|E_P| < 1$.

[12]Note that $TR/Q = AR = P$, where AR is the average revenue. Thus, the price that the firm receives per unit of the commodity is equal to the average revenue of the firm.

Table 3-2
Price Elasticity, Total Revenue, and Marginal Revenue

(1) P	(2) Q	(3) E_P	(4) $TR = P \cdot Q$	(5) $MR = \Delta TR/\Delta Q$
\$6	0	$-\infty$	\$ 0	—
5	100	-5	500	\$5
4	200	-2	800	3
3	300	-1	900	1
2	400	$-\frac{1}{2}$	800	-1
1	500	$-\frac{1}{5}$	500	-3
0	600	0	0	-5

MR is positive as long as *TR* increases (i.e., as long as demand is elastic) and negative when *TR* declines (i.e., when demand is inelastic).

The relationship between the price elasticity of demand and the total revenue and marginal revenues of the firm given in Table 3-2 is shown graphically in Figure 3-5. Note that since marginal revenue is defined as the change in total revenue per unit change in output or sales, the *MR* values given in column 5 of Table 3-2 are plotted *between* the various levels of output in the bottom panel of Figure 3-5. Note also that the *MR* curve starts at the same point as D_X on the vertical or price axis and at every point bisects (i.e., cuts in half) the distance of D_X from the price axis.[13]

There is an important and often-used relationship among marginal revenue, price, and the price elasticity of demand given by[14]

$$MR = P\left(1 + \frac{1}{E_P}\right) \tag{3-12}$$

[13]In terms of calculus, $MR = d(TR)/dQ$. Given demand function $Q = 600 - 100P$, $P = 6 - Q/100$, and $TR = PQ = (6 - Q/100)Q = 6Q - Q^2/100$. Therefore,

$$\frac{d(TR)}{dQ} = MR = 6 - \frac{Q}{50}$$

Setting

$$\frac{d(TR)}{dQ} = 0$$

we get $Q = 300$. That is, the *TR* curve has zero slope at $Q = 300$. To ensure that *TR* is a maximum rather than a minimum of $Q = 300$, we find

$$\frac{d^2(TR)}{dQ^2}$$

Since this is negative (that is, $-\frac{1}{50}$), *TR* is maximum at $Q = 300$ (see page 96).

[14]Since $TR = PQ$, in terms of calculus,

$$MR = \frac{d(PQ)}{dQ} = P + Q\frac{dP}{dQ} = P\left(1 + \frac{dP}{dQ} \cdot \frac{Q}{P}\right) = P\left(1 + \frac{1}{E_P}\right)$$

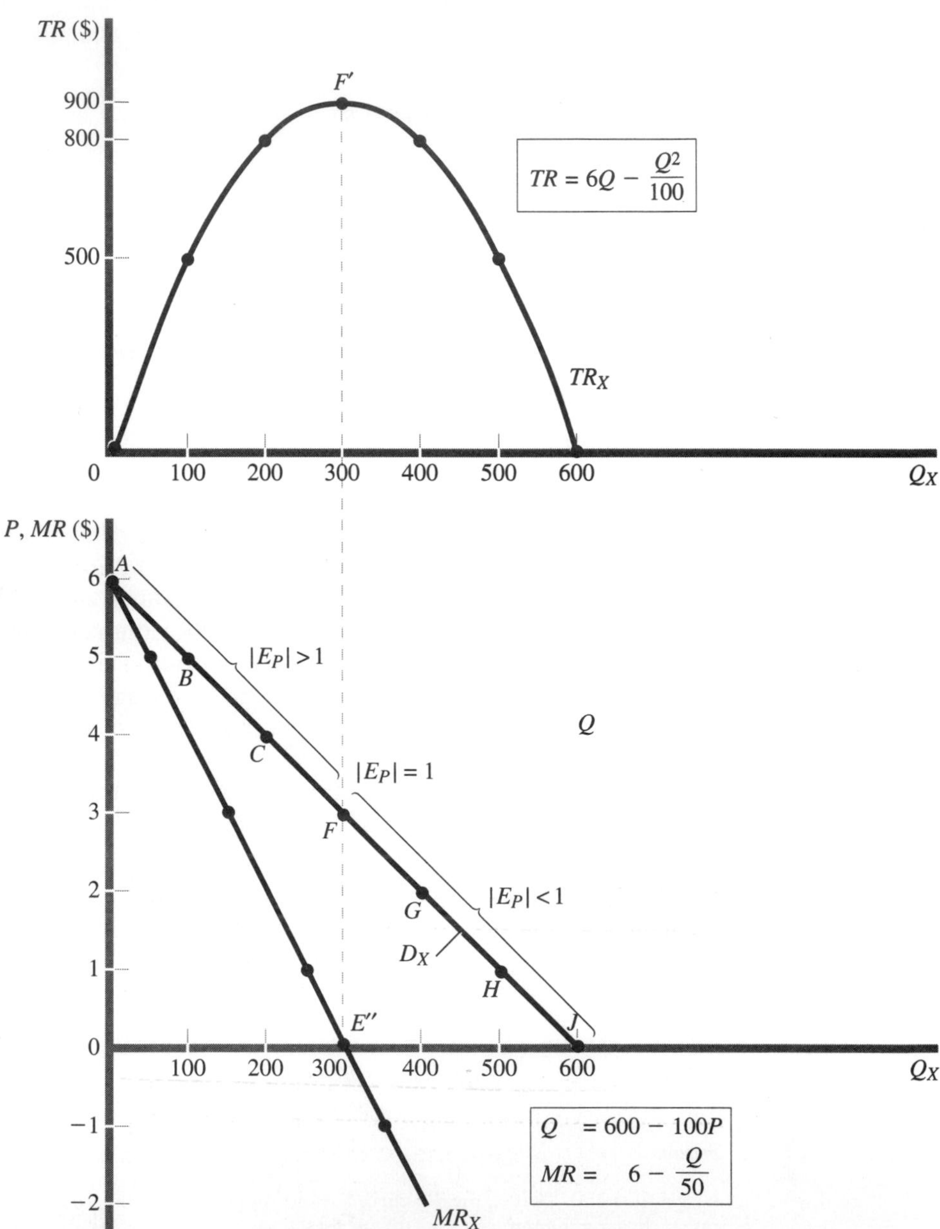

Figure 3-5
Demand, Total Revenue, Marginal Revenue, and Price Elasticity
As long as demand is price elastic (i.e., up to 300 units of output), a price reduction increases total revenue (*TR*), and marginal revenue (*MR*) is positive. At $Q = 300$, demand is unitary price elastic, *TR* is maximum, and $MR = 0$. When demand is price inelastic (i.e., for outputs greater than 300), a price reduction reduces *TR*, and *MR* is negative.

For example, from Table 3-2 we know that when $P = \$4$, $E_P = -2$. Substituting these values into Formula 3-12, we get

$$MR = \$4\left(1 + \frac{1}{-2}\right) = \$4\left(1 - \frac{1}{2}\right) = 2$$

The value of $MR = \$2$ when $P = \$4$ is confirmed by examining the bottom panel of Figure 3-5. At $P = \$3$, $E_P = -1$, and

$$MR = \$3\left(1 + \frac{1}{-1}\right) = 0$$

(see the bottom panel of Figure 3-5). At $P = \$2$, $E_P = -\frac{1}{2}$, and

$$MR = \$2\left(1 + \frac{1}{-0.5}\right) = -2$$

(see the bottom of panel of Figure 3-5).

The above relationships among E_P, TR, MR, and P hold for both the firm and the industry under any form of market organization. If the firm is a perfect competitor in the product market, it faces a horizontal or infinitely elastic demand curve for the commodity. Then the change in total revenue in selling each additional unit of the commodity (i.e., the marginal revenue) equals price. This is confirmed by using Formula 3-12. That is,

$$MR = P\left(1 + \frac{1}{-\infty}\right) = P$$

For example, in Figure 3-6, if the firm sells $3X$, its $TR = \$12$. If it sells $4X$, $TR = \$16$. Thus, $MR = P = \$4$, and the demand and marginal revenue curves that the firm faces coincide. (The perfectly competitive model will be examined in Chapter 9.) On the other hand, if the firm faced a vertical demand curve (so that the quantity demanded remains the same regardless of price), $E_P = 0$ throughout the demand curve. This is very rare in the real world.[15]

Factors Affecting the Price Elasticity of Demand

The price elasticity of demand for a commodity depends primarily on the availablity of substitutes for the commodity but also on the length of time over which the quantity response to the price change is measured. The size of the price elasticity of demand is larger the closer and the greater is the number of available substitutes for the commodity. For example, the demand for sugar is more price elastic than the demand for table salt because sugar has better and more substitutes (honey and saccharine) than salt. Thus, a given percentage increase in the

[15]If the demand curve assumes the shape of a rectangular hyperbola (so that total revenue is constant regardless of price), the price elasticity of demand is constant and is equal to -1 throughout the demand curve. For example, if $Q = P^b$, $dQ/dP = bP^{b-1}$ and $E_P = (dQ/dP)(P/Q) = (bP^{b-1})(P/Q) = bP^b/Q$; but since $Q = P^b$, $E_P = b = 1$ (the exponent of P) and is the same throughout the demand curve.

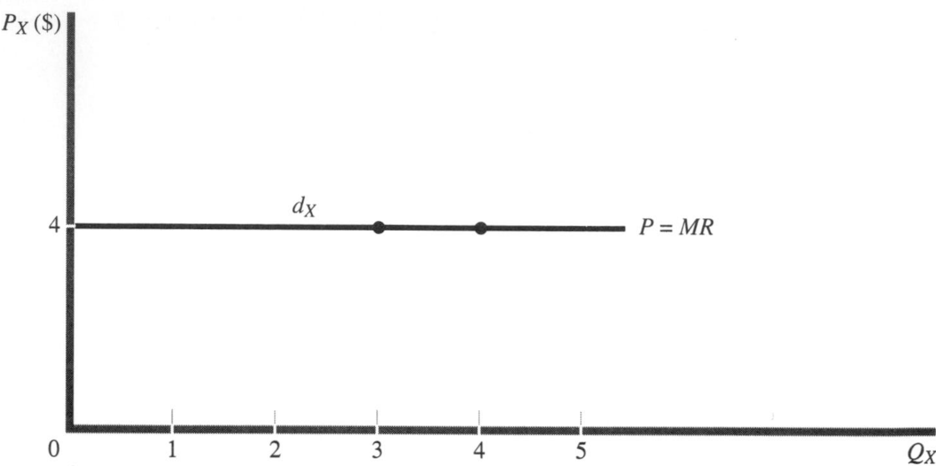

Figure 3-6
The Demand Curve Faced by a Perfectly Competitive Firm

The demand curve for the output of a perfectly competitive firm is horizontal or infinitely elastic. Thus, $P = MR$, and the demand curve and marginal revenue curves of the firm coincide.

price of sugar and salt elicits a larger percentage reduction per time period in the quantity demanded of sugar than of salt.

In general, the more narrowly a commodity is defined, the greater is its price elasticity of demand because the greater will be the number of substitutes. For example, the price elasticity for Coke is much greater than the price elasticity for soft drinks in general and still larger than the price elasticity of demand for all nonalcoholic beverages. If a commodity is defined so that it has very close substitutes, its price elasticity of demand is likely to be very large indeed and may be close to infinity. For example, if a producer of aspirin tried to increase the price above the general range of market prices for aspirin, he or she would stand to lose a very large portion of his or her sales as buyers can readily switch most of their purchases to competitors who sell very similar products.

The price elasticity of demand is also larger the longer is the time period allowed for consumers to respond to the change in the commodity price. The reason is that it usually takes some time for consumers to learn of the availability of substitutes and to adjust their purchases to the price change. For example, during the period immediately following the sharp increase in gasoline prices in 1974, the price elasticity of demand for gasoline was very low. Over the period of several years, however, the reduction in the quantity demanded of gasoline was much greater (i.e., the long-run price elasticity of demand for gasoline was much larger) than in the short run as consumers replaced their gas guzzlers with fuel-efficient, compact automobiles, switched to car pools and to public transportation, and took other steps to reduce gasoline consumption. Thus, for a given price change, the quantity response is likely to be much larger in the long run than in the short run, and so the price elasticity of demand is likely to be much greater in the long run than in the short run.[16]

[16]It is also said sometimes that the price elasticity of demand is larger the greater is the number of uses of the commodity, the smaller is the importance of the commodity in consumers' budgets (i.e., the smaller is the proportion of income that consumers spend on the commodity), and the more in the nature of a durable good is the commodity. Not everyone agrees with these statements, and, in fact, they are often contradicted by empirical studies.

Case Study 3-3

Price Elasticities of Demand in the Real World

Table 3-3 gives the estimated absolute values of the short-run and long-run price elasticities of demand (E_P) for selected commodities in the United States. The table shows that the long-run price elasticities of demand for most commodities are much larger than the corresponding short-run price elasticities.

Table 3-3
Estimated Short-Run and Long-Run Price Elasticity of Demand (E_P) for Selected Commodities, United States

	Elasticity	
Commodity	**Short Run**	**Long Run**
Radio and TV repairs	0.47	3.84
Motion pictures	0.87	3.67
Clothing*	0.90	2.90
China and glassware	1.54	2.55
Household natural gas†	1.40	2.10
Tobacco products	0.46	1.89
Electricity (household)	0.13	1.89
Foreign travel	0.14	1.77
Bus transportation (local)	0.20	1.20
Medical insurance	0.31	0.92
Jewelry and watches	0.41	0.67
Gasoline‡	0.20	0.60
Stationery	0.47	0.56

Source: H. S. Houthakker and L. S. Taylor, *Consumer Demand in the United States: Analyses and Projections* (Cambridge, Mass.: Harvard University Press, 1970).
*M. R. Baye, D. W. Jansen, and T. W. Lee, "Advertising in Complete Demand Systems," *Applied Economics,* vol. 24, 1992.
†G. R. Lakshmanan and W. Anderson, "Residential Energy Demand in the United States," *Regional Science and Urban Economics,* August 1980.
‡J. L. Sweeney, "The Response of Energy Demand to Higher Prices: What Have We Learned?" *American Economic Review,* May 1984.

item, such as vacations in the Caribbean, will increase very much when the economy is booming and fall sharply during recessionary periods. While somewhat sheltered from changing economic conditions, firms selling necessities may want to upgrade their product to share in the rise of incomes in the economy over time. Knowledge of income elasticity of demand is also important for a firm in identifying more precisely the market for its product (i.e., which type of consumers are most likely to purchase the product) and in determining the most suitable media for its promotional campaign to reach the targeted audience.

Case Study 3-4

Income Elasticities of Demand in the Real World

The third and last rows of Table 3-4 show, respectively, that the income elasticity of demand is 3.09 for foreign travel and −0.36 for flour. This means that a 1 percent increase in consumers' income leads to a 3.09 percent increase in expenditures on foreign travel but to a 0.36 percent *reduction* in expenditures on flour. Thus, foreign travel is a (strong) luxury while flour is a (weak) inferior good. Indeed, all of the other commodities shown in the table are luxuries, except tobacco products, china and glassware, and chicken and pork (which are necessities).

Note that the income elasticities given in Table 3-4 are measured as the percentage change in expenditures on the various commodities (rather than the percentage change in the *quantity* purchased of the various commodities). To the extent that prices are held constant, however, we get the same results as if the percentage change in quantities were used.

Table 3-4
Estimated Income Elasticity of Demand (E_I) for Selected Commodities, United States

Commodity	Income Elasticity	Commodity	Income Elasticity
Radio and TV repairs	5.20	Gasoline	1.36
Motion pictures	3.41	Beef*	1.06
Foreign travel	3.09	Tobacco products	0.86
Medical insurance	2.02	China and glassware	0.77
Electricity (household)	1.94	Chicken*	0.28
Bus transportation (local)	1.89	Pork*	0.14
Stationery	1.83	Flour	−0.36
Jewelry and watches	1.64		

Source: H. S. Houthakker and L. S. Taylor, *Consumer Demand in the United States: Analyses and Projections* (Cambridge, Mass.: Harvard University Press, 1970).

*D. B. Suits, "Agriculture," in W. Adams, ed., *Structure of American Industry* (New York: Macmillan, 1990).

3-4 CROSS-PRICE ELASTICITY OF DEMAND

The demand for a commodity also depends on the price of related (i.e., substitute and complementary) commodities. For example, if the price of tea rises, the demand for coffee increases (i.e., shifts to the right, and more coffee is demanded at each coffee price) as consumers substitute coffee for tea in consumption. On the other hand, if the price of sugar (a complement of coffee) rises, the demand for coffee declines (shifts to the left so that less coffee is demanded at each coffee price) because the price of a cup of coffee *with* sugar is now higher.

We can measure the responsiveness in the demand for commodity X to a change in the price of commodity Y with the **cross-price elasticity of demand** (E_{XY}). This is given by the percentage change in the demand for commodity X divided by the percentage change in the *price of commodity* Y, holding constant all the other variables in the demand function, including income and the price of commodity X. As with price and income elasticities, we have point and arc cross-price elasticity of demand. **Point cross-price elasticity of demand** is given by

$$E_{XY} = \frac{\Delta Q_X/Q_X}{\Delta P_Y/P_Y} = \frac{\Delta Q_X}{\Delta P_Y} \cdot \frac{P_Y}{Q_X} \tag{3-16}$$

where ΔQ_X and ΔP_Y refer, respectively, to the change in the quantity of commodity X and the change in the price of commodity Y.[19]

Note that the value of $\Delta Q_X/\Delta P_Y$ is given by a_4, the estimated coefficient of P_Y, in regression Equation 3-3.[20] Therefore, the formula for the point price elasticity of demand can be rewritten as

$$E_{XY} = a_4 \cdot \frac{P_Y}{Q_X} \tag{3-17}$$

where a_4 is the estimated coefficient of P_Y in the linear regression of Q_X on P_Y and other explanatory variables. For example, with $a_4 = 479$ in regression Equation 3-4, at $P_W = \$2.94$ (P_Y) and $Q_S = 10{,}312$ cwt (obtained by substituting the actual values of $P_S = \$5.60$, $N = 150.73$, $I = 1.76$, $P_W = \$2.94$, and $t = 1$ into Equation 3-4 for the United States in 1949), we have

$$E_{XY} = 479\left(\frac{2.94}{10{,}312}\right) = 0.14$$

This means that a 10 percent increase in the price of white potatoes would have resulted in only a 1.4 percent increase in the demand for sweet potatoes in the United States in 1949.

As with point price and income elasticities of demand, point cross-price elasticity of demand gives different results depending on whether the price of the

[19]In terms of calculus,

$$E_{XY} = \frac{\partial Q_X}{\partial P_Y} \cdot \frac{P_Y}{Q_X}$$

[20]That is, $\partial Q_X/\partial P_Y = a_4$ (the coefficient of P_Y) in Equation 3-3.

related commodity (P_Y) rises or falls. To avoid this, we usually measure **arc cross-price elasticity of demand** with Formula 3-18:

$$E_{XY} = \frac{\Delta Q_X}{\Delta P_Y} \cdot \frac{(P_{Y_2} + P_{Y_1})/2}{(Q_{X_2} + Q_{X_1})/2} = \frac{Q_{X_2} - Q_{X_1}}{P_{Y_2} - P_{Y_1}} \cdot \frac{P_{Y_2} + P_{Y_1}}{Q_{X_2} + Q_{X_1}} \tag{3-18}$$

where the subscripts 1 and 2 refer to the original and to the new levels of income and quantity, respectively, or vice versa.

If the value of E_{XY} is positive, commodities X and Y are substitutes because an increase in P_Y leads to an increase in Q_X as X is substituted for Y in consumption. Examples of substitute commodities are coffee and tea, coffee and cocoa, butter and margarine, hamburgers and hot dogs, Coca-Cola and Pepsi, and electricity and gas. On the other hand, if E_{XY} is negative, commodities X and Y are complementary because an increase in P_Y leads to a reduction in Q_Y and Q_X. Examples of complementary commodities are coffee and sugar, coffee and cream, hamburgers and buns, hot dogs and mustard, and cars and gasoline. The absolute value (i.e., the value without the sign) of E_{XY} measures the degree of substitutability and complementarity between X and Y. For example, if the cross-price elasticity of demand between coffee and tea is found to be larger than that between coffee and cocoa, this means that tea is a better substitute for coffee than cocoa. Finally, if E_{XY} is close to zero, X and Y are independent commodities. This may be the case with books and beer, cars and candy, pencils and potatoes, and so on.

The cross-price elasticity of demand is a very important concept in managerial decision making. Firms often use this concept to measure the effect of changing the price of a product they sell on the demand of other related products that the firm also sells. For example, the General Motors Corporation can use the cross-price elasticity of demand to measure the effect of changing the price of Chevrolets on the demand for Oldsmobiles. Since Chevrolets and Oldsmobiles are substitutes, lowering the price of the former will reduce the demand for the latter. On the other hand, a manufacturer of both razors and razor blades can use cross-price elasticity of demand to measure the increase in the demand for razor blades that would result if the firm reduced the price of razors.

A high positive cross-price elasticity of demand is often used to define an industry since it indicates that the various commodities are very similar. For example, the cross-price elasticity of demand between Chevrolets and Oldsmobiles is positive and very high and so they belong to the same (auto) industry. This concept is often used by the courts to reach a decision in business antitrust cases. For example, in the well-known *cellophane* case, the Du Pont Company was accused of monopolizing the market for cellophane. In its defense, Du Pont argued that cellophane was just one of many flexible packaging materials that included cellophane, waxed paper, aluminum foil, and many others. Based on the high cross-price elasticity of demand between cellophane and these other products, Du Pont successfully argued that the relevant market was not cellophane but flexible packaging materials. Since Du Pont had less than 20 percent of this market, the courts concluded in 1953 that Du Pont had not monopolized the market. This use of cross-price elasticity of demand is examined in greater detail in Chapter 12, which deals with business regulation and antitrust.

Case Study 3-5

Cross-Price Elasticities of Demand in the Real World

The first row of Table 3-5 shows that the cross elasticity of demand of margarine with respect to the price of butter is 1.53 percent. This means that a 1 percent increase in the price of butter leads to a 1.53 percent increase in the demand for margarine. Thus, margarine and butter are substitutes in the United States. On the other hand, the last row of Table 3-5 shows that the cross elasticity of demand of cereals with respect to fresh fish is −0.87. This means that a 1 percent increase in the price of cereals leads to a *reduction* in the demand for fresh fish by 0.87 percent. Thus, cereals (for example, bread) and fresh fish are complements. The table also shows the cross elasticity of demand of a few other selected commodities in the United States.

Table 3-5
Estimated Cross-Price Elasticity of Demand (E_{XY}) between Selected Commodities, United States

Commodity	Cross-Price Elasticity with Respect to Price of:	Cross-Price Elasticity
Margarine	Butter	1.53*
Natural gas	Electricity	0.80†
Pork	Beef	0.40*
Chicken	Pork	0.29*
Clothing	Food	−0.18‡
Entertainment	Food	−0.72§
Cereals	Fresh fish	−0.87¶

Source: *D. M. Heien, "The Structure of Food Demand: Interrelatedness and Duality," *American Journal of Agricultural Economics,* May 1982.
†G. R. Lakshmanan and W. Anderson, "Residential Energy Demand in the United States," *Regional Science and Urban Economics,* August 1980.
‡M. R. Baye, D. W. Jansen, and T. W. Lee, "Advertising in Complete Demand Systems," *Applied Economics,* vol. 24, 1992.
§E. T. Fujii et al., "An Almost Ideal Demand System for Visitor Expenditures," *Journal of Transport Economics and Policy,* May 1985.
¶A. Deaton, "Estimation of Own- and Cross-Price Elasticities from Household Survey Data," *Journal of Econometrics,* September–October 1987.

Case Study 3-6
Substitution between Domestic and Foreign Goods

Substitution between domestic and foreign goods and services has reached an all-time high in the world today and is expected to continue to increase sharply in the future. For homogeneous products such as a particular grade of wheat and steel, and for many industrial products with precise specifications such as computer chips, fiber optics, and specialized machinery, substitutability between domestic and foreign products is almost perfect. Here, a small price difference can lead quickly to large shifts in sales from domestic to foreign sources and vice versa. Even for differentiated products, such as automobiles and motorcycles, computers and copiers, watches and cameras, TV films and TV programs, soft drinks and cigarettes, soaps and detergents, commercial and military aircrafts, and most other products that are similar but not identical, substitutability between domestic and foreign products is very high and rising.

Despite the quality problems of the past, U.S.-made automobiles today are highly substitutable for Japanese and European automobiles, and so are most other products. Furthermore, with many parts and components imported from many nations and with production facilities and sales around the world often exceeding sales at home, even the distinction between domestic and foreign products is fast becoming obsolete. Should a Honda Accord produced in Ohio be considered American? What about a Chrysler minivan produced in Canada? Is a Kentucky Toyota or Mazda which uses nearly 50 percent of imported Japanese parts American? It is clearly becoming more and more difficult to define what is an American automobile even after the American Automobile Labeling Act of 1992, which requires all automobiles sold in the United States to indicate what percentage of the car's parts are domestic or foreign. Indeed, one could even ask if the question is relevant in a world growing more and more interdependent and globalized.

Source: "Honda's Nationality Proves Troublesome for Free-Trade Pact," *The New York Times,* October 9, 1992, p. 1; "Want a U.S. Car? Read the Label," *The New York Times,* September 18, 1994, Sec. 3, p. 6; and "Want to Buy American?" *U.S. News and World Report,* October 10, 1994, pp. 104–106.

3-5 USING ELASTICITIES IN MANAGERIAL DECISION MAKING

The analysis of the forces or variables that affect demand and reliable estimates of their quantitative effect on sales are essential for the firm to make the best operating decisions and to plan for its future growth. Some of the forces that affect demand are under the control of the firm, while others are not. A firm can usually set the price of the commodity it sells and decide on the level of its expenditures on advertising, product quality, and customers' service, but it has no control over the level and growth of consumers' incomes, consumers' price expectations, competitors' pricing decisions, and competitors' expenditures on advertising, product quality, and customers' service.

The firm can estimate the elasticity of demand with respect to all the forces or variables that affect the demand for the commodity that the firm sells. The firm needs these elasticity estimates in order to determine the optimal operational policies and the most effective way to respond to the policies of competing firms. For example, if the demand for the product is price inelastic, the firm would not want to lower its price since that would reduce its total revenue, increase its total costs (as more units of the commodity will be sold at the lower price) and, thus, face lower profits. Similarly, if the elasticity of the firm's sales with respect to advertising is positive and higher than for its expenditures on product quality and customers' service, then the firm may want to concentrate its sales efforts on advertising rather than on product quality and customers' service.

The elasticity of the firm's sales with respect to the variables outside the firm's control is also crucial to the firm in responding most effectively to competitors' policies and in planning the best growth strategy. For example, if the firm has estimated that the cross-price elasticity of the demand for its product with respect to the price of a competitor's product is very high, it will be quick to respond to a competitor's price reduction; otherwise, the firm would lose a great deal of its sales. However, the firm would think twice before lowering its price in such a case for fear of starting a price war. Furthermore, if the income elasticity is very low for the firm's product, management knows that the firm will not benefit much from rising incomes and may want to upgrade the quality of its product or move into new product lines with more income-elastic demand.

Thus, the firm should first identify all the important variables that affect the demand for the product it sells. Then the firm should obtain variable estimates of the marginal effect of a change in each variable on demand.[21] The firm would use this information to estimate the elasticity of demand for the product it sells with respect to each of the variables in the demand function. These are essential for optimal managerial decisions in the short run and in planning for growth in the long run.

For example, suppose that the Tasty Company markets coffee brand X and estimated the following regression of the demand for its brand of coffee:

$$Q_X = 1.5 - 3.0P_X + 0.8I + 2.0P_Y - 0.6P_S + 1.2A \tag{3-19}$$

where Q_X = sales of coffee brand X in the United States, in millions of pounds per year
P_X = price of coffee brand X, in dollars per pound
I = personal disposable income, in trillions of dollars per year
P_Y = price of the competitive brand of coffee, in dollars per pound
P_S = price of sugar, in dollars per pound
A = advertising expenditures for coffee brand X, in hundreds of thousands of dollars per year

Suppose also that this year, $P_X = \$2$, $I = \$2.5$, $P_Y = \$1.80$, $P_S = \$0.50$, and $A = \$1$. Substituting these values into Equation 3-19, we obtain

$$Q_X = 1.5 - 3(2) + 0.8(2.5) + 2(1.80) - 0.6(0.50) + 1.2(1) = 2$$

[21]This can be accomplished by regression analysis discussed in Chapter 4.

Thus, this year the firm would sell 2 million pounds of coffee brand X.

The firm can use the above information to find the elasticity of the demand for coffee brand X with respect to its price, income, the price of competitive coffee brand Y, the price of sugar, and advertising. Thus,

$$E_P = -3\left(\frac{2}{2}\right) = -3$$

$$E_I = 0.8\left(\frac{2.5}{2}\right) = 1$$

$$E_{XY} = 2\left(\frac{1.8}{2}\right) = 1.8$$

$$E_{XS} = -0.6\left(\frac{0.50}{2}\right) = -0.15$$

$$E_A = 1.2\left(\frac{1}{2}\right) = 0.6$$

The firm can then use these elasticities to forecast the demand for its brand of coffee next year. For example, suppose that next year the firm intends to increase the price of its brand of coffee by 5 percent and its advertising expenditures by 12 percent. Suppose also that the firm expects personal disposable income to rise by 4 percent, P_Y to rise by 7 percent, and P_S to fall by 8 percent. Using the level of sales (Q_X) of 2 million pounds this year, the elasticities calculated above, the firm's intended policies for next year, and the firm's expectations about the change in other variables given above, the firm can determine its sales next year (Q'_X) as follows:

$$\begin{aligned}
Q'_X &= Q_X + Q_X\left(\frac{\Delta P_X}{P_X}\right)E_P + Q_X\left(\frac{\Delta I}{I}\right)E_I + Q_X\left(\frac{\Delta P_Y}{P_Y}\right)E_{XY} + Q_X\left(\frac{\Delta P_S}{P_S}\right)E_{XS} + Q_X\left(\frac{\Delta A}{A}\right)E_A \\
&= 2 + 2(5\%)\,(-3) + 2(4\%)\,(1) + 2(7\%)\,(1.8) + 2(-8\%)\,(-0.15) + 2(12\%)(0.6) \\
&= 2 + 2(0.05)\,(-3) + 2(0.04)\,(1) + 2(0.07)\,(1.8) + 2(-0.08)\,(-0.15) + 2(0.12)(0.6) \\
&= 2\,(1 - 0.15 + 0.04 + 0.126 + 0.012 + 0.072) \\
&= 2(1 + 0.1) \\
&= 2(1.1) \\
&= 2.2, \text{ or } 2{,}200{,}000 \text{ pounds}
\end{aligned}$$

The Tasty Company could also use this information to determine that it could sell 2 million pounds of its brand of coffee next year (the same as this year) by increasing its price by 8.33 percent instead of by 5 percent (if everything else remained the same). The extra 3.33 percent increase in P_X would result in $2(0.033)(-3) = -0.198$, or 198,000 pounds less coffee sold than the 2.2 million pounds forecasted for next year with an increase in P_X of only 5 percent.

3-6 INTERNATIONAL CONVERGENCE OF TASTES

A rapid convergence of tastes is taking place in the world today. Tastes in the United States affect tastes around the world, and tastes abroad strongly influence tastes in the United States. Coca-Cola and jeans are only two of the most obvious U.S. products that have become household items around the world. One can see Adidas sneakers and Walkman personal stereos on joggers from Central Park in New York City to Tivoli Gardens in Copenhagen. You can eat a Big Mac in Piazza di Spagna in Rome or Gorky's Square in Moscow. We find Japanese cars and VCRs in New York and in New Dehli, French perfumes in Paris and in Cairo, and Perrier in practically every major (and not so major) city around the world. Texas Instruments and Canon calculators, Zenith and Hitachi portable PCs, and Xerox and Minolta copiers are found in offices and homes more or less everywhere. With more rapid communications and more frequent travels, the worldwide convergence of tastes has even accelerated. As a result, firms must increasingly think in terms of global production and marketing to remain competitive in today's rapidly shrinking world. Even small firms must constantly worry that new global products do not wipe out their entire product line overnight.

In his 1983 article "The Globalization of Markets" in the *Harvard Business Review,* Theodore Levitt asserted that consumers from New York to Frankfurt to Tokyo want similar products and that success in the future would require more and more standardized products and pricing around the world. In fact, in country after country, we are seeing the emergence of a middle-class consumer lifestyle based on a taste for comfort, convenience, and speed. In the food business, this means packaged, fast-to-prepare, and ready-to-eat products. This is the inevitable result of the information revolution, from people traveling more and more, and seeing the same movies and TV shows. Market researchers have discovered that similarities in living styles among middle-class people all over the world are much greater than once thought to be and are growing with rising incomes and education levels. With the tremendous improvement in telecommunications, transportation, and travel, the cross-fertilization of cultures and convergence of tastes can be expected only to accelerate in the future—with all its important implications for consumers, producers, and sellers of an increasing number and variety of products and services.

Case Study 3-7
Gillette Introduces the Sensor Razor—A Truly Global Product

As tastes become global, firms are responding more and more with truly global products. These are introduced more or less simultaneously in most countries of the world with little or no local variation. This is leading to what has been aptly called the "global supermarket." For example, in 1990, Gillette introduced its new Sensor Razor at the same time in most nations of the world and advertised it with virtually the same TV spots (ad campaign) in 19 countries in Europe and North America. By the end of 1993, Gillette had sold over 200 million of the razors and more than 6 billion twin-blade cartridges, and it had captured an incredible 33 percent of the global blade market. In 1994, Gillette introduced an upgrade of the Sensor Razor called "Excel Razor" with a high-tech edge and expected to increase its share of the world market even more.

The trend toward the global supermarket is rapidly spreading in Europe as borders fade. A growing number of companies are creating "Eurobrands"—a single product for most countries of Europe—and advertising them with "Euroads," which are identical or nearly identical across countries, except for language. Many national differences in taste will, of course, remain; for example, Nestlé markets more than 200 blends of Nescafé to cater to differences in tastes in different markets. But the converging trend in tastes around the world is unmistakable and is likely to lead to more and more global products. This is true not only in foods and inexpensive consumer products but also in automobiles, tires, portable computers, phones, and many other durable products. Teenagers represent by far the most global market of all today—they have the money and astonishing similarities in tastes regardless of where they live.

Source: "Building the Global Supermarket," *The New York Times,* November 18, 1988, p. D1; "Selling in Europe: Borders Fade," *The New York Times,* May 31, 1990, p. D1; "The Cutting Edge," *The Wall Street Journal,* April 6, 1992, p. R6; "Gillette's World View: One Blade Fits All," *The Wall Street Journal,* January 3, 1994, p. C3; and "Teens," *Fortune,* May 16, 1994, pp. 90–98.

Case Study 3-8
The New World Car by Ford

In fall 1994, Ford introduced its new Ford Contour and Mercury Mystique in the United States—the same basic midsize, compact car it introduced in Europe in 1993 under the name of Mondeo. This is Ford's new world car, which took six years to develop at a cost of $6 billion—twice what Ford spent to develop its vastly successful Taurus and four times more than Chrysler spent on its Dodge/Plymouth Neon. Ford insists, however, that by developing and producing a single basic car for Europe and the United States, it saved about 25 percent of developing and producing a separate car for each side of the Atlantic, as it had done in the past. Consumer tastes have now converged so much according to Ford that a single car will find lots of buyers everywhere, just as one menu is working around the world for McDonald's. Building a world car is a most ambitious undertaking; in the past, only Volkswagen's classic Beetle and Toyota's Corolla have come close.

For the exterior design, Ford commissioned clay models from its design studios in California, Michigan, England, and Italy—from which it then developed a consensus model. After showing the model to consumer clinics in the United States, however, Ford chose to change somewhat the front and rear styling and put a larger trunk and more chrome on the U.S. version of the car. Still, the European and American versions are very similar and share 75 percent common parts. This is a far cry from Ford's previous unsuccessful attempt in 1981 to build a common car for Europe and the United States (the Escort), which resulted in one of the grandest corporate foul-ups ever and led to very different European and American models sharing only two insignificant parts. Indeed, many people and most other auto producers seem to feel that a common car for the world market seems to violate the basic marketing wisdom of the nineties to get closer to customers. Ford, however, is confident that consumer tastes have converged so much around the world during the past decade as to ensure the success of a world car. For the Mondeo, success or failure depends on how well the car will sell. Early market reaction and sales in Europe seem to justify Ford's gamble.

Source: "Ford's $6 Billion Baby," *Fortune,* June 28, 1993, pp. 76–81; "Ford Sets Its Sights on a World Car," *The New York Times,* September 27, 1993, p. D1; and "One World, One Ford," *Forbes,* June 20, 1994, pp. 40–41.

SUMMARY

1. The demand for a commodity faced by a firm depends on the market or industry demand for the commodity, which in turn is the sum of the demand for the commodity of the individual consumers in the market. The demand for the commodity that a firm faces depends on the price of the commodity, the size of (i.e., the number of consumers in) the market, consumers' income, the price of related commodities, tastes, price expectations, the promotional efforts of the firm, and competitors' pricing and promotional policies. In general, the quantity response by a firm to a change in the price of the commodity will be some fraction of the total market response. The demand for durable goods is generally less stable than the demand for nondurable goods. The firm's demand for inputs or resources (producers' goods) is derived from the demand for the final commodities produced with the inputs.
2. The price elasticity of demand (E_P) measures the percentage change in quantity demanded of a commodity divided by the percentage change in its price, while holding constant all other variables in the demand function. We can measure point or arc price elasticity of demand. A linear demand curve is price elastic (that is, $|E_P| > 1$) above its geometric midpoint, is unitary elastic at its midpoint (that is, $|E_P| = 1$), and is inelastic (that is, $|E_P| < 1$) below the midpoint. For a decline in price, total revenue (TR) increases if demand is elastic, remains unchanged if demand is unitary elastic, and declines if demand is inelastic. The elasticity of demand is greater, the more and better are the substitutes available for the commodity and the greater is the length of time allowed for the quantity response by consumers to the price change.
3. The income elasticity of demand (E_I) measures the percentage change in the demand for a commodity divided by the percentage change in consumers' income, while holding constant all other variables in the demand function, including price. We can measure point or arc income elasticity of demand. Most goods are normal ($E_I > 0$). For inferior goods, $E_I < 0$. Those normal goods for which $E_I > 1$ are called "luxuries," while normal goods for which E_I is between zero and 1 are "necessities."

4. The cross-price elasticity of demand for commodity X with respect to commodity Y (E_{XY}) measures the percentage change in the demand for commodity X divided by the percentage change in the price of commodity Y, while holding constant all other variables in the demand function, including income and the price of commodity X. We can measure point or arc cross-price elasticity. Commodities X and Y are substitutes if E_{XY} is positive, complementary if E_{XY} is negative, and independent if E_{XY} is close to zero. A firm uses the cross-price elasticity of demand to estimate the effect of reducing the price of a commodity on the demand of other related commodities that the firm sells. A high cross-price elasticity of demand is also used to define an industry.
5. For the analysis of demand, the firm should first identify all the important variables that affect the demand for the product it sells. By using regression analysis (discussed in Chapter 4), the firm could then obtain reliable estimates of the effect of a change in each of these variables on demand for the product that it faces.
6. There is an increasing trend of converging tastes around the world today. Tastes in the United States affect tastes around the world, and tastes abroad strongly influence tastes in the United States. While some national differences will surely remain, the information revolution and cross-fertilization of cultures can be expected to accelerate the global convergence of tastes around the world. This has important implications for all firms.

DISCUSSION QUESTIONS

1. (*a*) If our main interest in managerial economics is the demand that a firm faces for its product, why do we study consumer demand theory? (*b*) What is the distinction between inferior goods and normal goods? Between the substitution effect and the income effect? Between a change in the quantity demanded and a change in demand?
2. (*a*) How many different types of demand functions are there? (*b*) In which type of demand are we most interested in managerial economics? Why? (*c*) Why do we then study the other types of demand?
3. (*a*) What are the most important determinants of the demand function that a firm faces for the commodity it sells? (*b*) What is meant by producers' goods? By derived demand? (*c*) Why is the demand for durable goods (both consumers' and producers') less stable than the demand for nondurable goods?
4. (*a*) What is the advantage of using the price elasticity rather than the slope of the demand curve or its inverse to measure the responsiveness in the quantity demanded of a commodity to a change in its price? (*b*) Why and how is the formula for arc price elasticity of demand different from the formula for point price elasticity of demand?

5. (*a*) State the relationship between the total revenue of a firm and the price elasticity of demand for a *price increase* along a linear demand curve. (*b*) Explain the reason for the relationship that you stated in part (*a*).
6. (*a*) Explain why a firm facing a negatively sloped demand curve would never produce in the inelastic portion of the demand curve. (*b*) When would the firm want to operate at the point where its demand curve is unitary elastic?
7. (*a*) Would you expect the price elasticity of demand to be higher for Chevrolet automobiles or for automobiles in general? Why? (*b*) Would you expect the price elasticity of demand for electricity for residential use to be higher or lower than for industrial use? Why? (*c*) Would you expect the price elasticity of demand for electricity to be higher or lower in the short run as compared with the long run? Why?
8. If there has been a 10 percent increase in consumers' income between two periods, what was the percentage change in the demand for foreign travel? For tobacco products? For flour? (*Hint:* Use the income-elasticity values in Table 3-4.)
9. Agricultural commodities are known to have a price-inelastic demand and to be necessities. How can this information allow us to explain why the income of farmers falls (*a*) after a good harvest? (*b*) In relation to the incomes in other sectors of the economy?
10. Suppose that the cross-price elasticity of demand between McIntosh and Golden Delicious apples is 0.8, between apples and apple juice is 0.5, between apples and cheese is −0.4, and between apples and beer is 0.1. What can you say about the relationship between each set of commodities?
11. (*a*) What other elasticities of demand are there besides price, income, and cross price? (*b*) What is the usefulness to the firm of the elasticity of demand for the variables over which the firm has some control? (*c*) Of the elasticity of demand over which the firm has no control? (*d*) Why is it essential for the firm to utilize the elasticity of all the variables included in the demand function?
12. (*a*) Why are tastes converging around the world? (*b*) What is the importance of this for U.S. firms?

PROBLEMS

1. John Smith, the research manager for marketing at the Chevrolet Division of the General Motors Corporation, has specified the following general demand function for Chevrolets in the United States:

$$Q_C = f(P_C, N, I, P_F, P_G, A, P_I)$$

where Q_C is the quantity demanded of Chevrolets per year, P_C is the price of Chevrolets, N is population, I is disposable income, P_F is the price of Ford automobiles, P_G is the price of gasoline, A is the amount of advertising for

Chevrolets, and P_I is credit incentives to purchase Chevrolets. Indicate whether you expect each independent or explanatory variable to be directly or inversely related to the quantity demanded of Chevrolets and the reason for your expectation.

*2. Suppose that John Smith, the manager of the marketing division of Chevrolet at GM, estimated the following regression equation for Chevrolet automobiles:

$$Q_C = 100{,}000 - 100P_C + 2{,}000N + 50I + 30P_F$$
$$-1{,}000P_G + 3A + 40{,}000P_I$$

where Q_C = quantity demanded per year of Chevrolet automobiles
P_C = price of Chevrolet automobiles, in dollars
N = population of the United States, in millions
I = per capita disposable income, in dollars
P_F = price of Ford automobiles, in dollars
P_G = real price of gasoline, in cents per gallon
A = advertising expenditures by Chevrolet, in dollars per year
P_I = credit incentives to purchase Chevrolets, in percentage points below the rate of interest on borrowing in the absence of incentives

(*a*) Indicate the change in the number of Chevrolets purchased per year (Q_C) for each unit change in the independent or explanatory variables. (*b*) Find the value of Q_C if the average value of P_C = \$9,000, N = 200 million, I = \$10,000, P_F = \$8,000, P_G = 80 cents, A = \$200,000, and if $P_I = 1$. (*c*) Derive the equation for the demand curve for Chevrolets; and (*d*) plot it.

3. Starting with the estimated demand function for Chevrolets given in Problem 2, assume that the average value of the independent variables changes to N = 225 million, I = \$12,000, P_F = \$10,000, P_G = 100 cents, A = \$250,000, and $P_I = 0$ (i.e., the incentives are phased out). (*a*) Find the equation of the new demand curve for Chevrolets and (*b*) plot this new demand curve, D'_C, and on the same graph, plot the demand curve for Chevrolets, D_C, found in Problem 2(*d*). (*c*) What is the relationship between D_C and D'_C? What explains this relationship?

4. The Ice Cream Parlor is the only ice cream parlor in Smithtown. Michael, the son of the owner, has just come back from college where he majors in business administration. In his course in managerial economics, Michael has just studied demand analysis and decides to apply what he has learned to estimate the demand for ice cream in his father's parlor during his summer vacation. Utilizing regression analysis, Michael estimates the following demand function:

$$Q_I = 120 - 20P_I$$

where the subscript I refers to ice cream portions served per day in his father's parlor, and P_I is the dollar price. Michael then sets out to (*a*) derive the demand schedule for ice cream and plot it, (*b*) find the point price elasticity of demand at each dollar price, from $P = \$6$ to $P = \$0$, and (*c*) find arc price elasticity of demand between consecutive dollar prices (i.e., between $P = \$6$ and $P = \$5$, $P = \$5$ and $P = \$4$, and so on). Show how Michael would get his results.

*5. Show how Michael could have found the price elasticity of demand (E_P) for ice cream graphically at, say, $P_I = \$4$ for the demand function given in Problem 4. Also show graphically that at $P_I = \$4$, E_P would be the same if the demand curve for ice cream were curvilinear but tangent to the linear demand curve at $P_I = \$4$.

6. For the demand function for ice cream given in Problem 4, (*a*) construct a table similar to Table 3-2 in the text, showing the quantity demanded, the total revenue, and the marginal revenue schedules of the Ice Cream Parlor. (*b*) Plot the demand, the total revenue, and the marginal revenue schedules from part (*a*) in a figure similar to Figure 3-5 in the text and indicate on it the range over which demand is elastic, inelastic, and unitary elastic. (*c*) Derive the equation for the *TR* and *MR* schedules for the parlor.

7. The total operating revenues of a public transportation authority are \$100 million while its total operating costs are \$120 million. The price of a ride is \$1, and the price elasticity of demand for public transportation has been estimated to be -0.4. By law, the public transportation authority must take steps to eliminate its operating deficit. (*a*) What pricing policy should the transportation authority adopt? Why? (*b*) What price per ride must the public transportation authority charge to eliminate the deficit if it cannot reduce costs?

*8. The coefficient of income in a regression of the quantity demanded of a commodity on price, income, and other variables is 10. (*a*) Calculate the income elasticity of demand for this commodity at income of \$10,000 and sales of 80,000 units. (*b*) What would be the income elasticity of demand if sales increased from 80,000 to 90,000 units and income rose from \$10,000 to \$11,000? What type of good is this commodity?

9. A researcher estimated that the price elasticity of demand for automobiles in the United States is -1.2, while the income elasticity of demand is 3.0. Next year, U.S. automakers intend to increase the average price of automobiles by 5 percent, and they expect consumers' disposable income to rise by 3 percent. (*a*) If sales of domestically produced automobiles are 8 million this year, how many automobiles do you expect U.S. automakers to sell next year? (*b*) By how much should domestic automakers increase the price of automobiles if they wish to increase sales by 5 percent next year?

10. The coefficient of the price of gasoline in the regression of the quantity demanded of automobiles (in millions of units) on the price of gasoline (in dollars) and other variables is -14. (*a*) Calculate the cross-price elasticity of demand between automobiles and gasoline at the gasoline price of \$1 per gallon and sales of automobiles of 8 (million units). (*b*) What would be the

cross-price elasticity of demand between automobiles and gasoline if sales of automobiles declined from 8 to 6 with an increase in the gasoline price from \$1 to \$1.20 per gallon?

*11. The management of the Mini Mill Steel Company estimated the following elasticities for a special type of steel they sell: $E_P = -2$, $E_I = 1$, and $E_{XY} = 1.5$, where X refers to steel and Y to aluminum. Next year, the firm would like to increase the price of the steel it sells by 6 percent. The management of the firm forecasted that income will rise by 4 percent next year, and the price of aluminum will fall by 2 percent. (*a*) If the sales of the firm this year are 1,200 tons of the special type of steel, how many tons of steel can the firm expect to sell next year? (*b*) By what percentage must the firm change the price of steel to keep its sales at 1,200 tons next year?

12. **Integrating Problem**

The research department of the Corn Flakes Corporation (CFC) estimated the following regression for the demand of the corn flakes it sells:

$$Q_X = 1.0 - 2.0P_X + 1.5I + 0.8P_Y - 3.0P_M + 1.0A$$

where Q_X = sales of CFC corn flakes, in millions of 10-ounce boxes per year

P_X = the price of CFC corn flakes, in dollars per 10-ounce box

I = personal disposable income, in trillions of dollars per year

P_Y = price of competitive brand of corn flakes, in dollars per 10-ounce box

P_M = price of milk, in dollars per quart

A = advertising expenditures of CFC corn flakes, in hundreds of thousands of dollars per year

This year, P_X = \$2, I = \$4, P_Y = \$2.50, P_M = \$1, and A = \$2. (*a*) Calculate the sales of CFC corn flakes this year; (*b*) calculate the elasticity of sales with respect to each variable in the demand function; (*c*) estimate the level of sales next year if the CFC reduces P_X by 10 percent, increases advertising by 20 percent, I rises by 5 percent, P_Y is reduced by 10 percent, and P_M remains unchanged. (*d*) By how much should the CFC change its advertising if it wants its sales to be 30 percent higher than this year?

APPENDIX

BEHIND THE MARKET DEMAND CURVE—THE THEORY OF CONSUMER CHOICE

In this appendix we present the theory of consumer choice. We will introduce indifference curves to show a consumer's tastes and the budget line to show the constraints under which the consumer operates. By the interaction of indifference curves (tastes) and the budget line (constraints), we define consumer's equilibrium, and from consumer-equilibrium points we then derive the consumer's demand curve for a commodity. Subsequently, we separate the income effect from the substitution effect of a price change. Finally, we present the theory of consumer choice mathematically. For a more detailed presentation of the theory of consumer choice, consult any text in microeconomic theory, such as my own (see the supplementary readings at the end of this chapter).

The Consumer's Tastes: Indifference Curves

If we assume, for simplicity, that a consumer spends all of his or her income on commodities X and Y, we can represent the tastes of the consumer with indifference curves. An *indifference curve* shows the various combinations of commodity X and commodity Y that yield equal utility or satisfaction to the consumer. For example, in Figure 3-7 indifference curve U_1 shows that 1 unit of commodity X and 4 units of commodity Y (point A) yield the same satisfaction as $2X$ and $2.5Y$ (point B), and $4X$ and $1.5Y$ (point C). On the other hand, points on higher indifference curves (U_2 and U_3) show higher levels of utility or satisfaction. Indifference curves give an ordinal (rank) rather than a cardinal measure of utility. That is, we know that $U_3 > U_2 > U_1$, but not by how much.

Indifference curves are negatively sloped because by consuming more of X, the individual would have to consume less of Y in order to remain on the same indifference curve (i.e., at the same level of satisfaction). The amount of Y that the individual would be willing to give up for an additional unit of X is called the

Figure 3-7
Indifference Curves

Indifference curve U_1 shows that the individual receives the same level of satisfaction from consuming $1X$ and $4Y$ (point A), $2X$ and $2.5\ Y$ (point B), and $4X$ and $1.5Y$ (point C). Indifference curve U_2 refers to a higher level of satisfaction than U_1, and U_3 to a still higher level. Indifference curves are negatively sloped, are convex to the origin, and cannot cross.

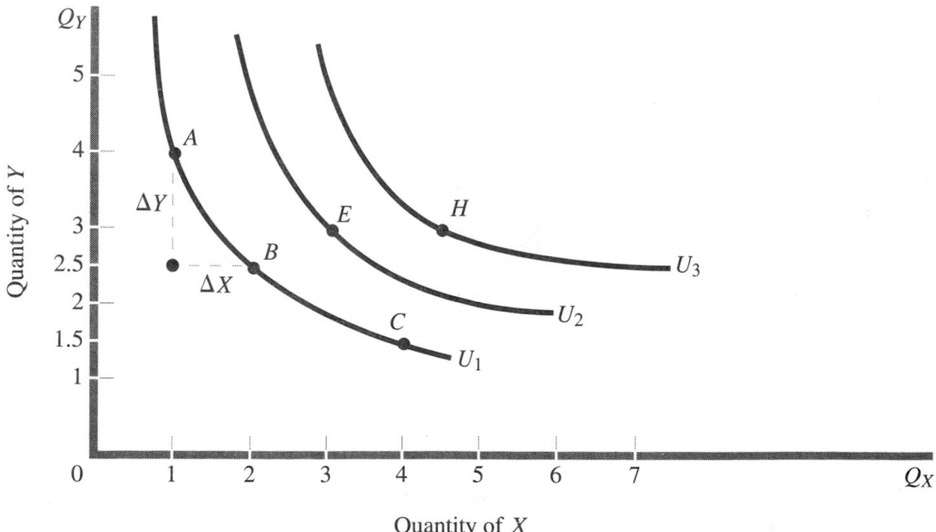

marginal rate of substitution (MRS). For example, starting from point A ($1X$, $4Y$) on U_1, the individual is willing to give up $1.5Y$ for an additional unit of X (and reach point B, which has $2X$ and $2.5Y$ and is also on U_1). Thus, the MRS between points A and B on U_1 is 1.5. Note that as we move down an indifference curve, the MRS declines (i.e., the individual is willing to give up less and less of Y for each additional unit of X). Declining MRS is reflected in the convex shape of indifference curves. Not only are indifference curves negatively sloped and convex to the origin, but they also cannot cross. If two indifference curves crossed, it would mean that one of them refers to a higher level of satisfaction than the other at one side of the intersection and to a lower level of satisfaction at the other side of the intersection. This is impossible because all points on the same indifference curve refer to the same level of satisfaction.

The Consumer's Constraints: The Budget Line

The constraints that a consumer faces can be shown graphically by the budget line. The *budget line* shows the various combinations of commodities X and Y that a consumer can purchase, given his or her money income and the prices of the two commodities. For example, suppose that the consumer's money income, $M = \$6$, and $P_X = P_Y = \$1$. Figure 3-8 shows that if the consumer spent all of his or her income on either X or Y, he or she could purchase either $6X$ (point F) or $6Y$ (point G). By joining points F and G by a straight line, we define budget line GF. Budget line GF shows all the combinations of X and Y that the individual

Figure 3-8
The Consumer's Budget Line

With money income, $M = \$6$, and $P_X = P_Y = \$1$, the consumer could purchase either $6X$ (point F) or $6Y$ (point G), or any combination of X and Y on GF (the budget line). With M and P_Y unchanged, the budget line would be GF' with $P_X = \$2$ and GF'' with $P_X = \$0.67$.

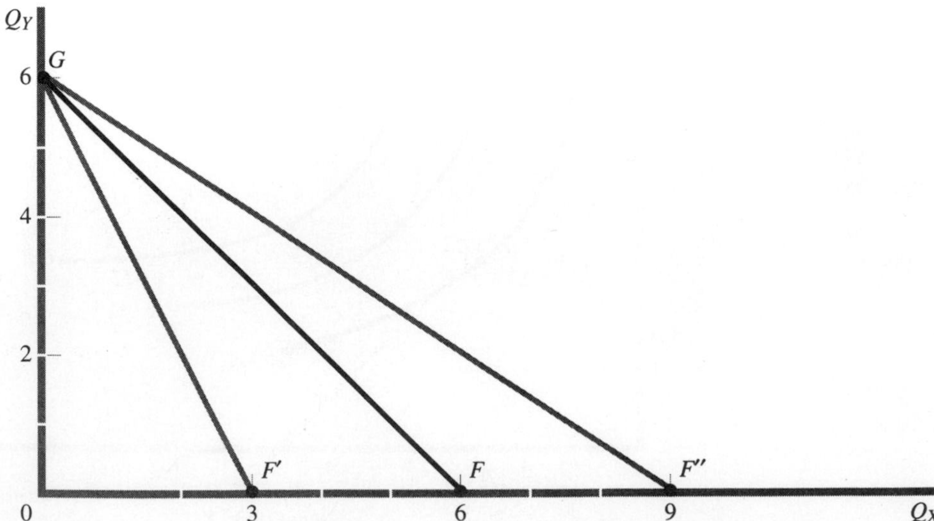

can purchase, given his or her money income and P_X and P_Y. With M and P_Y unchanged, the budget line would be GF' with $P_X = \$2$ and GF'' with $P_X = \$0.67$.

The Consumer's Equilibrium

A consumer is in equilibrium when, given his or her income and commodity prices, the consumer maximizes the utility or satisfaction from his or her expenditures. In other words, a consumer is in equilibrium when he or she reaches the highest indifference curve possible with his or her budget line. For example, Figure 3-9 shows that given $M = \$6$ and $P_X = P_Y = \$1$ (i.e., given budget line GF), the consumer is in equilibrium when he or she consumes $3X$ and $3Y$ (point E), where budget line GF is tangent to indifference curve U_2 (the highest indifference curve that the consumer can reach with his or her budget line).

Derivation of the Consumer's Demand Curve

Given the consumer's money income and the price of commodity Y, we can derive the consumer's demand curve for commodity X from the consumer's equilibrium points that result from different prices of commodity X. This is shown in Figure 3-10. The top panel of the figure shows that with $M = \$6$, $P_Y = \$1$, and $P_X = \$2$ (i.e., with budget line GF'), the individual is in equilibrium at point A

Figure 3-9
Consumer's Equilibrium

Given budget line GF, the consumer is in equilibrium when he or she consumes $3X$ and $3Y$ (point E), where budget line GF is tangent to the indifference curve U_2 (the highest indifference curve that the consumer can reach with his or her budget line).

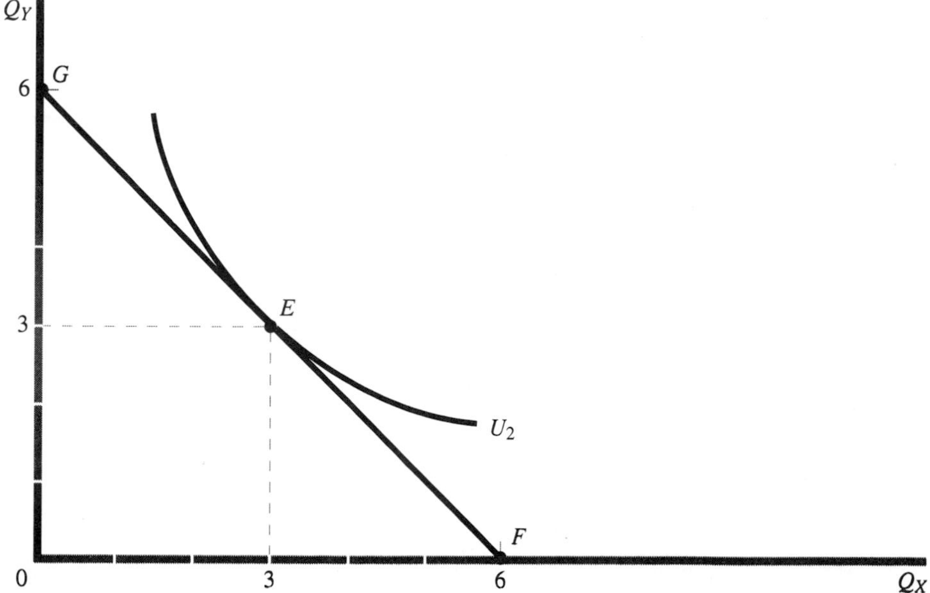

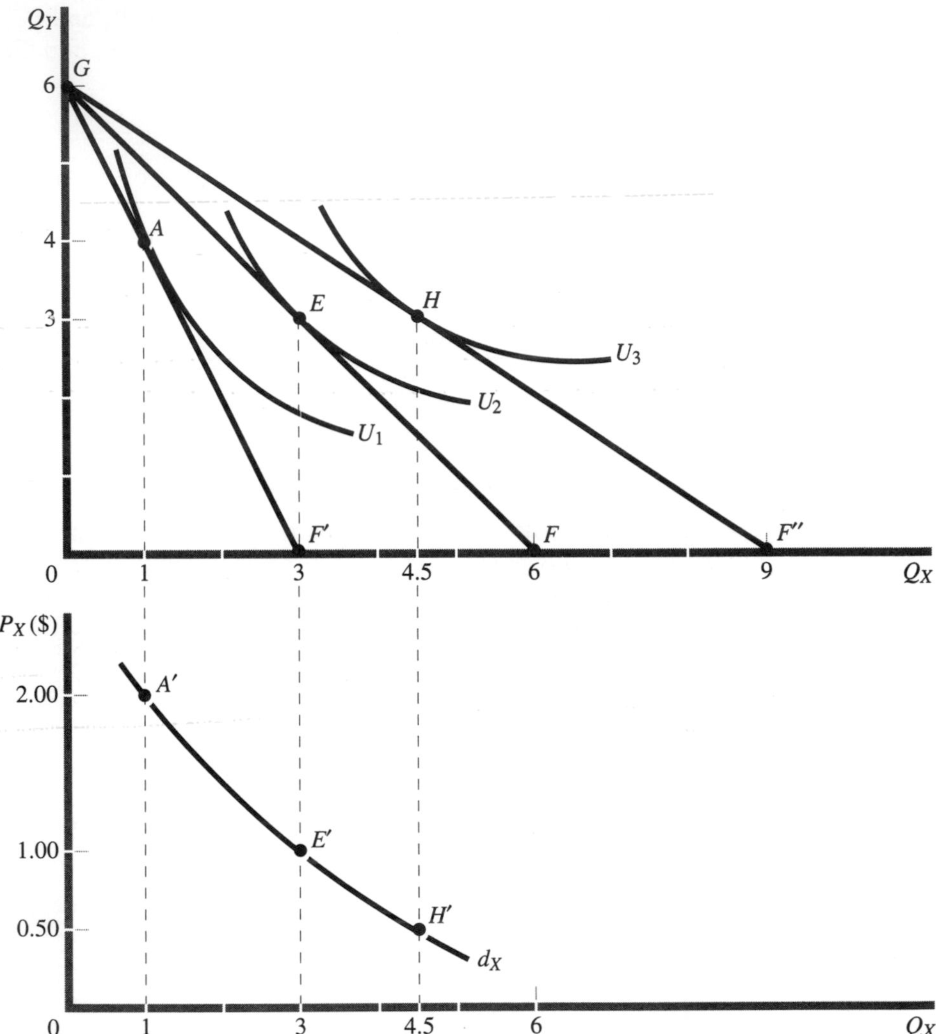

Figure 3-10
Derivation of the Consumer's Demand Curve
The top panel shows that with P_X = \$2, P_X = \$1, and P_X = \$0.67, we have budget lines *GF′*, *GF*, and *GF″*, and consumer equilibrium points *A*, *E*, and *H*, respectively. From equilibrium points *A*, *E*, and *H* in the top panel, we derive points *A′*, *E′*, and *H′* in the bottom panel. By joining points *A′*, *E′*, and *H′*, we derive d_X, the consumer's demand curve for commodity *X*.

(i.e., by consuming 1*X* and 4*Y*), where budget line *GF′* is tangent to indifference curve U_1. This gives point *A′* ($Q_X = 1$ at P_X = \$2) in the bottom panel. With *M* = \$6 and P_Y = \$1 but P_X = \$1, the individual would be in equilibrium at point *E* (3*X* and 3*Y*), where budget line *GF* is tangent to indifference curve U_2 (as in Figure 3-9). This gives point *E′* ($Q_X = 3$ at P_X = \$1) in the bottom panel. Finally, with *M* = \$6 and P_Y = \$1 but P_X = \$0.67, the individual would be in equilibrium at point H (4.5X and 3Y), where budget line GF'' is tangent to indifference curve U_3. This gives point H' ($Q_X = 4.5$ at $P_X = \$0.67$) in the bottom panel. By joining points A', E', and H' in the bottom panel of Figure 3-10, we derive d_X, the individual's demand curve for commodity X.

Income and Substitution Effects of a Price Change

We can use indifference curve analysis to separate the substitution from the income effect of the price change. This is shown in Figure 3-11. As in Figure 3-10, Figure 3-11 shows that with $M = \$6$, $P_Y = \$1$, and $P_X = \$2$, the individual is in equilibrium at point A and demands 1 unit of commodity X. On the other hand, with $M = \$6$, $P_Y = \$1$, and $P_X = \$1$, the individual is in equilibrium at point E and demands 3 units of X. The increase in the demand for commodity X from 1X to 3X represents the combined effect of the substitution and the income effects. The substitution effect postulates that when the price of X falls, the

Figure 3-11
Separation of the Substitution from the Income Effect of a Price Change
The individual is in equilibrium at point A with $P_X = \$2$ and at point E with $P_X = \$1$ (as in the top panel of Figure 3-10). To isolate the substitution effect, we draw hypothetical budget line G^*F^*, which is parallel to GF and tangent to U_1 at point J. The movement along U_1 from point A to point J is the substitution effect and results from the relative reduction in P_X only (i.e., with real income constant). The shift from point J on U_1 to point E on U_2 is then the income effect. The total effect ($AE = 2X$) equals the substitution effect ($AJ = 1X$) plus the income effect ($JE = 1X$).

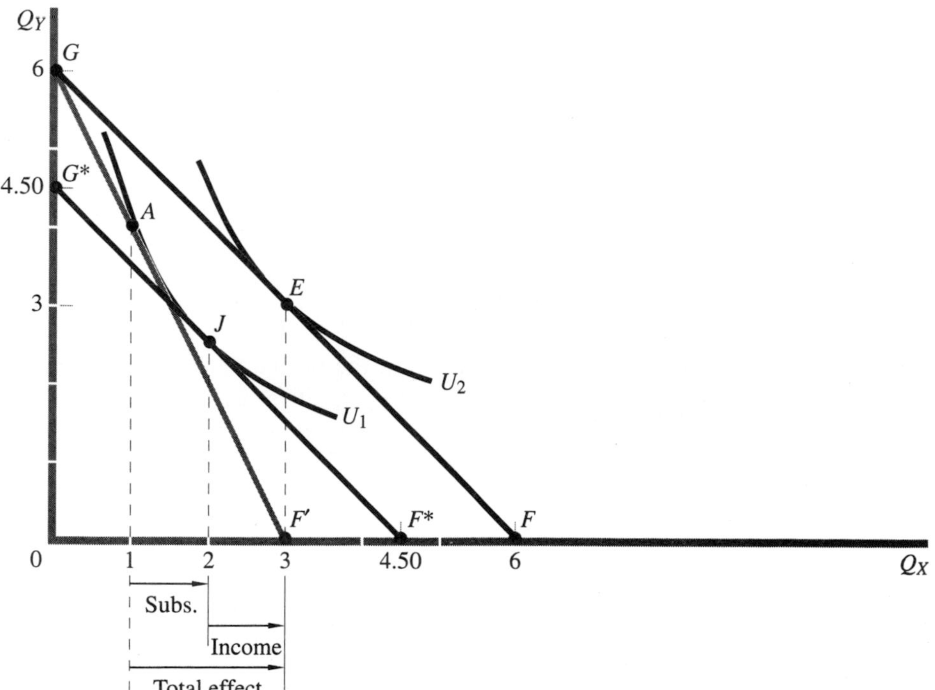

consumer will substitute X for Y in consumption. On the other hand, the income effect arises because when P_X falls but money income (M) and P_Y do not change, the individual's *real* income increases, and so he or she purchases more of X.

To separate the substitution from the income effect of the price change, we draw hypothetical budget line G^*F^*, which is parallel to budget line GF but tangent to indifference curve U_1 at point J. Hypothetical budget line G^*F^* involves the reduction in money income of \$1.50 = $GG^* = FF^*$ in order to keep the individual at the same level of real income that he or she had before the price change (i.e., in order to keep the individual on indifference curve U_1). The movement along indifference curve U_1 from point A to point J (equals $1X$) is then the substitution effect of the price change, while the shift from point J on U_1 to point E on U_2 (which also equals $1X$) is the income effect. The sum of the substitution and the income effects equals the total effect ($2X$) of the price change.

To be noted is that while the two effects are equal in Figure 3-11, the substitution effect is usually much larger than the income effect in the real world. The reason is that the consumer usually spends only a small proportion of his or her income on any one commodity. Thus, even a large change in the price of the commodity does not result in a large income effect. On the other hand, the substitution effect can be very large if the commodity has many good substitutes.

The Theory of Consumer Choice Mathematically

Suppose that a consumer spends all of his or her income on commodities X and Y. To reach equilibrium, the consumer must maximize utility (U) subject to his or her budget constraint. That is, he or she must

$$\text{maximize } U = f(Q_X, Q_Y) \qquad (3\text{-}20)$$

$$\text{subject to } M = P_XQ_X + P_YQ_Y \qquad (3\text{-}21)$$

This constrained maximization problem can be solved by the Lagrangian multiplier method (see page 58).

To do so, we first form the Lagrangian function:

$$L = f(Q_X, Q_Y) + \lambda(M - P_XQ_X - P_YQ_Y) \qquad (3\text{-}22)$$

To maximize L, we then find the partial derivative of L with respect to Q_X, Q_Y, and λ, and set them equal to zero. That is,

$$\frac{\partial L}{\partial Q_X} = \frac{\partial f}{\partial Q_X} - \lambda P_X = 0 \qquad (3\text{-}23)$$

$$\frac{\partial L}{\partial Q_Y} = \frac{\partial f}{\partial Q_Y} - \lambda P_Y = 0 \qquad (3\text{-}24)$$

$$\frac{\partial L}{\partial \lambda} = M - P_XQ_X - P_YQ_Y = 0 \qquad (3\text{-}25)$$

Solving Equations 3-23 and 3-24 for λ and setting them equal to each other, we get

$$\lambda = \frac{\partial f/\partial Q_X}{P_X} = \frac{\partial f/\partial Q_Y}{P_Y} \tag{3-26}$$

or

$$\lambda = \frac{MU_X}{P_X} = \frac{MU_Y}{P_Y} \tag{3-27}$$

where MU_X is the marginal or extra utility that the individual receives from consuming the last unit of commodity X and MU_Y is the marginal utility of Y. Thus, Equation 3-27 postulates that in order to maximize utility subject to the budget constraint (i.e., in order to be in equilibrium), the individual must spend his or her income so that the marginal utility of the last dollar spent on X equals the marginal utility of the last dollar spent on Y. Thus, λ is the marginal utility of the last dollar spent on X and Y when the consumer is in equilibrium.

From this equilibrium condition, we get one point on the individual's demand curves for commodity X and commodity Y. By changing the price of X and Y and repeating the process, we obtain other points of consumer equilibrium, and by joining these, we can derive the individual's demand curve for commodities X and Y (that is, d_X and d_Y).

Problem 1 Given $U = Q_X Q_Y$, $M = \$100$, $P_X = \$2$, and $P_Y = \$5$, derive d_X and d_Y by the Lagrangian multiplier method.

Problem 2 Show mathematically that if P_X, P_Y, and M in the last section are all multiplied by the constant k, the condition for consumer equilibrium remains unchanged.

SUPPLEMENTARY READINGS

For a problem-solving approach to demand analysis, see:

Salvatore, Dominick: *Theory and Problems of Managerial Economics,* Schaum Outline Series (New York: McGraw-Hill, 1989), Chap. 5.

For a more extensive problem-solving approach to demand theory, see:

Salvatore, Dominick: *Theory and Problems of Microeconomic Theory,* 3rd ed., Schaum Outline Series (New York: McGraw-Hill, 1992), Chaps. 2 through 5.

The complete presentation of consumer demand theory is found in:

Salvatore, Dominick: *Microeconomics,* 2nd ed. (New York: HarperCollins, 1994), Part II (Chaps. 3, 4, and 5).

A more advanced and mathematical presentation of demand theory is found in:

Henderson, James M., and **Richard E. Quandt:** *Microeconomic Theory: A Mathematical Approach,* 3rd ed. (New York: McGraw-Hill, 1980), Chaps. 2 and 3.

CHAPTER 4

Demand Estimation

KEY TERMS

Identification problem
Consumer surveys
Observational research
Consumer clinics
Market experiments
Scatter diagram
Regression analysis
Regression line
Least-squares method
Degrees of freedom (df)
Simple regression analysis
t statistic
Significance test
Critical value
t test
Confidence interval
Coefficient of determination (R^2)
Total variation
Explained variation
Unexplained variation
Coefficient of correlation
Multiple regression analysis
Adjusted R^2 ($\bar{R}^2$)
Analysis of variance
F statistic
Standard error (*SE*) of the regression
Multicollinearity
Heteroscedasticity
Cross-sectional data
Autocorrelation
Time-series data
Durbin-Watson statistic (*d*)

CHAPTER OUTLINE

In this chapter we build on the analysis of consumer demand theory examined in Chapter 3 to show how a firm can estimate the demand for the product it sells. We saw in Chapter 3 that the forces that affect demand are: the price of the commodity, consumers' incomes, the price of related (i.e., substitute and complementary) commodities, consumers' tastes, and other more specific forces that are important for the particular commodity. We also saw in Chapter 3 that reliable estimates of the quantitative effect on sales of all the significant forces that affect demand are essential for the firm to make the best operating decisions and for planning.

Important questions to which we seek an answer in this chapter are: How much will the revenues of the firm change after increasing the price of the commodity by a certain amount? How much will the quantity demanded of the commodity increase if consumers' incomes increase by a specific amount? If the firm doubles its advertising expenditures and/or if it provides a particular credit incentive to consumers? How much would the demand that a firm faces for its product fall if competitors lowered their prices, increased their advertising expenditures, and provided credit incentives? The answers to these and other questions are essential for a firm to achieve its objective of maximizing the value of the firm. They are just as important for not-for-profit organizations. For example, it is very crucial for a state university to know how much enrollment would decline with a 10 percent increase in tuition, how the socioeconomic composition of its student body would change, and how it would affect the number of out-of-state students.

In this chapter, we begin by examining some general difficulties encountered in deriving the demand curve for a product from market data (the so-called identification problem). Then, we briefly discuss some marketing research approaches to demand estimation. Subsequently, we focus on regression analysis as the most useful and common method of demand estimation. Finally, we discuss the estimation of the demand for U.S. imports and exports. In the next chapter, we will then examine methods of forecasting demand.

4-1 THE IDENTIFICATION PROBLEM

The demand curve for a commodity is generally estimated from market data on the quantity purchased of the commodity at various prices over time (i.e., using time-series data) or for various consuming units or markets at one point in time (i.e., using cross-sectional data). However, simply joining the price-quantity observations on a graph does not generate the demand curve for the commodity. The reason is that each price-quantity observation is given by the intersection of a different (but unobserved) demand and supply curve of the commodity.[1]

Over time or across different individuals or markets, the demand for the commodity shifts or differs because of changes or differences in tastes, incomes,

[1]From principles of economics and the appendix to Chapter 1, we know that the supply curve of a commodity shows the quantity supplied of the commodity per time period at various prices of the commodity, while holding constant all the other determinants of supply.

price of related commodities, and so on. Similarly, over time or across different sellers or markets, the supply curve shifts or is different because of changes or differences in technology, factor prices, and weather conditions (for agricultural commodities). The intersection (equilibrium) of the different but unknown demand and supply curves generates the different price-quantity points observed. If the demand and supply curves did not shift or differ, the commodity price would remain the same. Therefore, by simply joining the different price-quantity observations, we do not generate the demand curve for the commodity. The demand curve cannot be identified so simply. This is referred to as the **identification problem.**

For example, in Figure 4-1, only price-quantity points E_1, E_2, E_3, and E_4 are observed.[2] Each of these price-quantity observations, however, lies on a different demand and supply curve. These different demand curves result from changes in tastes, incomes, and price of related commodities over time (with time-series

[2]To derive a demand curve from market data, we need many more points, but in order to keep the figure simple, we assume that we have only the four price-quantity observations shown in Figure 4-1.

Figure 4-1
Price-Quantity Points and the Identification Problem

Observed price-quantity data points E_1, E_2, E_3, and E_4 result, respectively, from the intersection of unobserved demand and supply curves D_1 and S_1, D_2 and S_2, D_3 and S_3, and D_4 and S_4. Therefore, the dashed line connecting observed points E_1, E_2, E_3, and E_4 is not the demand curve for the commodity. To derive a demand curve for the commodity, say, D_2, we allow the supply to shift or to be different and correct, through regression analysis, for the forces that cause demand curve D_2 to shift or to be different (see points E_2 and E_2').

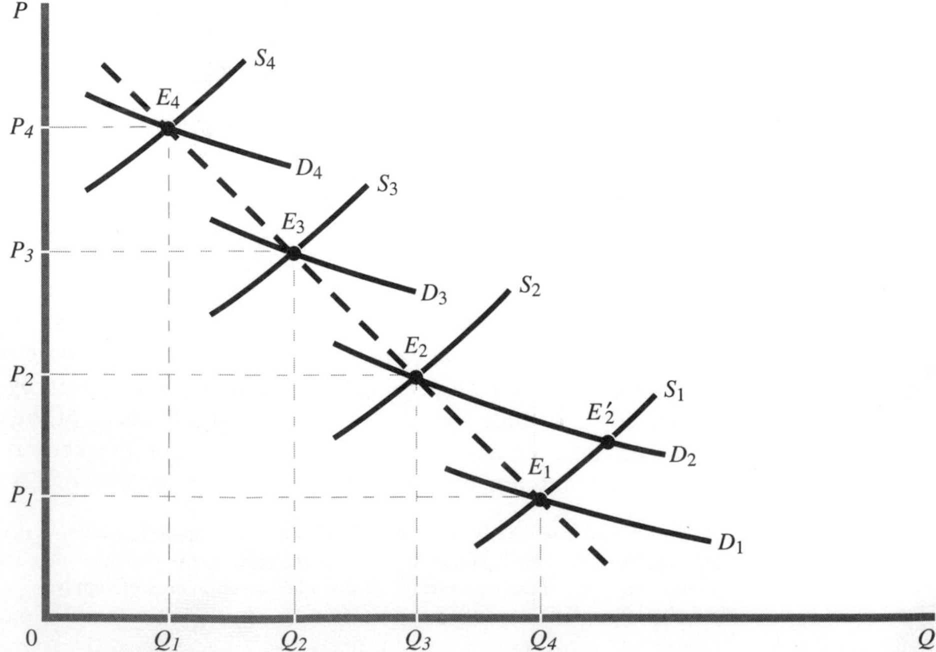

analysis), or from differences in tastes, incomes, and price of related commodities across different individuals or markets (with cross-sectional data). It is clear, therefore, that simply joining points E_1, E_2, E_3, and E_4 by a line as in Figure 4-1 does not generate the demand curve for the commodity. Thus, the dashed line connecting points E_1, E_2, E_3, and E_4 in Figure 4-1 is not the demand curve for the commodity.

In order to derive the demand curve for the commodity from the observed price-quantity data points, we should allow the supply curve of the commodity to shift or to differ, in an unrestricted manner, as shown in Figure 4-1, while we adjust or correct for the shifts or differences in the demand curve. That is, we must adjust or correct for the effect on the demand for the commodity resulting from changes or differences in consumers' incomes, in the price of related commodities, in consumers' tastes, and in other factors that cause the demand curve of the particular commodity to shift or to be different, so that we can isolate or identify the effect on the quantity demanded of the commodity resulting only from a change in its price. This price-quantity relationship, *after correction for all the forces that cause the demand curve to shift or to be different,* gives the true demand curve for the commodity (say, D_2, in Figure 4-1).

Note that in Figure 4-1, the dashed demand curves that we seek to identify are flatter or more elastic than the solid line joining the price-quantity observation points. Which of the dashed demand curves shown in Figure 4-1 we actually derive depends on the level at which we hold constant consumers' incomes, the price of related commodities, consumers' tastes, and other forces that cause the demand curve of the commodity to shift or to be different. For example, dashed demand curve D_3 is above and to the right of dashed demand curve D_2. This means that consumers' incomes and/or the price of substitute commodities are held constant at a higher level, while the price of complementary commodities are held constant at a lower level, than along market demand curve D_2. The opposite is true for demand curve D_1.

By including among the independent or explanatory variables the most important determinants of demand, regression analysis allows the researcher to disentangle the independent effects of the various determinants of demand, so as to isolate the effect of the price of the commodity on the quantity demanded of the commodity (i.e., to identify the demand curve for the commodity). Note that nothing is or should be done to correct for shifts or differences in supply. In fact, it is these uncorrected shifts or differences in supply, after having adjusted for shifts or differences in demand, that allow us to derive a particular demand curve. For example, in Figure 4-1, point E_2' on demand curve D_2 is derived by correcting the shifts or differences in demand while allowing the supply curve to shift from S_2 to S_1.

4-2 MARKETING RESEARCH APPROACHES TO DEMAND ESTIMATION

While regression analysis (to be discussed next) is by far the most useful and used method of estimating demand, marketing research approaches are also used. The most important of these are consumer surveys, consumer clinics, and market experiments. These approaches to demand estimation are discussed in detail in marketing courses. In this section we briefly examine these methods and point out their advantages and disadvantages and the conditions under which they might be useful to managers and economists.

Consumer Surveys and Observational Research

Consumer surveys involve questioning a sample of consumers about how they would respond to particular changes in the price of the commodity, incomes, the price of related commodities, advertising expenditures, credit incentives, and other determinants of demand. These surveys can be conducted by simply stopping and questioning people at a shopping center or by administering sophisticated questionnaires to a carefully constructed representative sample of consumers by trained interviewers.

In theory, consumer questionnaires can provide a great deal of useful information to the firm. In fact, they are often very biased because consumers are either unable or unwilling to provide accurate answers. For example, do you know how much your monthly beer consumption would change if the price of beer rose by 10 cents per 12-oz can or bottle? If the price of sodas fell by 5 cents? If your income rose by 20 percent? If a beer producer doubled its advertising expenditures? If the alcoholic content of beer were reduced by 1 percentage point? Even if you tried to answer these questions as accurately as possible, your reaction might be entirely different if actually faced with any of the above situations. Sometimes consumers provide a response that they deem more socially acceptable rather than disclose their true preferences. For example, no one would like to admit that he or she drinks 200 beers per month. Depending on the size of the sample and the elaborateness of the analysis, consumer surveys can also be expensive.

Because of the shortcomings of consumer surveys, many firms are supplementing or supplanting consumer surveys with **observational research.** This refers to the gathering of information on consumer preferences by watching them buying and using products. For example, observational research has led some automakers to conclude that many people think of their cars as art objects that are on display whenever they drive them. Observational research has also shown that consumers prefer to take several cold medicines, not just one. Observational research relies on product scanners which are increasingly found in stores and on people meters in homes. These make it possible for a company to learn overnight how a wide variety of products sell, the effectiveness of commercials, as well as television viewing patterns. Scanners and people meters, however, raise legal questions about privacy.

Observational research does not, however, render consumer surveys useless. Sometimes consumer surveys are the only way to obtain information about possible consumers' responses. For example, if a firm is thinking of introducing a new product or changing the quality of an existing one, the only way that the firm can test consumers' reactions is to directly ask them since no other data are available. From the survey, the researcher then typically tries to determine the demographic characteristics (age, sex, education, income, family size) of consumers who are most likely to purchase the product. The same may be true in detecting changes in consumer tastes and preferences and in determining consumers' expectations about future prices and business conditions. Consumer surveys can also be useful in detecting consumers' awareness of an advertising campaign by the firm. Furthermore, if the survey shows that consumers are unaware of price differences between the firm's product and competitive products, this may be a good indication that the demand for the firm's product is price inelastic.

Case Study 4-1

Micromarketing: Marketeers Zero In on Their Customers

More and more consumer-product companies are narrowing their marketing strategy from the region and city to the individual neighborhood and single store. The aim of such detailed point-of-sale information, or *micromarketing,* is to identify on a store-by-store basis the types of products with the greatest potential appeal for the specific customers in the area. Using census data and checkout scanners, Market Metrics, a marketing research firm, now collects consumer information at more than 30,000 supermarkets around the country. For example, for a particular grocery store in Georgia, Pennsylvania, Market Metrics found that potential customers were predominantly white, blue collar, and owned two cars, that they lived in households of three or four people and had an average income of $42,912, and that 26 percent of the people were below the age of 15. Based on these demographic and economic characteristics, Market Metrics determined that the strongest sellers in this market would be baby foods and grooming items, baking mixes, desserts, dry dinner mixes, cigarettes, laundry supplies, first-aid products, and milk. Less strong would be sales of artificial sweeteners, tea, books, film, prepared food, yogurt, wine, and liquor.

Such store-specific micromarketing is likely to become more and more common and necessary for successful retailing in the future. For example, Pepsi-Cola stocks more flavored soft drinks in stores where there are a lot of children, which represent the biggest market for flavored soft drinks. Indeed, as marketeers refine their tools, they are increasingly taking aim at the ultimate narrow target: the individual consumer. Thus, if you have shown an interest in a certain type of book, Waldenbooks will automatically send you information on new books in the field; the Quaker Oats Company tracks how your household redeems coupons and uses the information to refine the coupons it will offer you in the future; and Merrill Lynch & Co. provides detailed financial information about its customers to its brokers in order to help them promote the company's financial products. It is almost certain that marketing will be getting more and more personalized in the future.

Source: "Marketeers Zero In on Their Customers," *The Wall Street Journal,* March 18, 1991, p. B1; and "Segments of One," *The Wall Street Journal,* March 22, 1991, p. B4.

Case Study 4-2

With the Spread of Home TV Shopping, Retailing Will Never Be the Same Again

Home TV shopping is already a $2 billion-plus industry reaching over 60 million consumers and growing at about 20 percent per year. Although home TV shopping has been around for nearly two decades, it is only recently that it has been successfully used by big-name stores such as Macy's and even luxury merchants such as Saks Fifth Avenue to market a wide range of products appealing to the upscale urban and suburban consumers. Home shoppers are now younger, better educated, more affluent, and more style conscious than in the past, and a growing list of retailers are giving serious thought to the idea of producing "infomercials," launching shopping channels, or investing in interactive shopping ventures.

This does not mean that store shopping will disappear. Sociologists have identified a number of hidden dimensions in store shopping that solitary push-button home shopping cannot provide. Indeed, Americans use mall shopping for recreation, meeting friends, and even for exercise (walking). And the lack of reality is a major drawback of home shopping: customers cannot kick the tires, feel the fabric, or try on the shoes. However, as cable systems increase in number and more retailers participate, and as the medium upgrades and eventually becomes digital and interactive, as a sort of video mall where shoppers will browse through channels as through individual stores or catalogues, use the video telephone to ask questions, and charge orders on center accounts without the need to leave the comforts of home—retailing will never be the same again.

The rules of home shopping have also been sharply refined. They include: (1) Making merchandise seem special, limited, and available only through TV shopping; (2) describing scenarios, such as a cruise, where the merchandise can be used, and (3) using celebrities to glamorize inexpensive items, such as hair shampoos or makeup products. With new breakthroughs in digital signaling and satellite technology, cable advertising firms can now target viewers right down to specific zip codes and particular lifestyles.

Source: "Retailing Will Never Be the Same Again," *Business Week*, July 26, 1993, pp. 54–60; and "Cable Operators Refine Micromarketing," *The Wall Street Journal*, April 16, 1992, p. B8.

Consumer Clinics

Another approach to demand estimation is **consumer clinics.** These are laboratory experiments in which the participants are given a sum of money and asked to spend it in a simulated store to see how they react to changes in the commodity price, product packaging, displays, price of competing products, and other factors affecting demand. Participants in the experiment can be selected so as to closely represent the socioeconomic characteristics of the market of interest. Participants have an incentive to purchase the commodities they want the most because they are usually allowed to keep the goods purchased. Thus, consumer clinics are more realistic than consumer surveys. By being able to control the environment, consumer clinics also avoid the pitfall of actual market experiments (discussed next), which can be ruined by extraneous events.

Consumer clinics also have serious shortcomings, however. First, the results are questionable because participants know that they are in an artificial situation and that they are being observed. Therefore, they are not very likely to act normally, as they would in a real market situation. For example, suspecting that the researchers might be interested in their reaction to price changes, participants are likely to show more sensitivity to price changes than in their everyday shopping. Second, the sample of participants must necessarily be small because of the high cost of running the experiment. Inferring, however, a market behavior from the results of an experiment based on a very small sample can be dangerous. Despite these disadvantages, consumer clinics can provide useful information about the demand for the firm's product, particularly if consumer clinics are supplemented with consumer surveys.

Market Experiments

Unlike consumer clinics, which are conducted under strict laboratory conditions, **market experiments** are conducted in the actual marketplace. There are many different ways of performing market experiments. One method is to select several markets with similar socioeconomic characteristics, and change the commodity price in some markets or stores, packaging in other markets or stores, and the amount and type of promotion in still other markets or stores, and record the different responses (purchases) of consumers in the different markets. By using census data or surveys for various markets, a firm can also determine the effect of age, sex, level of education, income, family size, etc., on the demand for the commodity. Alternatively, the firm could change, one at a time, each of the determinants of demand under its control in a particular market over time and record consumers' responses.

The advantage of market experiments is that they can be conducted on a large scale to ensure the validity of the results and consumers are not aware that they are part of an experiment. Market experiments also have serious disadvantages, however. One of these is that in order to keep costs down, the experiment is likely to be conducted on too limited a scale and over a fairly short period of time, so that inferences about the entire market and for a more extended period of time are questionable. Extraneous occurrences, such as a strike or unusually bad weather, may seriously bias the results in uncontrolled experiments. Competitors could try to sabotage the experiment by also changing prices and other determinants of demand under their control. They could also monitor the experiment and gain very useful information that the firm would prefer not to disclose. Finally, a firm may permanently lose customers in the process of raising prices in the market where it is experimenting with a high price.

Despite these shortcomings, market experiments may be very useful to a firm in determining its best pricing strategy and in testing different packaging, promotional campaigns, and product qualities. Market experiments are particularly useful in the process of introducing a different product, where no other data exist. They may also be very useful in verifying the results of other statistical techniques used to estimate demand and in providing some of the data required for these other statistical techniques of demand estimation.

Case Study 4-3
Estimation of the Demand for Oranges by Market Experiment

In 1962, researchers at the University of Florida conducted a market experiment in Grand Rapids, Michigan, to determine the price elasticity and the cross-price elasticity of demand for three types of Valencia oranges: those from the Indian River district of Florida, those from the interior district of Florida, and those from California. Grand Rapids was chosen as the site for the market experiment because its size, demographic characteristics, and economic base were representative of other midwestern markets for oranges.

Nine supermarkets participated in the experiment, which involved changing the price of the three types of oranges, each day, for 31 consecutive days and recording the quantity sold of each variety. The price changes ranged within ±16 cents, in 4-cent increments, around the price of oranges that prevailed in the market at the time of the study. More than 9,250 dozen oranges were sold in the nine supermarkets during the 31 days of the experiment. Each of the participating supermarkets was provided with an adequate supply of each type of orange so that supply effects could be ignored. The length of the experiment was also sufficiently short so as to ensure no change in tastes, incomes, population, the rate of inflation, and determinants of demand other than price.

The results, summarized in Table 4-1, indicate that the price elasticity of demand for all three types of oranges was fairly high (the boldface numbers in the main diagonal of the table). For example, the price elasticity of demand for the Indian River oranges of −3.07 indicates that a 1 percent increase in their price leads to a 3.07 percent decline in their quantity demanded. More interestingly, the off-diagonal entries in the table show that while the cross-price elasticities of demand between the two types of Florida oranges were larger than 1, they were close to zero with respect to the California oranges. In other words, while consumers regarded the two types of Florida oranges as close substitutes, they did not view the California oranges as such. In pricing their oranges, therefore, producers of each of the two Florida varieties would have to carefully consider the price of the other (as consumers switch readily among them as a result of price changes) but need not be much concerned about the price of California oranges.

Table 4-1
Price Elasticity and Cross-Price Elasticity of Demand for Florida Indian River, Florida Interior, and California Oranges

	Price Elasticities and Cross-Price Elasticities		
Type of Orange	Florida Indian River	Florida Interior	California
Florida Indian River	**−3.07**	+1.56	+0.01
Florida Interior	+1.16	**−3.01**	+0.14
California	+0.18	+0.09	**−2.76**

Source: M. B. Godwin, W. F. Chapman, and W. T. Hanley, "Competition between Florida and California Valencia Oranges in the Fruit Market," *Bulletin 704* (Gainesville: University of Florida, December 1965).

4-3 INTRODUCTION TO REGRESSION ANALYSIS*

In order to introduce regression analysis, suppose that a manager wants to determine the relationship between the firm's advertising expenditures and its sales revenue. The manager wants to test the hypothesis that higher advertising expenditures lead to higher sales for the firm, and, furthermore, she wants to estimate the strength of the relationship (i.e., how much sales increase for each dollar increase in advertising expenditures). To this end, the manager collects data on advertising expenditures and on sales revenue for the firm over the past 10 years. In this case, the level of advertising expenditures (X) is the independent or explanatory variable, while sales revenues (Y) is the dependent variable that the manager seeks to explain. Suppose that the advertising-sales data for the firm in each of the past 10 years that the manager has collected are those in Table 4-2.

If we now plot each pair of advertising-sales values in Table 4-2 as a point on a graph, with advertising expenditures (the independent or explanatory variable) measured along the horizontal axis and sales revenues (the dependent

*Students familiar with regression analysis can use this and the next three sections as a review or skip them and go on directly to Section 4-7.

Table 4-2
Advertising Expenditures and Sales Revenues of the Firm (in millions of dollars)

Year (t)	1	2	3	4	5	6	7	8	9	10
Advertising expenditures (X)	10	9	11	12	11	12	13	13	14	15
Sales revenues (Y)	44	40	42	46	48	52	54	58	56	60

variable) measured along the vertical axis, we get the points (dots) in Figure 4-2. This is known as a **scatter diagram** since it shows the spread of the points in the X-Y plane. From Figure 4-2 (scatter diagram), we see that there is a positive relationship between the level of the firm's advertising expenditures and its sales revenues (i.e., higher advertising expenditures are associated with higher sales revenues) and that this relationship is approximately linear.

One way to estimate the approximate linear relationship between the firm's advertising expenditures and its sales revenues is to draw in, by visual inspection, the positively sloped straight line that "best" fits between the data points (so that the data points are about equally distant on either side of the line). By extending the line to the vertical axis, we can then estimate the firm's sales revenue with zero advertising expenditures. The slope of the line will then provide an estimate of the increase in the sales revenues that the firm can expect with each $1 million increase in its advertising expenditures. This will give us a rough estimate of the linear relationship between the firm's sales revenues (Y) and its advertising expenditures (X) in the form of Equation 4-1:

$$Y = a + bX \tag{4-1}$$

Figure 4-2
Advertising Expenditures and Sales Revenues of the Firm in Each of 10 Years

Advertising expenditure (X), the independent variable, is measured along the horizontal axis, while sales revenue (Y), the dependent variable, is measured along the vertical axis. Each point (dot) in the figure represents one of the advertising-sales combinations shown in Table 4-2.

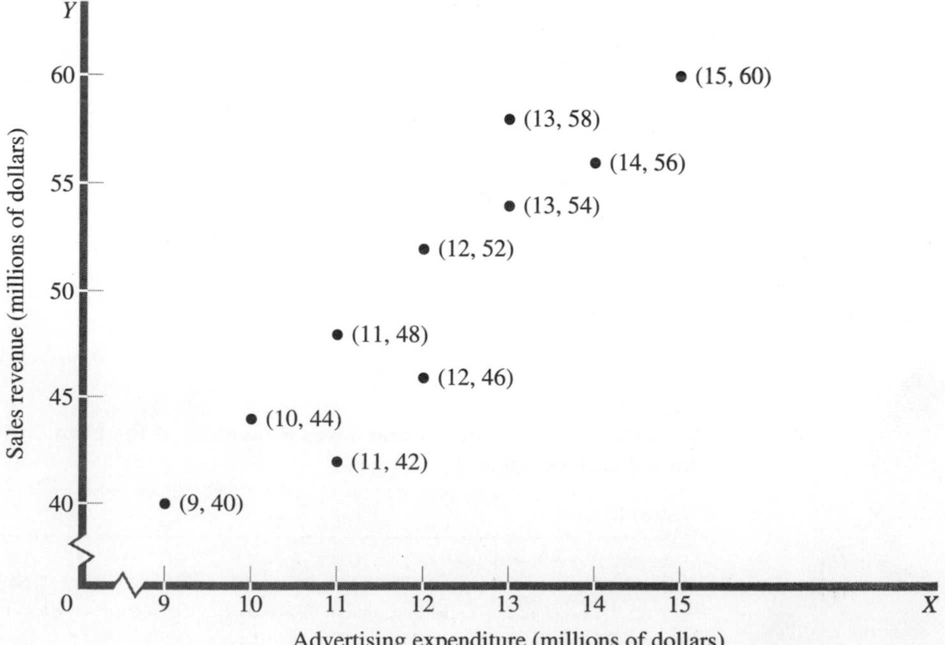

In Equation 4-1, a is the vertical intercept of the estimated linear relationship and gives the value of Y when $X = 0$, while b is the slope of the line and gives an estimate of the increase in Y resulting from each unit increase in X. The manager could then utilize this information to estimate how much the sales revenue of the firm would be if its advertising expenditures were anywhere between \$9 and \$15 million per year (the range of the advertising expenditures given in Table 4-2 and shown in Figure 4-2), or if advertising expenditures increased, say, to \$16 million per year, or fell to \$8 million per year.

The difficulty with the above visual fitting of a line to the data points in Figure 4-2 is that different researchers would probably fit a somewhat different line to the same data points and obtain somewhat different results. **Regression analysis** is a statistical technique for obtaining the line that best fits the data points according to an objective statistical criterion, so that all researchers looking at the same data would get exactly the same result (i.e., obtain the same line). Specifically, the **regression line** is the line obtained by minimizing the sum of the squared vertical deviations of each point from the regression line. This method is, therefore, appropriately called the "ordinary least-squares method," or "OLS" in short. The regression line fitted by such a **least-squares method** is shown in Figure 4-3.

Figure 4-3
Fitting a Regression Line

The regression line shown in the figure is the line that best fits the data points in the sense that the sum of the squared vertical deviations of the points from the line is a minimum.

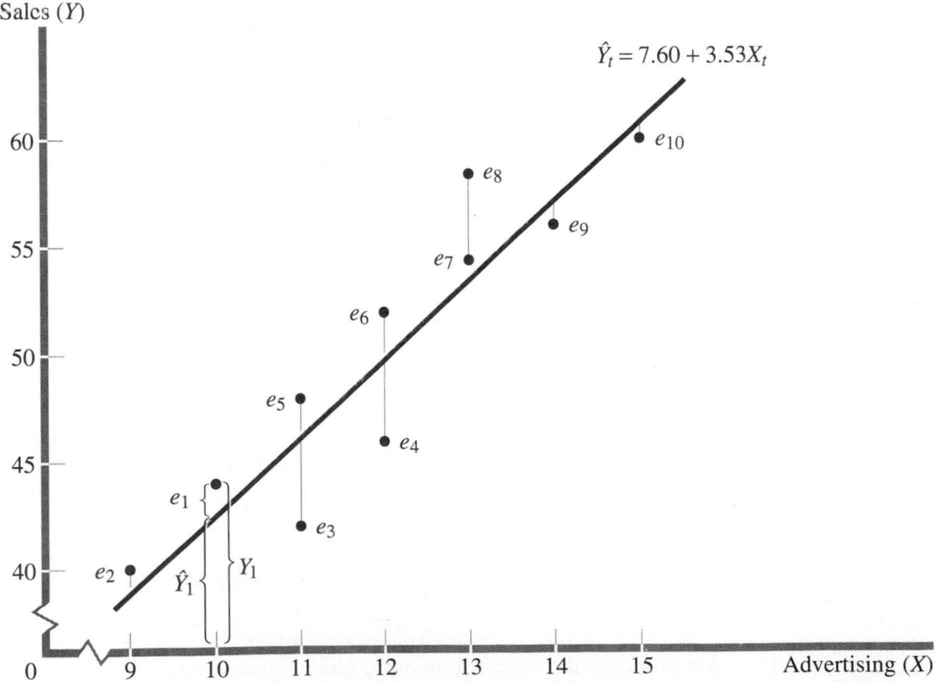

In Figure 4-3, Y_1 refers to the actual or observed sales revenue of $44 million associated with the advertising expenditures of $10 million in the first year for which the data was collected (see Table 4-2). The $\hat{Y}_1$ (reads: *Y* hat sub 1) shown in the figure is the corresponding sales revenues of the firm estimated from the regression line for the advertising expenditure of $10 million in the first year. The symbol e_1 in the figure is then the corresponding vertical deviation or error of the actual or observed sales revenue of the firm from the sales revenue estimated from the regression line in the first year. That is,

$$e_1 = Y_1 - \hat{Y}_1 \tag{4-2}$$

Errors of this type arise because (1) numerous explanatory variables with only slight or irregular effect on *Y* are not included in Equation 4-1, (2) of possible errors of measurement in *Y*, and (3) of random human behavior that leads to different results (say, different purchases of a commodity) under identical conditions.

Since there are 10 observation points in Figure 4-3, we have 10 such vertical deviations or errors. These are labeled e_1 to e_{10} in the figure. The regression line shown in Figure 4-3 is the line that best fits the data points in the sense that the sum of the squared (vertical) deviations from the line is minimum. That is, each of the 10 *e* values is first squared and then summed. The regression line is the line for which the sum of these squared deviations is a minimum.[3] How the value of $\hat{a}$ (the vertical intercept) and $\hat{b}$ (the slope coefficient) of the regression line that minimizes the sum of the squared deviations are actually obtained is shown next.

4-4 SIMPLE REGRESSION ANALYSIS

In this section we examine how to (1) calculate the value of *a* (the vertical intercept) and the value of *b* (the slope coefficient) of the regression line; (2) conduct tests of significance of parameter estimates; (3) construct confidence intervals for the true parameter; and (4) test for the overall explanatory power of the regression. While all these tasks are usually performed by the computer, we will do these operations by hand at first with very simple numbers in order to show exactly how regression analysis is performed and what it entails.

The Ordinary Least-Squares Method

We have seen in the previous section that a regression line is the line that best fits the data points in the sense that the sum of the squared deviations from the line is a minimum. The objective of regression analysis is to obtain estimates of *a* (the vertical intercept) and *b* (the slope) of the regression line:

$$\hat{Y}_t = \hat{a} + \hat{b}X_t \tag{4-3}$$

[3]The errors are squared before they are added in order to avoid the cancellation of errors of equal size but opposite signs. Squaring the errors also penalizes larger errors relatively more than smaller ones.

In Equation 4-3, $\hat{Y}_t$ is the estimate of the firm's sales revenues in year t obtained from the regression line for the level of advertising in year t (X_t), and $\hat{a}$ and $\hat{b}$ are estimates of parameters a and b, respectively. The deviation of error (e_t) of each observed sales revenue (Y_t) from its corresponding value estimated from the regression line ($\hat{Y}_t$) is then

$$e_t = Y_t - \hat{Y}_t = Y_t - \hat{a} - \hat{b}X_t \tag{4-4}$$

The sum of these squared errors or deviations can thus be expressed as

$$\sum_{t=1}^{n} e_t^2 = \sum_{t=1}^{n} (Y_t - \hat{Y}_t)^2 = \sum_{t=1}^{n} (Y_t - \hat{a} - \hat{b}X_t)^2 \tag{4-5}$$

The estimated values of a and b (that is, $\hat{a}$ and $\hat{b}$) are obtained by minimizing the sum of the squared deviations (i.e., by minimizing the value of Equation 4-5).[4] The value of $\hat{b}$ is given by

$$\hat{b} = \frac{\sum_{t=1}^{n} (X_t - \overline{X})(Y_t - \overline{Y})}{\sum_{t=1}^{n} (X_t - \overline{X})^2} \tag{4-6}$$

where $\overline{Y}$ and $\overline{X}$ are the mean or average values of the Y_t and the X_t, respectively. The value of $\hat{a}$ is then obtained from

$$\hat{a} = \overline{Y} - \hat{b}\overline{X} \tag{4-7}$$

Table 4-3 shows the calculation to determine the values of $\hat{a}$ and $\hat{b}$ for the advertising-sales data in Table 4-2. Substituting the values obtained from Table 4-3 into Equation 4-6, we get the value of $\hat{b}$:

$$\hat{b} = \frac{\sum_{t=1}^{n} (X_t - \overline{X})(Y_t - \overline{Y})}{\sum_{t=1}^{n} (X_t - \overline{X})^2} = \frac{106}{30} = 3.533$$

By then substituting the value of $\hat{b}$ found above and the values of $\overline{Y}$ and $\overline{X}$ found in Table 4-3 into Equation 4-7, we get the value of $\hat{a}$:

$$\hat{a} = \overline{Y} - \hat{b}\overline{X} = 50 - 3.533(12) = 7.60$$

Thus, the equation of the regression line is

$$\hat{Y}_t = 7.60 + 3.53X_t \tag{4-8}$$

[4]The values of $\hat{a}$ and $\hat{b}$ are obtained by finding the partial derivative of Equation 4-5 with respect to $\hat{a}$ and $\hat{b}$, setting the resulting two normal equations equal to zero, and solving them simultaneously to obtain Equation 4-6. [See Dominick Salvatore, *Theory and Problems of Statistics and Econometrics* (New York: McGraw-Hill, 1982), Chap. 6.]

Table 4-3
Calculations to Estimate Regression Line for Sales-Advertising Problem

t Year	X_t Advertising	Y_t Sales	$X_t - \bar{X}$	$Y_t - \bar{Y}$	$(X_t - \bar{X})(Y_t - \bar{Y})$	$(X_t - \bar{X})^2$
1	10	44	−2	−6	12	4
2	9	40	−3	−10	30	9
3	11	42	−1	−8	8	1
4	12	46	0	−4	0	0
5	11	48	−1	−2	2	1
6	12	52	0	2	0	0
7	13	54	1	4	4	1
8	13	58	1	8	8	1
9	14	56	2	6	12	4
10	15	60	3	10	30	9
$n = 10$	$\Sigma X_t = 120$ $\bar{X} = 12$	$\Sigma Y_t = 500$ $\bar{Y} = 50$	$\Sigma (X_t - \bar{X}) = 0$	$\Sigma (Y_t - \bar{Y}) = 0$	$\Sigma (X_t - \bar{X})(Y_t - \bar{Y}) = 106$	$\Sigma (X_t - \bar{X})^2 = 30$

This regression line indicates that with zero advertising expenditures (i.e., with $X_t = 0$), the expected sales revenue of the firm ($\hat{Y}_t$) is \$7.60 million. With advertising of \$10 million as in the first observation year (i.e., with X_1 = \$10 million), $\hat{Y}_1$ = \$7.60 + \$3.53(10) = \$42.90 million. On the other hand, with X_{10} = \$15 million, $\hat{Y}_{10}$ = \$7.60 + \$3.53(15) = \$60.55 million. Plotting these last two points (10, 42.90) and (15, 60.55) and joining them by a straight line, we obtain the regression line plotted in Figure 4-3.[5]

The estimated regression line could also be utilized to estimate that the firm's sales revenue with advertising expenditures of \$16 million would be \$7.60 + \$3.53(16) = \$64.08 million, or \$3.53 million higher than with advertising expenditures of \$15 million. Caution should, however, be exercised in using the regression line to estimate the sales revenue of the firm for advertising expenditures very different from those utilized in the estimation of the regression line itself. Strictly speaking, the regression line should be used only to estimate the sales revenues of the firm resulting from advertising expenditures that were within the range or that at least are near the advertising values that are used in the estimation of the regression line. Thus, not much confidence can usually be attached to the value of the estimated $\hat{a}$ coefficient, since this gives the sales revenues of the firm when advertising expenditures are zero (far off from the observed values). Because of this, we will concentrate our attention on the value of the $\hat{b}$, or slope, coefficient. The value of $\hat{b}$ measures the increase in the firm's sales revenues resulting from each unit (in this case, each \$1 million) increase in the advertising expenditures of the firm. That is, $\hat{b} = \Delta Y/\Delta X$. In the terminology of Chapter 2, $\hat{b}$ measures the marginal effect on Y (sales) from each unit change in X (advertising).[6]

[5]Note that the regression line goes through point ($\bar{X} = 12$, $\bar{Y} = 50$). This is always the case and will be useful in the analysis that follows.

[6]In terms of calculus, b is the derivative of Y with respect to X, or dY/dX.

Regression analysis is based on a number of crucial assumptions. These are that the error term (1) is normally distributed, (2) has zero expected value or mean, (3) has constant variance in each time period and for all values of X, and (4) its value in one time period is unrelated to its value in any other period. These assumptions are required so as to obtain unbiased estimates of the slope coefficient and to be able to utilize probability theory to test for the reliability of the estimates. How this is done is shown next.

Tests of Significance of Parameter Estimates

In the previous section, we estimated the slope coefficient ($\hat{b}$) from one sample of the advertising-sales data of the firm. If we had used a different sample (say, data for a different 10-year period), we would have obtained a somewhat different estimate of b. The greater is the dispersion of (i.e., the more spread out are) the estimated values of b (that we would obtain if we were to actually run many regressions for different data samples), the smaller is the confidence that we have in our single estimated value of the b coefficient.

To test the hypothesis that b is statistically significant (i.e., that advertising positively affects sales), we need first of all to calculate the standard error (deviation) of $\hat{b}$. The standard error of $\hat{b}$ ($s_{\hat{b}}$) is routinely provided as part of the computer printout of the regression analysis, but it is important to know how it is calculated and how it is used in tests of significance. The standard error of $\hat{b}$ is given by

$$s_{\hat{b}} = \sqrt{\frac{\sum (Y_t - \hat{Y}_t)^2}{(n-k)\sum (X_t - \overline{X})^2}} = \sqrt{\frac{\sum e_t^2}{(n-k)\sum (X_t - \overline{X})^2}} \tag{4-9}$$

where Y_t and X_t are the actual sample observations of the dependent and independent variables in year t, $\hat{Y}_t$ is the value of the dependent variable in year t estimated from the regression line, $\overline{X}$ is the expected value or mean of the independent variable, e is the error term or $Y_t - \hat{Y}_t$, n is the number of observations or data points used in the estimation of the regression line, and k is the number of estimated coefficients in the regression. The value of $n - k$ is called the **degrees of freedom (df).** Since in **simple regression analysis,** we estimate two parameters, $\hat{a}$ and $\hat{b}$, the value of k is 2, and the degrees of freedom is $n - 2$.

The value of $s_{\hat{b}}$ for our advertising-sales example can be calculated by substituting the values from Table 4-4 (an extension of Table 4-3) into Equation 4-9. In Table 4-4, the values of $\hat{Y}_t$ in column 4 are obtained by substituting the various advertising expenditures of column 2 into Equation 4-8. Column 5 is obtained by subtracting the values in column 4 from the corresponding values in column 3, column 6 is obtained by squaring the values in column 5, column 7 is repeated from Table 4-3.

Thus, the value of $s_{\hat{b}}$ is equal to

$$s_{\hat{b}} = \sqrt{\frac{\sum e_t^2}{(n-k)\sum (X_t - \overline{X})^2}} = \sqrt{\frac{65.4830}{(10-2)(30)}} = \sqrt{0.2728} = 0.52$$

Table 4-4
Calculations to Estimate the Standard Error of $\hat{b}$

(1) Year	(2) X_t	(3) Y_t	(4) $\hat{Y}_t$	(5) $Y_t - \hat{Y}_t = e_t$	(6) $(Y_t - \hat{Y}_t)^2 = e_t^2$	(7) $(X_t - \bar{X})^2$
1	10	44	42.90	1.10	1.2100	4
2	9	40	39.37	0.63	0.3969	9
3	11	42	46.43	−4.43	19.6249	1
4	12	46	49.96	−3.96	15.6816	0
5	11	48	46.43	1.57	2.4649	1
6	12	52	49.96	2.04	4.1616	0
7	13	54	53.49	0.51	0.2601	1
8	13	58	53.49	4.51	20.3401	1
9	14	56	57.02	−1.02	1.0404	4
10	15	60	60.55	−0.55	0.3025	9
$n = 10$	$\Sigma X_t = 120$ $\bar{X} = 12$	$\Sigma Y_t = 500$ $\bar{Y} = 50$			$\Sigma e_t^2 = 65.4830$	$\Sigma (X_t - \bar{X})^2 = 30$

Having obtained the value of $s_{\hat{b}}$, we next calculate the ratio $\hat{b}/s_{\hat{b}}$. This is called the ***t* statistic** or t ratio. The higher this calculated t ratio is, the more confident we are that the true but unknown value of b that we are seeking is not equal to zero (i.e., that there is a significant relationship between advertising and sales). For our sales-advertising example, we have

$$t = \frac{\hat{b}}{s_{\hat{b}}} = \frac{3.53}{0.52} = 6.79 \tag{4-10}$$

In order to conduct an objective or **significance test** for $\hat{b}$, we compare the calculated t ratio to the **critical value** of the t distribution with $n - k = 10 - 2 = 8$ df given by Table C-2.[7] This so-called ***t* test** of the statistical significance of the estimated coefficient is usually performed at the 5 percent level of significance. Thus, we go down the column headed 0.05 (referring to 2.5 percent of the area or probability in each tail of the t distribution, for a total of 5 percent in both tails) in Table C-2 until we reach 8 df. This gives the critical value of $t = 2.306$ for this two-tailed t test.

Since our calculated value of $t = 6.79$ exceeds the tabular value of $t = 2.306$ for the 5 percent level of significance with 8 df, we reject the null hypothesis that

[7]The t distribution is a bell-shaped, symmetrical distribution about its zero mean that is flatter than the standard normal distribution (see the figures on pages 644 and 645 in Appendix C at the end of the book) so that more of its area falls within the tails. While there is a single standard normal distribution, there is a different t distribution for each sample size, n. However, as n becomes larger, the t distribution approaches the standard normal distribution until, when $n > 30$, they are approximately equal. Thus, for large sample sizes, we can conduct significance tests using the normal distribution without concerning ourselves with degrees of freedom. In any event, a useful rule of thumb is that an estimated parameter is likely to be statistically significant at the 5 percent level if the calculated t statistic for the coefficient is greater than 2. Since in this case we have 10 observations or data points in our advertising-sales example, and we estimate two parameters ($\hat{a}$ and $\hat{b}$), the degrees of freedom is $n - k = 10 - 2 = 8$ and we use the t distribution to conduct our significance test.

there is no relationship between X (advertising) and Y (sales) and accept the alternative hypothesis that there is in fact a significant relationship between X and Y. To say that there is a statistically significant relationship between X and Y at the 5 percent level means that we are 95 percent confident that such a relationship exists. In other words, there is less than 1 chance in 20 (i.e., less than 5 percent chance) of being wrong, or accepting the hypothesis that there is a significant relationship between X and Y, when in fact there isn't. As mentioned earlier, this is called the "t test."

Other Aspects of Significance Tests and Confidence Intervals

While in the previous section we showed how to conduct statistical tests to show that the slope coefficient is different from zero at the 5 percent level of significance, other tests of significance are possible, and we can also construct confidence intervals for the true parameter from the estimated coefficient.

For example, we could test the hypothesis that the slope coefficient is different from zero at the 1 percent level of significance rather than at the 5 percent level. In that case we would be allowing for only 1 chance in 100 of being wrong (i.e., of accepting the alternative hypothesis that there is a relationship between X and Y when in fact no such relationship exists). To test the hypothesis at the 1 percent level, we go down the column headed 0.01 in Table C-2 until once again we reach 8 df. The critical value of t that we get from the t table is 3.355. Since the calculated t value of 6.79 exceeds this critical tabular value, we accept the hypothesis that there is in fact a significant relationship between X and Y at the 1 percent level also.

While tests of significance are sometimes conducted at the 1 percent or even at the 10 percent level of significance, it is more common, however, to use the 5 percent level. Note also that the greater is the number of the degrees of freedom (i.e., the greater is the number of observations or data points in relation to the number of estimated parameters in the regression analysis), the smaller are the critical t values in Table C-2 regardless of the level of significance that we choose. Therefore, the greater the number of the degrees of freedom, the more likely it is to accept the hypothesis that a statistically significant relationship exists between the independent variable(s) and the dependent variable.

Note that tests of significance are not usually conducted for the $\hat{a}$ coefficient (the vertical intercept) since this coefficient usually has little or no significance. Also note that in our presentation, we have tested only the hypothesis that $\hat{b}$ is significantly different from zero. Since $\hat{b}$ can be significantly different from zero by being either negative or positive, we conducted a two-tailed test. That is, we allowed for the possibility of $\hat{b}$ being significantly positive or significantly negative and examined areas (probabilities) under the t distribution in both tails. We could also test, however, the hypothesis that b is larger or smaller than some specified value. In those cases, we would conduct a single-tailed test and examine the area (probability) that the value of $\hat{b}$ falls only in the right or in the left tail of the t distribution (and look under the column headed 0.10 for the 5 percent test).

The above concepts can also be used to determine **confidence intervals** for the true b coefficient. Thus, using the tabular value of $t = 2.306$ for the 5 percent level of significance (2.5 percent in each tail) and 8 df in our advertising-sales example, we can say that we are 95 percent confident that the true value of b will be between

$$\hat{b} \pm 2.306\ (s_{\hat{b}})$$
$$3.53 \pm 2.306(0.52)$$
$$3.53 \pm 1.20$$

That is, we are 95 percent confident that the true value of b lies between 2.33 and 4.73. Similarly, we can say that we are 99 percent confident that the true value of b will be between $3.53 \pm 3.355(0.52)$, or 1.79 and 5.27 (the value of $t = 3.355$ is obtained by going down the column headed 0.01 in Table C-2 until we reach 8 df).

Test of Goodness of Fit and Correlation

Besides testing for the statistical significance of a particular estimated parameter, we can also test for the overall explanatory power of the entire regression. This is accomplished by calculating the coefficient of determination, which is usually denoted by R^2. The **coefficient of determination (R^2)** is defined as the proportion of the total variation or dispersion in the dependent variable (about its mean) that is explained by the variation in the independent or explanatory variable(s) in the regression. In terms of our advertising-sales example, R^2 measures how much of the variation in the firm's sales is explained by the variation in its advertising expenditures. The closer the observed data points fall to the regression line, the greater is the proportion of the variation in the firm's sales explained by the variation in its advertising expenditures, and the larger is the value of the coefficient of determination, or R^2.

We can calculate the coefficient of determination (R^2) by defining the total, the explained, and the unexplained or residual variation in the dependent variable, Y. The **total variation** in Y can be measured by squaring the deviation of each observed value of Y from its mean and then summing. That is,

$$\text{Total variation in } Y = \sum_{t=1}^{n} (Y_t - \overline{Y})^2 \tag{4-11}$$

Regression analysis breaks up this total variation in Y into two components: the variation in Y that is explained by the independent variable (X) and the unexplained or residual variation in Y. The **explained variation** in Y is given by Equation 4-12:

$$\text{Explained variation in } Y = \sum_{t=1}^{n} (\hat{Y}_t - \overline{Y})^2 \tag{4-12}$$

The values of $\hat{Y}_t$ in Equation 4-12 are obtained by substituting the various observed values of X (the independent variable) into the estimated regression equation. The mean of Y ($\overline{Y}$) is then subtracted from each of the estimated values of Y_t $(\hat{Y}_t)$. As indicated by Equation 4-12, these differences are then squared and added to get the explained variation in Y.

Finally, the **unexplained variation** in Y is given by Equation 4-13:

$$\text{Unexplained variation in } Y = \sum_{t=1}^{n} (Y_t - \hat{Y}_t)^2 \tag{4-13}$$

That is, the unexplained or residual variation in Y is obtained by first subtracting from each observed value of Y the corresponding estimated value of $\hat{Y}$, and then squaring and summing.

Summarizing, we have

Total variation = explained variation + unexplained variation

$$\sum (Y_t - \overline{Y})^2 = \sum (\hat{Y}_t - \overline{Y})^2 + \sum (Y_t - \hat{Y}_t)^2 \tag{4-14}$$

This breakdown of the total variation in Y into the explained and the unexplained variation is shown in Figure 4-4 for one particular observation or data point for our advertising-sales example.

Figure 4-4
Total, Explained, and Residual Variation

The total variation in the dependent variable, $\Sigma(Y_t - \overline{Y})^2$, is equal to the explained variation, $\Sigma(\hat{Y}_t - \overline{Y})^2$, plus the unexplained or residual variation, $\Sigma(Y_t - \hat{Y}_t)^2$. For the observation ($X = 13$, $Y = 58$), $Y_t - \overline{Y} = 58 - 50 = 8$, $\hat{Y}_t - \overline{Y} = 53.49 - 50 = 3.49$, and $Y_t - \hat{Y}_t = 4.51$ ($\hat{Y}_t = 53.49$ is the estimated value of Y_t for $X = 13$ in the fourth column of Table 4-4).

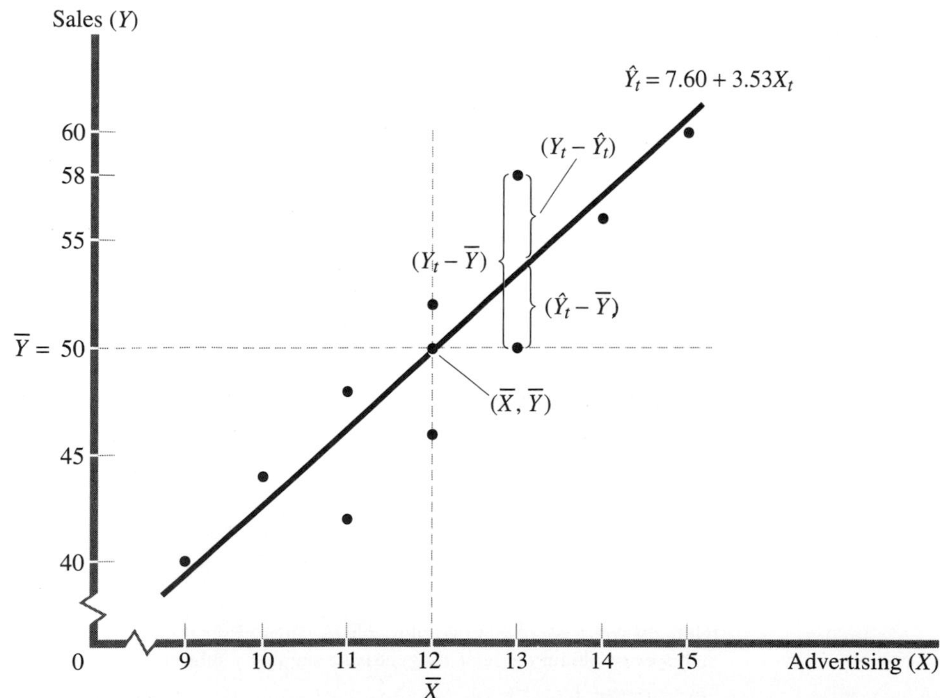

Now, the coefficient of determination, R^2, is defined as the ratio of the explained variation in Y to the total variation in Y. That is,

$$R^2 = \frac{\text{explained variation in } Y}{\text{total variation in } Y} = \frac{\sum (\hat{Y}_t - \overline{Y})^2}{\sum (Y_t - \overline{Y})^2} \tag{4-15}$$

If all the data points were to fall on the regression line (a most unusual occurrence), all the variation in the dependent variable (Y) would be explained by the variation in the independent or explanatory variable (X), and R^2 would be equal to 1 or 100 percent. At the opposite extreme, if none of the variation in Y were explained by the variation in X, R^2 would be equal to zero. Thus, the value of R^2 can assume any value from 0 to 1.

While the coefficient of determination is also routinely provided in the computer printout of the regression analysis, we will now show how to actually calculate R^2 for our advertising-sales problem. The calculations are shown in Table 4-5. From the bottom of column 4, we see that the total variation in Y (sales) is \$440 million. The explained variation is \$373.84 million, as shown at the bottom of column 7. Thus, the coefficient of determination for our advertising-sales problem is

$$R^2 = \frac{\$373.84}{\$440} = 0.85$$

This means that 85 percent of the total variation in the firm's sales is accounted for by the variation in the firm's advertising expenditures.

The last column of Table 4-5 gives the unexplained variation in Y (and has been copied from column 6 of Table 4-4). The unexplained variation in Y for our advertising-sales example is \$65.48 million. The sum of the explained and unexplained variation in Y (\$373.84 + \$65.48 = \$439.32) is equal to the total variation in Y (\$440), except for rounding errors.[8]

Two final things must be pointed out with respect to the coefficient of determination. The first is that in simple regression analysis the square root of the coefficient of determination (R^2) is the (absolute value of the) **coefficient of correlation,** which is denoted by r. That is,

$$r = \sqrt{R^2} \tag{4-16}$$

This is simply a measure of the degree of association or covariation that exists between variables X and Y. For our advertising-sales example,

$$r = \sqrt{R^2} = \sqrt{0.85} = 0.92$$

This means that variables X and Y vary together 92 percent of the time. The coefficient of correlation ranges in value between -1 (if all the sample observation points fall on a negatively sloped straight line) and 1 (for perfect positive linear

[8]Note that once we obtain two of the three values of the total, explained, and unexplained variation in Y, we can obtain the remaining measure simply by subtraction.

Table 4-5
Calculations to Estimate the Coefficient of Determination (R^2)

(1) Year	(2) Y_t	(3) $Y_t - \bar{Y}$	(4) $(Y_t - \bar{Y})^2$	(5) $\hat{Y}_t$	(6) $\hat{Y}_t - \bar{Y}$	(7) $(\hat{Y}_t - \bar{Y})^2$	(8) $(Y_t - \hat{Y}_t)^2$
1	44	−6	36	42.90	−7.10	50.4100	1.2100
2	40	−10	100	39.37	−10.63	112.9969	0.3969
3	42	−8	64	46.43	−3.57	12.7449	19.6249
4	46	−4	16	49.96	−0.04	0.0016	15.6816
5	48	−2	4	46.43	−3.57	12.7449	2.4649
6	52	2	4	49.96	−0.04	0.0016	4.1616
7	54	4	16	53.49	3.49	12.1801	0.2601
8	58	8	64	53.49	3.49	12.1801	20.3401
9	56	6	36	57.02	7.02	49.2804	1.0404
10	60	10	100	60.55	10.55	111.3025	0.3025
$n = 10$	$\Sigma Y_t = 500$ $\bar{Y} = 50$		$\Sigma (Y_t - \bar{Y})^2 = 440$			$\Sigma (\hat{Y}_t - \bar{Y})^2 = 373.8430$	$\Sigma (Y_t - \hat{Y})^2 = 65.4830$

correlation). It should be noted that the sign of the coefficient of correlation (r) is always the same as the sign of the estimated slope coefficient ($\hat{b}$).

As opposed to regression analysis, which implies that the variation in Y results from the variation in X, correlation analysis measures only the degree of association or covariation between the two variables, without any implication of causality or dependence. In short, we can find the correlation coefficient between any two variables, but we run a regression analysis only if we believe that the variation in one variable (the independent variable, X) affects or somehow results in some variation in Y (the dependent variable).

This brings us to the second point. That is, though regression analysis implies causality (i.e., that the variation in X causes the variation in Y), only theory can tell us if we can expect the variation in X to result in the variation in Y. In fact, it is possible that a high coefficient of determination (and correlation) between X and Y may be due to some other factor that affects both X and Y, which is not included in the regression analysis. For example, expenditures on food and housing may both depend on the level of consumers' income rather than on each other. In such a case, we would simply say that there is *correlation* or covariation between X and Y without identifying one variable (X) as the independent or explanatory variable.

4-5 MULTIPLE REGRESSION ANALYSIS

We now extend the simple regression model to multiple regression analysis. We will show how to estimate the regression parameters, how to conduct tests of their statistical significance, and how to measure and test the overall explanatory power of the entire regression.

The Multiple Regression Model

When the dependent variable that we seek to explain is hypothesized to depend on more than one independent or explanatory variable, we have **multiple regression analysis.** For example, the firm's sales revenue may be postulated to depend not only on the firm's advertising expenditures (as examined in Section 4-4) but also on its expenditures on quality control. The regression model can then be written as

$$Y = a + b_1X_1 + b_2X_2 \tag{4-17}$$

where Y is the dependent variable referring to the firm's sales revenue, X_1 refers to the firm's advertising expenditures, and X_2 to its expenditures on quality control. The coefficients, a, b_1, and b_2 are the parameters to be estimated.

The a coefficient is the constant or vertical intercept and gives the value of Y when both X_1 and X_2 are equal to zero. On the other hand, b_1 and b_2 are the slope coefficients. They measure the change in Y per unit change of X_1 and X_2, respectively. Specifically, b_1 measures the change in sales (Y) per unit change in advertising expenditures (X_1), while holding quality-control expenditures (X_2) constant. Similarly, b_2 measures the change in Y per unit change in X_2 while holding X_1 constant. That is, $b_1 = \Delta Y/\Delta X_1$, while $b_2 = \Delta Y/\Delta X_2$.[9] In our sales-advertising and quality-control problem we postulate that both b_1 and b_2 are positive, or that the firm can increase its sales by increasing its expenditures for advertising and quality control.

The model can also be generalized to any number of independent or explanatory variables (k'), as indicated in Equation 4-18:

$$Y = a + b_1X_1 + b_2X_2 + \cdots + b_{k'}X_{k'} \tag{4-18}$$

The only assumptions made in multiple regression analysis in addition to those made for simple regression analysis are that the number of independent or explanatory variables in the regression be smaller than the number of observations and that there be no perfect linear correlation among the independent variables.[10]

The process of estimating the parameters or coefficients of a multiple regression equation is in principle the same as in simple regression analysis, but since the calculations are much more complex and time-consuming, they are invariably done with computers. The computer also provides routinely the standard error of the estimates, the t statistics, the coefficient of multiple determination, and several other important statistics that are used to conduct other statistical tests of the results (to be examined later). All that is required is to be able to set up the regression analysis, feed the data into the computer, and interpret the results.

For example, if we regress the firm's sales (Y) on its expenditures for adver-

[9]In terms of calculus, $b_1 = \partial Y/\partial X_1$, while $b_2 = \partial Y/\partial X_2$. Thus, b_1 and b_2 are often referred to as the "partial regression coefficients."

[10]If the number of independent or explanatory variables (the X's) is equal to or larger than the number of observations, or if there is an exact linear relationship among some or all of the independent or explanatory variables, the regression equation cannot be estimated.

Table 4-6
Yearly Expenditures on Advertising and Quality Control, and Sales of the Firm (in millions of dollars)

Year (t)	1	2	3	4	5	6	7	8	9	10
Advertising (X_1)	10	9	11	12	11	12	13	13	14	15
Quality control (X_2)	3	4	3	3	4	5	6	7	7	8
Sales revenue (Y)	44	40	42	46	48	52	54	58	56	60

tising (X_1) and quality control (X_2) using the data in Table 4-6 (an extension of Table 4-2), we obtain the results given in Table 4-7.[11]

From the results shown in Table 4-7, we can write the following regression equation:

$$\hat{Y}_t = 17.944 + 1.873X_{1t} + 1.915X_{2t} \qquad (4\text{-}19)$$
$$t \text{ statistic} \qquad (2.663) \qquad (2.813)$$

The above results indicate that for each \$1 million increase in expenditures on advertising and quality control, the sales of the firm increase by \$1.87 million (the estimated coefficient of X_1) and \$1.92 million (the estimated coefficient of X_2), respectively. To perform t tests for the statistical significance of the estimated parameters or coefficients, we need to determine the critical value of t from the table of the t distribution. At the 0.05 level of significance for $n - k = 10 - 3 = 7$ df (where k is the number of estimated parameters, including the constant

[11]The results given in Table 4-7 are in the form provided by a standard computer program (TSP). Other computer programs (such as SORITEC, SPSS, and RATS) usually provide the same general information in a similar format. Different computer programs, however, usually give slightly different results because of differences in rounding.

Table 4-7
Computer Results of Regression of Y on X_1 and X_2

SMPL 1 - 10
10 Observations
LS // Dependent variable is Y

	COEFFICIENT	STANDARD ERROR	T STATISTIC
C	17.9437	5.91914	3.03147
X1	1.87324	0.70334	2.66335
X2	1.91549	0.68101	2.81272

R squared	0.930154	Mean of dependent var	50.00000
Adjusted R squared	0.910198	SD of dependent var	6.992061
SE of regression	2.095311	Sum of squared resid	30.73242
Durbin-Watson stat	1.541100	F statistic	46.61000
Log likelihood	−19.80301		

term), this is 2.365 and is obtained by going down the column headed 0.05 in Table C-2 (for the two-tailed test with 2.5 percent of the area under each tail of the t distribution) until we reach 7 df. Since the value of the calculated t statistic exceeds the critical t value of 2.365, we conclude that both parameters are statistically different from zero at the 5 percent level of significance.[12]

The Coefficient of Determination and Adjusted R^2

As in simple regression analysis, the coefficient of determination measures the proportion of the total variation in the dependent variable that is explained by the variation in the independent or explanatory variables in the regression. From Table 4-7, we see that for our example the coefficient of determination, or R^2, is 0.93. This means that variation in the firm's expenditures on advertising and quality control explain 93 percent of the variation in the firm's sales revenues. This is larger than the R^2 of 0.85 that we obtained for the simple regression of sales on advertising expenditures alone that we found on page 144. This was to be expected. That is, as more relevant independent or explanatory variables are included in the regression, we generally expect a larger proportion of the total variation in the dependent variable to be "explained."

However, in order to take into consideration that the number of degrees of freedom declines as additional independent or explanatory variables are included in the regression, we calculate the **adjusted R_2 ($\overline{R}^2$)** as

$$\overline{R}^2 = 1 - (1 - R^2)\left(\frac{n-1}{n-k}\right) \tag{4-20}$$

where n is the number of observations or sample data points and k is the number of parameters or coefficients estimated. For example, in the regression analysis of Y on X_1 and X_2, $n = 10$, $n - k = 10 - 3 = 7$, and $R^2 = 0.930154$. Substituting these values into Equation 4-20, we get the value of $\overline{R}^2 = 0.910198$ (the same as in the computer printout given by Table 4-7). This means that when due consideration is given to the fact that including the firm's expenditures on quality control as an additional explanatory variable in the regression reduces the degrees of freedom, the proportion of the total variation in sales explained by the regression is 91 percent rather than 93 percent. This is still larger than the 85 percent explained by advertising as the single independent variable in the simple regression.[13]

The inclusion of expenditures on quality control in the regression analysis also leads to a very different value of $\hat{b}_1$ (the estimated coefficient of advertising

[12]Note that since the t statistics were provided by the computer printout, we have presented those below the estimated coefficients rather than the standard errors (which are used to calculate the t statistics). We will follow this procedure in the rest of the text, unless otherwise indicated.

[13]Note that the adjustment (reduction) in R^2 to obtain $\overline{R}^2$ is smaller the larger the value of n is in relation to k.

expenditures in the multiple regression), as compared with the value of $\hat{b}$ (the estimated coefficient of advertising expenditures in the simple regression). The value of $\hat{b}$ was found to be 3.53 in Equation 4-8, while the value of $\hat{b}_1$ is 1.87 in Equation 4-19. Thus, omission of an important explanatory variable (expenditures for quality control, in this case) from the simple regression gives biased results for the estimated slope coefficient. Specifically, simple regression analysis attributes a much greater influence of advertising on sales than warranted. In other words, advertising gets "credited" for some of the influence on sales that is in fact due to expenditures on quality control. Thus, it is crucial to include in the regression analysis all *important* independent or explanatory variables.

Analysis of Variance

The overall explanatory power of the entire regression can be tested with the **analysis of variance.** This utilizes the value of the **F statistic,** or F ratio, which is also provided by the computer printout. Specifically, the F statistic is used to test the hypothesis that the variation in the independent variables (the X's) explains a significant proportion of the variation in the dependent variable (Y). Thus, we can use the F statistic to test the null hypothesis that all the regression coefficients are equal to zero against the alternative hypothesis that they are not all equal to zero.

The value of the F statistic is given by

$$F = \frac{\text{explained variation}/(k - 1)}{\text{unexplained variation}/(n - k)} \tag{4-21}$$

where, as usual, n is the number of observations and k is the number of estimated parameters or coefficients in the regression. It is because the F statistic is the ratio of two variances that this test is often referred to as the "analysis of variance." The F statistic can also be calculated in terms of the coefficient of determination as follows:

$$F = \frac{R^2/(k - 1)}{(1 - R^2)/(n - k)} \tag{4-22}$$

Using the values of $R^2 = 0.930154$, $n = 10$, and $k = 3$ for our example, we obtain $F = 46.61$, the same value as in the computer printout in Table 4-7.

To conduct the F test or analysis of variance, we compare the calculated or regression value of the F statistic with a critical value from the table of the F distribution. Two tables of the F distribution are presented in Appendix C at the end of the text. One is for the 5 percent level of significance, and the other is for the 1 percent level. The F distribution for each level of statistical significance is defined in terms of 2 df. These are $k - 1$ for the numerator (see Equations 4-2 and 4-22) and $n - k$ for the denominator. Thus, in our example, the degrees of freedom are $k - 1 = 3 - 1 = 2$ (the number of independent variables in the regression) for the numerator and $n - k = 10 - 3 = 7$ for the denominator.

To determine the critical value of the *F* distribution, we first move across Table C-3 of the *F* distribution (provided in Appendix C at the end of the text) until we reach 2 df for the numerator, and then move down in the table until we reach 7 df for the denominator. The critical value of *F* that we find in the table for the 5 percent level of significance is 4.74. Since the calculated value of the *F* statistic of 46.61 exceeds the critical value of 4.74 for the *F* distribution with 2 and 7 df, we reject at the 5 percent level of significance the null hypothesis that there is no statistically significant relationship between the independent variables and the dependent variable (i.e., we accept the alternative hypothesis at the 5 percent level of significance that not all coefficients are equal to zero).[14]

Point and Interval Estimates

The computer printout presented in Table 4-7 also gives the standard error of the entire regression (the value of 2.09531 labeled "*SE* of regression"). This is nothing else than the standard error of the dependent variable (Y) from the regression line.[15] The smaller the value of the **standard error (*SE*) of the regression,** the better is the "fit" of the regression line to the observation or sample points. The *SE* of the regression can be used to estimate confidence intervals for the dependent variable. Specifically, we can use the estimated regression given by Equation 4-19 to find a point estimate or forecast of Y, and then use the point estimate or forecast and the value of the *SE* of the regression to obtain interval estimates or forecasts of Y. For example, for $X_1 = 12$ and $X_2 = 5$, we obtain the point estimate (forecast) of

$$\hat{Y} = 17.944 + 1.915(12) + 1.873(5) = 50.289 \qquad (4\text{-}23)$$

The *approximate* 95 percent confidence interval estimate or forecast of Y is then given by

$$\begin{aligned} &50.289 \pm 2(SE) \\ &50.289 \pm (2)(2.095) \\ &50.289 \pm 4.190 \end{aligned} \qquad (4\text{-}24)$$

That is, we are 95 percent confident that the true value of Y will lie between 46.10 and 54.48.[16]

[14]To test the hypothesis at the 1 percent level of significance, we compare the calculated value of the *F* statistic to the critical *F* value from Table C-3 for the 1 percent level of statistical significance, with 2 and 7 df. In simple regression analysis, where there is only one independent variable, it can be shown that the *F* test is equivalent to the *t* test.

[15]This is not to be confused with the standard deviation (*SD*) of the dependent variable *itself* from its mean or expected value, that is also reported in Table 4-7.

[16]The Durbin-Watson statistic, which is also presented in Table 4-7, will be utilized on page 153.

4-6 PROBLEMS IN REGRESSION ANALYSIS

Regression analysis may face some serious problems. These are multicollinearity, heteroscedasticity, and autocorrelation. In this section, we discuss each of these in turn by examining the conditions under which they might arise, the tests available to detect their presence, and possible ways to overcome the difficulties that they create.

Multicollinearity

Multicollinearity refers to the situation where two or more explanatory variables in the regression are highly correlated. For example, suppose that the firm of Table 4-6 had kept its expenditures on quality control nearly constant as a fraction of its advertising expenditures over time (so that both types of expenditures would be highly collinear). In such a case, running a regression of sales on expenditures for advertising and for quality control would very likely have led to exaggerated standard errors and, therefore, to low t values for both estimated coefficients. This could lead to the conclusion that both slope coefficients are statistically insignificant, even though the R^2 may be very high.[17]

Serious multicollinearity can sometimes be overcome or reduced by (1) extending the sample size (i.e., collecting more data); (2) utilizing a priori information (for example, we may know from a previous study that $b_2 = 2b_1$); (3) transforming the functional relationship; and/or (4) dropping one of the highly collinear variables. An example of the last method may be the elimination of price as an explanatory variable in the regression model by using deflated (i.e., price-adjusted) values of the dependent and independent variables in the regression (see Problem 9). Dropping other variables that theory tells us should be included in the model would lead, however, to specification bias, which is even more serious than the multicollinearity problem.

Heteroscedasticity

Another serious problem that we may face in regression analysis is **heteroscedasticity.** This arises when the assumption that the variance of the error term is constant for all values of the independent variables is violated. This often occurs in **cross-sectional data** (i.e., data on a sample of families, firms, or other economic unit for a given year or other time period), where the size of the error may rise (the more common form) or fall with the size of an independent variable (see Figure 4-5*a* and *b*, respectively). For example, the error associated with the expenditures of low-income families is usually smaller than for high-income families

[17]To be sure, while the test for the statistical significance of the slope coefficients is biased, the value of the estimated coefficients is not (if the regression equation is otherwise properly specified by the inclusion of all important variables). Therefore, the regression results can still be used for forecasting purposes if the pattern of multicollinearity is expected to persist more or less unchanged during the forecasting period.

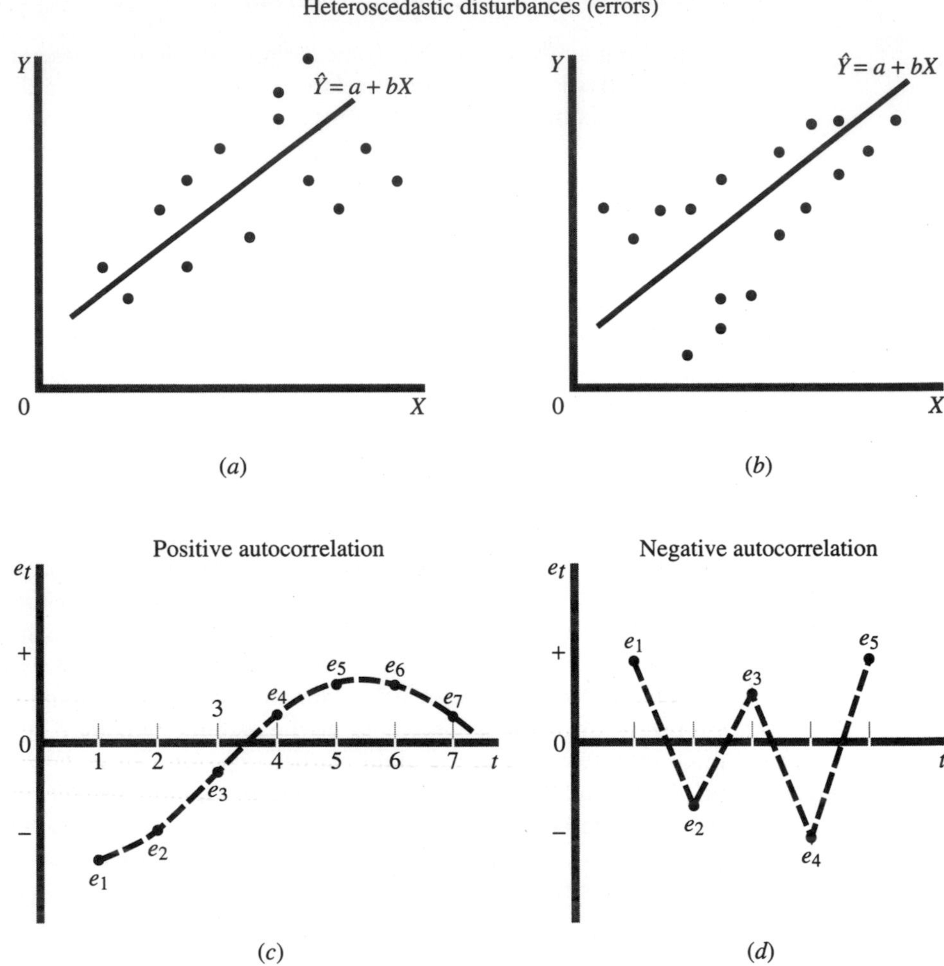

Figure 4-5
Heteroscedastic and Autocorrelated Disturbances

Part (*a*) shows heteroscedastic disturbances, where the size of the error or residual increases with the size of the value of *X*. Part (*b*) shows the opposite pattern of heteroscedastic disturbances (which is less common). Part (*c*) shows positive autocorrelation (i.e., a positive or negative error in one period is followed by another positive or negative error term, respectively, in the following period). Part (*d*) shows negative autocorrelation (which is less common).

because most of the expenditures of low-income families are on necessities, with little room for discretion. Thus, if data on family expenditures were used as an explanatory variable, the regression analysis would very likely face the problem of heteroscedasticity.

Heteroscedastic disturbances lead to biased standard errors and, thus, to incorrect statistical tests and confidence intervals for the parameter estimates. In cases where the pattern of errors or residuals points to the existence of heteroscedasticity, the researcher may overcome the problem by using the log of the explanatory variable that leads to heteroscedastic disturbances or by running a weighted least-squares regression. To run a weighted least-squares regression, we first divide the dependent and all independent variables by the variable that is responsible for the heteroscedasticity and then run the regression on the transformed variables.

Autocorrelation

Whenever consecutive errors or residuals are correlated, we have **autocorrelation,** or serial correlation. When consecutive errors have the same sign, we have positive autocorrelation (see Figure 4-5*c*). When they change sign frequently, we have negative autocorrelation (see Figure 4-5*d*). Autocorrelation is frequently found in **time-series data** (i.e., data where there is one observation on each variable for each time period). In economics, positive autocorrelation is more common than negative autocorrelation, and so we will deal only with the former in what follows. While estimated coefficients are not biased in the presence of autocorrelation, their standard errors are biased downward (so that the value of their t statistics is exaggerated). As a result, we may conclude that an estimated coefficient is statistically significant when, in fact, it is not. The value of $\bar{R}^2$ and of the F statistic will also be unreliable in the presence of autocorrelation.

Autocorrelation can arise from the existence of trends and cycles in economic variables, from the exclusion of an important variable from the regression, or from nonlinearities in the data. Autocorrelation can be detected by plotting the residuals or errors (as in Figure 4-5*c* and *d*) or, more usually, by using the **Durbin-Watson statistic (*d*)**. This is given by Formula 4-25 and is routinely provided in the computer printout of practically all regression packages. In Formula 4-25, e_t and e_{t-1} refer, respectively, to the error term in period t and in the previous time period $(t - 1)$. The value of d ranges between 0 and 4.

$$d = \frac{\sum_{t=2}^{n} (e_t - e_{t-1})^2}{\sum_{t=1}^{n} (e_t)^2} \tag{4-25}$$

The computed d statistic is then compared to a critical value from the Durbin-Watson (D-W) table (Table C-4) that is provided at the end of the book. The D-W test can be conducted either at the 5 percent or at the 1 percent level of significance. Across the top of the D-W table, we have k' (the number of explanatory variables in the regression), and moving downward on the table, we have n (the number of observations or sample data points). The D-W table starts at $n = 15$; therefore, we cannot use this method of testing for autocorrelation if we have fewer than 15 observations in our sample.

For each value of k' there are two columns in the D-W table, one headed d_L (for the lower value of d) and one headed d_U (for the upper value of d). If the calculated value of the d statistic exceeds the critical value of d_U in the table (for the appropriate value of k' and n), we conclude that there is no evidence of autocorrelation at the 5 or 1 percent level of significance. In general, a value of about $d = 2$ indicates the absence of autocorrelation. If the value of the D-W statistic falls between the critical value of d_L and d_U in the table, the test is inconclusive. Finally, if the value of the d statistic is smaller than the critical value of d_L given in the table, there is evidence of autocorrelation.

If the D-W test indicates the presence of autocorrelation, we must then adjust for its effect. The adjustment may involve the inclusion of time as an additional explanatory variable to take into consideration the trend that may exist in the data, the inclusion of an important missing variable into the regression, or the reestimation of the regression in nonlinear form. Sometimes, reestimating the regression for the *change* (i.e., using the first differences) in the dependent and independent variables and omitting the constant term may overcome autocorrelation. More complex methods also exist. These, however, are beyond the scope of this book.

4-7 DEMAND ESTIMATION BY REGRESSION ANALYSIS

While consumer surveys, consumer clinics, market experiments, and other marketing research approaches to demand estimation may be useful, by far the most common method of estimating demand in managerial economics is regression analysis. This method is usually more objective, provides more complete information, and is generally less expensive than properly conducted marketing approaches to demand estimation.

In this section, we summarize and review the method of estimating demand by regression analysis. Specifically, we discuss the specification of the model to be estimated, the data requirements, the possible functional forms of the demand equation, and the evaluation of the econometric results obtained.

Model Specification

The first step in using regression analysis to estimate demand is to specify the model to be estimated. This involves identifying the most important variables that are believed to affect the demand for the commodity under study. These will usually include the price of the commodity (P_X), consumers' income (I), the number of consumers in the market (N), the price of related (i.e., substitute and complementary) commodities (P_Y), consumers' tastes (T), and all the other variables, such as the level of advertising, the availability and level of credit incentives, and consumers' price expectations, that are thought to be important determinants of the demand for the particular commodity under study. These were discussed in detail in Chapter 3. Thus, we can specify the following general function of the demand for the commodity (Q_X), measured in physical units, where the dots at the end of Equation 4-26 refer to the other determinants of demand that are specific to the particular firm and commodity:

$$Q_X = f(P_X, I, N, P_Y, T, \ldots) \tag{4-26}$$

The variables that are specific to the demand function being estimated are determined from an in-depth knowledge of the market for the commodity. Thus, the demand function for expensive durable goods, such as automobiles and houses, which are usually purchased by borrowing money, must include credit terms or interest rates among the explanatory variables. The demand function for seasonal equipment, such as skiing equipment, air conditioners, swimming suits, and cold beverages, will have to include weather conditions, while the demand function for capital goods, such as machinery and factory buildings, will very likely have to include rates of profit, capital utilization, and wage increases among the explanatory variables. The researcher must avoid omitting important variables from the demand equation to be estimated; otherwise he or she will obtain biased results. At the same time, including too many explanatory variables (say, more than 5 or 6) may lead to econometric difficulties, such as having too few degrees of freedom (see page 139) and multicollinearity (see page 151).

Collecting Data on the Variables

The second step in using regression analysis to estimate the demand for a particular commodity is to collect the data for the variables in the model. Data can be collected for each variable over time (i.e., yearly, quarterly, monthly, etc.) or for different economic units (individuals, households, etc.) at a particular point in time (i.e., for a particular year, month, week, etc.). The former is called *time-series data,* while the latter is called *cross-sectional data.* Each type of data has specific advantages but leads to particular estimation problems.

The type of data actually utilized in demand estimation is often dictated by availability. Lack of data may also force the researcher to use a proxy for some of the variables for which no data are available. For example, a proxy for consumers' price expectations in each period might be the actual price changes from the previous period. The researcher could also try to measure consumers' expectations by consumer surveys. Finally, since it is usually very difficult to find reliable quantitative measures of tastes, the researcher may have to make sure (possibly by consumer surveys) that they have not changed during the period of the analysis. In that case, tastes can be dropped as an explicit explanatory variable from the actual estimation of the demand equation.

The most important sources of general published data that are likely to be useful in gathering the data for demand estimation are: the *Survey of Current Business,* the *Statistical Abstract of the United States,* the *Federal Reserve Bulletin,* and the *Annual Economic Report to the President.*

Specifying the Form of the Demand Equation

The third step in estimating demand by regression analysis is to determine the functional form of the model to be estimated. The simplest model to deal with, and the one which is often also the most realistic, is the linear model. For example, Equation 4-25 can be written in explicit linear form as

$$Q_X = a_0 + a_1P_X + a_2I + a_3N + a_4P_Y + \cdots + e \qquad (4\text{-}27)$$

In Equation 4-27, the *a*'s are the parameters (coefficients) to be estimated, and e is the error term. In such a linear model, the change in (i.e., the marginal effect on) the dependent variable (Q_X) for each 1-unit change in the independent or explanatory variables (given by the estimated coefficient for the variables) is constant regardless of the *level* of the particular variable (or other variables included in the demand equation). This leads to easy interpretation of the estimated coefficients of the regression.

There are cases, however, where a nonlinear relationship will fit the data better than the linear form. This may be revealed by plotting on a graph (scatter diagram) the dependent variable against each of the independent variables. The most common nonlinear specification of the demand equation is the power function. A demand equation in the form of a power function (including, for simplicity, only the price of the commodity and consumers' income as independent or explanatory variables) is

$$Q_X = a(P_X^{b_1})\,(I^{b_2}) \tag{4-28}$$

In order to estimate the parameters (i.e., coefficients a, b_1, and b_2) of demand Equation 4-28, we must first transform it into double log Equation 4-29, which is linear in the logarithms, and then run the regression on the log of the variables.[18]

$$\ln Q_X = \ln a + b_1 \ln P_X + b_2 \ln I \tag{4-29}$$

The estimated slope coefficients (that is, b_1 and b_2) in Equation 4-29 now represent percentage changes or average elasticities. Specifically, b_1 is the price elasticity of demand (E_P), while b_2 is the income elasticity of demand (E_I) for commodity X.[19] Thus, the advantage of the power formulation of the demand function is that the estimated coefficients give demand elasticities directly.[20] In the real world, both

[18]That is, first we find the logarithm of each of the variables (the computer usually does this) and then the regression is run on the logarithms of the variables, just as it was done before.

[19]Specifically,

$$E_P = \frac{\partial Q_X}{\partial P_X} \cdot \frac{P_X}{Q_X}$$

For Equation 4-28,

$$\frac{\partial Q_X}{\partial P_X} = b_1[a(P_X^{b_1-1})I^{b_2}]$$

Therefore,

$$E_P = b_1[a(P_X^{b_1-1})I^{b_2}] \cdot \frac{P_X}{Q_X} = \frac{b_1[a(P_X^{b_1})I^{b_2}]}{Q_X} = b_1 \cdot \frac{Q_X}{Q_X} = b_1$$

Similarly,

$$E_I = \frac{\partial Q_X}{\partial I} \cdot \frac{I}{Q_X}$$

For Equation 4-28,

$$\frac{\partial Q_X}{\partial I} = b_2[a(P_X^{b_1})I^{b_2-1}]$$

Therefore,

$$E_I = b_2[a(P_X^{b_1})I^{b_2-1}] \cdot \frac{I}{Q_X} = \frac{b_2[a(P_X^{b_1})I^{b_2}]}{Q_X} = b_2 \cdot \frac{Q_X}{Q_X} = b_2$$

[20]Note that while a_1 (which equals $\Delta Q_X/\Delta P_X$ in linear demand Equation 4-27) is independent of the level of P_X, b_1 (which equals E_P in demand Equation 4-28) depends on the level of P_X and also on the level of I (consumers' incomes). This is often realistic. For example, if commodity X were steaks, it is likely that the higher I is, the lower would be E_P because consumers may already be purchasing a large quantity of steaks at high incomes. Similarly, b_2 in demand Equation 4-28 depends on both the level of P_X and I.

the power and the linear forms of the demand function are usually estimated, and the one that gives better results (i.e., that fits the data better) is reported.

Testing the Econometric Results

The fourth and final step in the estimation of demand by regression analysis is to evaluate the regression results, as discussed in Sections 4-4 to 4-6. First, the sign of each estimated slope coefficient must be checked to see if it conforms to what is postulated on theoretical grounds. Second, t tests must be conducted on the statistical significance of the estimated parameters to determine the degree of confidence that we can have in each of the estimated slope coefficients. The (adjusted) coefficient of determination, $\bar{R}^2$ (see page 148), will then indicate the proportion of the total variation in the demand for the commodity that is "explained" by the independent or explanatory variables included in the demand equation.

Finally, the estimated demand equation must pass other econometric tests to make sure that such problems as multicollinearity, heteroscedasticity, and autocorrelation are not present (see Section 4-6). If any of these problems are detected from the tests, measures (also discussed in Section 4-6) must be applied to try to overcome these problems. In general, heteroscedasticity is more likely to be present if cross-sectional data are used to estimate demand, while autocorrelation is more likely to be prevalent when time-series data are used.

Case Study 4-4

Estimation of the Demand for Air Travel over the North Atlantic

J. M. Cigliano estimated the demand for air travel between the United States and Europe and between Canada and Europe, from 1965 to 1978. In what follows, we examine the demand for air travel between the United States and Europe only. Results are very similar for air travel between Canada and Europe. Cigliano estimated the following regression equation (the symbols for the variables have been changed to simplify the presentation):

$$\ln Q_t = 2.737 - 1.247 \ln P_t + 1.905 \ln GNP_t \qquad (4\text{-}30)$$

$$(-5.071) \qquad (7.286)$$

$$\bar{R}^2 = 0.97 \qquad D\text{-}W = 1.83$$

where Q_t = number of passengers per year traveling between the United States and Europe from 1965 to 1978 on IATA (International Air Transport Association) carriers, in thousands

P_t = average yearly air fare between New York and London (weighted by the seasonal distribution of traffic and adjusted for inflation)

GNP_t = U.S. gross national product in each year, adjusted for inflation

The numbers in parentheses below the estimated slope coefficients refer to the estimated t statistics or ratios.

Since all the variables in demand Equation 4-30 have been transformed into natural logarithms (a simple command in the regression package accomplished this) and the regression is run on the transformed variables, the estimated coefficients give demand elasticities directly. Specifically, the estimated coefficient of −1.247 for variable $\ln P_t$ gives the price elasticity of demand, while the estimated coefficient of 1.905 for variable $\ln GNP_t$ gives the *GNP* (income) elasticity of demand. These indicate, respectively, that a 10 percent increase in real average air fares would reduce the number of airline passengers by 12.47 percent, while a 10 percent rise in real *GNP* in the United States would increase the number of passengers by 19.05 percent. Thus, the demand for air travel between the United States and Europe is price elastic and is a luxury. Also to be noted is that since most airlines were flying at only $\frac{2}{3}$ to $\frac{4}{5}$ capacity during the period of the analysis, by lowering fares, airlines increased total revenue without incurring much higher costs (they simply filled empty seats), so that their profits increased.

We can have a great deal of confidence in the above regression results because (1) the signs of the estimated slope coefficients (elasticities) are as postulated by demand theory, (2) the very high t statistics reported below the estimated slope coefficients indicate that both are statistically significant at better than the 1 percent level, (3) the adjusted coefficient of determination ($\bar{R}^2$) indicates that air fares and *GNP* "explain" 97 percent of the variation in the log of the number of passengers flying between New York and London. Furthermore, (4) the multicollinearity problem between the two independent variables seems to have been avoided by deflating both air fares and *GNP* by the price index, and (5) the value of the Durbin-Watson *(D-W)* statistic indicates that the hypothesis of no autocorrelation cannot be rejected.*

Cigliano also found that the price elasticity of demand was much lower for first-class air travel (−0.447) than for economy-class travel (−1.826) and that within the economy class, it was much higher for short trips (−2.181), where good alternatives exist (automobile, bus, train), than for long trips. This meant that airlines increased their total revenues and profits by keeping the class distinctions and by charging relatively lower fares for short trips (to meet the competition from other modes of transportation) than for long trips.

*Even though the number of observations for each variable is only 14 and Table C-4 in the appendix starts from 15 observations, one can project that the *D-W* value obtained by the regression is well outside the critical value of d_U in Table C-4 for $n = 14$ (the number of observations) and $k' = 2$ (the number of explanatory variables).

Source: J. M. Cigliano, "Price and Income Elasticities for Airline Travel: The North Atlantic Market," *Business Economics*, September 1980, pp. 17–21.

4-8 ESTIMATING THE DEMAND FOR U.S. IMPORTS AND EXPORTS

Just like the demand for any domestic good or service (see Equation 4-26 on page 154), the demand for U.S. imports (Q_M) is a function of the dollar price of the imported commodity or service (P_M), U.S. consumers' incomes (I), the number of U.S. consumers (N), the dollar price of related (i.e., substitute and complementary) commodities or services in the United States (P_Y), the tastes of U.S. consumers (T), and all the other variables that are thought to be important determinants of the demand for the particular imported commodity or service under study. That is,

$$Q_M = f(P_M, I, N, P_Y, T, \ldots) \tag{4-31}$$

Note, however, that the dollar price of U.S. imports depends on prices in exporting nations (expressed in foreign currencies) and on the rate of exchange between the dollar and foreign currencies. For example, the dollar price of U.S. imports from the United Kingdom depends on the pound price of the commodity or service in the United Kingdom and the exchange rate between the dollar and the pound. If the exchange rate between the U.S. dollar and the British pound sterling (£) is 2, this means that the price of a music record that costs £10 in the United Kingdom is $20 to U.S. consumers. If the price of the record falls to £5 in the United Kingdom, U.S. consumers will have to pay only $10 for the record. The price of the British record to U.S. consumers can also fall to $10, even if the price remains at £10 in the United Kingdom, if the exchange rate between the dollar and the pound falls from $2 to £1 to $1 to £1. Exchange rates change very frequently in the real world.[21]

What is important is that the *dollar* price of U.S. imports can change because of a change in foreign-currency prices abroad or because of a change in exchange rates. Regardless of the reason for the change in the price of U.S. imports, we can measure the increase in quantity of U.S. imports resulting from a change in their *dollar* price by the price elasticity of demand for imports. This has been estimated to be about 1.06 for U.S. imports of manufactured goods, both in the short run and in the long run. That is, a 1 percent decline in the dollar price of U.S. imports of manufactured goods can be expected to lead to a 1.06 percent increase in the quantity demanded and thus leave their dollar value practically unchanged.

On the other hand, the price elasticity of demand for U.S. manufactured goods exports was estimated to be 0.48 in the short run and 1.67 in the long run. This means that a 1 percent decline in the price of U.S. exports can be expected to lead to an increase in the quantity of U.S. manufactured goods exports of 0.48 percent within a year or two of the price change and 1.67 percent in the long run (i.e., in a period of five years or so). Thus, a decline in U.S. export prices leads to U.S. earnings from manufactured exports to fall in the short run and to rise in the long run. Finally, the *income* elasticity of demand for imports was estimated to be 1.94 in the United States. This means that for each 1 percent increase in U.S. income or GDP, U.S. imports can be expected to increase by about 1.94 percent. Thus, U.S. imports are normal goods and can be regarded as luxuries. The income elasticity of imports for

[21]How exchange rates are determined and the reasons that they change are not important at this point and will be explained in Chapter 9.

the six largest industrial countries range from 0.35 for Japan to 2.51 for the United Kingdom.[22]

The demand for U.S. imports and exports also depends on the price of substitute and complementary commodities as well as tastes in the United States and abroad. The ability to substitute domestic for foreign goods and services at home and abroad has reached an all-time high in the world today and is expected to continue to increase sharply in the future because of (1) the sharp decline in transportation costs for most products, (2) increased knowledge of foreign products due to an international information revolution, (3) global advertising campaigns by multinational corporations, (4) the explosion of international travel, and (5) the rapid convergence of tastes internationally. For homogeneous products such as a particular grade of wheat and steel, and for many industrial products with precise specifications such as computer chips, fiber optics, and specialized machinery, substitutability between domestic and foreign products is almost perfect. Here, a small price difference can lead quickly to large shifts in sales from domestic to foreign sources and vice-versa. Indeed, so fluid is the market for such products that governments often step in to protect these industries from foreign competition.[23] Even for differentiated products, such as automobiles and motorcycles, computers and copiers, watches and cameras, TV films and TV programs, soft drinks and cigarettes, soaps and detergents, commercial and military aircraft, and most other products which are similar but not identical, substitutability between domestic and foreign products is very high and rising. Thus, a change in the price of substitute and complementary commodities or tastes at home or abroad will have a significant effect on the demand for imports and exports.

[22]See D. Salvatore, *International Economics,* 5th ed. (Englewood Cliffs, N.J.: Prentice-Hall, 1995), Chaps. 16 and 17.

[23]See D. Salvatore, *International Economics, op. cit.,* Chaps. 15 and 16.

Case Study 4-5

The Major Commodity Exports and Imports of the United States

Table 4-8 gives the value of the major commodity exports and imports of the United States in 1993. The major U.S. exports were automotive vehicles, parts, and engines (mostly from Canada, as part of the U.S.–Canada automotive agreement), foods and beverages (a great deal of which were grains), aircraft, chemicals, and computers. United States imports were dominated by automobile imports (mostly from Japan) and petroleum products. Very large were also imports of computers, foods and beverages, and semiconductors, chemicals, and metals.

Table 4-8
Major U.S. Commodity Exports and Imports in 1993
(in billions of dollars)

Exports		Imports	
Product	**Value**	**Product**	**Value**
Automotive, vehicles, parts, and engines	$52	Automotive, vehicles, parts, and engines	$102
Foods and beverages	41	Petroleum	51
of which grains	14	Computers, peripherals, and parts	38
Civilian aircraft, engines, and parts	33	Food and beverages	28
Chemicals, excluding medicinals	30	Semiconductors	19
Computers, peripherals and parts	29	Chemicals, excluding medicinals	18
Semiconductors	19	Nonferrous metals	18
Electricity generating machinery	17	Electricity generating machinery	17
Nonferrous metals	15	Iron and steel products	12
Telecommunications equipment	14	Civilian aircraft, engines, and parts	11
Energy products	13	Telecommunications equipment	11
Scientific, hospital, and medical equipment	11	Building materials, except metals	11

Source: U.S. Department of Commerce, *Survey of Current Business* (Washington, D.C.: Government Printing Office, June 1994), pp. 106 and 108.

Case Study 4-6

The Major Trade Partners of the United States

Table 4-9 gives data on the value and the percentage of total U.S. exports and imports of America's top 10 trade partners in 1993. The table shows that Canada, Japan, and Mexico are by far the largest trade partners of the United States. These three nations accounted for 41.5 percent of total U.S. exports and 44.3 percent of total U.S. imports in 1993. The closeness of Canada and Mexico to the United States goes a long way toward explaining their first- and third-ranked positions, respectively. Far away Japan, on the other hand, is the world's second largest industrial economy and one of the largest traders. Together, the largest 10 U.S. export markets absorbed 65 percent of total U.S. exports, while the 10 largest exporters to the United States accounted for 70 percent of total U.S. imports in 1993.

Table 4-9
America's Top Trade Partners in 1993

U.S. Exports to			U.S. Imports from		
Country	Value (billion $)	Percent of Total	Country	Value (billion $)	Percent of Total
Canada	$101.2	22.2	Canada	$113.3	19.2
Japan	46.7	10.2	Japan	107.2	18.2
Mexico	41.5	9.1	Mexico	40.4	6.9
U.K.	25.7	5.6	China	31.5	5.3
Germany	18.4	4.0	Germany	28.5	4.8
Taiwan	15.3	3.3	Taiwan	25.1	4.3
S. Korea	14.1	3.1	U.K.	21.5	3.6
France	13.2	2.9	S. Korea	17.1	2.9
Netherlands	12.6	2.8	France	15.2	2.6
Singapore	10.8	2.4	Italy	13.2	2.2

Source: U.S. Department of Commerce, *Survey of Current Business* (Washington, D.C.: Government Printing Office, June 1994), pp. 102 and 104.

Case Study 4-7

The Top U.S. Exporters

Table 4-10 gives data on the top U.S. exporters in 1993. They range from the General Motors Corporation, which exports nearly $15 billion, to Lockheed with more than $1.7 billion in exports. As a percentage of total company sales, Boeing comes first with exports of 57.8 percent of total sales, and Philip Morris is last with exports of 8.1 percent of total sales. Note that most U.S. top exporters also have production facilities abroad so that their total sales abroad are much higher than indicated by their exports.

Table 4-10
America's Top Exporters in 1993

Company	Major Export	Value of Exports (billion dollars)	Percent of Total Sales
General Motors	Motor vehicles and parts	$14,913	11.2
Boeing	Commercial aircraft	14,616	57.8
Ford Motors	Motor vehicles and parts	9,483	8.7
General Electric	Jet engines, turbines, plastics, locomotives	8,498	14.0
Chrysler	Motor vehicles and parts	8,397	19.3
IBM	Computers	7,297	11.6
Motorola	Communications equipment and semiconductors	4,990	29.4
Hewlett-Packard	Measurement and computation products and systems	4,738	23.3
Philip Morris	Tobacco, beer, food products	4,105	8.1
Caterpillar	Heavy machinery, engines, turbines	3,743	32.2
United Technologies	Jet engines, helicopters, cooling equipment	3,503	16.9
Du Pont	Specialty chemicals	3,500	10.7
Intel	Microcomputer components, modules, and systems	3,406	38.8
McDonnell-Douglas	Aerospace products, missiles, electronic systems	3,405	23.5
Archer Daniels	Protein meals, vegetable oils, flour, grain	2,900	29.6
Eastman Kodak	Imaging and health products	2,242	11.2
Raytheon	Electronic systems, engineering and construction projects	2,063	22.4
Compaq Computer	Computers and related equipment	1,922	26.7
Digital Equipment	Computers and related equipment	1,800	12.5
Lockheed	Aerospace products, electronics, missile systems	1,743	13.3

Source: Fortune, August 22, 1994, p. 132.

SUMMARY

1. Joining the price-quantity observations on a graph does not usually generate the demand curve for a commodity. The reason is that each price-quantity observation is the joint result (intersection) of a different (but unobserved) demand and supply curve for the commodity. The difficulty of deriving the demand curve for a commodity from observed price-quantity points is called the "identification problem." To derive the demand curve for a commodity from the price-quantity data points, we allow the supply curve to shift but correct for the forces that cause the demand curve to shift. This is done by regression analysis.

2. Besides regression analysis, a firm can estimate demand by consumer surveys, consumer clinics, and market experiments. Consumer surveys involve questioning a sample of consumers about how they would respond to particular changes in the price and other determinants of the demand for the commodity. Consumer clinics are laboratory experiments in which the participants are given a sum of money and asked to spend it in a simulated store to see how they react to changes in price, product packaging, displays, price of competing products, and other factors affecting demand. With market

experiments, the firm attempts to estimate the demand for the commodity by changing price and other determinants of demand in the actual marketplace. While these methods are sometimes the only ones available for estimating demand, they face serious shortcomings.

3. Regression analysis is a statistical technique for estimating the quantitative relationship between the economic variable that we seek to explain (the dependent variable) and one or more independent or explanatory variables. When there is only one independent or explanatory variable, we have simple regression analysis. Simple regression analysis usually begins by plotting the set of XY values on a scatter diagram and determining by inspection if there exists an approximate linear relationship. Estimating the regression line by simply drawing in a line between the observation points is imprecise and subjective.
4. The objective of regression analysis is to obtain estimates of a (the vertical intercept) and b (the slope) in order to derive the regression line that best fits the data points (in the sense that the sum of the squared vertical deviations of each observed point from the line is a minimum). A parameter estimate is statistically significant if the value of the calculated t statistic exceeds the critical value found from the table of the t distribution, at the appropriate degree of significance (usually 5 percent) and degrees of freedom. The t statistic is given by the estimated value of the parameter divided by the standard error (deviation) of the estimate. The degrees of freedom equal the sample size minus the number of parameters estimated. We can also construct confidence intervals for the true parameter from the estimated parameter. The coefficient of determination (R^2) measures the proportion of the explained to the total variation in the dependent variable in the regression analysis. The coefficient of correlation (r) measures the degree of association or covariation between variables. Regression analysis implies but does not prove causality.
5. When the dependent variable that we seek to explain is hypothesized to depend on more than one independent variable, we have multiple regression analysis. Here the calculations are invariably done with computers, which also provide the statistics to conduct statistical tests. In order to take into consideration the reduction in the degrees of freedom as additional independent variables are included in the regression, we calculate the adjusted R^2, $\bar{R}^2$. The analysis of variance can be used to test the overall explanatory power of the entire regression. This utilizes the F statistic, which is the ratio of the explained variance divided by $k - 1$ df to the unexplained variance divided by $n - k$ df, where k is the number of estimated parameters and n is the number of observations. If the value of the F statistic exceeds the critical value from the F table with $k - 1$ and $n - k$ df, we accept the hypothesis at the specified level of statistical significance that not all the regression coefficients are zero. The standard error of the regression can be used to make interval estimates or forecasts of the dependent variable.
6. Regression analysis may face some serious problems. Multicollinearity arises when two or more explanatory variables in the regression are highly corre-

lated. This may lead to insignificant coefficients even though $\overline{R}^2$ may be very high. This could be overcome by increasing the sample size, utilizing a priori information, transforming the function, or dropping one of the highly collinear variables. Heteroscedasticity arises in cross-sectional data when the error term is not constant. This leads to biased standard errors and incorrect statistical tests. It could be corrected by using the log of the variable that causes the problem or by weighted least squares. Autocorrelation often arises in time-series data when consecutive errors have the same sign or change sign frequently. This leads to exaggerated t statistics and unreliable $\overline{R}^2$ and F statistics. Autocorrelation can be detected by the Durbin-Watson test and may be corrected by including a time trend or an important missing variable in the regression, using a nonlinear form, running the regression on first differences in the variables, or with more complex techniques.

7. The process of estimating a demand equation by regression analysis involves four steps. First, the model must be specified. This involves determining the variables to include in the demand equation. These are dictated by demand theory and knowledge of the market for the commodity. Second, the data on each variable or its proxy must be obtained. Third, the researcher must decide on the functional form of the demand equation. The linear and the power-function formulations are most common, and often both are tried. In the power-function formulation, the estimated slope coefficients refer to elasticities rather than to marginal changes (as in the linear model). Finally, the regression results must be evaluated as to the sign of the estimated slope coefficients, the statistical significance of the coefficients, and the proportion of the total variation explained and to ensure that multicollinearity, heteroscedasticity, and autocorrelation do not bias the results.
8. As in the case of purely domestic goods and services, we can estimate the demand for imports and exports and obtain from them price and income elasticities. The only difference is that the domestic-currency prices of imports depend on foreign-currency prices and the exchange rate. The ability to substitute domestic for foreign goods and services is very high and increasing in today's world.

DISCUSSION QUESTIONS

1. (*a*) Why is the line connecting the observed price-quantity data points usually not the demand curve for the commodity? (*b*) How is the demand curve for a commodity derived or identified from observed price-quantity data points?
2. What are the major advantages and disadvantages of estimating demand by (*a*) consumer surveys, and (*b*) market experiments?
3. (*a*) What are the main advantages of regression analysis over the marketing research approaches of estimating demand? (*b*) What, if any, residual usefulness to the manager and economist do marketing research approaches have in demand estimation?

4. (*a*) What steps are usually involved in the estimation of a demand equation by regression analysis? (*b*) How does the researcher determine the demand model to estimate?
5. (*a*) How does a researcher go about obtaining the data to estimate a demand equation by regression analysis? (*b*) What are some of the most useful sources of published data in the United States today?
6. (*a*) How does the researcher determine the form of the demand equation to be estimated? (*b*) How are the estimated slope coefficients of the two most common forms of the demand equation interpreted?
7. (*a*) Why is it important to conduct a significance test of an estimated parameter? (*b*) How is this conducted? (*c*) What is meant by a confidence interval? (*d*) How is it determined?
8. (*a*) How can we test the overall explanatory power of a regression? (*b*) What is meant by the total, explained, and unexplained variation in the dependent variable? How are they measured? (*c*) What is meant by the coefficient of correlation? (*d*) Does regression analysis imply causality? Explain.
9. (*a*) What is the use of analysis of variance? (*b*) How is the analysis of variance conducted? (*c*) What is the relationship between the analysis of variance and the coefficient of determination?
10. With respect to multicollinearity, explain (*a*) what it is and why it is a problem, (*b*) how it can be detected, and (*c*) how it can be overcome.
11. With respect to autocorrelation, explain (*a*) what it is and why it is a problem, (*b*) how it can be detected, and (*c*) how it can be overcome.
12. (*a*) On what does the domestic-currency price of a nation's imports depend? (*b*) What would happen to the domestic-currency price of a nation's imports if the foreign-currency price of the nation's imports increases and the nation's currency depreciates (i.e., loses value in relation to the foreign currency)?

PROBLEMS

1. With the aid of a figure, show why (*a*) if the observed price-quantity data points fall more or less downward and to the right, we can derive the demand curve for the commodity, but (*b*) if the observed price-quantity data points are clustered or bunched together, we cannot derive the demand curve for the commodity.

*2. Draw two figures: (*a*) one showing that if the demand curve did not shift but the supply curve did, we could derive the demand curve for the commodity by simply connecting the observed price-quantity data points and (*b*) the other showing that if the supply curve did not shift but the demand curve did, we could derive the supply curve of the commodity by simply connecting the observed price-quantity data points. (*c*) In which sector of the economy is each of these cases most likely to occur? Why?

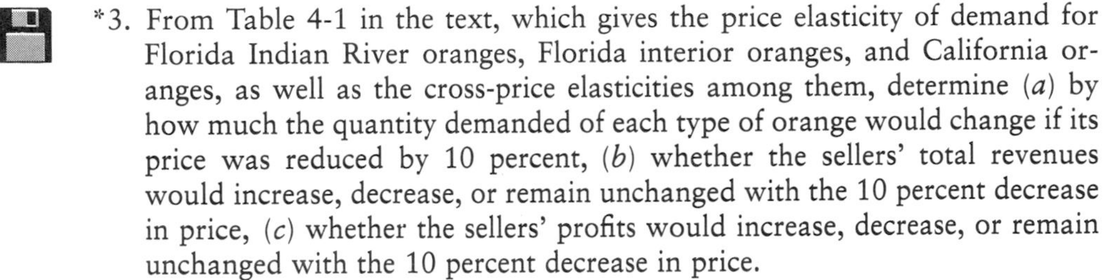

*3. From Table 4-1 in the text, which gives the price elasticity of demand for Florida Indian River oranges, Florida interior oranges, and California oranges, as well as the cross-price elasticities among them, determine (*a*) by how much the quantity demanded of each type of orange would change if its price was reduced by 10 percent, (*b*) whether the sellers' total revenues would increase, decrease, or remain unchanged with the 10 percent decrease in price, (*c*) whether the sellers' profits would increase, decrease, or remain unchanged with the 10 percent decrease in price.

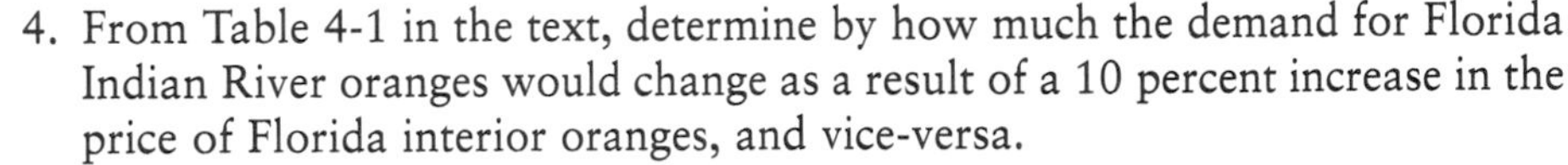

4. From Table 4-1 in the text, determine by how much the demand for Florida Indian River oranges would change as a result of a 10 percent increase in the price of Florida interior oranges, and vice-versa.

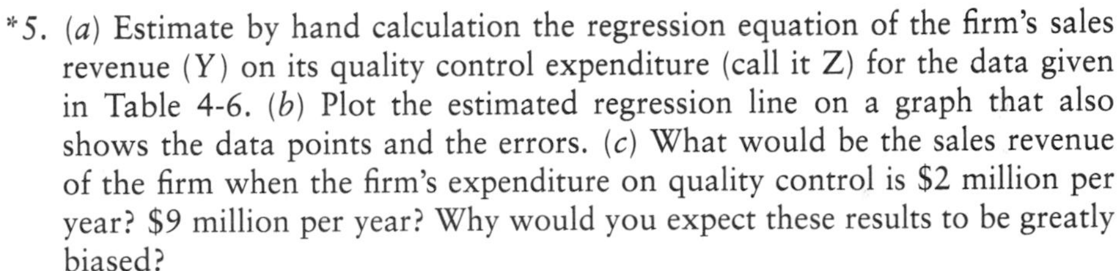

*5. (*a*) Estimate by hand calculation the regression equation of the firm's sales revenue (Y) on its quality control expenditure (call it Z) for the data given in Table 4-6. (*b*) Plot the estimated regression line on a graph that also shows the data points and the errors. (*c*) What would be the sales revenue of the firm when the firm's expenditure on quality control is $2 million per year? $9 million per year? Why would you expect these results to be greatly biased?

*6. From the following table giving the quantity demanded of a commodity (Y), its price (X_1), and consumers' income (X_2) from 1971 to 1990, (*a*) estimate the regression equation of Y on X_1 and X_2, (*b*) test at the 5 percent level for the statistical significance of the slope parameters, (*c*) find the unadjusted and the adjusted coefficients of determination, and (*d*) test at the 5 percent level for the overall statistical significance of the regression. Show all your results to three decimal places. [If you have not used the computer before, ask a fellow student to show you how to run the regression. If this is not possible, from the answer to part (*a*) of this question provided at the end of the book, answer parts (*b*), (*c*), and (*d*).]

Year	Y	X_1	X_2	Year	Y	X_1	X_2
1971	72	$10	$2,000	1981	144	6	3,000
1972	81	9	2,100	1982	180	4	3,099
1973	90	10	2,210	1983	162	5	3,201
1974	99	9	2,305	1984	171	4	3,308
1975	108	8	2,407	1985	153	5	3,397
1976	126	7	2,500	1986	180	4	3,501
1977	117	7	2,610	1987	171	5	3,689
1978	117	9	2,698	1988	180	4	3,800
1979	135	6	2,801	1989	198	4	3,896
1980	135	6	2,921	1990	189	4	3,989

7. If the regression of Y on X_1 and X_2 is run in double-log form for the data of Problem 6, the results are as follows:

$$\ln Y_t = -0.533 - \underset{(-3.304)}{0.389 \ln X_{1t}} + \underset{(4.042)}{0.769 \ln X_{2t}}$$

$$\bar{R}^2 = 0.95054 \qquad F = 183.582$$

Compare the above results with those of Problem 6. Which are better? Why?

8. In a study published in 1980, B. B. Gibson estimated the following price and income elasticities of demand for six types of public goods:

State Activity	Price Elasticity	Income Elasticity
Aid to needy people	−0.83	0.26
Pollution control	−0.99	0.77
Colleges and universities	−0.87	0.92
Elementary school aid	−1.16	1.14
Parks and recreational areas	−1.02	1.06
Highway construction and maintenance	−1.09	0.99

Source: B. B. Gibson, "Estimating Demand Elasticities for Public Goods from Survey Data," *American Economic Review,* December 1980, pp. 1068–1976.

(*a*) Do these public goods conform to the law of demand? For which public goods is demand price elastic? (*b*) What types of goods are these public goods? (*c*) If the price or cost of college and university education increased by 10 percent and, at the same time, incomes also increased by 10 percent, what would be the change in the demand for college and university education?

9. Following are the results of four regressions, in which M refers to the imports and Y to the GNP of the United States (both in billions of current dollars) from 1965 to 1980, and P is the consumer price index. Theory postulates that imports are directly related to the level of GNP and domestic prices.

1. $\hat{M} = -108.20 + \underset{(1.232)}{0.045Y} + \underset{(1.844)}{0.931P}$ $\quad R^2 = 0.9894 \quad \bar{R}^2 = 0.9877 \quad F = 604.621$

2. $\hat{M} = -69.97 + \underset{(32.08)}{0.112Y}$ $\quad R^2 = 0.9866 \quad F = 1029.40$

3. $\hat{M} = -555.84 + \underset{(42.18)}{13.81P}$ $\quad R^2 = 0.9922 \quad F = 1778.84$

4. $\widehat{M/P} = -1.39 + \underset{(12.22)}{0.202Y/P}$ $\quad R^2 = 0.9142 \quad F = 149.25$

Explain (*a*) why the first three regression results indicate the presence of serious multicollinearity and (*b*) how the fourth regression attempts to overcome the multicollinearity problem.

10. In their volume, *Consumer Demand in the United States: Analyses and Projections* (Cambridge, Mass.: Harvard University Press, 1970), p. 119, H. S. Houthakker and L. D. Taylor presented the following results for their estimated demand equation for local bus service over the period from 1929 to 1961 (excluding the 1942 through 1945 war years) in the United States:

$$Q_t = 22.819 + \underset{(12.23)}{0.0159X_t} - \underset{(16.84)}{0.1156P_t} - \underset{(15.83)}{86.106S_t} - \underset{(3.22)}{0.9841D_t}$$

$$R^2 = 0.996 \qquad D\text{-}W = 1.11$$

where Q_t = per capita personal consumption expenditures on bus transportation during year t, at 1954 prices
X_t = total per capita consumption expenditures during year t, at 1954 prices
P_t = relative price of bus transportation in year t, at 1954 prices
S_t = car stock per capita in year t
D_t = dummy variable to separate pre– from post–World War II years; $D_t = 0$ for years 1929 to 1941 and $D_t = 1$ for years 1946 to 1961

The numbers in parentheses below the estimated slope coefficients refer to the estimated t values.

Evaluate the above results (*a*) in terms of the signs and values of the coefficients, (*b*) for the statistical significance of the coefficients and the explanatory power of the regression, and (*c*) for the presence of possible econometric problems.

Note that a dummy variable is added to (if positive) or subtracted from (if negative) the value of the constant of the regression, thus causing the regression line to shift up or shift down, respectively, for the years to which the dummy variable refers. For a more detailed discussion of dummy variables, see D. Salvatore, *Statistics and Econometrics* (New York: McGraw-Hill, 1982, Section 8.2), or any other introductory econometrics text.

11. Suppose that during a given year: (1) the price of TV sets increases by 4 percent in Japan, (2) the dollar depreciates by 5 percent with respect to the yen (the Japanese currency), (3) consumers' incomes in the United States increase by 3 percent, (4) the price elasticity of demand for imported TV sets in the United States is −1.5, and (5) consumers' income elasticity of demand for TV sets in the United States is 2. (*a*) If the price of the imported TV set was \$300 in the United States at the beginning of the year, approximately how much would you expect the price of the same imported TV set to be in the United States at the end of the year? (*b*) By how much would the quantity demanded of imported TV sets in the United States change as a result of the change in price only? (*c*) By how much would the demand for imported TV sets in the United States change as a result of the increase in consumers' income alone? (*d*) By

how much would the demand for imported TV sets in the United States change as a result of both the change in price and incomes?

12. **Integrating Problem**

Starting with the data for Problem 6 and the data on the price of a related commodity for the years 1971 to 1990 given below, we estimated the regression for the quantity demanded of a commodity (which we now relabel $\hat{Q}_X$), on the price of the commodity (which we now label P_X), consumers' income (which we now label Y), and the price of the related commodity (P_Z), and we obtained the following results. (If you can, run this regression yourself; you should get results identical or very similar to those given below.)

Year	1971	1972	1973	1974	1975	1976	1977	1978	1979	1980
P_Z (\$)	14	15	15	16	17	18	17	18	19	20
Year	1981	1982	1983	1984	1985	1986	1987	1988	1989	1990
P_Z (\$)	20	19	21	21	22	23	23	24	25	25

$$\hat{Q}_X = 121.86 - 9.50P_X + 0.04Y - 2.21P_Z$$
$$(-5.12) \quad (2.18) \quad (-0.68)$$
$$R^2 = 0.9633 \qquad F = 167.33 \qquad D\text{-}W = 2.38$$

(*a*) Explain why you think we have chosen to include the price of commodity Z in the above regression. (*b*) Evaluate the above regression results. (*c*) What type of commodity is Z? Can you be sure?

SUPPLEMENTARY READINGS

For a problem-solving approach to demand estimation, see:

Salvatore, Dominick: *Theory and Problems of Managerial Economics,* Schaum Outline Series (New York: McGraw-Hill, 1988), Chap. 6.

For a discussion on demand estimation in general, see:

Schultz, Henry: *Theory and Measurement of Demand* (Chicago: University of Chicago Press, 1964).

Working, E. J.: "What Do Statistical 'Demand Curves' Show?" *Quarterly Journal of Economics,* 1927.

The use of regression analysis in demand estimation is discussed in:

Salvatore, Dominick: *Theory and Problems of Statistics and Econometrics,* Schaum Outline Series (New York: McGraw-Hill, 1982), Chaps. 7–10.

Gujarati, Damodar N.: *Basic Econometrics* (New York: McGraw-Hill, 1995).

Mason, Charlotte H., and William D. Perrault, Jr.: "Collinearity, Power, and Interpretation of Multiple Regression Analysis," *Journal of Marketing Research,* August 1991.

A discussion of marketing approaches to demand estimation is found in:

Pessemier, E. A.: "An Experimental Method for Estimating Demand," *Journal of Business,* October 1960.

Nevin, J. R.: "Laboratory Experiments for Establishing Consumer Demand: A Validation Study," *Journal of Marketing Research,* August 1974.

DeJong, Douglas V., and **Robert Foresythe:** "A Prospective on the Use of Laboratory Market Experimentation in Auditing Research," *Accounting Review,* January 1992.

For empirical estimates of demand utilizing regression analysis, see:

Houthakker, H. S., and **L. D. Taylor:** *Consumer Demand in the United States: Analyses and Projections* (Cambridge, Mass.: Harvard University Press, 1970).

For empirical estimates of demand for exports and imports, see:

Salvatore, Dominick: *International Economics,* 4th ed. (Englewood Cliffs, N.J.: Prentice-Hall, 1995), Chaps. 15 and 16.

CHAPTER 5

Demand Forecasting

KEY TERMS

Delphi method
Time-series data
Time-series analysis
Secular trend
Cyclical fluctuations
Seasonal variation
Irregular or random influences
Smoothing techniques
Moving average
Root-mean-square error *(RMSE)*
Exponential smoothing
Barometric forecasting
Leading economic indicators
Coincident indicators
Lagging indicators
Composite indices
Diffusion index
Endogenous variables
Exogenous variables
Structural (behavioral) equations
Definitional equations
Reduced-form equations

CHAPTER OUTLINE

Most business decisions are made in the face of risk or uncertainty. A firm must decide how much of each product to produce, what price to charge, and how much to spend on advertising, and it must also plan for the future growth of the firm. All these decisions are based on some forecast of the level of future economic activity in general and demand for the firm's product(s) in particular. The aim of economic forecasting is to reduce the risk or uncertainty that the firm faces in its short-term operational decision making and in planning for its long-term growth.

Forecasting the demand and sales of the firm's product usually begins with a macroeconomic forecast of the general level of economic activity for the economy as a whole or gross national product. The reason for this is that the demand and sales of most goods and services are strongly affected by business conditions. For example, the demand and sales of new automobiles, new houses, electricity, and most other goods and services rise and fall with the general level of economic activity. General forecasts of economic conditions for the economy as a whole are routinely provided by the President's Council of Economic Advisors, the U.S. Department of Commerce and other government agencies, economists working for private firms, and firms specializing in and selling their forecasting services to their clients (see Case Study 5-6).

The firm uses these macroforecasts of general economic activity as inputs for their microforecasts of the industry's and firm's demand and sales. The firm's demand and sales are usually forecasted on the basis of its historical market (industry) share and its planned marketing strategy (i.e., the introduction of new products and models, changes in relative prices, and promotional effort). From its general sales forecast, the firm can then forecast its sales by product line and region. These, in turn, are used to forecast the firm's operational needs for production (raw material, equipment, warehousing, workers), marketing (distributional network, sales force, promotional campaign), finances (cash flow, profits, need for and cost of outside financing), and personnel throughout the firm. The firm utilizes long-term forecasts for the economy and the industry to forecast expenditures on plant and equipment to meet its long-term growth plan and strategy.

Forecasting techniques range from the very naive that require little effort to very sophisticated ones that are very costly in terms of time and effort. Some forecasting techniques are basically qualitative, while others are quantitative. Some are based on examining only past values of the data series to forecast its future values; others involve the use of complex models based on a great deal of additional data and relationships. Some are performed by the firm itself; others are purchased from consulting firms. In this chapter we examine qualitative forecasts, time-series forecasts, forecasts based on smoothing techniques such as moving averages, barometric forecasts based on leading indicators, and econometric forecasts based on econometric models. In the appendix to this chapter, we then examine input-output forecasting. In each case we examine the advantages and limitations of the particular forecasting technique under study.

Some techniques, such as the barometric method, are more useful for short-term (monthly or quarterly) forecasts, while others, such as the input-output method, are more useful for long-term forecasting of one year or longer. Some may be more appropriate for forecasting at the macrolevel, while others are better for forecasting at the microlevel. Which forecasting method a firm chooses depends on (1) the cost of preparing the forecast and the benefit that results from its use, (2) the lead time in decision making, (3) the time period of the forecast (short term or long term), (4) the level of accuracy required, (5) the quality and availability of the data, and (6) the level of complexity of the relationships to be forecasted. In general, the greater the level of accuracy required and the more complex the relationships to be forecasted, the more sophisticated and expensive will be the forecasting exercise. By considering the advantages and limitations of each forecasting technique, managers can choose the method or combination of methods most useful to the firm.

5-1 QUALITATIVE FORECASTS

Surveys and opinion polls are often used to make short-term forecasts when quantitative data are not available. These qualitative techniques can also be very useful for supplementing quantitative forecasts that anticipate changes in consumer tastes or business expectations about future economic conditions. They can also be invaluable in forecasting the demand for a new product that the firm intends to introduce. In this section we briefly examine forecasting based on surveys, opinion polling, and soliciting a foreign perspective.

Survey Techniques

The rationale for forecasting based on surveys of economic intentions is that many economic decisions are made well in advance of actual expenditures. For example, businesses usually plan to add to plant and equipment long before expenditures are actually incurred. Consumers' decisions to purchase houses, automobiles, TV sets, washing machines, furniture, vacations, education, and other major consumption items are made months or years in advance of actual purchases. Similarly, government agencies prepare budgets and anticipate expenditures a year or more in advance. Surveys of economic intentions, thus, can reveal and can be used to forecast future purchases of capital equipment, inventory changes, and major consumer expenditures.

Some of the best-known surveys that can be used to forecast future economic activity in general and economic activity in various sectors of the economy are

1. *Surveys of business executives' plant and equipment expenditure plans.* These are conducted periodically by McGraw-Hill, Inc., the U.S. Department of Commerce, the Securities and Exchange Commission, and the National Industrial Conference Board. For example, the McGraw-Hill survey accounts for more than 50 percent of expenditures on new plant and equipment, is

conducted twice yearly, and is published in *Business Week* (a McGraw-Hill publication). The Department of Commerce survey is even more comprehensive: it is conducted quarterly and is published in its *Survey of Current Business.*

2. *Surveys of plans for inventory changes and sales expectations.* These are conducted periodically by the U.S. Department of Commerce, McGraw-Hill, Inc., Dun and Bradstreet, and the National Association of Purchasing Agents, and they report on business executives' plans for inventory changes and expectations about future sales.
3. *Surveys of consumers' expenditure plans.* These are conducted periodically by the Bureau of the Census and the Survey Research Center of the University of Michigan, and they report on consumer intentions to purchase specific products, including homes, consumer appliances, and automobiles. These results are often used to forecast consumer demand in general and the level of consumer confidence in the economy.

In general, the record of these surveys has been rather good in forecasting actual expenditures, except during periods of unexpected international political upheavals, such as war or threatened war. When used in conjunction with other quantitative methods, surveys can thus be very useful in forecasting economic activity in specific sectors of the economy and for the economy as a whole. U.S. firms now spend more than $1 billion each year to ask more than 50 million consumers for their opinions on a large variety of products and services that they sell. A growing number of consumers, however, are refusing to participate in market-research surveys because of the time involved, the loss of privacy, and the pressure of salespeople operating under the guise of market research. This leads to increasing difficulties in obtaining representative samples and to a trend toward the greater use of observational research (see Section 4-2).

Opinion Polls

While the results of published surveys of expenditure plans of businesses, consumers, and governments are useful, the firm usually needs specific forecasts of its own sales. The firm's sales are strongly dependent on the general level of economic activity and sales for the industry as a whole, but they also depend on the policies adopted by the firm. The firm can forecast its sales by polling experts within and outside the firm. There are several such polling techniques:

1. *Executive polling.* The firm can poll its top management from its sales, production, finance, and personnel departments on their views on the sales outlook for the firm during the next quarter or year. While these personal insights are to a large extent subjective, by averaging the opinions of the experts who are most knowledgeable about the firm and its products, the firm hopes to arrive at a better forecast than would be provided by these experts individually. Outside market experts could also be polled. To avoid a bandwagon

effect (whereby the opinions of some experts might be overshadowed by some dominant personality in their midst), the so-called **Delphi method** can be used. Here, experts are polled separately, and then feedback is provided without identifying the expert responsible for a particular opinion. The hope is that through this feedback procedure the experts can arrive at some consensus forecast.

2. *Sales force polling.* This is a forecast of the firm's sales in each region and for each product line that is based on the opinion of the firm's sales force in the field. The rationale is that these are the people closest to the market, and their opinion of future sales can provide very valuable information to the firm's top management.
3. *Consumer intentions polling.* Companies selling automobiles, furniture, household appliances, and other durable goods sometimes poll a sample of potential buyers on their purchasing intentions. Based on the results of the poll, the firm can then forecast its national sales for different levels of consumers' future disposable income.

Soliciting a Foreign Perspective

Many U.S. firms sell an increasing share of their output abroad and face rising competition at home and abroad from foreign firms. Thus, it becomes increasingly important for them to forecast changes in markets and products abroad because these affect not only the firm's exports but also its competitiveness at home. To get such an international perspective, an increasing number of U.S. firms are forming councils of distinguished foreign dignitaries and businesspeople, especially in Europe. The purpose is to get a global perspective on evolving events resulting from economic unification in Western Europe, restructuring in Eastern Europe, and economic liberalization in emerging markets or developing countries. The rationale is that there is no better way to forecast and figure out what is going to happen in Europe than to solicit the ideas of government and business leaders who live there.

For example, General Motors has found its European Advisory Council very useful in preparing for the mid-1990s. IBM has advisory councils in Europe, Asia, and Latin America and calls on them to help develop strategic plans for the future. The advantage of such foreign councils is that they do not have to spend time reviewing budgets or handling other fiduciary duties such as succession planning, but can devote their full attention to international issues that can have enormous impact on the firm's future as a global competitor. Firms' boards are usually so taken with immediate concerns and often lack in-depth knowledge of new developments abroad to be able to fully evaluate the effect of these developments on the future competitiveness of the firm at home and around the world. The input of such foreign councils thus becomes an invaluable tool to get a global perspective and plan longer-term domestic and foreign strategies for the firm.

Case Study 5-1

Forecasting the Number of McDonald's Restaurants Worldwide

Increased competition and lower profit margins at home are driving McDonald's and other large fast-food U.S. chains to expand abroad, where competition is weaker and profit margins are higher. Almost 5,000 of the nearly 15,000 McDonald's restaurants are now in more than 70 countries outside the United States, and McDonald's is now opening two restaurants abroad for every new one it opens at home. Using data on each country's population and per capita income, *Fortune Magazine* recently estimated the potential number of restaurants that McDonald's could build in each country if tastes were similar to U.S. tastes. The results for some countries are indicated in Table 5-1. *Fortune* came up with a total worldwide number of 42,000 restaurants. Note, however, that this estimate is based on the assumption that tastes in the rest of the world are the same as in the United States. Although tastes are converging, they are unlikely to ever become the same, and so this can be regarded as only a very rough "guestimate."

Table 5-1
McDonald's Actual and Potential Restaurants Around the World

Biggest Markets			Some Underpenetrated Markets		
Country	Current Number of Restaurants	Minimum Market Potential	Country	Current Number of Restaurants	Minimum Market Potential
Japan	1,070	6,100	China	23	784
Canada	694	1,023	Russia	3	685
Britain	550	1,794	India	0	489
Germany	535	3,235	South Africa	0	190
Australia	411	526	Pakistan	0	90
France	314	2,237	Colombia	0	79

Source: "McDonald's Conquers the World," *Fortune,* October 17, 1994, p. 104.

5-2 TIME-SERIES ANALYSIS

One of the most frequently used forecasting methods is time-series analysis or the analysis of time-series data. **Time-series data** refers to the values of a variable arranged chronologically by days, weeks, months, quarters, or years. The first step in time-series analysis is usually to plot past values of the variable that we seek to forecast (say, the sales of a firm) on the vertical axis and time on the horizontal axis in order to visually inspect the movement of the time series over time. **Time-series analysis** attempts to forecast future values of the time series by examining past observations of the data only. The assumption is that the time series will continue to move as in the past (i.e., the past pattern will continue unchanged or will be very similar in the future). For this reason, time-series analysis is often referred to as "naive forecasting."

In this section, we first examine the reasons that most time-series data fluctuate or vary over time and then examine how to utilize this information for forecasting future values of the time series.

Reasons for Fluctuations in Time-Series Data

If we plot most economic time-series data, we discover that they fluctuate or vary over time. This variation is usually caused by secular trends, cyclical fluctuations, seasonal variations, and irregular or random influences. These sources of variation are shown in Figure 5-1 and are briefly examined below:

1. **Secular trend** refers to a long-run increase or decrease in the data series (the straight solid line in the top panel of Figure 5-1). For example, many time series of sales exhibit rising trends over the years because of population growth and increasing per capita expenditures. Some, such as leaded gasoline, follow a declining trend as more and more automobiles on the road require unleaded gasoline.
2. **Cyclical fluctuations** are the major expansions and contractions in most economic time series that seem to recur every several years (the heavy dashed curved line in the top panel of Figure 5-1). For example, the housing construction industry follows long cyclical swings lasting 15 to 20 years, while the automobile industry seems to follow much shorter cycles.
3. **Seasonal variation** refers to the regularly recurring fluctuation in economic activity during each year (the heavy dashed curved line in the bottom panel of Figure 5-1) because of weather and social customs. Thus, housing starts are much more numerous in spring and summer than in winter and autumn (because of weather conditions), while retail sales are much greater during the last quarter of each year (because of the holidays) than in other quarters.
4. **Irregular or random influences** are the variations in the data series resulting from wars, natural disasters, strikes, or other unique events. These are shown by the solid line segments in the bottom panel of Figure 5-1.

The total variation in the time series of sales (not shown in Figure 5-1) is the result of all four factors operating together. Thus, the original sales data would show the seasonal and irregular variations superimposed on the cyclical fluctuations around the rising trend (the reader should try to sketch such original sales data). Since cyclical swings or business cycles can be of different duration and can arise from a variety of causes that even today are not yet fully understood, they are usually examined separately with qualitative techniques (see Section 5-4). Similarly, irregular or random influences in time series, by their very nature, cannot be examined systematically or forecasted. Thus, in this section we concentrate on forecasting the values of time-series data by using only the long-term trend and the seasonal variation in the data.

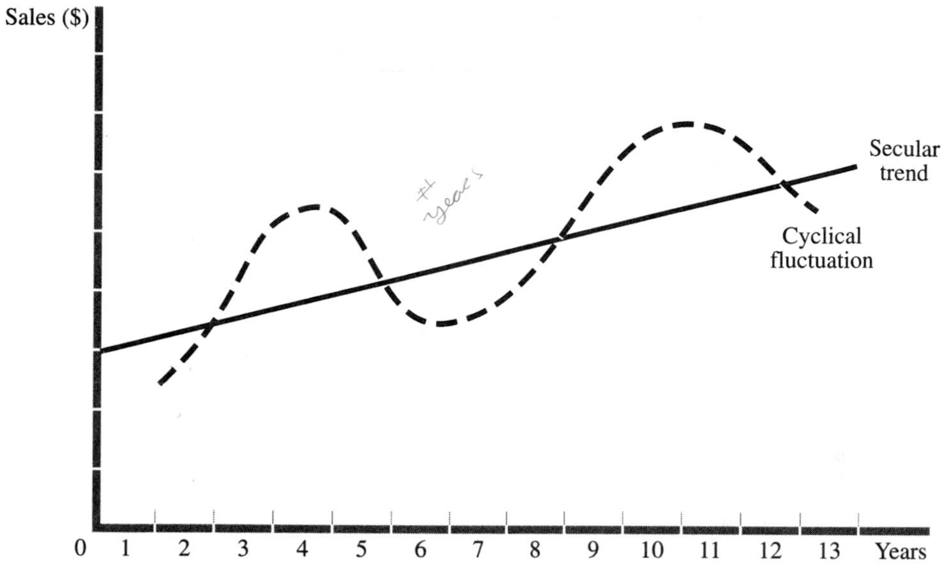

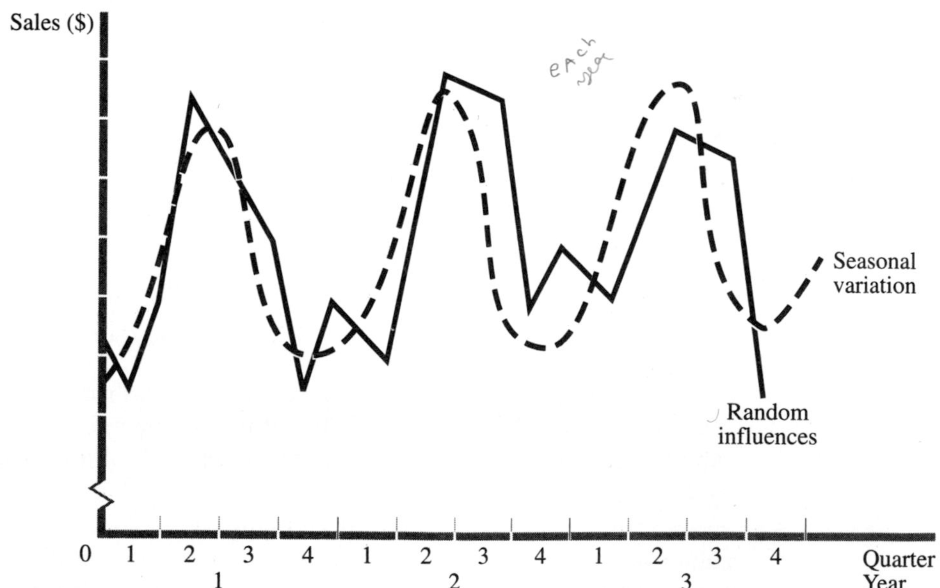

Figure 5-1
Trend, Cyclical, Seasonal, and Random Variations in Time-Series Data

The top panel shows the rising secular trend in the sales of the firm (the solid straight line) as well as the cyclical fluctuations above and below the trend during the course of several years (the dashed curved line). The bottom panel shows the seasonal variation in the data during each year (the dashed curved line) and the irregular or random influences (the solid line). The total variation in the time series is the result of all four forces working together.

Trend Projection

The simplest form of time-series analysis is projecting the past trend by fitting a straight line to the data either visually or, more precisely, by regression analysis. The linear regression model will take the form of

$$S_t = S_0 + bt \tag{5-1}$$

where S_t is the value of the time series to be forecasted for period t, S_0 is the estimated value of the time series (the constant of the regression) in the base period (i.e., at time period $t = 0$), b is the absolute amount of growth per period, and t is the time period in which the time series is to be forecasted.

For example, fitting a regression line to the electricity sales (consumption) data running from the first quarter of 1992 ($t = 1$) to the last quarter of 1995 ($t = 16$) given in Table 5-2, we get estimated regression Equation 5-2.

$$S_t = 11.90 + \underset{(4.00)}{0.394t} \qquad R^2 = 0.50 \tag{5-2}$$

Regression Equation 5-2 indicates that electricity sales in the city in the last quarter of 1991 (that is, S_0) are estimated to be 11.90 million kilowatt-hours and increase at the average rate of 0.394 million kilowatt-hours per quarter. The trend variable is statistically significant at better than the 1 percent level (inferred from the value of 4 for the t statistic given in parentheses below the estimated slope coefficient) and "explains" 50 percent in the quarterly variation of electricity consumption in the city (from $R^2 = 0.50$). Thus, based on the past trend, we can forecast electricity consumption (in million kilowatt-hours) in the city to be

$$S_{17} = 11.90 + 0.394(17) = 18.60 \quad \text{in the first quarter of 1996}$$
$$S_{18} = 11.90 + 0.394(18) = 18.99 \quad \text{in the second quarter of 1996}$$
$$S_{19} = 11.90 + 0.394(19) = 19.39 \quad \text{in the third quarter of 1996}$$
$$S_{20} = 11.90 + 0.394(20) = 19.78 \quad \text{in the fourth quarter of 1996}$$

These forecasts are shown by the dots on the dashed portion of the trend line extended into 1996 in Figure 5-2 (disregard for the moment the encircled points above and below the line). Note that the forecasted values of electricity sales read

Table 5-2
Seasonal Demand for (Sales of) Electricity (in millions of kilowatt-hours) in a U.S. City, 1992–1995

Time period	1992.1	1992.2	1992.3	1992.4	1993.1	1993.2	1993.3	1993.4
Quantity	11	15	12	14	12	17	13	16

Time period	1994.1	1994.2	1994.3	1994.4	1995.1	1995.2	1995.3	1995.4
Quantity	14	18	15	17	15	20	16	19

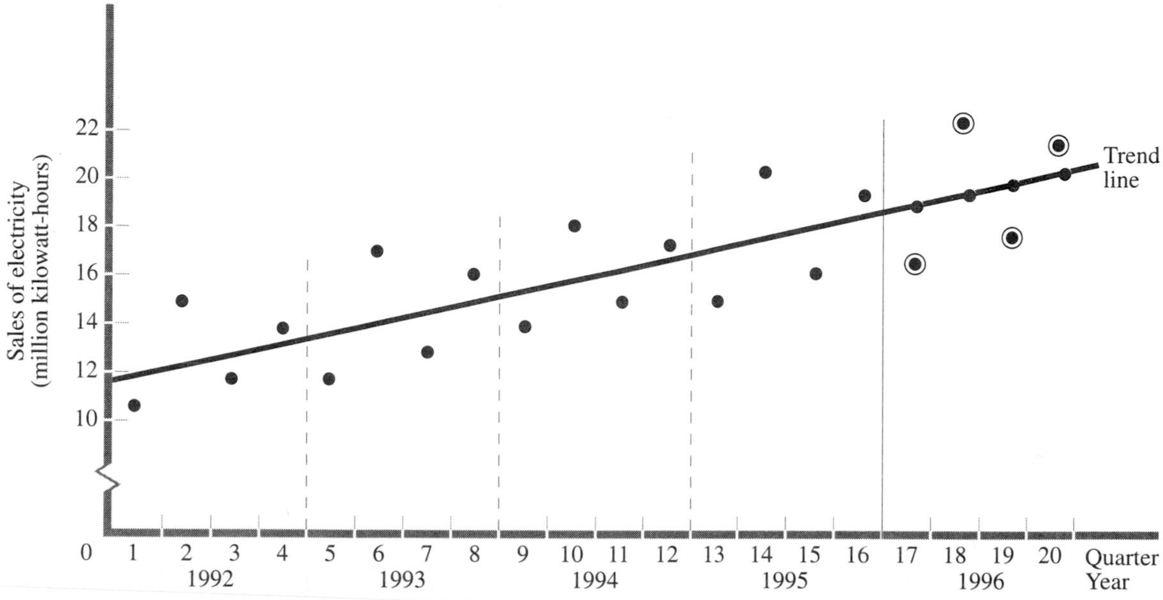

Figure 5-2
Forecasting by Trend Projection

Electricity sales for the first, second, third, and fourth quarters of 1996 can be read off the extended regression (trend) line (the dots on the dashed portion of the trend line) for quarters 17, 18, 19, and 20, respectively.

off the extended trend line take into consideration only the long-run trend factor in the data. By completely disregarding the very significant seasonal variation in the data (see the figure), the forecasted values are likely to be far off their actual future values. In Section 5-2, we will see how to incorporate this seasonal variation and significantly improve the forecast of future electricity consumption in the city. Before that, however, we will show how to fit a constant growth (percentage) rate trend to the same data.

While the assumption of a constant absolute amount of change per time period (here a quarter) may be appropriate in many cases, there are situations (such as the sales of many products) where a constant percentage change is more appropriate (i.e., fits the data better and gives better forecasts).[1] The constant percentage growth rate model can be specified as

$$S_t = S_0(1 + g)^t \tag{5-3}$$

where g is the constant percentage growth rate to be estimated.

To estimate g from Equation 5-3, we must first transform the time-series data into their natural logarithms and then run the regression on the transformed data.

[1]If uncertain, both the linear (i.e., the constant amount growth) and the exponential (constant percentage growth) trends can be tried, and the one that fits the data better is used for forecasting.

The transformed regression equation is linear in the logarithms and is given by

$$\ln S_t = \ln S_0 + t \ln (1 + g) \qquad (5\text{-}4)$$

Running regression Equation 5-4 for the data on electricity sales given in Table 5-2 transformed into logs,[2] we get

$$\ln S_t = 2.49 + \underset{(4.06)}{0.026t} \qquad R^2 = 0.50 \qquad (5\text{-}5)$$

In this case, the fit of Equation 5-5 is very similar to that of Equation 5-2 found earlier. Since the estimated parameters are now based on the logarithms of the data, however, they must be converted into their antilogs to be able to interpret them in terms of the original data. The antilog of $\ln S_0 = 2.49$ is $S_0 = 12.06$ (obtained by simply entering the value of 2.49 into any pocket calculator and pressing the key e^x for the antilog), and the antilog of $\ln (1 + g) = 0.026$ gives $(1 + g) = 1.026$. Substituting these values back into Equation 5-3, we get

$$S_t = 12.06(1.026)^t \qquad (5\text{-}6)$$

where $S_0 = 12.06$ million kilowatt-hours is the estimated sales of electricity in the city in the fourth quarter of 1991 (i.e., at $t = 0$) and the estimated growth rate is 1.026, or 2.6 percent, per quarter.

To estimate sales in any future quarter, we substitute into Equation 5-6 the value of t for the quarter for which we are seeking to forecast S and solve for S_t. Thus,

$$S_{17} = 12.06(1.026)^{17} = 18.66 \quad \text{in the first quarter of 1996}$$
$$S_{18} = 12.06(1.026)^{18} = 19.14 \quad \text{in the second quarter of 1996}$$
$$S_{19} = 12.06(1.026)^{19} = 19.64 \quad \text{in the third quarter of 1996}$$
$$S_{20} = 12.06(1.026)^{20} = 20.15 \quad \text{in the fourth quarter of 1996}$$

These forecasts are very similar to those obtained by fitting a linear trend.[3]

Seasonal Variation

As we have seen earlier, the forecasted values of electricity sales read off from the extended trend line in Figure 5-2 take into consideration only the long-run trend factor in the data. The data for the years 1992 to 1995, however, show strong seasonal variation, with sales in the first and third quarters of each year consistently below the corresponding long-run trend values, while sales in the second and fourth quarters are consistently above the trend values. By incorporating this sea-

[2]For example, the log of 11 (the value in Table 5-2 for the first quarter of 1992) is 2.40 (obtained by simply entering the value of 11 into any hand calculator and pressing the "ln" key).

[3]Note that the differences in the forecasts obtained by the use of exponential trend differ by increasing amounts from those obtained with a linear trend as the time series is forecasted further into the future. This is usually the case.

sonal variation, we can significantly improve the forecast of future electricity sales in the city. We can do this with the ratio-to-trend method or with dummy variables.

To adjust the trend forecast for the seasonal variation by the ratio-to-trend method, we simply find the average ratio by which the actual value of the time series differs from the corresponding estimated trend value in each quarter during the 1992 to 1995 period and then multiply the forecasted trend value by this ratio. The predicted trend value for each quarter in the 1992 to 1995 period is obtained by simply substituting the value of t corresponding to the quarter under consideration into Equation 5-2 and solving for S_t. It is also given in the computer printout for Equation 5-2. Table 5-3 shows the calculations for the seasonal adjustment of the electricity sales forecasted for each quarter of 1992 from the extended trend line examined earlier.

Multiplying the electricity sales forecasted earlier (from the simple extension of the linear trend) by the seasonal factors estimated in Table 5-3 (that is, 0.887 for the first quarter, 1.165 for the second quarter, and so on) we get the following new forecasts based on both the linear trend and the seasonal adjustment:

$$S_{17} = 18.60(0.887) = 16.50 \quad \text{in the first quarter of 1996}$$

$$S_{18} = 18.99(1.165) = 22.12 \quad \text{in the second quarter of 1996}$$

$$S_{19} = 19.39(0.907) = 17.59 \quad \text{in the third quarter of 1996}$$

$$S_{20} = 19.78(1.042) = 20.61 \quad \text{in the fourth quarter of 1996}$$

Table 5-3
Calculation of the Seasonal Adjustment of the Trend Forecast by the Ratio-to-Trend Method

Year	Forecasted	Actual	Actual/Forecasted
1992.1	12.29	11.00	0.895
1993.1	13.87	12.00	0.865
1994.1	15.45	14.00	0.906
1995.1	17.02	15.00	0.881
		Average:	0.887
1992.2	12.69	15.00	1.182
1993.2	14.26	17.00	1.192
1994.2	15.84	18.00	1.136
1995.2	17.42	20.00	1.148
		Average:	1.165
1992.3	13.08	12.00	0.917
1993.3	14.66	13.00	0.887
1994.3	16.23	15.00	0.924
1995.3	17.81	16.00	0.898
		Average:	0.907
1992.4	13.48	14.00	1.039
1993.4	15.05	16.00	1.063
1994.4	16.63	17.00	1.022
1995.4	18.20	19.00	1.044
		Average:	1.042

These forecasts are shown by the encircled points in Figure 5-2. Note that with the inclusion of the seasonal adjustment, the forecasted values for electricity sales closely replicate the past seasonal pattern in the time-series data along the rising linear trend.

Very similar results can be obtained by the inclusion of seasonal dummy variables in Equation 5-1. Taking the last quarter as the base-period quarter and defining dummy variable D_1 by a time series with 1's in the first quarter of each year and zero in the other quarters, D_2 by a time series with 1's in the second quarter of each year and zero in the other quarters, and D_3 by 1's in the third quarters and zero in the other quarters, we obtain the following results by running a regression of electricity sales on the seasonal dummy variables and the linear time trend:

$$S_t = 12.75 - 2.375D_{1t} + 1.750D_{2t} - 2.125D_{3t} + 0.375t \qquad R^2 = 0.99$$
$$(-10.83) \qquad (8.11) \qquad (-9.94) \qquad (22.25) \qquad\qquad (5\text{-}7)$$

Note that the estimated coefficients for the dummy variables and the trend variable are all statistically significant at better than the 1 percent level and that Equation 5-7 "explains" 99 percent of the variation in electricity sales (as compared with only 50 percent for Equation 5-2). Utilizing Equation 5-7 to forecast electricity sales for each quarter of 1996, we get[4]

$$S_{17} = 12.75 - 2.375 + 0.375(17) = 16.75 \quad \text{in the first quarter of 1996}$$
$$S_{18} = 12.75 + 1.750 + 0.375(18) = 21.25 \quad \text{in the second quarter of 1996}$$
$$S_{19} = 12.75 - 2.125 + 0.375(19) = 17.75 \quad \text{in the third quarter of 1996}$$
$$S_{20} = 12.75 \qquad\qquad + 0.375(20) = 20.25 \quad \text{in the fourth quarter of 1996}$$

These forecasted values are very similar to those obtained by the ratio-to-trend method. Thus, in this case the two methods are good alternatives for introducing the seasonal variation into the forecasts. It is important to remember, however, that these forecasts are based on the assumption that the past trend and seasonal patterns in the data will persist during 1996. If the pattern suddenly changes in a drastic manner, the forecasts are likely to be far off the mark. This is more likely the further into the future we attempt to forecast. In addition, it is very difficult or impossible to consider cyclical and irregular or random forces. Thus, time-series analysis cannot forecast turning points until after they have occurred. Even though these do not seem important in the historical data on electricity sales used in the example above, this may not be the situation in other real-world cases. Finally, time-series analysis does not examine the underlying forces

[4]Note that the dummy variable is added to (if positive) or subtracted from (if negative) the value of the constant of the regression (which refers to the fourth quarter, which is taken as the base). For a more detailed discussion of dummy variables, see D. Salvatore, *Statistics and Econometrics,* Schaum Outline Series (New York: McGraw-Hill, 1982), Sec. 8.2, or any other introductory econometrics text.

that cause the observed time series to fluctuate as it does over time. In any event, time-series analysis is seldom used alone but is most useful in conjunction with other forecasting methods.[5]

[5]There is a much more sophisticated method of time-series analysis called the "Box-Jenkins technique" (after its originators) which can improve on the time-series forecast. This method, however, is much more complex than the analysis presented above and is beyond the scope of this text. The interested reader is referred to the econometrics texts in the supplementary readings at the end of this chapter.

Case Study 5-2

Forecasting New-Housing Starts with Time-Series Analysis

Table 5-4 gives the number (in thousands) of new-housing units started in the United States from the first quarter of 1984 to the last quarter of 1989. Inspection of the data reveals that, except for 1986, housing starts generally declined over the years and were higher during the first quarter of each year, except for 1988.

To forecast housing starts in each quarter of 1990, we begin by regressing housing starts (H_t) on time (t), from $t = 1$ (the first quarter of 1984) to $t = 24$ (the last quarter of 1989) and get

$$H_t = 475.03 - 5.23t \qquad R^2 = 0.67 \qquad (5\text{-}8)$$
$$(-6.71)$$

Using these regression results to forecast new-housing starts for each quarter of 1990, we get

$$S_{25} = 475.03 - 5.23(25) = 344.28 \quad \text{in the first quarter of 1990}$$
$$S_{26} = 475.03 - 5.23(26) = 339.05 \quad \text{in the second quarter of 1990}$$
$$S_{27} = 475.03 - 5.23(27) = 333.82 \quad \text{in the third quarter of 1990}$$
$$S_{28} = 475.03 - 5.23(28) = 328.59 \quad \text{in the fourth quarter of 1990}$$

Table 5-4
New-Housing Starts in the United States: 1984.1-1989.4 (in thousand units)

1984.1	486.8	1985.1	440.4	1986.1	484.5	1987.1	444.7	1988.1	369.2	1989.1	379.3
1984.2	464.4	1985.2	435.7	1986.2	469.6	1987.2	401.4	1988.2	369.3	1989.2	338.1
1984.3	415.8	1985.3	421.9	1986.3	439.6	1987.3	404.7	1988.3	366.7	1989.3	334.4
1984.4	400.0	1985.4	433.3	1986.4	425.6	1987.4	383.2	1988.4	389.7	1989.4	333.3

Source: Economic Report of the President (Washington, D.C.: Government Printing Office), various issues.

that results in the smallest *RMSE* (weighted average error in the forecast). The formula for the root-mean-square error (*RMSE*) is

$$RMSE = \sqrt{\frac{\sum(A_t - F_t)^2}{n}} \tag{5-9}$$

where A_t is the actual value of the time series in period t, F_t is the forecasted value, and n is the number of time periods or observations. The forecast difference or error (that is, $A - F$) is squared in order to penalize larger errors proportionately more than smaller errors.

For example, column 4 in Table 5-5 shows $A_t - F_t$ for the three-quarter moving average forecast in column 3. Column 5 then shows $(A_t - F_t)^2$. The *RMSE* for the three-quarter moving average forecast in column 3 is then obtained by dividing the total of column 5 by 9 (the number of squared forecast errors) and finding the square root. That is,

$$RMSE = \sqrt{\frac{78.3534}{9}} = 2.95 \tag{5-10}$$

This compares with

$$RMSE = \sqrt{\frac{62.48}{7}} = 2.99 \tag{5-11}$$

for the five-quarter moving average forecast. Thus, the three-quarter moving average forecast is marginally better than the corresponding five-quarter moving average forecast. That is, we are a little more confident in the forecast of 21.33 than 20.6 for the thirteenth quarter (see Table 5-5).

Exponential Smoothing*

A serious criticism of using simple moving averages in forecasting is that they give equal weight to all observations in computing the average, even though intuitively we might expect more recent observations to be more important. Exponential smoothing overcomes this objection and is used more frequently than simple moving averages in forecasting.

With **exponential smoothing,** the forecast for period $t + 1$ (that is, F_{t+1}) is a weighted average of the actual and forecasted values of the time series in period t. The value of the time series at period t (that is, A_t) is assigned a weight (w) between 0 and 1 inclusive, and the forecast for period t (that is, F_t) is assigned the weight of $1 - w$.[6] The greater the value of w, the greater is the weight given to

*This section is a little more advanced than the others, but it can be skipped without loss of continuity.

[6]Note that the sum of the weights equals 1. That is, $w + (1 - w) = 1$. This is always the case.

the value of the time series in period t as opposed to previous periods.[7] Thus, the value of the forecast of the time series in period $t + 1$ is

$$F_{t+1} = wA_t + (1 - w)F_t \tag{5-12}$$

Two decisions must be made in order to use Equation 5-12 for exponential smoothing. First, it is necessary to assign a value to the initial forecast (that is, F_t) to get the analysis started. One way to do this is to let F_t equal the mean value of the entire observed time-series data. We must also decide on the value of w (the weight to assign to A_t). In general, different values of w are tried, and the one that leads to the forecast with the smallest root-mean-square error ($RMSE$) is actually used in forecasting.

For example, column 3 in Table 5-6 shows the forecasts for the firm's market share data given in columns 1 and 2 (the same as in Table 5-5) by using the average market share of the firm over the 12 quarters for which we have data (that is, 21.0) for F_1 (to get the calculations started) and $w = 0.3$ as the weight for A_t. Thus, F_2 (the second value in column 3) is

$$F_2 = 0.3(20) + (1 - 0.3)21 = 20.7 \tag{5-13}$$

The forecasts for other time periods (rounded off to the first decimal) are similarly obtained, until $F_{13} = 21.0$ for the thirteenth quarter.

[7]While F_{t+1} is calculated from the value of the time series and its forecast for period t only, the forecast for period t can be shown to depend on all past values of the time series, with weights declining exponentially for values further into the past. It is for this reason that this technique is called "exponential smoothing."

Table 5-6
Exponential Forecasts with w = 0.3 and w = 0.5, and Comparison

(1) Quarter	(2) Firm's Actual Market Share (A)	(3) Forecast with w = 0.3 (F)	(4) A − F	(5) (A − F)²	(6) Forecast with w = 0.5 (F)	(7) A − F	(8) (A − F)²
1	20	21.0	−1.0	1.00	21.0	−1.0	1.00
2	22	20.7	1.3	1.69	20.5	1.5	2.25
3	23	21.1	1.9	3.61	21.3	1.7	2.89
4	24	21.7	2.3	5.29	22.2	1.8	3.24
5	18	22.4	−4.4	19.36	23.1	−5.1	26.01
6	23	21.1	1.9	3.61	20.6	2.4	5.76
7	19	21.7	−2.7	7.29	21.8	−2.8	7.84
8	17	20.9	−3.9	15.21	20.4	−3.4	11.56
9	22	19.7	2.3	5.29	18.7	3.3	10.89
10	23	20.4	2.6	6.76	20.4	2.6	6.76
11	18	21.2	−3.2	10.24	21.7	−3.7	13.69
12	23	20.2	2.8	7.84	19.9	3.1	9.61
			Total:	87.19		Total:	101.50
13	—	21.0			21.5		

On the other hand, starting again with the average market share of the firm for the 12 quarters for which we have data (that is, 21.0) for F_1 but now using $w = 0.5$ as the weight for A_t, we get the exponential forecasts of the firm's market share shown in column 6 of Table 5-6. Thus, F_2 (the second value in column 6) is

$$F_2 = 0.5(20) + (1 - 0.5)21 = 20.5$$

The forecasts for the other time periods are similary obtained, until $F_{13} = 21.5$ for the thirteenth quarter.

The root-mean-square error (*RMSE*) for the exponential forecasts using $w = 0.3$ is

$$RMSE = \sqrt{\frac{87.19}{12}} = 2.70 \tag{5-14}$$

On the other hand, the *RMSE* for the exponential forecasts using $w = 0.5$ is

$$RMSE = \sqrt{\frac{101.5}{12}} = 2.91 \tag{5-15}$$

Thus, we are more confident in the exponential forecast of 21.0 for the thirteenth quarter obtained by using $w = 0.3$ than with the exponential forecast of 21.5 obtained by using $w = 0.5$ (see Table 5-6). Both exponential forecasts are also better than the three-quarter and the five-quarter moving average forecasts obtained earlier in Section 5-3. Since the best exponential forecast is usually better than the best moving average forecast, the former is generally used.[8]

[8]If the time-series data exhibit not only random variation but also a secular trend, the double exponential smoothing technique is required. This, however, is beyond the scope of this text. The interested reader can consult J. J. McAuley, *Economic Forecasting for Business* (Englewood Cliffs, N.J.: Prentice-Hall, 1986), Chap. 4, or C. W. Gross and R. T. Peterson, *Business Forecasting* (Boston: Houghton Mifflin, 1983), Chap. 3.

Case Study 5-3

Forecasting Copper Sales with Smoothing Techniques

The second column of Table 5-7 gives the index (with 1976 = 100) of the quantity of copper deliveries to customers in the United States per year from 1977 to 1988. Inspection of the data reveals no secular trend (and, of course, there is no seasonal variation) but a great deal of irregular or random variation. Thus, we can use exponential smoothing to forecast copper deliveries in the United States.

Starting with the average copper delivery from 1977 to 1988 (that is, 100), for F_1 and using $w = 0.3$ and $w = 0.7$ as the weights (we could have chosen any other value for w between 0.1 and 0.9) for actual copper deliveries in each year (A_t), we get the exponential forecasts (rounded off to the nearest integer) in columns 3 and 6, respectively, by using Equation 5-12 and using the *RMSE* of these forecasts to compare them.

Table 5-7
Exponential Forecasts of Index of Copper Deliveries in the United States (1976 = 100)

(1) Year	(2) Actual Copper Deliveries (A)	(3) Forecast with w = 0.3 (F)	(4) A − F	(5) $(A-F)^2$	(6) Forecast with w = 0.7 (F)	(7) A − F	(8) $(A-F)^2$
1977	103	100	3	9	100	3	9
1978	107	101	6	36	102	5	25
1979	118	103	15	225	106	12	144
1980	93	108	−15	225	114	−21	441
1981	103	104	−1	1	99	4	16
1982	76	104	−28	784	102	−26	676
1983	91	96	−5	25	84	7	49
1984	104	95	9	81	89	15	225
1985	97	98	−1	1	100	−3	9
1986	89	98	−9	81	98	−9	81
1987	103	95	8	64	92	11	121
1988	100	97	3	9	100	0	0
				Total: 1,541			Total: 1,796
1989		98			100		

Source: American Metal Market, *Metal Statistics* (New York: Fairchild, 1991), p. 64.

With $w = 0.3$,

$$RMSE = \sqrt{\frac{1{,}541}{12}} = 11.3 \tag{5-16}$$

With $w = 0.7$,

$$RMSE = \sqrt{\frac{1{,}796}{12}} = 12.2 \tag{5-17}$$

Thus, we are more confident in the exponential forecast of 98 for 1989 obtained by using $w = 0.3$ than in the exponential forecast of 100 obtained with $w = 0.7$.

5-4 BAROMETRIC METHODS

Until now we have examined secular trends, seasonal variations, and random influences in time-series data. Little if anything has been said about forecasting cyclical swings in the level of economic activity or business cycles. One way to forecast or anticipate short-term changes in economic activity or turning points in business cycles is to use the index of leading economic indicators. These are time series that tend to precede (lead) changes in the level of general economic activity, much as changes in the mercury in a barometer precede changes in weather conditions (hence the name "barometric methods"). **Barometric forecasting,** as conducted today, is primarily the result of the work conducted at the National Bureau of Economic Research (NBER) and the U.S. Department of Commerce.

A rise in **leading economic indicators** is used to forecast an increase in general business activity, and vice versa. For example, an increase in building permits precedes and can be used to forecast an increase in housing construction. Less obvious—but very important—an increase in stock prices, in general, precedes (i.e., it is a leading indicator for) an upturn in general business activity since stock prices reflect expectations of higher profits by business managers and others. On the other hand, a decline in contracts for plant and equipment usually precedes a slowdown in general economic activity. Thus, leading indicators normally tend to anticipate and are used to forecast turning points in the business cycle.

Although we are primarily interested in leading indicators, some time series move in step or coincide with movements in general economic activity and are therefore called **coincident indicators.** Still others follow or lag movements in economic activity and are called **lagging indicators.** The relative positions of leading, coincident, and lagging indicators in the business cycle are shown graphically in Figure 5-3. The figure shows that leading indicators precede business cycles' turning points (i.e., peaks and troughs), coincident indicators move in step with business cycles, while lagging indicators follow or lag turning points in business cycles.

Time-series data on more than 300 leading, coincident, and lagging indicators are provided in the *Survey of Current Business,* a monthly publication of the U.S. Department of Commerce. A shorter list of the 22 best indicators (11 leading, 4 coincident, and 7 lagging) together with their mean lead (−) or lag (+) time (in months) with respect to the actual cyclical peak or trough is given in Table 5-8. Our interest is primarily in the leading indicators. Table 5-8 also gives the lead

Figure 5-3
Economic Indicators

Leading indicators precede (lead) business cycles' turning points (i.e., peaks and troughs), *coincident indicators* move in step with business cycles, while *lagging indicators* follow or lag turning points in business cycles.

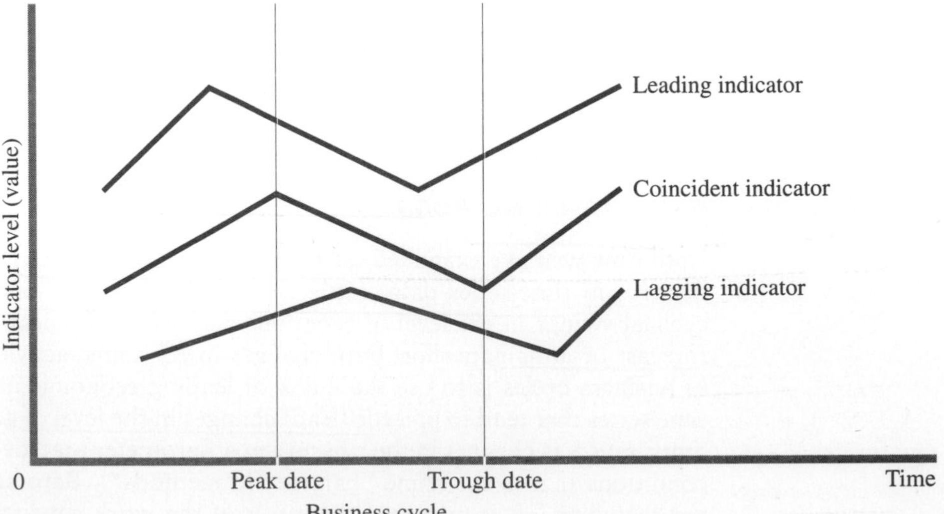

and lag times for the **composite indices** of the 11 leading, the 4 coincident, and the 7 lagging indicators. These are a weighted average of the individual indicators in each group, with the indicators that do a better job of forecasting given larger weights. As such, composite indices smooth out random variations and provide more reliable forecasts and fewer wrong signals than individual indicators.

Another method for overcoming the difficulty arising when some of the 11 leading indicators move up and some move down is the **diffusion index.** Instead of combining the 11 leading indicators into a composite index, the diffusion index gives the percentage of the 11 leading indicators moving upward. If all

Table 5-8
Short List of Leading, Coincident, and Lagging Indicators
(for reference peak of July 1990, the latest for which data are available)

	Mean Lead (−) or Lag (+)
LEADING INDICATORS (11 SERIES)	
Average weekly hours, manufacturing	−15
Average weekly initial claims for unemployment insurance (inverted)	−22
Manufacturers' new orders in 1987 dollars, consumer goods and materials	−2
Vendor performance, slower deliveries diffusion index	+1
Contracts and orders, plant and equipment in 1987 dollars	−7
Building permits, new private housing units	−21
Change in manufacturers' unfilled orders in 1987 dollars, durable goods (smoothed)	−3
Change in sensitive materials prices (smoothed)	+2
Index of stock prices, 500 common stocks	−1
Money supply M2 in 1987 dollars	−7
Index of consumer expectations	−18
COINCIDENT INDICATORS (4 SERIES)	
Employees on nonagricultural payrolls	−1
Personal income less transfer payments in 1987 dollars	−3
Index of industrial production	+2
Manufacturing and trade sales in 1987 dollars	−4
LAGGING INDICATORS (7 SERIES)	
Average duration of unemployment (inverted)	−13
Ratio, manufacturing and trade inventories to sales in 1987 dollars	+6
Change in index of labor cost per unit of output, manufacturing (smoothed)	+8
Average prime rate charged by banks	−14
Commercial and industrial loans outstanding in 1987 dollars	0
Ratio, consumer installment credit to personal income	−10
Change in consumer price index for services (smoothed)	+2
COMPOSITE INDICES	
Composite index of 11 leading indicators	−18
Composite index of 4 coincident indicators	−1
Composite index of 7 lagging indicators	−9

Source: U.S. Department of Commerce, Bureau of Economic Analysis, *Survey of Current Business* (Washington, D.C.: U.S. Government Printing Office, April 1994), p. C-29.

11 move up, the diffusion index is 100. If all move down, its value is 0. If only 7 move up, the diffusion index would be $(\frac{7}{11})(100)$, or 64. We usually forecast an improvement in economic activity when the diffusion index is above 50, and we will have greater confidence in our forecast the closer the index is to 100.

In general, barometric forecasting employs composite and diffusion indices rather than individual indicators, except when a firm seeks information about anticipated changes in the market for specific goods and services. Each month the Department of Commerce reports changes in the individual and composite indices. Although not much significance can be attached to individual monthly swings, three or four successive one-month declines in the composite index and a diffusion index of less than 50 percent are usually a prelude to recession (popularly defined as a decline in gross national product for two or more consecutive quarters). This can be seen from Figure 5-4. The top panel shows that the composite index of leading indicators turned down prior to the recessions of 1969 to 1970, 1973 to 1975, 1980, 1981 to 1982, and 1990 to 1991 (the shaded regions in the figure). Similarly, the bottom panel shows that the diffusion index for the 11 leading indicators was generally below 50 percent in the months preceding recessions (the shaded areas).

Figure 5-4
Composite and Diffusion Indices of the 11 Leading Indicators

(1968 through 1994) The top panel shows that the composite index of 11 leading indicators turned down prior to (i.e., led) the recessions of 1969 to 1970, 1973 to 1975, 1980, 1981 to 1982, and 1990 to 1991 (the shaded regions in the figure). The bottom panel shows that the diffusion index for the 11 leading indicators was generally below 50 percent in the months preceding recessions (the shaded areas). [*Source: U.S. Department of Commerce, Bureau of Economic Analysis,* Survey of Current Business *(Washington, D.C.: Government Printing Office, September 1994), p. C-8.]*

Composite index of the 11 leading indicators (1968-1994)

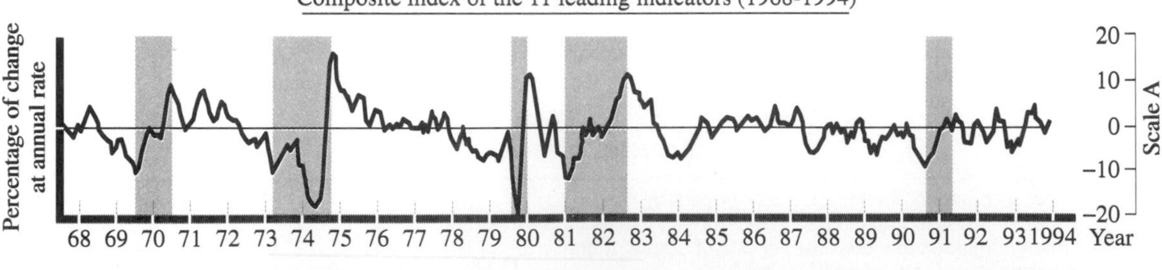

Diffusion index of the 11 leading indicators (1968-1994)

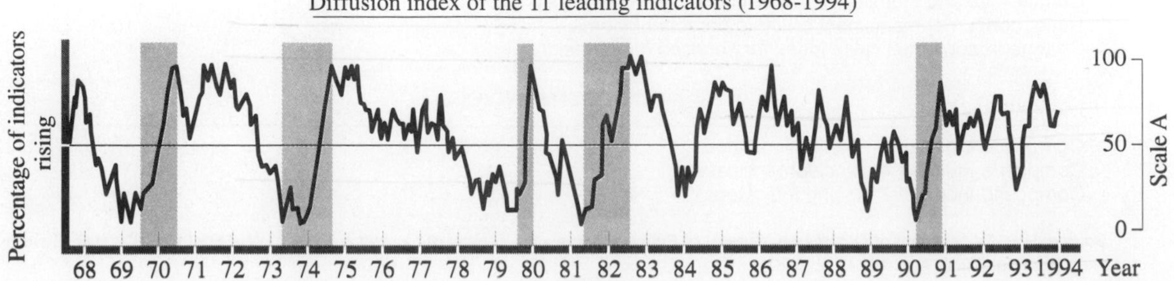

Although the composite and diffusion indices of leading indicators are reasonably good tools for predicting turning points in business cycles, they face a number of shortcomings. One is that on several occasions they forecasted a recession that failed to occur.[9] The variability in lead time can also be considerable. More importantly, barometric forecasting gives little or no indication of the *magnitude* of the forecasted change in the level of economic activity (i.e., it provides only a qualitative forecast of turning points). Thus, while barometric forecasting is certainly superior to time-series analysis and smoothing techniques (naive methods) in forecasting short-term turning points in economic activity, it must be used in conjunction with other methods (such as econometric forecasting—discussed in Section 5-5) to forecast the magnitude of change in the level of economic activity.

[9]At best, barometric forecasting is only 80 to 90 percent accurate in forecasting turning points.

Case Study 5-4

Forecasting the Level of Economic Activity with Composite and Diffusion Indices

Table 5-9 gives the monthly composite index (with 1987 = 100) and the diffusion index of the 11 leading indicators from January 1994 through December 1994. Note that the composite index increased in each month, except for July, September, and October 1994 (when it either remained unchanged or declined slightly), thus correctly anticipating continued economic expansion. Similarly, the diffusion index was above 50 in every month except for February, June, July, and October 1994, also signaling continued expansion.

Table 5-9
Composite and Diffusion Indices for the 11 Leading Indicators From January 1994 to December 1994

Month	Composite Index	Diffusion Index
January	100.5	77.3
February	100.7	45.5
March	101.3	81.8
April	101.4	54.5
May	101.5	63.6
June	101.7	45.5
July	101.7	40.9
August	102.3	77.3
September	102.3	59.1
October	102.2	45.5
November	102.5	63.6
December	102.6	59.1

Source: U.S. Department of Commerce, Bureau of Economic Analysis, *Survey of Current Business* (Washington, D.C.: Government Printing Office, January 1995), p. C-1.

5-5 ECONOMETRIC MODELS

The firm's demand and sales of a commodity as well as many other economic variables are increasingly being forecasted with econometric models. The characteristic that distinguishes econometric models from other forecasting methods is that they seek to identify and measure the relative importance (elasticity) of the various determinants of demand or other economic variables to be forecasted. By attempting to *explain* the relationship being forecasted, econometric forecasting allows the manager to determine the optimal policies for the firm. This is to be contrasted with the other forecasting techniques examined in this chapter which forecast demand, sales, or other economic variables on the basis of their past patterns or on the basis of some leading indicator alone.

Econometric forecasting frequently incorporates or utilizes the best features of other forecasting techniques, such as trend and seasonal variations, smoothing techniques, and leading indicators. Econometric forecasting models range from single-equation models of the demand that the firm faces for its product to large multiple-equation models describing hundreds of sectors and industries of the economy. Although our concern here is with forecasting the demand for a firm's product, macroforecasts of national income and major sectors of the economy are often used as inputs or explanatory variables in simple single-equation demand models of the firm. Therefore, we discuss both types of forecasting in this section, starting with single-equation models.

Single-Equation Models

The simplest form of econometric forecasting is with a single-equation model. The first step here is to identify the determinants of the variable to be forecasted. For example, in forecasting the demand for breakfast cereals, the firm will usually postulate that demand (Q) is a function of or depends on the price of breakfast cereals (P), consumers' disposable income (Y), the size of the population (N), the price of muffins (P_S—a substitute), the price of milk (P_C—a complement), and the level of advertising by the firm (A). Thus, we can write the following demand equation to be estimated:

$$Q = a_0 + a_1P + a_2Y + a_3N + a_4P_S + a_5P_C + a_6A + e \qquad (5\text{-}18)$$

Once the model has been estimated (i.e., the values of the a's determined) and evaluated (as discussed in Section 4-7), the firm must obtain forecasted values of the independent or explanatory variables of the model for the time period for which the dependent variable is to be forecasted. Thus, to forecast Q_{t+1} (i.e., the demand faced by the firm in the next period), the firm must obtain the values for P_{t+1}, Y_{t+1}, N_{t+1}, $P_{S_{t+1}}$, $P_{C_{t+1}}$, and A_{t+1}. By substituting these forecasted values of the independent variables into the estimated equation, we obtain the forecasted values of the dependent variable (Q_{t+1}). The forecasted value of the macroeconomic variables of the model (Y_{t+1} and N_{t+1}) are usually obtained from the U.S. Department of Commerce or from many private firms that specialize in making such forecasts (see Case Study 5-6). The microvariables in the model not under the control of the firm ($P_{S_{t+1}}$ and $P_{C_{t+1}}$) might be forecasted by time-series analysis or smoothing techniques, and the firm can experiment with various alternative forecasted values of the independent policy variables under its control (P_{t+1} and A_{t+1}). An example of econometric forecasting with a single-equation model is provided in Case Study 5-5.

Case Study 5-5

Forecasting the Demand for Air Travel over the North Atlantic

In Case Study 4-4, we reported the following estimated equation for air travel between New York and London for the period from 1965 to 1978:

$$\ln Q_t = 2.737 - 1.247 \ln P_t + 1.905 \ln GNP_t \qquad \overline{R}^2 = 0.97 \tag{5-19}$$

where Q_t = number of passengers per year traveling between the United States and Europe from 1965 to 1978 on IATA (International Air Transport Association) carriers, in thousands

P_t = average yearly air fare between New York and London (weighted by the seasonal distribution of traffic), in dollars, adjusted for inflation

GNP_t = U.S. gross national product in each year, in billions of dollars, adjusted for inflation

Suppose that in 1978 an airline company forecasted that in 1979 air fares (adjusted for inflation) between New York and London (that is, P_{t+1}) would be \$550 and real *GNP* (that is, GNP_{t+1}) would be \$1,480. The natural log of 550 (that is, ln 550) is 6.310 and ln 1,480 is 7.300. Substituting these values into Equation 5-19, we get

$$\ln Q_{t+1} = 2.737 - 1.247(6.310) + 1.905(7.300) = 8.775 \tag{5-20}$$

The antilog of 8.775 is 6,470 or 6,470,000 passengers forecasted for 1979. The accuracy of this forecast depends on the accuracy of the estimated demand coefficients and on the accuracy of the forecasted values of the independent or explanatory variables in the demand equation.

Multiple-Equation Models

Although single-equation models are often used by firms to forecast demand or sales, economic relationships may be so complex that a multiple-equation model may be required. This is particularly the case in forecasting macrovariables such as gross national product (*GNP*) or the demand and sales of major sectors or industries. Multiple-equation models may include only a few equations or hundreds of them. To show how multiple-equation models are used in forecasting, we start with a very simple three-equation (5-21, 5-22, and 5-23) model of the national economy that can be used to forecast *GNP*.

$$C_t = a_1 + b_1 GNP_t + u_{1t} \tag{5-21}$$

$$I_t = a_2 + b_2 \pi_{t-1} + u_{2t} \tag{5-22}$$

$$GNP_t \equiv C_t + I_t + G_t \tag{5-23}$$

where C = consumption expenditures
GNP = gross national product in year t
I = investment
π = profits
G = government expenditures
u = stochastic disturbance (random error term)
t = current year
$t - 1$ = previous year

Equation 5-21 postulates that consumption expenditures in year t (C_t) are a linear function of GNP in the same year (that is, GNP_t). Equation 5-22 postulates that investment in year t (I_t) is a linear function of profits in the previous year (that is, π_{t-1}). Finally, Equation 5-23 defines GNP in year t as the sum of consumption expenditures, investment, and government expenditures in the same year.

Variables C_t, I_t, and GNP_t (the left-hand variables or variables to the left of the equals signs in Equations 5-21, 5-22, and 5-23) are called **endogenous variables.** These are the variables that the model seeks to explain or predict from the solution of the model. **Exogenous variables,** on the other hand, are those determined outside the model. In the above model, π_{t-1} and G_t are the exogenous variables. Their values must be supplied from outside the model in order to be able to estimate the model. When (as in the above model) some of the endogenous variables also appear on the right of the equals signs, this means that they both affect and are in turn affected by the other variables in the model (i.e., they are simultaneously determined).

Equations 5-21 and 5-22 are called **structural (behavioral) equations** because they seek to explain the relationship between the particular endogenous variable and the other variables in the system. On the other hand, Equation 5-23 is a **definitional equation** or an identity and is always true by definition. Note that Equation 5-23 has no parameters or coefficients to be estimated. We will see that, given the value of the exogenous variables (π_{t-1} and G_t), we can solve the system and estimate the values of the endogenous variables. A change in the value of an exogenous variable will affect directly the endogenous variable in the equation in which it appears and indirectly the other endogenous variables in the system. For example, an increase in π_{t-1} leads to a rise in I_t directly (Equation 5-22). The induced increase in I_t then leads to an increase in GNP_t and, through it, in C_t as well.

Since the endogenous variables of the system (that is, C_t, I_t, and GNP_t) are both determined by and in turn determine the value of the other endogenous variables in the model (i.e., they also appear on the right-hand side in Equations 5-21 and 5-23), we cannot use the ordinary least-squares technique (OLS) to estimate the parameters of the structural equations (the *a*'s and the *b*'s in Equations

5-21 and 5-22). More advanced econometric techniques are required to obtain unbiased estimates of the coefficients of the model. These are beyond the scope of this book.[10] By assuming that these coefficients are correctly estimated by the appropriate estimating technique, we can show how the above simple macromodel can be used for forecasting the values of the endogenous variables. To do this, we substitute Equations 5-21 and 5-22 into Equation 5-23 (the definitional equation) and solve. This will give an equation for GNP_t that is expressed only in terms of π_{t-1} and G_t (the exogenous variables of the system). By then substituting the values of π_t (which is known in year $t + 1$) and the predicted or forecasted value of G_{t+1} into the solved equation, we get a forecast for GNP_{t+1}. That is, substituting Equation 5-21 into Equation 5-23, we get[11]

$$GNP_t = a_1 + b_1 GNP_t + I_t + G_t \tag{5-24}$$

By then substituting Equation 5-22 into 5-24, we get

$$GNP_t = a_1 + b_1 GNP_t + a_2 + b_2 \pi_{t-1} + G_t \tag{5-25}$$

Collecting the GNP_t terms to the left in Equation 5-25 and isolating GNP_t, we have

$$GNP_t(1 - b_1) = a_1 + a_2 + b_2 \pi_{t-1} + G_t \tag{5-26}$$

Dividing both sides of Equation 5-26 by $1 - b_1$, we finally obtain

$$GNP_t = \frac{a_1 + a_2}{1 - b_1} + \frac{b_2 \pi_{t-1}}{1} - b_1 + \frac{G_t}{1 - b_1} \tag{5-27}$$

Equation 5-27 is called a **reduced-form equation** because GNP_t is expressed only in terms of π_{t-1} and G_t (the exogenous variables of the model). By substituting into Equation 5-27 the value of π_t (which is known in year $t + 1$) and the predicted value of G_{t+1}, we obtain the forecasted value for GNP_{t+1}. The reduced-form equations for C_t and I_t can similarly be obtained (see Problem 11, with answer at the end of the book).

While the above very simple macromodel contains three endogenous and two exogenous variables, and two structural and one definitional equations, most large models of the U.S. economy contain hundreds of variables and equations. They require estimates of tens, if not hundreds, of exogenous variables and provide forecasts of an even greater number of endogenous variables, ranging from *GNP* to consumption, investment, and exports and imports by sector, as well as for numerous other real and financial variables. Firms usually obtain (purchase) macroforecasts for the entire economy and its major sectors from firms specializing in making such forecasts and use these macroforecasts as inputs in their own specific forecasting of the demand and sales of the firm's product(s).

[10]See D. Salvatore, *Theory and Problems of Statistics and Econometrics,* Schaum Outline Series (New York: McGraw-Hill, 1982), Chap. 10, and W. Baumol, *Economic Theory and Operations Analysis* (Englewood Cliffs, N.J.: Prentice-Hall, 1977), Chap. 10.

[11]The stochastic disturbances (i.e., the *u*'s in Equations 5-21 and 5-22) are omitted in the following equations because their expected values are zero.

Case Study 5-6

Econometric Forecasts with Large Econometric Models

Table 5-10 presents quarterly forecasts of real GDP, as well as yearly forecasts for real GDP, price rises (i.e., the rate of inflation), and the unemployment rate, for the U.S. economy for the year 1995 prepared in Fall 1994 by well-known econometric forecasters. Also included in the last row of Table 5-10 are the consensus forecasts. From the table we see that the forecasted percentage change in real GDP from the fourth quarter of 1994 to the fourth quarter of 1995 ranges from 3.5 for the Prudential Insurance Corporation to 1.7 for McGraw-Hill/DRI, for an average of 2.6 for all forecasts and for the consensus forecast. For prices, the range is from 3.8 for Georgia State University to 2.7 for Bankers Trust and Chemical Bank, for an average of 3.2 for all forecasts and 3.4 for the consensus forecast. The range for the unemployment rate is from 6.1 for Chemical Bank to 5.2 for Georgia State University, for an average of 5.6 for all forecasts and for the consensus forecast.

Most forecasts adjust the mechanical output of the econometric model for data revisions, past forecasting errors, feedback from users of the forecast, and for expected events (such as an anticipated strike or a presidential election) not considered by the model. The forecasting errors in these models are generally below 6 percent for GDP and less than 10 percent for the rate of inflation and unemployment.

Table 5-10
Macroforecasts for 1995 by Econometric Services

	Percentage Change in Real GDP (Annual Rate), 1995				Percentage Change, IV Q 1994–IV Q 1995		
	I	II	III	IV	Real GDP	Prices	Unemployment Rate, 1995
Bankers Trust	2.8	2.7	2.4	2.3	2.6	2.7	5.5
Business Week	2.2	2.6	2.4	2.2	2.4	3.5	5.3
Chemical Bank	1.8	2.2	2.7	2.5	2.3	2.7	6.1
DRI/McGraw-Hill	3.2	1.2	1.1	1.3	1.7	3.2	5.6
Georgia State University	2.8	3.3	3.0	2.8	3.0	3.8	5.2
Lehman Brothers	3.0	2.3	2.5	3.4	2.9	3.3	5.3
Nat'l Fed'n of Indep. Bus.	3.1	3.0	3.0	2.7	2.8	3.2	5.8
Prudential Insurance Co.	3.5	3.5	3.5	3.5	3.5	3.0	5.5
U.S. Chamber of Commerce	1.0	2.1	2.5	2.2	1.9	3.2	5.7
WEFA Group	2.8	2.4	2.7	2.4	2.6	3.0	5.8
Average	2.6	2.5	2.6	2.5	2.6	3.2	5.6
Consensus	2.8	2.6	2.4	2.3	2.6	3.4	5.6

Source: Business Week, December 26, 1994, p. 95.

Case Study 5-7
Risks in Demand Forecasting

Demand forecasting faces two major risks of grossly overestimating or underestimating demand. One risk arises from entirely unforeseen events, such as war, political upheavals, or natural disasters. The second risk arises from inadequate analysis of the market. For example, between 1983 and 1984, 67 new types of personal computers were introduced in the U.S. market, and most computer companies forecasted growth of shipments to be twice as large as those that actually took place. This led to many computer companies going out of business by 1986. Computer companies based their forecast of rapid growth on the fact that there were more than 50 million white-collar workers in the United States in 1983 but only 8 million PCs. More careful market analysis, however, would have shown that two-thirds of white-collar workers either did require a PC on their jobs or were already connected with inexpensive terminals to mainframe computers.

Another example is provided by the petroleum industry, which invested over $500 billion worldwide between 1980 and 1981 in the expectation that demand would grow from 52 million barrels of oil per day in 1979 to 60 million barrels by 1985 and that this would result in petroleum prices rising 50 percent. Instead, because of increased energy efficiency, the demand for petroleum declined to 46 million barrels per day by 1986, and this resulted in the collapse of petroleum prices and huge losses in drilling, production, refining, and shipping investments. Still another example of a costly but avoidable forecasting error was committed by video-game companies, which projected explosive growth based on the very small 10 percent overall market penetration in the United States. More careful analysis with available data, however, would have shown that 75 percent of upper-income families with children between the ages of 6 and 15 (the main target market for video games) already had video games.

All these costly forecasting errors could possibly have been avoided by (1) carefully defining the market for the product to include all potential users of the product and considering the possibility of product substitution, (2) dividing total industry demand into its main components and analyzing each component separately, (3) forecasting the main drivers or users of the product in each segment of the market and projecting how they are likely to change in the future, and (4) conducting sensitivity analyses of how the forecast would be affected by changes in any of the assumptions on which the forecast is based. Although uncertainties will remain, a manager that follows the above fourfold approach is more likely to be able to anticipate major changes in the demand for his product and to make better forecasts.

Source: "Four Steps to Forecast Total Market Demand," *Harvard Business Review,* July–August 1988, pp. 28–37.

SUMMARY

1. The aim of economic forecasting is to reduce the risk or uncertainty that the firm faces in its short-term operational decision making and in planning for its long-term growth. Forecasting techniques range from the very naive and

inexpensive to very sophisticated and expensive ones. By considering the advantages and limitations of various forecasting techniques, managers can choose the method or combinations of methods that are most suitable to the firm. Qualitative forecasts can be based on surveys of business executives' plans for plant and equipment expenditures, inventory changes and sales expectations, and surveys of consumer expenditure plans. Sales forecasts for the firm can also be based on polling executives, its sales force, and consumers. Firms often solicit an important foreign perspective from councils of foreign dignitaries and businesspeople.

2. One of the most frequently used forecasting methods is time-series analysis. Time-series data usually fluctuate over time because of secular trends, cyclical fluctuations, seasonal variations, and irregular or random influences. The simplest form of time-series analysis is trend projection. A linear trend assumes a constant absolute amount of change per time period. Sometimes an exponential trend (showing a constant percentage change per period) fits the data better. By incorporating the seasonal variation, we can significantly improve the trend forecast. This can be done by the ratio-to-trend method or by using dummy variables. It must be remembered, however, that time-series analysis is based on the assumption that the past pattern of movements in the data will continue unchanged in the future.
3. Naive forecasting also includes smoothing techniques, such as moving averages and exponential smoothing. These are useful when the time series exhibits little trend or seasonal variation but a great deal of irregular or random variation. With a moving average, the forecasted value of a time series in a given period is equal to the average value of the time series in a number of previous periods. With exponential smoothing, the forecast for a given period is a weighted average of the actual and forecasted values of the time series in the previous period. The exponential forecast is usually better than the moving average forecast. The weight chosen for the former is the one that minimizes the root-mean-square error (*RMSE*) of the forecast.
4. Turning points in the level of economic activity can be forecasted by using the composite index of the best 11 leading economic indicators. These are time series that tend to precede (lead) changes in the level of general economic activity. Composite indexes smooth out random variations and provide more reliable forecasts and fewer wrong signals than individual indicators. The diffusion index is also used. This gives the percentage of the 11 leading indicators that move upward. Barometric forecasting is only about 80 to 90 percent successful in forecasting turning points in economic activity, the variability in lead time can be considerable, and it cannot predict the magnitude of the changes. Thus, barometric forecasting should be used in conjunction with other methods.
5. Forecasting is increasingly being performed with econometric models. These seek to explain the relationship(s) being forecasted and are essential for devising optimal policies. Econometric forecasting models frequently incorporate other forecasting techniques and range from simple single-equation

models forecasting the firm's sales of a product to very large multiple-equation macromodels of the entire economy. Forecasting with single-equation models involves substituting into the estimated equation the predicted values of the independent or explanatory variables for the period of the forecast and solving for the forecasted values of the dependent variable. In multiple-equation models the estimated values of the exogenous variables (i.e., those determined outside the system) must be substituted into the estimated model to obtain forecasts of the endogenous variables.

DISCUSSION QUESTIONS

1. (*a*) What is meant by forecasting? Why is it so important in the management of business firms and other enterprises? (*b*) What are the different types of forecasting? (*c*) How can the firm determine the most suitable forecasting method to use?
2. (*a*) What is meant by qualitative forecasts? What are the most important forms of qualitative forecasts? (*b*) What is their rationale and usefulness? (*c*) What are the most important surveys of future economic activities? (*d*) What are the most important opinion polls of future economic activities? (*e*) Why is gaining a foreign perspective important? How do firms usually go about gaining this?
3. (*a*) What is meant by time-series data? What are the possible sources of variation in time-series data? (*b*) What is the basic assumption in time-series analysis? (*c*) How are the sources of variation reflected in the time-series data? (*d*) Why does time-series analysis deal primarily with trend and seasonal variations rather than with cyclical and irregular or random variations? (*e*) Why is time-series analysis often referred to as "naive forecasting"?
4. (*a*) What is meant by trend projection? (*b*) What does a linear trend measure? What is the other most common trend form used in time-series analysis? What does this show? Which is better? (*c*) Why might a forecast obtained by projecting a past trend into the future give very poor results even if past patterns remain unchanged?
5. (*a*) What are two methods of incorporating the past seasonal variation in the data into a trend forecast? (*b*) How is each accomplished? (*c*) Which is better?
6. (*a*) What is meant by smoothing techniques? (*b*) When are smoothing techniques useful in forecasting the future value of a time series? (*c*) What are two types of smoothing techniques? How is each undertaken?
7. (*a*) Which type of smoothing technique is generally better? (*b*) How do we determine which of two smoothing techniques is better? (*c*) How can we forecast the values of a time series that contains a secular trend as well as strong seasonal and random variations?

8. By how many months were the troughs of 1974, 1980, 1981, and 1991 in Figure 5-4 anticipated by (*a*) the composite index of the 11 leading indicators? (*b*) The diffusion index of the 11 leading indicators?
9. Is it possible for the composite index of the 11 leading indicators to rise but the diffusion index of the same 11 leading indicators to be below 50 percent for the same time period? Explain.
10. (*a*) What is meant by econometric forecasting? How is it conducted? (*b*) What are the advantages of econometric forecasting over other forecasting techniques?
11. If econometric forecasting is the best forecasting technique, what usefulness (if any) remains for other forecasting techniques?
12. (*a*) What is meant by endogenous and exogenous variables? (*b*) What is meant by structural, definitional, and reduced-form equations? What is their importance in a multiple-equation model? (*c*) If multiple-equation models require estimating or predicting the exogenous variables in order to forecast the endogenous variables, why can't we forecast the endogenous variables directly without the need for a model?

PROBLEMS

*1. The following table shows gasoline sales in the United States (in millions of barrels) from the first quarter of 1986 to the last quarter of 1989.

GASOLINE SALES IN THE UNITED STATES: 1986:1 TO 1989:4
(IN MILLIONS OF BARRELS)

1986.1	600.4	1987.1	610.8	1988.1	640.8	1989.1	639.3
1986.2	652.8	1987.2	679.5	1988.2	686.5	1989.2	681.0
1986.3	671.1	1987.3	681.2	1988.3	691.1	1989.3	685.5
1986.4	654.8	1987.4	667.6	1988.4	676.5	1989.4	677.7

Source: Survey of Current Business (Washington, D.C.: Government Printing Office), various issues.

(*a*) Estimate the linear trend in the data, and use it to forecast gasoline sales in the United States in each quarter of 1990. (*b*) Estimate the log-linear trend in the data, and use it to forecast gasoline sales in the United States in each quarter of 1990. (*c*) Which form of the trend fits the historical data better? Why would we expect both forecasts to be rather poor?

2. Adjust the linear trend projection found in Problem 1*a* for the seasonal variation in the data by using (*a*) the ratio-to-trend method and (*b*) dummy variables. (*c*) On the same graph, plot the original time series, the linear trend forecasts obtained in Problem 1*a*, and the forecasts obtained after adjustment for the seasonal variation by the ratio-to-trend method and by dummy variables.

*3. Adjust the trend forecasts of new-housing starts for each quarter of 1990 obtained from regression Equation 5-8 in Case Study 5-2 in the text by the use of dummy variables.

4. (*a*) Check the forecast of new-housing starts that was made for the four quarters of 1990 in Case Study 5-2 against data from the most recent *Survey of Current Business* available in your college library. (*b*) What is the most important reason for the difference between the forecasted and the actual number of new-housing starts in each quarter of 1990?

5. Using the index (with 1976 = 100) on new-housing starts in the United States per year from 1977 to 1988 given in the table below, forecast the index for 1989 using a three-year and a five-year moving average. Which of your estimates is better if the actual index of new-housing starts in the United States for 1989 is 89?

INDEX OF NEW-HOUSING STARTS IN THE UNITED STATES: 1977 TO 1988 (WITH 1976 = 100)

1977	1978	1979	1980	1981	1982	1983	1984	1985	1986	1987	1988
129	131	114	88	71	69	111	114	113	117	105	97

6. (*a*) Forecast the index of new-housing starts in the United States in 1989 by exponential smoothing with $w = 0.3$ and $w = 0.7$. (*b*) Which of these forecasts gives a better forecast for 1989? Which gives a better forecast on the average? (Skip this problem if "Exponential Smoothing" in Section 5-3 was not covered.)

7. The following table presents data on three leading indicators for a three-month period. Construct the composite index (with each indicator assigned equal weight) and the diffusion index.

Month	Leading Indicator *A*	Leading Indicator *B*	Leading Indicator C
1	100	200	30
2	110	230	27
3	120	240	33

8. The following table presents the monthly sales index of breakfast cereals of the Tasty Food Company for 1996 and three other time series for the same period. Indicate which time series is a (*a*) coincident indicator, (*b*) leading indicator (and the lead time), and (*c*) lagging indicator (and the lag time).

	Month											
	1	2	3	4	5	6	7	8	9	10	11	12
Index of cereal sales	110	130	125	120	130	135	150	140	150	130	120	110
Time series *A*	50	60	56	54	60	62	70	65	70	60	54	50
Time series *B*	140	130	145	150	170	160	165	170	145	143	136	135
Time series C	100	100	120	115	110	120	125	120	125	115	110	100

*9. Using estimated regression Equation 3-4 for the demand for sweet potatoes in the United States presented in Case Study 3-2, forecast the demand for sweet potatoes for (*a*) 1972 and (*b*) 1973 if the forecasted values of the independent or explanatory variables of the estimated demand equation are those given in the following table:

Year	P_S	N	Y	P_W
1972	4.10	208.78	3.19	2.41
1973	4.00	210.90	3.55	2.40

10. In their volume, *Consumer Demand in the United States: Analyses and Projections* (Cambridge, Mass.: Harvard University Press, 1970, p. 66), H. S. Houthakker and L. D. Taylor reported the following estimated demand equation for shoes in the United States over the period 1929 to 1961 (excluding the war years between 1942 and 1945):

$$Q_t = 19.575 + 0.0289X_t - 0.0923P_t - 99.568C_t - 4.06D_t$$
$$(9.3125) \quad (-1.7682) \quad (-9.8964) \quad (-3.50)$$
$$R^2 = 0.857 \qquad D\text{-}W = 1.86$$

where Q_t = per capita personal consumption expenditures on shoes and other footwear during year t, at 1954 prices
X_t = total per capita consumption expenditures during year t, at 1954 prices
P_t = relative price of shoes in year t, at 1954 prices
C_t = stock of automobiles per capita in year t
D_t = dummy variable to separate pre– from post–World War II years; $D_t = 0$ for years 1929 through 1941 and $D_t = 1$ for years 1946 to 1961

The numbers in parentheses below the estimated slope coefficients refer to the estimated t statistics.

Using the above estimated regression equation, forecast the demand for shoes for (*a*) 1962 and (*b*) 1972 if the forecasted values of the independent or explanatory variables are those given in the following table. (*c*) Why would you expect the error for the 1972 forecast to be larger than for the 1962 forecast?

Year	X	P	C
1962	1,646	20	0.4
1972	2,236	30	0.6

*11. In the simple macromodel given by Equations 5-21, 5-22, and 5-23 in Section 5-5, find the reduced-form equations for (*a*) C_t and (*b*) I_t.

12. **Integrating Problem**
In their article, "The Demand for Coffee in the United States: 1963–1977" *(Quarterly Review of Economics and Business,* Summer 1980, pp. 36–50), C. J. Huang, J. J. Siegfried, and F. Zardoshty estimated the following regression equation using quarterly data for the 58 quarters running from the first quarter of 1963 through the second quarter of 1977:

$$\ln Q_t = 1.2789 - \underset{(-2.14)}{0.1647} \ln P_t + \underset{(1.23)}{0.5115} \ln I_t + \underset{(0.55)}{0.1483} \ln P'_t - \underset{(-3.36)}{0.0089}T$$

$$-\underset{(-3.74)}{0.0961}D_{1t} - \underset{(-6.03)}{0.1570}D_{2t} - \underset{(-0.37)}{0.0097}D_{3t}$$

$$R^2 = 0.80 \qquad D\text{-}W = 2.08$$

where Q_t = quantity (in pounds) of coffee consumed per capita (for population over 16 years of age) in quarter t
P_t = relative price of coffee per pound in quarter t, at 1967 prices
I_t = per capita disposable personal income in quarter t, in thousands of 1967 dollars
P'_t = relative price of tea per quarter pound in quarter t, at 1967 prices
T = time trend; $T = 1$ for first quarter of 1963 to $T = 58$ for second quarter of 1977
D_{1t} = dummy variable equal to 1 for first quarter (spring) and 0 otherwise
D_{2t} = dummy variable equal to 1 for second quarter (summer) and 0 otherwise
D_{3t} = dummy variable equal to 1 for third quarter (fall) and 0 otherwise

The numbers in parentheses below the estimated coefficients are t statistics.

Using the above estimated regression equation for the seasonal demand for coffee in the United States and predicting that the values of the independent or explanatory variables in the demand equation from the third quarter of 1977 to the second quarter of 1978 are those indicated in the table below, forecast the demand for coffee for (*a*) the third quarter of 1977, (*b*) the fourth quarter of 1977, (*c*) the first quarter of 1978, and (*d*) the second quarter of 1978. (*e*) How much confidence can we have in these forecasts? What could cause the forecasting error to be very large?

Quarter	P	Y	P'
1977.3	1.86	3.57	1.10
1977.4	1.73	3.60	1.08
1978.1	1.60	3.63	1.07
1978.2	1.46	3.67	1.05

APPENDIX

INPUT-OUTPUT FORECASTING

A firm can also forecast sales by using input-output tables. *Input-output analysis* was introduced by Wassily Leontief and refers to the empirical study of the interdependence among the various industries and sectors of the economy. It shows the use of the output of each industry as inputs by other industries and for final consumption. For example, it shows how an increase in the demand for trucks will lead to an increase in the demand for steel, glass, tires, plastic, upholstery materials, and so on, and how the increase in the demand for these products will in turn lead to an increase in the demand for the inputs required to produce them (including trucks). Input-output analysis allows us to trace through all these interindustry input and output flows throughout the economy and to determine the total increase (direct and indirect) of all the inputs required to meet the increased demand for trucks.

The construction of such input-output tables is a very time-consuming and expensive undertaking. Most firms using input-output tables for forecasting purposes rely on the input-output tables periodically constructed by the Bureau of Economic Analysis (BEA) of the U.S. Department of Commerce. The most recent input-output table for the U.S. economy is for the year 1987 and refers to 95 industries and commodities, with a more detailed table for 480 industries and/or commodities also available. Thus, the most detailed input-output forecasting now possible is at the 480 industry-commodity level. Earlier input-output tables referred to the years 1982, 1977, 1972, 1967, 1963, 1958, and 1947. In this appendix we examine a simple input-output table, construct and explain the meaning of the direct requirements matrix and the total requirements matrix, show how input-output tables can be used for forecasting, examine some of the uses and shortcomings of input-output forecasting, and present (as Case Study 5-8) a portion of the actual input-ouput table of the U.S. economy and show how to use it for forecasting.

Input-Output Tables

Table 5-11 gives the input-output table for a very simple economy composed of three industries: *A*, *B*, and *C*. It shows the flow of inputs and outputs among the three industries. It also shows the final demand for the output of each industry, as well as the value added by each industry. The rows of Table 5-11 show the disposition of the output of each industry. For example, the first row shows that of the total output of $200 for industry *A*, $110 represents intermediate sales to firms in the same and other industries ($20 to firms in industry *A*, $60 to firms in industry *B*, and $30 to firms in industry *C*) to be used as inputs in the production activity of these industries, and $90 goes to consumers for final consumption.

On the other hand, the columns of the table indicate the input requirements of each industry, as well as the value added by the industry. For example, the first column indicates that industry *A* purchased $20 of its own output, $80 from

Table 5-11
Three-Sector Input-Output Flow Table

Supplying Industry	Producing Industry A	B	C	Final Demand	Total
A	20	60	30	90	200
B	80	90	20	110	300
C	40	30	10	20	100
Value added	60	120	40		220
Total	200	300	100	220	

industry *B*, and $40 from industry *C*, while $60 represents the value added (the profits, as well as the wages, interest payments, and taxes paid out) by industry *A*. Note that the total output of each industry (row total) equals the total costs of production, including value added (column total).

Direct Requirements Matrix

By dividing the input requirements shown in each column of Table 5-11 by the column total, we get the *direct requirements matrix*. This is shown by Table 5-12. For example, the coefficients of 0.1, 0.4, and 0.2 in column *A* of Table 5-12 are obtained by dividing the values of $20, $80, and $40 by the column total of $200 for industry *A* in Table 5-11. The coefficients in each column of Table 5-12 indicate the input requirements needed to produce each dollar of output by each industry. Thus, for each dollar of output, industry *A* requires inputs of $0.10 from industry *A*, $0.40 from industry *B*, and $0.20 from industry *C*. Hence, for industry *A* to increase its output by $100, it would require additional inputs of $10 from industry *A*, $40 from industry *B*, and $20 from industry *C*. But for industry *B* to increase output by $40, industry *B* would require additional inputs from industries *A* and *B*, as well as from industry *C* itself. These additional indirect or secondary input requirements are not taken into consideration by the direct requirements matrix.

Table 5-12
Direct Requirements Matrix

Supplying Industry	Producing Industry A	B	C
A	0.1	0.2	0.3
B	0.4	0.3	0.2
C	0.2	0.1	0.1

Total Requirements Matrix

The total (direct and indirect) input requirements needed to produce one additional dollar of output by each industry is obtained from the *total requirements matrix.*[12] For example, Table 5-13 gives the total requirements matrix derived from the direct requirements matrix of Table 5-12. Note that all the total (direct and indirect) input requirement coefficients in Table 5-13 exceed the corresponding direct input requirements in Table 5-12. The first column of Table 5-13 shows that for industry *A* the total input requirements needed to produce each dollar of output are \$1.47 from industry *A*, \$0.96 from industry *B*, and \$0.43 from industry *C*. Thus, for industry *A* to increase its output by \$100, it requires additional inputs of \$147 from industry *A*, \$96 from industry *B*, and \$43 from industry *C*.

By multiplying the total requirements matrix by the final demand for each commodity (the column vector of final demand in Table 5-11), we get the total demand for each commodity (the column vector of the total demand in Table 5-11). This is shown in Table 5-14. Specifically,

$$(1.47)(90) + (0.51)(110) + (0.60)(20) = 200$$
$$(0.96)(90) + (1.81)(110) + (0.72)(20) = 300$$
$$(0.43)(90) + (0.31)(110) + (1.33)(20) = 100$$

Forecasting with Input-Output Tables

We can now show how the total requirements matrix can be used for forecasting. Suppose that econometric forecasts indicate that next year the final demand for the output of industry *A* will increase from \$90 to \$100. Using the total requirements matrix of Table 5-14, we can now forecast the new total output of industries *A*, *B*, and *C* (rounded off to the nearest dollar) to be

$$(1.47)(100) + (0.51)(110) + (0.60)(20) = 215$$
$$(0.96)(100) + (1.81)(110) + (0.72)(20) = 310$$
$$(0.43)(100) + (0.31)(110) + (1.33)(20) = 104$$

These forecasts are internally consistent and can be used to construct a new input-output table showing the larger input demand of each industry that would result from the forecasted increase from \$90 to \$100 in the final demand of the output of industry *A*. This is shown by Table 5-15. The values in columns 2, 3, and 4 of the table are obtained by multiplying the total output of each industry

[12]The total requirements matrix is obtained by finding $(I - A)^{-1}$, where A is the direct requirements matrix, I is the identity matrix (i.e., a square matrix with 1's along the main or left-to-right diagonal and zeroes everywhere else), and the -1 refers to the inverse of matrix $(I - A)$. Finding the value of $(I - A)^{-1}$ is a complex operation and beyond the scope of this book. In the real world, it is not necessary to calculate the total requirements matrix because the Bureau of Economic Analysis of the U.S. Department of Commerce publishes it together with the input-output table of the U.S. economy (see Case Study 5-8).

Table 5-13
Total Requirements Matrix

Supplying Industry	Producing Industry		
	A	*B*	*C*
A	1.47	0.51	0.60
B	0.96	1.81	0.72
C	0.43	0.31	1.33

by the direct requirements coefficients of the industry given by Table 5-12. For example, the values in column *A* of Table 5-15 are obtained by multiplying the direct requirements of 0.1, 0.4, and 0.2 in Table 5-12 by $215.

Uses and Shortcomings of Input-Output Forecasting

Input-output analysis and forecasting has many uses and applications. It is used by firms to forecast the raw materials, labor, and capital requirements needed to meet a forecasted change in the demand for their products. It has been used by local governments to forecast the environmental impact of major development projects and programs and by the federal government to forecast the effect of the adoption of various disarmament proposals. It has been used to forecast employment changes in the various regions of the nation resulting from changes in the level of imports and exports, from energy and water shortages, and from population growth and immigration. It is also used by developing economies to evaluate the impact of various development schemes.

While input-output analysis and forecasting are very useful, they do face some serious shortcomings. One is that the direct and total requirements coefficients are assumed to be fixed and thus do not allow for input substitution in production. Commodity prices are also assumed to be constant so that commodity substitution in consumption cannot be considered either. Furthermore, input-output tables are usually available with a time lag of many years (e.g., in 1996 we still have to work with the 1987 input-output table of the U.S. economy), and while the input-output coefficients do not change very rapidly, over the course of many years they can become very biased. Finally, the reliability of the industry requirements forecasted by input-output tables depends on the reliability of the econometric forecasts of the demand for the final commodities on which they are

Table 5-14

Total Requirements Matrix	Final Demand Vector		Total Demand Vector
$\begin{bmatrix} 1.47 & 0.51 & 0.60 \\ 0.96 & 1.81 & 0.72 \\ 0.43 & 0.31 & 1.33 \end{bmatrix}$	$\begin{bmatrix} 90 \\ 110 \\ 20 \end{bmatrix}$	=	$\begin{bmatrix} 200 \\ 300 \\ 100 \end{bmatrix}$

Table 5-15
Revised Three-Sector Input-Output Flow Table

	Producing Industry				
Supplying Industry	*A*	*B*	*C*	**Final Demand**	**Total**
A	22	62	31	100	215
B	86	93	21	110	310
C	43	31	10	20	104

based. Despite these shortcomings, input-output analysis and forecasting retain a great deal of usefulness because they take into consideration the interrelationships among the various industries and sectors of the economy in an internally consistent manner.

Case Study 5-8
Using the Total Requirements Matrix for Forecasting in the United States

Table 5-16 (see pages 214–215) reproduces the first page of the total requirements matrix from the 1987 input-output table of the U.S. economy. From Table 5-16, we can see that each $1 increase in the final demand for new construction (column 11 of the table) requires $0.07938 of additional output of lumber and wood products (rows 20 and 21) and $0.00935 of paints and allied products (row 30), among other inputs. Thus, an increase of $1 million of final demand in new construction would require $79,380 of lumber and wood products, and $9,350 of paints and allied products. On the other hand, each row of Table 5-16 gives the additional output required from the particular industry resulting from each dollar increase in the final demand for the product of any industry (column). For example, each $1 increase in the final demand for agricultural products (other than livestock and livestock products, column 2 of the table) requires $0.08363 additional output of agricultural fertilizers and chemicals (row 27B).

Problem From Table 5-16, determine (*a*) by how much the output of the petroleum, refining, and related industries would have to increase for a $100,000 increase in the final demand for agricultural, forestry, and fishery services and (*b*) the additional output required from the glass and glass products industry resulting from a $200,000 increase in the final demand for new construction.

SUPPLEMENTARY READINGS

A discussion of the forecasting techniques examined in this chapter is found in:

Armstrong, J. S.: "Research on Forecasting: A Quarter Century Review, 1960–1984," *Interfaces,* vol. 16, January–February 1986.

McAuley, J. J.: *Economic Forecasting for Business* (Englewood Cliffs, N.J.: Prentice-Hall, 1986).

Granger, C. W.: *Forecasting in Economics and Business* (New York: Academic Press, 1989).

Willis, R. E.: *Guide to Forecasting for Planners and Managers* (Englewood Cliffs, N.J.: Prentice-Hall, 1987).

For qualitative forecasting, see:

Dunkelberg, W. C.: "The Use of Survey Data in Forecasting," *Business Economics,* vol. 21, January 1986.

A more advanced discussion of time-series analysis than presented in this chapter is found in:

Nelson, C. R.: *Applied Time Series Analysis for Managerial Forecasting* (San Francisco: Holden Day, 1973).

Box, G. E., and **G. M. Jenkins:** *Time Series Analysis: Forecasting and Control* (San Francisco: Holden Day, 1976).

Granger, C. W., and **P. Newbold:** *Forecasting Economic Time Series* (New York: Academic Press, 1986).

Granger, C. W., ed.: *Modeling Economic Series* (Oxford: Oxford University Press, 1990).

Harvey, A.: *The Econometric Analysis of Time Series* (Cambridge, Mass.: MIT Press, 1990).

Hamilton, J. D.: *Time Series Analysis* (Princeton, N.J.: Princeton University Press, 1994).

The double exponential smoothing technique is discussed in:

McAuley, J. J.: *Economic Forecasting for Business* (Englewood Cliffs, N.J.: Prentice-Hall, 1986), Chap. 4.

For a discussion of barometric methods, see:

Lahiri, K., and **J. Moore,** eds.: *Leading Economic Indicators: New Approaches and Forecasting Methods* (Cambridge, England: Cambridge University Press, 1991).

U.S. Department of Commerce, Bureau of Economic Analysis: *Business Conditions Digest* (Washington, D.C.: Government Printing Office, monthly).

U.S. Department of Commerce, Bureau of Economic Analysis: *Survey of Current Business* (Washington, D.C.: Government Printing Office, monthly).

Table 5-16

Total Requirements, Direct and Indirect, per Dollar of Delivery to Final Demand (at Producer's Prices), 1987

Commodity number	Each entry represents the output required, directly and indirectly, of the commodity named at the beginning of the row for each dollar of delivery to final demand of the commodity named at the head of the column	Livestock and livestock products	Other agricultural products	Forestry and fishery products	Agricultural, forestry, and fishery services	Metallic ores mining	Coal mining	Crude petroleum and natural gas	Nonmetallic minerals mining	New construction	Maintenance and repair construction	Ordnance and accessories
	Commodity number	1	2	3	4	5+6	7	8	9+10	11	12	13
1	Livestock and livestock products	1.31121	0.03283	0.03001	0.08195	0.00067	0.00045	0.00050	0.00061	0.00146	0.00149	0.00065
2	Other agricultural products	.39050	1.06613	.03557	.12721	.00079	.00058	.00056	.00068	.00222	.00226	.00072
3	Forestry and fishery products	.00213	.00092	1.01892	.00209	.00112	.00062	.00037	.00041	.00665	.00679	.00047
4	Agricultural, forestry, and fishery services	.09131	.08382	.14880	1.01938	.00079	.00060	.00147	.00067	.00681	.00694	.00052
5+6	Metallic ores mining	.00089	.00069	.00079	.00089	1.08507	.00134	.00061	.00184	.00377	.00375	.00485
7	Coal mining	.00362	.00220	.00151	.00256	.01578	1.12459	.00257	.01139	.00385	.00383	.00355
8	Crude petroleum and natural gas	.01734	.02007	.02738	.02529	.02745	.01668	1.04700	.02352	.01911	.01921	.00727
9+10	Nonmetallic minerals mining	.00511	.00981	.00309	.01289	.00289	.00256	.00111	1.04167	.01386	.01407	.00098
11	New construction	....	....	....	....	....	....	....	....	1.00010	....	....
12	Maintenance and repair construction	.02848	.02485	.02041	.02717	.03185	.02190	.03962	.02313	.01315	1.01322	.01631
13	Ordnance and accessories	.00006	.00005	.00329	.00006	.00006	.00004	.00003	.00011	.00020	.00020	1.02762
14	Food and kindred products	.21258	.00812	.05372	.02256	.00238	.00152	.00155	.00217	.00350	.00356	.00236
15	Tobacco products	(*)	....	....	(*)	....	....	....	....	....	....	....
16	Broad and narrow fabrics, yarn and thread mills	.00164	.00206	.00471	.00383	.00096	.00183	.00032	.00108	.00240	.00245	.00156
17	Miscellaneous textile goods and floor coverings	.00149	.00123	.00955	.00593	.00059	.00052	.00025	.00049	.00375	.00383	.00077
18	Apparel	.00022	.00016	.00024	.00034	.00028	.00058	.00014	.00051	.00046	.00047	.00071
19	Miscellaneous fabricated textile products	.00106	.00160	.00435	.00403	.00025	.00019	.00012	.00029	.00069	.00070	.00052
20+21	Lumber and wood products	.00704	.00825	.00370	.00512	.01238	.00674	.00376	.00385	→.07938	.08105	.00459
22+23	Furniture and fixtures	.00009	.00008	.00011	.00008	.00012	.00007	.00010	.00007	.00224	.00228	.00048
24	Paper and allied products, except containers	.01517	.00998	.00782	.01406	.00524	.00439	.00388	.00908	.01030	.01045	.00754
25	Paperboard containers and boxes	.00865	.00689	.00414	.01209	.00196	.00164	.00073	.00212	.00359	.00364	.00279
26A	Newspapers and periodicals	.00042	.00031	.00029	.00041	.00022	.00017	.00015	.00202	.00033	.00034	.00031
26B	Other printing and publishing	.00694	.00489	.00927	.00797	.00403	.00322	.00309	.00412	.00503	.00510	.00454
27A	Industrial and other chemicals	.01729	.01843	.01430	.03146	.04964	.01419	.01614	.02914	.01929	.02001	.01622
27B	Agricultural fertilizers and chemicals	.04315	→.08363	.03302	.16772	.00087	.00049	.00054	.00062	.00188	.00189	.00060
28	Plastics and synthetic materials	.00468	.00367	.00565	.00567	.00549	.00441	.00129	.00452	.00868	.00886	.00697
29A	Drugs	.00434	.00023	.00039	.00060	.00012	.00004	.00004	.00008	.00008	.00008	.00006
29B	Cleaning and toilet preparations	.00155	.00072	.00071	.00128	.00054	.00034	.00033	.00084	.00076	.00081	.00044
30	Paints and allied products	.00080	.00065	.00128	.00095	.00117	.00077	.00067	.00076	→.00935	.00954	.00110
31	Petroleum refining and related products	.02259	.02388	.04331	.02453	.03407	.02629	.00792	.02937	.02869	.02880	.00739
32	Rubber and miscellaneous plastics products	.01401	.01017	.00738	.01034	.01986	.01660	.00304	.01588	.01937	.01982	.01680
33+34	Footwear, leather, and leather products	.00059	.00014	.00046	.00045	.00009	.00008	.00006	.00010	.00021	.00021	.00015
35	Glass and glass products	.00374	.00096	.00197	.00208	.00134	.00074	.00052	.00114	.00407	.00414	.00125
36	Stone and clay products	.00315	.00375	.00215	.00353	.00776	.00649	.00644	.00923	.05991	.06047	.00498
37	Primary iron and steel manufacturing	.00762	.00569	.00745	.00605	.04067	.01940	.00805	.01587	.04262	.04069	.03645
38	Primary nonferrous metals manufacturing	.00588	.00357	.00524	.00416	.01146	.00765	.00276	.01367	.02822	.02867	.04737
39	Metal containers	.00629	.00089	.00383	.00180	.00054	.00030	.00022	.00040	.00086	.00088	.00035
40	Heating, plumbing, and fabricated structural metal products	.00255	.00232	.00227	.00216	.01045	.00676	.00298	.00818	.05362	.05423	.00247
41	Screw machine products and stampings	.00232	.00142	.00193	.00216	.00904	.00919	.00084	.00454	.00608	.00617	.01124
42	Other fabricated metal products	.00615	.00530	.01025	.00626	.00756	.00837	.00690	.00728	.02217	.02272	.02441
43	Engines and turbines	.00100	.00094	.00333	.00278	.00864	.00841	.00068	.00610	.00072	.00069	.00154
44+45	Farm, construction, and mining machinery	.00792	.00951	.00461	.00582	.02234	.04992	.00339	.02077	.00343	.00275	.00046
46	Materials handling machinery and equipment	.00028	.00029	.00019	.00036	.00608	.00461	.00016	.01216	.00282	.00287	.00019
47	Metalworking machinery and equipment	.00254	.00186	.00109	.00113	.00290	.00186	.00140	.00192	.00262	.00266	.00373

48	Special industry machinery and equipment	.00044	.00034	.00043	.00057	.00041	.00022	.00017	.00032	.00049	.00050	.00041
49	General industrial machinery and equipment	.00234	.00207	.00270	.00194	.01628	.02313	.00282	.01603	.00550	.00543	.01163
50	Miscellaneous machinery, except electrical	.00280	.00290	.00195	.00216	.00502	.00681	.00112	.00379	.00249	.00250	.00759
51	Computer and office equipment	.00043	.00036	.00052	.00068	.00057	.00028	.00022	.00062	.00068	.00069	.00178
52	Service industry machinery	.00055	.00047	.00055	.00068	.00070	.00043	.00054	.00040	.01186	.01209	.00038
53	Electrical industrial equipment and apparatus	.00167	.00144	.00145	.00139	.00734	.00707	.00293	.00765	.00798	.00810	.00428
54	Household appliances	.00015	.00014	.00022	.00021	.00015	.00010	.00016	.00012	.00267	.00272	.00008
55	Electric lighting and wiring equipment	.00143	.00134	.00107	.00143	.00189	.00200	.00111	.00143	.01732	.01767	.00103
56	Audio, video, and communication equipment	.00040	.00032	.00039	.00039	.00035	.00023	.00028	.00027	.00372	.00379	.02739
57	Electronic components and accessories	.00196	.00173	.00197	.00214	.00196	.00126	.00091	.00188	.00355	.00361	.04467
58	Miscellaneous electrical machinery and supplies	.00519	.00604	.00186	.00238	.00212	.00102	.00048	.00134	.00237	.00243	.00190
59A	Motor vehicles (passenger cars and trucks)	.00004	.00003	.00046	.00005	.00006	.00005	.00001	.00003	.00004	.00004	.00004
59B	Truck and bus bodies, trailers, and motor vehicles parts	.00477	.00478	.00436	.00610	.00607	.00250	.00088	.00177	.00337	.00342	.00284
60	Aircraft and parts	.00039	.00035	.00084	.00129	.00052	.00030	.00017	.00049	.00043	.00044	.11675
61	Other transportation equipment	.00061	.00032	.01753	.00094	.00112	.00079	.00012	.00025	.00042	.00042	.00026
62	Scientific and controlling instruments	.00068	.00040	.00214	.00056	.00134	.00048	.00031	.00062	.00313	.00319	.01599
63	Ophthalmic and photographic equipment	.00082	.00066	.00085	.00119	.00078	.00057	.00056	.00070	.00123	.00125	.00134
64	Miscellaneous manufacturing	.00101	.00079	.00082	.00152	.00088	.00058	.00043	.00099	.00235	.00240	.00071
65A	Railroads and related services; passenger ground transportation	.01947	.00802	.00504	.01207	.00989	.03300	.00251	.00694	.00804	.00800	.00385
65B	Motor freight transportation and warehousing	.05508	.03178	.01694	.03423	.01841	.01435	.00609	.02641	.03035	.03067	.01432
65C	Water transportation	.00343	.00179	.00419	.00330	.00272	.00342	.00182	.00217	.00193	.00194	.00084
65D	Air transportation	.00671	.00594	.00715	.02333	.00759	.00353	.00284	.00725	.00636	.00658	.01041
65E	Pipelines, freight forwarders, and related services	.00408	.00309	.00354	.00454	.00346	.00296	.00112	.00329	.00310	.00313	.00177
66	Communications, except radio and TV	.01348	.01010	.00723	.00881	.00756	.00538	.00534	.00752	.01314	.01329	.01117
67	Radio and TV broadcasting	.00013	.00008	.00008	.00014	.00008	.00008	.00014	.00008	.00012	.00012	.00027
68A	Electric services (utilities)	.02775	.01581	.00975	.01761	.11361	.03419	.01991	.05837	.01683	.01697	.01979
68B	Gas production and distribution (utilities)	.01027	.01148	.00654	.01454	.02918	.00682	.01317	.02748	.01047	.01048	.01106
68C	Water and sanitary services	.00534	.00650	.00227	.00355	.00408	.00370	.00227	.01163	.00251	.00252	.00238
69A	Wholesale trade	.11019	.06977	.05566	.10251	.04581	.05087	.01532	.04080	.07547	.07607	.04535
69B	Retail trade	.00619	.00583	.00417	.00728	.00487	.00263	.00232	.00259	.04162	.04242	.00185
70A	Finance	.03145	.02445	.02266	.02178	.02302	.01564	.01092	.02559	.02440	.02482	.01099
70B	Insurance	.02867	.03875	.02395	.01631	.01068	.00579	.00664	.00508	.00949	.00964	.00484
71A	Owner-occupied dwellings											
71B	Real estate and royalties	.10419	.11364	.03125	.04863	.03306	.04150	.20414	.02818	.02767	.02748	.02102
72A	Hotels and lodging places	.00349	.00268	.00378	.00351	.00373	.00166	.00166	.00984	.00447	.00455	.00380
72B	Personal and repair services (except auto)	.00329	.00294	.00351	.01025	.00210	.00136	.00112	.00305	.00233	.00237	.00189
73A	Computer and data processing services	.00591	.00473	.00820	.00977	.01162	.00394	.00277	.01494	.00874	.00888	.00477
73B	Legal, engineering, accounting, and related services	.01449	.01184	.03944	.02345	.02930	.01667	.01768	.01636	.07446	.07589	.01883
73C	Other business and professional services, except medical	.03171	.02950	.03419	.03432	.02232	.01579	.01309	.02178	.04852	.04930	.02671
73D	Advertising	.01627	.00988	.00980	.01639	.00990	.00934	.01686	.00945	.01454	.01460	.03236
74	Eating and drinking places	.00636	.00520	.00556	.00906	.00507	.00386	.00413	.00504	.00788	.00800	.00639
75	Automotive repair and services	.01253	.01040	.02350	.03384	.03590	.01335	.00560	.00662	.01908	.01942	.00638
76	Amusements	.00368	.00274	.00367	.01752	.00143	.00135	.00204	.00165	.00230	.00232	.00389
77A	Health services	.01156	.00031	.00048	.00091	.00001	(*)	.00001	.00001	.00002	.00002	.00001
77B	Educational and social services, and membership organizations	.00150	.00117	.00369	.00326	.00358	.00278	.00098	.00223	.00192	.00195	.00170
78	Federal Government enterprises	.00303	.00234	.00309	.00457	.00381	.00165	.00128	.00315	.00332	.00337	.00220
79	State and local government enterprises	.00112	.00085	.00119	.00144	.00138	.00050	.00026	.00053	.00078	.00079	.00058
80	Noncomparable imports	.00771	.00410	.00471	.00787	.00871	.00382	.01132	.00392	.00442	.00448	.00482
81	Scrap, used and secondhand goods	.00089	.00075	.00075	.00106	.00224	.00121	.00050	.00135	.00313	.00308	.00360
82	General government industry											
83	Rest of the world adjustment to final uses											
84	Household industry											
85	Inventory valuation adjustment											
	Total commodity output multiplier	**2.83998**	**1.92381**	**1.92452**	**2.17862**	**1.93812**	**1.72605**	**1.55934**	**1.70436**	**2.03525**	**2.04637**	**1.79317**

*Less than 0.000005.

Source: U.S. Department of Commerce, Bureau of Economic Analysis, *Survey of Current Business* (Washington, D.C.: Government Printing Office, May 1994), p. 72.

Econometric forecasting is discussed in:

Brandon, C., R. Fritz, and J. Xander: "Econometric Forecasts: Evaluation and Revision," *Applied Economics,* vol. 15, 1983.

Pindyck, R. S., and D. L. Rubinfeld: *Econometric Models and Economic Forecasts* (New York: McGraw-Hill, 1991), Chaps. 18–19.

Hamilton, J. D.: *Time Series Analysis* (Princeton, N.J.: Princeton University Press, 1994), Chap. 4.

Lawrence, D. B.: "Managerial Evaluation of Exogenous Forecast Sources," *Managerial and Decision Economics,* June 1991.

Leitch, G., and J. E. Tanner: "Economic Forecast Evaluation: Profit versus the Conventional Error Measure," *American Economic Review,* June 1991.

For more advanced techniques for estimating simultaneous equation models, see:

Salvatore, D.: *Theory and Problems of Statistics and Econometrics,* Schaum Outline Series (New York: McGraw-Hill, 1982), Chap. 10.

Gujarati, D.: *Basic Econometrics* (New York: McGraw-Hill, 1995), Chap. 17.

Pindyck R. S., and D. L. Rubinfeld: *Econometric Models and Economic Forecasts* (New York: McGraw-Hill, 1991), Chaps. 11–13.

Hamilton, J. D.: Time Series Analysis (Princeton, N.J.: Princeton University Press, 1994), Chap. 9.

For input-output analysis and forecasting, see:

Mohn, N. C. et al.: "Input-Output Modeling: New Sales Forecasting Tool," *University of Michigan Business Review,* July 1986.

Miller, R. E., and P. D. Blair: *Input-Output Analysis: Foundations and Extensions* (Englewood Cliffs, N.J.: Prentice-Hall, 1985).

U.S. Department of Commerce, Bureau of Economic Analysis: "Benchmark Input-Output Accounts for the U.S. Economy, 1987: Requirements Tables," *Survey of Current Business,* 1991.

INTEGRATING CASE STUDY TWO

Estimating and Forecasting the U.S. Demand for Electricity

Estimating and forecasting the demand for electricity is very important since it takes many years to build new capacity to meet future needs. Many such studies have been conducted during the past 20 years. One of these is by Halvorson, who used multiple regression analysis to estimate the market demand equation for electricity with cross-sectional data transformed into natural logarithms for the 48 contiguous states in the United States for the year 1969.

Table II-1 reports the estimated elasticity of demand for electricity for residential use in the United States with respect to the price of electricity, per capita income, the price of gas, and the number of customers in the market. While the results of the various studies differ somewhat, the results reported below indicate that the amount of electricity for residential use consumed in the United States would fall by 9.74 percent as a result of a 10 percent increase in the price of electricity, would increase by 7.14 percent with a 10 percent increase in per capita income, would increase by 1.59 percent with a 10 percent increase in the price of gas, and is proportional to the number of customers in the market. Thus, the market demand curve for electricity is negatively sloped, electricity is a normal good and a necessity, and gas is a substitute for electricity.

Table II-1
Elasticities of Demand for Electricity for Residential Use in the United States

Variable	Elasticity
Price	(−)0.974
Per capita income	0.714
Price of gas	0.159
Number of customers	1.000

Source: R. Halvorson, "Demand for Electric Energy in the United States," *Southern Economic Journal,* April 1976.

Using the above estimated demand elasticities and projecting the growth in per capita income, in the price of gas, in the number of customers in the market, and in the price of electricity, public utilities could forecast the growth in the demand for electricity in the United States so as to adequately plan new capacity to meet future needs. For example, if we assume that per capita income grows at 3 percent per year, the price of gas at 20 percent per year, the number of customers at 1 percent per year, and the price of electricity at 4 percent per year, we can forecast that the demand for electricity for residential use in the United States will expand at a rate of 2.43 percent per year. This is obtained by adding the products of the value of each elasticity by the projected growth of the corresponding variable, as indicated in the following equation:

$$
\begin{aligned}
Q &= (0.714)(3\%) + (0.159)(20\%) + (1.000)(1\%) - (0.974)(4\%) \\
&= 2.142 + 3.180 + 1.000 - 3.896 \\
&= 6.322 - 3.896 = 2.426
\end{aligned}
$$

With different projections on the yearly growth in per capita income, the price of gas, the number of customers in the market, and the price of electricity, we will get correspondingly different results.

The above results are shown in Figure II-1, where P_0 and Q_0 are the original price and quantity of electricity demanded in the United States on hypothetical demand curve D_0 in the base period (say, the current year). D' results from the projected increase in per capita income, D'' from the increase in the price of gas also, and D_1 from the increase in the number of customers in the market as well. Thus, D_1 takes into account or reflects the cumulative effect of all the growth factors considered.

Were the price of electricity to remain constant, the demand for electricity would rise by 6.322 percent per year (given by the movement from point A on D_0 to point G on D_1 in the figure). The projected increase in the price of electricity by 4 percent per year (from P_0 to P_1), by itself, will result in a decline in the quantity demanded of electricity by 3.896 percent (the movement from point G to point F on D_1). The net result of all forces at work gives rise to a net increase in Q of 2.426 percent per year (the movement from point A on D_0 to point F on D_1).

Data Resources, Wharton Econometrics, and the U.S. Department of Energy have forecasted growth in annual electricity demand of 2 to 3 percent to the turn of the century. To satisfy this increase in demand, from 100 to 200 new large electricity-generating power stations are required at the cost of hundreds of billions of dollars by the turn of the century. Since it takes from 6 to 12 years to build a new plant, electrical power companies have little time to waste. In the face of low electricity rates set by many of the nation's state regulatory commissions, however, electrical power companies prefer instead to charge higher electricity rates at times of peak demand and buying power from independent producers to avoid building the new plants. States adjacent to Canada, such as New York State, are importing (purchasing) increasing amounts of cheaper hydroelectric power from

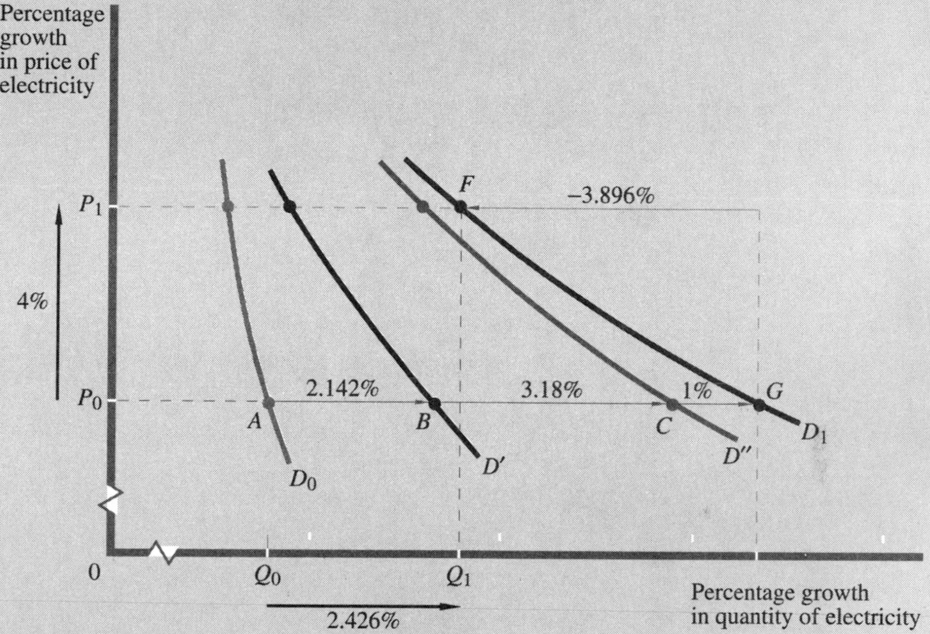

Figure II-1
Forecast of Electricity in the United States

P_0 and Q_0 are the original price and quantity of electricity demanded in the United States on demand curve D_0. D' results from projecting a 3 percent increase in per capita incomes, D'' by also projecting a 20 percent increase in the price of gas, and D_1 from a 1 percent increase in the number of customers in the market as well. If the price of electricity also increases by 4 percent (from P_0 to P_1), the demand for electricity increases by 2.426 percent per year (the movement from point *A* on D_0 to point *F* on D_1).

Canada. The electrical utility industry is now bracing for deregulation and competition. Demand studies have been conducted for practically every major commodity in the United States and are widely used by businesspeople and managers to forecast future demand. This, in turn, greatly affects investments in new plants and equipment and the general level of economic activity.

Source: R. Halvorson, "Demand for Electric Energy in the United States," *Southern Economic Journal,* April 1976; R. Barnes et al., "The Short-Run Residential Demand for Electricity," *The Review of Economics and Statistics,* November 1981; "Warding Off an Electricity Shortage," *The New York Times,* July 7, 1985, Sec. F, p. 3; "Making Power Cost-Effective," *The New York Times,* February 10, 1987, Sec. D, p. 1; "Electric Utilities Brace for an End to Monopolies," *The New York Times,* August 18, 1994, p. 1; and "A Makeover for Electric Utilities," *The New York Times,* February 3, 1995, p. D1.

PART THREE

Production and Cost Analysis

Part Three (Chapters 6 through 8) presents the theory and measurement of the firm's production and costs. These are what lie behind the firm's supply of the commodity. Chapter 6 examines production theory and measurement, or how firms combine inputs to produce goods and services. These concepts are then utilized and extended in Chapter 7 to derive the short-run and the long-run cost curves of the firm. Finally, Chapter 8 presents linear programming and examines its use in managerial economics. The rising importance of innovations and international competitiveness, as well as trade in parts and components, are examined throughout.

CHAPTER 6

Production Theory and Estimation

KEY TERMS

Production
Inputs
Fixed inputs
Variable inputs
Short run
Long run
Production function
Total product (*TP*)
Marginal product (*MP*)
Average product (*AP*)
Output elasticity
Law of diminishing returns
Stages I, II, III of production
Marginal revenue product
Marginal resource cost
Isoquant
Ridge lines
Marginal rate of technical substitution (*MRTS*)
Isocost line
Expansion path
Constant returns to scale
Increasing returns to scale
Decreasing returns to scale
Cobb-Douglas production function
Comparative advantage
Intra-industry trade
Product differentiation
Product innovation
Process innovation
Product cycle model
Just-in-time production system
Competitive benchmarking
Computer-aided design (CAD)
Computer-aided manufacturing (CAM)

CHAPTER OUTLINE

In Chapter 1, we defined the firm as an organization that combines and organizes labor, capital, ar d land or raw materials for the purpose of producing goods and services for sale. The aim of the firm is to maximize total profits or achieve some other related aim, such as maximizing sales or growth. The basic production decision facing the firm is how much of the commodity or service to produce and how much labor, capital, and other resources or inputs to use to produce that output most efficiently. To answer these questions, the firm requires engineering or technological data on production possibilities (the so-called production function) as well as economic data on input and output prices. This chapter provides the framework for understanding the economics of production of the firm and derives a set of conditions for efficient production.

The chapter begins with a discussion of the production function, which summarizes the engineering and technological production possibilities open to the firm. This general discussion is extended to the specific case where there is a single variable input or resource (Section 6-2) and examines how much of the variable input the firm should employ to maximize profits (Section 6-3). We then go on to examine the production function when there are two variable inputs (Section 6-4) and to develop the conditions for their efficient combination in production (Section 6-5). In Section 6-6, we then discuss returns to scale where all resources or inputs are variable. Section 6-7 discusses the empirical estimation of production functions. Finally, Section 6-8 deals with comparative advantage, technological progress, and innovations, and their importance for the domestic and international competitiveness of firms. In the appendix (which is optional), we use simple calculus to examine the conditions for maximizing output, minimizing costs, or maximizing profits. The many case studies presented throughout the chapter highlight the importance of production theory to the firm and its great relevance in managerial economics.

6-1 THE ORGANIZATION OF PRODUCTION AND THE PRODUCTION FUNCTION

In this section we examine first the organization of production and classify inputs into various broad categories, and then we define the meaning and usefulness of the production function in analyzing the firm's production activity.

The Organization of Production

Production refers to the transformation of inputs or resources into outputs of goods and services. For example, IBM hires workers to use machinery, parts, and raw materials in factories to produce personal computers. The output of a firm can either be a final commodity (such as a personal computer) or an intermediate product, such as semiconductors (which are used in the production of computers and other goods). The output can also be a service rather than a good. Examples of services are education, medicine, banking, communication, transportation, and many others. To be noted is that "production" refers to all of the activities involved in the production of goods and services, from borrowing to set up or expand production facilities, to hiring workers, purchasing raw materials, running quality control, cost accounting, and so on, rather than referring merely to the physical transformation of inputs into outputs of goods and services.

Inputs are the resources used in the production of goods and services. As a convenient way to organize the discussion, inputs are classified into labor (including entrepreneurial talent), capital, and land or natural resources. Each of these broad categories, however, includes a great variety of the basic input. For example, labor includes bus drivers, assembly-line workers, accountants, lawyers, doctors, scientists, and many others. Inputs are also classified as fixed or variable. **Fixed inputs** are those that cannot be readily changed during the time period under consideration, except perhaps at very great expense. Examples of fixed inputs are the firm's plant and specialized equipment (it takes several years for IBM to build a new factory to produce computer chips to go into its computers). On the other hand, **variable inputs** are those that can be varied easily and on very short notice. Examples of variable inputs are most raw materials and unskilled labor.

The time period during which at least one input is fixed is called the **short run,** while the time period when all inputs are variable is called the **long run.** The length of the long run (i.e., the time period required for all inputs to be variable) depends on the industry. For some, such as the setting up or expansion of a dry-cleaning business, the long run may be only a few months or weeks. For others, such as the construction of a new electricity-generating plant, it may be many years. In the short run, a firm can increase output only by using more of the variable inputs (say, labor and raw materials) together with the fixed inputs (plant and equipment). In the long run, the same increase in output could very likely be obtained more efficiently by also expanding the firm's production facilities (plant and equipment). Thus, we say that the firm operates in the short run and plans increases or reductions in its scale of operation in the long run. In the long run, technology usually improves, so that more output can be obtained from a given quantity of inputs, or the same output from less inputs.

The Production Function

Just as demand theory centers on the concept of the demand function, production theory revolves around the concept of the production function. A **production function** is an equation, table, or graph showing the maximum output of a commodity that a firm can produce per period of time with each set of inputs. Both inputs and outputs are measured in physical rather than in monetary units. Technology is assumed to remain constant during the period of the analysis.

For simplicity we assume here that a firm produces only one type of output (commodity or service) with two inputs, labor (L) and capital (K). Thus, the general equation of this simple production function is

$$Q = f(L, K) \tag{6-1}$$

Table 6-1
Production Function with Two Inputs

Capital (*K*)							
	6	10	24	31	36	40	39
	5	12	28	36	40	42	40
	4	12	28	36	40	40	36	Output (*Q*)
	3	10	23	33	36	36	33
↑	2	7	18	28	30	30	28
K	1	3	8	12	14	14	12
		1	2	3	4	5	6
		L →		Labor (*L*)			

Equation 6-1 reads: The quantity of output is a function of, or depends on, the quantity of labor and capital used in production. "Output" refers to the number of units of the commodity (say, automobiles) produced, "labor" refers to the number of workers employed, and "capital" refers to the amount of the equipment used in production. We assume that all units of L and K are homogeneous or identical. An explicit production function would indicate precisely the quantity of output that the firm would produce with each particular set of inputs of labor and capital. While our discussion will be in terms of a single output produced with only two inputs, the principles that we will develop are general and apply to cases where the firm uses more than two inputs and produces more than one output (the usual situation).

Table 6-1 gives a hypothetical production function which shows the outputs (the Q's) that the firm can produce with various combinations of labor (L) and capital (K). The table shows that by using 1 unit of labor ($1L$) and 1 unit of capital ($1K$), the firm would produce 3 units of output ($3Q$). With $2L$ and $1K$, output is $8Q$; with $3L$ and $1K$, output is $12Q$; with $3L$ and $2K$, output is $28Q$; with $4L$ and $2K$, output is $30Q$, and so on. Note also that labor and capital can be substituted for each other in production. For example, $12Q$ can be produced either with $3L$ and $1K$ or with $1L$ and $4K$.[1] Input prices will determine which of these two combinations of labor and capital is cheaper. The output that the firm will want to produce is the one that maximizes its total profits. These questions will be examined and answered later in the chapter.

The production relationships given in Table 6-1 are shown graphically in Figure 6-1, which is three-dimensional. In Figure 6-1, the height of the bars refers to the maximum output that can be produced with each combination of labor and capital shown on the axes. Thus, the top of all the bars forms the production surface for the firm.

If we assume that inputs and outputs are continuously or infinitesimally divisible (rather than being measured in discrete units), we would have an infinite number of outputs, each resulting from one of the infinite number of combinations

[1] $12Q$ could also be produced with $1K$ and $6L$ instead of $1K$ and $3L$ (see the last entry in the first row of the table), but the firm would certainly not want to use this combination of labor and capital. Similarly, $12Q$ could be produced with $1L$ and either $4K$ or $5K$, but the firm would not want to use the latter input combination.

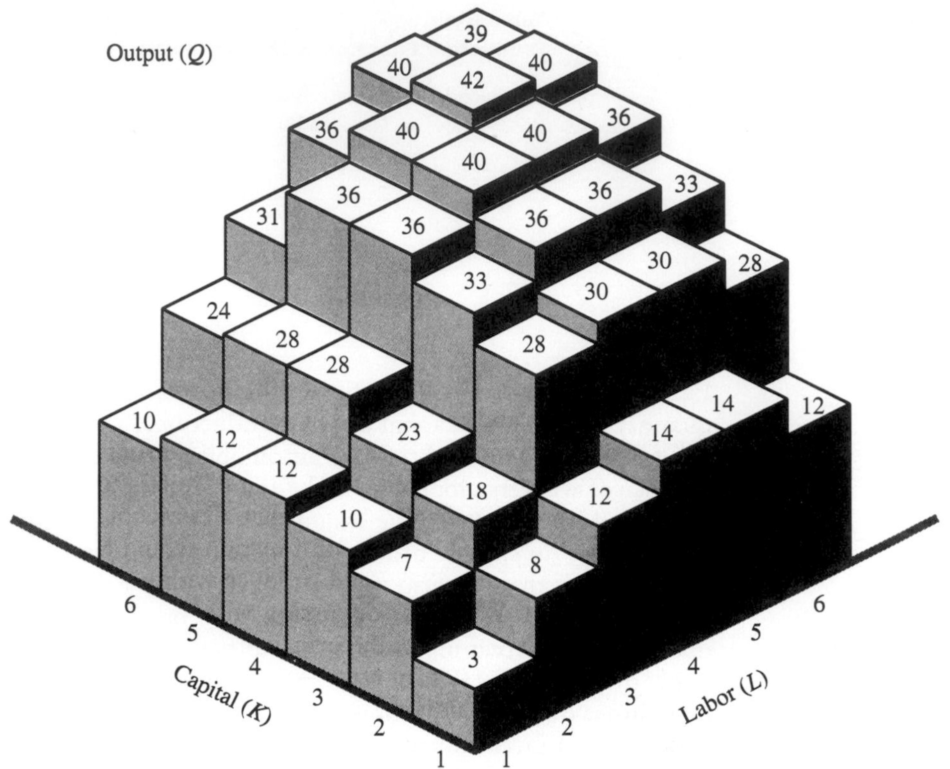

Figure 6-1
Discrete Production Surface

The height of the bars refers to the maximum output (Q) that can be produced with each combination of labor (L) and capital (K) shown on the axes. Thus, the tops of all the bars form the production surface for the firm.

of labor and capital that could be used in production. This is shown in Figure 6-2, in which the axes forming the base of the figure measure the labor and capital inputs, while the height of the surface gives the (maximum) level of output resulting from each input combination, all assumed to be continuously divisible.

For example, by keeping the quantity of capital used at K_1 in Figure 6-2 and increasing the quantity of labor used from zero to L_2 units (so that we are in the short run), the firm generates the output shown by the height of cross section K_1AB (with base parallel to the labor axis). On the other hand, by increasing the amount of labor used from zero to L_2 units but keeping capital constant at K_2 rather than K_1 (so that we are still in the short run), the firm generates the output shown by the top of cross section K_2CD. If instead the firm kept labor constant at L_1 and increased the quantity of capital used from zero to K_2 units, the firm's output would be the one shown by the top of cross section L_1EF (with base parallel to the capital axis). With labor constant at L_2, on the other hand, the firm's output generated by changing the quantity of capital used from zero to K_2 units would be the one shown by the height of cross section L_2CD.

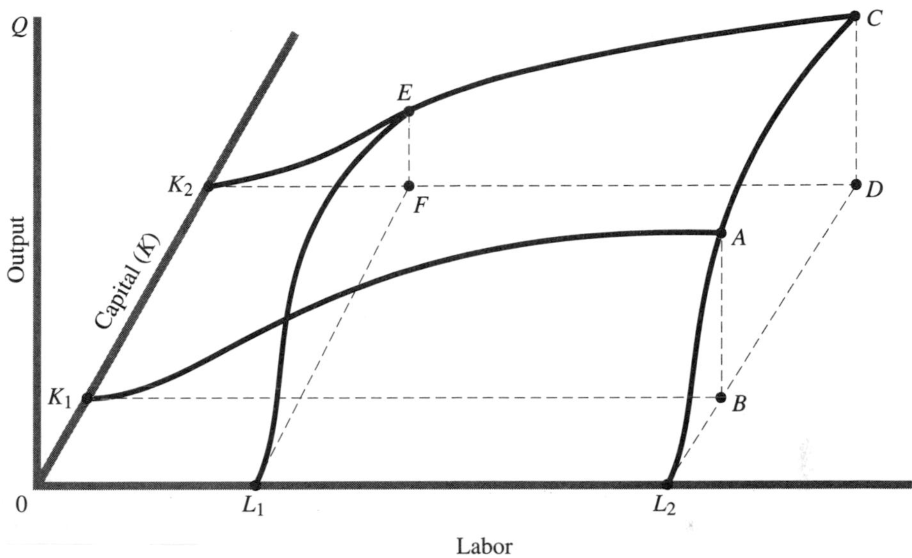

Figure 6-2
Continuous Production Surface

The horizontal and inclined axes measure, respectively, the labor and capital inputs, while the vertical axis measures the height of the surface or the maximum level of output resulting from each input combination—all assumed to be continuously divisible. The output generated by holding capital constant at K_1 and increasing labor from zero to L_2 units is given by the height of cross section K_1AB (with base parallel to the labor axis).

6-2 THE PRODUCTION FUNCTION WITH ONE VARIABLE INPUT

In this section, we present the theory of production when only one input is variable. Thus, we are in the short run. We begin by defining the total, the average, and the marginal product of the variable input and deriving from these the output elasticity of the variable input. We will then examine the law of diminishing returns and the meaning and importance of the stages of production. These concepts will be used in Section 6-3 to determine the optimal use of the variable input for the firm to maximize profits.

Total, Average, and Marginal Product

By holding the quantity of one input constant and changing the quantity used of the other input, we can derive the **total product** (*TP*) of the variable input. For example, by holding capital constant at 1 unit (i.e., with $K = 1$) and increasing the units of labor used from zero to 6 units, we generate the total product of labor given by the last row in Table 6-1, which is reproduced in column 2 of Table 6-2. Note that when no labor is used, total output or product is zero. With one unit of labor ($1L$), total product (TP) is 3. With $2L$, $TP = 8$. With $3L$, $TP = 12$, and so on.[2]

[2]The reason for the decline in *TP* when $6L$ is used will be discussed shortly.

Table 6-2
Total, Marginal, and Average Product of Labor, and Output Elasticity

(1) Labor (number of workers)	(2) Output or Total Product	(3) Marginal Product of Labor	(4) Average Product of Labor	(5) Output Elasticity of Labor
0	0	—	—	—
1	3	3	3	1
2	8	5	4	1.25
3	12	4	4	1
4	14	2	3.5	0.57
5	14	0	2.8	0
6	12	−2	2	−1

From the total product schedule we can derive the marginal and average product schedules of the variable input. The **marginal product (*MP*)** of labor (MP_L) is the change in total product or extra output per unit change in labor used, while the **average product (*AP*)** of labor (AP_L) equals total product divided by the quantity of labor used. That is,[3]

$$MP_L = \frac{\Delta TP}{\Delta L} \tag{6-2}$$

$$AP_L = \frac{TP}{L} \tag{6-3}$$

Column 3 in Table 6-2 gives the marginal product of labor (MP_L). Since labor increases by 1 unit at a time in column 1, the MP_L in column 3 is obtained by subtracting successive quantities of TP in column 2. For example, TP increases from 0 to 3 units when the first unit of labor is used. Thus, $MP_L = 3$. For an increase in labor from $1L$ to $2L$, TP rises from 3 to 8 units, so that $MP_L = 5$, and so on. Column 4 of Table 6-2 gives the AP_L. This equals TP (column 2) divided by L (column 1). Thus, with 1 unit of labor ($1L$), $AP_L = 3$. With $2L$, $AP_L = 4$, and so on.

Column 5 in Table 6-2 gives the **production** or **output elasticity** of labor (E_L). This measures the percentage change in output divided by the percentage change in the quantity of labor used. That is,

$$E_L = \frac{\%\Delta Q}{\%\Delta L} \tag{6-4}$$

By rewriting Equation 6-4 in more explicit form and rearranging, we get

$$E_L = \frac{\Delta Q/Q}{\Delta L/L} = \frac{\Delta Q/\Delta L}{Q/L} = \frac{MP_L}{AP_L} \tag{6-5}$$

[3]In terms of calculus, $MP_L = \partial TP/\partial L$.

That is, the output elasticity of labor is equal to the ratio of the MP_L to the AP_L.[4] For example, for the first unit of labor, $E_L = \frac{3}{3} = 1$. This means that from $0L$ to $1L$ (and with $K = 1$), TP or output grows proportionately to the growth in the labor input. For the second unit of labor, $E_L = 1.25$ (that is, TP or output grows more than proportionately to the increase in L), and so on.

Plotting the total, marginal, and average product of labor of Table 6-2 gives the corresponding product curves shown in Figure 6-3. Note that TP

[4]In terms of calculus,

$$E_L = \frac{\partial Q}{\partial L} \cdot \frac{L}{Q}$$

Figure 6-3
Total, Marginal, and Average Product of Labor Curves

The top panel shows the total product of labor curve. TP is highest between $4L$ and $5L$. The bottom panel shows the marginal and the average product of labor curves. The MP_L is plotted halfway between successive units of labor used. The MP_L curve rises up to $1.5L$ and then declines, and it becomes negative past $4.5L$. The AP_L is highest between $2L$ and $3L$.

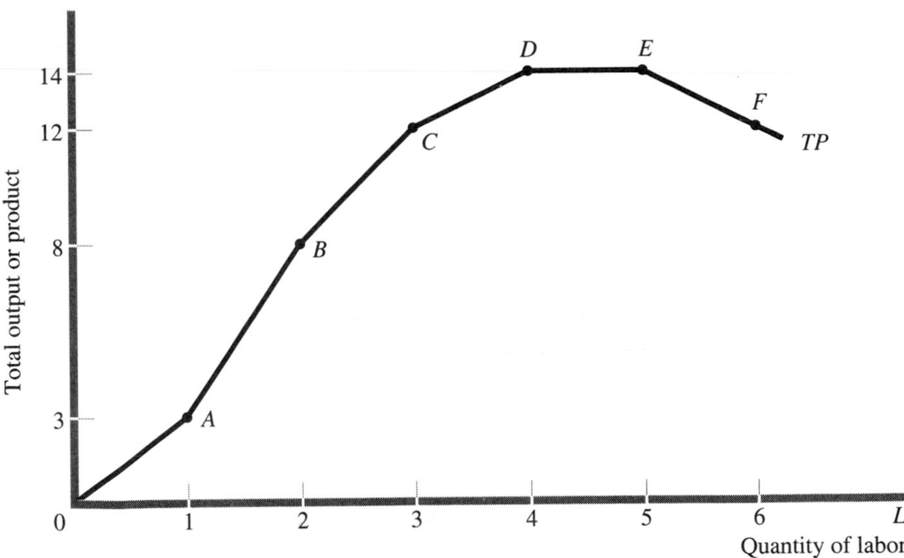

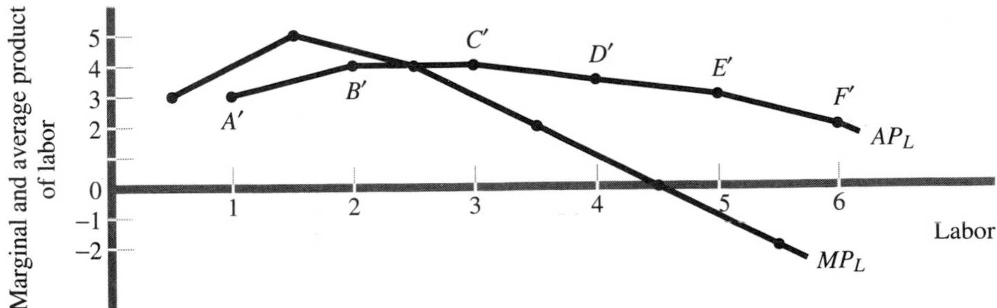

grows to 14 units with $4L$, remains at 14 units with $5L$, and then declines to 12 units with $6L$ (see the top panel of Figure 6-3). The reason for this is that with the addition of the sixth worker, workers begin to get in each other's way and total product declines. In the bottom panel, we see that AP_L rises to 4 units and then declines. Since the "marginal product of labor" refers to the change in total product per unit change in labor used, each value of the MP_L is plotted halfway between the quantities of labor used. Thus, the MP_L of 3 units of output that results by going from $0L$ to $1L$ is plotted at $0.5L$. The MP_L of 5 that results from increasing labor from $1L$ to $2L$ is plotted at $1.5L$, and so on. The MP_L curve rises to 5 units of output at $1.5L$ and then declines. Past $4.5L$, the MP_L becomes negative.

Had the firm kept capital fixed at $K = 2$, increasing the amount of labor used from $0L$ to $6L$ would have given the *TP* shown by the second row from the bottom in Table 6-1. This would correspond to the cross section at $K = 2$ in Figure 6-1. From this *TP* function and curve, we could then derive the MP_L and AP_L functions as done in Table 6-2 and shown in two-dimensional space in Figure 6-3. While the actual values of the *TP*, MP_L, and AP_L for $K = 2$ would differ from the corresponding ones with $K = 1$, the shape of the curves would generally be the same (see Problem 2, with answer at the end of the book).

The Law of Diminishing Returns and Stages of Production

In order to show graphically the relationship between the total product, on the one hand, and the marginal and average products of labor, on the other, we assume that labor time is continuously divisible (i.e., it can be hired for any part of a day). Then the *TP*, MP_L, and AP_L become smooth curves as indicated in Figure 6-4. The MP_L at a particular point on the *TP* curve is given by the slope of the *TP* curve at that point. From Figure 6-4, we see that the slope of the *TP* curve rises up to point *G* (the point of inflection on the *TP* curve), is zero at point *J*, and negative thereafter. Thus, the MP_L rises up to point G', is zero at point J', and negative afterward. On the other hand, the AP_L is given by the slope of a ray from the origin to the *TP* curve. From Figure 6-4, we see that the slope of the *TP* curve rises up to point *H* and falls thereafter but remains positive as long as *TP* is positive. Thus, the AP_L rises up to point H' and falls afterward. Note that at point *H* the slope of a ray from the origin to the *TP* curve (or AP_L) is equal to the slope of the *TP* curve (or MP_L). Thus, $AP_L = MP_L$ at point H' (the highest point on the AP_L curve). Note also that AP_L rises as long as MP_L is above it and falls when MP_L is below it.

From Figure 6-4, we can also see that up to point *G*, the *TP* curve increases at an increasing rate so that the MP_L rises. Labor is used so scarcely with the 1 unit of capital that the MP_L rises as more labor is used. Past point *G*, however, the *TP* curve rises at a decreasing rate so that the MP_L declines. The declining portion of the MP_L curve is a reflection of the **law of diminishing returns.** This postulates that as we use more and more units of the variable input with a given amount of the fixed input, after a point, we get diminishing returns (marginal product) from the variable input. In Figure 6-4, the law of diminishing returns

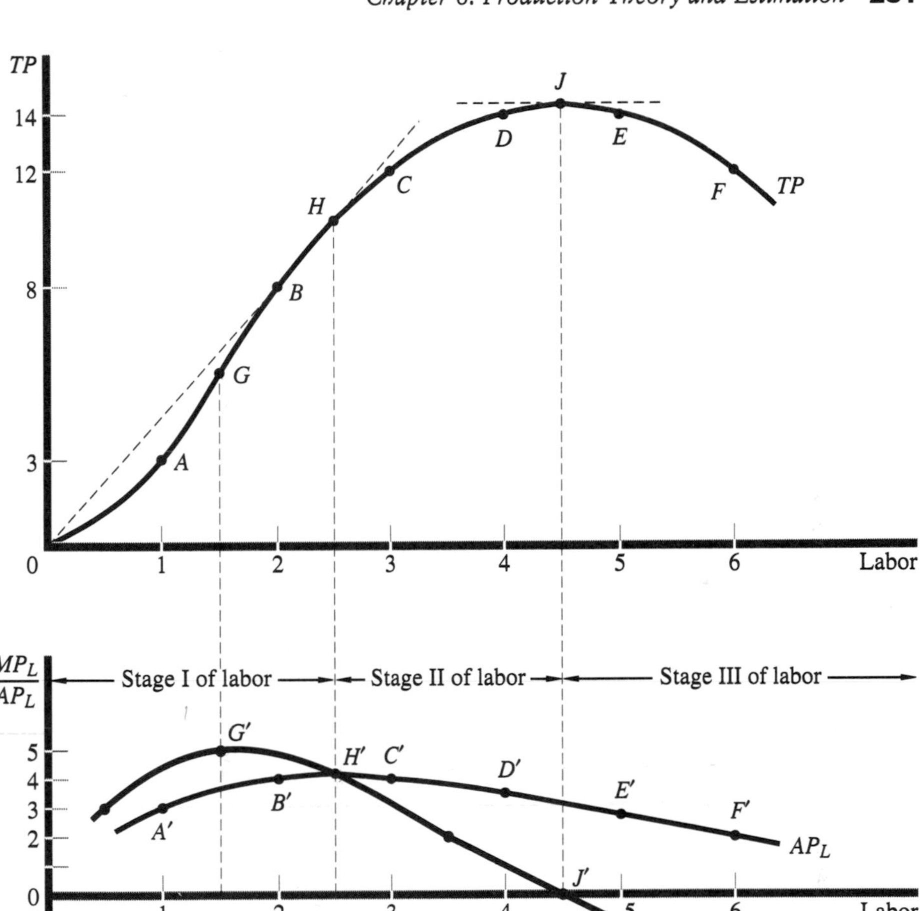

Figure 6-4
Total, Marginal, and Average Product Curves, and Stages of Production
With labor time continuously divisible, we have smooth *TP*, *MP*, and *AP* curves. The MP_L (given by the slope of the tangent to the *TP* curve) rises up to point G', becomes zero at J', and is negative thereafter. The AP_L (given by the slope of the ray from the origin to a point on the *TP* curve) rises up to point H' and declines thereafter (but remains positive as long as *TP* is positive). Stage I of production for labor corresponds to the rising portion of the AP_L. Stage II covers the range from maximum AP_L to where MP_L is zero. Stage III occurs when MP_L is negative.

begins to operate after $1.5L$ is used (after point G' in the bottom panel of Figure 6-4). Note that diminishing returns is not a theorem that can be proved or disproved with logic but is a physical law which has been found to be always empirically true. It states that after a point, we will invariably get diminishing returns from the variable input. That is, as the firm uses more and more units of the variable input with the same amount of the fixed input, each additional unit of the variable input has less and less of the fixed input to work with and, after a point, the marginal product of the variable input declines.

The relationship between the MP_L and AP_L curves in the bottom panel of Figure 6-4 can be used to define three stages of production for labor (the variable input). The range from the origin to the point where the AP_L is maximum (point H' at $2.5L$) is **stage I of production** for labor. **Stage II of production** for labor extends from the point where the AP_L is maximum to the point where the MP_L is zero (i.e., from point H' at $2.5L$ to point J' at $4.5L$). The range over which the MP_L is negative (i.e., past point J' or with more than $4.5L$) is **stage III of production** for labor. The rational producer would not operate in stage III of labor, even if labor time were free, because MP_L is negative. This means that a greater output or *TP* could be produced by using *less* labor! Similarly, he or she will not produce in stage I for labor because (as shown in more advanced texts) this corresponds to stage III of capital (where the *MP* of capital is negative).[5] Thus, the rational producer will operate in stage II where the *MP* of both factors is positive but declining. The precise point within stage II at which the rational producer operates will depend on the prices of inputs and output. This is examined in the next section.

6-3 OPTIMAL USE OF THE VARIABLE INPUT

How much labor (the variable input in our previous discussion) should the firm use in order to maximize profits? The answer is that the firm should employ an additional unit of labor as long as the extra revenue generated from the sale of the output produced exceeds the extra cost of hiring the unit of labor (i.e., until the extra revenue equals the extra cost). For example, if an additional unit of labor generates \$30 in extra revenue and costs an extra \$20 to hire, it pays for the firm to hire this unit of labor. By doing so, the firm adds \$30 to its revenues and \$20 to its costs, so that its total profits increase. It does not pay, however, for the firm to hire an additional unit of labor if the extra revenue it generates falls short of the extra cost incurred. This is an example or application of the general optimization principle examined in Chapter 2.

The extra revenue generated by the use of an additional unit of labor is called the **marginal revenue product** of labor (MRP_L). This equals the marginal product of labor (MP_L) times the marginal revenue (MR) from the sale of the extra output produced. That is,

$$MRP_L = (MP_L)(MR) \tag{6-6}$$

On the other hand, the extra cost of hiring an additional unit of labor or **marginal resource cost** of labor (MRC_L) is equal to the increase in the total cost to the firm resulting from hiring the additional unit of labor. That is,

$$MRC_L = \frac{\Delta TC}{\Delta L} \tag{6-7}$$

[5]Stage I of labor corresponds to stage III of capital only under constant returns to scale. This is the case where output changes in the same proportion as the change in all inputs (see Section 6-6).

Thus, a firm should continue to hire labor as long as $MRP_L > MRC_L$ and until $MRP_L = MRC_L$. We can examine the optimal use of labor (and profit maximization) by the firm facing the short-run production function discussed in Section 6-2 with the aid of Table 6-3.

Column 2 in Table 6-3 gives the marginal product of labor read off from the MP_L curve in stage II of production in the bottom panel of Figures 6-3 and 6-4. The fractional units of labor are based on the assumption that the firm can hire labor for the full or for half a day. Only the MP_L in stage II is given in column 2 because the firm would never produce in stage III of labor (where the MP_L is negative) or in stage I of labor (which corresponds to the stage of negative marginal product for capital). Column 3 gives the marginal revenue of \$10 from the sale of each additional unit of the commodity produced, on the assumption that the firm is small and can sell the additional units of the commodity at the given market price (P) of \$10. Column 4 gives the marginal revenue product of labor obtained by multiplying the MP_L in column 2 by the $MR = P$ of the commodity in column 3. Note that the MRP_L declines because the MP_L declines. Column 5 gives the marginal resource cost of labor on the assumption that the firm is small and can hire additional units of labor at the constant market wage rate (w) of \$20 for each half-day of work.

From Table 6-3, we see that the firm should hire 3.5 units of labor because that is where $MRP_L = MRC_L = \$20$. At less than $3.5L$, $MRP_L > MRC_L$, and the firm would be adding more to its total revenues than to its total cost by hiring more labor. For example, with $3L$, $MRP_L = \$30$, and this exceeds the MRC_L of \$20. By hiring more labor, the firm would increase its total profits. On the other hand, if the firm used more than $3.5L$, $MRP_L < MRC_L$, and the firm would be adding more to its total costs than to its total revenue, and its total profits would be lower. For example, with $4L$, $MRP_L = \$10$, while $MRC_L = \$20$. The firm could then increase its total profits by hiring less labor. Only with $3.5L$ will $MRP_L = MRC_L = \$20$, and the firm's profits are maximized. Thus, the optimal use of labor is 3.5 units. Note that the marginal revenue product of labor (MRP_L) schedule in column 4 of Table 6-3 represents the firm's demand schedule for labor. It gives the amount of labor demanded by the firm at various wage rates. For example, if the wage rate per day (w) were \$40, the firm would hire 2.5 units of

Table 6-3
Marginal Revenue Product and Marginal Resource Cost of Labor

(1) Units of Labor	(2) Marginal Product	(3) Marginal Revenue $= P$	(4) = (2) × (3) Marginal Revenue Product	(5) Marginal Resource Cost $= w$
2.5	4	\$10	\$40	\$20
3.0	3	10	30	20
3.5	2	10	20	20
4.0	1	10	10	20
4.5	0	10	0	20

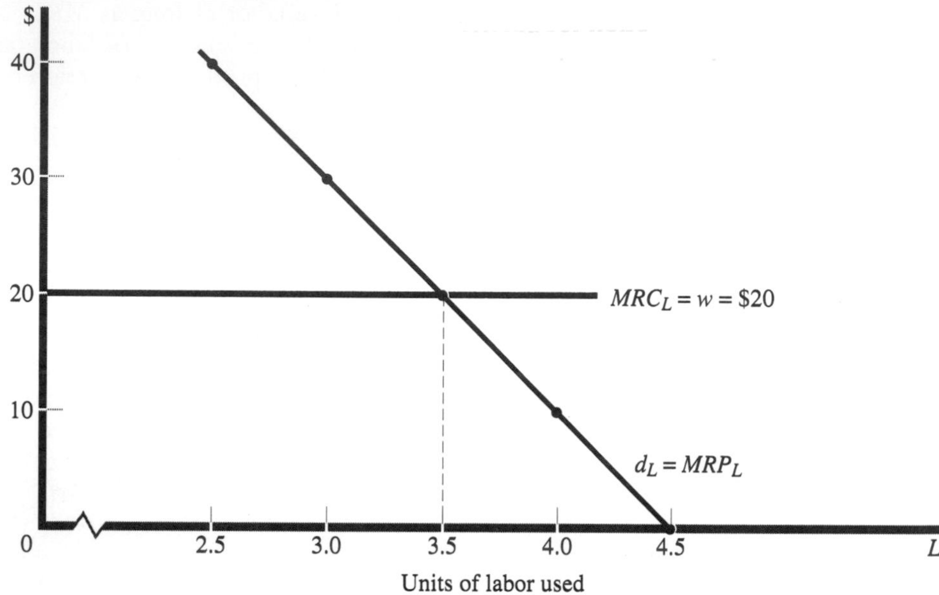

Figure 6-5
Optimal Use of Labor

It pays for the firm to hire more labor as long as the marginal revenue product of labor (MRP_L) exceeds the marginal resource cost of hiring labor (MRC_L), and until $MRP_L = MRC_L$. With $MRC_L = w = \$20$, the optimal amount of labor for the firm to use is 3.5 units. At 3.5L, $MRP_L = MRC_L = \$20$, and the firm maximizes total profits.

labor because that would be where $MRP_L = MRC_L = w = \$40$. If $w = \$30$, the firm would demand 3 units of labor. If $w = \$20$, the firm would demand 3.5L, and with $w = \$10$, the firm would demand 4L. This is shown in Figure 6-5, where $d_L = MRP_L$ represents the firm's demand curve for labor. The figure shows that if the wage rate per day (w) were constant at \$20, the firm would demand 3.5L, as indicated above.

The above discussion is applicable to any variable input, not just labor. To be noted is that the *MRP* of the variable input can be found not only by multiplying the marginal product of the input by the marginal revenue from the sale of the output produced but can also be obtained from the change in the total revenue that would result per unit change in the variable input used (see Problem 5, with answer at the end of the book).

6-4 THE PRODUCTION FUNCTION WITH TWO VARIABLE INPUTS

We will now go on to examine the production function when there are two variable inputs. This can be represented graphically by isoquants. In this section we define isoquants and discuss their characteristics. Isoquants will then be used in Section 6-5 to develop the conditions for the efficient combination of inputs in production.

Production Isoquants

An **isoquant** shows the various combinations of two inputs (say, labor and capital) that the firm can use to produce a specific level of output. A higher isoquant refers to a larger output, while a lower isoquant refers to a smaller output. Isoquants can be derived from Table 6-4, which repeats the production function of Table 6-1 with lines connecting all the labor-capital combinations that can be used to produce a specific level of output. For example, the table shows that 12 units of output (that is, 12*Q*) can be produced with 1 unit of capital (that is, 1*K*) and 3 units of labor (that is, 3*L*) or with 1*K* and 6*L*.[6] The output of 12*Q* can also be produced with 1*L* and 4*K*, and 1*L* and 5*K*. These are shown by the lowest isoquant in Figure 6-6. The isoquant is smooth on the assumption that labor and capital are continuously divisible. Table 6-4 also shows that 28*Q* can be produced with 2*K* and 3*L*, 2*K* and 6*L*, 2*L* and 4*K*, and 2*L* and 5*K* (the second isoquant marked 28*Q* in Figure 6-6). The table also shows the various combinations of *L* and *K* that can be used to produce 36*Q* and 40*Q* (shown by the top two isoquants in the figure). Note that to produce a greater output, more labor, more capital, or both more labor and capital are required.

Economic Region of Production

While the isoquants in Figure 6-6 (repeated below in Figure 6-7) have positively sloped portions, these portions are irrelevant. That is, the firm would not operate on the positively sloped portion of an isoquant because it could produce the same level of output with less capital and less labor. For example, the firm would not produce 36*Q* at point *U* in Figure 6-7 with 6*L* and 4*K* because it could produce 36*Q* by using the smaller quantities of labor and capital indicated by point *V* on the same isoquant. Similarly, the firm would not produce 36*Q* at point *W* with 4*L* and 6*K* because it could produce 36*Q* at point *Z* with less *L* and *K*. Since inputs are not free, the firm would not want to produce in the positively sloped range of isoquants.

[6]Since inputs are not free, a firm would produce 12*Q* with 1*K* and 3*L* rather than with 1*K* and 6*L*.

Table 6-4
Production Function with Two Variable Inputs

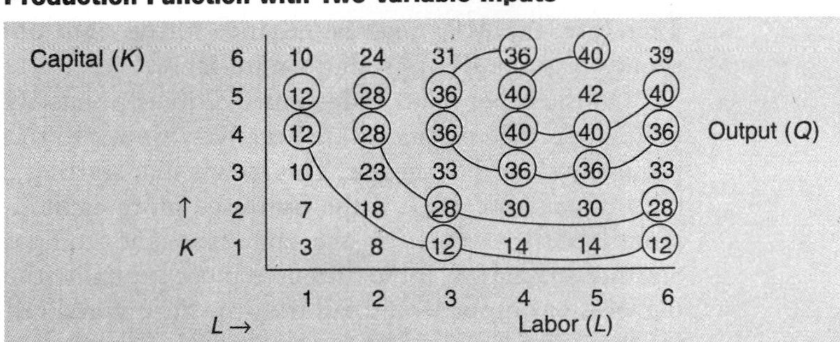

Capital (*K*) ↑ *K*							
	6	10	24	31	36	40	39
	5	12	28	36	40	42	40
	4	12	28	36	40	40	36
	3	10	23	33	36	36	33
	2	7	18	28	30	30	28
	1	3	8	12	14	14	12
L →		1	2	3	4	5	6

Labor (*L*) — Output (*Q*)

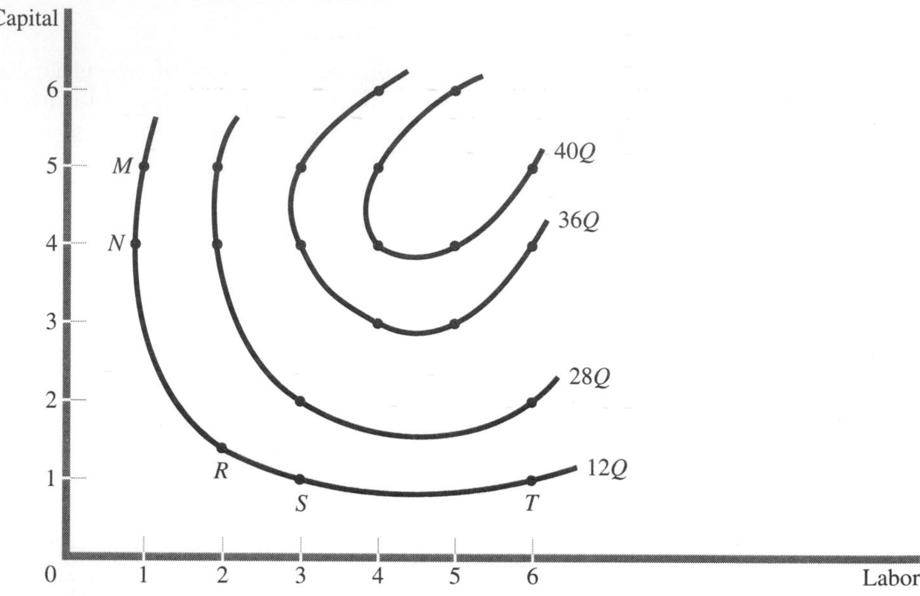

Figure 6-6
Isoquants

An isoquant shows the various combinations of two inputs that can be used to produce a specific level of output (Q). From Table 6-5, we can see that $12Q$ can be produced with $1L$ and $5K$ (point M), $1L$ and $4K$ (point N), $2L$ and $1.5K$ (point R), $3L$ and $1K$ (point S), or $6L$ and $1K$ (point T). Higher isoquants refer to higher levels of output.

Ridge lines separate the relevant (i.e., negatively sloped) from the irrelevant (or positively sloped) portions of the isoquants. In Figure 6-7, ridge line $0VI$ joins points on the various isoquants where the isoquants have zero slope. The isoquants are negatively sloped to the left of this ridge line and positively sloped to the right. This means that starting, for example, at point V on the isoquant for $36Q$, if the firm used more labor, it would also have to use more capital to remain on the same isoquant (compare point U to point V). Starting from point V, if the firm used more labor with the same amount of capital, the level of output would fall (i.e., the firm would fall back to a lower isoquant; see the dashed horizontal line in the figure). The same is true at all other points on ridge line $0VI$. Therefore, the MP_L must be negative to the right of this ridge line. This corresponds to stage III of production for labor.

On the other hand, ridge line $0ZI$ joins points where the isoquants have infinite slope. The isoquants are negatively sloped to the right of this ridge line and positively sloped to the left. This means that starting, for example, at point Z on the isoquant for $36Q$, if the firm used more capital, it would also have to use more labor to remain on the same isoquant (compare point W with point Z). Starting at point Z, if the firm used more capital with the same quantity of labor, the level of output would fall (i.e., the firm would fall back to a lower isoquant; see the dashed vertical line in the figure). The same is true at all other points on

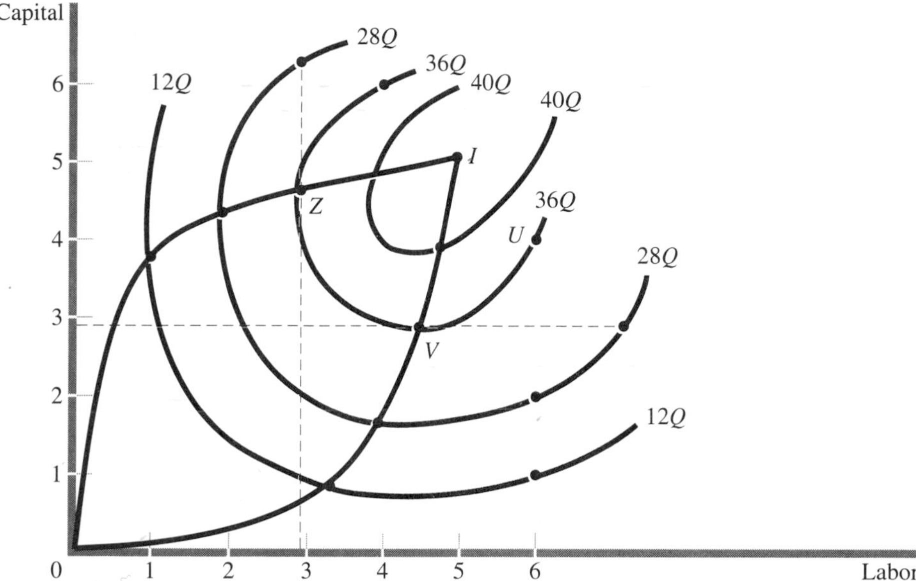

Figure 6-7
The Relevant Portion of Isoquants
The economic region of production is given by the negatively sloped segment of isoquants between ridge lines $0VI$ and $0ZI$. The firm will not produce in the positively sloped portion of the isoquants because it could produce the same level of output with both less labor and less capital.

ridge line $0ZI$. Therefore, the MP_K must be negative to the left of or above this ridge line. This corresponds to stage III of production for capital.

Thus, we conclude that the negatively sloped portion of the isoquants within the ridge lines represents the relevant economic region of production. This refers to stage II of production for labor and capital, where the MP_L and the MP_K are both positive but declining. Producers will never want to operate outside this region. As a result, in the rest of the chapter we will draw only the negatively sloped portion of isoquants.

Marginal Rate of Technical Substitution

We saw in the previous section that isoquants are negatively sloped in the economically relevant range. This means that if the firm wants to reduce the quantity of capital that it uses in production, it must increase the quantity of labor in order to remain on the same isoquant (i.e., produce the same level of output). For example, the movement from point N to point R on isoquant $12Q$ in Figure 6-8 indicates that the firm can give up $2.5K$ by adding $1L$. Thus, the slope of isoquant $12Q$ between points N and R is $-2.5K/1L$. Between points R and S, the slope of isoquant $12Q$ is $-\frac{1}{2}$, and so on.

The absolute value of the slope of the isoquant is called the **marginal rate of technical substitution** (*MRTS*). For a movement down along an isoquant, the

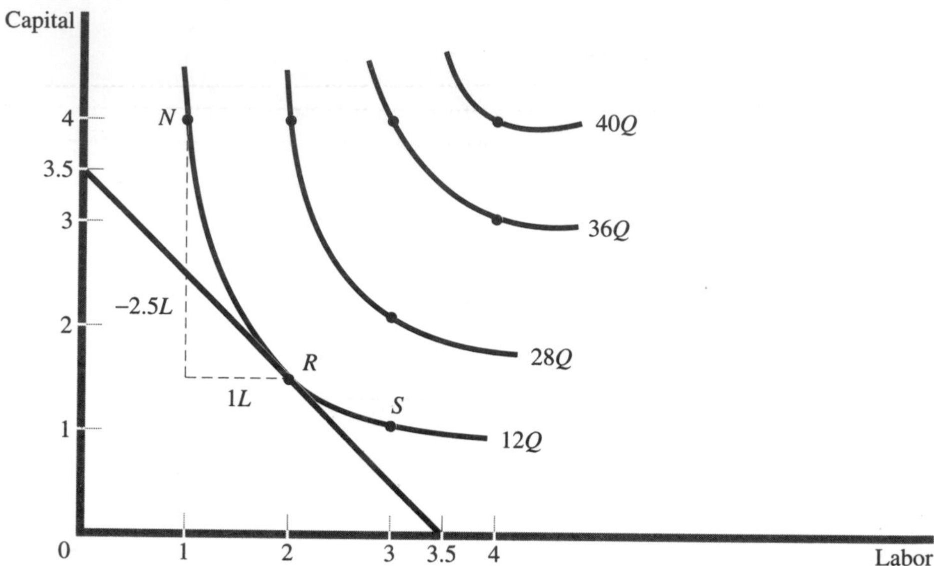

Figure 6-8
The Slope of Isoquants
The absolute value of the slope of an isoquant is called the *marginal rate of technical substitution* (*MRTS*). Between points *N* and *R* on isoquant 12*Q*, *MRTS* = 2.5. Between points *R* and *S*, *MRTS* = $\frac{1}{2}$. The *MRTS* at any point on an isoquant is given by the absolute slope of the tangent to the isoquant at that point. Thus, at point *R*, *MRTS* = 1.

marginal rate of technical substitution of labor for capital is given by $-\Delta K/\Delta L$. We multiply $\Delta K/\Delta L$ by -1 in order to express the *MRTS* as a positive number. Thus, the *MRTS* between points *N* and *R* on the isoquant for 12*Q* is 2.5. Similarly, the *MRTS* between points *R* and *S* is $\frac{1}{2}$. The *MRTS* at any point on an isoquant is given by the absolute slope of the isoquant at that point. Thus, the *MRTS* at point *R* is 1 (the absolute slope of the tangent to the isoquant at point *R*; see Figure 6-8).[7]

The *MRTS* of labor for capital is also equal to MP_L/MP_K. We can prove this by remembering that all points on an isoquant refer to the same level of

[7]The *MRTS* at a particular point on an isoquant when labor and capital are continuously divisible (so that the isoquant is a smooth curve) can be obtained by taking the total differential of the production function $Q = f(L, K)$, setting this total differential equal to zero (since output does not change along a given isoquant), and solving for dK/dL (the slope of the isoquant). That is,

$$dQ = \frac{\partial Q}{\partial L} \cdot dL + \frac{\partial Q}{\partial K} \cdot dK = 0$$

so that

$$\frac{dK}{dL} = (-)\frac{\partial Q/\partial L}{\partial Q/\partial K}$$

Since $\partial Q/\partial L = MP_L$ and $\partial Q/\partial K = MP_K$,

$$\frac{dK}{dL} = (-)\frac{MP_L}{MP_K} = MRTS$$

output. Thus, for a movement down a given isoquant, the gain in output resulting from the use of more labor must be equal to the loss in output resulting from the use of less capital. Specifically, the increase in the quantity of labor used (ΔL) times the marginal product of labor (MP_L) must equal the reduction in the amount of capital used ($-\Delta K$) times the marginal product of capital (MP_K). That is,

$$(\Delta L)(MP_L) = -(\Delta K)(MP_K) \tag{6-8}$$

so that

$$\frac{MP_L}{MP_K} = \frac{-\Delta K}{\Delta L} = MRTS \tag{6-9}$$

Thus, $MRTS$ is equal to the absolute slope of the isoquant and to the ratio of the marginal productivities.

Within the economically relevant range, isoquants are not only negatively sloped but also convex to the origin (see Figure 6-8). The reason for this is that as the firm moves down an isoquant and uses more labor and less capital, the MP_L declines and the MP_K increases (since the firm is in stage II of production for both labor and capital).[8] With the MP_L declining and the MP_K rising as we move down along an isoquant, the $MP_L/MP_K = MRTS$ will fall (thus, the isoquant is convex to the origin).

Perfect Substitutes and Complementary Inputs

The shape of an isoquant reflects the degree to which one input can be substituted for another in production. The smaller the curvature of an isoquant, the greater is the degree of substitutability of inputs in production. On the other hand, the greater the curvature of an isoquant, the smaller is the degree of substitutability.

At one extreme are isoquants that are straight lines, as shown in the left panel of Figure 6-9. In this case, labor and capital are perfect substitutes. That is, the rate at which labor can be substituted for capital in production (i.e., the absolute slope of the isoquant or $MRTS$) is constant. This means that labor can be substituted for capital (or vice versa) at the constant rate given by the absolute slope of the isoquant. For example, in the left panel of Figure 6-9, $2L$ can be substituted for $1K$ regardless of the point of production on the isoquant. In fact, point A on the labor axis shows that the level of output indicated by the middle isoquant can be produced with labor alone (i.e., without any capital). Similarly, point B on the capital axis indicates that the same level of output can be produced with capital only (i.e., without any labor). Examples of near-perfect input substitutability are oil and gas used to operate some heating furnaces, energy and time in a drying process, and fish meal and soybeans used to provide protein in a feed mix.

At the other extreme of the spectrum of input substitutability in production are isoquants that are at a right angle, as in the right panel of Figure 6-9. In this

[8]The MP_L also declines because less capital is used. On the other hand, the MP_K increases because more labor is also used.

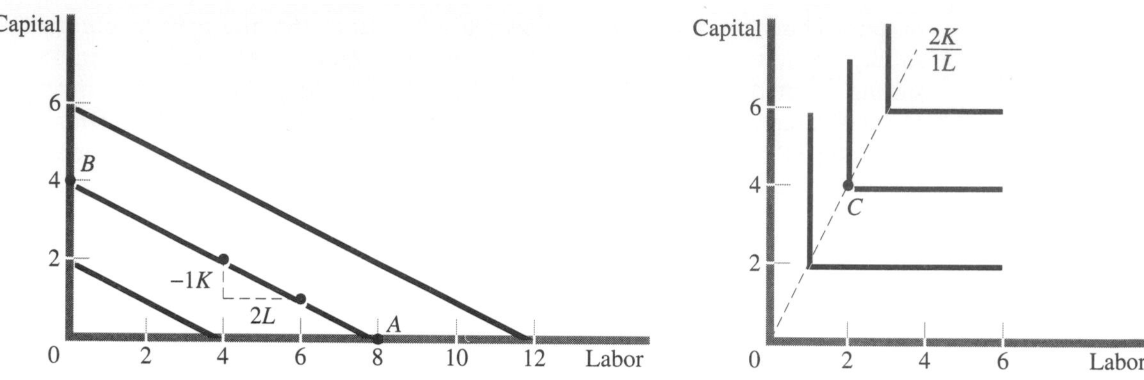

Figure 6-9
Perfect Substitutes and Complementary Inputs
When an isoquant is a straight line (so that its absolute slope or *MRTS* is constant), inputs are perfect substitutes. In the left panel, 2*L* can be substituted for 1*K* regardless of the point of production on the isoquant. With the right-angled isoquants in the right panel, efficient production can take place only with 2*K*/1*L*. Thus, labor and capital are perfect complements. Using only more labor or only more capital does not increase output (that is, $MP_L = MP_K = 0$).

case, labor and capital are perfect complements. That is, labor and capital must be used in the fixed proportion of 2*K*/1*L*. In this case there is zero substitutability between labor and capital in production. For example, starting at point C on the middle isoquant in the right panel of Figure 6-9, output remains unchanged if only the quantity of labor used is increased (that is, $MP_L = 0$ along the horizontal portion of the isoquant). Similarly, output remains unchanged if only the quantity of capital is increased (that is, $MP_K = 0$ along the vertical portion of the isoquant). Output can be increased only by increasing both the quantity of labor and capital used in the proportion of 2*K*/1*L*. Examples of perfect complementary inputs are certain chemical processes that require basic elements (chemicals) to be combined in a specified fixed proportion, engine and body for automobiles, two wheels and a frame for bicycles, and so on. In these cases, inputs can be used only in the fixed proportion specified (i.e., there is no possibility of substituting one input for another in production).

While perfect substitutability and perfect complementarity of inputs in production are possible, in most cases isoquants exhibit some curvature (i.e., inputs are imperfect substitutes), as shown in Figure 6-8. This means that in the usual production situation, labor can be substituted for capital to some degree. The smaller is the degree of curvature of the isoquant, the more easily inputs can be substituted for each other in production. In addition, when the isoquant has some curvature, the ability to substitute labor for capital (or vice versa) diminishes as more and more labor is substituted for capital. This is indicated by the declining absolute slope of the isoquant or *MRTS* as we move down along an isoquant (see Figure 6-8). The ability to substitute one input for another in production is extremely important in keeping production costs down when the price of an input increases relative to the price of another.

6-5 OPTIMAL COMBINATION OF INPUTS

As we have seen in the previous section, an isoquant shows the various combinations of labor and capital that a firm can use to produce a given level of output. In this section we examine isocosts. An **isocost line** shows the various combinations of inputs that a firm can purchase or hire at a given cost. By the use of isocosts and isoquants, we will then determine the optimal input combination for the firm to maximize profits. In this section, we will also examine input substitution in production as a result of a change in input prices.

Isocost Lines

Suppose that a firm uses only labor and capital in production. The total cost or expenditures of the firm can then be represented by

$$C = wL + rK \tag{6-10}$$

where C is total costs, w is the wage rate of labor, L is the quantity of labor used, r is the rental price of capital, and K is the quantity of capital used. Thus, Equation 6-10 postulates that the total costs of the firm (C) equals the sum of its expenditures on labor (wL) and capital (rK). Equation 6-10 is the general equation of the firm's isocost line or equal-cost line. It shows the various combinations of labor and capital that the firm can hire or rent at a given total cost. For example, if $C = \$100$, $w = \$10$, and $r = \$10$, the firm could either hire $10L$ or rent $10K$, or any combination of L and K shown on isocost line AB in the left panel of Figure 6-10. For each unit of capital the firm gives up, it can hire one additional unit of labor. Thus, the slope of the isocost line is -1.

By subtracting wL from both sides of Equation 6-10 and then dividing by r, we get the general equation of the isocost line in the following more useful form:

$$K = \frac{C}{r} - \frac{w}{r}L \tag{6-11}$$

where C/r is the vertical intercept of the isocost line and $-w/r$ is its slope. Thus, for $C = \$100$ and $w = r = \$10$, the vertical intercept is $C/r = \$100/\$10 = 10K$, and the slope is $-w/r = -\$10/\$10 = -1$ (see isocost line AB in the left panel of Figure 6-10).

A different total cost by the firm would define a different but parallel isocost line, while different relative input prices would define an isocost line with a different slope. For example, an increase in total expenditures to $C' = \$140$ with unchanged $w = r = \$10$ would give isocost line $A'B'$ in the right panel of Figure 6-10, with vertical intercept $C'/r = \$140/\$10 = 14K$ and slope of $-w/r = -\$10/\$10 = -1$. If total expenditures declined to $C'' = \$80$ with unchanged $w = r = \$10$, the isocost line would be $A''B''$, with vertical intercept of $C''/r = \$80/\$10 = 8K$ and slope of $-w/r = -\$10/\$10 = -1$. On thc other hand, with $C = \$100$ and $r = \$10$ but $w = \$5$, we would have isocost line AB^*, with vertical intercept of $C/r = \$100/\$10 = 10K$ and slope of $-w/r = -\$5/\$10 = -\frac{1}{2}$.

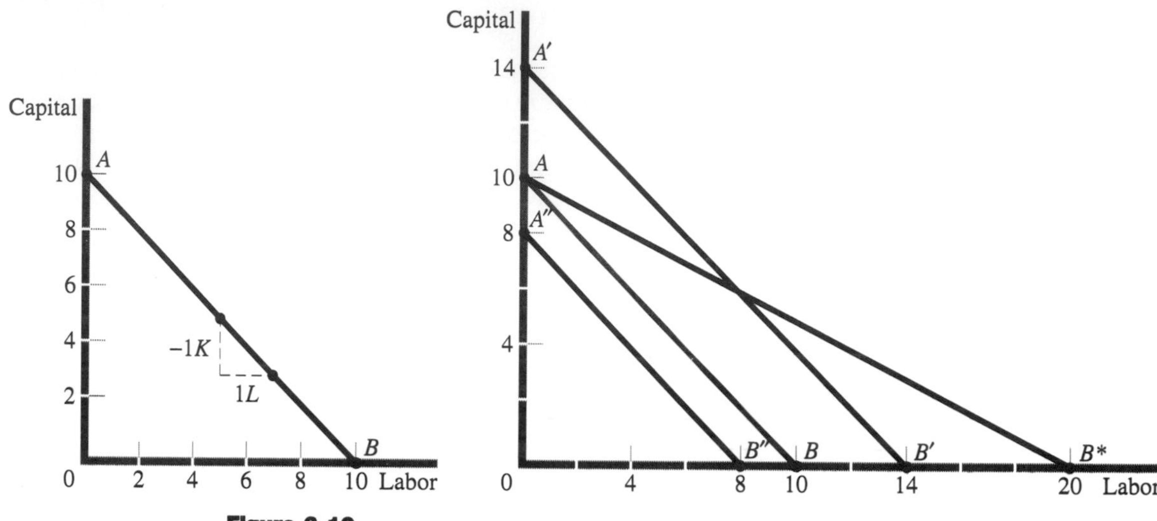

Figure 6-10
Isocost Lines

With total cost of $C = \$100$ and $w = r = \$10$, we have isocost line AB in the left panel, with vertical intercept of $C/r = \$100/\$10 = 10K$ and slope of $-w/r = -\$10/\$10 = -1$. With $C' = \$140$ and $w = r = \$10$, we have isocost line $A'B'$ in the right panel. With $C'' = \$80$ and $w = r = \$10$, the isocost line is $A''B''$ in the right panel. On the other hand, with $C = \$100$ and $r = \$10$ but $w = \$5$, we have isocost line AB^* in the right panel, with vertical intercept of $10K$ and slope of $-\frac{1}{2}$.

Optimal Input Combination for Minimizing Costs or Maximizing Output

The optimal combination of inputs needed for a firm to minimize the cost of producing a given level of output or maximize the output for a given cost outlay is given at the tangency point of an isoquant and an isocost. For example, Figure 6-11 shows that the lowest cost of producing 10 units of output (i.e., to reach isoquant $10Q$) is given by point E, where isoquant $10Q$ is tangent to isocost line AB. The firm uses $5L$ at a cost of \$50 and $5K$ at a cost of \$50 also, for a total cost of \$100 (shown by isocost AB). The output of $10Q$ can also be regarded as the maximum output that can be produced with an expenditure of \$100 (i.e., with isocost line AB).

Note that the firm could also produce $10Q$ at point G (with $3L$ and $11K$) or at point H (with $12L$ and $2K$) at a cost of \$140 (isocost $A'B'$). But this would not represent the least-cost input combination required to produce $10Q$. In fact, with an expenditure of \$140 (i.e., with isocost $A'B'$), the firm could reach isoquant $14Q$ at point F (see Figure 6-11). Similarly, the firm could produce $8Q$ efficiently at point D on isocost $A''B''$ at a cost of \$80 or inefficiently at points J and M on isocost AB at a cost of \$100. Thus, the optimal input combination needed to minimize the cost of producing a given level of output or the maximum output that the firm can produce at a given cost outlay is given at the tangency of an isoquant and an isocost.

Joining points of tangency of isoquants and isocosts (i.e., joining points of optimal input combinations) gives the **expansion path** of the firm. For example,

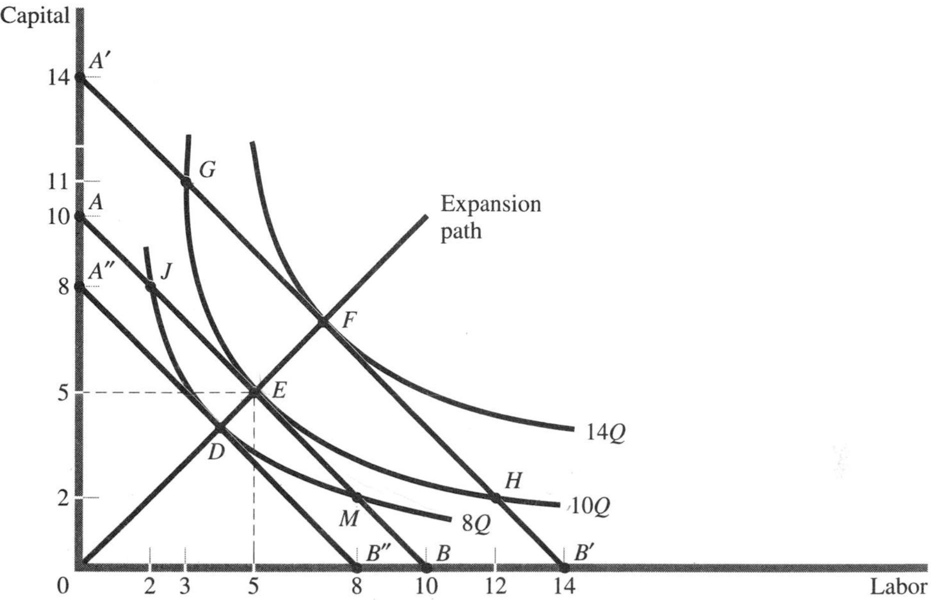

Figure 6-11
Optimal Input Combination

The optimal input combination is given by points *D*, *E*, and *F* at which isoquants 8*Q*, 10*Q*, and 14*Q* are tangent to isocosts *A″B″*, *AB*, and *A′B′*, respectively. By joining the origin with points *D*, *E*, and *F*, we get the expansion path of the firm. At the optimal input combinations (tangency points), the absolute slope of the isoquants ($MRTS = MP_L/MP_K$) equals the absolute slope of the isocost lines (w/r), so that $MP_L/w = MP_K/r$.

line 0*DEF* in Figure 6-11 is the expansion path for the firm. It shows that the minimum cost of reaching isoquants (i.e., producing) 8*Q*, 10*Q*, and 14*Q* are \$80, \$100, and \$140, given by points *D*, *E*, and *F*, respectively. It also shows that with total costs of \$80, \$100, and \$140 (i.e., with isocosts *A″B″*, *AB*, and *A′B′*) the maximum outputs that the firm can produce are 8*Q*, 10*Q*, and 14*Q*, respectively. To be noted is that not all expansion paths are straight lines through the origin as in Figure 6-11, though this is the case for most production functions estimated empirically (see Section 6-7).

With optimal input combinations (i.e., at the points of tangency of isoquants and isocost lines), the (absolute) slope of the isoquant or marginal rate of technical substitution of labor for capital is equal to the (absolute) slope of the isocost line or ratio of input prices. That is,

$$MRTS = \frac{w}{r} \tag{6-12}$$

Since the $MRTS = MP_L/MP_K$, we can rewrite the condition for the optimal combination of inputs as

$$\frac{MP_L}{MP_K} = \frac{w}{r} \tag{6-13}$$

Cross-multiplying, we get

$$\frac{MP_L}{w} = \frac{MP_K}{r} \tag{6-14}$$

Equation 6-14 indicates that to minimize production costs (or to maximize output for a given cost outlay), the extra output or marginal product per dollar spent on labor must be equal to the marginal product per dollar spent on capital. If $MP_L = 5$, $MP_K = 4$, and $w = r$, the firm would not be maximizing output or minimizing costs since it is getting more extra output for a dollar spent on labor than on capital. To maximize output or minimize costs, the firm would have to hire more labor and rent less capital. As the firm does this, the MP_L declines and the MP_K increases (since the firm is in stage II of production for L and K). The process would have to continue until condition 6-14 holds. If w were higher than r, the MP_L would have to be proportionately higher than the MP_K for condition 6-14 to hold. The same general condition for the optimal input combination would have to hold regardless of the number of inputs. That is, the *MP* per dollar spent on each input would have to be the same for all inputs.

Profit Maximization

In order to maximize profits, a firm should employ each input until the marginal revenue product of the input equals the marginal resource cost of hiring the input. With constant input prices, this means that the firm should hire each input until the marginal revenue product of the input equals the input price. This is a simple extension of the profit maximization condition discussed in Section 6-3 for the case of a single variable input. With labor and capital as the variable inputs, the firm will maximize profits by hiring labor and capital until the marginal revenue product of labor (MRP_L) equals the wage rate (w) and until the marginal revenue product of capital (MRP_K) equals the rental price of capital (r). That is, in order to maximize profits, a firm should hire labor and capital until

$$MRP_L = w \tag{6-15}$$

$$MRP_K = r \tag{6-16}$$

Hiring labor and capital so that Equations 6-15 and 6-16 hold implies that condition 6-14 for optimal input combination will also be satisfied. To see this, remember from Section 6-3 and Equation 6-6 that the marginal revenue product (*MRP*) of an input equals the marginal product of the input (*MP*) times the marginal revenue (*MR*) generated from the sale of the output. Thus, we can rewrite Equations 6-15 and 6-16 as

$$(MP_L)(MR) = w \tag{6-17}$$

$$(MP_K)(MR) = r \tag{6-18}$$

Dividing Equation 6-17 by Equation 6-18 gives

$$\frac{MP_L}{MP_K} = \frac{w}{r} \tag{6-19}$$

Cross-multiplying in Equation 6-19 gives the condition for the optimal combination of inputs given by Equation 6-14:

$$\frac{MP_L}{w} = \frac{MP_K}{r} \tag{6-14}$$

Note that there is an optimal input combination for each level of output (see points *D*, *E*, and *F* in Figure 6-11), but only at one of these outputs (the one where *MRP* of each input equals the input price) will the firm maximize profits. That is, to maximize profits, the firm must produce the profit-maximizing level of output with the optimal input combination. By hiring inputs so that Equations 6-15 and 6-16 are satisfied, however, both conditions are met at the same time. That is, the firm will be producing the best or profit-maximizing level of output with the optimal input combination.

Effect of Change in Input Prices

Starting from an optimal input combination, if the price of an input declines, the firm will substitute the cheaper input for other inputs in production in order to reach a new optimal input combination. For example, Figure 6-12 shows that with C = \$100 and $w = r =$ \$10, the optimal input combination is 5*K* and 5*L* given by point *E*, where isoquant 10*Q* is tangent to isocost *AB* (as in Figure 6-11). At point *E*, the capital-labor ratio (that is, *K*/*L*) is 1.

Figure 6-12
Input Substitution in Production

With *C* = \$100 and *w* = *r* = \$10, the optimal input combination to produce 10*Q* is 5*K* and 5*L* (point *E*, where isoquant 10*Q* is tangent to isocost *AB*). At point *E*, *K*/*L* = 1. If *r* remains at \$10 but *w* falls to \$5, the firm can reach isoquant 10*Q* with *C* = \$70. The optimal combination of *L* and *K* is then given by point *R* where isocost *A***B*′ is tangent to isoquant 10*Q*, and $K/L = \frac{3}{8}$.

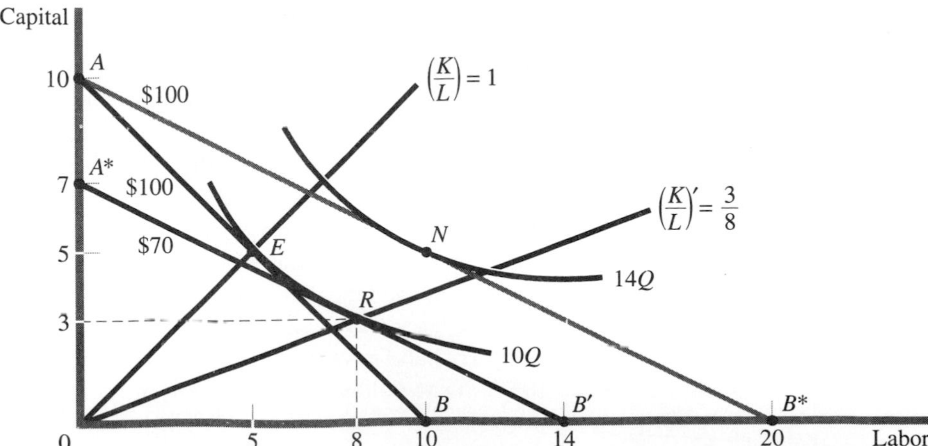

If r remains at \$10 but w falls to \$5, the isocost line becomes AB^*, and the firm can reach isoquant $14Q$ with $C = \$100$ (point N in Figure 6-12). The firm can now reach isoquant $10Q$ with $C = \$70$. This is given by isocost A^*B', which is parallel to AB^* (that is, $-w/r = -\frac{1}{2}$ for both) and is tangent to isoquant $10Q$ at point R. At point R, the firm uses $3K$ at a cost of \$30 and $8L$ at a cost of \$40, for a total cost of \$70. At point R, $K/L = \frac{3}{8}$ (as compared with $K/L = 1$ at point E before the reduction in w). Thus, with a reduction in w (and constant r), a lower C is required to produce a given level of output. To minimize the production cost of producing $10Q$, the firm will have to substitute L for K in production, so that K/L declines.

The ease with which the firm can substitute L for K in production depends on the shape of the isoquant. As we have seen in Section 6-4d, the flatter the isoquant, the easier it is to substitute L for K in production. On the other hand, if the isoquant is at a right angle (as in the right panel of Figure 6-9), no input substitution is possible (that is, $MRTS = 0$). Then, K/L will be constant regardless of input prices.

Case Study 6-1

Substitutability Between Gasoline Consumption and Driving Time

Higher highway speed reduces driving time but increases gasoline consumption by reducing gas mileage. The trade-off between gasoline consumption and traveling time for a trip of 360 miles can be represented by the isoquant shown in Figure 6-13. The isoquant shows that at 50 miles per hour, the 360 miles can be covered in 7.2 hours (that is, 7 hours and 12 minutes) with 10 gallons of gasoline, at 36 miles per gallon (point *A*). At 60 miles per hour, the 360 miles can be covered in 6 hours with 12 gallons of gasoline, at 30 miles per gallon (point *B*). Driving at 60 miles per hour saves 1 hour and 12 minutes of travel time but increases gasoline consumption by 2 gallons. At 72 miles per hour, the trip will take 5 hours and 15 gallons of gasoline, at 24 miles per gallon (point *C*). Driving at 72 miles per hour saves another 1 hour of travel time but increases gasoline consumption by another 3 gallons.

If the price of gasoline were \$2 per gallon and if the individual could have earned \$4 per hour by working rather than driving, the optimal combination of the inputs of gasoline and travel time would be at point *B* where the isoquant is tangent to isocost *DE*. At point *B*, the absolute slope of isocost *DE* is $\frac{1}{2}$ (the ratio of the price of 1 gallon of gasoline to the cost of 1 hour of driving time). The minimum cost for the trip is then \$48 (6 hours of driving time at \$4 per hour plus 12 gallons of gasoline at \$2 per gallon). If the price of gasoline fell from \$2 to \$1 per gallon, the optimal combination of driving time and gasoline would be given instead by point *C* where the isoquant is tangent to isocost line *FG*. At point *C* the absolute slope of isocost *FG* is $\frac{1}{4}$ and reflects the new relative price of gasoline (\$1 per gallon) and traveling time (\$4 per hour). The minimum cost of the trip would then be \$35 (5 hours of traveling time at \$4 per hour plus 15 gallons of gasoline at \$1 per gallon).

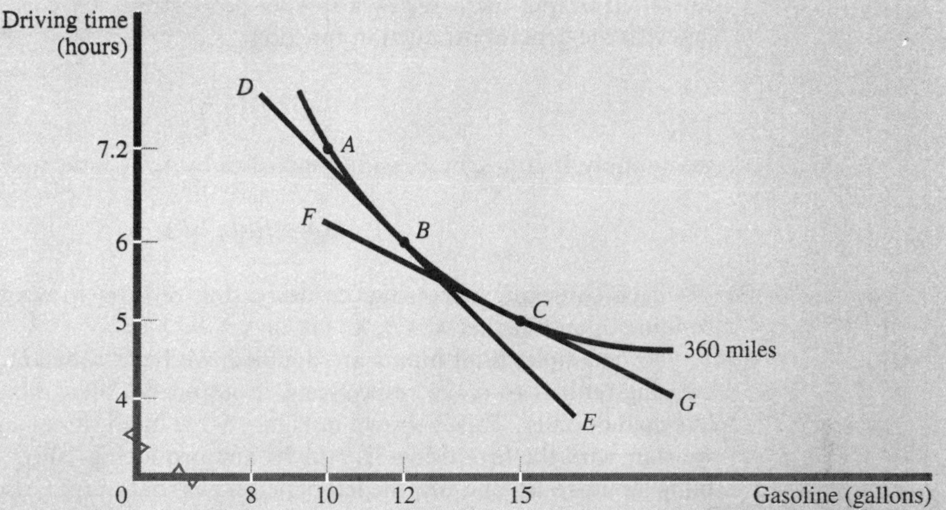

Figure 6-13
The Optimal Combination of Gasoline and Driving Time

At the gasoline price of $2 per gallon and foregone earnings of $4 per hour for driving, the minimum cost of a 360-mile trip is given by point *B*, at which the isoquant is tangent to isocost *DE*. The optimal driving speed is 60 miles per hour so that the trip would take 6 hours and 12 gallons of gasoline at a total cost of $48. If the price of gasoline falls to $1, the minimum cost of the trip is given by point *C*, at which the isoquant is tangent to isocost *FG*. The optimal driving speed is 72 miles per hour so that the trip would take 5 hours and 15 gallons of gasoline at a total cost of $35.

Thus, the repeal of the 55-mile-an-hour law in 1987 (which had been imposed in 1974 at the start of the petroleum crisis to save gasoline) seems a rational response to the decline in gasoline prices that has taken place since 1981. Opposition to the repeal of the 55-mile-an-hour law came primarily from those who believe that lower speed limits save lives. The reduction in gasoline price did, however, bring to a halt progress in energy efficiency.

Source: Charles A. Lave, "Speeding, Coordination, and the 55-MPH Limit," *American Economic Review,* December 1985, pp. 1159–1164; "U.S. Progress in Energy Efficiency Is Halting," *The New York Times,* February 27, 1989, p. 1; and "After 20 Years, America's Foot Is Still on the Gas," *The New York Times,* October 17, 1993, Sec. 3, p. 4.

6-6 RETURNS TO SCALE

"Returns to scale" refers to the degree by which output changes as a result of a given change in the quantity of all inputs used in production. We have three different types of returns to scale: constant, increasing, and decreasing. If the quantity of all inputs used in production is increased by a given proportion, we have **constant returns to scale** if output increases in the same proportion; **increasing returns to scale** if output increases by a greater proportion; and **decreasing returns**

to scale if output increases by a smaller proportion. That is, suppose that starting with the general production function

$$Q = f(L, K) \tag{6-1}$$

we multiply L and K by h, and Q increases by λ, as indicated in Equation 6-20:

$$\lambda Q = f(hL, hK) \tag{6-20}$$

We have constant, increasing, or decreasing returns to scale, respectively, depending upon whether $\lambda = h$, $\lambda > h$, or $\lambda < h$.

For example, if all inputs are doubled, we have constant, increasing, or decreasing returns to scale, respectively, if output doubles, more than doubles, or less than doubles. This is shown in Figure 6-14. In all three panels of Figure 6-14 we start with the firm using $3L$ and $3K$ and producing $100Q$ (point A). By doubling inputs to $6L$ and $6K$, the left panel shows that output also doubles to $200Q$ (point B), so that we have constant returns to scale; the center panel shows that output triples to $300Q$ (point C), so that we have increasing returns to scale, while the right panel shows that output only increases to $150Q$ (point D), so that we have decreasing returns to scale. Here h (the increase in L and K) is 100 percent, while λ (the increase in Q) is 100 percent in the left panel, 200 percent in the middle panel, and 50 percent in the right panel.

Increasing returns to scale arise because as the scale of operation increases, a greater division of labor and specialization can take place and more specialized and productive machinery can be used. Decreasing returns to scale, on the other hand, arise primarily because as the scale of operation increases, it becomes ever

Figure 6-14
Constant, Increasing, and Decreasing Returns to Scale

In all three panels of this figure we start with the firm using $3L$ and $3K$ and producing $100Q$ (point A). By doubling inputs to $6L$ and $6K$, the left panel shows that output also doubles to $200Q$ (point B), so that we have constant returns to scale; the center panel shows that output triples to $300Q$ (point C), so that we have increasing returns to scale; while the right panel shows that output only increases to $150Q$ (point D), so that we have decreasing returns to scale.

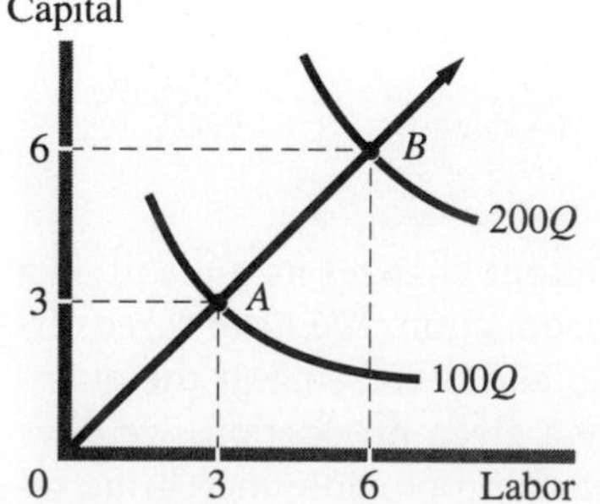

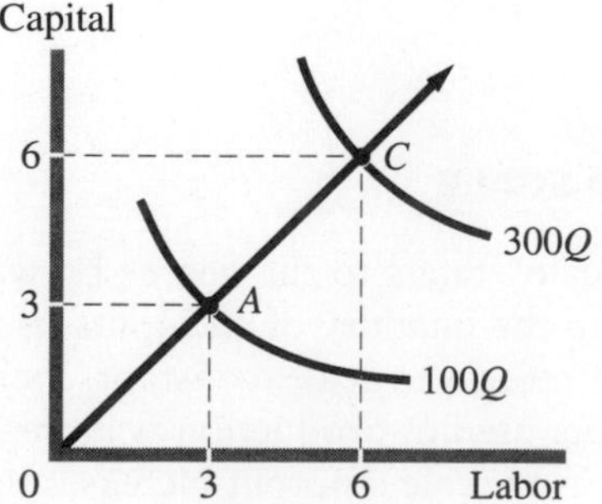

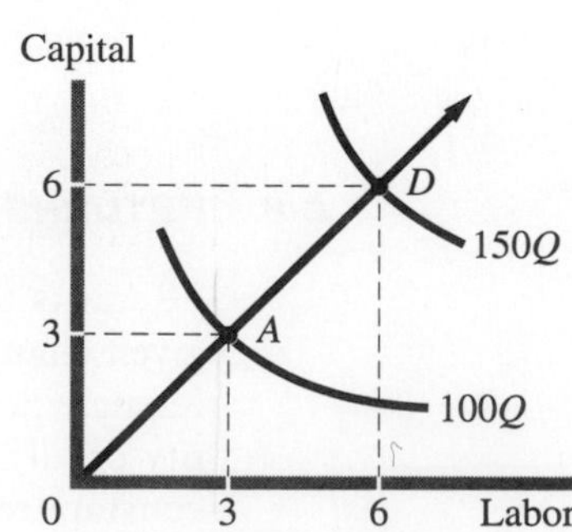

more difficult to manage the firm effectively and coordinate the various operations and divisions of the firm. In the real world, the forces for increasing and decreasing returns to scale often operate side by side, with the former usually overwhelming the latter at small levels of output and the reverse occurring at very large levels of output.

For example, in Table 6-1, we saw that with $1L$ and $1K$, we have $3Q$. With $2L$ and $2K$, we have $18Q$. Thus, we have increasing returns to scale over this range of outputs. However, doubling the amount of labor and capital used from $3L$ and $3K$ to $6L$ and $6K$ only increases output from 33 to 39 units, so that we have decreasing returns to scale over this larger range of outputs. In the real world, most industries seem to operate near the range of constant returns to scale where the forces of increasing and decreasing returns to scale are more or less in balance (see Case Study 6-2). But, as Case Study 6-3 shows, General Motors faces strong decreasing returns to scale and wants to shrink.

Case Study 6-2

Returns to Scale in U.S. Manufacturing Industries

Table 6-5 reports the estimated returns to scale in 18 manufacturing industries in the United States in 1957. A value of 1 refers to constant returns to scale, a value greater than 1 refers to increasing returns to scale, and a value less than 1 refers to decreasing returns to scale. The table shows that for a doubling of (i.e., with a 100 percent increase in) all inputs, output would rise by 111 percent in the furniture industry, by 109 percent in chemicals, but only by 95 percent in petroleum (the last entry in the second column of the table). While only the textile industry seems to face constant returns to scale exactly, most other industries are very close to it.

Table 6-5
Estimated Returns to Scale in U.S. Manufacturing in 1957

Industry	Returns to Scale	Industry	Returns to Scale
Furniture	1.11	Stone, clay, etc.	1.03
Chemicals	1.09	Fabricated metals	1.03
Printing	1.08	Electrical machinery	1.03
Food, beverages	1.07	Transport equipment	1.02
Rubber, plastics	1.06	Nonelectrical machinery	1.02
Instruments	1.04	Textiles	1.00
Lumber	1.04	Paper and pulp	0.98
Apparel	1.04	Primary metals	0.96
Leather	1.04	Petroleum	0.95

Source: J. Moroney, "Cobb-Douglas Production Functions and Returns to Scale in U.S. Manufacturing Industry," *Western Economic Journal,* December 1967, pp. 39–51.

Case Study 6-3
General Motors Decides Small Is Better

General Motors (GM), the largest corporation and car maker in the world, incurred losses of \$2 billion in 1990 and an incredible \$4.5 billion in 1991. This was the result of a bloated work force and management, low capacity utilization, too many divisions and models, and high-cost suppliers. For a corporation that had been extolled as the epitome of a successful corporation in 1946, this was a dramatic decline indeed! As the data on sales per employee in Table 6-6 seem to indicate, GM was too large and faced strong decreasing returns to scale. Chrysler, on the other hand, could still expand to take advantage of increasing returns to scale. Ford, with the largest sales per employee, seemed to be just about the right size in 1991.

As part of its reorganization plan announced in December 1991, GM closed 21 plants and shed 74,000 (50,000 blue-collar and 24,000 white-collar) workers from 1992 to 1994. The plants closed eliminated GM's excess capacity of 2 million cars and trucks per year and left GM with a 5 to 5.5 million capacity in its North American operation. It also left GM with about 33 percent of the U.S. car market—down from 46 percent in 1978 and 35 percent in 1991. The loss of GM market share during the past decade was larger than the entire Chrysler operation today and was captured by Japanese automobile imports and production in the United States. Just closing plants and reducing GM's size, however, was not sufficient. Nothing short of a complete change in corporate mentality was needed—and the job is not yet completed since GM's productivity still lags Ford's and Chrysler's.

Source: "Automobiles: GM Decides Smaller Is Better," *The Margin,* November/December 1988, p. 29; "GM Posts Record '91 Loss of \$4.45 Billion, Sends Tough Message to UAW on Closings," *The New York Times,* February 25, 1992, p. 3; and "GM's \$11 Billion Turnaround," *Fortune,* October 17, 1994, pp. 54–74.

Table 6-6
Total World Sales, Employees, and Sales per Employee at GM, Ford, and Chrysler, in 1991

	Sales (in billion dollars)	Employees (in thousands)	Sales per Employee (in thousand dollars)
General Motors	123.1	756	162.7
Ford	88.3	333	265.4
Chrysler	29.4	123	238.8

Source: The Economist, May 2, 1992, p. 78.

6-7 EMPIRICAL PRODUCTION FUNCTIONS

The production function most commonly used in empirical estimation is the power function of the form

$$Q = AK^aL^b \tag{6-21}$$

where Q, K, and L refer, respectively, to the quantities of output, capital, and labor, and A, a, and b are the parameters to be estimated empirically. Equation 6-21 is often referred to as the **Cobb-Douglas production function** in honor of Charles W. Cobb and Paul H. Douglas, who first introduced it in the 1920s.[9]

The Cobb-Douglas production function has several very useful properties. First, the marginal product of capital and the marginal product of labor depend on both the quantity of capital and the quantity of labor used in production, as is often the case in the real world.[10] Second, the exponents of K and L (that is, a and b) represent, respectively, the output elasticity of labor and capital (E_K and E_L), and the sum of the exponents (that is, $a + b$) measures the returns to scale. If $a + b = 1$, we have constant returns to scale; if $a + b > 1$, we have increasing returns to scale; and if $a + b < 1$, we have decreasing returns to scale.[11] Third, the Cobb-Douglas production function can be estimated by regression analysis by transforming it into

$$\ln Q = \ln A + a \ln K + b \ln L \tag{6-22}$$

which is linear in the logarithms. Finally, the Cobb-Douglas production function can easily be extended to deal with more than two inputs (say, capital, labor, and natural resources or capital, production labor, and nonproduction labor).

The Cobb-Douglas production function can be estimated either from data for a single firm, industry, or nation over time (i.e., using time-series analysis), or for a number of firms, industries, or nations at one point in time (i.e., using cross-sectional data). In either case, the researcher may face some difficulties. First, if the firm produces a number of different products, output may have to be measured in monetary rather than in physical units, and this will require deflating the value of output by the price index in time-series analysis or adjusting for price differences for firms and industries located in different regions in cross-sectional analysis. Second, only the capital consumed in the production of the output

[9]See C. W. Cobb and P. H. Douglas, "A Theory of Production," *American Economic Review,* March 1928, pp. 139–165.

[10]The equation for the marginal product of capital is

$$MP_K = \frac{\partial Q}{\partial K} = aAK^{a-1}L^b = a \cdot \frac{Q}{K}$$

Similarly, the equation for the marginal product of labor is

$$MP_L = \frac{\partial Q}{\partial L} = bAK^aL^{b-1} = b \cdot \frac{Q}{L}$$

The MP_K and MP_L are positive and diminishing throughout (i.e., the Cobb-Douglas production function exhibits only stage II of production for capital and labor).

[11]The output elasticity of capital is

$$E_K = \frac{\partial Q}{\partial K} \cdot \frac{K}{Q} = \frac{(aQ)}{K} \cdot \frac{K}{Q} = a$$

Similarly,

$$E_L = \frac{\partial Q}{\partial L} \cdot \frac{L}{Q} = \frac{(bQ)}{L} \cdot \frac{L}{Q} = b$$

and $E_K + E_L = a + b =$ returns to scale.

should be counted, ideally. Since machinery and equipment are of different types and ages (vintages) and productivities, however, the total stock of capital in existence has to be used instead. Third, in time-series analysis a time trend is also usually included to take into consideration technological changes over time, while in cross-sectional analysis we must ascertain that all firms or industries utilize the same technology (the best available).

Case Study 6-4

Output Elasticities in U.S. Manufacturing Industries

Table 6-7 reports the estimated output elasticities of capital (a), production workers (b), and nonproduction workers (c) for the same 18 manufacturing industries examined in Case Study 6-3. The value of $a = 0.205$ for furniture means that a 1 percent increase in the quantity of capital used (holding the number of production and nonproduction workers constant) results in a 0.205 percent increase in the quantity of furniture produced. The value of $b = 0.802$ means that a 1 percent increase in the number of production workers used (while holding the stock of capital and the number of nonproduction workers used constant) increases Q by 0.802 percent. Finally, the value of $c = 0.102$ means that a 1 percent increase in the number of nonproduction workers used (together with a constant amount of the other inputs) results in Q increasing by 0.102 percent. Increasing all three inputs at the same time by 1 percent leads to Q rising by $a + b + c = 0.205 + 0.802 + 0.102 = 1.11$ percent. This means that we have slightly increasing returns to scale in furniture production.

The values of a, b, and c reported in Table 6-7 were estimated by regression analysis with cross-sectional data for each of 18 industries for the year 1957, using a Cobb-Douglas production function extended to three inputs and transformed into natural logarithms. All estimated coefficients, with the exception of c for the rubber and plastics industry, were positive, as expected. Of the 54 estimated coefficients, 39 were statistically significant at the 5 percent level and all 18 regressions explained more than 95 percent of the variation in output (that is, R^2 exceeded 0.95). However, only the first four industries listed in the table and fabricated metals have returns to scale that are statistically different from 1 at the 5 percent level of significance. In all the other industries constant or near-constant returns to scale seemed to prevail.

Table 6-7
Output Elasticities of Capital (*a*), Production Workers (*b*), and Nonproduction Workers (*c*) in U.S. Manufacturing Industries in 1957

	Output Elasticity of			
Industry	Capital (*a*)	Production Workers (*b*)	Nonproduction Workers (*c*)	Returns to Scale (*a* + *b* + *c*)
Furniture	0.205	0.802	0.102	1.110
Chemicals	0.200	0.553	0.336	1.089
Printing	0.459	0.045	0.574	1.078
Food and beverages	0.555	0.439	0.076	1.070
Rubber and plastics	0.481	1.033	−0.458	1.056
Instruments	0.205	0.819	0.020	1.044
Lumber	0.392	0.504	0.145	1.041
Apparel	0.128	0.437	0.477	1.041
Leather	0.076	0.441	0.523	1.040
Stone, clay, etc.	0.632	0.032	0.366	1.030
Fabricated metals	0.151	0.512	0.364	1.027
Electrical machinery	0.368	0.429	0.229	1.026
Transport equipment	0.234	0.749	0.041	1.024
Nonelectrical machinery	0.404	0.228	0.389	1.021
Textiles	0.121	0.549	0.334	1.004
Paper and pulp	0.420	0.367	0.197	0.984
Primary metals	0.371	0.077	0.509	0.957
Petroleum	0.308	0.546	0.093	0.947

Source: J. Moroney, "Cobb-Douglas Production Functions and Returns to Scale in U.S. Manufacturing Industry," *Western Economic Journal,* December 1967, pp. 39–51.

6-8 COMPARATIVE ADVANTAGE, TECHNOLOGY, AND INTERNATIONAL COMPETITIVENESS

In this section we examine the meaning and importance of comparative advantage and the role that technological progress and innovations play in international competitiveness.

Comparative Advantage and International Trade

The law of **comparative advantage** postulates that even if a nation is less efficient or has an absolute disadvantage with respect to another in the production of all commodities, there is still a basis for mutually beneficial trade. The nation should specialize in the production of the commodities in which its absolute *disadvantage* is *smallest* (these are the commodities of its *comparative advantage*) and import the commodities in which its absolute *disadvantage* is *greatest* (these are the commodities of its *comparative disadvantage*). But how, you might ask, can a country that is less efficient than another in the production of all commodities be able to export anything to the more efficient nation? By input prices being sufficiently lower in the less efficient nation to make some of its commodities (those in which the nation has a comparative advantage) actually cheaper in terms of a common currency than in the other nation. Thus, India has a comparative advantage and exports labor-intensive commodities based on its relative abundance of cheap labor, while the United States has a comparative advantage and exports capital-intensive commodities based on its relative abundance of cheap capital.

A great deal of trade among developed countries today, however, is not trade in entirely different products manufactured with different input combinations under conditions of constant returns to scale. It is rather **intra-industry trade,** or trade in differentiated products produced under conditions of economies of scale. **Product differentiation** refers to products of the same industry that are similar but not identical, as, for example, the different types of automobiles on the market today. Such product differentiation satisfies the different tastes of different consumers. This is the reason that (as we have seen in Table 4-8), the United States both exports and imports chemicals, computers, automobiles, and many other products.

Intra-industry trade allows each nation to specialize in the production of some variations of the product for the domestic market and for export (thus achieving economies of scale), while importing other variations of the product from other nations at a lower price than it could produce them domestically. For example, Germany exports luxurious and expensive Mercedes automobiles to France and imports many economy Renaults from France. Nearly 50 percent of world trade and more than 60 percent of U.S. trade is now intra-industry trade.

Case Study 6-5

The Comparative Advantage of the United States, Europe, and Japan

The broad comparative advantage of a nation can be inferred from the excess in the percentage of the nation's exports over its imports relative to the total exports and imports of the nation in each product category. The rationale is that if a nation exports relatively more than it imports of a particular product, the nation must have a comparative advantage in that product.

Following this rule, we can infer from Table 6-8 that the United States has a comparative advantage in food (since U.S. food exports as a percentage of total U.S. exports exceed the percentage of U.S. food imports relative to total U.S. imports), but a comparative disadvantage in fuels, among primary commodities. In manufactures, the United States seems to have a comparative advantage in chemicals and office equipment, but a comparative disadvantage in motor vehicles and textiles. Europe seems to have a comparative advantage in motor vehicles and chemicals but a comparative disadvantage in food, fuels, office equipment, and textiles. Japan seems to have a very strong comparative advantage in motor vehicles and office equipment and an equally

Table 6-8
Composition of Exports and Imports of the United States, Europe, and Japan in 1990 and Their Revealed Comparative Advantage

	United States (% of total)		Europe (% of total)		Japan (% of total)	
	Exports	Imports	Exports	Imports	Exports	Imports
Primary commodities						
Food	12.0	6.5	10.9	12.4	0.7	16.6
Fuels	3.2	11.7	4.3	10.2	0.3	26.8
Manufacturers						
Motor vehicles	9.9	17.4	10.9	8.5	25.1	1.7
Office equipment	12.5	8.2	4.9	6.0	14.3	3.0
Textiles	1.8	6.8	6.6	7.1	2.7	5.2

Source: GATT, *International Trade, 1991–1992* (Geneva, 1992).

strong comparative disadvantage in food, fuels, chemicals, and textiles. Product differentiation is the reason for the high incidence of intra-industry trade. All three nations or group of nations have a comparative disadvantage in fuels (which they import from petroleum-exporting countries) and textiles (which they import from developing countries).

Meaning and Importance of Innovations

The introduction of innovations is the single most important determinant of a firm's long-term competitiveness at home and abroad. Innovations are basically of two types—**product innovation** (which refers to the introduction of new or improved products), and **process innovation** (the introduction of new or improved production processes). Contrary to popular belief, most innovations are incremental and involve more or less continuous small improvements in products or processes rather than a single, major technological breakthrough. Furthermore, most innovations involve the commercial utilization of ideas that may have been around for years. For example, it took a quarter of a century before firms (primarily Japanese ones) were able to perfect the flat video screen (invented in the mid-1960s by George Heilmeier of RCA) and introduce them commercially in portable PCs.

Innovations can be examined with isoquants. A new or improved product requires a new isoquant map showing the various combinations of inputs to produce each level of output of the new or improved product. On the other hand, a process innovation can be shown by a shift toward the origin of product isoquants, showing that each level of output can be produced with fewer inputs after the innovation than before. Unless a firm aggressively and continuously improves the product or the production process, it will inevitably be overtaken by other more innovative firms. This is how the Xerox Corporation, the inventor of the copier in 1959, lost its competitive edge to Japanese competitors in the 1970s before it shook off its complacency and learned again how to compete during the 1980s. To be successful in today's world, firms must adopt a global competitive strategy, which means that they must continuously scout the world for new product ideas and processes. It is also crucial for firms to have a presence, first through exports and then by local production, in the world's major markets. Larger sales mean economies of scale in production and distribution, and being able to spend more on research and development to stay ahead of the competition.

The introduction of innovations is also stimulated by strong domestic rivalry and geographic concentration—the former because it forces firms to constantly innovate or lose market share (and even risk being driven entirely out of the market), the latter because it leads to the rapid spread of new ideas and the development of specialized machinery and other inputs for the industry. It is sharp domestic rivalry and great geographic concentration that make Japanese firms in many high-tech industries such fierce competitors in world markets today.[12]

The risk in introducing innovations is usually high. For example, 8 out of 10 new products fail within a short time of their introduction. Even the most carefully introduced innovations can fail, as evidenced by the failure of RJR Nabisco Inc.'s "smokeless cigarette" and Coca-Cola's change of its 99-year-old recipe in 1985. In general, the introduction of a new product or concept (such as McDonald's hamburgers and Sony Walkmans) is more likely to succeed than changing an existing product (such as launching a new soup, cheese, or biscuit globally). Product innovations can also die from poor planning and unexpected production problems. This happened, for example, when Weyerhauser (encouraged by market testing, which showed that its product was better than competitors' products and could be produced more cheaply) introduced its UltraSoft diapers in 1990, but failed within a year because of unexpected production problems.[13]

[12]See Michael E. Porter, "The Competitive Advantage of Nations," *Harvard Business Review,* March–April 1990, pp. 75–93; Walter B. Wriston, "The State of American Management," *Harvard Business Review,* January–February 1990, pp. 78–83; and "Competition: How American Industry Stacks Up Now," *Fortune,* April 18, 1994, pp. 52–64.

[13]See "Diaper's Failure Shows How Poor Plans, Unexpected Woes Can Kill New Products," *The Wall Street Journal,* October 8, 1990, p. B11.

Case Study 6-6

How Do Firms Get New Technology?

Table 6-9 provides the result of a survey of 650 executives in 130 industries on the methods that U.S. firms use to acquire new technology on process and product innovations, arranged from the most important to the least important. From the table, we see that the most important method of acquiring product and process innovations is by independent research and development (R&D) by the firm. The other methods arranged in order of decreasing importance are: licensing technology by the firms that originally developed

Table 6-9
Methods of Acquiring New Technology

Method of Acquisition	Rank: Process Innovation	Rank: Product Innovation
Independent R&D	1	1
Licensing	2	3
Publications or technical meetings	3	5
Reverse engineering	4	2
Hiring employees of innovating firm	5	4
Patent disclosures	6	6
Conversations with employees of innovating firm	7	7

Source: R. E. Levin, "Appropriability, R&D Spending, and Technological Performance," *American Economic Review,* May 1988, pp. 424–428.

the technology; publications or technical meetings; reverse engineering (i.e., taking the competitive product apart and devising a method of producing a similar product); hiring employees of innovating firms; patent disclosures (i.e., from the detailed information available from the patent office, which can be used to develop a similar technology or product in such a way as not to infringe on the patent); or information from conversations with employees of innovating firms (who may inadvertently provide secret information in the course of general conversations). For product innovations, reverse engineering becomes more important than licensing, and hiring employees from innovating firms is more important than publications or technical meetings.

Innovations and the International Competitiveness of U.S. Firms

There was hardly a technological breakthrough during the past four decades, from TV to robots, from copiers to fax machines, from semiconductors to flat video screens, that was not made by an American firm or laboratory. According to the **product cycle model,** however, firms that first introduce an innovation eventually lose their export market and even their domestic market to foreign imitators who pay lower wages and generally face lower costs. In the meantime, however, technologically leading firms introduce even more advanced products and technologies.

The problem is that the period during which firms can exploit the benefits of successful innovations is becoming shorter and shorter before foreign imitators take the market away. In fact, in many cases, American discoveries such as the fax machine and the flat video screen were first introduced and exploited commercially by foreign (Japanese) firms. While many American firms remain world leaders in their industries (e.g., Boeing in commercial aircraft, IBM in mainframe computers, Hewlett-Packard in laser printers, Coca-Cola in soft drinks, and McDonald's in fast food—to mention only a few), firms in many other industries such as steel, automobiles, and consumer electronic products have lost competitiveness to foreign competitors, especially Japanese ones. One important reason for this is that American firms generally stress product innovation while Japanese firms stress process innovations. Thus, even when American firms are the first to introduce a new product, Japanese firms are soon able to produce it better and more cheaply, and in a few years outsell American competitors at home and abroad. This has happened in industry after industry from steel, to textiles, consumer electronic products, and automobiles.

During the 1970s and 1980s the Japanese became technological leaders in many fields and introduced many successful product and process innovations. For example, Toyota pioneered the **just-in-time production system,** which is based on every part or component becoming available just when needed. This avoids carrying costly inventories and double-handling of parts and greatly increases efficiency in general. The time required to develop new models and to switch production from one model to another at Toyota is a fraction of that at competing American automobile plants. American auto producers have learned a great deal from their Japanese competitors, but Japanese firms are not standing still and are constantly introducing new improvements in product quality and production technology.

Often Japanese firms are prepared to sustain millions of dollars of losses over many years while striving to succeed. American managers and investors, on the other hand, generally have a much shorter time horizon and are excessively concerned with quarterly statements and profits. Japanese firms also face far greater domestic rivalries and geographical concentration than their American counterparts, and thus a greater stimulus to innovate. Furthermore, as Japanese firms gained a global market share in many industries, their advantages became cumulative. Nevertheless, many American high-tech firms retain world leadership, and others have shown that they are fully capable of regaining lost competitiveness—as the following case study indicates.

Case Study 6-7

How Xerox Lost and Regained International Competitiveness

The Xerox Corporation was the first to introduce a copying machine in 1959, based on its patented xerographic technology. Until 1970, Xerox had no competition and thus had little incentive to reduce manufacturing costs, improve quality, and increase customers' satisfaction. Even when Japanese firms entered the low end of the market with better and cheaper copiers in 1970 and began to take over this segment of the market, Xerox did not respond, concentrating instead on the mid and high end of the market where profit margins were much higher. Xerox also used the profits from its copier business to expand into computers and office systems during the 1970s. It was not until 1979 that Xerox finally awakened to the seriousness of the Japanese threat. From **competitive benchmarking** missions to Japan to compare relative production efficiency and product quality, Xerox was startled to find that Japanese competitors were producing copiers of higher quality at far lower costs and were positioning themselves to move up the more profitable mid- and high-end segments of the market.

Faced with this life-threatening situation, Xerox, with the help of its Japanese subsidiary (Fuji Xerox), mounted a very strong response, which involved reorganization and integration of development and production, and an ambitious companywide quality-control effort. Employee involvement was greatly increased, suppliers were brought into the early stages of product design, and inventories and the number of suppliers were greatly reduced. Constant benchmarking was then used to test progress in the companywide quality-control program and customer satisfaction. By taking these drastic actions, Xerox was able to reverse the trend toward loss of market share to Japanese competitors, even at the low segment of the market, and it now has reinvented itself to become a digital document company.

Source: The MIT Commission on Industrial Productivity, *Made in America* (Cambridge, Mass.: The MIT Press, 1989), pp. 270–277; "Japan Is Tough, But Xerox Prevails," *The New York Times,* September 3, 1992, p. D1; and "Xerox: Well Documented," *The Economist,* October 1, 1994, pp. 88–89.

The New Computer-Aided Production Revolution and U.S. International Competitiveness

During the 1970s and the 1980s, U.S. firms in many industries steadily lost competitiveness to foreign firms, especially Japanese and German ones. Nevertheless, in 1990 U.S. labor productivity was still higher than the productivity of Japanese and German labor in many industries (see Case Study 6-8). Since then, a veritable revolution in production has been taking place in the United States, based on computer-aided design and computer-aided manufacturing, which greatly increased U.S. productivity and international competitiveness.

Computer-aided design (CAD) allows research and development engineers to design a new product or component on a computer screen, quickly experiment with different alternative designs, and test their strength and reliability—all on the screen! Then, **computer-aided manufacturing** (CAM) issues instructions to a network of integrated machine tools to produce a prototype of the new or changed product. These prototypes allow firms to avoid many possible production problems, greatly speed up the time required to develop and introduce new or improved products, and reduce the optimal lot size (i.e., the size of the production batch that minimizes production costs), thus greatly increasing the efficiency of the firm. This revolution has been taking place almost exclusively in the United States, based primarily on its world leadership and superiority in computer software and computer networks.

Case Study 6-8

Relative Labor Productivity in the United States, Japan, and Germany

Table 6-10 shows labor productivity in terms of value added per hour worked in various industries in Japan and Germany relative to the United States in 1990. Taking the labor productivity in the United States as 100, we can see from the table that Japan's labor was more productive than U.S. labor by an incredible 47 percent in steel, 24 percent in auto parts, 19 percent in metalworking, 16 percent in automobiles, and 15 percent in consumer electronics. On the other hand, U.S. labor was more productive than Japanese labor in computers, beer, soaps and detergents, and especially food. For all industries together, Japanese labor was, on the average, only 83 percent as productive as U.S. labor. Table 6-10 also shows that German labor was as productive as U.S. labor only in metalworking and steel and less productive in all other industries, especially in beer production. Overall, German labor was only 79 percent as productive as U.S. labor.

Table 6-10
Productivity of Japanese and German Labor Relative to U.S. Labor in 1990, with U.S. Index = 100

Industry	Japanese	German
Steel	147	100
Auto parts	124	76
Metalworking	119	100
Automobiles	116	66
Consumer electronics	115	76
Computer	95	89
Soap and detergents	94	76
Beer	69	44
Food	33	76
All industries	83	79

Source: McKinsey Global Institute, *Manufacturing Productivity* (Washington, D.C.: McKinsey Global Institute, 1993), Exhibit 1.

Case Study 6-9

The New U.S. Digital Factory

Welcome to the new American factory—an information age marvel that is responsible for a quantum leap in the speed, flexibility, and productivity of U.S. firms resulting from the ingenious marriage of computer software and computer networks in industries as diverse as construction equipment, automobiles, PCs, and electronic pagers. The so-called digital factory has unheard of agility that allows it to customize products down to 1 unit while achieving mass-production speed and efficiency. For example, as a Motorola salesperson specifies an order for a pager for a particular consumer, the digitized data flow to the assembly line where production begins immediately and is completed in a few minutes, so that the customer can have his or her customized pager the day after. This is sometimes called software-controlled continuous flow manufacturing—a process that is basically merging manufacturing and retailing. This much faster time-to-market and customizing capability is beginning to provide American firms with tremendous advantage over foreign competitors—including the Japanese, who seem bewildered by this new development. After years of losing the world competitive war, the United States is finally regaining some of the lost ground, and then some.

Computer-aided design (CAD) is dramatically increasing the pace of innovations. For example, a designer can call up on the screen a car door she may be working on, test opening and closing the door, running the window up and down, experiment with lighter materials, and direct machinery to make a prototype door. Such CAD allowed Chrysler to design and build its highly successful NEON subcompact car in 33 months instead of the usual 45 months. Even more exotically, scientists at Caterpillar, the largest earth-moving equipment builder in the world, test-drive huge machinery that they are developing in virtual reality before they are even built. CAD is even used to design and simulate entire assembly lines, and it can be used to send production orders to suppliers' machinery so that, in a sense, they become an extension of the firm's plant. In short, we are likely to be at the dawn of the biggest revolution in manufacturing since the perfection of the industrial lathe in the year 1800. And with the U.S. undisputed superiority in software, it is unlikely that foreign competitors can easily copy and match the new American manufacturing genius any time soon.

Source: "The Digital Factory," *Fortune,* November 14, 1994, pp. 92–110.

SUMMARY

1. "Production" refers to the transformation of inputs or resources into outputs of goods and services. Inputs are broadly classified into labor (including entrepreneurial talent), capital, and land or natural resources. Inputs can also be classified as fixed (if they cannot be readily changed during the time period under consideration) and variable (if they can be varied easily and on very short notice). The time period during which at least one input is fixed is called the "short run." If all inputs are variable, we are in the long run. A production function is an equation, table, or three-dimensional graph that shows the maximum output that a firm can produce per period of time with each set of inputs. If inputs and outputs are measured continuously, the production surface is smooth.

2. Total product (*TP*) is the output produced by using different quantities of an input with fixed quantities of the other(s). Marginal product (*MP*) is the change in total product per unit change in the variable input used.

Average product (*AP*) equals total product divided by the quantity of the variable input used. Output elasticity measures the percentage change in output or total product divided by the percentage change in the variable input used. The law of diminishing returns postulates that, after a point, the marginal product of a variable input declines. "Stage I of production" refers to the range of increasing average product of the variable input. "Stage II of production" is the range from the maximum average product of the variable input to where the marginal product of the input is zero. "Stage III of production" refers to the range of negative marginal product of the variable input.

3. The marginal revenue product (*MRP*) of the variable input equals the marginal product (*MP*) of the variable input times the marginal revenue (*MR*) from the sale of the extra output produced. The marginal resource cost (*MRC*) of a variable input is equal to the increase in total costs resulting from hiring an additional unit of the variable input. As long as *MRP* exceeds *MRC*, it pays for the firm to expand the use of the variable input because by doing so, it adds more to its total revenue than to its total cost (so that the firm's total profits rise). On the other hand, the firm should not hire those units of the variable inputs for which the *MRP* falls short of the *MRC*. The optimal use of the variable input is (i.e., the firm maximizes profits) where $MRP = MRC$ for the input.

4. An isoquant shows the various combinations of two inputs that can be used to produce a specific level of output. Ridge lines separate the relevant (i.e., the negatively sloped) from the irrelevant (or positively sloped) portions of the isoquants. The absolute slope of the isoquant is called the "marginal rate of technical substitution" (*MRTS*). This equals the ratio of the marginal products of the two inputs. As we move down along an isoquant, its absolute slope or *MRTS* declines so that the isoquant is convex to the origin. When isoquants are straight lines (so that their absolute slope or *MRTS* is constant), inputs are perfect substitutes. With right-angled isoquants, inputs can be combined only in fixed proportions (i.e., there is zero substitutability of inputs in production).

5. Given the wage rate of labor (w), the rental price of capital (r), and the total costs or expenditures of the firm (C), we can define the isocost line. This shows the various combinations of L and K that the firm can hire. With K plotted along the vertical axis, the Y intercept of the isocost line is C/r and its slope is $-w/r$. In order to minimize production costs or maximize output, the firm must produce where an isoquant is tangent to an isocost. There, $MRTS = w/r$, and $MP_L/w = MP_K/r$. Joining points of optimal input combinations where isoquants are tangent to isocosts, we get the expansion path of the firm. To maximize profits, a firm should hire each input until the marginal revenue product equals the marginal resource cost of the input. If the price of an input declines, the firm will substitute the cheaper for the more expensive input in order to reach a new optimal input combination.

6. "Constant," "increasing," and "decreasing returns to scale" refer to the situation where output changes, respectively, by the same, by a larger, and by a smaller proportion than inputs. Increasing returns to scale arise because of specialization and division of labor and from using specialized machinery. Decreasing returns to scale arise primarily because as the scale of operation increases, it becomes more and more difficult to manage the firm and coordinate its operations and divisions effectively. In the real world, most industries seem to exhibit near-constant returns to scale.
7. The most commonly used production function is the Cobb-Douglas in the form of $Q = AK^aL^b$, where a and b are the output elasticities of capital and labor, respectively. If $a + b = 1$, we have constant returns to scale; if $a + b > 1$, we have increasing returns to scale, and if $a + b < 1$, we have decreasing returns to scale. The Cobb-Douglas production function can be estimated from time-series or from cross-sectional data. In either case, difficulties may arise in the measurement of output and capital input. In time-series analysis we must also be concerned with technological change over time, and in cross-sectional analysis we must ascertain that all firms or industries utilize the same technology.
8. Comparative advantage is based on differences in relative input supplies and prices among nations. Most international trade today is intra-industry trade based on product differentiation and economies of scale. The introduction of innovations is the single most important determinant of a firm's long-term competitiveness. "Product innovations" refer to the introduction of new or improved products while "process innovations" refer to the introduction of new or improved production processes. The introduction of innovations is stimulated by taking a strong global view of competition, as well as the existence of strong domestic rivalry and geographic concentration. Many innovations die because of poor planning and unexpected production problems. During the 1970s and 1980s, American firms in many high-tech industries lost competitiveness, especially to Japanese firms, but since the turn of the decade they have regained some of it based on computer-aided design and computer-aided manufacturing.

DISCUSSION QUESTIONS

1. (*a*) What is meant by production, inputs, fixed inputs, variable inputs, short run, long run? (*b*) How long is the time period of the long run? (*c*) What is a production function? What is its usefulness in the analysis of the firm's production?
2. What is the relationship between the marginal product and the average product curves of a variable input?
3. (*a*) How is the law of diminishing returns reflected in the shape of the total product curve? (*b*) What is the relationship between diminishing returns and the stages of production?

4. If the total product curve increases at a decreasing rate from the very beginning (i.e., from the point where the variable input is zero), what would be the shape of the corresponding marginal and average product curves?

5. (*a*) What is meant by the marginal revenue product of an input? How is it calculated? Why does it decline as more units of the variable input are used? (*b*) What is meant by the marginal resource cost? When is this equal to the input price? (*c*) What is the principle for the optimal use of a variable input?

6. (*a*) Do isoquants refer to the short run or to the long run? Why? (*b*) In what way are isoquants similar to indifference curves? (*c*) In what way are isoquants different from indifference curves? (*d*) Why can't isoquants intersect?

7. (*a*) What does the shape of an isoquant show? Why is this very important in managerial economics? (*b*) Does petroleum as an energy source have good substitutes? How is this reflected in the shape of the isoquant for petroleum versus other energy sources? Why was this very important during the energy crisis of the 1970s?

8. (*a*) If two firms face the same wage and rental price of capital but spend different amounts on labor and capital, how do their isocost lines differ? What happens to their isocost lines if the wage rate increases? (*b*) If the wage rate increases, what happens to the capital-labor ratio used in production? Why? (*c*) What is the difference between the capital-labor ratio and the expansion path?

9. Minimum wage legislation in the United States requires that most firms pay workers no less than the legislated minimum wage per hour. Using marginal productivity theory, explain how a change in the minimum wage affects the employment of unskilled labor.

10. It is always better to hire a more qualified and productive worker than a less qualified and productive one regardless of cost. True or false? Explain.

11. Does the production function of Table 6-1 show constant, increasing, or decreasing returns to scale if the firm increases the quantity of labor and capital used from (*a*) $2L$ and $2K$ to $4L$ and $4K$? (*b*) $2L$ and $4K$ to $3L$ and $6K$?

12. If an estimated Cobb-Douglas production function is $Q = 10K^{0.6}L^{0.8}$, (*a*) what are the output elasticities of capital and labor? If the firm increases only the quantity of capital or only the quantity of labor used by 10 percent, by how much would output increase? (*b*) What type of returns to scale does this production function indicate? If the firm increases at the same time both the quantity of capital and the quantity of labor used by 10 percent, by how much would output increase?

13. (*a*) What is meant by an innovation? What are the different types of innovations? (*b*) What are some of the factors that determine the rate at which a firm introduces innovations?

PROBLEMS

1. Assuming that $L_1 = 1$ and $L_2 = 6$, while $K_1 = 1$ and $K_2 = 4$ in Figure 6-2, indicate the number of units of output to which (*a*) *FE*, (*b*) *BA*, and (*c*) *DC* refer by using Table 6-1.

*2. (*a*) From Table 6-1 construct a table similar to Table 6-2 showing the total product, the marginal product, and the average product of labor, as well as the output elasticity of labor, when capital is kept constant at 4 units rather than at 1 unit. (*b*) Draw a figure similar to Figure 6-4 showing the total product as well as the marginal and average products of labor from the results in part (*a*). (*c*) How do the results in parts (*a*) and (*b*) differ from those in Table 6-2 and Figure 6-4 in the text?

3. (*a*) From Table 6-1 construct a table similar to Table 6-2 showing the total product, and the marginal and the average products of capital, as well as the output elasticity of capital when labor is kept constant at 1 unit. (*b*) Draw a figure similar to Figure 6-4 showing the total product as well as the marginal and average products of capital from the results in part (*a*). (*c*) How much capital would a rational producer use?

4. Ms. Smith, the owner and manager of the Clear Duplicating Service located near a major university, is contemplating keeping her shop open after 4 P.M. and until 12 midnight. In order to do so, she will have to hire additional workers. She estimates that the additional workers hired will generate the following total output (where each unit of output refers to 100 pages duplicated). If the price of each unit of output is $10 and each worker hired must be paid a wage of $40 per day, how many workers should Ms. Smith hire?

Workers hired	0	1	2	3	4	5	6
Total product	0	12	22	30	36	40	42

*5. Find the marginal revenue product of labor for the data in Problem 4 from the change in total revenue resulting from the employment of each additional unit of labor, and show that the number of workers that Ms. Smith should hire is the same as that obtained in Problem 4.

6. From the production function given in the following table, draw a figure showing (*a*) the isoquants for 8, 12, and 16 units of output and (*b*) the ridge lines.

Capital (*K*)								
	6	4	8	14	16	13	11	
	5	6	12	16	18	15	14	
	4	7	13	16	20	18	16	Output (*Q*)
	3	8	12	14	16	16	14	
	2	4	7	12	13	12	8	
	1	1	3	8	7	6	5	
	0	1	2	3	4	5	6	
						Labor (*L*)		

7. Find the marginal rate of technical substitution for the isoquant for 8 units of output (*a*) between (1*L*, 3*K*) and (1.5*L*, 1.5*K*); (*b*) between (1.5*L*, 1.5*K*) and (3*L*, 1*K*); (*c*) at (1.5*L*, 1.5*K*); and (*d*) at (1*L*, 3*K*) and at (3*L*, 1*K*). (*e*) What is the relevant portion of the isoquant for 8 units of output? Why?

8. (*a*) Starting from Figure 6-8 in the text, and assuming that both the wage of labor (w) and the rental price of capital (r) are $2, draw a figure showing the optimal combination of labor and capital needed to produce 12 units of output. What is the capital-labor ratio at the optimal input combination? What are the total expenditures or costs of the firm required in order to produce 12 units of output with the optimal combination of labor and capital? (*b*) Answer the same questions as in part (*a*) if $w = \$1$ and $r = \$3$.

*9. Suppose that the marginal product of the last worker employed by a firm is 40 units of output per day and the daily wage that the firm must pay is $20, while the marginal product of the last machine rented by the firm is 120 units of output per day and the daily rental price of the machine is $30. (*a*) Why is this firm not maximizing output or minimizing costs in the long run? (*b*) How can the firm maximize output or minimize costs?

10. John Wilson, the owner of a fast-food restaurant, estimated that he can sell 1,000 additional hamburgers per day by renting more automated equipment to prepare food at a cost of $100 per day. Alternatively, he estimated that he could sell an extra 1,200 hamburgers per day by keeping the restaurant open for an additional two hours per day at a cost of $50 per hour. Which of these two alternative ways of increasing output should Mr. Wilson use?

*11. Draw a figure similar to Figure 6-14 in the text showing constant, increasing, and decreasing returns to scale by the quantity of inputs required to double output.

12. (*a*) What is the difference between technological progress and economies of scale? (*b*) Suppose that technological progress is not neutral (i.e., the productivity of each input does not grow proportionately) but is labor-saving (i.e., the productivity of labor increases proportionately less than the productivity of capital). How can this type of technological progress be shown by isoquants? (*c*) How can we show a capital-saving innovation?

13. **Integrating Problem**

The Rapid Transit Corporation in a city has estimated the following Cobb-Douglas production function using monthly observations for the past two years:

$$\ln Q = 2.303 + 0.40 \ln K + 0.60 \ln L + 0.20 \ln G$$
$$(3.40) \qquad (4.15) \qquad (3.05)$$
$$R^2 = 0.94 \qquad D\text{-}W = 2.20$$

where Q is the number of bus miles driven, K is the number of buses the firm operates, L is the number of bus drivers it employs each day, and G is the gallons of gasoline it uses. The numbers in parentheses below the estimated coefficients are t values. With respect to the above results, answer the following questions: (*a*) Estimate Q if $K = 200$, $L = 400$, and $G = 4{,}000$. (*b*) Rewrite the estimated production function in the form of a power function. (*c*) Find the marginal product of capital, labor, and gasoline at $K = 200$, $L = 400$, and $G = 4{,}000$. (*Hint:* Use the formulas in footnote 10.) Are the MP_K, MP_L, and MP_G positive? Are they diminishing? Why? (*d*) Find the value of the output elasticity of K, L, and G. By how much does output increase by increasing each input by 10 percent, one at a time? (*e*) Determine the economies of scale in production. By how much does output increase if the firm increases the quantity used of all inputs at the same time by 10 percent? (*f*) Suppose the firm operates 200 buses per day, with 400 drivers, and uses 4,000 gallons of gasoline, and the rental price of a bus (r) is \$40 per day, the wage rate of a driver (w) is \$30 per day, and the price of gasoline (g) is \$1 per gallon. Determine whether or not the firm is using the optimal combination of capital, labor, and gasoline. (*g*) If the firm operated 200 buses with 400 drivers and used 4,000 gallons of gasoline per day, and the average bus ride is 1 mile, what price would the firm have to charge for a bus ride in order to maximize profits? (*h*) Are the estimated coefficients of the Cobb-Douglas production function statistically significant at the 5 percent level? How much of the variation in Q does the estimated regression explain? Does the D-W statistic indicate the absence of autocorrelation? Does the regression face multicollinearity? Explain.

APPENDIX

PRODUCTION ANALYSIS WITH CALCULUS

In this appendix we use the Lagrangian multiplier method to examine the condition for a firm to be (1) maximizing output for a given cost outlay and (2) minimizing the cost of producing a given output.

Constrained Output Maximization

Suppose that a firm that uses labor (L) and capital (K) in production wants to determine the amount of labor and capital that it should use in order to maximize the output (Q) produced with a given cost outlay (C^*). That is, the firm wants to

Maximize $$Q = f(L, K) \tag{6-1}$$

Subject to $$C^* = wL + rK \tag{6-23}$$

where w is the wage of labor and r is the rental price of capital. This constrained maximization problem can be solved by the Lagrangian multiplier method (see Section 2-8).

To do so, we first form the Lagrangian function:

$$Z = f(L, K) + \lambda(C^* - wL - rK) \tag{6-24}$$

To maximize Z, we then find the partial derivatives of Z with respect to L, K, and λ and set them equal to zero. That is,

$$\frac{\partial Z}{\partial L} = \frac{\partial f}{\partial L} - \lambda w = 0 \tag{6-25}$$

$$\frac{\partial Z}{\partial K} = \frac{\partial f}{\partial K} - \lambda r = 0 \tag{6-26}$$

$$\frac{\partial Z}{\partial \lambda} = C^* - wL - rK = 0 \tag{6-27}$$

By substituting MP_L for $\partial f/\partial L$ and MP_K for $\partial f/\partial K$, transposing w and r to the right of the equals sign, and dividing Equation 6-25 by Equation 6-26, we have

$$\frac{MP_L}{MP_K} = \frac{w}{r} \tag{6-13}$$

or

$$\frac{MP_L}{w} = \frac{MP_K}{r} \tag{6-14}$$

That is, the firm should hire labor and capital so that the marginal product per dollar spent on each input (λ) is equal. This is the first-order condition for output maximization for the given cost outlay or expenditure of the firm. The second-order condition is for the isoquant to be convex to the origin.

Problem 1 Given: $Q = 100K^{0.5}L^{0.5}$, $C^* = \$1{,}000$, $w = \$30$, and $r = \$40$. Determine the amount of labor and capital that the firm should use in order to maximize output. What is this level of output?

Problem 2 Solve the above problem with $w = \$50$.

Constrained Cost Minimization

Suppose, on the other hand, that the firm of the previous section wants to determine the amount of labor and capital to use to minimize the cost of producing a given level of output (Q^*). The problem would then be

Minimize $$C = wL + rk \tag{6-10}$$

Subject to $$Q^* = f(L, K) \tag{6-28}$$

This constrained cost minimization problem can also be solved by the Lagrangian multiplier method.

To do so, we first form the Lagrangian function:

$$Z' = wL + rK + \lambda'[Q^* - f(L, K)] \tag{6-29}$$

To minimize Z', we then find the partial derivatives of Z' with respect to L, K, and λ', and set them equal to zero. That is,

$$\frac{\partial Z'}{\partial L} = w - \frac{\lambda' \partial f}{\partial L} = 0 \qquad (6\text{-}30)$$

$$\frac{\partial Z'}{\partial K} = r - \frac{\lambda' \partial f}{\partial K} = 0 \qquad (6\text{-}31)$$

$$\frac{\partial Z'}{\partial \lambda'} = Q^* - f(L, K) = 0 \qquad (6\text{-}32)$$

By substituting MP_L for $\partial f/\partial L$ and MP_K for $\partial f/\partial K$, transposing them to the right of the equal sign, and dividing Equation 6-30 by Equation 6-31, we have

$$\frac{w}{r} = \frac{MP_L}{MP_K} \qquad (6\text{-}33)$$

or

$$\frac{w}{MP_L} = \frac{r}{MP_K} \qquad (6\text{-}34)$$

Each term in Equation 6-34 equals λ' and refers to the marginal cost in terms of labor and capital. That is, Equation 6-34 postulates that to minimize the costs of producing Q^*, the firm should use labor and capital in such a way that the extra cost of producing an additional unit of output is the same whether the firm produces it with more labor or more capital. Note that Equation 6-33 and λ' are the inverse of Equation 6-13 and λ. This is the first-order condition for cost minimization. The second-order condition is that the isoquant must be convex to the origin.

Problem 1 Given: $Q = 100K^{0.5}L^{0.5}$, $w = \$30$, and $r = \$40$. Show how to determine the amount of labor and capital that the firm should use in order to minimize the cost of producing 1,444 units of output. What is this minimum cost?

Problem 2 Given: $Q = 100K^{0.5}L^{0.5}$, $w = \$50$, and $r = \$40$. Show how to determine the amount of labor and capital that the firm should use in order to minimize the cost of producing 1,118 units of output. What is this minimum cost?

Profit Maximization

In general, the firm will want to determine the amount of labor and capital needed to maximize profits rather than to maximize output or minimize costs. Total profit (π) is

$$\pi = TR - TC \qquad (6\text{-}35)$$

$$= P \cdot Q - wL - rK \qquad (6\text{-}36)$$

Since $Q = f(L, K)$, we can rewrite the profit function as

$$\pi = P \cdot f(L, K) - wL - rK \tag{6-37}$$

To determine the amount of labor and capital that the firm should use in order to maximize profits, we take the partial derivatives of Equation 6-37 with respect to L and K and set them equal to zero. That is,

$$\frac{\partial \pi}{\partial L} = \frac{P\partial f}{\partial L} - w = 0 \tag{6-38}$$

$$\frac{\partial \pi}{\partial K} = \frac{P\partial f}{\partial K} - r = 0 \tag{6-39}$$

Assuming that the price of the final commodity (P) is constant so that it is equal to marginal revenue (MR), we can rewrite Equations 6-38 and 6-39 as

$$(MP_L)(MR) = MRP_L = w \tag{6-40}$$

$$(MP_K)(MR) = MRP_K = r \tag{6-41}$$

That is, in order to maximize profits, the firm should hire labor and capital until the marginal revenue product of labor equals the wage rate, and until the marginal revenue product of capital is equal to the rental price of capital.

Dividing Equation 6-40 by Equation 6-41, we get Equation 6-19 that we found in Section 6-5c:

$$\frac{MP_L}{MP_K} = \frac{w}{r} \tag{6-19}$$

Cross-multiplying in Equation 6-19 gives the condition for the optimal combination of inputs given by Equation 6-14:

$$\frac{MP_L}{w} = \frac{MP_K}{r} \tag{6-14}$$

That is, hiring labor and capital so that Equations 6-40 and 6-41 hold implies that Equation 6-14 for optimal input combinations will also be satisfied.

Problem 1 Suppose that the production function of a firm is $Q = 100L^{0.5}K^{0.5}$ and $K = 100$, $P = \$1$, $w = \$30$, and $r = \$40$. Determine the quantity of labor that the firm should hire in order to maximize profits. What is the maximum profit of this firm?

Problem 2 Solve the above problem for $w = \$50$.

SUPPLEMENTARY READINGS

For a problem-solving approach to production theory and estimation, see:

Salvatore, Dominick: *Theory and Problems of Managerial Economics,* Schaum Outline Series (New York: McGraw-Hill, 1989), Chap. 7.

For a more extensive treatment of production theory, see:

Salvatore, Dominick: *Theory and Problems of Microeconomic Theory,* 3rd ed. (New York: McGraw-Hill, 1992), Chap. 6 and Secs. 8.1–8.3.

Salvatore, Dominick: *Microeconomics,* 2nd ed. (New York: HarperCollins, 1994), Chap. 6.

Baumol, William J.: *Economic Theory and Operations Analysis* (Englewood Cliffs, N.J.: Prentice-Hall, 1977), Chap. 11.

Other important recent writings on production theory are:

Mefford, Robert N.: "Introducing Management into the Production Function," *Review of Economics and Statistics,* January–February 1986, pp. 75–81.

Lane, S.: "The Determinants of Investments in New Technology," *American Economic Review,* May 1991, pp. 262–265.

On the empirical estimation of production functions, see:

Gold, B.: "Changing Perspectives on Size, Scale, and Returns: An Interpretative Survey," *Journal of Economic Literature,* March 1981, pp. 5–33.

Douglas, Paul H.: "The Cobb-Douglas Production Function Once Again: Its History, Its Testing, and Some New Empirical Values," *Journal of Political Economy,* October 1984, pp. 903–915.

Adler, Paul S.: "A Plant Productivity Measure for 'Hi-Tec' Manufacturing," *Interfaces,* November–December 1987, pp. 75–85.

Chew, W. Bruce: "No-Nonsense Guide to Measuring Productivity," *Harvard Business Review,* January–February 1988, pp. 110–118.

For technological progress and international competitiveness, see:

Comanor, William S., and **Takahiro Miyao:** "The Organization of Relative Productivity of Japanese and American Industry," *Managerial and Decision Economics,* June 1985, pp. 88–92.

Darrow, William P.: "An International Comparison of Flexible Manufacturing Systems," *Interfaces,* November–December 1987, pp. 86–91.

Porter, M. J.: *The Competitive Advantage of Nations* (New York: Free Press, 1990).

Rosenberg, Nathan, and **Edward W. Steinmueller:** "Why Are Americans such Poor Imitators?" *American Economic Review,* May 1988, pp. 229–234.

Salvatore, Dominick: *International Economics,* 5th ed. (New York: Macmillan, 1995), Chaps. 6–8, 13.

Salvatore, Dominick: *The Japanese Trade Challenge and the U.S. Response* (Washington, D.C.: Economic Policy Institute, 1990).

The MIT Commission on Industrial Productivity: *Made in America* (Cambridge, Mass.: The MIT Press, 1989), pp. 270–277.

CHAPTER 7

Cost Theory and Estimation

KEY TERMS

Explicit costs
Implicit costs
Alternative or opportunity costs
Economic costs
Accounting costs
Relevant cost
Incremental cost
Sunk costs
Total fixed costs (*TFC*)
Total variable costs (*TVC*)
Total costs (*TC*)
Average fixed cost (*AFC*)
Average variable cost (*AVC*)
Average total cost (*ATC*)
Marginal cost (*MC*)
Long-run total cost (*LTC*)
Long-run average cost (*LAC*)
Long-run marginal cost (*LMC*)
Planning horizon
Economies of scope
Learning curve
Foreign sourcing of inputs
New international economies of scale
Brain drain
Cost-volume-profit or breakeven analysis
Contribution margin per unit
Japanese cost-management system
Operating leverage
Degree of operating leverage (*DOL*)
Engineering technique
Survival technique

CHAPTER OUTLINE

We saw in Section 1-2 that the aim of a firm, in general, is to maximize profits. Total profits equal the positive difference between total revenue and total costs. The total revenue of the firm was examined in Part Two of the text, which dealt with demand analysis. In this chapter we examine costs and their importance in decision making. The firm's cost functions are derived from the optimal input combinations examined in the last chapter and show the minimum cost of producing various levels of output. Clearly, cost is a very important consideration in managerial decision making and cost analysis is an essential and major aspect of managerial economies.

The chapter begins by examining the nature of costs of production. These include explicit and implicit costs, relevant or opportunity costs, and incremental costs. We then derive the firm's short-run and long-run total, average, and marginal cost curves. Subsequently, we examine plant size and economies of scale, economies of scope, the learning curve, as well as international trade in inputs and the immigration of skilled labor. Finally, we discuss breakeven analysis and examine the empirical estimation of cost functions.

7-1 THE NATURE OF COSTS

One crucial distinction in the analysis of costs is between explicit and implicit costs. **Explicit costs** refer to the actual expenditures of the firm to hire, rent, or purchase the inputs it requires in production. These include the wages to hire labor, the rental price of capital, equipment and buildings, and the purchase price of raw materials and semifinished products. **Implicit costs,** on the other hand, refer to the value of the inputs owned and used by the firm in its own production activity. Even though the firm does not incur any actual expenditures to use these inputs, they are not free since the firm could sell or rent them out to other firms. The amount for which the firm could sell or rent out these owned inputs to other firms represents a cost of production of the firm owning and using them. Implicit costs include the highest salary that the entrepreneur could earn in his or her best alternative employment (say, in managing another firm for somebody else), and the highest return that the firm could receive from investing its capital in the most rewarding alternative use or renting its land and buildings to the highest bidder (rather than using them itself).

In economics, both explicit and implicit costs must be considered. That is, in measuring production costs, the firm must include the **alternative or opportunity costs** of all inputs, whether purchased or owned by the firm. The reason is that the firm could not retain a hired input if it paid a lower price for it than another firm. Similarly, it would not pay for a firm to use an owned input if the value (productivity) of the input is greater to another firm. These **economic costs** must be distinguished from **accounting costs,** which refer only to the firm's actual expenditures or explicit costs incurred for purchased or rented inputs. Accounting or historical costs are important for financial reporting by the firm and for tax purposes. For managerial decision-making purposes (with which we are primarily interested here), however, economic or opportunity costs are the **relevant cost** concept that must be used. Two examples will clarify this distinction and will highlight its importance in arriving at correct managerial decisions.

One example is from *inventory valuation.* Suppose that a firm purchased a raw material for \$100, but its price subsequently fell to \$60. The accountant would continue to report the cost of the raw material at its historical price of \$100, even after its price fell to \$60. The economist, however, would value the raw material at its current or replacement value. Failure to do so might lead to the wrong managerial decision. This would occur if the firm decided not to produce a commodity that would lead to a loss if the raw material were valued at its historical cost of \$100 but to a profit if the raw material were valued at its current or replacement value of \$60. The fact that the firm paid \$100 for the input is irrelevant to its current production decision since the firm could only obtain \$60 if it sold the input now. The \$40 reduction in the price of the raw material is a sunk cost which the firm should not consider in its current managerial decisions.

Another example is given by the *measurement of depreciation cost* for a long-lived asset. Suppose that a firm purchased a machine for \$1,000. If the estimated life of the machine is 10 years and the accountant uses a *straight-line depreciation method* (that is, \$100 per year), the accounting value of the machine is zero at the end of the tenth year. Suppose, however, that the machine can still be used for (i.e., it would last) another year and that the firm could sell the machine for \$120 at the end of the tenth year or use it for another year. The cost of using the machine is zero as far as the accountant is concerned (since the machine has already been fully depreciated), but it is \$120 for the economist. Again, incorrectly assigning a zero cost to the use of the machine would be wrong from an economics point of view and could lead to wrong managerial decisions.

In discussing production costs, we must also distinguish between marginal cost and incremental cost. Marginal cost refers to the change in total cost for a 1-unit change in output. For example, if total cost is \$140 to produce 10 units of output and \$150 to produce 11 units of output, the marginal cost of the eleventh unit is \$10. **Incremental cost,** on the other hand, is a broader concept and refers to the change in total costs from implementing a particular management decision, such as the introduction of a new product line, the undertaking of a new advertising campaign, or the production of a previously purchased component. The costs that are not affected by the decision are irrelevant and are called **sunk costs.**

7-2 SHORT-RUN COST FUNCTIONS

In this section we distinguish between fixed and variable costs and derive the firm's total and per-unit cost functions. These cost functions are derived from input prices and the optimal input combinations used to produce various levels of outputs (as explained in the previous chapter).

Short-Run Total and Per-Unit Cost Functions

In Section 6-1 we defined the short run as the time period during which some of the firm's inputs are fixed (i.e., cannot be readily changed, except perhaps at very great expense). The total obligations of the firm per time period for all fixed inputs are called **total fixed costs (*TFC*)**. These include interest payments on borrowed capital, rental expenditures on leased plant and equipment (or depreciation associated with the passage of time on owned plant and equipment), property taxes, and those salaries (such as for top management) that are fixed by contract and must be paid over the life of the contract whether the firm produces or not. **Total variable costs (*TVC*)**, on the other hand, are the total obligations of the firm per time period for all the variable inputs that the firm uses. Variable inputs are those that the firm can vary easily and on short notice. Included in variable costs are payments for raw materials, fuels, depreciation associated with the use of the plant and equipment, most labor costs, excise taxes, etc.[1] **Total costs (*TC*)** equal total fixed costs (*TFC*) plus total variable costs (*TVC*). That is,

$$TC = TFC + TVC \tag{7-1}$$

Within the limits imposed by the given plant and equipment, the firm can vary its output in the short run by varying the quantity used of the variable inputs. This gives rise to the *TFC*, *TVC*, and *TC* functions of the firm. These show, respectively, the minimum fixed, variable, and total costs of the firm to produce various levels of output in the short run. Cost functions show the minimum costs of producing various levels of output on the assumption that the firm uses the optimal or least-cost input combinations to produce each level of output. Thus, the total cost of producing a particular level of output is obtained by multiplying the optimal quantity of each input used times the input price and then adding all these costs. In defining cost functions, all inputs are valued at their opportunity cost, which includes both explicit and implicit costs. Input prices are assumed to remain constant regardless of the quantity demanded of each input by the firm.

From the total fixed, total variable, and total cost functions, we can derive the corresponding per-unit (average fixed, average variable, average total, and marginal) cost functions of the firm. **Average fixed cost (*AFC*)** equals total fixed costs (*TFC*) divided by the level of output (*Q*). **Average variable cost (*AVC*)** equals total variable costs (*TVC*) divided by output. **Average total cost (*ATC*)** equals total costs (*TC*) divided by output. Average total cost also equals average fixed cost plus average variable cost. Finally, **marginal cost (*MC*)** is the change in total costs or the change in total variable costs (*TVC*) per unit change in output.[2]

[1]An incremental-cost analysis, *semivariable costs* are often encountered. These are cost changes that arise if output falls outside some specified range. For example, by contract the firm may be able to reduce the salary of top management if output falls sharply or must pay bonuses for large increases in output.

[2]Since the difference between *TC* and *TVC* is *TFC*, which are fixed, the change in *TC* and the change in *TVC* per unit change in output (*MC*) are identical. In terms of calculus,

$$MC = \frac{d(TC)}{dQ} = \frac{d(TVC)}{dQ} \qquad \text{since } \frac{d(TFC)}{dQ} = 0$$

That is,

$$AFC = \frac{TFC}{Q} \tag{7-2}$$

$$AVC = \frac{TVC}{Q} \tag{7-3}$$

$$ATC = \frac{TC}{Q} = AFC + AVC \tag{7-4}$$

$$MC = \frac{\Delta TC}{\Delta Q} = \frac{\Delta TVC}{\Delta Q} \tag{7-5}$$

Short-Run Total and Per-Unit Cost Curves

Table 7-1 shows the hypothetical short-run total and per-unit cost schedules of a firm. These schedules are plotted in Figure 7-1. From column 2 to Table 7-1 we see that *TFC* are $60 regardless of the level of output. *TVC* (column 3) are zero when output is zero and rise as output rises. Up to point *G′* (the point of inflection in the top panel of Figure 7-1), the firm uses very little of the variable inputs with the fixed inputs and the law of diminishing returns is not operating. Thus, the *TVC* curve faces downward or rises at a decreasing rate. Past point *G′* (i.e., for output levels greater than 1.5 units in the top panel of Figure 7-1), the law of diminishing returns operates, and the *TVC* curve faces upward or rises at an increasing rate. Since *TC* = *TFC* + *TVC*, the *TC* curve has the same shape as the *TVC* curve but is $60 (the amount of the *TFC*) above it at each output level. These *TVC* and *TC* schedules are plotted in the top panel of Figure 7-1.

The *AFC* values given in column 5 are obtained by dividing the *TFC* values in column 2 by the quantity of output in column 1. *AVC* (column 6) equals *TVC* (column 3) divided by output (column 1). *ATC* (column 7) equals *TC* (column 4) divided by output (column 1). *ATC* also equals *AFC* plus *AVC*. *MC* (column 8) is given by the change in *TVC* (column 3) or in *TC* (column 4) per unit change

Table 7-1
Short-Run Total and Per-Unit Cost Schedules

(1) Quantity of Output	(2) Total Fixed Costs	(3) Total Variable Costs	(4) Total Costs	(5) Average Fixed Cost	(6) Average Variable Cost	(7) Average Total Cost	(8) Marginal Cost
0	$60	$ 0	$ 60	—	—	—	—
1	60	20	80	$60	$20	$80	$20
2	60	30	90	30	15	45	10
3	60	45	105	20	15	35	15
4	60	80	140	15	20	35	35
5	60	135	195	12	27	39	55

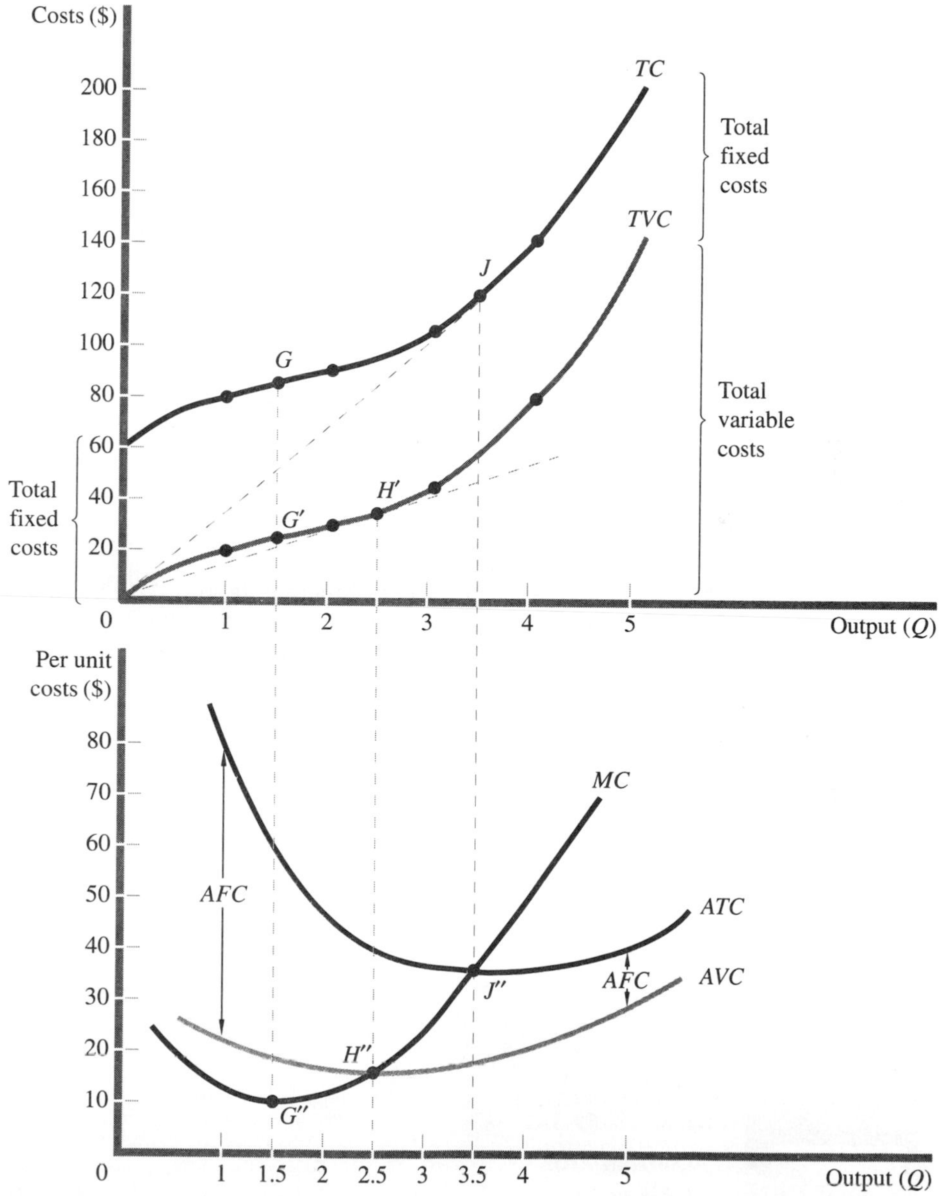

Figure 7-1

Short-Run Total and Per-Unit Cost Curves

The top panel shows that *TVC* is zero when output is zero and rises as output rises. At point *G′* the law of diminishing returns begins to operate. The *TC* curve has the same shape as the *TVC* curve and is above it by $60 (the *TFC*). The bottom panel shows U-shaped *AVC*, *ATC*, and *MC* curves. *AFC* = *ATC* − *AVC* and declines continuously as output rises. The *MC* curve reaches a minimum before the *AVC* and *ATC* curves and intercepts them from below at their lowest points.

in output (column 1). Thus, MC does not depend on TFC. These per-unit cost schedules are plotted in the bottom panel of Figure 7-1. *Note that MC is plotted halfway between the various levels of output.* From Table 7-1 and the bottom panel of Figure 7-1 we see that the AVC, ATC, and MC curves first fall and then rise (i.e., they are U-shaped). Since the vertical distance between the ATC and the AVC curves equals AFC, a separate AFC curve is not drawn. Note that AFC declines continuously as output expands as the given *total* fixed costs are spread over more and more units of output. Graphically, AVC is the slope of a ray from the origin to the TVC curve, ATC is equal to the slope of a ray from the origin to the TC curve, while the MC is the slope of the TC or TVC curves. Note that the MC curve reaches its minimum before (i.e., at a lower level of output) and intercepts from below the AVC and ATC curves at their lowest points.

We can explain the U shape of the AVC curve as follows. With labor as the only variable input, TVC for any output level (Q) equals the wage rate (w, which is assumed to be fixed) times the quantity of labor (L) used. Thus,

$$AVC = \frac{TVC}{Q} = \frac{wL}{Q} = \frac{w}{Q/L} = \frac{w}{AP_L} \quad (7\text{-}6)$$

Since the average physical product of labor (AP_L or Q/L) usually rises first, reaches a maximum, and then falls (see Section 6-2), it follows that the AVC curve first falls, reaches a minimum, and then rises. Since the AVC curve is U-shaped, the ATC curve is also U-shaped. The ATC curve continues to fall after the AVC curve begins to rise as long as the decline in AFC exceeds the rise in AVC.

The U shape of the MC curve can similarly be explained as follows:

$$MC = \frac{\Delta TVC}{\Delta Q} = \frac{\Delta(wL)}{\Delta Q} = \frac{w(\Delta L)}{\Delta Q} = \frac{w}{\Delta Q/\Delta L} = \frac{w}{MP_L} \quad (7\text{-}7)$$

Since the marginal product of labor (MP_L or $\Delta Q/\Delta L$) first rises, reaches a maximum, and then falls, it follows that the MC curve first falls, reaches a minimum, and then rises. Thus, the rising portion of the MC curve reflects the operation of the law of diminishing returns.

Case Study 7-1

Per-Unit Cost Curves in the Cultivation of Corn

Figure 7-2 shows the estimated *AVC*, *ATC*, and *MC* per thousand bushels of corn raised in Iowa farms in 1971. The *AVC*, *ATC*, and *MC* cost curves in the figure have the same general shape as the typical curves examined in the bottom panel of Figure 7-1. Note that once *MC* starts rising in the figure, it does so very rapidly. This is often the case in the real world.

Source: D. Suits, "Agriculture," in W. Adams, *The Structure of the American Economy* (New York: Macmillan, 1977), p. 17.

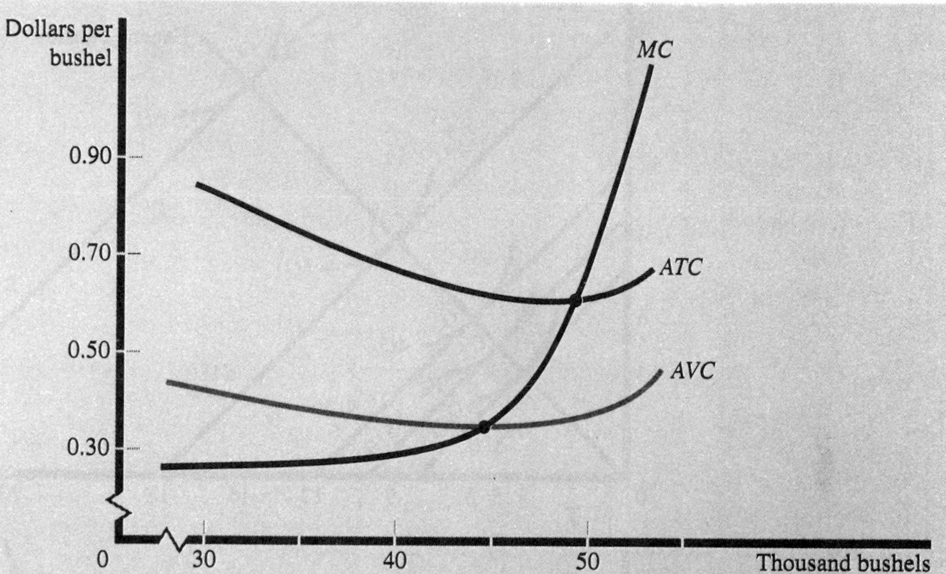

Figure 7-2
Estimated Per-Unit Cost Curves in Corn Cultivation
The estimated *ATC*, *AVC*, and *MC* curves in corn cultivation are U-shaped as are those shown in the bottom panel in Figure 7-1. Once the *MC* curve of corn starts rising, it does so very rapidly.

7-3 LONG-RUN COST CURVES

In this section we derive the firm's long-run total, average, and marginal cost curves. We then show the relationship between the firm's long-run average cost curve and the firm's short-run average cost curves.

Long-Run Total Cost Curves

In Section 6-1 we defined the long run as the time period during which all inputs are variable. Thus, all costs are variable in the long run (i.e., the firm faces no fixed costs). The length of time of the long run depends on the industry. In some service industries, such as dry-cleaning, the period of the long run may be only a few months or weeks. For others which are very capital intensive, such as the construction of a new electricity-generating plant, it may be many years. It all depends on the length of time required for the firm to be able to vary all inputs.

The firm's **long-run total cost** (*LTC*) curve is derived from the firm's expansion path and shows the minimum long-run total costs of producing various levels of output. The firm's long-run average and marginal cost curves are then derived from the long-run total cost curve. These derivations are shown in Figure 7-3.

The top panel of Figure 7-3 shows the expansion path of the firm. As explained on page 242, the expansion path shows the optimal input combinations

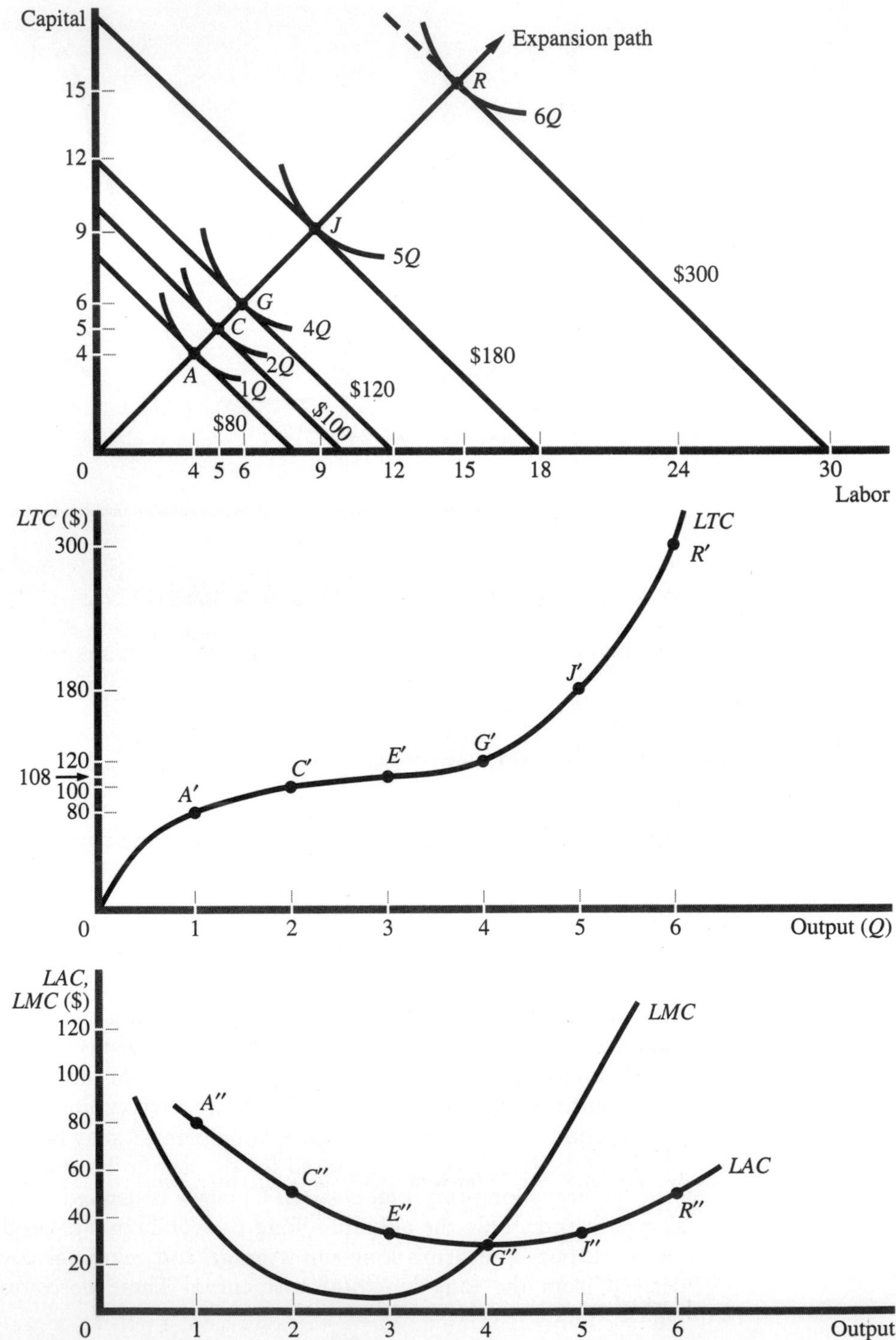

Capital
Expansion path
15
12
9
6
5
4
R
6Q
J
5Q
$300
G
C
4Q
2Q
A
1Q
$180
$120
$100
$80
0
4 5 6
9
12
15
18
24
30
Labor
LTC ($)
300
180
120
108
100
80
LTC
R′
J′
G′
E′
C′
A′
1
2
3
4
5
6
Output (Q)
LAC,
LMC ($)
120
100
80
60
40
20
LMC
LAC
A″
C″
E″
G″
J″
R″
Output

to produce various levels of output. For example, point A shows that in order to produce 1 unit of output ($1Q$), the firm uses 4 units of labor ($4L$) and 4 units of capital ($4K$). If the wage of labor (w) is \$10 per unit and the rental price of capital (r) is also \$10 per unit, the minimum total cost of producing $1Q$ is

$$(4L)(\$10) + (4K)(\$10) = \$80$$

This is shown as point A' in the middle panel, where the vertical axis measures total costs and the horizontal axis measures output. From point C on the expansion path in the top panel, we get point C' (\$100) on the LTC curve in the middle panel for $2Q$. Other points on the LTC curve are similarly obtained.[3] Note that the LTC curve starts at the origin because there are no fixed costs in the long run.

From the LTC curve we can derive the firm's **long-run average cost (LAC)** curve. LAC is equal to LTC divided by Q. That is,

$$LAC = \frac{LTC}{Q} \tag{7-8}$$

For example, the LAC to produce $1Q$ is obtained by dividing the LTC of \$80 (point A' on the LTC curve in the middle panel of Figure 7-3) by 1. This is the slope of a ray from the origin to point A' on the LTC curve and is plotted as point A'' in the bottom panel of Figure 7-3. Other points on the LAC curve are similarly obtained. Note that the slope of a ray from the origin to the LTC curve declines up to point G' (in the middle panel of Figure 7-3) and then rises. Thus, the LAC curve in the bottom panel declines up to point G'' ($4Q$) and rises thereafter.

It is important to keep in mind, however, that while the U shape of the short-run average cost (SAC) curve is based on the operation of the law of diminishing returns (resulting from the existence of fixed inputs in the short run), the U shape of the LAC curve depends on increasing, constant, and decreasing returns to scale, respectively, as will be explained in Section 7-4.

[3]Point E' on the LTC curve in the middle panel of Figure 7-3 is based on the assumption that $3Q$ is produced with $5.4L$ and $5.4K$ (not shown on the expansion path in the top panel in order not to clutter the figure), so that LTC = \$108. The shape of the LTC curve will be explained in terms of the LAC curve that is derived from it.

Figure 7-3
Derivation of the Long-Run Total, Average, and Marginal Cost Curves

From point A on the expansion path in the top panel, and w = \$10 and r = \$10, we get point A' on the long-run total cost (LTC) curve in the middle panel. Other points on the LTC curve are similarly obtained. The long-run average cost (LAC) curve in the bottom panel is given by the slope of a ray from the origin to the LTC curve. The LAC curve falls up to point G'' ($4Q$) because of increasing returns to scale and rises thereafter because of decreasing returns to scale. The long-run marginal cost (LMC) curve is given by the slope of the LTC curve and intersects the LAC curve from below at the lowest point on the LAC curve.

From the LTC curve we can also derive the **long-run marginal cost (LMC)** curve. This measures the change in LTC per unit change in output and is given by the slope of the LTC curve. That is,

$$LMC = \frac{\Delta LTC}{\Delta Q} \tag{7-9}$$

For example, increasing output from $0Q$ to $1Q$ increases LTC from \$0 to \$80. Therefore, LMC is \$80 and is plotted at 0.5 (i.e., halfway between $0Q$ and $1Q$) in the bottom panel of Figure 7-3. Increasing output from $1Q$ to $2Q$ leads to an increase in LTC from \$80 to \$100, or \$20 (plotted at 1.5 in the bottom panel), etc. Note that the relationship between LMC and LAC is the same as that between the short-run MC and ATC or AVC. That is, the LMC curve reaches its lowest point at a smaller level of output than the LAC curve and intersects the LAC curve from below at the lowest point on the LAC curve.

Long-Run Average and Marginal Cost Curves

The long-run average cost (LAC) curve shows the lowest average cost of producing each level of output when the firm can build the most appropriate plant to produce each level of output. This is shown in Figure 7-4. The top panel of Figure 7-4 is based on the assumption that the firm can build only four scales of plant (given by SAC_1, SAC_2, SAC_3, and SAC_4), while the bottom panel of Figure 7-4 is based on the assumption that the firm can build many more or an infinite number of scales of plant.

The top panel of Figure 7-4 shows that the minimum average cost of producing 1 unit of output ($1Q$) is \$80 and results when the firm operates the scale of plant given by SAC_1 (the smallest scale of plant possible) at point A''. The firm can produce $1.5Q$ at an average cost of \$70 by utilizing either the scale of plant given by SAC_1 or the larger scale of plant given by SAC_2 at point B^* (see the top panel of Figure 7-4). To produce $2Q$, the firm will utilize scale of plant SAC_2 at point C'' (\$50) rather than smaller scale of plant SAC_1 at point C^* (the lowest point on SAC_1, which refers to the average cost of \$67). Thus, the firm has more flexibility in the long run than in the short run. To produce $3Q$, the firm is indifferent between using plant SAC_2 or larger plant SAC_3 at point E^* (\$60). The minimum average cost of producing $4Q$ (\$30) is achieved when the firm operates plant SAC_3 at point G'' (the lowest point on SAC_3). To produce $5Q$, the firm operates either plant SAC_3 or larger plant SAC_4 at point J^* (\$60). Finally, the minimum cost of producing $6Q$ is achieved when the firm operates plant SAC_4 (the largest plant) at point R'' (\$50).

Thus, if the firm could build only the four scales of plant shown in the top panel of Figure 7-4, the long-run average cost curve of the firm would be $A''B^*C''E^*G''J^*R''$. If the firm could build many more scales of plant, the kinks at points B^*, E^*, and J^* would become less pronounced, as shown in the bottom panel of Figure 7-4. In the limit, as the number of scales of plants that the firm

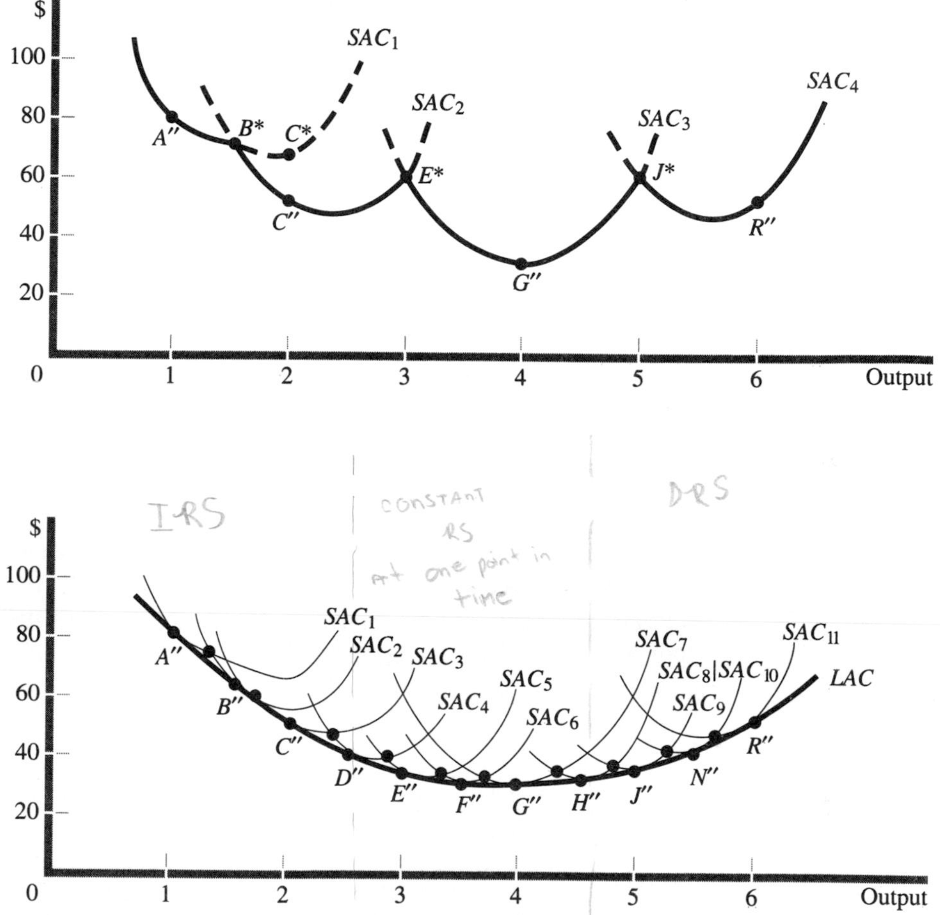

Figure 7-4
Relationship Between the Long-Run and Short-Run Average Cost Curves
In the top panel, the LAC curve is given by $A''B^*C''E^*G''J^*R''$ on the assumption that the firm can build only four scales of plant (SAC_1, SAC_2, SAC_3, and SAC_4). In the bottom panel, the LAC curve is the smooth curve $A''B''C''D''E''F''G''H''J''N''R''$ on the assumption that the firm can build a very large or infinite number of plants in the long run.

can build in the long run increases, the *LAC* curve approaches the smooth curve indicated by the *LAC* curve in the bottom panels of Figures 7-3 and 7-4. Thus, the *LAC* curve is the tangent or "envelope" to the *SAC* curves and shows the minimum average cost of producing various levels of output in the long run, when the firm can build any scale of plant. Note that only at point G'' (the lowest point on the *LAC* curve) does the firm utilize the optimal scale of plant at its lowest point. To the left of point G'', the firm operates on the declining portion of the relevant *SAC* curve, while to the right of point G'' the firm operates on the rising portion of the appropriate *SAC* curve (see the top panel of Figure 7-4).

The long run is often referred to as the **planning horizon** because the firm can build the plant that minimizes the cost of producing any anticipated level of output. Once the plant has been built, the firm operates in the short run. Thus, the firm plans for the long run and operates in the short run.[4]

[4]If the firm is uncertain about the level of demand and production in the future, it may want to build a more flexible plant for the *range* of anticipated outputs, rather than the optimal plant for producing a *particular* level of output at an even lower cost (see Problem 7, with answer in the back of the book).

Case Study 7-2

The Long-Run Average Cost Curve in Electricity Generation

Figure 7-5 shows the estimated *LAC* curve for a sample of 114 firms generating electricity in the United States in 1970. The figure shows that *LAC* is lowest at the output level of about 32 billion kilowatt-hours. The *LAC* curve, however, is nearly L-shaped (the reason for and significance of this are explained in Section 7-4). In order to avoid the increasing costs that they would incur in producing more power themselves to satisfy increasing consumer demand, electric power companies have been buying more and more power from independent power producers.

Source: L. Christensen and H. Green, "Economies of Scale in U.S. Electric Power Generation," *Journal of Political Economy,* August 1976, p. 674; and "Electric Utilities Brace for an End to Monopolies," *The New York Times,* August 18, 1994, p. 1.

Figure 7-5
The Long-Run Average Cost Curve in Electricity Generation
The figure shows the estimated *LAC* curve in the generation of electricity in the United States for a sample of 114 firms in 1970. The lowest *LAC* occurs at the output level of about 32 billion kilowatt-hours, but the *LAC* curve is nearly L-shaped.

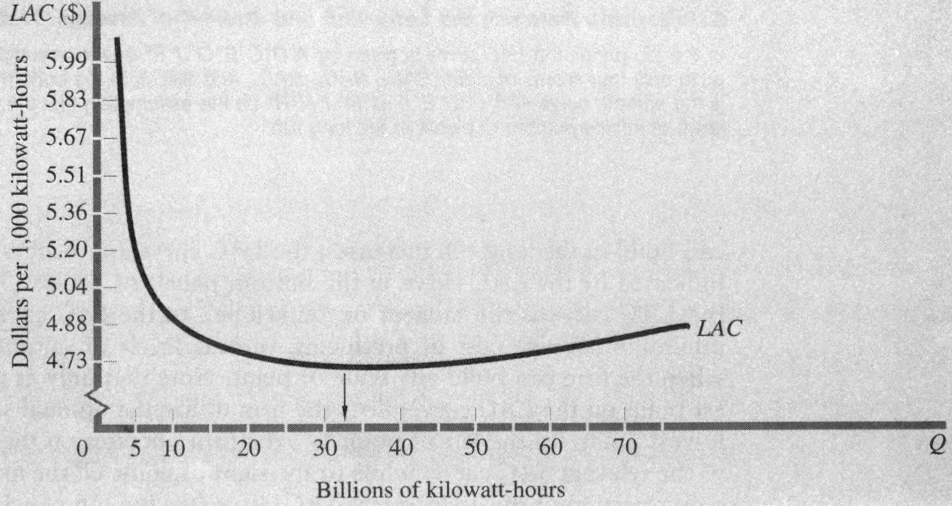

7-4 PLANT SIZE AND ECONOMIES OF SCALE

In the bottom panel of Figures 7-3 and 7-4, the *LAC* curve has been drawn as U-shaped. This is based on the assumption that economies of scale prevail at small levels of output and diseconomies of scale prevail at larger levels of output. As pointed out in Section 6-6, "economies of scale" refers to the situation where output grows proportionately faster than the use of inputs. For example, output more than doubles with a doubling of inputs. With input prices remaining constant, this leads to lower costs per unit. Thus, increasing returns of scale are reflected in a declining *LAC* curve. On the other hand, decreasing returns to scale refers to the situation where output grows at a proportionately slower rate than the use of inputs. With input prices constant, this leads to higher costs per unit. Thus, decreasing returns to scale are reflected in an *LAC* curve that is rising. The lowest point on the *LAC* curve occurs at the output level at which the forces for increasing returns to scale are just balanced by the forces for decreasing returns to scale.

Increasing returns to scale or decreasing costs arise because of technological and financial reasons.[5] At the technological level, economies of scale arise because as the scale of operation increases, a greater division of labor and specialization can take place and more specialized and productive machinery can be used. Specifically, with a large-scale operation, each worker can be assigned to perform a repetitive task rather than numerous different ones. This results in increased proficiency and the avoidance of the time lost in moving from one machine to another. At higher scales of operation, more specialized and productive machinery can also be used. For example, using a conveyor belt to unload a small truck may not be justified, but it greatly increases efficiency in unloading a whole train or ship. Furthermore, some physical properties of equipment and machinery also lead to increasing returns to scale. For example, doubling the diameter of a pipeline more than doubles the flow without doubling costs, doubling the weight of a ship more than doubles its capacity to transport cargo without doubling costs, and so on. Thus, per-unit costs decline. Firms also need fewer supervisors, fewer spare parts, and smaller inventories per unit of output as the scale of operation increases.

Besides the above technological reasons for increasing returns to scale or decreasing costs, there are financial reasons that arise as the size of the firm increases. Because of bulk purchases, larger firms are more likely to receive quantity discounts in purchasing raw materials and other intermediate (i.e., semi-processed) inputs than smaller firms. Large firms can usually sell bonds and stocks more favorably and receive bank loans at lower interest rates than smaller firms. Large firms can also achieve economies of scale or decreasing costs in advertising and other promotional efforts. For all these technological and financial reasons, the *LAC* curve of a firm is likely to decline as the firm expands and becomes larger.

Decreasing returns to scale, on the other hand, arise primarily because as the scale of operation increases, it becomes ever more difficult to manage the firm

[5]The technological forces for economies of scale are sometimes referred to as "plant economies" because they operate at the plant level. On the other hand, the financial reasons for economies of scale are often referred to as "firm economies" because they arise at the firm (as opposed to the plant) level.

effectively and coordinate the various operations and divisions of the firm. The number of meetings, the paperwork, and telephone bills increase more than proportionately to the increase in the scale of operation, and it becomes increasingly difficult for top management to ensure that their directives and guidelines are properly carried out by their subordinates. Thus, efficiency decreases and costs per unit tend to rise.

In the real world, the forces for increasing and decreasing returns to scale often operate side by side, with the former prevailing at small levels of output (so that the *LAC* curve declines) and the latter tending to prevail at much larger levels of output (so that the *LAC* curve rises). The lowest point on the *LAC* curve occurs when the forces for increasing and decreasing returns to scale just balance each other. In the real world, however, the *LAC* curve is often found to have a nearly flat bottom and to be L-shaped rather than U-shaped. This implies that economies of scale are rather quickly exhausted and constant or near-constant returns to scale prevail over a considerable range of outputs in many industries. In these industries, small firms coexist with much larger firms.[6]

There are some industries, however, where the *LAC* curve declines continuously as the firm expands output, to the point where a single firm could satisfy the total market for the product or service more efficiently than two or more firms. These cases are usually referred to as "natural monopolies" and often arise in the provision of electricity, public transportation, etc. (public utilities). In such cases the local government often allows a single firm to supply the service to the entire market but subjects the firm to regulation (i.e., regulates the price or rate charged for the service). These three possible shapes of the *LAC* curve (U-shaped, L-shaped, and constantly declining) are shown in Figure 7-6 and examined in various U.S. industries in Case Study 7-3.

[6]The inability to observe rising *LAC* in the real world may be due to the fact that firms avoid expanding output when *LAC* begins to rise rapidly.

Figure 7-6
Possible Shapes of the *LAC* Curve

The left panel shows a U-shaped *LAC* curve, which indicates first increasing and then decreasing returns to scale. The middle panel shows a nearly L-shaped *LAC* curve, which shows that economies of the scale quickly give way to constant returns to scale or gently rising *LAC*. The right panel shows a *LAC* curve that declines continuously, as in the case of natural monopolies.

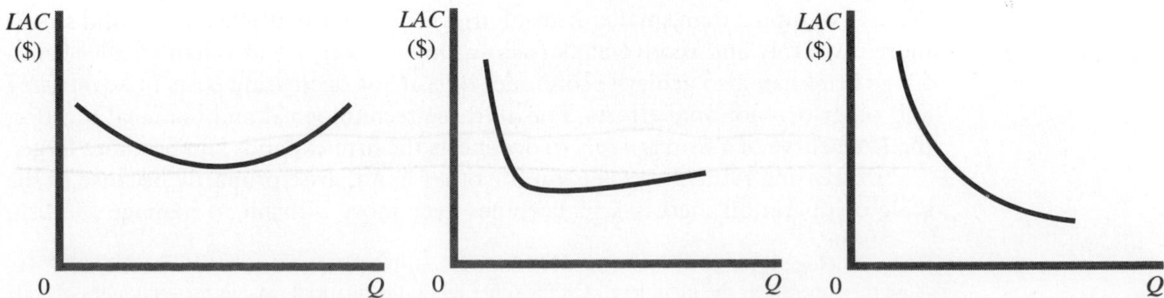

Economies of scale have to be distinguished from **economies of scope.** The latter refer to the lowering of costs that a firm often experiences when it produces two or more products together rather than each alone. A smaller commuter airline, for example, can profitably extend into providing cargo services, thereby lowering the cost of each operation alone. Another example is provided by a firm that produces a second product in order to utilize the by-products (which before the firm had to dispose of at a cost) arising from the production of the first product. Management must constantly be alert to the possibility of profitably extending its product line to exploit such economies of scope. One firm that is pushing economies of scale and economies of scope to the limit is Motorola—considered by many to be the best-managed firm in the world (see Case Study 7-4).

Case Study 7-3

The Shape of the Long-Run Average Cost Curve in Various U.S. Industries

Table 7-2 gives the long-run average cost for small firms as a percentage of the long-run average cost of large firms in six U.S. industries. The table shows that the *LAC* of small hospitals is 29 percent higher than for large hospitals. This implies that small hospitals operate in the declining portion of the *LAC* curve. For most other industries, the *LAC* of small firms is not much different from the *LAC* of large firms in the same industry. These results are consistent with the widespread near-constant returns to scale reported in Table 6-5 and, thus, with L-shaped or at least flat-bottomed *LAC* curves. Only in trucking does the *LAC* curve seem mildly U-shaped (since small firms have lower *LAC* costs than large ones). From Case Study 6-3, we can also infer that the *LAC* curve in automobile manufacturing is U-shaped with a flat bottom, with Ford near the bottom of the *LAC* curve, General Motors on the rising arm of the *LAC* curve (i.e., because of its large size, GM is incurring diseconomies of scale), while Chrysler, being much smaller than either GM or Ford, operated on the falling arm of the *LAC* curve in 1991. As indicated in Case Study 6-3, General Motors is shrinking to avoid diseconomies of scale.

Source: H. Cohen, "Hospital Cost Curves with Emphasis on Measuring Patient Care Output," in H. Klarman, ed., *Empirical Studies in Health Economics* (Baltimore: Johns Hopkins Press, 1979), pp. 279–293; F. Bell and N. Murphy, *Costs in Commercial Banking* (Boston: Federal Reserve Bank of Boston, Research Report No. 41, 1968); L. Christensen and W. Greene, "Economies of Scale in U.S. Electric Power Generation," *Journal of Political Economy,* August 1976; G. Eads, M. Nerlove, and W. Raduchel, "A Long-Run Cost Function for the Local Service Airline Industry," *The Review of Economics and Statistics,* August 1969; Z. Griliches, "Cost Allocation in Railroad Regulation," *The Bell Journal of Economics and Management Science,* Spring 1972; R. Koenker, "Optimal Scale and the Size Distribution of American Trucking Firms," *Journal of Transport Economics and Policy,* January 1977; "Automobiles: GM Decides Smaller Is Better," *The Margin,* November–December 1988, p. 28; and "GM's $11 Billion Turnaround," *Fortune,* October 17, 1994, pp. 54–74.

Table 7-2
***LAC* of Small Firms As a Percentage of *LAC* of Large Firms**

Industry	Percentage
Hospitals	129
Commercial banking	
Demand deposits	116
Installment loans	102
Electric power	112
Airline (local service)	100
Railroads	100
Trucking	95

Case Study 7-4
Can Motorola Avoid Diseconomies of Scale As It Grows by Leaps and Bounds?

Motorola, a leader in the worldwide revolution in wireless communications, is growing by leaps and bounds. In 1993 its sales jumped by 27.5 percent to $17 billion (with profits of $1 billion), propelling it to the twenty-third spot on the *Fortune 500* list, and 1994 was another knockout year. In fact, Motorola has been doubling in size every five years. The question is, Can Motorola keep avoiding excessive bureaucracy, complacency, and diseconomies of scale as it grows larger and larger?

Motorola is considered by many to be the best-managed company in the world today. It has been described as a titan of total quality management, an icon of innovation, a pioneer of self-directed teams, and a prince of profits; it is writing the book on reengineering, decentralization, job training, and on the breaking down of organizational boundaries and promoting cooperation between labor and management. Motorola is simply the best in the world in almost everything it does—including cellular phones, pagers, two-way radios, semiconductors, and other electronic gadgets. Motorola has an incredible 85 percent share of the world market in pagers, a 45 percent share of the world market for cellular phones, and $6 billion in semiconductor sales (making it the world's number 3 chip producer, after Intel and NEC), and it generates more than half of its revenues abroad. Contrary to many other large U.S. firms, this is a large company that sizzles. From a slowly declining electronics company, Motorola has become a world technological leader, beating the best of its Japanese competitors—and in the process becoming an industrial legend and management-books case study.

As it keeps growing, however, Motorola faces many new challenges. One is how to become more adept at marketing as its products become cheaper and more accessible to ordinary consumers (in the past, Motorola customers were primarily engineers and executives). Another challenge is how to tailor its approach to unfamiliar cultures as it ventures more and more onto the world market (Motorola expects to earn more than 75 percent of its income abroad in a few years). The most serious challenge that Motorola faces, however, is how to manage and hold its ever-growing business units together, how to continue to constantly renew itself, how to avoid becoming overconfident, and above all how to keep its workers motivated, energized, and constantly dissatisfied with past accomplishments and always striving to achieve more—so as to avoid the setting in of the dreaded diseconomies of scale.

Source: "Keeping Motorola on a Roll," *Fortune,* April 18, 1994, pp. 67–78.

7-5 LEARNING CURVES

As firms gain experience in the production of a commodity or service, their average cost of production usually declines. That is, *for a given level of output per time period,* the increasing *cumulative total output* over many time periods often provides the manufacturing experience that enables firms to lower their average cost of production. The **learning curve** shows the decline in the average input cost of production with rising cumulative total outputs over time. For example, it might take 1,000 hours to assemble the 100th aircraft, but only 700 hours to assemble the 200th aircraft because as managers and workers gain production experience, they become more efficient. Contrast this to economies of scale, which refer instead to declining average cost as the firm's output *per time period* increases.

Figure 7-7 shows a learning curve, which indicates that the average cost declines from about \$250 for producing the 100th unit of the product (point *F*), to about \$200 for producing the 200th unit (point *G*), and to about \$165 for the 400th unit (point *H*). Note that average cost declines at a decreasing rate so that the learning curve is convex to the origin. This is the usual shape of learning

Figure 7-7
Learning Curve

Learning curve *FGH* shows that the average cost is about \$250 for producing the 100th unit (point *F*), about \$200 for the 200th unit (point *G*), and about \$165 for the 400th unit (point *H*).

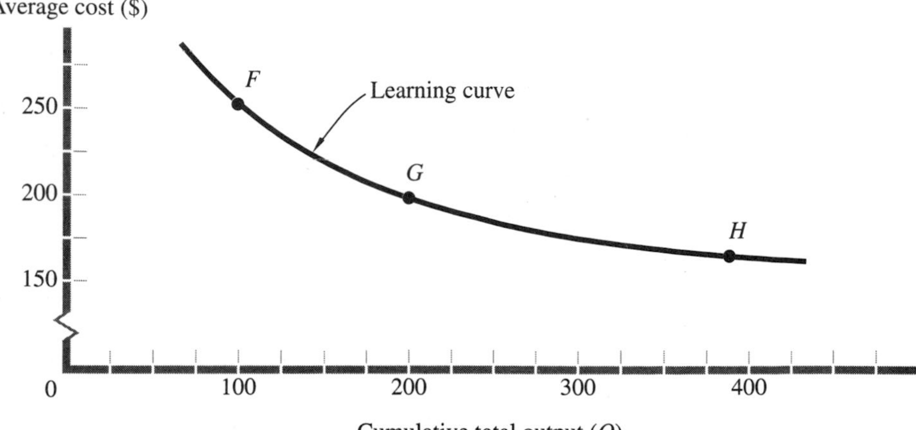

curves; that is, firms usually achieve the largest decline in average input costs when the production process is relatively new and less as the firm matures.

The learning curve can be expressed algebraically as follows:

$$C = aQ^b \tag{7-10}$$

where C is the average input cost of the Qth unit of output, a is the average cost of the first unit of output, and b will be negative because the average input cost declines with increases in cumulative total output. The greater the absolute value of b, the faster average input cost declines. Taking the logarithm of both sides of Equation 7-10 gives

$$\log C = \log a + b \log Q \tag{7-11}$$

In the above logarithmic form, b is the slope of the learning curve.

The parameter of the learning curve in the double-log form of Equation 7-11 (i.e., $\log a$ and b) can be estimated by regression analysis with historical data on average cost and cumulative output. Suppose that doing this gives the following result:

$$\log C = 3 - 0.3 \log Q \tag{7-12}$$

In Equation 7-12, C is expressed in dollars, $\log a = 3$ and $b = -0.3$. Thus, the average input cost of the 100th unit is

$$\log C = 3 - 0.3 \log 100$$

Since the log of 100 is 2 (obtained by simply entering the number 100 in your hand calculator and pressing the "log" key, we have

$$\begin{aligned}\log C &= 3 - 0.3(2)\\ &= 3 - 0.6\\ &= 2.4\end{aligned}$$

Since the antilog of 2.4 is 251.19, the average input cost (C) of the 100th unit of output is \$251.19.

The average input cost for the 200th unit is

$$\begin{aligned}\log C &= 3 - 0.3 \log 200\\ &= 3 - 0.3(2.30103)\\ &= 3 - 0.690309\\ &= 2.309691\end{aligned}$$

Therefore, $C = \$204.03$.

The student can determine in an analogous way that for the 400th unit, $C = \$165.72$. These are, in fact, the values shown by the learning curve in Figure 7-7.

Learning curves have been documented in many manufacturing and service sectors, ranging from the manufacturing of airplanes, appliances, shipbuilding, refined petroleum products, to the operation of power plants. They have also been used to forecast the needs for personnel, machinery, and raw materials, and for scheduling production, determining the price at which to sell output, and even to evaluate suppliers' price quotations. For example, in its early days as a computer-chip producer, Texas Instruments adopted an aggressive price strategy based on the learning curve. Believing that the learning curve in chip production was very steep, it kept unit prices very low in order to increase its cumulative total output very rapidly and thereby benefit from learning by doing. The strategy was very successful and the rest is history (Texas Instruments became one of the world's major players in this market).

How rapidly the learning curve (i.e., average input costs) declines can differ widely among firms and is greater the smaller the rate of employee turnover, the fewer the production interruptions (which would lead to "forgetting"), and the greater the ability of the firm to transfer knowledge from the production of other similar products. The average cost typically declines by 20 to 30 percent for each doubling of cumulative output for many firms. Firms, however, do not rely only on their production experience to lower costs and are looking farther and farther afield from their industry to gain creative insights on how to increase productivity (see Case Study 7-5). Indeed, tomorrow's firm is likely to be much more productive than today's firm by constantly rethinking its function and organization (see Case Study 7-6).

Case Study 7-5

To Reduce Costs, Firms Often Look Far Afield

In order to increase productivity and cut costs to better compete, firms often seek creative insights in industries far afield from their own. Of course, in a time of increased global competition, firms routinely scrutinize competitors' practices in their quest for innovative products and processes. But seeking inspiration only in one's own industry has limitations, and so more and more firms are increasingly looking in other industries and fields, "from outside the box," to come up with new products and better ways of doing things. For example, when Southwest Airlines wanted to improve the turnaround of its aircraft at airports, it did not examine other airlines' practices but went to the Indianapolis 500 to watch how pit crews fuel and service race cars in a matter of seconds. The result was that Southwest was able to cut its turnaround time by 50 percent. Such a drastic increase in productivity could hardly be accomplished by observing other airlines' practices. It is, of course, much more difficult to adapt techniques from other industries, but when it is accomplished, the potential rewards in terms of increased efficiency can be very great.

The key to finding useful insights in seemingly unrelated fields is to focus on processes. After all, all firms do basically the same things—hire employees, buy from suppliers, carry on production processes, sell to customers, and collect payments. For example, a firm seeking to speed its production process might look at Domino's Pizza, an outfit that takes an order, produces the pizza, delivers it, and collects the money—all in less than 30 minutes. A major gas utility firm discovered ways to greatly speed the delivery of its fuel to customers by observing how Federal Express delivers packages overnight. Similarly, a firm delivering gravel learned how to greatly speed deliveries by having truck drivers plug a card into a machine requesting the quantity of gravel to load without the need for the driver to get off the truck and waste a great deal of time filling order forms—just as automatic teller machines work at banks.

Source: "To Compete Better, Look Far Afield," *The New York Times*, September 18, 1994, Sec. 3, p. 11.

Case Study 7-6
Tomorrow's Factory

The factory of tomorrow will be generally smaller than today's factory and more flexible and able to shift gears quickly; it will be closer to markets, and it will be focused, producing one or a very few related products. Recent technological advances, such as computer-aided design and computer-aided manufacturing, have greatly reduced optimal lot sizes or the production runs necessary to achieve maximum production efficiency. By the turn of the century, the average factory is likely to employ from 400 to 600 workers, down from 1,200 workers today. Shorter production runs also mean that often it will not be wise for the firm to completely automate all of its production processes if the product will not be around long enough for the firm to recoup all of the capital invested in automation. Capital investment will also be dictated by the need for the firm to be flexible and able to shift quickly to the production of different or related products, as required by shifts in consumer demand.

Factories will also be located closer to markets in order to speed deliveries and, even more importantly, in order to have rapid customer feedback on product performance and anticipate changes in consumer tastes. The global firm of the future will have a manufacturing network of decentralized plants in each large, sophisticated regional market for its product, such as the United States, Europe, and Asia. The specific location of factories in each region will then depend on the availability of the manufacturing infrastructure (i.e., on where the labor force has the necessary skill and knowledge and on where there is easy accessibility to required raw materials, transportation, and communications).

By the turn of the century, factories are also likely to be more focused; that is, they are likely to specialize in the production of a single or a few related products rather than producing a myriad of different products, as in the past. In such a factory of the future, the line between departments will be blurred so that engineers, production people, and sales personnel will all work together on every aspect of the product, from its original design to its final sale. Furthermore, in order to respond to government regulations and customers' wishes, tomorrow's factory is likely to be more ecologically responsible than today's factory. Above all, the factory of the future will be incredibly efficient—just as today's farms, with only 1 percent of the labor force, are 100 times more productive than farms in past decades.

Source: "Tomorrow's Factory," *Management Review*, January 1993, pp. 19–23; and "The New Dynamics of Global Manufacturing Site Location," *Sloan Management Review*, Summer 1994, pp. 69–80.

7-6 MINIMIZING COSTS INTERNATIONALLY—THE NEW ECONOMIES OF SCALE

In this section we examine the growing importance of international trade in inputs as a way for firms to minimize costs internationally, as well as the ability of some U.S. firms to satisfy their needs for some skilled labor from abroad.

International Trade in Inputs

During the past decade or so, there has been a sharp increase in international trade in parts and components. Today, more products manufactured by international corporations have parts and components made in many different nations. The reason is to minimize production costs. For example, the motors of some Ford Fiestas are produced in the United Kingdom, the transmissions in France, the clutches in Spain, and the parts are assembled in Germany for sales throughout Europe. Similarly, Japanese and German cameras are often assembled in Singapore to take advantage of the much cheaper labor there.

Foreign sourcing of inputs is often not a matter of choice to earn higher profits, but simply a requirement to remain competitive. Firms that do not look abroad for cheaper inputs face loss of competitiveness in world markets and even in the domestic market. This is certainly the reason that $625 of the $860 total cost of producing an IBM PC was incurred for parts and components manufactured by IBM outside the United States or purchased from foreign producers during the mid-1980s (see Case Study 7-7). Such low-cost offshore purchase of inputs is likely to continue to expand rapidly in the future and is being fostered by joint ventures, licensing arrangements, and other nonequity collaborative arrangements. Indeed, this represents one of the most dynamic aspects of the global business environment of today.

Not only are more and more inputs imported, but more and more firms are opening production facilities in more and more nations. For example, Nestlé's, the largest Swiss company and the world's second largest food company, has production facilities in 59 countries, and America's Gillette has facilities in 22. In 1987, Ford had component factories and assembly plants in 26 different industrial sites in the United Kingdom, Germany, Belgium, France, Spain, and Portugal, and it employed more people abroad than in the United States (201,000 people abroad as compared with 181,000 in the United States). Bertelsmann AG, the $7 billion German media empire, not only owns printing plants around the world and the Literary Guild Book Club but also prints books at competitor's plants and sells them through Time-owned Book-of-the-Month Club.[7]

So widespread and growing is international trade in inputs and the opening of production facilities abroad that we are rapidly moving toward truly multinational firms with roots in many nations rather than in only one country, as in the past. And this affects not only multinationals. Indeed, more and more firms that until a few years ago operated exclusively in the domestic market are now purchasing increasing quantities of inputs and components and shifting some of their production to

[7]See W. H. Davidson and J. de la Torre, *Managing the Global Corporation* (New York: McGraw-Hill, 1989).

foreign nations. For example, Malachi Mixon, the American medical-equipment company, now buys parts and components in half a dozen countries, from China to Colombia, when ten years ago it did all of its shopping at home. The popular Mazda Miata automobile, which is manufactured in Japan, was conceived in Mazda's California design lab by an American engineer at the same time that Mazda opened production facilities for other models in the United States.

Case Study 7-7

Even the IBM PC Is Not All American!

Table 7-3 shows that of the total manufacturing cost of $860 for the IBM PC in 1985, $625 were for parts and components made abroad (of which, $230 were from U.S.–owned plants). While all the parts made overseas could be manufactured domestically, they would have cost more and would have led to higher PC prices in the United States (and reduced competitiveness of IBM PCs in international markets). Today, even a larger proportion of parts and components going into the IBM PC are made abroad. Indeed, IBM manufactured its new PS/55 laptop entirely in Japan in 1992!

Source: "America's High-Tech Crisis," *Business Week,* March 11, 1985, pp. 56–67, and "Selling Now in Tokyo: Thinnest IBM Portable," *The New York Times,* April 11, 1991, p. D1.

Table 7-3
Distribution of Manufacturing Costs for the IBM PC in the United States and Abroad

Total manufacturing cost:				$860
Portion made abroad:			$625	
In U.S.–owned plants		$230		
In foreign-owned plants		395		
Distribution of manufacturing costs:				
Monochrome monitor (Korea)	$ 85			
Semiconductors (Japan)	105			
Semiconductors (U.S.)	105			
Power supply (Japan)	60			
Graphics printer (Japan)	160			
Floppy disk drives (Singapore)	165			
Assembly of disk drives (U.S.)	25			
Keyboard (Japan)	50			
Case and final assembly (U.S.)	105			
	$860			

The New International Economies of Scale

Firms must constantly explore sources of cheaper inputs and overseas production in order to remain competitive in our rapidly shrinking world. Indeed, this process can be regarded as manufacturing's **new international economies of scale** in today's global economy. Just as companies were forced to rationalize operations within each country in the 1980s, they now face the challenge of integrating their operations for their entire system of manufacturing around the world in order to take advantage of these new international economies of scale.[8] What is important is for the firm to focus on those components that are indispensible to the company's competitive position over subsequent product generations and outsource other components in which outside suppliers have a distinctive production advantage.[9]

These new international economies of scale can be achieved in five basic areas: product development, purchasing, production, demand management, order fulfillment. In product development, the firm can design a core product for the entire world economy, building into the product the possibility of variations and derivatives to meet the needs of local markets. Firms can also achieve new economies of scale by purchasing raw materials, parts and components on a global rather than on a local basis, no matter where their operations are located. Firms can also coordinate production in low-cost manufacturing centers with final assembly in high-cost locations near markets. They can also forecast the demand for their products and undertake demand management on a world rather than on a national basis. Firms can also achieve important economies of scale by shipping products from the plants closest to customers more quickly and with smaller inventory on a global basis. These new international economies of scale are likely to become even more important in the future as we move closer and closer to a truly global economy.

Immigration of Skilled Labor

A survey of almost 300 employers by the National Science Foundation (NSF) in 1985 found that 28 percent of them had personnel shortages in science and engineering. This shortage persists today. Indeed, the NSF is now predicting a shortage of 675,000 scientists and engineers in the United States by the year 2006.[10] This is the result of fewer college-age people in the United States due to the lower birth rates of the 1970s and the declining percentage going into science and engineering. Shortages of skilled workers also exist in other fields. Many hospitals today are staffed by increasing numbers of foreign-born doctors and nurses. There are also shortages in mathematics and computer science. While government aid to higher education can induce more students to train in these fields in the long run, in the short run firms will have to turn more and more to foreign workers with the sought-after skills, and this trend is likely to accelerate during this decade.

[8]See "Manufacturing's New Economies of Scale," *Harvard Business Review,* May–June 1992, pp. 94–102, and "The New Dynamics of Global Manufacturing Site Location," *Sloan Management Review,* Summer 1994, pp. 69–80.

[9]See "Strategic Outsourcing," *Harvard Business Review,* November–December 1992, pp. 98–107, and "Strategic Outsourcing," *Sloan Management Review,* Summer 1994, pp. 43–55.

[10]See "Wanted: 675,000 Future Scientists and Engineers," *Science,* June 1989, pp. 1536–1538, and "Supply and Demand for Scientists and Engineers: A National Crisis in the Making," *Science,* April 1990, pp. 425–432.

Some of the projected shortfall in scientists, engineers, and other highly skilled professionals is also likely to be made up by the increasing number of foreign students who attend American universities—many of whom choose to remain in the United States after completing their studies. For example, in recent years more than 25 percent of the students earning doctorates in the United States have been foreigners. The figure is 30 percent in the physical sciences and 40 percent in mathematics and engineering. Changes in U.S. immigration laws in 1990 recognize that the United States now needs "the best and the brightest from other countries in order to compete in the cutthroat world of global markets."[11] The new law nearly triples (to 140,000) the number of yearly visas granted to sought-after experts and professionals. With the collapse of communism in the former Soviet Union in the late 1980s and early 1990s, a huge number of chemists, physicists, mathematicians, and computer scientists have been flocking to the United States, attracted by much higher paying jobs and better working conditions.[12]

It must be kept in mind, however, that while this represents a gain for the United States, such an inflow of highly skilled personnel represents a loss for the country of emigration. This has been aptly captured by the phrase **brain drain.** But in a world of global competition, the manager must forecast the firm's need for skilled labor and hire it from abroad when not available domestically. If that is not possible, the firm may have to consider moving some of its operations abroad.

7-7 COST-VOLUME-PROFIT ANALYSIS AND OPERATING LEVERAGE

In this section, we examine cost-volume-profit analysis (often called "breakeven analysis") and operating leverage. These simple analytical techniques are frequently used in managerial decision making and can be quite useful when applied under the proper set of circumstances.

Cost-Volume-Profit Analysis

Cost-volume-profit or breakeven analysis examines the relationship among the total revenue, total costs, and total profits of the firm at various levels of output. Cost-volume-profit or breakeven analysis is often used by business executives to determine the sales volume required for the firm to break even and the total profits and losses at other sales levels. The analysis utilizes a cost-volume-profit chart in which the total revenue (TR) and the total cost (TC) curves are represented by straight lines, as in Figure 7-8.

In the figure, total revenues and total costs are plotted on the vertical axis, whereas output or sales per time period are plotted on the horizontal axis. The

[11]See "The Hunt for New Americans," *Newsweek,* December 17, 1990, pp. 33–34; "Employers Are Looking Abroad for the Skilled and the Energetic," *The New York Times,* July 16, 1989, p. E4; and "The Immigrants," *Business Week,* July 13, 1992, pp. 114–122.

[12]See D. Salvatore, *International Economics,* 5th ed. (Englewood Cliffs, N.J.: Prentice-Hall, 1995), Sec. 12.6.

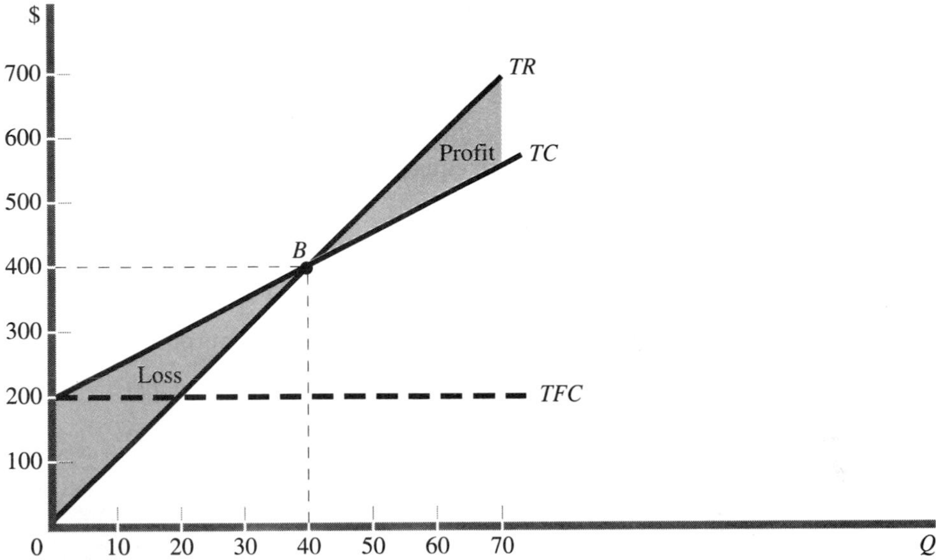

Figure 7-8
Linear Cost-Volume-Profit or Breakeven Chart

The slope of the total revenue (*TR*) curve refers to the product price of \$10 per unit. The vertical intercept of the total cost (*TC*) curve refers to the total fixed costs (*TFC*) of \$200, and the slope of the *TC* curve to the average variable cost of \$5. The firm breaks even with $TR = TC =$ \$400 at the output (Q) of 40 units per time period (point *B*). The losses that the firm incurs at smaller output levels and profits at larger output levels can be read off the figure.

slope of the *TR* curve refers to the constant price of \$10 per unit at which the firm can sell its output. The *TC* curve indicates total fixed costs (*TFC*) of \$200 (the vertical intercept) and a constant average variable cost of \$5 (the slope of the *TC* curve). This is often the case for many firms for small changes in output or sales. The firm breaks even (with $TR = TC =$ \$400) at $Q = 40$ per time period (point *B* in the figure). The firm incurs losses at smaller outputs and earns profits at higher output levels.

The cost-volume-profit or breakeven chart is a flexible tool to quickly analyze the effect of changing conditions on the firm. For example, an increase in the price of the commodity can be shown by increasing the slope of the *TR* curve, an increase in total fixed costs of the firm can be shown by an increase in the vertical intercept of the *TC* curve, and an increase in average variable costs by an increase in the slope of the *TC* curve. The chart will then show the change in the breakeven point of the firm and the profits or losses at other output or sales levels (see Problem 11).

Cost-volume-profit analysis can also be performed algebraically, as follows. Total revenue is equal to the selling price (P) per unit times the quantity of output or sales (Q). That is,

$$TR = (P)(Q) \tag{7-13}$$

Total costs equal total fixed costs plus total variable costs (TVC). Since TVC is equal to the average (per-unit) variable costs (AVC) times the quantity of output or sales, we have

$$TC = TFC + (AVC)(Q) \tag{7-14}$$

Setting total revenue equal to total costs and substituting Q_B (the breakeven output) for Q, we have

$$TR = TC \tag{7-15}$$

$$(P)(Q_B) = TFC + (AVC)(Q_B) \tag{7-16}$$

Solving Equation 7-16 for the breakeven output, Q_B, we get

$$(P)(Q_B) - (AVC)(Q_B) = TFC$$

$$(Q_B)(P - AVC) = TFC$$

$$Q_B = \frac{TFC}{P - AVC} \tag{7-17}$$

For example, with $TFC = \$200$, $P = \$10$, and $AVC = \$5$,

$$Q_B = \frac{\$200}{\$10 - \$5} = 40$$

This is the breakeven output shown on the cost-volume-profit chart in Figure 7-8. The denominator in Equation 7-17 (that is, $P - AVC$) is called the **contribution margin per unit** because it represents the portion of the selling price that can be applied to cover the fixed costs of the firm and to provide for profits.

More generally, suppose that the firm wishes to earn a specific profit and wants to estimate the quantity that it must sell to earn that profit. Cost-volume-profit or breakeven analysis can be used in determining the target output (Q_T) at which a target profit (π_T) can be achieved. To do so, we simply add π_T to the numerator of Equation 7-17 and have

$$Q_T = \frac{TFC + \pi_T}{P - AVC} \tag{7-18}$$

For example, if the firm represented in the cost-volume-profit chart in Figure 7-8 wanted to earn a target profit of \$100, the target output would be

$$Q_T = \frac{\$200 + \$100}{\$10 - \$5} = \frac{\$300}{\$5} = 60$$

To see that the output of $Q = 60$ does indeed lead to the target profit (π_T) of \$100, note that

$$TR = (P)(Q) = (\$10)(60) = \$600$$

$$TC = TFC + (AVC)(Q) = \$200 + (\$5)(60) = \$500$$

and

$$\pi_T = TR - TC = \$600 - \$500 = \$100$$

While linear cost-volume-profit charts and analysis can be very useful and are frequently used by business executives, government agencies, and not-for-profit organizations, care must be exercised to apply them only in cases *where the assumption of constant prices and average variable costs holds.*[13] Cost-volume-profit anaylsis also assumes that the firm produces a single product or a constant mix of products. Over time, the product mix changes, and it may be difficult to allocate the fixed costs among the various products. Despite these shortcomings, when properly used, cost-volume-profit analysis can be very useful in managerial decision making.

To be noted, however, is that sometimes Japanese firms turn cost-volume-profit analysis on its head. Instead of designing a new product and then estimating the cost of producing it (as American firms typically do), Japanese firms sometimes start with a target cost based on the market price at which the firm believes consumers will buy the product and then strive to produce the product at the specified targeted cost. Under such **Japanese cost-management systems,** the firm subtracts the desired profit from the expected selling price and then allocates targeted costs to each part, component, and process required to produce the product in such a way as to keep costs within the targeted level.

Operating Leverage

Operating leverage refers to the ratio of the firm's total fixed costs to total variable costs. The higher is this ratio, the more highly leveraged the firm is said to be. As the firm becomes more automated or more highly leveraged (i.e., substitutes fixed for variable costs), its total fixed costs rise but its average variable costs fall. Because of higher overhead costs, the breakeven output of the firm increases. This is shown in Figure 7-9.

In Figure 7-9, the intersection of TR and TC defines the breakeven output of $Q_B = 40$ (as in Figure 7-8). If the firm's total fixed costs rise from \$200 (the vertical intercept of TC) to \$300 (the vertical intercept of TC'), while average variable costs decline from $AVC = \$5$ (the slope of TC) to $AVC' = \$3.33$ (the slope of TC'), the breakeven output will rise to $Q_{B'} = 45$ (given by the intersection of TR and TC').

Figure 7-9 also shows that the higher is the ratio of total fixed costs to total variable costs (i.e., the more highly leveraged the firm is), the more sensitive are the firm's profits to changes in output or sales. For example, the increase in output or sales from 60 to 70 units increases profits from \$100 (the vertical distance between TR and either TC or TC') to \$150 with TC and to \$166.67 with TC'. The responsiveness or sensitivity of the firm's total profits (π) to a change in its output or sales (Q) can be measured by the **degree of operating leverage (DOL).**

[13]If prices and average variable costs are not constant, a nonlinear cost-volume-profit chart and analysis would have to be used. This is similar to the optimization analysis examined on page 41 and shown in Figure 2-4. The only difference is that the objective of the analysis shifts from the determination of the optimum price and output in optimization analysis to the determination of the output levels at which the firm breaks even or earns a target profit in cost-volume-profit analysis.

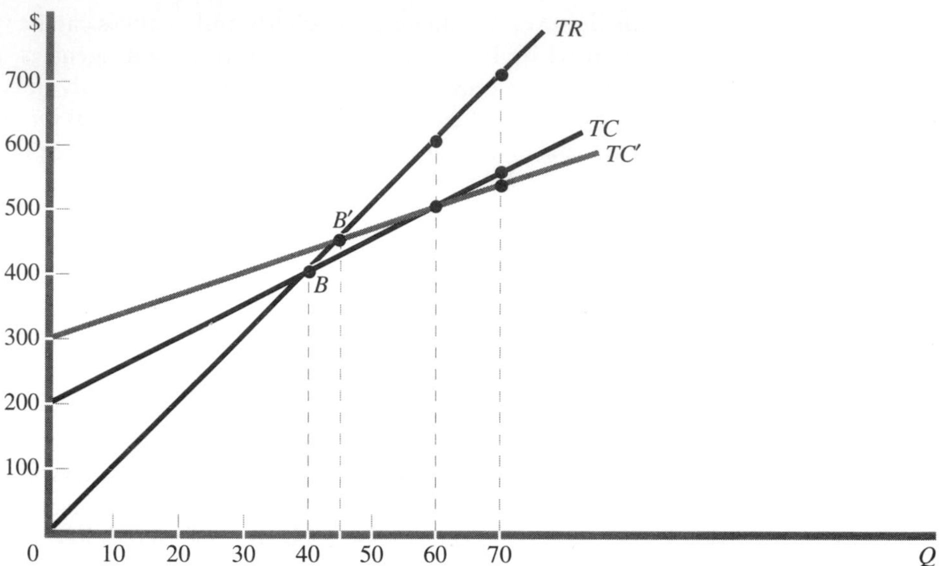

Figure 7-9
Operating Leverage, Breakeven Point, and Variability of Profits

The intersection of *TR* and *TC* defines the breakeven quantity of $Q_B = 40$ (as in Figure 7-8). With *TC*′ (i.e., if the firm becomes more highly leveraged), the breakeven quantity increases to $Q_{B'} = 45$ (given by the intersection of *TR* and *TC*′). The total profits of the firm are also more variable with *TC*′ than with *TC*.

This is nothing other than the sales elasticity of profit and is defined as the percentage change in profit divided by the percentage change in output or sales. That is,[14]

$$DOL = \frac{\%\Delta\pi}{\%\Delta Q} = \frac{\Delta\pi/\pi}{\Delta Q/Q} = \frac{\Delta\pi}{\Delta Q}\cdot\frac{Q}{\pi} \tag{7-19}$$

But $\pi = Q(P - AVC) - TFC$ and $\Delta\pi = \Delta Q(P - AVC)$. Substituting these values into Equation 7-19, we get

$$DOL = \frac{\Delta Q(P - AVC)Q}{\Delta Q[Q(P - AVC) - TFC]} = \frac{Q(P - AVC)}{Q(P - AVC) - TFC} \tag{7-20}$$

The numerator in Equation 7-20 is the total contribution to fixed costs and profits of all units sold by the firm, while the denominator is total (economic) profit.

[14]In terms of calculus,

$$DOL = \frac{\partial\pi}{\partial Q}\cdot\frac{Q}{\pi}$$

For example, for an increase in output from 60 to 70 units, the degree of operating leverage with TC is

$$DOL = \frac{60(\$10 - \$5)}{60(\$10 - \$5) - \$200} = \frac{\$300}{\$100} = 3$$

With TC' (i.e., when the firm becomes more highly leveraged), the degree of operating leverage becomes

$$DOL' = \frac{60(\$10 - \$3.33)}{60(\$10 - \$3.33) - \$300} = \frac{\$400}{\$100} = 4$$

Thus, the degree of operating leverage (DOL) increases as the firm becomes more highly leveraged or capital intensive. It is also higher the closer we are to the breakeven point because the base in measuring the percentage change in profits (the denominator in Equation 7-19) is close to zero near the breakeven point. Note that when the firm's sales and output are high (greater than 60 units in Figure 7-9), the firm makes larger profits when it is more highly leveraged (i.e., with TC'). But it also incurs losses sooner, and these losses rise more rapidly than when the firm is less highly leveraged (i.e., with TC). The larger profits of the more highly leveraged firm when output is high (greater than 60 units in Figure 7-9) can thus be regarded as the return for its greater risk.

Case Study 7-8

Breakeven Analysis for Lockheed's Tri-Star Airbus and Europe's Airbus Industrie

In 1971, Lockheed sought a government guarantee for a bank loan for $250 million in order to complete the development of the L-1001 Tri-Star Airbus, a wide-bodied commercial jet aircraft. The debate in the congressional hearings on the question of whether the Tri-Star program was economically sound proceeded almost entirely on the basis of estimated breakeven sales. Lockheed indicated that the breakeven point would be reached at sales of about 200 aircraft, at a price of $15.5 million each at 1968 prices. With firm orders for 103 aircraft and options for 75 others at the time of the congressional hearings, Lockheed was confident to be able to surpass the breakeven point and earn a profit. Based on this economic rationality of the project, the loan guarantee legislation was passed. In its calculations, however, Lockheed had not included among its fixed costs the cost of developing the technology and construction facilities to build the aircraft. Had it done so, breakeven sales would have been twice as large as those indicated by Lockheed in the congressional hearings. Since it was unrealistic (based on the total market for wide-bodied aircraft and competition from McDonnell-Douglas and Boeing) for Lockheed to sell that many aircraft, the inclusion of all costs in the calculations would have shown that the project was economically unsound. In the aircraft industry, where development costs are very high, very large sales are usually required before a firm can break even. Indeed, it took more than twenty-five years and $26 billion in subsidies by the governments of Germany, France, the United Kingdom, and Spain before Airbus Industrie began to break even in 1990.

Source: U. E. Reinhardt, "Break-Even Analysis for Lockheed Tri-Star: An Application of Financial Theory," *The Journal of Finance,* September 1973, pp. 821–838; "There Is No Stopping of Europe's Airbus Industrie Now," *The New York Times,* June 23, 1991, Sec. 3, p. 1; and "Boeing, Airbus in Cost Dogfight," *Financial Times,* July 12, 1994, p. 6.

7-8 EMPIRICAL ESTIMATION OF COST FUNCTIONS

Empirical estimates of cost functions are essential for many managerial decision purposes. Knowledge of short-run cost functions is necessary for the firm in determining the optimal level of output and the price to charge. Knowledge of long-run cost functions is essential in planning for the optimal scale of plant for the firm to build in the long run. In this section, we examine the most important techniques for estimating the firm's short-run and long-run cost curves, discuss some of the data and measurement problems encountered in estimation, and summarize the results of some empirical studies of short-run and long-run cost functions.

Data and Measurement Problems in Estimating Short-Run Cost Functions

The most common method of estimating the firm's short-run cost functions is regression analysis, whereby total variable costs are regressed against output and a few other variables, such as input prices and operating conditions, during the time period when the size of the plant is fixed. The total variable cost function rather than the total cost function is usually estimated because of the difficulty of allocating fixed costs to the various products produced by the firm. The firm's total cost function can then be obtained by simply adding the best estimate possible of the fixed costs to the total variable costs. The firm's average variable and marginal cost functions can be easily obtained from the total variable cost function as indicated in Section 7-2. While this sounds simple enough, the estimation of the firm's short-run cost functions is fraught with data and measurement difficulties.

As pointed out earlier in the chapter, the firm's cost functions are based on the assumption of constant input prices. If input prices increase, they will cause an upward shift of the entire cost function. Therefore, input prices will have to be included as additional explanatory variables in the regression analysis in order to identify their independent effect on costs. Other independent variables that may have to be included in the regression analysis are fuel and material costs, the quality of inputs, the technology used by the firm, weather conditions, and changes in the product mix and product quality. The actual independent or explanatory variables included in the regression (besides output) depend on the particular situation under examination. Thus, we can postulate that

$$C = f(Q, X_1, X_2, \ldots, X_n) \tag{7-21}$$

where C refers to total variable costs, Q is output, and the X's refer to the other determinants of the firm's costs. Using multiple regression analysis (see Section 4-5) allows us to isolate the effect on costs of changes in each of the independent or explanatory variables. By concentrating on the relationship between costs and output, we can then identify the firm's total variable cost curve.

One fundamental problem that arises in the empirical estimation of cost functions is that opportunity costs must be extracted from the available accounting cost data. That is, each input used in production must be valued at its opportunity cost based on what the input could earn in its best alternative use rather than the actual expenditures for the input. For example, if the firm owns the building in which it operates, the cost of utilizing the building is not zero but is equal to the rent that the firm would obtain by renting the building to the highest bidder. Similarly, inventories used in current production must be valued at current market prices rather than at historical cost. Finally, the part of the depreciation of fixed assets, such as machinery, that is based on the actual usage of the assets (as contrasted to the depreciation of the assets based on the passage of time alone) should be estimated and included in current production costs for each product. These data are often very difficult to obtain from the available accounting data.

Not only must costs be correctly apportioned to the various products produced by the firm but care must also be exercised to match costs to output over time (i.e., allocate costs to the period in which the output is produced rather than to the period when the costs were incurred). Specifically, the leads and lags in costs from the corresponding output must be adjusted so as to achieve a correct correspondence between costs and output. For example, while a firm may postpone all but emergency maintenance until a period of slack production, these maintenance costs must be allocated to the earlier production periods.

The manager must also determine the length of time over which to estimate cost functions. While daily, weekly, monthly, quarterly, or yearly data can be used, monthly data over a period of two or three years are usually utilized. The period of time must be long enough to allow for sufficient variation in output and costs but not long enough for the firm to change plant size (since the firm would then no longer be operating in the short run). Since output is usually measured in physical units (e.g., number of automobiles of a particular type produced per time period) while costs are measured in monetary units, the various costs must be deflated by the appropriate price index to correct for inflation. That is, with input prices usually rising at different rates, the price index for each category of inputs will have to be used to obtain their deflated values to use in the regression analysis.

The Functional Form of Short-Run Cost Functions

Economic theory postulates an S-shaped (cubic) TVC curve as indicated in the left panel of Figure 7-10, with corresponding U-shaped AVC and MC curves. The general equations for these functions are, respectively,[15]

$$TVC = a(Q) + bQ^2 + cQ^3 \tag{7-22}$$

$$AVC = \frac{TVC}{Q} = a + bQ + cQ^2 \tag{7-23}$$

$$MC = a + 2bQ + 3cQ^2 \tag{7-24}$$

[15]In the empirical estimation of these functions, a and c will be positive and b negative. Also, using calculus, $MC = d(TVC)/(dQ)$.

Figure 7-10
Theoretical and Empirical Approximation of *TVC*, *AVC*, and *MC* Curves

Economic theory postulates an S-shaped (cubic) *TVC* curve as indicated in the left panel, with corresponding U-shaped *AVC* and *MC* curves. The right panel shows a linear approximation to the cubic *TVC* curve, which often gives a better empirical fit of the data points over the observed range of outputs. Note that the *AVC* curve in the right panel becomes quite flat, approaching the value of *b* (the horizontal *MC* curve) as output expands.

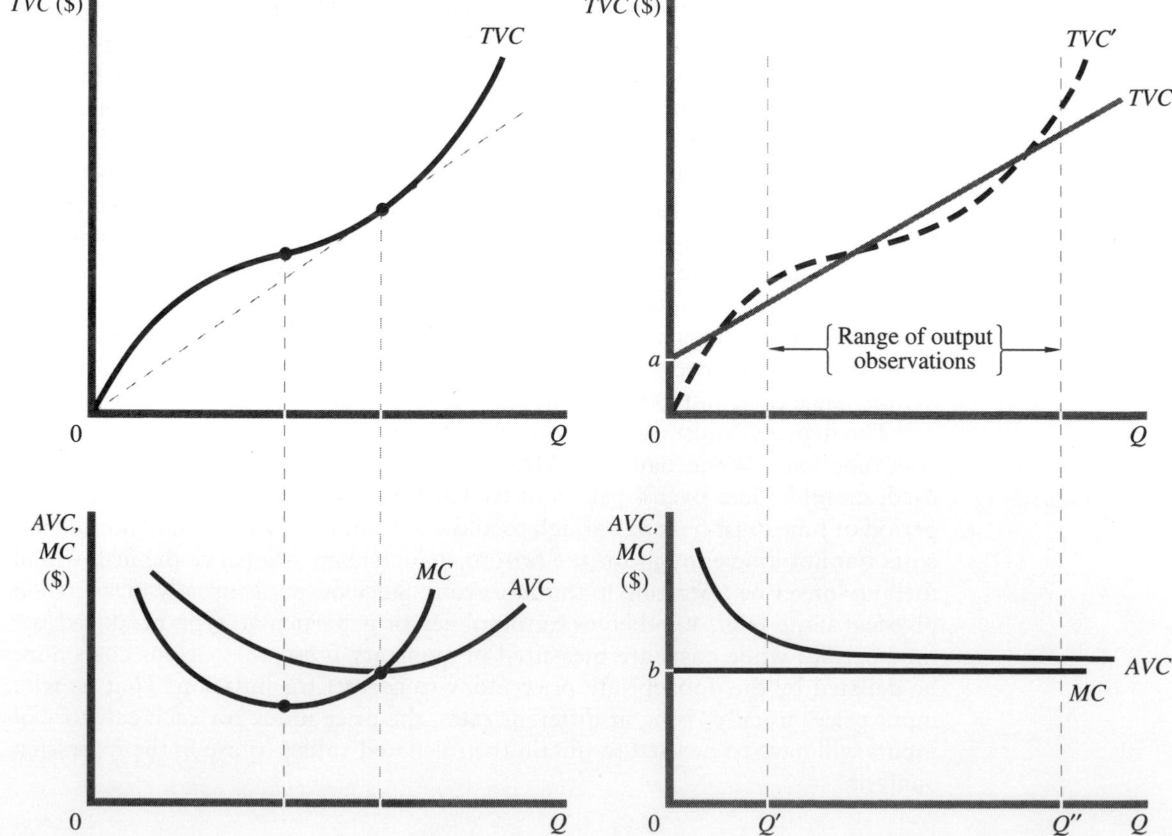

The right panel of Figure 7-10 shows a linear approximation to the cubic *TVC* curve, which often gives a good empirical fit of the data points over the observed range of outputs. The estimated equations of the linear approximation to the S-shaped or cubic *TVC* curve and of its corresponding *AVC* and *MC* curves are

$$TVC = a + bQ \tag{7-25}$$

$$AVC = \frac{a}{Q} + b \tag{7-26}$$

$$MC = b \tag{7-27}$$

Having estimated the parameters of the *TVC* curve (i.e., the values of a and b in Equation 7-25), we can use these estimated parameters to derive the corresponding *AVC* and *MC* functions of the firm, as indicated in Equations 7-26 and 7-27. Note that estimated parameter a (the constant in estimated Regression 7-25) cannot be interpreted as the fixed costs of the firm since we are estimating the *TVC* function. Since $Q = 0$ is usually far removed from the actual observed data points on the *TVC* curve (from Q' to Q'' in the right panel of Figure 7-10), no economic significance can be attached to the estimated parameter a. Note also that the *AVC* curve in the right panel becomes quite flat, approaching the value of b (the horizontal *MC* curve). This is often observed in the actual empirical estimation (see Case Study 7-9).[16] One possible explanation for this is that while the amount of capital (say, the number of machines) that the firm has is fixed in the short run, the firm may keep some machines idle when output is low and bring them into operation by hiring more labor when it wants to increase output. Since the ratio of machines to output as well as machines to labor tends to remain constant in the face of changes in output, the firm's *AVC* and *MC* tend to remain approximately constant.

Estimating Long-Run Cost Functions with Cross-Sectional Regression Analysis

The empirical estimation of long-run cost curves is even more difficult than the estimation of short-run cost curves. The objective of estimating the long-run cost curves is to determine the best scale of plant for the firm to build in order to minimize the cost of producing the anticipated level of output in the long run. Theoretically, long-run cost curves can be estimated with regression analysis utilizing either time-series data (cost-quantity observations for a given firm or plant over time) or cross-sectional data (cost-quantity data for a number of firms at a given point in time). In fact, time-series data are seldom used to estimate long-run cost functions because the period of observation must be sufficiently long for the firm to have changed its scale of plant several times. But this will inevitably also involve changes in the type of product that the firm produces and the technology it

[16]Another nonlinear theoretical form of the *TVC* curve that is often closely approximated by a linear *TVC* is the quadratic form. The quadratic *TVC* curve rises at an increasing rate (i.e., faces diminishing returns) throughout (and so do the corresponding *AVC* and *MC* curves).

uses to render the correct estimation of the firm's long-run cost curves with time-series analysis practically impossible.[17] Regression analysis using cross-sectional data is, therefore, used.

Regression analysis using cross-sectional data to estimate long-run cost curves also presents some difficulties, however. For one thing, firms in different geographical regions are likely to pay different prices for their inputs, and so input prices must be included together with the levels of output as independent explanatory variables in the regression.[18] It is even more difficult to reconcile the different accounting and operational practices of the different firms in the sample. For example, some firms pay lower wages but provide more benefits (better health insurance programs, longer vacation, etc.) than other firms that provide smaller benefits to their workers. If only wages are included in labor costs, the former firms will mistakenly seem to have lower labor costs than the latter firms. The various firms in the sample are also likely to follow very different depreciation policies.

It may also be very difficult to determine if each firm is operating the optimal scale of plant at the optimal level of output (i.e., at the point on its *SAC* curve which forms part of its *LAC* curve). Specifically, in order to be able to estimate *LAC* curve $A''C''G''R''$ in Figure 7-11, the firms represented by SAC_1, SAC_2, SAC_3, and SAC_4 must operate at points A'', C'', G'', and R'', respectively. If in fact the four firms are producing at points A^*, D^*, G'', and R^*, respectively, we would be

[17]This is on top of all the other difficulties encountered in the empirical estimation of short-run cost curves with regression analysis using time-series data discussed on page 302.

[18]Since cross-sectional data refer to one point in time, no adjustment for inflation is necessary.

Figure 7-11
Efficiency of Operation in Estimating the *LAC* Curve

In order to be able to estimate *LAC* curve $A''C''G''R''$, the firms represented by SAC_1, SAC_2, SAC_3, and SAC_4 must operate at points A'', C'', G'', and R'', respectively. If the firms operated their plants at points A^*, D^*, G'', and R^*, respectively, we would be estimating the dashed LAC' curve, which overestimates the degree of both the economies and diseconomies of scale.

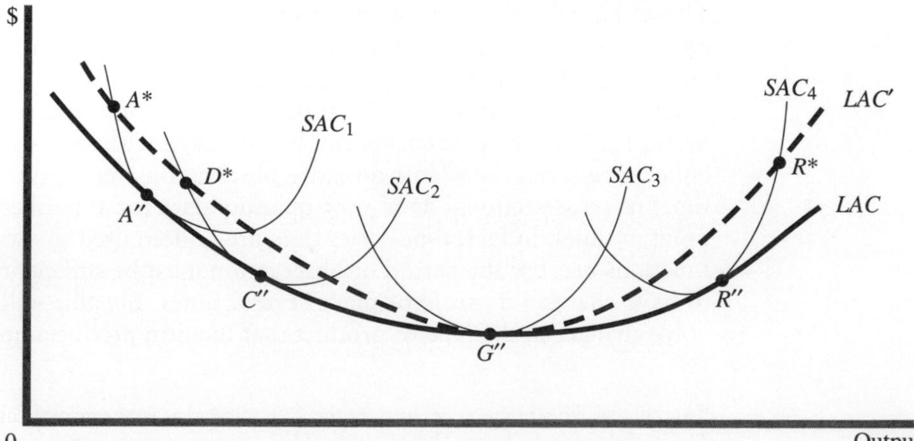

estimating the dashed *LAC′* curve, which overestimates the degree of both the economies and diseconomies of scale. As we will see in Case Study 7-9, estimated long-run average cost curves seem to indicate sharply increasing returns to scale (falling *LAC* curve) at low levels of output followed by near-constant returns to scale at higher levels of output (i.e., the *LAC* curve seems to be L-shaped or nearly so).

Estimating Long-Run Cost Functions with Engineering and Survival Techniques

When sufficient data are not available for cross-sectional regression estimation of the long-run cost curves (or as an independent check on that estimation), the engineering or the survival techniques are used. The **engineering technique** utilizes knowledge of the physical relationship between inputs and output expressed by the production function to determine the optimal input combination needed to produce various levels of output. By then multiplying the optimal quantity of each input by the price of the input, we obtain the long-run cost function of the firm, as shown in Figure 7-3. The engineering technique is particularly useful in estimating the cost functions of new products or improved products resulting from the application of new technologies, where historical data are not available.

The advantage of the engineering technique over cross-sectional regression analysis is that it is based on the present technology, thus avoiding mixing the old and current technology used by different firms in cross-sectional analysis. Neither does the problem of different input prices in different geographical regions arise. Many of the difficult cost-allocation and input-valuation accounting problems that plague regression estimation are also avoided. The engineering technique is not without problems, however. These arise because it deals only with the technical aspects of production without considering administrative, financing, and marketing costs; it deals with production under ideal rather than actual real-world conditions; and it is based on current technology, which may soon become obsolete. The engineering technique has been successfully applied to examine the cost-to-output relationship in many industrial sectors, such as petroleum refining and chemical production.[19] The results obtained seem to confirm those obtained with cross-sectional regression analysis. That is, the *LAC* curve seems to be L-shaped.

The **survival technique** was first expounded by John Stuart Mill in the 1850s and was then elaborated on by George Stigler a century later in the 1950s. In its original formulation, it simply postulated that if large and small firms coexist in the same industry, in the long run scale economies must be constant or nearly so. With large economies of scale over a wide range of outputs, large and more efficient firms (i.e., those with lower *LAC*) would drive smaller and less efficient firms out of business, thus leaving only large firms in the industry in the long run.

[19]See J. Haldi and D. Whitecomb, "Economies of Scale in Industrial Plants," *Journal of Political Economy,* August 1967, pp. 373–385.

Stigler made this concept more operational by proposing to classify firms in an industry according to size and calculate the share of the industry output of the firms in each size classification. If over time the share of the industry output coming from small firms declines while that coming from large firms increases, this is evidence of the presence of significant economies of scale. If the opposite is the case, we would have diseconomies of scale.

Stigler applied this technique to the steel industry and measured the share of industry output of the small, medium, and large firms in the years 1930, 1938, and 1951.[20] He found that the share of the industry output of small and large firms declined over time, while that of medium-sized firms increased. Thus, he concluded that the *LAC* curve in the steel industry was U-shaped but had a flat bottom (i.e., constant returns to scale operated over a wide range of outputs). Stigler also applied the technique to the automobile industry and concluded that economies of scale operated at small outputs, but constant returns to scale operated over the remaining range of outputs (i.e., the *LAC* curve seemed to be L-shaped).

While the survival technique is simple to apply, it implicitly assumes a highly competitive form of market structure in which survival depends only on economic efficiency. If, however, firms are sheltered from competition by government regulation or barriers to entry, inefficient firms can survive, and the survival principle will be distorted or inoperative. Market imperfections, such as product differentiation (i.e., the existence of different brands of a product) or locational advantages, may also allow some firms to survive even if they are relatively inefficient. Furthermore, the survival technique does not allow us to measure the *degree* of economies or diseconomies of scale.

[20]See George J. Stigler, "The Economies of Scale," *Journal of Law and Economics,* April 1958, pp. 251–274.

Case Study 7-9
Estimates of Short-Run and Long-Run Cost Functions

Table 7-4 summarizes the results of 16 empirical studies on short-run and long-run cost functions reported by A. A. Walters, the year the studies were published, and the method of estimation. The questionnaire's method is based on managers' answers to questions asked by the researcher on the firm's production costs. Most studies found that in the short run *MC* are constant (so that the *AVC* curve approaches the horizontal *MC* curve, as indicated in the right bottom panel of Figure 7-10) in the observed range of outputs. Most studies also indicate the presence of economies of scale (i.e., declining *LAC*) at all observed levels of output. Firms, however, seem to avoid expanding into the range of decreasing returns to scale in the long run. These results are similar to those reported in Case Studies 7-2 and 7-3.

Table 7-4
Results of Empirical Studies of Short-Run and Long-Run Cost Functions

Industry	Date	Method*	Period*†	Result
Manufacturing	1939	Q	SR	*MC* declining
Manufacturing	1946	Q	SR	*AVC* declining
Manufacturing	1952	Q	SR	*MC* below *AVC* at all outputs
Furniture	1936	TS	SR	*MC* constant
Steel	1940	TS	SR	*MC* constant
Hosiery	1941	TS	SR	*MC* constant
Dept. store	1942	TS	SR	*MC* declining or constant
Electricity‡	1960	TS	SR	*AVC* falls approaching constant *MC*
Manufacturing	1956	Q	LR	Small economies of scale
Manufacturing	1959	E	LR	Economies of scale
Metal	1959	E	LR	Economies of scale, then constant
Gas‡	1951	CS	LR	Economies of scale
Railways	1952	CS	LR	Economies or constant returns
Electricity‡	1952	CS	LR	Economies of scale
Electricity‡	1960	CS	LR	Economies of scale
Electricity	1961	CS	LR	Economies and then diseconomies

*Q = questionnaire, TS = time series, E = engineering, CS = cross section.
†SR = short run, LR = long run.
‡ = United Kingdom, otherwise United States.
Source: A. A. Walters, "Production and Cost Functions: An Econometric Survey," *Econometrica*, January 1963, pp. 48–50.

SUMMARY

1. "Explicit costs" refer to the actual expenditures of the firm required to purchase or hire inputs. "Implicit costs" refer to the value (imputed from their best alternative use) of the inputs owned and used by the firm. In managerial decisions both explicit and implicit costs must be considered. That is, the relevant costs include the alternative or opportunity costs of all inputs, whether purchased or owned by the firm. "Marginal cost" is the change in total cost per unit change in output, while "incremental cost" refers to the total increase in costs resulting from the implementation of a particular managerial decision. The costs that are not affected by the decision are called "sunk costs."

2. In the short run we have fixed and variable costs. Total costs equal total fixed costs plus total variable costs. The shape of the total variable cost curve follows from the law of diminishing returns. The total cost curve has the same shape as the total variable cost curve but is above it by the amount of the total fixed costs. Average total cost equals total costs divided by output. Average variable cost equals total variable costs divided by output. Average fixed cost equals average total cost minus average variable cost. Marginal cost is the change in total costs or total variable costs per unit change in output. The average total, average variable, and marginal cost curves are U-shaped. The

marginal cost curve reaches a minimum before the average total and average variable cost curves and intersects them from below at their lowest points.

3. The long-run total cost (*LTC*) curve is derived from the expansion path and shows the minimum total cost of producing various levels of output when the firm can build any desired scale of plant. The long-run average cost (*LAC*) equals LTC/Q, while the long-run marginal cost (*LMC*) equals $\Delta LTC/\Delta Q$. The U shape of the *LAC* curve results from the operation of increasing, constant, and decreasing returns to scale, respectively. The *LMC* curve intersects the *LAC* curve from below. The *LAC* curve is the tangent to or the envelope of the short-run average cost curves and shows the minimum long-run average cost of producing various levels of output. The firm plans in the long run and operates in the short run.
4. A U-shaped long-run average cost curve is based on the assumption that economies of scale prevail at small levels of output and diseconomies of scale prevail at larger levels of output. Increasing returns to scale arise because as the scale of operation increases, a greater division of labor and specialization can take place and more specialized and productive machinery can be used. A large firm can also take advantage of quantity discounts in the purchase of raw materials, lower borrowing costs, and economies in advertising. Decreasing returns to scale arise primarily because as the scale of operation increases, it becomes ever more difficult to manage the firm effectively and coordinate the various operations and divisions of the firm. In the real world, the *LAC* curve is often found to have a nearly flat bottom and to be L-shaped rather than U-shaped.
5. The learning curve shows the decline in the average cost of production with rising cumulative total outputs over time. The learning curve is negatively sloped and convex to the origin, indicating that average input costs decline at a decreasing rate as cumulative total output rises. Learning curves have been used to forecast the needs for personnel, machinery, and raw materials, and for scheduling production, determining the price at which to sell output, and even to evaluate suppliers' price quotations.
6. During the past decade, there has been a sharp increase in international trade in parts and components. More and more firms that until recently operated only in the domestic market are purchasing parts and components abroad in order to keep costs down and meet the competition. These are sometimes referred to as the "new international economies of scale." Similarly, an increasing number of American firms are filling their needs for some highly specialized skilled personnel with foreign-trained workers.
7. The firm can use cost-volume-profit or breakeven analysis to determine the output and sales level at which the firm breaks even or earns a desired target profit. The excess of the selling price of the product over the average variable cost of the firm is called the "contribution margin per unit" because it can be applied to cover the fixed costs of the firm and to earn a profit. Linear cost-volume-profit analysis is applicable only if prices and average variable costs

are constant. The operating leverage of the firm refers to the ratio of its total fixed costs to total variable costs. When a firm becomes more highly leveraged, its total fixed costs increase, its average variable costs decline, its breakeven output is larger, and its profitability becomes more variable. The degree of operating leverage or sales elasticity of profits measures the percentage change in the firm's total profits resulting from a 1 percent change in the firm's output or sales.

8. The most common method of estimating the firm's short-run cost functions is by regressing total variable costs on output, input prices, and other operating conditions, during the time period when the size of the plant is fixed. One fundamental problem that arises is that opportunity costs must be extracted from the available accounting cost data. Costs must be correctly apportioned to the various products produced, must be matched with output over time, and must be deflated by the appropriate price index to correct for inflation. Economic theory postulates an S-shaped (cubic) *TVC* curve, but a linear approximation often gives a better empirical fit. The long-run cost functions are estimated by cross-sectional regression analysis, by the engineering method, or by the survival technique. Each method has some advantages and disadvantages over the others. Empirical studies indicate that the *LAC* curve has a flat bottom or is L-shaped.

DISCUSSION QUESTIONS

1. (*a*) What is the distinction between economic costs and accounting costs? (*b*) Which are important for calculating the economic profits of the firm?
2. (*a*) What is the distinction between marginal cost and incremental costs? (*b*) How are sunk costs treated in managerial decision making? Why?
3. (*a*) Do fixed costs refer to the short run or to the long run? Why? (*b*) Why does the *ATC* curve reach its lowest point after the *AVC* curve? (*c*) Why does the *MC* curve intersect from below the *AVC* and *ATC* curves at their lowest points? (*d*) How can the *AFC, AVC, ATC,* and *MC* curves be derived geometrically?
4. If the total variable cost curve faced down or increased at a decreasing rate from zero output, (*a*) what would be the shape of the average variable cost, average total cost, and marginal cost curves? Why? (*b*) What would be the shape of the average fixed cost curve? (*c*) What type of production function would have cost curves of the shape indicated in part (*a*)?
5. The U shape of the short-run and long-run average cost curves are both based on the operation of the law of diminishing returns. True or false? Explain.
6. (*a*) Why is the long run often referred to as the "planning horizon" while the short run is called the "operational period"? What is the relationship between the two concepts? (*b*) Under what condition would the firm build a

plant that does not minimize the cost of producing a specific level of output in the long run?

7. On what does the U shape of the *SAC* and *LAC* curves depend?
8. What shape of the *LAC* curve has been found in many empirical studies? What does this mean for the survival of small firms in the industry?
9. (*a*) What is the meaning of the economies of scope? How do they differ from economies of scale? (*b*) What do learning curves show? How do they differ from economies of scale? What is the usefulness of learning curves as a managerial tool? What is the reason for rising international trade in inputs and the use of foreign skilled labor?
10. What are the aim, usefulness, and shortcomings of (*a*) cost-volume-profit analysis and (*b*) the concept of operating leverage?
11. If the total revenue (*TR*) and total cost (*TC*) curves of the firm are as shown in Figure 2-4, indicate (*a*) the outputs (*Q*) at which the firm breaks even and (*b*) the output at which the firm earns a profit (π) of $30. (*c*) What is the difference between the optimization analysis examined on page 41 and the cost-volume-profit analysis examined on page 296.
12. (*a*) How are the short-run cost functions of the firm estimated? (*b*) What difficulties are usually encountered? (*c*) What is the most common technique for estimating the long-run average cost curve? (*d*) What are some of the difficulties encountered? (*e*) What are the shapes of the short-run and long-run cost curves obtained from empirical studies?
13. What are the advantages and disadvantages of estimating the long-run average cost curve by the (*a*) engineering technique and (*b*) the survival technique? (*c*) Do the long-run average cost curves estimated by the engineering or survival techniques support or contradict the shape of the long-run average cost curves found by cross-sectional regression analysis?

PROBLEMS

*1. John McAuley, a lawyer working for a large law firm and earning $60,000 per year, is contemplating giving up his job and setting up his own law practice. He estimates that renting an office would cost $10,000 per year, hiring a legal secretary would cost $20,000 per year, renting the required office equipment would cost $15,000 per year, and purchasing the required supplies, paying for electricity, telephone, etc. would cost another $5,000. The lawyer estimated that his total revenues for the year would be $100,000, and he is indifferent between keeping his present occupation with the large law firm and opening his own law office. (*a*) How much would be the explicit costs of the lawyer for running his own law office for the year? (*b*) How much would the accounting costs be? The implicit costs? The economic costs? (*c*) Should the lawyer go ahead and start his own practice?

2. Given the following total cost schedule of a firm, (*a*) derive the total fixed cost and total variable cost schedules of the firm, and from them derive the average fixed cost, average variable cost, average total cost, and marginal cost schedules of the firm. (*b*) Plot all the schedules of part (*a*) on a figure similar to Figure 7-1.

Q	0	1	2	3	4	5
TC	$30	50	60	81	118	180

3. Airway Express has an evening flight from Los Angeles to New York with an average of 80 passengers and a return flight from New York to Los Angeles the next afternoon with an average of 50 passengers. The plane makes no other trip. The charge for the plane remaining in New York overnight is $1,200 and zero in Los Angeles. The airline is contemplating eliminating the night flight out of Los Angeles and replacing it with a morning flight. The estimated number of passengers is 70 in the morning flight and 50 in the return afternoon flight. The one-way ticket for any flight is $200. The operating cost of the plane for each flight is $11,000. The fixed costs for the plane are $3,000 per day whether it flies or not. (*a*) Should the airline replace its night flight from Los Angeles with a morning flight? (*b*) Should the airline remain in business?

4. Electric utility companies usually operate their most modern and efficient equipment continuously (i.e., around the clock) and use their older and less efficient equipment only to meet periods of peak electricity demand. (*a*) What does this imply for the short-run marginal cost of these firms? (*b*) Why do these firms not replace all their older with newer equipment in the long run?

5. Given that the wage rate of labor (w) is $10 per unit and the rental price of capital (r) is also $10 per unit, and that the amount of labor (L) and capital (K) used to produce various levels of output are as given in the following table, (*a*) draw a figure similar to Figure 7-3, which shows the expansion path of the firm, the long-run total cost curve, and the long-run average and marginal cost curves of the firm. On the panel showing the long-run average cost curve of the firm, draw four short-run average cost curves. (*b*) If the firm could build only the four plants indicated by the short-run average cost curves shown on your figure, what would be the long-run average cost of the firm? Under what conditions would the long-run average cost curve of the firm be a smooth curve?

L	0	2	3	3.45	4	6	9
K	0	2	3	3.45	4	6	9
Q	0	1	2	3	4	5	6

6. Draw a figure showing that the *LTC* curve is the "dual" of the total output curve. That is, when the total output curve increases at an increasing rate, the *LTC* curve increases at a decreasing rate, and when the

total output curve increases at a decreasing rate, the *LTC* curve increases at an increasing rate.

*7. Draw a figure showing the *LTC* curve for constant returns to scale. On a separate panel show the corresponding *LAC* and *LMC* curves. On still another panel show the *LAC* and *LMC* curves and two *SAC* curves.

*8. Draw a figure showing that the best plant for a range of outputs may not be the best plant to produce a specific level of output.

9. For the parameter of the learning curve given by Equation 7-12 in the text, (*a*) find the average cost of producing the first unit, the second unit, and the fourth unit. (*b*) At what rate does the average cost decline? What generalization can you come to regarding the rate of decline in average cost for different increases in output?

10. The Goldberg-Scheinman Publishing Company is publishing a new managerial economics text for which it has estimated the following total fixed and average variable costs:

Total fixed costs:	
Copy editing	$ 10,000
Typesetting	70,000
Selling and promotion	20,000
Total fixed costs	$100,000
Average variable costs:	
Printing and binding	$ 6
Administrative costs	2
Sales commissions	1
Bookstore discounts	7
Author's royalties	4
Average variable costs	$20
Project selling price	$30

(*a*) Determine the breakeven output and total sales revenues and draw the cost-volume-profit chart, and (*b*) determine the output that would generate a total profit of $60,000 and the total sales revenues at that output level; draw the cost-volume-profit chart. (*c*) Suppose that with a technological breakthrough in printing, the publisher was able to lower its *TFC* to $40,000. What would be its breakeven output? the output that would lead to a total profit of $60,000? Draw a chart to show your answer. (*d*) Suppose that total fixed costs remained at $100,000 but average variable costs declined to $10. What would be the publishers' breakeven output? the output that would lead to a total profit of $60,000? Draw a chart to show your answer. (*e*) If the publisher's total fixed costs remained at $100,000 and its average variable costs at $20 but the publisher charged a price of $40, what would be the breakeven output? the output at which the publisher earns a profit of $60,000? Draw a chart showing your answer.

*11. Two firms in the same industry sell their product at \$10 per unit, but one firm has TFC = \$100 and AVC = \$6 while the other has TFC' = \$300 and AVC' = \$3.33. (*a*) Determine the breakeven output of each firm. Why is the breakeven output of the second firm larger than that of the first firm? (*b*) Find the degree of operating leverage for each firm at $Q = 60$ and at $Q = 70$. Why is the degree of operating leverage greater for the second than for the first firm? Why is the degree of operating leverage greater at $Q = 60$ than at $Q = 70$?

12. The Microsoft Computer Company wants to estimate the average variable cost function of producing computer diskettes. The firm believes that AVC varies with the level of output and wages. Alan Anderson, the economist in the research department of the firm, collects monthly data on output (the number of diskettes produced), average variable costs, and wage rates paid by the firm over the past two years. He deflates cost and wages by their respective price indexes in order to eliminate inflationary influences. He then regresses total variable costs (TVC) on output (Q) and wages (W) and obtains the following result (where the numbers in parentheses are t values):

$$TVC = 0.14 + \underset{(2.8)}{0.80Q} + \underset{(3.8)}{0.036W} \qquad \bar{R}^2 = 0.92 \qquad D\text{-}W = 1.9$$

(3.3)

(*a*) If W = \$10, derive the AVC and MC functions of the firm. (*b*) What are the shapes of the AVC and MC curves of the firm? (*c*) Why did Anderson fit a linear rather than quadratic or cubic TVC function? (*d*) Was this the right choice? Why?

13. **Integrating Problem**

The manager of the Electronic Corporation has estimated the total variable costs and the total fixed cost functions for producing a particular type of camera to be

$$TVC = 60Q - 12Q^2 + Q^3$$
$$TFC = \$100$$

The corporation sells the cameras at the price of \$60 each. An engineering study just published estimated that by employing newly developed technology, the long-run total cost function would be

$$TC = 50 + 20Q + 2w + 3r$$

where w = wage rate and r = rental price of capital. The manager asks you to find (*a*) the average variable and marginal cost functions of the firm, the output level at which the two curves cross, and a plot of them (*Hint:* See Equations 7-22 to 7-24); (*b*) the breakeven output of the firm and the output at which the firm maximizes its total profits; and (*c*) the long-term average cost and long-run marginal cost functions with the new technology if w = \$20 and r = \$10, and plot them. Are these curves similar to those found in other empirical studies of the long-run costs? (*d*) Should the corporation adopt the new technology? If it did, what would be the profit-maximizing level of output if the firm can continue to sell its cameras at the price of $60 per unit?

APPENDIX

COST ANALYSIS WITH CALCULUS

The general equation of the firm's total cost (*TC*) function is

$$TC = d + aQ + bQ^2 + cQ^3 \tag{7-28}$$

In the empirical estimation of Equation 7-28, d, a, $c > 0$, and $b < 0$.

Dropping d, the total fixed costs from Equation 7-28, we get the general equation of the firm's total variable cost (*TVC*) function:

$$TVC = aQ + bQ^2 + cQ^3 \tag{7-29}$$

The average variable cost (*AVC*) function of the firm is then

$$AVC \quad \text{and} \quad \frac{TVC}{Q} = a + bQ + cQ^2 \tag{7-30}$$

The *AVC* is minimum at the point where

$$\frac{d(AVC)}{dQ} = b + 2cQ = 0 \tag{7-31}$$

and

$$Q = \frac{-b}{2c} \tag{7-32}$$

The second-order condition for a minimum is satisfied (so that the *AVC* curve is U-shaped) because

$$\frac{d^2(\text{AVC})}{dQ^2} = 2c > 0 \tag{7-33}$$

The firm's marginal cost (*MC*) function is

$$MC = \frac{d(TC)}{dQ} = \frac{d(TVC)}{dQ} = a + 2bQ + 3cQ^2 \tag{7-34}$$

The *MC* is minimum at the point where

$$\frac{d(MC)}{dQ} = 2b + 6cQ = 0 \tag{7-35}$$

so that

$$Q = \frac{-b}{3c} \tag{7-36}$$

Since the denominator of Equation 7-36 is larger than the denominator of Equation 7-32, the *MC* curve reaches its minimum point at a smaller level of output than the corresponding *AVC* curve.

The second-order condition for a minimum is satisfied (so that the *MC* curve is U-shaped) because

$$\frac{d^2(MC)}{dQ^2} = 6c > 0 \tag{7-37}$$

To show that the *MC* curve intersects the *AVC* curve at the lowest point of the latter, we set Equation 7-30 for the *AVC* curve equal to Equation 7-34 for the *MC* curve. We then solve for *Q* and find that this is equal to $-b/2c$ (the output at which the *AVC* curve is minimum). That is,

$$a + bQ + cQ^2 = a + 2bQ + 3cQ^2 \tag{7-38}$$

so that

$$bQ + 2cQ^2 = 0 \tag{7-39}$$

and

$$Q = \frac{-b}{2c} \tag{7-32}$$

To find the value of the *AVC* at its lowest point, we substitute Equation 7-32 for *Q* into Equation 7-30 for the *AVC* curve and solve for the *AVC*. That is,

$$AVC = a + b\left(\frac{-b}{2c}\right) + \frac{c(b^2)}{4c^2} \tag{7-40}$$

$$= \frac{4ac - b^2}{4c} \tag{7-41}$$

Problem 1 Given: $TC = 100 + 60Q - 12Q^2 + Q^3$. Find (*a*) the equations of the *TVC*, *AVC*, and *MC* functions and (*b*) the level of output at which *AVC* and *MC* are minimum, and prove that the *AVC* and *MC* curves are U-shaped. (*c*) Find the *AVC* and *MC* for the level of output at which the *AVC* curve is minimum.

Problem 2 Answer the same questions as in Problem 1 if

$$TC = 120 + 50Q - 10Q^2 + Q^3$$

SUPPLEMENTARY READINGS

For a problem-solving approach to the topics discussed in this chapter, see:

Salvatore, Dominick: *Theory and Problems of Managerial Economics,* Schaum Outline Series (New York: McGraw-Hill, 1989), Chap. 9.

For a more extensive treatment of cost theory, see:

Salvatore, Dominick: *Theory and Problems of Microeconomic Theory,* 3rd ed., Schaum Outline Series (New York: McGraw-Hill, 1992), Chap. 7.

Salvatore, Dominick: *Microeconomics,* 2nd ed. (New York: HarperCollins, 1994), Chap. 8

A discussion of economies of scale in some industries is found in:

Lieberman, Paul M.: "Market Growth, Economies of Scale and Plant Size in the Chemical Processing Industries," *Journal of Industrial Economics,* December 1987, pp. 175–191.

Aivazian, Varouj A., et al.: "Economies of Scale Versus Technological Change in the Natural Gas Transmission Industry," *Review of Economics and Statistics,* August 1987, pp. 556–561.

Beston, G. J., G. A. Hanweck, and **D. B. Humphrey:** "Scale Economies in Banking: A Restructuring and a Reassessment," *Journal of Money, Credit, and Banking,* November 1982, pp. 435–456.

Gold, B.: "Changing Perspective on Size, Scale, and Returns: An Interpretative Essay," *Journal of Economic Literature,* March 1981, pp. 5–33.

On economies of scope, see:

Teece, David J.: "Economies of Scope and the Scope of the Enterprise," *Journal of Economic Behavior and Organization,* September 1980, pp. 223–247.

The learning curve is discussed in:

Argote, Linda, and **Dennis Epple:** "Learning Curves in Manufacturing," *Science,* February 23, 1990, pp. 920–924.

Bailey, C. D., and **E. V. McIntyre:** "Some Evidence on the Nature of Relearning Curves," *Accounting Review,* April 1992, pp. 368–378.

For international trade in inputs and the immigration of skilled labor, see:

Davidson, W. H., and **J. de la Torre:** *Managing the Global Corporation* (New York: McGraw-Hill, 1989).

Salvatore, Dominick: *International Economics,* 5th ed. (Englewood Cliffs, N.J.: Prentice-Hall, 1995), Chap. 12.

Thompson, Arthur A.: "Strategies for Staying Cost Competitive," *Harvard Business Review,* January–February 1984, pp. 110–117.

Quinn, J. B., and **F. G. Hilmer:** "Strategic Outsourcing," *Sloan Management Review,* Summer 1994, pp. 43–67.

MacCormack, A. D., L. J. Newman III, and **D. B. Rosenfield:** "The New Dynamics of Global Manufacturing Site Location," *Sloan Management Review,* Summer 1994, pp. 69–80.

For a discussion of cost curves and estimation, see:

Daughety, Andrew F., and **Forrest D. Nelson:** "An Econometric Analysis of Changes in Cost and Production Structure of the Trucking Industry," *Review of Economics and Statistics,* February 1988, pp. 67–75.

Johannes, James M., et al.: "Estimating Regional Cost Differences: Theory and Evidence," *Managerial Decision Economics,* June 1985, pp. 70–79.

CHAPTER 8

Linear Programming

KEY TERMS

Linear programming
Production process
Feasible region
Optimal solution
Objective function
Inequality constraints
Nonnegativity constraints
Decision variables
Binding constraints
Slack variable
Simplex method
Primal problem
Dual problem
Shadow price
Duality theorem
Logistic management

CHAPTER OUTLINE

In this chapter we introduce linear programming. This is a very useful and powerful technique that is often used by large corporations, not-for-profit organizations, and government agencies to analyze very complex production, commercial, financial, and other activities. The chapter begins by examining the meaning of "linear programming," the assumptions on which it is based, and some of its applications. We then present the basic concepts of linear programming and examine its relationship to the production and cost theories discussed in Chapters 6 and 7. Subsequently, we show how linear programming can be used to solve complex constrained profit maximization and cost minimization problems, and we estimate the economic value or shadow price of each input. The theory is reinforced with six case studies of real-world applications of linear programming. Also discussed in this chapter is the use of linear programming and logistics in the world economy today. Finally, we show how to actually solve linear programming problems on personal computers using one of the simplest and most popular software packages or programs.

8-1 MEANING, ASSUMPTIONS, AND APPLICATIONS OF LINEAR PROGRAMMING

In this section we define "linear programming" and examine its origin, specify the assumptions on which it rests, and examine some of the situations to which it has been successfully applied.

The Meaning and Assumptions of Linear Programming

Linear programming is a mathematical technique for solving constrained maximization and minimization problems when there are many constraints and the objective function to be optimized, as well as the constraints faced, are linear (i.e., can be represented by straight lines). Linear programming was developed by the Russian mathematician L.V. Kantorovich in 1939 and extended by the American mathematician G. B. Dantzig in 1947. Its acceptance and usefulness have been greatly enhanced by the advent of powerful computers since the technique often requires vast calculations.

The usefulness of linear programming arises because firms and other organizations face many constraints in achieving their goals of profit maximization, cost minimization, or other objectives. With only one constraint, the problem can easily be solved with the traditional techniques presented in the previous two chapters. For example, we saw in Chapter 6 that in order to maximize output (i.e., reach a given isoquant) subject to a given cost constraint (isocost), the firm should produce at the point where the isoquant is tangent to the firm's isocost. Similarly, in order to minimize the cost of producing a given level of output, the firm seeks the lowest isocost that is tangent to the given isoquant. In the real world, however, firms and other organizations often face numerous constraints in trying to achieve their objective. For example, in the short run or operational period, a firm may not be able to hire more labor with some type of specialized skill, obtain more than a specified quantity of some raw material, purchase some advanced equipment, and it may be bound by contractual agreements to supply a minimum quantity of certain products, to keep labor employed for a minimum number of hours, to abide by some pollution regulations, and so on. To solve such constrained optimization problems, traditional methods break down and linear programming must be used.

Linear programming is based on the assumption that the objective function that the organization seeks to optimize (i.e., maximize or minimize), as well as the constraints that it faces, are linear and can be represented graphically by straight lines. This means that we assume that input and output prices are constant, that we have constant returns to scale, and that production can take place with limited technologically fixed input combinations. Constant input prices and constant returns to scale mean that average and marginal costs are constant and equal (i.e., they are linear). With constant output prices, the profit per unit is constant, and the profit function that the firm may seek to maximize is linear. Similarly, the total cost function that the firm may seek to minimize is also linear.[1] The limited technologically fixed input combinations that a firm can use to produce each commodity result in isoquants that are not smooth as shown in Chapter 6 but will be made up of straight line segments (as shown in the next section). Since firms and other organizations often face a number of constraints, and the objective function that they seek to optimize as well as the constraints that they face are often linear over the relevant range of operation, linear programming is applicable and very useful.

Applications of Linear Programming

Linear programming has been applied to a wide variety of constrained optimization problems. Some of these are

1. *Optimal process selection.* Most products can be manufactured by using a number of processes, each requiring a different technology and combination of inputs. Given input prices and the quantity of the commodity that the firm wants to produce, linear programming can be used to determine the optimal combination of processes needed to produce the desired level and output at the lowest possible cost, subject to the labor, capital, and other constraints that the firm may face. This type of problem is examined in Section 8-2.
2. *Optimal product mix.* In the real world, most firms produce a variety of products rather than a single one and must determine how to best utilize their plants, labor, and other inputs to produce the combination or mix of products that maximizes their total profits subject to the constraints they face. For example, the production of a particular commodity may lead to

[1]The total profit function is obtained by multiplying the profit per unit of output by the number of units of output and summing these products for all the commodities produced. The total cost function is obtained by multiplying the price of each input by the quantity of the input used and summing these products over all the inputs used.

the highest profit per unit but may not utilize all the firm's resources. The unutilized resources can be used to produce another commodity, but this product mix may not lead to overall profit maximization for the firm as a whole. The product mix that would lead to profit maximization while satisfying all the constraints under which the firm is operating can be determined by linear programming. This type of problem is examined in Section 8-3, and a real-world example of it is given in Case Study 8-1.

3. *Satisfying minimum product requirements.* Production often requires that certain minimum product requirements be met at minimum cost. For example, the manager of a college dining hall may be required to prepare meals that satisfy the minimum daily requirements of protein, minerals, and vitamins at a minimum cost. Since different foods contain various proportions of the various nutrients and have different prices, the problem can be very complex. This problem, however, can be solved easily by linear programming by specifying the total cost function that the manager seeks to minimize and the various constraints that he or she must meet or satisfy. The same type of problem is faced by a chicken farmer who wants to minimize the cost of feeding chickens the minimum daily requirements of certain nutrients; a petroleum firm that wants to minimize the cost of producing a gasoline of a particular octane subject to its refining, transportation, marketing, and exploration requirements; a producer of a particular type of bolt joints who may want to minimize production costs, subject to its labor, capital, raw materials, and other constraints. This type of problem is examined in Section 8-4 and a real-world example of it is given in Case Study 8-2.

4. *Long-run capacity planning.* An important question that firms seek to answer is how much contribution to profit each unit of the various inputs makes. If this exceeds the price that the firm must pay for the input, this is an indication that the firm's total profits would increase by hiring more of the input. On the other hand, if the input is underutilized, this means that some units of the input need not be hired or can be sold to other firms without affecting the firm's output. Thus, determining the marginal contribution (shadow price) of an input to production and profits can be very useful to the firm in its investment decisions and future profitability.

5. *Other specific applications of linear programming.* Linear programming has also been applied to determine (*a*) the least-cost route for shipping commodities from plants in different locations to warehouses in other locations, and from there to different markets (the so-called transportation problem); (*b*) the best combination of operating schedules, payload, cruising altitude, speed, and seating configurations for airlines; (*c*) the best combination of logs, plywood, and paper that a forest products company can produce from given supplies of logs and milling capacity; (*d*) the distribution of a given advertising budget among TV, radio, magazines, newspapers, billboards, and other forms of promotion to minimize the cost of reaching a specific number of customers in a particular socioeconomic group; (*e*) the best routing of

millions of telephone calls over long distances; (*f*) the best portfolio of securities to hold to maximize returns subject to constraints based on liquidity, risk, and available funds; and (*g*) the best way to allocate available personnel to various activities, and so on.

Although these problems are very different in nature, they all basically involve constrained optimization, and they can all be solved and have been solved by linear programming. This clearly points out the great versatility and usefulness of this technique. While linear programming can be very complex and is usually conducted by the use of computers, it is important to understand its basic principles and how to interpret its results. To this end, we present next some basic linear programming concepts before moving on to more complex and realistic cases.

8-2 SOME BASIC LINEAR PROGRAMMING CONCEPTS

Though linear programming is applicable in a wide variety of contexts, it has been more fully developed and more frequently applied in production decisions. Production analysis also represents an excellent point of departure for introducing some basic linear programming concepts. We begin by defining the meaning of a production process and deriving isoquants. By then bringing in the production constraints, we show how the firm can determine the optimal mix of production processes to use in order to maximize output.

Production Processes and Isoquants in Linear Programming

As pointed out in Section 8-1, one of the basic assumptions of linear programming is that a particular commodity can be produced with only a limited number of input combinations. Each of these input combinations or ratios is called a **production process** or activity and can be represented by a straight line ray from the origin in input space. For example, the left panel of Figure 8-1 shows that a particular commodity can be produced with three different processes, each utilizing a particular combination of labor (L) and capital (K). These are: process 1 with $K/L = 2$, process 2 with $K/L = 1$, and process 3 with $K/L = \frac{1}{2}$. Each of these processes is represented by the ray from the origin with slope equal to the particular K/L ratio used. Process 1 uses 2 units of capital for each unit of labor used, process 2 uses $1K$ for each $1L$ used, and process 3 uses $0.5K$ for each $1L$ used.

By joining points of equal output on the rays of processes, we define the isoquant for the particular level of output of the commodity. These isoquants will be made up of straight line segments and have kinks (rather than being smooth as in Chapter 6). For example, the right panel of Figure 8-1 shows that 100 units of output ($100Q$) can be produced with process 1 at point A (i.e., by using $3L$ and $6K$), with process 2 at point B (by using $4L$ and $4K$), or with process 3 at point C (with $6L$ and $3K$). By joining these points, we get the isoquant for $100Q$.

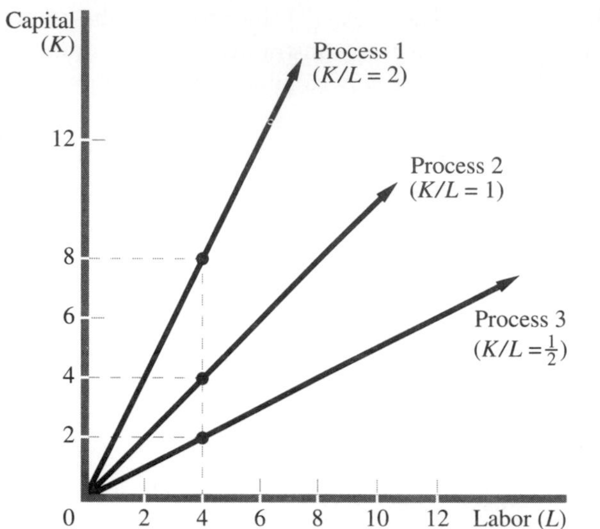

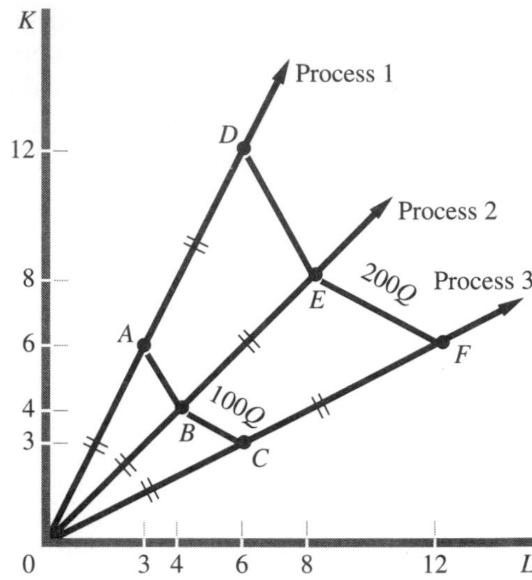

Figure 8-1
The Firm's Production Processes and Isoquants

The left panel shows production process 1 using $K/L = 2$, process 2 using $K/L = 1$, and process 3 using $K/L = \frac{1}{2}$ that a firm can use to produce a particular commodity. The right panel shows that 100 units of output (100*Q*) can be produced with 6*K* and 3*L* (point *A*), 4*K* and 4*L* (point *B*), or 6*L* and 3*K* (point *C*). Joining these points, we get the isoquant for 100*Q*. Because of constant returns to scale, using twice as many inputs along each production process (ray) results in twice as much output. Joining such points, we get the isoquant for 200*Q*.

Note that the isoquant is not smooth but has kinks at points *A*, *B*, and *C*.[2] Furthermore, since we have constant returns to scale, the isoquant for twice as much output (that is, 200*Q*) is determined by using twice as much of each input with each process. This defines the isoquant for 200*Q* with kinks at points *D* (6*L*, 12*K*), *E* (8*L*, 8*K*), and *F* (12*L*, 6*K*). Note that corresponding segments on the isoquant for 100*Q* and 200*Q* are parallel.

The Optimal Mix of Production Processes

If the firm faced only one constraint, such as isocost line *GH* in the left panel of Figure 8-2, the **feasible region,** or the area of attainable input combinations, is represented by shaded triangle **0*JN*.** That is, the firm can purchase any combination of labor and capital on or below isocost line *GH*. But since no production process is available that is more capital intensive than process 1 (i.e., which involves a *K*/*L* higher than 2) or less capital intensive than process 3 (i.e., with *K*/*L* smaller than $\frac{1}{2}$), the feasible region is restricted to the shaded area **0*JN*.** The best or **optimal solution** is at point *E* where the feasible region reaches the isoquant for 200*Q* (the highest possible). Thus, the firm produces the 200 units of output with process 2 by using 8*L* and 8*K*.

[2]The greater the number of processes available to produce a particular commodity, the less pronounced are these kinks and the more the isoquants approach the smooth curves assumed in Chapter 6.

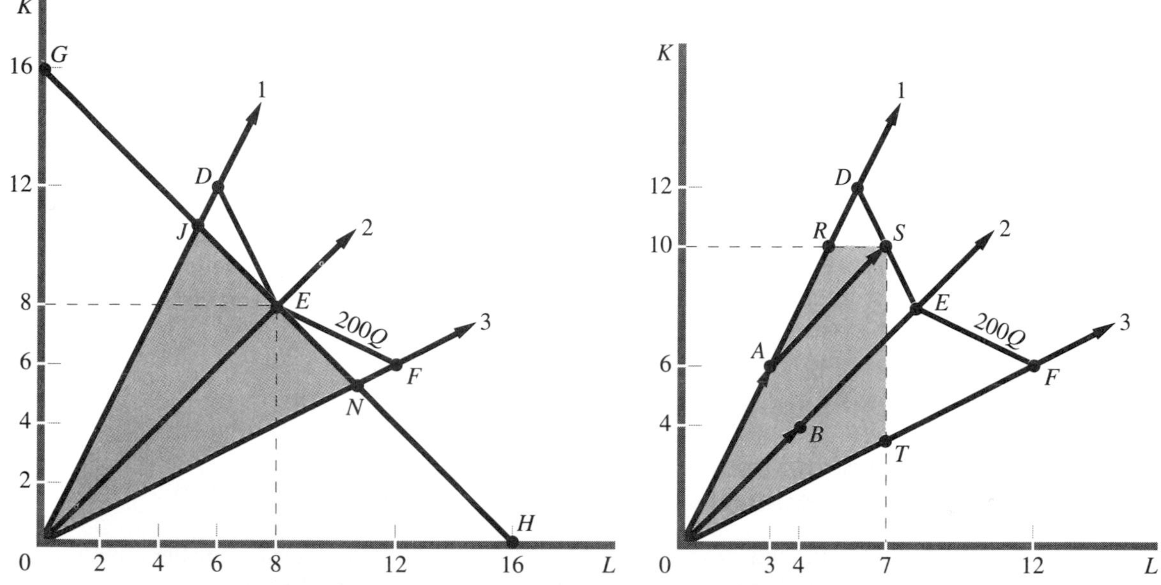

Figure 8-2
Feasible Region and Optimal Solution

With isocost line *GH* in the left panel, the feasible region is shaded triangle 0*JN*, and the optimal solution is at point *E* where the firm uses 8*L* and 8*K* and produces 200*Q*. The right panel shows that if the firm faces no cost constraint but has available only 7*L* and 10*K*, the feasible region is shaded area 0*RST* and the optimal solution is at point *S* where the firm produces 200*Q*. To reach point *S*, the firm produces 100*Q* with process 1 (0*A*) and 100*Q* with process 2 (0*B* = *AS*).

The right panel of Figure 8-2 extends the analysis to the case where the firm faces no *cost* constraint but has available only 7*L* and 10*K* for the period of time under consideration. The feasible region is then given by shaded area **0*RST*** in the figure. That is, only those labor-capital combinations in shaded area **0*RST*** are relevant. The maximum output that the firm can produce is 200*Q* and is given by point *S*. That is, the isoquant for 200*Q* is the highest that the firm can reach with the constraints it faces. To reach point *S*, the firm will have to produce 100*Q* with process 1 (**0*A***) and 100*Q* with process 2 (**0*B*** = *AS*).[3]

Note that when the firm faced the single isocost constraint (*GH* in the left panel of Figure 8-2), the firm used only one process (process 2) to reach the optimum. When the firm faced two constraints (the right panel), the firm required two processes to reach the optimum. From this, we can generalize and conclude that to reach the optimal solution, a firm will require *no more* processes than the number of constraints that the firm faces. Sometimes fewer processes will do. For example, if the firm could use no more than 6*L* and 12*K*, the optimum would be

[3] **0*A*** and **0*B*** are called "vectors." Thus, the above is an example of vector analysis, whereby vector **0*S*** (not shown in the right panel of Figure 8-2) is equal to the sum of vectors **0*A*** and **0*B***.

at point D ($200Q$), and this is reached with process 1 alone (see the left panel of Figure 8-2).[4]

From the left panel of Figure 8-2 we can also see that if the ratio of the wage rate (w) to the rental price of capital (r) increased (so that isocost line GH became steeper), the optimal solution would remain at point E as long as the GH isocost (constraint) line remained flatter than segment DE on the isoquant for $200Q$. If w/r rose so that isocost GH coincided with segment DE, the firm could reach isoquant $200Q$ with process 1, process 2, or any combination of process 1 and process 2 that would allow the firm to reach a point on segment DE. If w/r rose still further, the firm would reach the optimal solution (maximum output) at point D (see the figure).

8-3 PROCEDURE USED IN FORMULATING AND SOLVING LINEAR PROGRAMMING PROBLEMS

The most difficult aspect of solving a constrained optimization problem by linear programming is to formulate or state the problem in a linear programming format or framework. The actual solution to the problem is then straightforward. Simple linear programming problems with only a few variables are easily solved graphically or algebraically. More complex problems are invariably solved by the use of computers. It is important, however, to know the process by which even the most complex linear programming problems are formulated and solved and how the results are interpreted. To show this, we begin by defining some important terms and then using them to outline the steps to follow in formulating and solving linear programming problems.

The function to be optimized in linear programming is called the **objective function.** This usually refers to profit maximization or cost minimization. In linear programming problems, constraints are given by inequalities (called **inequality constraints**). The reason is that the firm can often use up to, but not more than, specified quantities of some inputs, or the firm must meet some minimum requirement. In addition, there are **nonnegativity constraints** on the solution to indicate that the firm cannot produce a negative output or use a negative quantity of any input. The quantities of each product to produce in order to maximize profits or inputs to use to minimize costs are called **decision variables.**

The steps followed in solving a linear programming problem are

1. Express the objective function of the problem as an equation and the constraints as inequalities.

[4]To reach any point on an isoquant between two adjacent production processes, we utilize the process to which the point is closer, in proportion to 1 minus the distance of the point from the process (ray). For example, if point S were one-quarter of the distance DE from point D along the isoquant for $200Q$, the firm would produce $1 - \frac{1}{4} = \frac{3}{4}$ of the $200Q$ (that is, $150Q$) with process 1 and the remaining $\frac{1}{4}$ with process 2 (see the figure). The amount of each input that is used in each process is then proportional to the output produced by each process.

2. Graph the inequality constraints, and define the feasible region.
3. Graph the objective function as a series of isoprofit (i.e., equal profit) or isocost lines, one for each level of profit or costs, respectively.
4. Find the optimal solution (i.e., the values of the decision variables) at the extreme point or corner of the feasible region that touches the highest isoprofit line or the lowest isocost line. This represents the optimal solution to the problem subject to the constraints faced.

In the next section we will elaborate on these steps as we apply them to formulate and solve a specific profit maximization problem. In the following section, we will then apply the same general procedure to solve a cost minimization problem.

8-4 LINEAR PROGRAMMING: PROFIT MAXIMIZATION

In this section, we follow the steps outlined in the previous section to formulate and solve a specific profit maximization problem, first graphically and then algebraically. We will also examine the case of multiple solutions.

Formulation of the Profit Maximization Linear Programming Problem

Most firms produce more than one product, and a crucial question to which they seek an answer is how much of each product (the decision variables) the firm should produce in order to maximize profits. Usually, firms also face many constraints on the availability of the inputs they use in their production activities. The problem is then to determine the output mix that maximizes the firm's total profit subject to the input constraints it faces.

In order to show the solution of a profit maximization problem graphically, we assume that the firm produces only two products: product X and product Y. Each unit of product X contributes \$30 to profit and to covering overhead (fixed) costs, and each unit of product Y contributes \$40.[5] Suppose also that in order to produce each unit of product X and product Y, the firm requires inputs A, B, and C in the proportions indicated in Table 8-1. That is, each unit of product X requires 1 unit of input A, one-half unit of input B, and no input C, while 1 unit of product Y requires $1A$, $1B$, and $0.5C$. Table 8-1 also shows that the firm has available only 7 units of input A, 5 units of input B, and 2 units of input C per time period. The firm then wants to determine how to use the available inputs to produce the mix of products X and Y that maximizes its total profits.

[5]The contribution to profit and overhead costs made by each unit of the product is equal to the difference between the selling price of the product and its average variable cost. Since the total fixed costs of the firm are constant, however, maximizing the total contribution to profit and to overhead costs made by the product mix chosen also maximizes the total profits of the firm.

Table 8-1
Input Requirements and Availability for Producing Products *X* and *Y*

	Quantities of Inputs Required per Unit of Output		Quantities of Inputs Available per Time Period
Input	Product *X*	Product *Y*	Total
A	1	1	7
B	0.5	1	5
C	0	0.5	2

The first step in solving a linear programming problem is to express the objective function as an equation and the constraints as inequalities. Since each unit of product *X* contributes \$30 to profit and overhead costs and each unit of product *Y* contributes \$40, the objective function that the firm seeks to maximize is

$$\pi = \$30Q_X + \$40Q_Y \tag{8-1}$$

where π is the total contribution to profit and overhead costs faced by the firm (henceforth simply called the "profit function"), and Q_X and Q_Y refer, respectively, to the quantities of product *X* and product *Y* that the firm produces. Thus, Equation 8-1 postulates that the total profit (contribution) function of the firm equals the per-unit profit contribution of product *X* times the quantity of product *X* produced plus the per-unit profit contribution of product *Y* times the quantity of product *Y* that the firm produces.

Let us now go on to express the constraints of the problem as inequalities. From the first row of Table 8-1, we know that 1 unit of input *A* is required to produce each unit of product *X* and product *Y* and that only 7 units of input *A* are available to the firm per period of time. Thus, the constraint imposed on the firm's production by input *A* can be expressed as

$$1Q_X + 1Q_Y \leqq 7 \tag{8-2}$$

That is, the 1 unit of input *A* required to produce each unit of product *X* times the quantity of product *X* produced plus the 1 unit of input *A* required to produce each unit of product *Y* times the quantity of product *Y* produced must be equal to or smaller than the 7 units of input *A* available to the firm. The inequality sign indicates that the firm can use up to, but no more than, the 7 units of input *A* available to it to produce products *X* and *Y*. The firm can use less than 7 units of input *A*, but it cannot use more.

From the second row of Table 8-1, we know that one-half unit of input *B* is required to produce each unit of product *X* and 1 unit of input *B* is required to produce each unit of product *Y*, and only 5 units of input *B* are available to the firm per period of time. The quantity of input *B* required in the production of product *X* is then $0.5Q_X$, while the quantity of input *B* required in the production of product *Y* is $1Q_Y$ and the sum of $0.5Q_X$ and $1Q_Y$ can be equal to, but it cannot be more than, the 5 units of input *B* available to the firm per time period. Thus, the constraint associated with input *B* is

$$0.5Q_X + 1Q_Y \leqq 5 \tag{8-3}$$

From the third row in Table 8-1, we see that input *C* is not used in the production of product *X*, one-half unit of input *C* is required to produce each unit of product *Y*, and only 2 units of input *C* are available to the firm per time period. Thus, the constraint imposed on production by input *C* is

$$0.5Q_Y \leqq 2 \tag{8-4}$$

In order for the solution to the linear programming problem to make economic sense, however, we must also impose nonnegativity constraints on the output of products *X* and *Y*. The reason for this is that the firm can produce zero units of either product, but it cannot produce a negative quantity of either product (or use a negative quantity of either input). The requirement that Q_X and Q_Y (as well as that the quantity used of each input) be nonnegative can be expressed as

$$Q_X \geqq 0 \qquad Q_Y \geqq 0$$

We can now summarize the linear programming formulation of the above problem as follows:

Maximize	$\pi = \$30Q_X + \$40Q_Y$	(objective function)
Subject to	$1Q_X + 1Q_Y \leqq 7$	(input *A* constraint)
	$0.5Q_X + 1Q_Y \leqq 5$	(input *B* constraint)
	$0.5Q_Y \leqq 2$	(input *C* constraint)
	$Q_X, Q_Y \geqq 0$	(nonnegativity constraint)

Graphic Solution of the Profit Maximization Problem

The next step in solving the linear programming problem is to treat the inequality constraints of the problem as equations, graph them, and define the feasible region. These are shown in Figure 8-3. Figure 8-3*a* shows the graph of the constraint imposed on the production of products *X* and *Y* by input *A*. Treating inequality constraint 8-2 for input *A* as an equation (i.e., disregarding the inequality sign for the moment), we have $1Q_X + 1Q_Y = 7$. With 7 units of input *A* available, the firm could produce 7 units of product *X* (that is, 7*X*) and no units of product *Y*, 7*Y* and 0*X*, or any combination of *X* and *Y* on the line joining these two points. Since the firm could use an amount of input *A* equal to or smaller than the 7 units available to it, inequality constraint 8-2 refers to all the combinations of *X* and *Y* on the line and in the entire shaded region below the line (see Figure 8-3*a*).

In Figure 8-3*b* we have limited the feasible region further by considering the constraints imposed by the availability of inputs *B* and *C*. The constraint on input *B* can be expressed as the equation $0.5Q_X + 1Q_Y = 5$. Thus, if $Q_X = 0$, $Q_Y = 5$, and if $Q_Y = 0$, $Q_X = 10$. All the combinations of product *X* and product *Y* falling

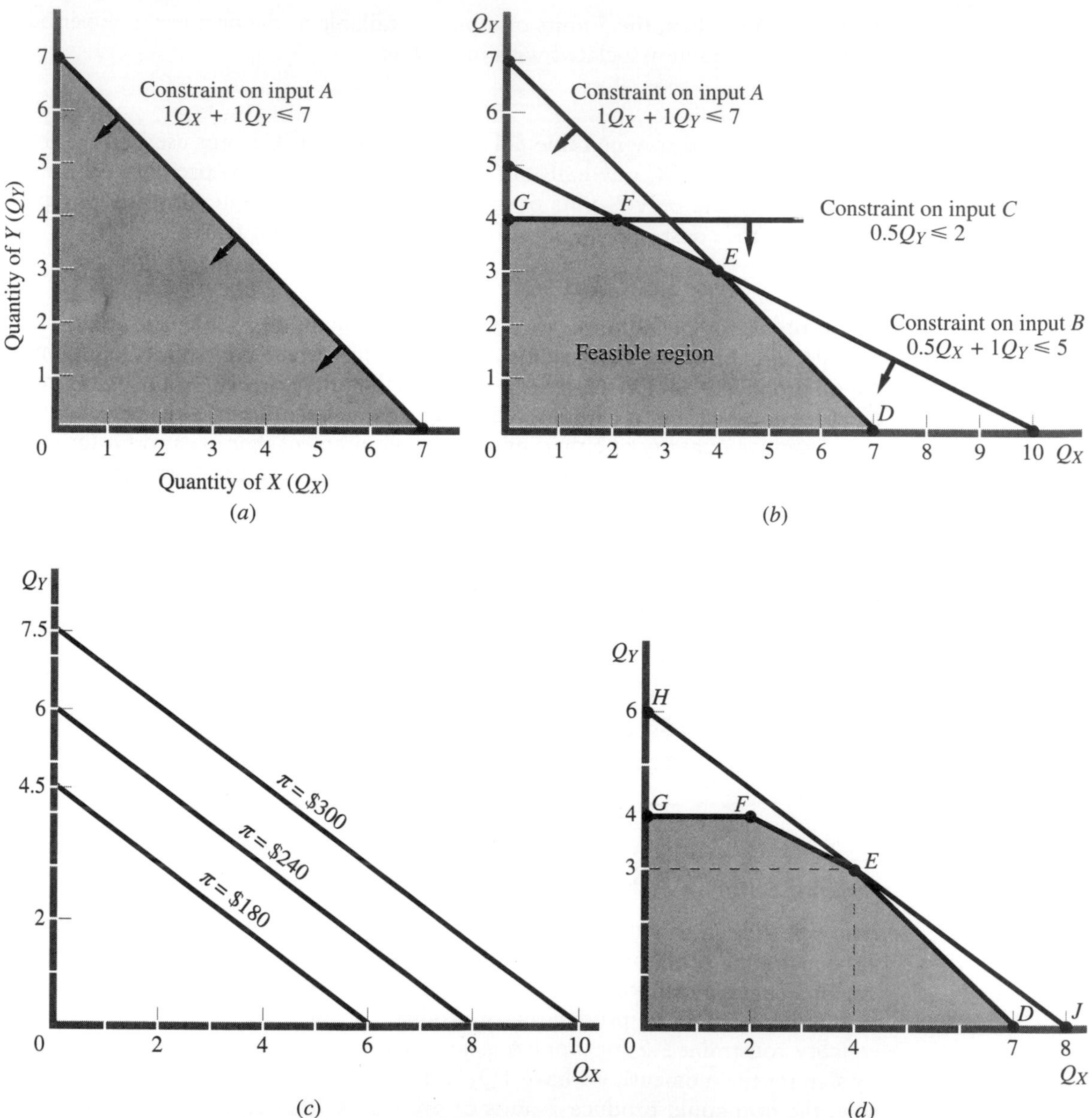

Figure 8-3
Feasible Region, Isoprofit Lines, and Profit Maximization

The shaded area in part *a* shows the inequality constraint from input *A*. The shaded area in part *b* shows the feasible region, where all the inequality constraints are simultaneously satisfied. Part *c* shows the isoprofit lines for $\pi = \$180$, $\pi = \$240$, and $\pi = \$300$. All three isoprofit lines have an absolute slope of \$30/\$40 or $\frac{3}{4}$, which is the ratio of the contribution of each unit of *X* and *Y* to the profit and overhead costs of the firm. Part *d* shows that π is maximized at point *E* where the feasible region touches isoprofit line *HJ* (the highest possible) when the firm produces 4*X* and 3*Y* so that $\pi = \$30(4) + \$40(3) = \$240$.

on or to the left of the line connecting these two points represent the inequality constraint 8-3 for input *B*. The horizontal line at $Q_Y = 4$ represents the constraint imposed by input *C*. Since input *C* is not used in the production of product *X*, there is no constraint imposed by input *C* on the production of product *X*. Since 0.5 unit of input *C* is required to produce each unit of product *Y* and only 2 units of input *C* are available to the firm, the maximum quantity of product *Y* that the firm can produce is 4 units. Thus, the constraint imposed by input *C* is represented by all the points on or below the horizontal line at $Q_Y = 4$. Together with the nonnegativity constraints on Q_X and Q_Y, we can, therefore, define the feasible region as the shaded region of 0*DEFG*, for which all the inequality constraints facing the firm are satisfied *simultaneously.*

The third step in solving the linear programming problem is to graph the objective function of the firm as a series of isoprofit (or equal) profit lines. Figure 8-3*c* shows the isoprofit lines for π equal to \$180, \$240, and \$300. The lowest isoprofit line in Figure 8-3*c* is obtained by substituting \$180 for π into the equation for the objective function and then solving for Q_Y. Substituting \$180 for π in the objective function, we have

$$\$180 = \$30Q_X + \$40Q_Y$$

Solving for Q_Y, we obtain

$$Q_Y = \frac{\$180}{\$40} - \left(\frac{\$30}{\$40}\right)Q_X \tag{8-5}$$

Thus, when $Q_X = 0$, $Q_Y = \$180/\$40 = 4.5$ and the slope of the isoprofit line is $-\$30/\$40$, or $-\frac{3}{4}$. This isoprofit line shows all the combinations of products *X* and *Y* that result in $\pi = \$180$. Similarly, the equation of the isoprofit line for $\pi =$ \$240 is

$$Q_Y = \frac{\$240}{\$40} - \left(\frac{\$30}{\$40}\right)Q_X \tag{8-6}$$

for which $Q_Y = 6$ when $Q_X = 0$ and the slope is $-\frac{3}{4}$. Finally, the isoprofit equation for $\pi = \$300$ is

$$Q_Y = \frac{\$300}{\$40} - \left(\frac{\$30}{\$40}\right)Q_X \tag{8-7}$$

for which $Q_Y = 7.5$ when $Q_X = 0$ and the slope is $-\frac{3}{4}$. Note that the slopes of all isoprofit lines are the same (i.e., the isoprofit lines are parallel) and are equal to −1 times the ratio of the profit contribution of product *X* to the profit contribution of product *Y* (that is, $-\$30/\$40 = -\frac{3}{4}$).

The fourth and final step in solving the linear programming problem is to determine the mix of products *X* and *Y* (the decision variables) that the firm should produce in order to reach the highest isoprofit line. This is obtained by superimposing the isoprofit lines shown in Figure 8-3*c* on the feasible region shown in Figure 8-3*b*. This is done in Figure 8-3*d*, which shows that the highest isoprofit line that the firm can reach subject to the constraints it faces is *HJ*. This is reached at point *E* where the firm produces 4*X* and 3*Y* and the total contribution to profit (π) is maximum at \$30(4) + \$40(3) = \$240. Note that point *E* is at the intersection of the constraint lines for inputs *A* and *B* but below the constraint line for input *C*. This means that inputs *A* and *B* are fully utilized, while input *C* is not.[6] In the terminology of linear programming, we then say that inputs *A* and *B* are **binding constraints,** while input *C* is nonbinding or is a **slack variable.**[7]

Extreme Points and the Simplex Method

In the previous section, we showed that the firm's optimal or profit maximization product mix is given at point *E*, a corner of the feasible region.[8] This example illustrates a basic theorem of linear programming. This is that in searching for the optimal solution, we need to examine and compare the levels of π at only the extreme points (corners) of the feasible region and can ignore all other points inside or on the borders of the feasible region. That is, with a linear objective function and linear input constraints, the optimal solution will always occur at one of the corners. In the unusual event that the isoprofit lines have the same slope as one of the segments of the feasible region, then all the product mixes along that segment will result in the same maximum value, and we have multiple optimal solutions. Since these include the two corners defining the segment, the rule that in order to find the optimal or profit-maximizing product mix, we only need to examine and compare the value of π at the corners of the feasible region holds up.

Figure 8-4 shows the case of multiple optimal solutions. In the figure, the new isoprofit line *H′J′* (\$240 = \$24Q_X + \$48Q_Y) has the absolute slope of \$24/\$48 = $\frac{1}{2}$, the same as segment *EF* of the feasible region. Thus, all the product mixes along *EF*, including those at corner points *E* and *F*, result in the same value of π = \$240. For example, at point *M* (3*X*, 3.5*Y*) on *EF*, π = \$24(3) + \$48(3.5) = \$240. Since π = \$240 at corner point *E* and at corner point *F* also, we can find the optimal solution of the problem by examining only the corners of the feasible region, even in a case such as this one where there are multiple optimal points.[9]

[6]From Figure 8-3*b* we can see that at point *E* only $1\frac{1}{2}$ out of the 2 units of input *C* available to the firm per time period are used.

[7]We will return to this in the algebraic solution to this problem in the following subsection and in our discussion of the dual problem and shadow prices in Section 8-6.

[8]At the other corners of the feasible region, the values of π are as follows: at corner point *D*(7, 0), π = \$30(7) = \$210; at point *F* (2, 4), π = \$30(2) + \$40(4) = \$220; at point *G* (0, 4), π = \$40(4) = \$160; and at the origin (0, 0), π = 0.

[9]At corner point *E* (4, 3), π = \$24(4) + \$48(3) = \$240; at corner point *F* (2, 4), π = \$24(2) + \$48(4) = \$240. Sometimes a constraint may be redundant. This occurs when the feasible region is defined only by the other constraints of the problem. For example, if the constraint equation for input C had been 0.5Q_Y = 3, the constraint line for input C would have been a horizontal straight line at Q_Y = 6 and fallen outside the feasible region of the problem (which in that case would have been defined by the constraint lines for inputs *A* and *B* only—see Figure 8-3*b*). There are other cases where a constraint may make the solution of the problem impossible. In that case (called "degeneracy"), the constraints have to be modified in order to obtain a solution to the problem (see Problem 7).

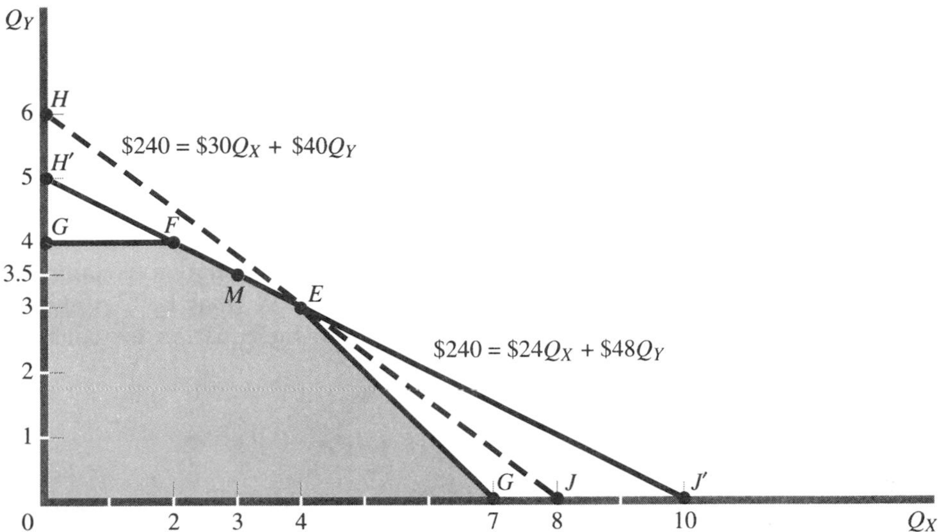

Figure 8-4
Multiple Optimal Solutions
The new isoprofit line *H′J′* ($240 = 24Q_X$ + 48Q_Y$) has the same absolute slope of $24/$48 = $\frac{1}{2}$ as segment *EF* of the feasible region. Thus, all the product mixes along *EF*, such as those indicated at point *M* and at corner points *E* and *F*, result in the same value of π = $240.

The ability to determine the optimal solution by examining only the extreme or corner points of the feasible region greatly reduces the calculations necessary to solve linear programming problems that are too large to solve graphically. These large linear programming problems are invariably solved by computers. All the computer programs available for solving linear programming problems start by arbitrarily picking one corner and calculating the value of the objective function at that corner, and then systematically moving to other corners that result in higher profits until they find no corner with higher profits. This is referred to as the "extreme-point theorem," and the method of solution is called the **simplex method.** The algebraic solution to the linear programming problem examined next provides an idea of how the computer proceeds in solving the problem.[10]

Algebraic Solution of the Profit Maximization Problem

The profit maximization linear programming problem that was solved graphically earlier can also be solved algebraically by identifying (algebraically) the corners of the feasible region and then comparing the profits at each corner. Since each corner is formed by the intersection of two constraint lines, the coordinates of the intersection point (i.e., the value of) Q_X and Q_Y at the corner can be found

[10]In 1984, N. Karmarkar of Bell Labs discovered a new algorithm or mathematical formula that can solve very large linear programming problems 50 to 100 times faster than with the simplex method. However, most routine linear programming problems are still being solved with the simplex method.

by solving simultaneously the equations of the two intersecting lines. This can be seen in Figure 8-5 (which is similar to Figure 8-3*b*).

In Figure 8-5, only corner points *D*, *E*, and *F* need to be considered. While the origin is also a corner point of the feasible region, profits are zero at this point because $Q_X = Q_Y = 0$. Corner point *G* (0*X*, 4*Y*) can also be dismissed because it refers to the same output of product *Y* as at corner point *F* but to less of product *X*. This leaves only corner points *D*, *E*, and *F* to be evaluated. Since corner point *D* is formed by the intersection of the constraint line for input *A* with the horizontal axis (along which $Q_Y = 0$, see Figure 8-5), the quantity of product *X* (that is, Q_X) at corner point *D* is obtained by substituting $Q_Y = 0$ into the equation for constraint *A*. That is, substituting $Q_Y = 0$ into

$$1Q_X + 1Q_Y \leqq 7$$

we get

$$Q_X = 7$$

Thus, at point *D*, $Q_X = 7$ and $Q_Y = 0$.

Figure 8-5
Algebraic Determination of the Corners of the Feasible Region

The quantity of products *X* and *Y* (that is, Q_X and Q_Y) at corner point *D* is obtained by substituting $Q_Y = 0$ (along the Q_X axis) into the constraint equation for input *A*. Q_X and Q_Y at corner point *E* are obtained by solving simultaneously the constraint equations for inputs *A* and *B*. Q_X and Q_Y at point *F* are obtained by solving simultaneously the equations for constraints *B* and *C*. Corner point *G* can be dismissed outright because it involves the same Q_Y as at point *F* but has $Q_X = 0$. The origin can also be dismissed since $Q_X = Q_Y = \pi = 0$.

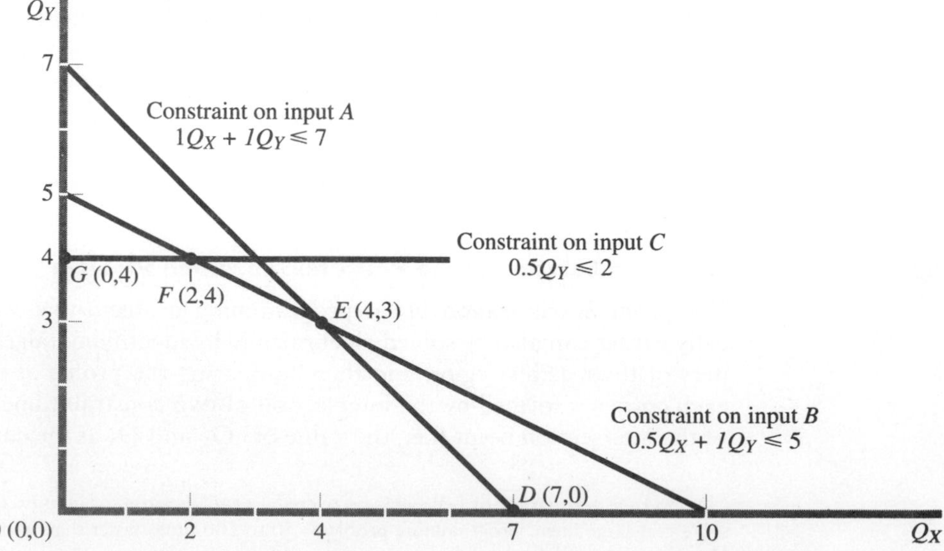

Corner point E is formed by the intersection of the constraint lines for inputs A and B (see Figure 8-5), which are, respectively,

$$1Q_X + 1Q_Y = 7$$

and

$$0.5Q_X + 1Q_Y = 5$$

Subtracting the second equation from the first, we have

$$\begin{array}{r} 1Q_X + 1Q_Y = 7 \\ \underline{0.5Q_X + 1Q_Y = 5} \\ 0.5Q_X \qquad\;\; = 2 \end{array}$$

so that $Q_X = 4$. Substituting $Q_X = 4$ into the first of the two equations, we get $Q_Y = 3$. Thus, $Q_X = 4$ and $Q_Y = 3$ at corner point E. These are the same values of Q_X and Q_Y determined graphically in Figure 8-3*b*.

Finally, corner point F is formed by the intersection of the constraint lines for inputs B and C, which are, respectively,

$$0.5Q_X + 1Q_Y = 5$$

and

$$0.5Q_Y = 2$$

Substituting $Q_Y = 4$ from the second equation into the first equation, we have

$$0.5Q_X + 4 = 5$$

so that $Q_X = 2$. Thus at corner point F, $Q_X = 2$ and $Q_Y = 4$ (the same as obtained graphically in Figure 8-3*b*).

By substituting the values of Q_X and Q_Y (the decision variables) at each corner of the feasible region into the objective function, we can then determine the firm's total profit contribution (π) at each corner. These are shown in Table 8-2, which (for the sake of completeness) also shows the levels of profit at the origin and at point G. The optimal or profit-maximizing point is at corner E at which $\pi = \$240$ (the same as obtained in the graphical solution in Figure 8-3*d*).

From the algebraic or graphical solution we can also determine which inputs are fully utilized (i.e., are binding constraints on production) and which are not (i.e., are slack variables) at each corner of the feasible region. For example, from

Table 8-2
Outputs of Products *X* and *Y*, and Profits at Each Corner of the Feasible Region

Corner Point	Q_X	Q_Y	$\$30Q_X + \$40Q_Y$	Profit
0	0	0	\$30(0) + \$40(0)	\$ 0
D	7	0	\$30(7) + \$40(0)	\$210
**E*	4	3	\$30(4) + \$40(3)	\$240
F	2	4	\$30(2) + \$40(4)	\$220
G	0	4	\$30(0) + \$40(4)	\$160

Figure 8-5 we can see that since corner point D is on the constraint line for input A but is below the constraint lines for inputs B and C, input A is a binding constraint on production, while inputs B and C represent slack variables. Since corner point E is formed by the intersection of the constraint lines for inputs A and B but is below the constraint line for input C, inputs A and B are binding constraints while input C is a slack variable or input. Finally, since corner point F is formed by the intersection of the constraint lines for inputs B and C but is below the constraint line for input A, inputs B and C are binding while input A is slack.[11]

Not only is a firm's manager interested in knowing the quantities of products X and Y that the firm must produce in order to maximize profits, but he or she is also interested in knowing which inputs are binding and which are slack at the optimal or profit-maximizing point. This information is routinely provided by the computer solution to the linear programming problem. The computer solution will also give the unused *quantity* of each slack input. The firm can then use this information to determine how much of each binding input it should hire in order to expand output by a desired amount, or how much of the slack inputs it does not need to hire or it can rent out to other firms (if it owns the inputs) at the profit-maximizing solution.

[11]We can similarly determine that at corner point G, only input C is binding, while at the origin all three inputs are slack.

Case Study 8-1

Maximizing Profits in Blending Aviation Gasoline by Linear Programming

One important application of linear programming is in the blending of aviation gasolines. Aviation gasolines are blended from carefully selected refined gasolines so as to ensure that certain quality specifications, such as performance numbers (*PN*) and Reid vapor pressure (*RVP*), are satisfied. Each of these specifications depends on a particular property of the gasoline. For example, *PN* depends on the octane rating of the fuel. Aircraft engines require a certain minimum octane rating to run properly and efficiently, but using higher-octane gasoline results in greater expense without increasing operating performance. In the problem at hand, three types of aviation gasoline, *M*, *N*, and *Q*, were examined, each with a stipulated minimum *PN* and maximum *RVP* rating, generated by combining four fuels (*A*, *B*, *D*, and *F*) in various proportions. The problem was to maximize the following objective function:

$$\pi = 0.36M + 0.089N + 1.494Q$$

subject to 32 inequality and nonnegativity constraints (based on the characteristics of each input and their availability, as well as on the condition that all outputs and inputs be nonnegative). The solution to the problem specified how each of the four inputs had to be combined in order to produce the mix of aviation gasolines that maximized profits. The maximum profit per day obtained was $15,249 on total net receipts of $69,067.

Source: A. Charnes, W. W. Cooper, and B. Mellon, "Blending Aviation Gasolines—A Study in Programming Interdependent Activities in an Integrated Oil Company," *Econometrica*, April 1952, pp. 135–159.

Case Study 8-2

Linear Programming as a Tool of Portfolio Management

Linear programming is now being applied even in portfolio management. In fact, more and more computer programs are being developed to help investors maximize their expected rates of return on their stock and bond investments subject to risk, dividend and interest, and other constraints. For example, one linear programming model can be used to determine when a bond dealer or other investor should buy, sell, or simply hold a bond. The model can also be used to determine the optimal strategy for an investor to follow in order to maximize portfolio returns for each level of risk exposure. Another use of linear programming is to determine the highest return that an investor can receive from holding portfolios with various proportions of different securities. Still another use of the model is in determining which of the projects that satisfy some minimum acceptance standard should be undertaken in the face of capital rationing (i.e., when all such projects cannot be accepted because of capital limitations).

The most complex portfolio management problems involving thousands of variables that leading financial management firms deal with, and which previously required hours of computer time with the largest computers to solve with the simplex method, can now be solved in a matter of minutes with the new algorithm developed by Karmarkar at Bell Labs (see footnote 10). More important for the individual investor and small firms is that more and more user-friendly computer programs are becoming available to help solve an ever-widening range of financial management decisions on personal computers (see Section 8-8). While in the final analysis these computer programs can never replace financial acumen, they can certainly help all investors improve their financial-planning decisions.

Source: P. R. Chandy and P. Kharabe, "Pricing in the Government Bond Market," *Interfaces,* September–October 1986, pp. 65–71.

8-5 LINEAR PROGRAMMING: COST MINIMIZATION

We now follow the steps outlined in Section 8-3 to formulate and solve a specific cost minimization problem, first graphically and then algebraically.

Formulation of the Cost Minimization Linear Programming Problem

Most firms usually use more than one input to produce a product or service, and a crucial choice they face is how much of each input (the decision variables) to use in order to minimize the costs of production. Usually firms also face a number of constraints in the form of some minimum requirement that they or the product or service that they produce must meet. The problem is then to determine the input mix that minimizes costs subject to the constraints that the firm faces.

In order to show how a cost minimization linear programming problem is formulated and solved, assume that the manager of a college dining hall is required to prepare meals that satisfy the minimum daily requirements of protein (P), minerals (M), and vitamins (V). Suppose that the minimum daily requirements have been established at $14P$, $10M$, and $6V$. The manager can use two basic foods (say, meat and fish) in the preparation of meals. Meat (food X) contains $1P$, $1M$, and $1V$ per pound. Fish (food Y) contains $2P$, $1M$, and $0.5V$ per pound. The price of X is \$2 per pound, while the price of Y is \$3 per pound. This information is summarized in Table 8-3. The manager wants to provide meals that fulfill the minimum daily requirements of protein, minerals, and vitamins at the lowest possible cost per student.

The above linear programming problem can be formulated as follows:

Minimize	$C = \$2Q_X + \$3Q_Y$	(objective function)
Subject to	$1Q_X + 2Q_Y \geqq 14$	(protein constraint)
	$1Q_X + 1Q_Y \geqq 10$	(minerals constraint)
	$1Q_X + 0.5Q_Y \geqq 6$	(vitamins constraint)
	$Q_X, Q_Y \geqq 0$	(nonnegativity constraint)

Specifically, since the price of food X is \$2 per pound while the price of food Y is \$3 per pound, the cost function (C) per student that the firm seeks to minimize is $C = \$2Q_X + \$3Q_Y$. The protein ($P$) constraint indicates that $1P$ (found in each unit of food X) times Q_X plus $2P$ (found in each unit of food Y) times Q_Y must be equal to *or larger than* the $14P$ minimum daily requirement that the manager must satisfy. Similarly, since each unit of foods X and Y contains 1 unit of minerals (M) and meals must provide a daily minimum of $10M$, the minerals constraint is given by $1Q_X + 1Q_Y \geqq 10$. Furthermore, since each unit of food X contains 1 unit of vitamins ($1V$) and each unit of food Y contains $0.5V$, and meals must provide a daily minimum of $6V$, the vitamins constraint is

Table 8-3
Summary Data for the Cost Minimization Problem

	Meat (Food *X*)		Fish (Food *Y*)
Price per pound	\$2		\$3
	Units of Nutrients per Pound of		Minimum Daily Requirement
Nutrient	**Meat (Food *X*)**	**Fish (Food *Y*)**	**Total**
Protein (*P*)	1	2	14
Minerals (*M*)	1	1	10
Vitamins (*V*)	1	0.5	6

$1Q_X + 0.5Q_Y \geqq 6$. Note that the inequality constraints are now expressed in the form of "equal to or larger than" since the minimum daily requirements must be fulfilled but can be exceeded. Finally, nonnegativity constraints are required to preclude negative values for the solution.

Graphic Solution of the Cost Minimization Problem

In order to solve graphically the cost minimization linear programming problem formulated above, the next step is to treat each inequality constraint as an equation and plot it. Since each inequality constraint is expressed as "equal to or greater than," all points on or *above* the constraint line satisfy the particular inequality constraint. The feasible region is then given by the shaded area above *DEFG* in the left panel of Figure 8-6. All points in the shaded area simultaneously satisfy all the inequality and nonnegativity constraints of the problem.

In order to determine the mix of foods *X* and *Y* (that is, Q_X and Q_Y) that satisfies the minimum daily requirements for protein, minerals, and vitamins at the lowest cost per student, we superimpose cost line *HJ* on the feasible region in the right panel of Figure 8-6. *HJ* is the lowest isocost line that allows the firm to reach the feasible region. Note that cost line *HJ* has an absolute slope of $\frac{2}{3}$, which is the ratio of the price of food *X* to the price of food *Y* and is obtained by solving the cost equation for Q_Y. Cost line *HJ* touches the feasible region at point *E*.

Figure 8-6
Feasible Region and Cost Minimization

The shaded area in the left panel shows the feasible region where all the constraints are simultaneously satisfied. *HJ* in the right panel is the lowest isocost line that allows the manager to reach the feasible region. The absolute slope of cost line *HJ* is $\frac{2}{3}$, which is the ratio of the price of food *X* to the price of food *Y*. The manager minimizes costs by using 6 units of food *X* and 4 units of food *Y* at point *E* at a cost of $C = \$2(6) + \$3(4) = \$24$ per student.

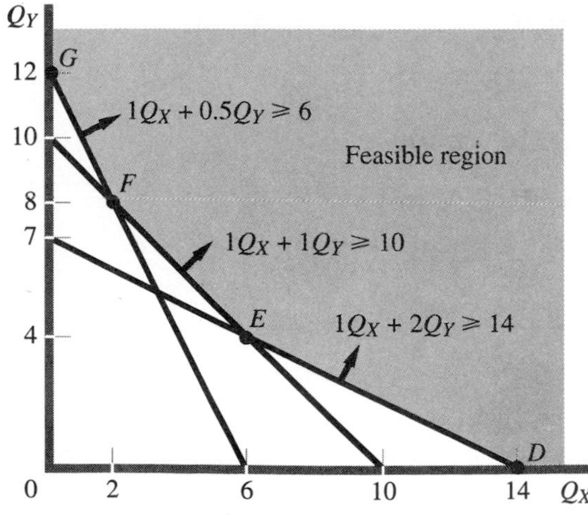

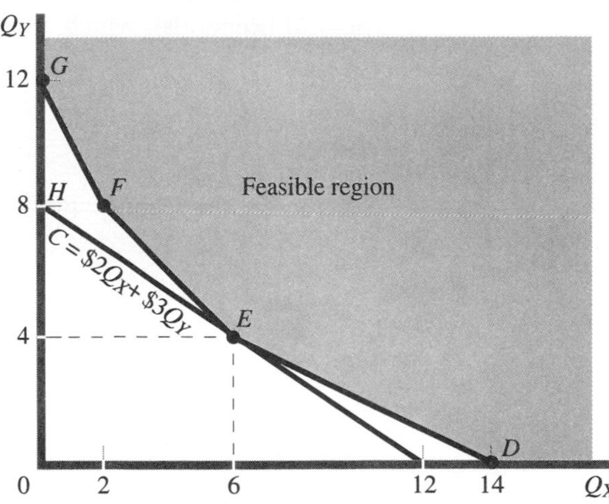

Thus, the manager minimizes the cost of satisfying the minimum daily requirements of the three nutrients per student by using 6 units of food X and 4 units of food Y at a cost of

$$C = (\$2)(6) + (\$3)(4) = \$24$$

Costs are higher at any other corner or point inside the feasible region.[12]

Note that point E is formed by the intersection of the constraint lines for nutrient P (protein) and nutrient M (minerals) but is above the constraint line for nutrient V (vitamins). This means that the minimum daily requirements for nutrients P and M are just met while the minimum requirement for nutrient V is more than met. Note also that if the price of food X increases from \$2 to \$3 (so that the ratio of the price of food X to the price of food Y is equal to 1), the lowest isocost line that reaches the feasible region would coincide with segment EF of the feasible region. In that case, all the combinations or mixes of food X and food Y along the segment would result in the same minimum cost (of \$30) per student. If the price of food X rose above \$3, the manager would minimize costs at point F.

Algebraic Solution of the Cost Minimization Problem

The cost minimization linear programming problem solved graphically above can also be solved algebraically by identifying (algebraically) the corners of the feasible region and then comparing the costs at each corner. Since each corner is formed by the intersection of two constraint lines, the coordinates of the intersection point (i.e., the values of Q_X and Q_Y at the corner) can be found by solving simultaneously the equations of the two intersecting lines, exactly as was done in solving algebraically the profit maximization linear programming problem.

For example, from the left panel of Figure 8-6, we see that corner point E is formed by the intersection of the constraint lines for nutrient P (protein) and nutrient M (minerals), which are, respectively,

$$1Q_X + 2Q_Y = 14$$

and

$$1Q_X + 1Q_Y = 10$$

Subtracting the second equation from the first, we have

$$\begin{array}{r} 1Q_X + 2Q_Y = 14 \\ \underline{1Q_X + 1Q_Y = 10} \\ 1Q_Y = \ \ 4 \end{array}$$

[12]At corner point D, $C = (\$2)(14) = \$28$; at point F, $C = (\$2)(2) + (\$3)(8) = \$28$; and at point G, $C = (\$3)(12) = \$36$.

Table 8-4
Use of Foods *X* and *Y*, and Costs at Each Corner of the Feasible Region

Corner Point	Q_X	Q_Y	$\$2Q_X + \$3Q_Y$	Cost
D	14	0	\$2(14) + \$3(0)	\$28
**E*	6	4	\$2(6) + \$3(4)	\$24
F	2	8	\$2(2) + \$3(8)	\$28
G	0	12	\$2(0) + \$3(12)	\$36

Substituting $Q_Y = 4$ into the second of the two equations, we get $Q_X = 6$. Thus, $Q_X = 6$ and $Q_Y = 4$ at corner point *E* (the same as we found graphically above). With the price of food *X* at \$2 and the price of food *Y* at \$3, the cost at point *E* is \$24. The values of Q_X and Q_Y and the costs at the other corners of the feasible region can be found algebraically in a similar manner and are given in Table 8-4. The table shows that costs are minimized at \$24 at corner point *E* by the manager using 6*X* and 4*Y*.

Since each unit of food *X* provides 1*P*, 1*M*, and 1*V* (see Table 8-3), the 6*X* that the manager uses at point *E* provide 6*P*, 6*M*, and 6*V*. On the other hand, since each unit of food *Y* provides 2*P*, 1*M*, and 0.5*V*, the 4*Y* that the manager uses at point *E* provide 8*P*, 4*M*, and 2*V*. The total amount of nutrients provided by using 6*X* and 4*Y* are then 14*P* (the same as the minimum requirement), 10*M* (the same as the minimum requirement), and 8*V* (which exceeds the minimum requirement of 6*V*). This is the same conclusion that we reached in the graphical solution.

Case Study 8-3
Cost Minimization Model for Warehouse Distribution Systems

A cost minimization model for a warehouse distribution system was developed for a firm that produced six different consumer products at six different locations and distributed the products nationally from 13 warehouses. The questions that the firm wanted to answer were (1) how many warehouses should the firm use, (2) where should these warehouses be located, and (3) which demand points should be serviced from each warehouse. Forty potential warehouse locations were considered for demand originating from 225 counties. While transportation costs represented the major costs of distributing the products, the model also considered other costs such as warehouse storage and handling costs, interest cost on inventory, state property taxes, income and franchise taxes, the cost of order processing, and administrative costs. The summary of the results comparing the distribution system in effect with the optimal distribution system is given in Table 8-5. The table shows that switching from the distribution system in effect (which utilized 13 warehouses) to the optimal distribution system (which utilized 32

Table 8-5
Comparison of Distribution System in Effect with Optimal Distribution System

Characteristic	Old System	Optimal System
Total variable cost (in millions)	$3.458	$3.054
Mean service distance (miles)	174	100
Number of warehouses	13	32

warehouses) would save the firm about $400,000 per year. This cost reduction arises because the decline in the mean transportation distance and transportation costs resulting from utilizing 32 warehouses exceeds the increase in the fixed costs of operating 32 warehouses as compared with operating 13 warehouses.

Source: D. L. Eldredge, "A Cost Minimization Model for Warehouse Distribution Systems," *Interfaces,* August 1982, pp. 113–119.

8-6 THE DUAL PROBLEM AND SHADOW PRICES

In this section, we examine the meaning and usefulness of dual linear programming and shadow prices. Then we formulate and solve the dual linear programming problem and find the value of shadow prices for the profit maximization problem of Section 8-4 and for the cost minimization problem for Section 8-5.

The Meaning of Dual and Shadow Prices

Every linear programming problem, called the **primal problem,** has a corresponding or symmetrical problem called the **dual problem.** A profit maximization primal problem has a cost minimization dual problem, while a cost minimization primal problem has a profit maximization dual problem.

The solutions of a dual problem are the **shadow prices.** They give the change in the value of the objective function per unit change in each constraint in the primal problem. For example, the shadow prices in a profit maximization problem indicate how much total profits would rise per unit increase in the use of each input. Shadow prices thus provide the imputed value or marginal valuation or worth of each input to the firm. If a particular input is not fully employed, its shadow price is zero because increasing the input would leave profits unchanged. A firm should increase the use of the input as long as the marginal value or shadow price of the input to the firm exceeds the cost of hiring the input.

Shadow prices provide important information for planning and strategic decisions of the firm. Shadow prices are also used (1) by many large corporations to correctly price the output of each division that is the input to another division, in order to maximize the total profits of the entire corporation, (2) by governments to appropriately price some government services, and (3) for planning in developing countries where the market system often does not function properly (i.e., where input and output prices do not reflect their true relative scarcity). The computer solution of the primal linear programming problem also provides the values of the shadow prices. Sometimes it is also easier to obtain the optimal value of the decision variables in the primal problem by solving the corresponding dual problem.

The dual problem is formulated directly from the corresponding primal problem as indicated below. We will also see that the optimal value of the objective function of the primal problem is equal to the optimal value of the objective function of the corresponding dual problem. This is called the **duality theorem.**

The Dual of Profit Maximization

In this section, we formulate and solve the dual problem for the constrained profit maximization problem examined in Section 8-4, which is repeated below for ease of reference.

Maximize	$\pi = \$30Q_X + \$40Q_Y$	(objective function)
Subject to	$1Q_X + 1Q_Y \leqq 7$	(input *A* constraint)
	$0.5Q_X + 1Q_Y \leqq 5$	(input *B* constraint)
	$0.5Q_Y \leqq 2$	(input *C* constraint)
	$Q_X, Q_Y \geqq 0$	(nonnegativity constraint)

In the dual problem we seek to minimize the imputed values, or shadow prices, of inputs *A*, *B*, and *C* used by the firm. Defining V_A, V_B, and V_C as the shadow prices of inputs *A*, *B*, and *C*, respectively, and *C* as the total imputed value of the fixed quantities of inputs *A*, *B*, and *C* available to the firm, we can write the dual objective function as

Minimize $$C = 7V_A + 5V_B + 2V_C \tag{8-8}$$

where the coefficients 7, 5, and 2 represent, respectively, the fixed quantities of inputs *A*, *B*, and *C* available to the firm.

The constraints of the dual problem postulate that the sum of the shadow price of each input times the amount of that input used to produce 1 unit of a particular product must be equal to or larger than the profit contribution of a unit of the product. Thus, we can write the constraints of the dual problem as

$$1V_A + 0.5V_B \geqq \$30$$
$$1V_A + 1V_B + 0.5V_C \geqq \$40$$

The first constraint postulates that the 1 unit of input *A* required to produce 1 unit of product *X* times the shadow price of input *A* (that is, V_A) plus 0.5 unit of input *B* required to produce 1 unit of input *X* times the shadow price of input *B* (that is, V_B) must be equal to or larger than the profit contribution of the 1 unit of product *X* produced. The second constraint is interpreted in a similar way.

Summarizing the dual cost minimization problem and adding the nonnegativity constraints, we have

$$\text{Minimize} \qquad C = 7V_A + 5V_B + 2V_C \qquad \text{(objective function)}$$

$$\begin{aligned} \text{Subject to} \qquad 1V_A + 0.5V_B \qquad\qquad &\geqq \$30 \\ 1V_A + \quad 1V_B + 0.5V_C &\geqq \$40 \\ V_A,\ V_B,\ V_C &\geqq \quad 0 \end{aligned}$$

The dual objective function is given by the sum of the shadow price of each input times the quantity of the input available to the firm. We have a dual constraint for each of the two decision variables (Q_X and Q_Y) in the primal problem. Each constraint postulates that the sum of the shadow price of each input times the quantity of the input required to produce 1 unit of each product must be equal to or larger than the profit contribution of a unit of the product. Note also that the direction of the inequality constraints in the dual problem is opposite that of the corresponding primal problem and that the shadow prices cannot be negative (the nonnegativity constraints in the dual problem).

That is, we find the values of the decision variables (V_A, V_B, and V_C) at each corner and choose the corner with the lowest value of C. Since we have three decision variables and this would necessitate a three-dimensional figure, which is awkward and difficult to draw and interpret, we will solve the above dual problem algebraically. The algebraic solution is simplified because in this case we know from the solution of the primal problem that input C is a slack variable so that V_C equals zero. Setting $V_C = 0$ and then subtracting the first from the second constraint, treated as equations, we get

$$\begin{aligned} 1V_A + \quad 1V_B &= \$40 \\ 1V_A + 0.5V_B &= \$30 \\ \hline 0.5V_B &= \$10 \end{aligned}$$

so that $V_B = \$20$. Substituting $V_B = \$20$ into the first equation, we get that $V_A = \$20$ also. This means that increasing the amount of input A or input B by 1 unit would increase the total profits of the firm by \$20, so that the firm should be willing to pay as much as \$20 for 1 additional unit of each of these inputs. Substituting the values of V_A, V_B, and V_C into the objective cost function (Equation 8-8), we get

$$C = 7(\$20) + 5(\$20) + 2(\$0) = \$240$$

This is the minimum cost that the firm would incur in producing $4X$ and $3Y$ (the solution of the primal profit maximization problem in Section 8-4). Note also that the maximum profits found in the solution of the primal problem (that is, $\pi = \$240$) equals the minimum cost in the solution of the corresponding dual problem (that is, $C = \$240$) as dictated by the duality theorem.

The Dual of Cost Minimization

In this section we formulate and solve the dual problem for the cost minimization problem examined in Section 8-5, which is repeated below for ease of reference.

Minimize	$C = \$2Q_X + \$3Q_Y$	(objective function)
Subject to	$1Q_X + 2Q_Y \geqq 14$	(protein constraint)
	$1Q_X + 1Q_Y \geqq 10$	(mineral constraint)
	$1Q_X + 0.5Q_Y \geqq 6$	(vitamins constraint)
	$Q_X, Q_Y \geqq 0$	(nonnegativity constraint)

The corresponding dual profit maximization problem can be formulated as follows:

Maximize $\pi = 14V_P + 10V_M + 6V_V$

Subject to

$$1V_P + 1V_M + 1V_V \leqq \$2$$
$$2V_P + 1V_M + 0.5V_V \leqq \$3$$
$$V_P, V_M, V_V \geqq 0$$

where V_P, V_M, and V_V refer, respectively, to the imputed value (marginal cost) or shadow price of the protein, mineral, and vitamin constraints in the primal problem, and π is the total imputed value or cost of the fixed amounts of protein, minerals, and vitamins that the firm must provide. The first constraint of the dual problem postulates that the sum of the 1 unit of protein, minerals, and vitamins available in 1 unit of product X times the shadow price of protein (that is, V_P), minerals (that is, V_M), and vitamins (that is, V_V), respectively, must be equal to or smaller than the price or cost per unit of product X purchased. The second constraint can be interpreted in a similar way. Note that the direction of the inequality constraints in the dual problem is opposite those of the corresponding primal problem and that the shadow prices cannot be negative.

Since we know from the solution of the primal problem that the vitamin constraint is a slack variable, so that $V_V = 0$, subtracting the first from the second constraint, treated as equations, we get the solution of the dual problem of

$$\begin{array}{rl} 2V_P + 1V_M &= 3 \\ 1V_P + 1V_M &= 2 \\ \hline 1V_P \quad\quad &= 1 \end{array}$$

Substituting $V_P = \$1$ into the second equation, we get $V_M = \$1$, so that

$$\pi = 14(\$1) + 10(\$1) + 6(\$0) = \$24$$

This is equal to the minimum total cost (C) found in the primal problem.

If the profit contribution resulting from increasing the protein and mineral constraints by 1 unit exceeds their respective marginal cost or shadow prices (that is, V_P and V_M), the total profit of the firm (that is, π) would increase by relaxing the protein and mineral constraints. On the other hand, if the profit contribution resulting from increasing the protein and mineral constraints by 1 unit is smaller than V_P and V_M, π would increase by *reducing* the protein and mineral constraints.

Case Study 8-4

Shadow Prices in Closing an Airfield in a Forest Pest Control Program

The Maine Forest Service conducts a large aerial spray program to limit the destruction of spruce-fir forests in Maine by spruce bud worms. Until 1984, 24 aircraft of three different types were flown from six airfields to spray a total of 850,000 acres in 250 to 300 infested areas. Spray blocks were assigned to airfields by partitioning the map into regions around each airfield. Aircraft types were then assigned to blocks on the basis of the block's size and distance from the airfield. In 1984, the Forest Service started using a linear programming model to minimize the cost of the spray program. The solution of the model also provided the shadow price of using each aircraft and operating each airfield. The spray project staff was particularly interested in the effect (shadow price) of closing one or more airfields. The solution of the dual of the cost minimization primal problem indicated that the total cost of the spray program of $634,000 for 1984 could be reduced by $24,000 if one peripheral airfield were replaced by a more centrally located airfield. The Forest Service, however, was denied access to the centrally located airfield because of environmental considerations. This shows the conflict that sometimes arises between economic efficiency and noneconomic social goals.

Source: D. L. Rumpf, E. Melachrinoudis, and T. Rumpf, "Improving Efficiency in a Forest Pest Control Spray Program," *Interfaces,* September–October 1985, pp. 1–11.

8-7 LINEAR PROGRAMMING AND LOGISTICS IN THE GLOBAL ECONOMY

Linear programming is also being used in the emerging field of **logistic management.** This refers to the merging at the corporate level of the purchasing, transportation, warehousing, distribution, and customer services functions, rather than dealing with each of them separately at divisions levels. Monitoring the movement of materials and finished products from a central place can reduce the shortages and surpluses that inevitably arise when these functions are managed separately. For example, it would be difficult for a firm to determine the desirability of a sales promotion without considering the cost of the inventory buildup to meet the anticipated increase in demand. Logistic management can, thus, increase the efficiency and profitability of the firm.

The merging of decision making for various functions of the firm involved in logistic management requires the setting up and solving of ever-larger linear programming problems. Linear programming, which in the past was often profitably used to solve specific functional problems (such as purchasing, transportation, warehousing, distribution, and customer functions) separately, is now increasingly being applied to solve all these functions together with logistic management. The new much faster algorithm developed by Karmarkar at Bell Labs as well as the development of ever-faster computers are greatly facilitating the development of logistic management. Despite its obvious merits, however, only about 10 percent of corporations now have expertise and are highly sophisticated in logistics, but things are certainly likely to change during this decade. Among the companies that are already making extensive use of logistic management are the 3M Corporation, Alpo Petfood Inc., Chrysler, the Minnesota Mining and Manufacturing Company, Land O'Lakes Foods, and Bergen Brunswing.[13]

Besides the development of the new faster algorithm and more powerful computers, two other forces are at work that will certainly lead to the rapid spread of logistics in the future. One is the growing use of just-in-time inventory management, which makes the buying of inputs and the selling of the product much more tricky and more closely integrated with all other functions of the firm. The second related reason is the increasing trend toward globalization of production and distribution in today's world. With production, distribution, marketing, and financing activities of the leading world corporations scattered around the world, the need for logistic management becomes even more important—and beneficial. For example, the 3M Corporation saved more than $40 million in 1988 by linking its American logistic operations with those in Europe (in preparation of the formation of the single market in 1992) and in the very rapidly growing Pacific Rim region. By centralizing several logistic functions, companies achieve greater flexibility in ordering inputs and selling products.

[13]Logistics: A Trendy Management Tool," *The New York Times,* December 24, 1989, Sec. 3, p. 12.

Case Study 8-5

Measuring the Pure Efficiency of Operating Units

A serious problem faced by any large business with hundreds or thousands of units is how to measure and maximize the real performance or pure efficiency of each store, branch, or office. There are, of course, many traditional methods of measuring and comparing the efficiency of each unit, such as sales, sales growth, profits, market share, labor and other costs per unit or the product or service, profit per employee, revenues per square foot, and so on. All of these methods, however, use overall average performance as the benchmark for comparison. Much more useful is to measure the real performance or pure efficiency of each unit after adjusting for all important differences between the specific unit and all the other units. For example, a particular unit may earn more profit than another unit, but when its better location, new equipment, and better trained labor force is taken into consideration, the unit may in fact be seen as underperforming in relation to another unit earning less but operating under much less favorable conditions.

The real performance or pure efficiency of a unit can now be measured more accurately with a relatively new operations research technique called *data envelopment analysis* (*DEA*), which utilizes the technical apparatus of linear programming. DEA takes into account all the most important measurable factors under which each unit or branch operates—the type of technology it uses, its level of capacity utilization, the degree of competition it faces, the quality of its inputs, and so on—in measuring the real performance or pure efficiency of each unit or branch. That is, DEA compares the performance of each unit or branch to that of a standardized peer unit or branch with similar attributes. Thus, DEA may show that a particular unit with high profits does operate with high efficiency. Another unit may have high profits but be underperforming in relation to its potential. A third unit may be earning low profits because of inefficiencies and, therefore, be a candidate for managerial help to bring it up to its potential. Still another unit may be efficient and earning low profits and, thus, be a candidate for closing or disinvestment. DEA has been very profitably used by such companies as Citibank, British Airways, and Pizza Hut, and it is increasingly being used to identify the best site or location for new units or branches of a firm. Although DEA was developed several decades ago, it is only with the advent of very powerful PCs since the early 1990s that it has become feasible because of its very high computational intensity.

Source: "Which Offices or Stores Really Perform Best? A New Tool Tells," *Fortune,* October 31, 1994, p. 38.

Case Study 8-6

Logistics at National Semiconductor, Saturn, and Compaq

Since the early 1990s, National Semiconductors, the world's thirteenth largest chipmaker, has become a logistics or supply-chain management expert, and, in the process, it has cut delivery time by 47 percent and reduced distribution costs by 2.5 percent at the same time that its sales increased by 34 percent. National Semiconductors achieved this feat by closing six warehouses around the globe and air-freighting its computer chips from its six production plants (four in the United States, one in England, and one in Israel) to its new world distribution center in Singapore, from where it fills orders from IBM, Toshiba, Compaq, Ford, Siemens, and its other large customers. Earlier, National Semiconductor's distribution network was a nightmare of waste, costly stockpiles, and an inefficient delivery system that often included as many as 10 stopovers for its chips on their way to customers.

From its very beginning Saturn has had a world-class logistics system that links suppliers, factories, and customers so efficiently that it maintains almost no inventory. Its central computer directs truck deliveries from its 339 suppliers located in 39 states at an average distance of more than 500 miles to its 56 receiving docks, 21 hours per day, 6 days per week, in a process that is so smooth that Saturn's assembly line had to be shut only once and for only 18 minutes in 4 years because of the lack of a component. Compaq estimated it lost from $500 million to $1 billion in sales in 1994 because its computers were not available in the location and at the time customers wanted them. Now it has set up a new logistics system to sharply increase the efficiency of its supply-chain management. For one thing, an on-board computer tells Compaq's truckers exactly where to go, the best route to take, and the time required. In short, there seems to be today much greater opportunities to cut costs from increasing supply-chain efficiency than from the manufacturing of the product in many cases. More and more, logistics is regarded as a crucial strategy for survival and growth in global competition.

Source: "Delivering the Goods," *Fortune,* November 28, 1994, pp. 64–78.

8-8 ACTUAL SOLUTION OF LINEAR PROGRAMMING PROBLEMS ON PERSONAL COMPUTERS

Linear programming problems are usually solved with computers rather than with graphical or algebraic techniques in the real world. One of the simplest and most popular software packages or programs to solve linear programming problems on personal computers is called LINDO (Linear Interactive Discrete Optimizer). In this section we show how to actually use LINDO to solve the maximization problem of Section 8-4. More complex problems are solved just as easily. Other programs are nearly as easy to use to solve linear programming problems.

On most computers, you access LINDO by simply typing: LINDO. The symbol ":" will then appear in the left-hand part of your screen. There, you type "max" or "min", followed by a space and then type the equation of the objective function that you seek to maximize or minimize. Then you press the "enter" key. The symbol "?" will then appear on the left-hand part of your screen. At that point you write the equation of your first inequality constraint and press the "enter" key. Note that in typing the equation of the inequality constraints, LINDO allows you to use the symbol "<" for *equal or smaller than* and the symbol ">" for *equal or larger than* since most keyboards do not have the symbols "≤" and "≥". After you have entered the equation of the first inequality constraint and pressed the "enter" key, another "?" appears on the left-hand part of your screen. There, you type the second inequality constraint and press the "enter" key. You repeat this process until you have entered all the inequality constraints. There is no need to enter the nonnegativity constraints.

After you have entered all the inequality constraints, you type "end" after the new "?" and then press the "enter" key. This indicates to LINDO that all the information for solving the linear programming problem has been entered. The symbol ":" will appear on the left-hand corner of your screen. There, you type the word "look" and press the "return" key. "ROW: ?" then appears on the left-hand corner of your screen. There you type "all" and press the "return" key. The objective function and the inequality constraints that you have entered followed by the word "END" and the symbol ":" then appear on the left-hand corner of your screen. This allows you to check that you have made no errors in entering the objective function and the inequality constraints. At this point you type the word "go" to get the solution to the problem.

What follows is the actual printout for entering and solving the problem of Section 8-4.

```
LINDO

:   max 30x+40y
?   1x+ 1y<7
? .5x+ 1y<5
?       .5y<2

? end
: look
ROW:
? all

MAX      30 X+40 Y
SUBJECT TO
   2)    1 X+1 Y <= 7
   3)   .5 X+1 Y <= 5
   4)       .5 Y <= 2
END

: go

   LP OPTIMUM FOUND AT STEP 2
      OBJECTIVE FUNCTION VALUE

1)          240.00000

VARIABLE      VALUE              REDUCED COST
  X            4.000000              0.000000
  Y            3.000000              0.000000

ROW           SLACK               DUAL PRICES
   2)          0.000000              20.00000
   3)          0.000000              20.00000
   4)          0.500000              0.000000

NO. ITERATIONS=  2

 DO RANGE (SENSITIVITY) ANALYSIS?
? no
: quit
STOP
```

Several clarifications are in order with regard to the above printout. First, we see that the results of the primal and dual problems in the above printout are the same as those found in Sections 8-4 and 8-6. Second, note that everything that we have typed is entered in lowercase letters (although this is not necessary), while everything done by LINDO is printed in capital letters. Third, the symbol "<" that we have entered is printed as "<=" by LINDO after we entered "look" and "all". Fourth, when LINDO asks if you wish to do sensitivity analysis, we answered "no" because we are not familiar with this more advanced type of analysis. Fifth, you can ignore the step at which the solution is found and the number of iterations performed appears in the printout.

Finally, we can change the model without having to retype the entire problem by simply typing "alter" instead of "quit" before the very end in the above printout. Then the word "ROW:" and "?" will appear on the screen. There, we simply enter the number of the row in which we wish to make a change in the problem. For example, if we wish to change the inequality constraint in row 3, we simply type "3" after the symbol "?". The symbols "VAR:" and "?" will then appear on the screen. There, we type the variable whose coefficient we wish to change. For example, if we want to change the coefficient of the variable *Y*, we simply type "y" after the "?". The words "NEW COEFFICIENT:" and "?" will then appear on the screen. There, we will enter the new coefficient we wish. For example, if we wish to change the coefficient of *Y* from 1 to 2, we simply type "2" after the "?". The symbol ":" will then appear on the screen. There, we enter the word "look" and continue exactly as above. LINDO will then provide the new solution to the revised linear programming problem in the format shown above.

SUMMARY

1. Linear programming is a mathematical technique for solving constrained maximization and minimization problems when there are many constraints and the objective function to be optimized as well as the constraints faced are linear (i.e., can be represented by straight lines). Linear programming has been applied to a wide variety of constrained optimization problems. Some of these are: the selection of the optimal production process to use to produce a product, the optimal product mix to produce, the least-cost input combination to satisfy some minimum product requirement, the marginal contribution to profits of the various inputs, and many others.

2. Each of the various input ratios that can be used to produce a particular commodity is called a "production process" or "activity." With only two inputs, production processes can be represented by straight-line rays from the origin in input space. By joining points of equal output on these rays or processes, we define the isoquant for a particular level of output of the commodity. These isoquants are formed by straight-line segments and have kinks rather than being smooth. A point on an isoquant which is not on a ray or process can be reached by the appropriate combination of the two adjacent processes. By adding the linear constraints of the problem, we can define the feasible region or all the input combinations that the firm can purchase and the optimal solution or highest isoquant that it can reach with the given constraints.

3. The function optimized in linear programming is called the "objective function." This usually refers to profit maximization or cost minimization. To solve a linear programming problem graphically, we (1) express the objective function as an equation and the constraints as inequalities; (2) graph the inequality constraints and define the feasible region; (3) graph the objective function as a series of isoprofit or isocost lines; and (4) find the optimal solution at the extreme point or corner of the feasible region that touches the highest isoprofit line or lowest isocost line.
4. Most firms produce more than one product, and the problem is to determine the output mix that maximizes the firm's total profit subject to the many constraints on inputs that the firm usually faces. Simple linear programming problems with only two decision variables (which product mix to produce) can be solved graphically. More complex problems with more than three decision variables can be solved only algebraically (usually with the use of computers by the simplex method). According to the extreme-point theorem of linear programming, the optimal solution can be found at a corner of the feasible region, even when there are multiple solutions. The computer solution also indicates the binding constraints and the unused quantity of each slack variable.
5. Most firms usually use more than one input to produce a product or service, and a crucial choice they face is how much of each input (the decision variables) to use in order to minimize costs of production subject to the minimum requirement constraints that it faces. In cost minimization linear programming problems, the inequality constraints are expressed in the form of "equal to or larger than" since the minimum requirements must be fulfilled but can be exceeded. Cost minimization linear programming problems are solved graphically when there are only two decision variables and algebraically (usually with computers) when there are more than two decision variables. The solution is usually found at a corner of the feasible region.
6. Every linear programming problem, called the "primal problem," has a corresponding or symmetrical problem called the "dual problem." A profit maximization primal problem has a cost minimization dual problem, while a cost minimization primal problem has a profit maximization dual problem. The solutions of a dual problem are the shadow prices. They give the change in the value of the objective function per unit change in each constraint in the primal problem. The dual problem is formulated directly from the corresponding primal problem. According to duality theory, the optimal value of the primal objective function equals the optimal value of the dual objective function.
7. Logistic management refers to the merging at the corporate level of the purchasing, transportation, warehousing, distribution, and customer services functions, rather than dealing with each of them separately at divisions levels. This increases the efficiency and profitability of the firm. Logistic management requires the setting up and solving of ever-larger linear program-

ming problems. The growing use of just-in-time inventory management and the increasing trend toward globalization of production and distribution in today's world are likely to lead to the rapid spread of logistic management in the future.

8. Linear programming problems are usually solved with computers rather than with graphical or algebraic techniques in the real world. One of the simplest and most popular software packages or programs to solve linear programming problems on personal computers is LINDO. The instructions on how to actually use LINDO are fairly easy to master, as shown on the actual computer program reproduced in Section 8-8.

DISCUSSION QUESTIONS

1. (*a*) In what way does linear programming differ from the optimization techniques examined in Chapter 2? (*b*) Why is the assumption of linearity important in linear programming? Is this assumption usually satisfied in the real world?
2. What three broad types of problems can linear programming be used to solve?
3. (*a*) In what way do the isoquants in linear programming differ from those of traditional production theory? (*b*) How can we determine the number of processes required to reach an optimal solution in linear programming?
4. Determine how much of the output of 200*Q* would be produced with each process in the right panel of Figure 8-2 if point *S* had been (*a*) one-quarter of distance *DE* from point *D* or (*b*) halfway between points *E* and *F* on *EF*.
5. (*a*) Why do only the corners of the feasible solution need to be examined in solving a linear programming problem? (*b*) Under what conditions is it possible to have multiple solutions? (*c*) Does this invalidate the extreme-point theorem?
6. (*a*) What is meant by the "profit contribution" in a linear programming problem? (*b*) Will maximizing the total profit contribution also maximize the total net profits of the firm? Why?
7. Suppose that a fourth constraint in the form of $1Q_X + 1Q_Y = 10$ were added to the profit maximization linear programming problem examined in Section 8-4. Would you be able to solve the problem? Why?
8. (*a*) Starting from the profit-maximizing solution at point *E* in Figure 8-3*d*, can the firm expand the production of both products by relaxing only one of the binding constraints? (*b*) How much should the firm be willing to pay to hire an additional unit of an input that represents a binding constraint on the solution? (*c*) What is the opportunity cost of a unit of the input that is slack at the optimal solution?

9. (*a*) In what way is the definition of the feasible region in a cost minimization linear programming problem different from that in a profit maximization problem? (*b*) What would happen if we added a fourth constraint in the left panel of Figure 8-6 that would be met by all points on or above a straight line connecting points *D* and *G*?
10. Starting from the left panel of Figure 8-6, what are the optimal solution and minimum cost if the price of food *X* remains at \$2 per unit but the price of food *Y* changes to (*a*) \$1, (*b*) \$2, (*c*) \$4, and (*d*) \$6?
11. What are the objective function and the constraints of the dual problem corresponding to the primal problem of (*a*) profit maximization subject to constraints on the availability of the inputs used in production? (*b*) cost minimization to produce a given output mix? (*c*) cost minimization to generate a given level of profits?
12. (*a*) Why is the solution of the dual problem useful? (*b*) What is the usefulness of shadow prices to the firm in a profit maximization problem? (*c*) What is the usefulness of shadow prices to the firm in a cost minimization problem? (*d*) What is meant by "duality theory"?
13. (*a*) What is logistic management? (*b*) What is the relationship of logistic management to linear programming? (*c*) What are the forces that are likely to lead to the rapid spread of logistic management in the future?

PROBLEMS

*1. Mark Oliver is bored with his job as a clerk in a department store and decides to open a dry-cleaning business. Mark rents dry-cleaning equipment which allows three different dry-cleaning processes: Process 1 uses capital (*K*) and labor (*L*) in the ratio of 3 to 1; process 2 uses $K/L = 1$; and process 3 uses $K/L = \frac{1}{3}$. The manufacturer of the equipment indicates that 50 garments can be dry-cleaned by using 2 units of labor and 6 units of capital with process 1, 3 units of labor and 3 units of capital with process 2, or 6 units of labor and 2 units of capital with process 3. The manufacturer also indicates that in order to double the number of garments dry-cleaned, inputs must be doubled with each process. The wage rate (w) for hired help for 1 day's work (a unit of labor) is \$50, and the rental price of capital (r) is \$75 per day. Suppose that Mark cannot incur expenses of more than \$750 per day. Determine the maximum number of garments that the business could dry-clean per day and the production process that Mark should utilize.

2. Starting from the solution to Problem 1 (shown at the end of the book), suppose that (*a*) the wage rate rises from \$50 to \$62.50 and the rental price of capital declines from \$75 to \$62.50. What would be the maximum output that Mark could produce if expenditures per day must remain at \$750? What process would he use to produce that output? (*b*) What would the value of w and r have to be in order for Mark to be indifferent between utilizing process 1 and process 2? Draw a figure showing your answer. What

would w and r have to be for Mark to utilize only process 1 to produce $100Q$? (*c*) If Mark could not hire more than 9 workers and rent more than 5 units of capital per day, what would be the maximum output that Mark could produce? What process or processes would he have to use in order to reach this output level? How many units of labor and capital would Mark use in each process if he used more than one process?

*3. The Petroleum Refining Company uses labor, capital, and crude oil to produce heating oil and automobile gasoline. The profit per barrel is $20 for heating oil and $30 for gasoline. To produce each barrel of heating oil, the company uses 1 unit of labor, $\frac{1}{2}$ unit of capital, and $\frac{1}{3}$ unit of crude oil, while to produce 1 barrel of gasoline, the company uses 1 unit of labor, 1 unit of capital, and 1 unit of crude oil. The company cannot use more than 10 units of labor, 7 units of capital, and 6.5 units of crude oil per time period. Find the quantity of heating oil and gasoline that the company should produce in order to maximize its total profits.

4. (*a*) Solve Problem 3 algebraically. (*b*) Which are the binding constraints at the optimal solution? Which is the slack input? How much is the unused quantity of the slack input? (*c*) What would the profit per barrel of heating oil and gasoline have to be in order to have multiple solutions along the segment of the feasible region formed by the constraint line from the capital input?

5. The Portable Computer Corporation manufactures two types of portable computers, type X, on which it earns a profit of $300 per unit, and type Y, on which it earns a profit of $400 per unit. In order to produce each unit of computer X, the company uses 1 unit of input A, $\frac{1}{2}$ unit of input B, and 1 unit of input C. To produce each unit of computer Y, the company uses 1 unit of input A, 1 unit of input B, and no input C. The firm can use only 12 units of input A and only 10 units of inputs B and C per time period. (*a*) Determine how many computers of type X and how many computers of type Y the firm should produce in order to maximize its total profits. (*b*) How much of each input does the firm use in producing the product mix that maximizes total profits? (*c*) If the profit per unit of computer X remains at $300, how much can the profit per unit of computer Y change before the firm changes the product mix that it produces to maximize profits?

*6. The National Ore Company operates two mines, A and B. It costs the company $8,000 per day to operate mine A and $12,000 per day to operate mine B. Each mine produces ores of high, medium, and low qualities. Mine A produces 0.5 ton of high-grade ore, 1 ton of medium-grade ore, and 3 tons of low-grade ore per day. Mine B produces 1 ton of each grade of ore per day. The company has contracted to provide local smelters with a minimum of 9 tons of high-grade ore, 12 tons of medium-grade ore, and 18 tons of low-grade ore per month. (*a*) Determine graphically the minimum cost at which the company can meet its contractual obligations. (*b*) How much are the company's costs at the other corners of the feasible region? (*c*) Which of the company's obligations are just met at the optimal point? Which is more than met? (*d*) If the cost of running mine A increased to $12,000 per day, how many days per month should the company run each mine in order to minimize the cost of meeting its contractual obligations? What would be the company's costs?

7. The Tasty Breakfast Company is planning a radio and television advertising campaign to introduce a new breakfast cereal. The company wants to reach at least 240,000 people, with no less than 90,000 of them having a yearly income of at least $40,000 and no fewer than 60,000 of age 50 or below. A radio ad costs $2,000 and is estimated to reach 10,000 people, 5,000 of whom have annual incomes of at least $40,000 and 10,000 of age 50 or lower. A TV ad costs $6,000 and is estimated to reach 40,000 people, 10,000 of whom have annual incomes of at least $40,000 and 5,000 of age 50 or lower. (*a*) Determine algebraically the minimum cost that allows the firm to reach its advertising goals. (*b*) Calculate how many in the targeted audience are reached by the radio ads and how many by the TV ads at the optimum point. Which advertising goals are just met? Which are more than met?

*8. (*a*) Formulate and (*b*) solve the dual for Problem 3 (the solution of which is provided at the end of the book).

9. For Problem 5, (*a*) formulate the dual problem and (*b*) solve it. (*c*) Indicate how the shadow prices could have been obtained from the primal solution.

10. For Problem 6, (*a*) formulate the dual problem and (*b*) solve it. (*c*) Indicate how the shadow prices could have been obtained from the primal solution.

11. For Problem 7, (*a*) formulate the dual problem and (*b*) solve it. (*c*) Indicate how the firm can use this information to plan its advertising campaign.

12. **Integrating Problem**

The Cerullo Tax Service Company provides two types of tax services: type *X* and type *Y*. Each involves 1 hour of a tax expert's time. With service *X*, the customer comes in or phones, asks questions, and is given answers. With tax service *Y*, the customer also gets tax material and a small-computer tax package. The tax firm charges $200 for service *X* and $300 for service *Y*. Service *X* requires 1 unit of labor, $\frac{1}{2}$ unit of capital, and no tax material. Service *Y* requires 1 unit of labor, 1 unit of capital, and $\frac{1}{2}$ unit of tax material. The firm can use no more than 9 units of labor (*L*), 6 units of capital (*K*), and 2.5 units of tax material (*R*) per hour. Suppose that the firm wants to know what combination of tax services *X* and *Y* to supply in order to maximize its total profits. (*a*) Formulate a linear programming problem; (*b*) solve it graphically; (*c*) check your answer algebraically; (*d*) determine which are the binding constraints and which is the slack constraint at the optimal point; (*e*) determine how much labor, capital, and tax materials are used to supply services *X* and *Y* at the optimal point; (*f*) indicate what would happen if the firm increased the price of service *Y* to $400; (*g*) formulate the dual problem; (*h*) solve the dual problem; (*i*) show how the same results could have been obtained from the original primal problem; and (*j*) indicate the usefulness to the firm of the results obtained from parts (*h*) and (*i*) in planning its expansion.

SUPPLEMENTARY READINGS

For a problem-solving approach to linear programming see:

Salvatore, Dominick: *Theory and Problems of Managerial Economics,* Schaum Outline Series (New York: McGraw-Hill, 1989), Chap. 9.

Dowling, Edward: *Introduction to Mathematical Economics* (New York: McGraw-Hill, 1991), Chaps. 13–15.

An excellent text on linear programming is:

Hillier, F., and G. J. Lieberman: *Introduction to Mathematical Programming* (New York: McGraw-Hill, 1990).

For the use of personal and mainframe computers for linear programming see:

Deniniger, R. A.: "Teaching Linear Programming on the Microcomputer," *Interfaces,* August 1982, pp. 30–33.

Harrison, T. P.: "Micro versus Mainframe Performance for a Selected Class of Mathematical Programming Problems," *Interfaces,* July–August 1985, pp. 14–19.

For some applications of linear programming, see:

Boquist, J. A., and W. T. Moore: "Estimating the Systematic Risk of an Industry Segment: A Mathematical Programming Approach," *Financial Management,* Winter 1983, pp. 11–18.

Haehling, V. L., et al.: "RRSP Flood: LP to the Rescue," *Interfaces,* July–August 1985, pp. 27–40.

Hays, J. W.: "Discount Rates in Linear Programming Formulations of the Capital Budgeting Problem," *Engineering Economist,* Winter 1984, pp. 113–126.

McNamara, J. R.: "A Linear Programming Model for Long-Range Capacity Planning in an Electric Utility," *Journal of Economics and Business,* Spring–Summer 1976, pp. 227–235.

Ronn, E. I.: "A New Linear Programming Approach to Bond Portfolio Management," *Journal of Financial and Quantitative Analysis,* December 1987, pp. 439–466.

Small, K. A.: "Trip Scheduling in Urban Transportation Analysis," *American Economic Review,* May 1992, pp. 482–486.

INTEGRATING CASE STUDY THREE

Production and Cost Functions in the Petroleum Industry, Duality, and Linear Programming

Introductory Comment In this part of the text (Chapters 6 through 8) we have examined production theory and estimation (Chapter 6), cost theory and estimation (Chapter 7), and linear programming (Chapter 8). We now integrate all these topics by starting with production theory, proceeding to cost theory, showing the duality or symmetry between production theory and cost theory, and finally, examining how all these topics are related to linear programming.

As indicated in Chapter 6, the production function most commonly used in empirical estimation is the Cobb-Douglas of the form:

$$Q = AK^aL^b$$

where Q, K, and L refer, respectively, to the quantities of output, capital, and labor, and A, a, and b are the parameters to be estimated. In order to use regression analysis for the estimation of the parameters, the Cobb-Douglas production function is transformed into

$$\ln Q = \ln A + a \ln K + b \ln L$$

which is linear in logarithms. Such a production function has been estimated for many industries, one of which is the petroleum industry. For the petroleum industry, $a = 0.31$ and $b = 0.64$.[1] Since $a + b = 0.31 + 0.64 = 0.95$ and is smaller than 1, it seems that the petroleum industry operates under slight diseconomies of scale. However, the difference in the estimated value of $a + b$ from 1 was not statistically significant at the 5 percent level, so that the hypothesis of constant returns to scale cannot be rejected.

The marginal product of labor and capital functions for the general formulation of the Cobb-Douglas production function are[2]

$$MP_K = \frac{\partial Q}{\partial K} = aAK^{a-1}L^b$$

[1]The labor input measures both production and nonproduction workers. They have been aggregated into a single labor input in order to simplify the analysis and deal with only two inputs, L and K.

[2]Those who do not know calculus can simply accept these results since

$$\frac{\partial Q}{\partial K} \cong \frac{\Delta Q}{\Delta K} = MP_K \quad \text{and} \quad \frac{\partial Q}{\partial L} \cong \frac{\Delta Q}{\Delta L} = MP_L$$

$$MP_L = \frac{\partial Q}{\partial L} = bAK^aL^{b-1}$$

For production efficiency,

$$\frac{MP_K}{r} = \frac{MP_L}{w}$$

where r is the rental price of capital and w is the wage rate of labor. Substituting the values of MP_K and MP_L for the Cobb-Douglas into the above condition, we get

$$\frac{aAK^{a-1}L^b}{r} = \frac{bAK^aL^{b-1}}{w}$$

Solving for K, we have

$$K = \frac{awL}{br}$$

This is the equation of the expansion path for the Cobb-Douglas and shows all efficient combinations of K and L. For the petroleum industry,

$$K = \frac{0.31w}{0.64r}L$$

By substituting the market values of w and r for the petroleum industry into the above equation, we get the equation of the expansion path for this industry. For example, if $w = \$20$ and $r = \$10$, $K \cong L$, which means that the expansion path is a straight line through the origin with slope of about 1.

We can derive the corresponding cost functions and show the duality between production and cost theory. The general equation of the total cost function can be written as

$$TC = rK + wL$$

Substituting the general equation of the expansion path (showing production efficiency) into the TC function, we have

$$TC = r\left(\frac{a}{b} \cdot \frac{w}{r}L\right) + wL$$

which can be rewritten as

$$TC = \left(\frac{a}{b} + 1\right)wL$$

The TC function, however, is usually expressed as a function of output (Q) rather than as a function of L. In order to remove L from the TC function and express TC as a function of Q, we substitute the general equation for the expansion path into the general equation of the Cobb-Douglas and obtain

$$Q = A\left(\frac{aw}{br}L\right)^a L^b = A\left(\frac{aw}{br}\right)^a L^{a+b}$$

Solving for L, we get

$$L^{a+b} = \frac{Q}{A}\left(\frac{aw}{br}\right)^{-a}$$

so that

$$L = \left(\frac{Q}{A}\right)^{1/(a+b)}\left(\frac{aw}{br}\right)^{-a/(a+b)}$$

Substituting the above value of L into the TC function, we get

$$TC = r\left(\frac{aw}{br}L\right) + w\left(\frac{Q}{A}\right)^{1/(a+b)}\left(\frac{aw}{br}\right)^{-a/(a+b)} = c\left(\frac{Q}{A}\right)^{1/(a+b)}$$

where c = constant. Thus,

$$TC = c\left(\frac{Q}{A}\right)^{1/(a+b)}$$

is the TC function associated with the Cobb-Douglas $Q = AK^aL^b$.

For the petroleum industry, $a + b \cong 1$, thus,

$$TC = c\frac{Q}{A} = c'Q$$

where $c' = C/A$ = constant. This means that TC is a linear function of Q, and

$$AC = \frac{TC}{Q} = c'$$

and
$$MC = \frac{d(TC)}{dQ} = \frac{\Delta TC}{\Delta Q} = c'$$

Thus, $AC = MC \cong c'$ (i.e., the AC and MC curves are horizontal and coincide) and we have (near) constant returns to scale and constant costs in this industry.

Since we have near-constant returns to scale and costs, petroleum prices remained fairly constant over long periods of time (especially before 1973); the petroleum industry faced many constraints on the inputs it used and the output mix to produce, so linear programming seemed a natural technique to apply in this industry in order to minimize production costs and maximize profits, subject to the many constraints faced by petroleum companies. In fact, one of the first successful applications of linear programming was in the petroleum industry. Large petroleum firms engage in exploration, extraction, refining, and marketing of petroleum products. Each phase can be and has been approached as a linear programming problem. In each phase, the firm seeks to optimize an objective function, such as maximizing the chance of finding petroleum deposits, minimizing extraction and production costs, and maximizing profits from sales. Each phase is subject to certain constraints, such as the availability of funds, technical personnel, specialized capital equipment in exploration and extraction, refining capacity, transportation, and marketing outlets in the other phases. For example, in refining, more than 10 chemically distinct blending stocks (semi-refined oils) are mixed together to produce gasoline of various knock ratings, vapor pressures, sulphur contents, etc. The firm wants to minimize the cost of producing the various types of gasoline subject to the availability of the blending stocks, refining capacity, transportation network, contract requirements, and so on. The problem is too complicated for traditional (graphical) analysis but is easily solved by linear programming with the use of computers.

Source: J. Moroney, "Cobb-Douglas Production Functions and Returns to Scale in U.S. Manufacturing Industry," *Western Economic Journal,* December 1967, pp. 39–51; A. Charnes, W. Cooper, and B. Mellon, "Blending Aviation Gasoline," *Econometrica,* April 1952; A. Manne, *Scheduling of Petroleum Refining Operations* (Cambridge, Mass.: Harvard University Press, 1956); and "Delivering the Goods," *Fortune,* November 28, 1994, pp. 64–78.

PART FOUR

Market Structure and Pricing Practices

Part Four (Chapters 9 through 11) brings together demand analysis (examined in Part Two) and production and cost analysis (examined in Part Three) in order to analyze how price and output are determined under various forms of market organization. Chapter 9 examines how price and output are determined under perfect competition, monopoly, and monopolistic competition, while Chapter 10 examines price and output decisions and strategic behavior under oligopoly. Chapter 11 then examines various pricing practices under monopoly, monopolistic competition, and oligopoly. Under perfect competition, commodity prices are determined exclusively by the interaction of the forces of market demand and supply, and the firm only determines the optimal level of output to produce. Crucial international interactions are also examined throughout this part.

CHAPTER 9

Market Structure: Perfect Competition, Monopoly, and Monopolistic Competition

KEY TERMS

Market
Market structure
Perfect competition
Monopoly
Monopolistic competition
Oligopoly
Imperfect competition
Price taker
Shut-down point
Short-run supply curve of the perfectly competitive firm
Foreign exchange market
Foreign exchange rate
Depreciation
Appreciation
Natural monopoly
Consumers' surplus
Deadweight loss
Differentiated product
Excess capacity
Overcrowding
Product variation
Selling expenses

CHAPTER OUTLINE

In this chapter we bring together demand analysis (examined in Part Two) and production and cost analysis (examined in Part Three) in order to analyze how price and output are determined under perfect competition, monopoly, and monopolistic competition. We begin the chapter by defining the meaning of markets and by identifying the various types of market structure. We then go on to examine the meaning of perfect competition and show how the equilibrium price and quantity are determined in a perfectly competitive market. Subsequently, we examine how a perfectly competitive firm determines the optimum level of output in the short run and in the long run. Here, we also examine competition in the international economy by showing the effect of imports on domestic prices and the effect of a change in the dollar exchange rate on the international competitiveness of U.S. firms. We then move on to examine monopoly. After identifying the sources of monopoly power, we examine how the monopolist determines the best level of output and price in the short run and in the long run and compare monopoly to perfect competition. Finally, we discuss the meaning and importance of monopolistic competition, show how the equilibrium price and quantity are determined in the short run and in the long run, and analyze product variation and selling expenses.

9-1 MARKET STRUCTURE AND DEGREE OF COMPETITION

The process by which price and output are determined in the real world is strongly affected by the structure of the market. A **market** consists of all the actual and potential buyers and sellers of a particular product. **Market structure** refers to the competitive environment in which the buyers and sellers of the product operate.

Four different types of market structure are usually identified. These are: perfect competition at one extreme, pure monopoly at the opposite extreme, and monopolistic competition and oligopoly in between. These different types of market structure or organization are defined and distinguished from one another in terms of the number and size of the buyers and sellers of the product, the type of product bought and sold (i.e., standardized or homogeneous as contrasted with differentiated), the degree of mobility of resources (i.e., the ease with which firms and input owners can enter or exit the market), and the degree of knowledge that economic agents (i.e., firms, suppliers of inputs, and consumers) have of prices and costs, and demand and supply conditions.

The above market characteristics are used to define the four different types of market structure, as follows:

Perfect competition is the form of market organization in which (1) there are many buyers and sellers of a product, each too small to affect the price of the product; (2) the product is homogeneous; (3) there is perfect mobility of resources; and (4) economic agents have perfect knowledge of market conditions.

Monopoly is the form of market organization in which a single firm sells a product for which there are no close substitutes. Entry into the industry is very difficult or impossible (as evidenced by the fact that there is a single firm in the industry).

Monopolistic competition refers to the case where there are many sellers of a differentiated product and entry into or exit from the industry is rather easy in the long run.

Oligopoly is the case where there are few sellers of a homogeneous or differentiated product. While entry into the industry is possible, it is not easy (as evidenced by the small number of firms in the industry).[1]

Monopoly, monopolistic competition, and oligopoly are often referred to as **imperfect competition** to distinguish them from perfect competition. The definitions of the various types of market structure presented above are examined in detail and explained when the particular market structure is analyzed. In this chapter we examine perfect competition, monopoly, and monopolistic competition. Oligopoly is examined in the next chapter.

9-2 PERFECT COMPETITION

In this section we discuss in detail the meaning of perfect competition, show that under perfect competition the market price and quantity of a product are determined exclusively by the forces of market demand and market supply for the product, and examine how the firm determines its best level of output in the short run and in the long run at the given market price. In the process we also derive the short-run competitive firm and market supply curves for the product.

Meaning and Importance of Perfect Competition

According to the first part of the definition of perfect competition presented above, there is a great number of buyers and sellers of the product, and each seller and buyer is too small in relation to the market to be able to affect the price of the product by his or her own actions. This means that a change in the output of a single firm will not *perceptibly* affect the market price of the product. Similarly, each buyer of the product is too small to be able to extract from the seller such things as quantity discounts and special credit terms.

[1]The above definitions of monopoly, monopolistic competition, and oligopoly are expressed in terms of the sellers of the product. Analogous types of market structure can be defined in terms of buyers of the product or input. These are monopsony, monopsonistic competition, and oligopsony. *Monopsony* refers to the market situation in which there is a single *buyer* of a commodity or input for which there are no close substitutes. *Monopsonistic* competition and *oligopsony* are defined in an analogous way. Monopsony and oligopsony are more common in input markets than in commodity markets. They sometimes exist in labor markets dominated by one or a few large employers, in local agricultural markets dominated by one or a few large processors, or in government purchases of large defense systems.

The product of each competitive firm is homogeneous, identical, or perfectly standardized. An example of this might be grade-A winter wheat. As a result buyers cannot distinguish between the output of one firm and the output of another, so they are indifferent from which firm they buy the product. This refers not only to the physical characteristics of the product but also the "environment" (such as the pleasantness of the seller and the selling location) in which the purchase is made.

Under perfect competition, there is perfect mobility of resources. That is, workers and other inputs can easily move geographically from one job to another and can respond very quickly to monetary incentives. No input required in the production of a product is monopolized by its owners or producers. In the long run firms can enter or leave the industry witbout much difficulty. That is, there are no patents or copyrights, "vast amounts" of capital are not necessary to enter the market, and already established firms do not have any lasting cost advantage over new entrants because of experience or size.

Finally, under perfect competition, consumers, resource owners, and firms in the market have perfect knowledge as to present and future prices, costs, and economic opportunities in general. Thus, consumers will not pay a higher price than necessary for the product. Price differences are quickly eliminated, and a single price will prevail throughout the market for the product. Resources are sold to the highest bidder. With perfect knowledge of present and future prices and costs, producers know exactly how much to produce.

Perfect competition, as defined above, has never really existed. Perhaps the closest we might come today to a perfectly competitive market is the stock market (see Case Study 9-1). Another case where we may have come close to satisfying the first three assumptions of perfect competition is in the market for such agricultural commodities as wheat and corn. The natural gas industry and the trucking industries also approach perfect competition. The fact that perfect competition in its pure form has never really existed in the real world does not reduce the great usefulness of the perfectly competitive model. As indicated in Chapter 1, a theory must be accepted or rejected on the basis of its ability to explain and to predict correctly and not on the realism of its assumptions. And the perfectly competitive model does give us some very useful (even if at times rough) explanations and predictions of many real-world economic phenomena when the assumptions of the perfectly competitive model are only approximately (rather than exactly) satisfied. In addition, this model helps us evaluate and compare the *efficiency* with which resources are used under different forms of market organization.

Case Study 9-1

Competition in the Stock Market

The stock market is as close as we come today to a perfectly competitive market. In most cases the price of a particular stock is determined by the market forces of demand and supply of the stock, and individual buyers and sellers of the stock have an insignificant effect on price (i.e., they are price takers). All stocks within each category are more or less homogeneous. The fact that a stock is bought and sold frequently is evidence that resources are mobile. Finally, information on prices and quantities is readily available.

In general, the price of a stock reflects all the publicly known information about the present and expected future profitability of the stock. This is known as the *efficient market hypothesis.* Funds flow into stocks, and resources flow into uses in which the rate of return, corrected for risk, is highest. Thus, stock prices provide the signals for the efficient allocation of investments in the economy. Despite the fact that the stock market is close to being a perfectly competitive market, imperfections occur even here. For example, the sale of $1 billion worth of stocks by IBM or any other large corporation will certainly affect (depress) the price of its stocks.

Today, more and more Americans trade foreign stocks, and more and more foreigners trade American stocks. This has been the result of a communications revolution that linked stock markets around the world into a huge global capital market and around-the-clock trading. While this provides immense new earning possibilities and sharply increased opportunities for portfolio diversification, it also creates the danger that a crisis in one market will very quickly spread to other markets around the world. This actually happened when the New York Stock Exchange collapsed in October 1987. In recent years, the New York Stock Exchange seems to have lost some of its former ability to predict changing economic conditions and its importance as the central source of capital for corporate America, as the latter borrowed increasing amounts from banks for takeovers and mergers.

Source: The New York Stock Exchange (New York: The New York Stock Exchange, 1987); "Does the Market Matter?" *Business Week,* October 30, 1989, pp. 24–26; "Let Markets Multiply," *Economist,* January 16, 1993, pp. 71–72; and "Luck or Logic? Debate Rages On Over 'Efficient Market Theory'," *The Wall Street Journal,* November 4, 1993, p. C1.

Price Determination under Perfect Competition

Under perfect competition, the price of a product is determined at the intersection of the market demand curve and the market supply curve of the product. The market demand curve for a product is simply the horizontal summation of the demand curves of all the consumers in the market, as explained on page 83. As we will see on page 373, the market supply curve of a product is similarly obtained from the horizontal summation of the supply curve of the individual producers of the product.

Given that the market price of a product is determined at the intersection of the market demand and supply curves of the product, the perfectly competitive firm is a **price taker.** That is, the perfectly competitive firm takes the price of the product as given and has no perceptible effect on that price by varying its own level of output and sales of the product. Since the products of all firms are homogeneous, a firm cannot sell at a price higher than the market price of the product, otherwise the firm would lose all its customers. On the other hand, there is no reason for the firm to sell at a price below the market price since it can sell any quantity of the product at the given market price. As a result, the firm faces a horizontal or infintely elastic demand curve for the product at the market price determined at the intersection of the market demand and supply curves of the product. For example, a small wheat farmer can sell any amount of wheat at the given market price of wheat. This is shown in Figure 9-1.

In Figure 9-1, D is the market demand curve for the product, and S is the market supply curve of the product. The equilibrium price of the product is $P = \$45$ and is determined at point E at the intersection of D and S. At a price higher than the equilibrium price, say, $P = \$55$, the quantity supplied of the product exceeds the quantity demanded of the product ($QS - QD = RN = 100$), and the price of the product will fall. As P falls, the quantity demanded of the product increases and the quantity supplied declines until the equilibrium price of $P = \$45$ is established, at which the quantity demanded is equal to the quantity supplied (that is, $QD = QS = 400$). On the other hand, at a price below the equilibrium price, $QD > QS$ (for example, at $P = \$35$, $QD - QS = JT = 100$), and P rises to the equilibrium $P = \$45$.

The equilibrium price and quantity can be determined algebraically by setting the market demand and supply functions equal to each other and solving for the equilibrium price. Substituting the equilibrium price into the demand or supply functions and solving for Q, we then get the equilibrium quantity. For

Figure 9-1
The Equilibrium Price and the Demand Level Faced by a Perfectly Competitive Firm

The equilibrium price of the product, $P = \$45$, is determined at the intersection of the competitive market demand and supply curves (i.e., at the intersection of D and S) at point E. The perfectly competitive firm is then a price taker and faces the infinitely elastic demand curve, d, at $P = \$45$. Since the firm can sell any quantity of the product at $P = \$45$, the change in total revenue per unit change in output or marginal revenue (MR) also equals \$45.

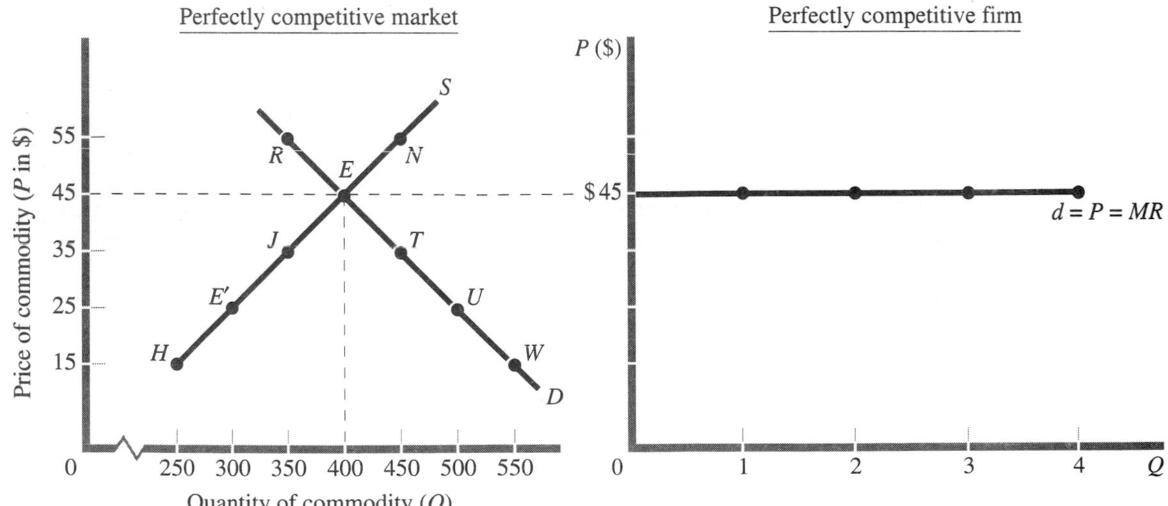

example, the equations for the market demand and supply curves for the product in Figure 9-1 are

$$QD = 625 - 5P \tag{9-1}$$

$$QS = 175 + 5P \tag{9-2}$$

Setting QD equal to QS and solving for P, we have

$$QD = QS$$
$$625 - 5P = 175 + 5P$$
$$450 = 10P$$
$$P = \$45$$

Substituting $P = \$45$ into the demand or supply functions and solving for Q, we have

$$QD = 625 - 5P = 625 - 5(45) = 400$$
$$QS = 175 + 5P = 175 + 5(45) = 400$$

Given the equilibrium price of $P = \$45$, a perfectly competitive firm producing the product faces the horizontal or infinitely elastic demand curve shown by d at $P = \$45$ in Figure 9-1. The perfectly competitive firm only determines what quantity of the product to produce at $P = \$45$ in order to maximize its total profits. How the firm does this is examined in the next section. For the moment, suppose that there are 100 identical firms in this market, each producing 4 units of the product at $P = \$45$. If one such firm expanded its output by 25 percent, the total quantity of product X sold in this market would rise by only 1 unit, from 400 to 401, and P would fall from \$45 to \$44.90. With 1,000 firms, P would fall only from \$45 to \$44.99, and with 10,000 firms to $P = \$44.999$. Of course, if all firms increase their output, the market supply curve of the product would shift to the right and intersect the market demand curve at a lower equilibrium price (see Problem 1). When only one firm changes its output, however, we can safely assume that it will have an imperceptible effect on the equilibrium price (i.e., the firm is a price taker), so that we can draw the demand curve for the product that the firm faces as horizontal. When the product price is constant, the change in the total revenue per unit change in output or marginal revenue (MR) is also constant and is equal to the product price. That is, for a perfectly competitive firm,

$$P = MR \tag{9-3}$$

Short-Run Analysis of a Perfectly Competitive Firm

We saw in Section 1-2 that the aim of a firm is to maximize profits. In the short run, some inputs are fixed, and these give rise to fixed costs, which go on whether the firm produces or not. Thus, it pays for the firm to stay in business in the short run even if it incurs losses, as long as these losses are smaller than its fixed costs.[2] Thus, the best level of output of the firm in the short run is the one at which the firm maximizes profits or minimizes losses.

The best level of output of the firm in the short run is the one at which the marginal revenue (MR) of the firm equals its short-run marginal cost (MC). As pointed out on page 42, as long as MR exceeds MC, it pays for the firm to expand output because by doing so the firm would add more to its total revenue than to its total costs (so that its total profits increase or its total losses decrease). On the other hand, as long as MC exceeds MR, it pays for the firm to *reduce* output because by doing so the firm will reduce its total costs more than its total revenue (so that, once again, its total profits increase or its total losses decline). Thus, the best level of output of any firm (not just a perfectly competitive firm) is the one at which $MR = MC$. Since a perfectly competitive firm faces a horizontal or infinitely elastic demand curve, $P = MR$, so that the condition for the best level of output can be restated as the one at which $P = MR = MC$.[3] This can be seen in Figure 9-2.

In the top panel of Figure 9-2, d is the demand curve for the output of the perfectly competitive firm shown in Figure 9-1, and the marginal and average total cost (that is, MC and ATC) curves are those of Figure 7-1. The best level of output of the firm is given at point E, where the MC curve intersects the firm's d or MR curve. At point E, the firm produces 4 units of output at $P = MR = MC =$ \$45. Since at point E, $P =$ \$45 and $ATC =$ \$35, the firm earns a profit of $EA =$ \$10 per unit and $EABC =$ \$40 in total (the shaded area). This is the largest total profit that the firm can earn. This can be proved as follows. Since at any output level smaller than $Q_X = 4$, $P = MR > MC$, the firm would be adding more to its total revenue than to its total costs (so that its total profits would increase) by expanding output. On the other hand, it does not pay for the firm to expand its output past point E (i.e., to be greater than $Q_X = 4$) because $MC > MR = P =$ \$45 and the firm would be adding more to its total costs than to its total revenues (so

[2]In the long run, of course, all costs are variable and the firm will not remain in business if it cannot cover at least all of its costs (so as to break even) and possibly earn a profit.

[3]This can be shown with calculus as follows. Total profits (π) equals total revenue (TR) minus total costs (TC). Taking the first derivative of π with respect to Q and setting it equal to zero, we have

$$\frac{d\pi}{dQ} = \frac{d(TR)}{dQ} - \frac{d(TC)}{dQ} = 0$$

Since

$$\frac{d(TR)}{dQ} = MR \quad \text{and} \quad \frac{d(TC)}{dQ} = MC$$

the above condition becomes $MR = MC$. But under perfect competition, the price is given to the firm and is constant. Therefore,

$$\frac{d(TR)}{dQ} = \frac{d(PQ)}{dQ} = P = MR$$

so that the first-order condition for maximization under perfect competition becomes $P = MR = MC$. For the second-order condition, see the appendix to this chapter.

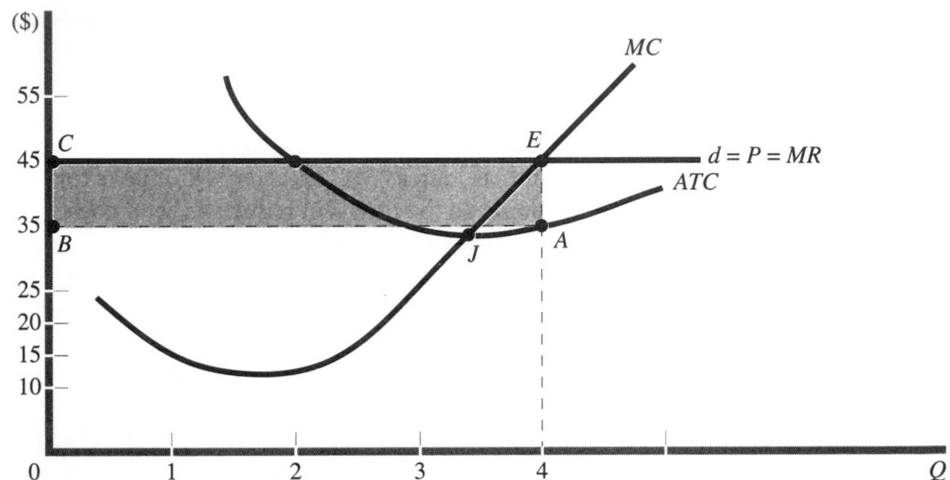

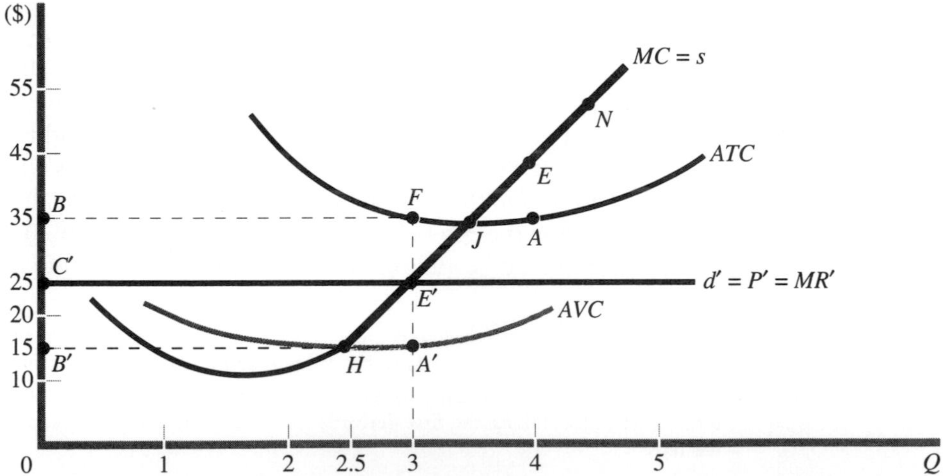

Figure 9-2
Short-Run Analysis of a Perfectly Competitive Firm

With d, the best level of output is 4 units and is shown in the top panel by point E, at which $P = MR = MC$, and the firm earns profit EA = \$10 per unit, and $EABC$ = \$40 in total. With d' in the bottom panel, the best level of output is 3 units, and is given by point E' at which the firm incurs a loss of FE' = \$10 per unit, and $FE'C'B$ = \$30 in total. At point E', the firm minimizes losses. The shut-down point is at point H. The rising portion of the MC curve above the AVC curve (shut-down point) is the firm's short-run supply curve (the heavy portion of the MC curve labeled s in the bottom panel).

that its total profits would decline). Thus, the best level of output for the firm is $Q_X = 4$, at which $MR = P = MC$ and the total profits of the firm are maximized.[4]

The bottom panel of Figure 9-2 shows that if the market price of the product is \$25 instead of \$35, so that the demand curve faced by the perfectly competitive firm is d' instead of d, the best level of output of the firm is 3 units, as indicated by point E', where $P = MR = MC$. At $Q_X = 3$, $P = \$25$ and $ATC = \$35$, so that the firm incurs the loss of $FE' = \$10$ per unit and $FE'C'B = \$30$ in total. If the firm stopped producing the product and left the market, however, it would incur the greater loss of $FA' = \$20$ per unit and $FA'B'B = \$60$ (its total fixed costs). Another way of looking at this is to say that at the best level of output of $Q = 3$, the excess of $P = \$25$ over the firm's average variable cost (AVC) of \$15 (also from Figure 7-1) can be applied to cover part of the firm's fixed costs (FA' per unit and $FA'B'B$ in total). Thus, the firm *minimizes its losses* by continuing to produce its best level of output. If the market price of the product declined to slightly below \$15, so that the demand curve facing the firm crossed the MC curve at point H (see the bottom panel of Figure 9-2), the firm would be indifferent whether to produce or not. The reason is that at point H, $P = AVC$ and the total losses of the firm would be equal to its total fixed costs whether it produced or not. Thus, point H is the **shut-down point** of the firm. Below point H, the firm would not even cover its variable costs, and so by going out of business, the firm would limit its losses to be equal to its total fixed costs.

Short-Run Supply Curve of the Competitive Firm and Market

From what has been said above, we can conclude that the rising portion of the firm's MC curve above the AVC curve or shut-down point is or represents the **short-run supply curve of the perfectly competitive firm** (the heavier portion of the MC curve labeled s in the bottom panel of Figure 9-2). The reason for this is that the perfectly competitive firm always produces where $P = MR = MC$, as long as $P > AVC$. Thus, at $P = \$55$, the firm produces 4.5 units (point N); at $P = \$45$, $Q = 4$; at $P = \$25$, $Q = 3$; and at $P = \$15$, $Q = 2.5$. That is, given P, we can determine the output supplied by the perfectly competitive firm by the point where $P = MC$. Thus, the rising portion of the competitive firm's MC curve abovc AVC shows a unique relationship between P and Q, which is the definition of the supply curve.

Given constant prices, the perfectly competitive market supply curve of the product is then obtained by the horizontal summation of the individual firm's supply curves. The market supply curve (S) shown in Figure 9-1 is based on the assumption that there are 100 firms identical to the one shown in Figure 9-2. Thus, S has the same shape as s, but its quantity scale is 100 times larger than for s. At the point where D and S cross, we then have the equilibrium price, which

[4]Note that at $Q_X = 3.5$ (point J on the ATC curve in the left panel of Figure 9-2), the profit *per unit* would be slightly higher than at point E, but total profits would be lower, and the aim of the firm is to maximize total profits—not profits per unit of output.

is given to the firm (see Figure 9-1). The circle is now complete—that is, we started with the market, moved on to the firm, and finally returned to the market in a way that is internally consistent and simultaneously determined.

Long-Run Analysis of a Perfectly Competitive Firm

In the long run all inputs and costs of production are variable, and the firm can construct the optimum or most appropriate scale of plant to produce the best level of output. The best level of output is the one at which price equals the long-run marginal cost (*LMC*) of the firm. The optimum scale of plant is the one with the short-run average total cost (*SATC*) curve tangent to the long-run average cost of the firm at the best level of output. If existing firms earn profits, however, more firms enter the market in the long run. This increases (i.e., shifts to the right) the market supply of the product and results in a lower product price until all profits are squeezed out. On the other hand, if firms in the market incur losses, some firms will leave the market in the long run. This reduces the market supply of the product until all firms remaining in the market just break even. Thus, when a competitive market is in long-run equilibrium, all firms produce at the lowest point on their long-run average cost (*LAC*) curve and break even. This is shown by point E^* in Figure 9-3.

Figure 9-3 shows that at $P = \$25$, the best level of output of the perfectly competitive firm is 4 units and is given by point E^*, at which $P = LAC$. Because of free or easy entry into the market, all profits and losses have been eliminated, so that $P = LMC =$ lowest *LAC*. Thus, for a competitive market to be in long-run equilibrium, all firms in the industry must produce where $P = MR = LMC =$ lowest *LAC* (point E^* in Figure 9-3), so that all firms break even. The perfectly

Figure 9-3
Long-Run Equilibrium of the Perfectly Competitive Firm and Industry
The best level of output of the perfectly competitive firm at $P = \$25$ is 4 units and is given by point E^*, at which $P = MR = LMC =$ lowest *LAC*. Because of free or easy entry into the market, all profits and losses have been eliminated, and the firm produces at the lowest point on its *LAC* curve. The firm operates the scale of plant given by *SATC* at its lowest point so that $SMC = LMC$ also.

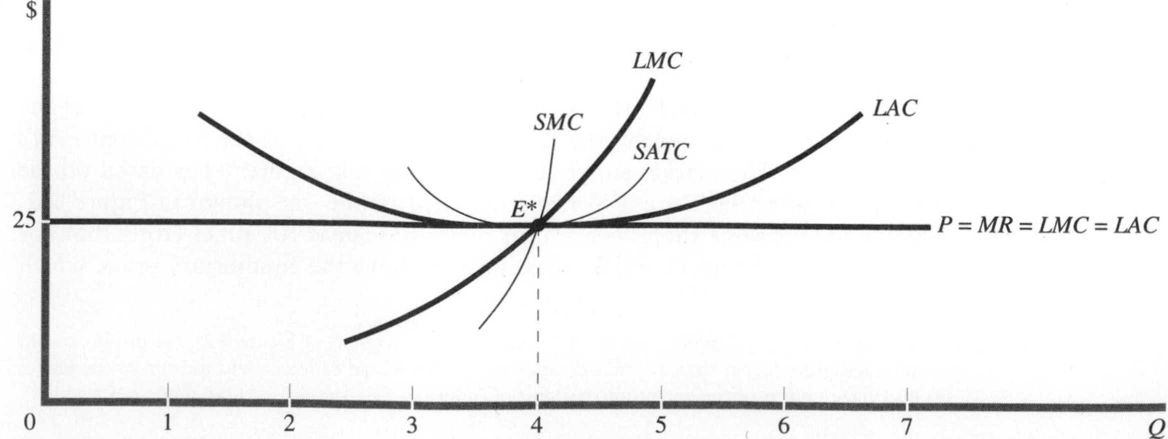

competitive firm operates the scale of plant represented by *SATC* at its lowest point (point E^*), so that its short-run marginal cost (*SMC*) equals *LMC* also.

When a perfectly competitive market is in long-run equilibrium, firms break even and earn zero economic profits. Therefore, the owner of the firm receives only a normal return on investment or an amount equal to what he or she would earn by investing his or her funds in the best alternative venture of similar risk. If the owner manages the firm, zero economic profits also include what he or she would earn in the best alternative occupation (i.e., managing the firm for someone else). Thus, zero economic profits means that the total revenues of the firm just cover all costs (explicit and implicit).

It should be noted that perfectly competitive firms need not have identical cost curves (although we assume so for simplicity), but the lowest point on their *LAC* curves must indicate the same cost per unit. If some firms used more productive inputs and, thus, had lower average costs than other firms in the industry, the more productive inputs would be able to extract from their employer higher rewards (payments) commensurate to their higher productivity, under the threat of leaving to work for others. As a result, their *LAC* curves would shift upward until the lowest point on the *LAC* curve of all firms is the same. Thus, competition in the input markets as well as in the commodity market will result in all firms having identical (minimum) average costs and zero economic profits when the industry is in long-run equilibrium.

In the real world, we seldom, if ever, observe markets that are in long-run equilibrium because consumer tastes are constantly changing, market demand curves are shifting, and the technology of production and the prices of inputs change (so that the market supply curve also shifts). Perfectly competitive markets, therefore, seldom if ever reach equilibrium. The fact, however, that they will always be gravitating or moving toward long-run equilibrium is extremely useful to managers in analyzing the effect of changes in market forces and in determining the optimum scale of plant and best level of output of the firm in the long run.

Case Study 9-2

Long-Run Adjustment in the U.S. Cotton Textile Industry

In a study of U.S. industries between the world wars Lloyd Reynolds found that the U.S. cotton textile industry was the one that came closest to being perfectly competitive. Cotton textiles were practically homogeneous, there were many buyers and sellers of cotton cloth, each was too small to affect its price, and entry into and exit from the industry was easy. Reynolds found that the rate of return on investments in the cotton textile industry was about 6 percent in the South and 1 percent in the North (because of higher costs for raw cotton and labor in the North), as contrasted to an average rate of return of 8 percent for all other manufacturing industries in the United States over the same period of time. Because of the lower returns in the textile industry than in other industries, the perfectly competitive model would predict that firms would leave the textile industry in the long run and enter other industries. The model would also predict that because returns were lower in the North than in the South, a greater contraction of the textile industry would take place in the North than in the South. Reynolds found that both of these predictions were borne out by the facts. Capacity in the U.S. textile industry declined by over 33 percent between 1925 and 1938, with the decline being larger in the North than in the South. Thus, managers of textile firms, cotton farms, and firms using cloth did seem to make use of this knowledge and did respond to these economic forces in their managerial decisions. Most U.S. textile firms were able to remain in business after World War II only as a result of U.S. restrictions on cheaper textile imports.

Source: L. Reynolds, "Competition in the Textile Industry," in W. Adams and T. Traywick, eds., *Readings in Economics* (New York: Macmillan, 1948), and "Apparel Makes Last Stand," *The New York Times*, September 26, 1990, p. D2.

9-3 COMPETITION IN THE GLOBAL ECONOMY

In this section we examine how international competition affects prices in the nation and how the value of the nation's currency affects the nation's international competitiveness, and how a competitive firm in the nation adjusts to international competition.

Domestic Demand and Supply, Imports, and Prices

Domestic firms in most industries face a great deal of competition from abroad. Most U.S.–made goods today compete with similar goods from abroad and in turn compete with foreign-made goods in foreign markets. Steel, textiles, cameras, wines, automobiles, television sets, computers, and aircraft are but a few of the domestic products that compete with foreign products for consumers' dollars in the U.S. economy today. International competition affects the price and the quantity sold by domestic firms, as shown by Figure 9-4.

In the figure, D_X and S_X refer to the domestic market demand and supply curves of commodity X. In the absence of trade, the equilibrium price is given by the intersection of D_X and S_X at point E, so that domestic consumers purchase $400X$ (all of which are produced domestically) at $P_X = \$5$. With free trade at the world price of $P_X = \$3$, the price of commodity X to domestic consumers will fall to the world price. The foreign supply curve of this nation's imports, S_F, is horizontal at $P_X = \$3$ *on the assumption that this nation's demand for imports is very small in relation to the foreign supply.* From the figure, we can see that domestic consumers will purchase AC or $600X$ at $P_X = \$3$ with free trade (and no transportation costs), as compared with $400X$ at $P_X = \$5$ in the absence of trade (given by point E). Figure 9-4 also shows that with free trade, domestic firms produce only AB or $200X$, so that BC or $400X$ is imported at $P_X = \$3$. Resources in the nation will then shift from the production of commodity X to the production of other commodities (thus benefiting domestic firms that produce those commodities) in which the nation is relatively more efficient or has a comparative advantage. With tariffs or other trade restrictions, the price of commodity X in

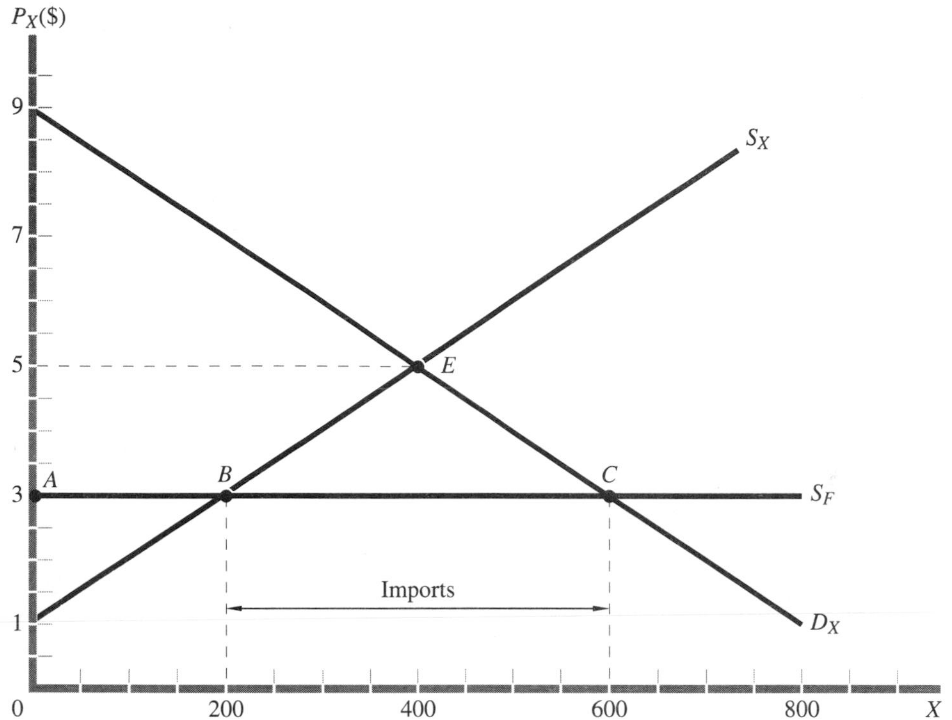

Figure 9-4
Consumption, Production, and Imports under Free Trade

In the absence of trade, equilibrium is at point E, where D_X and S_X intersect, so that $P_X = \$5$ and $Q_X = 400$. With free trade at the world price of $P_X = \$3$, domestic consumers purchase $AC = 600X$, of which $AB = 200X$ are produced domestically and $BC = 400X$ are imported.

the nation will be higher than the free-trade price of $3, and the nation's imports will be smaller than 400X. However, tariffs and other restrictions to the flow of international trade have been reduced sharply over the past decades and have been all but eliminated for trade among the 15-nation European Union (EU) and in North America (by the North American Free Trade Area, or NAFTA).

Case Study 9-3

Economic Profiles of the EU, NAFTA, and Japan

Table 9-1 provides an economic profile of the European Union (EU), the North American Free Trade Area (NAFTA) and their members, as well as Japan in 1993. The table shows that the EU and NAFTA are very similar in population, gross national product (GNP), and income or GNP per capita. Japan has about a little more than a third of the population, more than half of the GDP, and a higher GNP per capita than both the EU and NAFTA. The EU, however, is by far the largest trading bloc in the world.

Table 9-1
The European Union (EU), the North American Free Trade Area (NAFTA), and Japan

Country	Population (millions)	GDP (in billions of dollars)	GNP (per capita)	Exports* (in billions of dollars)	Imports* (in billions of dollars)
Austria	7.9	$ 185.2	$22,380	$ 69.1	$ 67.0
Belgium	10.0	218.8	20,880	151.6	145.2
Denmark	5.2	123.5	26,000	47.3	36.8
Finland	5.0	93.9	21,970	28.0	23.2
France	57.4	1,319.9	22,260	282.9	255.7
Germany	80.6	1,789.3	23,030	622.3	494.2
Greece	10.3	67.3	7,290	16.9	24.3
Ireland	3.5	43.3	12,210	27.4	23.1
Italy	57.8	1,223.0	20,460	221.8	224.4
Luxembourg	0.4	8.7	31,271	10.7	9.8
Netherlands	15.2	320.3	20,480	167.4	153.1
Portugal	9.8	79.5	7,450	20.9	31.4
Spain	39.1	574.8	13,970	97.7	98.2
Sweden	9.7	220.8	27,010	60.9	53.8
United Kingdom	57.8	903.1	17,790	237.4	249.8
EU Total	368.7	6,277.3	18,592†	2,062.3	1,890.0
Canada	27.4	493.6	20,440	161.4	164.7
Mexico	85.0	329.0	1,958	41.4	59.8
United States	255.4	5,920.2	22,240	661.7	725.3
NAFTA Total	367.8	6,742.8	18,483†	864.5	949.8
Japan	124.5	3,671.0	28,190	397.8	299.6

*Exports and imports refer to goods and services.
†Weighted average.
Source: World Bank, *World Bank Report* (1994), and International Monetary Fund, *International Financial Statistics* (1994).

The Dollar Exchange Rate and U.S. International Competitiveness

The market where a currency is exchanged for another is called the foreign exchange market. The **foreign exchange market** for any currency, say the U.S. dollar, is formed by all the locations (such as London, Tokyo, Frankfurt, as well as New York) where dollars are bought and sold for other currencies. These international monetary centers are connected by a telephone and telex network and are in constant contact with one another. The rate at which one currency is exchanged for another is called the **foreign exchange rate.** This is the price of a unit of the foreign currency in terms of the domestic currency. For example, the exchange rate (R) between the U.S. dollar and the British pound sterling (£) is the number of dollars required to purchase one pound. That is, $R = \$/£$. Thus, if $R = \$/£ = \$2$, this means that 2 dollars are required to purchase 1 pound.

Under a flexible exchange rate system of the type we have today, the dollar price of the pound (R) is determined (just like the price of any other commodity in a competitive market) by the intersection of the market demand and supply curves of pounds. This is shown in Figure 9-5, where the vertical axis measures the dollar price of pounds, or the exchange rate ($R = \$/£$), and the horizontal axis measures the quantity of pounds. The market demand and supply curves for pounds intersect at point E defining the equilibrium exchange rate of $R = 2$, at which the quantity of pounds demanded and the quantity supplied of pounds are equal at £300 million per day. At a higher exchange rate, the quantity of pounds supplied exceeds the quantity demanded, and the exchange rate will fall toward the equilibrium rate of $R = 2$. At an exchange rate lower than $R = 2$, the quantity of pounds demanded exceeds the quantity supplied, and the exchange rate will be bid up toward the equilibrium rate of $R = 2$.

Figure 9-5
The Foreign Exchange Market and the Dollar Exchange Rate
The vertical axis measures the dollar price of pounds ($R = \$/£$) and the horizontal axis measures the quantity of pounds. Under a flexible exchange rate system, the equilibrium exchange rate is $R = 2$ and the equilibrium quantity of pounds bought and sold is £300 million per day. This is given by point E at which the U.S. demand and supply curves for pounds intersect.

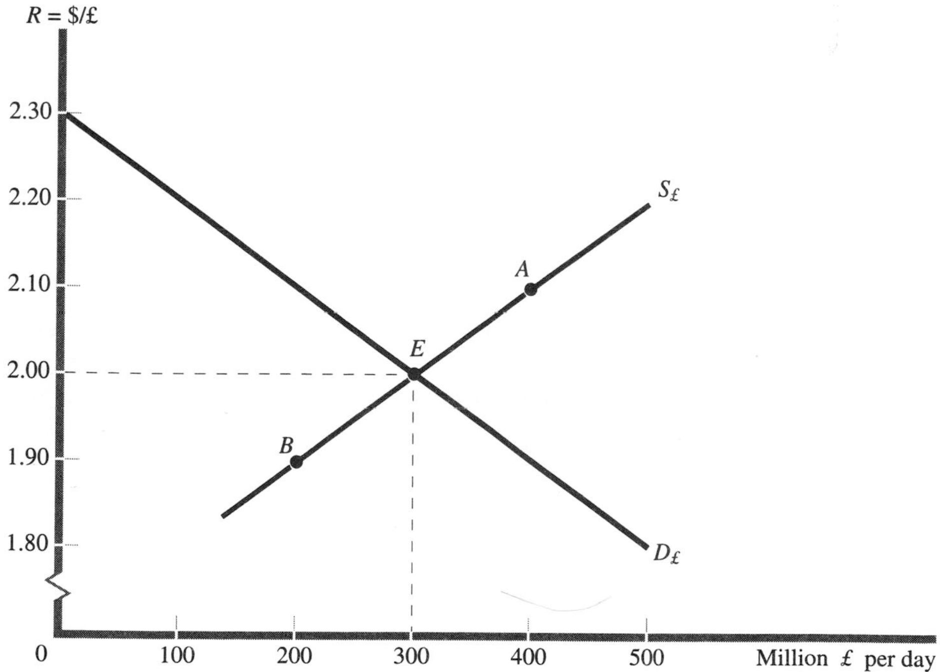

The U.S. demand for pounds is negatively inclined, indicating that the lower is the exchange rate (R), the greater is the quantity of pounds demanded by the United States. The reason is that the lower is the exchange rate (i.e., the fewer the number of dollars required to purchase 1 pound), the cheaper it is for the United States to import from and invest in the United Kingdom, and thus the greater is the quantity of pounds demanded by U.S. residents. On the other hand, the U.S. supply of pounds is usually positively inclined, indicating that the higher is the exchange rate (R), the greater is the quantity of pounds earned by or supplied to the United States. The reason is that at higher exchange rates, U.K. residents receive more dollars for each of their pounds. As a result, they find U.S. goods and investments cheaper and more attractive and spend more in the United States, thus supplying more pounds to the United States.

If the U.S. demand curve for pounds shifted up (for example, as a result of increased U.S. tastes for English goods) and intersected the U.S. supply curve for pounds at point A (see Figure 9-5), the equilibrium exchange rate would be $R = 2.10$, and the equilibrium quantity would be £400 million per day. The dollar is then said to have depreciated since it now requires \$2.10 (instead of the previous \$2) to purchase 1 pound. **Depreciation** thus refers to an increase in the domestic currency price of the foreign currency. On the other hand, if through time the U.S. demand for pounds shifted down so as to intersect the U.S. supply curve of pounds at point B (see Figure 9-5), the equilibrium exchange rate would fall to $R = 1.90$ and the dollar is said to have appreciated (because fewer dollars are now required to purchase 1 pound). An **appreciation** thus refers to a decline in the domestic currency price of the foreign currency. Shifts in the U.S. supply curve of pounds through time would similarly affect the equilibrium exchange rate and equilibrium quantity of pounds.

In the absence of interferences by national monetary authorities, the foreign exchange market operates just like any other competitive market, with the equilibrium price and quantity of the foreign currency determined at the intersection of the market demand and supply curves for the foreign currency. Sometimes, monetary authorities attempt to affect exchange rates by a coordinated purchase or sale of a currency on the foreign exchange market. For example, U.S. and foreign monetary authorities may sell dollars for foreign currencies to induce a dollar depreciation (which makes U.S. goods cheaper to foreigners) in order to reduce the U.S. trade deficit. These official foreign exchange market interventions are only of limited effectiveness, however, because the foreign exchange resources at the disposal of national monetary authorities are very small in relation to the size of daily transactions on the foreign exchange market (now estimated to be over \$1 billion per day!). Such a huge volume of transactions has been made possible by sharp improvements in telecommunications and the coming into existence of a 24-hour foreign exchange market around the world. In the meantime, the European Union (EU) plans to replace the 15 currencies of the member nations with a single currency, the ECU (European currency unit), by the turn of the century. The incentive is the huge savings that would result from avoiding foreign currency transactions among their national currencies.

Case Study 9-4
Foreign Exchange Quotations

Table 9-2 gives the exchange rate for various currencies with respect to the U.S. dollar for Thursday, January 19, 1995, and for Wednesday January 18, 1995—defined first as the dollar price of the foreign currency (as in the text) and then alternatively as the foreign currency price of the dollar. For example, next to Britain, we find that the exchange rate was \$1.5875/£1 on Thursday and \$1.5705 on Wednesday. On the same line, we find that the pound price of the dollar was £0.6299/\$ on Thursday and £0.6367 on Wednesday. On the next three lines under Britain, we find that the 30-day forward rate (i.e., the rate for a transaction entered upon today but with the foreign currency delivered in 30 days), the 90-day forward rate, and the 180-day forward rate). The 30-day forward rate of the pound is lower than the spot rate, meaning that the market expects the pound to be weaker in 30 days (and progressively weaker in 90 and 180 days, because the 90-day and 180-day forward rates are smaller than the spot rate by larger amounts than the 30-day forward rate).

Table 9-2
Foreign Exchange Quotations

EXCHANGE RATES

Thursday, January 19, 1995

The New York foreign exchange selling rates below apply to trading among banks in amounts of $1 million and more, as quoted at 3 p.m. Eastern time by Bankers Trust Co., Dow Jones Telerate Inc. and other sources. Retail transactions provide fewer units of foreign currency per dollar.

Country	U.S. $ equiv. Thur.	U.S. $ equiv. Wed.	Currency per U.S. $ Thur.	Currency per U.S. $ Wed.
Argentina (Peso)	1.00	1.00	1.00	1.00
Australia (Dollar)	.7673	.7618	1.3034	1.3128
Austria (Schilling)	.09292	.09271	10.76	10.79
Bahrain (Dinar)	2.6526	2.6524	.3770	.3770
Belgium (Franc)	.03201	.03163	31.24	31.62
Brazil (Real)	1.1785504	1.1827321	.85	.85
Britain (Pound)	1.5875	1.5705	.6299	.6367
30-Day Forward	1.5872	1.5703	.6300	.6368
90-Day Forward	1.5869	1.5699	.6302	.6370
180-Day Forward	1.5860	1.5691	.6305	.6373
Canada (Dollar)	.7026	.7039	1.4233	1.4208
30-Day Forward	.7014	.7026	1.4257	1.4232
90-Day Forward	.6994	.7007	1.4299	1.4272
180-Day Forward	.6965	.6978	1.4358	1.4331
Czech. Rep. (Koruna)				
Commercial rate	.0359712	.0361011	27.8000	27.7000
Chile (Peso)	.002462	.002464	406.25	405.85
China (Renminbi)	.118481	.118476	8.4402	8.4405
Colombia (Peso)	.001171	.001176	853.90	850.25
Denmark (Krone)	.1673	.1653	5.9760	6.0510
Ecuador (Sucre)				
Floating rate	.000425	.000425	2351.00	2355.00
Finland (Markka)	.21365	.21086	4.6806	4.7426
France (Franc)	.19069	.18852	5.2440	5.3045
30-Day Forward	.19076	.18858	5.2421	5.3028
90-Day Forward	.19094	.18874	5.2372	5.2982
180-Day Forward	.19122	.18904	5.2295	5.2900
Germany (Mark)	.6603	.6516	1.5143	1.5348
30-Day Forward	.6609	.6521	1.5130	1.5334
90-Day Forward	.6624	.6535	1.5096	1.5301
180-Day Forward	.6651	.6562	1.5034	1.5238
Greece (Drachma)	.004237	.004188	236.00	238.80
Hong Kong (Dollar)	.12920	.12920	7.7400	7.7398
Hungary (Forint)	.0089469	.0089726	111.7701	111.4500
India (Rupee)	.03188	.03188	31.37	31.37
Indonesia (Rupiah)	.0004514	.0004523	2215.50	2210.87
Ireland (Punt)	1.5713	1.5541	.6364	.6435
Israel (Shekel)	.3318	.3319	3.0140	3.0130
Italy (Lira)	.0006250	.0006184	1600.00	1616.95

Country	U.S. $ equiv. Thu.	U.S. $ equiv. Wed.	Currency per U.S. $ Thu.	Currency per U.S. $ Wed.
Japan (Yen)	.010096	.010033	99.04	99.6[illegible]
30-Day Forward	.010129	.010064	98.73	99.3[illegible]
90-Day Forward	.010200	.010131	98.04	98.71
180-Day Forward	.010325	.010253	96.86	97.5[illegible]
Jordan (Dinar)	1.4306	1.4327	.6990	.698[illegible]
Kuwait (Dinar)	3.3428	3.3417	.2992	.299[illegible]
Lebanon (Pound)	.000608	.000608	1644.50	1644.5[illegible]
Malaysia (Ringgit)	.3921	.3916	2.5505	2.5535
Malta (Lira)	2.7317	2.7386	.3661	.3652
Mexico (Peso)				
Floating rate	.1808318	.1858391	5.5300	5.3810
Netherland (Guilder)	.5890	.5812	1.6979	1.7205
New Zealand (Dollar)	.6430	.6411	1.5553	1.5599
Norway (Krone)	.1509	.1489	6.6270	6.7170
Pakistan (Rupee)	.0324	.0324	30.83	30.83
Peru (New Sol)	.4588	.4587	2.18	2.18
Philippines (Peso)	.04065	.04058	24.60	24.64
Poland (Zloty)	.41350000	.41203100	2.42	2.43
Portugal (Escudo)	.006389	.006309	156.52	158.50
Saudi Arabia (Riyal)	.26663	.26661	3.7504	3.7508
Singapore (Dollar)	.6897	.6880	1.4500	1.4535
Slovak Rep. (Koruna)	.0322789	.0322789	30.9800	30.9800
South Africa (Rand)				
Commercial rate	.2821	.2831	3.5443	3.5323
Financial rate	.2407	.2433	4.1550	4.1100
South Korea (Won)	.0012618	.0012598	792.50	793.80
Spain (Peseta)	.007582	.007488	131.90	133.55
Sweden (Krona)	.1347	.1335	7.4226	7.4906
Switzerland (Franc)	.7846	.7743	1.2745	1.2915
30-Day Forward	.7860	.7757	1.2722	1.2891
90-Day Forward	.7891	.7786	1.2673	1.2843
180-Day Forward	.7942	.7838	1.2590	1.2759
Taiwan (Dollar)	.038049	.038054	26.28	26.28
Thailand (Baht)	.03989	.03993	25.07	25.05
Turkey (Lira)	.0000200	.0000249	50000.00	40181.14
United Arab (Dirham)	.2723	.2723	3.6728	3.6726
Uruguay (New Peso)				
Financial	.170940	.170940	5.85	5.85
Venezuela (Bolivar)	.00589	.00589	169.87	169.87
SDR	1.46395	1.46901	.68308	.68073
ECU	1.24800	1.23390	....	....

Special Drawing Rights (SDR) are based on exchange rates for the U.S., German, British, French and Japanese currencies. Source: International Monetary Fund.

European Currency Unit (ECU) is based on a basket of community currencies.

Case Study 9-5

The Depreciation of the Dollar and the Profitability of U.S. Firms

A depreciation of the dollar, by making U.S. goods and services cheaper to foreigners in terms of their own (i.e., foreign) currency, allows U.S. firms to sell more abroad without lowering the dollar price of their products, and thus increases their profits and their share of foreign markets. U.S. firms also gain from receiving more dollars per foreign-currency unit of profits earned abroad. Against these benefits are the higher dollar prices that U.S. firms must pay for imported inputs. How much a U.S. firm gains from a depreciation of the dollar, therefore, depends on the amount of its foreign sales as compared to its expenditures on imported inputs. Of course, the opposite is true (i.e., U.S. firms receive lower dollar prices, lose market share abroad, and receive lower profits) when the dollar appreciates.

For example, the Black & Decker Corporation, a maker of power tools and appliances with about half of its sales abroad but few imported inputs, found that the depreciation of the dollar during 1990 led to about a 5 percent increase in its foreign sales and earnings. On the other hand, the Gillette Corporation, which has plants in many countries and uses almost exclusively local inputs to supply each market, benefited mostly through the repatriation of foreign profits as a result of the dollar depreciation during 1990. Merck & Company, which has plants in 19 nations and conducts most of its business in local currencies, is in a similar position. In between is the Digital Corporation, which found some of its price advantage abroad resulting from the depreciation of the dollar eaten away by the higher cost of its imported disk drives and circuit-board parts.

Source: "How Dollar's Plunge Aids Some Companies, Does Little for Others," *The Wall Street Journal,* October 22, 1990, p. A1, and "How Low the Dollar?" *The New York Times,* July 18, 1994, p. D1.

9-4 MONOPOLY

In this section we discuss the sources of monopoly, examine how the monopolist determines the best level of output and price in the short run and in the long run, and compare monopoly with perfect competition.

Sources of Monopoly

As defined in Section 9-1, monopoly is the form of market organization in which a single firm sells a product for which there are no close substitutes. Thus, the monopolist represents the market and faces the market's negatively sloped demand curve for the product. As opposed to a perfectly competitive firm, a monopolist can earn profits in the long run because entry into the industry is essentially blocked. Thus, monopoly is at the opposite extreme from perfect competition in the spectrum or range of market organizations.

There are four basic reasons that can give rise to monopoly. *First,* the firm may control the entire supply of raw materials required to produce the product. For example, until World War II, the Aluminum Company of America (Alcoa) controlled almost every source of bauxite (the raw material required to produce aluminum) and thus had a monopoly over the production of aluminum in the United States.

Second, the firm may own a patent or copyright which precludes other firms from using a particular production process or producing the same product. For example, when cellophane was first introduced, DuPont had monopoly power in its production based on patents. Similarly, Xerox had a monopoly on copying machines and Polaroid on instant cameras, when these products were first introduced. Patents are granted by the government for a period of 17 years as an incentive to inventors.

Third, in some industries, economies of scale may operate (i.e., the long-run average cost curve may fall) over a sufficiently large range of outputs as to leave only one firm supplying the entire market. Such a firm is called a **natural monopoly.** Examples of these are public utilities (electrical, gas, water, and local transportation companies). To have more than one such firm in a given market would lead to duplication of supply lines and to much higher costs per unit. To avoid this, local governments usually allow a single firm to operate in the market but regulate the price of the services provided, so as to allow the firm only a normal return on investment.

Fourth, a monopoly may be established by a government franchise. In this case, the firm is set up as the sole producer and distributor of a product or service but is subjected to governmental regulation. The best example of a monopoly established by government franchise is the post office. Local governments also require a license to operate many types of businesses, such as liquor stores, taxis, broadcasting, medical offices, and private health care clinics. The aim of these licenses is to ensure minimum standards of competency, but since the number of licenses is usually restricted, their effect is also to restrict competition and to provide monopoly profits to license owners.

Aside from regulated monopolies, cases of pure monopoly have been rare in the past and are forbidden today by U.S. antitrust laws. Even so, the pure monopoly model is often useful in explaining observed business behavior in cases approximating pure monopoly and also gives insights into the operation of other types of imperfectly competitive markets (i.e., monopolistic competition and oligopoly). To be noted is that a monopolist does not have unlimited market power. The monopolist faces indirect competition for the consumer's dollar from all other commodities. Furthermore, though there are no *close* substitutes for the product sold by the monopolist, substitutes may nevertheless exist. For example, even when Alcoa had a monopoly over the production and sale of aluminum in the United States, aluminum faced competition from steel, plastics, copper, and other materials. Fear of government prosecution and the threat of potential competition also act as a check on the monopolist's market power. In general, all monopoly power based on barriers to entry is subject to decay in the long run, except that based on government franchise.

Case Study 9-6

Economies of Scale, Government Franchise, and Monopoly Power in the Telecommunications Industry

Until 1982, when the American Telephone and Telegraph Company (AT&T) was ordered to divest itself of local telephone companies, AT&T had a monopoly over telephone services in the United States. Such a monopoly was based on economies of scale in providing local telephone service. After divestiture of its local telephone operations, AT&T was allowed to continue to provide long-distance telephone service, but it began to face increasing competition from MCI Communication Corporation, the Sprint Corporation, and other companies. By 1995, these competitors had captured about 40 percent of the $60 billion long-distance telephone market by charging lower rates and mounting very aggressive advertising campaigns. This shows how market power that is presumably unassailable can be eroded over time by government ruling and by competition. Furthermore, recognizing that telephones and computers had become inseparable (e.g., in data transmission), IBM entered the local telephone market in the early 1980s, and in 1991 AT&T acquired NCR, the fifth-largest computer company in the United States, in order to take advantage of the synergies (such as network computing) between computers and communications.

In 1994, AT&T (the world's largest telecommunications company) acquired for $12.6 billion McCaw Cellular Communications (the world's largest cellular-telephone company) in the nation's seventh-largest takeover ever, thus starting a race to build a national wireless-communications network or multimedia that includes communications, computers, and video technologies. With McCaw, AT&T is expected to aggressively compete in the $90 billion local telephone market by reaching customers directly and without paying (as it now does) billions of dollars in access charges to the seven local telephone companies (the so-called Baby Bells). Still prohibited from entering the long-distance telephone market, the local telephone companies responded with alliances of their own. The Bell Atlantic Corporation merged its cellular business with the Nynex Corporation and are discussing a possible deal with the Sprint Corporation (the nation's third-largest long-distance carrier). In the meantime, Sprint teamed up with three of the nation's biggest cable companies (Telecommunications Inc. of Denver, Comcast Corporation of Philadelphia, and Cox Enterprises of Atlanta). MCI Communications, the second-largest U.S. long-distance carrier, is also preparing to put together its own nationwide wireless network and is spending $2 billion to build local telephone networks in many of the nation's biggest cities. Time Warner Inc., the nation's second-largest cable company, has aligned itself with U.S. West (the Western Bell Company). These alliances are intended to further the goal of one-stop shopping for local and long-distance telephone calls, cable television, and high-speed data communications that are not currently available from any single company. With consolidation and increased competition, the price of multimedia services is likely to fall sharply in the future.

Source: "Long-Distance Risks of AT&T–MCI War," *The Wall Street Journal,* March 14, 1993, p. B9; "AT&T Completes Deal to Buy McCaw Cellular," *The New York Times,* September 20, 1994, p. D5; "Cellular Giants in Rush for Alliances," *The New York Times,* September 15, 1994, p. D1; "Sweeping Revision in Communication Is on the Horizon," *The New York Times,* October 26, 1994, p. 1; and "No-Holds-Barred Battle for Long-Distance Calls," *The New York Times,* January 21, 1995, p.1.

Short-Run Price and Output Determination under Monopoly

A monopolist, as contrasted to a perfect competitor, is not a price taker but can set the price at which it sells the product. In this section, we see how the monopolist sets the price to maximize profits or minimize losses in the short run. In the following section we see how the monopolist adjusts the scale of plant and sets the price in order to maximize profits in the long run.

Since a monopolist is the sole seller of a product for which there are no close substitutes, the monopolist faces the negatively sloped market demand curve for the product. This means that the monopolist can sell more units of the product only by lowering its price. Because of this, the marginal revenue is smaller than the product price and the marginal revenue curve is below the demand curve that the monopolist faces. This is shown in Figure 9-6.

In Figure 9-6, D is the market demand curve faced by the monopolist, and MR is the corresponding marginal revenue curve. To see why the MR curve is below the D curve, note that the monopolist can sell 100 units of the product at $P = \$15$ (point G on the D curve), so that $TR = \$1{,}500$. To sell 200 units, the monopolist must lower its price to $P = \$14$ on all units sold (point H), so that $TR = \$2{,}800$. The change in TR per unit change in output or MR is

$$MR = \frac{\Delta TR}{\Delta Q} = \frac{\$1{,}300}{100} = \$13$$

Figure 9-6
Short-Run Price and Output Determination by a Monopolist

The best level of output for the monopolist in the short run is 500 units and is given by point E, where $MR = MC$. At $Q = 500$, $P = \$11$ (point A on the D curve), and $ATC = \$8$ (point F), so that the monopolist earns a profit of $AF = \$3$ per unit and $AFBC = \$1{,}500$ in total (the shaded area).

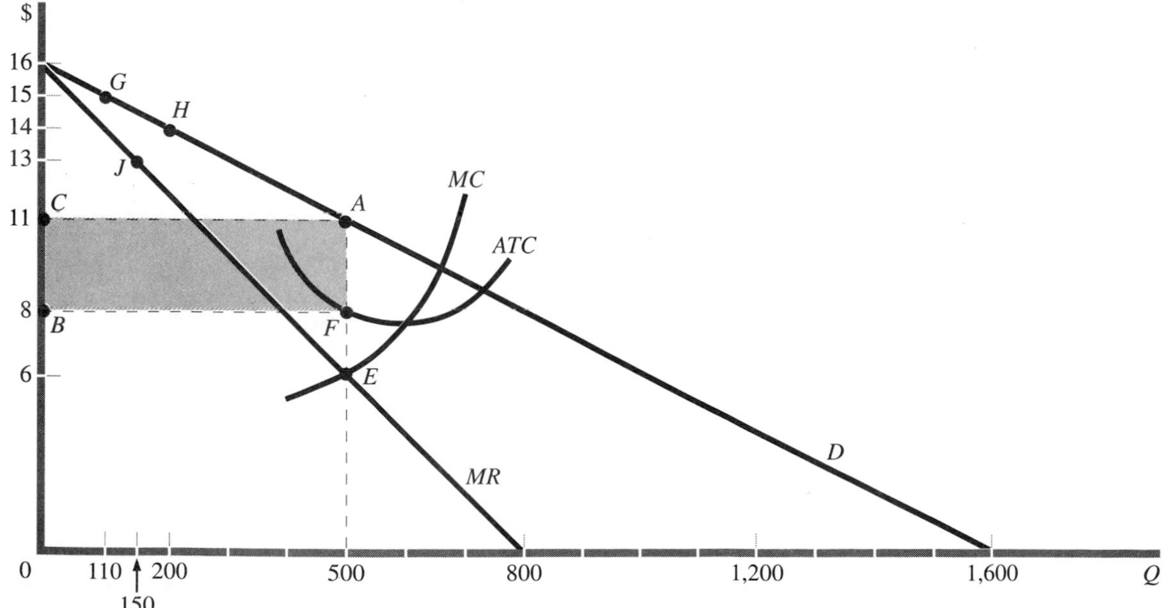

(point J, plotted halfway between 100 and 200 units of output on the MR curve in Figure 9-6). Thus, with D negatively sloped, the MR curve must be below it. From Figure 9-6 we can also see that when the demand curve (D) is linear the absolute slope of the MR curve is twice that of the D curve so that the MR curve lies everywhere halfway between the D curve and the price axis.[5]

The best level of output in the short run is 500 units and is given by point E in Figure 9-6 at which $MR = MC$. At $Q < 500$, $MR > MC$ and the total profits of the monopolist will increase by expanding output. On the other hand, at $Q > 500$, $MC > MR$ and the total profits of the monopolist will increase by *reducing* output. The price at which the monopolist should sell its best level of output is then given on the D curve. In Figure 9-6, $P = \$11$ at $Q = 500$. Since at $Q = 500$, $ATC = \$8$ (point F in the figure), the monopolist earns a profit of $AF = \$3$ per unit and $AFBC = \$1{,}500$ in total (the shaded area in the figure). This is the largest profit that the monopolist can earn in the short run. Note that, as contrasted with the case under perfect competition, $P > MR$ at the best level of output under monopoly because the demand curve is above the marginal revenue curve.

While the monopolist of Figure 9-6 is earning short-run profits, a monopolist (just like a perfect competitor) could also break even or incur losses in the short run. It all depends on the height of the ATC at the best level of output. If $ATC = P$ at the best level of output, the monopolist breaks even, and if $ATC > P$ at the best level of output, the monopolist incurs a loss. Again, as in the case of perfect competition, it pays for a monopolist to remain in business in the short run even if it incurs losses, as long as $P > AVC$. In that case, the excess of P over AVC can be used to cover part of the fixed costs of the monopolist. Were the monopolist to go out of business, it would incur the larger loss equal to its total fixed costs. Thus, the aim of the monopolist in the short run is the same as that of a perfect competitor, that is, to maximize profits or minimize losses.[6]

Long-Run Price and Output Determination under Monopoly

In the long run all inputs and costs of production are variable, and the monopolist can construct the optimal scale of plant to produce the best level of output.

[5]This can easily be shown mathematically, as follows. Let the monopolist's demand function be

$$Q = \frac{a - P}{b} \quad \text{or} \quad P = a - bQ$$

where a is the vertical or price intercept and $-b$ is the slope of the demand curve. Then $TR = PQ = (a - bQ)Q = aQ - bQ^2$ and

$$MR = \frac{d(TR)}{dQ} = a - 2bQ$$

Thus, the MR curve has the same vertical or price intercept as the D curve, but its absolute slope ($2b$) is twice the slope of the D curve (b).

[6]Note that since at the best level of output $MR = MC < P$ under monopoly and a given MR can be associated with different P's, depending on the price elasticity of demand, there is no unique relationship between P and Q under monopoly (i.e., we cannot derive the supply curve of the monopolist from the rising portion of its MC curve above the AVC curve, as was done for a perfectly competitive firm).

As in the case of perfect competition, the best level of output of the monopolist is given at the point at which $P = LMC$, and the optimum scale of plant is the one with the *SATC* curve tangent to the *LAC* curve at the best level of output. As contrasted with perfect competition, however, entrance into the market is blocked under monopoly, and so the monopolist can earn economic profits in the long run. Because of blocked entry, the monopolist is also not likely to produce at the lowest point on its *LAC* curve. This is shown in Figure 9-7.

Figure 9-7 shows that the best level of output for the monopolist in the long run is 700 units and is given by point E', at which $P = LMC$. At $Q = 700$, $P =$ \$9 (point A' on the *D* curve). The monopolist has had time in the long run to build the optimum scale of plant given by the *SATC* curve tangent to the *LAC* curve at $Q = 700$ (point F' in Figure 9-7). Operating the optimum scale of plant at F' at the best level of output of $Q = 700$, the monopolist has $SATC = LAC =$ \$5 (point F'). Thus, the monopolist is earning a long-run profit of $A'F' =$ \$4 per unit and $A'F'B'C' =$ \$2,800 in total (as compared to \$1,500 in the short run). Because entry into the market is blocked, the monopolist will continue to earn these profits in the long run as long as the demand it faces and its cost curves remain unchanged.

To be noted is that when the monopolist is in long-run equilibrium (point E' in Figure 9-7), it is also and necessarily in short-run equilibrium (i.e., $MR = SMC$),

Figure 9-7
Long-Run Price and Output Determination by the Monopolist

The best level of output for the monopolist in the long run is 700 units and is given by point E', at which $MR = LMC$. At $Q = 700$, $P =$ \$9 (point A' on the *D* curve). The monopolist operates the optimal scale of plant (given by the *SATC* curve in the figure) at point F' at an average cost of \$5. The monopolist earns a long-run profit of $A'F' =$ \$4 per unit, and $A'F'B'C' =$ \$2,800 in total.

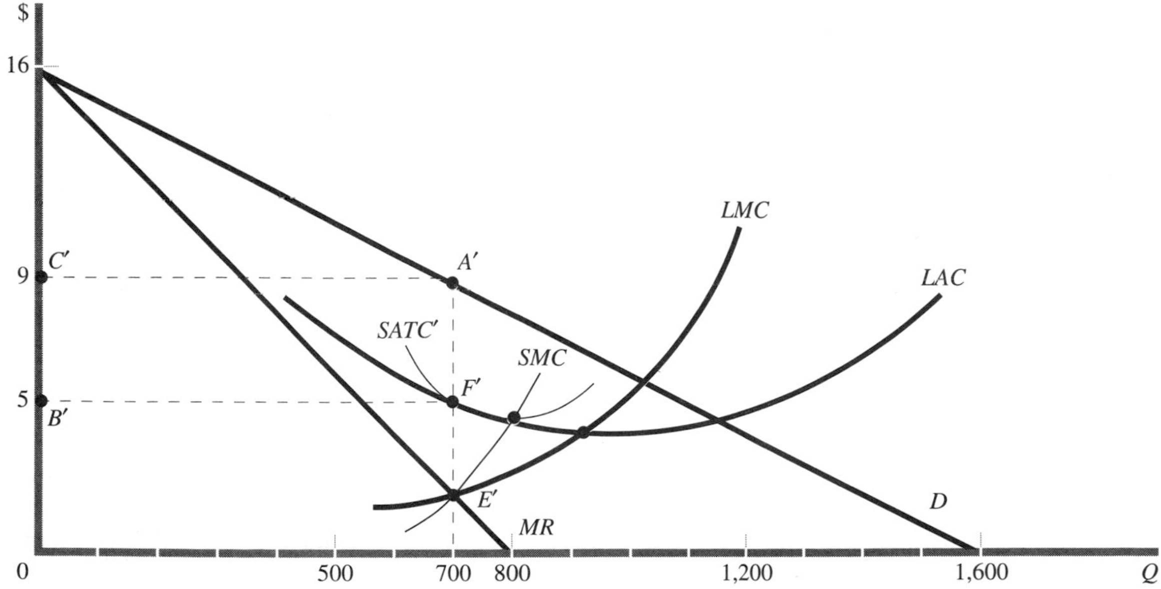

but the reverse is not true. Also to be noted is that the monopolist of Figure 9-7 does not produce at the lowest point on its *LAC* curve (as competition forces the perfectly competitive firm to do). Only in the unusual situation when the *MR* curve of the monopolist goes through the lowest point on its *LAC* curve would the monopolist (as the perfect competitor) produce at the lowest point on its *LAC* curve. In that case, however, the monopolist would still charge a price that is higher than its *LAC* and earn a profit in the long run.

Case Study 9-7

The Market Value of Monopoly Profits in the New York City Taxi Industry

New York City, as most other municipalities (cities) in the United States, requires a license (medallion) to operate a taxi. Since medallions are limited in number, this confers a monopoly power (i.e., the ability to earn economic profits) to owners of medallions. The value of owning a medallion is equal to the present discounted value of the future stream of earnings from the ownership of a medallion—a process called *capitalization.* For example, the number of medallions in New York City has remained fixed at 11,787 for almost half a century, and the value of a medallion has risen from $10 in 1937 to more than $130,000 today. The price of a medallion is lower (and sometimes much lower) in other cities, reflecting the lower earning power of a medallion in other cities. For example, it is $25,000 in Chicago (the next most expensive) where there are 4,600 medallions. Proposals to increase the number of medallions in New York City have been successfully blocked by a powerful taxi industry lobby. Were the city to freely grant a license to operate a taxi for the asking, the price of the medallion would drop to zero. While not doing that, New York City has allowed a sharp growth during the 1980s in the number of radio cabs, which can only respond to radio calls and cannot cruise the streets for passengers. This has, nevertheless, sharply increased competition in the New York City taxi industry and curtailed the further rise in the price of medallions. Despite the increased competition, however, taxi owners earned profits ranging from 32 percent to 40 percent ($15,500 to $21,300) per taxi in 1993.

Source: "Taxi Cab Regulation from Many Directions," *The New York Times,* November 24, 1986, p. B1; "Owners Bewail Flood of Cabs in New York," *The New York Times,* April 10, 1989, p. B1; and "Taxi Panel Rejects Calls for Fare Rise," *The New York Times,* April 1, 1994, p. B1.

Comparison of Monopoly and Perfect Competition

We saw on page 374 that when a perfectly competitive industry is in long-run equilibrium, each firm produces at the lowest point on its *LAC* curve and charges a price equal to the lowest *LAC,* so that each firm earns zero economic profits. Under monopoly, on the other hand, production is not likely to take place at the lowest point on the *LAC* curve, and because of blocked entry, the monopolist is also likely to earn profits in the long run. We cannot conclude from this, however, that perfect competition is necessarily "better" or more efficient than monopoly.

Perfect competition is more efficient than monopoly only if the lowest point on the *LAC* curve occurs at an output level that is very small in relation to the market demand, so as to allow many firms to operate and, if the product is homogeneous, so that perfect competition is possible. Often this is not the case. That is, a very large scale of operation is often required to produce most products efficiently, and this permits only a few firms to operate. For example, economies of scale operate over such a large range of outputs that steel, aluminum, automobiles, mainframe computers, aircraft, and many other products and services can be produced efficiently only by very large firms, so that a handful of such firms can meet the entire market demand for the product or service. Perfect competition under such conditions would either be impossible or lead to prohibitively high production costs. One could only imagine how high the cost per unit would be if automobiles were produced by 100 or more firms instead of by three or four very large firms.

There are also those who believe that the ability to earn profits in the long run due to restricted entry provides the monopolist with the resources and the incentive to undertake research and development. Since the greater part of the increase in the standards of living in industrial countries today arises from technological progress, this is a very important consideration. There is, however, a great deal of disagreement as to whether monopoly leads to more technological change than perfect competition. There are those who believe that a monopolist, sheltered as it is from competition, does not have much of an incentive to innovate and that many technological advances are in fact introduced by very small firms.

Only if we abstract from technological progress and if we assume that the technology used in the production of the product allows many firms to operate efficiently, can we prove that perfect competition is better than monopoly from the point of view of society as a whole. This can be shown with the aid of Figure 9-8.

In Figure 9-8, we assume that the *LMC* curve is constant and equal to the perfectly competitive firm's and the monopolist's *LAC*. Under perfect competition, the $LAC = LMC$ curve represents the market supply curve. The equilibrium price of $6 and the equilibrium quantity of 1,000 units are given by point *E*, at which the *D* and the *LMC* (the long-run market supply) curves under perfect competition cross. All the many competitive firms in the market together supply 1,000 units of the product at $P = \$6$ and break even. Consumers pay a total of $EJ0N = \$6{,}000$ for 1,000 units of the product. They would have been willing to pay $EJ0G = \$11{,}000$ (the total area under the *D* curve up to point *E*) if the product were sold 1 unit at a time and if the seller sold each unit at the highest price possible. The difference between what consumers would have been willing to pay for 1,000 units of the product (that is, $EJ0G = \$11{,}000$) and what they actually pay (that is, $EJ0N = \$6{,}000$) is called **consumers' surplus.** The consumers' surplus in this case is, thus, $ENG = \$5{,}000$.

Suppose that now the market were suddenly monopolized and the monopolist faced the same demand and cost conditions as the perfectly competitive firms. The best level of output of the monopolist is now 500 units (given by point E' at which $MR = LMC$). The monopolist would charge $P = \$11$ (point *H* on the *D*

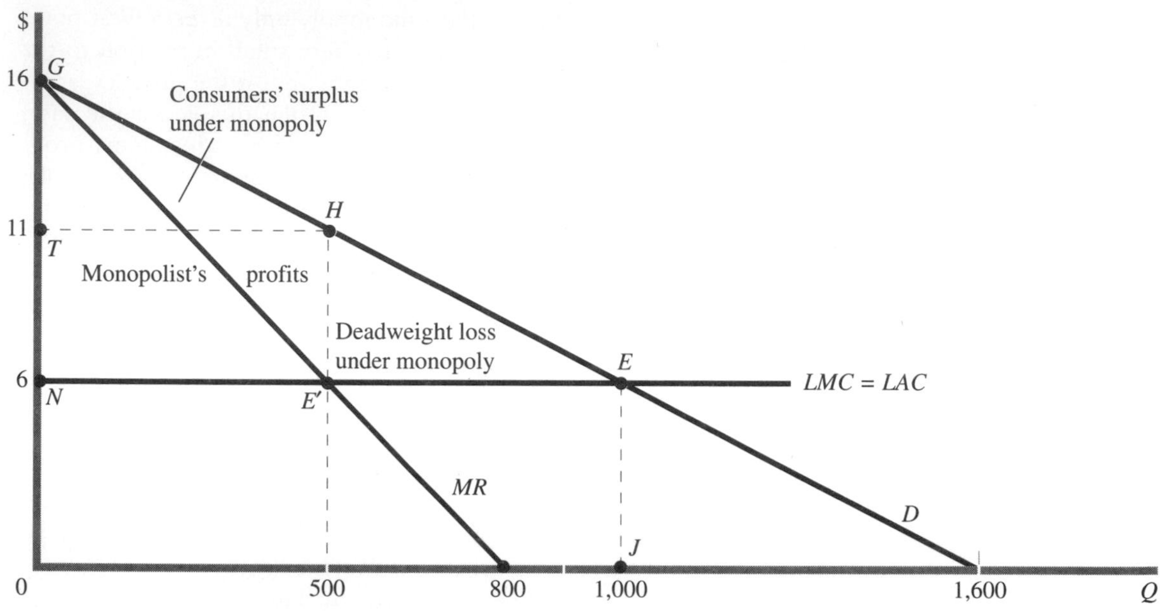

Figure 9-8
The Social Cost of Monopoly

Under perfect competition, the *LMC* = *LAC* curve represents the market supply curve. Therefore, equilibrium is at point *E*, at which *Q* = 1,000 units, *P* = \$6 (point *E* on the *D* curve), *ENG* = \$5,000 represents the consumers' surplus (i.e., the difference between what consumers are willing to pay and what they actually pay for 1,000 units of the product), and all firms break even. If the market is monopolized, the best level of output is 500 and is given by point *E′*, at which *MR* = *LMC*, and *P* = \$11 (point *H* on the *D* curve). The monopolist's profits are *HE′NT* = \$2,500, consumers' surplus is *HTG* = \$1,250, and the true deadweight loss to society (resulting from a less efficient use of resources) is *EE′H* = \$1,250.

curve) and earn profits of *HE′* = \$5 per unit and *HE′NT* = \$2,500 in total. Only *HTG* = \$1,250 of the original consumers' surplus of *ENG* = \$5,000 would remain to consumers. *HE′NT* = \$2,500 would be transferred to the monopolist in the form of profits, and *EE′H* = \$1,250 represents the true or **deadweight loss** from monopoly. The transfer of some of the consumers' surplus to the profits of the monopolist (*HE′NT*) does not necessarily represent a loss to society (for example, the monopolist could use the profits for research and development). There is no disagreement, however, that the deadweight loss (*EE′H*) is a true loss to society because consumers are willing to pay \$11 for the last unit produced under monopoly (point *H* on the *D* curve), but the cost of producing that unit is only \$6 (point *E′* on the *LMC* curve). The monopolist restricts output and charges too high a price. Some resources will be transferred to the production of other products which are valued less by society, and so triangle *EE′H* represents the loss of efficiency in the use of society's resources resulting from the monopolization of the market.

9-5 MONOPOLISTIC COMPETITION

In this section we discuss in detail the meaning and importance of monopolistic competition, show how the equilibrium price and quantity are determined in the short run and in the long run, and examine product variation and selling expenses.

Meaning and Importance of Monopolistic Competition

In Section 9-1 we defined *monopolistic competition* as the form of market organization in which there are many sellers of a heterogeneous or differentiated product, and entry into and exit from the industry are rather easy in the long run. **Differentiated products** are those which are similar but not identical and satisfy the same basic need. Examples are the numerous brands of breakfast cereals, toothpaste, cigarettes, detergents, cold medicines, etc., on the market today. The differentiation may be real (for example, the various breakfast cereals may have greatly different nutritional and sugar contents) or imaginary (for example, all brands of aspirin contain the same basic ingredients). Product differentiation may also be based on a more convenient location and/or more courteous service.

As the name implies, monopolistic competition is a blend of competition and monopoly. The competitive element results from the fact that in a monopolistically competitive market (as in a perfectly competitive market), there are many sellers of the differentiated product, each too small to affect others. The monopoly element arises from product differentiation (i.e., from the fact that the product sold by each seller is somewhat different from the product sold by any other seller). The resulting monopoly power is severely limited, however, by the availability of many close substitutes. Thus, if the seller of a particular brand of aspirin increased its price even moderately, it would stand to lose a great deal of its sales.

Monopolistic competition is most common in the retail and service sectors of our economy. Clothing, cotton textiles, and food processing are the industries that come close to monopolistic competition at the national level. At the local level, the best examples of monopolistic competition are fast-food outlets, shoe stores, gasoline stations, beauty salons, drug stores, video rental stores, and pizza parlors, all located in close proximity to one another. Firms in each of these businesses have some monopoly power over their competitors based on the uniqueness of their product, better location, better service, greater range of product varieties, slightly lower prices, etc., but their market power is severely limited by the availability of many close substitutes.

Since each firm sells a somewhat different product under monopolistic competition, we cannot derive the market demand curve and the market supply curve of the product as we did under perfect competition, and we do not have a single equilibrium price for the differentiated products but a cluster of prices. Our analysis must, therefore, necessarily be confined to that of the "typical" or "representative" firm. The graphical analysis will also be greatly simplified by assuming (with Edward Chamberlin, the originator of the monopolistically competitive model[7]) that all firms selling similar products face identical demand and cost curves. This is unrealistic since the production of differentiated products is likely to lead to somewhat different demand and cost curves. Making such an assumption, however, will greatly simplify the analysis.

As contrasted to a perfectly competitive firm, a monopolistically competitive firm can determine the characteristics of the products, the amount of selling expenses (such as advertising) to incur, as well as the price and quantity of the product. In the next section we assume first that the monopolistically competitive firm has already decided on the characteristics of the product and on the selling expenses to incur, so that we can concentrate on its pricing and output decisions in the short run and in the long run. Subsequently, we examine how the firm determines the optimal expenditures on product variation and selling effort.

[7]Edward H. Chamberlin, *The Theory of Monopolistic Competition* (Cambridge, Mass.: Harvard University Press, 1933).

Case Study 9-8

The Monopolistically Competitive Restaurant Market

The restaurant market in any city has all the characteristics of monopolistic competition. There are usually thousands of restaurants in any large city, catering to all types of foods, tastes, incomes, and sectors. Some restaurants are very luxurious and expensive, while others are simple and inexpensive. (The author recently had dinner at one of the best French restaurants in New York City with a distinguished economist after a conference—the bill was $234. Two days later he had dinner with a colleague at a small and unpretentious restaurant near campus for $17.50.) Some restaurants provide entertainment, while others do not. Some are located in the theater district and serve pre-theater dinner and after-theater supper, while others are located in residential areas of the city and cater to the family business. In one block in mid-Manhattan, the author recently counted 19 restaurants: 5 Italian, 4 French, 3 Chinese, and 1 Brazilian, Indian, Japanese, Korean, Mexican, Pakistani, and Spanish. In a recent issue of *New York Magazine* more than 300 restaurants of all types were advertised, and these are only a very small fraction of the restaurants located in the city. Entry into the restaurant business is also relatively easy (witness the hundreds of new restaurants that open each year and the about equal number that close in any large city during the same year). Since each restaurant offers a somewhat differentiated product, many advertise their existence, location, and menu, together with the usual claim (which no one really takes seriously) of superiority over all other restaurants in the same class.

Source: The New Yorker, January 1995.

Short-Run Price and Output Determination under Monopolistic Competition

Since a monopolistically competitive firm produces a differentiated product, the demand curve it faces is negatively sloped, but since there are many close substitutes for the product, the demand curve is highly price elastic. The price elasticity of demand is higher the smaller is the degree of product differentiation. As in the case of monopoly, since the demand curve facing a monopolistic competitor is negatively sloped and linear the corresponding marginal revenue curve is below it, with the same price intercept and twice the absolute slope. As in the case of firms in the other forms of market structure examined, the best level of output of the monopolistically competitive firm in the short run is given by the one at which marginal revenue equals marginal cost, provided that price (determined on the demand curve) exceeds the average variable cost. This is shown in Figure 9-9.

Figure 9-9 shows that the best level of output of the typical or representative monopolistically competitive firm in the short run is 6 units and is given by point E, at which $MR = MC$. At $Q < 6$, $MR > MC$, and the total profits of the firm increase by expanding output. At $Q > 6$, $MC > MR$, and the total profits of the firm increase by *reducing* output. To sell the best level of output (that is, 6 units), the firm charges a price of \$9 per unit (point A on the D curve). Since at $Q = 6$, $ATC = \$7$ (point F in the figure) the monopolistic competitor earns a profit of $AF = \$2$ per unit and $AFBC = \$12$ in total (the shaded area in the figure).[8] As in the case of a perfectly competitive firm and monopolist, the monopolistic competitor can earn profits, break even, or incur losses in the short run. If at the best level of output, $P > ATC$, the firm earns a profit; if $P = ATC$, the firm breaks even; and if $P < ATC$, the firm incurs losses, but it minimizes losses by continuing to produce as long as $P > AVC$. Finally, since the demand curve facing a monopolistic competitor is negatively sloped, $MR = MC < P$ at the best level of output so that (as in the case of monopoly) the rising portion of the MC curve above the AVC curve does not represent the short-run supply curve of the monopolistic competitor.

Long-Run Price and Output Determination under Monopolistic Competition

If firms in a monopolistically competitive market earn profits in the short run (or would earn profits in the long run by building optimal scales of plants to produce their best level of output), more firms will enter the market in the long run. This shifts the demand curve facing each monopolistic competitor to the left (as its market share decreases) until it becomes tangent to the firm's LAC curve. Thus, in the long run all monopolistically competitive firms break even and produce on the negatively sloped portion of their LAC curve (rather than at the lowest point, as in the case of perfect competition). This is shown in Figure 9-10.

[8]Note that Figure 9-9 is very similar to Figure 9-6 for the monopolist. The only difference is that the monopolistic competitor's D curve is more price elastic than the monopolist's D curve.

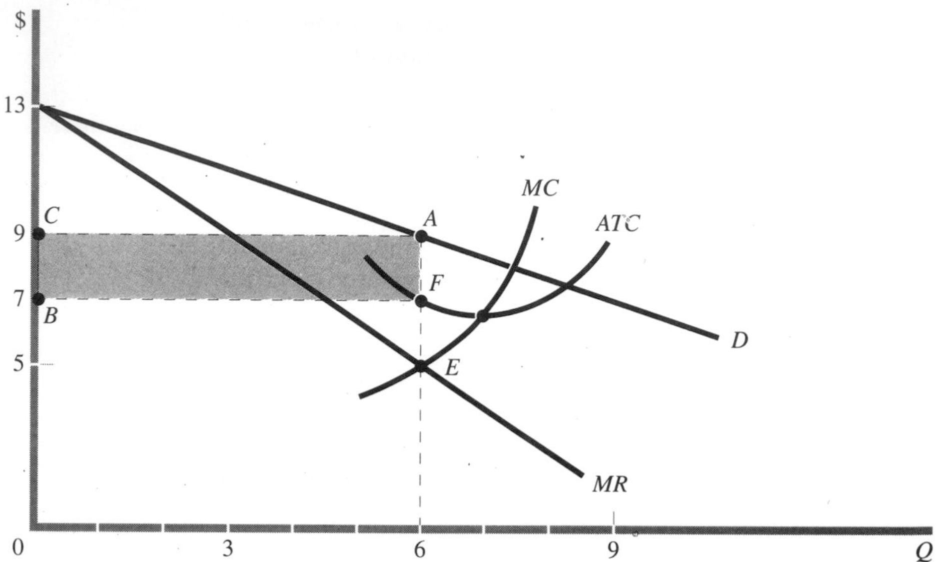

Figure 9-9
Short-Run Price and Output Determination under Monopolistic Competition

The best level of output of the monopolistic competitor in the short run is 6 units and is given by point E, where $MR = MC$. At $Q = 6$, $P = \$9$ (point A on the D curve) and $ATC = \$7$ (point F), so that the monopolistic competitor earns a profit of $AF = \$2$ per unit and $AFBC = \$12$ in total (the shaded area).

Figure 9-10
Long-Run Price and Output Determination under Monopolistic Competition

The best level of output of the monopolistically competitive firm in the long run is 4 units and is given by point E', at which $MR' = LMC = SMC'$ and $P = LAC = SATC' = \$6$ (point A'), so that the firm breaks even. This compares to the best level of output of 7 units given by point E'', at which $MR' = LMC$ and $P = LAC = \$5$ (point E'') under long-run perfectly competitive market equilibrium.

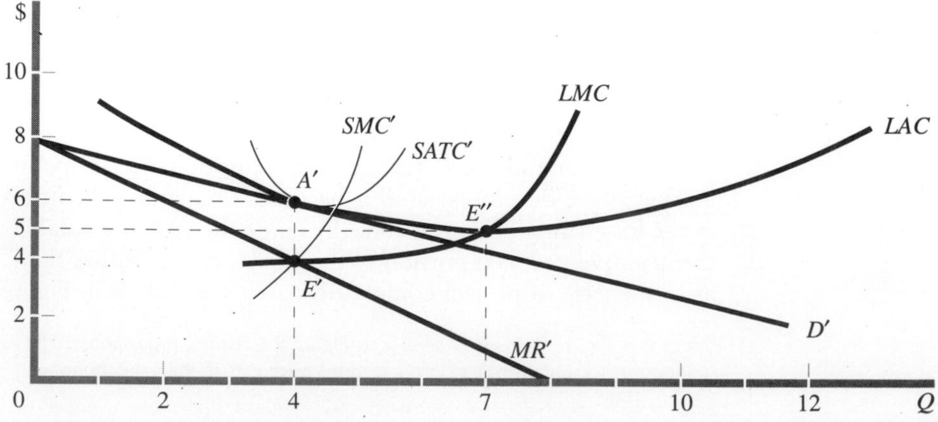

In Figure 9-10, D' is the demand curve facing a typical or representative monopolistically competitive firm in the long run. Demand curve D' is lower and more price elastic than demand curve D that the firm faced in the short run. That is, as more firms enter the monopolistically competitive market in the long run (attracted by the profits that can be earned), each monopolistic competitor is left with a smaller share of the market and a more price elastic demand curve because of the greater range of competition (products) that becomes available in the long run. Note that demand curve D' is tangent to the LAC and $SATC'$ curves at point A', the output at which $MR' = LMC = SMC'$ (point E' in the figure). Thus, the monopolistic competitor sells 4 units of the product at the price of \$6 per unit and breaks even in the long run (as compared to $Q = 6$ at $P = \$9$ and profits of \$2 per unit and \$12 in total in the short run). At any other price the monopolistically competitive firm would incur losses in the long run, and with a different number of firms it would not break even.[9]

The fact that the monopolistically competitive firm produces to the left of the lowest point on its LAC curve when it is in long-run equilibrium means that the average cost of production and price of the product under monopolistic competition is higher than under perfect competition (\$6 at point A' as compared with \$5 at point E'', respectively, in Figure 9-10). This difference is not large because the demand curve faced by the monopolistic competitor is very elastic. In any event, the slightly higher LAC and P under monopolistic competition than under perfect competition can be regarded as the cost of having a variety of differentiated products appealing to different consumer tastes, rather than a single undifferentiated product. The fact that each monopolistic competitor produces to the left of the lowest point on its LAC curve means that each firm operates with **excess capacity** and that there are many more firms (i.e., there is some **overcrowding**) when the market is organized along monopolistically competitive rather than along perfectly competitive lines.

Product Variation and Selling Expenses under Monopolistic Competition

Under monopolistic competition a firm can increase its expenditures on product variation and selling effort in order to increase the demand for its product and make it more price inelastic. **Product variation** refers to changes in some of the characteristics of the product that a monopolistic competitor undertakes in order to make its product more appealing to consumers. For example, producers may reduce the sugar content of breakfast cereals and include a small surprise gift in each package. **Selling expenses** are all those expenses that the firm incurs to advertise the product, increase its sales force, provide better servicing for its product, etc. Product variation and selling expenses can increase the firm's sales and profits, but they also lead to additional costs. A firm should spend more on product variation and selling

[9]Mathematically, we could determine the best level of output (Q) and price (P) for a monopolistic competitor in long-run equilibrium by setting the price equal to LAC and solving for Q and P (see point A' in Figure 9-10 and Problem 11 with answer at the end of the book).

effort as long as the *MR* from these efforts exceeds the *MC*, and until *MR* = *MC*. While spending more on product variation and selling effort can increase profits in the short run, monopolistically competitive firms will break even in the long run because of imitation by other firms and the entrance of new firms. This is shown in Figure 9-11.

In Figure 9-11, *D″* and *MR″* are demand and marginal revenue curves that are higher than *D′* and *MR′* in Figure 9-10 as a result of greater product variation and selling expenses. The *LAC* curve is that of Figure 9-10, while *LAC** and *LMC** are the long-run average and marginal cost curves resulting from greater product variation and selling expenses. Note that the vertical distance between *LAC** and *LAC* increases on the (realistic) assumption that to sell greater quantities of the product requires larger expenses per unit on product variation and selling effort. While these efforts can lead to larger short-run profits, however, our typical or representative firm will break even in the long run. This is shown by point *A** in Figure 9-11, at which $Q = 5$ and $P = LAC^* = \$8$, and $MR'' = LMC^*$ (point *E**). Note that at point *A** the firm charges a higher price and sells a greater quantity than at point *A′* in Figure 9-10, but the firm will nevertheless break even in the long run. If all firms selling similar products increase their expenses on product variation and selling effort, each firm may retain only its share of an expanding market in the long run.

Figure 9-11
Long-Run Equilibrium of the Monopolistically Competitive Firm with Selling Expenses

Curves *D″* and *MR″*, as well as *LAC** and *LMC**, are higher than in Figure 9-10 because of greater expenses on product variation and selling effort. While these efforts can increase the firm's profits in the short run, in the long run the firm breaks even. This is shown by point *A**, at which *Q* = 5 units and *P* = *LAC** = $8, and *MR″* = *LMC** (point *E**).

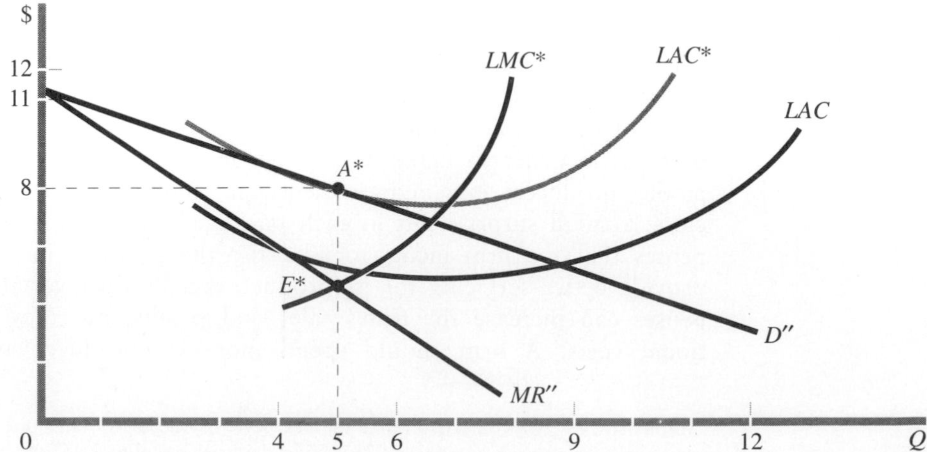

Case Study 9-9
Advertisers Are Taking on Competitors by Name

Since 1981 when the National Association of Broadcasters abolished its guidelines against making disparaging remarks against competitors' products, advertisers have taken their gloves off and have begun to praise the superior qualities of their products, not compared to "brand X" as before 1981 but by identifying competitors' products by name. The Federal Trade Commission welcomed the change because it anticipated that this would increase competition and lead to better-quality products at lower prices. Some of these hopes have in fact been realized. For example, the price of eyeglasses was found to be much higher in states that prohibited advertising by optometrists and opticians than in states that allowed such advertising, without any increase in the probability of having the wrong eyeglass prescription. Similarly, the price of an uncontested divorce dropped from $350 to $150 in Phoenix, Arizona, after the Supreme Court allowed advertising for legal services. Though less sportsmanlike and possibly resulting in legal suits, advertisers have been willing to take on competitors by name because the technique seems very effective. For example, Burger King sales soared when it began to attack McDonald's by name. However, Gillette has recently sued Wilkinson Sword, MCI sued AT&T, and Alpo Petfoods sued Ralston Purina over allegedly misleading ad claims. The stakes can be very high—just legal fees in battles between large companies can run as high as $200,000 per month! In the future, we are thus likely to see a return to comparison to "brand X" in many promotion campaigns. AT&T and MCI, however, do not seem ready for a truce in their long-running nasty campaign to take customers from each other for long-distance telephone service. In a recent TV ad, AT&T offered reason 117 for sticking with it rather than using MCI. MCI responded with an ad of its own in which it accused AT&T of either practicing deception or being lousy at math.

Source: "Advertisers Remove the Cover from Brand X," *U.S. News & World Report,* December 19, 1983, pp. 75–76; L. Benham, "The Effect of Advertising on the Price of Eyeglasses," *Journal of Law and Economics,* October 1973, pp. 337–352; "Lawyers Are Facing Surge in Competition as Courts Drop Curbs," *The Wall Street Journal,* October 18, 1978, p. 1; "A Comeback May Be Ahead for Brand X," *Business Week,* December 1989, p. 35; and "Long-Distance Risks of AT&T–MCI War," *The Wall Street Journal,* April 14, 1993, p. B9.

SUMMARY

1. The process by which price and output are determined in the real world is strongly affected by the structure of the market. A market consists of all the actual and potential buyers and sellers of a particular product. Market structure refers to the competitive environment in which the buyers and sellers of the product operate. Four different types of market structure are usually identified. These are: perfect competition at one extreme, pure monopoly at the opposite extreme, and monopolistic competition and oligopoly in between.
2. The perfectly competitive firm is a price taker (i.e., it faces an infinitely elastic demand curve for the product). The best level of output for a perfectly competitive firm in the short run is at the point where $P = MR = MC$,

provided that $P > AVC$. The rising portion of the firm's MC curve above the AVC curve is the competitive firm's short-run supply curve of the product. If input prices are constant, the market supply curve is obtained by the horizontal summation of the competitive firms' supply curves. In the long run the firm can construct the optimal scale of plant to produce the best level of output. If profits can be earned in the industry, more firms will enter the industry in the long run until all profits are eliminated and all firms produce at the lowest point on their LAC curve. If firms in the industry incur losses, some firms will leave the industry in the long run until the remaining firms break even.

3. Domestic firms in most industries face a great deal of competition from imports. International trade leads to a decline in the domestic price of the commodity, and to larger domestic consumption and lower domestic production of the commodity than in the absence of trade. The exchange rate refers to the dollar price of a unit of the foreign currency. In the absence of government intervention, the exchange rate of the dollar is determined by the intersection of the market demand and supply for the foreign currency. A depreciation of the dollar allows U.S. firms to increase foreign sales and profits but also to increase their cost of imported inputs.

4. Monopoly is the form of market organization in which a single firm sells a product for which there are no close substitutes. Thus, the monopolist faces the market's negatively sloped demand curve for the product and $MR < P$. As in the case of perfect competition, the best level of output for the monopolist in the short run is given by the point at which $MR = MC$, provided that $P > AVC$. In the long run, the monopolist will construct the optimal scale of plant to produce the best level of output (given by the point at which $P = LMC$). Because of blocked entry into the market, however, the monopolist can earn profits in the long run and is not likely to produce at the lowest point on the LAC curve. Perfect competition represents a better use of society's resources only when technology allows many firms to operate efficiently in the market.

5. Monopolistic competition is the form of market organization in which there are many sellers of a differentiated product and entry into and exit from the industry are rather easy in the long run. Monopolistic competition is most common in the retail sector of the economy. Because of the availability of many close substitutes, the demand curve faced by a monopolistically competitive firm is highly elastic. The best level of output in the short run is where $MR = MC$, provided $P > AVC$. Monopolistically competitive firms should spend on product variation and selling expenses until $MR = MC$. If monopolistically competitive firms earn profits in the short run, more firms enter the market in the long run. This shifts the demand curve facing each firm to the left until all firms break even. In monopolistic competition, P and LAC are somewhat higher than under perfect competition and firms operate with excess capacity.

DISCUSSION QUESTIONS

1. A certain car manufacturer regards his business as highly competitive because he is keenly aware of his rivalry with the other few car manufacturers in the market. Like the other car manufacturers, he undertakes vigorous advertising campaigns seeking to convince potential buyers of the superior quality and better style of his automobiles and reacts very quickly to claims of superiority by rivals. Is this the meaning of perfect competition from an economics point of view? Explain.
2. (*a*) Under what condition should a firm continue to produce in the short run if it incurs losses at the best level of output? (*b*) Are the normal returns on investment included as part of costs or as part of profits in managerial economics? Why?
3. (*a*) Is the market supply curve for a product more or less price elastic than the supply curve of one of the firms in the market? Why? (*b*) How is an increase in input prices shown on the firm's short-run marginal cost curve? Will this affect the competitive firm's short-run supply curve? (*c*) Is the competitive firm's short-run supply curve affected by a change in the firm's fixed costs? Why?
4. (*a*) What is the best level of output of a perfectly competitive firm in the long run? (*b*) What is the optimal scale of plant of a perfectly competitive firm when the firm is in long-run equilibrium? (*c*) What is the best level of output and the optimal scale of plant when the competitive market and firm are in long-run equilibrium?
5. (*a*) If a competitive firm is in short-run equilibrium, must it also be in long-run equilibrium? (*b*) If a competitive firm is in long-run equilibrium, must it also be in short-run equilibrium?
6. (*a*) How can an import tariff be shown in Figure 9-4? (*b*) What is the size of a prohibitive tariff (i.e., one that would stop all trade) in Figure 9-4?
7. Assuming a two-currency world, the U.S. dollar and the British pound sterling, what does a depreciation of the dollar mean for the pound? Explain.
8. (*a*) Can a monopolist incur losses in the short run? Why? (*b*) Can a monopolist earning short-run profits increase those profits in the long run? Why? (*c*) Would a monopolist ever operate in the inelastic portion of the demand curve it faces? Why?
9. Can we derive the supply curve of the monopolist from its marginal cost curve in the same way that it was derived for a prefectly competitive firm? Why?
10. Under what conditions can we be sure that perfect competition leads to a more efficient use of society's resources than monopoly? How prevalent are these conditions in the real world?
11. (*a*) What are the choice-related variables for a firm under monopolistic competition? (*b*) What is nonprice competition? (*c*) Product variation? (*d*) Selling expenses?

12. Many firms under monopolistic competition set their advertising budgets at a fixed percentage of their anticipated sales. Does this mean that these firms behave in a nonmaximizing manner? Why?

13. Excess capacity is inversely related to the price elasticity of demand faced by a monopolistically competitive firm. True or false? Explain.

PROBLEMS

*1. If the market demand and supply functions for pizza in Newtown were

$$QD = 10{,}000 - 1{,}000P$$
$$QS = -2{,}000 + 1{,}000P$$

(*a*) Determine algebraically the equilibrium price and quantity of pizza and (*b*) plot the market demand and supply curves, label the equilibrium point E, and draw the demand curve faced by a single pizza shop in this market on the assumption that the market is perfectly competitive. Show also the marginal revenue of the firm on the figure.

2. Starting with the market demand and supply functions in Problem 1, determine algebraically the new equilibrium price and quantity if (*a*) the demand function changes to $QD' = 12{,}000 - 1{,}000P$ or to $QD'' = 8{,}000 - 1{,}000P$, or (*b*) the market supply function changes to $QS^* = -4{,}000 + 1{,}000P$ or to $QS^{**} = 1{,}000P$. (*c*) Draw a figure for parts (*a*) and (*b*); label E' and E'', respectively, the equilibrium point resulting when the market demand changes to QD' or QD''; label E^* and E^{**}, respectively, the equilibrium point resulting when the market supply function changes to QS^* or QS^{**}; on the same figure, label F the equilibrium point resulting with QD' and QS^*, label G the equilibrium resulting with QD'' and QS^{**}, label H the equilibrium resulting with QD' and QS^{**}, and label J the equilibrium resulting with QD'' and QS^*.

*3. Emily Rivera, a consultant hired by the Unisex Hair Styling Corporation, a beauty salon in New York City, has estimated the cost curves shown in the following figure for hair styling. Determine the company's best level of output and its total profits if the price of hair styling is (*a*) \$18, (*b*) \$13, (*c*) \$9, (*d*) \$5, and (*e*) \$3.

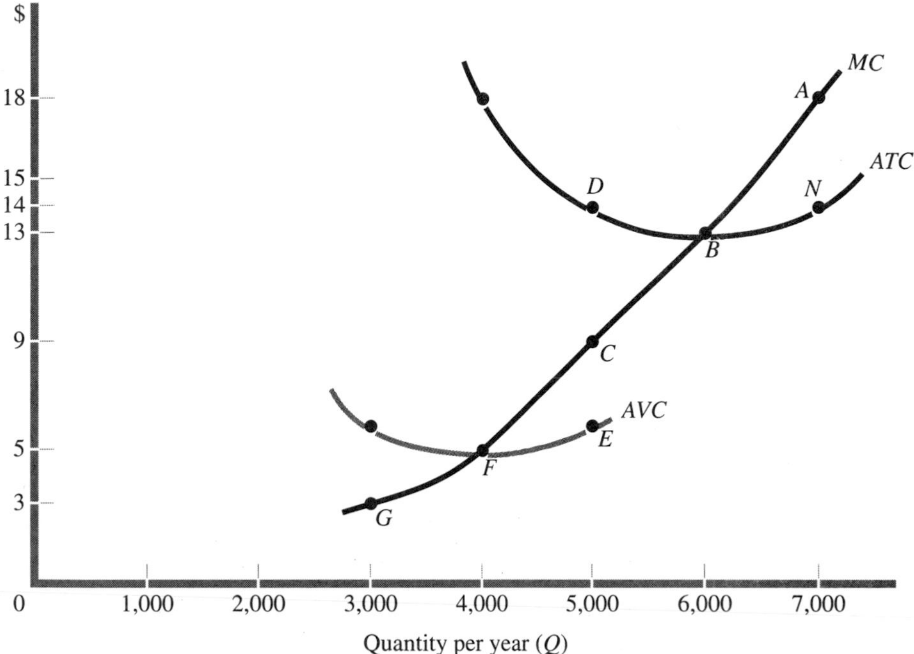

4. (*a*) Draw the supply curve for the perfectly competitive firm of Problem 3. Also draw the industry short-run supply curve on the assumptions that there are 100 identical firms in the industry and that factor prices remain unchanged as industry output expands (and thus more factors are used). (*b*) Explain the graph of part (*a*). (*c*) What quantity of the service will be supplied by each firm and the industry at the price of $9? At $18? At prices below $5?

*5. John Gilledeau, an economist in the research department of the Computer Parts Corporation, one of many producers of hard disks for personal computers, has estimated that short-run and long-run per-unit cost curves for the company given in the following figure. Suppose that the market is close to being perfectly competitive and that the company has the scale of plant indicated by SAC_1 and the short-run equilibrium price is $16. (*a*) What output will this firm produce and sell in the short run? Is the firm making a profit or a loss at this level of output? (*b*) Discuss the adjusted prices for this firm in the long run, *if only this firm* and no other firm in the industry *adjusted to the long run*. (*c*) Explain the long-run adjustment process for the firm and the market in the figure. (*d*) What implicit assumption about factor prices was made in the solution of part (*c*)? What would happen if input prices increase as more firms enter the market and demand more inputs?

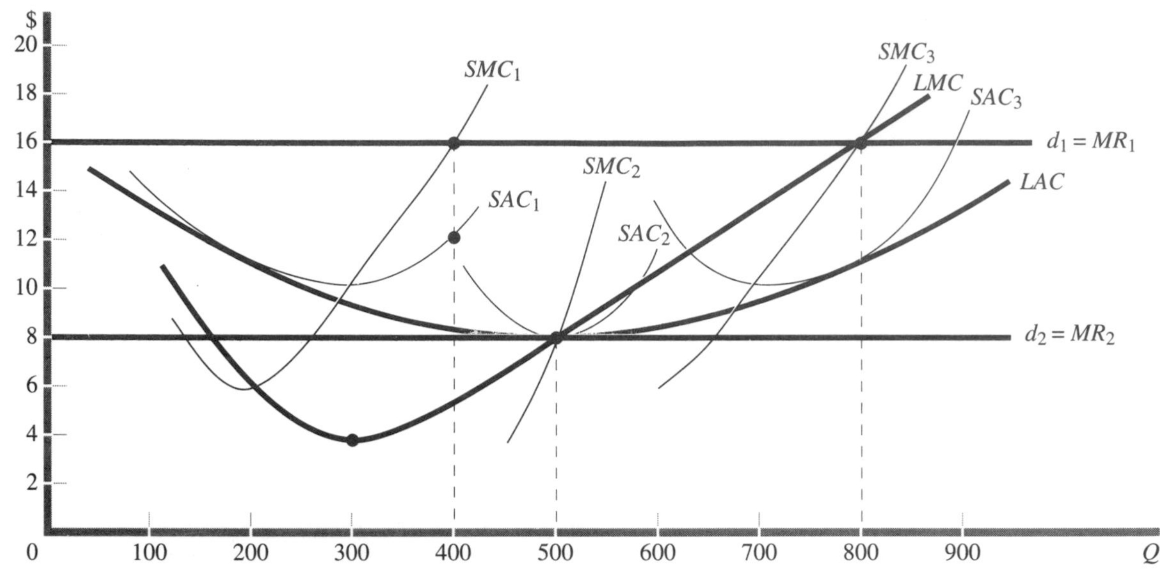

6. From Figure 9-4, determine the effect of a 33 percent import tariff on commodity *X*.

7. Starting from Figure 9-6 showing the short-run price and output determination by the monopolist, suppose that the average fixed costs of the monopolist increase by $5 and that its *AVC* is $6 less than the new *ATC* at the best level of output. Draw a figure showing the best level of output and price, the amount of profit or loss per unit and in total, and whether it pays for the monopolist to produce or not.

8. Starting from Figure 9-7 showing the monopolist in long-run equilibrium, draw a figure showing that (*a*) the monopolist would break even if costs rose sufficiently in the long run and (*b*) the change in demand that would result in the monopolist's producing at the lowest point on its *LAC* curve.

9. The Unisex International Haircutters, Inc., faces the following demand function for haircuts per day:

$$QD = 240 - 20P$$

(*a*) Draw a figure showing the demand curve and the corresponding marginal revenue curve of the firm. On the same figure draw a typical *MC*, *ATC*, and *AVC* curve showing that the best level of output is 80 haircuts per day, and that *ATC* = $10 and *AVC* = $6 at *Q* = 80. (*b*) How much profit or loss per haircut does the firm have? Does the firm remain in business in the short run? Why?

10. (*a*) Draw a figure similar to Figure 9-10 for the firm of Problem 1 showing the best level of output in the long run on the assumption that the demand curve facing the firm shifts in the long run but remains parallel to demand curve *D* in Problem 1. On the same figure show the best level of output and

price of the product if the market had been organized along perfectly competitive lines. (Omit the short-run per-unit cost curves from the figure to avoid overcrowding the figure.) (*b*) What is the amount of excess capacity of the monopolistically competitive firm in the long run? How does this affect the number of firms in the market? (*c*) Can you conclude from your figure in part (*a*) that perfect competition is more efficient than monopolistic competition?

*11. In Akron, Ohio, the movie market is monopolistically competitive. The demand function for daily attendance and the long-run average cost function at the Plaza Movie House are, respectively,

$$P = 9 - 0.4Q \qquad \text{and} \qquad AC = 10 - 0.06Q + 0.0001Q^2$$

(*a*) Calculate the price that the Plaza Movie House will charge for admission to movies in the long run. What will be the number of patrons per day at that price? (*b*) What is the value of the *LAC* that the firm will incur? How much profit will the firm earn?

12. **Integrating Problem**

Suppose that in a city there are 100 identical self-service gasoline stations selling the same type of gasoline. The total daily market demand function for gasoline in the market is $QD = 60{,}000 - 25{,}000P$, where P is expressed in dollars per gallon. The daily market supply curve is $QS = 25{,}000P$ for $P >$ \$0.60. (*a*) Determine algebraically the equilibrium price and quantity of gasoline. (*b*) Draw a figure showing the market supply curve and the market demand curve for gasoline, and the demand curve and the supply curve of one firm in the market on the assumption that the market is nearly perfectly competitive. (*c*) Explain why your figure of the market and the firm in part (*b*) is consistent. (*d*) Suppose that now the market is monopolized (for example, a centralized cartel is formed that determines the price and output as a monopolist would and allocates production equally to each member). Draw a figure showing the monopolist's equilibrium output and price. (*e*) How many gasoline stations would the monopolist operate? (*f*) Can we say that the monopoly leads to a less efficient use of resources than perfect competition? What is the amount of the dead-weight loss if any?

APPENDIX

PROFIT MAXIMIZATION WITH CALCULUS

A firm usually wants to produce the output that maximizes its total profits. Total profits (π) are equal to total revenue (TR) minus total costs (TC). That is,

$$\pi = TR - TC \tag{9-4}$$

where π, TR, and TC are all functions of output (Q).

Taking the first derivative of π with respect to Q and setting it equal to zero gives

$$\frac{d\pi}{dQ} = \frac{d(TR)}{dQ} - \frac{d(TC)}{dQ} = 0 \tag{9-5}$$

so that

$$\frac{d(TR)}{dQ} = \frac{d(TC)}{dQ} \tag{9-6}$$

Equation 9-6 indicates that in order to maximize profits, a firm must produce where marginal revenue (MR) equals marginal cost (MC). Since for a perfectly competitive firm P is constant and $TR = (P)(Q)$ so that

$$\frac{d(TR)}{dQ} = MR = P$$

the first-order condition for profit maximization for a perfectly competitive firm becomes $P = MR = MC$.

Equation 9-6 is only the first-order condition for maximization (and minimization). The second-order condition for profit maximization requires that the second derivative of π with respect to Q be negative. That is,

$$\frac{d^2\pi}{dQ^2} = \frac{d^2(TR)}{dQ^2} - \frac{d^2(TC)}{dQ^2} < 0 \tag{9-7}$$

so that

$$\frac{d^2(TR)}{dQ^2} < \frac{d^2(TC)}{dQ^2} \tag{9-8}$$

According to Equation 9-8, the algebraic value of the slope of the MC function must be greater than the algebraic value of the MR function. Under perfect competition, MR is constant (i.e., the MR curve of the firm is horizontal) so that Equation 9-8 requires that the MC curve be rising at the point where $MR = MC$ for the firm to maximize its total profits (or to minimize its total losses). With imperfect competition, the firm's demand curve (and therefore its MR curve) is negatively sloped, so that Equation 9-8 requires that the MC curve either be rising or falling less rapidly than the MR curve for the second-order condition for maximization to be satisfied.

For example, if the demand function faced by a firm is

$$Q = 90 - 2P$$

or

$$P = 45 - 0.5Q$$

so that

$$TR = PQ = (45 - 0.5Q)Q = 45Q - 0.5Q^2$$

and if

$$TC = Q^3 - 8Q^2 + 57Q + 2$$

the total profit function is then

$$\begin{aligned}\pi = TR - TC &= (45Q - 0.5Q^2) - (Q^3 - 8Q^2 + 57Q + 2)\\ &= 45Q - 0.5Q^2 - Q^3 + 8Q^2 - 57Q - 2\end{aligned}$$

To determine the level of output at which the firm maximizes π, we proceed as follows:

$$\frac{d\pi}{dQ} = -3Q^2 + 15Q - 12 = 0$$

$$= (-3Q + 3)(Q - 4) = 0$$

therefore,

$$Q = 1 \quad \text{and} \quad Q = 4$$

$$\frac{d^2\pi}{dQ^2} = -6Q + 15$$

At $Q = 1$,

$$\frac{d^2\pi}{dQ^2} = -6(1) + 15 = 9$$

and π is minimum. At $Q = 4$,

$$\frac{d^2\pi}{dQ^2} = -6(4) + 15 = -9$$

and π is maximum. Therefore, π is maximized at $Q = 4$, and from the original π function we can determine that

$$\pi = -(4)^3 + 7.5(4)^2 - 12(4) - 2$$

$$= -64 + 120 - 48 - 2$$

$$= \$6$$

Problem 1 Determine the best level of output for the above example by the *MR* and *MC* approach.

Problem 2 Determine the best level of output for a perfectly competitive firm that sells its product at $P = \$4$ and faces $TC = 0.04Q^3 - 0.9Q^2 + 10Q + 5$. Will the firm produce this level of output? Why?

SUPPLEMENTARY READINGS

For a problem-solving approach to the topics discussed in this chapter, see:

Salvatore, Dominick: *Theory and Problems of Managerial Economics,* Schaum Outline Series (New York: McGraw-Hill, 1989), Secs. 10.1 to 10.4.

For a more extensive theoretical analysis of perfect competition, monopoly, and monopolistic competition, see:

Salvatore, Dominick: *Microeconomics,* 2nd ed. (New York: HarperCollins, 1994), Chaps. 8 and 9, and Secs. 10.1 and 10.2.

Salvatore, Dominick: *Theory and Problems of Microeconomic Theory,* 3rd ed., Schaum Outline Series (New York: McGraw-Hill, 1992), Chaps. 9 and 10, and Secs. 11.1 to 11.3.

Other readings on markets and industrial structure are:

Scherer, F. M., and **David Ross:** *Industrial Market Structure and Economic Performance* (Boston: Houghton Mifflin, 1990).

Martin, Stephen: "Market Power or Efficiency?" *Review of Economics and Statistics,* February 1986, pp. 84–95.

Shapiro, Benson P., and **Thomas V. Bonoma:** "How to Segment Industrial Markets," *Harvard Business Review,* May–June 1984, pp. 104–110.

Shepard, W. G.: "Causes of Increased Competition in the U.S. Economy," *Review of Economics and Statistics,* November 1982, pp. 613–626.

Slade, M. E.:"Static Profitability as a Measure of Deviations from the Competitive Norm," *Managerial and Decision Economics,* June 1986, pp. 113–118.

Porter, Michael: "The Competitive Advantage of Nations," *Harvard Business Review,* March–April 1990, pp. 73–93.

The ground-breaking works on monopolistic competition and its evaluation are:

Chamberlin, Edward H.: *The Theory of Monopolistic Competition* (Cambridge, Mass.: Harvard University Press, 1962), Chaps. 4 and 5.

Stigler, George: *Five Lectures on Economic Problems* (New York: Macmillan, 1950), pp. 12–24.

Cohen, Kalman, and **Richard Cyert:** *Theory of the Firm* (Englewood Cliffs, N.J.: Prentice-Hall, 1975), pp. 225–230.

For the economic effects of product variation and advertising, see:

Lancaster, Kelvin: "Competition and Product Variety," *Journal of Business,* July 1980, pp. S79–S105.

Comanor, William S., and **Thomas A. Wilson:** "The Effect of Advertising on Competition: A Survey," *Journal of Economic Literature,* June 1979, pp. 453–476.

Tregarthen, Timothy: "Advertising: Friend or Foe?" *The Margin,* February 1988, pp. 10–11.

Stansell, R. S., C. P. Harper, and **R. P. Wilder:** "The Effects of Advertising Expenditures: Evidence from an Analysis of Major Advertisers," *Review of Business and Economic Research,* Fall 1984, pp. 86–95.

Stigler, George J.: "The Economics of Information," *Journal of Political Economy,* June 1961, pp. 213–225.

Stageman, Mark: "Advertising in Competitive Markets," *American Economic Review,* March 1991, pp. 210–233.

Feinberg, Fred M., Barbara E. Kahn, and **Leig McAlister:** "Market Share Response When Consumers Seek Variety," *Journal of Marketing Research,* May 1992, pp. 227–237.

For the effect of international competition and imports on domestic demand, supply, and prices, see:

Salvatore, Dominick: *International Economics,* 5th ed. (Englewood Cliffs, N.J.: Prentice-Hall, 1995), Secs. 4.2 and 4.9.

A detailed discussion of the foreign exchange market and exchange rate determination is found in:

Salvatore, Dominick: *International Economics,* 5th ed. (Englewood Cliffs, N.J.: Prentice-Hall, 1995), Chap. 14.

CHAPTER 10

Oligopoly and Strategic Behavior

KEY TERMS

Oligopoly
Duopoly
Pure oligopoly
Differentiated oligopoly
Nonprice competition
Limit pricing
Concentration ratios
Herfindahl index (*H*)
Theory of contestable markets
Kinked demand curve model
Collusion
Market-sharing cartel
Centralized cartel
Price leadership
Barometric firm
Sales maximization model
Strategic behavior
Game theory
Players
Strategies
Payoff
Payoff matrix
Dominant strategy
Nash equilibrium
Prisoners' dilemma
Repeated games
Tit-for-tat

CHAPTER OUTLINE

In this chapter we examine oligopoly and the strategic behavior of firms. We begin by discussing the meaning and sources of oligopoly, examining various models of oligopoly pricing and output, and evaluating the efficiency implications of oligopoly. We will see that there is no general theory of oligopoly but a number of models of various degrees of realism. We then go on to discuss the sales maximization model and the growth of global oligopolists. Subsequently, we examine the strategic behavior of firms with game theory. As we will see, game theory offers many insights into oligopolistic interdependence and the strategic behavior of firms that could not be examined with the traditional tools of economic analysis. After explaining the basic concepts of game theory and strategic behavior, we discuss the prisoners' dilemma and its applicability to the analysis of price and nonprice competition and cartel cheating. We then go on to examine multiple and strategic moves and the relationship between strategic behavior and international competitiveness.

10-1 OLIGOPOLY AND MARKET CONCENTRATION

In this section we examine the meaning and sources of oligopoly, discuss measures of market concentration, and present the theory of contestable markets.

Oligopoly: Meaning and Sources

In Section 9-1 we defined **oligopoly** as the form of market organization in which there are few sellers of a homogeneous or differentiated product. If there are only two sellers, we have a **duopoly.** If the product is homogeneous, we have a **pure oligopoly.** If the product is differentiated, we have a **differentiated oligopoly.** While entry into an oligopolistic industry is possible, it is not easy (as evidenced by the fact that there are only a few firms in the industry).

Oligopoly is the most prevalent form of market organization in the manufacturing sector of industrial nations, including the United States. Some of the oligopolistic industries in the United States are automobiles, primary aluminum, steel, electrical equipment, glass, breakfast cereals, cigarettes, and soaps and detergents. Some of these products (such as steel and aluminum) are homogeneous, while others (such as automobiles, cigarettes, breakfast cereals, and soaps and detergents) are differentiated. Oligopoly exists also when transportation costs limit the market area. For example, even though there are many cement producers in the United States, competition is limited to the few local producers in a particular area.

Since there are only a few firms selling a homogeneous or differentiated product in oligopolistic markets, the action of each firm affects the other firms in the industry and vice versa. For example, when General Motors introduced price rebates in the sale of its automobiles, Ford and Chrysler immediately followed with price rebates of their own. Furthermore, since price competition can lead to ruinous price wars, oligopolists usually prefer to compete on the basis of product-differentiation, advertising, and service. These are referred to as **nonprice com-**

petition. Yet, even here, if GM mounts a major advertising campaign, Ford and Chrysler are likely to soon respond in kind. When Pepsi mounted a major advertising campaign in the early 1980s, Coca-Cola responded with a large advertising campaign of its own.

From what has been said, it is clear that the distinguishing characteristic of oligopoly is the interdependence or rivalry among firms in the industry. This is the natural result of fewness. Since an oligopolist knows that its own actions will have a significant impact on the other oligopolists in the industry, each oligopolist must consider the possible reaction of competitors in deciding its pricing policies, the degree of product differentiation to introduce, the level of advertising to undertake, the amount of service to provide, etc. Since competitors can react in many different ways (depending on the nature of the industry, the type of product, etc.), we do not have a single oligopoly model but many—each based on the particular behavioral response of competitors to the actions of the first. Because of this interdependence, managerial decision making is much more complex under oligopoly than under other forms of market structure. In this chapter we present some of the most important oligopoly models. We must keep in mind, however, that each model is at best incomplete and more or less unrealistic.

The sources of oligopoly are generally the same as for monopoly. That is, (1) economies of scale may operate over a sufficiently large range of outputs as to leave only a few firms supplying the entire market; (2) huge capital investments and specialized inputs are usually required to enter an oligopolistic industry (say, automobiles, aluminum, steel, and similar industries), and this acts as an important natural barrier to entry; (3) a few firms may own a patent for the exclusive right to produce a commodity or to use a particular production process; (4) established firms may have a loyal following of customers based on product quality and service that new firms would find very difficult to match; (5) a few firms may own or control the entire supply of a raw material required in the production of the product; and (6) the government may give a franchise to only a few firms to operate in the market. The above are not only the sources of oligopoly but also represent the barriers to other firms entering the market in the long run. If entry were not so restricted, the industry could not remain oligopolistic in the long run. A further barrier to entry is provided by **limit pricing,** whereby existing firms charge a price low enough to discourage entry into the industry. By doing so, they voluntarily sacrifice short-run profits in order to maximize long-run profits.

Case Study 10-1

Brands: Thrive or Die

Private-label consumer products—which are becoming more and more like brand-name products in quality, looks, and taste but which cost from 15 percent to 40 percent less—are taking markets away from established brands and causing profit margins to fall. Private labels or store brands have already risen to 18 percent of supermarket sales volume, and their share could double by the turn of the decade. Brand names are fighting back with product improvements to justify higher prices, increased advertising, lower prices, and the introduction of their own private-label products.

For example, Hellmann's reduced the fat content of its mayonnaise, Heinz introduced a 20-ounce squeezable and recyclable plastic ketchup bottle, and Procter & Gamble introduced a diaper that is 50 percent thinner. Most makers of brand-name products have also increased their advertising expenditures to shore up brand loyalty, but consumers have become more skeptical and harder to reach. Makers of brand-name products have also reduced prices. For example, Philip Morris lowered the price of its premium Marlboro cigarettes by 20 percent in April 1994 to better compete with private-label cigarettes. Procter & Gamble cut prices of Pampers diapers by 5 percent and Luvs by 16 percent in May 1994, and this came on top of two other price cuts in less than a year. Finally, many brand-name product manufacturers such as Heinz, Borden, Campbell Soup, Nestlé, 3M, and every major U.S. cigarette maker are also churning out their own private-label versions of their brand-name products (even though margins are lower) in order to fight loss of market share, on the theory that "if you can't beat them, join them." But they have to be careful not to slight their prestigious brands or price their private labels too low, which would further erode their profit margins.

The brands that have fared best are those based on clear higher quality and superior technology and that have not gouged consumers on prices in the past. Examples of these are Gillette's Sensor razor and premium soft drink brands such as Coca-Cola and Pepsi. In the future, only the number 1 and number 2 brands plus a private label are likely to survive in any given market. There is simply no room on most store shelves for more brands. It's thrive or die! Makers of the number 3, 4, or 5 brands will either have to become the number 1 or number 2 brand, move to a private label, or leave the market.

Source: "How the Country's Biggest Brands Are Faring at the Supermarket," *The Wall Street Journal,* March 24, 1994, p. B1; "Discount Brands Flex Their Muscle," *The New York Times,* April 24, 1994, p. D1; "Big Companies Add Private-Label Lines that Vie with Their Premium Brands," *The Wall Street Journal,* May 21, 1994, p. B1; "Shoot Out at the Check-Out," *The Economist,* June 5, 1994, pp. 69–70; and "Brands: It's Thrive or Die," *Fortune,* August 23, 1994, pp. 52–65.

Concentration Ratios, the Herfindahl Index, and Contestable Markets

The degree by which an industry is dominated by a few large firms is measured by **concentration ratios.** These give the percentage of total industry sales of the 4, 8, or 12 largest firms in the industry (see Case Study 10-2). An industry in which the four-firm concentration ratio is close to 100 is clearly oligopolistic, and industries in which this ratio is higher than 50 or 60 percent are also likely to be oligopolistic. The four-firm concentration ratio for most manufacturing industries in the United States is between 20 and 80 percent. As discussed below in Case Study 10-1, however, concentration ratios must be used and interpreted with great caution since they may greatly overestimate the market power of the largest firms in an industry.

Another method of estimating the degree of concentration in an industry is the **Herfindahl index** (*H*). This is given by the sum of the squared values of the market shares of all the firms in the industry. The higher the Herfindahl index, the greater is the degree of concentration in the industry. For example, if there is only 1 firm in the industry, so that its market share is 100 percent, $H = 100^2 = 10{,}000$. If there are 2 firms in an industry, one with a 90 percent share of the market and the other with a 10 percent share, $H = 90^2 + 10^2 = 8{,}200$. If each firm had a 50 percent share of the market, $H = 50^2 + 50^2 = 5{,}000$. With 4 equal-sized firms in the industry, $H = 2{,}500$. With 100 equal-sized firms in the (perfectly competitive) industry, $H = 100$. This points to the advantage of the Herfindahl index over the concentration ratios discussed above. Specifically, the Herfindahl index uses information on all the firms in the industry—not just the share of the market by the largest 4, 8, or 12 firms in the market. Furthermore, by squaring the market share of each firm, the Herfindahl index appropriately gives a much larger weight to larger than to smaller firms in the industry. The Herfindahl index has become of great practical importance since 1982 when the Justice Department announced new guidelines for evaluating proposed mergers based on this index (see Section 12-5).

In fact, according to the **theory of contestable markets** developed during the 1980s, even if an industry has a single firm (monopoly) or only a few firms (oligopoly), it would still operate as if it were perfectly competitive if entry is "absolutely free" (i.e., if other firms can enter the industry and face exactly the same costs as existing firms) and if exit is "entirely costless" (i.e., if there are no sunk costs so that the firm can exit the industry without facing any loss of capital).[1] An example of this might be an airline that establishes a service between two cities already served by other airlines if the new entrant faces the same costs as existing airlines and could subsequently leave the market by simply reassigning its planes to other routes without incurring any loss of capital. When entry is absolutely free and exit is entirely costless, the market is contestable. Firms will then operate as if they were perfectly competitive and sell at a price which only covers their average costs (so that they earn zero economic profit) even if there is only one firm or a few of them in the market.

[1]See William J. Baumol, "Contestable Markets: An Uprising in the Theory of Industrial Structure," *American Economic Review,* March 1982, pp. 1–5.

Case Study 10-2

Industrial Concentration in the United States

Table 10-1 presents the four-firm and the eight-firm concentration ratios for various industries in the United States from the 1987 Census of Manufactures (the latest available).

There are several reasons, however, for using these concentration ratios cautiously. First, in industries where imports are significant, concentration ratios may greatly overestimate the relative importance of the largest firms in the industry. For example, since automobile imports are about 30 percent of the domestic market in the United States, the real four-firm concentration ratio in the automobile industry is not 90 percent (as indicated in the table below) but 63 percent (that is, 90 percent times 0.70). Second, con-

Table 10-1
Concentration Ratios in the United States, 1987

Industry	Four-Firm Ratio	Eight-Firm Ratio
Cigarettes	92	*D*
Electric lamps	91	94
Motor vehicles	90	95
Breakfast cereals	87	99
Household refrigerators	85	98
Primary aluminum	74	95
Aircraft	72	92
Tires	69	87
Soaps and detergents	65	76
Office machines	47	62
Steel mills	44	63
Household furniture	43	59
Cheese	43	55
Book publishing	38	62
Petroleum refining	32	52
Soft drinks	30	40
Cement	28	47
Newspapers	25	39
Men's clothing	19	29
Women's clothing	6	10

Source: U.S. Bureau of the Census, 1987 Census of Manufacturers, *Concentration Ratios in Manufacturing* (Washington, D.C.: Government Printing Office, 1992).

D = Data withheld to avoid disclosing company data.

centration ratios refer to the nation as a whole, while the relevant market may be local. For example, the four-firm concentration ratio for the cement industry is 28 percent, but because of very high transportation costs, only two or three firms may actually compete in many local markets. Third, how broadly or narrowly a product is defined is also very important. For example, concentration ratios in the computer industry as a whole are higher than in the personal computer segment of the market. Fourth, and as pointed out by the theory of contestable markets, concentration ratios do not give any indication of potential entrants into the market and of the degree of actual and potential competition in the industry. Thus, concentration ratios provide only one dimension of the degree of competition in the market, and while useful, they must be used with great caution. While the Herfindahl index is better than concentration ratios, it also faces the same problems and must, therefore, also be used with great caution.

10-2 OLIGOPOLY MODELS

In this section we present some of the most important oligopoly models. These are the kinked demand curve model, cartel arrangements, and price leadership model. As we will see, each of these models focuses on one particular aspect of oligopolistic interdependence but overlooks others. As a result, they have limited applicability and are more or less unrealistic. The section ends with a discussion of the efficiency implications of oligopoly.

The Kinked Demand Curve Model

The **kinked demand curve model** was introduced by Paul Sweezy in 1939 in an attempt to explain the price rigidity that was often observed in many oligopolistic models.[2] Sweezy postulated that if an oligopolist raised its price, it would lose most of its customers because other firms in the industry would not follow by raising their prices. On the other hand, an oligopolist could not increase its share of the market by lowering its price because its competitors would quickly match price cuts. As a result, according to Sweezy, oligopolists face a demand curve that has a kink at the prevailing price and is highly elastic for price increases but much less elastic for price cuts. In this model, oligopolists recognize their interdependence but act without collusion in keeping their prices constant even in the face of changed cost and demand conditions—preferring instead to compete on the basis of quality, advertising, service, and other forms of nonprice competition. The Sweezy model is shown in Figure 10-1.

In Figure 10-1, the demand curve facing the oligopolist is D or ABC and has a kink at the prevailing price of \$6 and quantity of 40 units (point B). Note that the D curve is much more elastic above the kink than below, on the assumption that competitors will not match price increases but quickly match price cuts. The marginal revenue curve is MR or $AGHJ$; AG is the segment of the marginal revenue curve corresponding to the AB portion of the demand curve; HJ corresponds to the BC portion of the demand curve. The kink at point B on the demand curve causes the BH discontinuity in the marginal revenue curve. The best level of output of the oligopolist with marginal cost curve MC is 40 units and is given by point E at which the MC curve intersects the vertical portion of the MR curve. The oligopolist will then charge the price of \$6 given by point B (at the kink on the demand curve). As in other forms of market organization, the firm under oligopoly can earn profits, break even, or incur losses in the short run, and it will continue to produce as long as $P > AVC$.[3]

From Figure 10-1 we can also see that the oligopolist's marginal cost curve can rise or fall anywhere within the discontinuous portion of the MR curve (i.e., from MC' to MC'') without inducing the oligopolist to change the prevailing price of \$6 and sales of 40 units (as long as $P > AVC$).[4] Only if the MC curve shifts above the MC' curve will the oligopolist be induced to increase its price and reduce quantity, or only if the MC curve shifts below MC'' will the oligopolist lower price and increase quantity. With a rightward or a leftward shift in the demand

[2]P. Sweezy, "Demand under Conditions of Oligopoly," *Journal of Political Economy,* August 1939, pp. 568–573.

[3]For the mathematical presentation of the model shown in Figure 10-1, see the appendix to this chapter.

[4]The shift in the oligopolist's MC curve will change only the level of profits or losses.

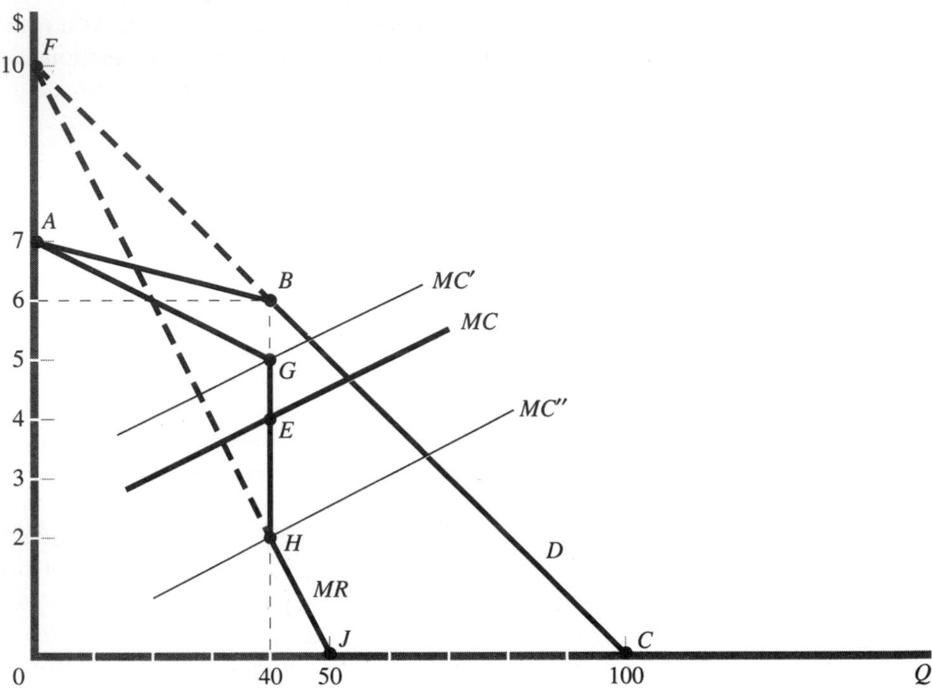

Figure 10-1
The Kinked Demand Curve Model

The demand curve facing the oligopolist is *D* or *ABC* and has a kink at the prevailing market price of \$6 and quantity of 40 units (point *B*), on the assumption that competitors match price cuts but not price increases. The marginal revenue curve is *MR* or *AGEHJ*. The best level of output of the oligopolist is 40 units and is given by point *E* at which the *MC* curve intersects the discontinuous portion of the *MR* curve. At $Q = 40$, $P = \$6$ (point *B* on the *D* curve). Any shift in the *MC* curve from *MC′* to *MC″* would leave price and output unchanged.

curve, sales will increase or fall, respectively, but the oligopolist will keep the price constant as long as the kink on the demand curve will remain at the same price and the *MC* curve continues to intersect the discontinuous or vertical portion of the *MR* curve.

When the kinked demand curve model was introduced nearly 60 years ago, it was hailed as a general theory of oligopoly. Subsequently, however, two serious criticisms were raised against the model. First, Stigler found no evidence that oligopolists readily matched price cuts but not price increases, thus seriously questioning the existence of the kink.[5] Thus, the model may be applicable only in a new industry and in the short run when firms have no clear idea as to how competitors might react to price changes. Even more serious is the criticism that while the kinked demand curve model can rationalize the existence of rigid prices, it cannot explain or predict at what price the kink will occur in the first place.

[5]G. J. Stigler, "The Kinky Oligopoly Demand Curve and Rigid Prices," *Journal of Political Economy,* October 1947, pp. 432–449.

Cartel Arrangements

In the kinked demand curve model, oligopolists did not collude to restrict or eliminate competition in order to increase profits. **Collusion** can be overt or explicit, as in centralized and market-sharing cartels, or tacit or implicit, as in price leadership models. Overt collusion as well as tacit collusion (if it can be proven) are illegal in the United States under the Sherman Antitrust Act of 1890, but they are legal in many parts of the world. U.S. corporations can, however, belong to international cartel arrangements, such as the International Air Transport Association (IATA), which sets uniform fares for transatlantic flights. Some cartel-like arrangements are also sanctioned by the U.S. government, as in the sale of certain farm products such as milk. Similarly, many professional associations, such as the American Medical Association and the New York Taxi and Limousine Commission, restrict entrance into their respective markets to ensure monopoly profits for their members. In this section we deal with overt collusion or cartels while in the next section we deal with tacit collusion or price leadership models.

There are two types of cartels: the centralized cartel and the market-sharing cartel. As the name implies, the **market-sharing cartel** gives each member the exclusive right to operate in a particular geographical area. The most notorious of the market-sharing cartels was the one under which Du Pont of the United States and Imperial Chemicals of the United Kingdom agreed in the early part of this century to divide the market for some chemicals, in such a way that Du Pont had the exclusive right to sell in North and Central America (except for British possessions) and Imperial Chemical had the exclusive rights in the British Empire and Egypt. The most well-known type of cartel, however, is the **centralized cartel.** This is a formal agreement among the oligopolistic producers of a product to set the monopoly price, allocate output among its members, and determine how profits are to be shared. This was attempted by OPEC, the Organization of Petroleum Exporting Countries (see Case Study 10-3). Figure 10-2 shows a simple two-firm centralized cartel.

In Figure 10-2, D is the total market demand curve, and MR is the corresponding MR curve for the homogeneous product produced by the two firms forming the centralized cartel. The $\Sigma\ MC$ curve for the entire cartel is obtained by summing horizontally the MC curves of the two firms. The centralized cartel authority will set $P = \$8$ and sell $Q = 50$ units (given by point E, at which MC intersects the MR curve of the cartel). To minimize production costs, the centralized authority will have to allocate 20 units of output to firm 1 and 30 units of output to firm 2 (given, respectively, by point E_1 at which $MC_1 = MR$ and by point E_2 at which $MC_2 = MR$).[6] If $MC_1 > MC_2$ at the point of production, the total costs of the cartel as a whole can be reduced by shifting production from firm 1 to firm 2 until $MC_1 = MC_2$. At the cartel price of $P = \$8$, firm 1 then earns a profit of $B_1F_1 = \$1$ per unit and \$20 in total (the shaded area) and firm 2 earns a profit of $B_2F_2 = \$2$ per unit and \$60 in total. The result would be the same for a multiplant monopolist operating plants 1 and 2. Firm 1, however, may

[6]For a mathematical analysis of the centralized and market-sharing cartel, see the appendix to this chapter.

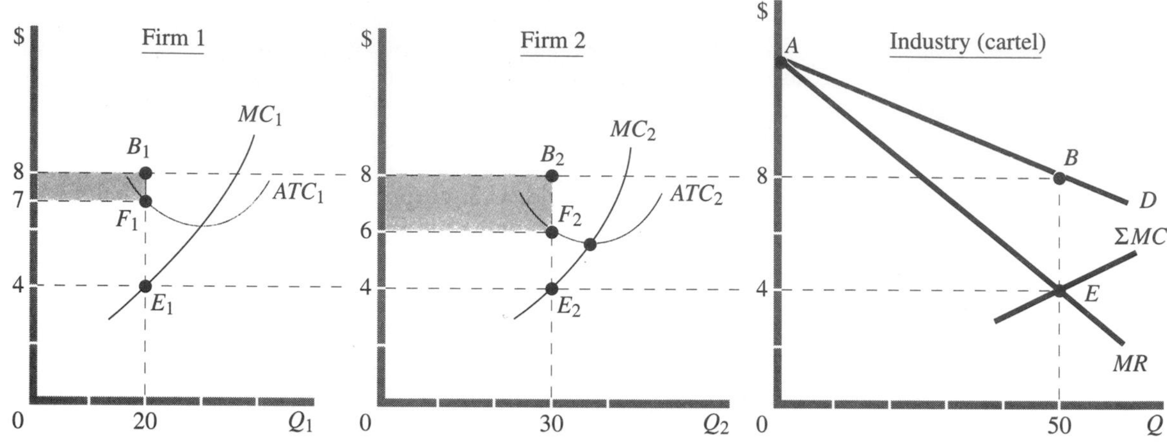

Figure 10-2
The Centralized Cartel

D is the total market demand curve, and *MR* is the corresponding marginal revenue curve for the two-firm centralized cartel. The Σ *MC* for the cartel is obtained by summing horizontally the *MC* curves of the two member firms. The centralized authority will set $P = \$8$ and sell $Q = 50$ units (given by point *E* at which the Σ *MC* curve intersects the *MR* curve). If firm 1 sells 20 units at a profit of \$1 per unit and \$20 in total (the shaded area) and firm 2 sells 30 units at a profit of \$2 per unit and \$60 in total, we have the monopoly solution. The share of profits of each firm could, however, be determined by bargaining.

demand a more equitable share of profits under the threat of withdrawing from the cartel, and herein lies an important weakness of most cartels and the reason for their failure. Cartel members also have a strong incentive to cheat by selling more than their quota. The existence of monopoly profits is also likely to attract other firms into the market. As indicated next, all these factors operated to bring OPEC to near collapse after 1985.

Case Study 10-3

The Organization of Petroleum Exporting Countries (OPEC) Cartel

It is often asserted that OPEC was able to sharply increase petroleum prices and profits for its members by restricting supply and behaving as a cartel. Twelve nations are presently members of OPEC: Algeria, Gabon, Indonesia, Iran, Iraq, Kuwait, Libya, Nigeria, Qatar, Saudi Arabia, the Arab Emirates, and Venezuela (Ecuador, the thirteenth member, withdrew in November 1992). As a result of supply shocks during the Arab-Israeli war in the fall of 1973 and the Iranian revolution during 1979 to 1980, OPEC was able to increase the price of petroleum from \$2.50 per barrel in 1973 to over \$40 per barrel in 1980. This, however, stimulated conservation in developed nations (by lowering thermostats, switching to small fuel-efficient automobiles, etc.), expanded exploration and production (by the United Kingdom and Norway in the North Sea, by the United

States in Alaska, and by Mexico in newly discovered fields), and the switching to other energy sources (such as coal). As a result, OPEC's share of world oil production fell from 55 percent in 1974 to less than 40 percent in 1994. Although OPEC meets regularly for the purpose of setting petroleum prices and production quotas, it has seldom succeeded in its effort under the conditions of excess supplies that have prevailed since 1980.

In general, the densely populated and low-petroleum-reserve countries such as Indonesia, Nigeria, and Iran want to change high prices in order to maximize short-run profits, while the sparsely populated and large-reserve countries, such as Saudi Arabia and Kuwait, prefer lower prices to discourage conservation and non-OPEC production in order to maximize long-run profits. Be that as it may, OPEC was unable to prevent a decline in petroleum prices to the $15 to $20 range and widespread cheating by its members during the 1980s. Thus, while OPEC is often given as the best example of a sometimes successful cartel, many economists are now convinced that OPEC never really controlled the world crude oil market. Under the conditions of tight supply that prevailed during the 1970s, OPEC was given credit for the sharp increase in petroleum prices, but when excess supplies arose, OPEC was uanble to prevent almost equally sharp price declines. Even the mini-oil shock resulting from Saddam Hussein's invasion of Kuwait in August 1990 was reversed with the quick victory in the Persian Gulf war, so that by the middle of 1991 oil prices were as low as before the invasion of Kuwait, and at the end of 1994 the price of oil was $18 a barrel.

Source: "OPEC's Painful Lessons," *The New York Times,* December 29, 1985, p. F3; "OPEC Sets New Policy Quotas," *The New York Times,* November 29, 1989, p. D1; "Gulf Victory: An Energy Defeat?" *The New York Times,* June 18, 1991, p. D1; and "OPEC Seeking to Raise Prices by Output Freeze," *The New York Times,* November 22, 1994, p. D2.

Price Leadership

One way of making necessary adjustments in oligopolistic markets without fear of starting a price war and without overt collusion is by **price leadership.** With price leadership, the firm that is recognized as the price leader initiates a price change and then the other firms in the industry quickly follow. The price leader is usually the largest or the dominant firm in the industry. It could also be the low-cost firm or any other firm (called the **barometric firm**) recognized as the true interpreter or barometer of changes in industry demand and cost conditions warranting a price change. An orderly price change is then accomplished by the other firms in the industry following the leader. In the dominant-firm price leadership model, the dominant firm sets the product price that maximizes its total profits, allows all the other firms (the followers) in the industry to sell all they want at that price, and then it comes in to fill the market. Thus, the follower firms behave as perfect competitors or price takers, and the dominant firm acts as the residual monopolistic supplier of the product. This is shown in Figure 10-3.

In Figure 10-3, D_T (*ABCFG*) is the total market demand curve for the homogeneous product sold in the oligopolistic market, and curve ΣMC_F is the horizontal summation of the marginal cost curves of the follower firms in the industry. Since the follower firms behave as perfect competitors, they produce where price (set by the leader) equals $\Sigma\ MC_F$. Then $D_T - \Sigma\ MC_F = D_L$ is the demand curve faced by the leader or dominant firm. For example, if the leader sets $P =$ \$7, the followers supply $HB = 50$ units of the product, leaving nothing to be supplied by the leader. This gives the vertical intercept (point H) on D_L. If the leader sets $P = \$6$, $\Sigma\ MC_F = JR = 40$ units, leaving $RC = JN = 20$ units to be supplied by the leader (point N on D_L). At $P = \$2$, $\Sigma\ MC_F = 0$ (point T), and the leader would face the total quantity demanded in the market (point F). Thus, the demand curve faced by the leader is D_L ($HNFG$) and its marginal revenue curve is MR_L. If the marginal cost curve of the leader is MC_L, the leader will set $P = \$6$ (given by point N on D_L at which $MC_L = MR_L$) in order to maximize its total

Figure 10-3
Price Leadership by the Dominant Firm

D_T ($ABCFG$) is the market demand curve for the product, and $\Sigma\ MC_F$ is the marginal cost curve of all the follower firms in the industry. Since the followers always produce where $P = \Sigma\ MC_F$, $D_T - \Sigma\ MC_F = D_L$ ($HNFG$) is the demand curve faced by the dominant leader firm, and MR_L is the corresponding marginal revenue curve. With MC_L as the marginal cost curve of the leader, the leader will set $P = \$6$ (given by point N at which $MC_L = MR_L$) in order to maximize its total profits. At $P = \$6$, the followers will supply $JR = 40$ units of the product and the leader $RC = JN = 20$ units.

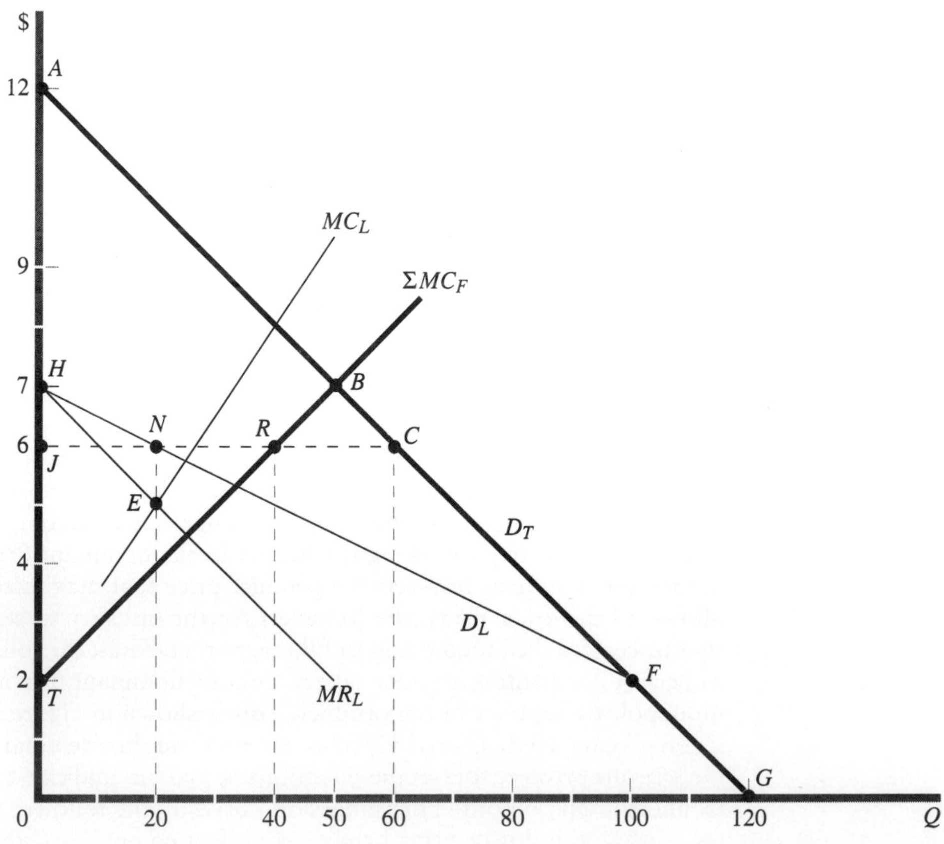

profits. At $P = \$6$, the followers will supply $JR = 40$ units (see the figure), and the leader fills the market by selling $RC = JR = 20$ units.

Among the firms that operate as price leaders in their respective industries in the U.S. economy were General Motors, U.S. Steel, Alcoa, American Tobacco, Goodyear Tire and Rubber, Gulf Oil, and the Chase Manhattan Bank (in setting the prime rate). For example, during the auto sales slumps of 1981 to 1982, 1985 to 1986, and 1990 to 1991, a cash rebate program initiated by one automaker was invariably matched by the others in a matter of days. The role of the price leader can also shift from one firm to another over time.

Efficiency Implications of Oligopoly

Most of our analysis of oligopoly until this point has referred to the short run. In the short run, an oligopolist, just as a firm under any other form of market organization, can earn a profit, break even, or incur a loss. Even if incurring a loss, it pays for an oligopolist to continue to produce in the short run as long as $P > AVC$. In the long run, the oligopolistic firm will leave the industry unless it can earn a profit (or at least break even) by constructing the best scale of plant to produce the anticipated best long-run level of output. However, in view of the uncertainty generally surrounding oligopolistic industries, it is even more difficult than under other forms of market organization for firms to determine their best level of output and plant in the long run.

In the long run, oligopoly may lead to the following harmful effects: (1) as in monopoly, price usually exceeds LAC so that profits in oligopolistic markets can persist in the long run because of restricted entry; (2) oligopolists usually do not produce at the lowest point on their LAC curve as perfectly competitive firms do; (3) because the demand curves facing oligopolists are negatively sloped, $P > LMC$ at the best level of output (except by the followers in a price leadership model by the dominant firm) and so there is an underallocation of the economy's resources to the firms in an oligopolistic industry; and (4) when oligopolists produce a differentiated product, too much may be spent on advertising and model changes.

The above statements on the harmful effects of oligopoly must be highly qualified, however. For technological reasons (economies of scale), many products (such as automobiles, steel, and aluminum) could not possibly be produced under conditions of perfect competition (or their cost of production would be prohibitive). In addition, oligopolists spend a great deal of their profits on research and development, and many economists believe that this leads to much faster technological advance and higher standards of living than if the industry were organized along perfectly competitive lines. Finally, some advertising is useful because it informs consumers, and some product differentiation has economic value in satisfying different consumers' tastes.

The reason that we cannot be more specific in evaluating the efficiency implications of oligopoly is that, as mentioned at the beginning of the chapter, we have no general theory of oligopoly but a number of specific models, each focusing on one particular aspect of oligopoly but overlooking others. This is unfortunate in view of the fact that oligopoly is the most prevalent form of market organization in production in all modern economies. It is also unlikely that major new developments will take place on the oligopoly theory front in the near future.

Case Study 10-4
Firm Size and Profitability

Do larger firms, because of their size and possible market power, earn larger profits than smaller firms? This question has been of great interest to both business and government and has been hotly debated over the years. To answer this question, we calculated the rank correlation between size (measured by sales) and profits in 1993 for the 20 largest U.S. industrial corporations from the data shown in Table 10-2. The rank correlation, which can range from 0 to 100 percent, was found to be 49 percent—which is not very high. Thus, profits are only weakly associated with size. It should be noted that life at the top is slippery—from 30 to 50 companies are displaced in a typical year from the *Fortune 500*.

Table 10-2
Sales and Profits for the 20 Largest U.S. Industrial Corporations

Company	Sales (in millions of dollars)	Profits (in millions of dollars)
General Motors	133,622	2,466
Ford Motor	108,521	2,529
Exxon	97,825	5,280
IBM	62,716	−8,101
General Electric	60,823	4,315
Mobil	56,576	2,084
Philip Morris	50,621	3,091
Chrysler	43,600	−2,551
Texaco	34,359	1,068
Du Pont	32,621	555
Chevron	32,123	1,265
Procter & Gamble	30,433	−656
Amoco	25,336	1,820
Boeing	25,285	1,244
Pepsico	25,021	1,588
Conagra	21,519	270
Shell Oil	20,853	781
United Technologies	20,736	487
Hewlett-Packard	20,317	1,177
Eastman Kodak	20,059	−1,515

Source: "The Fortune 500 Largest U.S. Industrial Corporations," *Fortune,* April 18, 1994, p. 220.

10-3 THE SALES MAXIMIZATION MODEL

In the study of market structure in this and in the previous chapter, we have assumed that the firm seeks to maximize profits or the value of the firm. This has been criticized as being much too narrow and unrealistic. In its place, broader theories of the firm have been proposed. The most prominent among these is the **sales maximization model** proposed by William Baumol, which postulates that managers of modern corporations seek to maximize sales after an adequate rate

Figure 10-4
The Sales Maximization Model

TR, *TC*, and π refer, respectively, to the total revenue, total cost, and total profits of the oligopolistic firm. $\pi = TR - TC$ and is maximized at \$90 when $Q = 40$ and $TR = \$240$. On the other hand, *TR* is maximum at \$250 when $Q = 50$ and $\pi = \$70$. A minimum profit requirement above \$70 would be binding, and the firm would produce less than 50 units of output. For example, if the minimum profit requirement were \$80, the firm would produce 47.5 units of output with *TR* of nearly \$250.

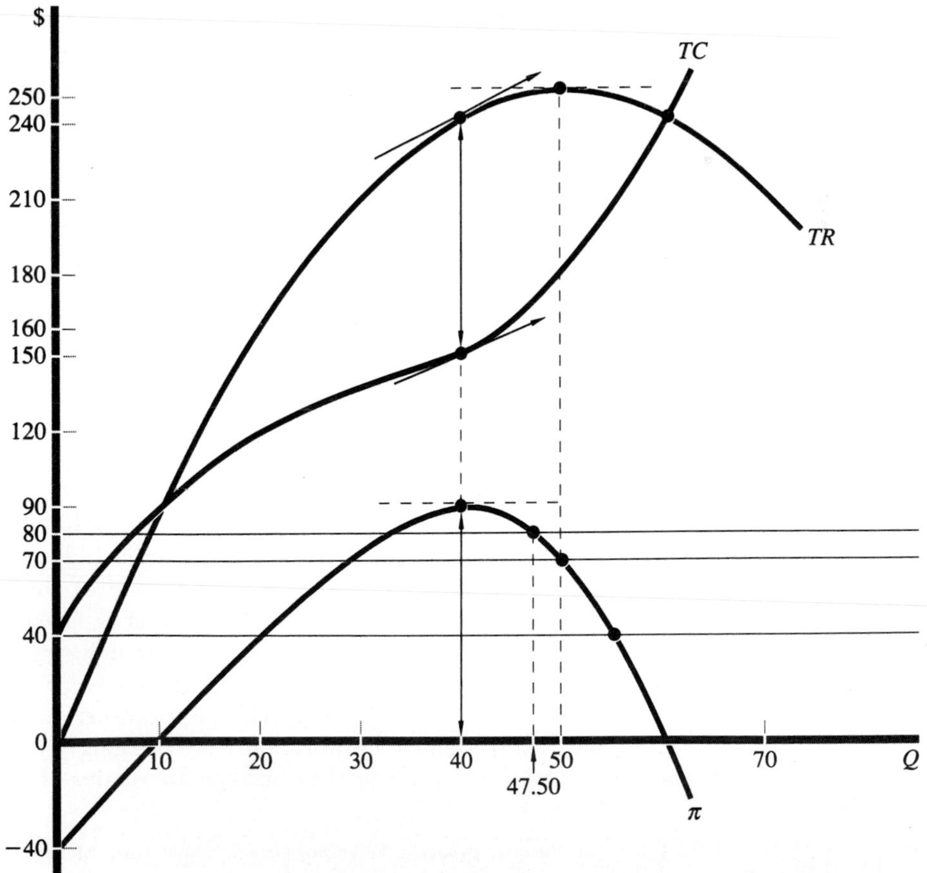

of return has been earned to satisfy stockholders.[7] Baumol argued that a larger firm may feel more secure, may be able to get better deals in the purchase of inputs and lower rates in borrowing money, and may have a better image with consumers, employees, and suppliers. Furthermore, and as pointed out in Section 1-2, some early empirical studies found that a strong correlation existed between executives' salaries and sales, but not between sales and profits. More recent studies, however, have found the opposite. The sales maximization model is presented here because it is particularly relevant in oligopolistic markets. The model can be shown with Figure 10-4.

In Figure 10-4, TR refers to the total revenue, TC to the total costs, and π to the total profits of the firm. $\pi = TR - TC$ and is maximized at \$90 at $Q = 40$ units where the positive difference between TR and TC is greatest (i.e., where the TR and TC curves are parallel). On the other hand, TR is maximum at \$250 where $Q = 50$, at which the slope of the TR curve or MR is zero and $\pi = \$70$ (see the figure). If the firm had to earn a profit of at least \$70 to satisfy the minimum profit constraint, the firm would produce 50 units of output and maximize TR at \$250 with $\pi = \$70$. The same would be true as long as the minimum profit requirement of the firm was equal to or smaller than \$70. With a minimum profit requirement between \$70 and \$90, however, the profit constraint would be binding. For example, to earn a profit of at least \$80, the firm would have to produce an output of about 47.50 units (see the figure). Finally, if the minimum profit requirement were higher than \$90, all that the firm could do would be to produce $Q = 40$ and maximize π at \$90 with $TR = \$240$.[8]

While these alternative and broader theories of the firm stress some relevant aspect of the operation of the modern corporation, they do not provide a satisfactory alternative to the theory of the firm postulated in Section 1-2. Indeed, the stiff competition prevailing in most product and resource markets as well as in managerial and entrepreneurial talent today forces managers to pay close attention to profits—lest the firm go out of business or they be replaced.

10-4 THE MARCH OF GLOBAL OLIGOPOLISTS

During the past decade the trend toward the formation of global oligopolies has accelerated as the world's largest corporations have been getting bigger and bigger through internal growth and mergers. Indeed, in more and more industries and sectors the pressure to become one of the largest global players seems irresistible. No longer are corporations satisfied to be the largest or the next-to-the-largest national company in their industry or sector. More and more corporations operate on the belief that their very survival requires that they become one of a handful of world corporations or global oligopolists in their sector. Many smaller corporations are merging with larger ones in the belief that either they grow or they become a casualty of the sharply increased

[7]W. J. Baumol, *Business Behavior, Value and Growth* (New York: Macmillan, 1959).

[8]For a mathematical presentation of the sales maximization mode, see the appendix to this chapter.

global competition. Strong impetus toward globalization has been provided by the sharp and rapid improvements in communications and transportation, the movement toward the globalization of tastes, and the reduction of barriers to international trade and investments.

The sector in which the size of the largest firm has grown the most during the past decades is international banking. From 1966 to 1994, the total deposits of the world's 10 largest banks grew from $87 billion to more than $4,000 billion. Even after accounting for the quadrupling of prices and exchange rate changes (to convert local currency values into dollar values), this meant that the size of the world's 10 largest banks increased by more than nine times during the past 30 years. It should also be pointed out that in 1966, 6 of the world's largest banks (including the first 4) were American. By 1995, the largest 8 banks were Japanese, the ninth was French, and the tenth was German. The largest American bank (Citicorp) was 29th! There is a great deal of disagreement, however, as to whether American banks are today too small to compete in the global market. It is often pointed out that after a certain size (already achieved by the largest 4 or 5 U.S. banks), stability and profitability are more important than size per se. Nevertheless, the growth in the size of the world's largest banks has been nothing but spectacular.[9]

Another sector where corporations have grown sharply in size and gone global has been in communications. The merger of Time Inc. and Warner Communications Inc. to form the world's largest communications company (American) and Japan's Sony Corporation's purchase of American Paramount Pictures for $3.4 billion in 1989 are only two of the latest examples of the growth and globalization that swept the communications industry worldwide during the 1980s. Most of the recent mergers involved the purchase of American companies by foreigners: Sony bought CBS Records, West Germany's Bertelsmann acquired RCA Records as well as Doubleday and Bantam Books, Ruppert Murdoch (from Australia but now residing in the United States) bought Harper & Row Publishers, Triangle Publications, and Twentieth-Century Fox. The reason given for most mergers in the communications industry is to become more competitive globally. "Competitive, according to the current conventional wisdom, means being equipped to become one of the five to eight giant corporations expected to dominate the world communications industry by the year 2000 or so. . . . These enterprises, the reasoning goes, will be able to produce and distribute information and entertainment in virtually any medium: books, magazines, news, television, movies, videos, cinemas, electronic data networks and so on."[10] This is expected to provide important synergies or cross benefits from joint operation.

The same growth toward globalization has occurred in industry. The total sales in real terms (i.e., after taking inflation into account) of the world's 25

[9]"The World's Biggest Commercial Banks," *Fortune,* July 31, 1989, p. 286; and "The World's Largest Commercial Banks," *Business Week,* September 30, 1994, p. R27.

[10]"Media Mergers: An Urge to Get Bigger and More Global," *The New York Times,* March 19, 1989, p. 7; and "American Banking Dinosaurs," *The Wall Street Journal,* March 18, 1992, p. A14.

largest *industrial* corporations increased 70 percent faster than the combined index of real total industrial production in all industrial countries from 1969 to 1979 and 50 percent faster from 1979 to 1990.[11] Thus, there has been a clear tendency for the largest industrial corporations to become relatively larger during the past two decades. The movement toward globalization is very clear in automobiles, where only a handful of global players survive. General Motors with 1993 sales of $134 billion and Ford with sales of $109 billion are the world's number one and number two largest industrial corporations. They are followed (with 1993 sales in billions of dollars) by Toyota (85), Daimler-Benz (59), Nissan (54), Volkwagen (46), Chrysler (44), Honda (36), Fiat (35), Renault (32), Peugeot (26), Mazda (20), BMW (18), and Volvo (14)—all in the world's largest 50 corporations—except for Mazda, which was 57th, BMW (64th), and Volvo (89th).[12] Even some of these are likely to merge. Globalization has proceeded even more rapidly in tires, where Goodyear (American), Bridgestone (Japanese), and Michelin (French) command more than half of the world's total sales, and further consolidation is expected.

The same type of globalization has been taking place in consumer products, food, drugs, electronics, and commercial aircraft. In 1989, Gillette introduced its new Sensor razor, which took 20 years and $300 million to develop, and is now marketing it in 19 countries around the world. Nestlé has production plants in 37 countries and sells its food products in more than 100 countries. America's Philip Morris, the world's largest tobacco and food company, Britain's Unilever, and Switzerland's Nestlé are among the world's 22 largest corporations, and America's RJR Nabisco, Sara Lee, and Pepsico are among the top 100. Coca-Cola has 40 percent of the U.S. market and an incredible 33 percent of the world's soft drink market. Despite the need to cater to local food tastes (Nestlé has more than 200 blends of Nescafé to cater to different local tastes), there is a clear trend toward global supermarkets. This has been the result of the cross-fertilization of cultures and convergences of tastes made possible by the tremendous improvements in communications and transportation. The same is true in drugs, chemicals, electronics, commercial aircraft, and other products, where a handful of huge corporations literally control the world market. It no longer makes any sense to talk about or be concerned only with national rather than global competition in these sectors. Bluntly, a large corporation can even be a monopolist in the national market and face deadly competition from larger and more efficient global oligopolists. The ideal global corporation is today strongly decentralized to allow local units to develop products that fit into the local cultures and yet at its core is very centralized to coordinate activities around the globe.[13]

[11]See *Fortune,* August 1970, May 1980, and July 1990.

[12]"The World's Largest Industrial Corporations," *Fortune,* July 25, 1994, pp. 113–114.

[13]"A View from the Top: Survival Tactics for the Global Business Arena," *Management Review,* October 1992, pp. 49–53.

Case Study 10-5
The Rising Competition in Global Banking

The late 1990s are likely to be an era of aggressively intensified competition in the high-stakes world of international banking, with only 6 to 10 of the 40 to 45 large international banks now aspiring to become global powerhouses attaining their goal. From the 1950s through the 1970s world banking was dominated by U.S. banks, while in the 1980s Japanese banks made a run for the top. During the 1990s, only Citicorp among U.S. banks is likely to make the mark and become the world's consumer bank. The reason is the weak capital base of U.S. banks and their soured loans to developing countries, on real estate, and for highly leveraged takeovers. In fact, in recent years, Chase Manhattan Bank, BankAmerica, Chemical Bank, and others have all sold or closed their operations abroad to cut losses. Japanese banks, while rich in assets, are poor on innovations and have recently been hit hard by rising interest rates, falling real estate and stock market prices, and intensified competition. Most future powerhouses in global banking are likely to be European (such as Germany's Deutsche Bank AG, Union Bank of Switzerland, Swiss Bank Corporation, and Britain's Barcley's Bank PLC) because they are well capitalized, were much less exposed to third-world problem loans, had much fewer bad real-estate and takeover credits, and have long been able to enter investment banking and insurance denied to U.S. banks.

With deregulation, each bank must increasingly compete with foreign banks at home and abroad to survive during the late 1990s. Global banks must be able to meet the rising financial needs for lending, underwriting, currency and security trading, insurance, financial advice, and other financial services for customers and investors with increasingly global operations. Global banks must also be highly innovative and introduce new financial products and technologies to meet changing customer needs. Overcapacity—too many banks chasing too few customers—will also increase competition. Large U.S. banks are strong on innovations but also need the right to operate without geographic and product constraints to be able to compete with foreign banks more successfully at home and abroad in the future.

Source: "Competition Rises in Global Banking," *The Wall Street Journal*, March 25, 1991, p. A1; and "International Banking Survey," *The Economist*, April 30, 1994, pp. 1–42.

Case Study 10-6
The Globalization of the Pharmaceutical Industry

The past few years have witnessed more than 15 mergers of large pharmaceutical companies. The largest of these were the merger of Bristol-Myers with Squibb, Marion with Merrel, Dow SmithKline with Beecham, Rhone-Poulec with Rorer, and Merck with Medco. As a result, the industry is today dominated by many global firms (the largest of which is U.S.'s Johnson & Johnson with 1993 sales of more than $14 billion). Competition is likely to lead to further consolidation and globalization of the industry during the rest of the 1990s. Some industry analysts are predicting that two-thirds of today's 20 largest U.S. drug companies will have merged, been bought or disappeared by the end of the decade. The same is likely to take place in Europe and Japan. The urge to merge even by today's largest industry players arises from the incredibly high cost of developing new drugs. It has been estimated that it now costs about $230 million (including failures and lost opportunity costs) to bring a new commercial drug to market. This is expected to rise to over $400 million by the end of the decade. Despite average profit rates of 13 to 14 percent, these huge development costs are becoming out of reach of even the largest drug companies. Hence the need for further consolidation and globalization in the industry.

Faced with growing competition at home and abroad, U.S. pharmaceutical companies are looking to increase sales abroad as never before. Nowhere is this more apparent than at Johnson & Johnson, which already has 175 operating units in 55 countries. Indeed, the company's fastest-growing drug in the United States (Hismanal, a nonsedating antihistamine) was discovered and developed by the company's Belgian unit and is now sold in 116 countries. While in the past, it licensed drugs to companies abroad in exchange for royalties (which are usually small), Johnson & Johnson now sells new drugs directly through its growing international sales force. Indeed, about half of the company's sales and 60 percent of profits are now generated outside the United States. Expansion abroad allows the firm to spread research costs over larger sales and reach a breakeven point on new drugs sooner.

Source: "Johnson and Johnson Looks Abroad," *The New York Times,* September 3, 1990, p. 27; "Drug Industry Still Has Room to Merge," *The Wall Street Journal,* June 25, 1991, p. A2; "Merck to Purchase Medco in $6 Billion Transaction," *The Wall Street Journal,* July 29, 1993, p. A3; and "Johnson & Johnson Is on a Roll," *Fortune,* December 26, 1994, pp. 178–192.

10-5 STRATEGIC BEHAVIOR AND GAME THEORY

In this section we explain the basic concepts, objectives, and usefulness of strategic behavior and game theory. We then go on to discuss the payoff matrix, the dominant strategy and Nash equilibrium, and examine their usefulness in the analysis of oligopolistic behavior.

Strategic Behavior and Game Theory: Meaning and Importance

Strategic behavior refers to the plan of action or behavior of an oligopolist, after taking into consideration all possible reactions of its competitors, as they compete for profits or other advantages. Since there are only a few firms in the industry, the actions of each affects the others, and the reaction of the others must be kept in mind by the first in charting its best course of action. Thus, each oligopolist changes the product price, the quantity of the product that it sells, the level of advertising, and so on, so as to maximize its profits after having considered all possible reactions of its competitors to each of its courses of action. The study of such strategic behavior is the subject matter of game theory.

Game theory was pioneered by the mathematician John von Neumann and the economist Oskar Morgenstern in 1944 and it was soon hailed as a breakthrough in the study of oligopoly.[14] In general, **game theory** is concerned with the choice of the best or optimal strategy in conflict situations. For example, game theory can help a firm determine the conditions under which lowering its price would not trigger a ruinous price war, whether the firm should build excess capacity to discourage entry into the industry even though this lowers the firm's short-run profits, and why cheating in a cartel usually leads to its collapse. In short, game theory shows how an oligopolistic firm makes strategic decisions to gain a competitive advantage over a rival or how it can minimize the potential harm from a strategic move by a rival.

Every game theory model includes players, strategies, and payoffs. The **players** are the decision-makers (here the managers of oligopolist firms) whose behavior we are trying to explain and predict. The **strategies** are the choices to change price, develop new products, undertake a new advertising campaign, build new capacity, and all other such actions that affect the sales and profitability of the firm and its rivals. The **payoff** is the outcome or consequence of each strategy. For each strategy adopted by a firm, there is usually a number of strategies (reactions) available to a rival firm. The payoff is the outcome or consequence of each combination of strategies by the two firms. The payoff is usually expressed in terms of the profits or losses of the firm that we are examining as a result of the firm's strategies and the rivals' responses. The table giving the payoffs from all the strategies open to the firm and the rivals' responses is called the **payoff matrix.**

Payoff Matrix for an Advertising Game

To see how players choose strategies to maximize their payoffs, let us begin with the simplest type of game in an industry (duopoly) composed of two firms, firm *A* and firm *B*, and a choice of two strategies for each—advertise or don't advertise. Firm *A*, of course, expects to earn higher profits if it advertises than if it doesn't. But the actual level of profits of firm *A* depends also on whether firm *B* advertises or not. Thus, each strategy by firm *A* (i.e., advertise or don't advertise) can be associated with each of firm *B*'s strategies (also to advertise or not to advertise).

The four possible outcomes for this simple game are illustrated by the payoff matrix in Table 10-3. The first number in each of the four cells refers to the payoff (profit) for firm *A*, while the second is the payoff (profit) for firm *B*. From Table 10-3, we see that if both firms advertise, firm *A* will earn a profit of 4, and firm *B* will earn a profit of 3 (the top left cell of the payoff matrix).[15] The bottom

[14] J. von Neumann and O. Morgenstern, *Theory of Games and Economic Behavior* (Princeton, N.J.: Princeton University Press, 1944). A more in-depth presentation of game theory with applications to economics and management is found in M. J. Osborne and A. Rubinstein, *A Course in Game Theory* (Cambridge, Mass.: MIT Press, 1994).

[15] The profits of 4 and 3 could refer, for example, to $4 million and $3 million, respectively.

Table 10-3
Payoff Matrix for an Advertising Game

		Firm *B*	
		Advertise	Don't Advertise
Firm *A*	Advertise	(4, 3)	(5, 1)
	Don't Advertise	(2, 5)	(3, 2)

left cell of the payoff matrix, on the other hand, shows that if firm *A* doesn't advertise and firm *B* does, firm *A* will have a profit of 2, and firm *B* will have a profit of 5. The other payoffs in the second column of the table can be similarly interpreted.

What strategy should each firm choose? Let us consider firm *A* first. If firm *B* does advertise (i.e., moving down the left column of Table 10-3), we see that firm *A* will earn a profit of 4 if it also advertises and 2 if it doesn't. Thus, firm *A* should advertise if firm *B* advertises. If firm *B* doesn't advertise (i.e., moving down the right column in Table 10-3), firm *A* would earn a profit of 5 if it advertises and 3 if it doesn't. Thus, firm *A* should advertise whether firm *B* advertises or not. Firm *A*'s profits would always be greater if it advertises than if it doesn't regardless of what firm *B* does. We can then say that advertising is the dominant strategy for firm *A*. The **dominant strategy** is the optimal choice for a player no matter what the opponent does.

The same is true for firm *B*. Whatever firm *A* does (i.e., whether firm *A* advertises or not), it would always pay for firm *B* to advertise. We can see this by moving across each row of Table 10-3. Specifically, if firm *A* advertises, firm *B*'s profit would be 3 if it advertises and 1 if it does not. Similarly, if firm *A* does not advertise, firm *B*'s profit would be 5 if it advertises and 2 if it doesn't. Thus, the dominant strategy for firm *B* is also to advertise.

In this case, both firm *A* and firm *B* have the dominant strategy of advertising, and this will, therefore, be the final equilibrium. Both firm *A* and firm *B* will advertise regardless of what the other firm does and will earn a profit of 4 and 3, respectively (the top left cell in the payoff matrix in Table 10-3). Note that in this case, the advertising solution or final equilibrium for both firms holds whether firm *A* or firm *B* chooses its strategy first, or if both firms decide on their best strategy simultaneously.

Nash Equilibrium

Not all games have a dominant strategy for each player, however. In fact, it is more likely in the real world that one or both players do not have a dominant strategy. An example of this is shown in the payoff matrix in Table 10-4. This is

Table 10-4
Payoff Matrix for the Advertising Game

		Firm *B*	
		Advertise	Don't Advertise
Firm *A*	Advertise	(4, 3)	(5, 1)
	Don't Advertise	(2, 5)	(6, 2)

the same as the payoff matrix in Table 10-3, except that the first number in the bottom right cell was changed from 3 to 6. Now firm *B* has a dominant strategy, but firm *A* does not. The dominant strategy for firm *B* is to advertise whether firm *A* advertises or not, exactly as above, because the payoffs for firm *B* are the same as in Table 10-3. Firm *A*, however, has no dominant strategy now. The reason is that if firm *B* advertises, firm *A* earns a profit of 4 if it advertises and 2 if it does not. Thus, if firm *B* advertises, firm *A* should also advertise. On the other hand, if firm *B* does not advertise, firm *A* earns a profit of 5 if it advertises and 6 if it does not.[16] Thus, firm *A* should advertise if firm *B* does, and it should not advertise if firm *B* doesn't. Firm *A* no longer has a dominant strategy. What firm *A* should do now depends on what firm *B* does.

In order for firm *A* to determine whether to advertise or not, firm *A* must first try to determine what firm *B* will do, and advertise if firm *B* does and not advertise if firm *B* does not. Since firm *A* knows the payoff matrix, it can figure out that firm *B* has the dominant strategy of advertising. Therefore, the optimal strategy for firm *A* is also to advertise (because firm *A* will earn a profit of 4 by advertising and 2 by not advertising—see the first column of Table 10-4). This is the Nash equilibrium, named after John Nash, the Princeton University mathematician and 1994 Nobel Prize winner who first formalized the notion in 1951.

The **Nash equilibrium** is the situation where each player chooses his or her optimal strategy, *given the strategy chosen by the other player.* In the above example, the high advertising strategy for firm *A* and firm *B* is the Nash equilibrium because, given that firm *B* chooses its dominant strategy of advertising, the optimal strategy for firm *A* is also to advertise. Note that when both firms had a dominant strategy, each firm was able to choose its optimal strategy regardless of the strategy adopted by its rival. Here, only firm *B* has a dominant strategy. Firm *A* does not. As a result, firm *A* cannot choose its optimal strategy independently of firm *B*'s strategy. Only when each player has chosen its optimal strategy given the strategy of the other player do we have a Nash equilibrium.

[16]This might result, for example, if firm *A*'s advertisement is not effective or if advertising adds more to firm *A*'s costs than to its revenues.

Case Study 10-7
Dell Computers and Nash Equilibrium

Dell Computers of Austin, Texas, a company created by 27-year-old Michael Dell in 1984, ended the 1994 fiscal year with revenues of more than $3.4 billion, making it the sixth largest computer company in the nation. By offering a 30-day money-back guarantee on the next day, free on-sight service through independent contractors for the first year of ownership and unlimited calls to a toll-free technical support line, Dell established a solid reputation for reliability, thus taking the fear and uncertainty out of mail-order computers. Dell will even mail a $25 check to any customer that does not get a Dell technician within five minutes of calling Dell's technical support line! Ordering a computer from Dell by mail is now like ordering a Big Mac at MacDonald's—you know exactly what you will get. By eliminating retailers, Dell was also able to charge lower prices than its larger and more established competitors. For example, Dell's selling and administrative expenses are 14 cents for each dollar of sales, compared with 24 cents for Apple and 30 cents for IBM. Dell ships comptuers by mail by adding only a 2 percent shipping charge to the sale price. When receiving a mail order, Dell technicians simply pick up the now-standard components from the shelf to assemble the particular PC ordered. It is simple, quick, and inexpensive. Thus, Dell has developed a dominant strategy—one that is optimal regardless of what competitors do. By doing so, Dell has become a kind of high-tech Wal-Mart.

Until recently, traditional computer firms such as IBM, Apple, Compaq, and others always thought that customers were willing to pay a substantial retail markup for the privilege of being able to go to a store and feel and touch the machine before buying it. Some still do. But by reducing fears and uncertainty from ordering computers through the mail, Dell was able to convince a growing number of customers to bypass the retailers and order directly from Dell by mail at lower prices. Today, roughly 20 percent of PCs are sold by mail in the United States. Given Dell's dominant and profitable strategy, IBM, Apple, Compaq, and Zenith quickly followed and set up their own mail-order departments and 800 phone lines in 1993 and 1994. Their dominant strategy of selling exclusively through retail outlets was knocked out by Dell's new market strategy, and so we now can say that the computer industry is in a Nash equilibrium. Given Dell's dominant strategy, the other major computer companies have decided to change their strategy and also sell by mail. This increased competition reduced profits at Dell.

Source: "Why Dell Is a Survivor," *Forbes,* October 12, 1992, pp. 82–91; "Compaq Also to Sell Its PC's Direct," *The New York Times,* March 12, 1993, p. D3; and "The Kid Bytes Back," *U.S. News & World Report,* December 12, 1994, pp. 70–76.

10-6 THE PRISONERS' DILEMMA, PRICE AND NONPRICE COMPETITION, AND CARTEL CHEATING

In this section, we first examine the meaning of the prisoners' dilemma and then see its applicability to explain oligopolistic behavior in the form of price and nonprice competition and cartel cheating.

The Prisoners' Dilemma

Oligopolistic firms often face a problem called the **prisoners' dilemma.** This refers to a situation in which each firm adopts its dominant strategy but each could do better (i.e., earn larger profits) by cooperating. To understand this, consider the following situation. Two suspects are arrested for armed robbery, and if convicted, each could receive a maximum sentence of 10 years imprisonment. However, unless one or both suspects confess, the evidence is such that they could be convicted only of possessing stolen goods, which carries a maximum sentence of 1 year in prison. Each suspect is interrogated separately, and no communication is allowed between the two suspects. The district attorney promises each suspect that by confessing, he will go free while the other suspect (who does not confess) will receive the full 10-year sentence. If both suspects confess, each gets a reduced sentence of 5 years' imprisonment. The (negative) payoff matrix in terms of years of detention is given in Table 10-5.

From Table 10-5, we see that confessing is the best or dominant strategy for suspect *A* no matter what suspect *B* does. The reason is that if suspect *B* confesses, suspect *A* receives a 5-year sentence if he confesses and a 10-year jail sentence if he does not. Similarly, if suspect *B* does not confess, suspect *A* goes free if he confesses and receives a 1-year jail sentence if he does not. Thus, the dominant strategy for suspect *A* is to confess. Confessing is also the best or dominant strategy for suspect *B*. The reason is that if suspect *A* confesses, suspect *B* gets a 5-year jail sentence if he also confesses and a 10-year jail sentence if he does not. Similarly, if suspect *A* does not confess, suspect *B* goes free if he confesses and gets 1 year if he does not. Thus, the dominant strategy for suspect *B* is also to confess.

With each suspect adopting his dominant strategy of confessing, each ends up receiving a 5-year jail sentence. But if each suspect did not confess, each would get only a 1-year jail sentence! Each suspect, however, is afraid that if he does not confess, the other will confess, so that he would end up receiving a 10-year jail sentence. Only if each suspect was sure the other would not confess and he himself does not confess would each get away with only a 1-year sentence. Since it is not possible to reach agreement not to confess (remember the suspects are already in jail and cannot communicate), each suspect adopts his dominant strategy to

Table 10-5
Negative Payoff Matrix (Years of Detention) for Suspect *A* and Suspect *B*

		Individual *B*	
		Confess	**Don't Confess**
Individual *A*	**Confess**	(5, 5)	(0, 10)
	Don't Confess	(10, 0)	(1, 1)

confess and receives a 5-year jail sentence. Note that even if an agreement not to confess could be reached, the agreement could not be enforced. Therefore, each suspect will end up confessing and receiving a 5-year jail sentence.

Price Competition and the Prisoners' Dilemma

The concept of the prisoners' dilemma can be used to analyze price and nonprice competition in oligopolistic markets, as well as the incentive to cheat (i.e., the tendency to secretly cut price or sell more than its allocated quota) in a cartel. Oligopolistic price competition in the presence of the prisoners' dilemma can be examined with the payoff matrix in Table 10-6.

The payoff matrix of Table 10-6 shows that if firm *B* charged a low price (say, $6), firm *A* would earn a profit of 2 if it also charged the low price ($6) and 1 if it charged a high price (say, $8). Similarly, if firm *B* charged a high price ($8), firm *A* would earn a profit of 5 if it charged the low price and 3 if it charged the high price. Thus, firm *A* should adopt its dominant strategy of charging the low price. Turning to firm *B*, we see that if firm *A* charged the low price, firm *B* would earn a profit of 2 if it charged the low price and 1 if it charged the high price. Similarly, if firm *A* charged the high price, firm *B* would earn a profit of 5 if it charged the low price and 3 if it charged the high price. Thus, firm *B* should also adopt its dominant strategy of charging the low price. However, both firms could do better (i.e., earn the higher profit of 3) if they cooperated and both charged the high price (the bottom right cell).

Thus, the firms are in a prisoners' dilemma: Each firm will charge the low price and earn a smaller profit because if it charges the higher price, it cannot trust its rival to also charge the high price. Specifically, suppose that firm *A* charged the high price in the expectation that firm *B* would also charge the high price (so that each firm would earn a profit of 3). Given that firm *A* has charged the high price, however, firm *B* has now an incentive to charge the low price because by doing so it can increase its profits to 5 (see the bottom left cell). The same is true if firm *B* started by charging the high price in the expectation that firm *A* would also do so. The net result is that each firm charges the low price and earns a profit of only 2. Only if the two firms learned to cooperate and both charged the high price would they earn the higher profit of 3 (and overcome their dilemma).

Table 10-6
Payoff Matrix for a Pricing Game

		Firm *B*	
		Low Price	High Price
Firm *A*	Low Price	(2, 2)	(5, 1)
	High Price	(1, 5)	(3, 3)

Nonprice Competition, Cartel Cheating, and the Prisoners' Dilemma

Although the payoff matrix of Table 10-6 was used above to examine oligopolistic price competition in the presence of the prisoners' dilemma, by simply changing the heading of the columns and rows of the payoff matrix, we can use the same payoff matrix to also examine nonprice competition and cartel cheating. For example, if we changed (penciled in) the heading of "low price" to "advertise" and changed the heading of "high price" to "don't adverstise" in the columns and rows of the payoff matrix of Table 10-6, we can utilize the same payoff matrix of Table 10-6 to analyze advertising as a form of nonprice competition in the presence of the prisoners' dilemma. We would then see that each firm would adopt its dominant strategy of advertising and (as in the case of charging a low price) would earn a profit of 2. Both firms, however, would do better by not advertising because they would then earn (as in the case of charging a high price) the higher profit of 3. The firms then face the prisoners' dilemma. Only by cooperating in not advertising would each increase its profits to 3. For example, when cigarette advertising on television was banned in 1971, all tobacco companies benefited by spending less on advertising and earning higher profits. While the intended effect of the law was not to encourage people to smoke, the law also had the unintended effect of solving the prisoners' dilemma for cigarette producers!

Similarly, if we now changed the heading of "low price" or "advertise" to "cheat" and the heading of "high price" or "don't advertise" to "don't cheat" in the columns and rows of the payoff matrix of Table 10-6, we could use the same payoffs in Table 10-6 to analyze the incentive for cartel members to cheat in the presence of the prisoners' dilemma. In this case, each firm adopts its dominant strategy of cheating and (as in the case of charging the low price or advertising) earns a profit of 2. But by not cheating, each member of the cartel would earn the higher profit of 3. The cartel members then face the prisoners' dilemma. Only if cartel members do not cheat will each share the higher cartel profits of 3. A cartel can prevent or reduce the probability of cheating by monitoring the sales of each member and punishing cheaters. However, the greater the number of members of the cartel and the more differentiated is the product, the more difficult it is for the cartel to do this and prevent cheating.

Case Study 10-8

The Airlines' Fare War and the Prisoners' Dilemma

In April 1992, American Airlines, the nation's largest carrier with 20 percent share of the domestic market, introduced a new simplified fare structure that included only four kinds of fares instead of 16, and it lowered prices for most business and leisure travelers. Coach fares were cut by an average of 38 percent, and first-class fares were lowered by 20 to 50 percent. Other domestic airlines quickly announced similar fare cuts. American and other carriers hoped that the increase in air travel resulting from the fare cuts would more than offset the price reductions and eventually turn losses into badly needed profits [during 1990 and 1991, domestic airlines lost more than $6 billion, Pan Am and

Eastern Airlines went out of business, and Continental, Trans World Airlines (TWA), and America West filed for bankruptcy protection].

Rather than establishing price discipline, however, American's new fare structure started a process of competitive fare cuts that led to another disastrous price war during the summer of 1992. It started when TWA, operating under protection from creditors and badly needing quick revenues, began to undercut American's fares by 10 to 20 percent as soon as they were announced. American and other airlines responded by matching TWA price cuts. Then, on May 26, 1992, Northwest, in an effort to stimulate summer leisure travel, announced that an adult and child could travel on the same flight within continental United States for the price of one ticket. The next day, American countered by cutting all fares by 50 percent. The other big carriers immediately matched American's 50 percent price cut for all summer travel. Another full-fledged price war had been unleashed.

Even though deep price cuts increased summer travel sharply, all airlines incurred losses (i.e., the low fares failed to cover the industry average cost). Three attempts to increase air fares by 30 percent above presale levels in the fall of 1992 failed when one or more of the carriers did not go along. Having become used to deep discounts, passengers were simply unwilling to pay higher fares, especially in a weak economy. Similar price wars erupted in summer 1993 and 1994. In the meantime, many airlines started to imitate Southwest Airlines and provided an increasing number of no-frills flights at deep discounts (billed as "peanuts fares") in the hope of greatly stimulating air travel and taking away passengers from competitors. But losses continue. In short, U.S. airlines are in a prisoners' dilemma and, unable to cooperate, face heavy losses.

Source: "American Air Cuts Most Fares in Simplification of Rate System," *The New York Times,* April 10, 1992, p. 1; "The Airlines Are Killing Each Other Again," *Business Week,* June 8, 1992, p. 32; "Airlines Tally the Damage from Summer's Fare War," *The New York Times,* September 12, 1992, p. 1; "Airlines Cut Fares by up to 45%," *The New York Times,* September 14, 1993, p. D1; and "Come Fly the Unfriendly Skies," *The Economist,* November 5, 1994, pp. 61–62.

10-7 EXTENSIONS OF GAME THEORY

In this section, we examine repeated games and games involving threats, commitments, credibility, and entry deterrence. These concepts greatly enrich game theory and provide an important element of realism and relevance.

Repeated Games and Tit-for-Tat

We have seen above how two firms facing the prisoners' dilemma can increase their profits by cooperating. Such cooperation, however, is not likely to occur in the type of prisoners' dilemma games discussed until now, which are played only once (i.e., that involve a single move or action by each player). Cooperation is more likely to occur in repeated games, or games involving many consecutive moves by each player. These types of games are more realistic in the real world. For example, oligopolists do not decide on their pricing strategy only once but many times over many years.

In **repeated games** (i.e., in games involving many consecutive moves and countermoves by each player), the best strategy for each player is tit-for-tat. **Tit-for-tat** behavior can be summarized as follows: Do to your opponent what he has just done to you. That is, you begin by cooperating and continue to cooperate as long as your opponent cooperates. If he betrays you, the next time you betray him back. If he then cooperates, the next time you also cooperate. This strategy is retaliatory enough to discourage noncooperation, but forgiving enough to allow a pattern of mutual cooperation to develop. In computer simulation as well as in actual experiments, a tit-for-tat behavior was found to be consistently the best strategy (i.e., the one that resulted in the largest benefit) for each player over time.[17]

For a tit-for-tat strategy to be best, however, certain conditions must be met. First, it requires a reasonably stable set of players. If the players change frequently, there is little chance for cooperative behavior to develop. Second, there must be a small number of players (otherwise, it becomes very difficult to keep track of what each is doing). Third, it is assumed that each firm can quickly detect (and is willing and able to quickly retaliate for) cheating by other firms. Cheating that can go undetected for a long time encourages cheating. Fourth, demand and cost conditions must be relatively stable (for if they change rapidly, it is difficult to define what is cooperative behavior and what is not). Fifth, we must assume that the game is repeated indefinitely, or at least a very large and *uncertain* number of times. If the game is played for a finite number of times, each firm has an incentive not to cooperate in the final period since it cannot be harmed by retaliation. However, each firm knows this and thus will not cooperate on the next-to-the-last move. Indeed, in an effort to gain a competitive advantage by being the first to start cheating, the entire situation will unravel, and cheating begins from the first move.[18]

There are, of course, times when a firm finds that it is to its advantage not to cooperate. For example, if a supplier is near bankruptcy, a firm may find every excuse for not paying its bills to the near-bankrupt firm (claiming, for example, that supplies were defective or did not meet specification) in the hope of avoiding payment altogether if the firm does go out of business. It is the necessity to deal with the same suppliers and customers in the future and their ability to retaliate for noncooperative behavior that often forces a firm to cooperate. With a tit-for-tat strategy, however, it is possible for firms to cooperate without actually resorting to collusion. As we will see in Chapter 12, this can be a nightmare for antitrust officials.

Threat, Commitments, and Credibility

Oligopolistic firms often adopt strategies to gain a competitive advantage over their rivals even if it means constraining their own behavior or temporarily reducing their own profits. For example, an oligopolist may threaten to lower its

[17]See R. Axelrod, *The Evolution of Cooperation* (New York: Basic Books, 1984).

[18]See D. Kreps, P. Milgron, J. Roberts, and R. Wilson, "Rational Cooperation in the Finitely Repeated Prisoners' Dilemma," *Journal of Economic Theory,* vol. 27, 1982, pp. 245–252.

Table 10-7
Payoff Matrix for Pricing Game with a Threat

		Firm *B*	
		Low Price	High Price
Firm *A*	Low Price	(2, 2)	(2, 1)
	High Price	(3, 4)	(5, 3)

prices if its rivals lower theirs, even if this means reducing its own profits. This threat can be made credible, for example, by a written commitment to customers to match any lower price by competitors.

For example, suppose that the payoff matrix of firms *A* and *B* is given by Table 10-7. This payoff matrix indicates that firm *A* has the dominant strategy of charging a high price. The reason is that if firm *B* charged a low price, firm *A* would earn a profit of 2 if it charged a low price and a profit of 3 if it charged a high price. Similarly, if firm *B* charged a high price, firm *A* would earn a profit of 2 if it charged a low price and a profit of 5 if it charged a high price. Therefore, firm *A* charges a high price regardless of what firm *B* does. Given that firm *A* charges a high price, firm *B* will want to charge a low price because by doing so it will earn a profit of 4 (instead of 3 with a high price). This is shown by the bottom left cell of Table 10-7. Now firm *A* can threaten firm *B* to lower its price and also charge a low price. However, firm *B* does not believe this threat (i.e., the threat is not credible) because by lowering its price, firm *A* would lower its profits from 3 (with a high price) to 2 with the low price (the top left cell in the table).

One way to make this threat credible is for firm *A* to develop a *reputation* for carrying out its threats—even at the expense of profits. This may seem irrational. However, if firm *A* actually carries out its threat several times, it would earn a reputation for making credible threats, and this is likely to induce firm *B* to also charge a high price, thus possibly leading to higher profits for firm *A* in the long run. In that case, firm *A* would earn a profit of 5 and firm *B* a profit of 3 (the bottom right cell) as opposed to a profit of 3 for firm *A* and 4 for firm *B* (the bottom left cell). Note that even if firm *B* earns a profit of 3 by charging the high price (as compared with a profit of 4 by charging the low price), this is still higher than the profit of 2 that it would earn if firm *A* carries out the threat of charging the low price if firm *B* does (see the top left cell of the table). By showing a commitment to carry out its threats, firm *A* makes its threats credible and increases its profits over time.

Entry Deterrence

One important strategy that an oligopolist can use to deter market entry is to threaten to lower its price and thereby impose a loss on the potential entrant. Such a threat, however, works only if it is credible. *Entry deterrence* can be examined with the payoff matrices of Tables 10-8 and 10-9. Let us start with the payoff matrix of Table 10-8.

The payoff matrix of Table 10-8 shows that firm *A*'s threat to lower its price is not credible and does not discourage firm *B* from entering the market. The reason is that firm *A* earns a profit of 4 if it charges the low price and a profit of 7 if it charges the high price. Unless firm *A* makes a credible commitment to fight entry even at the expense of profits, it would not deter firm *B* from entering the market. Firm *A* could make a credible threat by expanding its capacity before it is needed (i.e., to build excess capacity). The new payoff matrix might then look like the one indicated in Table 10-9.

The payoff matrix of Table 10-9 is the same as in Table 10-8, except that firm *A*'s profits are now lower when it charges a high price because idle or excess capacity increases firm *A*'s costs without increasing its sales. On the other hand, in the payoff matrix of Table 10-9, we assume that charging a low price would allow firm *A* to increase sales and utilize its newly built capacity so that costs and revenues increase, leaving firm *A*'s profits the same as in Table 10-8 (i.e., the same as before firm *A* expanded capacity).[19] Building excess capacity in anticipation of future needs now becomes a credible threat because with excess capacity firm *A* will charge a low price and earn

[19]Revenues and profits need not increase exactly by the same amount, so that profits can change even when firm *A* charges a low price. The conclusion would remain the same, however (i.e., firm *B* would be deterred from entering the market) as long as firm *A* earns a higher profit with a low price than with a high price after increasing its capacity.

Table 10-8
Payoff Matrix without Credible Entry Deterrence

		Firm *B*	
		Enter	**Do Not Enter**
Firm *A*	**Low Price**	(4, −2)	(6, 0)
	High Price	(7, 2)	(10, 0)

Table 10-9
Payoff Matrix with Credible Entry Deterrence

		Firm *B*	
		Enter	**Do Not Enter**
Firm *A*	**Low Price**	(4, −2)	(6, 0)
	High Price	(3, 2)	(8, 0)

a profit of 4 instead of a profit of 3 if it charged the high price. By now charging a low price, however, firm *B* would incur a loss of 2 if it entered the market, and so firm *B* would stay out. Entry deterrence is now credible and effective. An alternative to building excess capacity could be for firm *A* to cultivate a reputation for irrationality in deterring entry by charging a low price even if this means earning lower profits indefinitely.[20]

[20]For a more detailed analysis of the use of excess capacity to deter entry, see J. Tirole, *The Theory of Industrial Organization* (Cambridge, Mass.: MIT Press, 1988).

Case Study 10-9

Wal-Mart's Preemptive Expansion Marketing Strategy

Rapid expansion during the 1980s (from 153 stores in 1976 to more than 2,500 in 1994) propelled Wal-Mart, the discount retail-store chain started by Sam Walton in 1969, to become the nation's largest and most profitable retailer, at a time when most other retailers were making razor-thin profits or incurring losses as a result of stiff competition. How did Wal-Mart do it? By opening retail discount stores in small towns across America and adopting an everyday low-price strategy. The conventional wisdom had been that a discount retail outlet required a population base of at least 100,000 people to be profitable. Sam Walton showed otherwise—by relying on size, low costs, and high turnover, Wal-Mart earned high profits even in towns of only a few thousand people. Since a small town could support only one large discount store, Wal-Mart did not have to worry about competition from other national chains (which would drive prices and profit margins down). At the same time, Wal-Mart was able to easily undersell small local specialized stores out of existence (Wal-Mart has been labeled the "Merchant of Death" by local retailers), thereby establishing a virtual local retailing monopoly.

The success of Wal-Mart did not go unnoticed by other national discount retailers such as Kmart and Target, and so a frantic race started to open discount stores in rural America ahead of the competition. By adopting such an aggressive expansion or *preemptive investment strategy,* Wal-Mart has continued to expand at breathtaking speed and to beat the competition most of the time. Sales at Wal-Mart were in excess of $80 billion in 1994 and are projected to surpass $100 billion in a few years. Wal-Mart has also started opening stores in Canada and Latin America. As Wal-Mart expands to suburban areas and as a revitalized Kmart and Target push into rural areas, however, the paths of these mammoth chains are likely to cross more and more frequently across America for what promises to be one of retailing's fiercest fights in the 1990s.

Source: "3 Discounters on a Collision Course," *The New York Times,* September 23, 1991, p. D1; "Can Wal-Mart Keep Growing at Breakneck Speed?" *The New York Times,* August 9, 1992, p. F5; and "Wal-Mart to Continue International Expansion," *The Wall Street Journal,* June 4, 1994, p. 37.

10-8 STRATEGIC BEHAVIOR AND INTERNATIONAL COMPETITIVENESS

Game theory can also be used to examine strategic trade and industrial policies that a nation can use to gain a competitive advantage over other nations, particularly in the high-technology field. We can best show this by an example.

Suppose that Boeing (the American commercial aircraft company) and Airbus Industrie (a consortium of German, French, English, and Spanish companies) are both deciding whether to produce a new aircraft. Suppose also that because of the huge cost of developing the new aircraft, a single producer would have to have the entire world market for itself to earn a profit, say, of $100 million. If both firms produce the aircraft, each loses $10 million. This information is shown in Table 10-10. The case where both firms produce the aircraft and each incurs a loss of $10 million is shown in the top left cell of Table 10-10. If only Boeing produces the aircraft, Boeing makes a profit of $100 million while Airbus makes a zero profit (the top right cell of the table). On the other hand, if Boeing does not produce the aircraft while Airbus does, Boeing makes zero profit while Airbus makes a profit of $100 million (the bottom left cell). Finally, if neither firm produces the aircraft, each makes a zero profit (the bottom right cell).

Suppose that for whatever reason Boeing enters the market first and earns a profit of $100 million (we might call this the "first-mover advantage"). Airbus is now locked out of the market because it could not earn a profit. This is the case shown in the top right cell of the table. If Airbus entered the market, both firms would incur a loss (and we would have the case shown in the top left column of the table). Suppose that now European governments give a subsidy of $15 million per year to Airbus. Then Airbus will produce the aircraft even though Boeing is already producing the aircraft because with the $15 million subsidy Airbus would turn a loss of $10 million into a profit of $5 million. Without a subsidy, however, Boeing will then go from making a profit of $100 million (without Airbus in the market) to incurring a loss of $10 million afterward (we are still in the top left corner of the table, but with the Airbus entry changed from −10 without the subsidy to +5 with the subsidy). Because of its unsubsidized loss, Boeing will then stop producing the aircraft, thus leaving the entire market to Airbus, which

Table 10-10
Two-Firm Competition and Strategic Trade Policy

		Airbus	
		Produce	**Don't Produce**
Boeing	**Produce**	(−10, −10)	(100, 0)
	Don't Produce	(0, 100)	(0, 0)

will then make a profit of $100 million without any further subsidy (the bottom left cell of the table).[21]

The U.S. government could, of course, retaliate with a subsidy of its own to keep Boeing producing the aircraft. Except in cases of national defense, however, the U.S. government is much less disposed to grant subsidies to firms than European governments. While the real world is certainly much more complex than this, we can see how a nation could overcome a market disadvantage and acquire a strategic comparative advantage in a high-tech field by using an industrial and strategic trade policy. In fact, Airbus is now exploring the possibility of developing an aircraft capable of carrying 500 to 600 passengers, which would compete head on with the Boeing 747 (which can carry up to 475 passengers). This is why the United States is now insisting that the governments of France, Germany, England, and Spain sharply reduce development subsidies to Airbus (which, over the past decade amounted to more than $26 billion dollars). Boeing, however, continued to earn high profits even as it lost market share to Airbus.[22]

One serious shortcoming of this analysis is that it is usually very difficult to accurately forecast the outcome of government industrial and trade policies (i.e., get the data to fill a table such as Table 10-10). Even a small change in the table could completely change the results. For example, suppose that if both Airbus and Boeing produce the aircraft, Airbus incurs a loss of $10 million (as before) but Boeing now makes a profit of $10 million (without any subsidy), say, because of superior technology. Then, even if Airbus produces the aircraft with the subsidy, Boeing will remain in the market because it makes a profit without any subsidy. Then, Airbus would require a subsidy indefinitely year after year in order to continue to produce the aircraft. In this case giving a subsidy to Airbus does not seem to be such a good idea. Thus, it is extremely difficult to correctly carry out this type of analysis. We would have to be able to correctly forecast the precise outcome of different strategies, and this is very difficult to do. This is why most economists are wary of supporting the adoption of a full-fledged industrial policy and still regard free trade as the best policy for the United States.[23]

SUMMARY

1. Oligopoly is the form of market organization in which there are few sellers of a homogeneous or differentiated product, and entry into or exit from the industry is possible but difficult. Oligopoly is the most prevalent form of market organization in the manufacturing sector. The dis-

[21]This type of analysis was first introduced into international trade by James Brander and Barbara Spencer. See their "International R & D Rivalry and Industrial Strategy," *Review of Economic Studies,* October 1983, pp. 707–722; see also M. Porter, *The Competitive Advantage of Nations* (New York: The Free Press, 1990).

[22]"A Paper Dart Against Boeing," *The Economist,* June 11, 1994, pp. 61–62.

[23]"Remember Clinton's Industrial Policy? O.K. Now Forget It," *Business Week,* December 12, 1994, p. 53; and P. Krugman, "Is Free Trade Passe?" *The Journal of Economic Perspectives,* Fall 1987, pp. 131–144.

tinguishing characteristic of oligopoly is the interdependence or rivalry among the firms in the industry. The sources of oligopoly are similar to those of monopoly. The degree by which an industry is dominated by a few large firms is measured by concentration ratios and the Herfindahl index. According to the theory of contestable markets, vigorous competition can take place even among few sellers if entry into the market is absolutely free and exit is entirely costless.

2. The kinked demand curve model attempted to explain the price rigidity often encountered in oligopolistic markets by postulating a demand curve with a kink at the prevailing price. A centralized cartel can reach the monopoly solution. Another form of market collusion is the market-sharing cartel. An example of tacit collusion is price leadership by the dominant or barometric firm. Oligopoly may lead to many of the harmful effects of monopoly. In addition, oligopolists generally spend too much on advertising and model changes. However, economies of scale make large-scale production and oligopoly inevitable in many industries.
3. The sales maximization model postulates that oligopolistic firms seek to maximize sales after a satisfactory rate of profit has been earned to satisfy stockholders. In the past, evidence was introduced that executives' salaries were correlated more with sales than with profits (thus, providing support for the sales maximization model). More recently, the opposite has been found. In general, the profit maximization model provides the best vantage point from which to study the behavior of firms.
4. During the past decade, the trend toward the formation of global oligopolies has accelerated as the world's largest corporations have been getting bigger and bigger through internal growth and mergers. More and more, corporations operate on the belief that their very survival requires that they become one of a handful of world corporations, or global oligopolists, in their sector.
5. Strategic behavior is concerned with the choice of an optimal strategy in conflict situations and is analyzed with game theory. Every game theory model includes players, strategies, and payoffs. The dominant strategy is the best or optimal choice for a player no matter what the opponent does. The Nash equilibrium occurs when each player has chosen his or her optimal strategy, given the strategy chosen by the other player.
6. Oligopolistic firms often face a problem called the prisoners' dilemma. This refers to a situation in which each firm adopts its dominant strategy but could do better (i.e., earn a larger profit) by cooperating. Oligopolistic firms deciding on their pricing or advertising strategy, or on whether or not to cheat in a cartel, may face the prisoners' dilemma. In those cases, both firms would gain by shifting from a noncooperative to a cooperative game.
7. The best strategy for repeated or multiple-move prisoners' dilemma games is tit-for-tat, which refers to doing to your opponent what he or she has just done to you. A player must show a commitment to carry out a threat for it to be credible.

8. Just like firms, nations can behave strategically by protecting and subsidizing some high-tech industry in order to gain a competitive advantage over other nations. It is very difficult, however, to carry out a successful industrial policy, and so free trade remains the best policy in most cases.

DISCUSSION QUESTIONS

1. (*a*) What is the distinguishing characteristic of oligopoly in relation to other forms of market organization? What is the significance of this? (*b*) In which sector of the U.S. economy is oligopoly most prevalent? Why?
2. (*a*) What are the advantages of the Herfindahl index over concentration ratios? (*b*) What is the disadvantage of both?
3. What is the difference between limit pricing and contestable markets?
4. (*a*) What alleged pricing behavior of oligopolists does the kinked demand curve seek to explain? (*b*) How does the model seek to accomplish this? (*c*) What criticism does the model face?
5. (*a*) Why do we study cartels if they are illegal in the United States? (*b*) Why are cartels unstable, and why do they often fail? (*c*) In what way does OPEC resemble a cartel? How successful is it?
6. Since under price leadership by the dominant firm, the firms in the industry following the leader behave as perfect competitors or price takers by always producing where the price set by the leader equals the sum of their marginal cost curves, the followers break even in the long run. True or false? Explain.
7. (*a*) What does the sales maximization model postulate? (*b*) Under what conditions does this model give the same results as the profit maximization model? When does it not? (*c*) How relevant or useful is the sales maximization model? (*d*) What is the most important reason for the rise and rapid spread of global oligopolists?
8. Do we have a Nash equilibrium when each firm chooses its dominant strategy?
9. In what way is the prisoners' dilemma related to the choice of dominant strategies by the players in a game and to the concept of Nash equilibrium?
10. How can the concept of the prisoners' dilemma be used to analyze price competition?
11. How can introducing yearly style changes lead to a prisoners' dilemma for automakers?
12. (*a*) What is the meaning of "tit-for-tat" in game theory? (*b*) What conditions are usually required for tit-for-tat to be the best strategy?

PROBLEMS

1. Find the Herfindahl index for an industry composed of (*a*) three firms—one with 70 percent of the market, and the other two with 20 and 10 percent of the market, respectively; (*b*) one firm with a 50 percent share of the market and 10 other equal-sized firms; (*c*) 10 equal-sized firms.

*2. The research department of the Computer Supplies Corporation, a producer of computer diskettes, has estimated that the demand function facing the firm for price increases and price declines from the prevailing price are, respectively,

$$Q = 210 - 30P \qquad \text{and} \qquad Q' = 90 - 10P$$

The marginal and average total cost functions of the firm were also estimated to be, respectively,

$$MC = 3.5 + \frac{Q}{30} \qquad \text{and} \qquad ATC = 3.5 + \frac{Q}{60}$$

(*a*) Draw the demand, marginal revenue, marginal cost, and average total cost curves of the firm. (*b*) Determine the best level of output of the firm, the price at which the firm sells its output, as well as the profit per unit and in total. (*c*) Within what range can the *MC* curve of the firm shift without inducing it to change its price and output?

3. Suppose that the demand function for price increases for the firm in Problem 6 shifts to $Q^* = 150 - 30P$. (*a*) Draw a figure showing the best level of output, price, and profits per unit and in total. (*b*) Has the price of the firm changed or remained the same? Why?

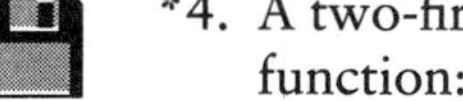

*4. A two-firm cartel producing industrial diamonds faces the following demand function:

$$Q = 120 - 10P \qquad \text{or} \qquad Q = 12 - 0.1P$$

The marginal cost and the average total cost functions of each firm are, respectively,

$$MC_1 = 4 + 0.2Q_1 \qquad \text{and} \qquad ATC_1 = 4 + 0.1Q_1$$
$$MC_2 = 2 + 0.2Q_2 \qquad \text{and} \qquad ATC_2 = 2 + 0.1Q_2$$

Draw a figure showing the best level of output and price for the cartel, the output of each firm to minimize the total costs of production for the cartel, and calculate the profits per unit and in total for each firm.

5. Plains, an isolated farming town, is cut in half by a highway, and each side of town has a supplier of fertilizer. John, one of the suppliers, learned that the other, Joe, was planning to open a store on his side of town. John was very concerned with this and called Joe to arrange a meeting in which he threatened to open another store on Joe's side of town. Joe took the threat

seriously and agreed at the meeting with John that each would remain only on his side of town, thus basically setting up a market-sharing cartel. Suppose that the total market demand for fertilizer in Plains is $Q = 120 - 10P$, where Q is in pounds and P is in dollars. John and Joe face MC and ATC functions equal to $MC = 0.2$ and $ATC = 0.1Q$. (*a*) Draw a figure showing the best level of output, price, and profit of each firm, and (*b*) explain why this market-sharing cartel reaches the monopoly solution. Is this realistic in the real world? Why?

6. Assume that (1) the 10 identical firms in a purely oligopolistic industry form a centralized cartel; (2) the total market demand function facing the cartel is $Q = 240 - 10P$, where P is given in dollars; and (3) each firm's marginal cost function is $MC = \$1$ for $Q > 4$ units, and factor prices remain constant. Find (*a*) the best level of output and price for this cartel, (*b*) how much each firm should produce if the cartel wants to minimize costs of production, and (*c*) how much profit the cartel will make if $ATC = \$12$ at the best level.

7. Assume that (1) two firms selling a homogeneous product share the market equally, (2) the total market demand schedule facing each firm is $Q = 240 - 10P$, and (3) the cost schedules of each firm are the ones shown below. (*a*) What would be the total profit of each firm if each were producing its best level of output? (*b*) What is the most likely result? (*c*) What other result is possible?

Q_1	40	50	60	80	Q_2	50	70	100
MC_1 (\$)	8	10	12	16	MC_2 (\$)	4	6	9
ATC_1 (\$)	13	12.30	12	13	ATC_2 (\$)	7	6	7

8. From the following payoff matrix, where the payoffs are the profits or losses of the two firms, determine (*a*) whether firm *A* has a dominant strategy, (*b*) whether firm *B* has a dominant strategy, (*c*) the optimal strategy for each firm, and (*d*) the Nash equilibrium, if there is one.

		Firm *B*	
		Low Price	High Price
Firm *A*	Low Price	(1, 1)	(3, −1)
	High Price	(−1, 3)	(4, 2)

*9. From the following payoff matrix, where the payoffs are the profits or losses of the two firms, determine (*a*) whether firm *A* has a dominant strategy, (*b*) whether firm *B* has a dominant strategy, (*c*) the optimal strategy for each firm, (*d*) the Nash equilibrium, and (*e*) under what conditions the above situation is likely to occur.

		Firm *B*	
		Small Cars	**Large Cars**
Firm *A*	**Large Cars**	(4, 4)	(−2, −2)
	Small Cars	(2, −2)	(4, 4)

*10. From the following payoff matrix, where the payoffs refer to the profits that firms *A* and *B* earn by cheating and not cheating in a cartel, determine (*a*) whether firms *A* and *B* face the prisoners' dilemma and (*b*) what would happen if we changed the payoff in the bottom left cell to (5, 5).

		Firm *B*	
		Cheat	**Don't Cheat**
Firm *A*	**Cheat**	(4, 3)	(8, 1)
	Don't Cheat	(2, 6)	(6, 5)

11. Given the following payoff matrix, (*a*) what would be the best strategy for each firm? (*b*) Why is the entry-deterrent threat by firm *A* to lower price not credible to firm *B*? (*c*) What could firm *A* do to make its threat credible without building excess capacity?

		Firm *B*	
		Enter	**Do Not Enter**
Firm *A*	**Low Price**	(3, −1)	(3, 1)
	High Price	(4, 5)	(6, 3)

12. What strategic, industrial, or trade policy would be required (if any) in the United States and in Europe if the entries in the top left cell of the payoff matrix in Table 10-10 were changed to (*a*) 10, 10? (*b*) 5, 0? (*c*) 5, −10?

13. **Integrating Problem**
In Bayonne, New Jersey, there is a large beauty salon and a number of smaller ones. The total demand function for hair styling per day is $Q = 180 - 10P$, where P is in dollars. The marginal cost function of all the small salons together is $\Sigma MC_F = 4 + 0.1Q$, and the marginal cost function of the dominant or leading salon is $MC_L = 7 + 0.1Q$. (*a*) Draw a figure showing D_T, ΣMC_F, MC_L, D_L, MR_T, MR_L, and the horizontal summation of ΣMC_F and MC_L. (*b*) Determine the best level of output and price for hair styling for the dominant and for the smaller salons if the large or dominant salon operates as the price leader. How many stylings will the large salon supply per day? How many will the small salons supply together? (*c*) If the large salon forms a centralized cartel, what would be the best level of output per day and price?

How much will be supplied by the dominant salon and by all the small salons together if the cartel wants to minimize the total costs of producing the best level of output for the cartel as a whole? (*d*) What would be the equilibrium output level and price if the large salon did not exist and the small salons operated as perfect competitors? (*e*) What would be the best level of output and price if the large salon did exist in the market but operated as a perfect competitor, just like the small salons?

APPENDIX

OLIGOPOLY THEORY WITH CALCULUS

In this appendix we examine mathematically some of the oligopoly models presented graphically in the text. The models that are presented with calculus in this appendix are the kinked demand curve model, the cartel model, the market-sharing cartel, and the sales maximization model.

The Kinked Demand Curve Model

Suppose that the demand functions for price increases and for price cuts facing an oligopolist are, respectively,

$$Q_1 = 280 - 40P_1 \quad \text{or} \quad P_1 = 7 - 0.025Q_1$$
$$Q_2 = 100 - 10P_2 \quad \text{or} \quad P_2 = 10 - 0.1Q_2$$

where Q is output and P is price in dollars.

Suppose that the firm's total cost function is

$$TC = 2Q + 0.025Q^2$$

We can calculate MR_1, MR_2, and MC as follows:

$$TR_1 = P_1Q_1 = (7 - 0.025Q_1)Q_1 = 7Q_1 - 0.025Q_1^2$$
$$MR_1 = \frac{d(TR_1)}{dQ_1} = 7 - 0.05Q_1$$
$$TR_2 = P_2Q_2 = (10 - 0.1Q_2)Q_2 = 10Q_2 - 0.1Q_2^2$$
$$MR_2 = \frac{d(TR_2)}{dQ_2} = 10 - 0.2Q_2$$
$$MC = \frac{d(TC)}{d(Q)} = 2 + 0.05Q$$

To find the kink, or point of intersection of demand curves D_1 and D_2, we set $Q_1 = Q_2 = Q$ and get

$$7 - 0.025Q = 10 - 0.1Q$$
$$0.075Q = 3$$
$$Q = 40$$

and $$P = 7 - 0.025(40) = \$6$$

The upper and lower limits of the MR gap are

$$MR_1 = 7 - 0.5(40) = 7 - 2 = 5$$
$$MR_2 = 10 - 0.2(40) = 10 - 8 = 2$$

Since $$MC = 2 + 0.05(40) = 4$$

the MC curve intersects the vertical portion of the MR curve. The total profits (π) of the firm are

$$\pi = TR - TC = PQ - 2Q - 0.025Q^2$$
$$= 6(40) - 2(40) - 0.025(40)^2 = \$120$$

The level of π could also have been found from

$$\pi = (P - ATC)Q$$

$$ATC = \frac{TC}{Q} = \frac{2Q + 0.025Q^2}{Q} = 2 + 0.025Q = 2 + 0.025(40) = 3$$

so that $$\pi = (6 - 3)(40) = \$120$$

The graphical solution for this problem is shown in Figure 10-1.

Problem The demand function for price increases and for price cuts for an oligopolist are, respectively,

$$Q_1 = 210 - 30P_1 \quad \text{or} \quad P_1 = 7 - \frac{Q_1}{30}$$

$$Q_2 = 90 - 10P_2 \quad \text{or} \quad P_2 = 9 - \frac{Q_2}{10}$$

The oligopolist's total cost function is

$$TC = 3.5Q + \frac{Q^2}{60}$$

(a) Derive the MR_1, MR_2, and MC functions facing the oligopolist. (b) Determine the price and output at the kink on the demand curve. (c) Determine the upper and lower limits of the MR gap and prove that MC falls in the MR gap. (d) Find the value of the total profits of the oligopolist.

The Centralized Cartel Model

Suppose that a two-firm cartel faces the following demand function:

$$Q = 120 - 10P \quad \text{or} \quad P = 12 - 0.1Q$$

and the total cost function of each member firm is, respectively,

$$TC_1 = 4Q_1 + 0.1Q_1^2 \quad \text{and} \quad TC_2 = 2Q_2 + 0.1Q_2^2$$

We can calculate MR, MC_1, and MC_2 as follows:

$$TR = PQ = (12 - 0.1Q)Q = 12Q - 0.1Q^2$$

$$MR = \frac{d(TR)}{dQ} = 12 - 0.2Q$$

$$MC_1 = \frac{d(TC_1)}{dQ_1} = 4 + 0.2Q_1 \quad \text{and} \quad MC_2 = \frac{d(TC_2)}{dQ_2} = 2 + 0.2Q_2$$

In order to add MC_1 and MC_2 horizontally to find $\Sigma\, MC$, we solve for Q_1 and Q_2 and get

$$Q_1 = -20 + 5MC_1 \quad \text{and} \quad Q_2 = -10 + 5MC_2$$

so that

$$Q = -30 + 10\,\Sigma\, MC$$

Solving for $\Sigma\, MC$, we have

$$\sum MC = \frac{Q + 30}{10} = 3 + 0.1Q$$

(Strictly speaking this is the average $\Sigma\, MC$ function and does not show the kink at $Q = 10$ in Figure 19 in the answer to Problem 4 at the end of the book.)

Setting $\Sigma\, MC = MR$, we get

$$3 + 0.1Q = 12 - 0.2Q$$

so that

$$9 = 0.3Q$$

and

$$Q = 30$$

Then

$$P = 12 - 0.1(30) = \$9$$

At $Q = 30$,

$$MR = 12 - 0.2(30) = 12 - 6 = \$6$$

Setting MC_1 and MC_2 equal to MR, we have

$$4 + 0.2Q_1 = 6 \quad \text{so that } Q_1 = 10$$

and

$$2 + 0.2Q_2 = 6 \quad \text{so that } Q_2 = 20$$

and

$$Q = Q_1 + Q_2 = 10 + 20 = 30$$

Therefore,

$$\pi_1 = TR_1 - TC_1 = PQ_1 - 4Q_1 - 0.1Q_1^2 = 9(10) - 4(10) - 0.1(10)^2$$
$$= 90 - 40 - 10 = \$40$$

$$\pi_2 = TR_2 - TC_2 = PQ_2 - 2Q_2 - 0.1Q_2^2 = 9(20) - 2(20) - 0.1(20)^2$$
$$= 180 - 40 - 40 = \$100$$

and

$$\pi = \pi_1 + \pi_2 = \$40 + \$100 = \$140$$

The graphical solution of this problem is shown in Figure 19 in the answer to Problem 4 at the end of the text.

Problem Solve the above problem again on the assumption that the demand function that the cartel faces increases to

$$Q' = 150 - 10P$$

The Market-Sharing Cartel

Suppose that the market demand function for a two-firm equal-market-sharing cartel is

$$Q = 120 - 10P$$

and that the total cost function of duopolist 1 is

$$TC' = 0.1Q^2$$

The half-share market faced by each duopolist is then

$$Q' = 60 - 5P \qquad \text{or} \qquad P' = 12 - 0.2Q$$

so that $$TR' = P'Q' = (12 - 0.2Q')Q' = 12Q' - 0.2Q'^2$$

and $$MR' = \frac{d(TR')}{dQ'} = 12 - 0.4Q'$$

The marginal and average total cost of each duopolist is

$$MC' = \frac{d(TC')}{dQ'} = 0.2Q' \qquad \text{and} \qquad ATC' = \frac{TC'}{Q'} = \frac{0.1Q'^2}{Q'} = 0.1Q'$$

Setting MC' equal to MR', we get

$$0.2Q' = 12 - 0.4Q'$$
$$0.6Q' = 12$$
$$Q' = 20$$

and $$P' = 12 - 0.2(20) = \$8$$

Therefore,

$$TR' = 12(20) - 0.2(20)^2 = 240 - 80 = \$160$$

and

$$\pi' = TR' - TC' = 160 - 0.1(20)^2 = 160 - 40 = \$120$$
$$\pi = 2(\pi') = \$240$$

Problem Determine mathematically the monopoly solution for the above problem.

The Sales Maximization Model

Suppose that the demand function faced by an oligopolist is

$$Q = 100 - 10P \qquad \text{or} \qquad P = 10 - 0.1Q$$

so that the total revenue function of the firm is

$$TR = PQ = (10 - 0.1Q)Q = 10Q - 0.1Q^2$$

If the total cost function of the firm is given by

$$TC = 70 + 2Q$$

then the total profit of the firm is

$$\pi = TR - TC = 10Q - 0.1Q^2 - 70 - 2Q = -70 + 8Q - 0.1Q^2$$

The firm maximizes profits where

$$\frac{d\pi}{dQ} = 8 - 0.2Q = 0$$

so that $Q = 40$ and $P = 10 - 0.1(40) = \$6$.

$$TR = 10(40) - 0.1(40)^2 = 400 - 160 = \$240$$
$$\pi = -70 + 8(40) - 0.1(40)^2 = -70 + 320 - 160 = \$90$$

On the other hand, the firm maximizes sales or total revenue where

$$\frac{d(TR)}{dQ} = 10 - 0.2Q = 0$$

so that $Q = 50$ and $P = 10 - 0.1(50) = \$5$.

$$TR = 10(50) - 0.1(50)^2 = 500 - 250 = \$250$$
$$\pi = -70 + 8(50) - 0.1(50)^2 = -70 + 400 - 250 = \$80$$

To find Q, P, and TR if the minimum profit constraint of the firm is $\pi = \$85$, we proceed as follows:

$$\pi = -70 + 8Q - 0.1Q^2 = \$85$$
$$0.1Q^2 - 8Q + 155 = 0$$

Using the quadratic formula to find the two roots of this equation, we have

$$Q = \frac{-b \mp \sqrt{b^2 - 4ac}}{2a} = \frac{8 \mp \sqrt{(-8)^2 - 4(0.1)(155)}}{2(0.1)}$$
$$= \frac{8 \mp \sqrt{2}}{0.2} = \frac{8 \mp 1.414}{0.2}$$
$$= 32.93 \quad \text{and} \quad 47.07$$

Taking the largest of these outputs, we have

$$P = 10 - 0.1(47.07) = \$5.29$$

and

$$TR = 10(47.07) - 0.1(47.07)^2 = 470.70 - 221.56 = \$249.14$$

so that

$$\begin{aligned} \pi &= -70 + 8(47.07) - 0.1(47.07)^2 \\ &= -70 + 376.56 - 221.56 \\ &= \$85 \qquad \text{(the minimum } \pi \text{ required)} \end{aligned}$$

Problem Given: $Q = 120 - 10P$ and $TC = 90 + 2Q$ for an oligopolistic firm, determine mathematically the output at which the firm maximizes its (*a*) total profits, and calculate P, TR, and π; (*b*) total revenue, and calculate P, TR, and π; and (*c*) total revenue, and calculate P, TR, and π if the firm faces the total profit constraint of \$155.

SUPPLEMENTARY READINGS

For a problem-solving approach to the topics discussed in this chapter, see:

Salvatore, Dominick: *Theory and Problems of Managerial Economics,* Schaum Outline Series (New York: McGraw-Hill, 1989), Sec. 10.5.

For a more extensive theoretical analysis of perfect competition, monopoly, and monopolistic competition, see:

Salvatore, Dominick: *Microeconomics,* 2nd ed. (New York: HarperCollins, 1994), Chap. 10.

Salvatore, Dominick: *Theory and Problems of Microeconomic Theory,* 3rd ed., Schaum Outline Series (New York: McGraw-Hill, 1992), Secs. 11.4 to 11.12 and 12.1 to 12.3.

For the theory of contestable markets, see:

Baumol, William J.: "Contestable Markets: An Uprising in the Theory of Industrial Structure, *American Economic Review,* March 1982, pp. 1–5.

Baumol, William J., John C. Panzar, and **Robert D. Willig:** *Contestable Markets and the Theory of Industrial Structure* (San Diego: Harcourt Brace Jovanovich, 1982).

Shepherd, William G.: "Contestability vs. Competition," *American Economic Review,* September 1984, pp. 572–587.

Oligopoly and the structure of U.S. industry are examined in:

Scherer, F. M., and **David Ross:** *Industrial Market Structure and Economic Performance,* 3rd ed. (Boston: Houghton Mifflin, 1990).

Adams, Walter, ed.: *The Structure of American Industry,* 8th ed. (New York: Macmillan, 1990).

Stiglitz, J., and **G. F. Mathewson,** eds.: *New Developments in the Analysis of Market Structure* (Cambridge, Mass.: MIT Press, 1986).

For game theory, see:

Von Neumann, John, and **Oskar Morgenstern:** *Theory of Games and Economic Behavior* (Princeton, N.J.: Princeton University Press, 1953).

Schotter, Andrew, and **Gerhart Schwodlauer:** "Economics and the Theory of Games: A Survey," *Journal of Economic Literature,* June 1980, pp. 479–527.

Axelrod, R.: *The Evolution of Cooperation* (New York: Basic Books, 1984).

Osborne, M. J., and **A. Rubinstein:** *A Course in Game Theory* (Cambridge, Mass.: MIT Press, 1994).

Global corporations and their strategic behavior are examined in:

Salvatore, Dominick: *International Economics,* 5th ed. (Englewood Cliffs, N.J.: Prentice-Hall, 1995), Chaps. 8 to 10.

Porter, M.: *The Competitive Advantage of Nations* (New York: Free Press, 1990).

Porter, M., ed.: *Competition in Global Industries* (Boston: Harvard Business School, 1986).

Wheelen, T., and **D. J. Hunger:** *Cases in Strategic Management and Business Policy* (Reading, Mass.: Addison-Wesley, 1987).

CHAPTER 11

Pricing Practices

KEY TERMS

Demand interrelationships
Price discrimination
First-degree price discrimination
Consumers' surplus
Second-degree price discrimination
Third-degree price discrimination
Dumping
Transfer pricing
Cost-plus pricing
Fully allocated average cost
Markup on cost
Profit margin
Incremental analysis
Limit pricing
Peak-load pricing
Two-part tariff
Tying
Bundling
Prestige pricing
Price lining
Skimming
Value pricing
Electronic scanners

CHAPTER OUTLINE

We saw in Chapters 9 and 10 that in order to maximize profits, a firm produces where marginal revenue (MR) equals marginal cost (MC) and then charges the price indicated on the demand curve it faces. This is true under all types of market structures, except perfect competition, where the firm is a price taker and maximizes profits by producing the output level at which $P = MR = MC$. Throughout our presentation, however, we assumed that the firm produced only one product, sold its product in only one market, was organized as a centralized entity, and had precise knowledge of the demand and cost curves it faced. None of these assumptions is generally true for most firms today. That is, most firms produce more than one product, sell products in more than one market, are organized (at least large corporations) into a number of decentralized or semiautonomous divisional profit centers, and have only a general rather than a precise knowledge of the demand and cost curves they face. As a result, our discussion of the pricing decision presented in the previous two chapters must be expanded to take into consideration actual pricing practices.

In this chapter, we examine the firm's pricing of multiple products, price discrimination or the pricing of products sold by the firm in different markets, transfer pricing or the pricing of (intermediate) products transferred between the firm's divisions, and cost-plus pricing (a rule of thumb used by firms because of lack of precise data on demand and cost curves but which, nevertheless, approximates the $MR = MC$ rule). We conclude the chapter with some other recent pricing practices.

11-1 PRICING OF MULTIPLE PRODUCTS

Most modern firms produce a variety of products rather than a single product. This requires that we expand our simple pricing rule examined in the previous two chapters to consider demand and product interdependencies. In this section, we examine the firm's pricing of multiple products with interdependent demands, plant capacity utilization and optimal product pricing, and the optimal pricing of joint products produced in fixed or in variable proportions.

Pricing of Products with Interrelated Demands

The products sold by a firm may be interrelated as substitutes or complements. For example, Oldsmobiles and Chevrolets produced by General Motors are substitutes, while the various options (such as air conditioning, power windows, etc.) produced by GM are complementary to its automobiles. In the pricing of interrelated products, a firm needs to consider the effect of a change in the price of one of its products on the demand for the others. The reason for this is that a reduction in the price of a product (say, Oldsmobiles) leads to a reduction in the demand for a substitute product (Chevrolets) sold by the same firm, and to an increase in the demand for complementary products (options for Oldsmobiles). Thus, profit maximization requires that the output levels and prices of the various products produced by the firm be determined jointly rather than independently.

Demand interrelationships influence the pricing decisions of a multiple product firm through their effect on marginal revenue. For a two-product (A and B) firm, the marginal revenue functions of the firm are[1]

$$MR_A = \frac{\Delta TR_A}{\Delta Q_A} + \frac{\Delta TR_B}{\Delta Q_A} \tag{11-1}$$

$$MR_B = \frac{\Delta TR_B}{\Delta Q_B} + \frac{\Delta TR_A}{\Delta Q_B} \tag{11-2}$$

From the two equations above, we see that the marginal revenue for each product has two components, one associated with the change in the total revenue from the sale of the product itself, and the other associated with the change in the total revenue from the other product. The second term on the right-hand side of each equation, thus, reflects the demand interrelationships. For example, the term $(\Delta TR_B)/(\Delta Q_A)$ in Equation 11-1 measures the effect on the firm's revenues from product B resulting from the sale of an additional unit of product A by the firm. Similarly, $(\Delta TR_A)/(\Delta Q_B)$ in Equation 11-2 measures the effect on the firm's total revenue from product A resulting from the sale of an additional unit of product B by the firm. If the second term on the right-hand side of each equation is positive, indicating that increased sales of one product stimulates sales of the other, the two products are complementary. If, on the other hand, the second term in each equation is negative, indicating that increased sales of one product leads to reduced sales of the other, the two products are substitutes. For example, increased sales of Oldsmobiles leads to increased sales of options for Oldsmobiles (complements) but reduced sales of Chevrolets (substitutes for Oldsmobiles).

Optimal pricing and output decisions on the part of the firm, therefore, require that the total effect (i.e., the direct as well as the cross-marginal effects) of the change in the price of a product on the firm be taken into consideration. Failure to do so leads to suboptimal pricing and output decisions. For example, suppose that products A and B are complements so that the term $(\Delta TR_B)/(\Delta Q_A)$ in Equation 11-1 is positive. If the firm disregards this term and produces where $MR_A = (\Delta TR_A)/(\Delta Q_A) = MC_A$, the firm will be producing too little of product A to maximize profits. On the other hand, suppose that products A and B are substitutes, so that $(\Delta TR_B)/(\Delta Q_A)$ is negative. If the firm disregards this term and produces where $MR_A = (\Delta TR_A)/(\Delta Q_A) = MC_A$, the firm will be producing too much of product A to be maximizing profits.

Plant Capacity Utilization and Optimal Product Pricing

One important reason that firms produce more than one product is to make fuller use of their plant and production capacities. A firm which would have idle capacity after producing the best level of output of a single product can search for

[1]In terms of calculus,

$$MR_A = \frac{\partial TR_A}{\partial Q_A} + \frac{\partial TR_B}{\partial Q_A} \quad \text{and} \quad MR_B = \frac{\partial TR_B}{\partial Q_B} + \frac{\partial TR_A}{\partial Q_B}$$

other products to produce so as to make fuller (which does not necessarily mean 100 percent) use of its plant and production capacity.[2] As long as the marginal revenue from these products exceeds their marginal cost, the profits of the firm will increase. Thus, instead of producing a single product at the point where $MR = MC$ and be left with a great deal of idle capacity, the firm will introduce new products (or different varieties of existing products), in the order of their profitability, until the marginal revenue of the least profitable product produced equals its marginal cost to the firm. The quantity produced of the more profitable products is then determined by the point at which their marginal revenue equals the marginal revenue and marginal cost of the last unit of the least profitable product produced by the firm. The price of each product is then determined on its respective demand curve. This process is shown in Figure 11-1.

[2]In fact, Clemens has convincingly argued that it is more realistic to regard the firm as selling its unique productive capacity than specific products. See Eli Clemens, "Price Discrimination and the Multiple Product Firm," *Review of Economic Studies,* no. 29, 1950–1951, pp. 1–11.

Figure 11-1
Optimal Outputs and Prices of Multiple Products by a Firm

D_A, D_B, and D_C are the demand curves for products *A*, *B*, and *C* sold by the firm, and MR_A, MR_B, and MR_C are the corresponding marginal revenue curves. The firm maximizes profits when $MR_A = MR_B = MR_C = MC$. This is shown by points E_A, E_B, and E_C, where the equal marginal revenue (*EMR*) curve, at the level at which $MR_C = MC$, crosses the MR_A, MR_B, and MR_C curves. Thus, $Q_A = 60$ and $P_A = \$16$; $Q_B = 90$ (from 150 − 60) and $P_B = \$15$; and $Q_C = 180$ (from 330 − 150) and $P_C = \$14$. Note that each successive demand curve is more elastic and that the price of each successive product is lower, while its *MC* is higher.

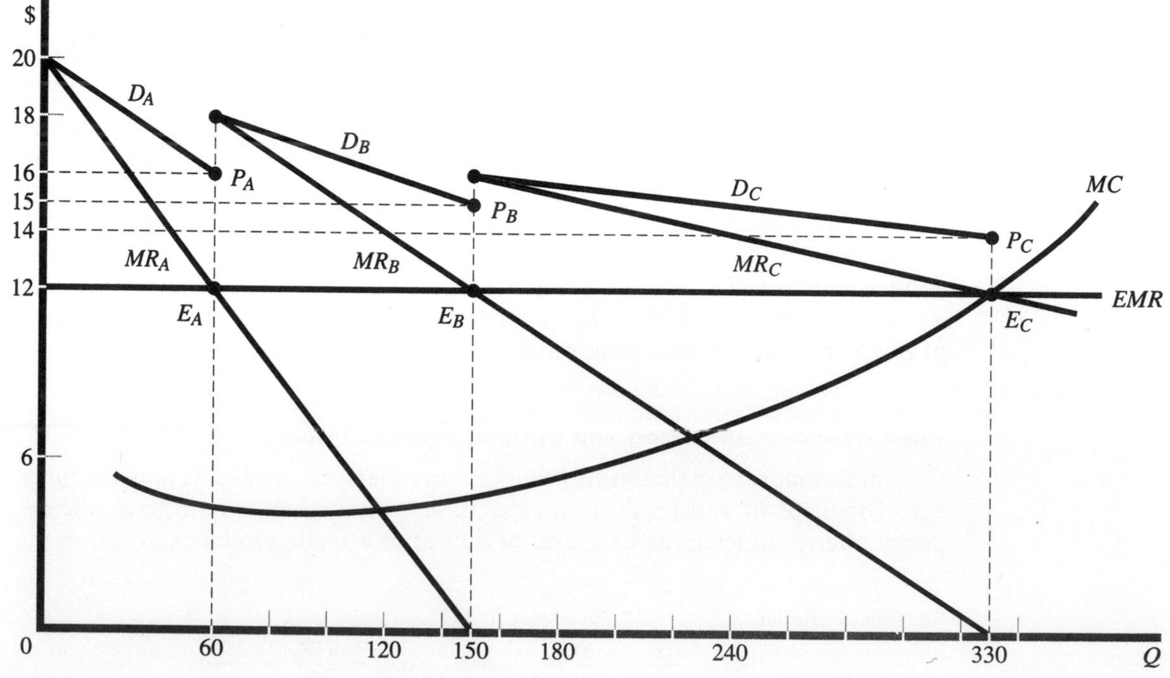

Figure 11-1 shows the situation of a firm selling three products (A, B, and C) with respective demand curves D_A, D_B, and D_C, and corresponding marginal revenue curves MR_A, MR_B, and MR_C. The firm maximizes profits when it produces the quantity of each product at which $MR_A = MR_B = MR_C = MC$. This is shown by points E_A, E_B, and E_C, at which the equal marginal revenue (EMR) line from the level at which $MR_C = MC$ crosses the MR_A, MR_B, and MR_C curves. Thus, in order to maximize profits, the firm should produce 60 units of product A and sell them at the price of $P_A = \$16$ on the D_A curve (see the figure); 90 units of product B (the horizontal distance between points E_B and E_A, or 150 − 60) and sell them at $P_B = \$15$ on the D_B curve; and 180 units of product C (from 330 − 150) and sell them at $P_C = \$14$ on the D_C curve. Note that each successive demand curve is more elastic and that the price of each successive product introduced is lower, while its marginal cost is higher (so that per-unit profits decline).

Several things must be pointed out with respect to the above analysis and figure. *First,* it would be profitable for the firm to introduce still other products until the price of the last product introduced is equal to its marginal cost (so that the firm would be a perfect competitor in the market for this product), or the firm's productive capacity has been reached. *Second,* it is assumed that the firm's production facilities can easily be adapted to the production of other products and that the firm's marginal cost curve reflects any increase in costs resulting from the introduction of additional products. *Third,* Figure 11-1 assumes that the demand curve for each product sold by the firm is independent rather than interrelated or that the figure shows the total and final effect of all demand interrelationships. *Fourth* (and related to the first point above), a firm may produce a product on which it makes little or no profit in order to offer a full range of products, to use it as a "loss leader" (i.e., to attract customers), to retain customers' goodwill, to keep channels of distribution open, or to keep the firm's resources in use while awaiting more profitable opportunities (as in the case of construction companies). For example, supermarkets earn very thin profit margins on staples (soaps, detergents, coffee, sodas, potatoes, etc.) which have very elastic demands and are heavily advertised, and earn much more on specialty products, which are often bought on impulse and with which customers have much less pricing experience.

Optimal Pricing of Joint Products Produced in Fixed Proportions

The products produced by a firm can be related not only in demand but also in production. Production interdependence arises when products are jointly produced. Products can be jointly produced in fixed or variable proportions. An example of joint production in fixed proportions is cattle raising, which provides both beef and hides in the ratio of one-to-one. An example of joint production with variable proportions is provided by petroleum refining, which results in gasoline, fuel oils, and other products in proportions which, within a range, can be varied by the firm. Such production interdependence must be considered by the firm in order to reach optimal output and pricing decisions. We will consider joint production in fixed proportions in this section and joint production in variable proportions in the next section.

When products are jointly produced in fixed proportions, they should be thought of as a single "production package." There is then no rational way of allocating the cost of producing the package to the individual products in the package. For example, the cost of raising cattle cannot be allocated in any rational way to beef and hides, since they are jointly produced. On the other hand, the jointly produced products may have independent demands and marginal revenues. For example, the demand and marginal revenue for beef are separate and independent of the demand and marginal revenue for hides. The best level of output of the joint product is then determined at the point where the vertical summation of the marginal revenues of the various jointly produced products equals the single marginal cost of producing the entire product package. This is shown in Figure 11-2.

In the left panel of Figure 11-2, D_A and D_B refer, respectively, to the demand curves of products *A* and *B*, which are jointly produced in the proportion of one-to-one. We could think of product *A* as beef and product *B* as hides which result

Figure 11-2
Optimal Output and Prices of Joint Products Produced in Fixed Proportions

In both panels, D_A and MR_A, and D_B and MR_B refer, respectively, to the demand and marginal revenue curves for products *A* and *B*, which are jointly produced in fixed proportions. The total marginal revenue (MR_T) curve is obtained from the vertical summation of the MR_A and MR_B curves. When the marginal cost of the jointly produced production package is *MC* (see the left panel), the best level of output of products *A* and *B* is 40 units and is given by point *E*, at which $MR_T = MC$. At $Q = 40$, $P_A = \$12$ on D_A and $P_B = \$5$ on D_B. On the other hand, with MC' (see the right panel), the best level of output of the joint product package is 60 units and is given by point E', at which $MR_T = MC'$. At $Q = 60$, $P'_A = \$10$ on D_A, but since MR_B is negative for $Q_B > 45$, the firm sells only 45 units of product *B* at $P'_B = \$4.50$ (at which TR_B is maximum at $MR_B = 0$) and disposes of the remaining 15 units of product *B*.

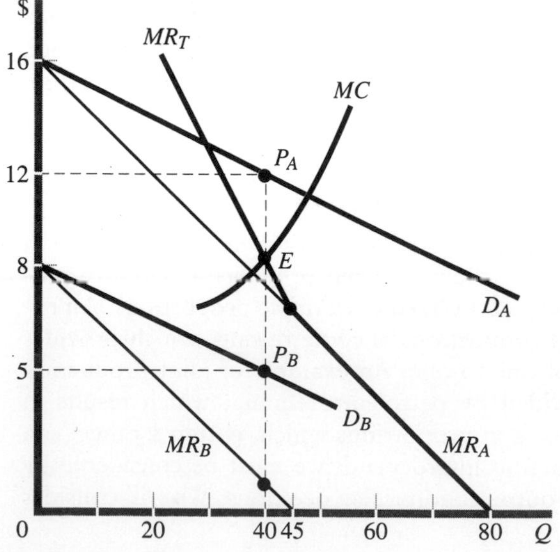

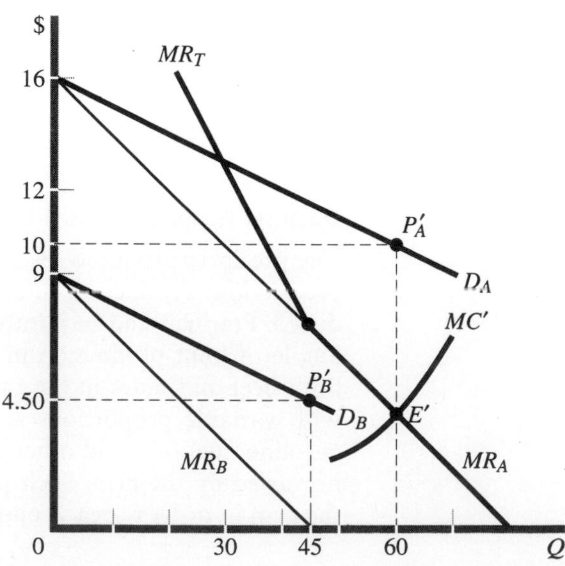

in the ratio of one-to-one from the slaughter of each cow. Thus, the horizontal axis of the figure measures at the same time the quantity (Q) of cattle, beef, and hides. Despite the fact that beef and hides are jointly produced, their demand curves are independent because they are unrelated in consumption. The corresponding marginal revenue curves are MR_A and MR_B in the figure. The total marginal revenue (MR_T) curve is obtained by summing vertically the MR_A and MR_B curves because the firm receives marginal revenues from the sale of both products. Note that starting at the output level of $Q = 45$ units, at which $MR_B = 0$, the MR_T curve coincides with the MR_A curve. The best level of output of both beef and hides is 40 units and is given by point E, at which the MC curve for cattle (both beef and hides together) crosses the MR_T curve of the firm. At $Q = 40$, $P_A = \$12$ on the D_A curve and $P_B = \$5$ on the D_B curve.

In the left panel of Figure 11-2, both MR_A and MR_B are positive at the best level of output of $Q = 40$. In contrast, in the right panel of Figure 11-2, MR_B is negative at the best level of output of $Q = 60$ given by point E', at which the lower MC' curve crosses the same MR_T curve. This means that selling more than 45 units of product B (hides) reduces the firm's total revenue and profits. In such a case the firm produces 60 units of the joint product (cattle), sells 60 units of product A (beef) at $P'_A = \$10$ but sells only 45 units of product B (hides) at $P'_B = \$4.50$ (at which TR_B is maximum and $MR_B = 0$). That is, the firm withholds from the market and disposes of the extra 15 units of product B jointly produced with the 60 units of product A in order not to sell them at a negative marginal revenue.[3] An example of this was provided by the destruction of excess pineapple juice that jointly resulted from the production of sliced pineapples for canning. Until use was found for it, the excess pineapple juice was simply destroyed in order not to depress its price below the point at which its marginal revenue became negative.[4]

Optimal Pricing and Output of Joint Products Produced in Variable Proportions

While the case of products that are produced jointly in fixed proportions (i.e., that are complementary in production) is possible, more common is the case of products that are jointly produced in variable proportions (i.e., that are substitutes in production). We can determine the profit-maximizing combination of products that are jointly produced in variable proportions with the aid of Figure 11-3.

In Figure 11-3, the curved lines are product transformation curves and show the various combinations of products A and B that the firm can produce at each

[3]For the mathematical analysis of optimal pricing of joint products produced in fixed proportions, see Problem 3, with answer at the end of the book.

[4]When the firm incurs a significant cost in disposing of the excess quantity of a jointly produced product, the cost is added to the MC function of the firm, thereby reducing the optimal level of output. Significant disposal costs, however, provide strong incentives for the firm to find uses for the excess products that are jointly produced.

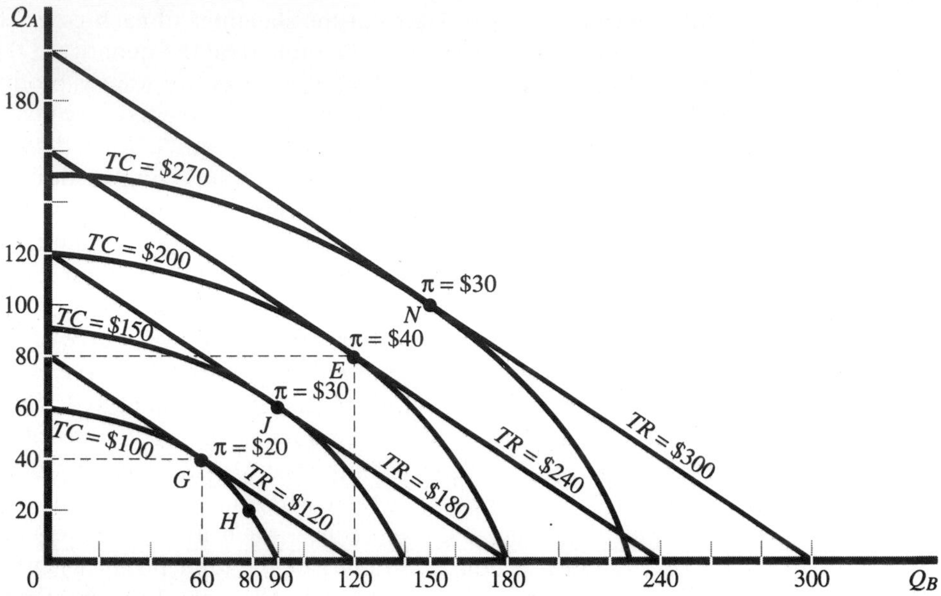

Figure 11-3
Profit Maximization with Joint Products Produced in Variable Proportions

The curved lines are product transformation curves showing the various combinations of products *A* and *B* that the firm can produce at each level of total cost (*TC*). The curvature arises because the firm's productive resources are not perfectly adaptable in the production of products *A* and *B* that give rise to the same total revenue (*TR*) to the firm when sold at constant prices. The tangency point of an isorevenue curve to a *TC* curve gives the combination of products *A* and *B* that leads to the maximum profit (π) for the firm for the specific *TC*. The overall maximum profit of the firm is π = $40. This is earned by producing and selling 80*A* and 120*B* (point *E*) with *TR* = $240 and *TC* = $200.

level of input use and total cost. For example, the lowest curve shows that with *TC* = $100, the firm can produce 40 units of product *A* and 60 units of product *B* (point *G*), 20 units of product *A* and 80 units of product *B* (point *H*), or any combination of products *A* and *B* shown on the curve. Higher product transformation curves refer to the various larger combinations of products *A* and *B* that can be produced at each higher level of *TC*. Production transformation curves are concave to the origin because the firm's production resources are not perfectly adaptable in (i.e., cannot be perfectly transferred between) the production of products *A* and *B*.

Figure 11-3 also shows isorevenue lines. They represent all combinations of outputs of products *A* and *B* that generate the same total revenue for the firm. For example, the lowest isorevenue line shows all the combinations of products *A* and *B* that lead to *TR* = $120 with P_A = $1.50 and P_B = $1.00. For example, at point *G* (40*A*, 60*B*), *TR* = (40)($1.50) + (60)($1.00) = $120. The higher isorevenue lines refer to the higher levels of *TR* that the firm receives by selling larger quantities of products *A* and *B* at constant P_A and P_B. The isorevenue lines are straight on the assumption that the prices of products *A* and *B* are constant (as in the case of a perfectly competitive firm).[5]

Looking at both the product transformation curves and the isorevenue lines in Figure 11-3, we can see that for a given *TC,* the firm maximizes profits by reaching the isorevenue line that is tangent to the particular *TC* curve. For example, with $TC = \$100$, the highest total profit (π) possible is \$20, which is reached by producing 40*A* and 60*B* and reaching the $TR = \$120$ isorevenue line. With $TC = \$150$, the maximum $\pi = \$30$, which is reached by producing 60*A* and 90*B* and reaching the $TR = \$180$ isorevenue line at point *J*. The overall highest profit that the firm can earn is $\pi = \$40$. This is reached by producing 80*A* and 120*B* at $TC = \$200$ and reaching the $TR = \$240$ isorevenue line at point *E* (see the figure).[6]

[5]Note that isorevenue lines are parallel and that their absolute slope is $P_B/P_A = \$1/\$1.50 = \frac{2}{3}$. If P_A and P_B are not constant, the isorevenue lines would not be straight, but the analysis remains basically the same.

[6]Note that this is an example of constrained maximization and can easily be solved by linear programming.

Case Study 11-1

Optimal Pricing and Output by Gillette

The Gillette Company is one of many firms producing and selling many varieties of many different products. The U.S. subsidiary of the Gillette Company sells many different types of razors, razor blades, shaving creams, deodorants, hair conditioners, and many other products for personal care, while Braun, the European subsidiary of the company, sells more than 400 other products. Many of these products are interdependent in demand or consumption as well as in production. For example, razor blades and shaving creams are complementary with razors, so that lowering the price of one product increases the quantity demanded of that product (as well as the total revenue from that product if its demand is price elastic) and also increases the demand and total revenue from complementary products. On the other hand, lowering the price of one type of razor reduces the demand for the other types of (substitute) razors sold by the company. Thus, the firm must keep these demand interdependencies in mind in devising the optimal pricing and output strategy for its many products. During the 1970s Gillette diversified into many other related and unrelated product lines in order to fully exploit demand interdependencies and to achieve fuller utilization of its productive resources. By 1977, Braun, the European subsidiary of Gillette, produced more than 600 products. That diversification, however, was not successful. It seems that producing a wide variety of unrelated products resulted in only small profits. Therefore, Gillette's top management ordered nearly one-third of the products (such as pocket calculators, digital watches, and small electrical appliances) produced by the company to be discontinued. Gillette was further reorganized in 1988 into a North Atlantic unit (responsible for blades and razors, and personal care and stationery businesses in North America and Europe) and another division (handling international operations outside Europe, as well as Braun small appliances), and further streamlined its product offerings.

In 1990, Gillette introduced its new and incredibly successful Sensor Razor, which cost over $200 million to develop and $100 million to advertise. In 1992, Gillette introduced the Sensor for Women, which captured 60 percent of the U.S. market. Then, in 1994, Gillette introduced an upgrade of the Sensor Razor called Excell Razor, which also became an immediate hit. But these were only the most conspicuous of the more than 20 new products that Gillette introduced each year.

Source: "Gillette After the Diversification that Failed," *Business Week*, February 28, 1977, pp. 58–62; "How a $4 Razor Ends up Costing $300 Million," *Business Week*, January 29, 1990, pp. 62–63; "A New Equal Right: The Close Shave," *Business Week*, March 29, 1993, pp. 58–59; and "Gillette to Launch Excell Razor in U.S., Backed by $80 Million Marketing Blitz," *The New York Times*, October 5, 1994, p. B9.

11-2 PRICE DISCRIMINATION

In this section we examine the optimal pricing of a product sold by the firm in multiple markets. First, we define the meaning of "price discrimination" and examine the conditions under which it arises. Then, we deal with first- and second-degree price discrimination. Finally, we examine third-degree price discrimination graphically and algebraically.

Meaning of and Conditions for Price Discrimination

Price discrimination refers to the charging of different prices for different quantities of a product, at different times, to different customer groups or in different markets, when these price differences are not justified by cost differences. For example, telephone companies usually charge a given price per call for a given number of calls and a lower price for additional batches of calls, charge higher prices for calls during business hours than in evenings and on holidays, and charge higher prices to businesses than to households. The incentive for this is that the firm can increase its total revenue and profits for a given level of sales and total costs by practicing price discrimination.

Other examples of price discrimination are (1) the practice of power (i.e., electrical and gas) companies of charging lower prices to commercial than to residential users; (2) the practice of the medical and legal professions of charging lower fees to low-income than to high-income people; (3) the charging of lower prices abroad than at home for a variety of products and services, ranging from books and medicines to movies; (4) the charging of lower prices for afternoon than for evening performances of movies, theaters, and sports events; (5) the charging of lower prices for children and the elderly for haircuts, public transportation, and airline tickets; (6) the charging of lower hotel rates for conventions, and so on. These examples are an indication of the pervasiveness of price discrimination in our economy.

To be remembered, however, is that price differences based on cost differences in supplying a product or service in different quantities, at different times, to different customer groups, or in different markets, are not forms of price discrimination. To be price discrimination, the price differences must not be justified or be based on cost differences. Also to be pointed out is that price discrimination does not have a negative connotation in economics (as contrasted with the case of law). That is, in economics, price discrimination is neutral and benefits some (those paying a price for the product lower than in the absence of price discrimination) and harms others, and as such, it is often difficult or impossible to determine whether, on balance, it is beneficial or harmful for society as a whole.

Three conditions must be met for a firm to be able to practice price discrimination. First, the firm must have some control over the price of the product (i.e., the firm must be an imperfect competitor). A perfectly competitive firm has no control over the price of the product it sells (i.e., it is a price taker) and thus cannot possibly practice price discrimination. Second, the price elasticity of demand for the product must differ for different quantities of the product, at different times, for different customer groups, or in different markets. As we will see later, if the price elasticities of demand are equal, the firm cannot increase its revenues and profits by practicing price discrimination. Third, the quantities of the product or service, the times when they are used or consumed, and the customer groups or markets for the product must be separable (i.e., the firm must be able to segment the market). Otherwise, individuals or firms will purchase the product or service where they are cheap and resell them where they are more expensive, thereby undermining the firm's effort to charge different prices for the same product (i.e., practice price discrimination). In the case of electricity, gas, and water consumption, meters on business premises or in homes keep the markets separate. Transportation costs and trade restrictions keep domestic and foreign markets separate. In the case of services, markets are naturally separated by the fact that most services (e.g., doctors' visits, legal advice, haircuts, public transportation passes for the elderly, etc.) cannot easily or possibly be transferred or resold to other people.

First- and Second-Degree Price Discrimination

There are three types of price discrimination: first, second, and third degree. By practicing any type of price discrimination, the firm can increase its total revenue and profits by capturing all or part of the consumer's surplus. **First-degree price discrimination** involves selling each unit of the product separately and charging the highest price possible for each unit sold. By doing so the firm extracts all of the consumers' surplus from consumers and maximizes the total revenue and profits from the sale of a particular quantity of the product. This is shown in Figure 11-4.

In Figure 11-4, *D* is the demand curve faced by a monopolistic firm. The firm can sell 40 units of the product at the price of \$2 per unit and receive a total revenue of \$80 (the area of rectangle *CF0G*). Consumers, however, are willing to pay *ACF0* = \$160 for 40 units of the product. That is, demand curve *D* indicates that the firm can sell the first unit of the product at the price of \$6. To sell additional units of the product, the firm would have to lower the price a little on each

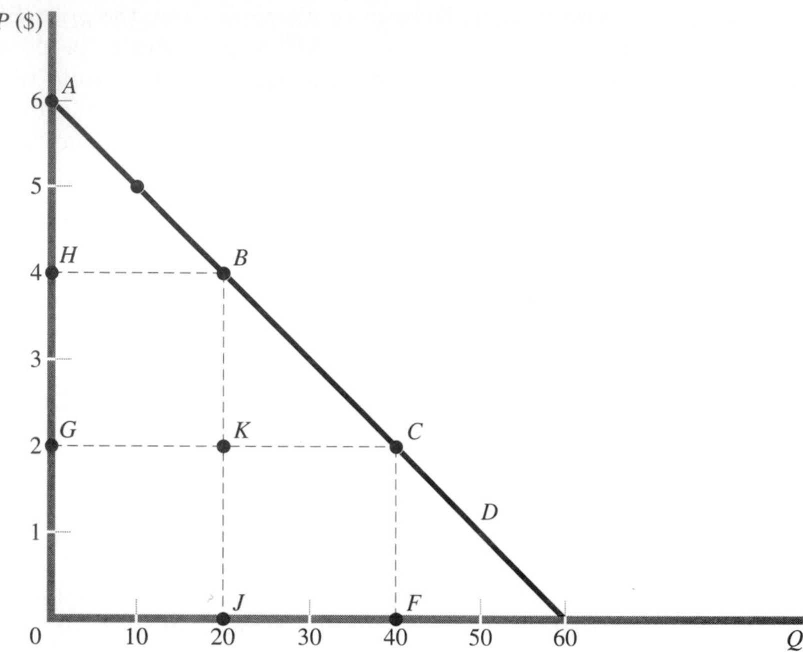

Figure 11-4
First- and Second-Degree Price Discrimination

With *D* as the demand curve faced by a monopolist, the firm could sell *Q* = 40 at *P* = \$2 for a *TR* = \$80 (the area of rectangle *CF0G*). Consumers, however, would be willing to pay *ACF0* = \$160 for 40 units of the product. The difference of \$80 (the area of triangle *ACG*) is the consumers' surplus. With first-degree price discrimination (i.e., by selling each unit of the product separately at the highest price possible), the firm can extract all the consumers' surplus from consumers. If, however, the firm charged the price of *P* = \$4 per unit for the first 20 units of the product and \$2 per unit on the next 20 units, the total revenue of the firm would be \$120 (the sum of the areas of rectangles *BJ0H* and *CFJK*), so that the firm would extract \$40 (the area of rectangle *BKGH*), or half of the consumers' surplus from consumers. This is second-degree price discrimination.

additional unit sold. For example, the firm could sell the second unit of the product for slightly less than \$6 per unit, it could sell the 20th unit at the price of \$4, and the 40th unit at the price of \$2 (see the figure). Thus, if the firm sold each unit of the product separately and charged the highest price possible, the firm would generate the total revenue of *ACF0* = \$160. In the absence of first-degree price discrimination, however, the firm will charge the price of \$2 (only as much as consumers are willing to pay for the 40th unit of the product) for all the 40 units of the product and receive a total revenue of only *CF0G* = \$80. The difference between what consumers are willing to pay (*ACF0* = \$160) and what they actually pay (*CF0G* = \$80) is the **consumers' surplus** (triangle *ACG* = \$80). Thus, by practicing first-degree price discrimination (i.e., by selling each unit of the product separately and charging the highest price possible for each unit), the firm can extract all the consumers' surplus from buyers and increase its total revenues from \$80 to \$160. Since the total cost of producing the 40 units of the product is not affected by the price at which the product is sold, the total profits of the firm rise sharply by practicing first-degree price discrimination.

First-degree price discrimination is seldom encountered in the real world, however, because to practice it, the firm needs to have precise knowledge of each individual consumer's demand curve and charge the highest possible price for each separate unit of the product sold. This is practically impossible. One situation where this does seem to occur is when independent colleges and universities adjust the amount of financial aid based on detailed data on family income, mortgage payments and savings, and charge the highest price possible. More practical and common is **second-degree price discrimination.** This refers to the charging of a uniform price per unit for a specific quantity or block of the product sold to each customer, a lower price per unit for an additional batch or block of the product, and so on. By doing so, the firm will extract part, but not all, of the consumers' surplus. For example, suppose that the firm of Figure 11-4 sets the price of \$4 per unit on the first 20 units of the product and the price of \$2 per unit on the next batch or block of 20 units of the product. The total revenue of the firm would then be $BJ0H = \$80$ from the first batch of 20 units of the product and $CFJK = \$40$ from the next batch or block of 20 units, for the overall total revenue of \$120 (as compared to \$160 with first-degree price discrimination and \$80 without any price discrimination). Thus, the firm can extract one-half or \$40 (the area of rectangle *BKGH*) of the total consumers' surplus from consumers by practicing second-degree price discrimination in this market. The remaining consumers' surplus of \$40 is given by the sum of the areas of triangles *ABH* and *BCK* (see the figure).

While second-degree price discrimination is more common than first-degree price discrimination, it is also somewhat limited to cases where products and services are easily metered, such as kilowatt-hours of electricity, cubic feet of gas and water, number of copies duplicated, minutes of CPU (central processing unit of computer) time used, and so on. Thus, second-degree price discrimination is often encountered in the pricing of electric, gas, water, and other public utilities, in the renting of photocopying machines, in the use of computers, and so on.

Third-Degree Price Discrimination Graphically

Third-degree price discrimination refers to the charging of different prices for the same product in different markets until the marginal revenue of the last unit of the product sold in each market equals the marginal cost of producing the product. For example, if the firm sells a product in two markets (market 1 and market 2), the firm will maximize its total profits by selling the product in each market until $MR_1 = MR_2 = MC$. If $MR_1 > MR_2$, it pays for the firm to redistribute sales from the second to the first market until the condition for profit maximization is met. On the other hand, if $MR_1 < MR_2$, it pays for the firm to transfer sales from the first to the second market until $MR_1 = MR_2$. As pointed out earlier, in order for the firm to be able to practice this or any other type of price discrimination, the firm must have some monopoly power, the price elasticity of demand for the product must be different in the different markets, and the markets must be separable. The rule that, in order to maximize total profits, the firm must sell in each market until $MR_1 = MR_2 = MC$ will then involve selling the product at a higher price in the market with the less elastic demand than in the market with the more elastic demand. This is shown in Figure 11-5.

Panel *a* in Figure 11-5 shows D_1 and MR_1 (the demand and marginal revenue curves for the product that the firm faces in market 1); panel *b* shows D_2 and MR_2 (the demand and marginal revenue curves that the firm faces in market 2); and panel *c* shows *D* and *MR* (the total demand and marginal revenue curves for the product that the firm faces in both markets together). The total market demand curve (*D*) is obtained from the horizontal summation of the demand curves in market 1 and in market 2 (that is, $D = \Sigma D_{1+2}$). Note that up to $Q = 60$, $D = D_1$. Similarly, the total marginal revenue curve (*MR*) is obtained from the horizontal summation of MR_1 and MR_2 (that is, $MR = \Sigma MR_{1+2}$). Note also that up to $Q = 30$, $MR = MR_1$.

The best level of output of the firm is 90 units of the product and is given by point *E* in panel *c*, at which $MR = \Sigma MR_{1+2} = MC = \$2$. To maximize profits, the firm should then sell 50 units of the product in the first market and the remaining 40 units of the product in the second market, so that $MR_1 = MR_2 =$

Figure 11-5
Third-Degree Price Discrimination

Panel *a* shows D_1 and MR_1 (the demand and marginal revenue curves faced by the firm in market 1), panel *b* shows D_2 and MR_2, and panel *c* shows *D* and *MR* (the total demand and marginal revenue curves for the two markets together). $D = \Sigma D_{1+2}$, and $MR = \Sigma MR_{1+2}$, by horizontal summation. The best level of output of the firm is 90 units and is given by point *E* in panel *c* at which $MR = MC = \$2$. The firm sells 50 units of the product in market 1 and 40 units in market 2, so that $MR_1 = MR_2 = MR = MC = \$2$ (see points E_1, E_2, and *E*). For $Q = 50$, $P_1 = \$7$ on D_1 in market 1, and for $Q_2 = 40$, $P_2 = \$4$ on D_2 in market 2. With an average total cost of \$3 per unit for $Q = 90$, the firm earns a profit of \$4 per unit and \$200 in total in market 1, and \$1 per unit and \$40 in total in market 2, for an overall total profit of \$240 in both markets. In the absence of price discrimination, $Q = 90$, $P = \$5$ (see panel *c*), so that profits are \$2 per unit and \$180 in total.

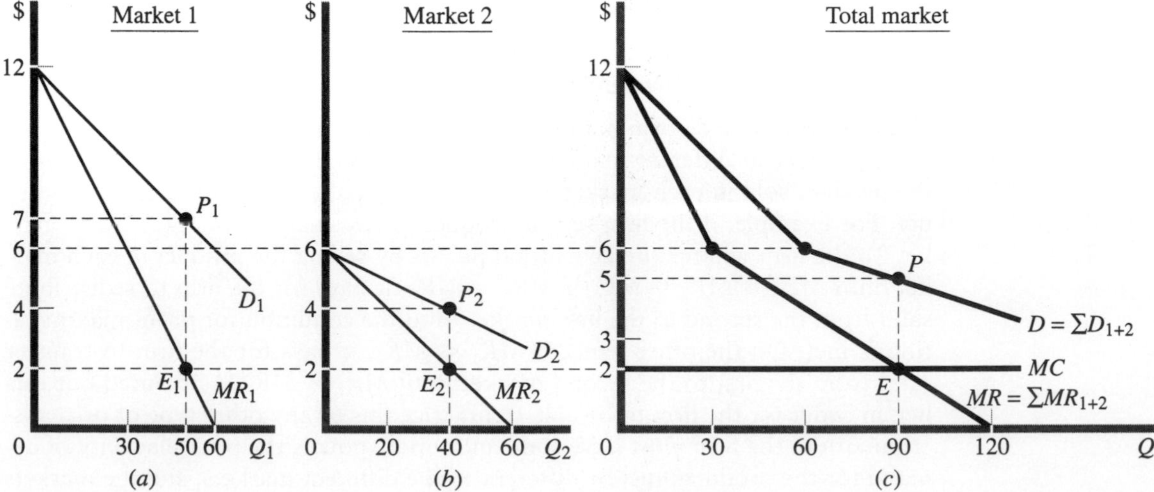

$MR = MC = \$2$ (see, respectively, points E_1, E_2, and E in the three panels of Figure 11-5). For $Q = 50$, $P_1 = \$7$ on D_1 in market 1, and for $Q_2 = 40$, $P_2 = \$4$ on D_2 in market 2. Note that the price is higher in the market with the more inelastic demand. Thus, the firm generates total revenues of \$350 in market 1 and \$160 in market 2, for an overall total revenue of \$510 in both markets together.

If the average total cost (ATC) of the firm is \$3 at the best level of output of 90 units (50 units for market 1 and 40 units for market 2), then the firm earns a profit of $P_1 - ATC = \$7 - \$3 = \$4$ per unit and \$200 in total in market 1, and $P_2 - ATC = \$4 - \$3 = \$1$ per unit and \$40 in total in market 2, for a total profit of \$240 in both markets together.[7] In the absence of price discrimination, the firm would sell the best level of output of $Q = 90$ at $P = \$5$ (see panel *c*) and generate a total revenue of \$450 (as compared to a $TR = \$510$ with third-degree price discrimination). With $ATC = \$3$ for $Q = 90$, the firm would earn a profit of $P - ATC = \$5 - \$3 = \$2$ per unit and \$180 in total. Thus, given the best level of output and costs, the firm can increase its total revenue and profits significantly by practicing third-degree price discrimination.

There are many examples of third-degree price discrimination in our economy. One of these is provided by electrical power companies, which usually charge higher rates to residential than to commercial users of electricity. The reason for this is that the price elasticity of demand for electricity is higher for the latter than for the former because the latter could generate their own electricity if its price rose above the cost of building and running their own power plants. This choice is generally not available to households. The commercial and residential markets for electricity are then kept separate or segmented by meters installed in offices and homes. Other examples of third-degree price discrimination are the higher air fares charged by airlines to business travelers than to vacationers, the higher prices that college bookstores charge students than professors for books, the higher price charged for milk to households than to cheese makers, the higher price charged by telephone companies during business hours than at other times, and the higher prices charged for many services to all customers, except children and the aged. In each case, the higher price is charged in the market with the less elastic demand (i.e., the one in which there are fewer substitutes for the product) and the markets are kept separated or segmented by various methods.

Third-Degree Price Discrimination Algebraically

The graphical analysis of price discrimination shown in Figure 11-5 can easily be shown algebraically.[8] From Figure 11-5, we can determine that the demand and marginal revenue functions of the firm in each market are, respectively,

$$Q_1 = 120 - 10P_1 \quad \text{or} \quad P_1 = 12 - 0.1Q_1 \quad \text{and} \quad MR_1 = 12 - 0.2Q_1$$

$$Q_2 = 120 - 20P_2 \quad \text{or} \quad P_2 = 6 - 0.05Q_2 \quad \text{and} \quad MR_2 = 6 - 0.1Q_2$$

[7]An $ATC = \$3$ for $Q = 90$ and a constant $MC = 2$ for any output level implies a total cost function of $TC = 90 + 2Q$, so that the TC curve (not shown in Figure 11-5) is a straight line with vertical intercept or total fixed costs of \$90 and a constant slope or marginal cost of \$2.

[8]For the analysis of third-degree price discrimination using calculus, see the appendix to this chapter.

would arise as to how much coal the coal mine should sell to the parent steel company and how much to outsiders, and at what prices. Similarly, the parent steel company must determine how much coal to purchase from its own coal mine and how much from outsiders, and at what prices. These are some of the most complex and troublesome questions that arise in the operation of large-scale enterprises today.

The appropriate pricing of intermediate products sold by one semiautonomous division of a large-scale enterprise to another or transfer pricing is of crucial importance to the efficient operation of the individual divisions of the enterprise as well as to the enterprise as a whole. There are two reasons for this. First, the price paid by a division of the enterprise for intermediate products produced by another division affects the output of each division and, therefore, the output of the entire enterprise. If wrong transfer prices are set, the various divisions of the firm involved in the transaction, and the firm as a whole, will not produce the optimum or profit-maximizing level of output. Second, transfer prices affect the profitability of the divisions involved in the transfer of the intermediate products, and, as such, they serve as incentives and rewards for the efficient operation of the various divisions of the enterprise. Too low transfer prices artificially reduce the profitability of the producing division and artificially increase the profitability of the purchasing division, and such prices can undermine the morale of the managers, officers, and workers of the former since salary increases and bonuses, and sometimes even their jobs, depend on the profitability of the division.

In what follows, we will examine how the appropriate transfer prices are determined in cases where an external market for the transfer or intermediate product does not exist, when it exists and is perfectly competitive, and when it exists and is imperfectly competitive. To simplify our discussion, we assume throughout that the firm has two divisions, a production division (indicated by the subscript p) and a marketing division (indicated by the subscript m). The production division sells the intermediate product to the marketing division, as well as to outsiders, if an outside market for the intermediate product exists. The marketing division purchases the intermediate product from the production division, completes the production process, and markets the final product for the firm. Also, to simplify the presentation, we will assume throughout that 1 unit of the transfer or intermediate product is required to produce each unit of the final product sold by the marketing division. While our discussion is necessarily limited in scope (since transfer pricing is covered in other business courses), it does indicate the nature of the problem and outlines the rules for optimal transfer pricing.

Transfer Pricing with No External Market for the Intermediate Product

When there is no external demand for the intermediate product, the production division can sell the intermediate product only internally to the marketing division of the firm, and the marketing division can purchase the intermediate product only from the production division of the firm. Since 1 unit of the intermediate product is used to produce each unit of the final product, the output of the intermediate product and of the final product are equal. Figure 11-6 shows how the transfer price of the intermediate product is determined when there is no external market for the intermediate product.

In Figure 11-6, MC_p and MC_m are the marginal cost curves of the production and marketing divisions of the firm, respectively, while MC is the vertical summation of MC_p and MC_m, and it represents the total marginal cost curve for the firm as a whole. The figure also shows the external demand curve for the final product sold by the marketing division, D_m, and its corresponding marginal revenue curve, MR_m. The firm's best or profit-maximizing level of output for the final product is 40 units and is given by point E_m, at which $MR_m = MC$. Therefore, $P_m = \$14$. Since 40 units of the intermediate product are required (i.e., are demanded by the marketing division of the firm in order to produce the best level of 40 units of the final product), the transfer price for the intermediate product, P_t, is set equal to the marginal cost of the intermediate product (MC_p) at $Q_p = 40$. Thus, $P_t = \$6$ and is

Figure 11-6
Transfer Pricing of the Intermediate Product with No External Market

MC, the marginal cost of the firm, is equal to the vertical summation of MC_p and MC_m, the marginal cost curves of the production and the marketing divisions of the firm, respectively. D_m is the external demand for the final product faced by the marketing division of the firm, and MR_m is the corresponding marginal revenue curve. The firm's best level of output of the final product is 40 units and is given by point E_m, at which $MR_m = MC$, so that $P_m = \$14$. Since the production of each unit of the final product requires 1 unit of the intermediate product, the transfer price for the intermediate product, P_t, is set equal to MC_p at $Q_p = 40$. Thus, $P_t = \$6$. With $D_p = MR_p = P_t = MC_p = \$6$ at $Q_p = 40$ (see point E_p), $Q_p = 40$ is the best level of output of the intermediate product for the production division.

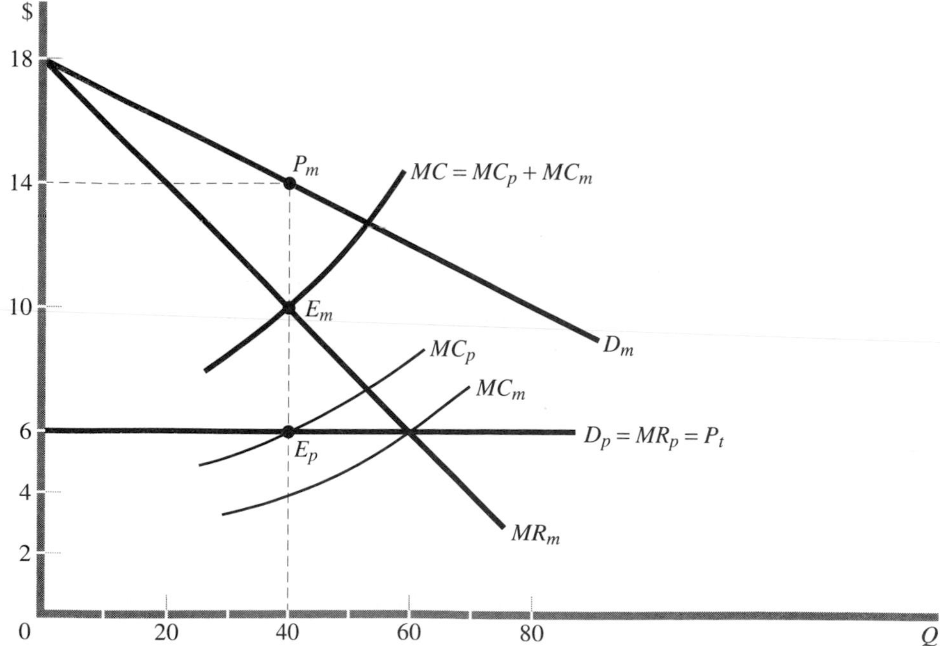

given by point E_p at which $Q_p = 40$. The demand and marginal revenue curves faced by the production division of the firm are then equal to the transfer price (that is, $D_p = MR_p = P_t$). Note that $Q_p = 40$ is the best level of output of the intermediate product by the production division of the firm because at $Q_p = 40$, $D_p = MR_p = P_t = MC_p = \$6$. Thus, we can conclude that the correct transfer price for an intermediate product for which there is no external market is the marginal cost of production.

Transfer Pricing with a Perfectly Competitive Market for the Intermediate Product

When an external market for the intermediate product does exist, the output of the production division need not be equal to the output of the final product. If the optimal output of the production division exceeds the quantity of the intermediate product demanded internally by the marketing division, the excess of the intermediate product produced can be sold on the external market for the intermediate product. On the other hand, if the marketing division of the firm demands more than the best level of output of the production division, the excess demand can be covered by purchases of the intermediate product in the external market. The transfer price, however, depends on whether or not the external market for the intermediate product is perfectly competitive. The determination of the transfer price when the external market is perfectly competitive is shown in Figure 11-7.

Figure 11-7 is identical to Figure 11-6, except that the marginal cost curve of the production division MC'_p is lower than in Figure 11-6. The production division then produces more of the intermediate product then the marketing division demands and sells the excess in the perfectly competitive external market for the intermediate product. With a perfectly competitive market for the intermediate product, the production division faces horizontal demand curve D_p for its output at the given market price P_t for the intermediate product. Since D_p is horizontal, $D_p = MR_p = P_t$ (see the figure). The best or profit-maximizing level of output of the intermediate product by the production division of the firm is 50 units and is given by point E'_p at which $D_p = MR_p = P_t = MC'_p = \$6$.

Since the marketing division can purchase the *intermediate* product either internally or externally at $P_t = \$6$, its total marginal cost curve is given by MC_t, which is the vertical sum of its own marginal cost of assembling and marketing the product (MC_m) and the price of the intermediate product (P_t). Thus, the best level of output of the *final* product by the marketing division of the firm is 40 units (the same as when there was no external market for the intermediate product) and is given by point E_m at which $MR_m = MC_t$. At $Q_m = 40$, $P_m = \$14$ (the same as in Figure 11-6).

Thus, the production division of the firm produces 50 units of the intermediate product and sells 40 units internally to the marketing division at $P_t = \$6$ and sells the remaining 10 units in the external market, also at $P_t = \$6$. The marketing division will not pay more than the external price of \$6 per unit for the

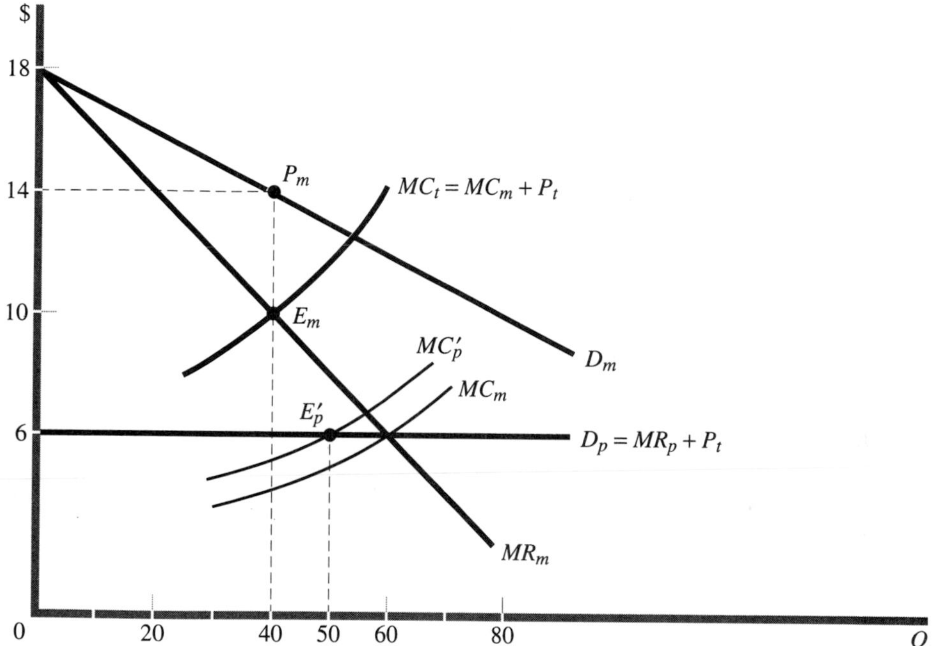

Figure 11-7
Transfer Pricing of the Intermediate Product with a Perfectly Competitive Market
This figure is identical to Figure 11-6, except that MC'_p is lower than MC_p. At the perfectly competitive external price of P_t = \$6 for the intermediate product, the production division of the firm faces $D_p = MR_p = P_t$ = \$6. Therefore, the best level of output of the intermediate product is $Q_p = 50$ and is given by point E'_p at which $D_p = MR_p = P_t = MC'_p$ = \$6. Since the marketing division can purchase the intermediate product (internally or externally) at P_t = \$6, its total marginal cost curve, MC_t, is equal to the vertical summation of MC_m and P_t. Thus, the best level of output of the final product by the marketing division is 40 units and is given by point E_m, at which $MR_m = MC_t$, so that P_m = \$14 (as in Figure 11-6).

intermediate product, while the production division will not sell the intermediate product internally to the marketing division for less than \$6 per unit. Thus, when a perfectly competitive external market for the intermediate product exists, the transfer price for intracompany sales of the intermediate product is given by the external competitive price for the intermediate product.

The analysis shown graphically in Figure 11-7 can also be undertaken algebraically, as follows. The demand and marginal revenue curves for the final product faced by the marketing division in Figure 11-7 can be represented algebraically as

$$Q_m = 180 - 10P_m \quad \text{or} \quad P_m = 18 - 0.1Q_m$$
$$\text{and} \quad MR_m = 18 - 0.2Q_m$$

Assuming that the marginal cost functions of the production and marketing divisions of the firm are, respectively,

$$MC'_p = 1 + 0.1Q_p \quad \text{and} \quad MC_m = 0.1Q_m$$

and that the perfectly competitive external price for the transfer product is P_t = \$6, we can find the best level of output of the intermediate product for the production division by setting its marginal cost equal to the transfer price. That is,

$$MC'_p = 1 + 0.1Q_p = \$6 = P_t$$

so that $$0.1Q_p = 5$$

and $$Q_p = 50$$

The best level of output of the *final product* for the marketing division is determined by finding the total marginal cost of the marketing division (MC_t) and setting it equal to its marginal revenue. That is,

$$MC_t = MC_m + P_t$$
$$= 0.1Q_m + 6$$

Then $$MC_t = 0.1Q_m + 6 = 18 - 0.2Q_m = MR_m$$
$$0.3Q_m = 12$$

so that $$Q_m = 40$$

and $$P_m = 18 - 0.1(40) = \$14$$

Thus, the production division sells 40 units of the intermediate product internally to the marketing division and the remaining 10 units on the external competitive market, all at P_t = \$6. The marketing division uses the 40 units of the intermediate product purchased internally from the production division at P_t = \$6 to produce 40 units of the final product to be sold on the external market for the final product at P_m = \$14. These are the same results obtained graphically in Figure 11-7, except that we have assumed linear rather than curvilinear *MC* functions in the above algebraic solution.

Transfer Pricing with an Imperfectly Competitive Market for the Intermediate Product

When an imperfectly competitive external market for the intermediate product exists, the transfer price of the intermediate product for intrafirm sales will differ from the price of the intermediate product on the imperfectly competitive external market. The determination of the internal and external prices of the intermediate product by the production division of the firm becomes one of third-degree price discrimination. This is shown in Figure 11-8.

Panel *a* of Figure 11-8 shows the marginal revenue of the marketing division of the firm (that is, MR_m) after subtracting from it the transfer price of the intermediate product (P_t), which is equal to the marginal cost of the production division (MC_p). Thus, the $MR_m - MC_p$ curve in the left panel shows the net marginal revenue of the marketing division. Panel *b* presents the negatively sloped demand curve for the intermediate product of the firm on the imperfectly competitive external market (D_e) and its corresponding marginal revenue curve (MR_e). In panel *c*, the MR_p curve is the total revenue curve of the production division of the firm, which is equal to the horizontal summation of the net marginal revenue curves for internal sales to the marketing division of the firm and to the external market (that is, $MR_p = MR_m - MC_p + MR_e$). The MC_p curve, on the other hand, shows the marginal cost to the production division of the firm of producing the intermediate product for internal sales to the marketing division of the firm and to the external market.

The best level of output of the intermediate product by the production division of the firm is 40 units and is given by point E_p, at which $MR_p = MC_p$ in panel *c*. The optimal distribution of the 40 units of the intermediate product produced by the production division of the firm is 20 units internally to the marketing division of the firm (given by point P_t in panel *a*) and 20 units to the external market (given by point E_e in panel *b*), so that $MR_m - MC_p = MR_e = MR_p = MC_p$ = \$4. Thus, the production division of the firm operates as the monopolist seller of the intermediate product in the segmented internal and external markets for the intermediate product. Setting the internal transfer price at $P_t = MC_p$ = \$4 ensures that the marketing division of the firm (in panel *a*) demands 20 units of the

Figure 11-8
Transfer Pricing of the Intermediate Product with an Imperfectly Competitive Market

Panel *a* presents the net marginal revenue ($MR_m - MC_p$) curve of the marketing division for the intermediate product, panel *b* shows the external demand and marginal revenue curves (that is, D_e and MR_e) for the intermediate product, while panel *c* shows the $MR_p = MR_m - MC_p + MR_e$ and MC_p curves of the production division. The best level of output of the intermediate product by the production division is 40 units and is given by E_p, at which $MR_p = MC_p$ in panel *c*. The optimal distribution of Q_p = 40 is 20 units to the marketing division and 20 units to the external market (given by points P_t and E_e, respectively), at which $MR_m - MC_p = MR_e = MR_p = MC_p$ = \$4. The transfer price to the marketing division is then $P_t = MC_p$ = \$4, and the price of the intermediate product for sales on the external market is P_e = \$6.

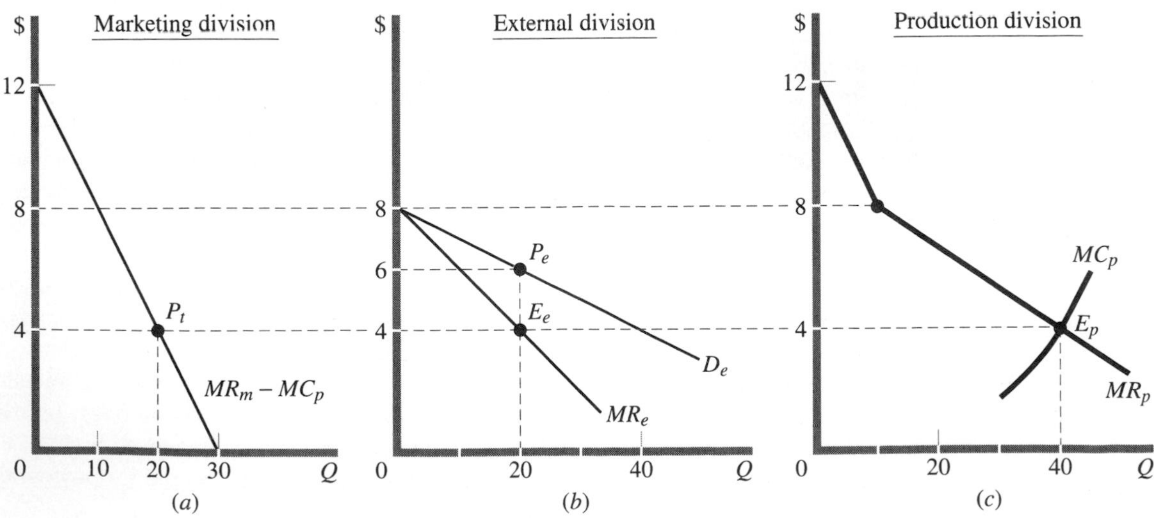

intermediate product, which leads to profit maximization for the marketing division and for the firm as a whole. With optimal sales of 20 units of the intermediate product in the external market (given by point E_e in panel *b*), the market-clearing price for the intermediate product is $P_e = \$6$.

Case Study 11-4
Transfer Pricing by Multinational Corporations

When an enterprise operates across national borders, additional profit opportunities and risks arise because of different rates of corporate taxes in different countries, currency fluctuations, import-export tariffs and subsidies, and so on. For example, by artificially overpricing intermediate products shipped to a semiautonomous division of the firm in a higher-tax nation and underpricing products shipped from the division in the high-tax nation, a multinational corporation can minimize its tax bill and increase its profits. Governments of high-tax countries seek to minimize the loss of tax and customs revenues resulting from transfer pricing by generally applying an "arm's length" test. "Arm's-length" is defined as the price an unrelated party would pay for the products under the same circumstances. This test, however, provides general guidance only and is vague on many issues. As a result, multinational corporations retain a great deal of leeway in setting transfer prices so as to minimize their overall taxes and maximize profits. This is especially true in developing countries since they generally have less effective legal controls on the transfer pricing practices of multinational corporations than developed countries. This seems to be the conclusion of a 1986 study on transfer pricing by multinationals operating in Bangladesh.

The authors of the study began by pointing out that multinational enterprises have many important advantages over local competitors. These include: economies of scale in production, high research and development expenditures by the parent company, sophisticated and efficient marketing techniques, access to sources of finance on a worldwide basis, superior marketing skills, and so on. Because of these important economic advantages, the authors expected that semiautonomous divisions of multinational corporations would have higher profit rates than local competitors. They found the reverse to be the case, however. The average net profit as a percentage of total sales of the division of multinational corporations was 3.4 percent as compared to 5.4 percent for their local competitors over the period 1975 to 1979 of the study. The authors then examined the price of intermediate products imported by semiautonomous divisions of multinational pharmaceutical corporations and the price of the same products imported by their local competitors and found that, on the average, the former were 194 percent higher than the latter. Since this difference was not due to differences in transportation costs, the authors concluded that multinational pharmaceutical firms operating in Bangladesh used transfer pricing to transfer large profits abroad.

The U.S. Internal Revenue Service, bolstered by new auditing powers, is investigating many American subsidiaries of foreign firms, especially Japanese ones, on the suspicion that they have underpaid U.S. corporate income taxes by as much as $12 billion. Indirect evidence of this is given by the fact that the ratio of income tax payments to total receipts of foreign-controlled U.S. corporations was less than half that of U.S. corporations. Even more incredible is the fact that of the nearly 37,000 foreign-owned companies filing returns in 1986, more than half reported no taxable income! Then starting in 1991, the IRS adopted an "advance pricing agreement" with an increasing number of multinational corporations on the range of prices at which to value the various products that these multinationals import to the United States, so as to avoid transfer price disputes. But such disputes continue.

Source: OECD, *Transfer Pricing and Multinational Enterprises* (Paris: OECD, 1979); M. P. Casey, "International Transfer Pricing," *Management Accounting,* October 1985, pp. 31–35; M. Z. Rahman and R. W. Scapens, "Transfer Pricing by Multinationals: Some Evidence from Bangladesh," *Journal of Business and Financial Accounting,* Autumn 1986, pp. 383–391; "I.R.S. Investigating Foreign Companies for Tax Cheating," *The New York Times,* February 10, 1990, p. 1; "Big Japan Concern Reaches an Accord on Paying U.S. Tax," *The New York Times,* November 11, 1992, p. 1; and "Why Do Foreign Companies Report such Low Profits on Their U.S. Operations?" *The Wall Street Journal,* November 2, 1994, p. A1.

11-5 PRICING IN PRACTICE

In this section we examine some of the actual pricing practices followed by firms in the real world. The most common of these is cost-plus pricing. Here, we explain this practice, examine its advantages and disadvantages, and show that it approximates the profit-maximizing pricing rule. We complete this section with an examination of incremental analysis in pricing, two-part tariff, tying, bundling, and other real-world pricing practices.

Cost-Plus Pricing

In the real world, firms may not be able (and it may be too expensive) to collect precise marginal revenue (MR) and marginal cost (MC) data to determine the optimal level of output and price at the point at which $MR = MC$. Therefore, firms have developed rules of thumb or short-cut methods for pricing their products. The most widely used of such pricing rules is **cost-plus pricing** (also called "markup pricing" and "full-cost pricing"). The usual method is for the firm to first estimate the average variable cost (AVC) of producing or purchasing and marketing the product for a normal or standard level of output (usually taken to be between 70 and 80 percent of capacity). The firm then adds to the AVC an average overhead charge (usually expressed as a percentage of AVC), so as to get the estimated fully allocated average cost (C). To this **fully allocated average cost,** the firm then adds a markup on cost (m) for profits.

The formula for the **markup on cost** can, thus, be expressed as

$$m = \frac{P - C}{C} \qquad (11\text{-}3)$$

where m is the markup on cost, P is the product price, and C is the fully allocated average cost of the product. The numerator of Equation 11-3 (that is, $P - C$) is called the **profit margin.** Solving Equation 11-3 for P, we get the price of the product in a cost-plus pricing scheme. That is,

$$P = C(1 + m) \tag{11-4}$$

For example, suppose that a firm takes 80 percent of its capacity output of 125 units as the normal or standard output, that it projects total variable and overhead costs for the year to be, respectively, \$1,000 and \$600 for the normal or standard output, and that it wants to apply a 25 percent markup on cost. Then the normal or standard output is 100 units, the $AVC = \$10$, and the average overhead cost is \$6. Thus, $C = \$16$ and $P = 16(1 + 0.25) = \$20$ with $m = (\$20 - \$16)/\$16 = 0.25$. Markups of 25 percent have been traditional in some major industries, such as automobiles, electrical equipment, and aluminum, in order for firms in these industries to achieve a target rate of return on investment for the normal or standard level of output.

Evaluation of Cost-Plus Pricing

The widespread use of cost-plus pricing in the real world can be explained by the several important advantages that it provides. First, cost-plus pricing generally requires less information and less precise data than the rule of setting price at the output level at which marginal revenue equals marginal cost. Second, cost-plus pricing seems easy and simple to use. This apparent simplicity, however, is misleading since it may be very difficult to correctly estimate and project total variable costs, and it may actually be impossible to appropriately allocate total overhead charges to the various products produced by the firm. Third, cost-plus pricing usually results in relatively stable prices when costs do not vary very much over time. This is an advantage because it is costly to change prices. Price changes may also lead to uncertain price responses in oligopolistic markets. Finally, cost-plus pricing can provide a clear justification for price increases when costs rise.

Despite the above important advantages and widespread use, cost-plus pricing is criticized on several important grounds. One criticism is that cost-plus pricing is based on accounting and historical costs, rather than on replacement and opportunity costs. While this is a serious criticism of how cost-plus pricing is usually conducted in practice, it is not a criticism of cost-plus pricing itself since the firm could (and should) base its calculations on the correct replacement or opportunity cost basis rather than on incorrect accounting and historical costs. Another important criticism is that cost-plus pricing is based on the average, rather than on the marginal, cost of production. To the extent, however, that marginal cost is constant or nearly constant over the normal or standard level of output of the firm, marginal cost is approximately equal to (the fully allocated) average cost. Therefore, cost-plus pricing would not lead to product prices that are much different from prices based on the $MR = MC$ rule.

Finally, cost-plus pricing is criticized because it ignores conditions of demand. Since it has been shown, however, that firms usually apply higher markups to products facing less elastic demand than to products with more elastic demand, it can be demonstrated that cost-plus pricing leads to approximately the profit-maximizing price. To show this, we begin with Equation 3-12, repeated below as Equation 11-5:

$$MR = P\left(1 + \frac{1}{E_p}\right) \tag{11-5}$$

where MR is the marginal revenue, P is the product price, and E_p is the price elasticity of demand. Solving for P, we get

$$P = \frac{MR}{1 + 1/E_p} = \frac{MR}{(E_p + 1)/E_p} = MR\frac{E_p}{E_p + 1} \tag{11-6}$$

Since profits are maximized where $MR = MC$, we can substitute MC for MR in the above equation and get

$$P = MC\frac{E_p}{E_p + 1}$$

To the extent that the firm's MC is constant over the normal or standard level of output, $MC = C$, where C is the fully allocated average cost of the product. Substituting C for MC into the above equation, we get

$$P = C\frac{E_p}{E_p + 1} \tag{11-7}$$

Setting Equations 11-4 and 11-7 equal to each other, we have

$$C(1 + m) = C\frac{E_p}{E_p + 1}$$

or

$$1 + m = \frac{E_p}{E_p + 1}$$

so that the optimal markup is

$$m = \frac{E_p}{E_p + 1} - 1 \tag{11-8}$$

From Equation 11-8 we can calculate that if $E_p = -1.5$, $m = 2$, or 200 percent; if $E_p = -2$, $m = 1$, or 100 percent; if $E_p = -3$, $m = 0.5$, or 50 percent; and if $E_p = -4$, $m = 0.33$, or 33 percent. We can thus conclude that the optimal markup is lower the greater is the price elasticity of demand of the product.[9]

This fact has often been observed in the real world.[10] That is, firms have been found to apply a higher markup to products with inelastic demand than to products with elastic demand, and when increased competition has increased the price elasticity of demand, they have been found to reduce their markup. For example,

[9]Note that an imperfectly competitive firm (i.e., one facing a negatively sloped demand) will operate only in the elastic portion of the demand curve for the product (i.e., in the range of the demand curve for which $E_p > |-1|$) so that MR is positive and equals MC.

[10]See R. M. Cyert and J. G. March, *A Behavioral Theory of the Firm* (Englewood Cliffs, N.J.: Prentice-Hall, 1963).

the markup on cost is much lower (between 10 and 12 percent) in the grocery business, where price elasticity of demand is very high, than for industrial machinery where the price elasticity is lower. We can, therefore, conclude that cost-plus pricing does take demand considerations into account in actual practice and does lead to approximately profit-maximizing prices. In a world of inadequate and imprecise data on demand and costs, firms may simply utilize cost-plus pricing as the rule-of-thumb method for determining the profit-maximizing prices.

Incremental Analysis in Pricing

Correct pricing and output decisions require **incremental analysis.** That is, a firm should change the price of a product or its output, introduce a new product, or a new version of a given product, accept a new order, etc., if the increase in total revenue or incremental revenue from the action exceeds the increase in total or incremental cost. For example, an airline should introduce a new flight if the incremental revenue from the flight exceeds the incremental cost. When excess capacity exists in the short run, overhead or fixed costs are irrelevant in determining whether or not a firm should undertake a particular course of action. Since overhead or fixed costs have already been covered, any action on the part of the firm that increases revenues more than costs leads to an increase in the total profits of the firm and should be undertaken.

If, on the other hand, the firm is already producing at capacity, lowering a product's price to increase sales or introducing a new product will lead to the expansion of all costs, including those for plant and equipment. In this case, full-cost and incremental-cost pricing lead to the same results. Even when the firm is operating with idle capacity, the long-run implications of a particular course of action must be taken into consideration in order for the firm to reach correct pricing and output decisions. For example, if a firm lowers the price of a product in order to increase sales or introduces a new product in order to take advantage of idle capacity, these actions may require the expansion of capacity if the firm expects the demand for its products to increase in the long run. Incremental analysis must, then, take these long-run effects into consideration.

Correct incremental analysis requires that all direct and indirect changes in revenues and costs resulting from a particular course of action be taken into consideration. For example, in calculating the incremental revenue from lowering the price of a product or from the introduction of a new product, the firm must consider all demand interrelationships between the product in question and all other complementary and substitute products sold by the firm. For example, the incremental revenue from lowering the price of photographic film by Kodak may very well be smaller than the incremental cost, but when the increase in sales of Kodak cameras resulting from the reduction in the price of the film is taken into consideration, the action may prove to be highly profitable for the firm. Similarly, increasing the production of a particular product or the introduction of a new product may lower the cost of a jointly produced product so much that the overall incremental cost from the action may be much lower than the overall incremental revenue, so that the decision may lead to much higher profits for the firm.

From what has been said above, it should be clear that a firm could not price all its products on an incremental basis since in the aggregate, the firm must also cover all its overhead and fixed costs, at least in the long run. But it is not necessary and it would be inappropriate for a firm to price each of its products on a fully allocated average cost basis. Particularly in the short run and in the presence of idle capacity, it would be very advantageous (i.e., it would increase total profits or reduce total losses) if the firm accepted a price on some additional sales that was below fully allocated average costs, as long as the price exceeded average incremental costs. Such incremental pricing policies provide the firm with much more flexibility and are clearly in evidence in the pricing policies followed by "excellently managed firms."[11] These firms take into consideration not only the short-run but also the long-run implications of their pricing policies, and they consider all important demand and production interrelationships.

[11]See J. S. Early, "Marginal Policies in Excellently Managed Firms: A Survey," *American Economic Review,* March 1956, pp. 44–70, and "Flexible Pricing," *Business Week,* December 12, 1977, pp. 66–76.

Case Study 11-5

Incremental Pricing at Continental Airlines

A classic example of incremental analysis is the decision process followed by Continental Airlines to add or to cancel a particular flight from its schedule. Continental and the airline industry in general face very high overhead costs for depreciation, interest charges, and ground, office, and flight crews. Continental followed the rule of adding a flight to its schedule as long as the increase in total revenue or the incremental revenue from the flight exceeded the increase in out-of-pocket expenses or incremental cost. The excess of incremental revenue over incremental cost would then make a contribution toward covering the firm's overhead or fixed costs. Great care was exercised to uncover all incremental revenues and costs in deciding whether or not to add a particular flight.

In determining the net incremental revenue from the flight, Continental considered not only the extra revenue that the flight itself was expected to generate but also the effect of adding the flight on competing and connecting flights. For example, the direct incremental revenue from the proposed flight might fall short of the incremental cost, but if the flight fed passengers into Continental's long-haul service and the overall direct and indirect incremental revenue exceeded the overall direct and indirect incremental costs, the airline would add the flight. Similarly, Continental sometimes scheduled late evening round-trip flights from New York to Houston without a single passenger to avoid the higher overnight hangar rental cost in New York than in Houston (its home base). On some of its routes, Continental also introduced fares sufficiently low to effectively discourage other airlines from entering the market and also servicing the route. This is an example of **limit**

pricing. Similarly, Continental charged higher fares in times of peak demand when older and less fuel efficient planes had to be brought into operation. This is an example of **peak-load pricing.** In recent years, incremental pricing has been greatly refined with the use of advanced computers and is now practiced by all airlines under the name of "yield management" (see Integrating Case Study Four at the end of this chapter).

Source: "Airline Takes the Marginal Route," *Business Week,* April 20, 1963, pp. 111–114; and "Continental Airlines Grounds Airbus Fleet in Cost-Cutting Move," *The Wall Street Journal,* December 22, 1994, p. C18.

Case Study 11-6

Peak-Load Pricing by Con Edison

Table 11-2 gives the higher price per kilowatt-hour (kWh) that Con Edison charged residential and commercial users of electricity for peak hours than for off-peak hours in New York City in 1995 during winter and summer months. Note that Con Edison practices peak-load pricing only for residential users and small businesses, not for large commercial users. Also to be noted is that peak-load pricing is different from third-degree price discrimination because higher peak electricity rates are based on or reflect the higher costs of generating electricity at peak hours when older and less efficient plants and equipment have to be brought into operation to meet peak demand.

Table 11-2
Electricity Rates Charged by Con Edison for Peak and Nonpeak Hours During 1995 (cents per kilowatt-hour)

RESIDENTIAL RATES (SINGLE RESIDENCE)		
	Peak Hours	Off-Peak Hours
Winter	14.36	3.75
Summer	33.01	3.75

COMMERCIAL RATES (SMALL BUSINESS)		
	Peak Hours	Off-Peak Hours
Winter	13.74	5.87
Summer	26.28	5.87

Source: Con Edison, New York City.

Two-Part Tariff, Tying, and Bundling

Two-part tariff refers to the pricing practice in which consumers pay an initial fee for the right to purchase a product or service, as well as a usage fee or price for each unit of the product they purchase. Oligopolistic and monopolistic firms sometimes use this pricing method as a way to increase their profits. Examples are provided by amusement parks where visitors are charged a general admission fee as well as a fee or price for each ride they take; telephone companies, which charge a monthly fee plus a message-unit fee; computer companies, which charge monthly rentals plus a usage fee for renting their mainframe computers; and golf and tennis clubs, which charge an annual membership fee plus a fee for each round or game played.[12]

Tying refers to the requirement that a consumer who buys or leases a product also purchase another product needed in the use of the first. For example, when the Xerox Corporation was the only producer of photocopiers in the 1950s, it required those leasing its machines to also purchase paper from Xerox. Similarly, until it was ordered by the court to discontinue the practice, IBM required by contract that the users of its computers purchase IBM punch cards. Sometimes tying of purchases is done to ensure that the correct supplies are used for the equipment to function properly or to ensure quality. More often, it is used as a form of two-part tariff to earn higher profits. The courts, however, often intervene to forbid these restrictions on competition. For example, McDonald's was forced to allow its franchises to purchase their materials and supplies from any McDonald's-approved supplier rather than only from McDonald's. This increased competition while still ensuring quality and protection of the brand name.[13]

Bundling is a common form of tying in which the firm requires customers buying or leasing one of its products or services to also buy or lease another product or service *when customers have different tastes* but the firm cannot price discriminate (as in tying). By selling or leasing the product or service as a package or bundle rather than separately, the monopolist can increase its total profits. This is examined in Case Study 11-7.

[12]For a more in-depth discussion of two-part tariff, see W. Oi, "A Disneyland Dilemma: Two-Part Tariff for a Mickey Mouse Monopoly," *Quarterly Journal of Economics,* February 1971, pp. 77–96.

[13]See B. Klein and L. F. Saft, "The Law and Economics of Franchise Tying Contracts," *Journal of Law and Economics,* May 1985, pp. 345–361.

Case Study 11-7

Bundling in the Leasing of Movies

Table 11-3 shows the prices that theater 1 and theater 2 would be willing to pay to lease movie *A* and movie *B*. If the film company cannot price discriminate and it leases each movie separately to the two theaters, it will have to lease each movie at the lower of the two prices at which each theater is willing to lease each film. Specifically, the film company would have to charge $10,000 for movie *A* and $3,000 for movie *B* for a total of $13,000 to lease both movies to each theater (if the film company charged more for each movie, one of the theaters would not lease the movie). But theater 1 would have been willing to pay $15,000 to lease both movies, and theater 2 would have been willing to pay $14,000 for both movies. The film company can thus lease both movies as a package or a bundle for $14,000 (the lowest of the total amounts at which the two theaters are willing to lease the two movies) rather than individually for $13,000 (without price discriminating between the two theaters).

Table 11-3
Maximum Price Each Theater Would Be Willing to Pay to Lease Each Film Separately or As a Bundle

	Theater 1	Theater 2
Movie *A*	$12,000	$10,000
Movie *B*	3,000	4,000

Such profitable bundling is possible only when one theater is willing to pay more for leasing one movie but less for leasing the other movie with respect to the other theater. If, in our example, theater 1 had been willing to pay only $9,000 or theater 2 only $8,000 to lease movie *A*, then the maximum price that the film company could charge either theater without price discrimination would be $12,000, whether it leased the movies as a bundle or separately. In that case, the relative valuation for the two movies would be the same for both theaters and bundling would not be profitable. For bundling to be profitable, one theater must be willing to pay more for one movie and less for another movie with respect to the other theater. This occurs only if the two theaters serve different audiences with different tastes and have different relative valuations for the two movies.

Source: R. L. Schmalensee, "Commodity Bundling by Single-Product Monopolies," *Journal of Law and Economics,* April 1982, pp. 67–71; and A. Lewbel, "Bundling of Substitutes or Complements," *International Journal of Industrial Organization,* no. 3, 1985, pp. 101–107.

Other Pricing Practices

There are many other pricing practices often used in the real world. Some of these are prestige pricing, price lining, skimming, and value pricing. A new pricing technology based on the use of electronic scanners is also spreading rapidly in supermarkets.

Prestige pricing refers to deliberately setting high prices to attract prestige-oriented consumers. For example, many people pay prices ranging from $30,000 to $70,000 to drive Mercedes rather than similar lower-priced automobiles for the prestige that they get from doing so. There are more people buying furs costing $5,000 than similar furs costing $2,000 because of the snob appeal they get from the more expensive furs. Consumers often pay high prices for some goods when very similar much lower price substitutes exist because they often equate price with quality. This occurs particularly in cases where it is difficult to obtain objective information on product quality. Recognizing this fact, producers sometimes package the same basic product differently—one to look as being of higher quality than another and selling the first at a much higher price.

Price lining is another pricing practice sometimes observed in the real world. This refers to the setting of a price target by a firm and then developing a product that would allow the firm to maximize total profits at that price. Thus, instead of deciding first on the type of product to produce and then on the price to charge so as to maximize the firm's total profits (as usual), the order is reversed with price lining. For example, GM has the Cadillac line of automobiles that sells at the highest price range and appeals to the wealthiest and most quality-conscious consumers. GM also has the Oldsmobile line of midsized automobiles that sells at a lower price range and appeals to consumers of average income. Finally, GM has the compact-car line that sells at the lowest price range. GM automobile lines compete with similar lines of automobiles from Ford, Chrysler, and imports which sell at similar price ranges. Trying to increase the quality and price of Oldsmobiles outside the established range would probably not be profitable because consumers have become accustomed to view Oldsmobiles as being of midrange in quality and at selling at a midrange price.

Skimming refers to the setting of a high price when a product is first introduced and gradually lowering its price subsequently. This occurs most often in durable goods such as refrigerators, washing machines, and personal computers. The reason and the rationale for this are that it is often difficult to determine exactly the strength of demand when a product is first introduced and, therefore, the best price to charge. Starting with a high price allows the firm to sell the product to those consumers who are willing to pay the high price. The firm then lowers the price, both to increase sales and to discourage entrants if the initial high price leads to very large profits. Skimming is particularly useful if the firm has initially limited production capacity. In that case, it pays for the firm to sell its limited output at the highest price it can fetch. As the firm becomes convinced that it can sell a greater quantity at a lower price, it will expand capacity and lower its price.

Value pricing refers to the selling of quality goods at much lower prices than previously. This is old-fashioned price cutting but with manufacturers redesigning the product to keep or enhance quality while lowering costs so as to still earn a profit. It is offering more for a lot less. For example, the PepsiCo Inc.'s Taco Bell chain saw its fourth quarter 1990 sales jump 15 percent in response to a "value" menu offering 59-cent tacos and 14 other items for either 59 cents or 79 cents. This forced McDonald's and Wendy's to respond with a value menu of their own. Similarly Toyota redesigned its lowest price automobile, the Tercel, to offer more horsepower and a quieter ride than its predecessor at a lower price and still make money on it. Value pricing is likely to spread in the future as companies cater to increasingly sophisticated but bargain-conscious consumers.

Pricing technology at supermarkets is being revolutionized by the use of **electronic scanners.** More than half of the nation's supermarkets already use such electronic scanners at checkout counters to ring up prices for barcoded items. The use of scanners drastically cuts costs by allowing supermarkets to avoid item-by-item pricing and repricing of grocery items and allowing them to use less skilled and less costly sales clerks at checkout counters. While it is expensive to install scanners, with profit margins already very thin, competition will very likely force all supermarkets to adopt this innovation in order to remain in business.

Case Study 11-8

No-Haggling Value Pricing by General Motors

During the past few years, General Motors (GM) has been moving toward no-haggling, value pricing for more of its cars. Although some Americans may find it stimulating, most consider the time-honored business of haggling over the price of a new car intimidating and even humiliating. One-price selling was first instituted at GM's Saturn division when it began building cars in 1990, but it has since spread to many other GM models. Ford has also started experimenting with one-price selling on a few of its vehicles. Dealers' great fear of one-price selling is that customers will simply take the offer elsewhere and use it to negotiate a better deal. Advocates of one-price selling respond that dealers can avoid being undercut by combining one-price selling with value pricing and accepting smaller profit margins. They believe that customers are not going to go to other dealers to hassle over $40 or $50 if they know that they are already getting good value for their money.

GM moved to value pricing for most of its cars with the 1994 model year. This involved the selling of well-equipped 1994 cars at lower prices than similarly equipped 1993 models. For example, the 1994 Pontiac Grand Prix was offered at a lower price than the 1993 model even though the newer model had dual airbags while the 1993 model came with no airbags. GM's hope, of course, was to increase market share and profits. The strategy seems to be working. For example, by lowering the price of a well-equipped Buick LeSabre from $21,000 for the 1993 model to $18,995 for a similarly equipped 1994 model, GM boosted sales of the model by about 15 percent. Thus, GM's objective is to move from a strategy of higher sticker price offset by big rebates to a strategy of lower prices without rebates. GM enforces this strategy by loading its cars with options and setting the recommended prices so close to the invoice price that dealers have little room to bargain. In fact, gross profit margins were already only 6.7 percent or $1,200 per new car sold in the United States in 1993, and net profit margins (after paying rent, commissions, and other selling costs) averaged only about $80 per new car sold.

Source: "GM Stresses Value Pricing for '94 Models," *The Wall Street Journal,* July 12, 1993, p. A3; and "Buying Without Haggling as Cars Get Fixed Prices," *The New York Times,* February 1, 1994, p. 1.

SUMMARY

1. When the firm produces more than one product, the firm must consider demand interdependence (substitutability and complementarity), which are reflected in the marginal revenue function of each product, for optimal pricing and output decisions. Firms produce more than one product in order to

make fuller use of their production facilities. They introduce new products in order of their profitability until $MR_A = MR_B = MC_C = MC$, where product C is the least profitable product for the firm. The best level of output of products that are jointly produced in fixed proportions is given by the point at which total marginal revenue (MR_T) equals the marginal cost for the joint products. Prices are then determined on the respective demand curves for the jointly produced products. A firm will sell a jointly produced product, however, only up to the point at which $MR = 0$. The optimal output of products that are jointly produced in variable proportions is given at the tangency point of the isorevenue line and the product transformation or total cost curve that leads to the overall maximum profits for the firm.

2. "Price discrimination" refers to the charging of different prices for different quantities of a product, at different times, to different customer groups, or in different markets, when these price differences are not justified by cost differences. Three conditions must be met for a firm to be able to practice price discrimination: (1) The firm must have some monopoly power, (2) the price elasticities of demand for the product in different markets must differ, and (3) the markets must be separable or can be segmented. "First-degree price discrimination" refers to the selling of each unit of the product separately and charging the highest price possible for each unit sold. "Second-degree price discrimination" refers to the charging of a uniform price per unit for a specific quantity or block of the product, a lower price per unit for an additional batch or block of the product, and so on. "Third-degree price discrimination" refers to the charging of different prices for the same product in different markets until the marginal revenue of the last unit of the product sold in each market equals the marginal cost of the product.
3. International price discrimination is called (persistent) dumping. Under this type of dumping the monopolist sells the commodity at a higher price at home (where the market demand curve is less elastic) than abroad where the monopolist faces competition from other nations and the market demand curve for the monopolist's product is more elastic.
4. "Transfer pricing" refers to the determination of the price of the intermediate products sold by one semiautonomous division of a firm to another semiautonomous division of the same enterprise. Appropriate transfer pricing is essential in determining the optimal output of each division and of the firm as a whole, and in evaluating divisional performance and determining divisional rewards. The correct transfer price for an intermediate product for which there is no external market is the marginal cost of production. When a perfectly competitive external market for the intermediate product exists, the transfer price for intracompany sales of the intermediate product is given by the external competitive price for the intermediate product. When an intermediate product can be sold in an imperfectly competitive market, the (internal) transfer price of the intermediate product is given at the point at which the net marginal revenue of the marketing division of the firm is equal to the marginal cost of the production division at the best total level of

output of the intermediate product, and the price charged in the external market is given on the external demand curve.

5. Because it may be too expensive or impossible to collect precise marginal revenue and marginal cost data, most firms use cost-plus pricing. This involves calculating the average variable cost of producing the normal or standard level of output (usually between 70 and 80 percent of capacity), adding an average overhead charge so as to get the fully allocated average cost for the product, and then adding to this a markup on cost for profits. Since firms usually apply higher markups for products facing less elastic demand than for products with more elastic demand, it can also be demonstrated that cost-plus pricing leads to approximately the profit-maximizing price. Correct pricing and output decisions by the firm involve incremental analysis or comparison of the incremental revenue to the incremental cost of the managerial decisions. Other real-world pricing practices are two-part tariff, tying, bundling, prestige pricing, price lining, value pricing, and skimming. Pricing technology at supermarkets is also being revolutionized by the use of electronic scanners.

DISCUSSION QUESTIONS

1. (*a*) What is meant by demand interrelationships for a multiproduct firm? (*b*) How are demand interrelationships measured? (*c*) Why must a multiproduct firm take into consideration demand interrelationships in its pricing and output decisions?
2. (*a*) Why do most firms produce more than one product? (*b*) What is the rule for profit maximization for a multiproduct firm? (*c*) Why would a firm produce a product on which it makes zero profits?
3. Why should jointly produced products in fixed proportions be (*a*) regarded as a single production package? (*b*) treated separately in demand?
4. (*a*) How can a firm determine the best level of output and price for products that are jointly produced in fixed proportions? (*b*) Under what circumstances would a firm produce a product and then destroy it?
5. While the case of products jointly produced in variable proportions is more common than the case of products jointly produced in fixed proportions, Figure 11-3 is based on a somewhat inappropriate assumption. Can you identify what that assumption is?
6. (*a*) How would the shape of the isorevenue lines in Figure 11-3 change if we did not assume that P_A and P_B are constant? (*b*) How does this change the analysis?
7. Quantity discounts are not a form of price discrimination because the firm saves on handling large orders. True or false? Explain.

8. (*a*) Why are first- and second-degree price discrimination less common than third-degree price discrimination? (*b*) Are lower airline fares at midweek an example of third-degree price discrimination? (*c*) Under what conditions would it not be useful to charge different prices in different markets (i.e., practice third-degree price discrimination) even if possible?

9. (*a*) Is persistent dumping good or bad for the receiving country? (*b*) Against what type of dumping would the nation want to protect itself? Why?

10. (*a*) What has stimulated the growth of the large-scale modern enterprise? (*b*) What organizational development was introduced in order to contain the tendency toward rising costs? (*c*) To what problem did this lead? (*d*) Why is it important to solve this problem?

11. How is the transfer price of an intermediate product determined when (*a*) there is no external market for the intermediate product, (*b*) a perfectly competitive external market for the intermediate product exists, and (*c*) when an imperfectly competitive external market for the intermediate product exists?

12. (*a*) Indicate in Figure 11-6 the shape and location of the total marginal cost curve of the marketing division of the firm. (*b*) Can you explain why such a curve was not shown in Figure 11-6?

13. What are (*a*) the advantages and (*b*) disadvantages of cost-plus pricing? (*c*) Why is incremental cost pricing the correct pricing method? Why is full-cost pricing equal to it?

14. What is meant by (*a*) two-part tariff? (*b*) Tying? (*c*) Bundling? (*d*) Prestige pricing? (*e*) Price lining? (*f*) Value pricing? (*g*) Skimming?

PROBLEMS

*1. The Bike Corporation of America produces four types of bicycles (*A*, *B*, *C*, and *F*) in declining order of sophistication, price, and profitability. In fact, in the sale of model *F*, the firm is a perfect competitor. Draw a figure showing the best level of output and price of each type of bicycle produced by the firm.

2. The Bel Monte Canning Company cans pineapples and sells the juice that results as a by-product of peeling and slicing pineapples. Each 10-pound basket of pineapples results in a 5-pound can of pineapples and in a 5-quart can of pineapple juice. The demand and marginal revenue functions that the firm faces for canned pineapple (product *A*) and pineapple juice (product *B*) are, respectively,

$$Q_A = 80 - 5P_A \quad \text{or} \quad P_A = 16 - 0.2Q_A$$
$$\text{and} \quad MR_A = 16 - 0.4Q_A$$
$$Q_B = 50 - 5P_B \quad \text{or} \quad P_B = 10 - 0.2Q_B$$
$$\text{and} \quad MR_B = 10 - 0.4Q_B$$

Two alternative marginal cost functions for the total pineapple "package" are, respectively.

$$MC = 8 + 0.1Q \quad \text{or} \quad MC' = \frac{2Q}{35}$$

Determine graphically the best level of output and price of canned pineapple and pineapple juice with each alternative MC function.

*3. Solve Problem 2 algebraically.

4. Suppose that the marginal cost functions in Figure 11-2 were not the ones indicated on that figure but were instead:

$$MC = 1 + 02.Q \quad \text{and} \quad MC' = 1 + 0.05Q$$

Solve the problem of Figure 11-2 mathematically.

5. The Dairy Farm Company, a small producer of milk and cheese, has estimated the quantities of milk and cheese that it can produce with three different levels of total expenditures or total costs. These are indicated in the following table. If the price of milk (product A) and the price of cheese (product B) that the firm receives are \$1 each per unit of the products, draw a figure showing the maximum total profit (π) that the firm can earn at each level of TC and the overall maximum profit that the firm can earn for the three different levels of TC.

TC = \$70		TC = \$90		TC = \$140	
Product A	Product B	Product A	Product B	Product A	Product B
80	0	100	0	130	0
70	40	90	60	110	70
50	70	70	90	80	120
20	90	30	120	40	150
0	95	0	130	0	160

6. Show graphically the maximum total profit that the firm of Problem 5 earns if the price of milk (product A) falls to \$0.50 while the price of cheese (product B) remains at \$1.

*7. The Saga Food Company produces one type of frozen dinner sold directly to consumers and to restaurants. The demand and marginal revenue functions for Saga's frozen dinner by consumers (market 1) and restaurants (market 2) are, respectively.

$$Q_1 = 160 - 10P_1 \quad \text{or} \quad P_1 = 16 - 0.1Q_1 \quad \text{and} \quad MR_1 = 16 - 0.2Q_1$$
$$Q_2 = 200 - 20P_2 \quad \text{or} \quad P_2 = 10 - 0.05Q_2 \quad \text{and} \quad MR_2 = 10 - 0.1Q_2$$

Saga's total cost function is

$$TC = 120 + 4Q$$

Draw a figure showing (1) the demand, marginal revenue, and marginal cost curves faced by the firm; (2) the best level of output of the firm and how the firm should distribute sales in each market in order to maximize total profits with third-degree price discrimination; (3) the price and total revenue of the firm in each market with third-degree price discrimination; (4) the profit per unit and in total with third-degree price discrimination; and (5) the output, price, total revenue, and profit per unit and in total in the absence of price discrimination.

8. Solve Problem 7 algebraically.

9. The Digital Clock Corporation is composed of two semiautonomous divisions—a production division which manufactures the moving mechanism for digital clocks and a marketing division which assembles and markets the clocks. There is no external market for the moving parts of the clocks manufactured by the production division. The external demand and marginal revenue functions for the finished product (i.e., the clock) sold by the marketing division of the firm are, respectively,

$$Q_m = 160 - 10P_m \quad \text{or} \quad P_m = 16 - 0.1Q_m \quad \text{and} \quad MR_m = 16 - 0.2Q_m$$

The marginal cost functions of the production and marketing divisions of the firm are, respectively,

$$MC_p = 3 + 0.1Q_p \quad \text{and} \quad MC_m = 1 + 0.1Q_m$$

Draw a figure showing (1) the firm's best level of output and price for the finished product (the clock) and (2) the transfer price and output of the intermediate product (the moving parts of the clock).

10. Starting with the given information of Problem 9, except that

$$MC'_p = 2 + 0.1Q_p$$

and that a perfectly competitive market exists for the intermediate product at P_t = \$6, determine graphically the profit-maximizing outputs for the production and marketing divisions of the firm and the optimal transfer price for the intermediate product and the price of the final product.

*11. Solve Problem 10 algebraically.

12. **Integrating Problem**
The California Instruments Corporation, a producer of electronic equipment, produces pocket calculators in a plant which is run autonomously. The plant has a capacity output of 200,000 calculators per year, and the plant's manager regards 75 percent of capacity as the normal or standard output. The projected total variable costs for the normal or standard level of output are \$900,000, while the total overhead or fixed costs are estimated to be 120 percent of total variable costs. The plant manager wants to apply a 20 percent markup on cost. (*a*) What price should the manager charge for the calculators? (*b*) If the price set is the profit-maximizing price, what is the

price elasticity of demand for calculators faced by the plant? (*c*) If the price elasticity of demand were −4, what would be the optimum markup on cost that the manager should apply? (*d*) If during the year the plant manager receives an order for an additional 20,000 of its calculators from a large municipal school system to be delivered in four months for the price of \$10, should the manager accept the order? (*e*) If California Instruments wants to add the pocket calculator produced by the plant to its own product line on a regular basis, what should be the transfer price of the pocket calculators? (*f*) Suppose that in the future the plant will sell pocket calculators to the marketing division of California Instruments and on the external imperfectly competitive market, where the price elasticity of demand is $E_p = -2$. What would be the net marginal revenue of the marketing division of the firm for the pocket calculators? At what price should the calculators be sold on the external market?

APPENDIX

THIRD-DEGREE PRICE DISCRIMINATION WITH CALCULUS

A monopolist selling a commodity in two separate markets must decide how much to sell in each market in order to maximize his or her total profits. The total profits of the monopolist (π) are equal to the sum of the total revenue that he or she receives from selling the commodity in the two markets (that is, $TR_1 + TR_2$) minus the total cost (TC) of producing the total output. That is,

$$\pi = TR_1 + TR_2 - TC \tag{11-9}$$

Taking the first partial derivative of π with respect to Q_1 (the quantity sold in the first market) and Q_2 (the amount sold in the second market) and setting them equal to zero, we get

$$\frac{\partial \pi}{\partial Q_1} = \frac{\partial TR_1}{\partial Q_1} - \frac{\partial TC}{\partial Q_1} = 0 \quad \text{and} \quad \frac{\partial \pi}{\partial Q_2} = \frac{\partial TR_2}{\partial Q_2} - \frac{\partial TC}{\partial Q_2} = 0 \tag{11-10}$$

or

$$MR_1 = MR_2 = MC \tag{11-11}$$

That is, in order to maximize his or her total profits, the monopolist must distribute sales between the two markets in such a way that the marginal revenue is the same in both markets and equals the common marginal cost. Equations 11-10 and 11-11 represent the first-order condition for profit maximization. The second-order condition is that

$$\frac{\partial^2 \pi}{\partial Q_1^2} < 0 \quad \text{and} \quad \frac{\partial^2 \pi}{\partial Q_2^2} < 0 \tag{11-12}$$

Since we know from Equation 3-12 that

$$MR = P\left(1 + \frac{1}{E_p}\right) \tag{11-13}$$

profit maximization requires that $MR_1 = MR_2$ or

$$P_1\left(1 + \frac{1}{E_{p1}}\right) = P_2\left(1 + \frac{1}{E_{p2}}\right) \tag{11-14}$$

where P_1 and P_2 are the prices in market 1 and market 2, respectively, and E_{p_1} and E_{p_2} are the coefficients of price elasticity of demand in market 1 and market 2 (which are negative). If $|E_{p_1}| < |E_{p_2}|$, Equation 11-14 will hold only if $P_1 > P_2$. That is, in order to maximize total profits, the monopolist must sell the commodity at a higher price in the market with the lower price elasticity of demand (see Figure 11-5).

For example, if

$$Q_1 = 120 - 10P_1 \quad \text{so that} \quad P_1 = 12 - 0.1Q_1$$

and

$$Q_2 = 120 - 20P_2 \quad \text{so that} \quad P_2 = 6 - 0.05Q_2$$

then

$$TR_1 = P_1Q_1 = (12 - 0.1Q_1)Q_1 = 12Q_1 - 0.1Q_1^2$$

and

$$TR_2 = P_2Q_2 = (6 - 0.05Q_2)Q_2 = 6Q_2 - 0.05Q_2^2$$

If $TC = 90 + 2(Q_1 + Q_2)$, then

$$\begin{aligned}\pi &= TR_1 + TR_2 - TC \\ &= 12Q_1 - 0.1Q_1^2 + 6Q_2 - 0.05Q_2^2 - 90 - 2(Q_1 + Q_2)\end{aligned}$$

and

$$\frac{\partial \pi}{\partial Q_1} = 12 - 0.2Q_1 - 2 = 0 \qquad \frac{\partial \pi}{\partial Q_2} = 6 - 0.1Q_2 - 2 = 0$$

so that

$$0.2Q_1 = 10 \qquad 0.1Q_2 = 4$$

and

$$Q_1 = 50 \qquad Q_2 = 40$$

Since

$$\frac{\partial^2 \pi}{\partial Q_1^2} = -0.2 < 0 \quad \text{and} \quad \frac{\partial^2 \pi}{\partial Q_2^2} = -0.1 < 0$$

the monopolist maximizes his or her total profits by selling $Q_1 = 50$ and $Q_2 = 40$. Then

$$P_1 = 12 - 0.1(50) = \$7 \quad \text{and} \quad P_2 = 6 - 0.05(40) = \$4$$

and

$$\pi = 12(50) - 0.1(50)^2 + 6(40) - 0.05(40)^2 - 90 - 2(50) - 2(40) = \$240$$

with third-degree price discrimination.

In the absence of price discrimination,

$$Q = Q_1 + Q_2 = 240 - 30P \qquad \text{and} \qquad P = 8 - 0.0333Q$$

$$TR = (P)(Q) = (8 - 0.0333Q)Q = 8Q - 0.0333Q^2$$

$$\pi = TR - TC$$

$$= 8Q - 0.0333Q^2 - 90 - 2Q$$

$$\frac{d\pi}{dQ} = 8 - 0.0667Q - 2 = 0$$

$$0.0667Q = 6$$

$$Q = 89.96 \cong 90$$

Since
$$\frac{d^2\pi}{dQ^2} = -0.0667 < 0$$

the monopolist maximizes profits at $Q = 90$ in the absence of price discrimination. Then

$$P = 8 - 0.0333Q = 8 - 0.0333(90) = 8 - 2.997 \cong \$5$$

and
$$\pi = 8(90) - 0.0333(90)^2 - 90 - 2(90) = \$180$$

Problem 1 Calculate the price that the monopolist would charge and the quantity of the product that he or she would sell with third-degree price discrimination in the above example if the monopolist's total cost curve were $TC = 20 + 4(Q_1 + Q_2)$. How much profit would the monopolist earn?

Problem 2 Estimate the price that the monopolist would charge and the quantity of the product that he or she would sell in the absence of third-degree price discrimination in Problem 1. How much profit would the monopolist earn?

SUPPLEMENTARY READINGS

For a problem-solving approach to the topics discussed in this chapter, see:

Salvatore, Dominick: *Theory and Problems of Managerial Economics,* Schaum Outline Series (New York: McGraw-Hill, 1989), Chap. 11.

Other readings on pricing are:

Scherer, F. M., and **David Ross:** *Industrial Market Structure and Economic Performance* (Boston: Houghton Mifflin, 1990).

Lazear, Edward P.: "Retail Pricing and Clearance Sales," *American Economic Review,* March 1986, pp. 14–32.

Manes, Rene P., Francoise Shoumaker, and **Peter A. Silhan:** "Demand Relationships and Pricing Decisions for Related Products," *Managerial and Decision Economics,* June 1984, pp. 120–122.

Nayle, Thomas: "Economic Foundations of Pricing," *Journal of Business,* January 1984, pp. 23–39.

Rao, Vithala R.: "Pricing Research in Marketing: The State of the Art," *Journal of Business,* January 1984, pp. 53–60.

Blinder, A. S.: "Why Are Prices Sticky? Preliminary Results from an Interview Study," *American Economic Review,* May 1991, pp. 89–96.

Hanson, W.: "The Dynamics of Cost-Plus Pricing," *Managerial and Decision Economics,* March–April 1992, pp. 149–161.

On transfer pricing, see:

Eccles, R. G.: *The Transfer Pricing Problem: A Theory for Practice* (Lexington, Mass.: D. C. Heath, 1985).

Rugaman, A. M., and **L. Eden,** eds.: *Multinationals and Transfer Pricing* (New York: St. Martin's, 1985).

Prusa, T. J.: "An Incentive Compatible Approach to the Transfer Pricing Problem," *Journal of International Economics,* February 1990, pp. 155–172.

Kant, C.: "Foreign Subsidiary, Transfer Pricing and Tariffs," *Southern Economic Journal,* July 1988, pp. 162–170.

Kim, S. H.: "International Transfer Pricing," in R. Z. Aliber and R. W. Click, eds., *Readings and International Business* (Cambridge, Mass.: MIT Press, 1993), pp. 407–421.

For a more extensive discussion of international price discrimination and dumping, see:

Salvatore, D.: *International Economics,* 5th ed. (Englewood Cliffs, N.J.: Prentice-Hall, 1995), Chap. 10.

See also the references for Chaps. 9 and 10.

INTEGRATING CASE STUDY FOUR

The Art of Devising Air Fares

Introductory Comment The following selection illustrates most of the concepts presented in this part of the text as they are actually applied in the real world, and, thus, it serves as an excellent integrating case study. It shows the importance of market structure in output and pricing decisions, price leadership, price discrimination, the pricing of multiple products, and how they are all interrelated to incremental analysis in pricing as it is actually conducted in a major industry today.

The Art of Devising Air Fares

In the airline business, it is sometimes called the "dark science." The latest round of fare wars, however, has put a spotlight on how carriers use state-of-the-art computer software, complex forecasting techniques, and a little intuition to divine how many seats and at what prices they will offer on any given flight.

The aim of this inventory, or yield management, is to squeeze as many dollars as possible out of each seat and mile flown. That means trying to project just how many tickets to sell at a discount without running out of seats for the business traveler, who usually books at the last minute and therefore pays full fare. Too many wrong projections can lead to huge losses of revenue, or even worse. The inability of People Express (airline) to manage its inventory of seats properly, for example, was one of the major causes of its demise.

"It's a sophisticated guessing game," said Robert E. Martens, vice president of pricing and production planning at American Airlines, the carrier that has the most sophisticated technology for yield management, according to airline analysts and consultants. "You don't sell a seat to a guy for $69 when he is willing to pay $400."

With the industry now adopting very low discount but nonrefundable fares, the complex task of managing seat inventory may become easier because airlines will be better able to predict how many people will show up for a flight. Some airlines have already seen a drop in their no-shows, which means they can overbook less and spare more customers from being bumped. The nonrefundable fares could also enable carriers to sell more discount seats weeks before a flight, rather than putting them on sale at the last minute in an effort to fill up the plane.

American's inventory operation illustrates just how complicated the process can be. At the airline's corporate headquarters, 90 yield managers are linked by terminals to five International Business Machines mainframe computers in Tulsa,

Oklahoma. The managers monitor and adjust the fare mixes on 1,600 daily flights as well as 528,000 future flights involving nearly 50 million passengers. Their work is hectic: A fare's average life span is two weeks, and industry-wide about 200,000 fares change daily.

Few Discounts on Fridays American and the other airlines base their forecasts largely on historical profiles on each flight. Business travelers, for example, book heavily on many Friday afternoon flights, but often not until the day of departure. The airlines reserve blocks of seats for those frequent fliers. Few, if any, discounts are made available. "Good luck in getting a 'Q fare' from New York to Chicago on Friday afternoon," said James J. Hartigan, president of United Airlines, using the industry parlance for the low-priced, supersaver ticket. "It's like winning the New York lottery." The same route on a midday on a Wednesday, however, begs for passengers, so the airline might discount more than 80 percent of its seats to draw leisure travelers and others with more flexible schedules.

Passengers Angered Many passengers, attracted by advertisements trumpeting deep discounts but unaware that fare allocations change from flight to flight, have expressed anger at the carriers and travel agents when the cheap seats were unavailable. To help clear up the confusion, Continental Airlines is now running ads noting the relative demand for certain routes, thus giving some sense of the supply of discount seats. Overbooking, too, is based on the computerized history of flights and their no-shows and involves myriad factors that include destination, time of day, and cost of ticket.

The airlines have used inventory management for decades, but its importance in helping carriers to enhance their revenue coincides with new software developed in the past three or four years, analysts and airline executives said. Some of the software has been developed in-house; other systems have been from such companies as the Unis Corporation and the Control Data Corporation. "It's probably the No. 1 management tool required to compete properly in this highly competitive airline environment," said Lee R. Howard, executive vice president of Airline Economics, a Washington-based consulting firm.

Effective inventory management alone can improve an airline's revenues by 5 to 20 percent annually, analysts estimated. Mr. Martens said American's system was worth "hundreds of millions of dollars" a year to the airline. The airline's total sales exceeded $6 billion last year. "The revenue implications for yield management are enormous," said Julius Maltudis, airline analyst at Salomon Brothers. Inventory management improves a carrier's load factor, or ratio of seats filled. Every 1 percent increase in the load factor translates into $10 million in revenues for the typical major carrier, analysts said.

"Crystal-Ball Gazing" As sophisticated as it is, however, yield management is still subject to variables beyond its control. "Yield management is about 70 percent technology and 30 percent crystal-ball gazing," said Robert W. Cuggin, assistant vice president of marketing development at Delta Airlines. Bad weather or a last-minute switch to a plane of a different size can wreak havoc with weeks of planning, he said.

At American, inventory management begins 330 days before departure. Yield managers use the profiles of a flight's history to parcel out an alphabet soup of fares, rationing full-fare seats first, then moving down the price scale. In the following weeks, the computer alerts the managers if sales in a particular fare class pick up unexpectedly. If a travel agent booked a large group of passengers in advance, for example, the computer would flag the large order, and yield managers would restrict or expand the number of seats in that category. Otherwise, managers begin checking all fare mixes regularly 180 days before departure, adding or subtracting seats in each according to demand.

The process continues right up to two hours before boarding, according to American's director of yield management, Dennis McKaige. Airlines typically put more discount seats on sale just before an advance purchase requirement expires, he said. Therefore, a new batch of cheap tickets that require a 30-day advance purchase might go on sale 31 days before departure. A cut-rate fare offered on Monday might be sold out by Wednesday, then suddenly reoffered hours before takeoff on Thursday if passenger projections based on previous flights fail to materialize, Mr. McKaige said.

There are some instances when an airline actually gives preference to discount travelers over customers paying full fare. American has recently developed software to increase the yield on flights through its hubs. American gives preference to a passenger flying on a discount fare from Austin, Texas, to London through Dallas, over another passenger paying full fare from Austin to Shreveport, Louisiana, through Dallas. The London passenger, who pays $241 each way, is worth more to the airline than the passenger flying to Shreveport, who pays the full fare of $87 each way. For the bargain hunter, finding a discount will increasingly depend on the season, day and time of travel, the destination, and the length of stay.

The New Fare Cuts Continental, a unit of Texas Air, ignited the latest round of rock-bottom fares in January with "Maxsaver tickets," which require a minimum two-day advance purchase and are nonrefundable. "The spread between our highest and lowest fares is much lower than other airlines," said James O'Donnel, vice president of marketing at Continental. "While our yield management job is no less important than other airlines', it is easier." Mr. O'Donnel said the carrier's system was more automated than those used by some of its competitors.

The two-day purchase requirement has siphoned off some business travelers who would otherwise have paid full fare. (American and several other airlines last week abandoned plans to raise their lowest discount fares and increase the advance purchase requirement on the cheapest tickets to 30 days, from 2. The airlines backed away from the change when support for the proposal collapsed.) Airline officials said that nonrefundable tickets were here to stay. Mr. Martens said that since the nonrefundable, Maxsaver-type fares were introduced, American's no-show rate had dropped "substantially below" the usual range of 12 to 15 percent. Passengers who are willing to commit themselves to a particular flight in exchange for lower prices allow yield managers to refine their operations by concentrating on the remaining coach seats.

Concluding Remarks

Yield management (i.e., the idea of selling as many tickets as possible at high fares and filling the rest of the seats at cut rates) is here to stay in the pricing of airline tickets and is constantly being refined with the use of ever more powerful computers and software. Indeed, yield management is considered the single most important technological improvement in airline management in the last decade and is often credited with making the difference between profit and loss for many airlines. Yield management is now spreading also to hotels, cruise lines, and truck rentals. The great variety and frequent changes in airfares is, however, creating great confusion and frustration for air travelers as they are routinely unable to book seats at the lowest advertised fares. This had led to increasing complaints of false advertisement, which the Transportation Department (the sole authority charged with regulating the airline industry since it was deregulated in 1978) started to investigate in 1995.

Source: Eric Schmidt, "The Art of Devising Air Fares," *The New York Times,* March 4, 1987, pp. D1–D2. Reprinted by permission of the New York Times Corporation. See also "Computers as Price Setters Complicate Travelers' Lives," *The New York Times,* January 24, 1994, p. 1; "Come Fly the Unfriendly Skies," *The Economist,* November 5, 1994, pp. 61–62; and "Special Offers by Airlines Come Under U.S. Review," *The New York Times,* January 23, 1995, p. 10.

P A R T   F I V E

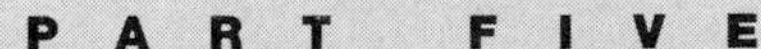

Regulation, Risk Analysis, and Capital Budgeting

Part Five (Chapters 12 through 14) examines regulation and antitrust, risk analysis, and long-term capital investment decisions. Chapter 12 on regulation and antitrust examines the rationale for government intervention in the economy, presents the method or vehicle by which the government intervenes in the economy, evaluates the cost and benefits of such intervention, and examines the regulation of international competition. Chapter 13 extends the basic model of the firm presented in Chapter 1 to include risk (both domestic and international). Finally, Chapter 14 examines capital budgeting, or the process by which firms make decisions involving costs and giving rise to revenues over a number of years. It also examines foreign capital inflows and the cost of capital in the United States.

CHAPTER 12

Regulation and Antitrust: The Role of Government in the Economy

KEY TERMS

Economic theory of regulation
Licensing
Patent
Public interest theory of regulation
Market failures
Externalities
External diseconomies of production
External economics of production
External diseconomies of consumption
External economies of consumption
Natural monopoly
Public utilities
Averch-Johnson (A-J) effect
Sherman Act (1890)
Clayton Act (1914)
Federal Trade Commission Act (1914)
Robinson-Patman Act (1936)
Wheeler-Lea Act (1938)
Celler-Kefauver Antimerger Act (1950)
Dissolution and divestiture
Injunction
Consent decree
Conscious parallelism
Predatory pricing
Import tariff
Import quota
Voluntary export restraint (VER)
Uruguay Round

CHAPTER OUTLINE

In this chapter we examine regulation and antitrust or the role of government in the economy. The traditional role of government of maintaining law and order and providing for national defense has greatly expanded over time, particularly during the past few decades, so that today it affects most industries, firms, and consumers. It is important, therefore, that managers be sufficiently familiar with business laws and regulations to know when to seek legal help in the conduct of their business and to be able to recognize when competitors are harming the firm through illegal business practices.

According to one theory of government involvement in the economy, regulation is the result of pressures from business, consumers, and environmental groups and results in regulation which supports business and protects consumers, workers, and the environment. This theory of regulation is examined in the first section of the chapter. According to more traditional theory, however, regulation is undertaken to ensure that the economic system operates in a manner consistent with the public interest and to overcome market failures. This is discussed in Sections 12-2 and 12-3 of this chapter. Section 12-4 summarizes our antitrust laws, which are designed to enhance competition and forbid anticompetitive actions on the part of business firms. Section 12-5 examines the enforcement of antitrust laws and the recent deregulation movement. Finally, Section 12-6 examines the regulation of international competition.

12-1 GOVERNMENT REGULATION TO SUPPORT BUSINESS AND TO PROTECT CONSUMERS, WORKERS, AND THE ENVIRONMENT

According to the **economic theory of regulation** (sometimes called the "capture theory of regulation") expounded by Stigler and others,[1] regulation is the result of pressure-group action and results in laws and policies to support business and to protect consumers, workers, and the environment. In this section, we examine regulations that shelter firms from competition and protect consumers against unfair business practices, workers against hazardous working conditions, and the environment against pollution and degradation.

Government Regulations That Restrict Competition

Hundreds of pressure groups from business, agriculture, trades, and the professions have been successful in having government (local, state, and federal) adopt many regulations which, in effect (though perhaps not always and entirely by intent), restrict competition and create artificial market power. These regulations include licensing, patents, restrictions on price competition, and restrictions on the free flow of international trade. These are briefly discussed in turn.

A license is often required to enter and remain in many businesses (such as operating a radio or TV station or a liquor store), professions (such as medicine or

[1]G. Stigler, "The Theory of Economic Regulation," *Bell Journal of Economics and Management Science,* Spring 1971, pp. 3–21; J. Buchanan and G. Tullock, *The Calculus of Consent* (Ann Arbor: University of Michigan Press, 1962); and R. Posner, "Theories of Economic Regulation," *Bell Journal of Economics and Management Science,* Autumn 1974, pp. 335–358.

law), and trades (such as driving a cab or being a dietitian). **Licensing** is usually justified to ensure a minimum degree of competence and to protect the public against fraud and harm in cases where it is difficult for the public to gather independent information about the quality of the product or service, and the potential for harm is quite large. Inevitably, however, licensing becomes a method to restrict entry into the business, profession, or trade and to restrict competition. Sometimes licensing seems to serve no other function than to restrict entry and competition.

Examples of this range from unnecessarily high standards for admission into some craft unions, the serious limitations that the American Medical Association (AMA) enforced for many decades on admissions into medical schools in this country and on the utilization of paramedical personnel to perform many routine functions, to the limitation on the number of customers that a trucking firm could have or on the size of the brush that a painter could use. Even when a clear need for licensing exists, the inevitable result is also to restrict entry and competition, thereby increasing prices to consumers and profits to license holders. This is an important reason that most business, professional, and trade associations strongly support licensing and regulation and actively lobby against deregulation. For example, prices and profits in the trucking industry declined sharply in the early 1980s as a result of deregulation of the trucking industry (as well as the recession in the economy) and the American Truckers' Association petitioned Congress to bring back regulation.

Patents are another means by which competition and entry into an industry, profession, or trade is restricted by government action. A **patent** is the right granted by the federal government to an inventor for the exclusive use of the invention for a period of 17 years. The patent holder (individual or firm) can use the patent directly or grant a license for others to use the invention in exchange for royalty payments. The granting of a limited monopoly to the inventor is aimed at encouraging inventions, but it also leads to output restrictions and higher prices. To be sure, the monopoly power resulting from a patent is limited, not only by time, but also because other firms try to develop similar products and processes. Sometimes this is not possible, however, because large firms often hold so many patents on a particular product or process as to completely dominate a field and exclude others long after the original patents have expired. This has been the case in such industries as aluminum, shoe manufacturing, photographic equipment, and many others. Even if restricted by antitrust action, this monopoly power is sometimes further reinforced by cross-licensing agreements, whereby a firm allows other firms in related fields to use some of its patents in exchange for being allowed to use theirs. The result is a cartel-like agreement indirectly made possible by the government, under which a few firms dominate technology in the field.

There are also many restrictions on price competition that are the direct result of government action. These include government-guaranteed parity prices in agriculture, trucking freight rates and airline fares before deregulation, ocean shipping rates, and many others. One aspect of the *Robinson-Patman Act* passed in 1936 to amend the *Clayton Act* (discussed in Section 12-4) also restricted price competition by forbidding selling more cheaply to one buyer or in one market than to others, or selling at "unreasonably low prices" with the intent of destroying competition or eliminating a competitor. The act sought to protect small retailers (primarily independent grocery stores and drug stores) from price competition from large chainstore retailers, based on the latter's ability to obtain lower prices and brokerage concession fees on bulk purchases from suppliers. Judging from the continuous decline in the number of small independent grocers, drug stores, and other retail businesses, and the expansion in the number and size of supermarkets, the act was not very successful, however.

There are many other actions undertaken by the government to directly support some sectors of the economy, particularly agriculture, transportation, and energy with subsidies and special tax treatment. Agriculture has been aided with price supports and many other programs costing billions of dollars per year to consumers and taxpayers. Railroads were granted free lands along their right-of-way as well as direct subsidies, the maritime industry has been greatly helped with large direct subsidies, airlines have greatly benefited from government-sponsored aerospace military research, and the energy (oil, gas, and coal) sectors have benefited from special depletion allowances. While all these actions on the part of the government in support of business have been justified on the basis of the national interest, they often represented the government response to strong lobbying pressure from industry seeking support to restrict entry and competition.

Case Study 12-1

Restrictions on Competition in the Pricing of Milk in New York City

Retail milk prices in New York State are kept artificially high by an antiquated law passed during the depression which requires milk dealers to obtain a license to operate in any local market in the state. The commissioner of agriculture, appointed by the governor, has the responsibility of granting these licenses, except in cases where they lead to "destructive competition in a market already adequately served." In practice, however, commissioners have not issued licenses if the licenses threatened the profits of established local dairies. The result is that retail milk prices in New York State are about 20 percent higher than in neighboring New Jersey. In 1986, the commissioner finally allowed a New Jersey dairy firm to sell milk in Staten Island (a borough of New York City), and immediately the price of milk in the borough declined by 20 percent. The commissioner, however, under strong pressure from local dairies (which contend that they cannot tolerate more competition because their costs are higher), rejected the application for a license from the same New Jersey dairy firm to sell milk in two other boroughs of New York City. This is but one clear case where government regulation restricts entry and competition and leads to higher prices for consumers and profits for firms in the industry. Thus, while deregulation has opened up many fields, such as airlines and telephones, it has left the dairy industry untouched.

Source: "The Price of Monopoly Milk," *The New York Times,* Februrary 10, 1986, p. 22; "The Milk Cartel," *The New York Times,* September 1, 1987, p. 22; and "Gloom on New York Farms as Milk Price Seesaws Low," *The New York Times,* May 31, 1991, p. B1.

Government Regulations to Protect Consumers, Workers, and the Environment

Government also intervenes in the economy in order to protect consumers against unfair business practices, workers against hazardous working conditions, and the environment against pollution and degradation. These laws and regulations are often passed or adopted in response to political pressure brought to bear by some consumer group, workers' association, or environmental group. Often these have the effect of restricting competition.

The first type of policy designed to protect consumers is that of *requiring truthful disclosure and forbidding the misrepresentation of products*. The *Food and Drug Act of 1906* forbids adulteration and mislabeling of foods and drugs sold in interstate commerce. The act was strengthened to also include cosmetics in 1938. More recent amendments require that drugs and chemical additives to food be proven safe for human use and that herbicides and pesticides be tested for toxicity. The *Federal Trade Commission Act of 1914* was designed to protect firms against unfair methods of competition based on product misrepresentation, but it also, and at the same time, provided significant protection to consumers. Among the practices that were forbidden by the act were misrepresenting (1) the price of products (such as claiming that prices have been slashed after first artificially raising them, or falsely claiming to be selling at below cost); (2) the origin of products (such as claiming that the product was manufactured in the United States when in fact it was produced abroad); (3) the usefulness of the product (such as claiming, for example, that a product can prevent arthritis when it does not); and (4) the quality of the product (such as claiming that glass is crystal). The act was amended by the *Wheeler-Lea Act of 1938,* which forbids false or deceptive advertisement of foods, drugs, corrective devices, and cosmetics entering interstate commerce. The federal laws have been supplemented by similar state and local laws and regulations. By authority of the *1990 Nutrition Labeling Act,* the Food and Drug Administration (FDA) mandated more strict labeling requirements on all foods sold in the United States (See Case Study 12-2).

A second type of regulation designed to protect consumers is the *truth-in-lending law.* This is based on the *Consumer Credit Protection Act of 1968,* which requires lenders to make a complete and accurate disclosure, in easy-to-understand language, of the precise terms of credit, particularly the absolute amount of interest and other credit charges and the annual interest rate on the unpaid balance. A third type of consumer protection is provided by the *Consumer Product Safety Commission,* which was established in 1972 to (1) protect consumers against risk and injury associated with the use of some products, (2) provide information to consumers for comparing and evaluating the relative safety in the use of various products, and (3) develop uniform safety standards for many products. During the first five years of operation, the commission recalled more than 20 million products but has been criticized by consumer groups for concentrating on unimportant products and by business for unreasonably high standards of product safety and for the very high cost of compliance.

Other laws designed to protect consumers are (1) the *Fair Credit Reporting Act of 1971,* which grants credit applicants the right to examine their credit file and to know the reason for the rejection of a credit application, and forbidding credit discrimination based on race, religion, sex, marital status, or age; (2) the *Warranty Act of 1975*, which requires warranties to be written in plain English, indicate which parts are covered, and explain how the consumer can exercise the rights granted by the warranty; (3) the *National Highway Traffic Safety Administration (NHTSA)*, which imposes safety standards on highway traffic; and (4) laws that require mail-order houses to fill orders within 30 days or refund the customer's money.

Some of the *laws and regulations protecting workers* are (1) the *Occupational Safety and Health Administration (OSHA)*, which specifies safety standards for noxious gases and chemicals, noise levels, and other hazards; (2) the *Equal Employment Opportunity Commission (EEOC)*, which regulates business hiring and firing practices; and (3) minimum wage laws, which put a floor on wages that businesses can pay to hired labor.

Environmental pollution and degradation are regulated by the *Environmental Protection Agency (EPA)*. Since its creation in 1970, the EPA has become one of the most powerful of the federal regulatory agencies and is credited with substantially reducing environmental deterioration (see Case Study 12-3). The EPA monitors the air, water, toxic chemicals, pesticides, and waste materials, and it oversees grants for sewage treatment plants throughout the United States. Business, however, has often bitterly complained about too stringent air and water pollution regulations. These have added several hundreds of billions of dollars to costs of production in less than two decades. The *Clean Air Act of 1990* requires a phased reduction in overall pollution and established a generalized market for pollution permits. Many other laws and regulations designed to protect consumers, workers, and the environment exist. Those listed above are only some of the most important ones.

Case Study 12-2

The FDA Steps Up Regulation of the Drug Industry

The passage of the *1990 Nutrition Labeling Act* empowered the Food and Drug Administration (FDA) to impose more stringent labeling, production, and quality standards on all foods and drugs sold in the United States. For example, in 1991, the FDA forced food companies to remove from their labels misleading claims regarding cholesterol and to discontinue their claims that bottled water was superior to tap water, and it ordered the removal of the word "fresh" in describing sauces and juices made from concentrate. In 1992, it pulled most breast implants off the market for safety reasons. In 1993, it forced the Warner-Lambert Corporation to temporarily halt production of its drugs and over-the-counter products (including Listerine, Rolaids, and Benadryl) that did not meet FDA specifications. These are only a few of the many actions that a more active FDA has taken since 1990. The cost of withdrawn drugs as a result of FDA action exceeded $150 million in 1993 alone. It is not that industry practices have deteriorated, but that the FDA has adopted a more rigorous and demanding standard since 1990. In the Warner-

Lambert case, the FDA found the company's plants did not meet the agency's production, quality control, and testing procedures. It found that the company's antianxiety drug Centrax did not dissolve as specified, Tedral (the asthma medicine) did not meet sustained-release requirements, and Ergostat (the migraine drug) was below potency in the FDA's lab tests. The FDA has also been sending hundreds of letters to the top executives of some of the nation's largest drug makers, such as Merck, Sandoz Pharmaceuticals, and American Home Products, warning them to rigorously follow the agency-defined acceptable production, testing, and marketing practices. The industry has certainly taken note, and compliance has increased sharply.

Source: "Strong Medicine," *Business Week,* September 6, 1993, pp. 20–21.

Case Study 12-3
Regulation Greatly Reduced Air Pollution

There is now clear evidence that regulations enforced by the Environmental Protection Agency (EPA) succeeded in sharply reducing the level of air pollution in some of America's largest and most congested cities. In hot weather, air pollutants react with sunlight to form ozone. Stagnant air then makes the problem worse. During the past few summers, however, the number of days of ozone advisories has declined sharply. For example, during summer 1993, Philadelphia had just 7 days of ozone advisories as compared with 23 during summer of 1988, even though summer 1993 was almost as hot as the summer of 1988. New York City had just 4 days of ozone advisories during the summer of 1993 as compared with 21 days during the summer of 1988, while Washington had just 1 day in summer 1993 as compared with 12 days in summer 1988. In Los Angeles, ozone readings have declined steadily over the past two decades. During the past decade, carbon-monoxide pollution went down 30 percent, sulfur dioxide declined 20 percent, and airborne lead fell almost 90 percent.

Great progress was also made against carbon monoxide, the most serious winter pollutant (which causes respiratory problems). For example, New York City was out of compliance with the EPA standard for carbon monoxide for 71 days during 1985 but none in 1992. Since automobiles and trucks are responsible for two-thirds of smog emission, the replacement of older more polluting cars with newer and less polluting ones was the biggest contributor to the sharply reduced level of air pollution in American cities. For example, the average 1995 automobile emits less than 1 percent of the pollution emitted by the average 1970 automobile. In fact, the effort to reduce pollution even further is reaching diminishing returns (in terms of sharply rising costs for each additional amount of pollution removed) and the quest for a near-zero-emission car may backfire if that increases car prices so much that people keep their older and more polluting cars longer.

Source: "Winning the War on Smog," *Newsweek,* August 23, 1993, p. 29.

12-2 EXTERNALITIES AND REGULATION

According to the **public interest theory of regulation,** government regulation is undertaken to overcome **market failures,** so as to ensure that the economic system operates in a manner consistent with the public interest. Market failures arise because of externalities and from the monopoly power that exists in imperfectly competitive markets. In this section, we examine externalities and ways to overcome them. Monopoly power, as another type of market failure, is examined in the rest of this chapter.

The Meaning and Importance of Externalities

The production and consumption of some products may give rise to some harmful or beneficial side effects that are borne by firms or people not directly involved in the production or consumption of the product. These are called **externalities.** We have external economies and diseconomies of production and consumption. **External diseconomies of production** are uncompensated costs imposed on some firms by the expansion of output by other firms. For example, the increased discharge of waste materials by some firms along a waterway may result in antipollution legislation that increases the cost of disposing of waste materials for all firms in the area. **External economies of production** are uncompensated benefits conferred on some firms by the expansion of output by other firms. An example of this arises when some firms train workers and some of these workers go to work for other firms (which, therefore, save on training costs). **External diseconomies of consumption** are uncompensated costs imposed on some individuals by the consumption expenditures of other individuals. For example, smoking in a public place has a harmful effect (i.e., imposes a cost) on nonsmokers in the place. Finally, **external economies of consumption** are uncompensated benefits conferred on some individuals by the increased consumption of a product by other individuals. For example, increased expenditures to maintain a lawn by a homeowner increases the value of the neighbor's home also.

When the private and social costs or benefits do not coincide (i.e., in the presence of externalities), too much or too little of a product or service is produced or consumed from society's point of view. Specifically, if social costs exceed private costs, too much of the product is being produced, while if social benefits exceed private benefits, too little of the product is being consumed. These are shown in Figure 12-1.

In the left panel of Figure 12-1, MPB_A refers to the marginal private benefit that individual A receives for each additional hour of typing technical material at home in the evening after a regular full-time day job. If individual A is willing to type for only 1 hour per evening, he or she will accept work only from the best-paying customer (that is, \$12). If individual A is willing to type for more hours per evening, he or she will have to accept work from customers who are willing to pay less and less, as indicated by the MPB_A curve. The left panel of Figure 12-1 shows also the MPC_A, or the marginal private cost, that individual A incurs in

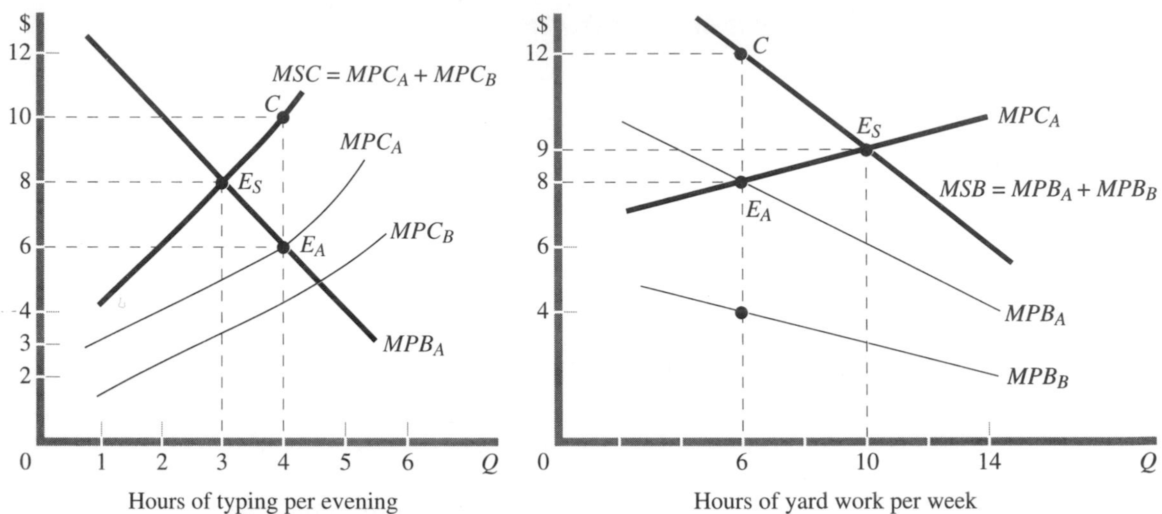

Figure 12-1
Private and Social Costs and Benefits of Production and Consumption

The left panel shows that the best number of hours of typing per evening for individual *A* is 4 and is given by point E_A, at which the marginal private benefit to individual *A* (MPB_A) equals the private marginal cost to individual *A* (MPC_A). Evening typing by individual *A*, however, also creates noise and a cost for individual *B*. The marginal social cost (*MSC*) is thus given by the vertical summation of the MPC_A and MPC_B curves. From society's point of view, the best level of typing by individual *A* is 3 hours per evening and is given by point E_S, at which $MPB_A = MSC =$ \$8. In the right panel, the best number of hours for individual *A* to work in his or her yard is 6 hours per week and is given by point E_A, at which $MPB_A = MPC_A$. Individual *A*'s yard work, however, generates an external benefit to individual *B*. The marginal social benefit, *MSB*, equals $MPB_A + MPB_B$. The best level of yard work by individual *A* is 10 hours per week, as shown by point E_S, at which $MSB = MPC_A = MSC =$ \$9.

typing each additional hour per evening. The best number of hours that individual *A* is then willing to type per evening is 4 and is given by point E_A, at which the MPB_A and MPC_A curves intersect.

By typing at home in the evening, however, individual *A* creates noise, which drives his or her neighbor to eat out or to go to a movie or a bar. Suppose that the private marginal cost imposed on individual *B* from each additional hour of evening typing by individual *A* is given by the MPC_B curve. The marginal social cost of evening typing by individual *A* is then given by the *MSC* curve, which is the vertical summation of the MPC_A and MPC_B curves. At the best number of 4 hours of evening typing by individual *A*, the *MSC* of \$10 (point C) exceeds the MPB_A of \$6 (point E_A). It is, therefore, economically inefficient from society's point of view for individual *A* to type 4 hours. From society's point of view, individual *A* should type only 3 hours per evening, which is given by point E_S, at which $MSC = MPB_A =$ \$8.[2]

[2]Since $MPB_B = 0$, $MPB_A = MSB$, where *MSB* refers to the marginal social benefit. Therefore, 3 hours of evening typing by individual *A* is socially efficient because $MSC = MSB$.

In the right panel of Figure 12-1, the MPB_A gives the marginal private benefit that individual *A* receives for each additional hour per week devoted to tending his or her yard (i.e., cutting grass, planting flowers, etc.), thereby increasing the value of individual *A*'s home and providing relaxation. The private marginal cost incurred by individual *A* for tending the yard (the depreciation on the lawn mowers, the cost of seeds, etc.) is given by the MPC_A curve. Therefore, the best number of hours to spend tending the yard is 6 hours per week and is given by point E_A, at which the MPB_A and MPC_A curves cross. By improving his or her yard, however, individual *A* also confers a benefit to individual *B* (i.e., it also increases the value of individual *B*'s home). If the marginal private benefit conferred on individual *B* is given by the MPB_B curve, the total marginal social benefit is then given by the *MSB* curve, which is the vertical summation of the MPB_A and the MPB_B curves. The best number of 6 hours per week spent working in the yard by individual *A* is not socially efficient, however, because $MSB = \$12$, while $MPC_A = MSC = \$8$. From society's point of view, the most efficient number of hours for individual *A* to work in his or her yard is 10 hours per week and is given by point E_S, at which $MPC_A = MSC = MSB = \$9$. In cases such as these where the private costs and benefits do not coincide with the social costs and benefits, government intervention in the economy is justified in order to induce the production and/or the consumption of the product or service until the marginal social cost is equal to the marginal social benefit (i.e., until $MSC = MSB$).

Policies to Deal with Externalities

One way that a market failure or inefficiency resulting from external economies can be overcome is by government prohibition or regulation. By forbidding an activity that gives rise to an external diseconomy, the external diseconomy can be avoided. For example, by prohibiting the use of automobiles, auto emissions can be eliminated. Similarly, by forbidding evening typing at home by individual *A* in the left panel of Figure 12-1, the noise externality that such typing creates for individual *B* would be avoided. Such prohibitions, however, also eliminate the benefit that results from the activities that give rise to the externalities. More reasonable, therefore, is regulation that allows the activity that leads to the externality up to the point at which the marginal social benefit from the activity is equal to the marginal social cost. For example, the government could allow individual *A* to type only 3 hours per evening in the left panel of Figure 12-1, so that the marginal private (and social) benefit of evening typing to individual *A* equals the marginal social cost (i.e., the marginal cost to individual *A* plus the marginal cost to individual *B*—see point E_S in the figure). Since direct regulation, however, often specifies the production technique to be used in order to limit the external diseconomies, it is usually not cost-efficient.

More efficient in limiting externalities to the level at which the marginal social benefit from an externality-producing activity is equal to the marginal social cost are taxes or subsidies. This is shown in Figure 12-2, which is an extension of Figure 12-1. In the left panel of Figure 12-2, the dashed MPC_{A+t} curve is obtained when the government imposes a tax of $t = \$3$ per hour of evening typing

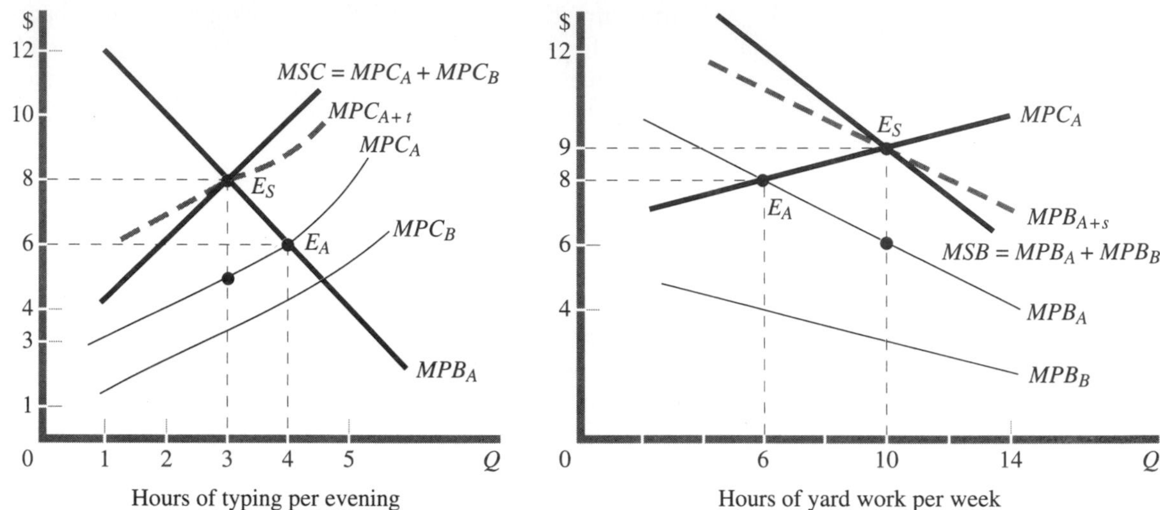

Figure 12-2
A Tax or Subsidy to Overcome a Negative or Positive Externality

The left panel shows that the socially optimal level of 3 hours of evening typing is reached when the government imposes a tax of $t = \$3$ per hour on evening typing on individual A. This shifts the MPC_A curve up by \$3 so that the MPC_{A+t} curve intersects the MPB_A curve at point E_S, at which $MPB_A = MSB = MSC$. The right panel shows that individual A can be induced to demand or consume the socially optimal home improvement that results from tending his or her yard for 10 hours per week by giving him or her a consumption subsidy of $s = \$3$ per hour. This shifts the MPB_A curve up by \$3, so that the MPB_{A+s} curve intersects the MPC_A curve at point E_S, at which $MSB = MPC_A = MSC$.

on individual A. Since the MPC_{A+t} curve intersects the MPB_A curve at point E_S, individual A will be induced to type the socially optimal number of hours per evening (3 hours), so that the marginal social benefit (MSB, which now coincides with MPB_A) equals the marginal social cost (that is, $MSC = MSC_A + MSC_B$).

In the right panel of Figure 12-2, the dashed MPB_{A+s} curve is obtained when the government gives individual A a subsidy of $s = \$3$ per hour for tending his or her yard. Since the MPB_{A+s} curve intersects the MPC_A curve at point E_S, individual A will be induced to work the socially optimal number of hours (that is, 10 hours) per week in his or her yard, so that the marginal social benefit ($MSB = MPB_A + MPB_B$) equals the marginal social cost ($MSC = MPC_A$).[3] Other taxes used to overcome negative externalities or external diseconomies (and raise revenues to provide government services) are liquor, cigarette, and gasoline taxes. Other subsidies used to correct for positive externalities or external economies are investment tax credits to promote investments, depletion allowances to promote natural resource development, and aid to education.

Besides prohibition and regulation, and taxes and subsidies, negative and positive externalities can sometimes be overcome by *voluntary payments*. For example, if a firm pollutes the air and produces a foul odor, the residents of the area

[3]The same result can be reached by a \$3 downward shift in the MPC_{A-S} curve, not shown in Figure 12-2.

can get together and contribute to the cost of introducing pollution-abatement equipment by the firm, or the firm can contribute to the cost of relocating the area residents.[4] This method, however, is impractical when there are many people residing in an area. Still another method of overcoming external diseconomies imposed by some firms is to allow or foster *mergers,* so that the external diseconomies are internalized and explicitly taken into consideration by the merged firm. For example, if a paper mill is located upstream from a brewery, the discharges from the paper mill into the stream represent an external diseconomy for the brewery since the latter incurs the additional cost of purifying the water that it uses in beer making. If the paper mill and the brewery merge, however, the cost of purifying the water for beer making becomes an explicit and direct cost that the merged firm will have to take into consideration in its production (milling and brewing) decisions.

A radically different method of limiting the amount of a negative externality to the level that is socially optimal is by the *sale of pollution rights* by the government. Under such a system, the government decides on the amount of pollution that it thinks is socially desirable (based on the benefits that result from the activities that generate the pollution) and then auctions off licenses to firms to generate pollution up to the specified amount. Pollution costs are thus internalized (i.e., considered as part of regular production costs) by firms, and the allowed amount of pollution is utilized in activities in which it is most valuable. This and other methods of dealing with externalities, however, are based on the assumption that the private and social benefits and costs of any activity leading to externalities can be measured or estimated fairly accurately. This is seldom the case. Nevertheless, the policies that we have examined do give an indication of what needs to be measured and the procedure for reaching socially optimal decisions or policies in cases involving externalities.

[4]See R. Coase, "The Problem of Social Cost," *Journal of Law and Economics,* October 1960, pp. 1–44.

Case Study 12-4

The Market for Dumping Rights

A market for dumping rights came into existence in 1977 when the Environmental Protection Agency (EPA) issued the first transferrable permit for dumping. Under such a system, the EPA decides how much pollution it wants to allow and then issues marketable rights for that quantity of pollution. Since these dumping rights are marketable (i.e., can be bought and sold by firms), they are likely to be used in those activities in which they are most valuable. For example, suppose that the EPA has imposed specific dumping restrictions on two firms. If the cost of reducing emission by 1 unit is $10,000 for one firm and $50,000 for a second firm, the first firm could sell the right to dump that unit of emission to the second firm for a price between $10,000 and $50,000. The result would be that both firms (and society) would gain without any overall increase in pollution. In fact, the only way that a new firm can build a plant that pollutes the air in an area that does not meet federal air-quality standards is to purchase the right to a specific amount of pollution from an already existing and polluting firm in the area. Since 1977 more than 2,000 such market exchanges for pollution rights have been carried out. In fact, we now have pollution-rights banks which act as brokers between firms that want to sell pollution rights and firms that want to purchase them. In 1980 the concept of marketable pollution rights was extended by the so-called bubble policy. Under this policy, a firm with several plants operating in a single air pollution area is given a total permissible emission level for all its plants rather than a limit for each one. This allows the firm to concentrate its emission reduction efforts in plants where it can be done more cheaply. The *Clean Air Act of 1990* requires a phased reduction in overall pollution and established a generalized market for pollution permits. The United States is now proposing the establishment of an international market where nations could purchase or sell pollution permits in order to cut the cost of reducing the greenhouse effect and resulting global warming.

Source: "A Market Place for Pollution Rights," *U.S. News & World Report,* November, 12, 1990, p. 79; "Blue Skies for Sale," *The Margin,* November–December 1990, pp. 34–35; "Emission Trading Goes Global," *Science,* February 1991, pp. 520–521; "New Rules Harness the Power of Markets to Curb Air Pollution," *The Wall Street Journal,* April 14, 1992, p. A1; and "Eastern Utilities in Unusual Pact: A Smog Tradeoff," *The New York Times,* March 16, 1994, p. 1.

12-3 PUBLIC UTILITY REGULATION

In this section we define public utilities and natural monopoly, and we examine the need for their regulation and the dilemma usually faced in determining the appropriate method and degree of regulation.

Public Utilities As Natural Monopolies

In some industries, economies of scale operate (i.e., the long-run average cost curve may fall) continuously as output expands, so that a single firm could supply the entire market more efficiently than any number of smaller firms. Such a large firm supplying the entire market is called a **natural monopoly.** The distinguishing characteristic of a natural monopoly is that the firm's long-run average cost curve is still declining when the firm supplies the entire market. Monopoly in this case is the natural result of a larger firm having lower costs per unit than smaller firms and being able to drive the latter out of business. Examples of natural monopolies are **public utilities** (electrical, gas, water, and local transportation companies). To have more than one such firm in a given market would lead to duplication of supply lines and to much higher costs per unit. To avoid this, local governments usually allow a single firm to operate in the market but regulate the price and quality of the services provided, so as to allow the firm only a normal risk-adjusted rate of return on its investment. This is shown in Figure 12-3.

In Figure 12-3, the *D* and *MR* curves are, respectively, the market demand and marginal revenue curves for the service faced by the natural monopolist, while the *LAC* and *LMC* curves are its long-run average and marginal cost

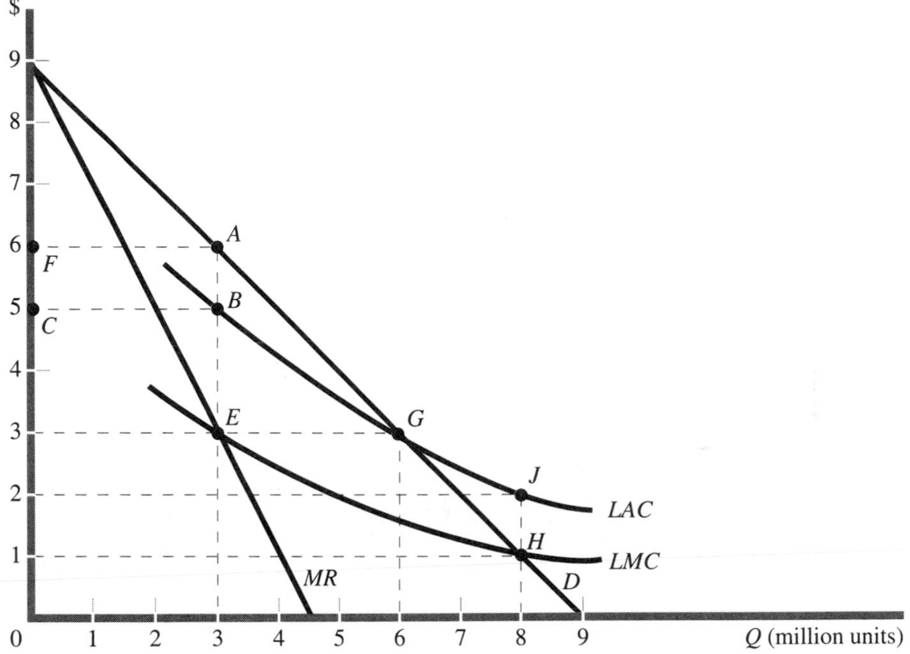

Figure 12-3
Natural Monopoly Regulation

A regulatory commission usually sets $P = LAC = \$3$ (point G), at which output is 6 million units per time period and public utility breaks even in the long run. At $Q = 6$ million, however, $P > LMC$, and more of the service is desirable from society's point of view. The best level of output from society's point of view is 8 million units per time period and is given by point H, at which $P = LMC = \$1$. However, that would result in a loss of \$1 (JH) per unit and \$8 million in total, and the public utility company would not supply the service in the long run without a subsidy of \$1 per unit.

curves. If unregulated, the best level of output of the monopolist in the long run would be 3 million units per time period and is given by point E, at which the LMC and MR curves intersect. For $Q = 3$ million units, the monopolist would charge the price of \$6 (point A on the D curve) and incur at $LAC = \$5$ (point B on the LAC curve), thereby earning a profit of \$1 (AB) per unit and \$3 million (the area of rectangle $ABCF$) in total. Note that at $Q = 3$ million units, the LAC curve is still declining. Note also that at the output level of 3 million units, $P > LMC$, so that more of the service is desirable from society's point of view. That is, the marginal cost of the last unit of the service supplied is smaller than the value of the service to society, as reflected by the price of the service. There is, however, no incentive for the unregulated monopolist to expand output beyond $Q = 3$ million units per time period because its profits are maximized at $Q = 3$ million.

To ensure that the monopolist earns only a normal rate of return on its investment, the regulatory commission usually sets the price at which $P = LAC$. In Figure 12-3, this is given by point G, at which $P = LAC = \$3$ and output is

6 million units per time period. While the price is lower and the output is greater than at point *A*, $P > LMC$ at point *G*. The best level of output from society's point of view would be 8 million units per time period, as shown by point *H*, at which $P = LMC = \$1$. At $Q = 8$ million, however, the $LAC = \$2$ (point *J* on the *LAC* curve), and the public utility company would incur a loss of \$1 (*HJ*) per unit and \$8 million per time period. As a result, the public utility would not supply the service in the long run without a per-unit subsidy of \$1 per unit. In general, regulatory commissions set $P = LAC$ (point *G* in Figure 12-3) so that the public utility company breaks even in the long run without a subsidy.

Difficulties in Public Utility Regulation

While the above discussion of public utility regulation seems fairly simple and straightforward, the actual determination of prices (rates) for public utility services by regulatory commissions (often called the *rate case*) is very complex. For one thing, it is very difficult to determine the value of the plant or fixed assets on which to allow a normal rate of return. Should it be the original cost of the investment or the replacement cost? More often than not, regulatory commissions decide on the former. Furthermore, since public utility companies supply the service to different classes of customers, each with different price elasticities of demand, many different rate schedules could be used to allow the public utility company to break even. Even more troublesome is the fact that a public utility company usually provides many services that are jointly produced, and so it is impossible to allocate costs in any rational way to the various services provided and customers served.

Regulation can also lead to inefficiencies. These result from the fact that, having been guaranteed a normal rate of return on investment, public utility companies have little incentive to keep costs down. For example, managers may decide on salary increases for themselves in excess of what they would get in their best alternative employment and provide luxurious offices and large expense accounts for themselves. Regulatory commissions must, therefore, scrutinize costs to prevent such abuses.

Other inefficiencies arise because if rates are set too high, public utilities will overinvest in fixed assets and use excessively capital-intensive production methods to avoid showing above-normal returns (which would lead to rate reductions). On the other hand, if public utility rates are set too low, public utility companies will underinvest in fixed assets (i.e., in plant and equipment) and overspend on variable inputs, such as labor and fuel, and tend to reduce the quality of services. Overinvestment or underinvestment in plant and equipment resulting from the wrong public utility rates being set is known as the **Averch-Johnson** or **A-J effect** (from Harvey Averch and Leland Johnson, who first identified this problem) and can lead to large inefficiencies.[5] And yet, it is very difficult indeed for regulatory commissions to come up with correct utility rates in view of the

[5]Harvey Averch and Leland Johnson, "Behavior of the Firm under Regulatory Constraint," *American Economic Review*, December 1962, pp. 1052–1069.

difficulty of valuing the fixed assets of public utilities and because of the long planning and gestation period of public utility investment projects.[6]

Finally, there is usually a lag of 9 to 12 months from the time the need for a rate change is recognized and the time it is granted. This *regulatory lag* results because public hearings must be conducted before a regulatory commission can approve a requested rate change. Since the members of the regulatory commissions are either political appointees or elected officials and are thus subject to political pressures from consumer groups, they usually postpone a rate increase as long as possible and tend to grant rate increases which are smaller than necessary. During inflationary periods, this leads to underinvestment in fixed assets and to the inefficiencies discussed above. To avoid these regulatory lags, rates are sometimes tied to fuel costs and are automatically adjusted as variable costs change.

[6]In recent years regulatory commissions have begun to pay more attention to the structure of rates so as to avoid undue price discrimination against any class of customers.

Case Study 12-5

Regulated Electricity Rate Increases for Con Edison

In February 1983, and after nearly six months of public hearings and deliberations, the New York Public Service Commission approved a 6.5 percent increase in electricity rates for the 2.7 million customers served by the Consolidated Edison Company. This rate increase, which took effect in March 1983, increased the basic monthly electricity charge by $2.60 in New York City and $3.75 in Westchester County, where the average resident uses more electricity. The increase in the monthly electricity charge was about half of the 12.4 percent that Con Edison had asked for and far lower than the 15.5 percent increase that the commission granted Con Edison in 1981. The commission indicated that the decision to grant rate increases that would generate additional revenues of only $240 million per year for Con Edison rather than the requested $491 million was based on the fact that the borrowing and operating costs of the public utility had fallen sharply since it had made the request for a rate increase as the result of the decline in fuel costs, interest rates, and inflation. Both Con Edison and consumer advocates immediately criticized the rate increase—the former as inadequate and the latter as too high. Because of even lower fuel costs, greater demand for electricity, and higher productivity increases than anticipated, the rate increase actually generated $267 million in additional revenues per year for Con Edison, and this represented a 15.2 percent return on its investment, instead of the projected 13.67 percent return. In 1986, the city administration threatened to sue Con Edison to have the excess profits returned to customers but dropped its plan when Con Edison agreed not to seek another rate increase until March 1987. In fact, Con Edison did not get another rate increase until 1992, and the rate increases that it got from 1992 to 1995 were very small.

Source: "Con Edison Wins 6.5% Rise in Rates, Half of its Request," *The New York Times,* February 24, 1983, p. B4; "Con Edison Puts Freeze on Its Electricity Rates," *The New York Times,* January 13, 1986, p. B1; and "Electric Rates," Con Edison, January 1992, 1993, 1994, and 1995.

12-4 ANTITRUST: GOVERNMENT REGULATION OF MARKET STRUCTURE AND CONDUCT

The late nineteenth century saw a rapid increase in concentration of economic power in the United States in the form of trusts. Under a trust agreement, the voting rights of the stock of the firms in an (oligopolistic) industry are transferred to a legal trust, which manages the firms as a cartel, restricting output, charging monopoly prices, and earning monopoly profits. The most notorious of these trusts were the Standard Oil Trust, the Tobacco Trust, and several railroad and coal trusts, all of which were in operation in the United States in the 1880s. Public indignation over the rapid increase in the concentration of economic power and the abuses that resulted from it led to the passage of antitrust laws, starting with the Sherman Act of 1890. The intent of these antitrust laws was to prevent monopoly or undue concentration of economic power, to protect the public against the abuses and inefficiencies resulting from monopoly or the concentration of economic power, and to maintain a workable degree of competition in the economy.

In this section we summarize the provisions of the most important antitrust laws. These are the **Sherman Act** (**1890**), the **Clayton Act** (**1914**), the **Federal Trade Commission Act** (**1914**), the **Robinson-Patman Act** (**1936**), the **Wheeler-Lea Act** (**1938**), and the **Celler-Kefauver Antimerger Act** (**1950**). The two basic statutes of antitrust legislation are the Sherman and the Clayton Acts. They prohibited "monopolization," "restraints of trade," and "unfair competition." Being very broad in nature, however, the Sherman and the Clayton Acts left a great deal to judicial interpretation based on economic analysis and led to the passage of the subsequent legislation to spell out more precisely what business behavior was in fact prohibited by the antitrust laws and close loopholes in the original legislation.

Sherman Act (1890)

This is the first federal antitrust law. Sections 1 and 2 state, respectively:

1. Every contract, combination in the form of a trust or otherwise, or conspiracy, in restraint of trade or commerce among the several states, and with foreign nations is hereby declared to be illegal.
2. Every person who shall monopolize, or combine or conspire with any other person or persons, to monopolize any part of the trade or commerce among the several states, or with foreign nations, shall be deemed guilty of a misdemeanor.

Thus, Section 1 made any contract or combination in restraint of trade (such as price fixing) illegal, while Section 2 made any attempt to monopolize a market illegal. In 1903, the Antitrust Division of the U.S. Department of Justice was established to enforce the act. A 1974 amendment to the Sherman Act made violations felonies rather than misdemeanors, increased maximum penalties from

$50,000 to $1 million for corporations and from $50,000 and one year in prison to $100,000 and three years in prison for individuals, and made it possible for those injured by antitrust violations to collect triple damages in civil suits.

Clayton Act (1914)

This act listed four types of unfair competition that were illegal: price discrimination, exclusive and tying contracts, intercorporate stock holdings, and interlocking directorates. Specifically:

1. Section 2 of the act makes it illegal for sellers to discriminate in price among buyers, when such discrimination has the effect of substantially lessening competition or tends to create a monopoly. Price discrimination is *otherwise* permissible when it is based on differences in grade, quality or quantities sold, or selling or transportation costs and when lower prices are offered in good faith to meet competition.
2. Section 3 of the act makes it illegal for sellers to lease, sell, or contract for the sale of a commodity on the condition that the lessee or buyer does not purchase, lease, or deal in the commodity of a competitor, if such an exclusive or tying contract substantially lessens competition or tends to create a monopoly.
3. Section 7 of the act makes it illegal for a corporation engaged in commerce to acquire the stocks of a competing corporation or the stocks of two or more corporations that compete with one another if such intercorporate stock holdings substantially lessen competition or tend to create a monopoly.
4. Section 8 of the act makes it illegal for the same individual to be on the board of directors of two or more corporations (interlocking directorate) if the corporations are competitive and if any has capital, surplus, or undivided profits in excess of $1 million.

Note that while price discrimination, exclusive and tying contracts, and intercorporate stock holdings are illegal only if they *substantially lessen competition or tend to create a monopoly,* interlocking directorates are illegal per se, without any need to show that they lead to a reduction in competition.

Federal Trade Commission Act (1914)

This act supplemented the Clayton Act and simply stated that "unfair methods of competition were unlawful." The act also established the Federal Trade Commission (FTC) to prosecute violators of the antitrust laws and to protect the public against false and misleading advertisements (see Section 12-1). Determination of what constitutes "unfair competition" beyond those specified by the Clayton Act was left to the FTC, but it was now no longer necessary to wait for private parties to sue at their own expense when injured by unfair and monopolistic practices.

Robinson-Patman Act (1936)

As pointed out in Section 12-1, this act, passed to amend the Clayton Act, made it illegal to sell more cheaply to one buyer or in one market than to others or to sell at "unreasonably low prices" with the intent of destroying competition or eliminating a competitor. The act sought to protect small retailers (primarily independent grocery stores and drug stores) from price competition from large chain-store retailers, based on the latter's ability to obtain lower prices and brokerage concession fees on bulk purchases from suppliers.

Wheeler-Lea Act (1938)

As pointed out in Section 12-1, this act amended the Federal Trade Commission Act and forbade false or deceptive advertisement of foods, drugs, corrective devices, and cosmetics entering interstate commerce. Its main purpose was to protect consumers against false or deceptive advertisement.

Celler-Kefauver Antimerger Act (1950)

This act closed a loophole in Section 7 of the Clayton Act, which made it illegal to acquire the stock of a competing corporation but allowed the purchase of the *assets* of a competing corporation. The Celler-Kefauver Antimerger Act closed this loophole by making it illegal to purchase not only the stock but also the assets of a competing corporation if such a purchase substantially lessens competition or tends to create a monopoly. Thus, the act forbids all types of mergers: horizontal (i.e., firms producing the same type of products, such as steel mills), vertical (firms at various stages of production, such as steel mills and coal mines), and conglomerate (firms in unrelated product lines, such as breakfast cereals and magazines) if their effect lessens competition substantially or tends to create a monopoly.

12-5 ENFORCEMENT OF ANTITRUST LAWS AND THE DEREGULATION MOVEMENT

In this section we discuss the enforcement of antitrust laws, first in general and then from the point of view of market structure and market conduct. Finally, we examine the recent deregulation movement.

Enforcement of Antitrust Laws: Some General Observations

The enforcement of antitrust laws has been the responsibility of the Antitrust Division of the Department of Justice and the Federal Trade Commission (FTC). In general, the Justice Department enforces the Sherman Act and Section 7 (the antimerger section) of the Clayton Act with criminal proceedings, while the FTC enforces other sections of the Clayton Act with civil proceedings. Antitrust action can be initiated by the Justice Department, the FTC, state attorneys general (based on states' antitrust legislation), and private parties (individuals and firms). Of the roughly 2,000 antitrust suits currently filed in the United States each year, over 90 percent are initiated by private parties.

Since U.S. antitrust laws are often broad and general, a great deal of judicial interpretation based on economic analysis has often been required in the enforcement of antitrust laws. The problems of defining what is meant by "substantially lessening competition," defining the relevant product and geographical markets, and deciding when competition is "unfair" have not been easy to determine and often could not be resolved in a fully satisfactory and uncontroversial way. The fact that many antitrust cases lasted many years, involved thousands of pages of testimony, and cost millions of dollars to prosecute is ample evidence of their great complexity. In one area, however, the antitrust laws are very clear: Price collusion among firms is clearly and unequivocably prohibited.

Antitrust violations or alleged violations have been resolved by (1) dissolution and divestiture, (2) injunction, or (3) consent decree. **Dissolution and divestiture** have been used in monopoly and antimerger cases. With these, the firm is ordered either to dissolve (thereby losing its identity) or to divest itself of (i.e., sell) some of its assets. An **injunction** is a court order requiring that the defendant refrain from certain anticompetitive actions or take some specified competitive actions. A **consent decree** is an agreement, without a court trial, between the defendant (without, however, admitting guilt) and the Justice Department under which the defendant agrees to abide by the rules of business behavior set down in the decree. Most antitrust actions have been settled with consent decrees. Antitrust violations have also been punished by fines and jail sentences (see the discussion of the Sherman Act in Section 12-4).

Enforcement of Antitrust Laws: Structure

Enforcement of the antitrust laws to break up or prevent the emergence of an anticompetitive industry structure involved the application of Section 2 of the Sherman Act prohibiting monopolization and attempts or conspiracies to monopolize, and application of Section 7 of the Clayton Act, and the Celler-Kefauver Act, which prohibit mergers that substantially lessen competition.

Until 1945, the Court held that size per se was not illegal. The illegal use of monopoly power was required for successful prosecution. Thus, in the 1911 Standard Oil case, the Supreme Court argued that Standard Oil of New Jersey had acquired and used a 90 percent control in the refining and sale of petroleum products by illegal actions (such as using profits from one market to sell at below cost in another market to drive competitors out) and ordered its dissolution into 30 independent firms. On the other hand, in the 1920 U.S. Steel case, the Supreme Court ruled that size, in and of itself, was no offense and in the absence of conclusive proof of illegal actions, refused to order the dissolution of U.S. Steel. The same was true in the International Harvester case in 1927.

Starting with the 1945 Alcoa case, however, the Supreme Court ruled that size per se was an offense, irrespective of illegal acts. The fact that Alcoa had achieved 90 percent control of the aluminum market by efficient operation and by maintaining low profit margins was no defense.[7] In the 1982 IBM and AT&T cases (see Case Study 12-6), however, the Court took an intermediate position in its interpretation of Section 2 of the Sherman Act. While the Court backed away from the ruling that size per se was illegal, it ruled that size, together with practices that by themselves or when used by smaller firms did not represent an offense, were illegal when used by a very large firm. Thus, the Court ordered AT&T to divest itself of 22 local telephone companies under a consent decree but decided to drop its case against IBM. Overall, Section 2 of the Sherman Act may have been more effective in preventing monopolization than in breaking it up after its occurrence.

The Court recognized that the structure of an industry was also affected by mergers. Section 7 of the Clayton Act and the Celler-Kefauver Act prohibit mergers that "substantially lessen competition" or tend to lead to monopoly. According to its 1984 guidelines, the Justice Department will not usually challenge a horizontal merger (i.e., a merger of firms in the same product line) if the postmerger Herfindahl index (defined in Section 10-4) is less than 1,000. If the postmerger index is between 1,000 and 1,800 and the increase in the index as a result of the merger is less than 100 points, the merger will usually also go unchallenged. But if the postmerger index is between 1,000 and 1,800 and the merger leads to an increase in the index of more than 100 points, or if the postmerger index is more than 1,800 and the merger leads to an increase in the index of more than 50 points, the Justice Department is likely to challenge the merger.

The above guidelines based on the Herfindahl index are not the only factors that the Justice Department considers in horizontal mergers, however. The Justice Department is more likely to bend its Herfindahl-index guidelines if the merger would prevent the failure of the acquired firm, if entry into the industry is easy, if the degree of foreign competition is strong, and if the acquisition would lead to substantial economies of scale.[8] Less clear-cut are the guidelines on vertical and conglomerate mergers. As a result of the relaxed guidelines and in the face of sharply increased foreign competition, especially from Japan, the number and size of corporate acquisitions in the United States increased sharply during the 1980s. For example, as many as 143 of the 500 largest corporations in the United States in 1980 had been purchased by 1989. These were made possible by the easy accessibility of funds and the hands-off antitrust policy of the 1980s. Most takeovers occurred by firms in the same line of business and made corporations more focused and efficient, after years of diversification. When conglomerates were taken over, the various business lines were often sold off to buyers in the same line of business.[9] Somewhat different is the new wave of mergers in the 1990s (see Case Study 12-7).

[7]For a more detailed discussion of this and other antitrust cases, see the readings in the selected bibliography at the end of the chapter.

[8]See "Symposium on Mergers and Antitrust," *Economic Perspectives,* Fall 1987, pp. 3–54.

[9]See Andrei Sheifer and Robert W. Vishny, "The Takeover Wave of the 1980s," *Science,* August 17, 1990, pp. 745–749.

Case Study 12-6
The IBM and AT&T Cases

In 1969, the Justice Department filed suit against IBM under Section 2 of the Sherman Act for monopolizing the computer market, for using exclusive and tying contracts, and for selling new equipment at below cost. The government sought the dissolution of IBM. After 13 years of litigation, more than 104,000 trial transcript pages, $26 million cost to the government (and $300 million incurred by IBM to defend itself), however, the Justice Department dropped its suit against IBM in 1982. The reason that the government decided to drop its case against IBM was that rapid technological change, increased competition in the field of computers, and changed marketing methods since the filing of the suit had so weakened the government case that the Justice Department felt it could not win. In 1995, IBM was a struggling giant in a highly competitive market rather than the near monopolist it had been accused of being in 1969.

In 1974, the Justice Department filed suit (also under Section 2 of the Sherman Act) against AT&T for illegal practices aimed at eliminating competitors in the market for telephone equipment and in the market for long-distance telephone service. At the time, AT&T was the largest private firm in the world. After 8 years of litigation and a cost of $25 million to the government (and $360 million incurred by AT&T to defend itself), the case was settled on January 8, 1982 (the same day that the government dropped its case against IBM). By consent decree, AT&T agreed to divest itself of the 22 local telephone companies (which represented two-thirds of its total assets) and lose its monopoly on long-distance telephone service. In return, AT&T was allowed to retain Bell Laboratories and its manufacturing arm, Western Electric, and was allowed to enter the rapidly growing fields of cable TV, electronic data transmission, video-text communications, and computers. The settlement also led to an increase in local telephone charges (which had been subsidized by long-distance telephone service by AT&T) and a reduction in long-distance telephone charges. By 1995, MCI and Sprint had captured nearly 40 percent of the long-distance telephone market and AT&T began to compete in the local telephone market after its acquisition of McCaw Cellular Communication in 1994 (see Case Study 9-4).

Source: "Windup for Two Super Suits," *Time*, January 18, 1982, pp. 38–40; "Ma Bell's Big Breakup," *Newsweek*, January 18, 1992, pp. 58–63; "Creative Destruction at IBM," *The Wall Street Journal*, January 6, 1994, p. A10; and "Sweeping Revision in Communication Is on the Horizon," *The New York Times*, October 26, 1994, p. 1.

Case Study 12-7
Antitrust and the New Merger Boom

A new merger boom is taking place in the 1990s that rivals in size and importance the merger boom of the second half of the 1980s. For example, 1994 was the biggest year for merger and acquisitions in history with deals valued at more than $339 billion (the previous record was $335 billion in 1988). Megadeals are announced almost weekly in telecommunications, defense, railroads, pharmaceuticals, retailing, health care, banking, entertainment, and in many other industries. There are several forces that fuel this urge to merger. The most important are massive technological changes, increased international competition, deregulation, and a lower antitrust profile. In some instances, the Justice Department even encourages mergers as a way to cut costs, especially in the health and defense fields. To be sure the Justice Department will still oppose consolidations that greatly reduce competition, but the government now seems to be primarily concerned with vertical mergers (say, between a large drug maker and a large drug distributor) that greatly reduce market competition.

Firms are under strong pressure today to reduce excessive capacity and cut costs, and to become a major player in the global marketplace. These pressures are likely to persist for years to come and so is the merger boom now sweeping corporate America. Besides the above-mentioned industries, mergers are also likely to come in such diverse fields as publishing, food, computers, consulting, and other industries. The present merger wave is different, however, from the junk-bond-financed and leveraged-buyout craze of the late 1980s. In the merger wave of the late 1980s, financiers took over companies in order to exploit or sell their assets. Most mergers today, on the other hand, are strategic alliances among companies in the same line of business to take advantage of new technologies, cut costs, and increase revenue, with the merging companies combining their stocks and without burdening them with excessive debt.

Whether, in fact, the present merger boom will lead companies to reduce costs and increase efficiency and revenue depends on the type of merger taking place. In the defense and the health care fields, the promise of reduced costs and increased efficiency can be realized. In others, it is not too certain. Often the acquiring company pays a premium over the market price because of synergies that the acquiring company's management sees but the market does not. When such synergies fail to materialize or do not live up to expectations, the acquiring company and its stockholders suffer.

Source: "Mergers Today, Trouble Tomorrow?" *Business Week,* September 12, 1994, pp. 30–32; "Shades of the Go-Go 80's: Takeovers in a Comeback," *The New York Times,* November 3, 1994, p. 1; "The New Merger Boom," *Fortune,* November 28, 1994, pp. 95–106; and "Mergers and Acquisitions Set Records, But Activity Lacked that '80s Pizzaz," *The Wall Street Journal,* January 3, 1995, p. R8.

Enforcement of Antitrust Laws: Conduct

Antitrust policy was also directed against anticompetitive industry conduct. The Court ruled against price collusion outright and against price discrimination if it substantially lessened competition or tended to create a monopoly. Specifically, the Court ruled as illegal not only cartels but also any informal understanding or collusion to share the market, fix prices, or establish price leadership schemes. **Conscious parallelism** (i.e., the adoption of similar policies by oligopolists in view of their recognized interdependence) was ruled to be illegal when reflecting collusion. Thus, the Supreme Court ruled against the three large tobacco companies in the 1946 Tobacco case (where conscious parallelism was believed to have been the result of collusion in the form of price leadership), but ruled to drop the suit in the 1954 Theater Enterprises case (where collusion could not be inferred from conscious parallelism).

The most difficult aspect in enforcing Section 1 of the Sherman Act has been to prove tacit or informal collusion. Sometimes the case was clearcut. For example, in 1936, the U.S. Engineer's Office received 11 closed bids to supply 6,000 barrels of cement, each quoting a price of $3.286854 per barrel! The probability of identical prices, down to the sixth decimal, occurring without some form of collusion is practically zero. One of the most important collusive agreements uncovered and successfully prosecuted was the "electrical machinery conspiracy" in which General Electric, Westinghouse, and a number of smaller companies producing electrical equipment pleaded guilty in 1961 to violation of antitrust laws for price fixing and dividing up the market. The companies were fined a total of $2 million and had to pay over $400 million in damages to customers in civil suits, 7 of their executives were sent to jail, and 23 others received suspended sentences.[10]

Predatory pricing was ruled to be illegal under Section 1 of the Sherman Act. **Predatory pricing** refers to the case where a firm uses the profits earned in one market to sell a product or service below its average variable cost in another market in order to drive competitors out of the latter market or to discourage the entrance of new firms by threatening to lower prices below costs. Besides predatory pricing, the Court ruled that any other form of price discrimination or price behavior that substantially lessened competition or tended to create a monopoly was illegal under the Clayton Act and the Robinson-Patman Act.

In determining illegal antitrust conduct, the definition of the relevant product market has been very important. For example, in the well-known *cellophane case,* the Du Pont Company was accused of monopolizing the market for cellophane. In its defense, Du Pont argued that cellophane was just one of many flexible packaging materials that included cellophane, waxed paper, aluminum foil, and many others. Based on the high cross-price elasticity of demand between cellophane and these other products, Du Pont successfully argued that the relevant market was not cellophane but flexible packaging materials. Since Du Pont had less than 20 percent of this market, the Supreme Court ruled in 1953 that Du Pont had not monopolized the market.

The Deregulation Movement

While the *public interest theory* postulates that regulation is undertaken to overcome market failures, so as to ensure that the economic system operates in a manner consistent with the public interest (see Section 12-2), the *economic theory of regulation* expounded by Stigler and others postulates that regulation is the result of pressure-group action and results in laws and policies that restrict competition and promote the interest of the firms that they are supposed to regulate (this is the "capture theory" discussed in Section 12-1).

Regulation is also attacked because of the heavy cost it imposes on society. One estimate has put this cost at more than $100 billion in the year 1979 (of which about 5 percent were administrative costs and the rest were the costs of

[10]"The Incredible Electrical Conspiracy," *Fortune,* April 1961, p. 132, and May 1961, p. 161.

compliance).[11] While these estimates have been challenged as grossly exaggerated,[12] compliance costs are surely very high, particularly in the area of social regulation, such as job safety, energy and the environment, and consumer safety and health.[13] In any event, since it is even more difficult to measure the full private and social benefits of regulation, it is practically impossible to determine on a strict benefit-cost basis whether regulation is economically justified.

Be that as it may, from the mid-1970s a growing deregulation movement has sprung up in the United States that has led to deregulation in air travel, trucking, railroads, banking, and telecommunications. The *Airline Deregulation Act of 1978* removed all restrictions on entry, scheduling, and pricing in domestic air travel in the United States, and so did the *Motor Carrier Act of 1980* in the trucking industry. The *Depository Institutions Deregulation and Monetary Control Act of 1980* allowed banks to pay interest on checking accounts and increased competition for business loans. The *Railroad Revitalization and Regulatory Reform Act of 1976* greatly increased the flexibility of railroads to set prices and to determine levels of service and areas of operation. The settlement of the *AT&T Antitrust Case in 1982* opened competition in long-distance telephone service and in telecommunications. Natural gas pipelines are now deregulated, and there is talk of deregulating the banking and electric power generation industries.

The general purpose of deregulation is to increase competition and efficiency in the affected industries and lead to lower prices without sacrificing the quality of service. Most observers would probably conclude that, on balance, the net effect has been positive. Competition has generally increased, and prices have fallen in industries that were deregulated. As expected, however, deregulation has also resulted in some difficulties and strains in the industries affected, to the point where some consumer groups and some firms in recently deregulated industries are asking Congress to reregulate the industries. Nowhere is this more evident than in the airline industry (see Case Study 12-8).

[11]Murray Weidenbaum, "The High Cost of Government Regulation," *Challenge*, November–December 1979, pp. 32–39.

[12]See William K. Tabb, "Government Regulation: Two Sides of the Story," *Challenge*, November–December 1980, pp. 40–48.

[13]Regulation often leads to inefficiencies because regulators do not specify the desired result but only the method of compliance (such as the type of pollution-abatement equipment to use) in the absence of adequate information and expertise. It would be much better if regulators specified the results wanted and left to industry the task of determining the most efficient way to comply. In recent years, there has been a movement along this direction (see Case Study 12-4).

Case Study 12-8

Deregulation of the Airline Industry: An Assessment

By 1995 all but one (America West) of the 15 air carriers that had been established since the 1978 deregulation had gone out of business or had merged with established carriers. Several mergers also took place among large established carriers, and Eastern Airline and Pan Am went out of business. The result was that by 1995 seven carriers handled more than 93 percent of all domestic air travel in the United States (as compared with 11 carriers handling 87 percent of the traffic in 1978). Since 1985, the market share of the top five carriers jumped from 61 percent to 75 percent. Instead of a large number of small and highly competitive airlines envisioned by deregulation, the airline industry has become even more concentrated than it was before deregulation. Entry into the industry is increasingly being restricted by established airlines by (1) long-term leasing of the limited number of gates at most airports, (2) frequent flier programs which increase passengers' loyalty to a given airline, (3) computerized reservations systems which give a competitive advantage in attracting loyal customers to the airlines owning the system, (4) the emergence of "hub and spoke" operations in which airlines funnel passengers through centrally located airports where one or two companies often dominate service.

It is true that airfares after adjusting for inflation have declined an average of 20 percent since deregulation and that this greatly stimulated domestic air travel (from about 250 million passengers in 1976 to over 450 million in 1994). It is also true that airlines could not possibly continue to charge fares as low as those charged during the latter part of the 1970s and the early part of the 1980s, and continue to incur huge losses. Nevertheless, the sharp reduction in the number of airlines is beginning to worry even the stoutest supporters of deregulation. Furthermore, while safety does not seem to have suffered and many small cities have not lost air service (as the opponents of deregulation had warned), delays at airports and passenger complaints about lost luggage, canceled flights, and general declines in the quality of service have increased significantly since deregulation. Bills are now pending in Congress on reimposing some regulation in the industry. The shift of regulatory authority from the Transportation Department to the Justice Department in 1989 also led to a tougher stance on mergers in the industry. But with the list of distressed airlines increasing, we are likely to see further consolidation in the industry.

Source: "Airline Deregulation," *Federal Reserve Bank of San Francisco Review,* March 9, 1990; "Death Struggle in the Sky," *Newsweek,* June 15, 1992, pp. 43–45; "Waiting Out the Airline Shake Out," *The New York Times,* May 22, 1992, p. 2; and "Come Fly the Unfriendly Skies," *The Economist,* November 5, 1994, pp. 61–62.

12-6 REGULATION OF INTERNATIONAL COMPETITION

There are many ways by which national governments regulate international trade. Some of these are tariffs, quotas, voluntary export restraints, antidumping duties, as well as technical, administrative, and other regulations. An **import tariff** is simply a tax on imports.[14] As such, it increases prices to domestic consumers, reduces the quantity demanded of the commodity at home and imports from abroad, and encourages the domestic production of import substitutes. The nation also collects tariff revenues. This is seen by examining Figure 12-4 (which is an extension of Figure 9-4).

In Figure 12-4, D_X and S_X refer to the domestic demand and supply curves of commodity X, while S_F is the horizontal foreign supply curve of the nation's imports (on the assumption that the nation is too small to affect the world price of commodity X). If the nation imposes a \$1 tariff on each unit of commodity X

[14]The U.S. Constitution forbids tariffs on exports.

Figure 12-4
The Effect of an Import Tariff on Consumption, Production, and Imports

D_X and S_X refer to the domestic demand and supply curves of commodity X, while S_F and S_F' refer, respectively, to the foreign supply curve of the nation's imports of commodity X with and without an import tariff of \$1 per unit. With the import tariff (i.e., with S_F') P_X = \$4 for domestic consumers (as compared with P_X = \$3 without the tariff), domestic consumers purchase $AC' = 500X$ (as compared with $AC = 600X$ without the tariff), domestic producers produce $AB' = 300X$ (instead of $AB = 200X$), and the government collects \$200 in revenues (\$1 per unit on each of the $200X$ imported).

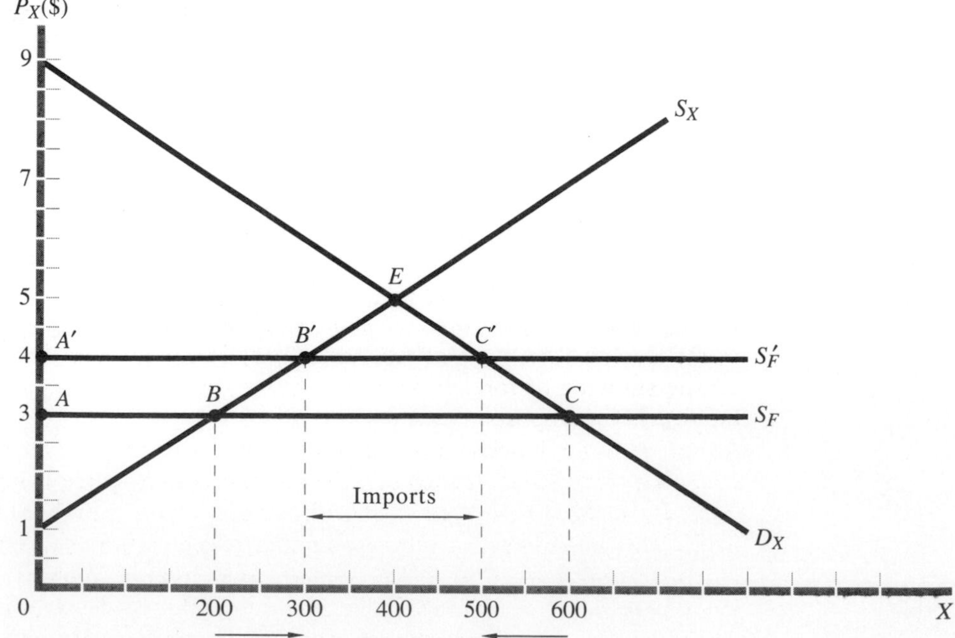

imported, the new foreign supply curve of imports to the nation shifts up to S'_F. From the figure, we see that with the tariff (i.e., with S'_F) P_X = \$4 for domestic consumers (as compared with P_X = \$3 without the tariff), domestic consumers purchase AC' = 500X (as compared with AC = 600X without the tariff), domestic producers produce AB' = 300X (instead of AB = 200X), and the government collects \$200 in revenues (\$1 per unit on each of the 200X imported).

An **import quota** of 200X would have the same effect as the \$1 tariff per unit of commodity X imported. While foreign producers could increase their exports by reducing the price of commodity X when they face an import tariff, however, they cannot with an equivalent import quota. Thus, an import quota is a more stringent restriction. In any event, import tariffs, quotas, and other trade restrictions protect domestic producers from foreign competition, thereby allowing them to produce more and charge higher prices. Import restrictions are invariably demanded by trade associations in order to protect their members from "unfair" foreign competition. In reality, they are often a convenient and effective way to restrict competition and increase prices.

Another form of trade restriction is the **voluntary export restraint (VER)**. This refers to the case where an importing country induces another nation to reduce its exports of a commodity "voluntarily," under the threat of higher all-around trade restrictions, when these exports threaten an entire domestic industry. Voluntary export restraints have been negotiated by the United States and other industrial countries to curtail exports of textiles, automobiles, steel, shoes, and other commodities from Japan and other nations. VERs have allowed industrial nations making use of them to save at least the appearance of continued support for the principle of free trade. When successful, VERs have all the economic effects of equivalent import tariffs, except that they are administered by the exporting country, and so the revenue effect or monopoly profits are captured by foreign exporters. Foreign exporters are also likely to fill their quota with higher-quality and higher-priced units of the product over time (see Case Study 12-9).

Another method of regulating (restricting) international trade is by antidumping complaints that are deliberately used to harass exporters to the nation (see Section 11-3). Still other methods are *safety regulations* for automobile and electrical equipment, *health regulations* for the hygienic production and packaging of imported food products, and *labeling requirements* showing origin and contents. While many of these regulations serve legitimate purposes, some (such as the French ban on scotch advertisement in France and the British restriction on the showing of foreign films on British television) are thinly veiled disguises for restricting imports.

The United States is now extending the reach of U.S. antitrust laws beyond U.S. borders to strike at such practices as bid rigging, price fixing, and other cartel behavior by foreign (particularly Japanese) companies that hurt U.S. international competitiveness in semiconductors, supercomputers, telecommunication equipment, aircraft, optical fibers, and other high-tech goods. Since 1984, the United States has also granted joint U.S. research-and-development ventures limited immunity from antitrust suits, including exemption from treble damages for private lawsuits against such ventures. The United States has also started to provide increasing support for "precompetitive generic technologies" in high-tech fields to counter strategic trade policies and targeting by other nations and regions, particularly Japan and the European Union.[15] These and other trade restrictions, however, are scheduled to be reduced as a result of the successful completion of the **Uruguay Round** of multilateral trade negotiations at the end of 1993 (see Case Study 12-10).

[15]"Antitrust Extension Is Weighted," *The New York Times,* April 16, 1990, pp. 54–55; "White House Reversing Policy Under Pressure, Begins to Pick High-Tech Winners and Losers," *The Wall Street Journal,*" May 13, 1991, p. A16; and "Uncle Sam's Helping Hand," *The Economist,* April 2, 1994, pp. 77–79.

Case Study 12-9
Voluntary Export Restraints on Japanese Automobiles to the United States

From 1977 to 1981, U.S. automobile production fell by about one-third, the share of imports rose from 18 to 29 percent, and nearly 300,000 autoworkers in the United States lost their jobs. In 1980 the Big Three U.S. automakers suffered combined losses of $4 billion. As a result, the United States negotiated an agreement with Japan which limited Japanese automobile exports to the United States to 1.68 million units per year from 1981 to 1983 and to 1.85 million units for 1984 and 1985. Japan "agreed" to restrict its automobile exports out of fear of still more stringent import restrictions by the United States.

U.S. automakers generally used the time from 1981 to 1985 wisely to lower breakeven points and improve quality, but the cost improvements were not passed on to consumers, and Detroit reaped profits of nearly $6 billion in 1983, $10 billion in 1984, and $8 billion in 1985. Japan gained by exporting higher-priced autos and earning higher profits. The big loser, of course, was the American public, which had to pay substantially higher prices for domestic and foreign automobiles. The U.S. International Trade Commission (USITC) estimated that the agreement resulted in a price $660 higher for U.S.–made automobiles and $1,300 higher for Japanese cars in 1984. The USITC also estimated that the total cost of the agreement to U.S. consumers was $15.7 billion from 1981 through 1984, and that 44,000 U.S. auto jobs were saved at a cost of more than $100,000 each. This was more than two to three times the yearly earnings of a U.S. autoworker.

Since 1985, the United States has not asked for a renewal of the VER agreement, but Japan unilaterally limited its auto exports (to 2.3 million from 1986 to 1991 and 1.65 million afterward) to avoid more trade frictions with the United States. Since the late 1980s, however, Japan has invested heavily to produce automobiles in the United States in so-called transplant factories, and by 1991 it was producing more than 1 million cars in the United States. By 1991, Japan had captured 31 percent of the U.S. auto market (18 percent from exports and 13 from production in the United States). Since then, however, the Japanese share of the U.S. auto market declined to 27 percent (in 1994) as a result of the increased efficiency of U.S. automakers (especially Ford and Chrysler) and the increase in the price of Japanese cars sold in the United States.

Source: U.S. International Trade Commission, *A Review of Recent Developments in the U.S. Automobile Industry Including an Assessment of the Japanese Voluntary Restraint Agreements* (Washington, D.C.: February 1985); J. de Melo and D. Tarr, "Welfare Costs of U.S. Quotas in Textiles, Steel, and Autos," *Review of Economics and Statistics,* March 1990, pp. 489–497; "U.S. Cars Come Back," *Fortune,* November 16, 1992, pp. 52–85; and "Sparking a Revival," *U.S. News & World Report,* June 14, 1993, pp. 69–73.

Case Study 12-10

Reductions of Trade Restrictions under the Uruguay Round

Following is the scheduled reduction in trade restrictions as a result of the successful completion of the Uruguay Round of multilateral trade negotiations in December 1993:

1. *Tariffs* Tariffs on industrial products are to be reduced from an average of 4.7 percent to 3 percent, and the share of goods with zero tariffs is to increase from 20 to 22 percent to 40 to 45 percent; tariffs were removed altogether on pharmaceuticals, construction equipment, medical equipment, paper products, and steel.
2. *Quotas* Nations are to replace quotas on agricultural imports and imports of textiles and apparel with less restrictive tariffs over a 10-year period; tariffs on agricultural products are to be reduced by 24 percent in developing nations and by 36 percent in industrial nations, and tariffs on textiles are to be cut by 25 percent.
3. *Antidumping* The agreement provides for tougher and quicker action to resolve disputes resulting from the use of antidumping laws but does not ban their use.
4. *Subsidies* The volume of subsidized agricultural exports are to be reduced by 21 percent over a 6-year period; government subsidies for industrial research are limited to 50 percent of applied research costs.
5. *Safeguards* Nations may temporarily raise tariffs or other restrictions against an import surge that severely harms a domestic industry, but countries are barred from administering health and safety standards unless they are based on scientific evidence and not simply on the desire to restrict trade. For example, a nation can keep out beef imports from cattle raised with growth hormones only by showing that the beef so produced is unsafe for human consumption.
6. *Intellectual property* The agreement provides for 20-year protection of patents, trademarks, and copyrights, but it allows a 10-year phase-in period for patent protection in pharmaceuticals for developing countries.
7. *Services* The United States failed to secure access to the markets of Japan, Korea, and many developing nations for its banks and security firms, and it did not succeed in having France and the European Community lift restrictions on the showing of American films and TV programs in Europe.

8. *Other industry provisions* The United States and Europe agreed to continue talking about further limiting government subsidies to civil aircraft makers, opening up the long-distance telephone market, and limiting European subsidies to steelmakers. The United States also indicated that it intends to continue negotiating the further opening of the Japanese computer-chip market.
9. *Trade-related investment measures* The agreement phases out the requirement that foreign investors (such as automakers) buy supplies locally or export as much as they import.
10. *World Trade Organization* The agreement calls for the establishment of the World Trade Organization (WTO) with authority in trade in industrial and agricultural products and services. Trade disputes are to be settled by a two-thirds vote rather than unanimously (which means that the guilty nation could block any action against it as was the case before).

The implementation of the Uruguay Round is expected to increase world trade by some $270 billion per year by the year 2002 and increase standards of living throughout the world as a result of the more efficient use of the labor, capital, and other resources.

Source: W. McKibbin and D. Salvatore, "The Global Economic Consequences of the Uruguay Round," *Open Economies Review,* March 1995, pp. 111–129.

SUMMARY

1. According to the economic theory of regulation expounded by Stigler and others, regulation arises from pressure-group action and results in laws and policies in support of business, and to protect consumers, workers, and the environment. Some of the policies designed to support business restrict entry and competition. These are licensing, patents, restrictions on price competition, import restrictions (tariffs and quotas), as well as subsidies and special tax treatments to aid such sectors as agriculture, transportation, airlines, and energy. Consumers are protected by requiring truthful disclosure by firms and by forbidding misrepresentation of products, and by laws requiring truth in lending, fairness in evaluating credit applications, clarity in warranties, safety on highways, and many others. Workers are protected by laws that specify safety standards, equal employment opportunity, and minimum wages, while air, water, and other environmental pollution are regulated by the Environmental Protection Agency.
2. According to the public interest theory of regulation, government regulation is undertaken to overcome market failures, so that the economic system can operate in a manner consistent with the public interest. One type of market failure is due to externalities. These are uncompensated costs and benefits borne or received by firms or individuals other than those producing or consuming the product or service. Thus, we have external economies and diseconomies of production and consumption. When private and social costs or benefits do not coincide (i.e., in the presence of externalities), too much or

too little of a product or service is being produced or consumed from society's point of view. In such cases, government intervention is justified in order to induce the production or consumption of the product or service until the marginal social cost is equal to the marginal social benefit. Market failures due to externalities can be overcome by prohibition or regulation, taxes or subsidies, by voluntary payments, by mergers, or the sale of pollution rights. Prohibition and regulation are preferred by regulatory agencies, but they are not the most efficient methods of dealing with externalities.

3. In some industries, economies of scale may operate continuously as output expands, so that a single firm can supply the entire market more efficiently than any number of smaller firms. Such natural monopolies are common in the provision of electrical, gas, water, and local transportation services (public utilities). In cases such as these, the government usually allows a single firm to operate but regulates it by setting $P = LAC$ (so that the firm breaks even and earns only a normal return on investment). Economic efficiency, however, requires that $P = LMC$, but this would result in a loss so that the company would not supply the service in the long run without a subsidy. Therefore, P is usually set equal to LAC. Public utility regulation faces many difficulties. These arise from the difficulty in determining the value of the fixed assets of the company, in setting rates for each type of customer, in allocating costs for the jointly produced services, in ensuring that public utilities keep costs as low as possible, from over or underinvestments in fixed assets (the Averch-Johnson effect), and from regulatory lags.

4. Starting with the Sherman Act of 1890, a number of antitrust laws were passed to prevent monopoly or undue concentration of economic power, protect the public against the abuses and inefficiencies resulting from monopoly or the concentration of economic power, and maintain a workable degree of competition in the American economy. *The Sherman Act (1890)* prohibited monopolization and restraints of trade in commerce among the states and with foreign nations. *The Clayton Act (1914)* prohibited price discrimination, exclusive and tying contracts, and intercorporate stock holdings if they substantially lessened competition or tended to create a monopoly, and prohibited outright interlocking directorates. *The Federal Trade Commission Act (1914)*, passed to supplement the Clayton Act, made unfair methods of competition illegal and established the Federal Trade Commission (FTC) to prosecute violators of the antitrust laws and protect the public against false and misleading advertisements. *The Robinson-Patman Act (1936)* sought to protect small retailers from price competition from large chain-store retailers, based on the latter's ability to obtain lower prices and brokerage concession fees on bulk purchases from suppliers if the intent was to destroy competition or eliminate a competitor. *The Wheeler-Lea Act (1938)* amended the Federal Trade Commission Act and forbade false or deceptive advertisement of foods, drugs, corrective devices, and cosmetics entering interstate commerce. *The Celler-Kefauver Antimerger Act (1950)* closed a loophole in the Clayton Act by making it illegal to acquire not only

the stock but also the assets of competing corporations if such purchases substantially lessen competition or tend to create a monopoly.

5. Enforcement of antitrust laws has been the responsibility of the Antitrust Division of the Department of Justice and the Federal Trade Commission (FTC). Antitrust violations have been resolved by (1) dissolution and divestiture, (2) injunction, or (3) consent decree. Fines and jail sentences have also been imposed. Starting with the 1945 Alcoa case, the Supreme Court ruled that size per se was an offense, irrespective of illegal acts. Today, both size and some anticompetitive behavior seem to be required for successful prosecution. The Court has generally challenged horizontal mergers between large direct competitors but not vertical and conglomerate mergers unless they would lead to increased horizontal market power. The Court has used the Sherman Act to prosecute not only attempts to set up a cartel but also any informal collusion to share the market, fix prices, or establish price leadership schemes. The Court has ruled that conscious parallelism is illegal when it reflects collusion. The Court has also attacked predatory pricing and price discrimination and other price behavior when it substantially lessened competition or tended to create a monopoly. Since the mid-1970s, the government has deregulated airlines and trucking and has reduced the level of regulation for financial institutions, telecommunications, and railroads in order to increase competition and avoid some of the heavy compliance costs of regulation. Deregulation seems to have led to increased competition and lower prices, but it has also resulted in some problems.
6. Nations regulate international trade by tariffs, quotas, voluntary export restraints, antidumping duties, as well as technical, administrative, and other regulations. An import tariff is simply a tax on imports. As such, it increases prices to domestic consumers, reduces the quantity demanded of the commodity at home and imports from abroad, and encourages the domestic production of import substitutes. The nation also collects tariff revenues. An import quota is a quantitative restriction on imports. A voluntary export restraint is used by an importing country to induce another nation to reduce its exports of a commodity "voluntarily," under the threat of higher all-around trade restrictions, when these exports threaten an entire domestic industry. Other regulations are antidumping duties and safety, health, and labeling regulations when they are used to restrict imports. Import restrictions are invariably demanded to protect their members from "unfair" foreign competition. In reality, they are often a convenient and effective way to restrict competition and increase prices. Trade restrictions are scheduled to be reduced as a result of the successful conclusion of the Uruguay Round.

DISCUSSION QUESTIONS

1. Name two theories that seek to explain the rationale for government intervention in the economy. What do they postulate? Which is the prevailing theory today?

2. (*a*) In what way do licensing, patents, import taxes, and import quotas restrict competition? (*b*) What are some of the direct restrictions on price competition resulting from government regulation?
3. What are the pros and cons of regulating oil and natural gas prices?
4. Why is it likely that in a system of private education (i.e., a system in which individuals pay for their own education) there will be underinvestment in education?
5. (*a*) How much of a tax of $3 per hour for evening typing imposed on individual *A* in the left panel of Figure 12-2 actually falls on (i.e., is actually paid by) individual *A* and how much of the tax does in fact fall on those who demand the typing services of individual *A*? (*b*) On what does the incidence of a per-unit tax (i.e., the relative share of the tax burden) depend in general?
6. (*a*) Why can a per-hour subsidy given to individual *A* for tending his or her yard be shown by a downward shift in the MPC_A curve in the right panel of Figure 12-2? (*b*) Explain why the result of a subsidy of $3 per hour given to individual *A* for tending his or her yard shown by shifting the MPC_A curve down by $3 is the same as the result obtained by shifting the MPB_A curve up by $3.
7. What is the basic difference between using a subsidy to induce producers to install antipollution equipment and a tax on producers who pollute?
8. (*a*) How could a regulatory commission induce a public utility company to operate as a perfect competitor in the long run? (*b*) To what difficulty would this lead? (*c*) What compromise does a regulatory commission usually adopt?
9. Given the difficulties that the regulation of public utilities faces, would it not be better to nationalize public utilities, as some European countries have done? Explain your answer.
10. (*a*) How does government decide whether to subject a very large firm to regulation or antitrust action? (*b*) Which are the basic antitrust laws? Why were other laws passed subsequently?
11. Has the Supreme Court interpreted size as illegal per se in enforcing the antitrust laws? Explain.
12. The settlement of the AT&T antitrust case in January 1982 involved both good news and bad news for AT&T and its customers. What was (*a*) the bad news and good news for AT&T? (*b*) the good news and bad news for users of telephone services?
13. From Figure 9-4, determine the effect of an import tariff of (*a*) $0.50 per unit and (*b*) $2 per unit.

PROBLEMS

1. The perfectly competitive industry demand and supply functions for a special type of computer memory chip are, respectively,

$$Qd = 7{,}000 - 5P \qquad \text{and} \qquad Qs = -2{,}000 + 10P$$

where P is in dollars. The production of each computer chip, however, results in a pollution cost of 10 cents. Draw a figure showing the equilibrium price and quantity for this special type of memory chip, as well as the socially optimal price and quantity.

*2. Draw a figure showing the corrective tax or subsidy that would induce the industry of Problem 1 to produce the socially optimal quantity of the product. What is the net price received by the producers?

3. Suppose that the production of each computer chip in Problem 1 results in an external benefit (economy of production) of 6 cents (instead of a pollution cost of 10 cents). Draw a figure showing the socially optimal price and quantity of the computer chips, as well as the corrective tax or subsidy needed to achieve them. What is the net price received by the producers?

4. The market demand and supply functions for canned soft drinks in Smithtown are, respectively,

$$Qd = 18{,}000 - 10{,}000P \qquad \text{and} \qquad Qs = 0.6 + 0.0001P$$

where P is in dollars. The market is nearly perfectly competitive. Since the consumption of each can of soft drink, however, leads to the need to collect and recycle empty soft drink cans, the demand curve showing the marginal social benefit of canned soft drinks has the same vertical intercept but twice the absolute slope of D. Draw a figure showing the equilibrium price and quantity, as well as the socially optimal price and quantity for cans of soft drinks in Smithtown.

*5. Draw a figure showing the corrective tax or subsidy that would induce consumers in Smithtown to consume the socially optimal number of cans of soft drinks. What is the net price now paid by consumers for each can of soft drink?

6. Suppose that each empty can of soft drink collected can be sold for scrap metal so that the demand curve showing the marginal social benefit of canned soft drinks has the same vertical intercept but half the absolute slope of D in Problem 4. Draw a figure showing the socially optimal price and quantity, as well as the corrective tax or subsidy needed to achieve them. What is the net price paid by consumers for each can of soft drink that they purchase?

*7. Suppose that the market demand curve for the public utility service shown in Figure 12-3 shifts to the right by 1 million units at each price level but the LAC and LMC curves remain unchanged. Draw a figure showing the price of the service that the public utility commission would set and the quantity of the service that would be supplied to the market at that price.

8. Suppose that the market demand curve for the public utility service shown in Figure 12-3 shifts to the right by 1 million units at each price level and, at the same time, the *LAC* curve of the public utility company shifts up by $1 throughout because of production inefficiencies that escape detection by the public utility commission. Draw a figure showing the price of the service that the public utility commission would set and the quantity of the service that would be supplied to the market at that price.

9. Sears sells under its trademark steel-belted tires manufactured by the Pneumatic Tire Company under an exclusive contract. Two years before that contract expires, the Pneumatic Tire Company merges with a nationally known firm that competes with Sears in the sale of steel-belted tires and breaks the contract with Sears. During the years before the Pneumatic Tire Company broke the contract, Sears sold on the average $100 million worth of tires with a net (i.e., after taxes, depreciation, etc.) profit margin of 30 percent. Sears expected to have the same revenue from the sale of tires in the remaining two years of the contract with the Pneumatic Tire Company, but after the latter breaks the contract and Sears starts to buy tires from another supplier, Sears's sales fall by 25 percent in the first year and by another 25 percent in the second year. Sears's net profit margin on tire sales, however, remains at 30 percent in both years. (*a*) Indicate which antitrust law Sears could accuse the Pneumatic Tire Company of having broken, and (*b*) measure the total economic loss that Sears can allege to have sustained from the Pneumatic Tire Company's breaking its contract with Sears.

10. Determine if the Justice Department would challenge a merger between two firms in an industry with 10 equal-sized firms, based on its Herfindahl-index guidelines only.

11. (Library research) Explain (*a*) in what way the U.S. trucking industry exemplified the capture theory hypothesis of government regulation prior to the passage of the *Motor Carrier Act of 1980* and (*b*) the result of the passage of the Motor Carrier Act in 1980.

*12. (Library research) During the 1970s the average rate of return on stockholders' equity in the U.S. banking industry was consistently higher than the average rate of return in other U.S. industries, while the opposite was the case in the 1980s. Identify the most important reasons for this.

13. **Integrating Problem**
    From the following figure referring to a natural monopolist, indicate: (*a*) The best level of output, price, and profits per unit and in total for the monopolist. (*b*) The best level of output and price with a lump sum tax that would eliminate all the monopolist's profits. (*c*) The best level of output, price, and profits per unit and in total with a $3 per unit tax collected from the monopolist. (*d*) The best level of output and profit per unit and in total if the government sets the price of the product or service at $10. (*e*) Which is the best method of controlling monopoly power. Why?

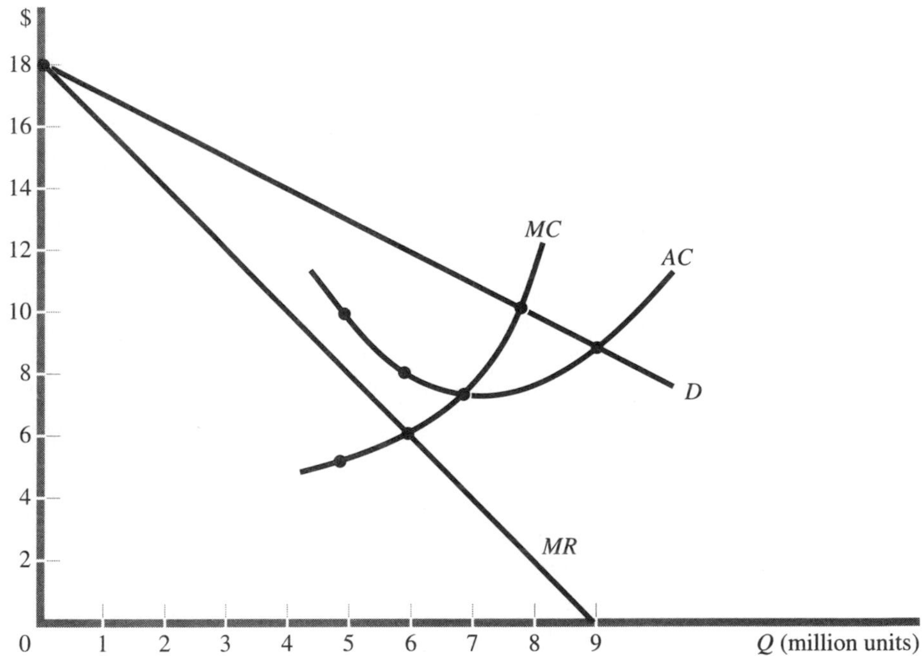

SUPPLEMENTARY READINGS

For a problem-solving approach to the topics examined in this chapter, see:

Salvatore, Dominick: *Theory and Problems of Managerial Economics,* Schaum Outline Series (New York: McGraw-Hill, 1989), Chap. 12.

The topics examined in this chapter are also discussed in:

Scherer, F. H., and **David Ross:** *Industrial Market Structure and Economic Performance* (Boston: Houghton Mifflin, 1990).

Wilcox, Clair, and **William G. Sheperd:** *Public Policies Toward Business* (Homewood, Ill.: Irwin, 1975).

For government regulations that restrict competition, see:

Buchanan, James, and **G. Tullock:** *The Calculus of Consent* (Ann Arbor: University of Michigan Press, 1962).

Posner, Richard: "Theories of Economic Regulation," *Bell Journal of Economics and Management Science,* Autumn 1974, pp. 335–358.

Stigler, George J.: "The Theory of Economic Regulation," *Bell Journal of Economics and Management Science,* Spring 1971, pp. 3–21.

Externalities are examined in:

Bator, Francis M.: "The Anatomy of Market Failure," *Quarterly Journal of Economics,* August 1958, pp. 351–379.

Coase, Ronald R.: "The Problem of Social Costs," *Journal of Law and Economics,* October 1960, pp. 1–44.

Misham, Ezra J.: "The Postwar Literature on Externalities: An Interpretative Essay," *Journal of Economic Literature,* March 1971, pp. 395–409.

Salvatore, Dominick: *Microeconomics,* 2nd ed. (New York: HarperCollins, 1994), Chap. 17.

For public utility regulation, see:

Kahn, Alfred E.: *The Economics of Regulation* (New York: Wiley, 1971).

Phillips, Charles F.: *The Regulation of Public Utilities* (Arlington, Va.: Public Utilities Report, 1984).

Averch, Harvey, and **Leland Johnson:** "Behavior of the Firm under Regulatory Constraint," *American Economic Review,* December 1962, pp. 1052–1069.

A more extensive discussion of antitrust laws and policies is found in:

Blair, Roger, and **David L. Kaserman:** *Antitrust Economics* (Homewood, Ill.: Irwin, 1985).

Stelzer, Irwin M.: *Selected Antitrust Cases* (Homewood, Ill.: Irwin, 1981). "Symposium on Mergers and Antitrust," *Economic Perspectives,* Fall 1987, pp. 3–54.

An evaluation of regulation and the recent deregulation movement is found in:

Peltzman, Sam: "The Economic Theory of Regulation after a Decade of Regulation, *Brookings Papers on Economic Activity,* 1989, pp. 2–41.

Morrison, Steven A., and **Clifford Winston:** "Enhancing the Performance of the Deregulated Air Transport System," *Brookings Papers on Economic Activity,* 1989, pp. 61–123.

Kahn, Alfred E.: "Surprises of Airline Deregulation," *American Economic Review,* May 1988, pp. 316–322.

Crandall, Robert W.: "Surprises from Telephone Deregulation and AT&T Divestiture," *American Economic Review,* May 1988, pp. 323–334.

Kane, Edward J.: "Interaction of Financial and Regulatory Innovation," *American Economic Review,* May 1988, pp. 328–334.

For regulation of international trade, see:

Salvatore, Dominick: *International Economics,* 5th ed. (Englewood Cliffs, N.J.: Prentice-Hall, 1995), Chaps. 9 and 10.

Salvatore, Dominick, ed.: *Protectionism and World Welfare* (New York: Cambridge University Press, 1993).

CHAPTER 13

Risk Analysis

KEY TERMS

Certainty, Risk, Uncertainty
State of nature
Probability
Probability distribution
Expected profit
Discrete probability distribution
Continuous probability distribution
Standard deviation (σ)
Variance (σ^2)
Standard normal distribution
Coefficient of variation (v)
Risk seeker, Risk neutral
Risk averter
Diminishing marginal utility of money
Util
Expected utility
Risk-adjusted discount rate
Risk-return trade-off function
Risk premium
Certainty-equivalent coefficient (α)
Decision tree
Conditional probability
Simulation
Sensitivity analysis
Maximin criterion
Minimax regret criterion
Foreign-exchange rate
Hedging, Forward contract
Futures contract
Asymmetric information
Adverse selection
Moral hazard
Information superhighway
Internet

CHAPTER OUTLINE

Until now we have examined managerial decision making under conditions of certainty. In such cases, the manager knows exactly the outcome of each possible course of action. Many managerial decisions are, indeed, made under conditions of certainty, especially in the short run. For example, suppose that the firm had borrowed \$100,000 at a 14 percent interest rate on a note that still has 30 days to maturity. Suppose also that the firm has just generated \$100,000 in surplus cash that it can invest in a 30-day Treasury bill with a yield of 10 percent. The manager of the firm can determine with certainty that the firm would earn \$329 more by using the cash to prepay the loan.[1]

In many managerial decisions, however, the manager often does not know the exact outcome of each possible course of action. For example, the return on a long-run investment depends on economic conditions in the future, the degree of future competition, consumer tastes, technological advances, the political climate, and many other such factors about which the firm has only imperfect knowledge. In such cases, we say that the firm faces "risk" or "uncertainty." Most strategic decisions of the firm are of this type. Thus, it is essential to extend the basic model of the firm presented in Chapter 1 to include risk and uncertainty.

We begin this chapter by distinguishing between risk and uncertainty and introducing some of the concepts essential for risk analysis. Then we examine methods for measuring risk and for analyzing the manager's attitude toward risk. Subsequently, we show how to adjust the valuation model of the firm for risk, and how to use decision trees and simulation to aid complex managerial decision making subject to risk. Finally, we examine decision making under uncertainty, including that resulting from fluctuating values of foreign currencies and from lack of information (or inadequate information).

13-1 RISK AND UNCERTAINTY IN MANAGERIAL DECISION MAKING

Managerial decisions are made under conditions of certainty, risk, or uncertainty. **Certainty** refers to the situation where there is only one possible outcome to a decision and this outcome is known precisely. For example, investing in Treasury bills leads to only one outcome (the amount of the yield), and this is known with certainty. The reason is that there is virtually no chance that the federal government will fail to redeem these securities at maturity or that it will default on interest payments. On the other hand, when there is more than one possible outcome to a decision, risk or uncertainty is present.

Risk refers to a situation where there is more than one possible outcome to a decision and the probability of each specific outcome is known or can be estimated. Thus, risk requires that the decision maker know all the possible outcomes of the decision and have some idea of the probability of each outcome's occurrence. For example, in tossing a coin, we can get either a head or a tail, and

[1]The \$329 higher earnings in prepaying the loan rather than investing in Treasury bills is obtained as follows:

$$(14\% - 10\%)(\$100{,}000)(30/365) = \$329$$

each has an equal (i.e., a 50-50) chance of occurring (if the coin is balanced). Similarly, investing in a stock or introducing a new product can lead to one of a set of possible outcomes, and the probability of each possible outcome can be estimated from past experience or from market studies. In general, the greater the variability (i.e., the greater the number and range) of possible outcomes, the greater is the risk associated with the decision or action.

Uncertainty is the case when there is more than one possible outcome to a decision and where the probability of each specific outcome occurring is not known or even meaningful. This may be due to insufficient past information or instability in the structure of the variables. In extreme forms of uncertainty not even the outcomes themselves are known. For example, drilling for oil in an unproven field carries with it uncertainty if the investor does not know either the possible oil outputs or their probability of occurrence.[2]

In the analysis of managerial decision making involving risk, we will utilize such concepts as strategy, states of nature, and payoff matrix.[3] A *strategy* refers to one of several alternative courses of action that a decision maker can take to achieve a goal. For example, a manager may have to decide on the strategy of building a large or a small plant in order to maximize profits or the value of the firm. **States of nature** refer to conditions in the future that will have a significant effect on the degree of success or failure of any strategy, but over which the decision maker has little or no control. For example, the economy may be booming, normal, or in a recession in the future. The decision maker has no control over the states of nature that will prevail in the future but the future states of nature will certainly affect the outcome of any strategy that he or she may adopt. The particular decision made will depend, therefore, on the decision maker's knowledge or estimation of how a particular future state of nature will affect the outcome or result of each particular strategy (such as investing in a large or in a small plant). Finally, a *payoff matrix* is a table that shows the possible outcomes or results of each strategy under each state of nature. For example, a payoff matrix may show the level of profit that would result if the firm builds a large or a small plant and if the economy will be booming, normal, or recessionary in the future.

[2]While it may be useful for pedagogical purposes to distinguish risk from uncertainty, it must be pointed out that both are part of a continuum, with certainty (complete knowledge) at one end of the continuum and complete ignorance at the other, and with risk and uncertainty in between.

[3]The concepts of strategy and payoff matrix were already encountered in Chapter 10 in the discussion of game theory.

Case Study 13-1

The Risk Faced by Coca-Cola in Changing Its Secret Formula

On April 23, 1985, the Coca-Cola Company announced that it was changing its 99-year-old recipe for Coke. Coke is the leading soft drink in the world, and the company took an unusual risk in tampering with its highly successful product. The Coca-Cola Company felt that changing its recipe was a necessary strategy to ward off the challenge from Pepsi-Cola, which had been chipping away at Coke's market lead over the years. The new Coke, with its sweeter and less fizzy taste, was clearly aimed at reversing Pepsi's market gains. Coca-Cola spent over $4 million to develop its new Coke and conducted taste tests on more than 190,000 consumers over a three-year period. These tests seemed to indicate that consumers preferred the new Coke by 61 percent to 39 percent over the old Coke. Coca-Cola then spent over $10 million on advertising its new product.

When the new Coke was finally introduced in May 1985, there was nothing short of a consumers' revolt against the new Coke, and in what is certainly one of the most stunning multimillion dollar about-faces in the history of marketing, the company felt compelled to bring back the old Coke under the brand name Coca-Cola Classic. The irony is that with the Classic and new Cokes sold side by side, Coca-Cola regained some of the market share that it had lost to Pepsi. While some people believe that Coca-Cola intended all along to reintroduce the old Coke and that the whole thing was part of a shrewd marketing strategy, most marketing experts are convinced that Coca-Cola had underestimated consumers' loyalty to the old Coke. This did not come up in the extensive taste tests conducted by Coca-Cola because the consumers tested were never informed that the company intended to *replace* the old Coke with the new Coke rather than sell them side by side. This case study clearly shows that even a well-conceived strategy is risky and can lead to results estimated to have a small probability of occurrence. Indeed, the failure rate for new products in the United States today is more than 50 percent. Coca-Cola is now fending off new challenges to its soft-drink market supremacy with its 1994 introduction of Frutopia line of fruit-based drinks, new sports elixir PowerAde, and generation-X inspired OK Soda, while keeping prices low to fight competition from Pepsi, its perennial archrival, and new archrival private-label colas, such as Cott.

Source: "Coca-Cola Changes Its Secret Formula in Use for 99 Years," *The New York Times,* April 24, 1985, p. 1; " 'Old' Coke Coming Back After Outcry by Faithful," *The New York Times,* July 11, 1985, p. 13; "Flops," *Business Week,* August 16, 1993, pp. 76–82; "Upstart Cott Challenges the Cola Kings," *Fortune,* August 8, 1994, p. 75; "Storm in a Soda Bottle," *The Economist,* August 6, 1994, p. 54; and "Behemoth on a Tear," *Business Week,* October 3, 1994, pp. 54–55.

Case Study 13-2
Why Companies Fail

Nearly 100,000 businesses failed in the United States during 1992. Of course, the number of business failures increases during recessions, but even during periods of buoyant economic conditions many businesses fail (for example, about 50,000 businesses failed in 1989). Although the reasons businesses fail are many and the details differ from case to case, several general underlying causes can be identified. *First,* many business failures arise because senior executives do not fully understand the fundamentals of their business or core expertise and business of the firm. Then the company drifts (often through mergers and acquisitions) into lines of business about which it knows little. This, for example, happened to Kodak when it diversified from its core camera and film business into pharmaceuticals and consumer health products.

The *second* basic reason for business failures is lack of vision or the inability of top management to anticipate or foresee serious problems that the business may face down the road. For example, U.S. automakers (General Motors, Ford, and Chrysler) failed to understand early enough the seriousness of the competitive challenge coming from Japan and almost willingly ceded the small-car market to Japan (because of the low profits per car earned in that market) in the erroneous belief that Japan would never be able to compete effectively in the medium-range segment of the market (where profit per automobile was much higher and American automakers were stronger). This resulted in huge losses for American automakers during the second half of the 1980s and early 1990s and almost drove Chrysler out of business (see Case Study 12-9). Another example is provided by Sears, which was unable or unwilling to understand the kind of sea change going on in consumer preferences that eventually propelled Wal-Mart to replace it as the nation's top marketeer. One indication of a vision failure is given when top management starts following every new management fad, without a clear understanding or reason for it. Most dangerous are latent or stealthy competitors, who as a result of some major and quick technological or market change can devastate the firm in its very core business. A clear example of this is IBM's inability to recognize early enough the importance and dramatic growth of the PC market in the mid-1980s and subsequent signing of Microsoft to develop the software and Intel to supply the chips for its PCs.

A *third* reason for business failures, especially during the late 1980s, is the loading of the firm with a heavy debt burden (usually to carry out a program of merger and acquisitions, often at overpriced terms) which then robs the firm of its strength in a market downturn. This is precisely what happened in 1991 and 1992 to the USG Corporation, the huge Chicago-based building product company. *Fourth,* business failures arise when firms vainly try to recapture their past glories and become stuck on obsolete strategies and are unable to respond to new and major competitive challenges. This is, to some extent, what happened to General Motors and IBM during the past decade before the brutal forces of the market shook them out of their complacency. It is often more difficult to keep a business great than to build it in the first place. *Finally,* a company may fail as a result of strikes and hostilities from unhappy workers.

Source: "Dinosaurs?" *Fortune,* May 3, 1994, pp. 36–42; and "Why Companies Fail," *Fortune,* November 14, 1994, pp. 52–68.

13-2 MEASURING RISK WITH PROBABILITY DISTRIBUTIONS

In the previous section we defined risk as the situation where there is more than one possible outcome to a decision and the probability of each possible outcome is known or can be estimated. In this section we examine the meaning and characteristics of probability distributions, and then we use these concepts to develop a precise measure of risk.

Probability Distributions

The **probability** of an event is the chance or odds that the event will occur. For example, if we say that the probability of booming conditions in the economy next year is 0.25, or 25 percent, this means that there is 1 chance in 4 for this condition to occur. By listing all the possible outcomes of an event and the probability attached to each, we get a **probability distribution.** For example, if only three states of the economy are possible (boom, normal, or recession) and the probability of each occurring is specified, we have a probability distribution such as the one shown in Table 13-1. Note that the sum of the probabilities is 1, or 100 percent, since one of the three possible states of the economy must occur with certainty.

The concept of probability distributions is essential in evaluating and comparing investment projects. In general, the outcome or profit of an investment project is highest when the economy is booming and smallest when the economy is in a recession. If we multiply each possible outcome or profit of an investment by its probability of occurrence and add these products, we get the expected value or profit of the project. That is,

$$\text{Expected profit} = E(\pi) = \overline{\pi} = \sum_{i=1}^{n} \pi_i \cdot P_i \tag{13-1}$$

where π_i is the profit level associated with outcome i, P_i is the probability that outcome i will occur, and $i = 1$ to n refers to the number of possible outcomes or states of nature. Thus, the **expected profit** of an investment is the weighted average of all possible profit levels that can result from the investment under the various states of the economy, with the probability of those outcomes or profits used as weights. The expected profit of an investment is a very important consideration in deciding whether or not to undertake the project or which of two or more projects is preferable.[4]

[4]While the discussion above is in terms of profits and we have defined the expected profit, the concepts are general. Specifically, the expected value or mean of the possible outcomes of any stategy or experiment is given by

$$\text{Expected value of } X = E(X) = \overline{X} = \sum_{i=1}^{n} X_i \cdot P_i$$

where X_i is outcome i, P_i is the probability of outcome i, and $i = 1$ to n refers to the number of possible outcomes.

Table 13-1
Probability Distribution of States of the Economy

State of the Economy		Probability of Occurrence
Boom		0.25
Normal		0.50
Recession		0.25
	Total	1.00

Table 13-2
Calculation of the Expected Profits of Two Projects

Project	(1) State of Economy	(2) Probability of Occurrence	(3) Outcome of Investment	(4) Expected Value (2) × (3)
A	Boom	0.25	$600	$150
	Normal	0.50	500	250
	Recession	0.25	400	100
		Expected profit from project A		$500
B	Boom	0.25	$800	$200
	Normal	0.50	500	250
	Recession	0.25	200	50
		Expected profit from project B		$500

For example, Table 13-2 presents the payoff matrix of project A and project B and shows how the expected value of each project is determined. In this case the expected value of each of the two projects is $500, but the range of outcomes for project A (from $400 in recession to $600 in boom) is much smaller than for project B (from $200 in recession to $800 in boom). Thus, project A is less risky than and, therefore, preferable to project B.[5]

[5]Note that the expected value of a probability distribution need not equal any of the possible outcomes (although in this case it does). The expected value is simply a weighted average of all the possible outcomes if the decision or experiment were repeated a very large number of times. Had the expected value of project A been lower than of project B, the manager would have had to decide whether the lower expected profit from project A was compensated by its lower risk. In Section 13-3 we will show how a manager makes such decisions.

Figure 13-1
Probability Distribution of Profits from Project A and Project B

The expected profit, $E(\pi)$, is $500 for both projects A and B, but the range of profits (and therefore the risk) is much smaller for project A than for project B. For project A the range of profits is from $400 in a recession to $600 in a boom. For project B, the range of profits is from $200 in a recession to $800 in a boom.

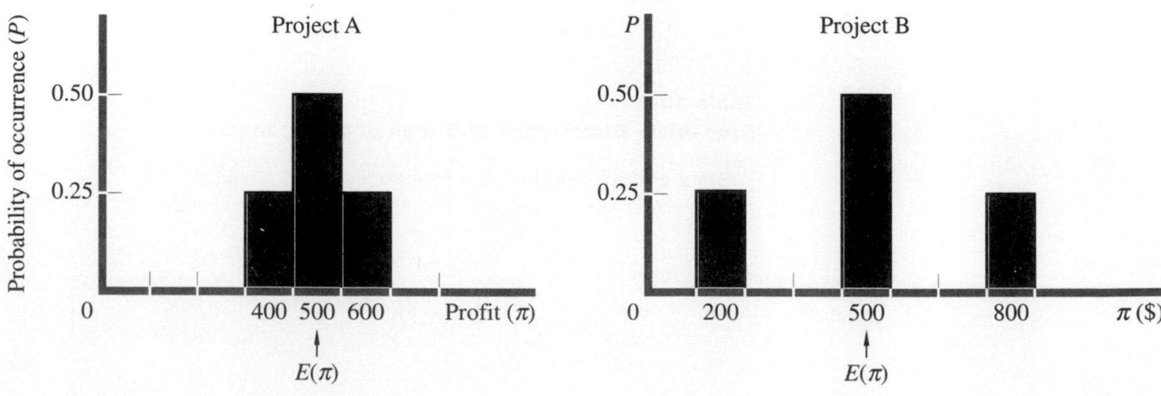

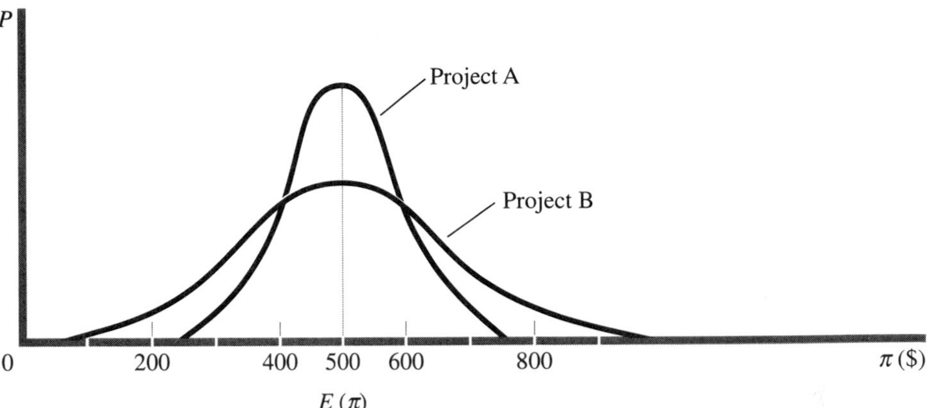

Figure 13-2
Continuous Probability Distribution of Profits from Project A and Project B

By specifying many states of nature, the steplike probability distribution of profits from project A and project B of Figure 13-1 becomes smooth and continuous, as shown above.

The expected profit and the variability in the outcomes of project A and project B are shown in Figure 13-1, where the height of each bar measures the probability that a particular outcome (measured along the horizontal axis) will occur. Note that the relationship between the state of the economy and profits is much tighter (i.e., less dispersed) for project A than for project B. Thus, project A is less risky than project B. Since both projects have the same expected profit, project A is preferable to project B if the manager is risk averse (the usual case).

In the above example, we identified only three possible states of the economy and obtained a steplike **discrete probability distribution** of profits. As we specify more and more different states of nature (gradients of boom, normal business conditions, and recession—and their respective probabilities and profits), each bar becomes thinner and thinner and approaches a vertical line in the limit. We will then approach the **continuous probability distributions** shown in Figure 13-2. Note that the probability distribution for project A is again tighter or less dispersed from its expected value than the probability distribution of project B and that it reflects the smaller risk associated with project A than with project B.[6]

An Absolute Measure of Risk: The Standard Deviation

We have seen above that the tighter or the less dispersed is a probability distribution, the smaller is the risk of a particular strategy or decision. The reason is

[6]With a continuous probability distribution there is theoretically an infinite number of outcomes, and so the probability of occurrence of each specific outcome is zero. We can determine, however, the probability that a particular outcome falls within a particular range, say, that profit will be between $400 and $500. This is given by the area under the curve within the range of outcomes (profits) specified. How this is done is shown in Section 13-2.

that there is a smaller probability that the actual outcome will deviate significantly from the expected value. We can measure the tightness or the degree of dispersion of a probability distribution by the standard deviation, which is indicated by the symbol σ (sigma). Thus, the **standard deviation** (σ) measures the dispersion of possible outcomes from the expected value. The smaller the value of σ, the tighter or less dispersed is the distribution, and the lower the risk.[7]

To find the value of the standard deviation (σ) of a particular probability distribution, we follow the three steps outlined below.

1. Subtract the expected value or the mean ($\overline{X}$) of the distribution from each possible outcome (X_i) to obtain a set of deviations (d_i) from the expected value. That is,

$$d_i = X_i - \overline{X} \tag{13-2}$$

2. Square each deviation, multiply the squared deviation by the probability of its expected outcome, and then sum these products. This weighted average of squared deviations from the mean is the **variance** of the distribution (σ^2). That is,

$$\text{Variance} = \sigma^2 = \sum_{i=1}^{n} (X_i - \overline{X})^2 \cdot P_i \tag{13-3}$$

3. Take the square root of the variance to find the standard deviation (σ):

$$\text{Standard deviation} = \sigma = \sqrt{\sum_{i=1}^{n} (X_i - \overline{X})^2 \cdot P_i} \tag{13-4}$$

As an example, we show in Table 13-3 how to calculate the standard deviation of the probability distribution of profits for project A and project B of Table 13-2. The expected value or mean ($\overline{\pi}$) was found earlier to be \$500 for each project. From Table 13-3, we see that the standard deviation of the probability distribution of profits for project A is \$70.71, while that for project B is \$212.13. These values provide a numerical measure of the absolute dispersion of profits from the mean for each project and confirm the greater dispersion of profits and risk for project B than for project A shown earlier graphically in Figures 13-1 and 13-2.

Measuring Probabilities with the Normal Distribution

The probability distribution of many strategies or experiments follows a normal distribution, so that the probability of a particular outcome falling within a specific range of outcomes can be found by the area under the **standard normal distribution** within the specified range. The figure of the standard normal distribution is given in Figure 13-3. This is a bell-like distribution, symmetrical about its

[7]If all the outcomes were identical, then σ and risk would be zero.

Table 13-3
Calculation of the Standard Deviation of Profits for Project A and Project B

PROJECT A

Deviation $(\pi_i - \overline{\pi})$	Deviation Squared $(\pi_i - \overline{\pi})^2$	Probability (P_i)	Deviation Squared Times Probability $(\pi_i - \overline{\pi})^2 \cdot P_i$
\$600 − \$500 = \$100	\$10,000	0.25	\$2,500
500 − 500 = 0	0	0.50	0
400 − 500 = −100	10,000	0.25	2,500
			Variance = σ^2 = \$5,000
			Standard deviation = $\sigma = \sqrt{\sigma^2} = \sqrt{\$5{,}000}$ = \$70.71

PROJECT B

Deviation $(\pi_i - \overline{\pi})$	Deviation Squared $(\pi_i - \overline{\pi})^2$	Probability (P_i)	Deviation Squared Times Probability $(\pi_i - \overline{\pi})^2 \cdot P_i$
\$800 − \$500 = \$300	\$90,000	0.25	\$22,500
500 − 500 = 0	0	0.50	0
200 − 500 = −300	90,000	0.25	22,500
			Variance = σ^2 = \$45,000
			Standard deviation = $\sigma = \sqrt{\sigma^2} = \sqrt{\$45{,}000}$ = \$212.13

zero mean, with standard deviation of 1, and with the area under the curve representing a total probability of 1. As shown in Figure 13-3, 68.26 percent of the total area under the standard normal curve is within plus or minus one standard deviation (that is, $\pm 1\sigma$) from its zero mean, 95.44 percent of the area is within $\pm 2\sigma$, and 99.74 percent of the area is within $\pm 3\sigma$.

To find the probability of a particular outcome falling within a specific range, we simply subtract the expected value or mean of the distribution from the outcome, divide by the standard deviation of the distribution, and look up the resulting value in Table C-1 on the standard normal distribution in Appendix C on statistical tables at the end of the book. For example, to find the probability that the profit from project A (assumed to be approximately normally distributed and with mean $\overline{\pi}$ = \$500 and standard deviation σ = \$70.71) falls between \$600 and \$500, we first find the value of z:

$$z = \frac{\pi_i - \overline{\pi}}{\sigma} = \frac{\$600 - \$500}{\$70.71} = 1.42 \qquad (13\text{-}5)$$

and then look up the value of $z = 1.42$ in Table C-1 in Appendix C.[8] Going down the column headed z to 1.4 and then moving across Table C-1 until we are

[8]More generally, the number of standard deviations (z) that a particular outcome (X_i) from its mean ($\overline{X}$) is given by $z = (X_i - \overline{X})/\sigma$.

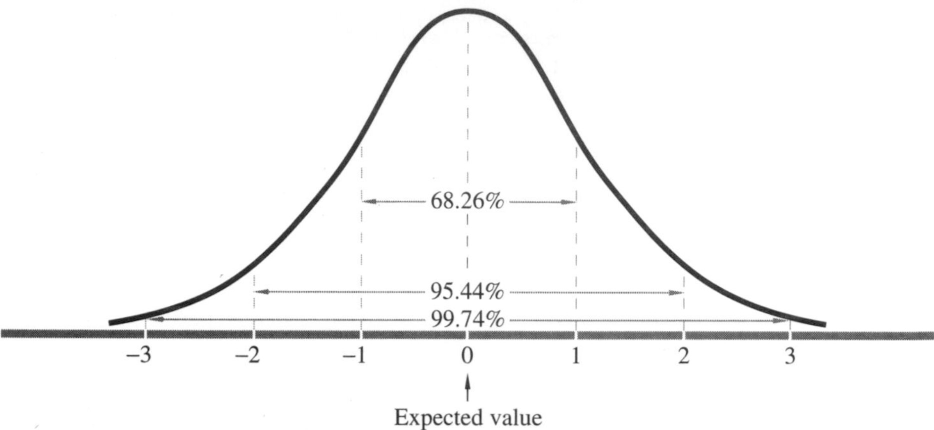

Figure 13-3
Areas under the Standard Normal Distribution

The total area under the standard normal distribution is equal to 1 or 100 percent, and its standard deviation is 1. Half of the area is to the left of its zero mean, and half is to the right. The areas under the curve within $\pm 1\sigma$, $\pm 2\sigma$, and $\pm 3\sigma$ are, respectively, 68.26 percent, 95.44 percent, and 99.74 percent.

directly below the column headed 0.02 (so as to have $z = 1.42$), we get the value of 0.4222. This means that the area under the standard normal curve between its zero mean and 1.42 standard deviations to the right of the mean is 0.4222, or 42.22 percent. Thus, the probability that the profit from project A falls between \$600 and \$500 is also 0.4222, or 42.22 percent.

Since the standard normal curve is symmetrical about its zero mean, the result would be the same if we had asked for the probability that profit would be between \$400 and \$500. The reason for this is that, aside from the negative sign, the value of z is the same, and so the area (probability) is also the same. That is,

$$z = \frac{\pi_i - \overline{\pi}}{\sigma} = \frac{\$400 - \$500}{\$70.71} = -1.42$$

and the probability that the profit from project A will be between \$400 and \$500 is 42.22 percent (by looking up the value of $z = 1.42$ in Table C-1). On the other hand, the probability of profit being below \$600 is 0.5 (the half of the area to the left of the zero mean under the standard normal curve corresponding to a profit of below \$500) plus 0.4222 (the area between $z = 0$ and $z = 1.42$, corresponding to a profit between \$500 and \$600). Thus, the probability of profits being below \$600 is 0.9222, or 92.22 percent. Finally, the probability of a profit higher than \$600 (or lower than \$400) is $1 - 0.9222$, which is 0.0778, or 7.78 percent. The probability of profit falling within any other range can be similarly found (see Problem 2, with answer at the end of the book).

A Relative Measure of Risk: The Coefficient of Variation

The standard deviation is not a good measure to compare the dispersion (relative risk) associated with two or more probability distributions with different expected values or means. The distribution with the largest expected value or mean may very well have a larger standard deviation (absolute measure of dispersion) but not necessarily a larger *relative* dispersion. To measure relative dispersion, we use the **coefficient of variation** (v). This is equal to the standard deviation of a distribution divided by its expected value or mean. That is,

$$\text{Coefficient of variation} = v = \frac{\sigma}{\overline{X}} \tag{13-6}$$

The coefficient of variation, thus, measures the standard deviation per dollar of expected value or mean. As such, it is dimension-free, or, in other words, it is a pure number that can be used to compare the relative risk of two or more projects. The project with the largest coefficient of variation will be the most risky.

For example, if the expected value or mean and standard deviation of project A were, respectively, $\overline{X}_A$ = \$5,000 and σ_A = \$707.11 (instead of the \$500 and \$70.71, respectively, calculated in Tables 13-2 and 13-3) while $\overline{X}_B$ = \$500 and σ_B = \$212.13 (as calculated in Tables 13-2 and 13-3), the standard deviation or absolute measure of dispersion for project A would be more than three times that for project B (\$707.11 for project A compared with \$212.13 for project B). However, the coefficient of variation (v) as a measure of relative dispersion or risk would still be smaller for project A than for project B. That is,

$$V_A = \frac{\sigma_A}{\overline{X}_A} = \frac{\$707.11}{\$5{,}000} = 0.14 \qquad \text{while} \qquad V_B = \frac{\sigma_B}{\overline{X}_B} = \frac{\$212.13}{\$500} = 0.42$$

Thus, project A would have less dispersion relative to its mean (i.e., it would be less risky) than project B.[9]

[9]Using the expected value or mean of \$500 and standard deviation of \$70.71 for project A found in Tables 13-2 and 13-3 to calculate the coefficient of variation for project A gives the same result as that obtained above. That is,

$$V_A = \frac{\sigma_A}{\overline{X}_A} = \frac{\$70.71}{\$500} = 0.14$$

In fact, in that case, since the expected value or mean of projects A and B would be equal (\$500), there would be no need to calculate the coefficient of variation to determine that project A is less risky than project B. Comparing the standard deviation of the two projects would suffice.

Case Study 13-3

RiskMetrics: J.P. Morgan's Method of Measuring Risk

Starting on October 11, 1994, J.P. Morgan, the large New York bank, began publishing daily the estimated volatility of more than 300 bonds, equity and currency prices, as well as the thousands of correlations among them. Morgan publishes not only the data but also the entire methodology it uses in measuring risk, including all the assumptions and the equations on which it is based. Morgan believes that its system, called "RiskMetrics," captures 95 percent of the risk involved in major global stock, bond, and currency markets. The information is made available free on the Internet (see Case Study 13-9), CompuServe, and Dow Jones/Telerate. Morgan's aim is to establish a common standard for measuring risk that will allow comparisons and become the benchmark by which banks, corporations, and institutional investors measure risk. Other banks and investment banks, such Bankers Trust, Goldman Sachs, Merrill Lynch, and Lehman Brothers also offer risk-management services to their clients, but only Morgan offers its risk calculations as well as its entire methodology to all and for free.

The importance of managing risk has sharply increased during the past decade as a result of the growing globalization of financial markets and the increasing complexity of the new financial instruments that have been created to cover such risk. Even the best risk-management strategy cannot ensure against occasional losses, but RiskMetrics can help firms or investors understand and measure the kind and amount of risks they face. For example, RiskMetrics allows a measure of the value at risk, or the amount of money a firm or investor can lose by holding position for a given period of time. It can also help in evaluating the performance of traders and money managers based on returns in relation to the amount of risks they assume. This is better than simply evaluating performance based on returns or risks separately, as done until now. Thus, a firm can use RiskMetrics to design its own risk-management system or purchase the software from a number of firms that have developed it using Morgan's data.

RiskMetrics requires additional refinements since it does not yet include commodities, corporate or mortgage securities, emerging-market securities, option-related securities, and event-risk, such as those associated with economic and political upheavals. Based as it is on general indexes, RiskMetrics also cannot be very useful in measuring individual-equity risks, without additional refinements and more specific data. It does, however, represent an important attempt to overcome the "block box" feeling that often surrounds risk-management services offered to investors, and it proposes an objective benchmark for measuring and managing risk in general.

Source: "Morgan Unveils the Way It Measures Market Risk," *The Wall Street Journal,* October 11, 1994, p. C1; and "A Framework for Risk Management," *Harvard Business Review,* November–December 1994, pp. 91–102.

13-3 UTILITY THEORY AND RISK AVERSION

Most managers, faced with two alternative projects of equal expected value of profit but different coefficients of variation or risk, will generally prefer the less risky project (i.e., the one with the smaller coefficient of variation). While it is true that some managers may very well choose the more risky project (i.e., are **risk seekers**) and some are indifferent to risk (i.e., are **risk neutral**), most managers are **risk averters.** The reason for this is to be found in the principle of **diminishing marginal utility of money.** The meaning of diminishing, constant, and increasing marginal utility of money can be explained with the aid of Figure 13-4.

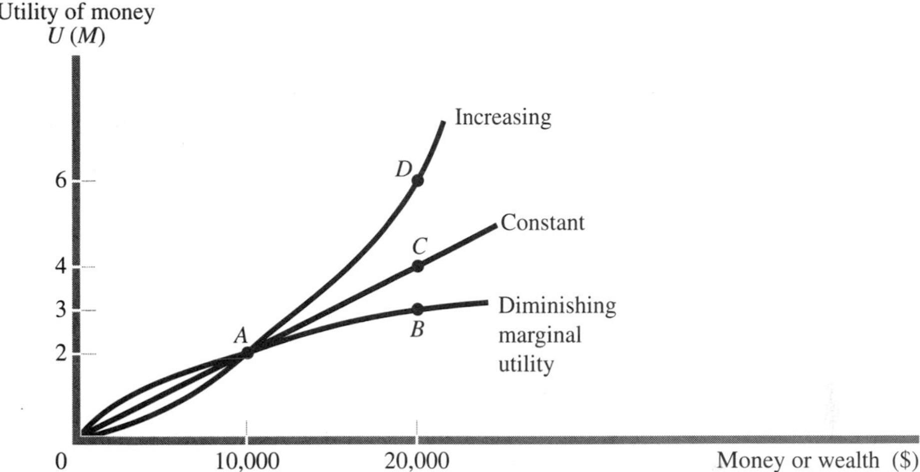

Figure 13-4
Diminishing, Constant, and Increasing Marginal Utility of Money

A $10,000 money income or wealth provides 2 utils of utility to a particular individual (point *A*), while $20,000 provides 3 utils (point *B*) if the total utility of money curve of the individual is concave or faces down (so that the marginal utility of money declines), 4 utils (point *C*) if the total utility curve is a straight line (so that the marginal utility is constant), and 6 utils (point *D*) if the total utility curve is convex or faces up (so that marginal utility increases). The individual would then be, respectively, a risk averter, face risk neutrality, or be a risk seeker.

In Figure 13-4, money income or wealth is measured along the horizontal axis while the utility or satisfaction of money (measured in **utils**) is plotted along the vertical axis.[10] From the figure, we can see that $10,000 in money or wealth provides 2 utils of utility to a particular individual (point *A*), while $20,000 provides 3 utils (point *B*), 4 utils (point C), or 6 utils (point *D*), respectively, depending on the *total* utility of money curve for this individual being concave or facing down, a straight line, or convex or facing up. If the *total* utility curve is concave or faces down, doubling the individual's income or wealth from $10,000 to $20,000 only increases his or her utility from 2 to 3 utils, so that the *marginal* utility of money (the slope of the total utility curve) diminishes for this individual. If the total utility of money curve is a straight line, doubling income also doubles utility, so that the marginal utility of money is constant. Finally, if the total utility of money curve is convex or faces up, doubling income more than doubles utility, so that the marginal utility of money income increases.

Most individuals are risk averters because their marginal utility of money diminishes (i.e., they face a total utility curve that is concave or faces down). To see why this is so, consider the offer to engage in a bet to win $10,000 if a head turns

[10]A *util* is a fictitious unit of utility. For the moment we assume that the utility or satisfaction that a particular individual receives from various amounts of money income or wealth can be measured in terms of utils.

up in the tossing of a coin or to lose \$10,000 if a tail comes up. The expected value of the money won or lost is

$$\begin{aligned}\text{Expected value of money} &= E(M)\\ &= 0.5(\$10{,}000) + 0.5(-\$10{,}000) \qquad (13\text{-}7)\\ &= 0\end{aligned}$$

Even though the expected value of such a *fair game* is zero, a risk averter (an individual facing diminishing marginal utility of money) would gain less utility by winning \$10,000 than he or she would lose by losing \$10,000. Starting from point *A* in Figure 13-4, we see that by losing \$10,000, the risk-averting individual loses 2 utils of utility but gains only 1 util of utility if he or she wins \$10,000. Even though the bet is fair (i.e., there is a 50-50 chance of winning or losing \$10,000), the **expected utility** of the bet is negative. That is,

$$\text{Expected utility} = E(U) = 0.5(1 \text{ util}) + 0.5(-2 \text{ utils}) = -0.5 \qquad (13\text{-}8)$$

In such a case, the individual will refuse a fair bet.[11] From this, we can conclude that a risk-averting manager will not necessarily accept an investment project with positive expected value or a positive net profit. To determine whether or not the manager should accept the project, we need to know his or her utility function of money.

For example, suppose that a manager has to decide whether or not to introduce a new product that has a 40 percent probability of providing a net return (profit) of \$20,000, and a 60 percent probability of resulting in a loss of \$10,000. Since the *expected monetary return* of such a project is positive (see Table 13-4), a risk-neutral or a risk-seeking manager would undertake the project. However, if the manager is risk averse (the usual case) and his or her utility function is as indicated in Figure 13-5, the manager would not

[11]With constant utility, $E(U) = 0.5(2 \text{ utils}) + 0.5(-2 \text{ utils}) = 0$, and the individual is risk neutral and indifferent to the bet. With increasing marginal utility, $E(U) = 0.5(4 \text{ utils}) + 0.5(-2 \text{ utils}) = 1$, and the individual is a risk seeker and would accept the bet.

Table 13-4
Expected Return of Project

State of Nature	(1) Probability	(2) Monetary Outcome	(3) Expected Return (1) × (2)
Success	0.40	\$20,000	\$8,000
Failure	0.60	−10,000	−6,000
		Expected return	\$2,000

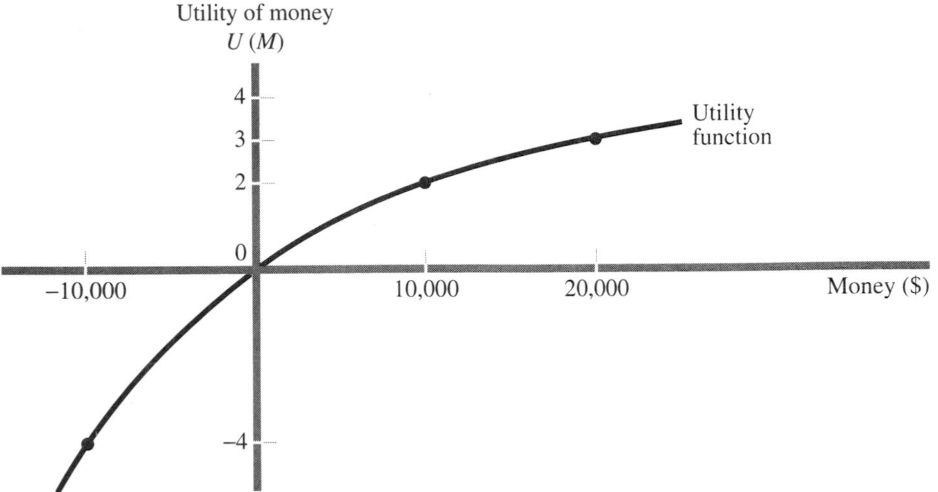

Figure 13-5
The Utility Function of a Risk-Averse Manager

A project with a 40 percent probability of providing a return of $20,000 (3 utils of utility) and a 60 percent probability of resulting in a loss of $10,000 (–4 utils of utility) has an expected utility of (0.4)(3 utils) + (0.6)(–4 utils) = –1.2 utils and would not be undertaken by the manager.

undertake the same project because the *expected utility* from the project is negative (see Table 13-5). Thus, even if the expected *monetary* return is positive, a risk-averse manager will not undertake the project if the expected *utility* from the project is negative.[12] Needless to say, different managers have different utility functions and face marginal utilities of money that diminish at different rates.

[12]Only for a risk-neutral manager does maximizing the expected monetary value or return correspond to maximizing expected utility. Thus, a risk-neutral manager need not go through the difficult task of attempting to derive his or her own utility function in order to reach correct managerial decisions.

Table 13-5
Expected Utility of Project

State of Nature	(1) Probability	(2) Monetary Outcome	(3) Associated Utility	(4) Expected Utility (1) × (3)
Success	0.40	$20,000	3	1.2
Failure	0.60	–10,000	–4	–2.4
			Expected utility	–1.2

Case Study 13-4

The Purchase of Insurance and Gambling by the Same Individual—A Seeming Contradiction

In the real world, we often observe individuals purchasing insurance and also gambling. For example, many people insure their homes against fire and also purchase lottery tickets. This behavior may seem contradictory. Why should the same individual act as a risk avoider (purchase insurance) and at the same time as a risk seeker (gamble)? One possible explanation for this seemingly contradictory behavior is provided by Friedman and Savage who postulate that the total utility of money curve may look like that in Figure 13-6. This total utility curve is concave or faces down (so that the marginal utility of money diminishes) at a particular level of money income, and it is convex or faces up (so that the marginal utility of money increases) at higher levels of income. An individual with an income at or near the point of inflection on the total utility curve (point *A*) will find it advantageous both to spend a small amount of money to insure himself or herself against the small chance of a large loss (say, through a fire that destroys his or her home) and to purchase a lottery ticket providing a small chance of a large win. Starting with an income level at or near *A*′, the individual would act as a risk avoider for declines in income and as a risk seeker for increases in income. Financial planners and brokers make use of these concepts in trying to assess their clients' tolerance for risk in providing financial advice.

Source: Milton Friedman and Leonard J. Savage, "The Utility Analysis of Choices Involving Risk," *Journal of Political Economy,* August 1948; "Finding the Right Levels of Risk," *The New York Times,* November 12, 1988, p. 36; "First of All Know Thyself," *The New York Times,* January 20, 1991, p. F13; and "Legal Gambling Faces Higher Odds," *The New York Times,* August 29, 1993, Sect. 3, p. 3.

Figure 13-6
Utility Function of an Individual Who Purchases Insurance and Gambles

An individual whose income is at or near point *A*′, which is directly below the point of inflection (point *A*) on the total-utility curve, will act as a risk averter and will spend a small amount of money to purchase insurance against the small chance of a large loss of income, and at the same time will act as a risk seeker and gamble a small amount of money (say, to purchase a lottery ticket) to have a small chance of a large win.

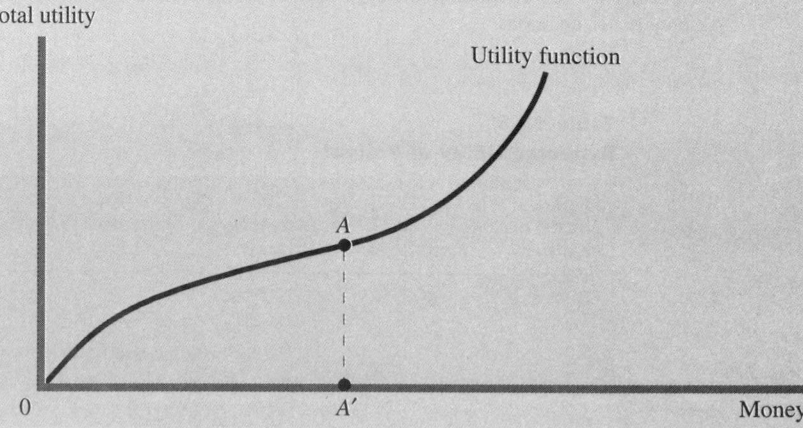

13-4 ADJUSTING THE VALUATION MODEL FOR RISK

In Section 1-2 of Chapter 1 we presented the valuation model for the firm:

$$\text{Value of the firm} = \sum_{t=1}^{n} \frac{\pi_t}{(1+r)^t} \tag{13-9}$$

where π_t refers to the expected profit in each of the n years considered, r is the appropriate discount rate used to calculate the present value of the future profits, and Σ refers to the sum of the present discounted value of future profits. In this section, we extend the above valuation model to deal with an investment project subject to risk. Two of the most commonly used methods of doing this are risk-adjusted discount rates and the certainty-equivalent approach.

Risk-Adjusted Discount Rates

One method of adjusting the valuation model of Equation 13-9 to deal with an investment project subject to risk is to use **risk-adjusted discount rates.** These reflect the manager's or investor's trade-off between risk and return, as shown, for example, by the **risk-return trade-off functions** of Figure 13-7. In the figure, risk, measured by the standard deviation of profit or returns, is plotted along the horizontal axis while the rate of return on investment is plotted along the vertical axis. The risk-return trade-off function or indifference curve labeled R (the middle curve in the figure) shows that the manager or investor is indifferent among a 10 percent rate of return on a riskless asset with $\sigma = 0$ (point A), a 20 percent rate of return on an investment with $\sigma = 1.0$ (point C), and a rate of return of 32 percent for a very risky asset with $\sigma = 1.5$ (point D).

The difference between the expected or required rate of return on a risky investment and the rate of return on a riskless asset is called the **risk premium** on the risky investment. For example, the middle risk-return trade-off function labeled R in Figure 13-7 shows that a risk premium of 4 percent is required to compensate for the level of risk given by $\sigma = 0.5$ (the 14 percent required on the risky investment with $\sigma = 0.5$ minus the 10 percent rate on the riskless asset). A 10 percent risk premium is required for an investment with risk given by $\sigma = 1.0$, and a 22 percent risk premium for an investment with $\sigma = 1.5$. The risk-return trade-off curve would be steeper (R' in Figure 13-7) for a more risk-averse manager or investor, and less steep (R'' in Figure 13-7) for a less risk-averse manager or investor. Thus, the more risk-averse manager facing curve R' would require a risk premium of 22 percent (point C') for an investment with risk given by $\sigma = 1.0$, while a less risk-averse investor with curve R'' would require a risk premium of only 4 percent for the same investment.

We can adjust the valuation model of the firm given by Equation 13-9 above to deal with an investment project subject to risk by using a risk-adjusted discount rate, as follows:

$$\text{Net present value of investment project} = \sum_{t=1}^{n} \frac{R_t}{(1+k)^t} - C_0 \tag{13-10}$$

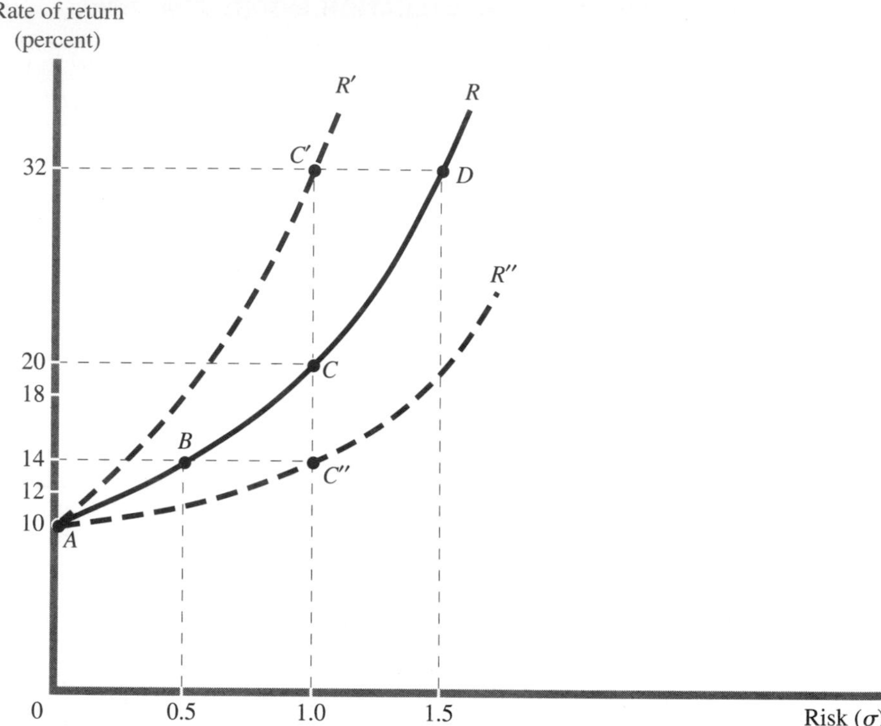

Figure 13-7
Risk-Return Trade-Off Functions

Risk-return trade-off function or indifference curve R indicates that the manager or investor is indifferent among a 10 percent rate of return on a riskless asset with $\sigma = 0$ (point A), a 14 percent rate of return on an investment with risk of $\sigma = 0.5$ (point B), a 20 percent rate of return on an investment with $\sigma = 1.0$, and a 32 percent rate of return on an investment with $\sigma = 1.5$. Thus, the risk premium is 4 percent (i.e., 14 to 10 percent) at point B, 10 percent at point C, and 22 percent at point D. A more risk-averse manager or investor (curve R') requires a higher premium, while a less risk-averse one (with curve R'') requires a smaller risk premium for each level of risk (σ).

where R_t refers to the net cash flow or return from the investment project in each of the n time periods considered, k is the risk-adjusted discount rate, Σ refers to the sum of the present discounted value of all the future net cash flows from the investment, and C_0 is the initial cost of the investment. Note that the risk-adjusted discount rate (k) in Equation 13-10 is equal to the risk-free discount rate (r) used in the valuation model of the firm of Equation 13-9 plus the risk premium involved. An investment project is undertaken if its NPV is greater than or equal to zero, or larger than that for an alternative project.

For example, suppose that a firm is considering undertaking an investment project that is expected to generate a net cash flow or return of $45,000 for the next five years and costs initially \$100,000. If the risk-adjusted discount rate of the firm for this investment project is 20 percent, we have[13]

$$
\begin{aligned}
NPV &= \sum_{t=1}^{5} \frac{R_t}{(1.20)^t} - C_0 \\
&= \sum_{t=1}^{5} \frac{\$45,000}{(1.20)^t} - \$100,000 \\
&= \$45,000\left(\sum_{t=1}^{5} \frac{1}{(1.20)^t}\right) - \$100,000 \\
&= \$45,000(2.9906) - \$100,000 \\
&= \$34,577
\end{aligned}
$$

If the firm perceived the above investment project as much more risky and used the risk-adjusted discount rate of 32 percent to adjust for the greater risk, the *NPV* of the investment project would be instead:

$$
\begin{aligned}
NPV &= \sum_{t=1}^{5} \frac{\$45,000}{(1.32)^t} - \$100,000 \\
&= \$45,000\left(\sum_{t=1}^{5} \frac{1}{(1.32)^t}\right) - \$100,000 \\
&= \$45,000(2.3452) - \$100,000 \\
&= \$5,534
\end{aligned}
$$

With the risk-adjusted discount rate of 32 percent, the investment project is still acceptable, but the *NPV* of the project is much lower than if the firm perceived the project as less risky and used the risk-adjusted discount rate of 20 percent. A risk-adjusted discount rate of 20 percent may be appropriate for the firm for the expansion of a given line of business, while the high rate of 32 percent might be required to reflect the much higher risk involved in moving into a totally new line of business. This method, however, has the serious shortcomings that risk-adjusted discount rates are subjectively assigned by managers and investors, and variations in net cash flows or returns are not explicitly considered. This approach is most useful for the evaluation of relatively small and repetitive investment projects. A better method for adjusting the valuation model for risk is the certainty-equivalent approach.

[13]The value of 2.9906 for

$$\sum_{t=1}^{5} \frac{1}{(1.20)^t}$$

in the calculations that follow is obtained from Table B-4 on the present value of an annuity in Appendix B at the end of the book. Specifically, the interest factor of 2.9906 is obtained by moving across Table B-4 until we reach the column headed 20 percent, and then moving down five rows for $n = 5$. A review of present value concepts is found in Appendix A. Students who are not familiar with present value concepts may want to read Appendix A at this time.

Certainty-Equivalent Approach

The risk-adjusted discount rate presented above modified the discount rate in the denominator of the valuation model to incorporate risk. The certainty-equivalent approach, on the other hand, uses a risk-free discount rate in the denominator and incorporates risk by modifying the numerator of the valuation model, as follows:

$$NPV = \sum_{t=1}^{n} \frac{\alpha R_t}{(1+r)^t} - C_0 \tag{13-11}$$

where R_t is the *risky* net cash flow or return from the investment (as in Equation 13-10), r is the *risk-free* discount rate, and α is the **certainty-equivalent coefficient.**[14] The latter is the certain sum (i.e., the sum received with certainty that is equivalent to the expected risky sum or return on the project) divided by the expected risky sum. That is,

$$\alpha = \frac{\text{equivalent certain sum}}{\text{expected risky sum}} = \frac{R_t^*}{R_t} \tag{13-12}$$

Specifically, the manager or investor must specify the certain sum that yields to him or her the same utility or satisfaction of (i.e., that is equivalent to) the expected risky sum or return from the investment. The value of α ranges from 0 to 1 for a risk-averse decision maker and reflects his or her attitude toward risk. A value of 0 for α means that the project is viewed as too risky by the decision maker to offer any effective return. On the other hand, a value of 1 for α means that the project is viewed as risk-free by the decision maker. Thus, the smaller the value of α, the greater is the risk perceived by the manager for the project.

For example, if the manager or investor regarded the sum of \$36,000 with certainty as equivalent to the expected (risky) net cash flow or return of \$45,000 per year for the next five years (on the investment project discussed in the previous section and costing initially \$100,000), the value of α is

$$\alpha = \frac{\$36{,}000}{\$45{,}000} = 0.8$$

Using the risk-free discount rate of 10 percent, we can then find the net present value of the investment project, as follows:[15]

[14]The other symbols have the same meaning as before.

[15]The interest factor of 3.7908 for

$$\sum_{t=1}^{5} \frac{1}{(1.10)^t}$$

in the calculations that follow is obtained from Table B-4 in Appendix B at the end of the book by moving across the table until we reach the column headed 10 percent, and then moving down five rows for $n = 5$.

$$NPV = \sum_{t=1}^{n} \frac{\alpha R_t}{(1+r)^t} - C_0$$
$$= \sum_{t=1}^{5} \frac{(0.8)(\$45{,}000)}{(1.10)^t} - \$100{,}000$$
$$= \$36{,}000\left[\sum_{t=1}^{5} \frac{1}{(1.10)^t}\right] - \$100{,}000 \qquad (13\text{-}11)$$
$$= \$36{,}000(3.7908) - \$100{,}000$$
$$= \$36{,}468.80$$

This is close to the result obtained by using the risk-adjusted discount rate of 20 percent in the previous section. If, on the other hand, the firm perceived the project as much more risky and applied the certainty-equivalent coefficient of 0.62, we would have

$$NPV = \sum_{t=1}^{5} \frac{(0.62)(\$45{,}000)}{(1.10)^t} - \$100{,}000$$
$$= \$27{,}900\left[\sum_{t=1}^{5} \frac{1}{(1.10)^t}\right] - \$100{,}000$$
$$= \$27{,}900(3.7908) - \$100{,}000$$
$$= \$5{,}763.32$$

This is close to the result obtained by using the risk-adjusted discount rate of 32 percent in the previous section.

Case Study 13-5

Adjusting the Valuation Model for Risk in the Real World

In a study published in 1977, Gitman and Forrester reported the results of a survey that they conducted on the capital budgeting techniques used by U.S. firms. Using a sample of 268 major U.S. firms, the authors asked, among other things, whether the firms did take risk into consideration in their investment decisions, and if so, which method they used. Of the 103 respondents (thus giving a response rate of 38 percent), 71 percent answered that they did take risk explicitly into consideration in their investment decisions, while 29 percent answered that they did not. Of the respondents that answered that they did take risk explicitly into consideration in their investment decisions, 43 percent indicated that they used the risk-adjusted discount rate method, and 26 percent answered that they used the certainty-equivalent approach. The remainder of 31 percent of the respondents indicated that they used other more subjective methods. Thus, the risk-adjusted discount rate method appears to be the most common method that major firms use to deal with risk. This is not surprising in view of the fact that the risk-adjusted discount rate method is one of the easiest approaches available for dealing with risk.

Source: L. G. Gitman and J. R. Forrester, "A Survey of Capital Budgeting Techniques Used by Major U.S. Firms," *Financial Management*, Fall 1977, pp. 66–71.

13-5 OTHER TECHNIQUES FOR INCORPORATING RISK INTO DECISION MAKING

Most real-world managerial decisions are much more complex than the ones examined above. Two methods of organizing and analyzing these more complex, real-world situations involving risk are decision trees and simulation. These are examined in turn.

Decision Trees

Managerial decisions involving risk are often made in stages, with subsequent decisions and events depending on the outcome of earlier decisions and events. A **decision tree** shows the sequence of possible managerial decisions and their expected outcome under each set of circumstances or states of nature. Since the sequence of decisions and events are represented graphically as the branches of a tree, this technique has been named "decision tree." The construction of decision trees begins with the earliest decision and moves forward in time through a series of subsequent events and decisions. At every point that a decision must be made or a different event can take place, the tree branches out until all the possible outcomes have been depicted. In the construction of decision trees, boxes are used to show decision points, while circles show states of nature. Branches coming out of boxes depict the alternative strategies of courses of action open to the firm. On the other hand, the branches coming out of circles show the various states of nature (and their probability of occurrence) that affect the outcome.

For example, Figure 13-8 shows a decision tree that a firm can use to determine whether to adopt a high-price or a low-price strategy (the box on the left of the figure). Since the firm has control over this strategy (i.e., whether to charge a high or a low price), no probabilities are attached to these branches (see section 1 of the figure). Next (section 2 of the figure) is the competitors' reaction to the firm's pricing strategy. This is an uncontrollable event for the firm, and so probabilities are attached to each possible price response of competitors. The firm estimates that if it adopts a high-price strategy (the top branch of the figure), there is a 60 percent probability that competitors will respond with a high price of their own, and 40 percent that they will respond with a low price. On the other hand, if the firm adopts a low-price strategy (the bottom branch of the figure), there is a 20 percent probability that competitors will respond with a high price, and

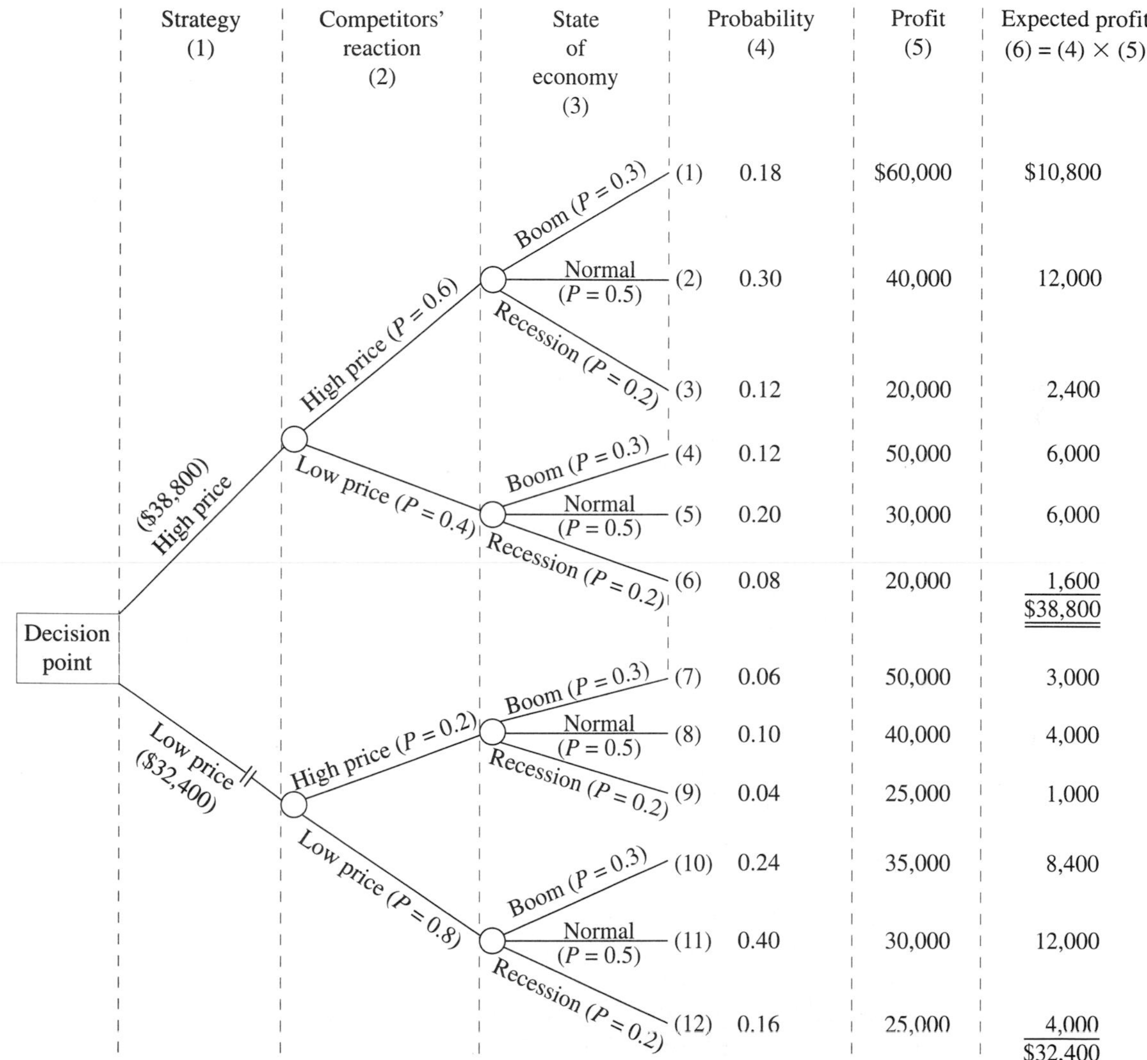

Figure 13-8
Decision Tree for Pricing Decisions

Starting at the left of the figure, we see that the firm can adopt either a high- or a low-price strategy (section 1 of the figure). Each of these strategies can lead to either a high- or a low-price response (reaction) by competitors, each with a particular probability of occurrence (section 2). Each strategy and the competitors' reaction can take place under each of three possible states of the economy (boom, normal, or recession) with specific probabilities of occurrence (section 3). The probability of each joint outcome is obtained by multiplying the probability of each state of the economy by the probability of each competitor's price response. The expected profit of each outcome (section 6) is then obtained by multiplying the probability of occurrence by its associated profit. Assuming that the firm already considered the difference in risk in estimating the net present value of profits of the two strategies, it will choose the high-price strategy. The low-price strategy is, thus, slashed off as suboptimal.

80 percent with a low price. Note that probabilities are entered in parentheses on the appropriate branches, and the sum of the probabilities of competitors' responses to each pricing strategy of the firm adds up to 1.0 or 100 percent.

Next we see that each pricing strategy on the part of the firm and competitors' price response (reaction) can occur under three states of the economy: boom, normal, and recession (section 3 of the figure), with probabilities of 30, 50, and 20 percent, respectively. Thus, we have 12 possible outcomes, 6 for the high-price strategy of the firm (the top branch of the figure), and 6 for the low-price strategy (the bottom branch). The probability of each of these 12 possible outcomes is shown in section 4 of the figure. The probability of occurrence of each possible outcome is a joint or **conditional probability** and is obtained by multiplying the probability of a particular state of the economy by the probability of a specific price reaction of competitors. For example, the probability of both booming conditions in the economy and a high price by competitors is equal to the probability of boom (0.3) times the probability of a high price by competitors (0.6). Thus, the probability of both boom and a high price by competitors (outcome 1) is 0.18 or 18 percent. Similarly, the probability of both normal conditions in the economy and high competitors' price (outcome 2) is given by 0.5 times 0.6, or 0.3 or 30 percent, and so on.

Section 5 of the figure then gives the estimated net present value of the profits of the firm associated with each of the 12 possible outcomes. By multiplying the probability of occurrence of each possible outcome by the profit associated with that particular outcome, we get the corresponding expected profit (section 6 of the figure). For example, the expected profit of boom and high competitors' price (outcome 1) is equal to the joint or conditional probability of occurrence (0.18) times the profit ($60,000), or $10,800. Similarly, the expected profit of outcome 2 (normal business conditions and high competitors' price) is equal to the probability of occurrence (0.30) times the profit ($40,000), or $12,000, and so on. By then adding the expected profit associated with each of the first 6 outcomes, we get the expected profit of $38,800 associated with the firm's high-price strategy (and noted in parentheses under this strategy in section 1 of the figure). Similarly, by adding all the expected profits associated with the last 6 outcomes, we get the expected profit of $32,400 associated with the firm's low-price strategy (and noted in parentheses under this strategy). Assuming that the firm already considered the difference in risk in estimating the net present value of profits of the two strategies, it will choose the high-price strategy. The low-price strategy is, thus, slashed off (in section 1) on the decision tree to indicate that it is suboptimal.

Several additional things need to be pointed out with respect to the above decision tree. First, the sum of the joint probabilities of the 6 possible outcomes (outcomes 1 through 6) resulting from the firm's high-price strategy is equal to 1, and so is the sum of the joint probabilities of the 6 possible outcomes (outcomes 7 through 12) resulting from the firm's low-price strategy. Second, while the construction of a decision tree starts at the left with the earliest decision and moves forward in time to the right through a series of subsequent events and decisions, the analysis of a decision tree begins at the right at the end of the sequence and works backward to the left. Third, while in the decision tree of Figure 13-8, the firm makes only one decision (the box leading to the high- and low-price strategies at the beginning of the tree at the left), there can be several decision points in between several states of nature (see the decision tree for Problem 10). Indeed, for many real-world business decisions, decision trees can become much more elaborate and complex than the one shown in Figure 13-8.

Simulation

Another method for analyzing complex, real-world decision-making situations involving risk is **simulation.** The first step in simulation is the construction of a mathematical model of the managerial decision-making situation that we seek to simulate. For example, an aerospace engineer constructs a miniature model plane and wind tunnel to test the strength and resistance of the model plane to change in wind speed and direction. This modeling mimics the essential features of the real-world situation and allows the engineer to simulate the effect of changes in wind speed and direction on a real aircraft. Similarly, the firm might construct a model for the strategy of expanding the output of a commodity. The model would specify in mathematical (i.e., equational) form the relationship between the output of the commodity and its price; output, input prices, and costs of production; output and depreciation; output, selling costs, and revenue; output, revenues, and taxes; and so on. The manager could then substitute likely values or best estimates for each variable into the model and estimate the firm's profit. By then varying the value of each variable substituted into the model, the firm can get an estimate of the effect of the change in the variable on the output of the model or profit of the firm. This simplest type of simulation is often referred to as **sensitivity analysis.**

In full-fledged simulation models, the model builder needs to estimate or specify the probability distribution of each variable in the model. For example, in order to fully simulate the strategy to expand output, the firm needs the probability distribution of output, commodity prices, input prices, costs of production, depreciation, selling costs, revenue, taxes, and so on. Randomly selected values of each variable of the model are then fed into the computer program to generate the present value of the firm's profits. This process is then repeated a large number of times. Each time (i.e., for each computer run), a new randomly selected value for each variable is fed into the computer program, and the net present value of the firm's profit is recorded. A large number (often in the hundreds) of such trials, or *iterations,* are conducted, so as to generate the probability distribution of the firm's profit. The probability distribution of the firm's profits so generated can then be used to calculate the expected profit of the firm and the standard deviation of the distribution of profits (as a measure of risk). Finally, the firm can use this information to determine the optimal strategy to adopt (as shown earlier in this chapter).

Full-scale simulation models are very expensive and are generally used only for large projects when the decision-making process is too complex to be analyzed by decision trees. The simulation techniques are very powerful and useful, however, because they explicitly and simultaneously consider all the interactions among the variables of the model. For the evaluation of alternative business strategies involving risk where millions of dollars are involved, computer simulation is becoming more and more widely used today.

13-6 DECISION MAKING UNDER UNCERTAINTY

In Section 13-1 we defined "uncertainty" as the case where there is more than one possible outcome to a decision and the probability of each specific outcome occurring is not known or even meaningful. As a result, decision making under uncertainty is necessarily subjective. Some specific decision rules are available, however, if the decision maker can identify the possible states of nature and estimate the payoff for each strategy. Two specific decision rules applicable under uncertainty are the maximin criterion and the minimax regret criterion. These are discussed next, as are some more informal and less precise methods of dealing with uncertainty.

The Maximin Criterion

The **maximin criterion** postulates that the decision maker should determine the worst possible outcome of each strategy and then pick the strategy that provides the best of the worst possible outcomes. The maximin criterion can be illustrated by applying it to the example in Table 13-4, where the firm could follow the strategy of introducing a new product that would provide a return of $20,000 if it succeeded or lead to a loss of $10,000 if it failed, or choose not to invest in the venture, with zero possible return or loss. This matrix is shown in Table 13-6. Note that no probabilities are given in Table 13-6 because we are now dealing with uncertainty. That is, we now assume that the manager does not know and cannot estimate the probability of success and failure of investing in the new product. Therefore, he or she cannot calculate the expected payoff or return and risk of the investment.

To apply the maximin criterion to this investment, the manager first determines the worst possible outcome of each strategy (row). This is −$10,000 in the case of failure for the investment strategy and 0 for the strategy of not investing. These worst possible outcomes are recorded in the last or maximin column of the table. Then he or she picks the strategy that provides the best (maximum) of the

Table 13-6
Payoff Matrix for Maximin Criterion

	State of Nature		
Strategy	**Success**	**Failure**	**Maximin**
Invest	$20,000	−$10,000	−$10,000
Do not invest	0	0	0*

*The strategy of not investing.

worst (minimum) possible outcomes (i.e., maximin). This is the strategy of not investing, which is indicated by the asterisk next to its zero return or loss in the last column of the table (as compared with the loss of $10,000 in the case of failure with the introduction of the new product). Thus, the maximin criterion picks the strategy of not investing, which has the maximum of the minimum payoffs.

By examining only the most pessimistic outcome of each strategy for the purpose of avoiding the worst of all possible outcomes, it is obvious that the maximin criterion is a very conservative decision rule and that the decision maker using it views the world pessimistically. This criterion is appropriate, however, when the firm has a very strong aversion to risk, as, for example, when the survival of a small firm depends on avoiding losses. The maximin criterion is also appropriate in the case of oligopoly, where the actions of one firm affect the others. Then, if one firm lowers its price, it can expect the others to soon lower theirs, thus reducing the profits of all.

The Minimax Regret Criterion

Another specific decision rule under uncertainty is the **minimax regret criterion.** This postulates that the decision maker should select the strategy that minimizes the maximum regret or opportunity cost of the wrong decision, whatever the state of nature that actually occurs. Regret is measured by the difference between the payoff of a given strategy and the payoff of the best strategy *under the same state of nature.* The rationale for measuring regret this way is that if we have chosen the best strategy (i.e., the one with the largest payoff) for the particular state of nature that has actually occurred, then we have no regret. But if we have chosen any other strategy, the regret is the difference between the payoff of the best strategy under the specific state of nature that has occurred and the payoff of the strategy chosen. After determining the maximum regret for each strategy under each state of nature, the decision maker then chooses the strategy with the minimum regret value.

To apply the minimax regret criterion, the decision maker must first construct a regret matrix from the payoff matrix. For example, Table 13-7 presents the payoff and regret matrices for the investment problem of Table 13-4 that we have been examining. The regret matrix is constructed by determining the maximum payoffs for each state of nature (column) and then subtracting each

Table 13-7
Payoff and Regret Matrices for the Maximum Regret Criterion

	State of Nature		Regret Matrix		
Strategy	**Success**	**Failure**	**Success**	**Failure**	**Maximum Regret**
Invest	$20,000	−$10,000	$ 0	$10,000	$10,000*
Do not invest	0	0	20,000	0	20,000

*The strategy with the minimum regret value.

payoff in the same column from that figure. These differences are the measures of regrets. For example, if the manager chooses to invest in the product and the state of nature that occurs is the one of success, he or she has no regret because this is the correct strategy. Thus, the regret value of zero is appropriately entered at the top of the first column in the regret matrix in Table 13-7. On the other hand, if the firm had chosen not to invest, so that it had a zero payoff under the same state of nature of success, the regret is $20,000. This regret value is entered at the bottom of the first column of the regret matrix. Moving to the state of failure column in the payoff matrix, we see that the best strategy (i.e., the one with the largest payoff) is not to invest. This has a payoff of zero. Thus, the regret value of this strategy is zero (the bottom of the second column in the regret matrix). If the firm undertook the investment under the state of nature of failure, it would incur a loss and a regret of $10,000 (the top of the second column of the regret matrix). Note that the regret value for the best strategy under each state of nature is always zero and that the other regret values in the regret matrix must necessarily be positive since we are always subtracting smaller payoffs from the largest payoff under each state of nature (column).

After constructing the regret matrix (with the maximum regret for each strategy under each state of nature), the decision maker then chooses the strategy with the minimum regret value. In our example, this is the strategy of investing, which has the minimum regret value of $10,000 (indicated by the asterisk in the maximum regret column of Table 13-7). This compares with the maximum regret of $20,000 resulting from the strategy of not investing. Thus, while the best strategy for the firm according to the maximin criterion is not to invest, the best strategy according to the minimax regret criterion is to invest. The choice as to which of these two decision rules the firm might apply under conditions of uncertainty depends on the firm's objectives and on the particular investment decision that it faces.

Other Methods of Dealing with Uncertainty

Besides the above formal investment criteria, there are a number of less formal methods that are commonly used by decision makers to reduce uncertainty or the dangers arising from uncertainty. Some of these are the acquisition of additional information, referral to authority, attempting to control the business environment, and diversification. We now briefly examine each of these in turn.

Decision makers often attempt to deal with uncertainty by gathering additional information. This can go a long way toward reducing the uncertainty surrounding a particular strategy or event and the dangers arising from it. Gathering more information is costly, however, and the manager should treat it as any other investment. That is, as pointed out in optimization analysis (see Section 2-3), the manager should continue to gather information until the marginal benefit (return) from it is equal to the marginal cost.

The decision maker can sometimes deal with uncertainty by requesting the opinion of a particular authority (such as the Internal Revenue Service on tax questions, the Securities and Exchange Commission on financial investments, the

Labor Relations Board on labor questions, or a particular professional association on matters of its particular competence). While this may remove uncertainty on some specific questions, one could hardly expect referrals to authority to eliminate the uncertainty inherent in most managerial decisions, especially those regarding long-term investments.

Another method by which decision makers sometimes seek to deal with uncertainty is by trying to control the business environment in which they operate. Thus, firms often attempt to gain monopoly control over a product by means of patents, copyrights, exclusive franchises, and so on. Competition through imitation as well as antitrust laws, however, severely limit firms' attempts to gain monopoly power, especially in the long run.

Diversification in the types of products produced, in the composition of security portfolios, and in different lines of business by a conglomerate corporation is another important method by which investors attempt to reduce risk. In such cases, if the demand for one product, the return on one particular asset, or the profit on one line of business falls, then the existence of the firm, the profitability of the entire portfolio, and the survival of the corporation, respectively, are not endangered. Diversification is an example of the old saying, "Don't put all your eggs in one basket," and it is a very important and common way of dealing with uncertainty.

Case Study 13-6

Spreading Risks in the Choice of a Portfolio

Since investors are risk averse, on the average, they will hold a more risky portfolio (stocks and bonds) only if it provides a higher return. Suppose for simplicity that there exist only two assets, with risk and return given by points *E* and *F* in Figure 13-9. If the risk of assets *E* and *F* are independent of each other, the investor can choose any mixed portfolio of assets *E* and *F* shown on the frontier or curve *ECF*. To understand the shape of frontier *ECF*, note that the return on a mixed portfolio will be between the return on asset *E* and on asset *F* alone, depending on the particular combination of the two assets in the portfolio. As far as risk is concerned, there are portfolios (such as that indicated by point *C*) on frontier *ECF* that have lower risks than those composed exclusively of either asset *E* or asset *F*. The reason for this can be gathered by assuming that the probability of a low return is $\frac{1}{2}$ on asset *E* and $\frac{1}{4}$ on asset *F*, and that, for the moment, we take the probability of a low return as a measure of risk. If these probabilities are independent of each other, the probability of a low return on both assets *E* and *F* at the same time is $(\frac{1}{2})(\frac{1}{4}) = \frac{1}{8}$, which is smaller than for either asset *E* or *F* separately. Given the risk-return trade-off function or indifference curve *R* from Figure 13-9, we can see that the optimum portfolio for this investor is the mixed portfolio indicated by point *C* in the figure, where risk-return indifference curve *R* is tangent to frontier *ECF*. Indeed, market evidence shows that a well-diversified portfolio containing various mixes of stocks,

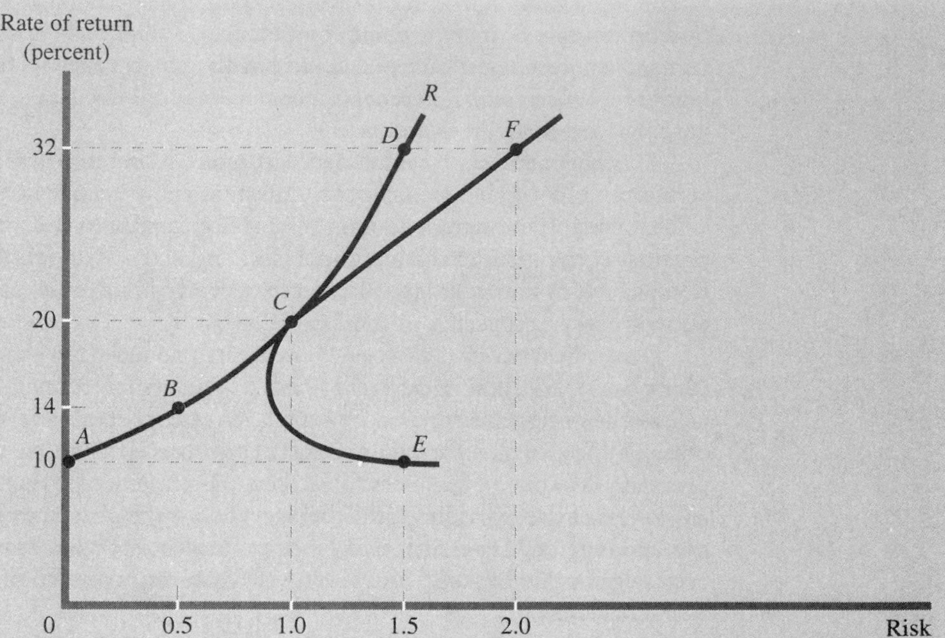

Figure 13-9
Choosing a Portfolio

The risk-return trade-off function or indifference curve *R* is the same as in Figure 13-7. It shows the various risk-return trade-off combinations among which the investor is indifferent. On the other hand, frontier *ECF* represents the combinations of risk and return that are obtainable with mixed portfolios of asset *E* and asset *F*, with independent risk. The optimum portfolio for the investor is represented by point *C*, where the risk-return trade-off function or indifference curve *R* is tangent to frontier *ECF*.

bonds, Treasury bills, real estate, and foreign securities can even out a lot of the ups and downs of investing without sacrificing much in the way of returns.

Source: H. M. Markowitz, "Portfolio Selection," *Journal of Finance,* March 1952, pp. 77–91; "Diversified Portfolios Are More Restful," *The Wall Street Journal,* January 25, 1990, p. C1; and "How to Keep Your Balance in Uncertain Markets," *The Wall Street Journal,* March 11, 1994, p. C1.

13-7 FOREIGN-EXCHANGE RISKS AND HEDGING

During the past decade, portfolios with domestic and foreign stocks enjoyed lower overall volatility and higher dollar returns than portfolios with U.S. stocks only. Many experts now recommend as much as 40 percent of a portfolio to be in foreign securities. Investing in foreign securities, however, gives rise to a foreign-exchange risk because the foreign currency can depreciate or decrease in value during the time of the investment.

For example, suppose that the return on British securities is 15 percent, compared with 10 percent at home. As a U.S. investor, you might then want to invest part of your portfolio in Britain. To do so, however, you must first exchange dollars for pounds (£), the currency of Britain, in order to make the investment. If the **foreign-exchange rate** is $2 to the pound (that is, $2/£1), you can, for example, purchase £10,000 of British securities for $20,000. In a year, however, the exchange rate might be $1.80/£1, indicating a 10 percent depreciation of the pound (i.e., each pound now buys 10 percent fewer dollars). In that case, you will earn 15 percent on your investment in terms of pounds, but lose 10 percent on the foreign-exchange transaction, for a net *dollar* gain of only 5 percent (as compared with 10 percent on U.S. securities). Of course, the exchange rate at the end of the year might be $2.20/£1, which means that the pound appreciated by 10 percent, or that you would get 10 percent more dollars per pound. In that case, you would earn 15 percent on the pound investment *plus* another 10 percent on the foreign-exchange transaction. As an investor (rather than a speculator), however, you will probably want to avoid the risk of a large foreign-exchange loss, and would not invest in Britain unless you can hedge or cover the foreign-exchange risk.

Hedging refers to the covering of a foreign-exchange risk. Hedging is usually accomplished with a **forward contract.** This is an agreement to purchase or sell a specific amount of a foreign currency at a rate specified today for delivery at a specific future date. For example, suppose that an American exporter expects to receive £1 million in 3 months. At today's exchange rate of $2/£1, the exporter expects to receive $2 million in three months. To avoid the risk of a large dollar depreciation by the time the exporter is to receive payment (and thus receive much fewer dollars than anticipated), the exporter hedges his foreign-exchange risk. He does so by selling £1 million forward at today's forward rate for delivery in three months, so as to coincide with the receipt of the £1 million from his exports. Even if today's forward rate is $1.98/£1, the exporter willingly "pays" 2 cents per pound to avoid the foreign-exchange risk. In 3 months, when the U.S. exporter receives the £1 million he will be able to immediately exchange it for $1.98 million by fulfilling the forward contract (and thus avoid a possible large foreign-exchange loss). An importer avoids the foreign-exchange risk by doing the opposite (see Problem 11).

Hedging can also be accomplished with a **futures contract.** This is a standardized forward contract for *predetermined quantities* of the currency and *selected calendar dates* (for example, for £25,000 for March 15 delivery). As such, futures contracts are more liquid than forward contracts. There is a forward market in many currencies and a futures market in the world's most important currencies (the U.S. dollar, German mark, Japanese yen, and British pound). Futures markets exist not only in currencies but also in many other financial instruments or derivatives (a broad class of transactions whose value is based on, or derived from, a financial market like stocks, interest rates, as well as currencies) and commodities (corn, oats, soybeans, wheat, cotton; cocoa, coffee, orange juice; cattle, hogs, pork bellies; copper, gold, silver, platinum). Hedging in forward or futures markets reduces transaction costs and risks and increases the volume of domestic and foreign trade in the commodity, currency, or other financial instrument. Of course, forward and futures contracts can also be used for speculation, where they can lead to very large wins or huge losses.

Case Study 13-7

Local-Currency and Dollar Stock Returns around the World

Table 13-8 shows that emerging markets offered the highest and the lowest stock returns both in the local currency and in terms of U.S. dollars during the first 11 months of 1994. Brazil was the top performer, both in local currency and in dollars. The table shows that Brazilian average stock return in 1994 was 1,162.2 percent in the local currency and 73.7 percent in terms of U.S. dollars (because of the sharp depreciation of the Brazilian currency with respect to the dollar during 1994). The table also shows that the five-year (1990–1994) average annual dollar return for Brazilian stock was nearly 31 percent. For Chile, returns were 39.1 percent in local currency and 44.0 percent in dollars in 1994 (because of a small appreciation of the Chilean currency during 1994), and the five-year average annual dollar return was 43.9 percent. Because of the strong depreciation of the Turkish currency during 1994, the average local-currency return of 25.0 percent became an average dollar return of −49.0 percent (making Turkey the worst performer). Of the five industrial countries listed in Table 13-8, only Japan had a positive return, both in terms of the local currency and in dollars during 1994. Japan, however, had the worst five-year average annual performance (−4.5 percent). The average stock return in the United States was −2.1 percent during 1994, but averaged 6.0 percent annually over the 1990–1994 period.

Table 13-8
Average Stock Returns Around the World, 1994 and 1990–1994

	1994		
	In Local Currency	**In Dollars**	**5-Year Average Annual Return in Dollars**
Emerging Market			
Brazil	1,162.2%	73.9%	30.7%
Chile	39.1	44.0	43.9
South Korea	28.3	30.3	−0.2
Turkey	25.0	−49.0	23.4
Hong Kong	−28.5	−28.6	−3.7
Industrial Country			
Japan	5.9%	19.4%	−4.5%
United States	−2.1	−2.1	6.0
Germany	−9.7	−0.2	6.0
United Kingdom	−9.8	−4.6	6.8
France	−11.7	−3.2	5.0

Source: "The Global Money Machine," *U.S. News & World Report,* December 12, 1994, p. 86.

Case Study 13-8

How Foreign Stocks Have Benefitted a Domestic Portfolio

Foreign stocks have provided higher returns and higher risks in comparison to U.S. stocks over the past decade. Therefore, a portfolio that includes domestic and foreign stocks can face reduced risk and higher returns than a portfolio that includes only domestic stocks. This is shown by Figure 13-10. The figure shows that a portfolio that included only (i.e., 100 percent) U.S. stocks faced relatively low volatility (measured by the standard deviation) as a measure of risk and provided an average annual dollar rate of return of about 15 percent from June 1984 to June 1994. A portfolio that included 20 percent foreign and 80 percent U.S. stocks would have provided a lower volatility and an average annual return of 16 percent over the past 10 years. For about the same volatility but 40 percent foreign stocks, the portfolio would have given an average annual rate of return of almost 17 percent. Finally, a portfolio of 100 percent foreign stocks would have provided an average annual dollar rate of return of over 18 percent but with much higher volatility (risk).

Source: "Three Steps to Intelligent Overseas Investing," *The Wall Street Journal,* October 13, 1994, p. C3.

Figure 13-10
Average Return and Risk for Portfolios of U.S. and Foreign Stocks

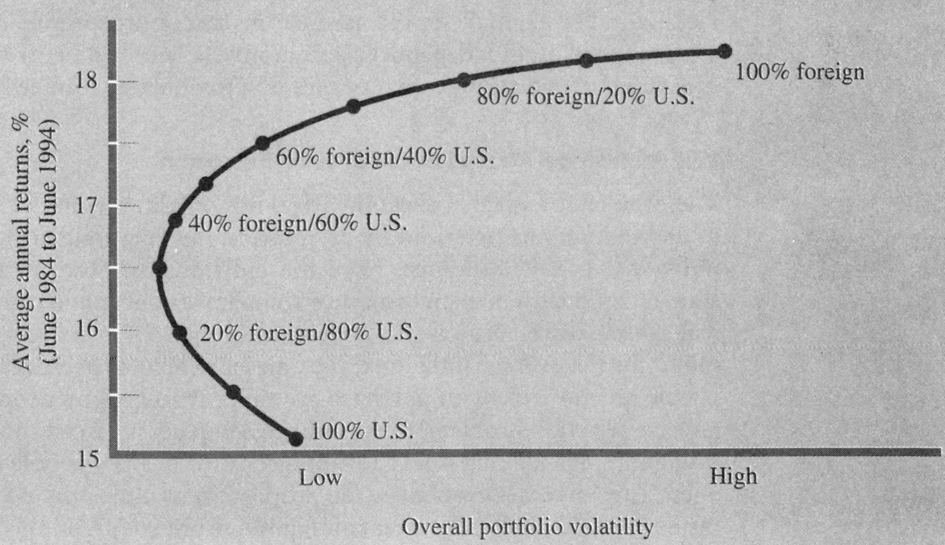

13-8 INFORMATION AND RISK

Risk often results from lack of or inadequate information. The relationship between information and risk can be analyzed by examining asymmetric information, adverse selection, and moral hazard.

Asymmetric Information and the Market for Lemons

One party to a transaction (i.e., the buyer or seller of a product or service) often has less information than the other party with regard to the quality of the product or service. This is a case of **asymmetric information.** An example of this is the market for "lemons" (i.e., a defective product, such as a used car, that will require a great deal of costly repairs and is not worth its price).

Specifically, sellers of used cars know exactly the quality of the cars that they are selling but prospective buyers do not. As a result, the market price for used cars will depend on the quality of the average used car available for sale. The owners of "lemons" would then tend to receive a higher price than their cars are worth, while the owners of high-quality used cars would tend to get a lower price than their cars are worth. The owners of high-quality used cars would therefore withdraw their cars from the market, thus lowering the average quality and price of the remaining cars available for sale. Sellers of the now above average quality cars withdraw their cars from the market, further reducing the quality and price of the remaining used cars offered for sale. The process continues until only the lowest-quality cars are sold in the market at the appropriate very low price. Thus, the end result is that low-quality cars drive high-quality cars out of the market. This is known as **adverse selection.**

The problem of adverse selection that arises from asymmetric information can be overcome or reduced by the acquisition of more information by the party lacking it. For example, in the used-car market, a prospective buyer can have the car evaluated at an independent automotive service center, or the used car dealer can *signal* above average quality cars by providing guarantees.

The Insurance Market and Adverse Selection

The problem of adverse selection arises not only in the market for used cars, but in any market characterized by asymmetric information, such as the market for individual health insurance. Here the individual knows much more about the state of her health than an insurance company can ever find out, even with a medical examination. As a result, when an insurance company sets the insurance premium for the average individual (i.e., an individual of average health), unhealthy people are more likely to purchase insurance than healthy people. Because of this adverse selection problem, the insurance company is forced to raise the insurance premium, thus making it less advantageous for healthy people to purchase insurance. This increases even more the proportion of unhealthy people in the pool of insured people, thus requiring still higher insurance premiums. In the end insurance premiums would have to be so high that even unhealthy people would stop buying insurance. Why buy insurance if the premium is as high as the cost of personally paying for an illness?

The problem of adverse selection arises in the market for any type of insurance (i.e., for accidents, fire, floods, and so on). In each case, only the above-risk people buy insurance, and this forces insurance companies to raise their premiums. The worsening adverse selection problem can lead to insurance premiums being so high that in the end no one would buy insurance. Insurance companies try to overcome the problem of adverse selection by requiring medical checkups, charging different premiums for different age groups and occupations, and offering different rates of coinsurance, amounts of deductibility, length of contracts, and so on.

The Problem of Moral Hazard

Another problem that arises in the insurance market is that of **moral hazard.** This refers to the increase in the probability of an illness, fire, or other accident when an individual is insured than when she is not. With insurance, the loss from an illness, fire, or other accident is shifted from the individual to the insurance company. Therefore, the individual will take fewer precautions to avoid the illness, fire, or other accident, and when a loss does occur, she will tend to inflate the amount of the loss. With auto insurance, an individual may drive more recklessly (thus increasing the probability of a car accident) and then is likely to exaggerate the injury and inflate the property damage that he suffers if he does get into an accident. Similarly with fire insurance, a firm may take fewer reasonable precautions (such as the installation of a fire detector system, thereby increasing the probability of a fire) than in the absence of fire insurance; and then the firm is likely to inflate the property damage suffered if a fire does occur.

If the problem of moral hazard is not reduced or somehow contained, it could lead to unacceptably high insurance rates and costs and thus defeat the very reason for insurance. One method by which insurance companies try to overcome the problem of moral hazard is by specifying the precautions that an individual or firm must take as a condition for buying insurance. For example, an insurance company might require yearly physical checkups as a condition for continuing to provide health insurance to an individual, increase insurance premiums for drivers involved in accidents, and the installation of a fire detector before providing fire insurance to a firm. By doing this, the insurance company tries to limit the possibility of illness, accident, or fire, and thereby reduce the number and amount of possible claims it will face. Another way used by insurance companies to overcome or reduce the problem of moral hazard is *coinsurance.* This refers to insuring only part of the possible loss or value of the property being insured. The idea is that if the individual or firm shares a significant portion of a potential loss with the insurance company, the individual or firm will be more prudent and will take more precautions to avoid losses from illness or accidents.

Case Study 13-9
The Internet and the Information Superhighway

Information available to consumers and firms is increasing by leaps and bounds as a result of the development of a national high-speed computer network. The goal is to build faster and more sophisticated computers (hardware) and programs (software) for running them and to link them throughout the nation via what has been aptly called an

information superhighway. This means that researchers, firms, and consumers could hook up with libraries, databases, and marketing information through a national high-speed computer network and have at their fingertips a vast amount of information as never before. Information technology is being applied to fields as diverse as science, manufacturing, finance, and marketing, and it is revolutionizing the way business is conducted. Creating such an information superhighway is a monumental and very expensive endeavor and may take decades to fully implement. It involves devising the needed hardware and software and then hooking everyone up to the network.

In a more limited sense, a *world* information superhighway is already here through the **Internet.** This is a collection of more than 48,000 computers throughout the world linked together in a service called the World Wide Web. To this Web are then connected more than 20 million people with nearly 4 million computers scattered in 159 nations around the world. Hundreds of thousands of individuals are joining the Web each month, and the network is expected to connect more than 200 million people and 100 million computers throughout the world by the turn of the decade. In short, through the Internet, the entire globe is becoming a single world marketplace.

Already more than 21,000 businesses are part of Internet. These include such corporate giants as AT&T, Ford, IBM, Merrill Lynch, J.P. Morgan, Bank of America, Dun and Bradstreet, J.C. Penney, Mitsubishi, as well as thousands of startup businesses, with many more joining or thinking of joining every day. The Internet is laying the groundwork for businesses dealing directly with suppliers, industrial customers, and potentially millions of online shoppers. For example, a consumer can examine thousands of multimedia documents from anywhere in the world, browse through a firm's catalogue, and in some cases, be able to click on a "buy" button and fill in an electronic order form, including shipping and credit-card information. This cuts a firm's cost of processing a telephone or mail order from $10 to $15 to less than $4. Dun and Bradstreet already sells and delivers credit reports over the Net. It is true that online shopping or "digital commerce" generated only about $200 million in revenue in 1994 in comparison to $1.5 trillion that U.S. consumers spend in stores and through mail orders, but the Internet is likely to change all that within a few years.

Source: "An Information Superhighway?" *Business Week,* February 1991, p. 28; "The Internet," *Business Week,* November 14, 1994, pp. 80–88; and "Trying to Find Gold with the Internet," *The New York Times,* January 3, 1995, p. C15.

SUMMARY

1. Most strategic managerial decisions are made in the face of risk or uncertainty. "Risk" refers to the situation where there is more than one possible outcome to a decision and the probability of each specific outcome is known or can be estimated. Under uncertainty, on the other hand, the probability of each specific outcome is not known or even meaningful. Managerial decisions involving risk utilize such concepts as strategy, states of nature, and payoff matrix.
2. The probability of an event is the chance or odds that the event will occur. A probability distribution lists all the possible outcomes of a decision and the

probability attached to each. The expected value of an event is obtained by multiplying each possible outcome of the event by its probability of occurrence and then adding these products. As the number of possible outcomes specified increases, we approach a continuous probability distribution. The standard deviation (σ) measures the dispersion of possible outcomes from the expected value and is used as an absolute measure of risk. The probability that an outcome will fall within a specified range of outcomes can be determined by measuring the area under the standard normal curve that lies within this range, for outcomes that are approximately normally distributed. A relative measure of risk is provided by the coefficient of variation (v), which is given by the standard deviation of the distribution divided by its expected value or mean.

3. While some managers are risk neutral or risk seekers, most are risk averters. Risk aversion is based on the principle of diminishing marginal utility of money, which is reflected in a total utility of money curve that is concave or faces down. A risk averter would not accept a fair bet, a risk-neutral individual would be indifferent to it, while a risk seeker would accept even some unfair bets. In managerial decisions subject to risk, a risk-averse manager seeks to maximize expected utility rather than monetary returns. The expected utility of a decision or strategy is the sum of the product of the utility of each possible outcome and the probability of its occurrence.
4. One method of adjusting the valuation model of the firm to deal with a project subject to risk is to use risk-adjusted discount rates. This involves adding a risk premium to the risk-free rate of interest or discount used to find the present value of the net cash flow or return of the investment. A similar method that explicitly incorporates the decision maker's attitude toward risk is the certainty-equivalent approach. This uses a risk-free discount rate in the denominator and incorporates risk by multiplying the net cash flow or return in the numerator of the valuation model by the certainty-equivalent coefficient. This is the ratio of the equivalent certain sum to the expected risky sum or net return from the investment.
5. Managerial decisions involving risk are often made in stages, with subsequent decisions or events depending on earlier decisions or events. Such decision processes can be analyzed with decision trees. The construction of a decision tree begins at the left with the earliest decision and moves forward in time to the right through a series of subsequent events and decisions. Boxes show decision points, and circles show possible states of nature. The analysis of decision trees starts at the right at the end of the sequence and moves backward to the left. For the evaluation of even more complex managerial decisions involving risk, simulation is often used. This involves the use of a computer program that explicitly and simultaneously considers all the interactions among the variables of the model to determine the expected outcome and risk of a particular business strategy.
6. One decision rule under uncertainty is the maximin criterion. This conservative and pessimistic rule postulates that the decision maker should determine

the worst possible outcome of each strategy and then pick the strategy that provides the best of the worst possible outcomes. Another decision rule under uncertainty is the minimax regret criterion. This postulates that the decision maker should select the strategy that minimizes the maximum regret or opportunity cost of the wrong decision, whatever the state of nature that occurs. Other more informal and less precise methods of dealing with uncertainty involve the acquisition of additional information, referral to authority, attempting to control the business environment, and diversification.

7. Including foreign securities in an investment portfolio can reduce risk (through diversification) and increase the rate of return, but also gives rise to a foreign-exchange risk because the foreign currency can depreciate during the time of the investment. Such foreign-exchange risk can be covered by hedging. This is usually accomplished with a forward or a futures contract. A forward contract is an agreement to purchase or sell a specific amount of a foreign currency at a rate specified today for delivery at a specific future date. A futures contract is a standardized forward contract for *predetermined quantities of the currency* and *selected calendar dates.*
8. Risk often results from lack of or inadequate information. The relationship between information and risk can be analyzed by examining asymmetric information, adverse selection, and moral hazard. Asymmetric information (i.e., when one party to a transaction has less information on the quality of the product or service offered for sale than the other party) gives rise to the problem of adverse selection (low-quality products or services driving high-quality products or services out of the market). The problem of adverse selection can be overcome by acquiring or providing more information. Moral hazard refers to the increased probability of a loss when an economic agent can shift some of its costs to others. Insurance companies try to overcome this problem by specifying the precautions that an individual or firm must take as a condition for insurance.

DISCUSSION QUESTIONS

1. What is the meaning of: risk, uncertainty, expected value, probability distribution, standard deviation, coefficient of variation?
2. What is the distinction between a discrete and a continuous probability distribution? How is the probability that an outcome will fall within a given range of outcomes determined? What is the usefulness of probability distributions in risk analysis?
3. What is the value of the standard deviation and coefficient of variation if all the outcomes of a probability distribution are identical? Why is this so? What does this mean? How does the maximization decision of a manager differ in the case of certainty and risk?
4. What is the meaning of diminishing, constant, and increasing marginal utility of money?

5. Why is maximization of the expected value not a valid criterion in decision making subject to risk? Under what conditions would that criterion be valid?
6. What is the expected utility of a project with a 40 percent probability of gaining 6 utils and a 60 percent probability of losing 1 util? Should the manager undertake this project? What if the payoff of the project were the same as above, except that the utility lost were 4 utils?
7. What is the meaning of a risk-adjusted discount rate? A risk-return trade-off function? A risk premium? What is their usefulness in adjusting the valuation model of the firm or of a project for risk?
8. What is the meaning of the certainty-equivalent coefficient? What is its relationship to utility theory and risk aversion? How is the certainty-equivalent coefficient used to adjust the valuation model for risk?
9. What is the number of possible outcomes in a decision tree depicting the choice between five different plant sizes, four possible ways that competitors may react under each of three different economic conditions? How is the probability of each outcome determined?
10. What is meant by "simulation"? By "sensitivity analysis"? When is simulation most useful and used?
11. Why is decision making under uncertainty necessarily subjective? Why is the maximin criterion a very conservative decision rule? Under what conditions might this decision rule be appropriate?
12. What is the rationale behind the minimax regret rule? What are some less formal and precise methods of dealing with uncertainty? When are these useful?
13. Why does an importer usually face a foreign-exchange risk? How can the importer hedge the foreign-exchange risk by purchasing the foreign currency today to have it by the time the foreign-currency payment is due? Why does hedging usually take place with a forward contract?
14. How does the adverse selection problem arise in the credit-card market? How do credit-card companies reduce the adverse selection problem that they face? To what complaint does this give rise?

PROBLEMS

1. An investor has two investment opportunities, each involving an outlay of $10,000. The present value of possible outcomes and their respective probabilities are

	Investment I		Investment II		
Outcome	$4,000	$6,000	$3,000	$5,000	$7,000
Probability	0.6	0.4	0.4	0.3	0.3

(*a*) Calculate the expected value of each investment. (*b*) Draw a bar chart for each investment. (*c*) Calculate the standard deviation of each project. (*d*) Determine which of the two investments the investor should choose.

*2. Using Table C-1 for the standard normal distribution in Appendix C at the end of the book, determine (*a*) that 68.26 percent of the area under the standard normal curve is found within plus or minus 1 standard deviation of the mean, 95.44 percent within $\pm 2\sigma$, and 99.74 percent within $\pm 3\sigma$; (*b*) the probability that profit will fall between \$500 and \$650 for project A in Section 13-2 of the text (with expected value of \$500 and standard deviation of \$70.71); (*c*) the probability that profit for project A will fall between \$300 and \$650, below \$300, above \$650.

3. A computer software company has to decide which of two advertising strategies to adopt: spot TV commercials or newspaper ads. The marketing department has estimated that sales and their probability under each alternative plan are as given in the table below:

Strategy A (TV Commercials)		Strategy B (Newspaper Ads)	
Sales	Probability	Sales	Probability
\$ 8,000	0.2	\$ 8,000	0.3
10,000	0.3	12,000	0.4
12,000	0.3	16,000	0.3
14,000	0.2		

The firm's profit is 50 percent of sales. (*a*) Calculate the expected profit under each promotion strategy. (*b*) Calculate the standard deviation of the distribution of profits for each promotion strategy. (*c*) Which of the two promotion strategies is more risky? (*d*) Which promotion strategy should the firm choose?

*4. An oil-drilling venture offers the chance of investing \$10,000 with a 20 percent probability of a return of \$40,000 if the venture is successful (i.e., oil is found). If unsuccessful, the \$10,000 investment will be lost. (*a*) What is the expected monetary return of this investment? (*b*) If the utility schedule of individuals A, B, and C is as indicated below, what is the expected utility of the project for each? Which individual(s) would invest in the venture? Why?

Money	−\$10,000	0	\$10,000	\$20,000	\$30,000	\$40,000
Utility of A	−5	0	4	7	9	10
B	−5	0	5	10	15	20
C	−5	0	6	13	21	30

5. A manager must determine which of two products to market. From market studies the manager constructed the following payoff matrix of the present value of all future net profits under all the different possible states of the economy:

	Product 1		Product 2	
State of the Economy	Probability	Profit	Probability	Profit
Boom	0.2	\$50	0.2	\$30
Normal	0.5	20	0.4	20
Recession	0.3	0	0.4	10

The manager's utility for money function is

$$U = 100M - M^2$$

where M refers to dollars of profit. (*a*) Is the manager a risk seeker, risk neutral, or a risk averter? Why? (*b*) If the manager's objective were profit maximization regardless of risk, which product should he or she introduce? (*c*) Evaluate the risk associated per dollar of profit with each product. (*d*) If the manager's objective were utility maximization, which product should he or she introduce?

*6. The manager of the Quality Products Company is faced with two alternative investment projects. Project A involves the introduction of a higher-quality version of its basic shaving cream, and project B, the introduction of a man's hair lotion (a new line of business for the company). The two projects involve the following expected streams of net cash flows and initial outlays:

	Net Cash Outflows			
Investment	Year 1	Year 2	Year 3	Initial Outlay
A	\$40,000	\$60,000	\$40,000	\$110,000
B	30,000	80,000	50,000	104,000

(*a*) Calculate the net present value of each investment project with the basic risk-free discount rate of 8 percent. (*b*) Which of the two projects should the manager adopt if the risk premium is 2 percent on project A and 6 percent on project B?

7. The Beach Resort Hotel must decide which of two vending machines, the Refreshing or the Cooling, to install on its beach front. The net cash flow remains the same for each machine in each of the four years that each machine lasts. The purchase price, the salvage value, and the payoff matrix for each machine are indicated in the table below:

	Refreshing			Cooling		
Purchase price		\$10,000			\$11,000	
Salvage value after 4 years		0			0	
Expected net cash flow in each of 4 years	\$6,000	\$5,000	\$4,000	\$7,000	\$5,000	\$3,000
Probability of occurrence	0.25	0.50	0.25	0.25	0.50	0.25

The risk-free discount rate is 10 percent. The risk premium applied by the hotel is as indicated below:

σ	Risk Premium
$ 0–$ 999	0%
1,000– 1,999	4
2,000– 2,999	10
3,000– 3,999	20

Prepare an analysis to determine which of the two machines the hotel should install.

8. Suppose that the certainty-equivalent coefficient for each machine of Problem 7 is as indicated below:

	Certainty-Equivalent Coefficient			
	Year 1	Year 2	Year 3	Year 4
Refreshing machine	0.90	0.85	0.75	0.70
Cooling machine	0.96	0.92	0.90	0.85

Calculate the net present value of each machine.

*9. The Fitness World Sporting Company wants to move into a new sales region and must determine which of two plants to build. It can build a large plant that costs $4 million or a small plant that costs $2 million. The company estimated that the probability that the economy will be booming, normal, or in a recession is 30 percent, 40 percent, and 30 percent, respectively. The company also estimated the present value of net cash flows for each type of plant under each state of the economy to be as indicated in the following payoff matrix. Construct a decision tree for the firm to show which of the two plants the company should build. Assume that the company is risk neutral.

		Large Plant	Small Plant
Present value	Boom	$10	$4
of net cash flows	Normal	6	3
(in millions)	Recession	2	2

10. Suppose that the Beauty Company faces the choice of introducing a new beauty cream or investing the same amount of money in Treasury bills with a return of $10,000. If the company introduces the beauty cream, there is an 80 percent probability that a competing firm will introduce a similar product and a 20 percent chance that it will not. Whether or not the competitor responds with a similar product, the company has a choice of charging a high, a medium, or a low price. In the absence of competition this is the end

of the story. In the presence of competition, the competitive firm can react to each price strategy of the Beauty Company with a high, medium, or low price of its own. The probability and the present value of the company's profit under each competitor's price response for the company strategy of high price (*HP*), medium price (*MP*), and low price (*LP*) are indicated in the table below. Construct a decision tree and determine whether the Beauty Company should introduce the new beauty cream or use its funds to purchase Treasury bills.

Competition	Company's Price Strategy	Competitor's Price Response	Probability	Present Value of Company's Profit
		HP	0.5	$12,000
	HP	*MP*	0.3	10,000
		LP	0.2	8,000
		HP	0.3	12,000
Yes	*MP*	*MP*	0.5	10,000
		LP	0.2	6,000
		HP	0.0	25,000
	LP	*MP*	0.4	15,000
		LP	0.6	10,000
	HP	—	—	40,000
No	*MP*	—	—	30,000
	LP	—	—	20,000

11. Given the following payoff matrix for investment projects A, B, and C, determine the best investment project for the firm according to (*a*) the maximin criterion and (*b*) the minimax regret criterion.

	State of Nature		
Project	Recession	Normal	Boom
A	$50	$75	$ 85
B	40	80	100
C	30	70	70

12. A U.S. firm imports $200,000 worth of British goods and agrees to pay in three months. The exchange rate is $2.00/£1 today and the three-month forward rate is $2.02/£1. Explain how the importer can hedge his foreign-exchange risk.

13. **Integrating Problem**
The Food Products Company has decided to introduce a new brand of breakfast cereals and is contemplating building either a $10 million or a $6 million plant to produce the new breakfast cereals. If the company builds the $10 million plant, there is a 70 percent chance that competitors will respond with a large increase in their advertising and a 30 percent probability that competitors will respond with a small increase in their advertising. On the

other hand, if the company builds the \$6 million plant, there is a 40 percent probability that competitors will respond with a large increase in their advertising and a 60 percent probability that competitors will respond with a small increase in their advertising.

Whether the company builds the \$10 million or the \$6 million plant and whether competitors will respond with a large or a small increase in their advertising, the general demand conditions that the company will face can be high, medium, or low. The probability and the net cash flow that the company faces under each plant it can build and competitors' responses are indicated in the table below. Since the variability of the net cash flows is higher with the \$10 million plant, the company uses the risk-adjusted discount rate of 20 percent to calculate the present value of the net cash flows. On the other hand, the company uses the risk-adjusted discount rate of 14 percent to calculate the present value of the net cash flows of the \$6 million plant.

Construct a decision tree, and determine whether the Food Products Company should build the \$10 million or the \$6 million plant. Round all calculations to the nearest dollar.

Plant	Competitors' Advertising Reaction	Conditions of Demand	Probability	Net Cash Flows for Year (in millions) 1	2	3
		High	0.4	\$6	\$6	\$5
	Large	Normal	0.4	4	5	4
		Low	0.2	3	4	2
\$10 million						
		High	0.4	7	7	7
	Small	Normal	0.4	5	5	5
		Low	0.2	4	4	4
		High	0.4	3	4	3
	Large	Normal	0.4	3	3	2
		Low	0.2	2	2	2
\$6 million						
		High	0.4	5	4	4
	Small	Normal	0.4	4	3	3
		Low	0.2	3	3	2

SUPPLEMENTARY READINGS

For a problem-solving approach to the analysis of risk, see:

Salvatore, Dominick: *Theory and Problems of Managerial Economics*, Schaum Outline Series (New York: McGraw-Hill, 1989), Sec. 2.2.

For the measuring of risk with probability distributions, see:

Salvatore, Dominick: *Theory and Problems of Statistics and Econometrics* (New York: McGraw-Hill, 1982), Chaps. 2 and 3.

Schaifer, R.: *Probability and Statistics for Business Decisions* (New York: McGraw-Hill, 1959).

Blume, M. E.: "On the Assessment of Risk," *Journal of Finance,* vol. 26, March 1971.

Arrow, Kenneth J.: "Risk Perception in Psychology," *Economic Inquiry,* vol. 20, 1982.

Bromiley, P.: Testing a Causal Model of Corporate Risk Taking and Performance," *Academy of Management Journal,* March 1991, pp. 37–59.

Skaperdas, S.: "Conflicts and Attitudes Toward Risk," *American Economic Review,* May 1991, pp. 116–120.

Utility theory and risk aversion are discussed in:

Salvatore, Dominick: *Microeconomics,* 2nd ed. (New York: HarperCollins, 1994), Appendix to Chap. 3.

Schoemaker, P. J. H.: "The Expected Utility Model: Its Variants, Purposes, Evidence and Limitations," *Journal of Economic Literature,* vol. 20, 1982.

For adjusting the valuation model for risk, see:

Crum, Roy L., and **Francis G. J. Derkinderen,** eds.: *Capital Budgeting Under Conditions of Uncertainty* (Boston: Martinus Nijhoff, 1981).

A discussion of decision trees is found in:

Magee, John F.: "Decision Trees for Decision Making," *Harvard Business Review,* vol. 42, 1964.

Hespos, Richard F., and **Paul A. Strassman:** "Stochastic Decision Trees for the Analysis of Investment Decisions," *Management Science,* 1965.

For decision making under uncertainty, see:

Neuman, John Von, and **Oscar Morgenstern:** *Theory of Games and Economic Behavior,* 3d ed. (Princeton, N.J.: Princeton University Press, 1953).

Markowitz, Harry: *Portfolio Selection: Efficient Diversification of Investments* (New York: Wiley, 1959).

Foreign-exchange risks and hedging are examined in:

Salvatore, Dominick: *International Economics,* 5th ed. (Englewood Cliffs, N.J.: Prentice-Hall, 1995) Chap. 14.

On the relationship between risk and information, see:

Ackerlof, George A.: "The Market for 'Lemons': Qualitative Uncertainty and the Market Mechanism," *Quarterly Journal of Economics,* August 1970, pp. 488–500.

Stiglitz, J. E.: "The Causes and Consequences of the Dependence of Quality on Price," *Journal of Economic Literature,* March 1987, pp. 1–48.

Pauly, Mark V.: "Taxation, Health Insurance, and Market Failure in the Medical Economy," *Journal of Economic Literature,* June 1986, pp. 629–675.

Arrow, Kenneth J.: "Uncertainty and the Welfare Economics of Medical Care," *American Economic Review,* December 1963, pp. 941–973.

CHAPTER 14

Long-Run Investment Decisions: Capital Budgeting

KEY TERMS

Capital budgeting
Net cash flow from a project
Time value of money
Net present value (*NPV*) of a project
Internal rate of return (*IRR*) on a project
Profitability index (*PI*)
Cost of debt
Dividend valuation model
Capital asset pricing model (*CAPM*)
Beta coefficient (β)
Composite cost of capital

CHAPTER OUTLINE

In previous chapters we were primarily interested in examining how firms organize production within existing facilities in order to maximize profits during a given year. In this chapter we shift attention to the analysis of a firm's investment opportunities. These may involve expansion of the firm's capacity in a given line of business or entrance into entirely different lines of business. The distinguishing characteristic of investment decisions is that they involve costs and give rise to revenues over a number of years rather than for one year only. Since $1 paid or received next year is worth less than $1 paid or received today, discounting and present value concepts need to be used in order to properly evaluate and compare different investment projects. These concepts are reviewed in Appendix A at the end of the book.[1]

In this chapter, we first present an overview of the capital budgeting process and then examine the various steps involved in capital budgeting and the key roles that the marketing, production, and financing departments of the firm play in the process. The chapter ends with a discussion of the relationship between cost of capital and international competitiveness.

14-1 CAPITAL BUDGETING: AN OVERVIEW

In this section we discuss the meaning and importance of capital budgeting, we classify the different types of investment projects, and we provide an overview of the capital budgeting process. In the remainder of the chapter, we will then provide a more detailed look at the various steps involved in capital budgeting.

Meaning and Importance of Capital Budgeting

Capital budgeting refers to the process of planning expenditures that give rise to revenues or returns over a number of years. Capital budgeting is of crucial importance to a firm. The application of new technological breakthroughs may lead to new and more efficient production techniques, changes in consumer tastes may make a firm's existing product line obsolete and give rise to the demand for entirely different products, and merger with other firms may significantly strengthen a firm's competitive position vis-à-vis its competitors. The firm's management must constantly be on the alert to explore these and other opportunities. The firm's profitability, growth, and its very survival in the long run depend on how well management accomplishes these tasks. Capital budgeting is also crucial because major capital investment projects are for the most part irreversible (e.g., after a specialized type of machinery has been installed, it has a very small secondhand value if the firm reverses its decision).

Capital budgeting is used not only to plan for the replacement of worn-out capital and equipment, for the expansion of production facilities, or for entering

[1]Since knowledge of compounding, discounting, and present value concepts is essential for understanding the material in this chapter, the student is urged to review or study the material in Appendix A before proceeding further with this chapter.

entirely new product lines but also in planning major advertising campaigns, employee training programs, research and development, decisions to purchase or rent production facilities or equipment, and any other investment project that would result in costs and revenues over a number of years. In general, firms classify investment projects into the following categories:

1. *Replacement.* Investments to replace equipment that is worn out in the production process.
2. *Cost reduction.* Investments to replace working but obsolete equipment with new and more efficient equipment, expenditures for training programs aimed at reducing labor costs, and expenditures to move production facilities to areas where labor and other inputs are cheaper.
3. *Output expansion of traditional products and markets.* Investments to expand production facilities in response to increased demand for the firm's traditional products in traditional or existing markets.
4. *Expansion into new products and/or markets.* Investments to develop, produce, and sell new products and/or enter new markets.
5. *Government regulation.* Investments made to comply with government regulations. These include investment projects required to meet government health and safety regulations, pollution control, and to satisfy other legal requirements.

In general, investment decisions to replace worn-out equipment are the easiest to make since management is familiar with the specifications, productivity, and operating and maintenance costs of existing equipment and with the time when it needs to be replaced. Investment projects to reduce costs and expand output in traditional products and markets are generally more complex and usually require more detailed analysis and approval by higher-level management. Familiarity with the product and the market, however, does not usually make these projects among the most challenging that management is likely to face. Investment projects to produce new products and move into new markets, on the other hand, are likely to be very complex because of the much greater risk involved. They are also likely to be the most essential and financially rewarding in the long run since a firm's product line tends to become obsolete over time and its traditional market may shrink or even disappear (witness the market for slide rules which have been practically replaced entirely by hand-held calculators during the past decade). Finally, investment projects to meet government regulations often give rise to special legal, evaluation, and monitoring problems requiring outside expert assistance.

From what has been said above, it is clear that the generation of ideas and proposals for new investment projects is crucial to the future profitability of the firm and to its very survival over time. In well-managed and dynamic firms, all employees are encouraged to come up with new investment ideas. Most large firms, however, are likely to have a research and development division especially entrusted with the responsibility of coming up with proposals for new investment projects. Such a division is likely to be staffed by experts in product development, marketing research, industrial engineering and so on, and they may regularly meet with the heads of other divisions in brainstorming sessions to examine new products, markets, and strategies.

While the final decision to undertake or not to undertake a major investment project is made by the firm's top management, especially for investment projects that involve entering into new product lines and markets, the capital budgeting process is likely to involve most of the firm's divisions. The marketing division will need to forecast the demand for the new or modified products that the firm plans to sell; the production, engineering, personnel, and purchasing departments must provide feasibility studies and estimates of the cost of the investment project; and the financing department must determine how the required investment funds are to be raised and their cost to the firm. Thus, capital budgeting can truly be said to integrate the operation of all the major divisions of the firm.

Overview of the Capital Budgeting Process

Capital budgeting is essentially an application of the general principle that a firm should produce the output or undertake an activity until the marginal revenue from the output or activity is equal to its marginal cost. In a capital budgeting framework, this principle implies that the firm should undertake additional investment projects until the marginal return from the investment is equal to its marginal cost. The schedule of the various investment projects open to the firm, arranged from the one with the highest to the lowest return, represents the firm's demand for capital. The marginal cost of capital schedule, on the other hand, gives the cost that the firm faces in obtaining additional amounts of capital for investment purposes.[2] The intersection of the demand and marginal cost curves for capital that the firm faces determines how much the firm will invest. This is shown in Figure 14-1.

In Figure 14-1, the various lettered bars indicate the amount of capital required for each investment project that the firm can undertake and the rate of return expected on each investment project. Thus, project *A* requires an investment of $2 million and is expected to generate an 18 percent rate of return. Project *B* requires an investment of $3 million (the total of $5 million minus the $2 million required for project *A* along the horizontal axis) and is expected to generate a 16 percent rate of return, and so on. The top of each bar, thus, represents the firm's demand for capital. Note that the projects are arranged from the one that is expected to provide the highest return to the firm to the one that is expected to provide the lowest return. The marginal cost of capital (*MCC*) curve shows that the firm can raise about $2 million of capital at the rate (cost) of 10 percent, but if it wants to raise additional amounts, it faces increasingly higher costs. How this *MCC* curve is derived and the reason for its shape are discussed in Section 14-4. At this point, we simply take it as a given to the firm.

[2]The cost of capital is the rate that the firm must pay on money raised externally (i.e., by borrowing or selling stock) and the opportunity cost or the return foregone on internal funds that the firm could have invested outside the firm. More will be said on this in Section 14-4.

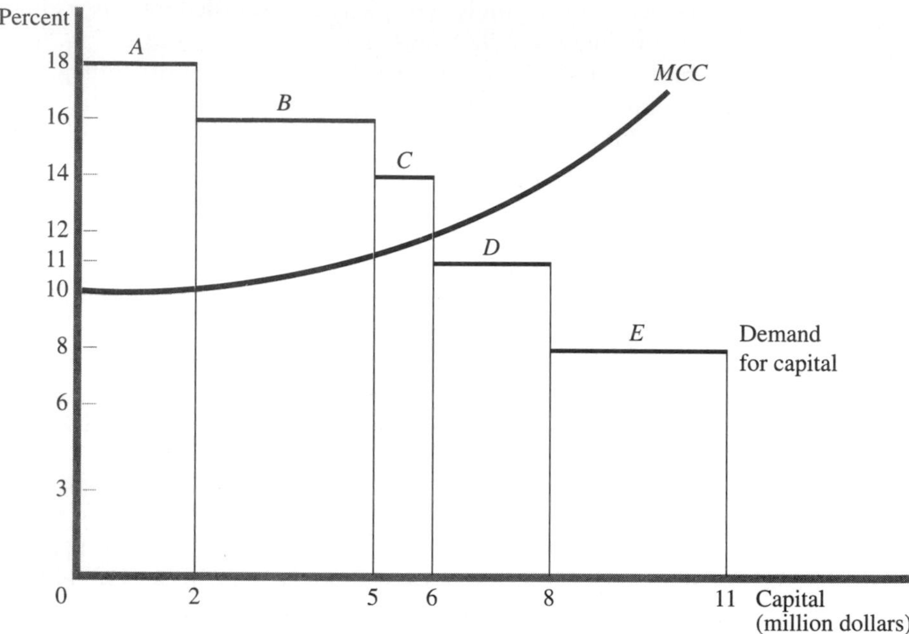

Figure 14-1
Graphical Overview of the Capital Budgeting Process
The various lettered bars indicate the amount of capital required for each investment project and the rate of return on the investment. The top of each bar, thus, represents the firm's demand for capital. The marginal cost of capital (*MCC*) curve shows the rising cost of raising additional amounts of capital that the firm faces. The firm will undertake projects *A*, *B*, and *C* because the expected rates of return on these projects exceed the cost of raising the capital to make these investments. On the other hand, the firm will not undertake projects *D* and *E* because the expected rates of return are lower than their capital costs.

Faced with the demand for capital and marginal cost of capital curves shown in Figure 14-1, the firm will undertake projects *A*, *B*, and *C* because the expected rates of return on these projects exceed the cost of capital to make these investments. Specifically, the firm will undertake project *A* because it expects a return of 18 percent from the project as compared with its capital cost of only 10 percent. Similarly, the firm undertakes project *B* because it expects a return of 16 percent as compared with a capital cost of between 10 and 11 percent for the project. The firm also undertakes project *C* because its expected return of 14 percent exceeds its capital cost of nearly 12 percent. On the other hand, the firm will not undertake projects *D* and *E* because the expected rate of return on these projects is lower than the cost of raising the capital to make these investments. For example, project *D* provides an expected return of only 11 percent as compared to a capital cost exceeding 12 percent. For project *E* the excess of capital cost over expected return is even greater. If the firm invested in projects *D* and *E*, it would face lower overall profits in the long run and the value of the firm would decline.

Case Study 14-1

Benefit-Cost Analysis and the SST

Based on benefit-cost analysis, the development of the supersonic transport plane (SST) was abandoned by the United States in 1971. The benefits were simply not large enough to justify the costs. The French and British governments, however, jointly continued to pursue the project and built the Concorde at a huge cost. Today, there are only a handful of such planes operated exclusively by the British and French national airlines. With operating costs more than 4 times higher than the Boeing 747, the Concorde must be classified as a clear market failure that would not fly without heavy government subsidies. Specifically, a one-way seat from New York to London or Paris on the Concorde would have to be priced at over $4,000 (as compared with less than $1,000 on the Boeing 747) for the Concorde to break even. This means that the passenger would be paying about $1,000 for each of the three hours saved by flying on the Concorde. Modern people may be hurried today but not that hurried! As it is, the British and French governments subsidize about half of the operating costs of the Concorde. Still, business is not brisk on the Concorde.

It seems that in their benefit-cost analysis, the British and French greatly overestimated the benefits arising from building and operating the Concorde and grossly underestimated the costs. This is a good example of how imprecise benefit-cost analysis can sometimes be. The question is why the British and French governments continue to heavily subsidize flying the Concorde now, thereby "throwing good money after bad." The answer may be national pride in being the only two nations flying a supersonic passenger plane. If that is the case, it is a very expensive source of national pride.

Interest seems now to have shifted from supersonic planes to the development of a super-jumbo jet capable of transporting from 600 to 800 passengers. Because of the incredible high cost of developing such a plane ($15 to $20 billion), Boeing is trying to organize a far-reaching international partnership so as to have such a plane flying early next century.

Source: "The Concorde's Destination," *The New York Times,* September 28, 1979, p. 26; and "Boeing, Partners to Press Ahead on Big Jetliner," *The Wall Street Journal,* January 10, 1994, p. A4.

Case Study 14-2

The Eurotunnel: Another Bad French-British Investment?

In 1987, the French and the British launched the Eurotunnel, another grandiose cooperative project to provide a rail link under the channel separating France and England, thereby cutting travel time from London to Paris to three hours and from London to Brussels to 3 hours and 15 minutes. The project was expected to cost $7 billion and be completed in 1993 and to generate enough revenues to pay the interest on the amount borrowed from a consortium of more than 200 banks and also provide a return to stockholders. As of the end of 1994, the Eurotunnel had still to begin operation, and its cost had more than doubled to $16 billion. This means that annual interest charges will be more than $800 million, or more than double what was originally estimated. The revenue side also seems to have been grossly overestimated, not only because of the delays of nearly two years in starting its operation but also from the competition from ferries, which have greatly improved service and cut prices.

There is then the problem that while high-speed rail links have been built on the French side of the tunnel, the British are still in the planning stages in establishing a high-speed rail link from the tunnel to London. This means that the trip from Paris to Brussels to London will take longer than originally scheduled. When such high-speed rail links have been built, rail transportation will be able to compete with air service between London and Paris and Brussels. It is true that actual flying time between London and Paris and Brussels is about one hour, but while train stations are in city centers, airports are outside cities and require about one hour travel time at each end. Furthermore, were it not for the large interest charges that Eurotunnel will have to pay, with its very low marginal cost of operation, the Eurotunnel could certainly beat the ferries on price competition. At this point, one may ask, what is the use of the benefit-cost analysis if it can be so egregiously wrong? The answer is that if the assumptions on which the analysis is based are wrong, the outcome will also be wrong. In other words: Garbage in, garbage out. Firms generally do a much better job than governments in their benefit-cost analysis.

Source: "More Money Down the Hole," *The Economist,* October 16, 1993, pp. 77–78; "£11 billion and Counting," *The Economist,* October 1, 1994, p. 74; and "Eurotunnel, Citing Start-Up Delays, Says Revenues to Fall Short of Forecasts," *The Wall Street Journal,* October 18, 1994, p. A2.

14-2 THE CAPITAL BUDGETING PROCESS

In this section we discuss how the firm projects the cash flows from an investment project, how it calculates the net present value of and the internal rate of return on the project, and how the two are related.

Projecting Cash Flows

One of the most important and difficult aspects of capital budgeting is the estimation of the **net cash flow from a project.** This is the difference between cash receipts and cash expenditures over the life of a project. Since cash receipts and expenditures occur in the future, a great deal of uncertainty is inevitably involved in their estimation. Some general guidelines must be followed in estimating cash flows. *First,* cash flows should be measured on an *incremental basis.* That is, the cash flow from a given project should be measured by the difference between the stream of the firm's cash flows with and without the project. Any increase in the expenditures or reduction in the receipts of other divisions of the firm resulting from the adoption of a given project must be considered. For example, the firm must subtract from the estimated gross cash receipts resulting from the introduction of a new product any anticipated reduction in the cash receipts of other divisions of the firm selling competitive products. *Second,* cash flows must be estimated on an *after-tax* basis, using the firm's marginal tax rate. *Third,* as a noncash expense, depreciation affects the firm's cash flow only through its effect on taxes.

A typical project involves making an initial investment and generates a series of net cash flows over the life of the project. The initial investment to add a new product line may include the cost of purchasing and installing new equipment, reorganizing the firm's production processes, providing additional working capital for inventory and accounts receivable, and so on. The net cash flows are equal to cash inflows minus cash outflows in each year during the life of the project. The cash inflows are, of course, the incremental sales revenues generated by the project plus the salvage value of the equipment at the end of its economic life, if any, and recovery of working capital at the end of the project. The cash outflows usually include the incremental variable costs, fixed costs, and taxes resulting from the project.

For example, suppose that a firm estimates that it needs to make an initial investment of $1 million in order to introduce a new product. The marketing division of the firm expects the life of the product to be five years. Incremental sales revenues are estimated to be $1 million during the first year of operation and to rise by 10 percent per year until the fifth year, when the product will be replaced. The production department projects that the incremental variable costs of producing the product will be 50 percent of incremental sales revenues and that the firm would also incur additional fixed costs of $150,000 per year. The finance department anticipates a marginal tax rate of 40 percent for the firm. The finance department of the firm would use the straight-line depreciation method so that the annual depreciation charge would be $200,000 per year for five years. The salvage value of the initial equipment is estimated to be $250,000, and the firm also expects to recover $100,000 of its working capital at the end of the fifth year. The cash flows from this project are summarized in Table 14-1.

Table 14-1
Estimated Cash Flow from Project

	Year				
	1	2	3	4	5
Sales	$1,000,000	$1,100,000	$1,210,000	$1,331,000	$1,464,100
Less: Variable costs	500,000	550,000	605,000	665,500	732,050
Fixed costs	150,000	150,000	150,000	150,000	150,000
Depreciation	200,000	200,000	200,000	200,000	200,000
Profit before taxes	$ 150,000	$ 200,000	$ 255,000	$ 315,500	$ 382,050
Less: Income tax	60,000	80,000	102,000	126,200	152,820
Profit after tax	$ 90,000	$ 120,000	$ 153,000	$ 189,300	$ 229,230
Plus: Depreciation	200,000	200,000	200,000	200,000	200,000
Net cash flow	$ 290,000	$ 320,000	$ 353,000	$ 389,300	$ 429,230
			Plus: Salvage value of equipment		250,000
			Recovery of working capital		100,000
			Net cash flow in year 5		$ 779,230

The question is now whether the firm should or should not undertake the investment. In order to answer this question, the firm must compare the net cash flow over the five years of the project indicated in Table 14-1 to the initial $1 million cost of the project. Since $1 received in future years is worth less than $1 spent today (this is referred to as the **time value of money**), the net cash flow from the project must be discounted to the present before comparing it to the initial cost of the investment. Alternatively, the firm could find the internal rate of return on the project. These methods of evaluating an investment project are next examined in turn.

Net Present Value (*NPV*)

One method of deciding whether or not a firm should accept an investment project is to determine the net present value of the project. The **net present value (*NPV*) of a project** is equal to the present value of the expected stream of net cash flows from the project, discounted at the firm's cost of capital, minus the initial cost of the project. As pointed out in Equation 13-10 in Chapter 13, the net present value (*NPV*) of a project is given by

$$NPV = \sum_{t=1}^{n} \frac{R_t}{(1 + k)^t} - C_0 \tag{14-1}$$

where R_t refers to the estimated net cash flow from the project in each of the n years considered, k is the risk-adjusted discount rate, Σ refers to "the sum of," and C_0 is the initial cost of the project. The value of the firm will increase if the *NPV* of the project is positive and decline if the *NPV* of the project is negative. Thus, the firm should undertake the project if its *NPV* is positive and should not undertake it if the *NPV* of the project is negative.

For example, if k (the risk-adjusted discount rate) or cost of capital of the project to the firm is 12 percent, the net present value of the project with the estimated net cash flow given in Table 14-1, and the initial cost of $1 million is

$$\begin{aligned} NPV = {} & \frac{\$290{,}000}{(1 + 0.12)^1} + \frac{\$320{,}000}{(1 + 0.12)^2} + \frac{\$353{,}000}{(1 + 0.12)^3} + \frac{\$389{,}300}{(1 + 0.12)^4} \\ & + \frac{\$779{,}230}{(1 + 0.12)^5} - \$1{,}000{,}000 \\ = {} & \$1{,}454{,}852 - \$1{,}000{,}000 \\ = {} & \$454{,}852 \end{aligned}$$

This project would thus add $454,852 to the value of the firm, and the firm should undertake it.[3] If the firm had used instead the risk-adjusted discount rates

[3]The values of the term $1/(1 + 0.12)^t$ for $t = 1$ to $t = 5$ in the above calculations can be obtained with a calculator and are equal to the first five terms in the column headed 12 percent in Table B-2 in Appendix B, as explained in Section A-2 in Appendix A at the end of the book.

of 10 percent and 20 percent, respectively, the net present value of the project would have been \$543,012 and \$169,078 (see the answer to Problem 3 at the end of the book). Thus, even if $k = 20$ percent, the firm should undertake the project.

Internal Rate of Return (*IRR*)

Another method of determining whether a firm should or should not accept an investment project is to calculate the internal rate of return on the project. The **internal rate of return (*IRR*) on a project** is the discount rate that equates the present value of the net cash flow from the project to the initial cost of the project. This is obtained by solving Equation 14-2 for k^*, the internal rate of return (*IRR*).

$$\sum_{t=1}^{n} \frac{R_t}{(1 + k^*)^t} = C_0 \tag{14-2}$$

While the internal rate of return ($IRR = k^*$) on a project can easily be obtained with a computer or a sophisticated hand-held calculator, it can also be obtained by trial and error by using Table B-2 in Appendix B at the end of the book. Specifically, we begin by using an arbitrary discount rate to calculate the present value of the net cash flows from the project. If the present value of the net cash flow exceeds the initial cost of the project, we increase the discount rate and repeat the process. On the other hand, if the present value of the net cash flows from the project is smaller than the initial cost of the project, we reduce the discount rate. The process is continued until the rate of discount is found that equates the present value of the net cash flow from the project to the initial cost of the project (so that Equation 14-2 holds). The discount rate found is the internal rate of return ($IRR = k^*$) on the project.

The firm should undertake the project if the internal rate of return on the project ($IRR = k^*$) exceeds or is equal to the marginal cost of capital or risk-adjusted discount rate (k) that the firm uses, and it should not undertake the project if the internal rate of return is smaller than the marginal cost of capital.[4] For example, using Table B-2, we can find that the present value of the net cash flow from the project shown in Table 14-1 is \$1,057,631 with $k = 24$ percent and \$961,986 with $k = 28$ percent, as compared to the initial cost of the project of \$1 million. Since the present value of the net cash flow from the project exceeds the initial cost of the project at $k = 24$ percent and is smaller at $k = 28$ percent, the internal rate of return on this project (k^*) must be between 24 and 28 percent. It is in fact 26.3 percent.[5]

[4]This is nothing else than the application of the marginal analysis presented in Figure 14-1, where the internal rates of return on the various projects open to the firm, arranged from the highest to the lowest, represent the firm's demand for capital.

[5]This was obtained with a hand calculator. Other investment criteria include the payback period and the average rate of return. Since they do not involve discounting the net cash flow from the investment, however, they are inferior to the *NPV* and *IRR* methods and are not discussed here.

Table 14-2
Net Present Value and Internal Rate of Return on Two Mutually Exclusive Investment Projects

	Project *A*	Project *B*
Initial cost	$1,000,000	$1,000,000
Net cash flow (years)		
Year 1	−100,000	350,000
Year 2	0	350,000
Year 3	500,000	350,000
Year 4	500,000	350,000
Year 5	1,400,000	350,000
Net present value (*NPV*) at 12% discount rate	$1,378,720	$1,261,680
Internal rate of return (*IRR*)	20.3%	22.1%

Comparison of *NPV* and *IRR*

When evaluating a single or independent project, the *NPV* and the *IRR* methods will always lead to the same accept-reject decision. The reason for this is that the *NPV* is positive only if the *IRR* on the project exceeds the marginal cost of capital or risk-adjusted discount rate used by the firm. Similarly, the *NPV* is negative only when the *IRR* is smaller than the marginal cost of capital. For mutually exclusive projects (i.e., when only one of two or more projects can be undertaken), however, the *NPV* and the *IRR* methods may provide contradictory signals as to which project will add more to the value of the firm. That is, the project with the higher *NPV* may have a lower *IRR* than an alternative project, and vice versa.

For example, Table 14-2 shows that project *A* has a higher net present value but a lower internal rate of return than project *B*. The reason this situation may arise is that under the *NPV* method, the net cash flows generated by the project are implicitly and conservatively assumed to be reinvested at the firm's cost of capital or risk-adjusted discount rate used by the firm. On the other hand, under the *IRR* method, the net cash flows generated by the project are implicitly assumed to be reinvested at the same higher internal rate of return earned on the project. Since there is no certainty that the firm can reinvest the net cash flows generated by a project at the same higher internal rate of return earned on the given project, it is generally better to use the *NPV* method in deciding which of two mutually exclusive investment projects to undertake. That is, it is preferable for the firm to undertake the project with the higher *NPV* rather than the one with the higher *IRR* when the two methods provide contradictory signals.

Case Study 14-3
Pennzoil's $3 Billion Capital Budgeting Challenge

In December 1987, after four years of litigation, Pennzoil settled its case against Texaco, the third largest U.S. energy company, for the staggering amount of $3 billion in cash. Texaco agreed to pay the $3 billion in cash to Pennzoil in lieu of an earlier $10.3 billion court judgment against Texaco for illegally inducing Getty Oil to break a merger agreement with Pennzoil. The $3 billion in cash that Pennzoil received from Texaco in 1988 (compared with Pennzoil's $2.6 billion in total assets and $1.9 billion sales prior to the settlement) catapulted Pennzoil from No. 394 to No. 220 among all publicly traded companies in the United States. The capital budgeting challenge faced by Pennzoil in 1988 was what to do with the $2.5 billion that it had left after paying $400 million in legal expenses and $100 million in taxes. Pennzoil had several options. One option was to put the money into Treasury bills, another option was to retire Pennzoil debt, a third option was to pay a one-time dividend of about $40, and a fourth option was to triple Pennzoil oil reserves through acquisitions. Of these four options, only the fourth provides the opportunity to avoid the large lump-sum tax penalty. The reason is that income from using the cash settlement to acquire oil and gas properties or similar assets would be taxed over the subsequent 20 or 30 years.

After scouting the economic landscape in general and the energy sector in particular, preparing various investment projects, and estimating the net present value and the internal rate of return of each, Pennzoil did a little of each of the above in 1989. It used $400 million to repurchase 5.3 million shares of its stock, raised the common stock dividend by 36 percent to $3 per share, and used nearly $2 billion of the remaining $2.2 billion (and the interest earned on the capital during 1988) to acquire an 8.8 percent stake in the Chevron Corporation (another petroleum company) to shelter it from taxes. Pennzoil argued that Chevron stock represented an investment in replacement property similar to that lost to Texaco and that such a property was, therefore, not to be treated as taxable property. The Internal Revenue Service (IRS), however, thought otherwise and Pennzoil finally settled at the end of 1994 by agreeing to pay $454 million ($265 million in additional taxes and $189 million in interest), or half of what the IRS had originally sought. Thus, comes to an end a 10-year investment-litigation saga.

Source: "A $3 Billion Question for Pennzoil," *The New York Times,* December 12, 1987, p. D1; "Problem Facing Pennzoil Company in Deciding Where to Invest," *The New York Times,* July 30, 1989, Sec. 3, p. 1; and "Pennzoil Agrees to Settle IRS's Texaco Claim," *The Wall Street Journal,* October 27, 1994, p. A4.

Case Study 14-4

Capital Budgeting for Investments in Human Capital

Expenditures on education, job training, migration to areas of better job opportunities, health, and so on are often referred to as "investments in human capital." As for other investments, these involve costs and provide returns. For example, college students incur out-of-pocket expenses or explicit costs for tuition, books, and living expenses and even larger implicit costs for the earnings foregone by attending college rather than working. A college education, however, also leads to higher lifetime earnings. Thus, the valuation model presented above can be used to determine the net present value of any investment in human capital, such as an investment in a college education.

Using the valuation model, it was estimated that the return to a college education was about 10 to 15 percent per year during the 1950s and the 1960s. This was substantially higher than the return on similarly risky investments (such as the purchase of a stock). Thus, getting a college education during the 1950s and 1960s, besides its intrinsic value, was also a good investment that made much economic sense. During the 1970s, however, and as a result of sharp tuition increases and lower starting salaries, the return to a college education declined to 7 or 8 percent per year. It rose somewhat during the 1980s and early 1990, except during the 1990–1991 recession.

These studies, however, face a number of statistical problems. For example, some of the expenditures included among the costs of attending college are more in the nature of consumption than investment (as, for example, when an engineering student takes a course in poetry). On the other hand, some of the higher lifetime earnings attributed to a college education may in fact result from the higher presumed intelligence of individuals attending college and would probably result even without a college education. There are then some benefits to a college education which are not easily measurable, such as college graduates suffering fewer mental problems, having happier marriages, and so on, than those without a college education. Despite these measurement difficulties, the concept and measurement of human capital is very important and commonly used (e.g., to determine damages to award to injury victims).

Source: Gary S. Becker, *Human Capital,* 2nd ed. (New York: Columbia University Press, 1975); Richard B. Freeman, "The Decline in the Economic Rewards to College Education," *The Review of Economics and Statistics,* February 1977, pp. 18–29; "The Soaring Payoff from Higher Education," *The Margin,* January/February 1990, p. 6; and "Schools Brief: Investing in People," *The Economist,* March 26, 1994, pp. 85–86.

14-3 CAPITAL RATIONING AND THE PROFITABILITY INDEX

We have seen in the previous section that in the case of mutually exclusive projects the *NPV* and the *IRR* methods may lead to contradictory investment signals. In that case the *NPV* method is generally preferable. Even the *NPV* investment rule, however, may lead to difficulties in the case of mutually exclusive investment projects of *unequal* size. That is, a smaller project may lead to a lower *NPV* than an alternative larger project, but the ratio of the present value of the net cash flows to the initial cost of the project (i.e., the profitability per dollar of investment) may be higher on the former than on the latter project.

In cases of capital rationing (i.e., when the firm cannot undertake all the projects with positive *NPV*), the firm should rank projects according to their profitability index and choose the projects with the highest profitability indexes rather than those with the highest *NPV*s. The **profitability index (*PI*)** of a project is measured by

$$PI = \frac{\sum_{t=1}^{n} [R_t/(1 + k)^t]}{C_0} \tag{14-3}$$

where R_t is the net cash flow in year t of the project, and C_0 is the initial cost of the project. With capital rationing, the firm should choose the projects with the highest relative profitability, or highest profitability per dollar of cost or investment (i.e., those whose *PI* exceeds 1 by the greatest amount) in order to avoid bias in favor of larger projects.

Table 14-3
Comparison of *NPV* and *PI* Rankings of Projects with Unequal Costs

	Project *A*	Project *B*	Project *C*
Present value of net cash flows (*PVNCF*)	\$2,600,000	\$1,400,000	\$1,400,000
Initial cost of project (C_0)	2,000,000	1,000,000	1,000,000
$NPV = PVNCF - C_0$	\$ 600,000	\$ 400,000	\$ 400,000
$PI = \frac{PVNCF}{C_0}$	1.3	1.4	1.4

For example, the data in Table 14-3 show that while project *A* has a higher *NPV* than either project *B* or *C* and would, therefore, be the only project undertaken according to the *NPV* investment rule if the firm could invest only \$2 million, the profitability indexes for projects *B* and *C* are greater than for project *A*, and the firm should undertake both of these projects instead of project *A*. That is, jointly, projects *B* and *C* increase the value of the firm by more than project *A*, but they would not be undertaken if the firm followed the *NPV* rule and could invest only \$2 million. While the above example is simplistic, it does show that with capital rationing, the profitability index or relative *NPV* rule may lead to a different *ranking* or order in which projects are to be undertaken. Of course, in the absence of capital rationing, the firm will undertake all projects with a positive *NPV* or profitability index larger than 1.

Capital rationing may arise for several reasons. First, undertaking all the projects with positive *NPV* may involve such rapid expansion as to strain the managerial, personnel, and other resources of the firm. As a result, top management may impose a limit on the number and size of the investment projects to be undertaken during a given period of time. Second, a firm may be reluctant to borrow heavily to supplement internal funds because of the risk to which the firm would be exposed in case of an unexpected economic downturn. Top management may also be reluctant to raise additional capital by selling stocks because of fear of losing control of the firm. Third, top management may arbitrarily limit the capital budget of its various divisions.

14-4 THE COST OF CAPITAL

In this section we examine how the firm estimates the cost of raising the capital to invest. As we have seen in Section 14-1, this is an essential element of the capital budgeting process. The firm can raise investment funds internally (i.e., from undistributed profits) or externally (i.e., by borrowing and from selling stocks). The cost of using internal funds is the opportunity cost or foregone return on these funds outside the firm. The cost of external funds is the lowest rate of return that lenders and stockholders require to lend to or invest their funds in the firm. In this section we examine how the cost of debt (i.e., the cost of raising capital by borrowing) and the cost of equity capital (i.e., the cost of raising capital by selling stocks) are determined. The estimation of the cost of debt is fairly straightforward. On the other hand, there are at least three methods of estimating the cost of equity capital. These are the risk-free rate plus premium, the dividend valuation model, and the capital asset pricing model (CAPM). These methods will be examined in turn. The estimation of the cost of capital to the firm is studied in detail in financial management courses. What follows is only an introduction to this topic.

The Cost of Debt

The **cost of debt** is the return that lenders require to lend their funds to the firm. Since the interest payments made by the firm on borrowed funds are deductible from the firm's taxable income, the *after-tax* cost of borrowed funds to the firm (k_d) is given by the interest paid (r) multiplied by 1 minus the firm's marginal tax rate, t. That is,

$$k_d = r(1 - t) \tag{14-4}$$

For example, if the firm borrows at a 12.5 percent interest rate and faces a 40 percent marginal tax rate on its taxable income, the after-tax cost of debt capital to the firm is

$$k_d = 12.5\%(1 - 0.40) = 7.5\%$$

To be noted is that if the firm has no taxable income after all costs are deducted during a particular year, the firm's after-tax cost of debt is equal to its pretax interest rate charged on borrowed funds. Also to be noted is that we are interested in the cost of new or marginal debt, not the average cost of debt, since it is the marginal cost of debt that is used to determine whether the firm should or should not undertake a particular investment project.

The Cost of Equity Capital: The Risk-Free Rate Plus Premium

As pointed out earlier, the cost of equity capital is the rate of return that stockholders require to invest in the firm. The cost of raising equity capital externally usually exceeds the cost of raising equity capital internally by the flotation costs (i.e., the cost of issuing the stock). For simplicity, we disregard these costs in the following analysis and treat both types of equity capital together. Since dividends paid on stocks (as opposed to the interest paid on bonds) are not deductible as a business expense (i.e., dividends are paid out after corporate taxes have been paid), there is no tax adjustment in determining the equity cost of capital.

One method employed to estimate the cost of equity capital (k_e) is to use the risk-free rate (r_f) plus a risk premium (r_p). That is,

$$k_e = r_f + r_p \tag{14-5}$$

The risk-free rate (r_f) is usually taken to be the six-month U.S. Treasury bill rate.[6] The reason for this is that the obligation to make payments of the interest and principal on government securities is assumed to occur with certainty. The risk

[6]Some security analysts prefer to use instead the long-term government bond rate for r_f.

premium (r_p) that must be paid in raising equity capital has two components. The first component results because of the greater risk that is involved in investing in a firm's securities (such as bonds) as opposed to investing in federal government securities. The second component is the additional risk resulting from purchasing the common stock rather than the bonds of the firm. Stocks involve a greater risk than bonds because dividends on stocks are paid only after the firm has met its contractual obligations to make interest and principal payments to bondholders. Since dividends vary with the firm's profits, stocks are more risky than bonds so that their return must include an additional risk premium. If the premiums associated with these two types of risk are labeled p_1 and p_2, we can restate the formula for the cost of equity capital as

$$k_e = r_f + p_1 + p_2 \tag{14-6}$$

The first type of risk (that is, p_1) is usually measured by the excess of the rate of interest on the firm's bonds (r) over the rate of return on government bonds (r_f). The additional risk involved in purchasing the firm's stocks rather than bonds (that is, p_2) is usually taken to be about 4 percentage points. This is the historical difference between the average yield (dividends plus capital gains) on stocks as opposed to the average yield on bonds issued by private companies. For example, if the risk-free rate of return on government securities is 8 percent and the firm's bonds yield 11 percent, the total risk premium (r_p) involved in purchasing the firm's stocks rather than government bonds is

$$r_p = p_1 + p_2 = (11\% - 8\%) + 4\% = 3\% + 4\% = 7\%$$

so that the firm's cost of equity capital is

$$k_e = r_f + p_1 + p_2 = 8\% + 3\% + 4\% = 15\%$$

The Cost of Equity Capital: The Dividend Valuation Model

The equity cost of capital to a firm can also be estimated by the **dividend valuation model.** To derive this model, we begin by pointing out that, with perfect information, the value of a share of the common stock of a firm should be equal to the present value of all future dividends expected to be paid on the stock, discounted at the investor's required rate of return (k_e). If the dividend per share (D) paid to stockholders is expected to remain constant over time, the present value of a share of the common stock of the firm (P) is then

$$P = \sum_{t=1}^{\infty} \frac{D}{(1 + k_e)^t} \tag{14-7}$$

If dividends are assumed to remain constant over time and to be paid indefinitely, Equation 14-7 is nothing else than an annuity (see Section A-4 in Appendix A at the end of the book) and can be rewritten as

$$P = \frac{D}{k_e} \tag{14-8}$$

If dividends are instead expected to increase over time at the annual rate of g, the price of a share of the common stock of the firm will be greater and is given by

$$P = \frac{D}{k_e - g} \tag{14-9}$$

Solving Equation 14-9 for k_e, we get the following equation to measure the equity cost of capital equation to the firm:

$$k_e = \frac{D}{P} + g \tag{14-10}$$

That is, the investor's required rate of return on equity is equal to the ratio of the dividend paid on a share of the common stock of the firm to the price of a share of the stock (the so-called dividend yield) plus the expected growth rate of dividend payments by the firm (g). The value of g is the firm's historic growth rate or the earnings growth forecasts of security analysts (based on the expected sales, profit margins, and competitive position of the firm) published in *Business Week, Forbes,* and other business publications.

For example, if the firm pays a dividend of \$20 per share on common stock that sells for \$200 per share and the growth rate of dividend payments is expected to be 5 percent per year, the cost of equity capital for this firm is

$$k_e = \frac{\$20}{\$200} + 0.05 = 0.10 + 0.05 = 0.15 \qquad \text{or } 15\%$$

The Cost of Equity Capital: The Capital Asset Pricing Model (CAPM)

Another method commonly used to estimate the equity cost of capital is the **capital asset pricing model** (CAPM). This takes into consideration not only the risk differential between common stocks and government securities but also the risk differential between the common stock of the firm and the average common stock of all firms or broad-based market portfolio. The risk differential between common stocks and government securities is measured by $(k_m - r_f)$, where k_m is the average return on all common stocks and r_f is the return on government securities.

The risk differential between the common stock of the firm and the common stock of all firms is given by the **beta coefficient (β)**. This is the ratio of the variability in the return on the common stock of the firm to the variability in the average return on the common stocks of all firms. Beta coefficients can be obtained by regressing the variability in the return of the stock of the firm on the variability in the average return of common stocks (as measured by the Standard & Poor's 500 Index or the New York Stock Exchange Index) over a given period of time. More commonly, beta coefficients for individual stocks are obtained from the Value Line Investment Survey, Merrill Lynch, or other brokerage firms.

A beta coefficient of 1 means that the variability in the returns on the common stock of the firm is the same as the variability in the returns on all stocks. Thus, investors holding the stock of the firm face the same risk as holding a broad-based market portfolio of all stocks. A beta coefficient of 2 means that the variability in the returns (i.e., risk of holding) on the stock of the firm is twice that of the average stock. On the other hand, holding a stock with a beta coefficient of 0.5 is half as risky as holding the average stock.

The cost of equity capital to the firm estimated by the capital asset pricing model (CAPM) is then measured by

$$k_e = r_f + \beta(k_m - r_f) \tag{14-11}$$

where k_e is the cost of equity capital to the firm, r_f is the risk-free rate, β is the beta coefficient, and k_m is the average return on the stock of all firms. Thus, the CAPM postulates that the cost of equity capital to the firm is equal to the sum of the risk-free rate plus the beta coefficient (β) times the risk premium on the average stock ($k_m - r_f$). Note that multiplying β by ($k_m - r_f$) gives the risk premium on holding the common stock of the particular firm.

For example, suppose that the risk-free rate (r_f) is 8 percent, the average return on common stocks (k_m) is 15 percent, and the beta coefficient (β) for the firm is 1. The cost of equity capital to the firm (k_e) is then

$$k_e = 8\% + 1(15\% - 8\%) = 15\%$$

That is, since a beta coefficient of 1 indicates that the stock of this firm is as risky as the average stock of all firms, the equity cost of capital to the firm is 15 percent (the same as the average return on all stocks). If $\beta = 1.5$ for the firm (so that the risk involved in holding the stock of the firm is 1.5 times larger than the risk on the average stock), the equity cost of capital to the firm would be

$$k_e = 8\% + 1.5(15\% - 8\%) = 18.5\%$$

On the other hand, if $\beta = 0.5$,

$$k_e = 8\% + 0.5(15\% - 8\%) = 11.5\%$$

In this example and in the examples using the risk-free rate plus premium and the dividend valuation model, the equity cost of capital was found to be the same (15 percent). This is seldom the case. That is, the different methods of estimating the equity cost of capital to a firm are likely to give somewhat different results. Firms are, thus, likely to use all three methods and then attempt to reconcile the differences and arrive at a consensus equity cost of capital for the firm.

The Weighted Cost of Capital

In general, a firm is likely to raise capital from undistributed profits, by borrowing, and by the sale of stocks, and so the marginal cost of capital to the firm is a weighted average of the cost of raising the various types of capital. Since the interest paid on borrowed funds is tax deductible while the dividends paid on stocks are not, the cost of debt is generally less than the cost of equity capital. The risk involved in raising funds by borrowing, however, is greater than the risk on equity capital because the firm must regularly make payments of the interest and principal on borrowed funds before paying dividends on stocks. Thus, firms do not generally raise funds only by borrowing but also by selling stock (as well as from undistributed profits).

Firms often try to maintain or achieve a particular long-term capital structure of debt to equity. For example, public utility companies may prefer a capital structure involving 60 percent debt and 40 percent equity, while auto manufacturers may prefer 30 percent debt and 70 percent equity. The particular debt/equity ratio that a firm prefers reflects the risk preference of its managers and stockholders and the nature of the firm's business. Public utilities accept the higher risk involved in a higher debt/equity ratio because of their more stable flow of earnings than automobile manufacturers. When a firm needs to raise investment capital, it borrows and sells stocks so as to maintain or achieve a desired debt/equity ratio.

The **composite cost of capital** to the firm (k_c) is then a weighted average of the cost of debt capital (k_d) and equity capital (k_e) as given by

$$k_c = w_d k_d + w_e k_e \tag{14-12}$$

where w_d and w_e are, respectively, the proportion of debt and equity capital in the firm's capital structure. For example, if the (after-tax) cost of debt is 7.5 percent, the cost of equity capital is 15 percent, and the firm wants to have a debt/equity ratio of 40:60, the composite or weighted marginal cost of capital to the firm will be

$$k_c = (0.40)(7.5\%) + (0.60)(15\%) = 3\% + 9\% = 12\%$$

This is the composite marginal cost of capital that we have used to evaluate all the proposed investment projects that the firm faced in Section 14-1 and Figure 14-1. That is, the proportion of debt to equity that the firm seeks to achieve or maintain in the long run is not usually defined for individual projects but for all the investment projects that the firm is considering. Note that the marginal cost of capital eventually rises (i.e., the *MCC* curve in Figure 14-1 becomes positively sloped) as the firm raises additional amounts of capital by borrowing and selling stocks because of the higher risk that lenders and investors face as the firm's debt/equity ratio rises.

Case Study 14-5

The Choice Between Equity and Debt

In a 1982 study published in *The Journal of Finance,* Paul Marsh used regression analysis to identify and determine the relative importance of the factors that influence firms' decisions to raise new capital by debt or equity. The author used data on 748 issues of debt and equity made by U.K. companies over the 1959 through 1970 period. The author found that (1) companies which are below their long-term debt targets are more likely to issue debt than equity; (2) smaller companies, those with few fixed assets, and those facing a greater risk of bankruptcy are more likely to issue equity than debt; (3) firms which have recently experienced unusually large increases in the value of their stocks tend to favor equity over debt; and (4) firms are more likely to issue equity than debt after periods of strong stock market performance, while they are more likely to issue debt than equity when interest rates are low and are expected to increase in the future. The author then tested the predictive ability of the model using a sample of 110 debt and equity issues made by U.K. companies between 1971 and 1974. The author found that the model classified 75 percent of the new issues correctly between debt and equity over the 1971 through 1974 period.

The above results seem to hold for the United States during the 1980s and early 1990s. Specifically, the U.S. companies that borrowed the most during the 1980s tended to be those that could best afford it. Furthermore, heavy borrowing during the 1980s does not seem to have itself reduced the international competitiveness of U.S. firms in comparison with their overseas rivals. The international competitiveness battle is not necessarily won by those who are less heavily leveraged but by those who are more productive—and debt can be a tool for increasing productivity.

Source: Paul Marsh, "The Choice Between Equity and Debt: An Empirical Study," *Journal of Finance,* March 1982, pp. 121–144; and "Don't Be Afraid of the Big Bad Debt," *Fortune,* April 22, 1991, pp. 121–128.

14-5 REVIEWING INVESTMENT PROJECTS AFTER IMPLEMENTATION

It is very important to review projects after they have been implemented. Such a review involves comparing the actual cash flow and return from a project with the expected or predicted cash flow and return on the project, as well as an explanation of the observed differences between predicted and actual results. In reviewing projects after their implementation, it is important, however, to recognize that some differences between predicted or estimated and actual results are to some extent inevitable in view of the uncertainty surrounding future cash flows. Some differences between predicted and actual results may also be due to entirely unforeseen events (such as the sharp increase in petroleum prices that occurred in the fall of 1973 and again in 1979) over which a firm has no control.

Comparing and explaining differences between the predicted and the actual results of an investment project after its implementation is, nevertheless, very useful. The reason is that if decision makers know that their investment projects will be reviewed and evaluated after implementation and compared with predicted outcomes, they are likely to draw up investment plans more carefully and also to work harder to ensure that their predictions are in fact fulfilled. It has been found, for example, that the best-run companies are those that place great importance on *postaudits* and that decision makers' estimates improve when they know that postaudit reviews are routinely conducted. Postaudit reviews must be used carefully, however, to avoid discouraging decision makers from proposing very risky but potentially very profitable investment projects.

Case Study 14-6
Capital Budgeting Techniques of Major U.S. Firms

Table 14-4 gives the result of a survey conducted on the capital budgeting techniques used by major U.S. firms in 1959 and in 1985. The firms surveyed could choose among the following capital budgeting techniques: net present value, internal rate of return, payback period, or other method. The first two methods (discussed in Section 14-2) are sophisticated in the sense that they consider the time value of money, while the third (i.e., the payback period) is unsophisticated because it simply involves the estimation of the number of years it takes for the project to generate enough revenue to fully cover the cost of the project, without discounting. The "other" methods used were also unsophisticated.

The table shows that 21 percent of firms surveyed used the net present value as their primary capital budgeting evaluating method in 1985 (up from 7 percent in 1959), 49 percent used the internal rate of return in 1985 (up from practically zero in 1959), 19 percent used the payback method in 1985 (down from 42 percent in 1959), and 11 percent used some other unsophisticated method in 1985 (down from 51 in 1959). Thus, in 1985, 70 percent of the firms surveyed used either the net present value or the internal rate of return as their primary capital budgeting evaluating method while the remaining 30 percent used either the payback period or some other unsophisticated method. This is to be contrasted with 93 percent of the firms surveyed using the payback period or other unsophisticated method as their primary evaluating method in 1959.

As far as their secondary evaluating method, 24 percent of the firms used the net present value in 1985 (up from 1 percent in 1959), 15 percent used the internal rate of return in 1985 (up from 1 percent in 1959), 35 percent used the payback period (up from 15 percent in 1959), and 26 percent used some other method (down from 85 percent in 1959). Thus, aside from the increase in the use of the payback period as the secondary evaluating method from 1959 to 1985, the capital budgeting evaluating method used by U.S. firms became much more sophisticated over time by the inclusion of the time value of money in the calculation, especially in the primary evaluating method used.

Table 14-4
Capital Budgeting Techniques Used (percent of respondents)

Primary Evaluating Method	1959	1985
Net present value	7	21
Internal rate of return	—	49
Payback period	42	19
Other	51	11

Secondary Evaluating Method	1959	1985
Net present value	1	24
Internal rate of return	1	15
Payback period	15	35
Other	82	26

Source: Suk H. Kim, Trevor Crick, and Seung H. Kim, "Do Executives Practice What Academics Preach?" *Management Accounting,* November 1986, pp. 49–52.

14-6 THE COST OF CAPITAL AND INTERNATIONAL COMPETITIVENESS

During most of the 1980s, the cost of capital was much higher in the United States than in Japan and in many other major industrial nations, and this was one of the factors that undermined the international competitiveness of U.S. firms during this period. Having to pay even one additional percentage point in interest charges to borrow money could add hundreds of thousands or even millions of dollars to the capital cost of a large firm and undermines its ability to compete both at home and abroad with foreign firms facing lower interest charges.[7] Table 14-5 shows the average nominal and real (i.e., inflation-adjusted) lending rates charged by banks for short- and medium-term loans to the private sector in the United States and Japan from 1981 to 1993. Japan is now the main competitor of the United States in most high-tech goods both at home and around the world. Long-term lending rates are related to short- and medium-term rates and generally move in tandem with them.

Table 14-5 shows that nominal lending rates were higher in the United States than in Japan in every year from 1981 to 1993. Real (i.e., inflation-adjusted) lending rates where higher from 1981 to 1984 and this was the period of greatest loss of U.S. international competitiveness to Japan. While there were other forces at work, the higher cost of capital in the United States relative to Japan was certainly one important contributing factor. Since 1985, U.S.–Japanese real lending rate differentials were mixed and U.S. firms recaptured some of the competitiveness that they had lost during the early 1980s.

[7]To be noted is that Japanese firms, just like their U.S. counterparts, borrowed heavily during the 1980s. Thus, it was the higher real cost of capital rather than the borrowing itself that undermined the international competitiveness of U.S. firms vis-à-vis Japanese firms during the 1980s.

Table 14-5
Real and Nominal Bank Lending Rates in the United States and Japan (in percentages per year: 1981–1989)

	United States			Japan			U.S.–Japanese Differentials	
Year	Nominal	CPI*	Real	Nominal	CPI	Real	Nominal	Real
1981	18.9	10.3	8.6	7.9	4.9	3.0	11.0	5.6
1982	14.9	6.2	8.7	7.3	2.7	4.6	7.6	4.1
1983	10.8	3.2	7.6	7.1	1.9	5.2	3.7	2.4
1984	12.0	4.3	7.7	6.8	2.2	4.5	5.2	3.2
1985	9.9	3.6	3.3	6.6	2.0	4.6	3.3	−1.3
1986	8.4	1.9	6.5	6.0	0.6	5.4	2.4	1.1
1987	8.2	3.7	4.5	5.2	0.1	5.2	3.0	−0.7
1988	9.3	4.0	5.3	5.0	0.7	4.3	4.3	1.0
1989	10.9	4.8	6.1	5.3	2.3	3.0	5.6	3.1
1990	10.1	5.4	4.7	7.0	3.1	3.9	3.1	0.8
1991	8.5	4.2	4.3	7.5	3.3	4.2	1.0	0.1
1992	6.3	3.0	3.3	6.2	1.7	4.5	0.1	−1.3
1993	6.0	3.0	3.0	4.4	1.3	3.1	1.6	−0.1

*CPI refers to the consumer price index as a measure of the rate of inflation.
Source: IMF, *International Financial Statistics Yearbook* (Washington, D.C.: IMF, 1994).

The reason for higher nominal and real interest or lending rates in the United States than in Japan is the much higher saving rates in Japan than in the United States. With the demand for borrowing higher in the United States than in Japan relative to the supply of loanable funds available in each nation, it should not be surprising that interest rates were higher in the former than in the latter. One of the reasons for the higher demand for borrowing in the United States was the huge federal budget deficit that the United States faced during the entire period of the 1980s. Indeed, without a huge inflow of loanable funds from other nations (especially Japan), interest rates would have been much higher. In order to continue to attract the huge capital inflow to finance the large budget deficit, however, interest rates had to remain somewhat above their level in Japan and other large industrial nations. Higher interest rates also required somewhat higher returns on stock to attract domestic and foreign equity capital. In addition, higher interest rates in the United States kept the international value of the dollar higher than it would otherwise have been and thus further contributed to the loss of international competitiveness of U.S. firms.

Conditions seem to have changed drastically since 1990, however, when the cost of capital in Japan increased so sharply as to eliminate for the most part the advantage that Japanese firms had enjoyed over American firms during the 1980s. While it is too soon to say, many in Japan believe that the days of extremely low-cost capital are over in Japan. If this turns out to be true it will lead to a more level playing field in international competition between U.S. and Japanese firms. Interest rates have also risen in Germany (the other main competitor of the United States) relative to the United States since 1990 in order to finance the rebuilding of East Germany.

SUMMARY

1. In this chapter we examined capital budgeting. This refers to the process of planning expenditures that give rise to revenues or returns over a number of years. Investment projects can be undertaken to replace worn-out equipment, reduce costs, expand output of traditional products in traditional markets, expand into new products and/or markets, or meet government regulations. The firm's profitability, growth, and its very survival in the long run depend on how well management accomplishes these tasks. Capital budgeting integrates the operation of all the major divisions of the firm. The basic principle involved in capital budgeting is for the firm to undertake additional investment projects until the marginal return from the investment is equal to its marginal cost.

2. The net cash flow from a project is the difference between cash receipts and cash expenditures over the life of a project. Net cash flows should be measured on an incremental and after-tax basis, and depreciation charges should be used only to calculate taxes. A firm should undertake a project only if the net present value (*NPV*) of the project is positive. The *NPV* is equal to the present value of the estimated stream of net cash flows from the project,

discounted at the firm's cost of capital, minus the initial cost of the project. Alternatively, the project should be undertaken only if the internal rate of return (*IRR*) on the project exceeds the cost of capital to the firm. The *IRR* is the rate of discount that equates the present value of the net cash flows from the project to the initial cost of the project. For a single or independent project, the *NPV* and *IRR* methods will always lead to the same accept-reject investment decision. For mutually exclusive projects, however, they may provide contradictory signals. In that case the project with the higher *NPV* should be chosen.

3. In cases of capital rationing (i.e., when the firm cannot undertake all the projects with positive *NPV*), the firm should rank projects according to their relative profitability rather than according to their *NPV*. The profitability index (*PI*) of a project is measured by the ratio of the present value of the net cash flows from a project to the cost of the investment. Capital rationing may be imposed by top management to avoid overexpansion, overborrowing, and possibly losing control of the firm by selling more stocks to raise additional capital.
4. A firm can raise investment funds internally or externally. The cost of using internal funds is the foregone return on these funds outside the firm. The cost of external funds is the rate of return that lenders and stockholders require to lend or invest funds in the firm. Since interest paid on borrowed funds is tax deductible, the after-tax cost of borrowed funds is given by the interest paid times 1 minus the firm's marginal tax rate. The cost of equity capital can be measured by (1) the risk-free rate plus a risk premium for holding the firm's stock rather than government bonds; (2) the dividend per share of the stock divided by the price of the stock, plus the expected growth rate of dividend payments; and (3) the risk-free rate plus the beta coefficient (β) times the risk premium on the average stock. This last named is the capital asset pricing model (CAPM). β is the ratio of the variability on the return on the stock of the firm to the variability in the average return on all stocks. Firms generally use more than one method to estimate the equity cost of capital. The composite cost of capital is the weighted average of the cost of debt and equity capital.
5. It is very important to review projects after they have been implemented. Such a review involves comparing the actual cash flow and return from the project with the expected or predicted cash flow and return, as well as an explanation of the observed differences between predicted and actual results. This is useful because if decision makers know that their investment projects will be evaluated, they are likely to draw up investment plans more carefully and to work harder to ensure that their predictions are in fact fulfilled.
6. During most of the 1980s, the cost of capital was much higher in the United States than in Japan and in many other major industrial nations, and this was one of the factors that undermined the international competitiveness of U.S. firms during this period. Higher interest rates also required somewhat higher returns on stock to attract domestic and foreign equity capital. It also

kept the international value of the dollar higher than it would otherwise have been and thus further contributed to the loss of international competitiveness of U.S. firms. During the early 1990s, however, interest rates rose faster in Japan and Germany, thus reducing or eliminating this competitive disadvantage of U.S. firms.

DISCUSSION QUESTIONS

1. In what way can it be said that capital budgeting is nothing more than the application of the theory of the firm to investment projects?
2. What general guidelines should a firm follow in properly estimating the net cash flow from an investment?
3. (*a*) What is the difference between the profit flow and the cash flow from an investment project? (*b*) Why do firms use the net cash flow to estimate the net present value of a project?
4. (*a*) How are depreciation charges taken into consideration in estimating the net cash flow from a project? (*b*) Why?
5. (*a*) What effect does the use of a higher risk-adjusted discount rate have on the net present value of a project? (*b*) Why?
6. What is the relationship between the *NPV* and the *IRR* methods of evaluating investment projects?
7. (*a*) When can the *NPV* and the *IRR* methods of evaluating investment projects provide contradictory results? (*b*) How can this arise? (*c*) Which method should then be used? Why?
8. (*a*) Why might a firm face capital rationing? (*b*) What investment criteria should the firm follow when it faces capital rationing? (*c*) Why?
9. Explain (*a*) why the cost of debt capital is usually lower than equity capital to the firm and (*b*) why firms do not rely exclusively on debt financing.
10. (*a*) How can a firm raise equity capital internally? (*b*) What is the cost to the firm of this type of capital? (*c*) Must the firm pay dividends to raise equity capital internally or externally? (*d*) Why is internal equity capital generally less costly to the firm than external equity capital?
11. (*a*) Why are government securities taken to be risk free? What is used as the risk-free rate? (*b*) What additional risks do the stockholders of a firm face in comparison to holders of government securities? (*c*) Why do different firms choose different debt/equity ratios?
12. (*a*) Why is the marginal cost schedule of most firms upward sloping? (*b*) What is the relationship between the cost of capital and public utility regulation?
13. In what ways do higher interest rates in the United States than abroad interfere with the international competitiveness of U.S. firms?

PROBLEMS

*1. As a result of a great deal of analysis and input from its various divisions, the Computer Software Corporation has concluded that it can undertake the projects indicated in the following table, and it has estimated that it could raise $2.5 million of capital at the rate (cost) of 9 percent, an additional $3 million at 12 percent, and another $3.5 million at 16 percent. Draw a figure to show which projects the firm should undertake and which it should not.

Capital Projects	Required Investment (millions)	Rate of Return
A	$1.0	18%
B	2.0	16
C	1.5	13
D	2.5	11
E	2.0	9

2. (*a*) Redraw Figure 14-1, and draw on it a smooth curve approximating the firm's demand curve for capital and marginal cost curve of capital. (*b*) Under what conditions would these smooth curves hold? (*c*) How much would the firm invest with these smooth curves? What would be the return on and cost of the last dollar invested?

*3. Show the calculations needed to estimate the net present value of the project discussed in Section 14-2 and Table 14-1 if the firm uses the risk-adjusted discount rate of (*a*) 10 percent and (*b*) 20 percent. (*c*) By how much would the value of the firm increase if the firm uses the risk-adjusted discount rates of 10 percent and 20 percent?

4. Gregory Burton, the manager of the Toybest Company, would like to introduce a new toy, and he has received the following estimates of costs and sales from the various divisions of the firm. The cost of purchasing, delivering, and installing the new machinery that is required to manufacture the toy is estimated to be $10 million. The expected life of the toy is four years. Incremental sales revenues are estimated to be $10 million in the first year of operation, are expected to rise by 20 percent in the second year and another 20 percent in the third year, but they are expected to remain unchanged in the fourth and final year. The incremental variable costs of producing the toy are estimated to be 40 percent of incremental sales revenues. The firm is also expected to incur additional fixed costs of $1 million per year. The marginal tax rate of the firm is 40 percent. The firm uses the straight-line depreciation method. The machinery purchased will have no salvage value but the firm is expected to recuperate $1.5 million of its working capital at the end of the four years. (*a*) Construct a table similar to Table 14-1 summarizing the cash flows from the project. (*b*) Calculate the net present value of the project if the firm uses the risk-adjusted discount rate of 20 percent. (*c*) Should the firm undertake the project? If so, by how much would the value of the firm increase?

*5. Suppose that the net cash flow from the investment project of Problem 4 is \$5 million in each year and the firm does not recover any working capital at the end of the four years. Use Table B-4 in Appendix B at the end of the book to determine whether the firm should undertake the project if the firm uses the risk-adjusted discount rate of 20 percent.

6. Determine the internal rate of return for the project of Problem 4.

7. The Cosmetics Company has to decide whether to introduce beauty cream *A* or beauty cream *B* on the market. The initial cost of introducing each cream is \$1 million and the net cash flows generated by each are indicated in the following table. Using the discount rate of 10 percent, determine (*a*) the net present value and (*b*) the internal rate of return on investment projects *A* and *B*. (*c*) Which project (cream) should the firm undertake? Why?

NET PRESENT VALUE AND INTERNAL RATE OF RETURN ON TWO MUTUALLY EXCLUSIVE INVESTMENT PROJECTS

	Project *A*	Project *B*
Initial cost	\$1,000,000	\$1,000,000
Net cash flows (years)		
Year 1	300,000	−100,000
Year 2	300,000	10,000
Year 3	300,000	300,000
Year 4	300,000	300,000
Year 5	300,000	1,400,000

8. John Piderit, the general manager of the Western Tool Company, is considering introducing some new tools to the company's product line. The top management of the firm has identified three types of tools (referred to as projects *A*, *B*, and *C*). The various divisions of the firm have provided the data given in the following table on these three possible projects. The company has a limited capital budget of \$2.4 million for the coming year. (*a*) Which project(s) would the firm undertake if it used the *NPV* investment criterion? (*b*) Is this the correct decision? Why?

	Project *A*	Project *B*	Project *C*
Present value of net cash flows (*PVNCF*)	\$3,000,000	\$1,750,000	\$1,400,000
Initial cost of project (C_0)	2,400,000	1,300,000	1,100,000

9. The Optical Instruments Corporation can sell bonds at an interest rate of 9 percent. The interest rate on government securities is 7 percent. Calculate the cost of equity capital for this firm.

10. The MacBurger Company, a chain of fast-food restaurants, expects to earn \$200 million after taxes for the current year. The company has a policy of paying out half of its net after-tax income to the holders of the company's 100 million shares of common stock. A share of the common stock of the

company currently sells for eight times current earnings. Management and outside analysts expect the growth rate of earnings and dividends for the company to be 7.5 percent per year. Calculate the cost of equity capital to this firm.

*11. Suppose that the Eldridge Manufacturing Company pays an interest rate of 11 percent on its bonds, the marginal income tax rate that the firm faces is 40 percent, the rate on government bonds is 7.5 percent, the return on the average stock of all firms in the market is 11.55 percent, the estimated beta coefficient for the common stock of the firm is 2, and the firm wishes to raise 40 percent of its capital by borrowing. Determine (*a*) the cost of debt, (*b*) the cost of equity capital, and (*c*) the composite cost of capital for this firm.

12. **Integrating Problem**
The Laundromat Corporation is considering opening another coin-operated laundry in a city. It has estimated that opening the laundry would involve an initial cost of $100,000 and would generate a net cash flow of $32,000 in each of five years, with no salvage value for the equipment and no recovery of operating expenses at the end of the five years. The corporation estimates that it would have to pay a rate of interest of 12 percent on its bonds and that it would face a marginal income tax rate of 40 percent. The interest on government securities is 10 percent. During the current year, the corporation expects to pay a dividend of $20 dollars on each share of its common stock, which sells for 10 times current earnings. Management and outside analysts expect the growth rate of earnings and dividends of the corporation to be 7 percent per year. The return on the average stock of all firms in the market is 14 percent, and the estimated beta coefficient for the common stock of the corporation is 1.25. The corporation wants to maintain a capital structure of 30 percent debt. Determine (*a*) the internal rate of return for the proposed project, (*b*) the cost of debt for the corporation, (*c*) the cost of equity capital by the risk-free rate plus premium method, (*d*) the cost of equity capital by the dividend valuation model, (*e*) the cost of equity capital by the capital asset pricing model, (*f*) the composite cost of capital if the firm uses the average of the cost of equity capital determined by each of the three methods, and (*g*) whether or not the corporation should undertake the project.

SUPPLEMENTARY READINGS

For a problem-solving approach to capital budgeting, see:

Salvatore, Dominick: *Theory and Problems of Managerial Economics,* Schaum Outline Series (New York: McGraw-Hill, 1989), Secs. 1–3.

A general discussion of capital budgeting is found in:

Bierman, H., and **S. Smidt:** *The Capital Budgeting Decision* (New York: Macmillan, 1988).

Kwan, Clarence, and **Yufei Yuan:** "Optimal Sequential Selection in Capital Budgeting: A Shortcut," *Financial Management,* Spring 1988, pp. 54–59.

Miller, Edward M.: "The Competitive Market Assumption and Capital Budgeting Criteria," *Financial Management,* Winter 1987, pp. 22–28.

Mukherjee, Tarun K., and **Glenn V. Henderson:** "The Capital Budgeting Process: Theory and Practice," *Interfaces,* March–April 1987, pp. 78–90.

Ross, Marc: "Capital Budgeting Practices of Twelve Large Manufacturers," *Financial Management,* Winter 1986, pp. 15–22.

Howarth, R. B., and **R. B. Norgaard:** "Environmental Valuation under Sustainable Development," *American Economic Review,* May 1992, pp. 473–477.

The cost of capital is examined in:

Modigliani, F., and **M. H. Miller:** "The Cost of Capital, Corporation Finance and the Theory of Investment," *American Economic Review,* June 1958, pp. 261–297.

Markowitz, H. M.: "Portfolio Selection," *Journal of Finance,* March 1952, pp. 77–91.

Fisher, L., and **J. H. Lorie:** "Rates of Return on Investments in Common Stock: 1926–1965," *Journal of Business,* July 1968, pp. 291–316.

Harris, R. S.: "Using Analysts' Growth Forecasts to Estimate Shareholder Required Rates of Return," *Financial Management,* Spring 1986, pp. 58–67.

Sick, Gordon A.: "A Certainty-Equivalent Approach to Capital Budgeting," *Financial Management,* Winter 1986, pp. 23–32.

Harris, M., and **A. Raviv:** "The Theory of Capital Structure," *Journal of Finance,* March 1991, pp. 297–355.

Talmor, E., and **H. E. Thompson:** "Technology, Dependent Investments, and Discounting Rules for Corporate Investment Decisions," *Managerial and Decision Economics,* March–April 1992, pp. 101–109.

For the presentation and evaluation of the capital asset pricing model, see:

Levy, H.: "The Capital Asset Pricing Model," *The Economic Journal,* March 1983, pp. 145–165.

Ross, S.: "The Current Status of the Capital Asset Pricing Model," *Journal of Finance,* June 1982, pp. 895–901.

Shanken, J.: "The Arbitrage Pricing Model: Is It Testable?" *Journal of Finance,* December 1982, pp. 1129–1140.

For the effect of international interest rate differentials on international competitiveness see:

Madura, Jeff: *International Financial Management* (St. Paul: West Publishing, 1989), Chap. 1.

Salvatore, Dominick: *International Economics,* 5th ed. (Englewood Cliffs, N.J.: Prentice-Hall, 1995), Chaps. 14 and 19.

INTEGRATING CASE STUDY FIVE

Regulation, Risk, Capital Budgeting, and the Price of International Telephone Calls

Introductory Comment The following selection illustrates how regulation of international telephone services around the world keeps rates on international telephone services higher than in the United States and what AT&T is doing to force a reduction in those rates. This integrating case shows how regulation, risk, capital budgeting, and the pricing of international telephone services are interrelated, and thus it serves as an excellent integrating case study.

In Italy, hundreds of times each day, American tourists venture into public phone booths and get ripped off—not by criminals but by the Società Italiana per l'Esercizio delle Telecommunicazioni, Italy's state-owned telephone monopoly. The Italian government administers one of the developed world's shoddiest public phone systems, with delapidated equipment and interminable customer delays. Worse, it charges extortionate rates. A peak-time call of five minutes from Venice to Chicago costs $14, more than double the cost of making the same connection using AT&T in the opposite direction. This scandalous situation is not unique to Italy. State-owned phone monopolies still rule everywhere in continental Europe, and everywhere they gouge the consumer for the benefit of the bureaucrats: The European telephone systems are vast patronage machines. To dramatically lower rates and introduce more modern digital switching would mean, as it did at AT&T, cutting many jobs.

Free enterprise to the rescue in the form of America's AT&T, the unlikely trustbuster. The U.S. communications giant has learned one lesson exceptionally well since divestiture in 1984: that cutting rates increases traffic, which leads to higher profits. Explains Chairman Robert Allen: "We have found out in very dramatic ways that as rates come down, usage goes up, and this then leads to demand for more features and more applications." Since divestiture, AT&T's international and domestic long-distance rates have fallen by 40 percent and more, while gross profit margins from its telecommunications business—primarily long-distance services—have risen steadily from 47 percent in 1985 to 62 percent in 1989, its last reporting year. The volume of international traffic from the United States is rising by about 20 percent per year. For the telephone business, that is little less than spectacular when compared with 10 percent growth in the domestic long-distance market and virtually zero growth in local calls.

To handle all the new traffic, AT&T has been investing heavily. It is spending over $150 million a year on new seabed fiber cabling, doubling its call-handling capacity to Europe in 1991. A new $400 million transatlantic fiber cable can handle 80,000 calls simultaneously. Using just half that capacity while billing the calls at 1 cent per minute, an operator could recover the investment in two years. To be sure, there are other costs besides amortizing the cable, but the 1-cent figure gives you some idea of what kind of markups are built into your $3-a-minute call from Milan. As it is in the United States, AT&T in Europe is resigned to the fact that it must pay some tribute to the local telephone company to gain "access" to the customer. But it thinks current access charges are way out of line. Not surprisingly, AT&T ran into a brick wall when it tried to persuade each European phone company to cut the wholesale rate it charges AT&T to complete calls on its network. So backward are the telephone companies in continental Europe that they do not even price their services as intelligent monopolists would. A greedy monopolist would offer discounts for night calling to draw in new traffic at next to zero marginal cost. Yet Germany, Belgium, Switzerland, and Denmark, to name just a few, have no night discounts for transatlantic calls.

So it is going to be an uphill battle for AT&T's monopoly-busting. In the meantime, transatlantic telephone service will continue as a sort of grant-in-aid by U.S. consumers to European governments. Here's what happens now: Because rates from Europe to the United States are on average 30 percent higher than rates going the other way, far more transatlantic calls originate here than there. In 1989, for example, the United States sent 350 million minutes of calls to West Germany while taking only 150 million minutes going the other way. For the 200-million-minute difference, U.S. long-distance companies sent off a check to the German telephone monopoly for $167 million. This compensation, figured at 80 cents a minute, is far in excess of Germany's true cost of completing the calls. Thus, the U.S. consumer is subsidizing Germany. Happily, AT&T has an ally in the U.S. Federal Communications Commission, which has been applying heavy pressure on the European governments over the last year. After much stalling, the Germans finally got the message and agreed, later this year, to cut wholesale rates by 17 percent, from $1.60 a minute to $1.33. (The compensation rate is half that; retail rates are much higher.)

AT&T is now asking the FCC to assist by threatening to use tougher and riskier tactics. If any nation were too recalcitrant in cutting long-distance charges, then the FCC would unilaterally chop the per-minute compensation. The foreign telephone monopoly would start getting smaller checks, like them or lump them. The FCC has not decided whether to attempt this tactic. While AT&T continues its frontal assault on rates, it has quietly dropped a few parachutists behind enemy lines. With the permission of the local monopolists, it is offering discounted, U.S.-like rates on certain calls originating in Europe. The battle plan seems to be this: Offer the rates initially only to Americans traveling abroad and to Europeans calling certain U.S. corporations, so that the local telephone ministry does not feel threatened. Then wait for word to leak out to Europeans about what a great deal they are missing. At that point the local bureaucrats may find themselves fighting an insurrection at home as well as an invasion from abroad.

One way AT&T offers cheaper rates is through its international toll-free 800 service. An employee in Dusseldorf can call headquarters in Los Angeles via an

800 number and cut as much as 40 percent off the cost of calling through the German network. Traffic has tripled in two years. Another way AT&T is offering cut-price international service is through its USA Direct service, aimed mainly at individuals. USA Direct allows anyone traveling abroad to pick up a phone, dial a local access number, and patch through to an AT&T operator, who completes the call to the United States. That five-minute call from Venice to Chicago for which the Italian government charges $14 costs just $11 collect or $8 on the AT&T card. Last year USA Direct accounted for over $200 million in calls. MCI is introducing a similar service. To get the European phone companies to allow toll-free connections to USA Direct and the international 800 service, AT&T had to agree not to market directly to Europeans. But it didn't promise to keep the terrific rates for Americans a state secret. "Europeans are starting to demand more openness and competition," says Chairman Allen. "This can only benefit AT&T."

On the equipment side, AT&T's great strength, both in the United States and Europe, is not its vaunted 5ESS digital switch, which is little more than a giant computer, but rather the proprietary software that makes possible services like 800 and 900 numbers, call forwarding, telemarketing, and teleconferencing—all the stuff of dreams in much of Europe. Fully 40 percent of the engineers working at Bell Labs are engaged in writing software. The European equipment makers are so worried that Pierre Suard, chief executive of France's giant Alcatel N.V., is enlisting European executives to band together to fight AT&T's growth in Europe. Telefónica de España S.A., Spain's largest telecommunications manufacturer, told Suard to get lost, but Italy's Telettra S.P.A. recently agreed to swap shares with Alcatel to fortify a defensive cartel. "This approach by Alcatel flies in the face of free trade and of Europe 1992," says Allen. "They are fighting an inevitable trend. We know the European market and know we will be able to win there."

Allen goes on to say, with evident relish, that AT&T's opportunities abroad are "virtually limitless." From almost a standing start in 1984, AT&T's international revenues doubled, to $6 billion last year, or 17 percent of total revenues. Within a decade, Allen says, AT&T should be earning half its revenues outside the United States. And in the process of making itself rich, it will benefit many a European and U.S. consumer.

Concluding Remarks

Pressure is now mounting to dismantle the legal OPEC-like cartel by which national telecommunications companies have cooperated until now to keep the price of international telephone calls very high and far above actual costs. For one thing, AT&T on this side of the Atlantic and British Telecom in Europe are creeping into continental European markets with lower rates. Secondly, European corporations, which now pay from two to three times more than American and British corporations for international phone services, are now clamoring for lower rates. In response to these pressures and as a result of rapidly changing technology, the European Commission decided in 1994 to open the international telephone market to competition throughout the European Union by 1998. Governments have already started privatizing their national telephone companies through stock sales—the largest to which will be that of Germany's Deutsche Bundespost Telekom (DBT) in 1996. From 1995 to 1998, $55 billion in telecommunications stock sales are expected across Europe. The process, however, is likely to be long and difficult. The major European telephone companies are now rushing to form alliances with other European and American telephone companies. Eventually, this could trigger massive consolidations around four or five telephone superpowers: AT&T and its WorldPartners alliance; the British Telecom and American MCI alliance; the French Telecom, DBT, and American Sprint group; Unisource—the alliance among the Dutch, Swedish, and Swiss phone companies; and Japan's NTT. As these alliances take shape, price wars will be inevitable and are likely to result in sharply lower prices for international telephone calls.

Source: "An Unlikely Trustbuster," *Forbes,* February 18, 1991, pp. 100–104. Reprinted by permission of *Forbes* Magazine. "The Global Free for All," *Business Week,* September 26, 1994, pp. 118–126; "Sky-High Overseas Phone Bills May Drop," *The Wall Street Journal,* September 20, 1994, p. B2; "European Phone Companies Reach Out for Partners," *The Wall Street Journal,* November 30, 1994, p. B4; and "Europe Begins Liberalizing Phone Sector," *The Wall Street Journal,* December 5, 1994, p. A9F.

Appendixes

APPENDIX A

Compounding Discounting, and Present Value

In this appendix, we examine compounding, discounting, and the present value of money. These concepts are widely used in all aspects of business and economics and especially in managerial economics. Specifically, it is important to recognize that \$1 received today is worth more than \$1 received next year because \$1 deposited in a bank today will earn interest and grow to more than \$1 by the end of the year. Similarly, \$1 received next year is worth less than \$1 received today because an amount less than \$1 deposited in a bank today will grow (with the interest earned) to \$1 by the end of the year. This is often referred to as the *time value of money.*

A-1 FUTURE VALUE AND COMPOUNDING

The process of determining the amount to which a sum will accumulate or grow over a specified number of periods of time at a given interest rate per time period is called *compounding*. For example, \$100 deposited in a bank savings account that pays 12 percent interest per year will grow to (\$100)(1.12) = \$112 by the end of the year. If the \$112 is left on deposit for another year, it will grow to (\$112)(1.12) = \$125.44 by the end of the second year.

We can easily derive a formula for determining the amount to which a sum will accumulate or grow at the end of any number of years when the account is left untouched and each year's interest is compounded on the previous year's ending balance. We can derive the formula for determining the future or compound value of a sum by defining the following terms:

PV = present value or beginning amount deposited
i = interest rate earned on the account, expressed as a decimal per year
FV_n = future value or ending amount of the account at the end of n years, after the interest has been added or compounded

At the end of the first year,

$$FV_1 = PV + PV(i) = PV(1 + i) \tag{A-1}$$

For example, \$100 deposited in a savings account that pays 12 percent (i.e., 0.12) interest per year will have grown by the end of the year to

$$FV_1 = \$100(1 + 0.12) = \$100(1.12) = \$112$$

This is equal to the \$100 deposit plus the \$12 interest earned and is shown in the first row of Table A-1.

At the end of the second year,

$$FV_2 = FV_1(1 + i) = PV(1 + i)(1 + i) = PV(1 + i)^2$$

Table A-1
Compound Interest Calculations

Year	Beginning Amount (*PV*)	1 + *i*	Ending Amount (*FV*)
1	$100.00	1.12	$112.00
2	112.00	1.12	125.44
3	125.44	1.12	140.49
4	140.49	1.12	157.35
5	157.35	1.12	176.23

Thus, by the end of the second year the $100 deposited will have grown to

$$FV_2 = \$100(1.12)^2 = \$100(1.2544) = \$125.44$$

This is shown in the second row of Table A-1.

Continuing, we see that FV_3, the balance after three years, is

$$FV_3 = FV_2(1 + i) = PV(1 + i)(1 + i)(1 + i) = PV(1 + i)^3$$

Thus, by the end of the third year the $100 will have grown to

$$FV_3 = \$100(1.12)^3 = \$100(1.4049) = \$140.49$$

This is shown in the third row of Table A-1.

Generalizing, we can say that FV_n, the future value at the end of n years, is

$$FV_n = PV(1 + i)^n \qquad \text{(A-2)}$$

For example, by the end of five years the $100 deposited in the savings account paying 12 percent interest compounded annually will have grown to

$$FV_5 = \$100(1.12)^5 = \$100(1.7623) = \$176.23$$

The value of 1.7623 for $(1.12)^5$ was obtained by (1.12)(1.12)(1.12)(1.12)(1.12). Such a time-consuming calculation is not necessary, however, because a table has been constructed for the compound value of the interest factor $(1 + i)^n$ for many values of i and n. This is Table B-1 in Appendix B.

In Table B-1, $FVIF_{i,n}$ (the future value interest factor) equals $(1 + i)^n$. Thus, $FV_n = PV(1 + i)^n = PV(FVIF_{i,n})$. For $i = 12$ percent and $n = 5$, the $FVIF_{12,5}$ is obtained by moving across Table B-1 until we reach the column headed 12 percent and then moving down five rows for $n = 5$. The value we get is 1.7623 (the same obtained by multiplying 1.12 by itself five times). Thus,

$$FV_5 = \$100(FVIF_{12,5}) = \$100(1.7623) = \$176.23$$

(the same amount found in the fifth row of Table A-1 above).

Using Table B-1, we can find that if the interest rates had been 10 percent and 14 percent, respectively, the $100 deposit would have grown by the end of the fifth year to

$$FV_5 = \$100(FVIF_{10,5}) = \$100(1.6105) = \$161.05$$

and $$FV_5 = \$100(FVIF_{14,\,5}) = \$100(1.9254) = \$192.54$$

On the other hand, with the interest rate of 12 percent, the \$100 would have grown by the end of the tenth year to

$$FV_{10} = \$100(FVIF_{12,\,10}) = \$100(3.1058) = \$310.58$$

Thus, the higher the interest rate, the greater is the rate of growth of the deposit, and the greater the number of years that the sum is left on deposit, the larger will be the amount accumulated or compounded.

A-2 PRESENT VALUE AND DISCOUNTING

The *present value* of a sum due in n years is the amount which, if invested today at a specified rate of interest, would grow to the future sum in n years. For example, since \$100 invested today at 12 percent interest per year will grow to \$176.23 in five years (see Section A-1 and Table A-1), \$100 is the present value of \$176.23 due in five years when the interest rate is 12 percent per year. Thus, finding the present value, or *discounting,* is the reverse of finding the future value of compounding. The interest rate used in such calculations is called the *discount rate* because the present value is smaller than the future value by the specific percentage each year.

The formula to find the present value (PV) can easily be derived from Equation A-2, which was used to find the future value (FV). Specifically, by solving equation

$$FV_n = PV(1 + i)^n$$

for PV, we get

$$PV = \frac{FV_n}{(1 + i)^n} = FV_n\left[\frac{1}{(1 + i)^n}\right] \tag{A-3}$$

The term in square brackets in Equation A-3 is called the *present value interest factor* ($PVIF$). Table B-2 in Appendix B gives the value of the present value interest factor for each value of i and n (that is, $PVIF_{i,\,n}$). For example, by moving across Table B-2 until we reach the column headed 12 percent and then moving down five rows for $n = 5$, we get the value of $PVIF_{12,\,5} = 0.5674$, to be used to find the present value of \$176.23 to be received in five years and discounted at the annual rate of 12 percent. That is,

$$\begin{aligned} PV &= FV_n(PVIF_{i,\,n}) \\ &= FV_5(PVIF_{12,\,5}) \\ &= \$176.23(0.5674) \\ &= \$99.99 \qquad \text{or } \$100 \end{aligned}$$

Using Table B-2 we can find that if the discount rate had been 10 percent and 14 percent, respectively, the \$176.23 to be received in five years would have a present value of

$$PV = FV_5(PVIF_{10,\,5}) = \$176.23(0.6209) = \$109.42$$

and

$$PV = FV_5(PVIF_{14,\,5}) = \$176.23(0.5194) = \$91.53$$

On the other hand, with the discount rate of 12 percent, \$176.23 to be received in 10 years would have a present value of

$$PV = FV_{10}(PVIF_{12,\,10}) = \$176.23(0.3220) = \$56.75$$

Thus, the higher the discount rate and the longer the discounting period, the smaller is the present value of a sum to be received in the future. From Table B-2, it can be seen that the present value of a sum to be received in 25 years or more and discounted at the rate of 10 percent or more per year is less than $\frac{1}{10}$ of the value of the future sum.

A-3 FUTURE VALUE OF AN ANNUITY

An *annuity* is a fixed sum that is received at the end of each year for a specified number of years in the future. The value of an annuity is the sum to which such year-end receipts would accumulate or grow if left in an account at a specified rate of interest compounded annually. For example, the future value of a five-year annuity (FVA_5) of \$100 left in an account paying 12 percent interest compounded annually is \$635.28. This is obtained as follows:

$$FVA_5 = \underbrace{\$100(1.12)^4}_{\text{from year 1}} + \underbrace{\$100(1.12)^3}_{\text{from year 2}} + \underbrace{\$100(1.12)^2}_{\text{from year 3}} + \underbrace{\$100(1.12)^1}_{\text{from year 4}} + \underbrace{\$100(1.12)^0}_{\text{from year 5}} = \$635.28$$

Note that since the first sum is received at the end of the first year, interest is compounded for only four years on this sum. Interest is compounded for three years on the second sum, two years on the third sum, one year on the fourth sum, and zero years on the fifth sum (since it is received at the end of the fifth year).

More generally, letting FVA_n be the future value of the annuity, R the yearly receipts, and n the number of years of the annuity, we can derive the formula for FVA_n as follows:

$$\begin{aligned} FVA_n &= R(1+i)^{n-1} + R(1+i)^{n-2} + \cdots + R(1+i)^1 + R(1+i)^0 \\ &= R[(1+i)^{n-1} + (1+i)^{n-2} + \cdots + (1+i)^1 + (1+i)^0] \\ &= R\sum_{t=1}^{n}(1+i)^{n-t} = R\sum_{t=1}^{n}(1+i)^{t-1} \qquad \text{(A-4)} \\ &= R(FVIFA_{i,\,n}) \end{aligned}$$

where $FVIFA_{i,\,n}$ is the future value interest factor for an annuity with interest i compounded annually for n years. Table B-3 in Appendix B gives the values of $FVIFA_{i,\,n}$ for various values of i and n. For example, by moving across Table B-3 until we reach the column headed 12 percent and then moving down five rows for $n = 5$, we get the value of $FVIFA_{12,5} = 6.3528$ to be used to find the future value of \$635.28 for $i = 12$ percent and $n = 5$ years. That is,

$$\begin{aligned} FVA_n &= R(FVIFA_{i,n}) \\ &= \$100(FVIFA_{12,5}) \\ &= \$100(6.3528) \\ &= \$635.28 \end{aligned}$$

This is the same answer that we obtained above by long-hand calculation. From Table B-3, we can see that the value of $FVIFA_{i,n}$ is always equal to or larger than n.

A-4 PRESENT VALUE OF AN ANNUITY

The present value of a five-year annuity (PVA_5) of \$100 discounted at the annual rate of 12 percent is \$360.48. This is obtained as follows:

$$PVA_5 = \frac{\$100}{(1.12)^1} + \frac{\$100}{(1.12)^2} + \frac{\$100}{(1.12)^3} + \frac{\$100}{(1.12)^4} + \frac{\$100}{(1.12)^5} = \$360.48$$

This means that investing \$360.48 today at 12 percent will return exactly \$100 at the end of each of the next five years.

More generally, letting PVA_n be the present value of the annuity, R the yearly receipts, and n the number of years of the annuity, we can derive the formula for PVA_n as follows:

$$\begin{aligned} PVA_n &= \frac{R}{(1+i)^1} + \frac{R}{(1+i)^2} + \cdots + \frac{R}{(1+i)^n} \\ &= R\left[\frac{1}{(1+i)^1} + \frac{1}{(1+i)^2} + \cdots + \frac{1}{(1+i)^n}\right] \\ &= R\sum_{t=1}^{n} \frac{1}{(1+i)^t} \qquad \text{(A-5)} \\ &= R(PVIFA_{i,n}) \end{aligned}$$

where $PVIFA_{i,n}$ is the present value interest factor for an annuity discounted at the annual rate of i for n years. Table B-4 in Appendix B gives the values of $PVIFA_{i,n}$ for various values of i and n. For example, for $i = 12$ percent and $n = 5$ years, $PVIFA_{12,5} = 3.6048$. Thus, the present value of a five-year annuity of \$100 discounted at the annual rate of 12 percent is

$$\begin{aligned} PVA_n &= R(PVIFA_{i,n}) \\ &= \$100(PVIFA_{12,5}) \\ &= \$100(3.6048) \\ &= \$360.48 \end{aligned}$$

This is the same answer that we obtained above by long-hand calculation. From Table B-4, we can see that the value of $PVIFA_{i,n}$ is always smaller than n.

A-5 COMPOUNDING AND DISCOUNTING PERIODS

Until now we assumed that interest was compounded or earned annually or at the end of each year. Some bonds, however, compound or pay interest semiannually, some banks pay interest quarterly, and some cash receipts and payments occur monthly. The more frequently interest is compounded or earned, the larger will be the future value of a sum and the smaller its present value for a given interest rate.

For example, a sum deposited at 12 percent interest compounded *semiannually* will earn 6 percent interest at the end of every six months or half year. Thus, \$100 deposited at the beginning of the year will grow to \$100(1.06) = \$106 at the end of the first six months and then by another 6 percent, or to \$106(1.06) = \$112.36, by the end of the second six-month period (i.e., by the end of the first year), as compared to \$112 at the rate of 12 percent compounded annually. Thus, a 12 percent interest rate compounded semiannually is equivalent to an *effective* annual rate of (\$112.36/\$100) − 1 = 0.1236, or 12.36 percent, compounded annually. The more frequently interest is compounded or earned, the greater is the effective annual rate corresponding to a given *nominal or stated* annual rate (i.e., interest rate compounded annually).

To find the future value of a sum when compounding occurs more frequently than once a year, we use the following formula:

$$FV_n = PV\left(1 + \frac{i}{m}\right)^{mn} \tag{A-6}$$

where m is the number of times per year that compounding occurs. Equation A-6 is obtained by dividing i by m and multiplying n by m in Equation A-2. For example, for \$100 deposited for 1 year at the nominal or stated interest rate of 12 percent compounded semiannually, $m = 2$ so that i/m = 12 percent/2 = 6 percent, and $mn = 2(1) = 2$. From Table B-1 in Appendix B, we find that $FVIF_{6,2} = 1.1236$, so that \$100 grows to \$100(1.1236) = \$112.36 (the same result obtained above by long-hand calculation).

If the \$100 had been deposited for 5 years at the nominal or stated interest rate of 12 percent compounded semiannually, $m = 2$, i/m = 12 percent/2 = 6 percent, $mn = 2(5) = 10$, so that $FVIF_{6,10} = 1.7908$, and \$100 grows to \$100(1.7908) = \$179.08 (as compared with \$176.23 found in Section A-1 for \$100 deposited at 12 percent per year compounded annually). Finally, for \$100 deposited for five years at the nominal or stated interest rate of 12 percent compounded quarterly, we have $m = 4$, i/m = 12 percent/4 = 3 percent, $mn = 4(5) = 20$, so that $FVIF_{3,20} = 1.8061$, and \$100 grows to \$100(1.8061) = \$180.61.

The same method is used in discounting. For example, to find the present value of \$176.23 to be received in five years and discounted semiannually at the nominal or stated annual rate of 12 percent, $m = 2$, i/m = 12 percent/2 =

6 percent, $mn = 2(5) = 10$, $PVIF_{6,10} = 0.5584$ (from Table B-2 in Appendix B), so that the present value of \$176.23 is \$176.23(0.5584) = \$98.41 (as compared with \$100 found with annual discounting in Section A-2). The same general procedure is used to find the future or present value of an annuity with other than annual compounding or discounting.

A-6 DETERMINING THE INTEREST RATE

Sometimes we know the present value and the future value of a sum or an annuity and we want to determine or solve for the implied rate of interest. For example, suppose you borrow \$100 and promise to repay \$176.23 at the end of five years. Since \$100 is the present value of \$176.23, the implied rate of interest that you are paying can be found as follows:

$$PVA_5 = FV_n \frac{1}{(1+i)^n} = FV_n(PVIF_{i,n}) \qquad \text{(A-7)}$$

$$\$100 = \$176.23(PVIF_{i,5})$$

$$\frac{\$100}{\$176.23} = PVIF_{i,5}$$

$$PVIF_{i,5} = 0.5674$$

By then moving across the fifth row (for $n = 5$ years) in Table B-2 in Appendix B, we find that 0.5674 is under the 12 percent column. Thus, you are paying a 12 percent interest rate.

Similarly, if you borrow \$100,000 today to purchase a home and sign a mortgage agreement to pay \$12,750 at the end of each of the next 25 years, the implied interest rate that you are paying can be found by first recognizing that \$100,000 is the present value of a 25-year, \$12,750 annuity. Thus,

$$PVA_n = R(PVIFA_{i,n}) \qquad \text{(A-8)}$$

$$\$100{,}000 = \$12{,}750(PVIF_{i,25})$$

$$\frac{\$100{,}000}{\$12{,}750} = PVIF_{i,25}$$

$$PVIF_{i,25} = 7.8431$$

By then moving across the twenty-fifth row (for $n = 25$ years) in Table B-4 in Appendix B, we find that 7.8431 is under the 12 percent column. Thus, you are paying a 12 percent interest rate on your mortgage loan.

If the yearly payments in the above mortgage loan had been \$13,000 instead of \$12,750, the implied interest rate that you would be paying can be found as follows:

$$\frac{\$100{,}000}{\$13{,}000} = 7.6923 = PVIF_{i,25}$$

Moving across the twenty-fifth row in Table B-4, we find 7.8431 under the 12 percent column and 6.8729 under the 14 percent column. Since $PVIF_{i,\,25} = 7.6923$ lies between these two values, the implied interest rate is between 12 percent and 14 percent and is found by interpolation to be

$$i = 12\% + \frac{7.8431 - 7.6923}{(7.8431 - 7.6923) + (7.6923 - 6.8729)}(14\% - 12\%)$$

$$= 12\% + \frac{0.1508}{0.9702}(2\%)$$

$$= 12.31\%$$

A-7 PERPETUITIES

Sometimes we are interested in finding the present value of an annuity for an infinite number of years, or *perpetuity.* The present value of a perpetuity of R equal cash flows and interest rate i is given by

$$PVA_\infty = \sum_{t=1}^{\infty} \frac{R}{(1 + i)^t} = R\sum_{t=1}^{\infty} \frac{1}{(1 + i)^t}$$

However, it can be shown that the above expression reduces to

$$PVA_\infty = \frac{R}{i} \tag{A-9}$$

For example, the present value of \$100 to be received each year in perpetuity, discounted at 12 percent, is \$100/0.12 = \$833.33. At $i = 10$ percent, the present value of the perpetuity would be \$100/0.1 = \$1,000, and at $i = 14$ percent, it would be \$100/0.14 = \$714.29.

APPENDIX B

Interest Factor Tables

Table B-1
Compound Value of $1: $FVIF_{i,n} = (1 + i)^n$

Period	1%	2%	3%	4%	5%	6%	7%	8%	9%	10%
1	1.0100	1.0200	1.0300	1.0400	1.0500	1.0600	1.0700	1.0800	1.0900	1.1000
2	1.0201	1.0404	1.0609	1.0816	1.1025	1.1236	1.1449	1.1664	1.1881	1.2100
3	1.0303	1.0612	1.0927	1.1249	1.1576	1.1910	1.2250	1.2597	1.2950	1.3310
4	1.0406	1.0824	1.1255	1.1699	1.2155	1.2625	1.3108	1.3605	1.4116	1.4641
5	1.0510	1.1041	1.1593	1.2167	1.2763	1.3382	1.4026	1.4693	1.5386	1.6105
6	1.0615	1.1262	1.1941	1.2653	1.3401	1.4185	1.5007	1.5869	1.6771	1.7716
7	1.0721	1.1487	1.2299	1.3159	1.4071	1.5036	1.6058	1.7138	1.8280	1.9487
8	1.0829	1.1717	1.2668	1.3686	1.4775	1.5938	1.7182	1.8509	1.9926	2.1436
9	1.0937	1.1951	1.3048	1.4233	1.5513	1.6895	1.8385	1.9990	2.1719	2.3579
10	1.1046	1.2190	1.3439	1.4802	1.6289	1.7908	1.9672	2.1589	2.3674	2.5937
11	1.1157	1.2434	1.3842	1.5395	1.7103	1.8983	2.1049	2.3316	2.5804	2.8531
12	1.1268	1.2682	1.4258	1.6010	1.7959	2.0122	2.2522	2.5182	2.8127	3.1384
13	1.1381	1.2936	1.4685	1.6651	1.8856	2.1329	2.4098	2.7196	3.0658	3.4523
14	1.1495	1.3195	1.5126	1.7317	1.9799	2.2609	2.5785	2.9372	3.3417	3.7975
15	1.1610	1.3459	1.5580	1.8009	2.0789	2.3966	2.7590	3.1722	3.6425	4.1772
16	1.1726	1.3728	1.6047	1.8730	2.1829	2.5404	2.9522	3.4259	3.9703	4.5950
17	1.1843	1.4002	1.6528	1.9479	2.2920	2.6928	3.1588	3.7000	4.3276	5.0545
18	1.1961	1.4282	1.7024	2.0258	2.4066	2.8543	3.3799	3.9960	4.7171	5.5599
19	1.2081	1.4568	1.7535	2.1068	2.5270	3.0256	3.6165	4.3157	5.1417	6.1159
20	1.2202	1.4859	1.8061	2.1911	2.6533	3.2071	3.8697	4.6610	5.6044	6.7275
21	1.2324	1.5157	1.8603	2.2788	2.7860	3.3996	4.1406	5.0338	6.1088	7.4002
22	1.2447	1.5460	1.9161	2.3699	2.9253	3.6035	4.4304	5.4365	6.6586	8.1403
23	1.2572	1.5769	1.9736	2.4647	3.0715	3.8197	4.7405	5.8715	7.2579	8.9543
24	1.2697	1.6084	2.0328	2.5633	3.2251	4.0489	5.0724	6.3412	7.9111	9.8497
25	1.2824	1.6406	2.0938	2.6658	3.3864	4.2919	5.4274	6.8485	8.6231	10.834
26	1.2953	1.6734	2.1566	2.7725	3.5557	4.5494	5.8074	7.3964	9.3992	11.918
27	1.3082	1.7069	2.2213	2.8834	3.7335	4.8223	6.2139	7.9881	10.245	13.110
28	1.3213	1.7410	2.2879	2.9987	3.9201	5.1117	6.6488	8.6271	11.167	14.421
29	1.3345	1.7758	2.3566	3.1187	4.1161	5.4184	7.1143	9.3173	12.172	15.863
30	1.3478	1.8114	2.4273	3.2434	4.3219	5.7435	7.6123	10.062	13.267	17.449
40	1.4889	2.2080	3.2620	4.8010	7.0400	10.285	14.974	21.724	31.409	45.259
50	1.6446	2.6916	4.3839	7.1067	11.467	18.420	29.457	46.901	74.357	117.39
60	1.8167	3.2810	5.8916	10.519	18.679	32.987	57.946	101.25	176.03	304.48

Table B-1
(Continued)

Period	12%	14%	15%	16%	18%	20%	24%	28%	32%	36%
1	1.1200	1.1400	1.1500	1.1600	1.1800	1.2000	1.2400	1.2800	1.3200	1.3600
2	1.2544	1.2996	1.3225	1.3456	1.3924	1.4400	1.5376	1.6384	1.7424	1.8496
3	1.4049	1.4815	1.5209	1.5609	1.6430	1.7280	1.9066	2.0972	2.3000	2.5155
4	1.5735	1.6890	1.7490	1.8106	1.9388	2.0736	2.3642	2.6844	3.0360	3.4210
5	1.7623	1.9254	2.0114	2.1003	2.2878	2.4883	2.9316	3.4360	4.0075	4.6526
6	1.9738	2.1950	2.3131	2.4364	2.6996	2.9860	3.6352	4.3980	5.2899	6.3275
7	2.2107	2.5023	2.6600	2.8262	3.1855	3.5832	4.5077	5.6295	6.9826	8.6054
8	2.4760	2.8526	3.0590	3.2784	3.7589	4.2998	5.5895	7.2058	9.2170	11.703
9	2.7731	3.2519	3.5179	3.8030	4.4355	5.1598	6.9310	9.2234	12.166	15.916
10	3.1058	3.7072	4.0456	4.4114	5.2338	6.1917	8.5944	11.805	16.059	21.646
11	3.4785	4.2262	4.6524	5.1173	6.1759	7.4301	10.657	15.111	21.198	29.439
12	3.8960	4.8179	5.3502	5.9360	7.2876	8.9161	13.214	19.342	27.982	40.037
13	4.3635	5.4924	6.1528	6.8858	8.5994	10.699	16.386	24.758	36.937	54.451
14	4.8871	6.2613	7.0757	7.9875	10.147	12.839	20.319	31.691	48.756	74.053
15	5.4736	7.1379	8.1371	9.2655	11.973	15.407	25.195	40.564	64.358	100.71
16	6.1304	8.1372	9.3576	10.748	14.129	18.488	31.242	51.923	84.953	136.96
17	6.8660	9.2765	10.761	12.467	16.672	22.186	38.740	66.461	112.13	186.27
18	7.6900	10.575	12.375	14.462	19.673	26.623	48.038	85.070	148.02	253.33
19	8.6128	12.055	14.231	16.776	23.214	31.948	59.567	108.89	195.39	344.53
20	9.6463	13.743	16.366	19.460	27.393	38.337	73.864	139.37	257.91	468.57
21	10.803	15.667	18.821	22.574	32.323	46.005	91.591	178.40	340.44	637.26
22	12.100	17.861	21.644	26.186	38.142	55.206	113.57	228.35	449.39	866.67
23	13.552	20.361	24.891	30.376	45.007	66.247	140.83	292.30	593.19	1178.6
24	15.178	23.212	28.625	35.236	53.108	79.496	174.63	374.14	783.02	1602.9
25	17.000	26.461	32.918	40.874	62.668	95.396	216.54	478.90	1033.5	2180.0
26	19.040	30.166	37.856	47.414	73.948	114.47	268.51	612.99	1364.3	2964.9
27	21.324	34.389	43.535	55.000	87.259	137.37	332.95	784.63	1800.9	4032.3
28	23.883	39.204	50.065	63.800	102.96	164.84	412.86	1004.3	2377.2	5483.8
29	26.749	44.693	57.575	74.008	121.50	197.81	511.95	1285.5	3137.9	7458.0
30	29.959	50.950	66.211	85.849	143.37	237.37	634.81	1645.5	4142.0	10143.
40	93.050	188.88	267.86	378.72	750.37	1469.7	5455.9	19426.	66520.	*
50	289.00	700.23	1083.6	1670.7	3927.3	9100.4	46890.	*	*	*
60	897.59	2595.9	4383.9	7370.1	20555.	56347.	*	*	*	*

**FVIF* > 99,999.

Table B-2
Present Value of $1: $PVIF_{i,n} = 1/(1+i)^n = 1/FVIF_{i,n}$

Period	1%	2%	3%	4%	5%	6%	7%	8%	9%	10%
1	.9901	.9804	.9709	.9615	.9524	.9434	.9346	.9259	.9174	.9091
2	.9803	.9612	.9426	.9246	.9070	.8900	.8734	.8573	.8417	.8264
3	.9706	.9423	.9151	.8890	.8638	.8396	.8163	.7938	.7722	.7513
4	.9610	.9238	.8885	.8548	.8227	.7921	.7629	.7350	.7084	.6830
5	.9515	.9057	.8626	.8219	.7835	.7473	.7130	.6806	.6499	.6209
6	.9420	.8880	.8375	.7903	.7462	.7050	.6663	.6302	.5963	.5645
7	.9327	.8706	.8131	.7599	.7107	.6651	.6227	.5835	.5470	.5132
8	.9235	.8535	.7894	.7307	.6768	.6274	.5820	.5403	.5019	.4665
9	.9143	.8368	.7664	.7026	.6446	.5919	.5439	.5002	.4604	.4241
10	.9053	.8203	.7441	.6756	.6139	.5584	.5083	.4632	.4224	.3855
11	.8963	.8043	.7224	.6496	.5847	.5268	.4751	.4289	.3875	.3505
12	.8874	.7885	.7014	.6246	.5568	.4970	.4440	.3971	.3555	.3186
13	.8787	.7730	.6810	.6006	.5303	.4688	.4150	.3677	.3262	.2897
14	.8700	.7579	.6611	.5775	.5051	.4423	.3878	.3405	.2992	.2633
15	.8613	.7430	.6419	.5553	.4810	.4173	.3624	.3152	.2745	.2394
16	.8528	.7284	.6232	.5339	.4581	.3936	.3387	.2919	.2519	.2176
17	.8444	.7142	.6050	.5134	.4363	.3714	.3166	.2703	.2311	.1978
18	.8360	.7002	.5874	.4936	.4155	.3503	.2959	.2502	.2120	.1799
19	.8277	.6864	.5703	.4746	.3957	.3305	.2765	.2317	.1945	.1635
20	.8195	.6730	.5537	.4564	.3769	.3118	.2584	.2145	.1784	.1486
21	.8114	.6598	.5375	.4388	.3589	.2942	.2415	.1987	.1637	.1351
22	.8034	.6468	.5219	.4220	.3418	.2775	.2257	.1839	.1502	.1228
23	.7954	.6342	.5067	.4057	.3256	.2618	.2109	.1703	.1378	.1117
24	.7876	.6217	.4919	.3901	.3101	.2470	.1971	.1577	.1264	.1015
25	.7798	.6095	.4776	.3751	.2953	.2330	.1842	.1460	.1160	.0923
26	.7720	.5976	.4637	.3607	.2812	.2198	.1722	.1352	.1064	.0839
27	.7644	.5859	.4502	.3468	.2678	.2074	.1609	.1252	.0976	.0763
28	.7568	.5744	.4371	.3335	.2551	.1956	.1504	.1159	.0895	.0693
29	.7493	.5631	.4243	.3207	.2429	.1846	.1406	.1073	.0822	.0630
30	.7419	.5521	.4120	.3083	.2314	.1741	.1314	.0994	.0754	.0573
35	.7059	.5000	.3554	.2534	.1813	.1301	.0937	.0676	.0490	.0356
40	.6717	.4529	.3066	.2083	.1420	.0972	.0668	.0460	.0318	.0221
45	.6391	.4102	.2644	.1712	.1113	.0727	.0476	.0313	.0207	.0137
50	.6080	.3715	.2281	.1407	.0872	.0543	.0339	.0213	.0134	.0085
55	.5785	.3365	.1968	.1157	.0683	.0406	.0242	.0145	.0087	.0053

Table B-2
(Continued)

Period	12%	14%	15%	16%	18%	20%	24%	28%	32%	36%
1	.8929	.8772	.8696	.8621	.8475	.8333	.8065	.7813	.7576	.7353
2	.7972	.7695	.7561	.7432	.7182	.6944	.6504	.6104	.5739	.5407
3	.7118	.6750	.6575	.6407	.6086	.5787	.5245	.4768	.4348	.3975
4	.6355	.5921	.5718	.5523	.5158	.4823	.4230	.3725	.3294	.2923
5	.5674	.5194	.4972	.4761	.4371	.4019	.3411	.2910	.2495	.2149
6	.5066	.4556	.4323	.4104	.3704	.3349	.2751	.2274	.1890	.1580
7	.4523	.3996	.3759	.3538	.3139	.2791	.2218	.1776	.1432	.1162
8	.4039	.3506	.3269	.3050	.2660	.2326	.1789	.1388	.1085	.0854
9	.3606	.3075	.2843	.2630	.2255	.1938	.1443	.1084	.0822	.0628
10	.3220	.2697	.2472	.2267	.1911	.1615	.1164	.0847	.0623	.0462
11	.2875	.2366	.2149	.1954	.1619	.1346	.0938	.0662	.0472	.0340
12	.2567	.2076	.1869	.1685	.1372	.1122	.0757	.0517	.0357	.0250
13	.2292	.1821	.1625	.1452	.1163	.0935	.0610	.0404	.0271	.0184
14	.2046	.1597	.1413	.1252	.0985	.0779	.0492	.0316	.0205	.0135
15	.1827	.1401	.1229	.1079	.0835	.0649	.0397	.0247	.0155	.0099
16	.1631	.1229	.1069	.0930	.0708	.0541	.0320	.0193	.0118	.0073
17	.1456	.1078	.0929	.0802	.0600	.0451	.0258	.0150	.0089	.0054
18	.1300	.0946	.0808	.0691	.0508	.0376	.0208	.0118	.0068	.0039
19	.1161	.0829	.0703	.0596	.0431	.0313	.0168	.0092	.0051	.0029
20	.1037	.0728	.0611	.0514	.0365	.0261	.0135	.0072	.0039	.0021
21	.0926	.0638	.0531	.0443	.0309	.0217	.0109	.0056	.0029	.0016
22	.0826	.0560	.0462	.0382	.0262	.0181	.0088	.0044	.0022	.0012
23	.0738	.0491	.0402	.0329	.0222	.0151	.0071	.0034	.0017	.0008
24	.0659	.0431	.0349	.0284	.0188	.0126	.0057	.0027	.0013	.0006
25	.0588	.0378	.0304	.0245	.0160	.0105	.0046	.0021	.0010	.0005
26	.0525	.0331	.0264	.0211	.0135	.0087	.0037	.0016	.0007	.0003
27	.0469	.0291	.0230	.0182	.0115	.0073	.0030	.0013	.0006	.0002
28	.0419	.0255	.0200	.0157	.0097	.0061	.0024	.0010	.0004	.0002
29	.0374	.0224	.0174	.0135	.0082	.0051	.0020	.0008	.0003	.0001
30	.0334	.0196	.0151	.0116	.0070	.0042	.0016	.0006	.0002	.0001
35	.0189	.0102	.0075	.0055	.0030	.0017	.0005	.0002	.0001	*
40	.0107	.0053	.0037	.0026	.0013	.0007	.0002	.0001	*	*
45	.0061	.0027	.0019	.0013	.0006	.0003	.0001	*	*	*
50	.0035	.0014	.0009	.0006	.0003	.0001	*	*	*	*
55	.0020	.0007	.0005	.0003	.0001	*	*	*	*	*

*The factor is zero to four decimal places.

Table B-3
Future Value of an Annuity of $1 for *n* Periods:
$FVIFA_{i,n} = \sum_{t=1}^{n}(1+i)^{t-1}$

Number of Periods	1%	2%	3%	4%	5%	6%	7%	8%	9%	10%
1	1.0000	1.0000	1.0000	1.0000	1.0000	1.0000	1.0000	1.0000	1.0000	1.0000
2	2.0100	2.0200	2.0300	2.0400	2.0500	2.0600	2.0700	2.0800	2.0900	2.1000
3	3.0301	3.0604	3.0909	3.1216	3.1525	3.1836	3.2149	3.2464	3.2781	3.3100
4	4.0604	4.1216	4.1836	4.2465	4.3101	4.3746	4.4399	4.5061	4.5731	4.6410
5	5.1010	5.2040	5.3091	5.4163	5.5256	5.6371	5.7507	5.8666	5.9847	6.1051
6	6.1520	6.3081	6.4684	6.6330	6.8019	6.9753	7.1533	7.3359	7.5233	7.7156
7	7.2135	7.4343	7.6625	7.8983	8.1420	8.3938	8.6540	8.9228	9.2004	9.4872
8	8.2857	8.5830	8.8923	9.2142	9.5491	9.8975	10.259	10.636	11.028	11.435
9	9.3685	9.7546	10.159	10.582	11.026	11.491	11.978	12.487	13.021	13.579
10	10.462	10.949	11.463	12.006	12.577	13.180	13.816	14.486	15.192	15.937
11	11.566	12.168	12.807	13.486	14.206	14.971	15.783	16.645	17.560	18.531
12	12.682	13.412	14.192	15.025	15.917	16.869	17.888	18.977	20.140	21.384
13	13.809	14.680	15.617	16.626	17.713	18.882	20.140	21.495	22.953	24.522
14	14.947	15.973	17.086	18.291	19.598	21.015	22.550	24.214	26.019	27.975
15	16.096	17.293	18.598	20.023	21.578	23.276	25.129	27.152	29.360	31.772
16	17.257	18.639	20.156	21.824	23.657	25.672	27.888	30.324	33.003	35.949
17	18.430	20.012	21.761	23.697	25.840	28.212	30.840	33.750	36.973	40.544
18	19.614	21.412	23.414	25.645	28.132	30.905	33.999	37.450	41.301	45.599
19	20.810	22.840	25.116	27.671	30.539	33.760	37.379	41.446	46.018	51.159
20	22.019	24.297	26.870	29.778	33.066	36.785	40.995	45.762	51.160	57.275
21	23.239	25.783	28.676	31.969	35.719	39.992	44.865	50.422	56.764	64.002
22	24.471	27.299	30.536	34.248	38.505	43.392	49.005	55.456	62.873	71.402
23	25.716	28.845	32.452	36.617	41.430	46.995	53.436	60.893	69.531	79.543
24	26.973	30.421	34.426	39.082	44.502	50.815	58.176	66.764	76.789	88.497
25	28.243	32.030	36.459	41.645	47.727	54.864	63.249	73.105	84.700	98.347
26	29.525	33.670	38.553	44.311	51.113	59.156	68.676	79.954	93.323	109.18
27	30.820	35.344	40.709	47.084	54.669	63.705	74.483	87.350	102.72	121.09
28	32.129	37.051	42.930	49.967	58.402	68.528	80.697	95.338	112.96	134.20
29	33.450	38.792	45.218	52.966	62.322	73.639	87.346	103.96	124.13	148.63
30	34.784	40.568	47.575	56.084	66.438	79.058	94.460	113.28	136.30	164.49
40	48.886	60.402	75.401	95.025	120.79	154.76	199.63	259.05	337.88	442.59
50	64.463	84.579	112.79	152.66	209.34	290.33	406.52	573.76	815.08	1163.9
60	81.669	114.05	163.05	237.99	353.58	533.12	813.52	1253.2	1944.7	3034.8

Table B-3
(Continued)

Number of Periods	12%	14%	15%	16%	18%	20%	24%	28%	32%	36%
1	1.0000	1.0000	1.0000	1.0000	1.0000	1.0000	1.0000	1.0000	1.0000	1.0000
2	2.1200	2.1400	2.1500	2.1600	2.1800	2.2000	2.2400	2.2800	2.3200	2.3600
3	3.3744	3.4396	3.4725	3.5056	3.5724	3.6400	3.7776	3.9184	4.0624	4.2096
4	4.7793	4.9211	4.9934	5.0665	5.2154	5.3680	5.6842	6.0156	6.3624	6.7251
5	6.3528	6.6101	6.7424	6.8771	7.1542	7.4416	8.0484	8.6999	9.3983	10.146
6	8.1152	8.5355	8.7537	8.9775	9.4420	9.9299	10.980	12.135	13.405	14.798
7	10.089	10.730	11.066	11.413	12.141	12.915	14.615	16.533	18.695	21.126
8	12.299	13.232	13.726	14.240	15.327	16.499	19.122	22.163	25.678	29.731
9	14.775	16.085	16.785	17.518	19.085	20.798	24.712	29.369	34.895	41.435
10	17.548	19.337	20.303	21.321	23.521	25.958	31.643	38.592	47.061	57.351
11	20.654	23.044	24.349	25.732	28.755	32.150	40.237	50.398	63.121	78.998
12	24.133	27.270	29.001	30.850	34.931	39.580	50.894	65.510	84.320	108.43
13	28.029	32.088	34.351	36.786	42.218	48.496	64.109	84.852	112.30	148.47
14	32.392	37.581	40.504	43.672	50.818	59.195	80.496	109.61	149.23	202.92
15	37.279	43.842	47.580	51.659	60.965	72.035	100.81	141.30	197.99	276.97
16	42.753	50.980	55.717	60.925	72.939	87.442	126.01	181.86	262.35	377.69
17	48.883	59.117	65.075	71.673	87.068	105.93	157.25	233.79	347.30	514.66
18	55.749	68.394	75.836	84.140	103.74	128.11	195.99	300.25	459.44	700.93
19	63.439	78.969	88.211	98.603	123.41	154.74	244.03	385.32	607.47	954.27
20	72.052	91.024	102.44	115.37	146.62	186.68	303.60	494.21	802.86	1298.8
21	81.698	104.76	118.81	134.84	174.02	225.02	377.46	633.59	1060.7	1767.3
22	92.502	120.43	137.63	157.41	206.34	271.03	469.05	811.99	1401.2	2404.6
23	104.60	138.29	159.27	183.60	244.48	326.23	582.62	1040.3	1850.6	3271.3
24	118.15	158.65	184.16	213.97	289.49	392.48	723.46	1332.6	2443.8	4449.9
25	133.33	181.87	212.79	249.21	342.60	471.98	898.09	1706.8	3226.8	6052.9
26	150.33	208.33	245.71	290.08	405.27	567.37	1114.6	2185.7	4260.4	8233.0
27	169.37	238.49	283.56	337.50	479.22	681.85	1383.1	2798.7	5624.7	11197.9
28	190.69	272.88	327.10	392.50	566.48	819.22	1716.0	3583.3	7425.6	15230.2
29	214.58	312.09	377.16	456.30	669.44	984.06	2128.9	4587.6	9802.9	20714.1
30	241.33	356.78	434.74	530.31	790.94	1181.8	2640.9	5873.2	12940.	28172.2
40	767.09	1342.0	1779.0	2360.7	4163.2	7343.8	22728.	69377.	*	*
50	2400.0	4994.5	7217.7	10435.	21813.	45497.	*	*	*	*
60	7471.6	18535.	29219.	46057.	*	*	*	*	*	*

*FVIFA > 99,999.

Table B-4
Present Value of an Annuity of $1 for *n* Periods:

$$PVIFA_{i,n} = \sum_{t=1}^{n} \frac{1}{(1+i)^t}$$

Number of Payments	1%	2%	3%	4%	5%	6%	7%	8%	9%
1	0.9901	0.9804	0.9709	0.9615	0.9524	0.9434	0.9346	0.9259	0.9174
2	1.9704	1.9416	1.9135	1.8861	1.8594	1.8334	1.8080	1.7833	1.7591
3	2.9410	2.8839	2.8286	2.7751	2.7232	2.6730	2.6243	2.5771	2.5313
4	3.9020	3.8077	3.7171	3.6299	3.5460	3.4651	3.3872	3.3121	3.2397
5	4.8534	4.7135	4.5797	4.4518	4.3295	4.2124	4.1002	3.9927	3.8897
6	5.7955	5.6014	5.4172	5.2421	5.0757	4.9173	4.7665	4.6229	4.4859
7	6.7282	6.4720	6.2303	6.0021	5.7864	5.5824	5.3893	5.2064	5.0330
8	7.6517	7.3255	7.0197	6.7327	6.4632	6.2098	5.9713	5.7466	5.5348
9	8.5660	8.1622	7.7861	7.4353	7.1078	6.8017	6.5152	6.2469	5.9952
10	9.4713	8.9826	8.5302	8.1109	7.7217	7.3601	7.0236	6.7101	6.4177
11	10.3676	9.7868	9.2526	8.7605	8.3064	7.8869	7.4987	7.1390	6.8052
12	11.2551	10.5753	9.9540	9.3851	8.8633	8.3838	7.9427	7.5361	7.1607
13	12.1337	11.3484	10.6350	9.9856	9.3936	8.8527	8.3577	7.9038	7.4869
14	13.0037	12.1062	11.2961	10.5631	9.8986	9.2950	8.7455	8.2442	7.7862
15	13.8651	12.8493	11.9379	11.1184	10.3797	9.7122	9.1079	8.5595	8.0607
16	14.7179	13.5777	12.5611	11.6523	10.8378	10.1059	9.4466	8.8514	8.3126
17	15.5623	14.2919	13.1661	12.1657	11.2741	10.4773	9.7632	9.1216	8.5436
18	16.3983	14.9920	13.7535	12.6593	11.6896	10.8276	10.0591	9.3719	8.7556
19	17.2260	15.6785	14.3238	13.1339	12.0853	11.1581	10.3356	9.6036	8.9501
20	18.0456	16.3514	14.8775	13.5903	12.4622	11.4699	10.5940	9.8181	9.1285
21	18.8570	17.0112	15.4150	14.0292	12.8212	11.7641	10.8355	10.0168	9.2922
22	19.6604	17.6580	15.9369	14.4511	13.1630	12.0416	11.0612	10.2007	9.4424
23	20.4558	18.2922	16.4436	14.8568	13.4886	12.3034	11.2722	10.3711	9.5802
24	21.2434	18.9139	16.9355	15.2470	13.7986	12.5504	11.4693	10.5288	9.7066
25	22.0232	19.5235	17.4131	15.6221	14.0939	12.7834	11.6536	10.6748	9.8226
26	22.7952	20.1210	17.8768	15.9828	14.3752	13.0032	11.8258	10.8100	9.9290
27	23.5596	20.7069	18.3270	16.3296	14.6430	13.2105	11.9867	10.9352	10.0266
28	24.3164	21.2813	18.7641	16.6631	14.8981	13.4062	12.1371	11.0511	10.1161
29	25.0658	21.8444	19.1885	16.9837	15.1411	13.5907	12.2777	11.1584	10.1983
30	25.8077	22.3965	19.6004	17.2920	15.3725	13.7648	12.4090	11.2578	10.2737
35	29.4086	24.9986	21.4872	18.6646	16.3742	14.4982	12.9477	11.6546	10.5668
40	32.8347	27.3555	23.1148	19.7928	17.1591	15.0463	13.3317	11.9246	10.7574
45	36.0945	29.4902	24.5187	20.7200	17.7741	15.4558	13.6055	12.1084	10.8812
50	39.1961	31.4236	25.7298	21.4822	18.2559	15.7619	13.8007	12.2335	10.9617
55	42.1472	33.1748	26.7744	22.1086	18.6335	15.9905	13.9399	12.3186	11.0140

Table B-4
(Continued)

Number of Payments	10%	12%	14%	15%	16%	18%	20%	24%	28%	32%
1	0.9091	0.8929	0.8772	0.8696	0.8621	0.8475	0.8333	0.8065	0.7813	0.7576
2	1.7355	1.6901	1.6467	1.6257	1.6052	1.5656	1.5278	1.4568	1.3916	1.3315
3	2.4869	2.4018	2.3216	2.2832	2.2459	2.1743	2.1065	1.9813	1.8684	1.7663
4	3.1699	3.0373	2.9137	2.8550	2.7982	2.6901	2.5887	2.4043	2.2410	2.0957
5	3.7908	3.6048	3.4331	3.3522	3.2743	3.1272	2.9906	2.7454	2.5320	2.3452
6	4.3553	4.1114	3.8887	3.7845	3.6847	3.4976	3.3255	3.0205	2.7594	2.5342
7	4.8684	4.5638	4.2883	4.1604	4.0386	3.8115	3.6046	3.2423	2.9370	2.6775
8	5.3349	4.9676	4.6389	4.4873	4.3436	4.0776	3.8372	3.4212	3.0758	2.7860
9	5.7590	5.3282	4.9464	4.7716	4.6065	4.3030	4.0310	3.5655	3.1842	2.8681
10	6.1446	5.6502	5.2161	5.0188	4.8332	4.4941	4.1925	3.6819	3.2689	2.9304
11	6.4951	5.9377	5.4527	5.2337	5.0286	4.6560	4.3271	3.7757	3.3351	2.9776
12	6.8137	6.1944	5.6603	5.4206	5.1971	4.7932	4.4392	3.8514	3.3868	3.0133
13	7.1034	6.4235	5.8424	5.5831	5.3423	4.9095	4.5327	3.9124	3.4272	3.0404
14	7.3667	6.6282	6.0021	5.7245	5.4675	5.0081	4.6106	3.9616	3.4587	3.0609
15	7.6061	6.8109	6.1422	5.8474	5.5755	5.0916	4.6755	4.0013	3.4834	3.0764
16	7.8237	6.9740	6.2651	5.9542	5.6685	5.1624	4.7296	4.0333	3.5026	3.0882
17	8.0216	7.1196	6.3729	6.0472	5.7487	5.2223	4.7746	4.0591	3.5177	3.0971
18	8.2014	7.2497	6.4674	6.1280	5.8178	5.2732	4.8122	4.0799	3.5294	3.1039
19	8.3649	7.3658	6.5504	6.1982	5.8775	5.3162	4.8435	4.0967	3.5386	3.1090
20	8.5136	7.4694	6.6231	6.2593	5.9288	5.3527	4.8696	4.1103	3.5458	3.1129
21	8.6487	7.5620	6.6870	6.3125	5.9731	5.3837	4.8913	4.1212	3.5514	3.1158
22	8.7715	7.6446	6.7429	6.3587	6.0113	5.4099	4.9094	4.1300	3.5558	3.1180
23	8.8832	7.7184	6.7921	6.3988	6.0442	5.4321	4.9245	4.1371	3.5592	3.1197
24	8.9847	7.7843	6.8351	6.4338	6.0726	5.4510	4.9371	4.1428	3.5619	3.1210
25	9.0770	7.8431	6.8729	6.4642	6.0971	5.4669	4.9476	4.1474	3.5640	3.1220
26	9.1609	7.8957	6.9061	6.4906	6.1182	5.4804	4.9563	4.1511	3.5656	3.1227
27	9.2372	7.9426	6.9352	6.5135	6.1364	5.4919	4.9636	4.1542	3.5669	3.1233
28	9.3066	7.9844	6.9607	6.5335	6.1520	5.5016	4.9697	4.1566	3.5679	3.1237
29	9.3696	8.0218	6.9830	6.5509	6.1656	5.5098	4.9747	4.1585	3.5687	3.1240
30	9.4269	8.0552	7.0027	6.5660	6.1772	5.5168	4.9789	4.1601	3.5693	3.1242
35	9.6442	8.1755	7.0700	6.6166	6.2153	5.5386	4.9915	4.1644	3.5708	3.1248
40	9.7791	8.2438	7.1050	6.6418	6.2335	5.5482	4.9966	4.1659	3.5712	3.1250
45	9.8628	8.2825	7.1232	6.6543	6.2421	5.5523	4.9986	4.1664	3.5714	3.1250
50	9.9148	8.3045	7.1327	6.6605	6.2463	5.5541	4.9995	4.1666	3.5714	3.1250
55	9.9471	8.3170	7.1376	6.6636	6.2482	5.5549	4.9998	4.1666	3.5714	3.1250

APPENDIX C

Statistical Tables

Table C-1
Areas under the Standard Normal Distribution

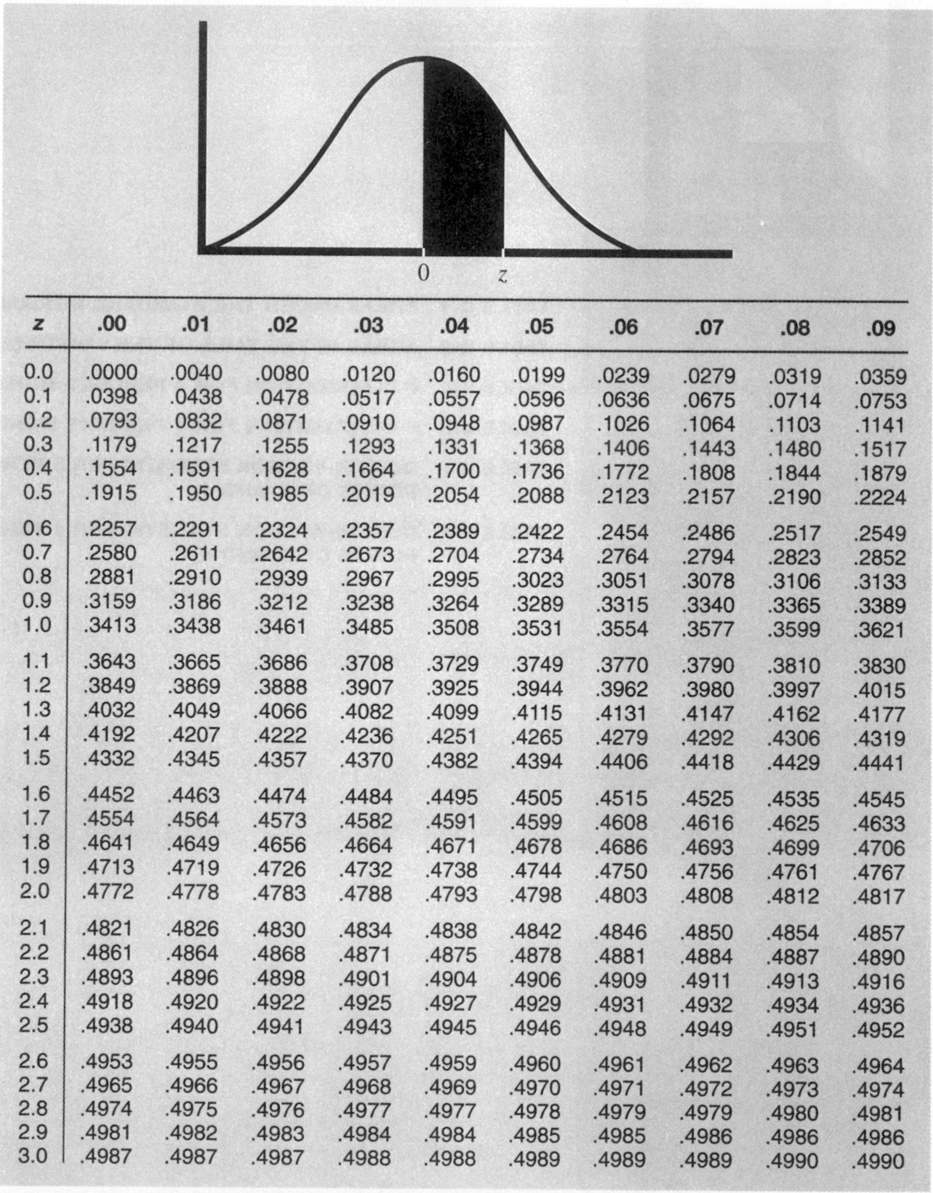

z	.00	.01	.02	.03	.04	.05	.06	.07	.08	.09
0.0	.0000	.0040	.0080	.0120	.0160	.0199	.0239	.0279	.0319	.0359
0.1	.0398	.0438	.0478	.0517	.0557	.0596	.0636	.0675	.0714	.0753
0.2	.0793	.0832	.0871	.0910	.0948	.0987	.1026	.1064	.1103	.1141
0.3	.1179	.1217	.1255	.1293	.1331	.1368	.1406	.1443	.1480	.1517
0.4	.1554	.1591	.1628	.1664	.1700	.1736	.1772	.1808	.1844	.1879
0.5	.1915	.1950	.1985	.2019	.2054	.2088	.2123	.2157	.2190	.2224
0.6	.2257	.2291	.2324	.2357	.2389	.2422	.2454	.2486	.2517	.2549
0.7	.2580	.2611	.2642	.2673	.2704	.2734	.2764	.2794	.2823	.2852
0.8	.2881	.2910	.2939	.2967	.2995	.3023	.3051	.3078	.3106	.3133
0.9	.3159	.3186	.3212	.3238	.3264	.3289	.3315	.3340	.3365	.3389
1.0	.3413	.3438	.3461	.3485	.3508	.3531	.3554	.3577	.3599	.3621
1.1	.3643	.3665	.3686	.3708	.3729	.3749	.3770	.3790	.3810	.3830
1.2	.3849	.3869	.3888	.3907	.3925	.3944	.3962	.3980	.3997	.4015
1.3	.4032	.4049	.4066	.4082	.4099	.4115	.4131	.4147	.4162	.4177
1.4	.4192	.4207	.4222	.4236	.4251	.4265	.4279	.4292	.4306	.4319
1.5	.4332	.4345	.4357	.4370	.4382	.4394	.4406	.4418	.4429	.4441
1.6	.4452	.4463	.4474	.4484	.4495	.4505	.4515	.4525	.4535	.4545
1.7	.4554	.4564	.4573	.4582	.4591	.4599	.4608	.4616	.4625	.4633
1.8	.4641	.4649	.4656	.4664	.4671	.4678	.4686	.4693	.4699	.4706
1.9	.4713	.4719	.4726	.4732	.4738	.4744	.4750	.4756	.4761	.4767
2.0	.4772	.4778	.4783	.4788	.4793	.4798	.4803	.4808	.4812	.4817
2.1	.4821	.4826	.4830	.4834	.4838	.4842	.4846	.4850	.4854	.4857
2.2	.4861	.4864	.4868	.4871	.4875	.4878	.4881	.4884	.4887	.4890
2.3	.4893	.4896	.4898	.4901	.4904	.4906	.4909	.4911	.4913	.4916
2.4	.4918	.4920	.4922	.4925	.4927	.4929	.4931	.4932	.4934	.4936
2.5	.4938	.4940	.4941	.4943	.4945	.4946	.4948	.4949	.4951	.4952
2.6	.4953	.4955	.4956	.4957	.4959	.4960	.4961	.4962	.4963	.4964
2.7	.4965	.4966	.4967	.4968	.4969	.4970	.4971	.4972	.4973	.4974
2.8	.4974	.4975	.4976	.4977	.4977	.4978	.4979	.4979	.4980	.4981
2.9	.4981	.4982	.4983	.4984	.4984	.4985	.4985	.4986	.4986	.4986
3.0	.4987	.4987	.4987	.4988	.4988	.4989	.4989	.4989	.4990	.4990

Example: For $z = 1.96$, shaded area is 0.4750 out of total area of 1.

Table C-2
Areas in the Tails of the *t* Distribution

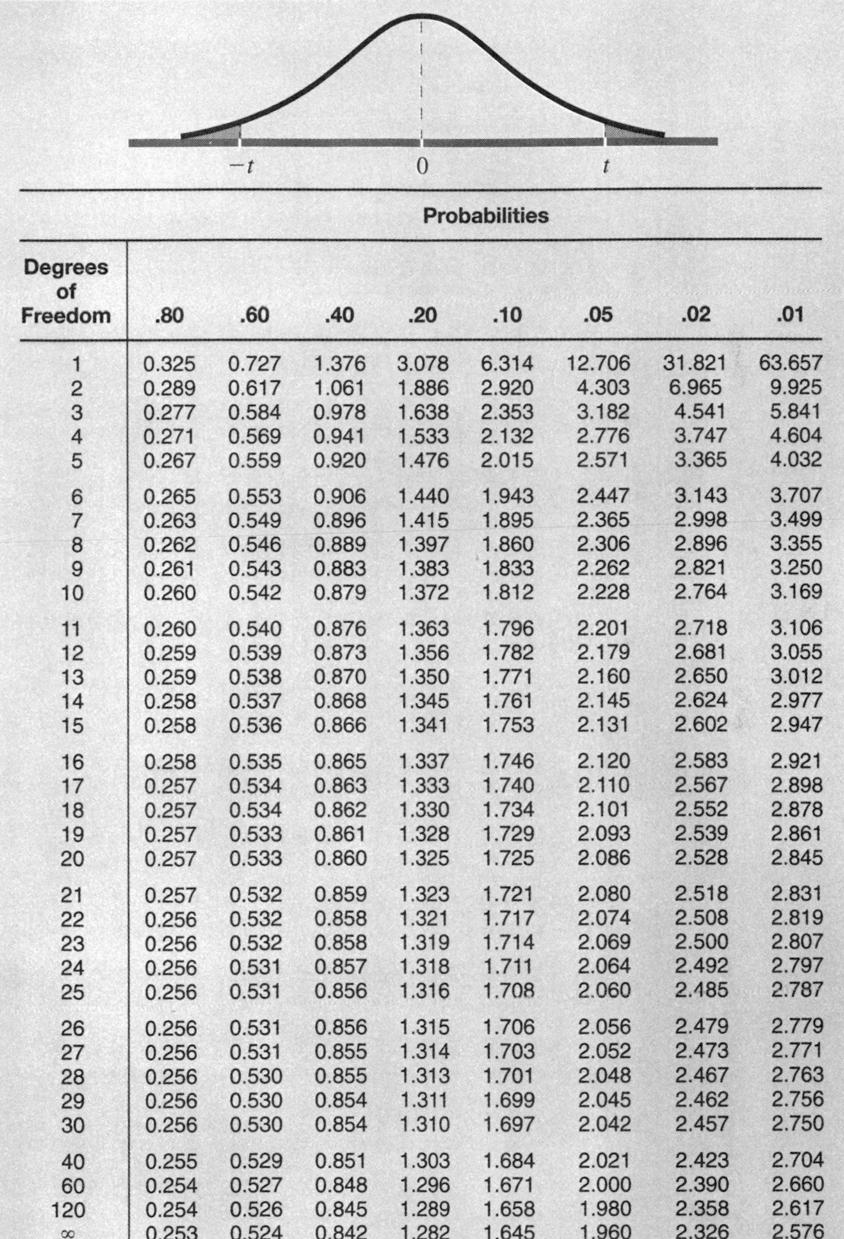

Degrees of Freedom	Probabilities .80	.60	.40	.20	.10	.05	.02	.01
1	0.325	0.727	1.376	3.078	6.314	12.706	31.821	63.657
2	0.289	0.617	1.061	1.886	2.920	4.303	6.965	9.925
3	0.277	0.584	0.978	1.638	2.353	3.182	4.541	5.841
4	0.271	0.569	0.941	1.533	2.132	2.776	3.747	4.604
5	0.267	0.559	0.920	1.476	2.015	2.571	3.365	4.032
6	0.265	0.553	0.906	1.440	1.943	2.447	3.143	3.707
7	0.263	0.549	0.896	1.415	1.895	2.365	2.998	3.499
8	0.262	0.546	0.889	1.397	1.860	2.306	2.896	3.355
9	0.261	0.543	0.883	1.383	1.833	2.262	2.821	3.250
10	0.260	0.542	0.879	1.372	1.812	2.228	2.764	3.169
11	0.260	0.540	0.876	1.363	1.796	2.201	2.718	3.106
12	0.259	0.539	0.873	1.356	1.782	2.179	2.681	3.055
13	0.259	0.538	0.870	1.350	1.771	2.160	2.650	3.012
14	0.258	0.537	0.868	1.345	1.761	2.145	2.624	2.977
15	0.258	0.536	0.866	1.341	1.753	2.131	2.602	2.947
16	0.258	0.535	0.865	1.337	1.746	2.120	2.583	2.921
17	0.257	0.534	0.863	1.333	1.740	2.110	2.567	2.898
18	0.257	0.534	0.862	1.330	1.734	2.101	2.552	2.878
19	0.257	0.533	0.861	1.328	1.729	2.093	2.539	2.861
20	0.257	0.533	0.860	1.325	1.725	2.086	2.528	2.845
21	0.257	0.532	0.859	1.323	1.721	2.080	2.518	2.831
22	0.256	0.532	0.858	1.321	1.717	2.074	2.508	2.819
23	0.256	0.532	0.858	1.319	1.714	2.069	2.500	2.807
24	0.256	0.531	0.857	1.318	1.711	2.064	2.492	2.797
25	0.256	0.531	0.856	1.316	1.708	2.060	2.485	2.787
26	0.256	0.531	0.856	1.315	1.706	2.056	2.479	2.779
27	0.256	0.531	0.855	1.314	1.703	2.052	2.473	2.771
28	0.256	0.530	0.855	1.313	1.701	2.048	2.467	2.763
29	0.256	0.530	0.854	1.311	1.699	2.045	2.462	2.756
30	0.256	0.530	0.854	1.310	1.697	2.042	2.457	2.750
40	0.255	0.529	0.851	1.303	1.684	2.021	2.423	2.704
60	0.254	0.527	0.848	1.296	1.671	2.000	2.390	2.660
120	0.254	0.526	0.845	1.289	1.658	1.980	2.358	2.617
∞	0.253	0.524	0.842	1.282	1.645	1.960	2.326	2.576

Note: The probabilities given in the table are for two-tailed tests. Thus, a probability of 0.05 allows for 0.025 in each tail. For example, for the probability of 0.05 and 21 df, $t = 2.080$. This means that 2.5 percent of the area under the t distribution lies to the right of $t = 2.080$, and 2.5 percent to the left of $t = -2.080$.

Source: From table III of Fisher and Yates, *Statistical Tables for Biological, Agricultural and Medical Research,* 6th ed., 1974, published by Longman Group Ltd., London (previously by Oliver & Boyd, Edinburgh), by permission of the authors and publishers.

Table C-3
***F* Distribution for 5 Percent Significance**

Degrees of Freedom for Denominator	Degrees of Freedom for Numerator																		
	1	2	3	4	5	6	7	8	9	10	12	15	20	24	30	40	60	120	∞
1	161	200	216	225	230	234	237	239	241	242	244	246	248	249	250	251	252	253	254
2	18.5	19.0	19.2	19.2	19.3	19.3	19.4	19.4	19.4	19.4	19.4	19.4	19.5	19.5	19.5	19.5	19.5	19.5	19.5
3	10.1	9.55	9.28	9.12	9.01	8.94	8.89	8.85	8.81	8.79	8.74	8.70	8.66	8.64	8.62	8.59	8.57	8.55	8.53
4	7.71	6.94	6.59	6.39	6.26	6.16	6.09	6.04	6.00	5.96	5.91	5.86	5.80	5.77	5.75	5.72	5.69	5.66	5.63
5	6.61	5.79	5.41	5.19	5.05	4.95	4.88	4.82	4.77	4.74	4.68	4.62	4.56	4.53	4.50	4.46	4.43	4.40	4.37
6	5.99	5.14	4.76	4.53	4.39	4.28	4.21	4.15	4.10	4.06	4.00	3.94	3.87	3.84	3.81	3.77	3.74	3.70	3.67
7	5.59	4.74	4.35	4.12	3.97	3.87	3.79	3.73	3.68	3.64	3.57	3.51	3.44	3.41	3.38	3.34	3.30	3.27	3.23
8	5.32	4.46	4.07	3.84	3.69	3.58	3.50	3.44	3.39	3.35	3.28	3.22	3.15	3.12	3.08	3.04	3.01	2.97	2.93
9	5.12	4.26	3.86	3.63	3.48	3.37	3.29	3.23	3.18	3.14	3.07	3.01	2.94	2.90	2.86	2.83	2.79	2.75	2.71
10	4.96	4.10	3.71	3.48	3.33	3.22	3.14	3.07	3.02	2.98	2.91	2.85	2.77	2.74	2.70	2.66	2.62	2.58	2.54
11	4.84	3.98	3.59	3.36	3.20	3.09	3.01	2.95	2.90	2.85	2.79	2.72	2.65	2.61	2.57	2.53	2.49	2.45	2.40
12	4.75	3.89	3.49	3.26	3.11	3.00	2.91	2.85	2.80	2.75	2.69	2.62	2.54	2.51	2.47	2.43	2.38	2.34	2.30
13	4.67	3.81	3.41	3.18	3.03	2.92	2.83	2.77	2.71	2.67	2.60	2.53	2.46	2.42	2.38	2.34	2.30	2.25	2.21
14	4.60	3.74	3.34	3.11	2.96	2.85	2.76	2.70	2.65	2.60	2.53	2.46	2.39	2.35	2.31	2.27	2.22	2.18	2.13
15	4.54	3.68	3.29	3.06	2.90	2.79	2.71	2.64	2.59	2.54	2.48	2.40	2.33	2.29	2.25	2.20	2.16	2.11	2.07
16	4.49	3.63	3.24	3.01	2.85	2.74	2.66	2.59	2.54	2.49	2.42	2.35	2.28	2.24	2.19	2.15	2.11	2.06	2.01
17	4.45	3.59	3.20	2.96	2.81	2.70	2.61	2.55	2.48	2.45	2.38	2.31	2.23	2.19	2.15	2.10	2.06	2.01	1.96
18	4.41	3.55	3.16	2.93	2.77	2.66	2.58	2.51	2.46	2.41	2.34	2.27	2.19	2.15	2.11	2.06	2.02	1.97	1.92
19	4.38	3.52	3.13	2.90	2.74	2.63	2.54	2.48	2.42	2.39	2.31	2.23	2.16	2.11	2.07	2.03	1.98	1.93	1.88
20	4.35	3.49	3.10	2.87	2.71	2.60	2.51	2.45	2.39	2.35	2.28	2.20	2.12	2.08	2.04	1.99	1.95	1.90	1.84
21	4.32	3.47	3.07	2.84	2.68	2.57	2.49	2.42	2.37	2.32	2.25	2.18	2.10	2.05	2.01	1.96	1.92	1.87	1.81
22	4.30	3.44	3.05	2.82	2.66	2.55	2.46	2.40	2.34	2.30	2.23	2.15	2.07	2.03	1.98	1.94	1.89	1.84	1.78
23	4.28	3.42	3.03	2.80	2.64	2.53	2.44	2.37	2.32	2.27	2.20	2.13	2.05	2.01	1.96	1.91	1.86	1.81	1.76
24	4.26	3.40	3.01	2.78	2.62	2.51	2.42	2.36	2.30	2.25	2.18	2.11	2.03	1.98	1.94	1.89	1.84	1.79	1.73
25	4.24	3.39	2.99	2.76	2.60	2.49	2.40	2.34	2.28	2.24	2.16	2.09	2.01	1.96	1.92	1.87	1.82	1.77	1.71
30	4.17	3.32	2.92	2.69	2.53	2.42	2.33	2.27	2.21	2.16	2.09	2.01	1.93	1.89	1.84	1.79	1.74	1.68	1.62
40	4.08	3.23	2.84	2.61	2.45	2.34	2.25	2.18	2.12	2.08	2.00	1.92	1.84	1.79	1.74	1.69	1.64	1.58	1.51
60	4.00	3.15	2.76	2.53	2.37	2.25	2.17	2.10	2.04	1.99	1.92	1.84	1.75	1.70	1.65	1.59	1.53	1.47	1.39
120	3.92	3.07	2.68	2.45	2.29	2.18	2.09	2.02	1.96	1.91	1.83	1.75	1.66	1.61	1.55	1.50	1.43	1.35	1.25
∞	3.84	3.00	2.60	2.37	2.21	2.10	2.01	1.94	1.88	1.83	1.75	1.67	1.57	1.52	1.46	1.39	1.32	1.22	1.00

Source: M. Merrington and C. M. Thompson, "Tables of Percentage Points of the Inverted Beta (*F*) Distribution," *Biometrica,* vol. 33, 1943, p. 73.

Table C-3

***F* Distribution for 1 Percent Significance**

Degrees of Freedom for Denominator	Degrees of Freedom for Numerator																		
	1	2	3	4	5	6	7	8	9	10	12	15	20	24	30	40	60	120	∞
1	4,052	5,000	5,403	5,625	5,746	5,859	5,928	5,982	6,023	6,056	6,106	6,157	6,209	6,235	6,261	6,287	6,313	6,339	6,366
2	98.5	99.0	99.2	99.2	99.3	99.3	99.4	99.4	99.4	99.4	99.4	99.4	99.4	99.5	99.5	99.5	99.5	99.5	99.5
3	34.1	30.8	29.5	28.7	28.2	27.9	27.7	27.5	27.3	27.2	27.1	26.9	26.7	26.6	26.5	26.4	26.3	26.2	26.1
4	21.2	18.0	16.7	16.0	15.5	15.2	15.0	14.8	14.7	14.5	14.4	14.2	14.0	13.9	13.8	13.7	13.7	13.6	13.5
5	16.3	13.3	12.1	11.4	11.0	10.7	10.5	10.3	10.2	10.1	9.89	9.72	9.55	9.47	9.38	9.29	9.20	9.11	9.02
6	13.7	10.9	9.78	9.15	8.75	8.47	8.26	8.10	7.98	7.87	7.72	7.56	7.40	7.31	7.23	7.14	7.06	6.97	6.88
7	12.2	9.55	8.45	7.85	7.46	7.19	6.99	6.84	6.72	6.62	6.47	6.31	6.16	6.07	5.99	5.91	5.82	5.74	5.65
8	11.3	8.65	7.59	7.01	6.63	6.37	6.18	6.03	5.91	5.81	5.67	5.52	5.36	5.28	5.29	5.12	5.03	4.95	4.86
9	10.6	8.02	6.99	6.42	6.06	5.80	5.61	5.47	5.35	5.26	5.11	4.96	4.81	4.73	4.65	4.57	4.48	4.40	4.31
10	10.0	7.56	6.55	5.99	5.64	5.39	5.20	5.06	4.94	4.85	4.71	4.56	4.41	4.33	4.25	4.17	4.08	4.00	3.91
11	9.65	7.21	6.22	5.67	5.32	5.07	4.89	4.74	4.63	4.54	4.40	4.25	4.10	4.02	3.94	3.86	3.78	3.69	3.60
12	9.33	6.93	5.95	5.41	5.06	4.82	4.64	4.50	4.39	4.30	4.16	4.01	3.86	3.78	3.70	3.62	3.54	3.45	3.36
13	9.07	6.70	5.74	5.21	4.97	4.62	4.44	4.30	4.19	4.10	3.96	3.82	3.66	3.59	3.51	3.43	3.34	3.25	3.17
14	8.86	6.51	5.56	5.04	4.70	4.46	4.28	4.14	4.03	3.94	3.80	3.66	3.51	4.43	3.35	3.27	3.18	3.09	3.00
15	8.68	6.36	5.42	4.89	4.56	4.32	4.14	4.00	3.89	3.80	3.67	3.52	3.37	3.29	3.21	3.13	3.05	2.96	2.87
16	8.53	6.23	5.29	4.77	4.44	4.20	4.03	3.89	3.78	3.69	3.55	3.41	3.26	3.18	3.10	3.02	2.93	2.84	2.75
17	8.40	6.11	5.19	4.67	4.34	4.10	3.93	3.79	3.68	3.59	3.46	3.31	3.16	3.08	3.00	2.92	2.83	2.75	2.65
18	8.29	6.01	5.09	4.58	4.25	4.01	3.84	3.71	3.60	3.51	3.37	3.23	3.08	3.00	2.92	2.84	2.75	2.66	2.57
19	8.19	5.93	5.01	4.50	4.17	3.94	3.77	3.63	3.52	3.43	3.30	3.15	3.00	2.92	2.84	2.76	2.67	2.58	2.49
20	8.10	5.85	4.94	4.43	4.10	3.87	3.70	3.56	3.46	3.37	3.23	3.09	2.94	2.86	2.78	2.68	2.61	2.52	2.42
21	8.02	5.78	4.87	4.37	4.04	3.81	3.64	3.51	3.40	3.31	3.17	3.03	2.88	2.80	2.72	2.64	2.55	2.46	2.36
22	7.95	5.72	4.82	4.31	3.99	3.76	3.59	3.45	3.35	3.26	3.12	2.98	2.83	2.75	2.67	2.58	2.50	2.40	2.31
23	7.88	5.66	4.76	4.26	3.94	3.71	3.54	3.41	3.30	3.21	3.07	2.93	2.78	2.70	2.62	2.54	2.45	2.35	2.26
24	7.82	5.61	4.72	4.22	3.90	3.67	3.50	3.36	3.26	3.17	3.03	2.89	2.74	2.66	2.58	2.49	2.40	2.31	2.21
25	7.77	5.57	4.68	4.18	3.86	3.63	3.46	3.32	3.22	3.13	2.99	2.85	2.70	2.62	2.53	2.45	2.36	2.27	2.17
30	7.56	5.39	4.51	4.02	3.70	3.47	3.30	3.17	3.07	2.98	2.84	2.70	2.55	2.47	2.30	2.39	2.21	2.11	2.01
40	7.31	5.18	4.31	3.83	3.51	3.29	3.12	2.99	2.89	2.80	2.66	2.52	2.37	2.29	2.20	2.11	2.02	1.92	1.80
60	7.08	4.98	4.13	3.65	3.34	3.12	2.95	2.82	2.72	2.63	2.50	2.35	2.20	2.12	2.03	1.94	1.84	1.73	1.60
120	6.85	4.79	3.95	3.48	3.17	2.96	2.79	2.66	2.56	2.47	2.34	2.19	2.03	1.94	1.86	1.76	1.66	1.53	1.38
∞	6.63	4.61	3.78	3.32	3.02	2.80	2.64	2.51	2.41	2.32	2.18	2.04	1.88	1.79	1.70	1.59	1.47	1.32	1.00

Source: M. Merrington and C. M. Thompson, "Tables of Percentage Points of the Inverted Beta (*F*) Distribution," *Biometrica,* vol. 33, 1943, p. 73.

Table C-4
Durbin-Watson Statistic for 5 Percent Significance Points of d_L and d_U

	$k' = 1$		$k' = 2$		$k' = 3$		$k' = 4$		$k' = 5$	
n	d_L	d_U	d_L	d_U	d_L	d_U	d_L	d_U	d_L	d_U
15	1.08	1.36	0.95	1.54	0.82	1.75	0.69	1.97	0.56	2.21
16	1.10	1.37	0.98	1.54	0.86	1.73	0.74	1.93	0.62	2.15
17	1.13	1.38	1.02	1.54	0.90	1.71	0.78	1.90	0.67	2.10
18	1.16	1.39	1.05	1.53	0.93	1.69	0.82	1.87	0.71	2.06
19	1.18	1.40	1.08	1.53	0.97	1.68	0.86	1.85	0.75	2.02
20	1.20	1.41	1.10	1.54	1.00	1.68	0.90	1.83	0.79	1.99
21	1.22	1.42	1.13	1.54	1.03	1.67	0.93	1.81	0.83	1.96
22	1.24	1.43	1.15	1.54	1.05	1.66	0.96	1.80	0.86	1.94
23	1.26	1.44	1.17	1.54	1.08	1.66	0.99	1.79	0.90	1.92
24	1.27	1.45	1.19	1.55	1.10	1.66	1.01	1.78	0.93	1.90
25	1.29	1.45	1.21	1.55	1.12	1.66	1.04	1.77	0.95	1.89
26	1.30	1.46	1.22	1.55	1.14	1.65	1.06	1.76	0.98	1.88
27	1.32	1.47	1.24	1.56	1.16	1.65	1.08	1.76	1.01	1.86
28	1.33	1.48	1.26	1.56	1.18	1.65	1.10	1.75	1.03	1.85
29	1.34	1.48	1.27	1.56	1.20	1.65	1.12	1.74	1.05	1.84
30	1.35	1.49	1.28	1.57	1.21	1.65	1.14	1.74	1.07	1.83
31	1.36	1.50	1.30	1.57	1.23	1.65	1.16	1.74	1.09	1.83
32	1.37	1.50	1.31	1.57	1.24	1.65	1.18	1.73	1.11	1.82
33	1.38	1.51	1.32	1.58	1.26	1.65	1.19	1.73	1.13	1.81
34	1.39	1.51	1.33	1.58	1.27	1.65	1.21	1.73	1.15	1.81
35	1.40	1.52	1.34	1.58	1.28	1.65	1.22	1.73	1.16	1.80
36	1.41	1.52	1.35	1.59	1.29	1.65	1.24	1.73	1.18	1.80
37	1.42	1.53	1.36	1.59	1.31	1.66	1.25	1.72	1.19	1.80
38	1.43	1.54	1.37	1.59	1.32	1.66	1.26	1.72	1.21	1.79
39	1.43	1.54	1.38	1.60	1.33	1.66	1.27	1.72	1.22	1.79
40	1.44	1.54	1.39	1.60	1.34	1.66	1.29	1.72	1.23	1.79
45	1.48	1.57	1.43	1.62	1.38	1.67	1.34	1.72	1.29	1.78
50	1.50	1.59	1.46	1.63	1.42	1.67	1.38	1.72	1.34	1.77
55	1.53	1.60	1.49	1.64	1.45	1.68	1.41	1.72	1.38	1.77
60	1.55	1.62	1.51	1.65	1.48	1.69	1.44	1.73	1.41	1.77
65	1.57	1.63	1.54	1.66	1.50	1.70	1.47	1.73	1.44	1.77
70	1.58	1.64	1.55	1.67	1.52	1.70	1.49	1.74	1.46	1.77
75	1.60	1.65	1.57	1.68	1.54	1.71	1.51	1.74	1.49	1.77
80	1.61	1.66	1.59	1.69	1.56	1.72	1.53	1.74	1.51	1.77
85	1.62	1.67	1.60	1.70	1.57	1.72	1.55	1.75	1.52	1.77
90	1.63	1.68	1.61	1.70	1.59	1.73	1.57	1.75	1.54	1.78
95	1.64	1.69	1.62	1.71	1.60	1.73	1.58	1.75	1.56	1.78
100	1.65	1.69	1.63	1.72	1.61	1.74	1.59	1.76	1.57	1.78

Note: n = number of observations; k' = number of independent variables.

Source: J. Durbin and G. S. Watson, "Testing for Serial Correlation in Least Squares Regression," *Biometrica,* vol. 38, 1951, pp. 159–177. Reprinted with the permission of the authors and the trustees of *Biometrica.*

Table C-4
Durbin-Watson Statistic for 1 Percent Significance Points of d_L and d_U

	$k' = 1$		$k' = 2$		$k' = 3$		$k' = 4$		$k' = 5$	
n	d_L	d_U	d_L	d_U	d_L	d_U	d_L	d_U	d_L	d_U
15	0.81	1.07	0.70	1.25	0.59	1.46	0.49	1.70	0.39	1.96
16	0.84	1.09	0.74	1.25	0.63	1.44	0.53	1.66	0.44	1.90
17	0.87	1.10	0.77	1.25	0.67	1.43	0.57	1.63	0.48	1.85
18	0.90	1.12	0.80	1.26	0.71	1.42	0.61	1.60	0.52	1.80
19	0.93	1.13	0.83	1.26	0.74	1.41	0.65	1.58	0.56	1.77
20	0.95	1.15	0.86	1.27	0.77	1.41	0.68	1.57	0.60	1.74
21	0.97	1.16	0.89	1.27	0.80	1.41	0.72	1.55	0.63	1.71
22	1.00	1.17	0.91	1.28	0.83	1.40	0.75	1.54	0.66	1.69
23	1.02	1.19	0.94	1.29	0.86	1.40	0.77	1.53	0.70	1.67
24	1.04	1.20	0.96	1.30	0.88	1.41	0.80	1.53	0.72	1.66
25	1.05	1.21	0.98	1.30	0.90	1.41	0.83	1.52	0.75	1.65
26	1.07	1.22	1.00	1.31	0.93	1.41	0.85	1.52	0.78	1.64
27	1.09	1.23	1.02	1.32	0.95	1.41	0.88	1.51	0.81	1.63
28	1.10	1.24	1.04	1.32	0.97	1.41	0.90	1.51	0.83	1.62
29	1.12	1.25	1.05	1.33	0.99	1.42	0.92	1.51	0.85	1.61
30	1.13	1.26	1.07	1.34	1.01	1.42	0.94	1.51	0.88	1.61
31	1.15	1.27	1.08	1.34	1.02	1.42	0.96	1.51	0.90	1.60
32	1.16	1.28	1.10	1.35	1.04	1.43	0.98	1.51	0.92	1.60
33	1.17	1.29	1.11	1.36	1.05	1.43	1.00	1.51	0.94	1.59
34	1.18	1.30	1.13	1.36	1.07	1.43	1.01	1.51	0.95	1.59
35	1.19	1.31	1.14	1.37	1.08	1.44	1.03	1.51	0.97	1.59
36	1.21	1.32	1.15	1.38	1.10	1.44	1.04	1.51	0.99	1.59
37	1.22	1.32	1.16	1.38	1.11	1.45	1.06	1.51	1.00	1.59
38	1.23	1.33	1.18	1.39	1.12	1.45	1.07	1.52	1.02	1.58
39	1.24	1.34	1.19	1.39	1.14	1.45	1.09	1.52	1.03	1.58
40	1.25	1.34	1.20	1.40	1.15	1.46	1.10	1.52	1.05	1.58
45	1.29	1.38	1.24	1.42	1.20	1.48	1.16	1.53	1.11	1.58
50	1.32	1.40	1.28	1.45	1.24	1.49	1.20	1.54	1.16	1.59
55	1.36	1.43	1.32	1.47	1.28	1.51	1.25	1.55	1.21	1.59
60	1.38	1.45	1.35	1.48	1.32	1.52	1.28	1.56	1.25	1.60
65	1.41	1.47	1.38	1.50	1.35	1.53	1.31	1.57	1.28	1.61
70	1.43	1.49	1.40	1.52	1.37	1.55	1.34	1.58	1.31	1.61
75	1.45	1.50	1.42	1.53	1.39	1.56	1.37	1.59	1.34	1.62
80	1.47	1.52	1.44	1.54	1.42	1.57	1.39	1.60	1.36	1.62
85	1.48	1.53	1.46	1.55	1.43	1.58	1.41	1.60	1.39	1.63
90	1.50	1.54	1.47	1.56	1.45	1.59	1.43	1.61	1.41	1.64
95	1.51	1.55	1.49	1.57	1.47	1.60	1.45	1.62	1.42	1.64
100	1.52	1.56	1.50	1.58	1.48	1.60	1.46	1.63	1.44	1.65

Note: n = number of observations; k' = number of independent variables.
Source: J. Durbin and G. S. Watson, "Testing for Serial Correlation in Least Squares Regression," *Biometrica,* vol. 38, 1951, pp. 159–177. Reprinted with the permission of the authors and the trustees of *Biometrica.*

APPENDIX D

Answers to Selected (Asterisked) Problems

CHAPTERS 1 THROUGH 14

CHAPTER 1

3. $$PV = \frac{\$100}{(1.15)^1} + \frac{\$100}{(1.15)^2} + \frac{\$800}{(1.15)^2}$$
$$= \frac{\$100}{1.15} + \frac{\$100}{1.3225} + \frac{\$800}{1.3225}$$
$$= \$86.96 + \$75.61 + \$604.91$$
$$= \$767.48$$

(The computer-generated solution gives $767.47 as the answer because of a difference in rounding. The same may be true for some of the other solutions.)

5. $$\text{Project 1: } PV = \frac{\$100{,}000}{1.10} + \frac{\$100{,}000}{(1.10)^2} + \frac{\$100{,}000}{(1.10)^3} + \frac{\$100{,}000}{(1.10)^4}$$
$$= \frac{\$100{,}000}{1.10} + \frac{\$100{,}000}{1.21} + \frac{\$100{,}000}{1.331} + \frac{\$100{,}000}{1.4641}$$
$$= \$316{,}986.55$$

$$\text{Project 2: } PV = \frac{\$75{,}000}{1.10} + \frac{\$75{,}000}{(1.10)^2} + \frac{\$75{,}000}{(1.10)^3} + \frac{\$75{,}000}{(1.10)^4}$$
$$+ \frac{\$75{,}000}{(1.10)^5} + \frac{\$75{,}000}{(1.10)^6}$$
$$= \$326{,}644.55$$

The manager should choose project 2.

8. The explicit costs are $6,000 for tuition, plus $2,000 for the room, plus $1,500 for meals, plus $500 for books and supplies, for a total of $10,000 per year. The implicit costs are given by the sum of $15,000 which the student could have earned by getting a job instead of going to college and the $1,000 of interest foregone on the $10,000 of expenses for a year, for a total of $16,000. The total economic cost of attending college for a year by this student equals the sum of its explicit costs of $10,000 and the implicit costs of $16,000, or $26,000.

CHAPTER 2

3. (*a*) The average profit ($\overline{\pi}$) and marginal profit ($\dot{\pi}$) schedules are derived in Table 1.

   (*b*) The π, $\overline{\pi}$, and $\dot{\pi}$ schedules of Table 1 are plotted in Figure 1.

   (*c*) The slope of a ray from the origin to the π curve, or $\overline{\pi}$, is negative at first but rises up to almost $Q = 3$, after which it declines, becomes zero at $Q = 4$, and negative thereafter (because π is once again negative). On the other hand, the slope of the π curve, or $\dot{\pi}$, is zero at $Q = 1$, but it rises

Table 1

Q	π	$\overline{\pi} = \pi/Q$	$\dot{\pi} = \Delta\pi/\Delta Q$
0	$-20	—	—
1	−50	$−50	$−30
2	0	0	50
3	30	10	30
4	0	0	−30

up to $Q = 2$ (the point of inflection) and declines thereafter, in such a way that $\dot{\pi}$ is zero at $Q = 1$ and $Q = 3$ (where the π curve has zero slope). As the $\overline{\pi}$ curve rises, reaches its highest point, and declines, the $\dot{\pi}$ curve is above it, intersects it, and is below it, respectively. Note that $\overline{\pi}$ is highest at a smaller level of output than the one ($Q = 3$) at which π is maximum.

6. (*a*) In Figure 2, the profit-maximizing output is $Q = 3$. This is the level of output at which the MC curve intersects the MR curve from below. We can explain why the firm maximizes total profits (π) at $Q = 3$ by showing that it pays for the firm to expand an output smaller than 3 units and reduce a larger output. For example, at $Q = 2$, $MR > MC$. Therefore, the firm is adding more to its TR than to its TC, and so π increases by expanding output. On the other hand, at $Q = 4$, $MR < MC$. Therefore,

Figure 1

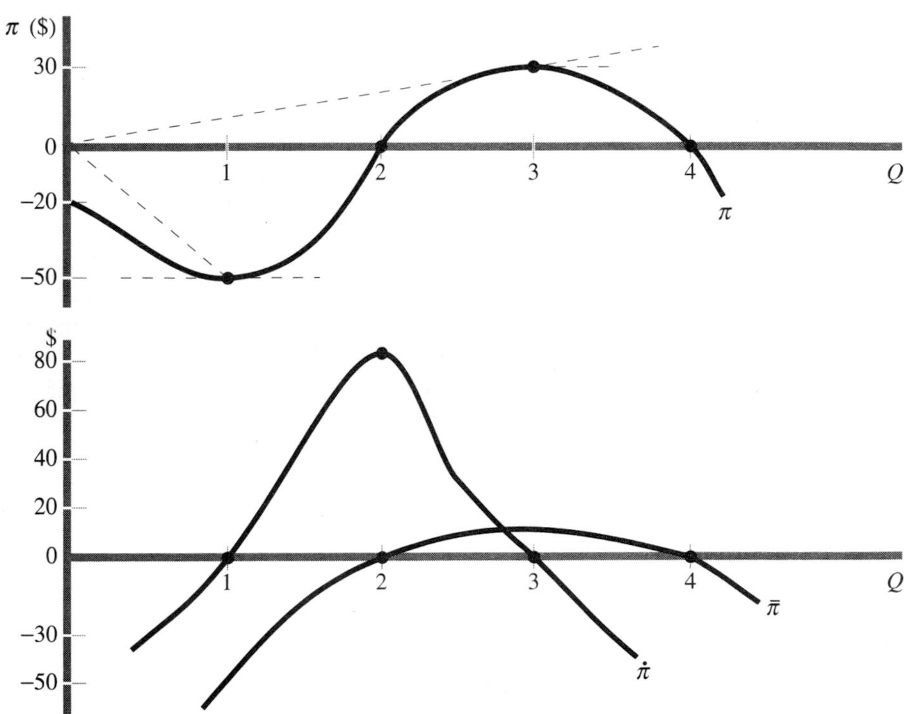

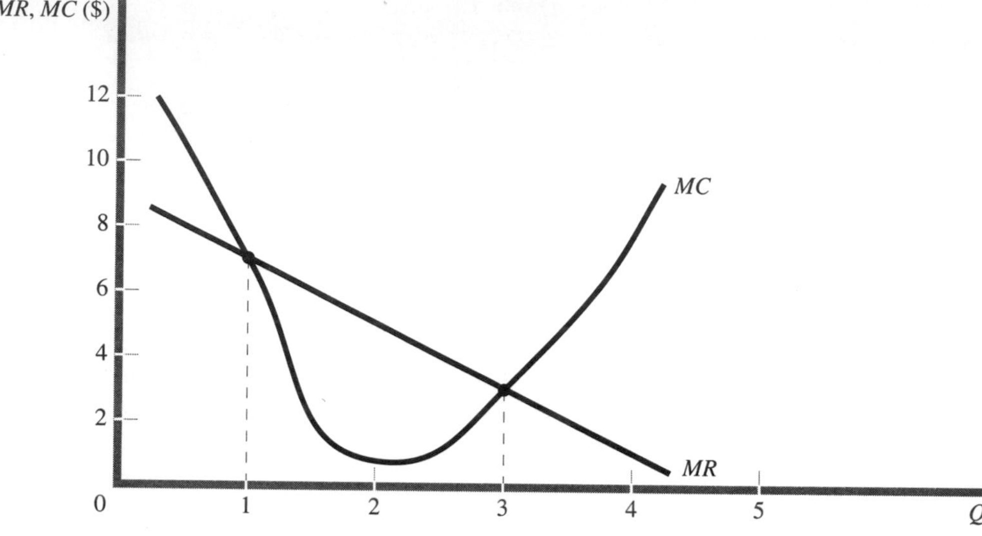

Figure 2

the firm is adding less to its *TR* than to its *TC*, and so increases by *reducing* output. At $Q = 3$, $MR = MC$. Therefore, the firm is adding as much to *TR* as to *TC* and π is maximum. Note, however, that $MR = MC$ at $Q = 1$ also. But at $Q = 1$, the firm has produced all the (fractional) units of the commodity for which $MC > MR$, and so the firm maximizes its total loss. To distinguish between the loss-maximizing and the profit-maximizing level of output (since at both levels of output $MR = MC$), we seek the level of output at which $MR = MC$ *and* the *MC* curve intersects the *MR* curve from below. This corresponds to looking for the level of output at which the π curve has zero slope and faces down (i.e., its slope diminishes, from positive, to zero, to negative).

(*b*) The answer to part (*a*) is an example of marginal analysis and optimization behavior in general because it shows that an organization (say, a business firm) should pursue an activity (say, expand output) as long as the marginal benefit (say, marginal revenue) from the activity exceeds the marginal cost and until the marginal benefit equals the marginal cost. By doing so, the organization (firm) maximizes the benefit (total profit) from the activity. Marginal analysis, therefore, is a most important tool of optimizing behavior on the part of any organization, and especially of a business firm.

8. (*a*)
$$\begin{aligned}\pi &= TR - TC\\ &= 22Q - 0.5Q^2 - \left(\tfrac{1}{3}Q^3 - 8.5Q^2 + 50Q + 90\right)\\ &= 22Q - 0.5Q^2 - \tfrac{1}{3}Q^3 + 8.5Q^2 - 50Q - 90\\ &= -\tfrac{1}{3}Q^3 + 8Q^2 - 28Q - 90\end{aligned}$$

To maximize π, we set $d\pi/dQ = 0$ and show that $d^2\pi/dQ^2 < 0$ at Q where $d\pi/dQ = 0$:

$$\frac{d\pi}{dQ} = -Q^2 + 16Q - 28 = 0$$

$$(Q - 2)(-Q + 14) = 0$$

$$Q = 2 \quad \text{and} \quad Q = 14$$

$$\frac{d^2\pi}{dQ^2} = -2Q + 16$$

At $Q = 2$, $d^2\pi/dQ^2 = -2(2) + 16 = 12 > 0$, and π is minimum. At $Q = 14$, $d^2\pi/dQ^2 = -2(14) + 16 = -12 < 0$, and π is maximum.

(*b*) To find the maximum profit that the firm could earn, we substitute $Q = 14$ into the π function found in part (*a*). That is,

$$\begin{aligned}\pi &= -\tfrac{1}{3}Q^3 + 8Q^2 - 28Q - 90 \\ &= -\tfrac{1}{3}(14)^3 + 8(14)^2 - 28(14) - 90 \\ &= -914.67 + 1{,}568 - 392 - 90 \\ &= \$171.33\end{aligned}$$

11. (*a*) To determine the level of output of commodity X and commodity Y that will maximize the total profit of the firm for the following function:

$$\pi = 144X - 3X^2 - XY - 2Y^2 + 120Y - 35$$

we set the partial derivative of π with respect to X and Y equal to zero and solve. That is,

$$\frac{\partial\pi}{\partial X} = 144 - 6X - Y = 0$$

$$\frac{\partial\pi}{\partial Y} = -X - 4Y + 120 = 0$$

Multiplying the first expression by -4, rearranging the second, and adding, we get

$$\begin{array}{r} -576 + 24X + 4Y = 0 \\ 120 - X - 4Y = 0 \\ \hline -456 + 23X = 0 \end{array}$$

Therefore, $X = 19.83$. Substituting $X = 19.83$ into the first expression of the partial derivative set equal to zero, and solving for Y, we get

$$144 - 6(19.83) - Y = 0$$

Therefore, $Y = 144 - 118.98 = 25.02$. Thus, the firm maximizes π when it sells 19.83 units of commodity X and 25.02 units of commodity Y.

(*b*) To determine the maximum amount of the total profit of the firm, we substitute the values of $X = 19.83$ and $Y = 25.02$ into the original function and obtain

$$\pi = 144(19.83) - 3(19.83)^2 - 19.83(25.02) - 2(25.02)^2$$
$$+ 120(25.02) - 35$$
$$= \$2{,}895.09$$

CHAPTER 3

2. (*a*) The number of Chevrolets purchased per year (Q_C) declines by 100 units for each \$1 increase in the price of Chevrolets (P_C), increases by 2,000 units for each 1 million increase in population (N), increases by 50 units for each \$1 increase in per capita disposable income (I), and increases by 30 units for each dollar increase in the price of Fords (P_F). On the other hand, Q_C declines by 1,000 for each 1 cent increase in the price of gasoline (P_G), increases by 3 units for each \$1 increase in advertising expenditures on Chevrolets (A), and increases by 40,000 units for each 1 percentage point reduction in the rate of interest charged to borrow to purchase Chevrolets (P_I).

(*b*) To find the value of Q_C, we substitute the average value of the independent or explanatory variables into the estimated demand function. Thus, for $P_C = \$9{,}000$, $N = 200$ million, $I = \$10{,}000$, $P_F = \$8{,}000$, $P_G = 80$ cents, $A = \$200{,}000$, and $P_I = 1$ percentage point, we have

$$Q_C = 100{,}000 - 100(9{,}000) + 2{,}000(200) + 50(10{,}000)$$
$$+ 30(8{,}000) - 1{,}000(80) + 3(200{,}000) + 40{,}000(1)$$
$$= 100{,}000 - 900{,}000 + 400{,}000 + 500{,}000 + 240{,}000$$
$$- 80{,}000 + 600{,}000 + 40{,}000$$
$$= 900{,}000$$

(*c*) To derive the equation for the demand curve for Chevrolets, we substitute into the estimated demand equation the average value of all the independent or explanatory variables given above, with the exception of P_C. Thus, the equation of the demand curve for Chevrolets is

$$Q_C = 100{,}000 - 100P_C + 2{,}000(200) + 50(10{,}000) + 30(8{,}000)$$
$$- 1{,}000(80) + 3(200{,}000) + 40{,}000(1)$$
$$= 1{,}800{,}000 - 100P_C$$

(*d*) To derive the demand curve for Chevrolets (D_C), we substitute the hypothetical values of \$12,000, \$9,000, and \$6,000 for P_C into the equation of the demand curve found in part (*c*). This gives, respectively, $Q_C = 600{,}000$, $Q_C = 900{,}000$, and $Q_C = 1{,}200{,}000$. Plotting these price-quantity values, we get the demand curve for Chevrolets, D_C, shown in Figure 3.

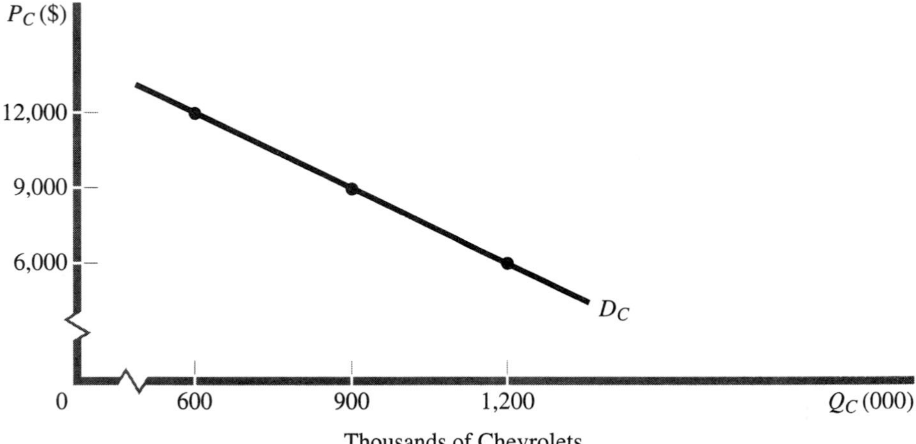

Figure 3

5. Figure 4 shows how Michael could have found the price elasticity of demand for ice cream graphically at P_I = $4. We can also use Figure 4 to show that the price elasticity of demand at P_I = $4 would have been the same if the demand curve for ice cream had been curvilinear but tangent to the linear demand curve given in Problem 4 at P_I = $4. For linear demand curve D_I, E_P at P_I = $4 is given by

$$E_P = \frac{P}{P - A} = \frac{\$4}{\$4 - \$6} = \frac{\$4}{-\$2} = -2$$

where P is the price of the commodity at which we want to find E_P, and A is the price of the commodity at which $Q = 0$ (see footnote 10 in Section 3-2

Figure 4

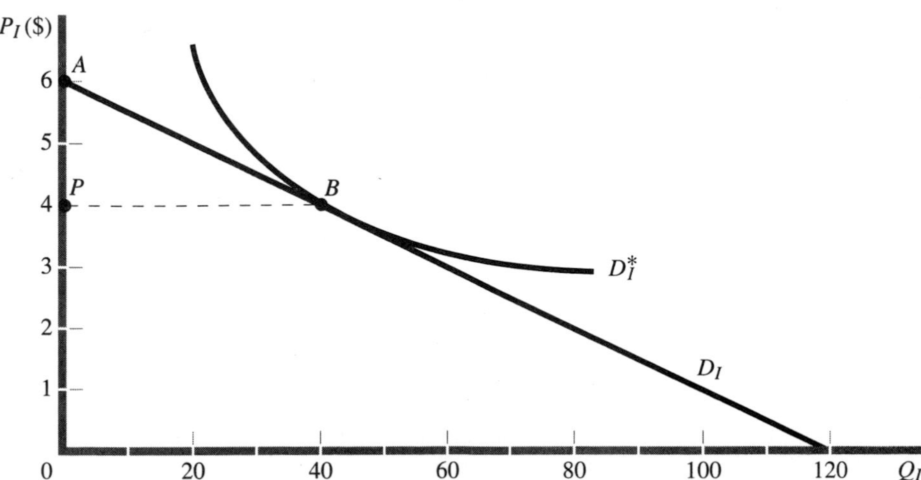

in the text). The value of E_P at other points on D_I can be similarly obtained. If the demand curve were curvilinear (D_I^* in Figure 4) and tangent to D_I at P_I = \$4, $E_P = -2$ at P_I = \$4, as for D_I.

8. (*a*) The income elasticity of demand (E_I) is given by

$$\frac{\Delta Q}{\Delta I} \cdot \frac{I}{Q}$$

where ΔQ is the change in quantity, and ΔI is the change in income. The estimated coefficient of I in the regression of Q on I and other explanatory variables is 10. That is,

$$\frac{\Delta Q}{\Delta I} = 10$$

Thus, with income of \$10,000 and sales of 80,000 units, E_I = 10(10,000/80,000) = 1.25.

(*b*) For an increase in sales from 80,000 to 90,000 units and an increase in consumers' income from \$10,000 to \$11,000,

$$E_I = \frac{Q2 - Q1}{I2 - I1} \cdot \frac{I2 + I1}{Q2 + Q1}$$

$$= \frac{90{,}000 - 80{,}000}{\$11{,}000 - \$10{,}000} \cdot \frac{\$11{,}000 + \$10{,}000}{90{,}000 + 80{,}000} = 1.24$$

Since E_I is positive, the good is normal, and since E_I exceeds 1, the good is a luxury.

11. (*a*) Since $E_P = -2$, if the firm increased the price of steel by 6 percent, its sales would change by (−2)(6 percent) = −12 percent. With E_I = 1, the forecasted increase in income of 4 percent, by itself, would result in a (1)(4 percent) = 4 percent increase in the steel sold by the firm. Finally, since E_{XY} = 1.5, a *reduction* in the price of aluminum of 2 percent, by itself, will result in a (1.5)(−2) = −3 percent change in steel sales. Therefore, the net effect of a 6 percent increase in the price of steel by the firm, a 4 percent increase in income, and a 2 percent reduction in the price of aluminum would result in a net decline in the sales of the firm of −12 percent + 4 percent − 3 percent = −11 percent. Thus, the steel sales of the firm next year would be 1,200 − (1,200)(−11 percent) = 1,200 − 132 = 1,068 tons.

(*b*) By themselves (i.e., without any increase in the price of steel), the increase in income and the reduction in the price of aluminum would result in a 1 percent increase in the steel sales of the firm. Thus, in order to keep sales unchanged, the firm can only increase the price of the steel so that, by itself, it would reduce the demand for steel by 1 percent. Since the price elasticity of demand of the steel is −2, the firm can increase the price of the steel by only 0.5 percent.

CHAPTER 4

2. (*a*) See Figure 5.

   (*b*) See Figure 6.

   (*c*) Because of changing and varying weather conditions, the supply curve of agricultural commodities is likely to shift much more than the demand curve (since most foods are necessities). Thus, it may be easier to derive or identify the demand curve than the supply curve of agricultural commodities from the observed price-quantity data points. The same may be true in the markets for commodities, such as pocket calculators, where very rapid technological change shifted the supply curve of pocket calculators in a very short time during which demand conditions did not change much. In the case of most industrial commodities, however, the demand curve is more likely to shift than the supply curve because of business cycles. Thus, it may be easier to derive or identify the supply curve than the demand curve from the observed price-quantity data points.

3. (*a*) Since the price elasticity of demand for Florida Indian River oranges is −3.07, a 10 percent decrease in the price of these oranges would increase their quantity demanded by (−10 percent) (−3.07) = 30.7 percent. Since the price elasticity of demand for Florida interior oranges is −3.01, a 10 percent decrease in the price of these oranges would increase their quantity demanded by (−10 percent) · (−3.01) = 30.1 percent. Since the price elasticity of demand for California oranges is −2.76, a 10 percent decrease in the price of these oranges would increase their quantity demanded by (−10 percent) · (−2.76) = 27.6 percent.

   (*b*) Since the demand for all three types of oranges is price elastic, a decline in price will increase the total revenue of the sellers of all three types

Figure 5

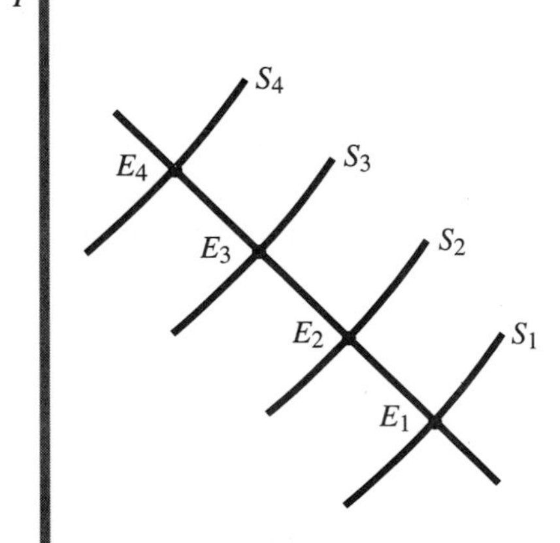

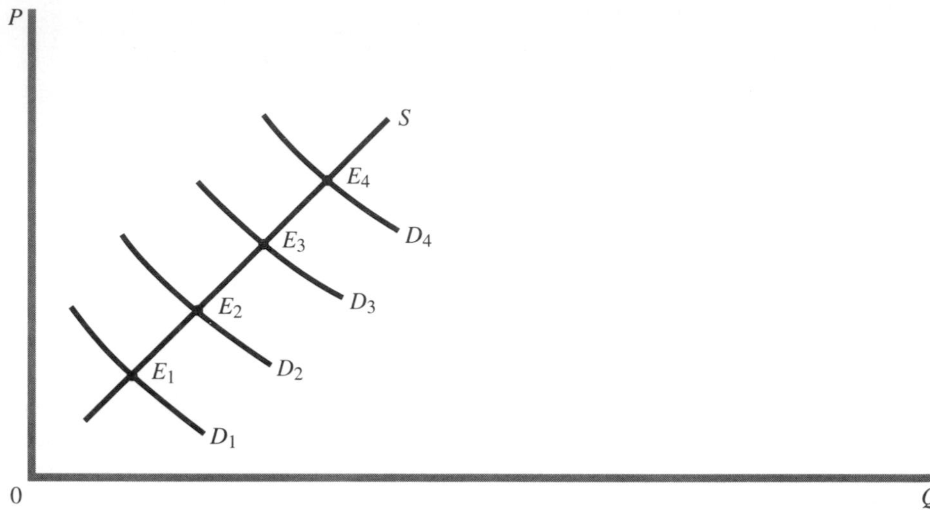

Figure 6

of oranges because the percentage increase in quantity sold exceeds the percentage decrease in their prices. Specifically, for the sellers of Florida Indian River oranges, the 10 percent decrease in price would result in an increase in the quantity sold of 30.7 percent, so that their total revenue would increase by 30.7 percent − 10 percent = 20.7 percent. For the sellers of Florida interior oranges, the 10 percent decrease in price would result in an increase in the quantity sold of 30.1 percent, so that their total revenue would increase by 30.1 percent − 10 percent = 20.1 percent. For the sellers of California oranges, the 10 percent decrease in price would result in an increase in the quantity sold of 27.6 percent, so that their total revenue would increase by 27.6 percent − 10 percent = 17.6 percent.

(*c*) Total profits are equal to the total revenue minus the total costs. We know from part (*b*) that the sellers' total revenue increases, but their total costs will also increase (to grow, transport, and sell more oranges). Their profits will increase if the increase in their total revenue exceeds the increase in their total costs. Since we do not know by how much total costs increase by selling more oranges, we cannot answer this question more precisely.

5. (*a*) Table 2 shows the calculations to find *a* and *b* for the data in Table 4-6 in the text on sales revenues of the firm (Y) and its expenditures on quality control (for simplicity, label this Z rather than X_2 here).

$$\hat{b} = \frac{\sum_{t=1}^{n} (Z_t - \overline{Z})(Y_t - \overline{Y})}{\sum_{t=1}^{n} (Z_t - \overline{Z})^2} = \frac{110}{32} = 3.44$$

Table 2
Calculations to Estimate Regression Line of Sales on Quality Control

Year	Y_t	Z_t	$Y_t - \bar{Y}$	$Z_t - \bar{Z}$	$(Z_t - \bar{Z})(Y_t - \bar{Y})$	$\Sigma(Z_t - \bar{Z})^2$
1	44	3	−6	−2	12	4
2	40	4	−10	−1	10	1
3	42	3	−8	−2	16	4
4	46	3	−4	−2	8	4
5	48	4	−2	−1	2	1
6	52	5	2	0	0	0
7	54	6	4	1	4	1
8	58	7	8	2	16	4
9	56	7	6	2	12	4
10	60	8	10	3	30	9
$n = 10$	$\Sigma Y_t = 500$ $\bar{Y} = 50$	$\Sigma Z_t = 50$ $\bar{Z} = 5$	$\Sigma(Y_t - \bar{Y}) = 0$	$\Sigma(Z_t - \bar{Z}) = 0$	$\Sigma(Z_t - \bar{Z})(Y_t - \bar{Y}) = 110$	$\Sigma(Z_t - \bar{Z})^2 = 32$

By then using the value of $\hat{b}$ found above and the values of Y and Z found in Table 2, we get the value of $\hat{a}$

$$\hat{a} = \overline{Y} - \hat{b}\overline{Z} = 50 - 3.44(5) = 32.80$$

Thus, the equation of the regression line is

$$\hat{Y}_t = 32.80 + 3.44Z_t$$

(*b*) With quality-control expenditures of \$3 million as in the first observation year (i.e., with Z_1 = \$3 million), Y_1 = \$32.80 + \$3.44(3) = \$43.12 million. On the other hand, with Z_{10} = \$8 million, Y_{10} = \$32.80 + \$3.44(8) = \$60.32 million. Plotting these two points [(3, 43.12) and (8, 60.32)] and joining them by a straight line, we have the regression line plotted in Figure 7.

(*c*) If the firm's expenditure on quality control were \$2 million, its estimated sales revenue would be

$$\hat{Y}_t = 32.80 + 3.44(2) = \$39.68 \text{ million}$$

On the other hand, if the firm's expenditure on quality control were \$9 million, its estimated sales revenue would be

$$\hat{Y}_t = 32.80 + 3.44(9) = \$63.76 \text{ million}$$

These results are greatly biased because, as we have seen in the text, the sales revenues of the firm also depend in an important way on its advertising expenditures. By including only the firm's quality-control expenditures in estimating the regression line, we obtain biased estimates for the *a* and *b* parameters and, therefore, biased values for the forecast of the firm's sales revenues. The same, of course, is the case when sales revenues are regressed only on the firm's advertising expenditures (as was done in

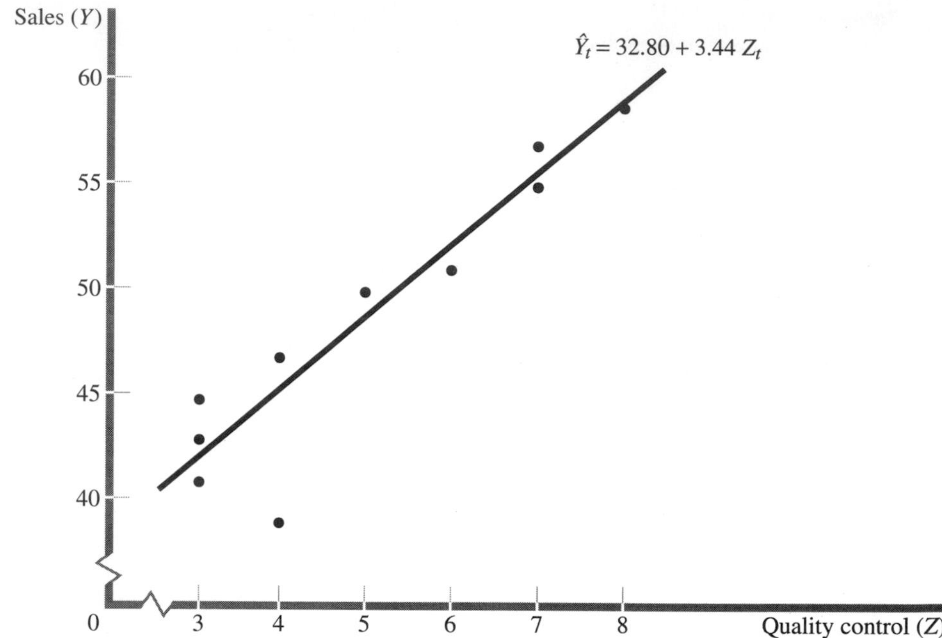

Figure 7

the text). The only reason for running these simple regressions is to make it easier for the student to understand how regression analysis is performed and how its results are interpreted.

6. (*a*)

$$\hat{Y}_t = 114.074 - 9.470X_{1t} + 0.029X_{2t}$$
$$(-5.205) \qquad (4.506)$$
$$R^2 = 0.96822 \qquad \bar{R}^2 = 0.96448 \qquad F = 258.942$$

The value of $b_1 = -9.47$ indicates that a \$1 decline in the price of the commodity will lead to a 9.47-unit increase in the quantity demanded of the commodity. On the other hand, the value of $b_2 = 0.029$ indicates that a \$100 increase in consumer's income will increase the quantity demanded of the commodity by 2.9 units.

(*b*) Since the t statistic for both b_1 and b_2 exceeds the critical t value of 2.110 for 17 df, both slope coefficients are statistically significant at the 5 percent level.

(*c*) The unadjusted and adjusted coefficients of determination are $R^2 = 0.96822$ and $\bar{R}^2 = 0.96448$, respectively. This means that the variation in price and income explains 96.82 percent of the variation in the quantity demanded of the commodity when no adjustment is made for degrees of freedom and 96.45 percent when such an adjustment is made.

(*d*) Since the value of the F statistic exceeds the critical F value of 3.59 with $k - 1 = 3 - 1 = 2$ and $n - k = 20 - 3 = 17$ df, we accept the hypothesis that the regression explains a significant proportion of the variation in the quantity demanded of the commodity (Y) at the 5 percent level of significance.

CHAPTER 5

1. (*a*) Regressing gasoline sales (S_t) on time, from $t = 1$ from the first quarter of 1986 to $t = 16$ for the last quarter of 1989, we get

$$S_t = 636.52 + \underset{(2.01)}{3.0309t} \quad R^2 = 0.28$$

Using these regression results to forecast gasoline sales (in millions of gallons) for each quarter of 1990, we get

$S_{17} = 636.52 + 3.0309(17) = 688.05$ in the first quarter of 1990
$S_{18} = 636.52 + 3.0309(18) = 691.08$ in the second quarter of 1990
$S_{19} = 636.52 + 3.0309(19) = 694.11$ in the third quarter of 1990
$S_{20} = 636.52 + 3.0309(20) = 697.14$ in the fourth quarter of 1986

(*b*) Regressing the logarithm of gasoline sales ($\ln S_t$) on time, from $t = 1$ for the first quarter of 1986 to $t = 16$ for the last quarter of 1989, we get

$$\ln S_t = 6.46 + \underset{(2.33)}{0.0047t} \quad R^2 = 0.28$$

Since the estimated parameters are based on the logarithms of the data, however, they must be converted into their antilogs to be interpreted in terms of the original data. The antilog of $\ln S_0 = 6.46$ is $S_0 = 639.06$ and the antilog of $\ln(1 + g) = 0.0047$ gives $1 + g = 1.0047$. Substituting these values back into the equation, we get

$$S_t = 639.06(1.0047)^t$$

where $S_0 = 639.06$ million barrels is the estimated sales of gasoline in the United States in the fourth quarter of 1985 (i.e., at $t = 0$) and the estimated growth rate is 1.0047, or 0.47 percent per quarter.

To estimate sales (in millions of barrels) in any future quarter, we substitute into the above equation the value of t for the quarter for which we are seeking to forecast S and solve for S_t. Thus,

$S_{17} = 639.06(1.0047)^{17} = 692.09$ in the first quarter of 1990
$S_{18} = 639.06(1.0047)^{18} = 695.34$ in the second quarter of 1990
$S_{19} = 639.06(1.0047)^{19} = 698.61$ in the third quarter of 1990
$S_{20} = 639.06(1.0047)^{20} = 701.89$ in the fourth quarter of 1990

(*c*) Since the value of the t statistic is higher for the constant logarithmic trend than for the linear trend, the latter seems to fit the data marginally better. However, both fits are very poor (i.e., they "explain" less than 30 percent of the variation in the quarterly sales of gasoline).

If we used either trend projection to forecast gasoline sales for 1990, they would be very poor because they do not take into consideration the strong seasonal factor in the data.

3. Taking the last quarter as the base-period quarter and defining dummy variable D_1 by a time series with ones in the first quarter of each year and zero in other quarters, D_2 by a time series with ones in the second quarter of each year and zero in other quarters, and D_3 by ones in the third quarter and zero in other quarters, we obtain the following results by running a regression of housing starts on the seasonal dummy variables and the linear time trend:

$$S_t = 464.160 + 24.972D_{1t} + 9.070D_{2t} - 1.998D_{3t} - 4.998t \qquad \bar{R}^2 = 0.67$$
$$\qquad (1.66) \qquad (0.61) \qquad (-0.13) \qquad (-6.48)$$

None of the estimated coefficients for the dummy variables are statistically significant at the 5 percent level and the regression "explains" 67 percent of the variation in new housing starts (the same as for regression 5-8).

With none of the estimated coefficients for the dummy variables statistically significant at the 5 percent level, we would not be justified in using this method for introducing the seasonal variation into the forecasts. If we did, however, we would get the following forecasts for housing starts in each quarter of 1990:

$$S_{25} = 464.160 + 24.972 - 4.998(25) = 364.18 \qquad \text{in 1990.1}$$
$$S_{26} = 464.160 + 9.070 - 4.998(26) = 338.28 \qquad \text{in 1990.2}$$
$$S_{27} = 464.160 - 1.998 - 4.998(27) = 327.22 \qquad \text{in 1990.3}$$
$$S_{28} = 464.160 - 4.998(28) = 324.22 \qquad \text{in 1990.4}$$

These forecasted values differ somewhat from and are less acceptable than those obtained by the ratio-to-trend method shown in Case Study 5-1.

9. (a) By substituting the given values of the independent or explanatory variables and $t = 24$ for 1972 in the estimated demand equation, we get the quantity demanded (sales) of sweet potatoes in the United States in 1972 of

$$QDs = 7{,}609 - 1{,}606(4.10) + 59(208.78) + 947(3.19) + 479(2.41) - 271(24)$$
$$= 11{,}013.74 \quad \text{in thousands (11.01 millions) hundredweight}$$

(*b*) By substituting the given values of the independent or explanatory variables and $t = 25$ for 1973 in the estimated demand equation, we get the quantity demanded (sales) of sweet potatoes in the United States in 1973 of

$$\begin{aligned} QDs &= 7{,}609 - 1{,}606(4.00) + 59(210.90) + 947(3.55) \\ &\quad + 479(2.40) - 271(25) \\ &= 11{,}364.55 \quad \text{in thousands (11.36 millions) hundredweight} \end{aligned}$$

Of course, the accuracy of these results depends on the accuracy of the forecasted values of the independent or explanatory variables. The greater the errors in forecasting the latter, the greater will be the forecasting error in the former.

11. (*a*) The reduced-form equation for C_t is obtained by substituting Equation 5-23 for GNP_t into Equation 5-21 for C_t. That is, substituting Equation 5-23 for GNP_t into Equation 5-21 for C_t (and omitting u_{1t} because its expected value is zero), we get

$$\begin{aligned} C_t &= a_1 + b_1(C_t + I_t + G_t) && (5\text{-}24') \\ &= a_1 + b_1C_t + b_1I_t + b_1G_t && (5\text{-}24'') \end{aligned}$$

By then substituting Equation 5-22 for I_t into Equation 5-24″ (and omitting u_{2t}), we have

$$\begin{aligned} C_t &= a_1 + b_1C_t + b_1(a_2 + b_2\pi_{t-1}) + b_1G_t && (5\text{-}25') \\ &= a_1 + b_1C_t + b_1a_2 + b_1b_2\pi_{t-1} + b_1G_t && (5\text{-}25'') \end{aligned}$$

Collecting the C_t terms to the left in Equation 5-25″ and isolating C_t, we have

$$C_t(1 - b_1) = a_1 + b_1a_2 + b_1b_2\pi_{t-1} + b_1G_t \qquad (5\text{-}26')$$

Dividing both sides of Equation 5-26′ by $1 - b_1$, we finally obtain

$$C_t = \frac{a_1}{1 - b_1} + \frac{b_1a_2}{1 - b_1} + \frac{b_1b_2\pi_{t-1}}{1 - b_1} + \frac{b_1G_t}{1 - b_1} \qquad (5\text{-}27')$$

Equation 5-27′ is the reduced-form equation for C_t. It is expressed only in terms of π_{t-1} and G_t (the exogenous variables of the model) and can be used in forecasting C_{t+1} by substituting the known value of π_t and the predicted value of G_{t+1} into Equation 5-27′ and solving for C_{t+1}.

(*b*) Equation 5-22 is already in reduced form because π_{t-1} is exogenous (i.e., it is known in period t). The lagged (and therefore known) value of a variable is sometimes known as a "predetermined variable."

CHAPTER 6

2. (*a*) See Table 3.

   (*b*) See Figure 8.

Table 3
Total, Marginal, and Average Products of Labor, and Output Elasticity

(1) Labor (Number of Workers)	(2) Output or Total Product	(3) Marginal Product of Labor	(4) Average Product of Labor	(5) Output Elasticity of Labor
0	0	—	—	—
1	12	12	12	1
2	28	16	14	$\frac{8}{7}$
3	36	8	12	$\frac{2}{3}$
4	40	4	10	$\frac{2}{5}$
5	40	0	8	0
6	36	−4	6	$-\frac{2}{3}$

Figure 8

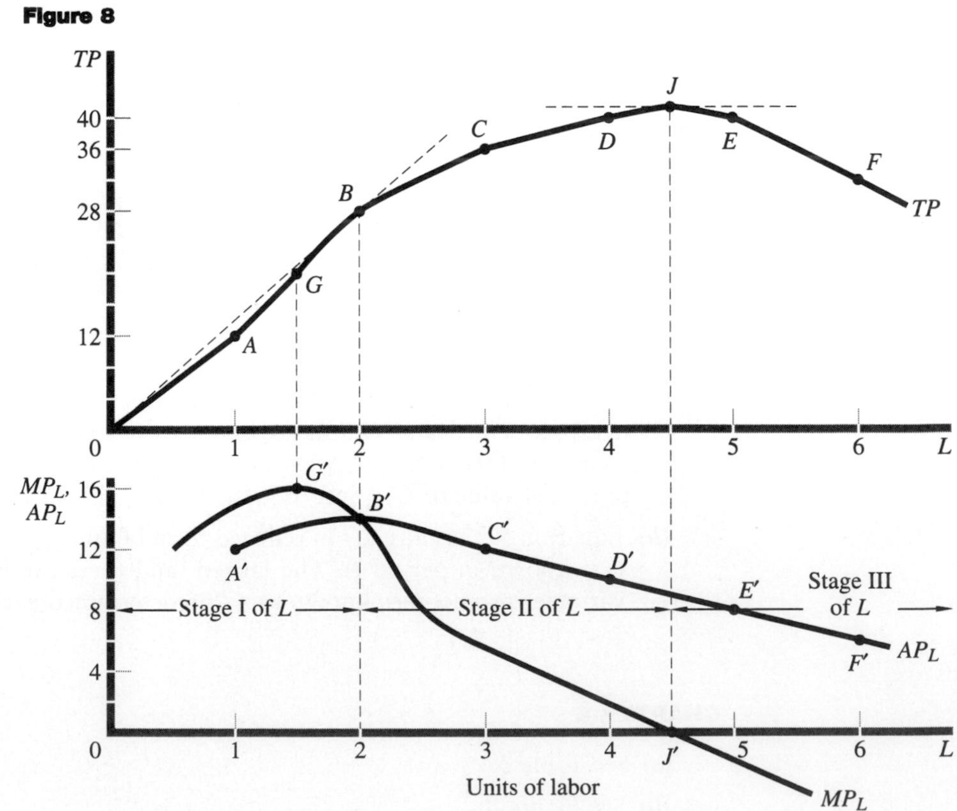

(*c*) When capital is fixed at 4 units rather than 1 unit, the MP_L and AP_L are both greater than when capital is held constant at 1 unit. This is reasonable. With more capital to work with, each unit of labor is more productive, so that both the MP_L and the AP_L are higher, and diminishing returns sets in later (i.e., after more units of labor have been used).

5. We can find the marginal revenue product of each additional worker hired by calculating the change in total revenue that results from the sale of the output produced by the additional worker. This is shown in Table 4.

   Since Mr. Smith can hire additional workers at the given daily wage (w) of \$40, $MRC = w =$ \$40 (column 6 in Table 4), and the firm's total profits will be maximum when it hires five workers so that $MRP = MRC =$ \$40. The result is the same as that obtained in Problem 4, where the MRP was obtained by multiplying the MP of labor by the MR or P of the commodity. This is shown in Figure 9. Note that the MRP values are plotted at the midpoint of each additional unit of labor used in Figure 9.

9. (*a*) The firm is not maximizing output or minimizing costs (i.e., the firm is not using the optimal input combination) because $MP_L/w = 40/\$20 = 2$ is not equal to $MP_K/r = 120/\$30 = 4$.

   (*b*) The firm can maximize output or minimize costs by hiring fewer workers and renting more machines. Since the firm produces in stage II of production for both labor and capital, as the firm employs fewer workers, the MP of the last remaining worker rises. On the other hand, as the firm rents more machines, the MP of the last machine rented declines. This process should continue until $MP_L/w = MP_K/r$. One such point of output maximization or cost minimization might be where

$$\frac{MP_L}{w} = \frac{60}{\$20} = \frac{MP_K}{r} = \frac{90}{\$30} = 3$$

11. Figure 10 shows constant, increasing, and decreasing returns to scale from the quantity of inputs required to double output. The left panel shows constant returns to scale. Here, doubling inputs from $3L$ and $3K$ to $6L$ and $6K$ doubles output from 100 (point A) to 200 (point B). Thus, $0A = AB$ along

Table 4

(1) Number of Workers (*L*)	(2) *TP*	(3) *P*	(4) *TR* = (*TP*)(*P*)	(5) $MRP_L = \Delta TR/\Delta L$	(6) $MRC_L = w$
0	0	\$10	\$ 0	—	\$40
1	12	10	120	\$120	40
2	22	10	220	100	40
3	30	10	300	80	40
4	36	10	360	60	40
5	40	10	400	40	40
6	42	10	420	20	40

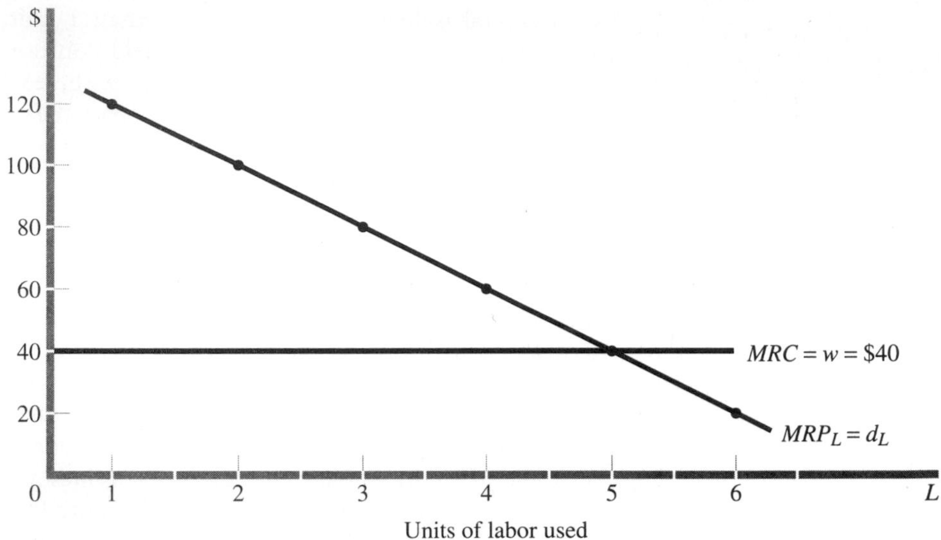

Figure 9

ray $0E$. The middle panel shows increasing returns to scale. Here, output can be doubled by less than doubling the quantity of inputs. Thus, $0A > AC$, and the isoquants become closer together. The right panel shows decreasing returns to scale. Here, output changes proportionately less than labor and capital, and $0A < AD$.

Figure 10

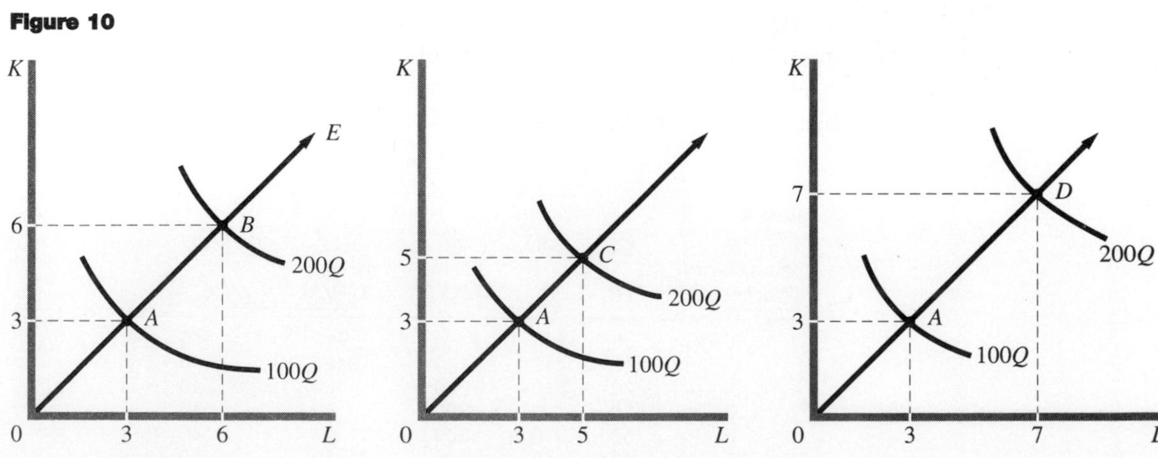

CHAPTER 7

1. (*a*) The explicit costs are \$10,000 + \$20,000 + \$15,000 + \$5,000 = \$50,000.

   (*b*) The accounting costs would be equal to the explicit costs of \$50,000. The implicit costs are \$60,000 (the earnings that would be foregone from his present occupation). The economic costs are the sum of the explicit costs of \$50,000 and implicit costs of \$60,000, or \$110,000.

   (*c*) Since the estimated total revenues from opening his own law practice are \$100,000 while the total estimated economic costs are \$110,000, John McAuley should not start his own law practice.

7. With constant returns to scale, the *LTC* curve is a straight line through the origin. This is shown in the left panel of Figure 11. Since the *LTC* curve is a straight line through the origin, $LAC = LMC$ and equals the constant slope of the *LTC* curve. This is shown in the middle panel of Figure 11. Finally, since the *LAC* is horizontal the *SAC* curves are tangent to the *LAC* curve at the lowest points on the *SAC* curves (see the right panel of Figure 11).

8. See Figure 12. The figure shows that to produce output level Q_2, the plant represented by *SAC* is better (i.e., it leads to lower per-unit costs) than the plant indicated by *SAC*′. However, for outputs smaller than Q_1 or larger than Q_3, plant *SAC*′ leads to lower per-unit costs. Thus, if the firm is not sure that its output will be between Q_1 and Q_3, it may prefer to build plant *SAC*′.

11. (*a*) The breakeven output (Q_B) for the first firm and the second firm ($Q_{B'}$) are

$$Q_B = \frac{TFC}{P - AVC} = \frac{\$100}{\$10 - \$6} = 25$$

$$Q_{B'} = \frac{TFC'}{P - AVC'} = \frac{\$300}{\$10 - \$3.33} = 45$$

These are shown in Figure 13. The breakeven output of the second firm (i.e., the more highly leveraged firm) is larger than that for the first firm because the second firm has larger overhead costs. Thus, it takes a greater level of output for the second firm to cover its larger overhead costs.

Figure 11

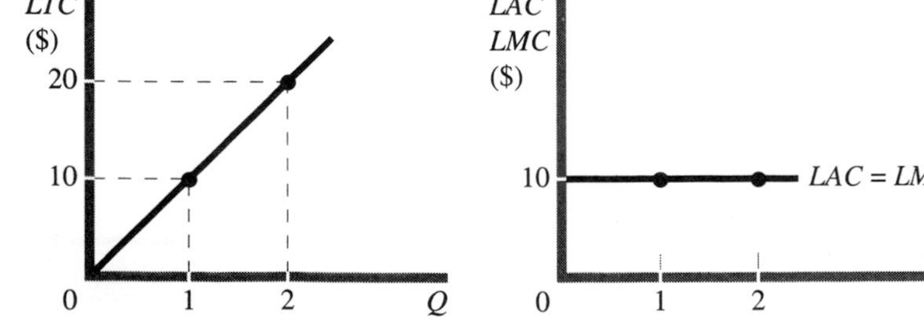

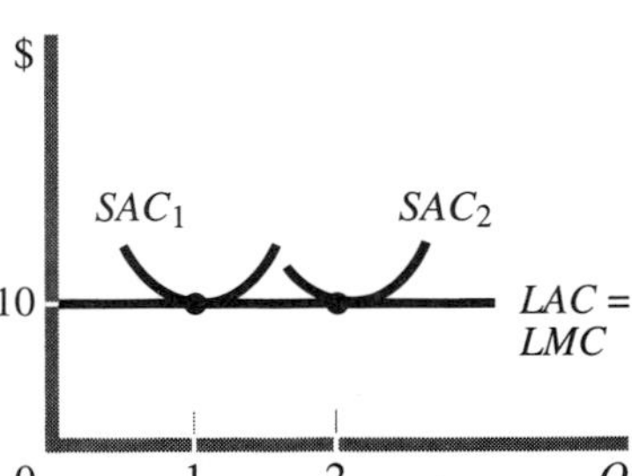

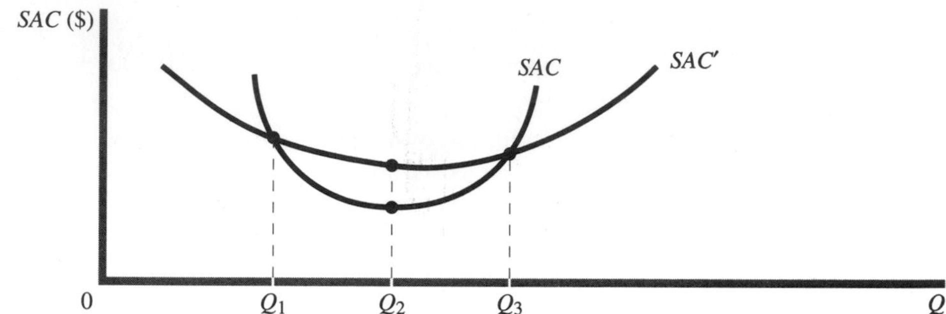

Figure 12

(*b*) At $Q = 60$, the degree of operating leverage of firm 1 (DOL) and firm 2 (DOL') are

$$DOL = \frac{Q(P - AVC)}{Q(P - AVC) - TFC} = \frac{60(\$10 - \$6)}{60(\$10 - \$6) - \$100}$$

$$= \frac{\$240}{\$140} = 1.71$$

$$DOL' = \frac{Q(P - AVC')}{Q(P - AVC') - TFC'} = \frac{60(\$10 - \$3.33)}{60(\$10 - \$3.33) - \$300}$$

$$= \frac{\$400}{\$100} = 4$$

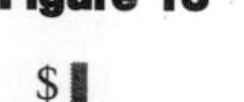

Figure 13

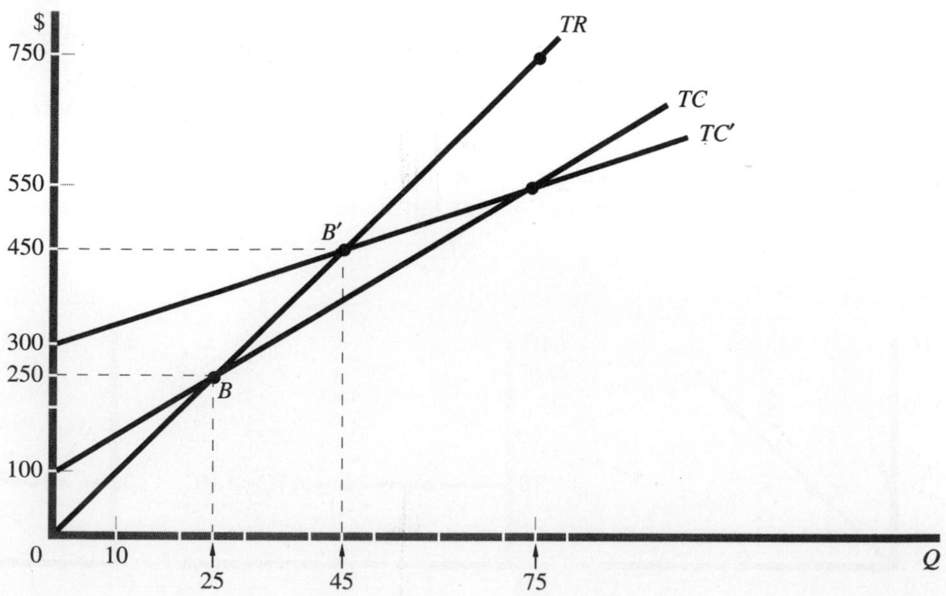

Thus, the more highly leveraged firm has a higher *DOL* (i.e., a greater variability of profits) than the less highly leveraged firm. The reason for this is that firm 2 has a larger contribution margin per unit (that is, $P - AVC$) than firm 1. Graphically, this is reflected in a larger difference between the slopes of *TR* and *TC'* than between *TR* and *TC*. At $Q = 70$, *DOL* and *DOL'* are, respectively,

$$DOL = \frac{70(\$10 - \$6)}{70(\$10 - \$6) - \$100} = \frac{\$280}{\$180} = 1.56$$

$$DOL' = \frac{70(\$10 - \$3.33)}{70(\$10 - \$3.33) - \$300} = \frac{\$467}{\$167} = 2.8$$

Thus, the larger the level of output, the smaller are *DOL* and *DOL'*. The reason for this is that the farther we are from the breakeven point, the smaller is the percentage change in profits (since the level of profits is higher).

CHAPTER 8

1. The three production processes as well as the isoquants for 50 garments (50*Q*) and 100*Q* dry cleaned are shown in the left panel of Figure 14. For maximum expenditures of \$750 per day and $w = \$50$ and $r = \$75$, the isocost is *GH* with absolute slope of $w/r = \$50/\$75 = \frac{2}{3}$ in the right panel of Figure 14. The feasible region is the shaded area 0*JN*, and the optimal solution is given by point *E* at which Mark uses 6*L* and 6*K* with process 2 and reaches the isoquant for 100*Q*.

Figure 14

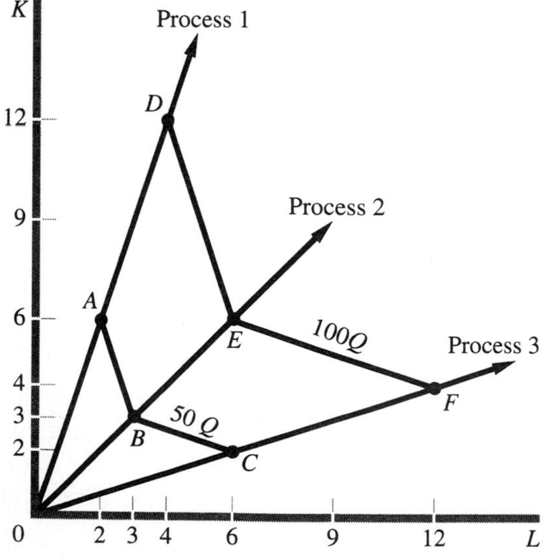

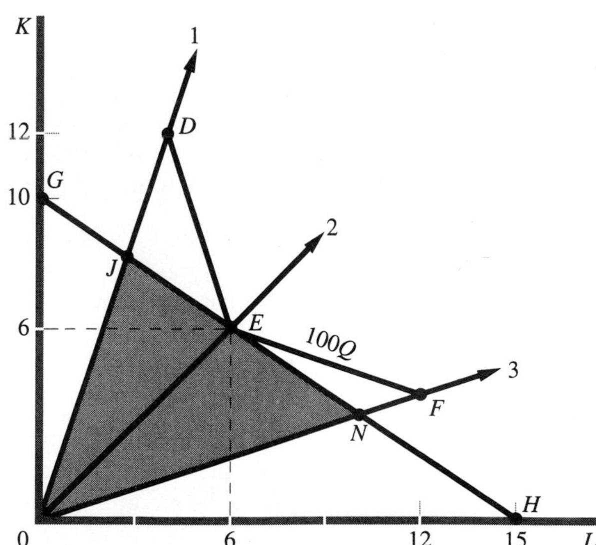

3. Letting heating oil be product X and gasoline be product Y; letting the labor input be L, the capital input be K, and the crude oil input be R, we can formulate the linear programming problem as follows:

$$
\begin{aligned}
&\text{Maximize} && \pi = \$20Q_X + \$30Q_Y && \text{(objective function)}\\
&\text{Subject to} && 1Q_X + 1Q_Y \leqq 10 && \text{(input } L \text{ constraint)}\\
& && \tfrac{1}{2}Q_X + 1Q_Y \leqq 7 && \text{(input } K \text{ constraint)}\\
& && \tfrac{1}{3}Q_X + 1Q_Y \leqq 6.5 && \text{(input } R \text{ constraint)}\\
& && Q_X, Q_Y \geqq 0 && \text{(nonnegativity constraint)}
\end{aligned}
$$

Treating each inequality constraint as an equation and plotting it, we get feasible region $0DEFG$ in part a of Figure 15. The isoprofit lines for $\pi =$ \$180, \$240, and \$300 are plotted in part b of Figure 15. Superimposing the isoprofit lines in part b on the feasible region in part a, we get the optimal solution at corner point E in part c of Figure 15. At optimal point E, the firm produces $6X$ and $4Y$ and maximizes its total profits at

$$\pi = \$20(6) + \$30(4) = \$240$$

6. (*a*) This problem can be formulated as follows:

$$
\begin{aligned}
&\text{Minimize } C = \$8{,}000A + \$12{,}000B && \text{(objective function)}\\
&\text{Subject to } 0.5A + 1B \geqq 9 && \text{(high-grade ore constraint)}\\
&\qquad\qquad\quad 1A + 1B \geqq 12 && \text{(medium-grade ore constraint)}\\
&\qquad\qquad\quad 3A + 1B \geqq 18 && \text{(low-grade ore constraint)}\\
&\qquad\qquad\qquad\;\; A, B \geqq 0 && \text{(nonnegativity constraint)}
\end{aligned}
$$

Treating each inequality constraint as an equation and plotting it, we get feasible region $DEFG$ in part a of Figure 16. Part b of Figure 16 shows that HJ is the lowest isocost line that allows the company to reach the feasible region. The absolute slope of isocost line HJ is $\frac{2}{3}$, which is the ratio of the cost of operating mine A to the cost of operating mine B. The company minimizes costs by operating mine A and mine B for six days each per month (point E) at a cost of

$$C = \$8{,}000(6) + \$12{,}000(6) = \$120{,}000$$

(*b*) At corner point D (18, 0), $C = \$8{,}000(18) + \$12{,}000(0) = \$144{,}000$. At corner point F (3, 9), $C = \$8{,}000(3) + \$12{,}000(9) = \$132{,}000$. At corner point G (0, 18), $C = \$8{,}000(0) + \$12{,}000(18) = \$216{,}000$.

(*c*) Since the optimal point E is formed by the intersection of the constraint lines for the high- and medium-grade ores but is above the constraint line for the low-grade ore, the minimum monthly requirements for the high- and the medium-grade ores are just met while the minimum requirement for the low-grade ore is more than met.

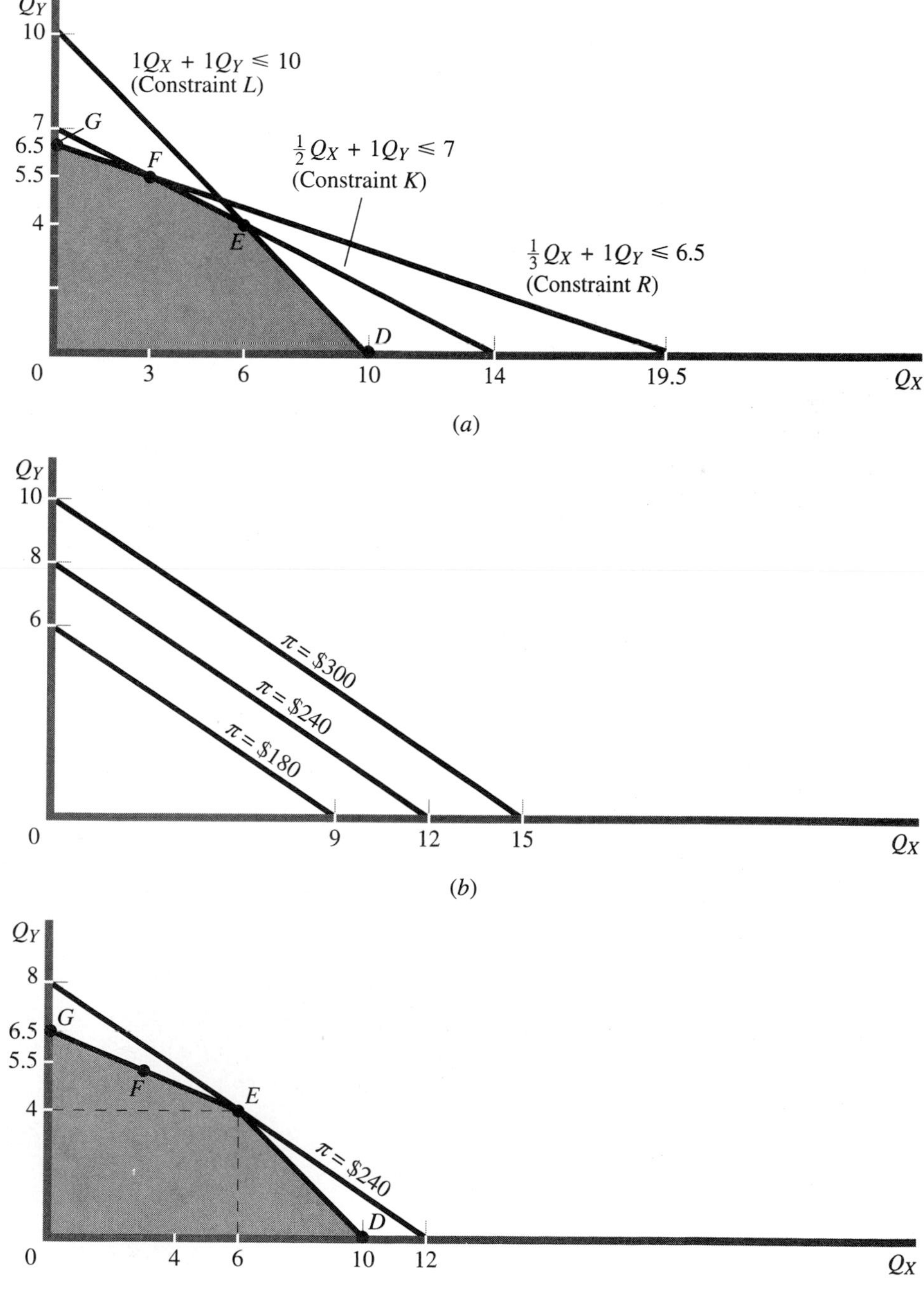

Q_Y
10
7
6.5
5.5
4
G
F
E
D
$1Q_X + 1Q_Y \leq 10$
(Constraint L)
$\frac{1}{2}Q_X + 1Q_Y \leq 7$
(Constraint K)
$\frac{1}{3}Q_X + 1Q_Y \leq 6.5$
(Constraint R)
0
3
6
10
14
19.5
Q_X
(a)
Q_Y
10
8
6
$\pi = \$300$
$\pi = \$240$
$\pi = \$180$
0
9
12
15
Q_X
(b)
Q_Y
8
6.5
5.5
4
G
F
E
D
$\pi = \$240$
0
4
6
10
12
Q_X
(c)

Figure 15

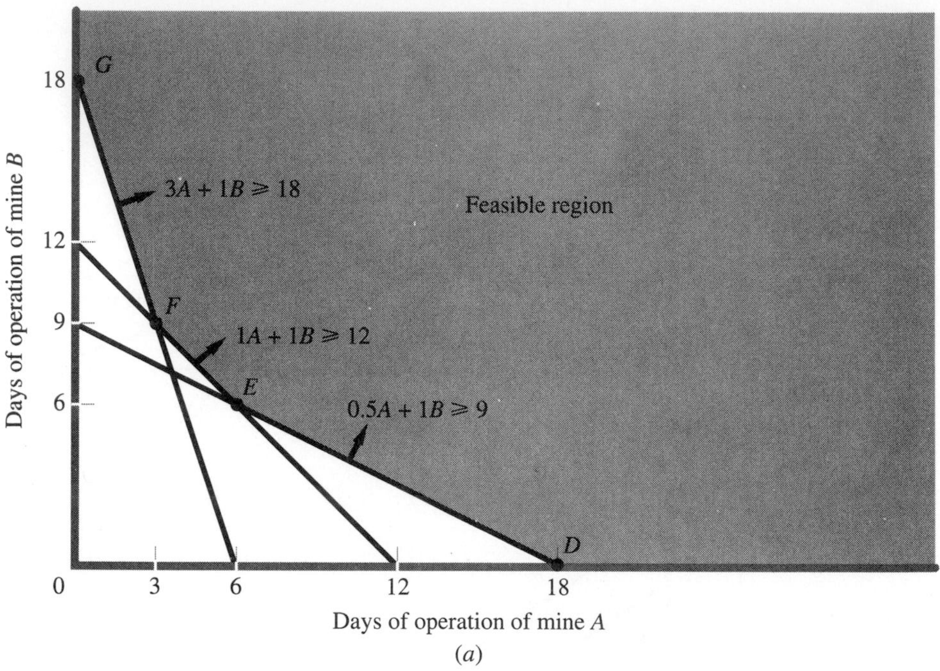
18
G
3A + 1B ≥ 18
Feasible region
12
F
9
1A + 1B ≥ 12
E
6
0.5A + 1B ≥ 9
D
0
3
6
12
18
Days of operation of mine B
Days of operation of mine A

(*a*)

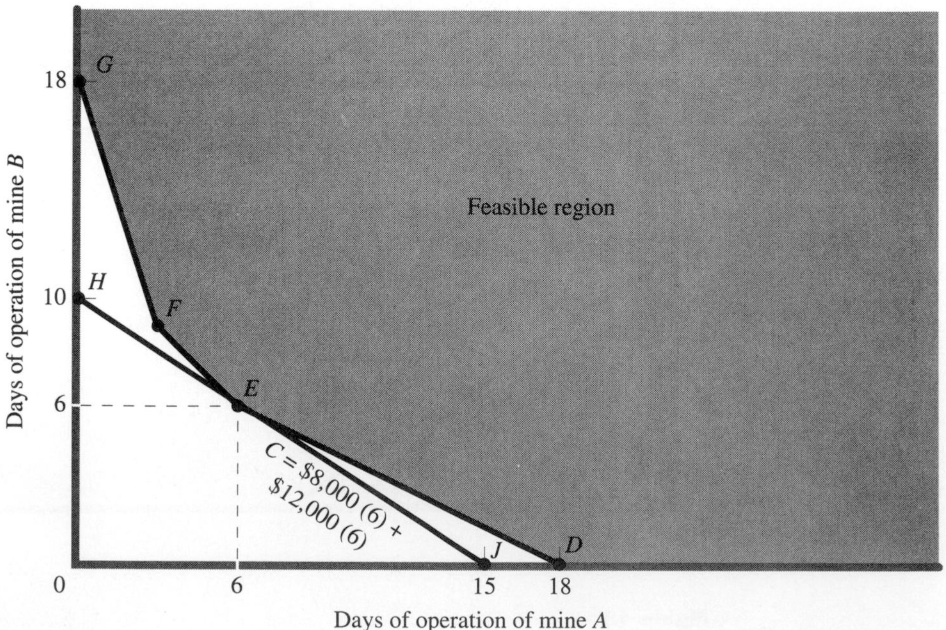
18
G
Feasible region
H
10
F
E
6
C = $8,000 (6) + $12,000 (6)
J
D
0
6
15
18
Days of operation of mine B
Days of operation of mine A

Figure 16

(*d*) If the cost of running mine A increased to \$12,000 per day (so that the ratio of the cost of running mine A to running mine B became 1), the lowest isocost line that reaches the feasible region would coincide with segment EF of the feasible region. In that case, all the combinations of days of operation of mines A and B along segment EF would result in the same minimum cost of meeting the contractual obligations of the company. These costs would be $C = \$12{,}000(6) + \$12{,}000(6) = \$144{,}000$.

8. (*a*) Problem 3 was a constrained profit maximization problem. The formulation of that problem, provided in the answer to Problem 3, is

$$\begin{aligned} &\text{Maximize } \pi = \$20Q_X + \$30Q_Y && \text{(objective function)} \\ &\text{Subject to } 1Q_X + 1Q_Y \leqq 10 && \text{(input } L \text{ constraint)} \\ &\tfrac{1}{2}Q_X + 1Q_Y \leqq 7 && \text{(input } K \text{ constraint)} \\ &\tfrac{1}{3}Q_X + 1Q_Y \leqq 6.5 && \text{(input } R \text{ constraint)} \\ &Q_X, Q_Y \geqq 0 && \text{(nonnegativity constraint)} \end{aligned}$$

Defining V_L, V_K, and V_R as the shadow price of labor (L), capital (K), and crude oil (R), respectively, and C as the total cost of the firm, we can formulate the following dual cost minimization problem:

$$\begin{aligned} &\text{Minimize} && C = 10V_L + 7V_K + 6.5V_R \\ &\text{Subject to} && 1V_L + \tfrac{1}{2}V_K + \tfrac{1}{3}V_R \geqq \$20 \\ &&& 1V_L + 1V_K + 1V_R \geqq \$30 \\ &&& V_L, V_K, V_R \geqq 0 \end{aligned}$$

(*b*) Since we know from the solution of the primal problem that input R is a slack variable, so that $V_R = 0$, subtracting the first from the second constraints, treated as equations, we get the solution of the dual problem of

$$\begin{aligned} 1V_L + 1V_K &= \$30 \\ 1V_L + \tfrac{1}{2}V_K &= \$20 \\ \hline \tfrac{1}{2}V_K &= \$10 \end{aligned}$$

so that $V_K = \$20$. Substituting $V_K = \$20$ into the first equation, we get $V_L = \$10$, and

$$C = 10(\$10) + 7(\$20) + 6.5(\$0) = \$240$$

This minimum total cost is equal to the maximum total profit in the solution of the primal problem.

CHAPTER 9

1. (*a*)

$$QD = QS$$
$$10{,}000 - 1{,}000P = -2{,}000 + 1{,}000P$$
$$12{,}000 = 2{,}000P$$
$$P = \$6 \quad \text{(equilibrium price)}$$

Substituting the equilibrium price into either the market demand or supply function, we get the equilibrium quantity. That is,

$$QD = 10{,}000 - 1{,}000(\$6) = 4{,}000$$

or

$$QS = -2{,}000 + 1{,}000(\$6) = 4{,}000$$

(*b*) See Figure 17.

3. (*a*) When $P = \$18$, the best or optimum level of output is 7,000 units (given by point *A*). The firm earns \$4 of profit per unit (*AN*) and a total profit of \$28,000. This represents the maximum total profit that the firm can make at this price.

(*b*) When $P = \$13$, the best level of output is 6,000 units (point *B*), and the firm breaks even.

(*c*) When $P = \$9$, the best level of output is 5,000 units (point *C*). At this level of output, the firm incurs a loss of \$5 per unit (*CD*) and \$25,000 in total. If the firm went out of business, however, it would incur a total loss to its *TFC* of \$40,000 (obtained by multiplying the *AFC* of *DE* or \$8 per unit times 5,000 units). Thus, the firm would minimize its total losses in the short run by staying in business.

(*d*) When $P = \$5$, the best level of output is 4,000 (point *F*). However, since $P = AVC$ and thus $TR = TVC$ (= \$20,000), the firm is indifferent

Figure 17

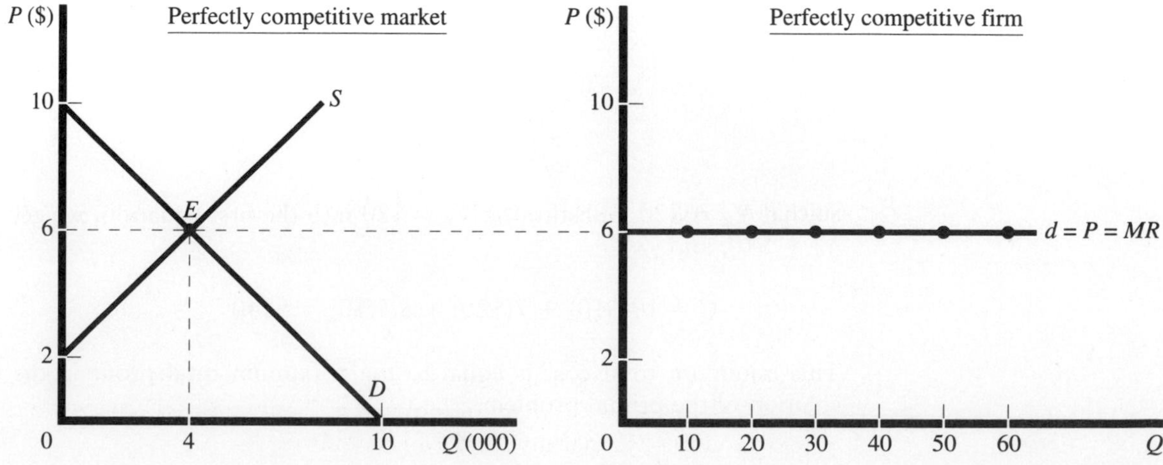

whether it produces or not. In either case, the firm would incur a short-run loss equal to its *TFC* of \$40,000. Point *F* is thus the shut-down point.

(*e*) Since *P* is smaller than *AVC*, *TR* (\$9,000) does not cover *TVC* (\$18,000). Therefore, the firm would incur a total loss equal to its *TFC* (\$40,000) *plus* the \$9,000 amount by which *TVC* exceeds *TR* (\$18,000 − \$9,000 = \$9,000). Thus, it pays for the firm to shut down and minimize its total losses at \$40,000 (its *TFC*) over the period of the short run.

5. (*a*) The best or optimum level of output for this firm in the short run is given by the point where $P = SMC_1$. At this level of output (400 units), the firm earns a profit of \$4 per unit and \$1,600 in total.

(*b*) If only this firm adjusts to the long run (a simplifying and unrealistic assumption for a perfectly competitive market), this firm will produce where $P = SMC_3 = LMC$. The firm will build the scale of plant indicated by SAC_3 and will produce and sell 800 units of output. The firm will earn a profit of \$5 per unit and \$4,000 in total per time period. Note that since we are dealing with a perfectly competitive firm, we can safely assume that if only this firm expanded its output, the effect on the equilibrium price would be imperceptible.

11. (*a*) Since the movie market is monopolistically competitive, $P = LAC$ in the long run. Thus,

$$9 - 0.04Q = 10 - 0.06Q + 0.001Q^2$$
$$1 - 0.02Q + 0.001Q^2 = 0$$
$$10{,}000 - 200Q + Q^2 = 0$$

which can be factored as

$$(Q - 100)\,(Q - 100) = 0$$

so that $Q = 100$. Substituting $Q = 100$ into the demand function, we have

$$P = 9 - 0.04(100) = \$5$$

(*b*) At $Q = 100$,

$$AC = 10 - 0.06(100) + 0.0001(100)^2$$
$$= 10 - 6 + 1$$
$$= \$5$$

Since $P = LAC = \$5$, the Plaza Movie House breaks even in the long run.

CHAPTER 10

2. (*a*) See Figure 18.

(*b*) The best level of output is 30 units and is given by point *E* at which $MR^* = MC$. At $Q = 30$, $P = \$6$ (point *B* in Figure 18), $ATC = \$4$, and profits are $BN = \$2$ per unit and \$60 in total.

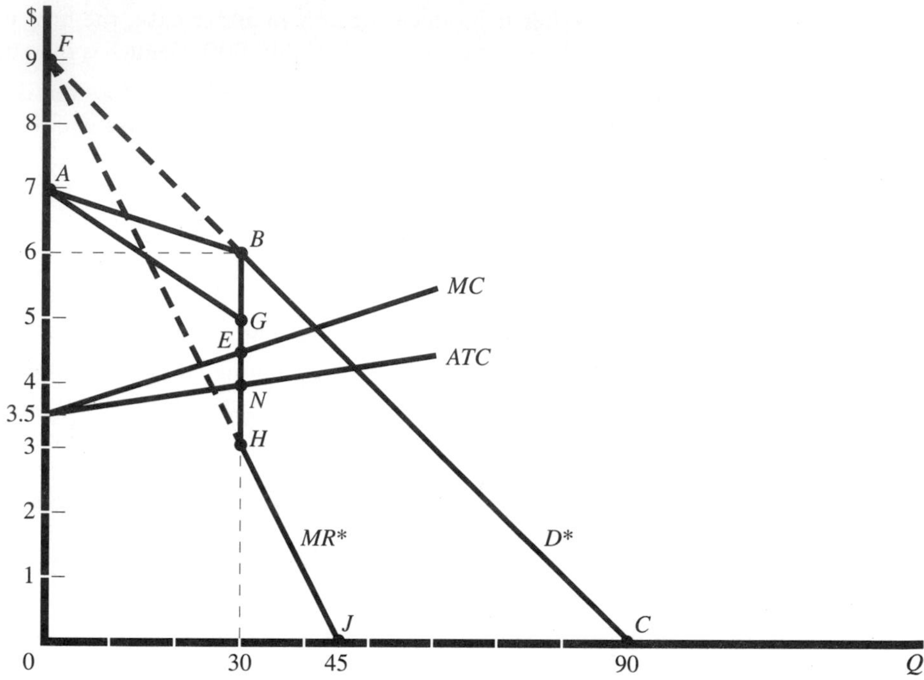

Figure 18

(*c*) The firm's *MC* curve can shift up to *MC* = \$5 and down to *MC* = \$3 (i.e., within the vertical segment *GH* of the *MR* curve) without inducing the firm to change its best level of output of 30 units and price of \$6.

4. See Figure 19. The best level of output for the cartel is 30 units and is given by point *E* at which $\Sigma MC = MR$. For $Q = 30$, the output of firm 1 is 10 units (given by point E_1 at which $MC_1 = MR$), and the output of firm 2 is 20 units (given by point E_2 at which $MC_2 = MR$). The profits are $B_1F_1 = \$4$ per unit and \$40 in total (the shaded area for firm 1), and $B_2F_2 = \$5$ per unit and \$100 in total for firm 2.

9. (*a*) If firm B produces small cars, firm A will earn a profit of 4 if it produces large cars and has a payoff of −2 (i.e., incurs a loss of 2) if it produces small cars. If firm B produces large cars, firm A will incur a loss of 2 if its also produces large cars and it earns a profit of 4 if it produces small cars. Therefore, firm A does not have a dominant strategy.

   (*b*) If firm A produces large cars, firm B will earn a profit of 4 if it produces small cars and has a payoff of −2 (i.e., incurs a loss of 2) if it also produces large cars. If firm A produces small cars, firm B will incur a loss of 2 if its also produces small cars and it earns a profit of 4 if it produces large cars. Therefore, firm B does not have a dominant strategy.

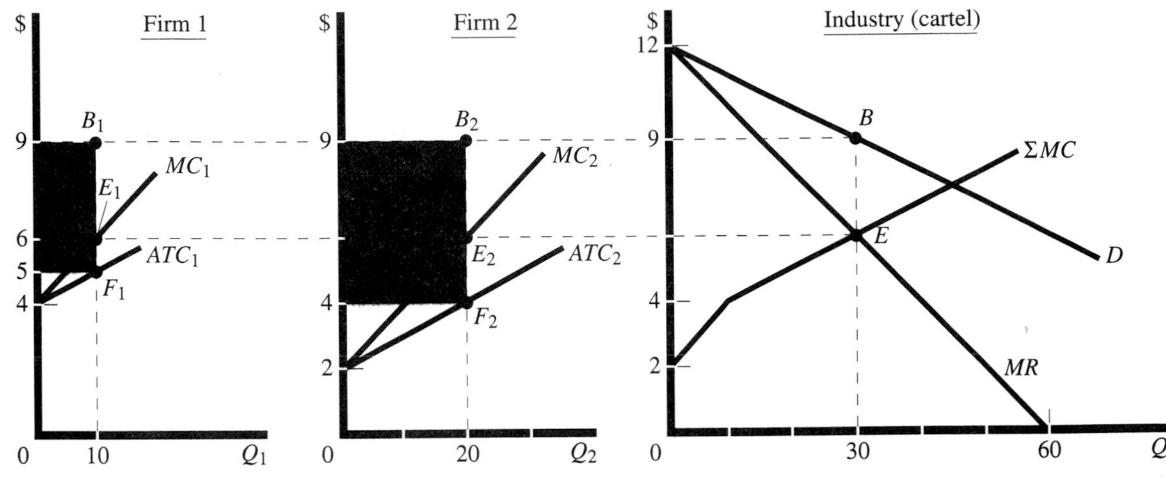

Figure 19

(*c*) The optimal strategy is for one firm to produce small cars and the other to produce large cars. In that case, each firm earns a profit of 4. If both firms produce either small cars or large cars, each incurs a loss of 2.

(*d*) In this case we have two Nash equilibria: either firm A produces large cars and firm B produces small cars (the top left cell in the given payoff matrix), or firm A produces small cars and firm B produces large cars (the bottom right cell in the payoff matrix).

(*e*) A situation such as that indicated in the payoff matrix of this problem might arise if each firm does not have the resources to invest in the plant and equipment necessary to produce both large and small cars, and the demand for either small or large cars is not sufficient to justify the production of small or large cars by both firms. Specifically, if both firms produced the same type of car, the oversupply of that type of car will result in low car prices and losses for both firms.

10. (*a*) Each firm adopts its dominant strategy of cheating (the top left cell), but could do better by cooperating not to cheat (the bottom right cell). Thus the firms face the prisoners' dilemma.

(*b*) If the payoff in the bottom right cell were changed to (5,5), the firms would still face the prisoners' dilemma by cheating.

CHAPTER 11

1. See Figure 20.
3. Adding the MR_A and MR_B functions together, we get

$$MR_T = MR_A + MR_B = 16 - 0.4Q_A + 10 - 0.4Q_B = 26 - 0.8Q$$

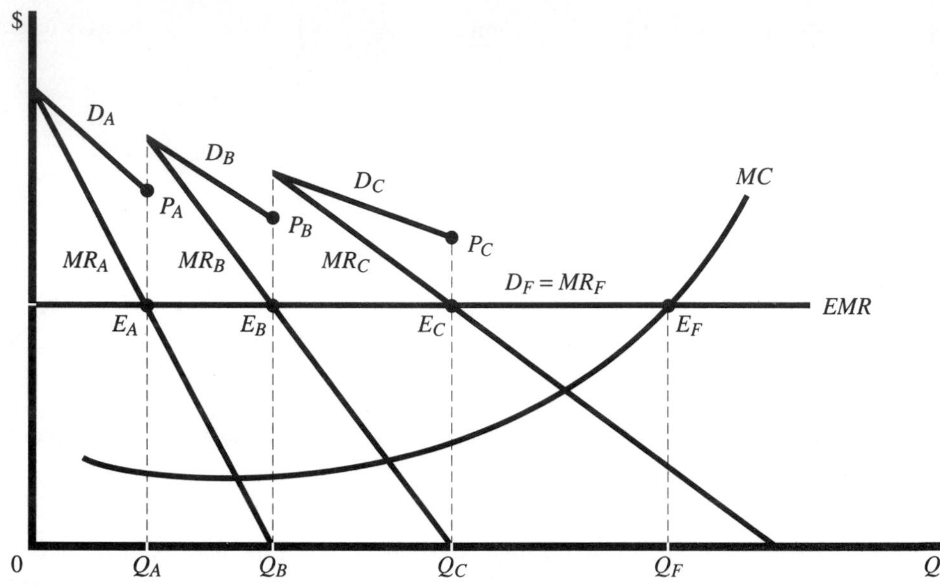

Figure 20

Setting $MR_T = MC$, we get

$$MR_T = 26 - 0.8Q = 8 + 0.1Q = MC$$
$$0.9Q = 18$$
$$Q = 20$$

Since at $Q = 20$,

$$MR_A = 16 - 0.4(20) = 8 > 0$$

and

$$MR_B = 10 - 0.4(20) = 2 > 0$$

$Q = 20$ is the profit-maximizing level of output and sales of each product. On the other hand, with MC', we have

$$MR_T = 26 - 0.8Q = \frac{2Q}{35} = MC'$$
$$0.8Q + \frac{2Q}{35} = 26$$
$$\frac{(28 + 2)Q}{35} = 26$$
$$30Q = 910$$
$$Q = 30.3$$

However, setting $MR_B = 0$, we get

$$MR_B = 10 - 0.4Q_B = 0$$
$$Q_B = 25$$

Therefore, $MR_B < 0$ for $Q_B = Q > 25$, and so $MR_T = MR_A$ for $Q > 25$. Setting MR_A equal to MC', we have

$$MR_A = 16 - 0.4Q = \frac{2Q}{35} = MC'$$

$$0.4Q + \frac{2Q}{35} = 16$$

$$\frac{(14 + 2)Q}{35} = 16$$

$$16Q = 560$$
$$Q = 35$$

Thus, the best level of *sales* (as opposed to output) is 35 units of product A but only 25 units of product B (i.e., the firm disposes of or keeps off the market 10 units of product B in order not to sell it at $MR_B < 0$). At sales of $Q_A = 35$, $P_{A'} = 16 - 0.2(35) = \$9$. At sales of $Q_B = 25$, $P_{B'} = 10 - 0.2(25) = \$5$.

7. See Figure 21. D_1 and MR_1 in part *a* are the demand and marginal revenue curves that the firm faces in market 1, D_2 and MR_2 in part *b* are the demand and marginal revenue curves that the firm faces in market 2, and D and MR in part *c* are the overall total demand and marginal revenue curves faced by the firm for the two markets together. $D = \Sigma D_{1+2}$, and $MR = \Sigma MR_{1+2}$, by horizontal summation. The total cost function, $TC = 120 + 4Q$, indicates that the firm faces total fixed costs of \$120 and a marginal cost of \$4. The best level of output of the firm is 120 units and is given by point E in part *c* at which $MR = MC = \$4$. With third-degree price discrimination, the firm should sell 60 units of the product in each market, so that $MR_1 = MR_2 = MR = MC = \$4$ (points E_1, E_2, and E). For $Q_1 = 60$, $P_1 = \$10$ (on D_1) in market 1, so that $TR_1 = \$600$. For $Q_2 = 60$, $P_2 = \$7$ (on D_2) in market 2, so that $TR_2 = \$420$. Thus, the overall total revenue of the firm is $TR = TR_1 + TR_2 = \$600 + \$420 = \$1{,}020$. For $Q = 120$, $TC = 120 + 4(120) = \$600$, so that

$$ATC = \frac{TC}{Q} = \frac{\$600}{120} = \$5$$

Thus, the firm earns a profit of $P_1 - ATC = \$10 - \$5 = \$5$ per unit and \$300 in total in market 1, and a profit of $P_2 - ATC = \$7 - \$5 = \$2$ per unit and \$120 in total in market 2. Thus, the overall total profit of the firm is $\pi = \pi_1 + \pi_2 = \$300 + \$120 = \$420$. In the absence of third-degree price discrimination, $Q = 120$, $P = \$8$ (in part *c*), $TR = (8)(120) = \$960$, and profits are \$3 per unit and \$360 in total.

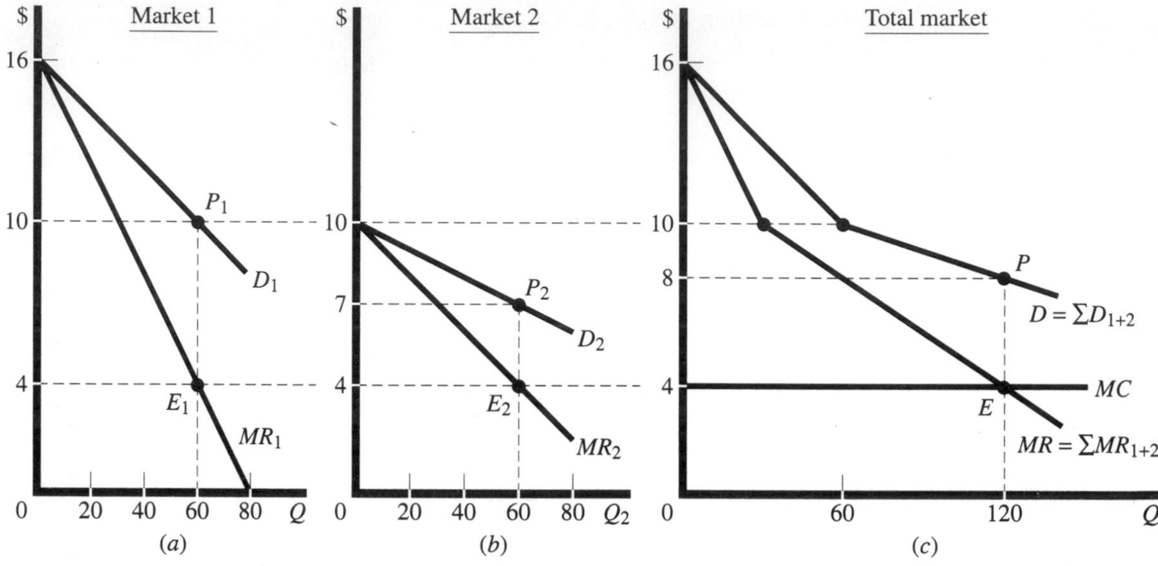

Figure 21

11. The demand and marginal revenue curves for the final product faced by the marketing division of the firm in Figure 22 can be represented algebraically as

$$Q_m = 160 - 10P_m \quad \text{or} \quad P_m = 16 - 0.1Q_m \quad \text{and} \quad MR_m = 16 - 0.2Q_m$$

The marginal cost functions of each division are, respectively,

$$MC_p' = 2 + 0.1Q_p \quad \text{and} \quad MC_m = 1 + 0.1Q_m$$

Since $P_t = \$6$, the total marginal cost function of the marketing division (MC_t) is

$$MC_t = MC_m + P_t = 1 + 0.1Q_m + 6 = 7 + 0.1Q_m$$

The best level of output of the intermediate product by the production division is given by the point at which $MC_p' = P_t$. Thus,

$$MC_p' = 2 + 0.1Q_p = 6 = P_t$$

so that
$$0.1Q_p = 4$$
and
$$Q_p = 40$$

The best level of output of the *final product* by the marketing division is given by the point at which $MC_t = MR_m$. Thus,

$$MC_t = 7 + 0.1Q_m = 16 - 0.2Q_m = MR_m$$

so that
$$0.3Q_m = 9$$
and
$$Q_m = 30$$
$$P_m = 16 - 0.1(30) = \$13$$

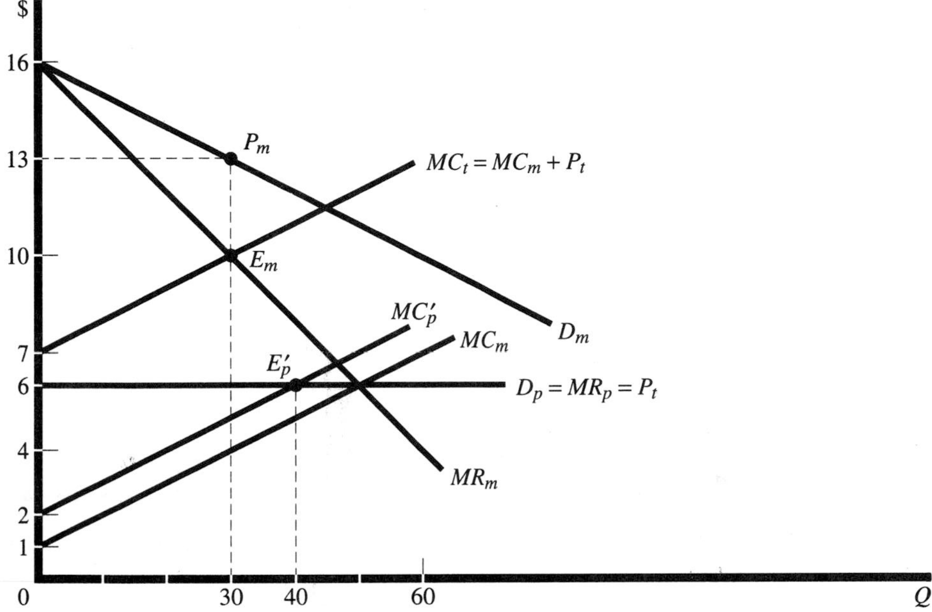

Figure 22

CHAPTER 12

2. Figure 23 shows that a corrective tax of \$300 per unit collected from producers will make S'' the new industry supply curve. With S', P = \$800 and Q = 3,000 (given by the intersection of the D and S' curves at point E'). Producers now receive a net price of \$500 (P = \$800 minus the \$300 tax per unit).

5. Figure 24 shows that the corrective tax of \$0.40 per can of soft drink imposed on consumers will make D'' the new market demand curve. With D', P = \$1.00 and Q = 4,000 (given by the intersection of D'' and S at point E'). Consumers now pay \$1.00 plus the \$0.40 tax per can for soft drinks, or a net price of \$1.40 (as compared with the price of \$1.20 before the imposition of the tax).

7. In Figure 25, D and D' are, respectively, the original and new market demand curves. With the new demand curve D' and the unchanged LAC curve, the regulatory commission would set $P' = LAC$ = \$2 (point G'), and the public utility company would supply 8 million units of the service per time period (as compared with $P = LAC$ = \$3 with Q = 6 million units per time period shown by point G on D). In either case, the public utility company breaks even.

12. During the 1970s, entrance into the banking industry in the United States was highly restricted, and banks were not allowed to pay interest on checking deposits or higher than specified interest rates on savings deposits (the so-called Regulation Q). Banks were also the only financial institutions that

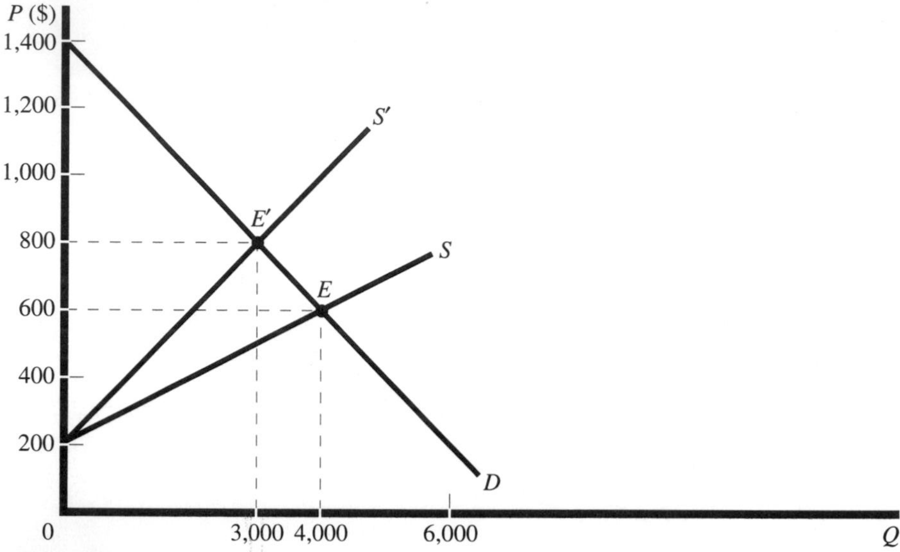

Figure 23

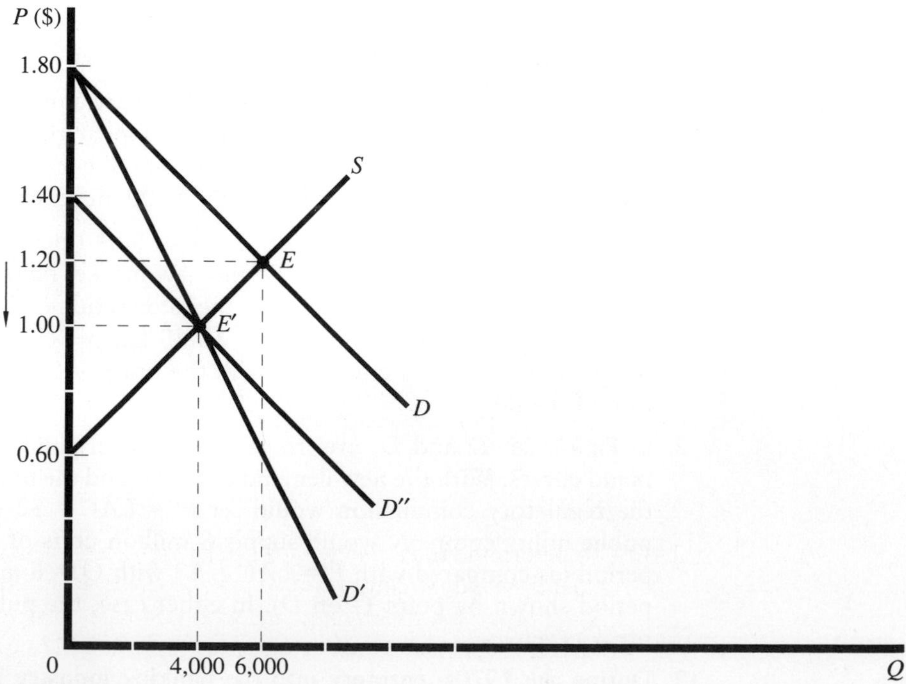

Figure 24

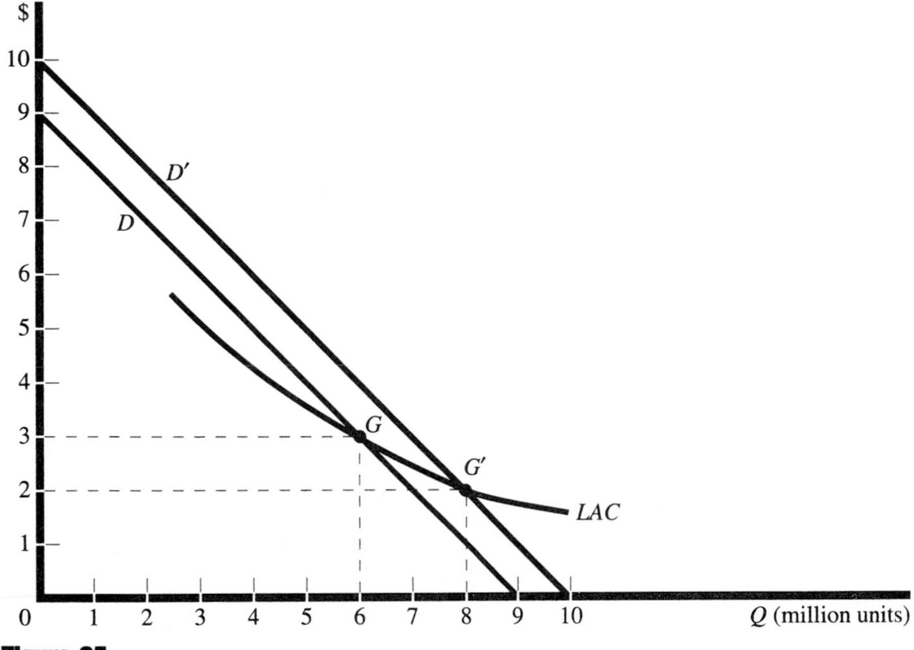

Figure 25

could make commercial loans. In the face of such restrictions on competition, the banking industry earned rates of return on stockholders' equity during the 1970s that were higher than the average rates of return (about 15 percent) in other industries. During the 1980s, however, the reverse was the case. That is, the banking industry earned rates of return that were consistently lower than for other U.S. industries. One reason for this was that the *Depository Institutions Deregulation and Monetary Control Act of 1980* deregulated many aspects of banking in the United States and greatly increased the competition for business loans. Another reason was that many of the loans that large U.S. commercial banks made in developing countries (primarily to such Latin American countries as Brazil, Argentina, and Venezuela) had to be written off as noncollectible.

CHAPTER 13

2. (*a*) To determine that the area under the standard normal distribution within $\pm 1\sigma$ is 68.26 percent, we look up the value of $z = 1.0$ in Table C-1. This is 0.3413. This means that the area to the right of the zero mean of the standard normal distribution to $z = 1$ is 0.3413, or 34.13 percent. Because of symmetry, the area between the mean and $z = -1$ is also 0.3413, or 34.13 percent. Therefore, the area between $z = \pm 1\sigma$ under the standard normal distribution is double 0.3413, which is 0.6826, or 68.26 percent. From Table C-1, we get the value of 0.4772 for $z = 2$.

Thus, the area under the standard normal curve between $z = \pm 2\sigma$ is 2(0.4772), which equals 0.9544, or 95.44 percent. From Table C-1, we get the value of 0.4987 for $z = 3$. Thus, the area under the standard normal curve between $z = \pm 3\sigma$ is 0.9974, or 99.74 percent.

(*b*) For \$650,

$$z = \frac{\$650 - \$500}{\$70.71} = 2.12$$

which from Table C-1 gives 0.4830, or 48.30 percent.

(*c*) For \$300,

$$z = \left|\frac{\$300 - \$500}{\$70.71}\right| = \frac{\$200}{\$70.71} = 2.83$$

which from Table C-1 gives 0.4977. This is the area between \$300 and \$500 (i.e., the probability that profit will fall between \$300 and \$500). Therefore, the probability that profit will fall between \$300 and \$650 is equal to the probability that profit will fall between \$300 and \$500 (49.77 percent) plus the probability that profit will fall between \$500 and \$650 (found earlier to be 48.30 percent), or 98.07. The probability that profit will be lower than \$300 is equal to 1.0 minus 0.9977, which is 0.0023, or 0.23 percent. The probability that profit will be higher than \$650 is 1.0 − 0.9830, which is 0.017, or 1.7 percent.

4. (*a*) The expected monetary return of this investment (R) is

$$\begin{aligned}\text{Expected return} &= E(R) = 0.2(\$40{,}000) + 0.8(-\$10{,}000)\\ &= \$8{,}000 - \$8{,}000\\ &= 0\end{aligned}$$

(*b*) The expected utilities of the project for individuals *A*, *B*, and *C* are

$$\begin{aligned}E(U)\text{ of }A &= 0.2(10\text{ utils}) + 0.8(-5\text{ utils})\\ &= 2\text{ utils} - 4\text{ utils} = -2\text{ utils}\\ E(U)\text{ of }B &= 0.2(20\text{ utils}) + 0.8(-5\text{ utils})\\ &= 4\text{ utils} - 4\text{ utils} = 0\text{ util}\\ E(U)\text{ of }C &= 0.2(30\text{ utils}) + 0.8(-5\text{ utils})\\ &= 6\text{ utils} - 4\text{ utils} = 2\text{ utils}\end{aligned}$$

Only individual *C* (the only individual for whom the marginal utility for money increases) will invest in the venture because only for him or her is the expected utility of the project positive. Because the marginal utility for money increases, individual *C* is a risk seeker. Individual *B* is indifferent to the venture because the expected utility of the project is zero. For individual *B*, the marginal utility for money is constant, so that he or she is risk neutral. Individual *A* will not invest in the venture because the expected utility of the project is negative. For individual *A*, the marginal utility for money diminishes, so that he or she is a risk averter.

6. (*a*) The net present values of project A and project B at the risk-free discount rate of 8 percent are

$$NPV_A = \sum_{t=1}^{n} \frac{R_t}{(1+r)^t} - C_0$$

$$= \frac{\$40{,}000}{1.08} + \frac{\$60{,}000}{(1.08)^2} + \frac{\$40{,}000}{(1.08)^3} - \$110{,}000$$

$$= \frac{\$40{,}000}{1.08} + \frac{\$60{,}000}{1.1664} + \frac{\$40{,}000}{1.259712} - \$110{,}000$$

$$= \$37{,}037.04 + \$51{,}440.33 + \$31{,}753.29 - \$110{,}000$$

$$= \$10{,}230.66$$

$$NPV_B = \frac{\$30{,}000}{1.08} + \frac{\$80{,}000}{(1.08)^2} + \frac{\$50{,}000}{(1.08)^3} - \$104{,}000$$

$$= \$27{,}777.78 + \$68{,}587.11 + \$39{,}691.61 - \$104{,}000$$

$$= \$32{,}056.50$$

(*b*) With a risk premium of 2 percent for project A, the risk-adjusted discount rate is $8 + 2 = 10$ percent. Thus,

$$NPV_A = \frac{\$40{,}000}{1.10} + \frac{\$60{,}000}{(1.10)^2} + \frac{\$40{,}000}{(1.10)^3} - \$110{,}000$$

$$= \frac{\$40{,}000}{1.10} + \frac{\$60{,}000}{1.21} + \frac{\$40{,}000}{1.331} - \$110{,}000$$

$$= \$36{,}363.64 + \$49{,}586.78 + \$30{,}052.59 - \$110{,}000$$

$$= \$6{,}003.01$$

On the other hand, with a risk premium of 6 percent for project B, the risk-adjusted discount rate is $8 + 6 = 14$ percent. Thus,

$$NPV_B = \frac{\$30{,}000}{1.14} + \frac{\$80{,}000}{(1.14)^2} + \frac{\$50{,}000}{(1.14)^3} - \$104{,}000$$

$$= \frac{\$30{,}000}{1.14} + \frac{\$80{,}000}{1.2996} + \frac{\$50{,}000}{1.481544} - \$104{,}000$$

$$= \$26{,}315.79 + \$61{,}557.40 + \$33{,}748.58 - \$104{,}000$$

$$= \$17{,}621.77$$

Even though project B is more risky than project A, it still gives a higher risk-adjusted NPV than project A. Therefore, the manager should undertake project B rather than project A.

9. The decision tree for the Fitness World Sporting Company to build either a large or a small plant is given in Figure 26. Being risk neutral, the company should choose the strategy with the largest expected present value. Thus, it should build the large plant. This results in the expected net present value of

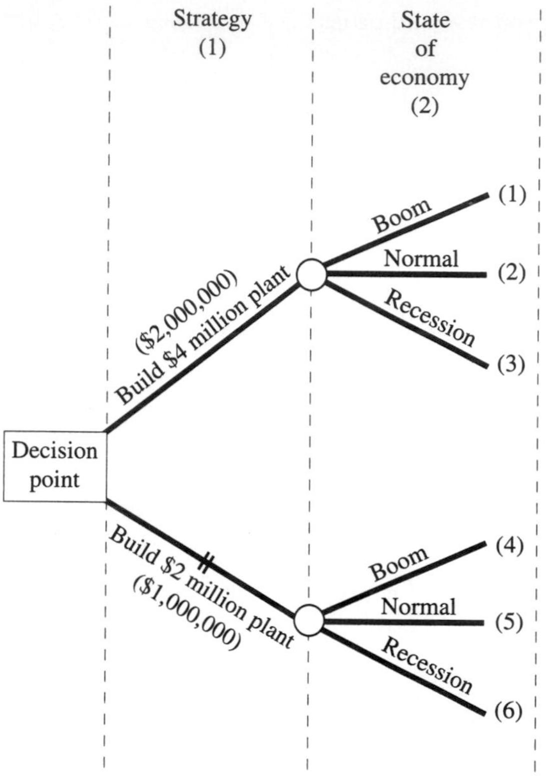

Strategy (1)	State of economy (2)		Probability (3)	Percent value of net cash flow (4)	Expected cash flows (5) = (3) × (4)
Build $4 million plant ($2,000,000)	Boom	(1)	0.30	$10,000,000	$3,000,000
	Normal	(2)	0.40	6,000,000	2,400,000
	Recession	(3)	0.30	2,000,000	600,000
			Expected present value of cash flows		$6,000,000
			Less cost		4,000,000
			Expected net present value		$2,000,000
Build $2 million plant ($1,000,000)	Boom	(4)	0.30	$4,000,000	$1,200,000
	Normal	(5)	0.40	3,000,000	1,200,000
	Recession	(6)	0.30	2,000,000	600,000
			Expected present value of cash flows		$3,000,000
			Less cost		2,000,000
			Expected net present value		$1,000,000

Decision point

Figure 26

$2,000,000 as compared with $1,000,000 for the small plant. The strategy of building the small plant is then slashed off on the decision tree to indicate that it is suboptimal.

CHAPTER 14

1. In Figure 27, the top of the lettered bars gives the firm's demand for capital, while the step *MCC* curve gives the marginal cost of capital to the firm. From Figure 27 we can determine that the firm should undertake projects *A*, *B*, and *C* because the rates of return expected from these projects exceed the marginal cost of raising the capital required to undertake them. On the other hand, the firm would not undertake projects *D* and *E* because the rates of return that these projects are expected to generate are below the cost of capital.

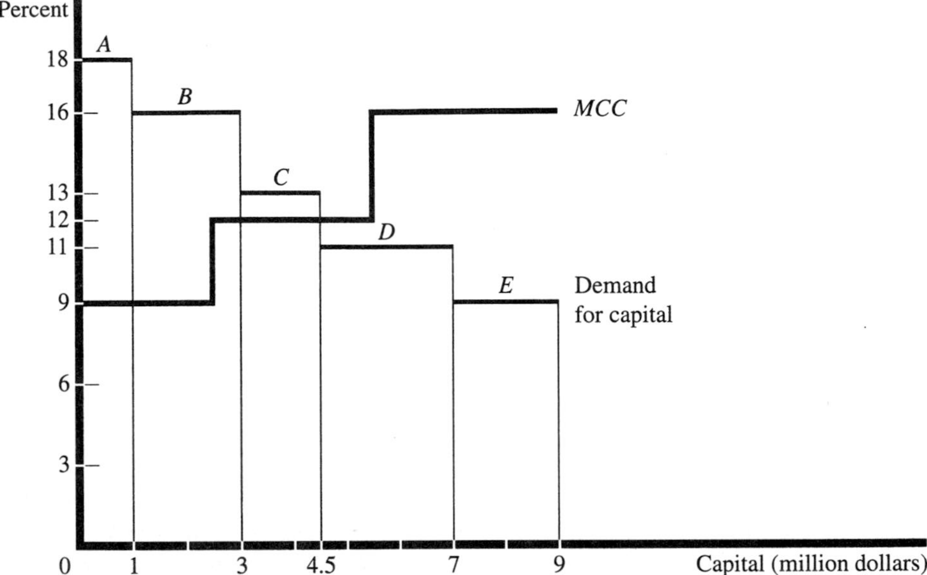

Figure 27

3. (*a*) If the firm uses the risk-adjusted discount rate (k) of 10 percent, the net present value (NPV) of the project is

$$
\begin{aligned}
NPV &= \frac{\$290{,}000}{(1.10)^1} + \frac{\$320{,}000}{(1.10)^2} + \frac{\$353{,}000}{(1.10)^3} + \frac{\$389{,}300}{(1.10)^4} \\
&\quad + \frac{\$779{,}230}{(1.10)^5} - \$1{,}000{,}000 \\
&= \frac{\$290{,}000}{1.1} + \frac{\$320{,}000}{1.21} + \frac{\$353{,}000}{1.331} + \frac{\$389{,}300}{1.4641} \\
&\quad + \frac{\$779{,}230}{1.61051} - \$1{,}000{,}000 \\
&= \$263{,}636 + \$264{,}463 + \$265{,}214 + \$265{,}897 \\
&\quad + \$483{,}841 - \$1{,}000{,}000 \\
&= \$1{,}543{,}051 - \$1{,}000{,}000 \\
&= \$543{,}051
\end{aligned}
$$

(*b*) If the firm uses instead the risk-adjusted discount rate (k) of 20 percent, the net present value (NPV) of the project is

$$NPV = \frac{\$290{,}000}{(1.20)^1} + \frac{\$320{,}000}{(1.20)^2} + \frac{\$353{,}000}{(1.20)^3} + \frac{\$389{,}300}{(1.20)^4} + \frac{\$779{,}230}{(1.20)^5} - \$1{,}000{,}000$$

$$= \frac{\$290{,}000}{1.2} + \frac{\$320{,}000}{1.44} + \frac{\$353{,}000}{1.728} + \frac{\$389{,}300}{2.0736} + \frac{\$779{,}230}{2.48832} - \$1{,}000{,}000$$

$$= \$241{,}657 + \$222{,}222 + \$204{,}282 + \$187{,}741 + \$313{,}155 - \$1{,}000{,}000$$

$$= \$1{,}169{,}067 - \$1{,}000{,}000$$

$$= \$169{,}067$$

The same value could have been obtained more readily by multiplying the net cash flow from the project in each year by the present value interest factor (*PVIF*) for $i = k = 20$ percent and from $n = t = 1$ to $n = t = 5$ given in Table B-2 in Appendix B, as explained in Appendix A at the end of the book.

(*c*) The value of the firm would increase by $543,051 (the net present value of the project) if the firm used the risk-adjusted discount rate of 10 percent and would increase by $169,067 if the firm used the risk-adjusted discount rate of 20 percent. Since the net present value of the project is positive in either case, the firm should undertake the project.

5. The net present value of the project is obtained from

$$NPV = \sum_{t=1}^{n} \frac{R_t}{(1+k)^t} - C_0$$

$$= \sum_{t=1}^{4} \frac{\$5{,}000{,}000}{(1+0.20)^t} - \$10{,}000{,}000$$

$$= \$5{,}000{,}000(PVIFA_{20,4}) - \$10{,}000{,}000$$

$$= \$5{,}000{,}000(2.5887) - \$10{,}000{,}000$$

$$= \$12{,}943{,}500 - \$10{,}000{,}000$$

$$= \$2{,}943{,}500$$

Since $NPV > 0$ the firm should undertake the project.

Note that $PVIFA_{20,4}$ refers to the present value interest factor of an annuity of $1 for 4 years discounted at 20 percent (see Section A-4 of Appendix A).

11. (*a*) The cost of debt (k_d) is given by the interest rate that the firm must pay on its bonds (r) times 1 minus the firm's marginal income tax rate. That is,

$$k_d = r(1 - t) = 11\%(1 - 0.4) = 6.6\%$$

(*b*) The cost of equity capital (k_e) found by the capital asset pricing model (CAPM) is given by

$$k_e = r_f + \beta(k_m - r_f)$$

where r_f is the risk-free rate (i.e., the interest rate on government securities), k_m is the return on the average stock of all firms in the market, and β is the estimated beta coefficient for the common stock of this firm. With $r_f = 7.5$ percent, $k_m = 11.55$ percent, and $\beta = 2$, the cost of equity capital for this firm found with the CAPM is

$$k_e = 7.5\% + 2(11.55\% - 7.5\%) = 15.6\%$$

(*c*) The composite cost of capital (k_c) is given by

$$k_c = w_d k_d + w_e k_e$$

where w_d and w_e are, respectively, the proportion of debt and equity capital in the firm's capital structure. With $w_d = 0.4$, $w_e = 0.6$, $k_d = 6.6$ percent, and the cost of equity capital of $k_e = 15.6$ percent, the composite cost of capital for this firm is

$$k_c = 0.4(6.6\%) + 0.6(15.6\%) = 12.0\%$$

Glossary

Accounting costs Historical explicit costs.
Adjusted R^2 ($\bar{R}^2$) The coefficient of multiple determination adjusted for the reduction in degrees of freedom as more independent variables are included in the regression.
Adverse selection The situation where low-quality products or services drive high-quality products or services out of the market as a result of asymmetric information between buyers and sellers.
Alternative or opportunity costs The cost to the firm of using a purchased or owned input, which is equal to what the input could earn in its best alternative use.
Analysis of variance A test of the overall explanatory power of the regression utilizing the F statistic.
Appreciation A decrease in the domestic-currency price of the foreign currency.
Arc cross-price elasticity of demand The cross-price elasticity of demand for commodity X between two price levels of commodity Y; it is measured by

$$\frac{Q_{X_2} - Q_{X_1}}{P_{Y_2} - P_{Y_1}} \cdot \frac{P_{Y_2} + P_{Y_1}}{Q_{X_2} + Q_{X_1}}$$

Arc income elasticity of demand The income elasticity of demand between two levels of income; it is measured by

$$\frac{Q_2 - Q_1}{I_2 - I_1} \cdot \frac{I_2 + I_1}{Q_2 + Q_1}$$

Arc price elasticity of demand The price elasticity of demand between two points on the demand curve; it is measured by

$$\frac{Q_2 - Q_1}{P_2 - P_1} \cdot \frac{P_2 + P_1}{Q_2 + Q_1}$$

Asymmetric information The situation where one party to a transaction has more information than the other party on the quality of the product or service offered for sale.
Autocorrelation The problem that can arise in regression analysis with time-series data, where consecutive errors have the same sign or change sign frequently; it leads to exaggerated t statistics and to an unreliable R^2 and F statistic.

Average fixed cost (*AFC*) Total fixed costs divided by output.

Average product (*AP*) The total product divided by the quantity of the variable input used.

Average total cost (*ATC*) Total costs divided by output. Also equals *AFC* + *AVC*.

Average variable cost (*AVC*) Total variable costs divided by output.

Averch-Johnson (A-J) effect The overinvestments and underinvestments in plant and equipment resulting when public utility rates are set too high or too low.

Bandwagon effect The situation where some people demand a commodity because other people purchase it (i.e., in order to "keep up with the Joneses").

Barometric firm The oligopolistic firm that is recognized as the true interpreter or barometer of changes in demand and cost conditions warranting a price change in the industry.

Barometric forecasting The method of forecasting turning points in business cycles by the use of leading economic indicators.

Benchmarking Finding out, in an open and above-board way, how other firms may be doing something better (cheaper) so that your firm can copy, and possibly improve on, their technique.

Beta coefficient (β) The ratio of the variability of the return on the common stock of the firm to the variability of the average return on all stocks.

Binding constraint A variable that is fully utilized at a particular point.

Brain drain The emigration of highly skilled workers from poorer nations to the United States and other leading industrial countries in Europe.

Broadbanding The elimination of multiple salary grades to foster movement among jobs within the firm.

Bundling The form of tying in which the firm requires customers buying or leasing one of its products or services to also buy or lease another product or service when customers have different tastes but the firm cannot price discriminate (as in tying).

Business profit The revenue of the firm minus its explicit or accounting costs.

Capital asset pricing model (CAPM) The method of measuring the equity cost of capital as the risk-free rate plus the beta coefficient (β) times the risk premium on the average stock.

Capital budgeting The process of planning expenditures that give rise to revenues or returns over a number of years.

Celler-Kefauver Antimerger Act (1950) The law that closed a loophole in the Clayton Act by making it illegal to acquire not only the stock but also the assets of competing corporations if such purchases substantially lessen competition or tend to create a monopoly.

Centralized cartel A formal agreement among oligopolists to set the monopoly price, allocate output among member firms, and share profits.

Certainty The situation where there is only one possible outcome to a decision and this outcome is known precisely; risk free.
Certainty-equivalent coefficient (α) The ratio of the certain sum equivalent to the expected risky sum or net return from the investment that is used to adjust the valuation model for risk.
Change in demand A shift in the demand curve of a commodity as a result of a change in the consumer's income, in the price of related commodities, tastes, or in any of the determinants of demand other than the price of the commodity.
Change in the quantity demanded The movement along a particular demand curve resulting from a change in the price of the commodity, while holding everything else constant.
Circular flow of economic activity The flow of resources from resource owners to business firms and the reverse flow of goods and services from the latter to the former. Money flows from firms to resource owners to pay for resources and back to firms in payment for goods and services.
Clayton Act (1914) The law that prohibits price discrimination, exclusive and tying contracts, and intercorporate stock holdings if they substantially lessen competition or tend to create a monopoly and that prohibits outright interlocking directorates.
Cobb-Douglas production function A production function of the form $Q = AK^aL^b$ where Q, K, and L are physical units of output, labor, and capital, and A, a, and b are the parameters to be estimated empirically.
Coefficient of correlation (r) The measure of the degree of covariation between two variables; the positive or negative square root of the coefficient of determination in simple regression analysis.
Coefficient of determination (R^2) The proportion of the explained to the total variation in the dependent variable in regression analysis.
Coefficient of variation (v) The standard deviation of the distribution divided by the expected value or mean.
Coincident indicators Time series that move in step or coincide with movements in the level of general economic activity.
Collusion A formal or informal agreement among oligopolists to adopt policies to restrict or eliminate competition and increase profits.
Comparative advantage The theory which postulates that mutually beneficial international trade can be based on international differences in relative abundance and cheapness of inputs.
Competitive benchmarking The comparison of the efficiency of a firm's production methods relative to its competitors.
Composite cost of capital The weighted average of the cost of debt and equity capital to the firm.
Composite indexes Indexes formed by a weighted average of the individual indicators. There are composite indexes for the 12 leading, the 4 roughly coincident, and the 6 lagging indicators.
Computer-aided design (CAD) The technique that allows research and development engineers to design a new or changed product or component on a computer screen.

Computer-aided manufacturing (CAM) The technique that allows research and development engineers to issue instructions to a network of integrated machine tools to produce a prototype of the new or changed product.

Concentration ratios The percentage of total industry sales of the 4, 8, and 20 largest firms in the industry.

Conditional probability The probability that an event will occur given that another event has already occurred.

Confidence interval The range within which we are confident (usually at the 95 percent level) that the true value of the parameter lies.

Conscious parallelism The adoption of similar policies by oligopolistic firms in view of their recognized interdependence.

Consent decree An agreement, without a court trial, between the defendant (without, however, admitting guilt) and the Justice Department under which the defendant agrees to abide by the rules of business behavior set down in the decree.

Constant returns to scale The case where output changes in the same proportion as inputs.

Constrained optimization The maximizing or the minimizing of an objective function subject to some constraints.

Consumer clinics Laboratory experiments in which the participants are given a sum of money and asked to spend it in a simulated store to see how they react to changes in the commodity price and other determinants of demand.

Consumer demand theory The study of the determinants of consumer demand for a commodity.

Consumer surveys The questioning of a sample of consumers about how they would respond to particular changes in the price and other determinants of the demand for the commodity.

Consumers' surplus The difference between what consumers are willing to pay for a specific quantity of a product and what they actually pay.

Continuous probability distribution The smooth bell-like curve that can be used to determine the probability that an outcome will fall within a specific range of outcomes.

Contribution margin per unit The excess of the selling price of the product over the average variable costs of the firm (that is, $P - AVC$), which can be applied to cover the fixed costs of the firm and to provide profits.

Cost of debt The net (after-tax) interest rate paid by a firm to borrow funds.

Cost-plus pricing The most common pricing practice by firms today, whereby a markup is added to the fully allocated average cost of the product.

Cost-volume-profit or breakeven analysis A method of determining the output at which a firm breaks even or earns a target profit from the total revenue and total cost functions of the firm.

Critical value The value found from the table of a distribution (say, the t distribution) that is used to conduct a significance test.

Cross-price elasticity of demand (E_{XY}) The percentage change in the demand for commodity X divided by the percentage change in the price of commodity Y, while holding constant all other variables in the demand function.

Cross-sectional data Data on a sample of families, firms, or other economic units at a particular point in time, say, for a given year.
Cyclical fluctuations The major expansions and contractions in most economic time series that recur every number of years.

Deadweight loss The loss of efficiency in the use of society's resources arising from monopoly.
Decision tree A graphical technique used for showing and analyzing the sequence of possible managerial decisions and their expected outcome under each set of circumstances or states of nature.
Decision variables The variables that the firm can vary in order to optimize the objective function.
Decreasing returns to scale The case where output changes by a smaller proportion than inputs.
Definitional equations The equations in a multiple-equation model that are identities and true by definition.
Degree of operating leverage (*DOL*) The percentage change in the firm's profits divided by the percentage change in output or sales; the sales elasticity of profits.
Degrees of freedom (df) The number of data points or sample observations minus the number of estimated parameters in regression analysis.
Delphi method The forecasting method based on polling the firm's top executives or outside experts separately and then providing feedback in the hope that they would reach a consensus forecast.
Demand function faced by a firm The relationship that identifies the determinants of the demand for a commodity faced by a firm. These include the price of the commodity, the number of consumers in the market, consumers' incomes, the price of related commodities, tastes, and other forces that are specific to the particular industry and firm.
Demand interrelationship The relationship of substitutability or complementarity among the products produced by the firm.
Depreciation An increase in the domestic-currency price of the foreign currency.
Derivative of Y with respect to X (dY/dX) The limit of the ratio $\Delta Y/\Delta X$, as ΔX approaches zero; that is, $dY/dX = \lim_{\Delta X \to 0} \Delta Y/\Delta X$.
Derived demand The firm's demand for the inputs or factors of production required in the production of the commodity that the firm sells.
Differentiated oligopoly An oligopoly where the products of the firms in the industry are differentiated.
Differentiated products Products that are similar but not identical and that satisfy the same basic need.
Differentiation The process of determining the derivative of a function.
Diffusion index An index that measures the percentage of the 12 leading indicators moving upward.
Diminishing marginal utility of money The decline in the extra utility received from each dollar increase in income.

Discrete probability distribution The steplike bar chart showing the probability of each possible outcome of a decision or strategy.
Dissolution and divestiture A court order in monopoly and antimerger cases under which the firm is ordered to dissolve (thereby losing its identity) or to divest itself of (i.e., sell) some of its assets.
Dividend valuation model The method of measuring the equity cost of capital to the firm with the ratio of the dividend per share of the stock to the price of the stock, plus the expected growth rate of dividend payments.
Dominant strategy The best or optimal strategy for a player regardless of what the other player does.
Dual problem The inverse of the primal linear programming problem.
Duality theorem The postulate that the optimal value of the primal objective function is equal to the optimal value of the dual objective function.
Dumping It refers to international price discrimination or the sale of the commodity at a lower price abroad than at home.
Duopoly An oligopoly of two firms.
Durable goods Goods that can be stored, as well as other products that provide services not only during the year that they are purchased but also in subsequent years.
Durbin-Watson statistic (d) The statistic used for the test to detect auto-correlation.

Econometrics The empirical estimation and testing of economic relationships and models.
Economic costs Alternative or opportunity costs.
Economic profit The revenue of the firm minus its economic costs.
Economic theory The study of microeconomics and macroeconomics.
Economic theory of regulation The theory that regulation results from pressure-group action to support business and to protect consumers, workers, and the environment.
Economies of scope The lowering of costs that a firm often experiences when it produces two or more products together rather than producing each product separately.
Electronic scanners The automatic ringing up of prices for bar-coded items at supermarket checkout counters.
Endogenous variables Those variables whose values are determined by the solution of a multiple-equation model.
Engineering technique The method of estimating the long-run average cost curve of the firm from the determination of the optimal input combinations used to produce various levels of output from the present technology and from input prices.
Excess capacity The difference between the quantity that a monopolistically competitive firm and a perfectly competitive firm would sell when the market is in long-run equilibrium.
Exogenous variables Those variables whose values are determined outside (and must be provided to solve) a multiple-equation model.

Expansion path The line joining tangency points of isoquants and isocosts with input prices held constant and which shows optimal input combinations.
Expected profit A weighted average of all possible profit levels that can result from an investment, with the probability of occurrence of each profit level used as weights.
Expected utility The sum of the product of the utility of each possible outcome of a decision or strategy and the probability of its occurrence.
Expected value The sum of the products of each possible outcome of a decision or strategy and the probability of its occurrence.
Explained variation The sum of the squared deviations of each *estimated* value of the dependent variable ($\hat{Y}$) from its mean ($\overline{Y}$).
Explicit costs The actual expenditures of the firm required to hire or purchase inputs.
Exponential smoothing The smoothing technique in which the forecast for a period is a *weighted* average of the actual and forecasted values of the time series in the previous period.
External diseconomies of consumption Uncompensated costs imposed on some individuals by the consumption expenditures of some other individual.
External diseconomies of production Uncompensated costs imposed on some firms by the expansion of output by other firms.
External economies of consumption Uncompensated benefits conferred on some individuals by the consumption expenditures of some other individual.
External economies of production Uncompensated benefits conferred on some firms by the expansion of output by other firms.
Externalities Harmful or beneficial effects borne or received by firms or individuals other than those producing or consuming a product or service.

***F* statistic** The ratio of the explained variance divided by $k - 1$ df to the unexplained variance divided by $n - k$ df, where k is the number of estimated parameters and n is the number of observations.
Fair game A game or bet in which there is a 50-50 chance of winning or losing.
Feasible region The area that includes all the solutions that are possible with the given constraints.
Federal Trade Commission Act (1914) A supplement to the Clayton Act which made unfair methods of competition illegal and which established the Federal Trade Commission (FTC) to prosecute violators of the antitrust laws and protect the public against false and misleading advertisements.
Firm An organization that combines and organizes resources for the purpose of producing goods and/or services for sale.
First-degree price discrimination The selling of each unit of a product separately and charging the highest price possible for each unit sold.
Fixed inputs Inputs that cannot be changed readily during the time period under consideration.
Foreign-exchange market The market where national currencies are bought and sold.

Foreign-exchange rate The price of a unit of a foreign currency in terms of the domestic currency.
Foreign sourcing of inputs The purchase of parts and components abroad in order to keep production costs down and meet the competition.
Forward contract An agreement to purchase or sell a specific amount of a foreign currency at a rate specified today for delivery at a specified future date.
Fully allocated average cost The sum of the average variable cost of producing the normal or standard level of output and an average overhead charge.
Functional areas of business administration studies The academic disciplines of accounting, finance, marketing, personnel, and production.
Futures contract A standardized forward contract for predetermined quantities of the currency and selected calendar dates.

Game theory The theory that examines the choice of the best or optimal strategies in conflict situations.
Giffen good An inferior good for which the positive substitution effect is smaller than the negative income effect so that less of the good is purchased when its price falls.

Hedging The covering of a foreign-exchange risk.
Herfindahl index (H) A measure of concentration in an industry given by the sum of the squared values of the market shares of all the firms in the industry.
Heteroscedasticity The problem that can arise in regression analysis on cross-sectional data, where the error term is not constant; it leads to biased standard errors and incorrect statistical tests.

Identification problem The difficulty of deriving the demand curve for a commodity from observed price-quantity points that result from the intersection of different and unobserved demand and supply curves for the commodity.
Imperfect competition Monopoly, monopolistic competition, and oligopoly.
Implicit costs The value (from their best alternative use) of the inputs owned and used by the firm.
Import quota A quantitative restriction on imports.
Import tariff A per-unit tax on imports.
Income effect The increase in the quantity demanded of a commodity resulting only from the increase in real income that accompanies a price decline.
Income elasticity of demand (E_I) The percentage change in the demand for a commodity divided by the percentage change in consumers' income, while holding constant all the other variables in the demand function.
Increasing returns to scale The case where output changes by a larger proportion than inputs.
Incremental analysis The comparison of the incremental revenue to the incremental cost in managerial decision making.

Incremental costs The toal increase in costs from implementing a particular managerial decision.

Individual's demand curve The graphical relationship between the price and the quantity demanded of a commodity by an individual per time period.

Individual's demand schedule The tabular relationship between the price and the quantity demanded of a commodity by an individual per time period.

Inequality constraints Limitations on the use of some inputs or certain minimum requirements that must be met.

Inferior goods Goods of which the consumer purchases less with an increase in income.

Information superhighway The ability of researchers, firms, and consumers to hook up with libraries, databases, and marketing information through a national high-speed computer network and have at their fingertips a vast amount of information as never before.

Injunction A court order requiring that the defendant refrain from certain anticompetitive actions or take some specified competitive actions.

Inputs Resources used in the production of goods and services.

Internal rate of return (*IRR*) on a project The rate of discount that equates the present value of the net cash flows to the initial cost of a project.

Internationalization of economic activity The setting up of production facilities and/or the purchase of components and parts, as well as the sale of commodities in other nations.

Internet A collection of thousands of computers, businesses, and millions of people throughout the world linked together in a service called World Wide Web.

Intra-industry trade International trade in differentiated products.

Irregular or random influences The unpredictable variations in the data series resulting from wars, natural disasters, strikes, or other unforeseen events.

Isocost line It shows the various combinations of two inputs that the firm can hire with a given total cost outlay.

Isoquant A curve showing the various combinations of two inputs that can be used to produce a specific level of output.

Iteration A computer run or trial of a simulation model with one set of randomly chosen values of the variables of the model.

Japanese cost-management system The production system where the firm starts with a target cost based on the market price at which the firm believes consumers will buy the product and then strives to produce the product at the specified targeted cost.

Just-in-time production system The production system introduced by Toyota in which every part and component of a product becomes available just when needed.

Kinked demand curve model The model that seeks to explain price rigidity by postulating a demand curve with a kink at the prevailing price.

Lagging indicators Time series that follow or lag movements in the level of general economic activity.
Lagrangian function A function formed by the original objective function that the firm seeks to maximize or minimize plus λ (the Lagrangian multiplier) times the constraint function set equal to zero.
Lagrangian multiplier method A technique for solving a constrained optimization problem by forming a Lagrangian function and treating it as an unconstrained problem.
Law of demand The inverse relationship between the price and the quantity demanded of a commodity per time period.
Law of diminishing returns A physical law, which has been found to be always empirically true, that after a point, the marginal product of a variable input declines.
Leading economic indicators Time series that tend to precede (lead) changes in the level of general economic activity.
Learning curve The curve showing the decline in average cost with rising cumulative total outputs over time.
Learning organization An organization that values continuing learning, both individual and collective, and believes that competitive advantage derives from and requires continuous learning in our information age.
Least-squares method The statistical technique for estimating a regression line which minimizes the sum of the squared vertical deviations or errors of the observed points from the regression line.
Licensing The requirement of a franchise or permission to enter or remain in a business, profession, or a trade.
Limit pricing The charging of lower than the profit-maximizing price by a firm in order to discourage the entrance of other firms into the market.
Linear programming A mathematical technique for solving constrained maximization and minimization problems when there are many constraints and the objective function to be optimized as well as the constraints faced are linear.
Logistic management The merging at the corporate level of the purchasing, transportation, warehousing, distribution, and customer services functions, rather than dealing with each of them separately at division levels.
Long run The time period when all inputs are variable.
Long-run average cost (LAC) The minimum per-unit cost of producing any level of output when the firm can build any desired scale of plant; $LAC = LTC/Q$.
Long-run marginal cost (LMC) The change in long-run total costs per unit change in output; $LMC = \Delta LTC/\Delta Q$.
Long-run total cost (LTC) The minimum total costs of producing various levels of output when the firm can build any desired scale of plant.

Macroeconomics The study of the total or aggregate level of output, income, employment, consumption, investment, and prices for the economy *viewed as a whole*.

Managerial economics The application of economic theory and the tools of decision science to examine how an organization can achieve its aims or objectives most efficiently.
Marginal analysis The postulate that optimization occurs when the marginal benefit of an activity equals the marginal cost.
Marginal cost (*MC*) The change in total costs or in total variable costs per unit change in output.
Marginal product (*MP*) The change in total product per unit change in the variable input used.
Marginal rate of technical substitution (*MRTS*) The absolute value of the slope of the isoquant. It equals the ratio of the marginal products of the two inputs.
Marginal resource cost The increase in total cost from hiring an additional unit of the variable input.
Marginal revenue (*MR*) The change in total revenue per unit change in quantity sold.
Marginal revenue product The marginal product of the variable input times the marginal revenue from the sale of the extra output produced.
Market All the actual and potential buyers and sellers of a particular product.
Market demand function The relationship that identifies the determinants of the total or aggregate demand for a commodity.
Market experiments Attempts by the firm to estimate the demand for the commodity by changing price and other determinants of the demand for the commodity in the actual marketplace.
Market failure Economic inefficiencies arising from the existence of monopoly power in imperfectly competitive markets, from externalities, and from the existence of public goods.
Market-sharing cartel An agreement among oligopolists to divide the market.
Market structure The competitive environment in which the buyers and sellers of the product operate.
Markup on cost The ratio of the profit margin to the fully allocated average cost of the product.
Mathematical economics The study of the formal (equational) relationships among economic variables in economic models and their theoretical implications.
Maximin criterion The decision rule under uncertainty that postulates that the decision maker should determine the worst possible outcome of each strategy and then pick the strategy that provides the best of the worst possible outcomes.
Microeconomics The study of the economic behavior of *individual* decision-making units, such as individual consumers, resource owners, and business firms, in a free-enterprise system.
Minimax regret criterion The decision rule under uncertainty that postulates that the decision maker should select the strategy that minimizes the maximum regret or opportunity cost of the wrong decision, whatever the state of nature that occurs.
Model A formal or mathematical statement of an economic theory.

Monopolistic competition The form of market organization where there are many sellers of a differentiated product and entry into or exit from the industry is rather easy in the long run.
Monopoly The form of market organization in which a single firm sells a product for which there are no close substitutes.
Moral hazard The increased probability of a loss when an economic agent can shift some of its costs to others.
Moving average The smoothing technique in which the forecasted value of a time series in a given period is equal to the average value of the time series in a number of previous periods.
Multicollinearity The problem in regression analysis that arises when two or more explanatory variables are highly correlated; it leads to exaggerated standard errors and biased statistical tests.
Multiple regression The regression analysis with more than one independent or explanatory variable.

Nash equilibrium The equilibrium situation where each player has chosen his or her optimal strategy, given the strategy chosen by the other player.
Natural monopoly The case where economies of scale result in a single firm's supplying the entire market.
Net cash flow from a project The difference between cash receipts and cash expenditures over the life of a project.
Net present value (*NPV*) of a project The present value of the estimated stream of net cash flows from the project, discounted at the firm's cost of capital, minus the initial cost of the project.
Networking The forming of temporary strategic alliances where each firm contributes its best competency.
New international economies of scale The increased productivity resulting from the firm's integration of its entire system of manufacturing operations around the world.
Nonnegativity constraints Limits that preclude negative values for the solution in a linear programming problem.
Nonprice competition Competition based on product variation, advertising, and service rather than on price.
Normal goods Goods of which the consumer purchases more with an increase in income.

Objective function The function to be optimized in linear programming.
Observational research The gathering of information on consumer preferences by watching them buying and using products.
Oligopoly The form of market organization in which there are few sellers of a homogeneous or differentiated product and entry into or exit from the industry is difficult.

Operating leverage The ratio of the firm's total fixed costs to its total variable costs.
Optimal solution The best of the feasible solutions.
Output elasticity The percentage change in output or total product divided by the percentage change in the variable input used.
Overcrowding The larger number of firms present in a monopolistically competitive market than if the market were perfectly competitive because of excess capacity in monopolistically competitive markets.

Partial derivative The marginal effect on the dependent or left-hand variable of a multivariate function resulting from changing one of the independent or right-hand variables while holding all the others constant.
Patent The right granted to an inventor by the federal government for the exclusive use of an invention for a period of 17 years.
Payoff The outcome or consequence of each combination of strategies by the players in game theory.
Payoff matrix A table that shows the possible outcome or result of each strategy under each state of nature.
Peak-load pricing The firm's charging of a higher price during peak times than at off-peak times.
Perfect competition The form of market organization in which there are many firms selling a homogeneous or identical product and each firm is too small to affect the price of the commodity.
Planning horizon The period of time of the long run when the firm can build any desired scale of plant.
Players The decision makers in the theory of games (here the oligopolistic firms or its managers) whose behavior we are trying to explain and predict.
Point cross-price elasticity of demand The cross-price elasticity of demand for commodity X at a particular price of commodity Y; it is measured by

$$\frac{\Delta Q_X}{\Delta P_Y} \cdot \frac{P_Y}{Q_X}$$

Point income elasticity of demand The income elasticity of demand at a particular level of income; it is measured by

$$\frac{\Delta Q}{\Delta I} \cdot \frac{I}{Q}$$

Point price elasticity of demand The price elasticity of demand at a particular point on the demand curve; it is measured by

$$\frac{\Delta Q}{\Delta P} \cdot \frac{P}{Q}$$

Predatory pricing Selling at below average variable cost in order to drive a competitor out of the market or discourage new entrants.

Prestige pricing The pricing method of deliberately setting high prices to attract prestige-oriented consumers.

Price discrimination The charging of different prices for different quantities of a product, at different times, to different customer groups, or in different markets, when these price differences are not justified by cost differences.

Price elasticity of demand (E_P) The percentage change in the quantity demanded of a commodity divided by the percentage change in its price, while holding constant all the other variables in the demand function.

Price leadership The form of market collusion in oligopolistic firms whereby the firm that serves as the price leader initiates a price change and the other firms in the industry soon match it.

Price lining The pricing practice of setting a price target and then developing a product that would allow the firm to maximize total profits at that price.

Price taker The situation under perfect competition whereby each firm has no effect on the price of the product it sells and can sell any quantity at the given market price.

Primal problem The original maximization (e.g., profit) or minimization (e.g., cost) linear programming problem.

Principal-agent problem The problem that arises because the agents (managers) of a firm may seek to maximize their own benefits (such as salaries) rather than the profits or value of the firm, which is the owners' or principals' interest.

Prisoners' dilemma The situation where each player in an oligopolistic game adopts his or her dominant strategy but could do better by cooperating.

Probability The chance or odds that an event will occur.

Probability distribution The list of all possible outcomes of a decision or strategy and the probability attached to each.

Process innovation The introduction of a new or improved production process.

Producers' goods The raw materials, capital equipment, and other inputs used by the firm to produce the goods and services demanded by consumers.

Product cycle model The theory that firms which introduce an innovation eventually lose their export market and even their domestic market to foreign imitators facing lower production costs.

Product differentiation Products that are similar, but not identical.

Product innovation The introduction of a new or improved product.

Product variation Differences in some of the characteristics of differentiated products.

Production The transformation of inputs or resources into output of goods and services.

Production function An equation, table, or graph that shows the maximum output that a firm can produce per period of time with each set of inputs.

Production process The various capital/labor ratios that a firm can use to produce a commodity; it is depicted by a ray from the origin in input space.

Profit margin The difference between the price and the fully allocated average cost of the product.

Profitability index (*PI*) The ratio of the present value of the net cash flows from a project to its initial cost.

Public interest theory of regulation The theory that regulation is undertaken to ensure that the economic system operates in a manner consistent with the public interest and to overcome market failures.

Public utilities Natural monopolies supplying electricity, water, gas, local telephone, and local transportation services.

Pure oligopoly An oligopoly in which the products of the firms in the industry are homogeneous.

Reduced-form equations The equations that represent the solution of a multiple-equation model and express the endogenous variables of the model in terms of the exogenous variables only.

Reengineering The radical redesign of all of the firm's processes to achieve major gains in speed, quality, service, and profitability.

Regression analysis A statistical technique for estimating the quantitative relationship between the economic variable that we seek to explain (the dependent variable) and one or more independent or explanatory variables.

Regression line The line obtained by minimizing the sum of the squared vertical deviations of all data points from the line.

Relevant costs The costs that should be considered in making a managerial decision; opportunity costs.

Repeated games Prisoners' dilemma games of more than one move.

Ridge lines The lines that separate the relevant (i.e., the negatively sloped) from the irrelevant (or positively sloped) portions of the isoquant.

Risk The situation where there is more than one possible outcome to a decision and the probability of each possible outcome is known or can be estimated.

Risk-adjusted discount rate The higher rate of discount used to calculate the present value of the net cash flow or return of an investment project in order to compensate for risk.

Risk averter An individual for whom the marginal utility of money diminishes; he or she would not accept a fair bet.

Risk neutral An individual for whom the marginal utility of money is constant; he or she is indifferent to a fair bet.

Risk premium The excess in the expected or required rate of return on a risky investment over the rate of return on a riskless asset in order to compensate for risk.

Risk-return trade-off function A curve showing the various risk-return combinations among which a manager or investor is indifferent.

Risk seeker An individual for whom the marginal utility of money increases; he or she would accept a fair bet and even some unfair bets.

Robinson-Patman Act (1936) The law that protects small retailers from price competition from large chain-store retailers, based on the latter's ability to obtain

lower prices and brokerage concession fees on bulk purchases from suppliers if the intent is to destroy competition or eliminate a competitor.
Root-mean-square error (*RMSE*) The measure of the weighted average error of a forecast.

Sales maximization model The model that postulates that oligopolistic firms seek to maximize sales after an adequate rate of profit has been earned to satisfy stockholders.
Satisficing behavior The theory of the firm that postulates that managers are not able to maximize profits but can strive only for some satisfactory goal in terms of sales, profits, growth, market share, and so on.
Scatter diagram A figure with the plots of the data points.
Seasonal variation The regularly recurring fluctuations in economic activity during each year because of weather and social customs.
Second-degree price discrimination The charging of a uniform price per unit for a specific quantity or block of a product, a lower price per unit for an additional batch or block of the product, and so on.
Second derivative The derivative of the derivative; it is found by the same rules of differentiation used to find the (first) derivative.
Secular trend The long-run increase or decrease in a data series.
Selling expenses Expenditures (such as advertising) that a firm incurs in order to induce consumers to purchase more of its product.
Shadow price The marginal valuation of an input or output to the firm.
Sherman Act (1890) The law that prohibits monopolization and restraints of trade in commerce among the states and with foreign nations.
Short run The time period when at least one input is fixed.
Short-run supply curve of the perfectly competitive firm The rising portion of the firm's short-run marginal cost curve above its average variable cost curve.
Shut-down point The level of output at which the price of the product equals the average variable cost of the firm.
Significance test The test to determine if there is a statistically significant relationship between the dependent and the independent variable(s) in regression analysis.
Simple regression analysis The regression analysis with only one independent or explanatory variable.
Simplex method A mathematical technique for solving linear programming problems.
Skimming Setting a high price when a product is first introduced and then gradually lowering its price later.
Slack variable A variable that is not fully utilized at a particular point.
Smoothing techniques A method of naive forecasting in which future values of a time series are forecasted on the basis of some average of its past values only.
Snob effect The situation where some people demand a smaller quantity of a commodity as more people consume it, in order to be different and exclusive.

Stage I of production The range of increasing average product of the variable input.
Stage II of production The range from the maximum average product of the variable input to where the marginal product of the input is zero.
Stage III of production The range of negative marginal product of the variable input.
Standard error (*SE*) of the regression The standard error of the dependent variable (*Y*) from the regression line.
Strategic behavior The plan of action of a player or oligopolist, after taking into consideration all possible reactions of the others, as they compete for profits or other advantages.
Strategies The potential choices that can be made by the players (firms) in the theory of games.
Structural (behavioral) equations The equations that seek to explain (i.e., to identify the determinants of) the relationships of the model.
Substitution effect The increase in the quantity demanded of a commodity resulting only from the decline in its price and independent of the change in real income.
Sunk costs The costs that are not affected by a particular managerial decision.
Survival technique The method of determining the existence of increasing, decreasing, or constant returns to scale depending on whether the share of industry output coming from large firms (as compared to the share of industry output coming from small firms) increases, decreases, or remains the same over time.

***t* statistic** The ratio of the value of the estimated parameter to its standard deviation or error.
***t* test** The significance test for an estimated parameter using the *t* distribution.
Theory of contestable markets The theory that postulates that even if an industry has only one or a few fims, it would still operate as if it were perfectly competitive if entry is absolutely free and exit is entirely costless.
Theory of the firm The postulate that the primary goal or objective of the firm is to maximize wealth or the value of the firm.
Third-degree price discrimination The charging of different prices for the same product in different markets until the marginal revenue of the last unit of the product sold in each markt equals the marginal cost of the product.
Time-series analysis The technique of forecasting future values of a time series by examining past observations of the time-series data only.
Time-series data The values of a variable arranged chronologically by days, weeks, months, quarters, or years.
Time value of money The recognition that $1 received or paid in the future is worth less than $1 paid or received today.
Tit-for-tat The strategy in repeated prisoners' dilemma games of doing to your opponent what he or she has just done to you.
Total costs (*TC*) Total fixed costs plus total variable costs.

Total fixed costs (*TFC*) The total obligations of the firm per time period for all the fixed inputs used.
Total product (*TP*) The ouptut produced by using different quantities of an input with fixed quantities of other(s).
Total quality management (*TQM*) The effort to constantly improve the quality of products and the firm's processes so as to consistently deliver increasing value to customers. It constantly asks how something can be done cheaper, faster, or better by benchmarking and teamwork.
Total revenue (*TR*) The price per unit of the commodity times the quantity sold.
Total variable costs (*TVC*) The total obligations of the firm per time period for all the variable inputs the firm uses.
Total variation The sum of the squared deviations of each *observed* value of the dependent variable (Y) from its mean ($\overline{Y}$).
Transaction costs The extra cost (beyond the price of the purchase) in terms of money, time, or inconvenience of conducting a transaction. Firms exist to avoid many transaction costs.
Transfer pricing The determination of the price of intermediate products sold by one semiautonomous division of a firm to another semiautonomous division of the same enterprise.
Two-part tariff The pricing practice in which consumers pay an initial fee for the right to purchase a product or service, as well as a usage fee or price for each unit of the product they purchase.
Tying The requirement that a consumer who buys or leases a product also purchases another product needed in the use of the first.

Unexplained variation The sum of the squared deviations of each *observed* value of the dependent variable (Y) from its corresponding *estimated* value ($\hat{Y}$).
Uruguay Round The multilateral trade agreement concluded in December 1993 under which trade restrictions are to be reduced.

Value of the firm The present value of all expected future profits of the firm.
Value pricing The selling of quality goods at lower prices than previously.
Variable inputs Inputs that can be varied easily and on a very short notice.
Voluntary export restraint A restriction on exports "voluntarily agreed-upon by a nation under the threat of higher all-around trade restrictions by the importing nation."

Wheeler-Lea Act (1938) The amendment to the Federal Trade Commission Act which forbids false or deceptive advertisement of foods, drugs, corrective devices, and cosmetics entering interstate commerce.

Indexes

Name Index

Subject Index